APPLYING
International Financial Reporting Standards

2ND EDITION

ERNST & YOUNG
Quality In Everything We Do

APPLYING International Financial Reporting Standards

2ND EDITION

KEITH ALFREDSON
Consultant

KEN LEO
Consultant

RUTH PICKER
Ernst & Young

JANICE LOFTUS
University of Adelaide

KERRY CLARK
Ernst & Young

VICTORIA WISE
Deakin University

With contributions from MATT DYKI
University of Melbourne

WILEY
John Wiley & Sons Australia, Ltd

Second edition published in 2009 by
John Wiley & Sons Australia, Ltd
42 McDougall Street, Milton, Qld 4064

Typeset in 9.5/11 pt ITC Giovanni LT Book

National Library of Australia
Cataloguing-in-Publication entry

Title:	Applying international financial reporting standards/ Keith Alfredson ... [et al.].
Edition:	2nd ed.
ISBN:	9780470819678 (pbk.)
Notes:	Includes index.
Subjects:	Accounting — Standards. Financial statements — Standards.
Other Authors/ Contributors:	Alfredson, Keith.
Dewey Number:	657.0218

Typeset in India by Aptara

Printed in Singapore by
Craft Print International Ltd

10 9 8 7

FROM THE PROFESSION

Ernst & Young is delighted to support *Applying International Financial Reporting Standards*, 2nd edition — a definitive guide to International Financial Reporting Standards (IFRSs). The year 2005 was a significant milestone in the accounting profession's history — almost 100 countries adopted one set of international standards for the first time. The challenge for these countries is to achieve global consistency in applying these standards. For example, a French company must account for a business combination in the same way as an Australian or New Zealand company. By contrast, in the past each of these countries had its own national accounting standards and interpretations were determined at the country level.

This text is an important contribution to the goal of global consistency. It is an invaluable guide to applying IFRSs, written by a distinctive combination of authoritative academics and experienced accounting practitioners.

This text is abundant with practical examples and is groundbreaking in providing such examples in many areas such as business combinations and financial instruments. I am sure that the book will be instructive not only to those learning about accounting standards for the first time but also to qualified accountants grappling with the new world of applying IFRSs.

In recent years the role of relevant and reliable financial reporting has been elevated, unfortunately as a result of corporate collapses or misdeeds. Never in my experience has financial reporting been in the media headlines as much as in the past few years. The opportunity for the accounting profession now is to ensure that our financial reporting standards are appropriate, well understood and consistently applied. The International Accounting Standards Board (IASB) has played its part in implementing a stable platform of IFRSs. The rest is up to us.

I commend the book to you, as you play your part in understanding and applying IFRSs.

James M. Millar
Area Managing Partner Oceania, CEO Australia
Ernst & Young
Sydney

March 2009

BRIEF CONTENTS

CONTENTS

PREFACE

With the completion of the stable platform of international accounting standards in 2004, the International Accounting Standards Board (IASB) established itself as a world leader in the preparation of accounting standards. The financial reporting standards issued by the IASB have now been adopted by an ever increasing number of countries throughout the world. Further, in recent years, we have seen acceptance of these standards by the regulators in the United States.

As evidenced by the current financial crisis, in business, a global perspective is required. For universities, educating students to become a part of a global business environment requires placing more emphasis on understanding accounting principles rather than applying specific local jurisdictional regulations.

Applying International Financial Reporting Standards, 2nd edition has been written to meet the needs of accounting students and practitioners in understanding the complexities of International Financial Reporting Standards.

This is the second edition of this book. That there is a second edition is due to the acceptance of the book by academics and practitioners throughout the world. We have welcomed the comments and suggestions received from various people and have tried to ensure that these are reflected in this edition.

There are two main reasons for the publication of a new edition. The first is that there have been major changes to a number of accounting standards since the first edition. In particular, these standards are:

- IFRS 3 *Business Combinations*
- IAS 1 *Presentation of Financial Statements*
- IAS 14 *Segment Reporting*
- IAS 27 *Consolidated and Separate Financial Statements*
- IAS 39 *Financial Instruments: Recognition and Measurement.*

The chapters covering these accounting standards now reflect these changes.

The second reason for a new edition is that users of the book have asked for chapters to be added to the book dealing with accounting standards not covered in the first edition. Four new chapters have thus been added to the book. Accounting standards for which new chapters have been added are:

- IFRS 6 *Exploration for and Evaluation of Mineral Resources*
- IAS 18 *Revenue*
- IAS 19 *Employee Benefits*
- IAS 41 *Agriculture*.

The addition of a chapter on revenue was considered critical to providing an understanding of one of the key elements in the *Framework*.

In writing this book, we have endeavoured to ensure that the following common themes flow throughout the text:

- *Accounting standards are underpinned by a conceptual framework.* Accounting standards are not simply a rulebook to be learned by rote. An understanding of the conceptual basis of accounting, and the rationale behind the principles espoused in particular standards, is crucial to their consistent application in a variety of practical applications.
- *The IASB financial reporting standards are principles-based.* Although a specific standard is a standalone document, the principles in any standard relate to and are interpreted in conjunction with other standards. To appreciate the application of a specific standard, an understanding of the reasoning within other standards is required. We have endeavoured where applicable to refer to other accounting standards that are connected in principle and application. In particular, extensive references are made to the Basis for Conclusions documents accompanying each standard issued by the IASB. This material, although not integral to the standards, explains the reasoning process used by the IASB and provides indicators of changes in direction being proposed by the IASB.
- *Accounting standards have a practical application.* The end product of the standard-setting process must be applied by accounting practitioners in a variety of organisational structures and practical settings. While a theoretical understanding of a standard is important, practitioners should

be able to apply the relevant standard. The author of each chapter has demonstrated the practical application of the accounting standards by providing case studies, examples and journal entries (where relevant). The references to practical situations require the reader to pay close attention to the detailed information discussed, but such a detailed examination is essential to an understanding of the standards. Having only a broad overview of the basic principles is insufficient.

Many people have been directly and indirectly involved in the writing of this book. Our task was made possible by the discussions and debates we have had with many colleagues and with staff associated with the standard-setting bodies, particularly at the IASB. We thank them for their patience and tolerance, as well as the impartation of their knowledge. Writing a book takes time, and this has left less time for family and friends. We thank them also for their support and understanding. We also extend a special thank you to Matt Dyki, University of Melbourne, who created the fact sheets that appear at the end of the textbook.

Finally, in a time when the world with its increasing sophistication seems to produce situations and pronouncements that have added complexity, we hope that this book assists in the life-long learning process that ourselves and the readers of this book are continuously engaged in.

Keith Alfredson
Ken Leo
Ruth Picker
Janice Loftus
Kerry Clark
Victoria Wise

February 2009

ABOUT THE AUTHORS

Keith Alfredson

Keith Alfredson, BCom(Hons), AAUQ, FAICD, FCA, FCPA, is a graduate of the University of Queensland. On graduation in 1963 he joined Arthur Andersen, becoming a partner in 1974 and retiring in 1997. He specialised in the audit of large publicly listed and privately owned entities in addition to acting as an expert on technical accounting issues. He was Arthur Andersen's representative on the Australian Urgent Issues Group. In 1998, he became a Senior Fellow in the Department of Accounting and Business Information Systems of The University of Melbourne. In May 2000, he was appointed the first full-time chairman of the Australian Accounting Standards Board, a position he held until May 2003. During that period he also acted as chairman of the Urgent Issues Group.

Ken Leo

Ken Leo, BCom (Hons), MBA (Qld), AAUQ, FCPA, is Professor of Accounting at Curtin University of Technology, Western Australia. During his 40 years as an academic, he has taught company accounting to undergraduate and postgraduate students. He has been involved in writing books published by John Wiley since 1981, and has also written books and monographs for other organisations including CPA Australia, Group of 100 and the Australian Accounting Research Foundation. As a founding member of the Urgent Issues Group in 1995, he served on this body until 2001. He subsequently served on the AASB from 2002 to 2007, including being deputy chairman of the AASB for some of that time.

Ruth Picker

Ruth Picker, BA, FCA, FSIA, FCPA, is Global Director, Global IFRS Services with Ernst & Young. Ruth has had 25 years' experience with Ernst & Young and held various leadership roles during this time. Up until June 2009, Ruth was Managing Partner — Melbourne and the Oceania Team Leader of Climate Change and Sustainability Services. Prior to this role Ruth was a senior partner in the Technical Consulting Group, Global IFRS and the firm's Professional Practice Director (PPD) responsible for directing the firm's accounting and auditing policies with the ultimate authority on accounting and auditing issues. She is a member of Ernst & Young's global International Financial Reporting Standards (IFRS) Policy Committee.

Ruth's authoritative insight and understanding of accounting policy and regulation was acknowledged through her appointment to the International Financial Reporting Interpretations Committee (IFRIC), the official interpretative arm of the International Accounting Standards Board. She is currently a member of the IFRIC and the only Australian on that body.

Ruth was responsible for the preparation of Ernst & Young's Corporate Governance Series (which includes guidance for directors and results of numerous corporate governance surveys) and subsequent advice to a number of entities in both the private and public sectors on the application of corporate governance.

Ruth has conducted numerous 'Directors' Schools' for listed company boards. These schools were designed by Ruth and are aimed at enhancing the financial literacy of listed company board members.

She is a frequent speaker and author on accounting issues and has been actively involved in the Australian accounting standard-setting process, being a past member and former deputy chair of the Australian Accounting Standards Board (AASB) and having served on the Urgent Issues Group for 3 years. She has been a long-standing lecturer and Task Force member for the Securities Institute of Australia, serving that organisation for 17 years.

Her written articles have been published in a number of publications, and she is frequently quoted in the media on accounting and governance issues.

In November 2000, Ruth was awarded the inaugural 'Lynne Sutherland Award' — an Ernst & Young award created to recognise those people at Ernst & Young who contribute to the development and retention of women and who support and enhance the ability of Ernst & Young to attract and retain talented people.

Janice Loftus

Janice Loftus, BBus, MCom (Hons), is a senior lecturer in accounting at The University of Sydney. Her teaching interests are in the area of financial accounting and she has written several study guides for distance learning programs. Janice's research interests are in the area of financial reporting. She co-authored Accounting Theory Monograph 11 on solvency and cash condition with Professor M. C. Miller. She has numerous publications on international financial reporting standards, risk reporting, solvency, earnings management, social and environmental reporting, and developments in standard setting in Australian and international journals. Janice co-authored *Accounting: Building Business Skills* published by John Wiley & Sons. She is the editor of *Financial Reporting, Regulation and Governance*. Prior to embarking on an academic career, Janice held several senior accounting positions in Australian and multi-national corporations.

Kerry Clark

Kerry Clark, BCom, CA, Executive Director — Technical Consulting Group, Global IFRS, has had 17 years' experience with Ernst & Young and is currently on secondment to the Ernst & Young Calgary office in Canada assisting many of Canada's largest oil and gas companies in their conversion to IFRSs. Prior to this she was a key member of the Technical Consulting Group, Global IFRS in the Ernst & Young Melbourne office in Australia where she was responsible for advising clients on the application of IFRSs to complex transactions. Kerry has been involved in the authoring of many Ernst & Young publications and *Charter* magazine articles and assisted Ruth Picker in conducting 'Directors' Schools' for listed company boards. She has also spoken on accounting issues in many different forums.

Victoria Wise

Victoria Wise, BCom, MEcon, PhD, FCPA, FPNA, is a Professor in the School of Accounting and Corporate Governance at the University of Tasmania, Hobart. During her 20 years as an academic she has taught financial accounting and auditing to undergraduate, honours and postgraduate students. Victoria has more than 130 publications including books and book chapters, refereed and professional journal articles and conference proceedings. Her journal articles focus on International Financial Reporting Standards, corporate governance and regulatory issues, and public sector and small business financial reporting. Her current research interests include corporate regulation and governance.

ACKNOWLEDGEMENTS

The authors and publisher would like to thank the following copyright holders, organisations and individuals for their permission to reproduce copyright material in this book.

Images

• **IASB:** Copyright © 2009 International Accounting Standards Committee Foundation. All rights reserved. No permission granted to reproduce or distribute • **p. 51:** 'Main market fact sheet, October 2008' © London Stock Exchange PLC • **p. 126:** Ernst & Young • **p. 250:** Deloitte Touche Tohmatsu • **pp. 370, 371:** From *Intangible: management, measurement and reporting* by Baruch Lev, The Brookings Institution Press, Washington DC, 2001, pp. 9, 18 • **p. 390:** © Skandia Insurance Company Ltd • **p. 391:** 'Management challenges', from the *Systematic Intellectual Capital Report 2002*, p. 10, www.systematic.com • **pp. 777, 780:** Reproduced by permission of Ernst & Young (EYGM Limited) © 2009 EYGM Limited. All rights reserved • **p. 955:** Peter Gerhardy, School of Commerce, Flinders University.

Text

• **AASB:** © Commonwealth of Australia 2009. All legislation herein is reproduced by permission but does not purport to be the official or authorised version. It is subject to Commonwealth of Australia copyright. The *Copyright Act 1968* permits certain reproduction and publication of Commonwealth legislation. In particular, s.182A of the Act enables a complete copy to be made by or on behalf of a particular person. For reproduction or publication beyond that permitted by the Act, permission should be sought in writing from the Commonwealth available from the Australian Accounting Standards Board. Requests in the first instance should be addressed to the Administration Director, Australian Accounting Standards Board, PO Box 204, Collins Street West, Melbourne, Victoria, 8007 • **IASB:** Copyright © 2009 International Accounting Standards Committee Foundation. All rights reserved. No permission granted to reproduce or distribute • **pp. 1, 3–4, 5, 6, 7–9, 11:** Copyright © 2009 International Accounting Standards Committee Foundation. All rights reserved. No permission granted to reproduce or distribute • **p. 28:** From 'September 2006: FASB issues fair value measurement standard' from the IASPlus website © Deloitte Touche Tohmatsu. Reproduced with permission • **pp. 28–9:** This text extract was originally published in the 'New definition of fair value' from *Heads Up*, 27 September 2006, Vol. 13, Iss. 12, p. 2, which is prepared by the National Office Accounting Standards and Communications Group of Deloitte LLP, and is being reproduced here with the permission of Deloitte LLP's subsidiary, Deloitte Development LLC, Copyright © 2006 Deloitte Development LLC. All rights reserved. Please see www.deloitte.com/us/about for a detailed description of the legal structure of Deloitte LLP and its subsidiaries, and further information and disclaimers applicable to this text extract and other *Heads Up* publications • **pp. 37, 42, 49, 55, 65–6, 256–7, 275, 424, 466, 473, 677–8, 1086:** © Nokia • **pp. 38–9:** © ICRC — International Committee of the Red Cross • **p. 47:** From article '$5 billion: Virgin float offer swamped' © Scott Rochfort, *The Age, Business*, 6 December 2003 • **pp. 48–9:** 'Main market fact sheet, October 2008 © London Stock Exchange PLC • **pp. 50–1:** Extracted from *ANZ renounceable rights issue prospectus*, November 2003 © ANZ • **pp. 56, 380, 386–7:** © Christian Dior • **pp. 59, 308–10, 440–1, 471–2, 476, 770–2:** © Wesfarmers Limited • **pp. 63–4, 767–70:** © ANZ • **pp. 103, 105–7:** © Deutsche Telekom • **pp. 103, 104–5, 785–98:** © Telstra Corporation Limited • **pp. 108, 1086–7, 1135–6:** © Bayer • **pp. 110–1, 111–3, 524–7:** © Qantas Airways Limited • **p. 124:** Ernst & Young • **pp. 197, 202, 208, 219–20:** © BlueScope Steel Limited • **pp. 200, 210, 213, 214:** 'e-GAAP update No. 3/2005 (April 2005) share based payments — new and complex IFRS equivalent standard' by Colin Parker FCA (www.gaap.com.au) • **pp. 319, 424, 817:** © Accounting Standards Board Ltd (ASB). Reproduced with the kind permission of the Financial Reporting Council. All rights reserved • **pp. 324, 577, 593, 671, 673, 675, 676, 677, 685–6, 690–1, 731–5:** © BHP Billiton • **p. 364:** From 'Internally generated intangible assets: framing the discussion' by E Jenkins & W Upton, *Australian Accounting Review*, Vol. 11, No. 2 © 2001. Reproduced with the permission of CPA Australia Ltd • **p. 365, 369, 379, 382:** From *Intangible: management, measurement and reporting* by Baruch Lev, The Brookings Institution Press, Washington DC, 2001 • **pp. 366, 812, 813, 1077–8, 1152:** Portions of various documents, copyright by the Financial Accounting

Standards Board, 401 Merritt 7, PO Box 5116, Norwalk, CT 06856-5116, USA, are reproduced with permission. Complete copies of these documents are available from the FASB • **pp. 381, 385, 479–9:** © Swatch Group • **pp. 394–5:** 'Hail the "age of access"' by David James, *BRW*, 27 April 2001. Reproduced with the permission of Journalists Copyright and Fairfax • **p. 395** 'Assets: standard deviation part two' by Nick Tabakoff, *BRW*, 21 May 1999 © Nick Tabakoff/Fairfax • **pp. 395–7:** 'Sporting glory — the great intangible' by Rosalind Whiting & Kyla Chapman, *Australian CPA*, February 2003, pp. 24–7 • **p. 398:** From 'A history of most popular brands' by Sue Peacock, *The West Australian*, 14 February 2004, p. 73 • **pp. 1136–7:** © Amalgamated Holdings Limited • **pp. 415, 416:** © Danisco • **pp. 424–5:** From *Accounting for identifiable intangibles and goodwill* by Ken Leo & Jennie Radford, ASCPA, Melbourne © 1995. Reproduced with the permission of CPA Australia Ltd • **pp. 426–8:** Graphs and accompanying text from 'SFAS 141: the first 5 years. The S&P 100's reporting of acquired intangible assets 2002–2007' © Intangible Business Limited. Reproduced with permission • **p. 499:** © Deloitte Touche Tohmatsu • **p. 499:** EFRAG — European Financial Reporting Advisory Group • **p. 553:** From 'Bunnings to sell, lease back $200m of stores' by Cathy Bolt, *The West Australian*, 17 February 2007 • **pp. 566–7:** Reproduced by permission of Ernst & Young (EYGM Limited) © 2009 EYGM Limited. All rights reserved • **pp. 570–1:** © Rio Tinto • **pp. 572–3:** © BP International Limited • **p. 576:** © Woodside Energy Ltd • **pp. 631–2:** From 'Extract from the EECS's database of enforcement decisions', April 2007 © CESR • **pp. 633–4:** © Lighthouse Caledonia Ltd • **pp. 635–6, 636–8:** © Foster's Group Limited • **p. 672:** © Dresdner Bank Group • **pp. 764–6:** © Queensland Cotton • **p. 1060:** © The American Accounting Association • **p. 1064:** *Advanced accounting*, second edition, by Jeter & Chaney, Copyright © 2004 John Wiley & Sons, Inc. Reprinted with the permission of John Wiley & Sons, Inc. • **pp. 1151, 1153, 1154, 1156:** All ASB material is reproduced by kind permission of the Accounting Standards Board UK. For further information please visit www.frc.org.uk/asb or call +44 20 7492 2300 • **pp. 1179, 1180** Copyright 1978 by AICPA, reproduced with permission. Opinions of the authors are their own and do not necessarily reflect the policies of the AICPA.

Every effort has been made to trace the ownership of copyright material. Information that will enable the publisher to rectify any error or omission in subsequent editions will be welcome. In such cases, please contact the Permissions Section of John Wiley & Sons Australia, Ltd.

Part 1

Framework

1 The IASB and its conceptual *Framework*

LEARNING OBJECTIVES

When you have studied this chapter, you should be able to:

- understand the structure of the IASB and its standard-setting role
- understand the purpose of a conceptual framework — who uses it and why
- explain the difference between general purpose financial statements and special purpose financial reports
- understand the IASB's current objectives of general purpose financial statements and proposed changes to these objectives
- explain the qualitative characteristics of information in the current conceptual framework and proposed changes to these characteristics
- define the basic elements in financial statements — assets, liabilities, equity, income and expenses
- understand the principles for recognising the elements of financial statements
- understand the accrual basis and going concern assumptions
- be aware of the various bases for measuring the elements of financial statements.

1.1 THE INTERNATIONAL ACCOUNTING STANDARDS BOARD (IASB)

The purpose of this section is to provide an understanding of the structure of the IASB and its role in the determination of International Financial Reporting Standards (IFRSs). Much of this information has been obtained from the website of the IASB www.iasb.org. To keep up to date with what the IASB is doing, this website should be regularly visited, along with the Deloitte IAS Plus website www.iasplus.com.

1.1.1 Formation of the IASB

In 1972, at the 10th World Congress of Accountants in Sydney Australia, a proposal was put forward for the establishment of an International Accounting Standards Committee (IASC). In 1973, the IASC was formed, with nine countries — Canada, the United Kingdom, the United States, Australia, France, Germany, Japan, the Netherlands and Mexico — sponsoring the committee. By December 1998, the membership of the IASC had expanded and the committee had completed its core set of accounting standards.

However, the IASC was seen as having a number of shortcomings:

- It had weak relationships with national standard setters; this was due in part to the fact that the representatives on the IASC were not representative of the national standard setters but rather of national professional accounting bodies.
- There was a lack of convergence between the IASC standards and those adopted in major countries, even after 25 years of trying.
- The board was only part time.
- The board lacked resources and technical support.

In 1998, the committee responsible for overseeing the operations of the IASC began a review of the IASC's operations. The results of the review were recommendations that the IASC be replaced with a smaller, full-time International Accounting Standards Board (IASB). In 1999, the IASC board approved the constitutional changes necessary for the restructuring of the IASC. A new International Accounting Standards Committee Foundation was established and its trustees appointed. By early 2001, the members of the IASB and the Standards Advisory Council (SAC) were appointed, as were technical staff to assist the IASB.

The IASB initially adopted the International Accounting Standards, with some modifications, as issued by the IASC. As standards were revised or newly issued by the IASB, they were called International Financial Reporting Standards. Hence, the term 'IFRS' includes both IFRS and IAS accounting standards, as well as interpretations.

1.1.2 The standard-setting structure of the IASB and the IASC Foundation

Available on the IASB website is a document entitled *IASB and the IASC Foundation: Who we are and what we do*. The document states that the structure is an 'independent standard-setting board (IASB), appointed and overseen by a geographically and professionally diverse group of Trustees (IASC Foundation) who are accountable to the public interest, supported by an external advisory council (SAC) and an interpretations committee (IFRIC) to offer guidance where divergence in practice occurs'. This structure can be seen diagrammatically in figure 1.1.

1.1.3 Objectives of the IASC Foundation and the IASB

The constitution of the IASC Foundation was first approved in March 2000 by the board and the members of the former IASC. The constitution requires the trustees of the foundation to review the constitution every five years. Under the current constitution, paragraph 2 sets out the following objectives of the IASC Foundation:

(a) to develop, in the public interest, a single set of high quality, understandable and enforceable global accounting standards that require high quality, transparent and comparable information in financial statements and other financial reporting to help participants in the world's capital markets and other users make economic decisions;

(b) to promote the use and rigorous application of those standards;
(c) in fulfilling the objectives associated with (a) and (b), to take account of, as appropriate, the special needs of small and medium-sized entities and emerging economies; and
(d) to bring about convergence of national accounting standards and International Accounting Standards and International Financial Reporting Standards to high quality solutions.

The duties of the trustees are set out in paragraph 15 of the Constitution, and include:

- appointing the members of the IASB
- appointing the members of the International Financial Reporting Interpretations Committee (IFRIC) and the Standards Advisory Council (SAC)
- approving the budget of the IASC Foundation.

The key responsibilities of the IASB are then to develop and issue IFRSs and approve the interpretations of IFRIC.

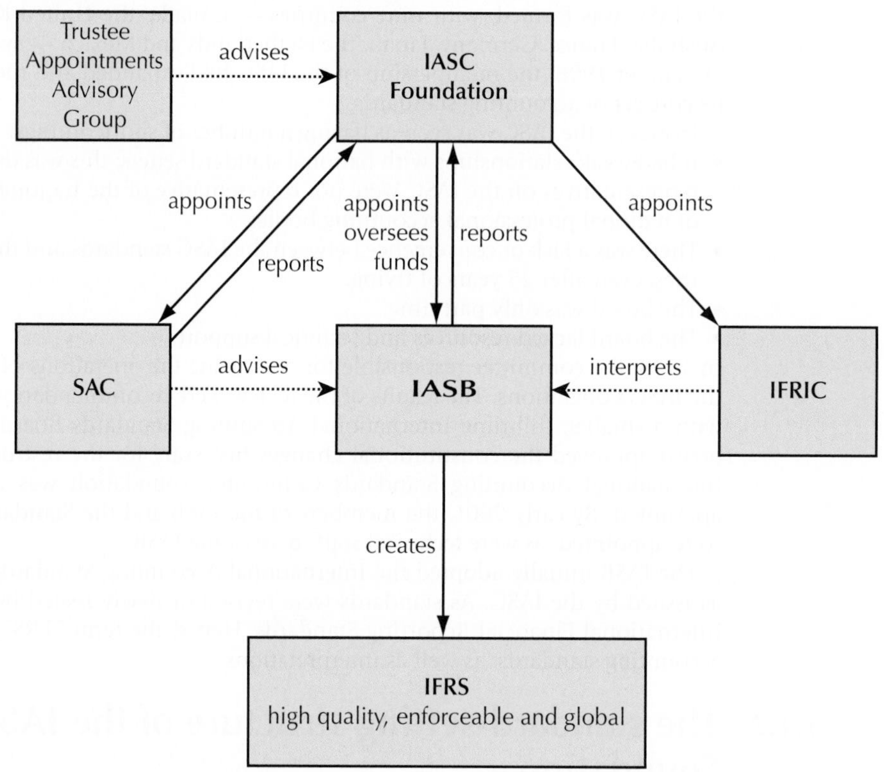

FIGURE 1.1 The IASB and the IASC Foundation
Source: www.iasb.org.

1.1.4 Role of the IASB

Paragraphs 18–32 of the IASC Foundation's constitution deal with matters relating to the IASB. Some key parts of these paragraphs are outlined in the sections below.

Membership and voting

- The IASB shall comprise 14 members of whom 12 will be full-time members.
- The main qualifications for membership shall be professional competence and practical experience.
- The mix of members will not be based on geographical criteria, but the trustees will ensure that the IASB is not dominated by any particular constituency or geographical interest.
- The IASB should comprise a mix of people with recent practical experience among auditors, preparers, users and academics.

As at January 2009, the IASB members were as follows:

Sir David Tweedie (Chairman)	Scotland
Thomas E Jones	USA
Professor Mary E Barth (part-time)	USA
Stephen Cooper (part-time)	UK
Philippe Danjou	France
Jan Engström	Sweden
Gilbert Gélard	France
Robert P Garnett	South Africa
James J Leisenring	USA
Warren McGregor	Australia
John Smith (part-time)	USA
Tatsumi Yamada	Japan
Zhang Wei-Guo	China

- The IASB is expected to liaise with national standard setters and other official bodies to promote the convergence of national accounting standards and IFRSs.
- Each member of the IASB has one vote. In the event of a tied vote, the chairman has an additional casting vote.
- The publication of an exposure draft, IAS, IFRS or interpretation requires the approval by nine of the 14 members of the IASB. Other decisions of the IASB, such as the publication of a discussion paper, are decided based on a majority vote at a meeting attended by at least 60% of the members.

Due process

The constitution in paragraph 31 requires the IASB to:
- publish an exposure draft (ED) on all projects
- normally publish a discussion paper for public comment on major projects
- consider holding public hearings to discuss proposed standards
- consider undertaking field tests, both in developed countries and in emerging markets to ensure that proposed standards are practicable and workable in all environments.

In March 2006, the trustees approved the publication of the booklet *Due Process Handbook for the IASB*, which is downloadable from the IASB website. In an address to the European Parliament in April 2008, the chairman of the trustees, Mr Gerrit Zalm, a former deputy prime minister and minister of finance in the Netherlands, noted that the IASB had taken the following steps to enhance its due process and accountability. It:

- broadcasts over the Internet all of its meetings and meetings of its working groups
- posts on its Website enhanced observer notes to enable interested parties to follow the IASB's deliberations
- provides a minimum of one year between the approval and the required application of new IFRSs or major amendments to IFRSs
- emphasises consultation through the increased use of discussion papers, working groups, and longer comment periods
- has introduced feedback statements, impact assessments and two-year post-implementation reviews, and provides greater oral feedback to interested parties.

In preparing the IFRSs, the IASB has complete responsibility for all technical matters including the preparation and issuing of standards and exposure drafts, including any dissenting opinions on these, as well as final approval of interpretations by IFRIC. The IASB has full discretion over its technical agenda and over the assignment of projects, potentially to national standard setters. The authoritative text of the work of the IASB is that published by the IASB in the English language.

IASB meetings are normally held every month and last between three and five days. The meetings are open to the public. Interested parties can attend the meetings in person, or may listen and view the meeting via the IASB webcast. Subsequent to each meeting, the decisions are summarised in the form of a publication called *IASB Update* which is available on the IASB website www.iasb.org.

1.1.5 International Financial Reporting Interpretations Committee (IFRIC)

Paragraphs 33–37 of the IASC Foundation constitution deal with the role of IFRIC. IFRIC shall comprise 14 voting members appointed by the trustees. The members will comprise a group of people who are the 'best available combination of technical expertise and diversity of international business and market experience in the practical application of International Financial Reporting Standards (IFRSs) and analysis of financial statements prepared in accordance with IFRSs'. The chairman, who may be a member of the IASB or senior member of the technical staff, has a right to participate in IFRIC's discussion but no right to vote. Each IFRIC member has one vote, and approval of interpretations requires that not more than four voting members vote against the final interpretation.

The specific role of IFRIC is detailed in paragraph 37 of the constitution:

(a) interpret the application of International Accounting Standards (IASs) and International Financial Reporting Standards (IFRSs) and provide timely guidance on financial reporting issues not specifically addressed in IASs and IFRSs, in the context of the IASB *Framework*, and undertake other tasks at the request of the IASB;
(b) in carrying out its work under (a) above, have regard to the IASB's objective of working actively with national standard-setters to bring about convergence of national accounting standards and IASs and IFRSs to high quality solutions;
(c) publish after clearance by the IASB Draft Interpretations for public comment and consider comments made within a reasonable period before finalising an Interpretation; and
(d) report to the IASB and obtain the approval of nine of its members for final Interpretations.

In January 2007, the trustees approved the publication of the booklet *Due Process Handbook for the IFRIC* which is downloadable from the IASB website. This booklet details:

- identification of issues
- setting the agenda
- IFRIC meetings and voting
- development of a draft interpretation
- the IASB's role in the issue of a draft interpretation
- the comment period and deliberation
- the IASB's role in an interpretation.

1.1.6 Standards Advisory Committee (SAC)

Paragraphs 38–40 of the constitution deal with the role of the SAC. Paragraph 38 states the purpose of the SAC:

> Provides a forum for participation by organisations and individuals, with an interest in international financial reporting, having diverse geographical and functional backgrounds, with the objective of:
> (a) giving advice to the IASB on agenda decisions and priorities in the IASB's work,
> (b) informing the IASB of the views of the organizations and individuals on the Council on major standard-setting projects, and
> (c) giving other advice to the IASB or the Trustees.

The SAC shall have 30 or more members with a diversity of geographical and professional backgrounds. Members are appointed for renewable terms of three years by the trustees. The SAC should meet at least three times a year, and meetings are open to the public. The chairman of the SAC must be independent of the IASB and its staff.

The current *Terms of Reference and Operating Procedures* of the SAC were proposed by the SAC on 7 July 2004 and approved by the trustees in March 2005. This document is downloadable from the IASB website.

1.1.7 Adoption of IFRSs around the world

Figure 1.2 contains a diagram from the IASB website at August 2008 showing the adoption of IFRSs on a worldwide basis. As the IASB's website notes in regards to the diagram: 'More than 100 countries now require or permit the use of IFRSs or are converging with the International Accounting Standards Board's (IASB) standards. The picture below shows the level of IFRS adoption at present. Darker areas indicate countries that require or permit IFRSs. Lighter areas are countries seeking convergence with the International Accounting Standards Board (IASB) or pursuing adoption of IFRSs.'

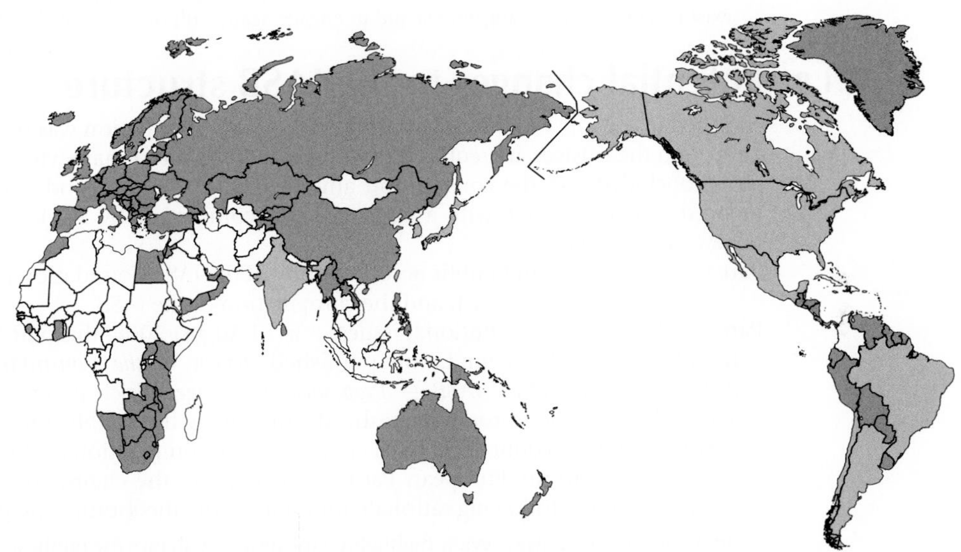

FIGURE 1.2 Adoption of IFRSs on a worldwide basis
Source: www.iasb.org. Map redrawn by MAPgraphics Pty Ltd.

In his address to the European Parliament in April 2008, the chairman of the trustees, Mr Gerrit Zalm, made the following comments on the adoption of IFRSs on a worldwide basis:

> When I joined the Trustees, I characterized the IASC Foundation's work as a romantic project. Although accounting is not frequently associated with romantic thoughts, I can think of no other international body that has come so far in setting a global standard. As the latest financial crisis demonstrates, the world's capital markets are linked together, and IFRSs can play a powerful role in providing transparency and comparability for investors, public authorities, and other participants in the world's capital markets. For me, this was and is a project worth pursuing.
>
> The progress has been steady. More than 100 countries have agreed to require or permit the adoption of International Financial Reporting Standards (IFRSs) or have established timelines towards the adoption of IFRSs. I have been struck by the speed of change. In the last year, Brazil, Canada, China, and India have all committed to formal timelines to adopt IFRSs, and Japan established 2011 as its target for convergence to IFRSs.
>
> What has been equally encouraging — and even surprising — has been the openness of attitude of the United States towards IFRSs. In November 2007, the US Securities and Exchange Commission (SEC) agreed to eliminate the reconciliation requirement, with immediate effect, for those non-US companies using IFRSs as prepared by the IASB. At the same time, the SEC is giving serious consideration to a proposal to permit US companies to use IFRSs. While the SEC is still in the process of considering this proposal, I believe that it is reasonable to expect that US companies will be permitted to use IFRSs in the near future.
>
> For me, as a European and a former Finance Minister involved with the adoption of IFRSs in the European Union, this is a proud moment. The European Union's strategy to adopt an international standard, rather than a particularly European one, has been validated. Not too long ago, some Americans would say, 'If you wanted to adopt a widely accepted international accounting standard, then adopt US GAAP.' Now, the view is quite the opposite. The United States, even the US standard-setter,

is calling for the adoption of IFRSs, not on the basis that it will be US GAAP under another name, but on the basis it remains a principles-based set of standards instead of a more rules-based system. This is a major shift.

The IASB and its counterpart in the United States also deserve credit for the progress made on the Memorandum of Understanding (MoU), without which the change in US attitudes would not be possible. The IASB is only halfway through its MoU work, and to fulfill our end of the agreement, the work on the MoU must continue. The Trustees are committed to providing the IASB with the necessary resources to complete the MoU work.

The advances in IFRS adoption in Europe, the United States, and elsewhere mean that the IASC Foundation operates in a different world from the one that it faced in May 2000 when it inherited its original Constitution. As we prepare to embark on the organisation's second Constitution Review, we see it as an opportunity for the Trustees, to assess the continued appropriateness and relevance of the existing governance arrangements and to engage again with our key stakeholders.

1.1.8 Potential changes to the IASB structure

As noted in section 1.4, the constitution of the IASC Foundation was originally approved in May 2000, and the trustees are required to undertake a constitutional review every five years. Changes were concluded and the constitution amended in 2005. A second constitutional review commenced in January 2008 with a target date for completion by 2010. The trustees have split the review into two parts:

Part 1: Governance and public accountability of the IASC Foundation (including the creation of a monitoring group), and the composition of the IASB.

Part 2: Remaining constitutional issues — as of August 2008, this part had not been started.

In July 2008, IASC Foundation published *Review of the Constitution: Public Accountability and the Composition of the IASB — Proposals for Change*, which is downloadable from the IASB website. The two major proposals in this document are the establishment of a monitoring group to increase public accountability, and changes in the composition of the IASB.

In his address to the European Parliament in 2008, the chairman of the trustees, Mr Gerrit Zalm, provided the following rationale for establishing the monitoring group.

> In particular, the strategy review highlighted the need to enhance the public accountability of the IASC Foundation, if the IASB were to become the world's accounting standard-setter, a clear organisational objective. As a European and former politician like you, I can understand why you find it unusual that a body overseen by a self-appointed group of Trustees, but not formally reporting to any public authority, is de facto setting law in Europe and elsewhere. Furthermore, as parliamentarians, you have no ability to amend the standards that come before you.
>
> Indeed, members of the European Parliament face the same situation as parliamentarians and national regulators throughout the world when it comes to the adoption of IFRSs. One of my chief objectives as Chairman of the Trustees is to avoid future carve-outs of IFRSs. To address the 'peculiar' situation that I described, on an operational level, the Trustees and the IASB are seeking to engage key interested parties, including the members of the European Parliament, at the earliest stages possible in a consultation.

He then gave the following details concerning the monitoring group.

> More importantly from a systemic level, we Trustees are recommending the establishment of a Monitoring Group to end the practice of self-appointment and to create a formal link to public authorities, including the European Commission. The establishment of such a link is aimed at providing public authorities greater comfort with our governance arrangements and operations. Specifically, we are recommending the creation of the Monitoring Group, along with a proposal to increase the size of the IASB and add a geographical element to its composition, as one of the two issues to be fast-tracked as part of the Constitution Review.
>
> Under the new Monitoring Group arrangement, the governance of the IASC Foundation would remain with the Trustees, and the responsibilities of the Trustees and the independence of the standard-setting function, as laid out in the existing Constitution, would remain fundamentally unchanged.
>
> However, this Monitoring Group, a representative group of public officials responsible for the adoption and promotion of IFRSs throughout the world's capital markets, would have a monitoring function to ensure that the Trustees are fulfilling their constitutional obligations and that the selection of Trustees is conducted in an appropriate and transparent manner.
>
> The Monitoring Group would be responsible for approving the selection of Trustees after an agreed nominations process administered by the IASC Foundation. The Trustees or a subgroup of the Trustees shall meet the Monitoring Group at least once annually, and more frequently as appropriate. The Monitoring Group will also have the authority to request meetings with the Trustees or separately with

the chairman of the Trustees (with the chairman of the IASB, as appropriate) regarding any area of work of either the Trustees or the IASB.

At these meetings, the Trustees would report to the Monitoring Group regularly to enable it to verify that the Trustees are fulfilling the requirements set out in the Constitution.

This would include a review of Trustee procedures for:

- appointing members to the IASB
- reviewing the strategy of the IASC Foundation and the IASB and its effectiveness, including consideration, but not determination, of the IASB's agenda
- reviewing the IASB's compliance with its operating procedures, consultative arrangements and due process
- ensuring the adequacy of the financing arrangements for the IASB and other IASC Foundation activities.

Our proposal for the composition of the Monitoring Group that we are putting forward for consultation is as follows:

- the responsible member of the European Commission,
- the managing director of the International Monetary Fund,
- the chair of the IOSCO Emerging Markets Committee,
- the chair of the IOSCO Technical Committee (or deputy chair in cases where either the Chairman of the Japan Financial Services Agency or Chairman of the US Securities and Exchange Commission is the chair of the IOSCO Technical Committee),
- the chairman of the Japan Financial Services Agency,
- the chairman of the US Securities and Exchange Commission, and
- the president of the World Bank

Of course, we will be open to the Committee's input and comments of other parties on the appropriate composition, as well as other aspects, of the Monitoring Group.

However, I believe that it is essential for the group's credibility that participation remains at the highest levels at public authorities responsible for the adoption of IFRSs throughout the world.

His comments on changes to the composition of the IASB were as follows.

When it comes to the IASB, the Trustees still believe that the Constitution's emphasis on 'professional competence and practical experience' is appropriate. However, to account for the growing acceptance of IFRSs, we are also recommending the expansion of the IASB to 16 members.

The expansion to 16 is justified on the following grounds:

- IASB members needed for liaison: As the IASB becomes the global standard-setter, the liaison and communications task for IASB members continues to grow. This needs to be shared broadly, while permitting time for IASB members to work with staff and relevant internal working groups in developing international accounting standards.
- Diversity as providing legitimacy: While professional competence (particularly technical expertise) and practical experience are the foremost criteria for IASB selection, the diversity of IASB members (professional and geographical) provides legitimacy in the eyes of many who adopt the standards.
- Diversity as enabling new perspectives: The introduction of IASB members from different backgrounds has enabled the IASB to account for issues that may not have been raised in the past.

In expanding the IASB to 16 members, the Trustees believe that the Constitution should also reflect in a positive manner the need for a broad geographical spread of the IASB's membership, like that defined for the Trustees. At the same time, the Constitution should provide sufficient flexibility to account for emerging economies and changing economic weight. Therefore, the Trustees are proposing that the 16 members be distributed in the following manner:

- four IASB members from the Asia/Oceania region;
- four IASB members from Europe;
- four IASB members from North America; and
- four IASB members appointed from any area, subject to maintaining overall geographical balance.

The establishment of clear geographic minimums will give further assurance that the distribution of IASB members will remain balanced in the future.

Further publications on changes to the constitution should be followed by reviewing the IASB website www.iasb.org.

1.2 THE CONCEPTUAL *FRAMEWORK* OF THE IASB

In 1989 the International Accounting Standards Committee (IASC), the predecessor to the IASB, adopted the *Framework for the Preparation and Presentation of Financial Statements* (hereafter referred to as the *Framework*). In 2001, the IASB 're-adopted' the *Framework*.

1.2.1 Purpose and status of the *Framework*

The *Framework* describes the basic concepts that underlie financial statements prepared in conformity with International Financial Reporting Standards. The *Framework* serves as a guide to the IASB in developing IFRSs and as a guide to resolving accounting issues that are not addressed directly in an IFRS.

However, the *Framework* is not itself a standard. Therefore, it does not define principles for any particular accounting recognition, measurement or disclosure matter. Nor does the *Framework* override any specific IASB standard if there appears to be a conflict. The *Framework*:

- defines the objective of financial statements
- identifies the qualitative characteristics that make information in financial statements useful
- defines the basic elements in financial statements and the concepts for recognising and measuring them in financial statements.

1.2.2 How is the *Framework* used?

Since the *Framework* is not a standard, who uses it and how do they use it? The *Framework* has a variety of uses.

1. Most importantly, the *Framework* guides the IASB in deliberating and establishing IFRSs and interpretations of these standards. In the absence of a framework, each board member inevitably would debate accounting standards questions premised on his or her own professional experience — their personal frameworks. Unfortunately, as in any debate, different premises can lead to different equally logical conclusions. For example, a board member who felt that accounting should smooth earnings volatility to help financial analysts assess long-term trends might favour a deferral-and-amortisation approach for certain kinds of costs. Another board member, however, who felt that assets must have clear future benefits in terms of expected cash flows to the entity might reject a deferral-and-amortisation approach. Both board members would have logic on their side. The difference, of course, is in the premises to their reasoning. The *Framework* provides a set of 'givens' in the debate over accounting standards. The members of the IASB change from time to time. New board members have an obligation to accept the *Framework* as a given or, if they disagree with some aspects of the *Framework*, to work to change these aspects.
2. Basing a set of accounting standards on the underlying *Framework* helps ensure that the body of standards is internally consistent, at least to the maximum extent possible. For instance, one of the things the *Framework* does is define the basic elements in financial statements — assets, liabilities, equity, income and expenses. When an accounting issue that comes before the IASB involves whether to accrue a provision (liability and related expense) for a contingency of uncertain amount or timing — such as a pending lawsuit — the *Framework* definition of a liability becomes a 'given', and the debate should centre on whether the particular contingency in question meets the agreed definition of a liability.
3. Preparers and auditors of financial statements use the *Framework* as a point of reference to resolve an accounting question in the absence of a standard or interpretation that specifically deals with the question. It is not possible for any set of accounting standards to provide clear answers to all accounting questions — and certainly not a principles-based body of accounting standards such as that promulgated by the IASB. Judgement is required in answering specific questions that the standards do not address. The *Framework* establishes boundaries for the exercise of judgement in preparing financial statements.
4. The *Framework* establishes precise terminology by which people can discuss accounting questions. To illustrate, agreement on the definition of 'liability' helps in deciding whether things known variously as obligations, commitments, contingencies, provisions, accruals and the like qualify for recognition as liabilities in the statement of financial position. Consider a company that has chosen to self-insure for fire losses. (Self-insure means the company has decided to retain all or some portion of its risk of loss from fire damage to its property rather than to pay an insurance premium for an insurance company to take on the risk.) Assume that an uninsured fire loss is expected to occur once every three years, and the first year goes by without a loss. An accounting question arises as to whether it is appropriate for the company to accrue one-third of the estimated loss as an expense of the first year and as a liability at the end of the first year. Without a conceptual framework, the company might well analyse the question in

terms of earnings volatility. If the once-in-every-three-years fire loss is recognised in its entirety in measuring profit in the year it occurs, with no loss recognised in the other two years, earnings will appear volatile. Wishing to avoid reporting earnings volatility, the company might conclude that accrual of one-third of the expected fire loss as an expense and a year-end obligation for the loss is appropriate in the first year. By defining the elements in financial statements rigorously, the *Framework* focuses the debate on whether the obligation meets the definition of a liability. (Incidentally, accruals for self-insured losses that have not yet happened would fail the test for liability under the existing *Framework* because the *Framework* defines a liability in terms of a present obligation arising from a past event. In the case of our self-insured company, the loss event would be an actual fire. A loss event has not yet occurred by the end of the first year, so there is no liability under the *Framework* at that date. Simply put, the entity does not owe anything to anyone.)

5. The *Framework* reduces the volume of standards. Without the *Framework*, each accounting question would have to be answered ad hoc, and there would be pressure from the preparers, auditors and users of financial statements for more detailed standards. The *Framework* provides direction for resolving questions without the need for increasingly specific standards.
6. By providing parameters for the exercise of judgement, the *Framework* reduces the need for interpretations and other detailed implementation guidance.
7. By adding rigour and discipline, the *Framework* enhances public confidence in financial statements. Users of financial statements make comparisons, and comparability is diminished if financial statement preparers use their own judgement on an ad hoc, company-by-company basis. No matter how well intentioned that judgement may be, financial statements can lose credibility if they lack a conceptual underpinning.

1.2.3 Authority of the *Framework*

The IASB addressed the role of the *Framework* in its *Preface to International Financial Reporting Standards*, adopted by the board in May 2002:

> IFRSs are based on the Framework, which addresses the concepts underlying the information presented in general purpose financial statements. The objective of the Framework is to facilitate the consistent and logical formulation of IFRSs. The Framework also provides a basis for the use of judgement in resolving accounting issues (para. 8).

Further, the preface described the due process steps that the IASB follows in developing an International Financial Reporting Standard. Step one noted in the preface is:

> The staff are asked to identify and review all of the issues associated with the topic and to consider the application of the Framework to the issues (para. 18(a)).

Despite these benefits, can preparers and auditors of financial statements choose to ignore it since it is not a standard? Until recently, the *Framework* might appropriately have been called 'non-binding'. According to paragraph 16 of IAS 1 *Presentation of Financial Statements*:

> An entity whose financial statements comply with IFRSs shall make an explicit and unreserved statement of such compliance in the notes. An entity shall not describe financial statements as complying with IFRSs unless they comply with all the requirements of IFRSs.

Because the *Framework* is not mentioned in that requirement of IAS 1, some people concluded that it lacked authority. Whether that view was ever accurate, it is certainly no longer the case. As a result of the inclusion of the following two paragraphs to IAS 8 *Accounting Policies, Changes in Accounting Estimates, and Errors*, the IASB clarified that the *Framework* cannot be ignored. IAS 8 is an authoritative, binding standard, and it states that the *Framework* is the first place to which a preparer or auditor must look in the absence of a specific standard or interpretation:

> 10. In the absence of an IFRS that specifically applies to a transaction, other event or condition, management shall use its judgement in developing and applying an accounting policy that results in information that is:
> (a) relevant to the economic decision-making needs of users; and
> (b) reliable, in that the financial statements:
> (i) represent faithfully the financial position, financial performance and cash flows of the entity;

(ii) reflect the economic substance of transactions, other events and conditions, and not merely the legal form;
(iii) are neutral, that is, free from bias;
(iv) are prudent; and
(v) are complete in all material respects.

11. In making the judgement described in paragraph 10, management shall refer to, and consider the applicability of, the following sources in descending order:
(a) the requirements in IFRSs dealing with similar and related issues; and
(b) the definitions, recognition criteria and measurement concepts for assets, liabilities, income and expenses in the *Framework*.

It should be noted that the IASB and the Financial Accounting Standards Board (FASB) in the United States are currently undertaking a joint project to develop a common conceptual framework for financial reporting. Whereas the IASB gives certain authority to the *Framework*, as outlined above, the FASB's Concepts Statements have the same authoritative status as accounting textbooks and journal articles. The boards have not yet reached a consensus on the eventual authority to be given to the revised conceptual framework, although agreement has been reached on the view that the framework will not override the accounting standards.

1.2.4 Background to development of the conceptual framework

As noted earlier, the IASB *Framework* was approved by the IASC board in April 1989 for publication in July 1989, and adopted by the IASB in April 2001. The IASB has not yet put its own stamp on the conceptual underpinnings of its own standards. The IASB is currently involved in a joint project with the FASB in the United States to revise the conceptual framework for both boards.

Proposed changes to the *Framework* as a result of the IASB's joint project with the FASB to amend the conceptual framework are also referred to in this chapter. The overall objective of this joint project between the FASB and the IASB is to develop a common conceptual framework that is both complete and internally consistent. The boards want to develop a framework that will provide a sound foundation for developing future accounting standards that are principles-based, internally consistent, internationally converged, and lead to financial reporting that provides the information needed for investment, credit and similar decisions. The improved conceptual framework, which will deal with a wide range of issues, will build on the existing IASB and FASB frameworks and consider developments since the boards issued their original framework documents.

1.3 GENERAL PURPOSE FINANCIAL STATEMENTS

The *Framework* addresses general purpose financial statements, which are the financial statements that an entity prepares and presents at least annually to meet the common information needs of a wide range of users external to the entity. Therefore, the *Framework* does not necessarily apply to special purpose financial reports such as reports to regulatory agencies or financial institutions.

The *Framework,* as developed by the IASB, focuses on the financial statements of business entities, which would include both privately owned and state-owned business entities. The *Framework* does not necessarily apply to the financial statements of governments, government non-business units or other not-for-profit entities, although most of the concepts in the *Framework* would seem to be equally relevant to those types of entities.

The *Framework* in paragraph 6 acknowledges that some parties who use the general purpose financial statements of an entity may have the power to obtain information in addition to that contained in the financial statements. For example, a major lender often can negotiate to obtain whatever special information it deems necessary to make its lending decision. Nonetheless, that major lender still has a use for the general purpose financial statements After all, lenders are bankers, not accountants, and even a lender with clout is likely to look to the accounting standard setters to define the accounting principles and presentation formats on which borrowers' financial statements should be based. Furthermore, many present and potential investors, creditors, vendors, and others who seek financial information about the entity do not have the same power as the major lender to get special information. They must rely on the general purpose financial statements to meet their information needs.

1.4 OBJECTIVES OF GENERAL PURPOSE EXTERNAL FINANCIAL REPORTING

Another important step in developing the conceptual framework was to determine the objective of financial reporting. The IASB's *Framework* deals only with the objective of general purpose external financial statements, i.e. financial statements intended to meet the information needs common to a range of users who are unable to command the preparation of reports tailored to satisfy their own particular needs.

The main objective of general purpose external financial reporting is 'to provide information useful to users for making and evaluating decisions on the allocation of scarce resources'. A second objective is that reports should be presented by management and governing bodies in such a manner as to discharge their accountability for the resources entrusted to them. The *Framework*, paragraph 12, states the objective of financial statements as follows:

> The objective of financial statements is to provide information about the financial position, financial performance and cash flows of an entity that is useful to a wide range of users in making economic decisions.

The *Framework* lists users and their needs under seven categories:

- *investors and their advisers*, who need information to help them decide whether to buy, hold or sell their risky investments, such as shares
- *employees and their representative groups*, who are interested in the stability and profitability of their employers as well as their ability to provide employment opportunities and to pay wages, leave packages and retirement benefits
- *lenders*, who need information as to the entity's ability to repay loans and interest when due
- *suppliers and other trade creditors*, who are interested in knowing whether the entity will be able to pay amounts owing when due
- *customers*, who have an interest in whether the entity will continue in the long term
- *governments and their agencies*, who are interested in the activities of the entity as well as its ability to pay taxes
- *the public*, especially if the entity makes a substantial contribution to the local economy.

1.4.1 Financial position

One of the objectives of financial statements is to provide information about an entity's financial position:

- What assets does the entity own?
- What does it owe?
- What are the residual equity interests in the entity's net assets?

The financial position of an entity is affected by the economic resources it controls, its financial structure (proportion of equity to liabilities), its liquidity and solvency (ability to pay its debts), and its capacity for adaptation (ability to convert assets to cash, and so adapt to changes in its environment). The statement of financial position presents this kind of information.

1.4.2 Performance

Performance is the ability of an entity to earn a profit on the resources that have been invested in it. Information about the amount and variability of profits helps in forecasting future cash flows from the entity's existing resources and in forecasting potential additional cash flows from additional resources that might be invested in the entity.

The *Framework* in paragraph 19 states that information about performance is primarily provided in a statement of comprehensive income, but that explanation is somewhat out of date. IAS 1 (revised after the *Framework* was written) added a fourth basic financial statement, the statement showing changes in equity. It is important to look to both the statement of comprehensive income and the statement of changes in equity in assessing performance because several IFRSs provide that certain items of income and expense should be reported directly in equity. These items are recognised in the statement of comprehensive income, reported after the disclosure of the profit for the period. Examples of income and expense items required by the accounting standards to be reported initially directly in equity are shown on the next page.

- Changes in fair value of available-for-sale financial assets (investments in equity and debt securities) are reported directly in equity until the financial asset is sold, at which time the cumulative fair value change is removed from equity and flowed through the statement of comprehensive income (IAS 39 *Financial Instruments: Recognition and Measurement*).
- Under IAS 16 *Property, Plant and Equipment*, subsequent to initial recognition, property, plant and equipment assets may be measured using either the cost model or the revaluation model. Under the revaluation model, major classes of property, plant and equipment (such as land, buildings and equipment) are remeasured to fair value at each reporting date, with changes in fair value taken directly to a 'revaluation reserve' and the increments and decrements reported in other comprehensive income.
- Foreign currency translation adjustments arising when the financial statements of a foreign operation are translated from the foreign currency into the reporting company's currency are reported directly in equity under IAS 21 *The Effects of Changes in Foreign Exchange Rates*.

An entity's performance is of particular interest to equity investors (shareholders) and providers of long-term debt capital. For them, the statement of comprehensive income and the statement of changes in equity are paramount, because the company's ability to provide a return on their capital investment depends on the company's operating performance, not on its current bank account and near-term collections of receivables. On the other hand, short-term creditors (vendors, suppliers, employees and so on) are generally more interested in current financial condition and liquidity, so they are more likely to focus on the statement of financial position and statement of cash flows.

1.4.3 Changes in financial position

Users of financial statements seek information about the sources and uses of an entity's cash and cash equivalents such as bank deposits during the reporting period. Cash comes into and goes out of an entity from three broad categories of activity: its operations (producing and selling its goods and services), its investing activities (buying and selling long-lived assets and financial investments), and its financing activities (raising and repaying debt and equity capital). The statement of cash flows provides this kind of information. In a sense, the statement of comprehensive income and the statement of changes in equity analyse changes in the equity section of the statement of financial position while the statement of cash flows provides insight into changes in all of the other line items in the statement of financial position.

Ultimately, all investors, creditors, and other capital providers to an entity want to get cash out of their investment. They can do that in various ways. They receive cash when they receive dividend or interest payments. They receive cash when the principal on their debt investments is paid when due. They receive cash when their receivables are paid off. They receive cash when they sell their investment securities. The statement of cash flows helps them assess the prospects of receiving cash from the entity.

Investors can even receive cash without selling their investments by using their securities as collateral on borrowings. In that case, the one who lends to the investor is interested in the entity's prospects of generating cash because that affects the liquidity of the collateral.

1.4.4 Notes and supplementary schedules

The financial statements also contain notes and supplementary schedules and other information that (a) explain items in the statement of financial position and statement of comprehensive income, (b) disclose the risks and uncertainties affecting the entity, and (c) explain any resources and obligations not recognised in the statement of financial position. The notes also sometimes contain information that meets disclosure requirements arising under national laws or regulations.

The *Framework* does not spell out a list of specific topics that should be covered in the notes to an entity's financial statements. No single standard does that, although many individual standards require specific items of disclosure.

1.4.5 Exposure draft May 2008 — The objective of financial reporting

In May 2008, the IASB and FASB jointly issued *Exposure Draft of An improved Conceptual Framework for Financial Reporting: Chapter 1: The Objective of Financial Reporting, Chapter 2: Qualitative Characteristics and Constraints of Decision-useful Financial Reporting Information*.

Paragraph OB2 of the ED states the objective of general purpose financial reporting:

> The objective of general purpose financial reporting is to provide financial information about the reporting entity that is useful to present and potential equity investors, lenders and other creditors in making decisions in their capacity as capital providers. Information that is decision-useful to capital providers may also be useful to other users of financial reporting who are not capital providers.

In reaching this conclusion, the boards made a number of key decisions:

- Financial statements should reflect the perspective of the entity rather than the perspective of the entity's equity investors. The focus is then on the entity's resources and the changes in them rather than on the shareholders as owners of the entity. Shareholders are providers of resources as are those who provide credit resources to the entity. Under the entity perspective, the reporting entity is deemed to have substance of its own, separate from that of its owners (ED, para. BC1.12).
- The key users of financial statements are capital providers — investors and lenders. As noted in paragraph OB6 of the ED, an entity obtains economic resources from capital providers in exchange for claims on those resources. Because of these claims, capital providers have the most critical and immediate need for economic information about the entity. These parties also have common information needs. The focus on these users of information, as opposed to other potential users such as government, regulatory bodies, employees and customers is a narrowing of the user groups in comparison to the groups considered in the current *Framework*. As noted in paragraph BC1.18 of the ED, the boards concluded that specifying a group of primary users provided a focus for the objective and the remainder of the conceptual framework. Absence of such a focus could result in a framework that was abstract and vague.
- Capital providers require information that is decision-useful. As noted in paragraph OB9 of the ED, the decisions made by capital providers are:
  - how to allocate resources to a particular entity
  - how to protect or enhance their investments
  - assessment of the entity's ability to generate net cash flows
  - assessment of management's ability to protect and enhance the capital providers' investments — this includes the stewardship role of management, and management's responsibilities including protecting the entity's resources from unfavourable economic events such as price changes and technological and social change.

Before the objective of general purpose external financial reporting can be implemented in practice, the basic qualitative characteristics of financial reporting information need to be specified. It is also necessary to define the basic elements — assets, liabilities, equity, income and expenses — used in financial statements. These aspects of the conceptual framework are considered next.

1.5 QUALITATIVE CHARACTERISTICS OF FINANCIAL REPORTING INFORMATION

1.5.1 The current *Framework*

What characteristics should financial information have to be included in general purpose external financial statements? The current *Framework* asserts that there are four main qualitative characteristics that information should have to be selected as the subject matter of general purpose financial statements: relevance, reliability, comparability and understandability. It is also pointed out that these qualitative characteristics may need to be balanced against one another. The relative importance of the characteristics in different cases is a matter of professional judgement.

Note that much of the thinking in the current *Framework* regarding qualitative characteristics has been made compulsory via the issue of IAS 8 discussed below. The desired qualitative characteristics of financial reporting information as contained in the current *Framework* can be expressed diagrammatically as in figure 1.3.

Relevance

To have *relevance*, financial information must have a quality that influences users' economic decisions by (a) helping them to form predictions about the outcomes of past, present or future events, and/or (b) confirming or correcting their past evaluations. In other words, for information to be relevant, it must have *predictive value*, and/or *feedback value* in the sense that it confirms or denies past assessments by the user. Note that having predictive value does not mean that the financial information must be in the form of an explicit forecast or budget.

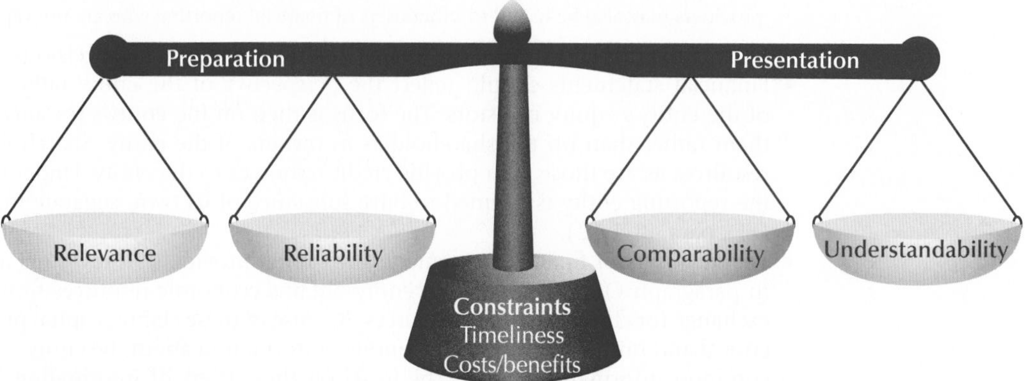

FIGURE 1.3 Qualitative characteristics of financial reporting information, discussed in the current *Framework*

The *Framework* points out that information about financial position and past performance is often used as the basis for predicting future financial position and performance and other matters in which users are directly interested, such as future dividends and wage payments, future share prices, and the ability of the reporting entity to pay its debts when they fall due. The predictive ability of information may be improved if unusual or infrequent transactions and events are reported separately in the statement of comprehensive income.

For information to be relevant, its nature and *materiality* must also be considered. In some cases, the nature of the information alone is enough to determine its relevance, such as money lost through embezzlement by staff. In other cases, both the nature and materiality are important. The *Framework* states that information is material if its omission or misstatement has the potential to adversely affect the economic decisions made by users of a particular set of general purpose financial statements, or the rendering of accountability by preparers.

Any assessment of materiality needs to be made in relation not only to individual items but also to classes of similar items. For instance, errors in individual items may be immaterial by themselves, but material in aggregate. A practical aspect to materiality is the immediate expensing of small costs incurred for the purchase of assets on the grounds that the amount paid is not significant enough to affect decisions. Small expenditures for non-current assets, for example, tools, are often expensed immediately, rather than depreciated over their useful lives, to save the clerical costs of recording depreciation and because the effects on performance and financial position measures over their useful lives are not large enough to affect decisions. Another example of the application of materiality is the common practice by large companies of rounding amounts to the nearest thousand dollars in their financial statements.

Materiality is a relative matter: what is material for one entity may be immaterial for another. A \$10 000 error may not be important in the financial statements of a multimillion-dollar company, but it may be critical to a small business. The materiality of an item may depend not only on its relative size but also on its nature. For example, the discovery of a \$10 000 bribe is a material event even for a large company. Judgements as to the materiality of an item or event are often difficult. Accountants make judgements based on their knowledge of the company and on past experience, and users of financial statements must generally rely on the accountants' judgements.

It is argued in the *Framework* that materiality is not a primary qualitative characteristic, which information must have if it is to be useful. Rather, materiality provides a threshold or cut-off point in determining whether information is relevant for inclusion in financial statements.

Reliability

Information is reliable if it is free from material error and bias and able to be depended on to represent faithfully the transactions or events that it claims to represent or is reasonably expected to represent. An important consequence of the reliability characteristic is the establishment of minimum criteria before assets, liabilities, income and expenses can be recognised in financial statements. Such criteria for recognising these elements place great importance on reliable measurement. Without such measurement, information cannot be considered free from bias, that is, neutral, or be a faithful representation of the transactions and events that have occurred.

Generally, information that is reliable is supported by adequate evidence, such as source documents (e.g. contracts, purchase orders, invoices or cheques). However, lack of documentary evidence is not a sufficient reason to ignore measurement in some cases. Examples of difficulties in measurement arise in the cases of internally generated intangible assets and underground mineral, oil or gas reserves. It is important that information included in general purpose external financial statements is a faithful representation of the transactions and events being reported. This means that, to balance relevance and reliability, disclosure of the uncertainties surrounding the information should help to avoid the risk of error by users.

If financial information is to be reliable, it is important that the substance rather than the form of transactions or events is reported. In considering substance over form, the *Framework* argues that the accountant must be concerned more with the economic substance rather than the legal form of a transaction. For example, certain types of equipment leases are to be handled in the accounting records as if the entity had purchased the items rather than acquiring them under a lease. In substance, the transaction is treated and reported as a purchase of the item even though legal ownership of the item may never be contemplated.

Sometimes, a concept of prudence has been discussed in accounting literature as a desirable characteristic of financial information. This concept is explained in terms of a desire to exercise care and caution when dealing with uncertainties in the measurement process. Consequently, the accountant is cautious not to overstate assets and profits and not to understate liabilities and expenses. In the *Framework*, prudence is included in the concept of reliability.

Comparability

In the presentation of general purpose external financial statements, users need to be able to compare aspects of an entity over time, and between entities at one time and over time. Comparability is more effective when different entities use the same accounting practices. The *Framework* states that an important implication of the qualitative characteristic of comparability is that users will be informed of the accounting policies used in the preparation of the financial statements, plus any changes to those policies and the effect of those changes. This implies the measurement and reporting of transactions and events with consistency over time and between entities.

Alternative accounting policies exist in the treatment of many items, such as inventories and cost of sales, non-current assets and depreciation, intangible assets such as patents, copyrights and goodwill, and leasing transactions. The standard setters have expressed their position regarding the consistency of accounting methods in accounting standard IAS 8 *Accounting Policies, Changes in Accounting Estimates and Errors*, which states that an entity must select and apply its accounting policies in a consistent manner from one period to another. Consistency of practices between entities is also desired. Any change made in an accounting policy by an entity must be disclosed by stating the nature of the change, the reasons the change provides reliable and more relevant information, and the effect of the change in monetary terms on each financial statement item affected. For example, a change in policies may be disclosed in a note such as this:

> During the year, the company changed from the first-in first-out to the weighted average cost method of accounting for inventory because the weighted average cost method provides a more relevant measure of the entity's financial performance. The effect of this change was to increase cost of sales by $460 000 for the current financial year.

Note that the need for consistency does not require a given accounting method to be applied throughout the entity. An entity may very well use different inventory methods for different types of inventory and different depreciation methods for different kinds of non-current assets. (Different inventory costing and depreciation methods are discussed in later chapters.) Furthermore, the need for consistency should not be allowed to hinder the introduction of better accounting methods. Consistency from year to year or entity to entity is not an end in itself, but a means for achieving greater comparability in the presentation of information in general purpose financial statements. The need for comparability should not be confused with mere uniformity or consistency. It is not appropriate for an entity to continue to apply an accounting policy if the policy is not in keeping with the qualitative characteristics of relevance and reliability.

Understandability

When information is included in general purpose external financial statements, it is obvious that the users of those reports must be able to comprehend their meaning; hence, the *Framework* lists the final qualitative characteristic of financial statements to be understandability. Understandability, however, does not necessarily imply simplicity. It is assumed that readers of reports have a reasonable knowledge of business and economic activities and accounting, and that they are willing to study the information with reasonable diligence. The *Framework* makes it clear that information about complex matters should still be included if it is considered relevant to the decision-making needs of users, even if it is too difficult for some users to understand. If users find that the information is too complex for their understanding, it is expected they will seek professional help and advice.

Constraints on relevant and reliable information

The *Framework* also suggests that there are two constraints which must be imposed on the preparation of relevant and reliable information.

The first of these is *timeliness*. Information may lose its relevance if there is an undue delay in reporting it. Hence, the time taken to gather and report financial information is seen as a constraint on providing relevant information. The need for timely reporting raises a question about the frequency of reports (yearly, half-yearly, quarterly) and also the length of time that can be allowed between the end of the reporting period and the publication of general purpose external financial statements for users. Any delays in publication cause the information in these reports to be less relevant.

The second constraint is *costs versus benefits*. This means weighing up the costs incurred in generating the information against the benefits to be obtained from having the information. Costs are incurred in collection, storage, retrieval, presentation, analysis and interpretation, and loss of competitive position, most of which are incurred by the reporting entity. Nevertheless, these costs will generally flow in a number of direct and indirect ways to other parties, such as consumers. The benefits are enjoyed directly by parties external to the entity, namely shareholders, investors and creditors. There is little chance that the costs of preparation will be borne ultimately by all those parties who enjoy the benefits.

Assessing whether the costs of reporting outweigh or fall short of the benefits is difficult to measure, and becomes a matter for professional judgement by preparers, standard setters and regulators. The cost versus benefits constraint is also a consideration in determining the reporting requirements for different entities. For example, the cost of compliance with a particular accounting standard may not be burdensome for a large company, but may be excessive for a smaller entity. Hence, we need to ask whether there should be differential reporting requirements. This has been the policy of the regulators to some extent in the past. For example, differential reporting requirements are a feature of current accounting standards, in that application of the standards applies mainly to those entities classified as reporting entities. In the case of external reporting by companies, accounting standards apply mainly to public companies and large proprietary companies.

1.5.2 Exposure draft May 2008 — Qualitative characteristics and constraints on decision-useful financial reporting information

In chapter 2 of the exposure draft, the objective of general purpose financial reporting is determined to be providing decision-useful financial information to capital providers. Chapter 2 of the exposure draft is concerned with the attributes of that information that make it decision useful. The following discusses both the qualitative characteristics of useful information and the constraints on providing useful information. The qualitative characteristics are divided into fundamental qualitative characteristics and enhancing qualitative characteristics.

Fundamental qualitative characteristics

For financial information to be decision useful, it must possess two fundamental qualitative characteristics:

- relevance, and
- faithful representation.

Paragraph QC3 of the ED contains details about the qualitative characteristic of *relevance*:

- Information is relevant if it is capable of making a difference in the decisions made by the capital providers as users of financial information.
- Information is capable of making a difference if the information has predictive value, confirmatory value or both. Predictive value occurs where the information is useful as an input into the users' decision models and affects their expectations about the future. Confirmatory value arises where the information confirms or changes past or present expectations based on previous evaluations.
- To be capable of making a difference, it is not necessary that the information has actually made a difference in the past or will make a difference in the future. Information may be capable of making a difference whether the users use it or not.

Paragraph QC7 of the ED contains information about *faithful representation*. Faithful representation is attained when the depiction of an economic phenomenon is complete, neutral, and free from material error. This results in the depiction of the economic substance of the underlying transaction. Note the following in relation to these characteristics:

- A depiction is *complete* if it includes all information necessary for faithful representation.
- *Neutrality* is the absence of bias intended to attain a predetermined result. Providers of information should not influence the making of a decision or judgement to achieve a predetermined result.
- As information is provided under conditions of uncertainty and judgements must be made, there is not necessarily certainty about the information provided. It may be necessary to disclose information about the degree of uncertainty in the information in order that the disclosure attains faithful representation.

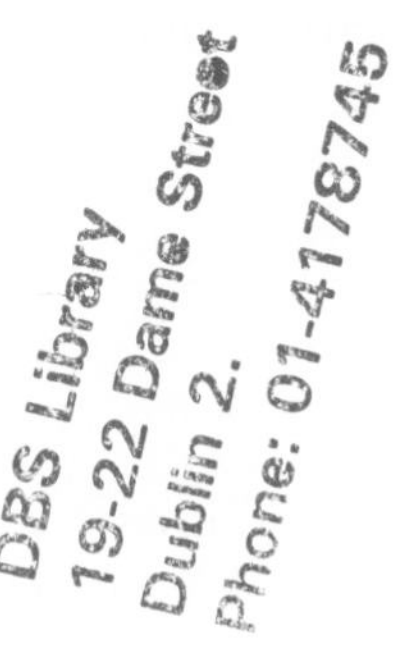

Whereas the current *Framework* places emphasis on reliability as a key qualitative characteristic, the ED proposes the use of faithful representation. As explained in paragraph BC2.13 of the ED, the boards noted that there are a variety of notions as to what is meant by reliability. The boards believe that the term faithful representation provides a better understanding of the quality of information required.

As explained in paragraphs QC12–QC14 of the ED, relevance is concerned with the relationship between the economic phenomena and the decisions of capital providers. Relevance is not concerned with how the information is depicted in the financial statements. Once the criterion of relevance is applied to information to determine which economic information should be contained in the financial statements, the criterion of faithful representation is applied to determine how to depict those phenomena in the financial statements. The two characteristics work together. Either irrelevance (the economic phenomenon is not connected to the decision to be made) or unfaithful representation (the depiction is not decision useful) results in information that is not decision useful.

Enhancing qualitative characteristics

The ED provides four enhancing qualitative characteristics: comparability, verifiability, timeliness and understandability. These characteristics are *complementary* to the fundamental characteristics. The enhancing characteristics distinguish *more useful* information from *less useful* information (ED, para. QC15). In relation to these enhancing qualities, note:

- *Comparability* is the quality of information that enables users to identify similarities in and differences between two sets of economic phenomena. Making decisions about one entity may be enhanced if comparable information is available about similar entities — for example, profit for the period per share.
- *Verifiability* is a quality of information that helps assure users that information faithfully represents the economic phenomena that it purports to represent. Verifiability is achieved if different independent observers could reach the same general conclusions that the information represents the economic phenomena or that a particular recognition or measurement model has been appropriately applied.
- *Timeliness* means having information available to decision makers before it loses its capacity to influence decisions. If such capacity is lost, then the information loses its relevance. Information may continue to be timely after it has been initially provided, for example, in trend analysis.
- *Understandability* is the quality of information that enables users to comprehend its meaning. Information may be more understandable if it is classified, characterised and presented clearly and concisely. As noted in paragraph QC24 of the ED, users of financial statements are assumed

to have a reasonable knowledge of business and economic activities and to be able to read a financial report.

Constraints

Paragraph QC27 of the ED notes two constraints that limit the information provided by financial reporting: materiality and cost.

1. Information is *material* if its omission or misstatement could influence the decisions that users make on the basis of an entity's financial information. Material requires judgement by the preparer of the information.
2. The provision of information requires *costs* to be incurred. The benefits of supplying information should always be greater than the costs. Costs include costs of collecting and processing information, costs of verifying information, and costs of disseminating information. The non-provision of information also imposes costs on the users of financial information as they seek alternative sources of information.

Materiality is considered, for example, when determining whether some information has sufficient predictive or confirmatory value. In assessing the costs and benefits of some information, a decision may be made to sacrifice one or more of the qualitative characteristics to some degree to reduce the cost.

Figure 1.4 provides a diagrammatical representation of the qualitative characteristics and constraints proposed in the exposure draft.

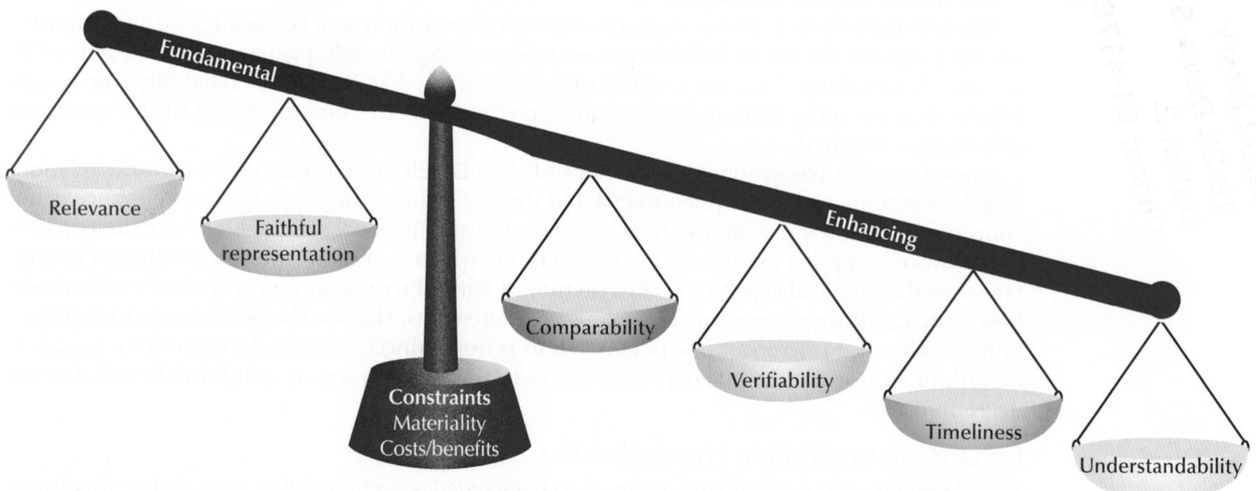

FIGURE 1.4 Qualitative characteristics and constraints proposed in the exposure draft (May 2008)

1.6 DEFINITIONS OF ELEMENTS IN FINANCIAL STATEMENTS

The current *Framework* provides definitions of important elements underlying financial statements, namely assets, liabilities, equity, income and expenses.

1.6.1 Assets in the current *Framework*

An *asset* is defined in paragraph 49(a) of the current *Framework* as 'a resource controlled by the entity as a result of past events and from which future economic benefits are expected to flow to the entity'. This definition identifies three essential characteristics of an asset:

1. The resource must contain *future economic benefits*; that is, it must have the potential to contribute, directly or indirectly, to the flow of cash and cash equivalents to the entity. An asset can cause future economic benefits to flow to the entity in a number of ways:
   - it can be exchanged for another asset

- it can be used to settle a liability
- it can be used singly or in combination with other assets to produce goods or services to be sold by the entity.

2. The entity must have *control* over the future economic benefits in such a way that the entity has the capacity to benefit from the asset in the pursuit of the entity's objectives, and can deny or regulate the access of others to those benefits.
3. There must have been a *past event*; that is, an event or events giving rise to the entity's control over the future economic benefits must have occurred.

An asset may have other characteristics, but the *Framework* does not consider them essential for an asset to exist. For instance, assets are normally acquired at a cost incurred by the entity, but it is not essential that a cost is incurred in order to determine the existence of an asset. Similarly, it is not essential that an asset is tangible, that is, has a physical form (see para. 56 of the *Framework*). Assets such as receivables, brands, copyrights and patents represent future economic benefits without the existence of any physical substance. Such assets may be classified as intangible assets. Furthermore, assets can be exchanged normally for other assets, but this does not make exchangeability an essential characteristic of an asset. Finally, it is not essential that an asset is legally owned by the reporting entity. Control by the entity often results from legal ownership, but the absence of legal rights or ownership does not preclude the existence of control, for example, a lease (see para. 57 of the *Framework*).

1.6.2 Assets in the proposed framework

Following discussions between the IASB and the FASB, several shortcomings were identified with the existing definition of an asset (see the Conceptual Framework Project Update on the FASB website www.fasb.org for more details):

- The existing definitions place too much emphasis on identifying the future flow of economic benefits, instead of focusing on the item that presently exists, an economic resource.
- Some users misinterpret the term 'control' and use it in the same sense as that used for purposes of consolidation accounting. The term should focus on whether the entity has some rights or privileged access to the economic resource.
- The definitions place undue emphasis on identifying the past transactions of events that gave rise to the asset, instead of focusing on whether the entity had access to the economic resource at the reporting date.

The current working definition of an asset being considered by the IASB and FASB is (see Project Update 28/07/08):

> An asset of an entity is a present economic resource to which, through an enforceable right or other means, the entity has access or can limit the access of others.

This definition places emphasis not only on the existence of a present economic resource but also on the need for an enforceable right that limits the access of others to that resource. Thus, it is expected that assets will be seen in future more in the context of legally enforceable rights to the resource. Some further terms being considered to amplify the asset definition are:

- *Present* means both the economic resource *and* the enforceable right or other means by which the entity has access or can limit the access of others exist on the date of the financial statements.
- An *economic resource* is something that is scarce and capable of producing cash inflows or reducing cash inflows, directly or indirectly, alone or together with other economic resources.
- An *enforceable right* is legally enforceable or enforceable by equivalent means (such as by a professional association). It enables the entity to use the present economic benefit directly or indirectly, and precludes or limits its use by others.

1.6.3 Liabilities in the current *Framework*

A *liability* is defined in paragraph 49(b) of the current *Framework* as 'a present obligation of the entity arising from past events, the settlement of which is expected to result in an outflow from the entity of resources embodying economic benefits'. There are a number of important aspects concerning this definition:

- A legal debt constitutes a liability, but a liability is not restricted to being a legal debt. Its essential characteristic is the existence of a *present obligation*, being a duty or responsibility of the entity to act or perform in a certain way. A present obligation may arise as an obligation imposed by notions of equity or fairness (referred to as an 'equitable' obligation), and by custom or normal business practices (referred to as a 'constructive' obligation), as well as those resulting from legally enforceable contracts. For example, an entity may decide as a matter of policy to rectify faults in its products even after the warranty period has expired. Hence, the amounts that are expected to be spent in respect of goods already sold are liabilities.

It is not sufficient for an entity merely to have an intention to sacrifice economic benefits in the future. A present obligation needs to be distinguished from a future commitment. A decision by management to buy an asset in the future does not give rise to a present obligation. An obligation normally arises when the asset is delivered, or the entity has entered into an irrevocable agreement to buy the asset, with a substantial penalty if the agreement is revoked.

- A liability must result in the *giving up of resources* embodying economic benefits that require settlement in the future. The entity must have little, if any, discretion in avoiding this sacrifice. This settlement in the future may be required on demand, at a specified date, or when a specified event occurs. Thus, a guarantee under a loan agreement is regarded as giving rise to a liability in that a sacrifice is required when a specified event occurs, for example, default under the loan.

  Settlement of a present obligation may occur in a number of ways:
  - by paying cash
  - by transferring other assets
  - by providing services
  - by replacing that obligation with another obligation
  - by converting that obligation to equity
  - by a creditor waiving or forfeiting his or her rights.
- A final characteristic of a liability is that it must have resulted from a *past transaction* or event. For example, the acquisition of goods and the work done by staff give rise to accounts payable and wages payable respectively. Wages to be paid to staff for work they will do in the future is not a liability as there is no past transaction or event and no present obligation.

1.6.4 Liabilities in the proposed framework

In the FASB conceptual framework Project Update 28/07/2008 (see www.fasb.org), the following shortcomings of the current definition of a liability are listed:

- Some users misinterpret the term 'expected' to mean that there must be a high likelihood of future outflow of economic benefits for the definition to be met; this excludes liability items with a low likelihood of a future outflow of economic benefits.
- The definition places too much emphasis on identifying the future outflow of economic benefits, instead of focusing on the item that presently exists, an economic obligation.
- The definitions place too much emphasis on identifying the past transactions or events that gave rise to the liability, instead of focusing on whether the entity has an economic obligation at the reporting date.
- It is unclear how the definition applies to contractual obligations.

The proposed working definition of a liability is:

> A liability of an entity is a present economic obligation that is enforceable against the entity.

One of the key areas of debate will be the level of enforceability — is it restricted to legal means or can it include moral or social ties, thus including equitable and constructive obligations as well as legal obligations? Currently the boards refer to 'legal or equivalent means'. Unless equivalent compulsion is clearly defined, some users may find it difficult to distinguish legal compulsion from economic compulsion. Possibly one way of viewing whether a liability exists is to note that every liability is the asset of another entity or entities. If another entity cannot recognise an asset, then a liability to that entity does not exist.

1.6.5 Equity in the current *Framework*

Paragraph 49(c) of the *Framework* defines *equity* as 'the residual interest in the assets of the entity after deducting all its liabilities'. Defining equity in this manner shows clearly that it cannot be defined independently of the other elements in the statement of financial position. The characteristics of equity are as follows:

- Equity is a residual, that is, something left over. In other words:

$$\text{Equity} = \text{Assets} - \text{Liabilities}$$

- Equity increases as a result of profitable operations, that is, the excesses of income over expenses, and by contributions by owners. Similarly, equity is diminished by unprofitable operations and by distributions to owners (drawings and dividends).
- Equity is influenced by the measurement system adopted for assets and liabilities and by the concepts of capital and capital maintenance adopted in the preparation of general purpose external financial statements. (These aspects are discussed later in the chapter.)
- Equity may be subclassified in the statement of financial position, for example, into contributed funds from owners, retained earnings, other reserves representing appropriations of retained earnings, and reserves representing capital maintenance adjustments.

At the time of writing, the IASB/FASB has not proposed a new definition of equity. On 28 February 2008, the IASB published *Discussion Paper: Financial Instruments with Characteristics of Equity* that includes the FASB's November 2007 document *Preliminary Views: Financial Instruments with Characteristics of Equity*. That document details three approaches to distinguishing equity instruments and non-equity instruments, but the IASB has not yet formed any preliminary views.

1.6.6 Income in the current *Framework*

The *Framework* defines *income* in paragraph 70(a) as:

> Increases in economic benefits during the accounting period in the form of inflows or enhancements of assets or decreases of liabilities that result in increases in equity, other than those relating to contributions from equity participants.

Note that this definition of income is linked to the definitions of assets and liabilities. The definition of income is wide in its scope, in that income in the form of inflows or enhancements of assets can arise from providing goods or services, investing in or lending to another entity, holding and disposing of assets, and receiving contributions such as grants and donations. To qualify as income, the inflows or enhancements of assets must have the effect of increasing equity, excluding capital contributions by owners. Also excluded are certain increases in equity under various inflation accounting models that require the recognition of capital maintenance adjustments.

Another important aspect of the definition is that, if income arises as a result of an increase in economic benefits, it is necessary for the entity to *control* that increase in economic benefits. If control does not exist, then no asset exists. Income arises once control over the increase in economic benefits has been achieved and an asset exists, provided there is no equivalent increase in liabilities. For example, in the case of magazine subscriptions received in advance, no income exists on receipt of the cash because an equivalent obligation also has arisen for services to be performed through supply of magazines to clients in the future.

Income can exist also through a reduction in liabilities that increase the entity's equity. An example of a liability reduction is if a liability of the entity is 'forgiven'. Income arises as a result of that forgiveness, unless the forgiveness of the debt constitutes a contribution by owners.

Under the current *Framework*, income encompasses both revenue and gains. A definition of revenue is contained in paragraph 7 of IAS 18 *Revenue* as follows:

> The gross inflow of economic benefits during the period arising in the course of the ordinary activities of an entity when those inflows result in increases in equity, other than increases relating to contributions from equity participants.

Thus revenue represents income which has arisen from 'the ordinary activities of an entity'. On the other hand, *gains* represent income that does not necessarily arise from the ordinary activities of the entity; for example, gains on the disposal of non-current assets or on the revaluation of marketable securities. Gains are usually disclosed in the statement of comprehensive income net of any related expenses, whereas revenues are reported at a gross amount. As revenues and gains are both income, there is no need to regard them as separate elements under the *Framework*.

At the time of writing, no proposals have come from the IASB/FASB to amend the definition of income.

1.6.7 Expenses in the current *Framework*

Paragraph 70(b) of the *Framework* contains the following definition of *expenses*:

> Expenses are decreases in economic benefits during the accounting period in the form of outflows or depletions of assets or incurrences of liabilities that result in decreases in equity, other than those relating to distributions to equity participants.

To qualify as an expense, a reduction in an asset or an increase in a liability must have the effect of decreasing the entity's equity. The purchase of an asset does not decrease equity and therefore does not create an expense. An expense arises whenever the economic benefits in the asset are consumed, expire or are lost. Like income, the definition of expenses is expressed in terms of changes in assets, liabilities and equity. This concept of expense is broad enough to encompass items that have typically been reported in financial statements as 'losses', for example, losses on foreign currency transactions, losses from fire, flood, etc., or losses on the abandonment of a research project. Losses are expenses that may not arise in the ordinary course of the entity's activities.

At the time of writing, no proposals have come from the IASB/FASB to amend the definition of expenses.

1.7 RECOGNITION OF THE ELEMENTS

There are recognition criteria to be followed in the preparation and presentation of financial statements in practice. These criteria have been set down as part of the *Framework*. *Recognition* means the process of incorporating in the statement of financial position or statement of comprehensive income an item that meets the definition of an element. In other words, it involves the inclusion of dollar amounts in the entity's accounting system. Note that an item must satisfy the definition of an element before it is 'recognised'.

1.7.1 Asset recognition in the current *Framework*

The *Framework* states in paragraph 89 that an asset should be recognised in the statement of financial position when it is probable that the future economic benefits will flow to the entity and the asset has a cost or other value that can be measured reliably. Consideration of the definition of an asset, as discussed in section 1.6.1, helps to determine whether an asset exists. Here, emphasis is placed on criteria for determining *when to record* an asset in the entity's accounting records. An asset is to be recognised only when both the probability and the reliable measurement criteria are satisfied. The term 'probability' refers to the degree of certainty that the future economic benefits will flow to the entity. The benefits should be more likely rather than less likely. For example, some development costs are not recognised as an asset because it is not 'probable' that future economic benefits will eventuate.

Even if such probability of future benefits is high, recognition of an asset cannot occur unless some cost or other value is capable of reliable measurement. Without such a measurement, the qualitative characteristic of 'reliability' will not be achieved. In practice, reliable measurement of internally generated goodwill has been difficult, and therefore such goodwill has not been recognised as an asset. Similarly, reliable measurement of an entity's mineral reserves is difficult. It is argued in the *Framework* that assets that cannot be measured reliably may nevertheless be disclosed in notes to the financial statements, particularly if knowledge of the item is considered relevant to evaluating the entity's financial position, performance and cash flows.

1.7.2 Asset recognition in the proposed framework

At the time of writing, this issue has not been clarified. However, because 'reliability' is being replaced by 'faithful representation' and 'verifiability', asset recognition criteria will change. It is expected that the measurement of an asset will need to be a faithful representation of the economic phenomena, and that the measurement must be verifiable.

1.7.3 Liability recognition in the current *Framework*

Once the existence of a liability has been established in accordance with the definition as discussed in section 1.6.3, criteria must then exist for the recognition of a liability in an entity's accounting records. The *Framework* paragraph 91 states that a liability is recognised in the statement of financial position when it is probable that an outflow of resources embodying economic benefits will result from settling the present obligation and the amount at which the settlement will take place can be measured reliably.

As with the recognition of assets, 'probable' means that the chance of the outflow of economic benefits being required is likely. The additional need for reliable measurement is an attempt to measure, in monetary terms, the amount of economic benefits that will be sacrificed to satisfy the obligation. Any liabilities that are not recognised in the accounting records because they do not satisfy the recognition criteria may be disclosed in notes to the financial statements, if considered relevant. Further discussion of the recognition of liabilities is provided in chapter 4.

1.7.4 Liability recognition in the proposed framework

At the time of writing, this issue has not been clarified. However, because 'reliability' is being replaced by 'faithful representation' and 'verifiability', liability recognition criteria will change. It is expected that the measurement of a liability will need to be a faithful representation of the economic resources given up, and that the measurement must be verifiable.

1.7.5 Income recognition in the current *Framework* and standards

In accordance with the *Framework* paragraph 92, income is recognised in the statement of comprehensive income when an increase in future economic benefits relating to an increase in an asset or a decrease in a liability can be measured reliably.

As with the recognition criteria for assets and liabilities, probability of occurrence and reliability of measurement are presented as the two criteria for income recognition. For many entities, the majority of income in the form of revenues results from the provision of goods and services during the reporting period. There is little uncertainty that the income has been earned since the entity has received cash or has an explicit claim against an external party as a result of a past transaction. However, the absence of an exchange transaction often raises doubts as to whether the income has achieved the required degree of certainty. In situations of uncertainty, the *Framework* requires the income to be recognised as long as it is 'probable' that it has occurred and the amount can be measured reliably.

As stated previously, income includes both revenues and gains. The standard setters have provided further requirements for the recognition of revenues in accounting standard IAS 18 *Revenue*, which deals with the recognition of different types of revenue that can arise in an entity. The standard requires all revenue recognised in the entity's financial statements to be measured at the fair value of the consideration received or receivable. Separate recognition criteria are then provided for each different category of revenue. See chapter 3 for a detailed discussion of revenue recognition.

1.7.6 Income recognition in the proposed framework

At the time of writing, this issue has not been clarified. However, because 'reliability' is being replaced by 'faithful representation' and 'verifiability', recognition criteria for all types of income including revenues and all contributions and government grants will change. It is expected that the measurement of an item of income will need to be a faithful representation of the appropriate economic phenomena, and that the measurement must be verifiable.

In addition, the IASB and FASB have been working on a joint project to clarify revenue recognition criteria. The objective of the project is to develop a single coherent asset and liability model for revenue recognition. In such a model, revenue is a function of changes in assets and liabilities and is not based on the notions of realisation and the completion of an earnings process (FASB *Action Alert*, No. 7-44, 1 November 2007). The IASB and FASB have been considering the implications of a model focusing on contract assets and contract liabilities. Under this model, revenue is defined as an increase in a contract asset or a decrease in a contract liability that results from the provision of goods and services to a customer. Hence, revenue is recognised when:

- an entity obtains a contract in which the underlying rights exceed the underlying obligations (because this would result in a new contract asset)

- the entity subsequently satisfies its obligations in the contract by providing goods or services to the customer (because this would either increase a contract asset or decrease a contract liability).

The amount of revenue that is recognised under the model is derived from the increase in the exit price of the contract asset or decrease in the exit price of the contract liability (see IASB *Update*, November 2007).

At the time of writing, no decisions have been made with respect to revenue and revenue recognition. However, the IASB and FASB are thinking along revolutionary lines as they continue to amend and develop the conceptual framework.

1.7.7 Expense recognition in the current *Framework*

Just as the income recognition criteria have been developed in the *Framework* as a guide to the timing of income recognition, the expense recognition criteria have been developed to guide the timing of expense recognition. The formulators of the *Framework* view expenses in terms of decreases in future economic benefits in the form of reductions in assets or increases in liabilities of the entity (see the definition of expenses in section 1.6.7). In addition to the probability criteria for expense recognition, the *Framework* states that expenses are recognised in the statement of comprehensive income when a decrease in future economic benefits related to a decrease in an asset or an increase in a liability can be measured reliably. This means that an expense is recognised simultaneously with a decrease in an asset or an increase in a liability. An expense is also recognised in the statement of comprehensive income when the entity incurs a liability without the recognition of any asset, for example, wages payable.

In years past, the process of recognising expenses was referred to as a 'matching process', whereby an attempt was made to associate each cost with the income recognised in the current period. Costs that were 'associated' with the revenue were then said to be 'matched' and written off to expenses. This idea of matching expenses with income has been dropped in the *Framework* in favour of assessing the probability of a decrease in economic benefits that can be measured reliably. Matching is no longer the expense recognition criterion under the *Framework*.

1.7.8 Expense recognition in the proposed framework

At the time of writing, this issue has not been discussed in any detail. However, because 'reliability' is being replaced by 'faithful representation' and 'verifiability', recognition criteria for all types of expenses will change. It is expected that the measurement of an expense will need to be a faithful representation of the appropriate economic phenomena, and that the measurement must be verifiable. In addition, it is expected that amendments to the definition and recognition of expenses will flow from the current IASB and FASB considerations of the definition and recognition of revenue, as referred to above, in due course.

1.8 ASSUMPTIONS UNDERLYING FINANCIAL STATEMENTS

Two underlying assumptions are noted in the *Framework*, namely the accrual basis and going concern assumptions. These are also referred to in IAS 1 *Presentation of Financial Statements*, paragraphs 25–28.

1.8.1 The accrual basis assumption

The *Framework*, paragraph 22, states that the *accrual basis of accounting* is used in the preparation of general purpose external financial statements. Under this assumption, the effects of all transactions and other events are recognised in the accounting records when they occur, rather than when cash or its equivalent is received or paid. Financial statements prepared on the accrual basis inform users not only of past transactions involving the receipt and payment of cash but also of obligations to pay cash in the future and of amounts owing to the entity in the form of receivables. It is argued that the accrual basis, therefore, provides better information for users in their decision-making processes.

1.8.2 The going concern assumption

Financial statements are prepared under the assumption that the entity will continue to operate for the foreseeable future. Past experience indicates that the continuation of operations in the future is highly probable for most entities. Thus, it is assumed that an entity will continue to operate at least long enough to carry out its existing commitments. This assumption is called the *going concern assumption* or sometimes the *continuity assumption*.

Adoption of the going concern assumption has important implications in accounting. For example, it is an assumption used by some to justify the use of historical costs in accounting for non-current assets and for the systematic allocation of their costs to depreciation expense over their useful lives. Because it is assumed that the assets will not be sold in the near future but will continue to be used in operating activities, current market values of the assets are sometimes assumed to be of little importance. If the entity continues to use the assets, fluctuations in their market values cause no gain or loss, nor do they increase or decrease the usefulness of the assets. The going concern assumption also supports the inclusion of some assets, such as prepaid expenses and acquired goodwill, in the statement of financial position even though they may have little, if any, sales value.

If management intends to liquidate the entity's operations, the going concern assumption is set aside and financial statements are prepared on the basis of expected liquidation (forced sale) values. Thus, assets are reported at their expected sales values and liabilities at the amount needed to settle them immediately. Paragraph 25 of IAS 1 details disclosures required when an entity does not prepare financial statements on a going concern basis.

1.9 MEASUREMENT

Paragraph 99 of the *Framework* states that measurement is 'the process of determining the monetary amounts at which the elements of the financial statements are to be recognised and carried in the balance sheet [statement of financial position] and income statement [statement of comprehensive income]'. Because the concepts of equity, income and expenses are highly dependent on the concepts of assets and liabilities, measurement of the former depends on measurement of the latter. In other words, emphasis is placed on measuring assets and liabilities; the measurement of equity, income and expenses then follows. Measurement is very important in accounting in that it is the process by which valuations are placed on all elements reported in financial statements. Measurements thus have an important effect on the economic decisions made by users of those financial statements. The *Framework* in paragraph 100 points out that a number of different measurement bases may be used for assets, liabilities, income and expenses in varying degrees and in varying combinations in financial statements. They include the following, the most common of which, in practice, is the historical cost basis:

- *Historical cost*. Under the historical cost measurement basis, an asset is recorded at the amount of cash or cash equivalents paid or the fair value of the consideration given to acquire it at its acquisition date. Liabilities are recorded at the amount of the proceeds received in exchange for an obligation, or at the amount of cash to be paid out in order to satisfy the liability in the normal course of business.
- *Current cost*. For an asset, current cost represents the amount of cash or cash equivalents that would be paid if the same or equivalent asset was acquired currently. A liability is recorded at the amount of cash or cash equivalents needed to settle the obligation currently.
- *Realisable or settlement value*. For an asset, the realisable value is the amount of cash or cash equivalents that could be obtained currently by selling the asset in an orderly disposal, or in the normal course of business. A liability is measured as the amount of cash or cash equivalents expected to be paid to satisfy the obligation in the normal course of business.
- *Present value*. The present value of an asset means the discounted future net cash inflows or net cash savings that are expected to arise in the normal course of business. The present value of a liability is the discounted future net cash outflows that are expected to settle the obligation in the normal course of business.

As mentioned above, the measurement basis most commonly adopted by entities is the historical cost basis. Nevertheless, other bases are used from time to time. For example, to comply with IAS 2 *Inventories*, inventories are to be measured at the lower of cost and net realisable value.

The use of fair value, defined as the value determined between knowledgeable, willing buyers and sellers in an arm's length transaction, is also referred to in many accounting standards. Accounting standards that require the use of fair value in some circumstances include:

- IFRS 1 *First-time Adoption of International Financial Reporting Standards*
- IFRS 2 *Share-based Payment*
- IFRS 3 *Business Combinations*
- IFRS 5 *Non-current Assets Held for Sale and Discontinued Operations*
- IAS 11 *Construction Contracts*
- IAS 16 *Property, Plant and Equipment*
- IAS 17 *Leases*
- IAS 18 *Revenue*
- IAS 19 *Employee Benefits*
- IAS 20 *Accounting for Government Grants and Disclosure of Government Assistance*
- IAS 26 *Accounting and Reporting by Retirement Benefit Plans*
- IAS 33 *Earnings per Share*
- IAS 36 *Impairment of Assets*
- IAS 38 *Intangible Assets*
- IAS 39 *Financial Instruments: Recognition and Measurement*
- IAS 40 *Investment Property*
- IAS 41 *Agriculture.*

In November 2005, the IASB issued *Discussion Paper: Measurement Bases for Financial Accounting — Measurement on Initial Recognition* prepared by the Canadian Accounting Standards Board. On 15 September 2006, the FASB issued Statement of Financial Accounting Standards (SFAS) No. 157 *Fair Value Measurements* providing guidance on the application of fair value to measure assets and liabilities. As noted on the Deloitte IAS Plus website www.iasplus.com, some points about SFAS 157 include:

> - Fair value is the price that would be received to sell an asset or paid to transfer a liability in an orderly transaction between market participants in the market in which the reporting entity transacts.
> - Fair value should be based on the assumptions market participants would use when pricing the asset or liability.
> - FAS 157 establishes a fair value hierarchy that prioritises the information used to develop those assumptions. The fair value hierarchy gives the highest priority to quoted prices in active markets and the lowest priority to unobservable data, for example, the reporting entity's own data. Fair value measurements would be separately disclosed by level within the fair value hierarchy.
> - FAS 157 is effective for financial statements issued for fiscal years beginning after 15 November 2007, and interim periods within those fiscal years. Early adoption is permitted.

The three-level fair value hierarchy is as follows:

> **Level 1** inputs are observable inputs that reflect quoted prices for identical assets or liabilities in active markets the reporting entity has the ability to access at the measurement date.
>
> **Level 2** inputs are observable inputs other than quoted prices for identical assets or liabilities in active markets at the measurement date.
>
> **Level 3** inputs are unobservable inputs, for example, inputs derived through extrapolation or interpolation that cannot be corroborated by observable data. However, the fair value measurement objective remains the same. Therefore, unobservable inputs should be adjusted for entity information that is inconsistent with market expectations. Unobservable inputs should also consider the risk premium a market participant (buyer) would demand to assume the inherent uncertainty in the unobservable input.

In the Deloitte publication *Heads Up* (27 September 2006, Vol. 13, Iss. 12), the following information relating to the use of fair value was given:

> Statement 157 emphasizes that fair value is **market based** rather than entity specific; fair values must rest on assumptions that market participants would use in pricing the asset or liability. Thus, the optimism that often characterizes an asset owner must be replaced with the skepticism that typically characterizes a risk averse buyer.
>
> Example
>
> Company X (X) is testing land and a manufacturing facility to be held and used for the purposes of a Statement 144 impairment test. In testing the assets for recoverability under Step 1 of the impairment test, X projects the cash flows it expects to realize from operating the assets. Step 1 of the test indicates

that the carrying value of the assets is not recoverable. Company X then discounts the same cash flows (under an income approach) for Step 2 of the test and arrives at a value of $40 million. Simply using cash flows based on X's intended use of the facility may not comply with Statement 157's new definition of fair value. The new definition reminds entities that, even though they may intend to use the land and manufacturing facility for the foreseeable future, they must consider market-participant-based information, and the $40 million may not represent fair value. For example, if recent sales of comparable facilities in the area have closed at a significantly lower amount, say $30 million, the fair value of the land and buildings must consider such market-based information.

In November 2006, the IASB published *Discussion Paper: Fair Value Measurements,* setting out its preliminary views on providing consistency in the measurement of fair value. The IASB used SFAS 157 as the starting point for its deliberations. Since then the IASB has continued to debate various aspects of fair value, but, at the time of writing, the IASB has still not reached consensus on many issues relating to fair value, including whether to keep the term 'fair value' or abandon it, and whether, in measuring an exit-price fair value, the entity should take the viewpoint of the entity or that of an independent marker participant.

1.9.1 Concepts of capital

Scant attention has been given to the concept of capital in accounting in the last 30 years, but it was a topic that received considerable focus during the current value debates of the 1960s to the early 1980s. It was argued then, and now, that before an entity can determine its income for any period, it must adopt not only a measurement basis for assets and liabilities but also a concept of capital. Two main concepts of capital are discussed in the *Framework,* namely financial capital and physical capital.

Financial capital

Under the financial capital concept, capital is synonymous with the net assets or equity of the entity, measured either in terms of the actual number of calculated dollars by subtracting the total of liabilities from assets, or in terms of the purchasing power of the dollar amount recorded as equity. Profit exists only after the entity has maintained its capital, measured as either the dollar value of equity at the beginning of the period, or the purchasing power of those dollars in the equity at the beginning of the period.

Physical capital

Under the physical capital concept, capital is seen not so much as the equity recorded by the entity but as the operating capability of the entity's assets. Profit exists only after the entity has set aside enough capital to maintain the operating capability of its assets. A number of different measurement systems have been devised in the past to provide alternatives to the conventional historical cost system, which is the system predominantly used in practice.

These alternatives, which represent different combinations of the measurement of assets and liabilities and the concept of capital maintenance, include:

- the *general price level accounting system,* which had its origins in Germany after World War I when inflation reached excessive levels — this system modifies the conventional historical cost system for the effects of inflation and therefore follows a financial capital concept
- *current value systems,* which attempt to measure the changes in the current values of assets and liabilities — these systems include measures of the current buying or input prices of net assets, and/or measures of the current selling or realisable values of net assets. Capital may be measured as either financial or physical.

SUMMARY

The *Framework* describes the basic concepts that underlie financial statements prepared in conformity with International Financial Reporting Standards. It serves as a guide to the IASB in developing accounting standards and in resolving accounting issues that are not addressed directly in an accounting standard.

The *Framework* identifies the principal classes of users of an entity's general purpose financial statements and states that the objective of financial statements is to provide information — about the financial position, performance and changes in financial position of an entity — that is useful in making economic decisions. It specifies the qualities that make financial information useful, namely understandability, relevance, reliability and comparability. The *Framework* also defines the basic elements in financial statements (assets, liabilities, equity, income and expenses) and discusses the criteria for recognising and measuring them.

In recent years, the IASB has undertaken a joint project with the FASB to develop a new conceptual framework. A number of steps in this project have reached the discussion paper and exposure draft stage. Current indications are that preparers and users of financial statements can expect major changes in the conceptual framework. If these changes are sufficiently substantial it could mean subsequent major changes in many current accounting standards. This is a project to watch carefully as the underlying concepts of accounting are debated and decisions made by the standard setters.

Discussion questions

1. What is meant by 'IFRSs'?
2. Discuss why a company may consider changing to preparing its financial statements under IFRSs.
3. Discuss the due process undertaken by the IASB in preparing IFRSs.
4. Distinguish between the roles of the IASC Foundation, the IASB and the SAC.
5. Discuss the changes proposed in 2008 by the trustees of the IASC Foundation to the IASC Foundation constitution.
6. Discuss proposals in the IASB/FASB *Discussion Paper: Preliminary Views on an Improved Conceptual Framework for Financial Reporting — The Reporting Entity.*
7. Specify the objectives of general purpose external financial reporting, the nature of users, and the information to be provided to users to achieve the objectives as provided in the *Framework*.
8. Discuss the changes to the objectives of financial reporting as contained in the IASB/FASB *Exposure Draft of An improved Conceptual Framework for Financial Reporting: Chapter 1: The Objective of Financial Reporting.*
9. From the current *Framework*, outline the qualitative characteristics of financial reporting information to be included in general purpose financial statements.
10. Discuss the proposed changes to the qualitative characteristics of information contained in the IASB/FASB *Exposure Draft of An improved Conceptual Framework for Financial Reporting: Chapter 2: Qualitative Characteristics and Constraints of Decision-useful Financial Reporting Information.*
11. Discuss the importance of the accrual basis and going concern assumptions to the practice of accounting.
12. Discuss the essential characteristics of an asset as contained in the *Framework* and how these might change as a result of the IASB/FASB discussions.
13. Discuss the essential characteristics of a liability as contained in the *Framework* and how these might change as a result of the IASB/FASB discussions.
14. A government gives a piece of land to a company at no charge. The company builds a factory on the land and agrees to employ a certain number of people at the factory for a certain period of time. Considering the definition of income in the *Framework*, do you think the fair value of the land is income to the company?
15. Discuss the difference, if any, between income, revenue and gains.
16. Explain what the IASB *Framework* is and how it is used in financial reporting.
17. (a) Explain what relevance and reliability mean and the role they play in the IASB *Framework*.
    (b) Explain why an item must first meet a financial statement element's definition before we can consider that element's recognition criteria.
18. Define 'equity', and explain why the IASB does not prescribe any recognition criteria for equity.
19. In relation to the following multiple choice questions, discuss your choice of correct answer:
    (a) Which of the following statements about the IASB *Framework* is incorrect?
        (i) The *Framework* considers timeliness and materiality to be constraints on relevant and reliable information.
        (ii) The *Framework* states that the elements directly related to the measurement of financial position are assets, liabilities and equity.
        (iii) The *Framework* applies to the financial statements of all commercial, industrial and business reporting entities.

(iv) In accordance with the *Framework*, income is recognised when an increase in future economic benefits related to an increase in an asset or a decrease in a liability has arisen that can be measured reliably.

(b) The *Framework*'s four principal qualitative characteristics include:
- (i) Understandability and materiality.
- (ii) Reliability and timeliness.
- (iii) Comparability and reliability.
- (iv) Substance over form and comparability.

(c) Which of the following statements about the *Framework*'s definition of expenses is correct?
- (i) Expenses include distributions to owners.
- (ii) Expenses are always in the form of outflows or depletions of assets.
- (iii) Expenses exclude losses.
- (iv) Expenses are always decreases in economic benefits.

(d) In accordance with the *Framework*, a lender should recognise the forgiveness of its $20 000 interest-free loan as:
- (i) An increase in income and a decrease in a liability.
- (ii) An increase in an expense and a decrease in an asset.
- (iii) An increase in an asset and an increase in income.
- (iv) An increase in an expense and a decrease in a liability.

STAR RATING

★ BASIC

★★ MODERATE

★★★ DIFFICULT

Problems

Problem 1.1 ★

RELEVANT INFORMATION FOR AN INVESTMENT COMPANY

A year ago you bought shares of stock in an investment company. The investment company in turn buys, holds and sells shares of business enterprises. You want to use the financial statements of the investment company to assess its performance over the past year.

(a) What financial information about the investment company's holdings would be most relevant to you?

(b) Compare the reliability of the financial statements if the investment company buys only shares in listed companies with their reliability if the company invests in shares of private high-tech companies.

(c) The investment company earns profits from appreciation of its investment securities and from dividends received. How would the concepts of recognition in the *Framework* apply here?

Problem 1.2 ★

MEANING OF 'PROBABLE FUTURE BENEFITS'

The *Framework* includes 'probable future economic benefits' as a condition for recognising an element of financial statements. How would you interpret 'probable' in this context?

Problem 1.3 ★

MEASURING INVENTORIES OF GOLD AND SILVER

IAS 2 *Inventories* allows producers of gold and silver to measure inventories of these commodities at selling price even before they have sold them, which means a profit is recognised at production. In nearly all other industries, however, profit is recognised only when the inventories are sold to outside customers. What concepts in the *Framework* might the IASB have considered with regard to accounting for gold and silver production?

Problem 1.4 ★

RECOGNISING A LOSS FROM A LAWSUIT

The law in your community requires store owners to shovel snow and ice from the pavement in front of their shops. You failed to do that, and a pedestrian slipped and fell, resulting in serious and costly injury. The pedestrian has sued you. Your lawyers say that while they will vigorously defend you in the lawsuit, you should expect to lose $25 000 to cover the injured party's costs. A court decision, however, is not expected for at least a year. What aspects of the *Framework* might help you in deciding the appropriate accounting for this situation?

Problem 1.5 FINANCIAL STATEMENTS OF A REAL ESTATE INVESTOR

★ An entity purchases a rental property for $10 000 000 as an investment. The building is fully rented and is in a prosperous area. At the end of the current year, the entity hires an appraiser who reports that the fair value of the building is $15 000 000 plus or minus 10%. Depreciating the building over 50 years would reduce the carrying amount to $9 800 000.

(a) What are the relevance and reliability accounting considerations in deciding how to measure the building in the entity's financial statements?

(b) Does the *Framework* lead to measuring the building at $15 000 000? Or at $9 800 000? Or at some other amount?

Problem 1.6 NEED FOR THE *FRAMEWORK* VS. INTERPRETATIONS

★ Applying the *Framework* is subjective and requires judgement. Would the IASB be better off to abandon the *Framework* entirely and instead rely on a very active interpretations committee that develops detailed guidance in response to requests from constituents?

Problem 1.7 CONSERVATISM

★ 'When I studied accounting, we were taught always to be conservative in recognition or measurement. When in doubt, don't put the asset on the statement of financial position or, if it's there, write it down at the first sign of trouble. Never recognise profit until a sale takes place.' How do this person's comments relate to the *Framework*?

Problem 1.8 AUTHORITATIVENESS OF THE *FRAMEWORK*

★ Was the IASB wise in using IAS 8 to make the *Framework* the mandatory source of guidance on an accounting question in the absence of a special standard dealing with the subject? What are the pluses and minuses of doing this?

Problem 1.9 MEANING OF 'DECISION USEFUL'

★ What is meant by saying that accounting information should be 'decision useful'?

Problem 1.10 PERFORMANCE OF A BUSINESS ENTITY

★ A financial analyst says: 'I advise my clients to invest for the long term. Buy good stocks and hang onto them. Therefore I am interested in a company's long-term earning power. Accounting standards that result in earnings volatility obscure long-term earning power. Accounting should report earning power by deferring and amortising costs and revenues.' How does the *Framework* relate to this analyst's view of financial statements?

Problem 1.11 GOING CONCERN

★ What measurement principles might be most appropriate for a company that has ceased to be a going concern (e.g. it is in bankruptcy and the receiver is seeking buyers for its assets)?

Problem 1.12 ECONOMIC CONSEQUENCES OF ACCOUNTING STANDARDS

★ After the OPEC oil embargo of 1973, the US government passed a law aimed at encouraging domestic exploration for oil and gas in order to make the US less dependent on foreign suppliers. At about the same time, the FASB proposed an accounting standard that would have required oil and gas exploration companies to charge to expense, immediately, all unsuccessful exploration costs (no oil or gas discovered). Some exploration companies had been capitalising and amortising such unsuccessful costs. They said the FASB's proposed new standard would cause them to report losses, their sources of venture capital would disappear, and they would stop their exploration activities, which is contrary to government economic policy. How does the *Framework* relate to the accounting question? Focus on the issue of neutrality.

Problem 1.13

ASSESSING PROBABILITIES IN ACCOUNTING RECOGNITION

★ The *Framework* defines an asset as a resource from which future economic benefits are expected to flow. 'Expected' means it is not certain, and involves some degree of probability. At the same time the *Framework* establishes, as a criterion for recognising an asset, that 'it is probable that any future economic benefit associated with the item will flow to or from the entity.' Again, an assessment of probability is required. Is there a redundancy, or possibly some type of inconsistency, in including the notion of probability in both the asset definition and recognition criteria?

Problem 1.14

PURCHASE ORDERS

★ An airline places a non-cancellable order for a new aeroplane with one of the major commercial aircraft manufacturers at a fixed price, with delivery in 30 months and payment in full to be made on delivery.

(a) Under the *Framework*, do you think the airline should recognise any asset or liability at the time it places the order?

(b) One year later, the price of this aeroplane model has risen by 5%, but the airline had locked in a fixed, lower price. Under the *Framework*, do you think the airline should recognise any asset (and gain) at the time when the price of the aeroplane rises? If the price fell by 5% instead of rising, do you think the airline should recognise a liability (and loss) under the *Framework*?

Problem 1.15

DEFINITIONS OF ELEMENTS

★ Explain how you would account for the following items/situations, justifying your answer by reference to the *Framework*'s definitions and recognition criteria:

(a) A trinket of sentimental value only.

(b) You are guarantor for your friend's bank loan:

- (i) You have no reason to believe your friend will default on the loan.
- (ii) As your friend is in serious financial difficulties, you think it likely that he will default on the loan.

(c) You receive 1000 shares in X Ltd, trading at \$4 each, as a gift from a grateful client.

(d) The panoramic view of the coast from your café's windows, which you are convinced attracts customers to your café.

(e) The court has ordered your firm to repair the environmental damage it caused to the local river system. You have no idea how much this repair work will cost.

Problem 1.16

DEFINITIONS AND RECOGNITION CRITERIA

★ Explain how you would account for the following items, justifying your answer by reference to the definitions and recognition criteria in the *Framework*. Also state, where appropriate, which ledger accounts should be debited and credited.

(a) Letters from your children, which are of great sentimental value.

(b) (i) Your firm has been sued for negligence — likely you will lose the case.
(ii) Your firm has been sued for negligence — likely you will win the case.

(c) Obsolete plant now retired from use.

(d) Donation of \$10 000 cheque.

Problem 1.17

DEFINITIONS AND RECOGNITION CRITERIA

★ Glasgow Accounting Services has just invoiced one of its clients \$3600 for accounting services provided to the client. Explain how Glasgow Accounting Services should recognise this event, justifying your answer by reference to relevant *Framework* definitions and recognition criteria.

Problem 1.18

ASSETS

★ Lampeter Cosmetics has spent \$220 000 this year on a project to develop a new range of chemical-free cosmetics. As yet, it is too early for Lampeter Cosmetics' management to be able to predict whether this project will prove to be commercially successful. Explain whether Lampeter Cosmetics should recognise this expenditure as an asset, justifying your answer by reference to the *Framework* asset definition and recognition criteria.

Problem 1.19 ASSET DEFINITION AND RECOGNITION

★ On 28 May 2009, $20 000 cash was stolen from Fremantle Ltd's night safe. Explain how Fremantle should account for this event, justifying your answer by reference to relevant *Framework* definitions and recognition criteria.

Problem 1.20 REVENUE RECOGNITION

★ Toucan is a telecommunications provider. One of its products is a mobile phone service, the contract terms of which require the customer to pay 12 months' rental charge in advance at $120 per month. Toucan's policy is to record the rental as revenue on receipt of the customer's payment. Its financial statements at 30 June 2009 classify the full amount of rental received during the year as revenue. Toucan's auditor has advised that the rental revenue is overstated and must be adjusted. Explain how Toucan should adjust the rental revenue recorded at 30 June 2009, justifying your answer by reference to relevant *Framework* definitions and recognition criteria.

References

Deloitte 2006, *Heads Up*, Volume 13, Issue 12, September 27.

International Accounting Standards Board 2008, *Exposure Draft of An improved Conceptual Framework for Financial Reporting: Chapter 1: The Objective of Financial Reporting. Chapter 2: Qualitative Characteristics and Constraints of Decision-useful Financial Reporting Information.*

— 2008, *Discussion Paper: Preliminary Views on an Improved Conceptual Framework for Financial Reporting — The Reporting Entity.*

— 2008, *Discussion Paper: Financial Instruments with Characteristics of Equity.*

— 2007, *Exposure Draft of a Proposed IFRS for Small and Medium-sized Entities.*

— 2006, *Discussion Paper: Fair Value Measurements.*

— 2005, *Discussion Paper: Measurement Bases for Financial Accounting — Measurement on Initial Recognition*, prepared by staff of the Canadian Accounting Standards Board.

— 2004, *Framework for the Preparation and Presentation of Financial Statements.*

International Accounting Standards Committee Foundation 2008, *Review of the constitution: public accountability and the composition of the IASB — proposals for change.*

— 2007, *Constitution.*

— 2007, *Due process handbook for the IFRIC.*

— 2006. *Due process handbook for the IASB.*

Part 2

Elements

2 Shareholders' equity: share capital and reserves

LEARNING OBJECTIVES

When you have studied this chapter, you should be able to:

- distinguish between different forms of corporate entities
- understand the key features of the corporate structure
- account for the issue of both par value and no-par shares
- account for share placements
- account for rights issues
- account for options
- account for bonus issues
- understand the rationale behind share buy-backs and the accounting treatment thereof
- account for movements in retained earnings, including dividends
- understand the nature of reserves other than retained earnings
- prepare note disclosures in relation to equity, as well as a statement of changes in equity.

2.1 SHAREHOLDERS' EQUITY

The purpose of this chapter is to introduce the various components of the equity section of the statement of financial position, namely contributed capital and reserves. The element of capital will differ depending on the nature of the organisation, whether a sole proprietorship, partnership or company. Reserves comprise equity attributable to the owners of the entity other than amounts directly contributed by the owners. An example of the equity section of the statement of financial position of a for-profit entity is shown in figure 2.1. It contains an extract from the consolidated balance sheet of Nokia Corporation as at 31 December 2007. The accounts were prepared in accordance with International Financial Reporting Standards (IFRSs), and the extract relating to the shareholders' equity of the group is shown in figure 2.1. Note that the two key components are share capital and reserves.

December 31	Notes	2007 EURm	2006 EURm
SHAREHOLDERS' EQUITY AND LIABILITIES			
Capital and reserves attributable to equity holders of the parent			
Share capital	21	246	246
Share issue premium		644	2 707
Treasury shares, at cost		(3 146)	(2 060)
Translation differences		(163)	(34)
Fair value and other reserves	20	23	(14)
Reserve for invested non-restricted equity		3 299	—
Retained earnings		13 870	11 123
		14 773	11 968
Minority interests		2 565	92
Total equity		17 338	12 060

FIGURE 2.1 Shareholders' equity of Nokia
Source: Nokia (2007, p. 9).

With a sole proprietor, having a single owner means there is little reason for distinguishing between capital (potentially the initial investment in the business) and profits retained in the business for investment purposes.

Traditionally with partnerships, the rights and responsibilities of the partners are specified in a partnership agreement. This document details how the profits and losses of the partnership are to be divided between the partners, including rules relating to distributions on dissolution of the partnership. In accounting for partnerships, a distinction is generally made for each partner between a capital account, to which amounts invested by a partner are credited, and a current account or retained earnings account, to which a partner's share of profits are credited and from which any drawings are debited. As with a sole proprietorship, there generally is no real distinction between capital contributed and profits retained (unless there is some other specification in the partnership agreement, which is unlikely). Both amounts represent the ongoing investment by the partners. On dissolution of the partnership, the distribution to partners is unaffected by whether an equity balance is capital or retained earnings.

With companies, the situation is different because their formation is generally governed by legislation, and there is normally a clear distinction made between contributed capital and profits retained in the entity. However, it must be understood that, although the laws governing companies in a particular country may require a distinction between capital and other forms of owners' equity, from an accounting point of view there is no real difference between the various classifications of owners' equity. In other words, apart from any legal restrictions such as applying to the distribution of dividends, whether an entity has \$200 000 of capital and \$100 000 of retained earnings, or \$100 000 of capital and \$200 000 of retained earnings, is of no real importance. In essence, the entity has \$300 000 of equity.

This chapter concentrates on the company as the organisational form of interest, with the major account reflecting contributed equity being share capital. However, as noted above, there is no reason, apart from legal reasons specific to a particular jurisdiction, for the organisational form to require major differences in accounting for the equity of an entity.

2.2 TYPES OF COMPANIES

Generally, companies can be distinguished by the nature of the ownership, and the rights and responsibilities of the shareholders. Two types of companies are examined in this section: not-for-profit companies and for-profit companies.

2.2.1 Not-for-profit companies

'Not-for-profit' is not defined in International Financial Reporting Standards. In Australia, whose accounting standards are equivalent to international standards, a not-for-profit entity is defined as an 'entity whose principal objective is not the generation of profit'.

An example of the equity section of the statement of financial position (balance sheet) of a not-for-profit entity is shown in figure 2.2, which contains the equity section and two explanatory notes relating to this section from the 2007 balance sheet of the International Committee of the Red Cross (ICRC). These financial statements are prepared in accordance with IFRSs. As noted in section 2 of the notes to the 2007 consolidated financial statements: 'Currently, the IFRS do not contain specific guidelines for non-profit organizations and non-governmental organizations concerning the accounting treatment and the presentation of the consolidated financial statements.'

FIGURE 2.2 Extract from the balance sheet and notes to the accounts at 31 December 2007 (in Swiss franc '000) of the International Committee of the Red Cross

	Notes	2007	2006 (restated)
Restricted Reserves			
Total funds and foundations		21 759	19 790
Total funding of field operations	24	5 386	(21 976)
Total Restricted Reserves		27 145	(2 186)
Unrestricted Reserves			
Total reserves designated by the Assembly	25	406 138	364 018
Total other unrestricted reserves	26	14 400	14 400
Total Unrestricted Reserves		420 538	378 418
Total RESERVES		447 683	376 232

Note 25. Reserves designated by the assembly

(in KCHF)	Future operations	Operational risks	Assets replacement	Financial risks	Human resources	Specific projects	Total
Balance as at 31 December 2005	147 691	26 166	125 354	14 933	10 694	4 516	329 354
Use/release during 2006		(395)	(192)	(6 000)	(841)	(3 220)	(10 648)
Allocations 2006	22 299	1 265	13 191	6 361	1 352	844	45 312
Balance as at 31 December 2006	169 990	27 036	138 353	15 294	11 205	2 140	364 018
Use/release during 2007		(1 188)	(338)	(6 367)	(10 980)	(1 398)	(20 271)
Allocations 2007	21 302	3 654	21 937	5 936	8 555	1 007	62 391
Balance as at 31 December 2007	191 292	29 502	159 952	14 863	8 780	1 749	406 138

The future operations reserve is intended for situations with insufficient operational funding, which is estimated at an average of 2.5 months of expenditure in cash, kind and services over the previous five years, including both at headquarters and in the field. The theoretical level is KCHF 195 032 (in 2006: KCHF 176 308).

FIGURE 2.2 *(continued)*

26. Other unrestricted reserves

(in KCHF)	2007	2006
General reserves	12 500	12 500
Retained surplus at beginning of year	1 900	1 900
Total	**14 400**	**14 400**

Source: International Committee of the Red Cross (2007, pp. 390, 407).

Not-for-profit companies can be divided into government or public sector companies and private not-for-profit sector entities:

- Entities may be established by the government to undertake various activities of the government, such as the supply of water or electricity, the provision of communications and the running of an airline. The government may own all the issued shares of the company, or a controlling interest in the entity. For the government enterprise to be classified as not-for-profit, the primary objective of the entity must be something other than the earning of profit.
- Organisations such as charities may form a company as their preferred organisational structure to limit their liability. The company may be limited by guarantee, whereby members undertake to contribute a guaranteed amount in the event the company goes into liquidation, but have no rights to dividends or distributions on liquidation. Alternatively, the company may be a non-public company, sometimes called a proprietary company or a closed corporation, where the shares are held by a limited number of shareholders and the shares are not available for purchase by the public.

2.2.2 For-profit companies

For-profit companies may take a number of forms:

- Proprietary or closed corporations may be established with limited membership and restrictions on obtaining funds from the public. In some countries, a distinction is made between large and small proprietary companies, with the size being measured in relation to accounting numbers such as gross revenue and gross assets as well as other variables such as the number of employees. Where a proprietary company is classified as large, there is an increased responsibility in relation to the disclosure of information.
- Public companies or open corporations generally have a large number of issued shares, with the ownership being widespread. These companies rely on the public for subscription to share offers as well the provision of debt funding via secured loans such as debentures or through unsecured loans.

For-profit companies may be:

- listed — their shares are traded on a stock exchange
- unlisted — the shares are traded through brokers and financial institutions
- limited by guarantee — the members undertake to contribute a guaranteed amount in the event of the company going into liquidation
- unlimited — members are liable for all the debts of the company
- no-liability — members are not required to pay any calls on their shares if they do not wish to continue being shareholders in the company.

The exact rights and responsibilities of shareholders in relation to the different forms of companies will differ according to the relevant companies legislation and other laws specific to the country or countries in which the company operates.

As noted by Nobes & Parker (2002, pp. 21–3) the types of organisations and ownership differ substantially across countries:

> In Germany, France and Italy, capital provided by banks is very significant, as are small family-owned businesses. By contrast, in the United States and the United Kingdom there are large numbers of companies that rely on millions of private shareholders for finance . . .
>
> A proposed grouping of countries into types by financial system has been formalized by Zysman (1983) as follows:
>
> 1. capital market systems (e.g. United Kingdom, United States)
> 2. credit-based government systems (e.g. France, Japan)
> 3. credit-based financial institution systems (e.g. Germany).

A further point of comparison between 'equity' and 'credit' countries is that, in the latter countries, even the relatively few listed companies may be dominated by shareholders who are bankers, governments or founding families. For example, in Germany, the banks in particular are important owners of companies as well as providers of debt finance . . . In such countries as Germany, France or Italy, the banks or the state will, in many cases, nominate directors and thus be able to obtain information and affect decisions.

Table 2.1 shows the distribution of the world's largest 500 companies by country, measured by revenue. The United States and Japan contain the largest number of top companies. Table 2.2 shows the major stock exchanges of the world and the market capitalisation of the

TABLE 2.1 Share of the world's top 500 companies (distribution by revenue)

Australia	8	Malaysia	1
Austria	2	Mexico	5
Belgium	5	Netherlands	13
Belgium/Netherlands	1	Norway	2
Brazil	5	Poland	1
Britain	34	Portugal	1
Britain/Netherlands	1	Russia	5
Canada	14	Saudi Arabia	1
China	29	Singapore	1
Denmark	2	South Korea	15
Finland	2	Spain	11
France	39	Sweden	6
Germany	37	Switzerland	14
India	7	Taiwan	6
Ireland	2	Thailand	1
Italy	10	Turkey	1
Japan	64	United States of America	153
Luxembourg	1		
			500

Source: Fortune magazine (2008).

TABLE 2.2 Major stock exchanges at October 2008

Region	Exchange	Domestic market capitalisation (USD millions)	Share turnover velocity (%)
Americas	NASDAQ	2 579 456.0	401.8
Americas	NYSE	10 312 695.0	236.6
Asia–Pacific	ASX	683 444.0	116.7
Asia–Pacific	Bombay SE	606 119.5	29.1
Asia–Pacific	Hong Kong Exchanges	1 228 468.1	89.2
Asia–Pacific	Korea Exchange	474 949.5	183.3
Asia–Pacific	National Stock Exchange India	570 351.4	74.6
Asia–Pacific	Shanghai SE	1 341 028.8	104.6
Asia–Pacific	Shenzhen SE	343 319.0	214.4
Asia–Pacific	Tokyo SE	2 884 409.8	151.2
Europe–Africa–Middle East	Deutche Bőrse	1 097 030.0	226.2
Europe–Africa–Middle East	London SE	2 042 144.8	157.1
Europe–Africa–Middle East	JSE	445 860.0	62.9
Europe–Africa–Middle East	Swiss Exchange	865 596.8	129.1

Source: Based on statistics from the World Federation of Exchanges website www.world-exchanges.org/WFE.

companies on those exchanges. Many companies list on a number of stock exchanges; Nokia, for example, is quoted on the following stock exchanges:

- HEX, Helsinki (quoted since 1915)
- Stockholmsborsen (quoted since 1983)
- Frankfurter Wertpapierborse (quoted since 1988)
- New York Stock Exchange (quoted since 1994).

Countries with larger capital markets tend to dominate the overall world market, as movements in these markets have immediate effects on other economies. Note, however, that the size of a country's market does not necessarily correlate with the sophistication of the accounting and regulatory regimes of that country.

2.3 KEY FEATURES OF THE CORPORATE STRUCTURE

The choice of the company as the preferred form of organisational structure brings with it certain advantages, such as limited liability to shareholders. It also comes with certain disadvantages, such as making the entity subject to increasing government regulation including the forced and detailed disclosure of information about the company. Some features of the company structure that affect the subsequent accounting for a company are described below.

The use of share capital

The ownership rights in a company are generally represented by shares; that is, the share capital of a company comprises a number of units or shares. Each share represents a proportional right to the net assets of the company and, within a class of shares, all shares have the same equal rights. These shares are generally transferable between parties. As a result, markets have been established to provide investors with an ability to trade in shares. Where active markets exist, such as with organised stock exchanges, the fair value of a company's shares at a point in time may be reliably determined. A further advantage of transferability is that a change in ownership by one shareholder selling shares to a new investor does not have an effect on the continued existence and operation of the company.

Besides the right to share equally in the net assets, and hence the profits and losses of a company, each share has other rights, including:

- *the right to vote for directors of the company*. This establishes the right of shareholders to have a say as owners in the strategic direction of the company. Where there are a large number of owners in a company, there is generally a separation between ownership and management. The shareholders thus employ professional managers (the directors) to manage the organisation, these managers then providing periodic reports to the shareholders on the financial performance and position of the company. Some directors are executive directors, being employed as executives in the company, while others have non-executive roles. The directors are elected at the annual general meeting of the company, and shareholders exercise their voting rights to elect the directors. The shareholders may vote in person, or by proxy. In relation to the latter, a shareholder may authorise another party to vote on his or her behalf at the meeting; the other party could be the chairman of the company's board.
- *the right to share in assets on the winding-up or liquidation of the company*. The rights and responsibilities of shareholders in the event of liquidation are generally covered in legislation specific to each country, as are the rights of creditors to receive payment in preference to shareholders.
- *the right to share proportionately in any new issues of shares of the same class*. This right is sometimes referred to as the pre-emptive right. It ensures that a shareholder is able to retain the same proportionate ownership in a company, and that this ownership percentage cannot be diluted by the company issuing new shares to other investors, possibly at prices lower than the current fair value. However, the directors may be allowed to make limited placements of shares under certain conditions.

Limited liability

When shares are issued, the maximum amount payable by each shareholder is set. Even if a company incurs losses or goes into liquidation, the company cannot require a shareholder to provide additional capital. In some countries, shares are issued with a specific amount stated on the share certificate, this amount being called the par value of the share. For example, a company may issue one million shares each with a par value of $1, the company then receiving share capital of $1 million.

Par value shares may also be issued at a premium. For example, where a company requires share capital of $2 million, one million $1 shares may be issued at a premium of $1 per share; in this case, each shareholder is required to pay $2 per share. Similarly, par value shares may be issued at a discount. For example, where a company issues $1 shares at a discount of 20c, the company requires each shareholder to pay 80c per share. The only real purpose of the par value is to establish the maximum liability of the shareholder in relation to the company. Legislation in some countries restricts the issue of shares at a discount, and also establishes the subsequent uses of any share premium received on a share.

Note that the par value does not represent a fair or market value of the share. At the issue date, it would be expected that the par value, plus the premium or minus the discount, would represent the market value of the share. In some countries, such as Australia, the use of par value shares has been replaced by the issue of shares at a specified price with no par value. For example, a company may issue 1000 shares in 2007 at $3 per share, and in 2010 it may issue another 1000 shares at $5 per share. In 2010, the company then has 2000 shares and a share capital of $8000. The issue price becomes irrelevant subsequent to the issue, the key variables being the number of shares issued and the amount of share capital in total. The liability of each shareholder is limited to the issue price of the shares at the time of issue.

The feature of limited liability protects shareholders by limiting the contribution required of shareholders. This then places limitations on the ability of creditors to access funds for the repayment of company debts. To protect creditors, many countries have enacted legislation that prohibits companies from distributing capital to shareholders in the form of dividends. Dividends are then payable only from profits, not out of capital.

Different forms of capital

Shares are issued with specific rights attached. Shares are then given different names to signify differences in rights.

The most common form of share capital is the ordinary share or common stock. These shares have no specific rights to any distributions of profit by the company, and ordinary shareholders are often referred to as 'residual' equity holders in that these shareholders obtain what is left after all other parties' claims have been met. An example of a company that has only one class of share is Nokia. Information on its shares as at 31 December 2007 was provided in its 2007 annual report in the notes to the financial statements of the parent company. Part of this information is shown in figure 2.3.

Shares and share capital

Nokia has one class of shares. Each Nokia share entitles the holder to one vote at General Meetings of Nokia. On December 31, 2007, the share capital of Nokia Corporation was EUR 245 896 461.96 and the total number of shares issued was 3 982 811 957. On December 31, 2007, the total number of shares included 136 862 005 shares owned by Group companies representing approximately 3.4% of the share capital and the total voting rights. To align the Articles of Association of Nokia with the new Finnish Companies Act, effective as of September 1, 2006, the Annual General Meeting held on May 3, 2007, amended the Articles of Association to the effect that the provisions on minimum and maximum share capital as well as on the par value of a share were removed.

Share capital and shares December 31, 2007	**2007**	**2006**	**2005**	**2004**	**2003**
Share capital, EURm	246	246	266	280	288
Shares (1 000, par value EUR 0.06)	3 982 811	4 095 043	4 433 887	4 663 761	4 796 292
Shares owned by the Group (1 000)	136 862	129 312	261 511	176 820	96 024
Number of shares excluding shares owned by the Group (1 000)	3 845 949	3 965 730	4 172 376	4 486 941	4 700 268
Number of registered shareholders[1]	103 226	119 143	126 352	142 095	133 991

[1]Each account operator is included in the figure as only one registered shareholder.

FIGURE 2.3 Share capital, Nokia
Source: Nokia (2007, p. 52).

Another form of share capital is the preference share. As the name implies, holders of preference shares generally have a preferential right to dividends over the ordinary shareholders. Note firstly that the name of the instrument does not necessarily indicate the rights associated with that instrument. As is discussed in chapter 5, some preference shares are in reality not equity but liabilities, or they may be compound instruments being partially debt and partially equity. Secondly, the rights of preference shareholders may be very diverse. Some preference shares have a fixed dividend; for example, a company may issue preference shares at $10 each with a 4% dividend per annum, thus entitling the shareholder to a 40c dividend per annum. Other common features of preference shares are:

- *cumulative versus non-cumulative shares*. Where a preference share is cumulative, if a dividend is not declared in a particular year, the right to the dividend is not lost but carries over to a subsequent year. The dividends are said to be in arrears. With non-cumulative shares, if a dividend is not paid in a particular year, the right to that dividend is lost.
- *participating versus non-participating shares*. A participating share gives the holder the right to share in extra dividends. For example, if a company has issued 8% participating preference shares and it pays a 10% dividend to the ordinary shareholders, the preference shareholders may be entitled to a further 2% dividend.
- *convertible versus non-convertible shares*. Convertible preference shares may give the holder the right to convert the preference shares into ordinary shares. The right to convert may be at the option of the holder of the shares or at the option of the company itself. As explained in chapter 5, convertible preference shares may need to be classified into debt and equity components.
- *converting preference shares*. With convertible preference shares, whether a conversion into ordinary shares ever occurs depends upon the exercise of an option, but with converting preference shares the terms of issue are such that the shares must convert into ordinary shares at a specified point of time. As explained in chapter 5, converting preference shares may need to be classified as debt.
- *redeemable versus non-redeemable shares.* Subsequent to their issue, redeemable preference shares may be bought back from the shareholders by the company at a price generally established in the terms of issue of the shares. The option to redeem is normally held by the company.

Returns to shareholders

As already noted, the shareholders of ordinary shares have no specific rights to dividends, being residual equity holders. Whether a dividend is paid depends on the decisions made by the directors. Regulations in some countries may specify from which equity accounts the dividends can be paid, or whether the company has to meet solvency tests before paying dividends. In some cases, the directors may be allowed to propose a dividend at year-end, but this proposal may have to be approved by the shareholders in the annual general meeting.

2.4 CONTRIBUTED EQUITY: ISSUE OF SHARE CAPITAL

Once a business has decided to form a public company, it will commence the procedures necessary to issue shares to the public. The initial offering of shares to the public to invest in the new company is called an initial public offering (IPO). To arrange the sale of the shares, the business that wishes to float the company usually employs a promoter, such as a stockbroker or a financial institution, with expert knowledge of the legal requirements and experience in this area. Once the promoter and the managers of the business agree on the structure of the new company, a prospectus is drawn up and lodged with the regulating authority. The prospectus contains information about the current status of the business and its future prospects.

In order to ensure that the statements in the prospectus are accurate, a process of due diligence is undertaken by an accounting firm and a report attached. To ensure that the sale of shares is successful, an underwriter may be employed. The role of the underwriter is to advise on such matters as the pricing of the issue, the timing of the issue and how the issue will be marketed. One of the principal reasons for using an underwriter is to ensure that all the shares are sold, as the underwriter agrees to acquire all shares that are not taken up by the public.

The costs of issuing the shares can then be quite substantial and could amount to 10% of the amount raised. The costs include costs associated with preparing and printing the relevant documentation and marketing the share issue, as well as the fees charged by the various experts consulted which could include accountants, lawyers and taxation specialists. Accounting for these costs is covered in paragraph 37 of IAS 32 *Financial Instruments: Presentation*:

> An entity typically incurs various costs in issuing or acquiring its own equity instruments. Those costs might include registration and other regulatory fees, amounts paid to legal, accounting and other professional advisers, printing costs and stamp duties. The transaction costs of an equity transaction are accounted for as a deduction from equity (net of any related income tax benefit) to the extent they are incremental costs directly attributable to the equity transaction that otherwise would have been avoided. The costs of an equity transaction that is abandoned are recognised as an expense.

The costs are then treated as a reduction in share capital such that the amount shown in share capital immediately after the share issue is the net amount available to the company for operations. The accounting for share issue costs is demonstrated in the next section.

Any costs associated with the formation of the company that cannot be directly related to the issue of the shares, such as registration of the company name, are expensed as the cost is incurred. These outlays do not meet the definition of an asset as there are no expected future economic benefits associated with these outlays that can be controlled by the company.

2.4.1 Issue of no-par shares

ILLUSTRATIVE EXAMPLE 2.1

Issue of no-par shares

Qatar Ltd issues 500 no-par shares for cash at $10 each, incurring share issue costs of $450. Qatar Ltd records on its share register the number of shares issued, and makes the following journal entry:

Cash	Dr	5 000	
Share Capital	Cr		5 000
(Issue of 500 $10 shares)			
Share Capital	Dr	450	
Cash	Cr		450
(Share issue costs)			

If cash is collected from applicants for shares before the shares are issued, the company records the cash received in a cash trust account, and raises an application account to record the balance prior to the issue of the shares. For example, if application monies of $5000 were collected during the month of January and the shares were issued at the end of January, the journal entries would be:

January				
1–30	Cash Trust	Dr	5 000	
	Application	Cr		5 000
	(Monies received from applicants for shares)			
31	Application	Dr	5 000	
	Share Capital	Cr		5 000
	(Issue of shares applied for)			
	Cash	Dr	5 000	
	Cash Trust	Cr		5 000
	(Transfer from cash trust on issue of shares)			

The reason for raising the cash trust account is that there may be a minimum number of applications that have to be received in order for the share issue to proceed. When the minimum subscription is not received or applicants are allotted fewer shares than they applied for, application monies collected are paid back to the applicants via the cash trust account.

Shares in limited liability companies are generally issued on a fully paid basis, but, in some cases, shares may be issued so that part of the issue price is payable immediately and part is required to be paid later. In this case, at the appropriate date the company has to make a call on the shareholders for the subsequent payment.

ILLUSTRATIVE EXAMPLE 2.2

Calls on no-par shares

Armenia Ltd issues 500 no-par shares at $10, the terms of issue requiring the shareholders to pay $6 immediately and $4 in 1 year's time. The initial journal entry is:

Cash	Dr	3 000	
Share Capital	Cr		3 000
(Issue of shares)			

The following journal entry is made in 1 year's time:

Call	Dr	2 000	
Share Capital	Cr		2 000
(Call of $4 on 500 shares)			

When the call money is received from shareholders, the following journal entry is made:

Cash	Dr	2 000	
Call	Cr		2 000
(Receipt of call money)			

Directors may be given the power under the regulations governing the company's operations to forfeit shares where the call is not paid. For example, assume that in illustrative example 2.2 the holders of 10 shares declined to pay the $4 call. The company then forfeits the shares, and the following journal entry is made:

Share Capital	Dr	100	
Call	Cr		40
Forfeited Shares Account	Cr		60
(Forfeiture of 10 shares called to $10 and paid to $6 per share)			

Depending on the regulations in the country in which the company is incorporated, the balance in the forfeited shares account may be refunded to the shareholders and the shares cancelled; in this case the account is classified as a liability. If the balance in the forfeited shares account is retained by the company, the account could be called 'Forfeited Shares Reserve' and be included in equity. Alternatively, the company could decide to reissue the shares. For example, the shares could be reissued as fully paid to $10 per share on payment of $8 per share, with the forfeited shares account being used to fund the difference as well as any costs of reissue. Assuming all the shares were reissued, incurring costs of $5, and any balance of the reserve being returned to the former shareholders, the journal entries are shown below.

Cash	Dr	80	
Forfeited Shares Account	Dr	20	
Share Capital	Cr		100
(Reissue of shares)			
Forfeited Shares Account	Dr	40	
Share Issue Costs Payable	Cr		5
Payable to Shareholders	Cr		35
(Share issue costs and monies refundable to shareholders)			
Share Issue Costs Payable	Dr	5	
Payable to Shareholders	Dr	35	
Cash	Cr		40
(Payment of amounts owing)			

2.4.2 Issue of par value shares

Shares issued at a premium

Where shares are issued at a premium, the excess over the par value is credited to an equity account which may be called share premium, additional paid-in capital or share capital in excess of par. The share premium is then a component of contributed equity.

ILLUSTRATIVE EXAMPLE 2.3

Issue of par value shares at a discount

Bhutan Ltd issues 5000 shares of $1 par value at a premium of $2 per share. The journal entry is:

Cash	Dr	15 000	
Share Capital	Cr		5 000
Share Premium	Cr		10 000
(Issue of shares at a premium)			

Shares issued at a discount

Where shares are issued at a discount, the account used in relation to the discount can be the same as that used for a premium, or it can be a separate discount account. The accounting treatment will vary depending on the regulations governing discounts in particular jurisdictions.

ILLUSTRATIVE EXAMPLE 2.4

Issue of par value shares at a discount

Iran Ltd issued 5000 shares of $2 par value at a 50c discount. The journal entry is:

Cash	Dr	7 500	
Discount on Shares	Dr	2 500	
Share Capital	Cr		10 000
(Issue of shares at a discount)			

2.4.3 Oversubscriptions

An issue of shares by a company may be so popular that it is oversubscribed; that is, there are more applications for shares than shares to be issued. Some investors may then receive an allotment of fewer shares than they applied for, or may not be allotted any shares at all.

An example of shares being oversubscribed was reported in the Melbourne newspaper *The Age* in relation to the share offer made by the airline Virgin Blue in 2003 (see figure 2.4).

$5 billion: Virgin float offer swamped

Virgin Blue's public share offer has tapped into growing interest in the sharemarket, with applications of more than $5 billion for only $558 million of stock.

Investors apparently shrugged off any concerns about a threat to Virgin's growth plans and sharemarket float from Qantas's fledgling discount offshoot, JetStar.

Virgin claims its public offer closed more than 10 times oversubscribed and at the top of its price range.

With Virgin Blue set to start trading on the Australian Stock Exchange with $2.3 billion market capitalisation, the two questions lingering yesterday were whether Sir Richard Branson would reduce his 29.1 per cent stake, and what publicity stunt the Virgin founder had in store for Monday's listing ceremony.

Sir Richard hinted that he might well increase the shares available through the float to 29 per cent of Virgin Blue, which would cut his interest to 25.1 per cent, when he paid credit to the '250 institutions worldwide and many thousands of our customers' who applied for shares.

'Although we have been told by our advisers that demand was over 10 times subscribed at the $2.25 price, we have decided not to price the offering any higher to hopefully allow for a decent aftermarket for the many staff and supporters of Virgin Blue,' Sir Richard said in a statement.

With the float costing Virgin Blue about $20 million, advisers Goldman Sachs, JBWere and Credit Suisse First Boston will get 2.5 per cent of the funds raised plus a 0.5 per cent bonus, worth an estimated $16.7 million.

FIGURE 2.4 Oversubscription of shares
Source: Rochfort, S (2003).

In most cases, excess application monies are simply refunded to the applicants. When this happens, the appropriate journal entries are:

Application	Dr	XXX	
Share Capital	Cr		XXX
(Issue of shares applied for)			
Application	Dr	XXX	
Cash	Dr	XXX	
Cash Trust	Cr		XXX
(Transfer from cash trust and refund of excess application money)			

Depending on the company's constitution or the terms of the prospectus, an entity may retain the excess application money as an advance on future calls. In this case the journal entry is:

Application	Dr	XXX	
Calls in Advance	Cr		XXX
Share Capital	Cr		XXX
(Issue of shares)			

ILLUSTRATIVE EXAMPLE 2.5

Oversubscription of shares

China Ltd was incorporated on 1 July 2010. The directors offered to the general public 100 000 ordinary shares for subscription at an issue price of $2. The company received applications for 200 000 shares. The directors then decided to issue 150 000 shares, returning the balance of application money to the unsuccessful applicants.

The appropriate journal entries are:

Cash Trust	Dr	400 000	
Application	Cr		400 000
(Money received on application)			
Application	Dr	300 000	
Share Capital	Cr		300 000
(Issue of shares)			
Cash	Dr	300 000	
Application	Dr	100 000	
Cash Trust	Cr		400 000
(Transfer of cash on issue of shares and refund of excess application money)			

2.5 CONTRIBUTED EQUITY: SUBSEQUENT MOVEMENTS IN SHARE CAPITAL

Having floated the company, the directors may at a later stage decide to make changes to the share capital. These changes may result in both increases and decreases in the share capital of the company. For example, the London Stock Exchange reported the information shown in figure 2.5 in relation to equity capital issues on the exchange.

FIGURE 2.5 New and further issues on the London Stock Exchange

	Main market UK listed		Main market international		Grand total	
October 2008	**No. of co's/issues**	**Money raised (£m)**	**No. of co's/issues**	**Money raised (£m)**	**No. of co's/issues**	**Money raised (£m)**
New companies						
Public offer	1	1.15	0	0.00	1	1.15
Placing	0	0.00	0	0.00	0	0.00
Placing and public offer	0	0.00	0	0.00	0	0.00
Introduction	2	0.00	0	0.00	2	0.00
Totals	**3**	**1.15**	**0**	**0.00**	**3**	**1.15**
Further issues						
Public offer	4	0.86	0	0.00	4	0.86
Placing	6	87.15	0	0.00	6	87.15
Placing and public offer	0	0.00	1	140.40	1	140.40
Rights issues	0	0.00	0	0.00	0	0.00
Employee shares/options	6	0.00	6	0.00	12	0.00
Totals	**16**	**88.01**	**7**	**140.40**	**23**	**228.41**
Grand totals	**19**	**89.16**	**7**	**140.40**	**26**	**229.56**

FIGURE 2.5 *(continued)*

Year to date	Main market UK listed		Main market international		Grand total	
	No. of co's/issues	Money raised (£m)	No. of co's/issues	Money raised (£m)	No. of co's/issues	Money raised (£m)
New companies						
Public offer	15	1 907.63	8	1 674.71	23	3 582.33
Placing	6	541.08	1	1 264.92	7	1 805.99
Placing and public offer	0	0.00	0	0.00	0	0.00
Introduction	25	0.00	3	0.00	28	0.00
Totals	**46**	**2 448.70**	**12**	**2 939.62**	**58**	**5 388.33**
Further issues						
Public offer	151	426.65	0	0.00	151	426.65
Placing	65	3 920.81	9	209.77	74	4 130.58
Placing and public offer	19	4 957.69	1	140.40	20	5 098.10
Rights issues	13	23 112.59	1	415.20	14	23 527.79
Employee shares/options	104	0.00	37	0.00	141	0.00
Totals	**352**	**32 417.75**	**48**	**765.37**	**400**	**33 183.12**
Grand totals	**398**	**34 866.45**	**60**	**3 704.99**	**458**	**38 571.44**

Source: London Stock Exchange (2008).

In its 2005 annual report, Nokia reported the authorisation given by shareholders to increase the entity's share capital. This authorisation is shown in figure 2.6.

The Board of Directors had been authorized by Nokia shareholders at the Annual General Meeting held on March 25, 2004 to decide on an increase of the share capital by a maximum of EUR 55 500 000 offering a maximum of 925 000 000 new shares. In 2005, the Board of Directors did not increase the share capital on the basis of this authorization. The authorization expired on March 25, 2005.

At the Annual General Meeting held on April 7, 2005 Nokia shareholders authorized the Board of Directors to decide on an increase of the share capital by a maximum of EUR 53 160 000 within one year from the resolution of the Annual General Meeting. The increase of the share capital may consist of one or more issues offering a maximum of 886 000 000 new shares with a par value of EUR 0.06 each. The share capital may be increased in deviation from the shareholders' pre-emptive rights for share subscription provided that from the company's perspective important financial grounds exist such as financing or carrying out of an acquisition or another arrangement or granting incentives to selected members of the personnel. In 2005, the Board of Directors did not increase the share capital on the basis of this authorization. The authorization is effective until April 7, 2006.

At the end of 2005, the Board of Directors had no other authorizations to issue shares, convertible bonds, warrants or stock options.

The Board of Directors proposes to the Annual General Meeting convening on March 30, 2006 that the Board of Directors be authorized to resolve to increase the share capital of the company by issuing new shares, stock options or convertible bonds in one or more issues. The increase of the share capital through issuance of new shares, subscription of shares pursuant to stock options and conversion of convertible bonds into shares, may amount to a maximum of EUR 48 540 000 in total.

As a result of share issuance, subscription of shares pursuant to stock options and conversion of convertible bonds into shares an aggregate maximum of 809 000 000 new shares with a par value of EUR 0.06 may be issued. The authorization is proposed to be effective until March 30, 2007, or in the event that the new Companies Act has been approved by the time of the Annual General Meeting, and enters into force latest on March 30, 2007, this authorization is proposed to be effective until June 30, 2007.

FIGURE 2.6 An authorisation to increase share capital, Nokia
Source: Nokia (2005, p. 45).

2.5.1 Placements of shares

Rather than issue new shares through an issue to the public or current shareholders, the company may decide to place the shares with specific investors such as life insurance companies and superannuation funds. The advantages to the company of a placement of shares are:

- *speed* — a placement can be effected in a short period of time
- *price* — because a placement is made to other than existing shareholders, and to a market that is potentially more informed and better funded, the issue price of the new shares may be closer to the market price at the date of issue
- *direction* — the shares may be placed with investors who approve of the directions of the company, or who will not interfere in the formation of company policies
- *prospectus* — in some cases, a placement can occur without the need for a detailed prospectus to be prepared.

There are potential disadvantages to the existing shareholders from private placements in that the current shareholders will have their interest in the company diluted as a result of the placement. In some countries, the securities regulations place limits on the amounts of placements of shares without the approval of existing shareholders. Further disadvantages to current shareholders can occur if the company places the shares at a large discount. Again, securities laws are generally enacted to ensure that management cannot abuse the placement process and that current shareholders are protected.

ILLUSTRATIVE EXAMPLE 2.6

Placement of shares

Thailand Ltd placed 5000 no-par ordinary shares at $5 each with Turkey Ltd.

The entry in the journals of Thailand Ltd is:

Cash	Dr	25 000	
Share Capital	Cr		25 000
(Placement of shares)			

2.5.2 Rights issues

A rights issue is an issue of new shares with the terms of issue giving existing shareholders the right to an additional number of shares in proportion to their current shareholding; that is, the shares are offered pro rata. For example, an offer could be made to each shareholder to buy two new shares on the basis of every 10 shares currently held. If all the existing shareholders exercise their rights and take up the shares, there is no change in each shareholder's percentage ownership interest in the company.

Rights issues may be renounceable or non-renounceable. If renounceable, existing shareholders may sell their rights to the new shares to another party during the offer period. As shown on its website in November 2003, the ANZ Bank in Australia issued a prospectus for a 2-for-11 fully underwritten renounceable rights issue to existing shareholders of ANZ of approximately 276.7 million new ordinary shares at an issue price of A$13 per new ordinary share to raise approximately A$3597 million as a part of the purchase price for the acquisition of the National Bank of New Zealand Group. On page 14 of the prospectus, the ANZ Bank (2003) listed the choices available to the eligible shareholders:

- take up the rights in full: the shareholders would thereby apply for the new shares on the appropriate application form, attaching a cheque or money order for $13 per share applied for. The bank noted (page 8) that until the new ordinary shares were allotted, ANZ would hold the application monies in a bank account.
- sell the rights in full on the Australian or New Zealand stock exchanges (ASX or NZSX). The shareholders would then instruct their stockbrokers to sell the rights. The prospectus specified the dates on which rights trading would conclude, and shareholders with unsold rights would have to make a final decision on whether to acquire the new shares themselves or forgo the

opportunity to take up the new shares. In the event of the rights being unsold, and the existing shareholders not taking up the new shares, the underwriters would deal with the rights.

- sell part of the rights on ASX or NZSX and take up the balance
- transfer all or part of the rights to another person other than via ASX or NZSX. The existing shareholder would then forward to the ANZ a completed renunciation form, the transferee's application form and cheque or money order.
- do nothing. In this case, the underwriters would endeavour to sell the rights to institutional investors at a minimum of $13 per share, with the proceeds less brokerage and other expenses being paid to the existing shareholders.

If the rights issue is non-renounceable, a shareholder is not allowed to sell his or her rights to the new shares and must either accept or reject the offer to acquire new shares in the company.

A major difference between an issue of shares to the public and a rights issue is that with the former, the offer comes from the applicant (the prospective shareholder) and it is for the company to accept or reject the offer. With a rights issue, the prospectus constitutes an offer, which may be accepted or rejected by the existing shareholder.

The graph in figure 2.7 shows the relative amounts of money raised by companies listed on the London Stock Exchange by new issues versus rights issues as at October 2008.

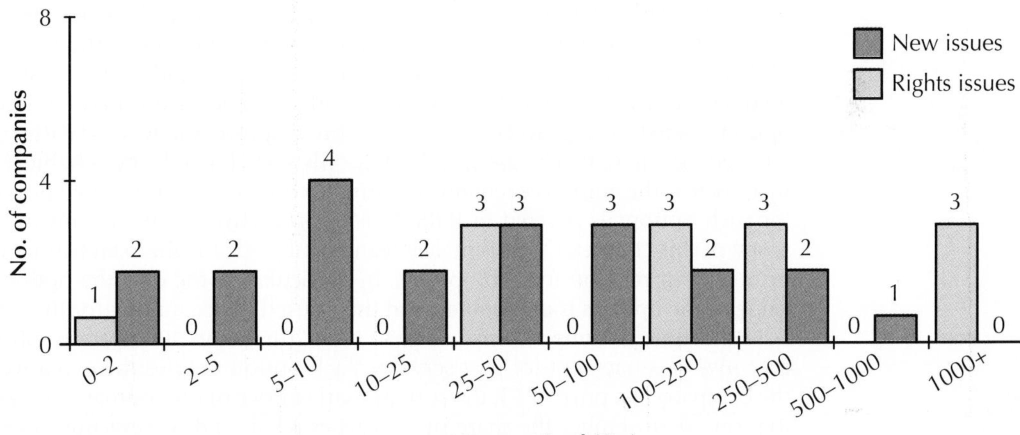

FIGURE 2.7 Rights issues versus new issues on the London Stock Exchange
Source: London Stock Exchange (2008).

ILLUSTRATIVE EXAMPLE 2.7

Rights issue

Pakistan Ltd planned to raise $3.6 million from shareholders through a renounceable one-for-six rights issue. The terms of the issue were 6 million no-par shares to be issued at 60c each, applications to be received by 15 April 2009. The rights issue was fully underwritten. By the due date, the company had received applications for 5 million shares from existing shareholders or parties to whom they had sold their rights. The underwriter acquired the other 1 million shares, and the shares were issued on 20 April 2009.

The journal entries in the company's records are:

15 April	Cash Application (Application monies)	Dr Cr	3 000 000	 3 000 000
	Receivable from Underwriter Application (Amount due from underwriter)	Dr Cr	600 000	 600 000

20 April	Cash	Dr	600 000	
	Receivable from Underwriter	Cr		600 000
	(Receipt from underwriter)			
	Application	Dr	3 600 000	
	Share Capital	Cr		3 600 000
	(Issue of shares)			

2.5.3 Options

A company-issued share option is an instrument that gives the holder the right but not the obligation to buy a certain number of shares in the company by a specified date at a stated price. For example, a company could issue options that gave an investor the right to acquire shares in the company at $2 each, with the options having to be exercised before 31 December 2010. The option holder is taking a risk in that the share price may not reach $2 (the option is 'out of the money') or the share price may exceed $2 (the option is 'in the money').

Where the option holder exercises the option, the company increases its share capital as it issues the shares to the option holder. The company could issue these options to its employees as a part of their remuneration package; or in conjunction with another share issue, rights issue or placement as an incentive to take up the shares offered. The option may be issued free. In the case of options issued to employees, for example, the employees may receive the options as payment for past service. Alternatively, the options may only vest; that is, be exercisable if certain conditions are met, such as the employee remaining with the company for a specified period of time. Accounting for such options is covered in IFRS 2 *Share-based Payment*, the details of which are beyond the scope of this chapter. One of the key features of IFRS 2 is the establishment of the measurement principles in relation to such options. In particular, at the date the options are granted, the fair value of the options is determined and this is used in accounting for the options.

To illustrate: assume a company at 30 June 2010 issues 100 options valued at $1 each to a key executive as a payment for past services. Each option entitles the executive to acquire a share in the company at a price of $3, the current market price of the company shares being $2.90. Assume that on 30 November the share price reaches $3.10 and the executive exercises the option. The journal entries required are shown below.

30 June	Wages Expense	Dr	100	
	Options	Cr		100
	(Options granted to executive)			
30 November	Cash	Dr	300	
	Options	Dr	100	
	Share Capital	Cr		400
	(Exercise of options issued)			

If the share price did not reach $3 within the specified life of the option, then the options would lapse. According to IFRS 2, paragraph 16, the company is then allowed to transfer the balance of the options account to other equity accounts.

Where the options are sold to investors, the company will record an increase in equity. For example, assume A Ltd issued 20 000 options at 50c each to acquire shares in A Ltd at $4 per share. The initial entry recorded by A Ltd is:

	Cash	Dr	10 000	
	Options*	Cr		10 000
	(Issue of options)			

*This account may be called 'Options Reserve' or simply 'Other Equity'.

Options generally have to be exercised by a specific date. Assume that in the case of A Ltd the options had to be exercised by 30 June 2010, and the holders of 18 000 options exercised their rights to acquire A Ltd shares. The journal entries required are:

	Cash Share Capital (Issue of shares on exercise of options)	Dr Cr	72 000	 72 000
	Options Share Capital (Exercise of options)	Dr Cr	9 000	 9 000

Note that the issue price of those options exercised is treated as part of share capital; in essence, these shareholders are paying $4.50 for their shares in A Ltd. However, the journal entries shown may not always be the appropriate ones. The journal entries that need to be made when options are issued may be affected in particular jurisdictions by legal and taxation implications. For example, in Australia it is possible to 'taint' share capital by transferred amounts to that account from retained earnings or other reserves. This affects the subsequent taxation of dividends and returns of capital. The choice of equity accounts used and accounting for movements between these accounts must always be taken after gaining an understanding of legal and taxation effects.

For the options not exercised, the entity could transfer the options balance of $1000 to share capital or a reserve account including retained earnings. Again, legal and taxation implications should be considered in choosing the appropriate accounts to be used. For the example above where the holders of 2000 options did not exercise those options, the journal entry required when the options lapse is:

	Options Options Reserve (Transfer of lapsed options)	Dr Cr	1 000	 1 000

2.5.4 Share warrants

Another form of option is the company-issued warrant. The difference between a warrant and an option is that the warrant is generally attached to another form of financing. For example, the warrant may be attached to an issue of debt, or be given as an incentive to acquire a large parcel of shares in a share issue as an incentive to be involved in the capital raising. The warrants may be detachable or non-detachable. If the latter, then they cannot be traded separately from the shares or debt package to which they were attached. In either case, the warrant has a value and accounting for the issue of warrants is the same as that shown in the previous section for options.

2.5.5 Bonus issues

A bonus issue is an issue of shares to existing shareholders in proportion to their current shareholdings at no cost to the shareholders. The company uses its reserves balances or retained earnings to make the issue. The bonus issue is a transfer from one equity account to another, so it does not increase or decrease the equity of the company. Instead, it increases the share capital and decreases another equity account of the company.

To illustrate: assume a company has a share capital consisting of 500 000 shares. If it makes a 1-for-20 bonus issue from its $100 000 general reserve, it will issue 25 000 shares pro rata to its current shareholders. The journal entry required is:

	General Reserve Share Capital (Bonus issue of 25 000 shares from general reserve)	Dr Cr	100 000	 100 000

Although the bonus issue does not have any effect on the equity of the company, empirical evidence from research into the stockmarket effects of bonus issues shows that share prices tend to increase as a result of bonus issues. The explanation for this effect is that the bonus issue is generally an indicator of future dividend increases. Other reasons for a company making a bonus issue include defending against a takeover bid, particularly following the revaluation of the entity's assets; providing a return to the shareholders; or lowering the current price of the company's shares in the expectation that a lower price per share may make them more tradeable.

2.5.6 Share-based transactions

A company may acquire assets, including other entities, with the consideration for the acquisition being shares in the company itself. Accounting for this form of transaction is covered in chapter 11. Accounting for share-based payments is covered in chapter 6.

2.6 SHARE CAPITAL: SUBSEQUENT DECREASES IN SHARE CAPITAL

A company may decrease the number of shares issued by buying back some of its own shares. The extent to which a company may buy back its own shares and the frequency with which it may do so are generally governed by specific laws within a jurisdiction. A key feature of such regulations is the protection of creditors, as the company is reducing equity by using cash that would have been available to repay debt. Companies may undertake a share buy-back to:

- increase the worth per share of the remaining shares
- manage the capital structure by reducing equity
- most efficiently manage surplus funds held by the company, rather than pay a dividend or reinvest in other ventures.

IFRSs do not prescribe any accounting treatment for share buy-backs. Consider the situation where an entity has issued the following no-par shares over a period of years:

200 000 shares at $1.00	$200 000
100 000 shares at $1.50	150 000
200 000 shares at $2.00	400 000
500 000 shares	$750 000

Assume the total equity of the entity consists of:

Share capital	$ 750 000
Asset revaluation surplus	20 000
Retained earnings	230 000
	$ 1 000 000

If the company now buys back 50 000 shares for $2.20 per share, a total of $110 000, what accounts should be affected by the buy-back? Is it necessary to determine which shares from past issues have been repurchased?

In essence, the composition of the $1 million equity of the entity is relatively unimportant — it is all equity. The composition is only important if there are tax or dividend distribution issues associated with particular accounts. In the absence of such considerations, whether the equity is share capital or retained earnings is irrelevant. This is demonstrated below:

	Equity composition A	or	Equity composition B
Share capital (500 000 shares)	$ 750 000		$ 550 000
Asset revaluation surplus	20 000		150 000
Retained earnings	230 000		300 000
	$1 000 000		$ 1 000 000

The composition of equity here is *per se* irrelevant. Hence, in accounting for the share buy-back, it is immaterial what accounts are affected. The $110 000 write-off could conceivably be taken totally against share capital or retained earnings, or proportionally against all three components of equity. One possible entry is:

	Share Capital	Dr	100 000	
	Retained Earnings	Dr	10 000	
	Cash	Cr		110 000
	(Buy-back of 50 000 shares for $110 000)			

If the shares had been issued at a specific par value, then it would be necessary to identify which particular parcel of shares had been repurchased. The share capital would be reduced by the relevant number of shares repurchased times the par value, and the share premium reduced by the appropriate amount relating to that raised on the original issue of shares not identified as being repurchased. However, any remaining balance could be adjusted against any equity account other than share capital and share premium account.

An example of a repurchase of shares is that undertaken by Nokia and reported in note 15 of its 2005 annual report. This is shown in figure 2.8.

At the Annual General Meeting held on March 25, 2004, Nokia shareholders authorized the Board of Directors to repurchase a maximum of 230 million Nokia shares. In 2005, Nokia repurchased 54 million Nokia shares on the basis of this authorization.

At the Annual General Meeting held on April 7, 2005, Nokia shareholders authorized the Board of Directors to repurchase a maximum of 443 200 000 Nokia shares, representing less than 10% of the share capital and the total voting rights, and to resolve on the disposal of a maximum of 443 200 000 Nokia shares. In 2005, a total of 261 010 000 Nokia shares were repurchased under this buy-back authorization, as a result of which the unused authorization amounted to 182 190 000 shares on December 31, 2005. No shares were disposed of in 2005 under the respective authorization. The shares may be repurchased under the buy-back authorization in order to carry out the company's stock repurchase plan. In addition, the shares may be repurchased in order to develop the capital structure of the company, to finance or carry out acquisitions or other arrangements, to settle the company's equity-based incentive plans, to be transferred for other purposes, or to be cancelled. The authorization to dispose of the shares may be carried out pursuant to terms determined by the Board in connection with acquisitions or in other arrangements or for incentive purposes to selected members of the personnel. The Board may resolve to dispose the shares in another proportion than that of the shareholders' pre-emptive rights to the company's shares, provided that from the company's perspective important financial grounds exist for such disposal. These authorizations are effective until April 7, 2006.

The Board of Directors proposes to the Annual General Meeting convening on March 30, 2006 that the Board of Directors be authorized to repurchase a maximum of 405 million Nokia shares by using unrestricted shareholders' equity. Further, the Board of Directors proposes that the Annual General Meeting authorize the Board of Directors to resolve to dispose a maximum of 405 million Nokia shares. These authorizations are proposed to be effective until March 30, 2007, or in the event that the new Companies Act has been approved by the time of the Annual General Meeting, and enters into force latest on March 30, 2007, these authorizations are proposed to be effective until June 30, 2007.

FIGURE 2.8 Repurchase of shares, Nokia
Source: Nokia (2005, p. 45).

In some countries, when shares are reacquired, they are held in treasury for reissue instead of being cancelled. Such shares are then referred to as 'treasury shares', and are essentially the same as unissued share capital. For example, if an entity acquires 10 000 of its own shares at $12 per share, it would pass the following entry to record this repurchase:

	Treasury Shares	Dr	12 000	
	Cash	Cr		12 000
	(Repurchase of shares)			

In Nokia's 2007 balance sheet (see figure 2.1), the treasury shares are shown as a reduction in total equity because the share capital of the entity has effectively been reduced by the repurchase of the shares. In Christian Dior's 2005 annual report, the fashion house reports treasury shares as part of its current assets. This accounting treatment is explained in note 2.9 to Dior's annual report, shown in figure 2.9.

Treasury shares are recorded at acquisition cost.

Shares held under French market regulations governing stock price adjustments, shares held for employee stock option plans and shares held by subsidiaries on a short-term basis are recorded as assets in the balance sheet.

Shares held under stock option plans are attributed to these plans, for their duration; these shares are recorded as 'less than a year' in the balance sheet when the corresponding options can be exercised immediately or in a period less than a year, and stay classified as 'more than a year' until this date.

When the market value of the treasury shares . . . becomes less than the acquisition price, a provision for depreciation equal to the amount of the difference is recorded.

For treasury shares allocated to option plans, the calculation of depreciation is made on a per-plan basis when the market value of the share is greater than the option exercise price and in relation to the average cost price for all plans in question when the market value of the share is less than the option exercise price. Moreover, when the value of the shares allocated to option plans, net of depreciation, is greater than the exercise price stipulated by each of the plans, a provision for risks and charges is recorded for the amount of the difference.

In case of disposal of treasury shares, the cost price of the disposed parcel is established according to the first-in first-out (FIFO) method.

Treasury Shares held for a long-term basis or for the purpose of future cancellation or exchange are deducted from shareholders' equity, including the realized capital gains and losses.

FIGURE 2.9 Treasury shares, Christian Dior
Source: Christian Dior Group (2005, p. 77).

2.7 RESERVES

'Reserves' is the generic term for all equity accounts other than contributed equity. A major component is the retained earnings account. This account accumulates the annual profit or loss earned by an entity, and is the primary account from which appropriations are made in the form of dividends. As noted in paragraph 88 of IAS 1 *Presentation of Financial Statements,* this standard requires all items of income and expense recognised in a period to be included in profit or loss unless another standard requires otherwise. Hence, in general, the retained earnings account will accumulate the profit or loss earned over the life of the entity. However, as paragraph 89 also notes, other standards require some gains and losses to be reported directly as changes in equity. Some examples are:

- revaluation of property, plant and equipment (see chapter 9)
- particular foreign exchange differences (see chapter 26)
- remeasurements of available-for-sale financial assets (see chapter 5).

These gains and losses are then recognised as part of reserves. As noted in paragraph 81 of IAS 1, entities are required to disclose movements in these accounts as other comprehensive income for the period.

2.7.1 Retained earnings

'Retained earnings' has the same meaning as 'retained profits' and 'accumulated profit or loss'. The key change in this account is the addition of the profit or loss for the current period. The main other movements in the retained earnings account are:

- dividends paid or declared
- transfers to and from reserves
- changes in accounting policy and errors (see IAS 8 *Accounting Policies, Changes in Accounting Estimates and Errors,* discussed in detail in chapter 17).

Dividends are a distribution from the company to its owners. It is generally the case, under companies legislation, that dividends can be paid only from profits, and not from capital. In some jurisdictions, companies must comply with a solvency test before paying dividends. The purpose in both situations is to protect the creditors, as any money paid to shareholders is money unavailable for paying creditors.

Dividends are sometimes divided into interim and final dividends. Interim dividends are paid during the financial year, while final dividends are declared by the directors at year-end for payment sometime after balance date. In some companies, the eventual payment of the final dividends is subject to approval of the dividend by the annual general meeting. With the final dividend, there is some debate as to when the company should raise a liability for the dividend, particularly where payment of the dividend is subject to shareholder approval. Some would argue that until approval is received there is only a contingent liability, the entity not having a present obligation to pay the dividend until approval is received. Others argue that there is a constructive obligation existing at balance date and, given customary business practice, the entity has a liability at the end of the reporting period.

In this regard, paragraphs 12 and 13 of IAS 10 *Events after the Reporting Period* state:

> 12. If an entity declares dividends to holders of equity instruments (as defined in IAS 32 *Financial Instruments: Presentation*) after the reporting period, the entity shall not recognise those dividends as a liability at the end of the reporting period.
> 13. If dividends are declared (i.e. the dividends are appropriately authorised and no longer at the discretion of the entity) after the reporting period but before the financial statements are authorised for issue, the dividends are not recognised as a liability at the end of the reporting period because no obligation exists at this time. Such dividends are disclosed in the notes in accordance with IAS 1 *Presentation of Financial Statements*.

If the dividends are not declared at the end of the reporting period, no liability is recognised at the end of the reporting period. When shareholder approval is required for dividends declared prior to the end of the reporting period, a liability should be recognised only once the annual general meeting approves the dividends, because before that date the entity does not have a present obligation. Until that occurs, the declared dividend is only a contingent liability. (See chapter 4 for further discussion on provisions and contingencies.) It is expected that companies that prefer to raise a liability at year-end will change their regulations or constitution so that dividends can be declared without the need for shareholder approval.

ILLUSTRATIVE EXAMPLE 2.8

Dividends

During the period ending 30 June 2009, the following events occurred in relation to Oman Ltd:

2008	
25 Sept.	Annual general meeting approves the final dividend of $10 000.
30 Sept.	Oman Ltd pays the final dividend to shareholders.
2009	
10 Jan.	Oman Ltd pays an interim dividend of $8 000.
30 June	Oman Ltd declares a final divided of $12 000, this dividend requiring shareholder approval at the next AGM.

Required

Prepare the journal entries to record the dividend transactions of Oman Ltd.

Solution

2008				
25 Sept.	Dividends Declared	Dr	10 000	
	Dividends Payable	Cr		10 000
	(Dividend of $10 000 authorised by annual meeting)			
30 Sept.	Dividends Payable	Dr	10 000	
	Cash	Cr		10 000
	(Payment of dividend)			
2009				
10 Jan.	Interim Dividend Paid	Dr	8 000	
	Cash	Cr		8 000
	(Payment of interim dividend)			

Notes:

1. No entry is required in relation to the final dividend of $12 000. A contingent liability would be recorded in the notes to the 2009 financial statements.
2. The journal entries contain temporary accounts such as 'Dividends declared' and 'Interim dividend paid'. These accounts are useful in preparing the statement of changes in equity (see section 2.8.2) as well as in the worksheet used in the preparation of consolidated financial statements (see chapter 22). At the end of the reporting period, these temporary accounts are transferred to retained earnings:

	Retained Earnings	Dr	18 000	
	Dividends Declared	Cr		10 000
	Interim Dividend Paid	Cr		8 000
	(Closing entry)			

2.7.2 Other components of equity

Some examples of reserves other than retained earnings are shown below.

Asset revaluation surplus

IAS 16 *Property, Plant and Equipment* allows entities a choice in the measurement of these assets. In particular, entities may choose between measuring the assets at cost (the cost model) or at fair value (the revaluation model). If the fair value basis is chosen, revaluation increments are recognised directly in equity via an asset revaluation surplus. (Details of the accounting under a fair value basis for property, plant and equipment is covered in chapter 9.)

The requirement to use the asset revaluation surplus is effectively a measure adopted by the IASB to stop the increase in the fair value of the assets being recognised immediately in the profit or loss for the period. It may be argued that this is an application of the prudence concept in that the fair values of the assets may decline in a later period, and to allow the recognition in current period profits of movements in the fair values of assets would introduce volatility into the profit numbers. However, certain movements in the asset revaluation surplus are required by IAS 1 to be disclosed as a component of other comprehensive income in the statement of comprehensive income.

Having created an asset revaluation surplus, an entity is not restricted in its subsequent disposition. It may be used for payment of dividends or be transferred to other reserve accounts including retained earnings. Amounts recognised directly in the asset revaluation surplus cannot subsequently be recognised in profit or loss for the period even when the revalued asset is disposed of.

Foreign currency translation differences

These differences arise when foreign operations are translated from one currency into another currency for presentation purposes. (Details of the establishment of this account can be found in chapter 26.) The changes in wealth as a result of the translation process are thereby not taken through the profit or loss for the period income, and are recognised in profit only if and when the investor disposes of its interest in the foreign operation.

Fair value differences

Under IAS 39 *Financial Instruments: Recognition and Measurement*, paragraph 55, gains and losses on available-for-sale financial assets are recognised directly in equity until the financial asset is derecognised. At this time, the cumulative gain or loss previously recognised in equity is recognised in profit or loss. This is a situation where the IASB allows the recycling of reserves to income, an accounting treatment unavailable with other reserves.

ILLUSTRATIVE EXAMPLE 2.9

Reserves

As an example of the disclosure of reserves, the consolidated balance sheet of Wesfarmers at 30 June 2008 contained the information shown in figure 2.10. Note the disclosures relating to the nature and purpose of reserves.

26 RESERVES	Consolidated						Parent		
	Restructure tax reserve $m	Capital reserve $m	Foreign currency translation reserve $m	Hedging reserve $m	Available for sale reserve $m	Total $m	Restructure tax reserve $m	Hedging reserve $m	Total $m
Balance at 1 July 2006	110	24	(3)	49	10	190	110	1	111
Remeasurement of financial instruments – gross	—	—	—	92	(31)	61	—	8	8
Tax effect of remeasurement	—	—	—	(28)	(1)	(29)	—	(2)	(2)
Transfer to net profit – gross	—	—	—	(5)	—	(5)	—	(5)	(5)
Tax effect of transfer to net profit	—	—	—	2	—	2	—	1	1
Currency translation differences	—	—	8	—	—	8	—	—	—
Balance at 30 June 2007	110	24	5	110	(22)	227	110	3	113
Tax losses in relation to the 2001 simplification plan	40	—	—	—	—	40	40	—	40
Remeasurement of financial instruments – gross	—	—	—	73	23	96	—	77	77
Tax effect of remeasurement	—	—	—	(23)	3	(20)	—	(23)	(23)
Ineffective cash flow hedges taken to net profit – gross	—	—	—	1	—	1	—	—	—
Currency translation differences	—	—	(14)	—	—	(14)	—	—	—
Balance at 30 June 2008	150	24	(9)	161	4	330	150	57	207

Nature and purpose of reserves
Restructure tax reserve
The restructure tax reserve is used to record the recognition of tax losses arising from the equity restructuring of the Group under the 2001 ownership simplification plan. These tax losses were generated on adoption by the Group of the tax consolidation regime.

Capital reserve
The capital reserve was used to accumulate capital profits. The reserve can be used to pay dividends or issue bonus shares.

Hedging reserve
This reserve records the portion of the gain or loss on a hedging instrument in a cash flow hedge that is determined to be an effective hedge.

Foreign currency translation reserve
The foreign currency translation reserve is used to record exchange differences arising from the translation of the financial statements of foreign subsidiaries.

Available for sale reserve
This reserve records fair value changes on available for sale investments.

FIGURE 2.10 Reserves
Source: Wesfarmers (2008, p. 114).

Entities may make transfers between these reserve accounts, or between reserve accounts and other equity accounts such as retained earnings. Where there is a bonus share dividend, a transfer may be made between reserve accounts and share capital. When accounting for retained earnings, as when accounting for dividends, temporary accounts (namely 'Transfer to/from reserve') are used, these being closed at the end of the period to retained earnings. Chapter 9 discusses in detail the application of the revaluation model to property, plant and equipment and the use of that model. IAS 16 *Property, Plant and Equipment* requires the use of an asset revaluation surplus account in accounting for a revaluation increment. Although not specifically stated in IAS 16, increases in an asset revaluation surplus cannot be made via transfers from other reserves or retained earnings because the surplus arises as a result of applying the revaluation model. Paragraph 41 of IAS 16 covers the accounting for an asset revaluation surplus subsequent to its creation. There is no requirement that an asset revaluation surplus must be transferred to retained earnings on derecognition of a revalued asset. IAS 16, however, allows transfers from the surplus account when a revalued asset is derecognised or progressively as the asset is used by the entity.

ILLUSTRATIVE EXAMPLE 2.10

Reserve transfers

During the period ending 30 June 2010, the following events occurred in relation to the company Malaysia Ltd:

10 Jan.	$10 000 transferred from retained earnings to general reserve
18 Feb.	$4 000 transferred from asset revaluation surplus to retained earnings
15 June	Bonus share dividend of $50 000, half from general reserve and half from retained earnings

Required

Prepare the journal entries to record these transactions.

Solution

2010				
10 Jan.	Transfer to General Reserve	Dr	10 000	
	General Reserve	Cr		10 000
	(Transfer to general reserve)			
18 Feb.	Asset Revaluation Surplus	Dr	4 000	
	Transfer from Asset Revaluation Surplus	Cr		4 000
	(Transfer from asset revaluation surplus)			
15 June	General Reserve	Dr	25 000	
	Bonus Dividend Paid	Dr	25 000	
	Share Capital	Cr		50 000
	(Bonus issue of shares)			
30 June	Retained Earnings	Dr	31 000	
	Transfer from Asset Revaluation Surplus	Dr	4 000	
	Transfer to General Reserve	Cr		10 000
	Bonus Dividend Paid	Cr		25 000
	(Closing entry)			

2.8 DISCLOSURE

Disclosures in relation to equity are detailed in IAS 1 *Presentation of Financial Statements*. The disclosures relate to specific items of equity as well as the preparation of a statement of changes in equity.

2.8.1 Specific disclosures

The specific disclosures illustrated in figure 2.11 are required by paragraphs 79, 137 and 138 of IAS 1.

	IAS 1 para.
Note 21: Company information Hong Kong Ltd is a public company registered in Barcelona, Spain. The company's principal activities are the manufacture of woollen goods, ranging from clothing to furnishings for homes and offices. The company is a subsidiary of China Ltd.	*138(a), (b), (c)*
Note 22: Share capital and reserves	
The company has only one class of share capital, namely ordinary shares. Details in relation to these shares are:	*79(a)*
• 2 million shares have been authorised for issue by the company	*(i)*
• 500 000 shares have been issued fully paid to €3, and 250 000 shares have been issued at €4, but are paid only to €3 per share	*(ii)*
• the shares issued are no-par shares.	*(iii)*
Number of shares issued at 1 January 2010 — 500 000 Issued during 2010 — 250 000 Number of shares issued at 31 December 2010 — 750 000	*(iv)*
There are no restrictions on dividends payable to the shareholders.	*(v)*
There are no shares held by subsidiaries or associates of Hong Kong Ltd, and the company has not repurchased any shares issued.	*(vi)*
The company has issued 50 000 options to current shareholders, each option entitling the holder to buy an ordinary share in Hong Kong Ltd at €2.70, the options having to be exercised by 30 June 2011.	*(vii)*
Reserves The plant maintenance reserve of €140 000 was established to inform those with a financial interest in the company that it had a major claim on future funds in relation to the need to maintain the plant in accordance with Spanish government regulations. The asset revaluation surplus of €95 000 has arisen as the company uses the revaluation model to measure its landholdings. Retained earnings accumulates the annual profit or loss of the entity, other than gains or losses taken directly to equity, and the balance at reporting date represents the undistributed profits of the entity.	*79(b)*
Note 23: Dividends The directors of Hong Kong Ltd in December 2010 proposed dividends of €1 per share for fully paid shares and €0.75 for the partly paid shares, giving a total proposed dividend of €687 500. These dividends have not been recognised in the accounts because their payment is subject to approval by the shareholders at the annual general meeting.	*137(a)*

FIGURE 2.11 Specific disclosures on equity required by IAS 1

2.8.2 Statement of changes in equity

Paragraph 106 of IAS 1 requires the preparation of a statement of changes in equity. This paragraph requires the statement to show the following:

(a) total comprehensive income for the period, showing separately the total amounts attributable to owners of the parent and to non-controlling interests;
(b) for each component of equity, the effects of retrospective application or retrospective restatement recognised in accordance with IAS 8; and
(c) [deleted]
(d) for each component of equity, a reconciliation between the carrying amount at the beginning and the end of the period, separately disclosing changes resulting from:
  (i) profit or loss;
  (ii) each item of other comprehensive income: and
  (iii) transactions with owners in their capacity as owners, showing separately contributions by and distributions to owners and changes in ownership interests in subsidiaries that do not result in a loss of control.

These requirements can be met in a number of ways, including using a columnar format. The statement of changes in equity must contain the information in paragraph 106 of IAS 1. The information required by paragraph 107 in relation to dividends may be included in the statement of changes in equity or disclosed in the notes.

Figure 2.12 is a pro-forma statement of changes in equity using a non-columnar format. Figure 2.13 uses the information disclosed by the ANZ Bank in Australia in its 2008 annual report to illustrate the use of this format. In figure 2.14, the statement of changes in equity disclosed in the 2007 annual report of Nokia Ltd demonstrates a columnar format for this statement.

FIGURE 2.12 Pro-forma note disclosures relating to the statement of changes in equity in accordance with IAS 1, para. 106

Statement of changes in equity for the year ended 30 June 2010 millions

	Note	Consolidated		Attributable to shareholders of the parent		The company	
		2010	2009	2010	2009	2010	2009
Comprehensive income							
Attributable to:							
Owners of the parent							
Non-controlling interest							
Share capital							
Balance at start of year							
Dividend reinvestment plan							
Group employee share acquisition scheme							
Group share option scheme							
New issues							
Share buy-back							
Balance at end of year							
Reserves							
Asset revaluation surplus							
Balance at start of year							
Revaluation increment							
Transfers							
Balance at end of year							

FIGURE 2.12 *(continued)*

	Note	Consolidated		Attributable to shareholders of the parent		The company	
		2010	2009	2010	2009	2010	2009
Foreign currency translation differences							
Balance at start of year							
Currency translation adjustments							
Balance at end of year							
Business combination valuation reserve							
Balance at start of year							
Increments — new business combinations							
Transfers to other reserves							
Balance at end of year							
Retained earnings							
Total income and expense for the period							
Balance of retained earnings at start of year							
Total available for appropriation							
Dividends paid or declared							
Balance of retained earnings at end of year							
Total equity at end of year							

FIGURE 2.13 Illustrative statement of changes in equity for ANZ Ltd

Statements of recognised income and expense for the year ended 30 September				
	Consolidated		**The Company**	
	2008 $m	**2007 $m**	**2008 $m**	**2007 $m**
Total recognised income and expense for the year attributable to minority interests	8	7	—	—
Total recognised income and expense for the year attributable to shareholders of the Company	3 375	3 856	3 352	3 471
28. Share capital				
Ordinary share capital				
Balance at start of year	8 946	8 271	8 946	8 271
Dividend reinvestment plan[1]	1 019	442	1 019	442
DRP underwriting	1 487	—	1 487	—
ANZ employee share acquisition plan[2]	80	57	80	57
Treasury shares[3,4]	(10)	(55)	(10)	(55)
ANZ share option plan[2]	67	132	67	132
Conversion of StEPS	1 000	—	1 000	—
Consideration for purchase of ETrade Australia	—	99	—	99
Balance at end of year	12 589	8 946	12 589	8 946

1 Refer to note 7 for details of plan.
2 Refer to note 46 for details of plan.
3 On-market purchase of shares for settlement of amounts due under share-based compensation plans. In addition, 2 356 857 shares were issued during the September 2008 year to the Group's Employee Share Trust for settlement of amounts due under share-based compensation plans.
4 As at 30 September 2008, there were 4 374 248 Treasury shares outstanding (2007: 2 592 893).

(continued)

FIGURE 2.13 *(continued)*

	Consolidated		The Company	
	2008 $m	2007 $m	2008 $m	2007 $m
Notes to the financial statements				
29: Reserves and Retained Earnings				
a) Foreign currency translation reserve				
Balance at beginning of year	(1 209)	(646)	(407)	(116)
Currency translation adjustments, net of hedges after tax	393	(563)	254	(291)
Total foreign currency translation reserve	(816)	(1 209)	(153)	(407)
b) Share option reserve[1]				
Balance at beginning of year	70	63	70	63
Share-based payments	14	7	14	7
Transfer of options lapsed to retained earnings[3]	(1)	—	(1)	—
Total share option reserve	83	70	83	70
c) Available-for-sale revaluation reserve				
Balance at start of year	97	2	93	(3)
Valuation gain/(loss) recognised after tax	(305)	109	(272)	100
Cumulative (gain)/loss transferred to the income statement	60	(14)	63	(4)
Transfer on step acquisition of associate	60	—	60	—
Total available-for-sale revaluation reserve	(88)	97	(56)	93
d) Hedging reserve				
Balance at start of year	153	227	80	40
Adjustment on adoption of AASB 2005-1[2]	—	(141)	—	—
Restated balance at beginning of year	153	86	80	40
Gain/(loss) recognised after tax	(39)	74	(34)	40
Transfer (to)/from income statement	(35)	(7)	5	—
Total hedging reserve	79	153	51	80
Total reserves	(742)	(889)	(75)	(164)

1 Further information about share based payments to employees is disclosed in note 46 to the financial statements.
2 Under the provisions of AASB 2005-1, hedge accounting is not available for the NZ revenue hedges, effective 1 October 2006 (refer note 1E (ii)).
3 The transfer of balances from the share option and capital reserves to retained earnings represent items of a distributable nature.

	Consolidated 2008 $m	Consolidated 2007 $m	The Company 2008 $m	The Company 2007 $m
Retained earnings				
Restated balance at start of year	13 082	11 084	9 436	8 173
Adjustment on adoption of AASB 2005-1[2]	—	141	—	—
Restated balance at beginning of year	13 082	11 225	9 436	8 173
Profit attributable to shareholders of the Company	3 319	4 180	3 336	3 551
Adjustment on step acquisition of associate	1	—	—	—
Transfer of options lapsed from share option reserve[1, 3]	1	—	1	—
Actuarial gain/(loss) on defined benefit plans after tax[4]	(79)	77	(60)	75
Ordinary share dividends paid	(2 506)	(2 363)	(2 506)	(2 363)
Preference share dividends paid	(46)	(37)	—	—
Retained earnings at end of year	13 772	13 082	10 207	9 436
Total reserves and retained earnings	13 030	12 193	10 132	9 272

1 Further information about share based payments to employees is disclosed in note 46 to the financial statements.
2 Under the provisions of AASB 2005-1, hedge accounting is not available for the NZ revenue hedges, effective 1 October 2006 (refer note 1E (ii)).
3 The transfer of balances from the share option, general and capital reserves to retained earnings represent items of a distributable nature.
4 ANZ has taken the option available under AASB 119 to recognise actuarial gains/losses on defined benefit superannuation plans directly in retained profits (refer note 1F (vi) and note 45).

Source: Compiled from information provided in the annual report of ANZ Ltd (2008, pp. 62, 109, 111–2).

FIGURE 2.14 Statement of changes in equity for Nokia Ltd

Consolidated statements of changes in shareholders' equity, IFRS

EURm	Number of shares (1000's)	Share capital	Share issue premium	Treasury shares	Translation differences	Fair value and other reserves	Reserve for invested non-restrict equity	Retained earnings	Before minority interests	Minority interests	Total
Balance at December 31, 2004	**4 486 941**	**280**	**2 366**	**(2 022)**	**(126)**	**13**	**—**	**13 874**	**14 385**	**168**	**14 553**
Tax benefit on stock options exercised			(2)						(2)		(2)
Translation differences					406				406	31	437
Net investment hedge losses					(211)				(211)		(211)
Cash flow hedges, net of tax						(132)			(132)		(132)
Available-for-sale investments, net of tax						(57)			(57)		(57)
Other decrease, net								(55)	(55)	1	(54)
Profit								3 616	3 616	74	3 690
Total comprehensive income		—	(2)	—	195	(189)	—	3 561	3 565	106	3 671
Stock options exercised	125		2						2		2
Stock options exercised related to acquisitions			(1)						(1)		(1)
Share-based compensation[1]			79						79		79
Acquisition of treasury shares	(315 174)			(4 268)					(4 268)		(4 268)
Reissuance of treasury shares	484			10					10		10
Cancellation of treasury shares		(14)	14	2 664				(2 664)	—		—
Dividend								(1 463)	(1 463)	(69)	(1 532)
Total of other equity movements		(14)	94	(1 594)	—	—	—	(4 127)	(5 641)	(69)	(5 710)
Balance at December 31, 2005	**4 172 376**	**266**	**2 458**	**(3 616)**	**69**	**(176)**	**—**	**13 308**	**12 309**	**205**	**12 514**
Tax benefit on stock options exercised			23						23		23
Excess tax benefit on share-based compensation			14						14		14
Translation differences					(141)				(141)	(13)	(154)
Net investment hedge gains, net of tax					38				38		38
Cash flow hedges, net of tax						171			171		171
Available-for-sale investments, net of tax						(9)			(9)		(9)
Other decrease, net								(52)	(52)	(1)	(53)
Profit								4 306	4 306	60	4 366
Total comprehensive income		—	37	—	(103)	162	—	4 254	4 350	46	4 396
Stock options exercised	3 046	0	43						43		43
Stock options exercised related to acquisitions			(1)						(1)		(1)

(continued)

FIGURE 2.14 *(continued)*

Share-based compensation[1]			219						219		219
Settlement of performance and restricted shares	2 236		(69)	38					(31)		(31)
Acquisition of treasury shares	(212 340)			(3 413)					(3 413)		(3 413)
Reissuance of treasury shares	412			4					4		4
Cancellation of treasury shares		(20)	20	4 927				(4 927)	—		—
Dividend								(1 512)	(1 512)	(40)	(1 552)
Acquisition of minority interests									—	(119)	(119)
Total of other equity movements		(20)	212	1 556	—	—		(6 439)	(4 691)	(159)	(4 850)
Balance at December 31, 2006	**3 965 730**	**246**	**2 707**	**(2 060)**	**(34)**	**(14)**	**—**	**11 123**	**11 968**	**92**	**12 060**
Excess tax benefit on share-based compensation			128						128		128
Translation differences					(167)				(167)	16	(151)
Net investment hedge gains, net of tax					38				38		38
Cash flow hedges, net of tax						(11)			(11)		(11)
Available-for-sale investments, net of tax						48			48		48
Other decrease, net								(40)	(40)		(40)
Profit								7 205	7 205	(459)	6 746
Total comprehensive income		—	128	—	(129)	37	—	7 165	7 201	(443)	6 758
Stock options exercised	57 269	0	46				932		978		978
Stock options exercised related to acquisitions			(3)						(3)		(3)
Share-based compensation			228						228		228
Settlement of performance and restricted shares	3 138		(104)	58			9		(37)		(37)
Acquisition of treasury shares	(180 590)			(3 884)					(3 884)		(3 884)
Reissuance of treasury shares	403			7					7		7
Cancellation of treasury shares				2 733				(2 733)	—		—
Share premium reduction and transfer			(2 358)				2 358		—		—
Dividend								(1 685)	(1 685)	(75)	(1 760)
Minority interest on formation of Nokia Siemens Networks									—	2 991	2 991
Total of other equity movements		0	(2 191)	(1 086)	—	—	3 299	(4 418)	(4 396)	2 916	(1 480)
Balance at December 31, 2007	**3 845 950**	**246**	**644**	**(3 146)**	**(16 3)**	**23**	**3 299**	**13 870**	**14 773**	**2 565**	**17 338**

1 In 2005 and 2006, share-based compensation is shown net of deferred compensation recorded related to social security costs on share-based payments. Dividends declared per share were EUR 0.53 for 2007 (EUR 0.43 for 2006 and EUR 0.37 for 2005), subject to shareholders' approval.

Source: Nokia (2007, p. 12).

SUMMARY

The corporate form of organisational structure is a popular one in many countries, particularly because of the limited liability protection that it affords to shareholders. These companies' operations are financed by a mixture of equity and debt. In this chapter the focus is on the equity of a corporate entity. The components of equity recognised generally by companies are share capital, other reserves and retained earnings. Share capital in particular is affected by a variety of financial instruments developed in the financial markets, offering investors instruments with an array of risk-return alternatives. Each of these equity alternatives has its own accounting implications. The existence of reserves is driven by traditional accounting as well as the current restrictions in some accounting standards for some wealth increases to be recognised directly in equity rather than in current income. Even though definite distinctions are made between the various components of equity, it needs to be recognised that they are all equity and differences relate to jurisdictional differences in terms of restrictions on dividend distribution, taxation effects and differences in rights of owners. IAS 1 requires detailed disclosures in relation to each of the components of equity.

Discussion questions

1. Discuss the nature of a reserve. How do reserves differ from the other main components of equity?
2. A company announces a final dividend at the end of the financial year. Discuss whether a dividend payable should be recognised.
3. The telecommunications industry in a particular country has been a part of the public sector. As a part of its privatisation agenda, the government decided to establish a limited liability company called Telecom Plus, with the issue of 10 million $3 shares. These shares were to be offered to the citizens of the country. The terms of issue were such that investors had to pay $2 on application and the other $1 per share would be called at a later time. Discuss:
   (a) the nature of the limited liability company, and in particular the financial obligations of acquirers of shares in the company
   (b) the journal entries that would be required if applications were received for 11 million shares.
4. Why would a company wish to buy back its own shares? Discuss.
5. A company has a share capital consisting of 100 000 shares issued at $2 per share, and 50 000 shares issued at $3 per share. Discuss the effects on the accounts if:
   (a) the company buys back 20 000 shares at $4 per share
   (b) the company buys back 20 000 shares at $2.50 per share.
6. A company has a share capital consisting of 100 000 shares having a par value of $1 per share and issued at a premium of $1 per share, and 50 000 shares issued at $2 par and $1 premium. Discuss the effects on the accounts if:
   (a) the company buys back 20 000 shares at $4 per share
   (b) the company buys back 20 000 shares at $2.50 per share.
7. Discuss the nature of a rights issue, distinguishing between a renounceable and a non-renounceable issue.
8. What is a private placement of shares? What are the advantages and disadvantages of such a placement?
9. Discuss whether it is necessary to distinguish between the different components of equity rather than just having a single number for shareholders' equity.
10. For what reasons may a company make an appropriation of its retained earnings?

STAR RATING
★ BASIC
★★ MODERATE
★★★ DIFFICULT

Exercises

Exercise 2.1

RESERVES AND DIVIDENDS

★ Prepare journal entries to record the following unrelated transactions of a public company:
(a) payment of interim dividend of $30 000

(b) transfer of $52 000 from the asset revaluation surplus to the general reserve
(c) transfer of $34 000 from the general reserve to retained earnings
(d) payment of 240 000 bonus shares, fully paid, at $2 per share from the general reserve.

Exercise 2.2 **DIVIDENDS**

★ India Ltd's share capital currently consists of 40 000 ordinary shares issued with a par value of $5 per share, and 20 000 10% preference shares issued at $10 each. In relation to the preference shares, dividends have not been paid for the 2 years prior to the current year. The company plans to pay out $100 000 in dividends in the current period, meeting all past obligations (where applicable) to shareholders.

Determine how much each class of shares should receive under the following situations:

(a) the preference shares are non-cumulative and non-participating
(b) the preference shares are cumulative and non-participating
(c) the preference shares are cumulative and participating. Assume that the participation agreement requires that the ordinary shareholders receive the same percentage of dividend as the preference shareholders, and that any balance of dividends to be paid is shared in proportion to the issued share capital of each class.

Exercise 2.3 **RIGHTS ISSUE**

Laos Ltd had share capital of one million $1 shares, fully paid. As it needed finance for certain construction projects, the company's management decided to make a non-renounceable rights issue to existing shareholders of 200 000 new shares at an issue price of $5 per share. The rights issue was to be fully underwritten by Finance Brokers Ltd. The prospectus was issued on 15 February 2009 and applications closed on 15 March 2009. Costs associated with the rights issue and the eventual issue of the shares were $10 000.

(a) If 80% of the rights were exercised by the due date, provide journal entries made by Laos Ltd in relation to the rights issue and the eventual share issue.
(b) If the rights issue was not underwritten and any unexercised rights lapsed, what would be the required journal entries?

Exercise 2.4 **SHARE ISSUE, OPTIONS**

★ Jordan Ltd has the following shareholders' equity at 1 January 2010:

Share capital — 500 000 shares	$1 240 000
Asset revaluation surplus	350 000
Retained earnings	110 000

On 1 March the company decided to make a public share issue to raise $600 000 for new capital development. The company issued a prospectus inviting applications for 200 000 $3 shares, payable in full on application. Shareholders who acquired more than 10 000 shares were allowed to buy options at 50 cents each. These options enabled the owner to buy shares in Jordan Ltd at $3.50 each, the acquisition having to occur before 31 December 2010.

By 25 March the company had received applications for 250 000 shares and for 20 000 options. The shares and options were allotted on 2 April, and money returned to unsuccessful applicants on the same day. All applicants who acquired options also received shares.

By 31 December 2010, the company's share price had reached $3.75. Holders of 18 000 options exercised their options in December. The remaining options lapsed.

Required

Prepare the journal entries in the records of Jordan Ltd in relation to the equity transactions in 2010.

Exercise 2.5 ★★

ISSUE OF ORDINARY AND PREFERENCE SHARES

Prepare journal entries and ledger accounts to record the following transactions for Kuwait Ltd:

2011	
01 April	A prospectus was issued inviting applications for 100 000 ordinary shares at an issue price of $1.50, fully payable on application. The prospectus also offered 100 000 10% preference shares at an issue price of $2, fully payable on application. The issue was underwritten at a commission of $4500, being $500 relating to the issue of ordinary shares and the balance for preference shares. All unsuccessful application monies were to be returned to the applicants.
10 April	Applications closed with the ordinary issue oversubscribed by 40 000 shares and the preference shares undersubscribed by 15 000 shares.
15 April	100 000 ordinary shares were allotted and applications for 40 000 shares were rejected and money refunded. 100 000 preference shares were also allotted.
20 April	The underwriter paid for the shares allocated to her, less the commission due.

Exercise 2.6 ★★

RIGHTS ISSUE, PLACEMENT OF SHARES

The shareholders' equity of Iraq Ltd on 1 January 2010 was:

Share capital — 200 000 shares fully paid	$400 000
General reserve	200 000
Retained earnings	100 000

The following transactions occurred during the year ended 31 December 2010:

1. On 1 February 2010, a renounceable one-for-two rights issue was made to existing shareholders. The issue price was $2 per share, payable in full on application. The issue was underwritten for a commission of $5000. The issue closed fully subscribed on 31 March, the holders of 40 000 shares having transferred their rights. The underwriting commission was paid on 5 March.
2. On 30 June 2010, 10 000 shares were privately placed with Asian Investments Ltd at $2 per share.

Required

Prepare the general journal entries to record the above transactions.

Problems

Problem 2.1 ★

DIVIDENDS, CALLS ON SHARES AND BONUS ISSUE

The equity of Japan Ltd at 1 January 2011 was as follows:

Share capital		
600 000 shares fully paid	$600 000	
400 000 shares issued for $1 and paid to 50c	200 000	$ 800 000
General reserve		200 000
Plant maintenance reserve		50 000
Retained earnings		80 000
Total equity		$1 130 000

The following events occurred during the year:

25 June	Interim dividend of 10c per share paid, with partly paid shares receiving a proportionate dividend.
10 July	Call of 50c per share on the partly paid shares.
31 July	Collection of call money.
15 Sept.	Bonus share issue of one share for each 10 shares held, at $1 per share, allocated from general reserve.
31 Dec.	Directors announce that a dividend of 20c per share will be paid in September, subject to approval at the February annual general meeting. Transfer of plant maintenance reserve to general reserve. The company earned a profit of $60 000

Required

(a) Prepare the journal entries to give effect to the above events.
(b) Prepare the equity section of the statement of financial position at 31 December 2011.

Problem 2.2 SHARE ISSUE, OPTIONS

★★ On 30 June 2009, the equity accounts of Brunei Ltd consisted of:

175 000 'A' ordinary shares, issued at $2.50 each, fully paid	$ 437 500
50 000 6% cumulative preference shares, issued at $3 and paid to $2	100 000
Options (20 000 at 56c each)	11 200
Accumulated losses	(6 250)

As the company had incurred a loss for the year ended 30 June 2009, no dividends were declared for that year. The options were exercisable between 1 March 2010 and 30 April 2010. Each option allowed the holder to buy one 'A' ordinary share for $4.50.

The following transactions and events occurred during the year ended 30 June 2010:

2009 25 July	The directors made the final call of $1 on the preference shares.
31 August	All call monies were received except those owing on 7500 preference shares.
7 September	The directors resolved to forfeit 7500 preference shares for non-payment of the call. The constitution of the company directs that forfeited amounts are not to be refunded to shareholders. The shares will not be reissued.
1 November	The company issued a prospectus offering 30 000 'B' ordinary shares payable in two instalments: $3 on application and $2 on 30 November 2011. The offer closed on 30 November.
30 November	Applications for 40 000 'B' ordinary shares were received.
1 December	The directors resolved to allot the 'B' ordinary shares pro rata with all applicants receiving 75% of the shares applied for. Excess application monies were allowed to be held. The shares were duly allotted.
5 December	Share issue costs of $5200 were paid.
2010 30 April	The holders of 15 000 options applied to purchase shares. All monies were sent with the applications. All remaining options lapsed. The shares were duly issued.

Required

(a) Prepare general journal entries to record the above transactions.

(a) If Brunei Ltd buys back 25 000 preference shares for $3.50 per share, what factors would its accountant have to consider in determining how best to record the transaction in the accounts?

Problem 2.3 ★★

ISSUE OF OPTION AND SHARES, FORFEITURE OF SHARES

Prepare ledger accounts to record the following transactions for Nepal Ltd:

2011 01 July	A prospectus was issued inviting applications for 100 000 ordinary shares at an issue price of $3, with $2 payable on application and the balance payable on 10 June 2012. The prospectus also offered 50 000 10% preference shares at $2, fully payable on application. The issue was underwritten at a commission of $6500, allocated equally between the classes of shares.
21 July	Applications closed with the ordinary share issue oversubscribed by 20 000 and the preference shares undersubscribed by 15 000.
31 July	All shares were allotted, and application money refunded to unsuccessful applicants for ordinary shares.
14 Aug.	The underwriter paid amounts less commission.
01 Dec.	The directors resolved to give each ordinary shareholder, free of charge, one option for every two shares held. The options are exercisable prior to 1 June 2012 and allow each holder to acquire one ordinary share at an exercise price of $2.70. Options not exercised prior to that date lapse.
2012 01 June	The holders of 40 000 options elected to exercise those options and 40 000 shares were issued.
10 June	The balance payable on the ordinary shares was received from holders of 95 000 ordinary shares.
15 June	The shares on which call money was not received were forfeited.
25 June	The forfeited shares were placed with a financial institution, paid to $3 on payment of $2.80. The cash was received from the financial institution, and any balance in the forfeited shares account returned to the former shareholders. Reissue costs amounted to $550.

Problem 2.4 ★★

BUY-BACK OF SHARES

Vietnam Ltd decided to repurchase 10% of its ordinary shares under a buy-back scheme for $5.60 per share. At the date of the buy-back, the equity of Vietnam Ltd consisted of:

Share capital — 4 million shares fully paid	$4 000 000
General reserve	600 000
Retained earnings	1 100 000

The costs of the buy-back scheme amounted to $3500.

Required

(a) Prepare the journal entries to account for the buy-back. Explain the reasons for the entries made.

(b) Assume that the buy-back price per share was equal to 70c per share. Prepare journal entries to record the buy-back, and explain your answer.

(c) Assume that, instead of the share capital shown above, Vietnam Ltd had issued 1 million shares at a par value of $1 and a share premium of $3 per share. Rework your answers to (a) and (b) under this new scenario.

Problem 2.5 RIGHTS ISSUE, CALL ON SHARES, ISSUE OF OPTIONS

★★ The share capital of Syria Ltd on 30 June 2010 was:

120 000 'A' ordinary shares issued at $1.50, paid to 75c	$ 90 000
50 000 'B' ordinary shares issued at $2.00, fully paid	100 000
100 000 9% preference shares issued at $1, paid to 80c	80 000
	$270 000

The following transactions occurred during 2010 and 2011:

2010 01 Nov.	The company makes a one-for-five rights offer to its 'B' ordinary shareholders. The rights are renounceable, and allow holders to obtain 'B' ordinary shares for $2.25 per share, payable in full on application.
30 Nov.	The holders of 40 000 'B' ordinary shares accept the rights offer by the expiry date. The shares are duly allotted.
2011 16 Jan.	A call of 75c per share is made on all 'A' ordinary shares. All call money except that owed by the holder of 10 000 shares is received by 31 January.
05 Feb.	Shares on which calls are unpaid are forfeited and cancelled.
17 Mar.	To assist with cash flow difficulties, the company issued a prospectus inviting offers for 50 000 options to acquire 'A' ordinary shares at an issue price of 60c per option, payable in full on application. Each option, exercisable prior to 31 December 2011, allows the holder to acquire one 'A' ordinary share for $1.78.
31 Mar.	Offers had been received for 35 000 options and these were duly allotted.
31 Dec.	The holders of 25 000 options had exercised their options, with money paid on exercise, and 25 000 'A' ordinary shares were issued. The remaining options lapsed. Costs of issuing the shares amounted to $2000.

Required

Prepare journal entries to record the above transactions in the records of Syria Ltd.

Problem 2.6 SHARE ISSUE, OPTIONS, STATEMENT OF CHANGES IN EQUITY

★★★ On 30 June 2009, the equity accounts of Taiwan Ltd consisted of:

120 000 ordinary shares, issued at $2.50 each, fully paid	$300 000
Options (80 000 at 50c each)*	40 000
General reserve	30 000
Forfeited shares reserve	2 000
Retained earnings	75 000

*The options were exercisable between 1 May 2010 and 31 May 2010. Each option allowed the holder to buy one ordinary share for $3 each.

Additional information

The following transactions and events occurred during the year ended 30 June 2010:

- The final 6c per share dividend for the year ended 30 June 2009 was paid on 27 September 2009. Shareholder approval to pay the dividend had been obtained at the annual general meeting on 20 September.
- On 1 October, the directors issued a prospectus offering 40 000 ordinary shares at an issue price of $2.80, payable $2 on application and 80c as a future call. The closing date for application was 31 October 2009. The share issue was underwritten by Support Stockbrokers for a fee of $2500, payable on 15 November 2009.
- By 31 October 2009, applications for 50 000 shares had been received.
- On 5 November 2009, the directors allotted the shares pro rata, with applicants receiving 80% of their requested shares. The company's constitution allows excess application monies to be retained and used to offset future calls payable.
- On 15 November 2009, the underwriting fee was paid.
- On 31 December 2009, the directors announced an interim dividend of 3c per share payable in cash on 1 February.
- To raise funds for expansion, the directors sold a parcel of 80 000 ordinary shares to Safe Superannuation Fund on 28 April 2010 at an issue price of $2.90 per share.
- By 31 May 2010, the holders of 65 000 options had indicated that they wished to purchase shares. On 2 June 2010, 65 000 ordinary shares were issued with monies being payable by 21 June. Options not exercised duly lapsed.
- All outstanding monies were received with respect to shares issued to option holders.
- Profit for the year was $69 420. On 30 June 2010, the directors decided to:
  - transfer $30 000 to the general reserve
  - declare a final 5c per share dividend. Shareholder approval for this dividend will be sought at the annual general meeting in September 2010.

Required

(a) Prepare general journal entries, including any closing entries required, to record the above transactions. (Narrations are not required, but show all workings.)

(b) Prepare a statement of changes in equity for the year ended 30 June 2010.

(c) Taiwan Ltd has recognised a 'Forfeited shares reserve' as part of equity. Explain how and why such a reserve would be created.

Problem 2.7 ★★★ SHARES, OPTIONS, DIVIDENDS AND RESERVE TRANSFERS

The equity of Maldives Ltd at 30 June 2010 consisted of:

400 000 ordinary 'A' shares issued at $2.00, fully paid	$ 800 000
300 000 ordinary 'B' shares issued at $2.00, called to $1.20	360 000
50 000 6% preference shares issued at $1.50, fully paid	75 000
Share options issued at 60c, fully paid	24 000
Retained earnings	318 000

The options were exercisable before 28 February 2011. Each option entitled the holder to acquire two ordinary 'C' shares at $1.80 per share, the amount payable on notification to exercise the option.

The following transactions occurred during the year ended 30 June 2011:

2010	
15 Sept.	The preference dividend and the final ordinary dividend of 16c per fully paid share, both declared on 30 June 2010, were paid. The directors do not need any other party to authorise the payment of dividends.
01 Nov.	A one-for-five renounceable rights offer was made to ordinary 'A' shareholders at an issue price of $1.90 per share. The expiry date on the offer was 30 November 2010. The issue was underwritten at a commission of $3000.

(continued)

30 Nov.	Holders of 320 000 shares accepted the rights offer, paying the required price per share, with the renounced rights being taken up by the underwriter. Ordinary 'A' shares were duly issued.
10 Dec.	Money due from the underwriter was received.
2011 10 Jan.	The directors transferred $35 000 from retained earnings to a general reserve.
28 Feb.	As a result of options being exercised, 70 000 ordinary 'C' shares were issued. Unexercised options lapsed.
30 Apr.	The directors made a call on the ordinary 'B' shares for 80c per share. Call money was payable by 31 May.
31 May	All call money was received except for that due on 15 000 shares.
18 June	Shares on which the final call was unpaid were forfeited.
26 June	Forfeited shares were reissued, credited as paid to $2, for $1.80 per share, the balance of the forfeited shares account being refundable to the former shareholders.
27 June	Refund paid to former holders of forfeited shares.
30 June	The directors declared a 20c per share final dividend to be paid on 15 September 2011.

Required

(a) Prepare general journal entries to record the above transactions.
(b) Prepare the equity section of the statement of financial position as at 30 June 2011.

Problem 2.8 DIVIDENDS, SHARE ISSUES, SHARE BUY-BACKS, OPTIONS AND MOVEMENTS IN RESERVES

★★★

Singapore Ltd, a company whose principal interests were in the manufacture of fine leather shoes and handbags, was formed on 1 January 2008. Prior to the 2011 period, Singapore Ltd had issued 110 000 ordinary shares:

- 95 000 $30 shares were issued for cash on 1 January 2008
- 5000 shares were exchanged on 1 February 2009 for a patent that had a fair value at date of exchange of $240 000
- 10 000 shares were issued on 13 November 2010 for $50 per share.

At 1 January 2011, Singapore Ltd had a balance in its retained earnings account of $750 000, while the general reserve and the asset revaluation surplus had balances of $240 000 and $180 000 respectively. The purpose of the general reserve is to reflect the need for the company to regularly replace certain of the shoe-making machinery to reflect technological changes.

During the 2011 financial year, the following transactions occurred:

15 Feb.	Singapore Ltd paid a $25 000 dividend that had been declared in December 2010. Liabilities for dividends are recognised when they are declared by the company.
10 May	10 000 shares at $55 per share were offered to the general public. These were fully subscribed and issued on 20 June 2011. On the same date, another 15 000 shares were placed with major investors at $55 per share.
25 June	The company paid a $20 000 interim dividend.
30 June	The company revalued land by $30 000, increasing the asset revaluation surplus by $21 000 and the deferred tax liability by $9000.

01 July	The company early adopted IAS X in relation to insurance. The transitional liability on initial adoption was $55 000 more than the liability recognised under the previous accounting standard. This amount was recognised directly in retained earnings.
22 July	Singapore Ltd repurchased 5000 shares on the open market for $56 per share. The repurchase was accounted for by writing down share capital and retained earnings by an equal amount.
16 Nov.	Singapore Ltd declared a 1-for-10 bonus issue to shareholders on record at 1 October 2011. The whole of the general reserve was used to create this bonus issue.
01 Dec.	The company issued 100 000 options at 20 cents each, each option entitling the holder to acquire an ordinary share in Singapore Ltd at a price of $60 per share, the options to be exercised by 31 December 2012. No options had been exercised by 31 December 2011.
31 Dec.	Singapore Ltd calculated that its profit for the 2011 year was $150 000. It declared a $30 000 final dividend, transferred $40 000 to the general reserve, and transferred $30 000 from the asset revaluation surplus to retained earnings.

Share issue costs amount to 10% of the worth of any share issue.

Required

(a) Prepare the general journal entries to record the above transactions.
(b) Prepare the statement of changes in equity for Singapore Ltd for the year ended 31 December 2011.

Problem 2.9 ★★★

SHARE ISSUES, OPTIONS, RIGHTS ISSUES, DIVIDENDS, RESERVE TRANSFERS

The equity of Yemen Ltd on 30 June 2009 (end of the reporting period) consisted of:

280 000 ordinary shares, issued at $2.40 each and called to $2.40	$ 672 000
Calls in arrears (24 000 shares × 80c)	(19 200)
General reserve	290 000
Retained earnings	53 780

Additional information

The following transactions and events relating to share issues and options occurred during the year ended 30 June 2010:

- On 15 July 2009, the directors forfeited the shares on which the call was outstanding. Forfeited shares are not to be reissued and the company's constitution requires that any forfeited amounts be refunded to the former shareholders. Refund cheques were sent on 26 July 2009. Any outstanding dividends were still payable to former shareholders.
- On 1 August 2009, a rights offer (offering 5% preference shares at an issue price of $2.80 per share) was made to existing shareholders on the basis of one preference share for every two ordinary shares held. Shares were payable in full on allotment and rights were renounceable. The issue was underwritten for a fee of $5000.
- The rights offer closed undersubscribed on 31 August 2009, and rights in respect of 40 000 shares were transferred to the underwriter. On 1 September 2009, the shares were allotted. The underwriter paid for its allotment of shares, net of its fee, on 10 September 2009. All other monies were received by 21 September 2009.
- On 1 March 2010, the directors offered for sale 100 000 options at 10c each. Each option gave the holder the right to purchase one ordinary share for $2.80 each. Options were exercisable between 1 April 2011 and 30 June 2011. The option offer closed with 80 000 applications being received. Options were duly allotted on 2 April 2010.

The following transactions and events relating to dividends and reserve transfers occurred during the year ended 30 June 2010:

- On 29 September 2009, the final dividend of 10c per share for the year ended 30 June 2009 was paid. The dividend had been declared on 28 June 2009. Shareholder approval is not required for a declaration of dividends.
- On 2 January 2010, the directors declared and paid an ordinary interim share dividend of one ordinary share, valued at $3, for every four ordinary shares held. The dividend was funded from the general reserve.
- On 30 June 2010, the directors transferred $30 000 from the general reserve to retained earnings, declaring the 5% preference dividend as well as a final ordinary dividend of 8c per share. The loss for the year ended 30 June 2010 was $36 000.

Required

(a) Prepare general journal entries to record the transactions relating to share issues and options for the year ending 30 June 2010.

(b) Prepare general journal entries, including any closing entries required, to record the transactions relating to dividends and reserve transfers for the year ended 30 June 2010.

(c) If the company's constitution required all dividends to be approved by the shareholders at the annual general meeting before they could be paid, explain how and why your recording of the dividend payment on 29 September 2009 would change. Assume shareholder approval was granted on 20 September 2009.

Problem 2.10 ★★★ OPTIONS, SHARES, DIVIDENDS, RESERVES

The statement of changes in equity for Philippines Ltd for the year ended 30 June 2011 was as shown below:

PHILIPPINES LTD Statement of Changes in Equity for the year ended 30 June 2011	
Profit for the period	$ 69 420
Other comprehensive income	0
Total comprehensive income for the period	$ 69 420
Movements of changes in equity during the period ending 30 June 2007 were:	
Share capital	
Balance at 1 July 2010	$ 300 000
Issue of 40 000 ordinary shares @ $2.00	80 000
Share issue costs: public issue	(2 500)
Issue of 80 000 ordinary shares @ $2.90 to public	232 000
Issue of 50 000 ordinary shares @ $3.00 on exercise of options costing 40c	170 000
Calls in advance on issue of 80 000 shares @ $2.90 to public	20 000
Balance at 30 June 2011	$ 779 500
Options	
Balance at 1 July 2010	$ 24 000
Transfer to share capital on exercise	(20 000)
Transfer to reserve on lapse	(4 000)
Balance at 30 June 2011	$ 0
General reserve	
Balance at 1 July 2010	$ 110 000
Bonus issue of shares	(80 000)
Transfer from retained earnings	30 000
Balance at 30 June 2011	$ 60 000

Options reserve	
Balance at 1 July 2010	$ 0
Transfer of lapsed options	$ 4 000
Balance at 30 June 2011	4 000
Retained earnings	
Balance at 1 July 2010	$ 75 000
Dividends declared	(8 000)
Dividends paid	(4 000)
Transfer to general reserve	(30 000)
Profit for the period	69 420
Balance at 30 June 2011	$ 102 420

Required

Provide journal entries in relation to:

(a) issue of shares on exercise of options, and related transfers to/from reserves
(b) issue of shares to public
(c) dividends
(d) movements in general reserve.

Note: None of the entries should contain the account Retained Earnings.

Problem 2.11 DIVIDENDS, SHARE-ISSUES, OPTIONS, RESERVE TRANSFERS

★★★

Mongolia Ltd's equity as at 30 June 2008 was as follows:

120 000 ordinary A shares, issued at $1.10, fully paid	$132 000
150 000 ordinary B shares, issued at $1.20, called to 70c	105 000
100 000 8% cumulative preference shares, issued at $1, fully paid	100 000
Calls in advance (30 000 shares)	15 000
Share issue costs	(11 200)
General reserve	160 000
Retained earnings	158 000
Total equity	$658 800

The general journal is used for all entries.

The following events occurred after 30 June 2008:

2008 30 Sep.	The final 10c per share ordinary dividend and the preference dividend, both declared on 25 June 2008, were paid. Shareholder approval is not required for payment of dividends.
31 Oct.	A prospectus was issued inviting offers to acquire 1 option for every 2 ordinary A shares held at a price of 80c per option, payable by 30 November 2008. Each option entitles the holder to 1 ordinary A share at a price of 70c per share and are exercisable in November 2010. Any options not exercised by 30 November 2010 will lapse.
30 Nov.	Offers and monies were received for 50 000 options, and these were issued.
2009 15 Jan.	The final call on ordinary B shares was made, payable by 15 February 2009.
15 Feb.	All call monies were received.

(continued)

20 Apr.	50 000 preference shares were repurchased at $1.10 per share. The repurchase was accounted for by writing down Preference Share Capital by $50 000 and Retained Earnings by the balance.
30 June	The profit for the year was $44 000. The directors decided to transfer $20 000 from the general reserve to retained profits and declared a 10c per share dividend and the preference dividend, both payable on 30 September 2009.
30 Sept.	The final ordinary and preference dividends declared on 30 June 2009 were paid.
15 Dec.	A 5c/share interim ordinary dividend was declared and paid.
2010 31 Jan.	The directors made a 1-for-5 renounceable rights offer to ordinary B shareholders at an issue price of $1.50 per share. The offer's expiry date was 28 February 2010.
28 Feb.	Holders of 120 000 shares accepted the rights offer. Shares were issued, with monies payable by 15 March 2010.
15 Mar.	All monies were received.
30 June	Profit for the year was $56 000. The directors, in lieu of declaring a final dividend, made a 1-for-10 bonus issue from the general reserve to all shareholders. Ordinary A shares were valued at $1.20 each, ordinary B shares were valued at $1.60 each and preference shares were valued at $1.15 each.
30 Nov.	Holders of 40 000 options exercised their options, and 40 000 ordinary A shares were issued. Monies were payable by 20 December 2010.
20 Dec.	All monies were received.
2011 10 Jan.	A 5c per share interim ordinary dividend was declared and paid.
30 June	Profit for the year was $48 000. The directors declared a 10c per share final dividend and the preference dividend, both payable on 30 September 2011.

Required

(a) Prepare general journal entries and closing entries to record the above transactions and events.

(b) Prepare the following general ledger accounts (T format) for the period 30 June 2008 to 30 June 2011:
- Share capital (Ordinary A)
- Share capital (Ordinary B)
- Share capital (Preference).

Problem 2.12 ★★★

DIVIDENDS, SHARE ISSUES, FORFEITURE OF SHARES

On 30 June 2007 the equity of Malaysia Ltd was as follows:

50 000 5% cumulative preference shares, issued at $1.20, fully paid	$ 60 000
100 000 ordinary shares, issued at $1.15, fully paid	115 000
Options (15 000 @ 50c)	7 500
Share issue costs	(2 610)
General reserve	123 100
Retained earnings	136 340

Each option entitles the holder to acquire 1 ordinary share at a price of $1.10 per share, exercisable by 31 March 2008. Any options not exercised by this date will lapse. The books are balanced 6-monthly.

The following events occurred during the year ended 30 June 2008:

2007 15 Aug.	The final 8c per share ordinary dividend and the final preference dividend, both declared on 30 June 2007, were paid in cash. Shareholder approval is required for payment of dividends and was obtained at the annual general meeting of 2 August.
01 Oct.	A prospectus was issued offering 60 000 ordinary shares at an issue price of $1.20 per share, payable 35c on application, 35c on allotment and 50c on a first and final call. The closing date for applications was 31 October 2007. The issue was underwritten at a commission of $1500.
31 Oct.	Applications were received for 75 000 shares by this date.
02 Nov.	The directors allotted 4 shares for every 5 applied for, with allotment monies due by 30 November 2007. In accordance with the constitution, surplus application monies were kept as an advance on future calls and allotment monies. The underwriting commission was paid.
30 Nov.	All allotment monies owing were received by this date.
2008 05 Jan.	An interim 5c per share ordinary dividend was paid in cash.
31 Jan.	The first and final call was made, with monies due by 28 February 2008.
28 Feb.	$28 500 call monies were received by this date.
20 Mar.	The shares on which the call was unpaid were forfeited. The company is entitled to keep any balance arising from forfeiture of shares.
31 Mar.	12 000 shares were allotted as a result of 12 000 options having been exercised, with allotment monies due by 30 April 2008.
30 Apr.	All allotment monies were received by this date.
31 May.	A 1-for-4 bonus issue was made from the general reserve, with the shares valued at $1.20 each.
30 June	A 10c per share final dividend was declared, payable on 15 August 2008. Net profit for the year ended 30 June 2008 was $29 460.

Required

(a) Prepare general journal entries and closing entries to record the above transactions.

(b) Prepare the Options and Retained Earnings ledger accounts for the period 30 June 2007 to 30 June 2008.

References

ANZ Bank 2003, *Prospectus*, Australia and New Zealand Banking Group Limited, www.anz.com.au.

—2008, *2008 annual report*, Australia and New Zealand Banking Group Limited, www.anz.com.au.

Dior 2005, *Full annual report 2004*, Christian Dior Group, Paris, www.dior-finance.com/en.

Fortune magazine 2008, 'Fortune global 500', 21 July, available from http://money.cnn.com/magazines/fortune/global500/2008.

International Committee of the Red Cross 2007, *ICRC annual report 2007*, Switzerland, www.icrc.org.

London Stock Exchange 2008, *Main market, market statistics*, www.londonstockexchange.com/en_gb.

Nobes, C & Parker, R 2002, *Comparative international accounting* 7th edn, Pearson Education Limited, England.

Nokia 2007, *Nokia in 2007*, Nokia Corporation, Finland, www.nokia.com.

—2005, *Nokia in 2005*, Nokia corporation, Finland, www,nokia.com. www.anz.com.au.

Rochfort, S 2003, '$5 billion: Virgin float offer swamped', *The Age*, 6 December.

Wesfarmers 2008, *2008 annual report*, Wesfarmers Limited, www.wesfarmers.com.au.

3 Revenue

ACCOUNTING STANDARDS IN FOCUS

IAS 18 *Revenue*

LEARNING OBJECTIVES

When you have studied this chapter you should be able to:

- understand the background to the development of IAS 18 *Revenue*
- understand the definition of 'income' under the *Framework*
- distinguish between the definitions of 'income' and 'revenue'
- understand the scope of IAS 18
- explain and apply the meaning of 'fair value' when applied to the measurement of revenue
- explain and apply the recognition criteria for revenue, distinguishing between the sale of goods and the rendering of services
- explain and apply the revenue recognition criteria for interest, royalties and dividends
- understand the practical application of IAS 18
- analyse the revenue recognition issues arising in specific industries in practice
- understand the relationship between IAS 18 and other standards and interpretations, in particular IFRIC 13 *Customer Loyalty Programmes*
- describe the disclosure requirements of IAS 18
- understand and interpret the disclosures made by companies applying IAS 18
- describe expected future developments in accounting for revenue.

3.1 INTRODUCTION TO IAS 18

IAS 18 *Revenue* was issued by the IASC in December 1993. It replaced IAS 18 *Revenue Recognition* (issued in December 1982) and was confirmed as being included in the core set of standards to be issued by the IASB in April 2001.

IAS 18 was not amended substantially by the IASB when it was issued in 2001 and it, therefore, remains essentially a very old standard. Unfortunately, IAS 18 is not entirely consistent with the *Framework* and is also internally inconsistent — with an Appendix that sometimes contradicts the body of the standard. Indeed, the original IAS 18 was written prior to the *Framework* (which was first issued in 1989). As a result, revenue recognition has been a problematic area for companies for many years. The International Financial Reporting Interpretations Committee (IFRIC) and its predecessor, the Standing Interpretations Committee (SIC), have received numerous requests for clarification of the standard and have issued six interpretations and numerous agenda decisions related to revenue since 1998.[1]

Understanding that revenue is such an important measure for companies and that it has been a problematic area for so long, the IASB, jointly with the Financial Accounting Standards Board (FASB) in the United States, added a significant project on revenue recognition to their agenda, finally issuing a Discussion Paper in December 2008. An overview of the Discussion Paper is provided at the end of this chapter.

3.2 THE DEFINITION OF INCOME

The *Framework*, paragraph 69 states that:

> Profit is frequently used as a measure of performance or as the basis for other measures, such as return on investment or earnings per share. The elements directly related to the measurement of profit are income and expenses.

Put simply, profit equals income less expenses. Income and expenses are the two *elements* of performance (as represented by the statement of comprehensive income (income statement)) according to the *Framework* (para. 47).

Paragraph 70 of the *Framework* defines income as:

> Increases in economic benefits during the accounting period in the form of inflows or enhancements of assets or decreases of liabilities that result in increases in equity, other than those relating to contributions from equity participants.

Put simply, an increase in an asset or a decrease in a liability will result in income, unless the increase or decrease results from an equity contribution (such as cash raised through share capital).

The definition of income is very broad, being based, in effect, on statement of financial position (balance sheet) movements. The elements of the statement of financial position (assets, liabilities and equity) are defined first in the *Framework*, before the elements of the statement of comprehensive income. Therefore, the statement of comprehensive income is derived from the statement of financial position according to a strict reading of the *Framework*. This is known as 'the asset/liability' model (see further in section 3.6.1).

Because of this broad definition, income is further dissected into revenue and gains.

3.3 THE DISTINCTION BETWEEN INCOME AND REVENUE

3.3.1 Income dissected

Paragraph 74 of the *Framework* states that income encompasses both revenue and gains:

> Revenue arises in the course of the ordinary activities of an entity and is referred to by a variety of different names including sales, fees, interest, dividends, royalties and rent.

[1]Agenda decisions indicate why IFRIC has not proceeded to issue an interpretation on an issue despite a request for clarification. This is usually because the request does not meet all the criteria for issuing an interpretation. Often IFRIC's agenda decision will explain where IFRIC thinks the answer to a particular question lies in the relevant standards.

Paragraph 75 of the *Framework* states:

> Gains represent other items that meet the definition of income and may, or may not, arise in the course of the ordinary activities of an entity. Gains represent increases in economic benefits and as such are no different in nature from revenue. Hence, they are not regarded as constituting a separate element in this *Framework*.

Gains include, for example:

- gains on disposal of non-current assets (see chapter 9)
- unrealised gains on the upward revaluation of property, plant and equipment under IAS 16 *Property, Plant and Equipment* (see chapter 9)
- unrealised gains on the upward revaluation of financial assets that are classified as 'available-for-sale' under IAS 39 *Financial Instruments* (see chapter 5).

Because the definition of income includes both revenue and gains, these are not defined as separate elements under the *Framework*. The only distinguishing feature of revenue in the *Framework* is the reference to 'ordinary activities of an entity' in paragraph 74. Therefore, revenue is essentially a *classification* of income to distinguish between an entity's ordinary activities and other activities.

Despite the explanation in the *Framework* as to why revenue needs no definition, IAS 18 does define revenue in paragraph 7 as:

> The gross inflow of economic benefits during the period arising in the course of the ordinary activities of an entity when those inflows result in increases in equity, other than increases relating to contributions from equity participants.

This definition is consistent with the *Framework*'s definition of income and its distinguishing feature of ordinary activities for revenue. However, it adds another distinguishing feature — gross inflows.

3.3.2 Ordinary activities and gross inflows

Ordinary activities are not defined in the *Framework* or in IAS 18. In past accounting standards, a distinction was made between ordinary, abnormal and extraordinary items of income or expenses; however, this distinction and the concepts of abnormal or extraordinary items no longer exist under IFRSs. Thus, the meaning of 'ordinary' is left to entities to determine for themselves. Most companies interpret ordinary as relating to their core business operations, but this is not without some controversy.

Revenue is a gross concept, whereas gains tend to be net (although this is not always the case; for example, unrealised gains on the upward revaluation of certain assets can be gross). IAS 1, in the paragraphs dealing with offsetting, discusses this. Paragraph 34 states:

> IAS 18 *Revenue* defines revenue and requires an entity to measure it at the fair value of the consideration received or receivable, taking into account the amount of any trade discounts and volume rebates the entity allows. An entity undertakes, in the course of its ordinary activities, other transactions that do not generate revenue but are incidental to the main revenue-generating activities. An entity presents the results of such transactions, when this presentation reflects the substance of the transaction or other event, by netting any income with related expenses arising on the same transaction. For example:
>
> a) An entity presents gains and losses on the disposal of non-current assets, including investments and operating assets, by deducting from the proceeds on disposal the carrying amount of the asset and related selling expenses.

IAS 16 paragraph 68 *prohibits* gains from the disposal of property, plant and equipment from being classified as revenue. This is quite puzzling, considering that the netting requirement in IAS 1 applies also to the disposal of *operating* assets. Operating assets would be part of the entity's ordinary activities, so why would their disposal not meet the revenue classification? Presumably this is because the disposal of the asset would not be considered ordinary, whereas the continued operation of the asset would.

The logic for the link between ordinary activities and netting is not clearly articulated in IFRSs, and the potentially arbitrary nature of this distinction was highlighted in an issue presented to IFRIC in 2007. IFRIC was faced with the question of whether an entity could hold an asset for a dual purpose (both renting out and sale) as part if its ordinary activities. The question was posed by an entity in the automotive industry that rented out its cars but also sold those cars if customers wanted to purchase them. IAS 16 prohibited gains on the sale of those cars from being classified as revenue. IFRIC referred the matter to the IASB, which subsequently decided to amend IAS 16 in its 2007 Annual Improvements Process. The IASB proposed that if an entity in the course of its ordinary activities routinely sells property, plant and equipment that it has held for rental to others, it should transfer such assets to inventories at their carrying amount when they cease to be rented and are held for sale. The proceeds of such assets should then be recognised as revenue in accordance with IAS 18. As outlined in the IASB's 2007 exposure draft on *Proposed Improvements to International Financial Reporting Standards,* in the IASB's view, the recognition of gross selling revenue, rather than a net gain or loss on sale of these assets, would better reflect the ordinary activities of such entities.

Once an item *is* classified as revenue, the question of gross or net can still arise. This is addressed in paragraph 8 of IAS 18, which states that revenue includes only the gross inflows received and receivable by the entity on its *own account*. Amounts collected on behalf of third parties, such as sales taxes, are not economic benefits that flow to the entity and do not result in increases in equity. This is because the amounts must be passed onto the third party. Therefore, they do not meet the definition of revenue. Similarly, in an agency relationship, amounts collected on behalf of the principal are not gross inflows flowing to the agent and thus do not meet the definition of revenue. Rather, the revenue is the amount of commission received or receivable by the agent.

Also, IAS 18 requires revenue to be recognised net of trade discounts or volume rebates. This is nothing to do with an agency relationship and the *definition* of revenue but rather to do with how revenue is *measured* (see section 3.5).

Figure 3.1 summarises the distinction between income and revenue.

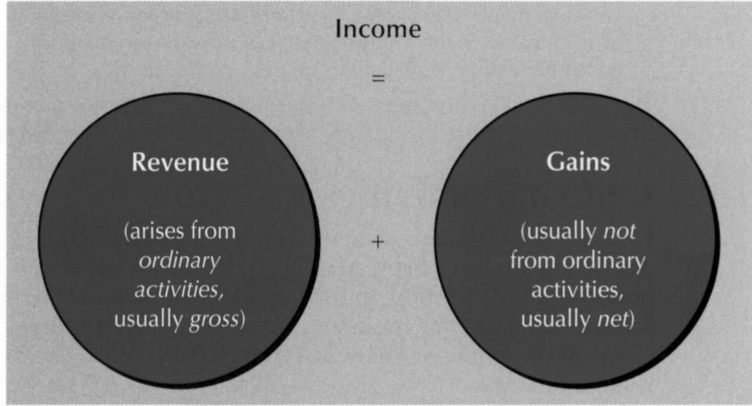

FIGURE 3.1 Distinguishing income from revenue

3.4 THE SCOPE OF IAS 18

Paragraph 1 of IAS 18 states that it applies in:

> Accounting for revenue arising from the following transactions and events:
> a) the sale of goods;
> b) the rendering of services; and
> c) the use by others of entity assets yielding interest, royalties and dividends.

Goods include goods produced by the entity for the purpose of sale, such as products made by a manufacturer and goods purchased for resale, such as products purchased by a retailer or land held for resale.

The rendering of services typically involves the performance by an entity of a contractually agreed task over an agreed period of time. Examples include consulting services, maintenance services and accounting services. Services in respect of construction contracts are not included in the scope of IAS 18 but rather are included in the scope of IAS 11 *Construction Contracts*.

IAS 18 does not deal with revenue arising from:

(a) lease agreements (see IAS 17 *Leases* (refer chapter 13))
(b) dividends arising from investments which are accounted for under the equity method (see IAS 28 *Investments in Associates* (refer chapter 27))
(c) insurance contracts within the scope of IFRS 4 *Insurance Contracts*
(d) changes in the fair value of financial assets and financial liabilities or their disposal (see IAS 39 *Financial Instruments: Recognition and Measurement* (refer chapter 5))
(e) changes in the value of other current assets
(f) the initial recognition of and changes in the fair value of biological assets related to agricultural activity (see IAS 41 *Agriculture* (refer chapter 16))

(g) the initial recognition of agricultural produce (see IAS 41)
(h) the extraction of mineral ores.

3.5 MEASUREMENT AT FAIR VALUE

3.5.1 Measurement requirement

Paragraph 19 of IAS 18 states that:

> Revenue shall be measured at the fair value of the consideration received or receivable.

'Fair value' is defined in paragraph 7 as:

> The amount for which an asset could be exchanged, or a liability settled, between knowledgeable, willing parties in an arm's length transaction.

The amount of revenue arising from a transaction is usually determined by agreement between the entity and the buyer or user of the asset. Paragraph 10 states that:

> It is measured at the fair value of the consideration received or receivable taking into account the amount of any trade discounts and volume rebates allowed by the entity.

Illustrative example 3.1 illustrates the measurement of revenue where there are trade discounts or volume rebates.

ILLUSTRATIVE EXAMPLE 3.1

Measurement of revenue where there are trade discounts or volume rebates

Company Z sells packaging materials. Customers that purchase quantities in excess of a specified volume are entitled to a discount of 10% on their purchases. On 1 March 2010, Customer D purchased packaging materials in excess of the specified volume. The normal selling price per kilogram of packaging materials is $5 per kilogram. Customer D purchases 30 kilograms.

Without the volume discount, Customer D would have paid $150. With the volume discount, Customer D will pay $135. Company Z therefore measures its revenue from sales to Customer D at $135. Assuming it is a cash sale the journal entry would be:

Cash	Dr	135	
Revenue	Cr		135

If IAS 18 did not require the volume discount to be deducted in measuring the fair value of revenue, Company Z would need to record the following journal entry:

Cash	Dr	135	
Expenses (discount allowed)	Dr	15	
Revenue	Cr		150

The question of whether the expense could be netted against the revenue for disclosure purposes would then arise. Since IAS 18 requires a net measurement in the first place this question does not arise.

3.5.2 How to apply the fair value measurement requirement

In most cases, it is straightforward to calculate the fair value of the consideration received or receivable because usually the consideration is in the form of cash. The amount of cash to be paid is typically specified in an agreement.

Sometimes, however, the amount to be paid is deferred for a period of time. In other cases, the consideration may not be in the form of cash, but rather may be a swap for other goods or services. IAS 18 deals specifically with these cases.

Deferred consideration

Deferred consideration may take the form of interest-free credit provided to a buyer or acceptance of a note receivable bearing a below-market interest rate. In such cases, the fair value of the consideration will be less than the nominal amount of the cash receivable. IAS 18 specifies that these types of transactions are to be accounted for as financing transactions and that the fair value of the consideration should be determined by discounting all future receipts using an imputed rate of interest. The imputed rate of interest is the more clearly determinable of either:

(a) the prevailing rate for a similar instrument of an issuer with a similar credit rating, or
(b) a rate of interest that discounts the nominal amount of the instrument to a current cash sales price of the goods or services.

The difference between the fair value and the nominal amount of the consideration is recognised as interest revenue in accordance with paragraphs 29 and 30 of IAS 18 and in accordance with IAS 39.

Illustrative example 3.2 illustrates how deferred consideration should be measured under IAS 18.

ILLUSTRATIVE EXAMPLE 3.2

Measurement of deferred consideration

Company B sells furniture and offers an interest-free period of 12 months to certain qualifying customers. Customer G qualifies for the interest-free period and purchases furniture on 30 June 2011. The current cash sales price of the furniture is $20 000. Customer G will pay $20 000 on 30 June 2012 (i.e. in 1 year's time).

The end of Company B's reporting period is 30 June. Company B determines that an appropriate discount rate for imputing interest to the transaction is 4% per annum. It determines that the present value of $20 000 to be received in 1 year's time is $19 230.

At 30 June 2011, Company B would record the following journal entry:

Receivable	Dr	20 000	
Revenue	Cr		19 230
Deferred Interest	Cr		770

For the year ended 30 June 2012, Company B would record the following journal entries:

Deferred Interest	Dr	770	
Interest Revenue	Cr		770
(To recognise interest earned on the transaction in the statement of comprehensive income)			
Cash	Dr	20 000	
Receivable	Cr		20 000
(To recognise receipt of cash)			

Exchanges or swaps

The requirements for measuring consideration where goods or services are exchanged or swapped depend on whether the swap or exchange is for goods or services of a similar nature and value.

(a) If the swap or exchange *is* for goods or services of a similar nature and value, then IAS 18 states that this transaction does *not* generate revenue.
(b) If the swap or exchange *is not* for goods or services of a similar nature and value, then IAS 18 states that this transaction *does* generate revenue.

The rationale for this is not explained in the standard but can be deduced by applying the definition of revenue in IAS 18. In (a), there is no increase in equity because one asset is replaced by another with a similar value. In (b), there is an increase in equity to the extent that the replacement asset exceeds the value of the original asset. In the case of (b), IAS 18 requires the revenue to be measured at the fair value of the goods or services received, adjusted by the amount of any cash transferred.

Illustrative example 3.3 illustrates how swaps and exchanges are accounted for under IAS 18.

ILLUSTRATIVE EXAMPLE 3.3

Accounting for swaps and exchanges

Company S swaps a container of its milk for a container of milk of Company R in order to be able to deliver to a customer located closer to Company R's distribution centre. The value of the container of milk is $100, which is the same for both Company S and Company R. Company S would record the following journal entry.

Inventory – Container 2	Dr	100	
Inventory – Container 1	Cr		100

No revenue is recorded in this transaction because the swap or exchange is for goods of a similar nature and value.

The following week, Company S swaps a container of milk (with a value of $100) with Company D in exchange for a container of cream. The value of Company D's container of cream is $120. Company S also pays Company D $12. Company S would record the following journal entry:

Inventory – Container of Cream	Dr	120	
Revenue	Cr		108
Cash	Cr		12
Cost of Sales	Dr	100	
Inventory – Container of Milk	Cr		100

This transaction does generate revenue because the swap *is not* for goods of a similar nature and value. The revenue is measured gross, at the fair value of the goods received, adjusted by the amount of any cash transferred.

The requirements of IAS 18 are in contrast with those in IAS 16 *Property, Plant and Equipment*. IAS 16 addresses the measurement of the cost of property, plant and equipment acquired in an exchange transaction. It requires all exchanges to be measured at fair value unless (a) the exchange transaction lacks commercial substance or (b) the fair value of neither the asset received nor the asset given up is reliably measurable. IAS 38 *Intangible Assets* has similar requirements. However, neither of these standards addresses whether revenue arises on such exchanges. Arguably, as these exchanges are likely to be outside the ordinary activities of an entity, any difference between the two values will be treated as a gain (or loss), not as revenue.

SIC 31 *Revenue — Barter Transactions Involving Advertising Services* addresses an issue that arose during the 'dot.com' boom in the late 1990s. It deals with the circumstances under which a seller can reliably measure revenue at the fair value of advertising services received or provided in a barter transaction. It sets a number of tests that need to be met before the seller can recognise revenue at fair value, basically by reference to similar non-barter transactions.

3.6 THE RECOGNITION CRITERIA

IAS 18 sets out specific recognition criteria for the sale of goods, the rendering of services and interest, royalties and dividends.

Before considering these criteria, it is important to understand (1) the recognition criteria for income generally, (2) the main objective of IAS 18 and (3) the identification of the transaction to which the recognition criteria should be applied.

3.6.1 The recognition criteria for income generally

Paragraph 92 of the *Framework* identifies the recognition criteria for income. It states:

> Income is recognised in the income statement when an increase in future economic benefits related to an increase in an asset or a decrease of a liability has arisen that can be measured reliably. This means, in effect, that recognition of income occurs simultaneously with the recognition of increases in assets or decreases in liabilities.

Theoretically, this means that once an asset is recognised or a liability reduced or derecognised, under the *Framework*'s asset/liability model, income is recognised simultaneously.

Illustrative example 3.4 gives a simple example to illustrate the asset/liability model.

ILLUSTRATIVE EXAMPLE 3.4

Explaining the asset/liability model

Assume Company A sells goods to Customer B for $100. Customer B enters into an agreement to buy the goods from Company A on 1 February for $100. Company A delivers the goods on 15 February. Customer B pays for the goods on 28 February.

On the agreement date (1 February), Company A has undertaken to deliver the goods to Customer B and Customer B has promised to pay for them. Company A has an obligation to deliver the goods and a right to receive payment once delivery has been made. However, until Company A delivers the goods it does not have an asset under the *Framework* because it does not control the right to receive payment until delivery. Similarly, Customer B has no liability under the *Framework* because it has no obligation to pay until delivery has been made. The agreement is thus an executory contract (also known as an agreement equally proportionately unperformed) at agreement date because neither party to the contract has performed their obligations. In the case of such agreements, no asset or liability exists under the *Framework*.

On the delivery date (15 February), Company A has performed under the agreement and is now entitled to receive payment. Company A thus has an asset under the *Framework*. As the right to receive payment is not an equity contribution, the increase in the asset meets the definition of income, and Company A would record the following journal entry:

Asset – Receivable from Customer B	Dr	100	
Income	Cr		100

On the payment date (28 February), Company A receives the cash from Customer B and records the following entry:

Cash	Dr	100	
Asset – Receivable from Customer B	Cr		100

The right to receive cash is replaced by the cash received.

This example illustrates how basic accrual accounting fits within the asset/liability model of the *Framework*.

Now assume that the agreement states that from 15 February, when Company A delivers the goods, it must continue to maintain them for a year for Customer B. Customer B still pays for the goods on 28 February; however, Customer B is entitled to a refund of 20% of the amount paid if Company A does not satisfactorily maintain the goods for the year as required.

Under the asset/liability model, Company A has an obligation to maintain the goods and to refund the cash as from 15 February. Thus, it would record the following entry:

Asset – Receivable from Customer B	Dr	100	
Liability (obligation to maintain goods and refund cash)	Cr		20
Income	Cr		80

Under the *Framework*, the definition of income is not met for 100% of the amount receivable because, while there has been an increase in an asset, there has also been an increase in a liability. The measurement of these amounts is not addressed in the *Framework*.

On the payment date (28 February), Company A receives the cash from Customer B and records the following entry:

Cash	Dr	100	
Asset – Receivable from Customer B	Cr		100

The right to receive cash is replaced by the cash received as in the previous case. However, Company A still has a liability as described above. When this liability is settled, for example when the maintenance period is complete or over the period of the maintenance agreement (this is discussed further in section 3.6.5), Company A records the following entry:

Liability (obligation to maintain goods and refund cash)	Dr	20	
Income	Cr		20

The *definition* of income is met because there has been a reduction in a liability. The *recognition criteria* for income have also been met simultaneously with the reduction of the liability because the reduction of the liability can be reliably measured at that point.

Thus, under the asset/liability model, income is recognised in two parts — the first when the receivable from Customer B is recognised, and the second when the liability to Customer B is settled.

In practice, this is no different from traditional models such as an earnings model that 'defers' revenue in order to record revenue only when it is earned. In the example above, the liability to Customer B would likely be described as 'deferred income' under an earnings model and released to income either over the maintenance agreement period or at the end of the period depending on the terms of the agreement. Under the *Framework*, 'deferred income' is not a liability; rather, the obligation to perform under the agreement is a liability. Because the measurement of this liability is not addressed in the *Framework*, in practice, there is no difference between the asset/liability model and the earnings model in this case.

However, another approach that exists in practice is to record 100% of the revenue and then provide for the cost of meeting the obligation. This gives a different outcome from the asset/liability model.

Many of the difficulties that have arisen in practice stem from (1) lack of distinction between the *definition* of income and the *recognition* criteria and (2) lack of clarity as to what model applies under IAS 18. This is discussed further below.

3.6.2 The objective of IAS 18

We have seen that while there is a distinction between the *definition* of income and the *recognition criteria* for income under the *Framework*, under the asset/liability model of the *Framework*, the only key difference between the two is the test of reliable measurement. If there is an increase in an asset or a decrease in a liability resulting in an increase in equity, income *exists*. Provided it can be reliably measured, it is recognised there and then.

This is where IAS 18 comes into play. The key stated purpose of IAS 18 is to identity *when* revenue should be recognised (Objective paragraph). It states that:

> Revenue is recognised when it is probable that future economic benefits will flow to the entity and these benefits can be measured reliably.

(Note that these are also the recognition criteria for the recognition of assets.) It then goes on to specify the circumstances in which these criteria will be met.

This means that IAS 18 does not strictly follow the asset/liability model, because it imposes additional revenue recognition criteria beyond those in the *Framework* for recognition of income.

In illustrative example 3.4, for example, once the liability is settled, income is recognised immediately. IAS 18 sets out further criteria to determine whether, in fact, revenue is recognised at that point. However, this is not always inconsistent with the asset/liability model. In effect, consistent with the asset/liability model, it helps entities to determine *whether* the liability is settled at a point in time or over a period of time.

However, the wording used in IAS 18 is unhelpful in this regard because it mixes up definitions and recognition criteria as we will see shortly.

3.6.3 Identifying the transaction

Paragraph 13 deals with identification of the transaction to which the recognition criteria should be applied. It states:

> The recognition criteria in this Standard are usually applied separately to each transaction. However, in certain circumstances, it is necessary to apply the recognition criteria to the separately identifiable components of a single transaction in order to reflect the substance of the transaction.

Examples include the selling price of a product that includes an amount for subsequent servicing (as in illustrative example 3.4), and a sale agreement that includes a repurchase agreement such that the sale is effectively negated.

These types of arrangements are sometimes referred to as 'multiple element arrangements' and are discussed further in section 3.8.

3.6.4 Sale of goods

Paragraph 14 of IAS 18 states:

> Revenue from the sale of goods shall be recognised when all of the following conditions have been satisfied:
> (a) the entity has transferred to the buyer the significant risks and rewards of ownership of the goods;
> (b) the entity retains neither continuing managerial involvement to the degree usually associated with ownership nor effective control over the goods sold;
> (c) the amount of revenue can be measured reliably;
> (d) it is probable that the economic benefits associated with the transaction will flow to the entity; and
> (e) the costs incurred or to be incurred in respect of the transaction can be measured reliably.

Note that (a) and (b) fundamentally address whether the seller or the buyer has the asset in question that has purportedly been sold. In (a) a risks and rewards approach is applied to identifying whose asset it is, while in (b), a control approach is applied. Neither strictly applies the definition of an asset under the *Framework*. These approaches are both currently used in IFRS literature, unfortunately not consistently. See figure 3.2.

FIGURE 3.2 Control vs. risks and rewards

Unfortunately 'control' is not defined in the *Framework* and is used throughout IFRSs without consistency. Sometimes control refers to the power to govern so as to obtain benefits from an entity (IAS 27 — see chapter 21). Sometimes it refers to the exposure to risks as well as benefits and the residual risks of an entity (SIC-12 *Consolidation — Special Purpose Entities*). In IAS 17 *Leases* (see chapter 13), the concept of control of an asset is linked to who has the risks and rewards incidental to ownership (even though this concept is not referred to as 'control'). In IAS 39 *Financial Instruments: Recognition and Measurement* (see chapter 5), there is a distinction between risks and rewards of ownership of an asset and control of that asset. Control in this case is referred to in terms of the entity's ability to sell the asset. If the entity is able to sell the asset then IAS 39 regards the entity as having control of the asset. In IAS 39, it is possible to *not* have the risks and rewards of ownership of an asset but still control it (para. 23). In IFRIC 4 *Determining Whether an Arrangement Contains a Lease,* the concept of *control of the use* of an asset is central. This is because a lease is defined as a *right of use* of an asset. IFRIC 4 contains conditions that must be met in order for an entity to control the right of use of an asset. These include the ability to operate the asset while obtaining more than a significant amount of output from the asset, or the ability to control physical access to the asset while obtaining more than a significant amount of

FIGURE 3.2 *(continued)*

> output from the asset. Note, however, that these conditions will indicate whether or not the arrangement *is a lease* (i.e. whether a right of use has been given to an entity). Whether the lease transfers the risks and rewards of ownership of the asset to the entity (i.e. whether it is a finance lease or an operating lease) is a second question. Then we have to go back to IAS 17, which appears to equate risks and rewards of ownership with control!

The recognition criteria in the *Framework* are repeated in (c) and (d). A new concept not included in the *Framework* is introduced in (e) — reliable measurement of costs. The rationale for this criterion is not explained and it appears to have little to do with revenue.

Returning to our discussion of the asset/liability model, we can see that paragraph 14 has some similarities in that (c) and (d) are the same *recognition* criteria as for assets. The additional criteria in (a) and (b) deal with the asset purportedly sold and to some extent repeat the *definition* of an asset. However, by not using the same terminology as the *Framework*, confusion is bound to arise, not to mention the fact that definitional concepts are mixed up in the recognition criteria in paragraph 14.

Paragraphs 15–19 discuss the recognition criteria in (a) and (d) in more detail. Most of the discussion relates to the transfer of the risks and rewards of ownership. In essence, the focus is on whether or not the asset has been transferred to the buyer.

Paragraph 15 states that, in most cases, the transfer of the risks and rewards of ownership coincides with the transfer of legal title or the passing of possession to the buyer. This is the case for most retail sales but not always.

Paragraph 16 states that if an entity retains significant risks of ownership, the transaction is not a sale and revenue is not recognised. Examples of such situations include:

(a) when the entity retains an obligation for unsatisfactory performance not covered by normal warranty provisions

(b) when the receipt of revenue by the seller is contingent on the buyer on-selling the goods

(c) when the goods are shipped subject to installation and the installation is a significant part of the contract which has not yet been completed by the entity

(d) when the buyer has the right to rescind the purchase.

Under the asset/liability model, these situations would result either in no asset recognised by the seller, or in a liability being recognised for all or some of the obligation or contingency created. This could result in the same outcome as IAS 18, but this depends on whether an asset is recognised and on whether any liability recognised equals the asset or is less than the asset. For example, in (a), IAS 18 prohibits any revenue recognition, whereas the asset/liability model would permit revenue recognition to the extent that the amount of the warranty obligation is less than the amount receivable from the customer. A similar situation applies in (c). However, in (b) and (d), both IAS 18 and the asset/liability model would result in no revenue recognition because under the asset/liability model a receivable from the customer would not be recognised (the definition of an asset would not be met).

Paragraph 17 states that if an entity retains only an insignificant risk of ownership, the transaction is a sale and revenue is recognised. For example a retailer may offer a refund if a customer is not satisfied.

> Revenue in such cases is recognised at the time of sale provided the seller can reliably estimate future returns and recognises a liability for returns based on previous experience and other relevant factors.

This approach is similar to the asset/liability model although it is not clear under paragraph 17 whether the liability is a liability for costs or an allocation of the amount of revenue received. This is discussed further in section 3.8.

Paragraph 18 addresses criterion (d) — the probability that economic benefits will flow to the entity. In some cases, economic benefits may not be probable until the consideration is received or until an uncertainty is removed[2]. A distinction needs to be made between an uncertainty that *precludes* revenue recognition and an uncertainty that affects the *measurement* of revenue. An example of an uncertainty that *precludes* revenue recognition would be a government restriction on remitting consideration from a sale in a foreign country. In this case, as under the asset/liability model,

[2]Note that 'probable' is not defined in the *Framework*, but it is defined as meaning 'more likely than not' in IAS 37, paragraph 23.

no receivable and thus no revenue is recognised until the government grants permission because the test of probability of inflow of economic benefits is not met until that point.

An example of an uncertainty that affects the *measurement* of revenue would be an uncertainty regarding the collectability of an amount already included in revenue. Such an amount is recognised as an expense (commonly referred to as a 'provision for doubtful debts') rather than as an adjustment of the amount of revenue already recognised.

Paragraph 19 talks about the matching of revenue and expenses, which is somewhat of an antiquated concept and attempts to explain criterion (e) of the recognition criteria. It is curious that a standard on revenue recognition deals with cost deferral. This appears to be a derivation of US GAAP, which includes requirements in respect of cost deferral in some of its literature on revenue recognition.

3.6.5 Rendering of services

Paragraph 20 of IAS 18 states:

> When the outcome of a transaction involving the rendering of services can be estimated reliably, revenue associated with the transaction shall be recognised by reference to the stage of completion of the transaction at the end of the reporting period. The outcome of a transaction can be estimated reliably when all the following conditions are satisfied:
> (a) the amount of revenue can be measured reliably;
> (b) it is probable that the economic benefits associated with the transaction will flow to the entity;
> (c) the stage of completion of the transaction at the end of the reporting period can be measured reliably; and
> (d) the costs incurred for the transaction and the costs to complete the transaction can be measured reliably.

The recognition of revenue by reference to the stage of completion of a transaction is often referred to as the percentage of completion method. This method is applied in accounting for construction contracts under IAS 11 *Construction Contracts*. Under this method, revenue is recognised in the accounting periods in which the services are rendered.

Paragraphs (a) and (b) of the recognition criteria are the same as for the sale of goods. Paragraph 23 contains more guidance on 'reliable measurement' in respect of the rendering of services. It states:

> An entity is generally able to make reliable estimates after it has agreed to the following with the other parties to the transaction:
> (a) each party's enforceable rights regarding the service to be provided and received by the parties;
> (b) the consideration to be exchanged; and
> (c) the manner and terms of settlement.
>
> It is also usually necessary for the entity to have an effective internal financial budgeting and reporting system. The entity reviews and, when necessary, revises the estimates of revenue as the service is performed. The need for such revisions does not necessarily indicate that the outcome of the transaction cannot be estimated reliably.

Paragraph 24 sets out a number of methods that may be used to determine the stage of completion of a transaction. These include:

(a) surveys of work performed
(b) services performed to date as a percentage of total services to be performed
(c) the proportion that costs incurred to date bear to the estimated total costs of the transaction.

In respect of (c), only costs that reflect services performed to date are included in costs incurred to date. Paragraph 24 also states that progress payments and advances received from customers often do *not* reflect the services performed.

Illustrative example 3.5 illustrates how the percentage of completion method is applied.

ILLUSTRATIVE EXAMPLE 3.5

Application of the percentage of completion method

On 1 March 2011, Company H enters into an agreement with Customer J to renovate Customer J's offices. The agreement states that the total consideration to be paid for the renovation will be \$450 000. Company H expects that its total costs for the renovation will be \$380 000. As at the end of its reporting period, 30 June, 2011, Company H had incurred labour costs of $110 000 and materials costs of $150 000. Of the materials costs, $45 000 is in respect of materials that have not yet been used in the renovation. All labour costs are in respect of services performed on the renovation project. As at 30 June 2011, Customer J had made progress payments to Company H of $265 000.

Company H calculates the percentage of completion using paragraph 24(c) of IAS 18 as follows:

Total costs incurred to date	$260 000	
Less		
Costs in respect of services not yet performed	45 000	
Total	215 000	(a)
Total estimated costs	380 000	(b)
Percentage complete	57%	(a) / (b)
Total estimated revenue under the agreement	450 000	(c)
Revenue to be recognised at 30 June 2011	254 605	57% × (c)

Note that payments made by Customer J cannot be used as a basis for calculating the percentage completion under IAS 18 (paragraph 24). Also note that Company H will show a loss on this project as at 30 June 2011 (revenue of $254 605 less costs incurred to date of $260 000 equals a loss of $5395). This is because it has incurred materials costs of $45 000 that are not permitted to be used in the percentage of completion calculation because they are in respect of services that have not yet been performed. The materials will need to be used in the provision of future services on the project. However, under paragraph 19 of IAS 18, Company H could argue that it should defer the costs of $45 000 until the services are provided. If Company H deferred the costs, then it would recognise a profit of $39 605.

Sometimes it is not possible to calculate the percentage of completion of services provided as precisely as in illustrative example 3.5. For example, an entity might charge fees for admission to an event or for tuition over a period of time. Paragraph 25 of IAS 18 addresses this issue and states:

> For practical purposes, when services are performed by an indeterminate number of acts over a specified period of time, revenue is recognised on a straight-line basis over the specified period unless there is evidence that some other method better represents the stage of completion. When a specific act is much more significant than any other acts, the recognition is postponed until the significant act is executed.

So, for example, tuition fees would be recognised on a straight-line basis over the period of instruction. Admission fees to an event would be recognised when the event is staged.

How does this relate to the asset/liability model? Take the example of tuition fees. Assume an entity enters into an agreement to provide tuition for 1 year and charges an upfront fee of $12 000. Under the asset/liability model the entity would record the following journal entry on day 1 of the agreement.

Cash	Dr	12 000	
Liability (obligation to provide tuition)	Cr		12 000

As the services are provided, the entity would record the following entry:

Liability (obligation to provide tuition)	Dr	XX	
Revenue	Cr		XX

The asset/liability model does not prescribe how the various assets and liabilities are to be measured. Under IAS 18, the first entry would be the same except that the credit would likely be described as 'deferred revenue'. Under IAS 18, the second and following entries are also the same as under the asset/liability model (except for the description of the liability) and, in addition, IAS 18 prescribes that the amount recognised would be $1000 per month (i.e. on a straight-line basis over the period of the agreement).

In the asset/liability model, the credit recognised at inception of the agreement is known as a 'performance obligation'. While the terminology used is different, the concept of not recognising revenue until performance of the service has occurred is consistent between the two approaches.

The Appendix to IAS 18 provides numerous examples of transactions involving the rendering of services. From the examples, it is clear that the *performance of the service* is the critical requirement for revenue recognition.

Paragraph 26 addresses situations where the outcome of the transaction involving the rendering of services cannot be estimated reliably. If this is the case, then arguably one of the recognition criteria (paragraph 20(a)) is not met. Note that ALL the recognition criteria must be met in order for revenue to be recognised. Curiously, despite this, IAS 18 still permits revenue to be recognised in this case, but only to the extent of 'the expenses recognised that are recoverable'. The explanation for this is given partly in paragraph 27, which states that 'as the outcome of the transaction cannot be estimated reliably, no profit is recognised'. This directly contradicts the concept of revenue being a gross amount rather than the net gain or loss in a transaction. Arguably, if revenue is a gross concept, and one of the fundamental revenue recognition criteria is reliable measurement, if this criterion is not met then no revenue should be recognised at all. Paragraph 26 in effect focuses on cost recovery rather then revenue recognition and implies that recoverable costs can be deferred.

Paragraph 28 further exacerbates the problem by stating that if it is not probable that the costs incurred will be recovered, revenue is not recognised and the costs incurred are recognised as an expense. While these paragraphs attempt to address whether or not the outcome of a transaction can be reliably determined, by focusing on costs rather than revenue they create an inconsistency with the fundamental revenue recognition criteria.

3.6.6 Interest, royalties and dividends

Paragraph 29 of IAS 18 states:

> Revenue arising from the use by others of entity assets yielding interest, royalties and dividends shall be recognised on the basis set out in paragraph 30 when:
> (a) it is probable that the economic benefits associated with the transaction will flow to the entity; and
> (b) the amount of revenue can be measured reliably.

This merely repeats the revenue recognition criteria.

Paragraph 30 states:

> Revenue shall be recognised on the following bases:
> (a) interest shall be recognised using the effective interest method as set out in IAS 39, paragraphs 9 and AG5–AG8;
> (b) royalties shall be recognised on an accrual basis in accordance with the substance of the relevant agreement; and
> (c) dividends shall be recognised when the shareholder's right to receive payment is established.

The effective interest method is explained in chapter 5. Royalties accrue in accordance with the terms of the relevant agreement and are usually recognised on that basis unless it is more appropriate to recognise revenue on some other systematic basis (para. 33). For example, an agreement might state that an author is entitled to be paid royalties twice a year, that the author must deliver the manuscript by a certain date in order to earn the first royalty, and that the book must be published in order to earn the second royalty. In this case, there are two critical events that indicate when each royalty is earned, and revenue would be recognised on those dates. On the other hand, once the book has been published, royalties would be payable on an ongoing basis based on the sales of the book. Once a reliable measure for, say, each month's sales can be determined, royalties could be calculated on that basis and recognised as revenue on a monthly basis.

In respect of dividends, paragraph 32 makes a distinction between dividends paid from pre- and post-acquisition profits. This is discussed further in chapter 22. Dividends paid from pre-acquisition profits are not recognised as revenue by the recipient but rather are deducted from the cost of the relevant investment. Dividends paid from post-acquisition profits are recognised as revenue by the recipient. This concept has recently been amended by changes to IAS 27. These are not discussed here.

3.7 PRACTICAL EXAMPLES OF APPLYING IAS 18

The Appendix to IAS 18 (which is not a part of the standard) provides numerous examples of transactions involving the sale of goods and the rendering of services. Students should be cautious of some of the specific additional revenue recognition criteria provided in these examples because these are not always consistent with the standard and appear to be based on US GAAP rather than on IAS 18. For example, example 9 in the Appendix dealing with real estate sales indicates that the seller considers the ability of the buyer to complete payment. This contradicts paragraph 24 of IAS 18. Example 9 was recently removed by IFRIC as part of its new interpretation *Agreements for the Construction of Real Estate*, which was issued in late 2008.

3.7.1 Examples in respect of the sale of goods

The following practical illustrative examples (3.6–3.12) further illustrate the application of IAS 18. In most of the examples one or two of the revenue recognition criteria in paragraph 14 are relatively more important to the transaction in question and these are highlighted in the examples. In all cases reliable measurement is assumed.

ILLUSTRATIVE EXAMPLE 3.6

Sales of goods where the buyer delays delivery

Company A sells goods to Customer B. Customer B requests Company A to hold delivery of the goods while it is preparing its site to be ready for delivery. Customer B formally accepts responsibility for the goods on the invoice date on the basis that that would be the usual delivery date.

Assuming the other revenue recognition criteria are met, Company A recognises revenue on the invoice date because at that date it has transferred the significant risks and rewards of ownership to Customer B and it is probable that future economic benefits will flow (i.e. Customer B will pay for the goods because it has formally accepted responsibility for them even though they have not yet been delivered).

Example 1 in the Appendix to IAS 18 provides further indicators of whether this transfer has occurred; however, these do not alter the fundamental revenue recognition criteria.

ILLUSTRATIVE EXAMPLE 3.7

Goods shipped subject to minor conditions

Company A sells goods to Customer B. On the delivery date, Company A invoices Customer B and is obliged to install the goods. The installation is minor and involves connecting the goods to an electric socket and testing that the goods perform when connected.

The key issue here is whether the installation requirement is a major or minor performance obligation of Company A. If it is a minor performance obligation with little likelihood that it will not be met then Company A has transferred the significant risks and rewards of ownership to Customer B on delivery, and it is probable that future economic benefits will flow (i.e. Customer B will pay for the goods even though installation is not complete because the installation is minor and unlikely to result in non-performance of the goods).

In this case, the performance obligation is minor and therefore Company A recognises revenue on the delivery date.

ILLUSTRATIVE EXAMPLE 3.8

Goods shipped subject to major conditions

Company A sells goods to Customer B. On the delivery date, Company A invoices Customer B and is obliged to install the goods. The installation is major and involves a few days' worth of work plus testing that the goods perform when installed.

In this case, the installation requirement is a major performance obligation. If Company A does not meet the obligation, Customer B would not accept the goods and would not pay for them. Thus, Company A has not transferred the significant risks and rewards of ownership to Customer B on delivery, and it is not probable that future economic benefits will flow (i.e. Customer B will not accept or pay for the goods until installation is complete because the installation is major and could result in non-performance of the goods if not properly performed).

ILLUSTRATIVE EXAMPLE 3.9

Consignment sales

Company A sells goods to Customer B. The agreement between the two parties states that Customer B will hold those goods on consignment and will only pay for the goods to the extent that Customer B on-sells the goods to third parties.

In this case, Company A has not transferred the significant risks and rewards of ownership to Customer B on delivery, and it is not probable that future economic benefits will flow nor, indeed, can it be argued that revenue can be reliably measured because Customer B will only pay for those goods that it on-sells to third parties. Until Company B on-sells the goods, it has no requirement to pay anything to Company A.

Accordingly, Company A does not recognise any revenue until Customer B has on-sold the goods.

ILLUSTRATIVE EXAMPLE 3.10

Sales with a right of return

Company A sells goods to Customer B. The agreement between the two parties states that Customer B has the right to return the goods within 5 days of delivery.

The key issue here is whether the right of return is limited or unlimited. If it is a limited right, then Company A has transferred the significant risks and rewards of ownership to Customer B once that right expires, and at that date it is probable that future economic benefits will flow (i.e. Customer B will pay for the goods once the right of return period expires).

If it is an unlimited right (e.g. if Customer B can return the goods at any time in the future), then Company A has not transferred the significant risks and rewards of ownership to Customer B. In effect, Customer B has the right to rescind the purchase and Company A is obliged to take the goods back at any time. Thus, Company A does not recognise any revenue. Example 5 in the Appendix to IAS 18 indicates that this should be accounted for as a financing transaction. This means that Company A will record the cash received for the 'sale' with the credit being recorded as a borrowing rather than as revenue (i.e. Dr Cash; Cr Borrowing).

ILLUSTRATIVE EXAMPLE 3.11

Instalment sales

Company A sells goods to Customer B. The agreement between the two parties states that Customer B pays for the goods in instalments, the first being paid on delivery and the rest being paid over 2 years from the date of delivery. The risks and rewards of the asset pass to Customer B at the date of delivery.

In this case, the revenue *recognition* criteria are met at the date of delivery. However, payment for the goods, other than the first instalment, is deferred. In accordance with IAS 18, paragraph 11, the *measurement* of the fair value of the consideration should be determined by discounting all future receipts using an imputed rate of interest.

Refer to illustrative example 3.2 for an illustration of how to apply this method.

ILLUSTRATIVE EXAMPLE 3.12

Payments in advance

Company A sells goods to Customer B. The agreement between the two parties states that Customer B pays for the goods in advance of delivery which will occur in 12 months' time. The risks and rewards of the goods pass to Customer B at the date of delivery.

Customer B pays $20 000 to Company A on 1 July 2011. Company A delivers the goods to Customer B on 1 July 2012.

Although this situation is not addressed in IAS 18, arguably it is exactly the reverse of the situation in illustrative example 3.11. Revenue is not recognised until the date of delivery and the advance payment should be treated as a financing transaction with interest accruing on it.

Company A would record the following journal entries, assuming the appropriate interest rate is 4%.

1 July 2011			
Cash	Dr	20 000	
Interest Expense	Dr	800	
Deferred Revenue (or obligation to deliver goods)	Cr		20 800
(To record the cash received in advance of delivery and accrued interest expense)			
1 July 2012			
Deferred Revenue	Dr	20 800	
Revenue	Cr		20 800
(To record the revenue recognised on the date of delivery at the fair value of the consideration which includes accrued interest)			

3.7.2 Examples in respect of the rendering of services

The following practical illustrative examples (3.13–3.17) further illustrate the application of IAS 18. In most of the examples one or two of the revenue recognition criteria in paragraph 20 are relatively more important to the transaction in question and these are highlighted in the examples. In all cases reliable measurement is assumed.

ILLUSTRATIVE EXAMPLE 3.13

Servicing fees included in the price of a product

Company A sells goods to Customer B. Customer B enters into an agreement to buy the goods from Company A for $30 000 on 1 February. Company A delivers the goods on 15 February. Customer B pays for the goods on 28 February.

The agreement states that from 15 February, when Company A delivers the goods, it must continue to maintain them for a year for Customer B. Customer B still pays for the goods on 28 February; however, it is entitled to a refund of 20% of the amount paid if Company A does not satisfactorily maintain the goods for the year as required.

As discussed in illustrative example 3.4, under the asset/liability model, Company A has an obligation to maintain the goods and to refund the cash as from 15 February. Thus, it would record the following entry:

Asset – Receivable from Customer B	Dr
Liability (obligation to maintain goods and refund cash)	Cr
Income	Cr

Under the *Framework,* the definition of income is not met for 100% of the amount receivable because, while there has been an increase in an asset, there has also been an increase in a liability. The measurement of these amounts is not addressed in the *Framework.*

Under IAS 18, the same principle applies; however, the language used focuses on the stage of completion of the transaction rather than on any performance obligation. Example 11 in the Appendix to IAS 18 states that the identifiable amount for subsequent servicing is deferred and recognised as revenue over the period during which the service is performed. It also states that 'the amount deferred is that which will cover the expected costs of the services under the agreement, together with a reasonable profit on those services'. This requirement is presumably intended to achieve an estimate of the fair value of the services. Note that this does not equate to providing for the *cost* of meeting the obligation.

Thus, assuming Company A estimates the fair value of the services to be $8000, under IAS 18, Company A would record the following journal entries:

Feb. 15	Asset – Receivable from Customer B	Dr	30 000	
	Deferred Revenue	Cr		8 000
	Revenue	Cr		22 000
	(To record the sale of goods to Customer B and the obligation to deliver services)			
Feb. 28	Cash	Dr	30 000	
	Asset – Receivable from Customer B	Cr		30 000
	(To record the receipt of cash from Customer B)			

Over the period of the maintenance agreement Company A records the following entry:

Deferred Revenue	Dr	8 000	
Revenue	Cr		8 000
(To record revenue as the services are provided to Customer B)			

ILLUSTRATIVE EXAMPLE 3.14

Commissions and upfront fees

Company A is an insurance agent and provides insurance advisory services to Customer B. Company A receives a commission from Insurance Company I when Company A places Customer B's insurance policy with Insurance Company I.

The key issue with commissions is whether the revenue is recognised in full upfront or over an actual or implied service period.

In this example, Company A would record its commission revenue in full upfront if its only service was to place the related insurance policy with Customer B. However, if Company A is required to render further services to Customer B over the life of the policy then part of the commission would be deferred and recognised as revenue over the period during which the policy is in force.

Usually it can be determined from the relevant arrangement whether further services are required. However, this is not always as simple as it sounds. In May 2006, IFRIC decided to take an item onto its agenda dealing with initial fees received by a fund manager. These fees are typically received by a fund manager when an investor makes an investment in a fund and are not refundable regardless of how long the investor remains in the relevant fund. Subsequent to the receipt of the initial fee, the fund manager will also receive an ongoing fee (usually a percentage of assets under management) from the fund for ongoing fund management. Units in the fund may be sold by an in-house adviser (i.e. belonging to the same group as the fund) or by an independent adviser.

The issue is whether the upfront fee should be recognised in full as revenue upfront or should be spread over the life of the investment.

IFRIC agreed that paragraph 13 of IAS 18 was relevant (refer section 3.3) and thus considered whether part of the upfront fee related to any actual or implied ongoing service obligation. The fact that the fee was not refundable did not necessarily mean that there was no ongoing service obligation. IFRIC noted that the upfront fee (usually a set percentage of the initial investment) was the same regardless of whether the investment was placed by an in-house manager or an independent adviser. If it was placed by an independent adviser, there was no link between the initial advice and the ongoing fund management. However, if it was placed by an in-house adviser there could be an implicit link between the initial advice and the ongoing fund management.

IFRIC was unable to reach agreement on this issue for various reasons, the key reason being that it was unable to determine whether the initial fee represented a separate service. The fact that an independent adviser earned the same fee as the in-house adviser did not necessarily mean that a separate service had been provided by the in-house adviser.

IFRIC agreed that if the upfront fee was clearly higher than the market rate for such a fee and was in substance related to ongoing services then the fee should be deferred. However it could not agree on the accounting in circumstances where the upfront fee was at market rate and how the link, if any, to ongoing services should be determined.

IFRIC removed the item from its agenda after debating it for three consecutive meetings because it was evident that it would be unable to reach a consensus. Illustrative example 3.15 shows just how difficult revenue recognition issues can be in practice.

ILLUSTRATIVE EXAMPLE 3.15

Placement fees for arranging a loan[3]

Company A is a financial adviser and provides advisory services to Customer B. Company A receives a placement fee from Financial Services Company F when Company A places Customer B's loan with Company F.

In this case, the service is provided with the completion of a significant act (in accordance with paragraph 25 of IAS 18, i.e. the placement of the loan). As there is no further service obligation, Company A recognises its placement fee as at the date the loan is formally arranged.

[3]This chapter does not deal with more complex revenue recognition issues in the financial services industry. Chapter 5 addresses accounting for financial instruments which should be studied prior to considering this topic.

ILLUSTRATIVE EXAMPLE 3.16

Membership fees

Company A is a sports club that charges membership fees. An upfront membership fee is payable on joining the club. In addition, an annual fee is also charged, at the commencement of each year. Both fees are non-refundable.

Again, the key question is whether the upfront fee contains any actual or implied ongoing service obligation. The upfront fee joining fee would usually not contain any ongoing service obligation and would provide membership only. If this is the case, then the joining fee would be recognised as revenue upfront. The annual fee would cover other services to be provided over the year — the key service being use of the facilities. Thus, the annual fee would be deferred and recognised as revenue over the year.

Note that example 17 in the Appendix to IAS 18 makes reference to collectability as a criterion for revenue recognition in the case of membership fees. This is inconsistent with paragraph 22 of IAS 18 which indicates that collectability is a *measurement* issue, not a *recognition* issue.

ILLUSTRATIVE EXAMPLE 3.17

Subscription fees

Company A is a publisher that charges non-refundable subscription fees. The subscription fee is payable each year in advance and entitles the customer to 12 magazines, one per month.

In this case, Company A clearly has an obligation to deliver the magazines each month and thus should recognise revenue when each month's magazine is despatched to the customer.

3.8 REVENUE RECOGNITION ISSUES IN VARIOUS INDUSTRIES IN PRACTICE

3.8.1 Understanding multiple-element arrangements

Before addressing various industry issues, it is important to understand the principles of determining revenue in multiple-element transactions.

For example, in the telecommunications industry, it is common for entities to provide 'bundled' arrangements to customers. For example, a company might provide a telephone handset free of charge to a customer who subscribes for a service contract with the company. These types of arrangements are known as multiple-element arrangements and are addressed in paragraph 13 of IAS 18. Paragraph 13 requires the entity to identify the components of the transaction.

IFRIC 13 *Customer Loyalty Programmes*, which was published in June 2007 and effective for annual reporting periods beginning on or after 1 July 2008, makes it clear that paragraph 13 applies an *allocation* approach to revenue recognition. This means that the total amount of the consideration is allocated between the various components of the arrangement. Thus, if two or more goods or services are to be delivered at different times, paragraph 13 requires revenue to be allocated to each delivered and undelivered element of the transaction. The revenue in respect of the *delivered* element is recognised immediately, whereas the revenue in respect of the *undelivered* element is deferred and recognised when that element is delivered. This is in contrast to providing for the *costs* of items that have yet to be delivered. IFRIC clarified that paragraph 19 of IAS 18 applies to expected costs on items that *have already been delivered*. In other words, paragraph 19 does not deal with revenue recognition; it deals with expected costs to be incurred once revenue has already been recognised. This clarification is most helpful and alleviates some of the confusion referred to in illustrative example 3.4.

Table 3.1 summarises the principles explained in IFRIC 13.

TABLE 3.1 Revenue allocation in multiple element arrangements, application of paragraphs 13 and 19 of IAS 18		
	IAS 18 paragraph 13	**IAS 18 paragraph 19**
Key principle	Separate the transaction into its component parts. Identify the delivered and undelivered elements of the transaction. *Allocate* the total consideration between these elements.	Provide for the costs, if any, expected *after* the items have been delivered and revenue has been recognised.
Recognise revenue	For each component, when it is delivered.	N/A. Does not deal with revenue recognition.
Total amount of revenue	Equals the fair value of the consideration in accordance with paragraph 9 of IAS 18.	N/A. Does not deal with revenue recognition.
Does the total amount of revenue change over the life of the transaction?	No. The total amount determined at inception of the transaction is *allocated* to the various components. The timing of recognition may change but the total consideration does not change.	N/A. Does not deal with revenue recognition.

For example, assume Company A provides a bundled service offering to Customer B. It charges Customer B $3000 for upfront advice and two ongoing services — 'on-call' advice and access to Company A's databases over a 2-year period.

Customer B pays the $3000 upfront.

Company A determines that, if it were to charge a separate fee for each service if sold separately, the fee would be:

Upfront advice	$ 200
On-call advice	$2600
Access to databases	$ 800

While IFRIC 13 does not prescribe a method for allocating the consideration between the various components, a commonly accepted method is the relative fair value approach. In this example the approach results in the following allocation.

	Fair value of each component if sold separately $	Allocation of fair value to total consideration $	Allocated amount $
Upfront advice	200	200/3 600 × 3 000	166
On-call advice	2 600	2 600/3 600 × 3 000	2 167
Access to databases	800	800/3 600 × 3 000	667
Total	3 600		3 000

Company A would record the following journal entry at inception of the agreement:

Cash	Dr	3 000	
Revenue – Upfront Advice	Cr		166
Deferred Revenue – On-call Advice	Cr		2 167
Deferred revenue – Access to Databases	Cr		667

The deferred revenue for each of the undelivered elements (i.e. the on-call advice and the access to databases) will be recognised when those services are delivered. Because both the on-call advice and the access to databases are available to Customer B continuously over the period of the agreement, the revenue should be recognised in accordance with paragraph 25 of IAS 18 (i.e. on a straight-line basis).

Since this agreement is for 2 years, in each year (assuming the financial year coincides with the agreement year) Company A would record the following entry:

Deferred Revenue – On-call Advice	Dr	1 083.50	
Deferred Revenue – Access to Databases	Dr	333.50	
Revenue	Cr		1 417.00

By the end of the 2 years, Company A would have recorded a total of revenue of $3000, made up as follows:

Year 1	
Revenue – upfront advice	$ 166
Revenue – on-call advice and access to databases	1 417
Year 2	
Revenue – on-call advice and access to databases	1 417
Total	3 000

This equals the total consideration agreed to at the inception of the agreement. Therefore, the allocation process does not alter the *amount* of revenue recognised; it only affects the *timing* of revenue recognition.

(This should be distinguished from the case of deferred consideration where the amount of revenue *is* affected because the *payment is deferred* and this affects the fair value of the consideration).

3.8.2 Telecommunications

Numerous revenue recognition issues arise in the telecommunications industry, including multiple-element arrangements such as those described above, upfront connection fees, the sale of handsets via distributors and fees from third-party content providers.

Multiple-element arrangements

While IFRIC was asked to deal specifically with subscriber acquisition costs in the telecommunications industry in 2006, it declined to take the item onto its agenda on the basis that the IASB would address the issue more broadly as part of its revenue recognition project. The question posed was whether, in an arrangement where a handset is provided 'free' to a customer together with a contract for services, the cost of the handset to the provider could be recorded as a customer acquisition cost and capitalised as an asset. The principle articulated subsequently in IFRIC 13 discussed above makes it clear how the revenue side of the transaction should be accounted for but it does not address whether the costs can be deferred, nor does it specifically address how to determine whether components are separate or part of the multiple-element arrangement.

The key question is whether the provision of the handset forms part of a multiple-element arrangement or whether it is a separate transaction. This is often dependent on the facts and circumstances of the particular arrangement. If the provision of the handset is considered to be a separate transaction (e.g. because it is provided to the customer by a distributor who has no right of return to the telecommunications company and bears all the risks and rewards associated with the provision of the handset to the customer) then the cost of the handset to the telecommunications company should be treated as an expense when it is provided because there is no relationship to ongoing service revenue.

However, if the provision of the handset is considered to be an integral part of the service arrangement with the customer (e.g. because it is provided to the customer as part of its services agreement with the telecommunications company) then the cost of the handset to the telecommunications company could be deferred on the basis that the revenue from the entire arrangement is recognised over the period of the agreement.

Telstra Corporation Limited applies the former view in accounting policy note 2.12(d) to its 2008 financial statements, as illustrated in figure 3.3.

2. Summary of accounting policies (continued)

2.12 Intangible assets (continued)

(d) Deferred expenditure

Deferred expenditure mainly includes costs incurred for basic access installation and connection fees for in place and new services, and direct incremental costs of establishing a customer contract.

Significant items of expenditure are deferred to the extent that they are recoverable from future revenue and will contribute to our future earning capacity. Any costs in excess of future revenue are recognised immediately in the income statement. Handset subsidies are considered to be separate units of accounting and expensed as incurred.

We amortise deferred expenditure over the average period in which the related benefits are expected to be realised.

FIGURE 3.3 Deferred expenditure of Telstra Corporation
Source: Telstra (2008, p. 115).

The Deutsche Telekom Group also applies the former view in its accounting policy note to its 2007 financial statements, although with a different reason, as illustrated in figure 3.4

Deutsche Telekom sells handsets separately and in connection with service contracts. As part of the strategy to acquire new customers, it sometimes sells handsets, in connection with a service contract, at below its acquisition cost. Because the handset subsidy is part of the Company's strategy for acquiring new customers the loss on the sale of handset it recognized at the time of the sale.

FIGURE 3.4 Handset subsidies, Deutsche Telekom Group
Source: Deutsche Telekom (2007, p. 123).

Upfront connection fees

As explained in illustrative example 3.14, the key issue with fees received for connecting a customer to the telecommunications network is whether the revenue is recognised in full upfront or over an actual or implied service period. Most telecommunications companies consider the fee to form part of a multiple-element service arrangement with the customer, as illustrated in figures 3.5 and 3.6.

Sale of handsets via distributors

The key issue here is whether the distribution channels used by telecommunications companies are agents for the telecommunications company or whether they act in their own right as principals in a transaction with customers. Paragraph 8 of IAS 18 makes it clear that where an entity acts as an agent it recognises only its commission received but it gives no guidance on how to determine whether an entity is an agent or a principal in a transaction. In practice, this is addressed by identifying who bears the risks and rewards of the goods to be provided. Say, for example, a distributor sells handsets to customers and at the same time signs them up to a service agreement with the telecommunications company. The telecommunications company provides the handsets to the distributor and pays a commission to the distributor when it signs up a customer to a services agreement with the telecommunications company. The customer can return the handset to the distributor if it is faulty and the distributor must replace the handset at its own cost. This indicates that the distributor acts as a principal in respect of the handset but as an agent in respect of the services. From the telecommunications company's perspective, the revenue, if any, it receives from the sale of the handsets to the distributor is recognised at the date of sale (and related costs are expensed) rather than being recognised over the service period as discussed in the section on multiple-element arrangements above.

Fees from third-party content providers

The agent vs. principal question is also fundamental in cases where third parties provide content (such as ringtones, transport updates and games) to mobile phone customers. The content can either be purchased separately by the customer or included in a price plan.

The telecommunications company usually receives a fee from the third party content provider for every subscriber to that content. The question is whether the telecommunications company should record gross revenue from the sale of services including the content, with an expense for the cost of the content, or the net amount (i.e. the amount attributable to the content provided to the customer less the cost of the content to the telecommunications company).

The answer, again, lies in analysing the facts and circumstances of each arrangement. In general terms, where the telecommunications company is simply acting as a vehicle for the third party's content and the third party is directly responsible to the customer for issues such as accuracy of the data provided, then the telecommunications should only record the net amount as revenue.

Alternatively, if the telecommunications company brands the content as its own and takes full responsibility to the customer for its accuracy then it should record the revenue gross.

Summary of revenue recognition issues

The following extracts (figure 3.5 and figure 3.6) from the accounting policy notes to the financial statements of Telstra Corporation Limited and Deutsche Telekom Group provide a good summary of revenue recognition issues in the telecommunications industry.

FIGURE 3.5 Revenue recognition of Telstra Corporation

2.17 Revenue recognition

Sales revenue

Our categories of sales revenue are recorded after deducting sales returns, trade allowances, discounts, sales incentives, duties and taxes.

(a) Rendering of services

Revenue from the provision of our telecommunications services includes telephone calls and other services and facilities provided, such as internet and data.

We record revenue earned from:

- telephone calls on completion of the call; and
- other services generally at completion, or on a straight line basis over the period of service provided, unless another method better represents the stage of completion.

Installation and connection fee revenues are deferred and recognised over the average estimated customer life that are not considered to be separate units of accounting. Incremental costs directly related to these revenues are also deferred and amortised over the customer contract life in accordance with note 2.12(d).

In relation to basic access installation and connection revenue, we apply our management judgement to determine the estimated customer contract life. Based on our reviews of historical information and customer trends, we have determined that our average estimated customer life is 5 years (2007: 5 years).

(b) Sale of goods

Our revenue from the sale of goods includes revenue from the sale of customer equipment and similar goods. This revenue is recorded on delivery of the goods sold.

Generally we record the full gross amount of sales proceeds as revenue, however if we are acting as an agent under a sales arrangement, we record the revenue on a net basis, being the gross amount billed less the amount paid to the supplier. We review the facts and circumstances of each sales arrangement to determine if we are an agent or principal under the sale arrangement.

(c) Rent of network facilities

We earn rent mainly from access to retail and wholesale fixed and mobile networks and from the rent of dedicated lines, customer equipment, property, plant and equipment and other facilities. The revenue from providing access to the network is recorded on an accrual basis over the rental period.

FIGURE 3.5 *(continued)*

(d) Construction contracts
We record construction revenue on a percentage of contract completion basis. The percentage of completion of contracts is calculated based on estimated costs to complete the contract.

Our construction contracts are classified according to their type. There are three types of construction contracts, these being material intensive, labour intensive and short duration. Revenue is recognised on a percentage of completion basis using the appropriate measures as follows:
- (actual costs/planned costs) × planned revenue – for material intensive projects;
- (actual labour hours/planned labour hours) × planned revenue – for labour intensive projects; and
- short duration projects are those that are expected to be completed within a month and revenues and costs are recognised on completion.

(e) Advertising and directory services
Classified advertisement and display advertisements are published on a daily, weekly and monthly basis for which revenues are recognised at the time the advertisement is published.

All of our Yellow Pages and White Pages directory revenues are recognised on delivery of the published directories using the delivery method. We consider our directories delivered when they have been published and delivered to customers' premises. Revenue from online directories is recognised over the life of service agreements, which is on average one year. Voice directory revenues are recognised at the time of providing the service to customers.

(f) Royalties
Royalty revenue is recognised on an accrual basis in accordance with the substance of the relevant agreements.

(g) Interest revenue
We record interest revenue on an accruals basis. For financial assets, interest revenue is determined by the effective yield on the instrument.

Revenue arrangements with multiple deliverables
Where two or more revenue-generating activities or deliverables are sold under a single arrangement, each deliverable that is considered to be a separate unit of accounting is accounted for separately. When the deliverables in a multiple deliverable arrangement are not considered to be separate units of accounting, the arrangement is accounted for as a single unit.

We allocate the consideration from the revenue arrangement to its separate units based on the relative fair values of each unit. If the fair value of the delivered item is not available, then revenue is allocated based on the difference between the total arrangement consideration and the fair value of the undelivered item. The revenue allocated to each unit is then recognised in accordance with our revenue recognition policies described above.

Source: Telstra (2008, p. 117).

FIGURE 3.6 Revenue recognition of Deutsche Telekom Group

Revenues include all revenues from the ordinary business activities of Deutsche Telekom. Revenues are recorded net of value-added tax and other taxes collected from customers that are remitted to governmental authorities. They are recognized in the accounting period in which they are earned in accordance with the realization principle. Customer activation fees are deferred and amortized over the estimated average period of customer retention, unless they are part of a multiple-element arrangement, in which case they are a component of the arrangement consideration to be paid by the customer. Activation costs and costs of acquiring customers are deferred, up to the amount of deferred customer activation fees, and recognized over the average customer retention period.

For **multiple-element arrangements,** revenue recognition for each of the elements identified must be determined separately. The framework of the Emerging Issues Task Force Issue No. 00-21 "Accounting for Revenue Arrangements with Multiple Deliverables" (EITF 00-21) was applied to account for multiple-element revenue agreements entered into after January 1, 2003, as permitted by IAS 8.12. EITF 00-21 requires in principle that arrangements involving the delivery of bundled

(continued)

FIGURE 3.6 *(continued)*

products or services be separated into individual units of accounting, each with its own separate earnings process. Total arrangement consideration relating to the bundled contracts is allocated among the different units based on their relative fair values (i.e., the relative fair value of each of the accounting units to the aggregated fair value of the bundled deliverables). If the fair value of the delivered elements cannot be determined reliably but the fair value of the undelivered elements can be determined reliably, the residual value method is used to allocate the arrangement consideration.

Payments to customers, including payments to dealers and agents (discounts, provisions) are generally recognized as a decrease in revenue. If the consideration provides a benefit in its own right and can be reliably measured, the payments are recognized as expenses.

Revenue from systems integration contracts requiring the delivery of customized products is recognized by reference to the stage of completion, as determined by the ratio of project costs incurred to date to estimated total contract costs, with estimates regularly revised during the life of the contract. A group of contracts, whether with a single customer or with several customers, is treated as a single contracts when the group of contracts is negotiated as a single package, the contracts are closely interrelated and the contracts are performed concurrently on in a continuous sequence. When a contract covers a number of assets, the construction of each asset is treated separately when separate proposals have been submitted for each asset, each asset has been negotiated separately and can be accepted or rejected by the customer separately, and the costs and revenues of each asset can be identified. Receivables from these contracts are classified in the balance sheet item "trade and other receivables." Receivables from these contracts are calculated as the balance of the costs incurred and the profits recognized, less any discount and recognized losses on the contract; if the balance for a contract is negative, this amount is reported in liabilities. If the total actual and estimated expenses exceed revenues for a particular contract, the loss is immediately recognized.

Revenue recognition in Deutsche Telekom's operating segments is as follows:

Mobile Communications Europe and Mobile Communication USA.
Revenue generated by the operating segments Mobile Communications Europe and Mobile Communications USA include revenues from the provision of mobile services, customer activation fees, and sales of mobile handsets and accessories. Mobile services revenues include monthly service charges, charges for special features, call charges, and roaming charges billed to T-Mobile-customers, as well as other mobile operators. Mobile services revenues are recognized based upon minutes of use and contracted fees less credits and adjustments for discounts. The revenue and related expenses associated with the sale of mobile phones, wireless data devices, and accessories are recognized when the products are delivered and accepted by the customer.

Broadband/Fixed Network.
The Broadband/Fixed Network operating segment provides its customers with narrow and broadband access to the fixed network as well as Internet access. It also sells, leases, and services telecommunications equipment for its customers and provides additional telecommunications services. The Broadband/Fixed Network operating segment also conducts business with national and international network operators and with resellers (wholesale including resale). Service revenues are recognized when the services are provided in accordance with contractual terms and conditions. Revenue and expenses associated with the sale of telecommunications equipment and accessories are recognized when the products are delivered, provided there are no unfulfilled company obligations that affect the customer's final acceptance of the arrangement. Revenue from rentals and operating leases is recognized monthly as the entitlement to the fees accrues. Revenues from customer activation fees are deferred over the average customer retention period. Revenues also result from charges for advertising and e-commerce. Advertising revenues are recognized in the period that the advertisements are exhibited. Transaction revenues are recognized upon notification from the customer that qualifying transactions have occurred and collection of the resulting receivable is reasonably assured.

FIGURE 3.6 *(continued)*

Business Customers.

Business Services. Telecommunication Services include Network Services, Hosting & ASP Services, and Broadcast Services. Contracts for network services, which consist of the installation and operation of communication networks for customers, have an average duration of approximately three years. Customer activation fees and related costs are deferred and amortized over the estimated average period of customer retention. Revenues for voice and data services are recognized under such contracts when used by the customer. When an arrangement contains a lease, the lease is accounted for separately in accordance with IFRIC 4 and IAS 17. Revenues from Hosting & ASP Services and Broadcast Services are recognized as the services are provided.

Enterprise Services. Enterprise Services derives revenues from Computing & Desktop Services, System Integration and Telecommunication Services. Revenue is recognized when persuasive evidence of sales arrangement exists, products are delivered or services are rendered, the sales price or fee is fixed or determinable and collectibility is reasonably assured.

The terms of contracts awarded by Enterprise Services generally range from less than one year to ten years.

Revenue from Computing & Desktop Services is recognized as the services are provided using a proportional performance model. Revenue is recognized ratably over the contractual services period for fixed-price contracts and on an output or consumption basis for all other service contracts. Revenue from service contracts billed on the basis of time and material used is recognized at the contractual hourly rates as labor hours are delivered and direct expenses are incurred.

Revenue from hardware sales or sales-type leases is recognized when the product is shipped to the customer, provided there are no unfulfilled company obligations that affect the customer's final acceptance of the arrangement. Any costs of these obligations are recognized when the corresponding revenue is recognized.

Revenue from rentals and leases is recognized on a straight-line basis over the rental period.

Revenue from systems integration contracts requiring the delivery of customized products is generally recognized by reference to the stage of completion, as determined by the ratio of project costs incurred to date to estimated total contract costs, with estimates regularly revised during the life of the contract. For contracts including milestones, revenues are recognized only when the services for a given milestone are provided and accepted by the customer, and the billable amounts are not contingent upon providing remaining services.

Revenue for Telecommunication Services rendered by Enterprise Services is recognized in accordance with the methods described under Business Services.

When an arrangement contains a lease, the lease is accounted for separately in accordance with IFRIC 4 and IAS 17.

Source: Deutsche Telekom (2007, pp. 128–30).

3.8.3 Pharmaceutical

The following extracts (figure 3.7 and figure 3.8) from the financial statements of AstraZeneca PLC and Bayer AG provide a good summary of revenue recognition issues in the pharmaceutical industry. Note that some of the specific revenue recognition criteria for licence revenue recognition in multiple-element arrangements are based on US GAAP.

Revenue

Sales exclude inter-company sales and value-added taxes and represent net invoice value less estimated rebates, returns and settlement discounts. Sales are recognised when the significant risks and rewards of ownership have been transferred to a third party. In general this is upon delivery of the products to wholesalers. However, when a product faces generic competition particular attention is given to the possible levels of returns and, in cases where the circumstances are such that the level of returns (and, hence, revenue) cannot be measured reliably, sales are only recognised when the right of return expires which is generally on ultimate prescription of the product to patients.

FIGURE 3.7 Revenue recognition of AstraZeneca

Source: AstraZeneca (2007, p. 121).

Net sales and other operating income

Revenues from the sale of products and the rendering of services are recognized when

- the significant risks and rewards of ownership of the goods have been transferred to the customer,
- the company retains neither continuing managerial involvement to the degree usually associated with ownership nor effective control over the goods sold,
- the amount of income and costs incurred or to be incurred can be measured reliably, and
- it is sufficiently probable that the economic benefits associated with the transaction will flow to the company.

Sales are stated net of sales taxes, other taxes and sales deductions. The latter are estimated amounts for cash discounts, rebates and product returns. They are deducted at the time the sales are recognized, and appropriate provisions are recorded. Sales deductions are estimated primarily on the basis of historical experience, specific contractual terms and future expectations of sales development in each business segment. It is unlikely that estimation parameters other than these could affect sales deductions in a way that would be material to the Buyer Group's business operations. The potential for variability in provisions for future sales deductions is not material in relation to the Group's reported operating results. Adjustments to provisions for rebates, cash discounts or returns for sales made in prior periods were not significant in relation to income before income taxes in the year under report.

Provisions for rebates in 2007 amounted to 1.4 percent of total net sales (2006: 1.6 percent). In addition to rebates, Group companies offer cash discounts for prompt payment in some countries. Provisions for cash discounts as of December 31, 2007 and December 31, 2006 were less than 0.1 percent of total net sales for the respective year.

Sales are reduced for expected returns of defective goods or in respect of contractual arrangements to return saleable products on the date of sale or at the time when the amount of future returns can be reasonably estimated. Provisions for product returns as of December 31, 2007 were 0.3 percent of total net sales for the year (December 31, 2006: 0.1 percent). If future products returns cannot be reasonably estimated and are significant to the sale transaction, the revenues and the related cost of sales are deferred until an estimate may reasonably be made or when the right to return the goods has expired.

Some of the Bayer Group's revenues are generated on the basis of licensing agreements under which third parties are granted right to is products and technologies. Payments relating to the sale or outlicensing of technologies or technological expertise — once the respective agreements have become effective — are immediately recognized in income if all rights relating to the technologies and all obligations resulting from them have been relinquished under the contract terms and Bayer has no continuing obligation to perform under the agreement. However, if rights to the technologies continue to exist or obligations resulting from them have yet to be fulfilled, the payments received are recorded in line with the actual circumstances. Upfront payments and similar non-refundable payments received under these agreements are recorded as other liabilities and recognized in income over the estimated performance period stipulated in the agreement. Revenues such as license fees or rentals are recognized according to the same principles.

License or research and development collaboration agreements may consist of multiple elements and provide for varying consideration terms, such as upfront payments and milestone or similar payments. They therefore have to be assessed to determine whether separate delivery of the individual elements of such arrangements requires more than one unit of account. The delivered elements are separated if

- they have value to the customer on a stand-alone basis,
- there is objective and reliable evidence of the fair value of the undelivered element(s) and
- the arrangement includes a general right of return relative to the delivered element(s) and delivery or performance of the as yet undelivered element(s) is probable and substantially within the control of the company.

If all three criteria are fulfilled, the appropriate revenue recognition rule is then applied to each separate accounting unit.

FIGURE 3.8 Revenue recognition of Bayer Group

Source: Bayer (2007, p. 108).

3.8.4 Retail

The following extracts (figure 3.9 and figure 3.10) from the financial statements of Esprit and Woolworths Limited provide a good summary of revenue recognition issues in the retail industry.

(n) Revenue recognition

Revenue comprises the fair value for the sale of goods and services, net of value-added tax, returns, rebates and discounts and after eliminating sales within the Group. Revenue is recognized as follows:

(i) Sales of goods — wholesale

Sales of goods are recognized on the transfer of risks and rewards of ownership, which generally coincides with the time when the goods are delivered to the customer and title has been passed.

(ii) Sales of goods — retail

Sales of goods are recognized on sale of a product to the customer. Retail sales are mainly in cash or by credit card.

(iii) Licensing income

Licensing income is recognized on an accrual basis in accordance with the substance of the relevant agreements.

(iv) Interest income

Interest income is recognized on a time proportion basis using the effective interest method.

FIGURE 3.9 Revenue recognition of Esprit
Source: Esprit (2008, p. 110).

(i) Sales revenue

Sales revenue represents the revenue earned from the provision of products and rendering of services to parties external to the consolidated entity and Company. Sales revenue is only recognised when the significant risks and rewards of ownership of the products, including possession, have passed to the buyer and for services when a right to be compensated has been attained and the stage of completion of the contract can be reliably measured.

Revenue is recognised on a commission only basis where Woolworths acts as an agent rather than a principal in the transaction. Revenue is recognised net of returns.

Revenue from the sale of customer gift cards is recognised when the card is redeemed and the customer purchases the goods by using the card. Where a revenue transaction involves the issue of a voucher that may be subsequently redeemed, the future expected cost of settling the obligation is provided for.

(ii) Rental income

Rental income is recognised on a straight-line basis over the term of the lease.

(iii) Financing income

Interest income is recognised in the income statement as it accrues, using the effective interest method. Dividend income is recognised in the income statement on the date the entity's right to receive payment is established, which in the case of quoted securities is the ex-dividend date.

FIGURE 3.10 Revenue recognition of Woolworths Limited
Source: Woolworths (2008, p. 84).

It should be noted that in the case of customer gift cards, the future cost is provided for rather than allocating revenue between components of the transaction. This is likely because the gift card is sold as a separate transaction and is not part of a multiple-element arrangement. Strictly speaking, the revenue should be described as being deferred rather than the cost being provided for as discussed in section 3.7.

3.8.5 Airline

The airline industry has been significantly affected by the issue of IFRIC 13 *Customer Loyalty Programmes.* IFRIC 13 requires that when an entity offers customer loyalty award credits as part of a sales transaction the award credits must be identified as part of the sale transaction. The fair value of the consideration received or receivable in respect of the initial sale must be allocated between the award credits and the other components of the sale (para. 5). As discussed above, this is an *allocation* of the total fair value of the consideration between the amounts.

Note that IFRIC 13 only applies where the award credits are granted as *part of a sales transaction*. If , for example, a voucher is given to a customer regardless of a sale then that would be regarded as a marketing expense and would not be caught by IFRIC 13.

Some airlines previously accounted for their frequent flyer programs by providing for the incremental cost of flying the passenger when the award credits are redeemed, rather than by allocating the consideration between the components. This means the airlines recognised all the revenue at the time of the sales transaction and at the same time provided for the expected incremental cost.

The following extracts (figures 3.11, 3.12 and 3.13) illustrate the impact of IFRIC 13 on three different airlines. Qantas early adopted IFRIC 13 in its 2008 financial statements and clearly explained the impact of the change in its accounting policy. Singapore Airlines stated that it already applies the method required by IFRIC 13. British Airways stated that it would need to change its accounting policy in order to comply with IFRIC 13. Both Qantas and British Airways previously used the cost accrual method.

FIGURE 3.11 Revenue recognition of Qantas Group

(G) Revenue Recognition

Passenger, Freight and Tours and Travel Revenue

Passenger, freight and tours and travel revenue is included in the income Statement at the fair value of the consideration received net of sales discount, passenger and freight interline/IATA commission and goods and services tax (GST). Passenger recoveries (including fuel surcharge on passenger tickets) are disclosed as part of net passenger revenue. Freight fuel surcharge is disclosed as part of net freight revenue. Other sales commissions paid by Qantas are included in expenditure. Passenger, freight and tours and travel sales are credited to revenue received in advance and subsequently transferred to revenue when passengers or freight are uplifted or when tours and travel air tickets and land content are utilised. Unused tickets are recognised as revenue using estimates regarding the timing of recognition based on the terms and conditions of the ticket. Changes in these estimation methods could have a material impact on the financial statements of Qantas.

Frequent Flyer Revenue

Revenue received in relation to points earning flights is allocated, based on fair value, between the flight and points earned by members of the Qantas Frequent Flyer program. The value attributed to the awarded points is deferred as a liability, within revenue received in advance, until the points are ultimately utilised.

Revenue received from third parties for the issue of Qantas Frequent Flyer points is also deferred as a liability, within revenue received in advance.

As members of the program redeem points for an award, revenue is brought to account within the Income Statement. Revenue is recognised at point of redemption where non-flight rewards are awarded. Revenue in relation to flight awards is recognised when the passenger is uplifted.

The value attributed to points that are expected to expire (breakage) is recognised as revenue when the risk expires i.e. based on the number of points that have been redeemed relative to the total number expected to be redeemed.

Changes in breakage expectations are accounted for prospectively in accordance with Note 1(C). During the year, there has been no material change to breakage expectations.

Contract Work Revenue

Revenue from the rendering of services associated with contracts is included in contract work revenue.

Where services performed are in accordance with contractually agreed terms over a short period and are task specific, revenue is recognised when the service has been performed or when the resulting ownership of the goods passes to the customer.

Revenue on long-term contracts to provide goods or services is recognised in proportion to the stage of completion of the contract when the stage of contract completion can be reliably measured and otherwise on completion of the contract.

FIGURE 3.11 *(continued)*

Other Income

Income resulting from claims for liquidated damages is recognised as other income when all performance obligations are met, including when a contractual entitlement exists, it can be reliably measured (including the impact of the receipt, if any, on the underlying assets' carrying value) and it is probable that the economic benefits will accrue to the Qantas Group.

Revenue from aircraft charter and leases, property income, Qantas Club membership fees, Frequent Flyer revenue relating to other carries, freight terminal and service fees, commission revenue, age availed surplus revenue and other miscellaneous income is recognised as other income at the time service is provided.

Finance Income

Interest revenue is recognised as it accrues, taking into account the effective yield on the financial asset.

Asset Disposals

The gain or loss on the disposal of assets is recognised at the date the significant risks and rewards of ownership of the asset passes to the buyer, usually when the purchaser takes delivery of the asset. The gain or loss on disposal is calculated as the difference between the carrying amount of the asset at the time of disposal and the net proceeds on disposal.

Aircraft Financing Fees

Fees relating to linked transactions involving the legal form of a lease are recognised as revenue only when there are no significant obligations to perform, or refrain from performing, significant activities, management determines there are no significant limitations on use of the underlying asset and the possibility of reimbursement is considered remote. Where these criteria are not met, fees are brought to account as revenue or expenditure over the period of the respective lease or on a basis which is representative of the pattern of benefits derived from the leasing transactions, with the unamoritised balance being held as a deferred lease benefit.

Dividend Revenue

Dividends/distributions from controlled entities are recognised as revenue by Qantas when dividends are declared by the controlled entities. Dividends/distributions from associates, jointly controlled entities and other investments are recognised when dividends are paid.

Dividend/distribution revenue is recognised net of any franking credits or withholding tax.

2. Change in Accounting Policy

On 1 July, 2007, the Qantas Group revised its accounting policy in relation to accounting for Qantas Frequent Flyer points and their associated expiry. This accounting policy change effects the early adoption of Interpretation 13.

The previous accounting policy created a provision for the cost of the obligation to provide travel rewards to members arising from travel on points earning services. This provision excluded the costs of the number of points that were estimated to expire. The provision was calculated as the present value of the expected incremental direct cost (being the cost of meals and passenger expenses) of providing the travel rewards.

The new accounting policy requires revenue received in relation to points earning flights to be split. The allocation between the value of the flight and the value of the points awarded is undertaken at fair value. The value attributable to the flight is then recognised on passenger uplift, while the value attributed to the awarded points is deferred as a liability until the points are ultimately utilised.

The value attributed to the points that are expected to expire is recognised as revenue as the risk expires i.e. based on the number of points that have been redeemed relative to the total number expected to be redeemed.

The impact of the adoption of Interpretation 13 on the Balance Sheet at 1 July 2006 and 30 June 2007 and the Income Statement for the year ended 30 June 2007 is shown in the following tables.

(continued)

FIGURE 3.11 *(continued)*

Qantas Group	Previously Reported 1 July 2006 $M	Effect of Adoption of Interpretation 13 $M	Revised 1 July 2006 $M	Previously Reported 30 June 2007 $M	Effect of Adoption of Interpretation 13 $M	Revised 30 June 2007 $M
Total current assets[1]	4 948.4	—	4 948.4	5 587.4	—	5 587.4
Total non-current assets[1]	14 234.9	—	14 234.9	13 906.3	—	13 906.3
Total assets[1]	19 183.3	—	19 183.3	19 493.7	—	19 493.7
Current Liabilities						
Payables	1 985.3	—	1 985.3	2 005.7	—	2 005.7
Revenue received in advance	2 282.8	481.0	2 763.8	2 533.6	515.7	3 049.3
Interest-bearing liabilities	440.8	—	440.8	863.7	—	863.7
Other financial liabilities	139.2	—	139.2	337.2	—	337.2
Provisions	469.0	(28.4)	440.6	534.4	(34.0)	500.4
Current tax liabilities	72.4	—	72.4	153.6	—	153.6
Deferred lease benefits/ income	37.5	—	37.5	29.3	—	29.3
Total current liabilities	5 427.0	452.6	5 879.6	6 457.5	481.7	6 939.2
Non-current Liabilities						
Revenue received in advance	708.5	312.6	1 021.1	701.5	348.2	1 049.7
Interest-bearing liabilities	5 334.8	—	5 334.8	4 210.9	—	4 210.9
Other financial liabilities	352.2	—	352.2	702.3	—	702.3
Provisions	479.7	(38.9)	440.8	481.9	(36.6)	445.3
Deferred tax liabilities	701.2	(217.9)	483.3	675.6	(238.1)	437.5
Deferred lease benefits/ income	98.8	—	98.8	69.0	—	69.0
Total non-current liabilities	7 675.2	55.8	7 731.0	6 841.2	73.5	6 914.7
Total liabilities	13 102.2	508.4	13 610.6	13 298.7	555.2	13 853.9
Net assets	6 081.1	(508.4)	5 572.7	6 195.0	(555.2)	5 639.8
Equity						
Issued capital	4 382.2	—	4 382.2	4 481.2	—	4 481.2
Treasury shares	(23.8)	—	(23.8)	(32.6)	—	(32.6)
Reserves	329.3	—	329.3	148.2	—	148.2
Retained earnings	1 388.5	(508.4)	880.1	1 593.3	(555.2)	1 038.1
Equity attributable to members of Qantas	6 076.2	(508.4)	5 567.8	6 190.1	(555.2)	5 634.9
Minority interest	4.9	—	4.9	4.9	—	4.9
Total equity	6 081.1	(508.4)	5 572.7	6 195.5	(555.2)	5 639.8

[1]Interpretation 13 has not impacted assets and accordingly the individual categories appearing on the face of the Balance Sheet have not been disclosed here.

FIGURE 3.11 *(continued)*

Sales and Other Income	Previously Reported Year Ended 30 June 2007 $M	Effect of Adoption of Interpretation 13 $M	Revised Year Ended 30 June 2007 $M
Net passenger revenue[1]	11 968.2	(48.1)	11 920.1
Net freight revenue	902.5	—	902.5
Tours and travel revenue[1]	775.1	—	775.1
Contract work revenue	434.3	—	434.3
Other[1]	1 086.3	(57.9)	1 028.4
Sales and other income	15 166.4	(106.0)	15 060.4
Expenditure			
Manpower and staff related	3 334.7	—	3 334.7
Aircraft operating – variable[1]	2 608.4	—	2 608.4
Fuel	3 336.8	—	3 336.8
Selling and marketing[1]	726.7	(34.9)	691.8
Property	350.5	—	350.5
Computer and communication[1]	319.5	—	319.5
Tours and travel	641.7	—	641.7
Capacity hire	303.2	—	303.2
Ineffective and non-designated derivatives – closed positions	67.6	—	67.6
Other[1]	644.7	—	644.7
Depreciation and amortisation	1 362.7	—	1 362.7
Non-cancellable operating lease rentals	415.3	—	415.3
Share of net profit of associates and jointly controlled entities	(46.5)	—	(46.5)
Expenditure	14 065.3	(34.9)	14 030.4
Operating result	1 101.1	(71.1)	1 030.0
Ineffective and non-designated derivatives – open positions	(54.1)	—	(54.1)
Profit before related income tax expense and net finance costs	1 047.0	(71.1)	975.9
Finance income	244.0	—	244.0
Finance costs	(258.9)	4.1	(254.8)
Net finance costs	(14.9)	4.1	(10.8)
Profit before related income tax expense	1 032.1	(67.0)	965.1
Income tax expense	(312.5)	20.2	(292.3)
Profit for the year	719.6	(46.8)	672.8

[1]Previously reported balances have been reclassified as a result of the implementation of a common chart of accounts throughout the Qantas Group.

Source: Qantas (2008, pp. 81–2, 87–8).

Note that the main impact is to reduce revenue recognised, increase revenue received in advance and reduce selling and marketing costs. This reflects the change from recognising all the revenue and accruing for costs versus recognising an element of the revenue and deferring the element relating to the award credits to be redeemed in the future.

FIGURE 3.12 Revenue recognition of Singapore Airlines

INT FRS 113: Customer Loyalty Programmes
The interpretation addresses accounting for loyalty award credits granted to customers who buy other goods or services, and the accounting for the entity's obligations to provide free or discounted goods or services to customers when the award credits are redeemed.

(continued)

FIGURE 3.12 *(continued)*

Loyalty award should be viewed as separately identifiable goods or services for which customers are implicitly paying and measured based on the allocated proceeds which represent the value of the award credits. The proceeds allocated to the award credits are deferred until the entity fulfills its obligations by supplying the free or discounted goods or services upon the redemption of the award credits.

The adoption of this interpretation should not result in a change in accounting policy of the Company as the current accounting treatment of the Company's award credits granted under the frequent flyer programme ("KrisFlyer") is closely aligned with the treatment as set out in the interpretation.

Source: Singapore Airlines (2008, p. 89).

FIGURE 3.13 Revenue recognition of British Airways

Revenue

Passenger and cargo revenue is recognised when the transportation serviced is provided. Passenger tickets net of discounts are recorded as current liabilities in the 'sales in advance of carriage' account until recognised as revenue. Unused tickets are recognised as revenue using estimates regarding the timing of recognition based on the terms and conditions of the ticket and historical trends. Other revenue is recognised at the time the service is provided. Commission costs are recognised at the same time as the revenue to which they relate and are charged to cost of sales.

Revenue recognition — mileage programmes

The Group operates two principal loyalty programmes. The airline frequent flyer programme operates through the airline's 'Executive Club' and allows frequent travellers to accumulate 'BA Miles' mileage credits that entitle them to a choice of various awards, primarily free travel. The estimated direct incremental cost of providing free redemption services, including British Airways' flights, in exchange for redemption of miles earned by members of the Group's 'Executive Club' is accrued as members of the scheme accumulate mileage. These costs are charged to cost of sales.

In addition, 'BA Miles' are sold to commercial partners to use in promotional activity. The fair value of the miles sold is deferred and recognised as revenue on redemption of the miles by the participants to whom the miles are issued. The cost of providing free redemption services is recognised when the miles are redeemed.

The Group also operates the AIRMILES scheme, operated by the Company's wholly-owned subsidiary Airmiles Travel Promotions Limited. The scheme allows companies to purchase miles for use in their own promotional activities. Miles can be redeemed for a range of benefits, including flights on British Airways and other carriers. The fair value of the miles sold is deferred and recognised as revenue on redemption of the miles by the participants to whom the miles are issued. The cost of providing free redemption services is recognised when the miles are redeemed.

New standards, amendments and interpretations not yet effective

The IASB and IFRIC issued the following standards and interpretations with an effective date after the date of these financial statements:

IFRIC 13 'Customer Loyalty Programmes', effective for annual periods beginning on or after July 1, 2008. IFRIC 13 addresses accounting by entities that operate or otherwise participate in customer loyalty programmes for their customers. IFRIC 13 applies to sales transactions in which the entities grant their customers award credits that, subject to meeting any further qualifying conditions, the customers can redeem in the future for free or discounted goods or services. The interpretation requires that an entity recognises credits that it awards to customers as a separately identifiable component of revenue, which would be deferred at the date of the initial sale. IRFIC 13 will become mandatory for the Group's consolidated financial statements beginning April 1, 2009 with earlier application permitted. The Group expects to early adopt IFRIC 13 from April 1, 2008 with initial adoption expected to result in a reduction in opening shareholders' equity.

Source: British Airways (2008, pp. 82, 87).

3.9 INTERACTION BETWEEN IAS 18 AND OTHER STANDARDS AND INTERPRETATIONS

We have seen in the foregoing sections that IAS 18 interacts with numerous standards and IFRIC interpretations, the most significant being IAS 39 in respect of the recognition of revenue for financial instruments (see chapter 5), IAS 1 in respect of disclosures, IAS 16 and IAS 38 in respect of gain recognition on the sale of non-current assets and accounting for exchanges or swaps of non-current assets, and IFRIC 13 in respect of the principle of revenue recognition in multiple-element arrangements. Another significant standard is IAS 11 *Construction Contracts*. IAS 11 requires use of the percentage completion method of revenue recognition for construction contracts that fall within its scope. IAS 11, paragraph 3 defines a construction contract as 'a contract specifically negotiated for the construction of an asset or a combination of assets'. Typical construction contracts that meet this definition are contracts for the construction of residential houses. In these cases, the buyer usually owns the land and contracts with a builder to build a house on that land. The builder applies IAS 11 and recognises revenue on a percentage of completion basis (as described in illustrative example 3.5) as the house is being built.

In 2007, IFRIC was asked to address the situation described as 'pre-completion sales' of constructed assets. The typical example of this is where a developer builds a residential apartment block and sells the apartments 'off-the-plan' (i.e. before they are built). The question asked was whether these types of contracts were construction contracts to be accounted for under IAS 11 or whether they should be accounted for under the general requirements of IAS 18. In 2008, IFRIC issued an interpretation titled *Agreements for the Construction of Real Estate*.

The principles of the interpretation are as follows:

(a) Identify the components of the transaction by applying paragraph 13 of IAS 18.
(b) For the component that is a construction contract as defined in IAS 11, apply IAS 11 (i.e. percentage completion method of revenue recognition).
(c) If the arrangement is not a construction contract but nevertheless the risks and rewards of ownership transfer to the buyer on a continuous basis, apply the percentage completion method under IAS 18 (i.e. there is a continuous transfer of the risks and rewards of ownership and control of the goods in respect of which the services have been provided). This is to cater for situations where the substance of the arrangement is a construction contract but it does not meet the definition of a construction contract in IAS 11 (these situations are expected to be rare).
(d) If the arrangement is not a construction contract and the risks and rewards of ownership do not transfer on a continuous basis, then IAS 18 also applies, but the percentage completion method of revenue recognition is not appropriate.

IFRIC had expressed some concerns with the concept of 'continuous transfer' and whether it was an acceptable interpretation of paragraph 14 of IAS 18 in respect of the sale of goods. The staff reported that IASB members have not objected to this notion. Nevertheless, IFRIC members believed that it was unlikely that many arrangements (that are not construction contracts) would meet the test of continuous transfer because all the conditions of paragraph 14 of IAS 18 would need to be met in respect of the partially completed work-in-progress. In other words, for example, if the tests in paragraph 14 were met, the buyer would be left with the partially completed work-in-progress should the developer fail and the buyer would have managerial control over the project. This is not the case in most off-the-plan sales where the buyer's risk is usually limited to their deposit. Notwithstanding these concerns, IFRIC agreed to retain the notion of 'continuous transfer', but expected that few arrangements would meet the required conditions.

The interpretation is effective for annual reporting periods beginning on or after 1 January 2009. It will apply retrospectively.

Note that for many entities that undertake off-the-plan real estate sales, the effect of the interpretation will be to discontinue the percentage of completion method of revenue recognition. Revenue will only be recognised on completion and delivery of the apartments in accordance with paragraph 14 of IAS 18.

3.10 DISCLOSURE REQUIREMENTS OF IAS 18

Paragraph 35 of IAS 18 requires an entity to disclose:

(a) the accounting policies adopted for revenue recognition, including how it determined the stage of completion of transactions

(b) the amount of each significant category of revenue recognised during the period (i.e. sale of goods, rendering of services, interest, royalties and dividends)

(c) the amount of revenue arising from exchanges of goods and services.

Any related contingencies must also be disclosed in accordance with IAS 37 *Provisions, Contingent Liabilities and Contingent Assets*. These might include, for example, contingent liabilities arising from claims or penalties related to non-performance.

IAS 1 (refer chapter 18) requires revenue to be disclosed in the statement of comprehensive income. The breakdown of revenue as required by IAS 18 may be disclosed in the statement or in the notes.

The example provided in figure 3.10 illustrates the comprehensive disclosures made in practice in respect of paragraph 35(a). Disclosures required in respect of paragraphs 11(b) and (c) are simple and do not cause any significant issues in practice.

3.11 EXPECTED FUTURE DEVELOPMENTS

As we have seen, accounting for revenue is a complex area, with IAS 18 being unhelpful in many respects.

Understanding that revenue is such an important measure for companies and that it has been a problematic area for so long, the IASB, jointly with the FASB, added a significant project on revenue recognition to their agenda, finally issuing a discussion paper in December 2008.

The discussion paper (DP) is titled *Preliminary Views on Revenue Recognition in Contracts with Customers*. It focuses on contracts with customers and thus excludes areas such as agriculture where fair value movements do not relate to contracts with customers.

The key principle in the discussion paper is that when an entity becomes a party to a contract with a customer it should account for its rights and obligations under that contract on a net basis. The principle is based on the asset/liability model of the *Framework* except that it prescribes a net basis for recognising assets and liabilities under the contract, whereas the *Framework* implies a gross basis. The discussion paper is also consistent with the asset/liability model in that it focuses on performance obligations rather than 'deferred revenue'.

The DP is also consistent with IFRIC 13 in that it proposes the revenue allocation method, and it does not propose that revenue should be remeasured unless there is an onerous contract (as defined in IAS 37).

Comments on the discussion paper were due by mid-2009. An exposure draft will follow. A final standard is not expected for some years.

SUMMARY

IAS 18 *Revenue* was issued by the IASC in December 1993 and was confirmed as being included in the core set of standards to be issued by the International Accounting Standards Board (IASB) in April 2001.

IAS 18 was not amended substantially by the IASB when it was issued in 2001. It, therefore, remains essentially a very old standard. Unfortunately, it is not entirely consistent with the *Framework* and is also internally inconsistent — with an Appendix that sometimes contradicts the body of the standard. As a result, revenue recognition has been a problematic area for companies for many years, with many requests for interpretations by the SIC and IFRIC.

The definition of *income* in the *Framework* is very broad, being based, in effect, on statement of financial position movements. This is known as 'the asset/liability' model. The definition of income includes both revenue and gains, with different criteria for each. IAS 18 deals only with revenue while other relevant standards deal with gains.

IAS 18 addresses revenue arising from:

(a) the sale of goods

(b) the rendering of services, and

(c) the use by others of entity assets yielding interest, royalties and dividends.
with different recognition criteria for each category. In all cases, IAS 18 requires that revenue be measured at the fair value of the consideration received or receivable.

Many issues arise in the practice of applying IAS 18, including accounting for deferred consideration, swaps and exchanges of goods; identifying when services are provided; identifying whether multiple-element arrangements exist; accounting for upfront fees; and distinguishing between different types of real estate agreements.

Discussion questions

1. What are the key distinctions between 'income' and 'revenue'? Why do you think the IASB made these distinctions?
2. What is the 'asset/liability' model for the definition and recognition of income under the *Framework*? Does it give a different outcome from other models permitted under IAS 18?
3. In what respects is IAS 18 inconsistent with the *Framework*?
4. What are the recognition criteria for income under the *Framework*? How do these differ from the key stated purpose of IAS 18?
5. What is a multiple-element transaction? Give two examples of these and discuss how IAS 18 applies to such transactions.
6. Compare and contrast the revenue recognition criteria for the sale of goods with those for the rendering of services.
7. Compare and contrast paragraphs 13 and 19 of IAS 18.

STAR RATING
★ BASIC
★★ MODERATE
★★★ DIFFICULT

Exercises

Exercise 3.1 ★

DEFINITIONS

State which of the following meets the definition of 'revenue' under IAS 18 for Company Z, a retailer of toys. Give reasons for your answer:
1. Sales tax collected on behalf of the taxing authority.
2. Gain on the sale of an investment property.
3. Amounts receivable from customers who have purchased toys.
4. Gain on the sale of equity securities held as investments.
5. Revaluation increment on the revaluation of operating properties under IAS 16.

Exercise 3.2 ★

DEFINITIONS, SCOPE

State whether each of the following is true or false:
1. 'Income' means the same as 'revenue'.
2. 'Gains' are always recognised net under IFRSs.
3. 'Revenue' must always be in respect of an entity's ordinary operations.
4. 'Gains' must always be outside of an entity's ordinary operations.
5. 'Deferred revenue' meets the definition of a liability under the *Framework*.
6. Services provided under a construction contract are accounted for under IAS 18.

Exercise 3.3 ★

MEASUREMENT

State whether each of the following is true or false:
1. Revenue is measured at the fair value of the consideration given by the seller.
2. Revenue is measured at the amount for which an asset could be exchanged, or a liability settled, between knowledgeable, willing parties in an arm's length transaction.
3. If payment for the goods or services is deferred, the fair value of the consideration will be less than the nominal amount of the cash receivable.
4. A swap or exchange for goods or services of a similar nature and value generates revenue.
5. Collectability of amounts due from customers is a measurement issue, not a recognition issue.

Exercise 3.4

★

RECOGNITION

What is an 'executory contract'? How does this affect the dates on which revenue is recognised under the *Framework*?

Exercise 3.5

★★

MEASUREMENT — DATES FOR RECOGNITION

Company R sells plastic bottles. Wholesale customers that purchase more than 10 000 bottles per month are entitled to a discount of 6% on their purchases. On 1 March 2011, Customer P ordered 10 crates of bottles from Company R. Each crate contains 2000 bottles. The normal selling price per crate is $400. Company R delivered the 10 crates on 15 March 2011. Customer P paid for the goods on 15 April 2011. The end of Company R's reporting period is 30 June.

Required

Prepare the journal entries to record this transaction by Company R for the year ended 30 June 2011.

Exercise 3.6

★★

REVENUE RECOGNITION — SALE OF GOODS

In each of the following situations, state at which date, if any, revenue will be recognised:

1. A contract for the sale of goods is entered into on 1 May 2011. The goods are delivered on 15 May 2011. The buyer pays for the goods on 30 May 2011. The contract contains a clause that entitles the buyer to rescind the purchase at any time. This is in addition to normal warranty conditions.
2. A contract for the sale of goods is entered into on 1 May 2011. The goods are delivered on 15 May 2011. The buyer pays for the goods on 30 May 2011. The contract contains a clause that entitles the buyer to return the goods up until 30 June 2011 if the goods do not perform according to their specification.
3. A contract for the sale of goods is entered into on 1 May 2011. The goods are delivered on 15 May 2011. The contract contains a clause that states that the buyer shall only pay for those goods that it sells to a third party for the period ended 31 August 2011. Any goods not sold to a third party by that date will be returned to the seller.
4. Retail goods are sold with normal provisions allowing the customer to return the goods if the goods do not perform satisfactorily. The goods are invoiced on 1 May 2011 and the customer pays cash for them on that date.

Exercise 3.7

★★★

REVENUE RECOGNITION — RENDERING OF SERVICES

In each of the following situations, state at which date/s, if any, revenue will be recognised:

1. A contract for the rendering of services is entered into on 1 May 2011. The services are delivered on 15 May 2011. The buyer pays for the services on 30 May 2011.
2. A contract for the rendering of services is entered into on 1 May 2011. The services are delivered continuously over a 1-year period commencing on 15 May 2011. The buyer pays for all the services on 30 May 2011.
3. A contract for the rendering of services is entered into on 1 May 2011. The services are delivered continuously over a 1-year period commencing on 15 May 2011. The buyer pays for the services on a monthly basis, commencing on 15 May 2011.
4. Company A is an insurance agent and provides insurance advisory services to Customer B. Company A receives a commission from Insurance Company I when Company A places Customer B's insurance policy with Insurance Company I, on 1 April 2011. Company A has no further obligation to provide services to Customer B.
5. Company A is an insurance agent and provides insurance advisory services to Customer B. Company A receives a commission from Insurance Company I when Company A places Customer B's insurance policy with Insurance Company I, on 1 April 2011. Company A is required to provide ongoing services to Customer B until 1 April 2012. Additional amounts are charged for these services. All amounts are at market rates.
6. Company A receives a non-refundable upfront fee from Customer B for investment advice, on 1 March 2011. Under the agreement with Customer B Company A must provide ongoing management services until 1 March 2012. An additional amount is charged for these services. The upfront fee is higher than the market rate for equivalent initial investment advice services.

Problems

Problem 3.1

REVENUE RECOGNITION — RENDERING OF SERVICES

★★

On 1 February 2011, Company Z entered into an agreement with Customer S to develop a new database system (both hardware and software) for Customer S. The agreement states that the total consideration to be paid for the system will be $860 000. Company Z expects that its total costs for the system will be $670 000. As the end of its reporting period, 30 June 2011, Company Z had incurred labour costs of $130 000 and materials costs of $360 000. Of the materials costs, $60 000 is in respect of materials that have not yet been used on the system. Of the labour costs, $25 000 is an advance payment to a sub-contractor who had not performed his work on the project as at 30 June 2011. As at 30 June 2011, Customer S had made progress payments to Company Z of $500 000.

Company Z has determined that IAS 11 does not apply to this transaction and calculates the percentage of completion using paragraph 24(c) of IAS 18.

Required

Calculate the revenue to be recognised by Company Z for the year ended 30 June 2011 and prepare the journal entries to record the transactions described. Assume all of Company Z's costs are paid for in cash.

Problem 3.2

AGENT VS. PRINCIPAL QUESTION

★★

Discuss how an entity would determine whether it acts as an agent or principal in sales transactions. In your answer, discuss the distinguishing features between an agency versus principal relationship and the consequences for revenue recognition.

Problem 3.3

MULTIPLE-ELEMENT ARRANGEMENT

★★

Company A provides a bundled service offering to Customer B. It charges Customer B $35 000 for initial connection to its network and two ongoing services — access to the network for 1 year and 'on-call troubleshooting' advice for that year.

Customer B pays the $35 000 upfront, on 1 July 2011. Company A determines that, if it were to charge a separate fee for each service if sold separately, the fee would be:

Connection fee	$ 5 000
Access fee	$12 000
Troubleshooting	$23 000

The end of Company A's reporting period is 30 June.

Required

Prepare the journal entries to record this transaction in accordance with IAS 18 for the year ended 30 June 2012, assuming Company A applies the relative fair value approach. Show all workings.

Problem 3.4

TELECOMMUNICATIONS MULTIPLE-ELEMENT ARRANGEMENT

★★★

Company A is a telecommunications company that offers a variety of services to its customers including fixed-line telephone services, mobile phone services and Internet services. It uses numerous distributors to sell its mobile phone services. Customers purchase a phone handset from the distributor and at the same time can sign up to a contract with Company A for a period of 12 months or 24 months for the provision of network access for a fixed fee. Calls are charged separately if they exceed a certain limit per month. If the customer enters into a 12 month contract, the handset is sold to them for 40% less than the quoted market price. If the customer enters into a 24 month contract, the handset is sold to them for 50% less than the quoted market price. The distributor earns a commission from Company A based on a percentage of the consideration for each contract entered into — 12% for a 12-month contract and 15% for a 24-month contract.

Company A sells its handsets to its distributors at 50% less than fair value on the basis that the distributor will use the handset to entice customers to enter into the contracts with Company A.

If the customer has any problems with the handset during or after the period of the contract (up to a maximum of 2 years), the customer has recourse to the distributor who must replace the handset at its own cost. In the case of a handset manufactured by Company A, the distributor will source the handset from Company A, who will sell it to the distributor at 50% less than fair value.

The distributor sells handsets to customers even if they don't sign up to any services agreement with Company A. In such cases, the customers are charged the market price for the handsets. The distributor also sells other handsets (i.e. not only those of Company A).

Company A has determined that the distributor is acting as its agent in respect of the service contracts but not in respect of its handsets.

Additional information	
Handset cost to Company A	$100
Handset fair value	$160
12-month contract, price charged to customers	$50 per month, all paid upfront
24-month contract, price charged to customers	$40 per month, all paid upfront

Required

Discuss the revenue recognition issues that arise out of the transactions described (a) for Company A and (b) for the distributor. Ignore discounting.

References

AstraZeneca 2007, *Annual report 2007*, AstraZeneca PLC, London, www.astrazeneca.com.

Bayer Group 2007, *Annual report 2007*, Bayer AG, Germany, www.bayer.com.

British Airways 2008, *2007/08 annual report and accounts*, British Airways PLC, London, www.ba.com.

Deutsche Telekom Group 2007, *Annual report 2007*, Deutsche Telekom AG, Germany, www.deutschetelekom.com.

Esprit 2008, *Annual report 2008*, Esprit Holdings Limited, Germany, www.espritholdings.com.

IASB 2007, *Exposure draft of proposed improvements to international financial reporting standards*, October, www.iasb.org.

– 2007, *IFRIC Update*, January 2007, www.iasb.org.

– 2006, *IFRIC Update*, March 2006, www.iasb.org.

Qantas Limited 2008, *Annual report 2008*, Qantas Airways Limited, www.qantas.com.

Singapore Airlines 2008, *Annual report 2007–08*, Singapore Airlines Limited, Singapore, www.singaporeair.com.

Telstra Corporation 2008, *Annual report 2008*, Telstra Corporation Limited, www.telstra.com.au.

Wesfarmers Ltd 2008, *Annual report 2008*, Wesfarmers Limited, www.wesfarmers.com.au.

Woolworths Limited 2007, *Annual report 2008*, Woolworths Limited, www.woolworthslimited.com.au.

4 Provisions, contingent liabilities and contingent assets

ACCOUNTING STANDARDS IN FOCUS

IAS 37 *Provisions, Contingent Liabilities and Contingent Assets*

LEARNING OBJECTIVES

When you have studied this chapter, you should be able to:

- understand the concept of a provision
- understand how to distinguish provisions from other liabilities
- understand the concept of a contingent liability
- describe how to distinguish a provision from a contingent liability
- explain when a provision should be recognised
- explain how a provision, once recognised, should be measured
- apply the definitions, recognition and measurement criteria for provisions and contingent liabilities to practical situations
- understand the concept of a contingent asset
- describe the disclosure requirements for provisions and contingent liabilities
- describe the disclosure requirements for contingent assets.

4.1 INTRODUCTION TO IAS 37

IAS 37 deals with the recognition, measurement and presentation of provisions and contingent assets and contingent liabilities. The standard contains specific requirements regarding the recognition of restructuring provisions and onerous contracts.

The standard:

- defines provisions and specifies recognition criteria and measurement requirements for the recognition of provisions in financial statements
- defines contingent liabilities and contingent assets and prohibits their recognition in the financial statements but requires their disclosure when certain conditions are met
- requires that where provisions are measured using estimated cash flows the cash flows be discounted to their present value at the reporting date and specifies the discount rate to be used for this purpose
- prohibits providing for future operating losses
- defines onerous contracts and requires the estimated net loss under onerous contracts to be provided for
- specifies recognition criteria for restructuring provisions and identifies the types of costs that may be included in restructuring provisions
- requires extensive disclosures relating to provisions, recoveries, contingent liabilities and contingent assets.

4.1.1 Scope

IAS 37 prescribes the accounting and disclosure for all provisions, contingent liabilities and contingent assets except:

(a) those resulting from financial instruments (see chapter 5) and those arising in insurance entities from contracts with policyholders

(b) those resulting from executory contracts, except where the contract is onerous (Executory contracts are contracts under which neither party has performed any of its obligations or both parties have partially performed their obligations to an equal extent.)

(c) those covered by another IAS. For example, certain types of provisions are also addressed in standards on:

- construction contracts (see IAS 11 *Construction Contracts*)
- income taxes (see IAS 12 *Income Taxes*, covered in chapter 7)
- leases (see IAS 17 *Leases*, covered in chapter 13. However, as IAS 17 contains no specific requirements to deal with operating leases that have become onerous, IAS 37 applies to such cases.)
- employee benefits (see IAS 19 *Employee Benefits*)
- insurance contracts (see IFRS 4 *Insurance Contracts*).

Some amounts sometimes described as provisions may relate to the recognition of revenue; for example, where an entity gives guarantees in exchange for a fee. This may also be described as 'deferred revenue'. IAS 37 does not address the recognition of revenue. IAS 18 *Revenue* identifies the circumstances in which revenue is recognised and provides practical guidance on the application of the recognition criteria (see chapter 3).

Sometimes the term 'provision' is also used in the context of items such as depreciation, impairment of assets and doubtful debts. These are adjustments to the carrying amounts of assets and are not addressed in IAS 37. Refer to IAS 36 *Impairment of Assets*, which is covered in chapter 12.

Other IASs specify whether expenditures are treated as assets or as expenses. These issues are not addressed in IAS 37. Accordingly, IAS 37 neither prohibits nor requires capitalisation of the costs recognised when a provision is made. Refer to IAS 38 *Intangible Assets*, which deals partly with this issue, and is covered in chapter 10.

IAS 37 applies to provisions for restructuring (including discontinued operations). Where a restructure meets the definition of a discontinued operation, additional disclosures may be required by IFRS 5 *Non-current Assets Held for Sale and Discontinued Operations*. IFRS 3 *Business Combinations* deals with accounting for restructuring provisions arising in business combinations. This chapter covers the relevant requirements of IFRS 3.

4.2 DEFINITION OF A PROVISION

Paragraph 49 of the *Framework* defines a liability as:

> a present obligation of the entity arising from past events, the settlement of which is expected to result in an outflow from the entity of resources embodying economic benefits.

A provision is a subset of liabilities (i.e. it is a type of liability). Paragraph 10 of IAS 37 defines a provision as:

> a liability of uncertain timing or amount.

It is this *uncertainty* that distinguishes provisions from other liabilities.

The *Framework* states that an essential characteristic of a liability is that the entity has a present obligation. An obligation is a duty or responsibility to act or perform in a certain way. Obligations may be legally enforceable as a consequence of a binding contract, for example. This is normally the case with amounts payable for goods or services received, which are described as 'payables' or 'trade creditors'. However, legal enforceability is not a necessary requirement to demonstrate the existence of a liability. An entity may have an equitable or constructive obligation, arising from normal business practice or custom, to act in an equitable manner. Alternatively, the obligation is construed from the circumstances. Determining whether an equitable or constructive obligation exists is often more difficult than identifying a legal obligation. IAS 37 does not specifically acknowledge the concept of an equitable obligation; however, it does define a constructive obligation, in paragraph 10, as:

> an obligation that derives from an entity's actions where:
> (a) by an established pattern of past practice, published policies or a sufficiently specific current statement, the entity has indicated to other parties that it will accept certain responsibilities; and
> (b) as a result, the entity has created a valid expectation on the part of those other parties that it will discharge those responsibilities.

A present obligation exists only where the entity has no realistic alternative but to make the sacrifice of economic benefits to settle the obligation.

For example, assume that an entity makes a public announcement that it will match the financial assistance provided by other entities to victims of a natural disaster and, because of custom and moral considerations, has no realistic alternative but to provide the assistance. (In this case the events have already taken place — the natural disaster — and the public announcement is the obligating event).

Importantly, a decision by the entity's management or governing body does not, by itself, create a constructive obligation. This is because the management or governing body would retain the ability to reverse that decision. A present obligation would come into existence when the decision was communicated publicly to those affected by it. This would result in the valid expectation that the entity would fulfil the obligation, thus leaving the entity with little or no discretion to avoid the sacrifice of economic benefits.

4.3 DISTINGUISHING PROVISIONS FROM OTHER LIABILITIES

A provision may arise from either a legal or constructive obligation. As stated previously, the key distinguishing factor is the uncertainty relating to either the timing of settlement or the amount to be settled.

Paragraph 11 of IAS 37 gives an example of the distinction between liabilities and provisions as follows. It states that trade payables and accruals are liabilities because:

> (a) trade payables are liabilities to pay for goods or services that have been received or supplied and have been invoiced or formally agreed with the supplier; and
> (b) accruals are liabilities to pay for goods or services that have been received or supplied but have not been paid, invoiced or formally agreed with the supplier, including amounts due to employees (for example, amounts relating to accrued vacation pay). Although it is sometimes necessary to estimate the amount or timing of accruals, the uncertainty is generally much less than for provisions.
>
> Accruals are often reported as part of trade and other payables, whereas provisions are reported separately.

Note, however, that employee benefits are addressed specifically by IAS 19 *Employee Benefits*, and are not included in the scope of IAS 37.

Some examples of typical provisions include provisions for warranty, restructuring provisions and provisions for onerous contracts. These are discussed in more detail later in this chapter.

4.4 DEFINITION OF A CONTINGENT LIABILITY

Paragraph 10 of IAS 37 defines a contingent liability as:

(a) a possible obligation that arises from past events and whose existence will be confirmed only by the occurrence or non-occurrence of one or more uncertain future events not wholly within the control of the entity; or

(b) a present obligation that arises from past events but is not recognised because:

  (i) it is not probable that an outflow of resources embodying economic benefits will be required to settle the obligation; or

  (ii) the amount of the obligation cannot be measured with sufficient reliability.

The definition of a contingent liability is interesting because it encompasses two distinctly different concepts. The first, part (a) of the definition, is the concept of a *possible* obligation. This fails one of the essential characteristics of a liability — the requirement for the existence of a present obligation. If there is no present obligation, only a possible one, there is no liability. Hence, part (a) of the definition does not meet the definition of a liability such that one could argue that the term 'contingent *liability*' is misleading, because items falling into category (a) are not liabilities by definition.

Part (b) of the definition, on the other hand, deals with liabilities that fail the recognition criteria. They are present obligations, so they meet the essential requirements of the definition of liabilities, but they do not meet the recognition criteria (probability of outflow of economic benefits and reliability of measurement).

4.5 DISTINGUISHING A CONTINGENT LIABILITY FROM A PROVISION

Contingent liabilities are not recognised in the financial statements but must be disclosed in the financial statements unless the possibility of an outflow in settlement is remote.

Paragraph 12 of IAS 37 states that:

> In a general sense, all provisions are contingent because they are uncertain in timing or amount. However, within this Standard the term 'contingent' is used for liabilities and assets that are not recognised because their existence will be confirmed only by the occurrence or non-occurrence of one or more uncertain future events not wholly within the control of the entity. In addition, the term 'contingent liability' is used for liabilities that do not meet the recognition criteria.

The following example (figure 4.1) illustrates the difference between a contingent liability and a provision. Note, however, that financial guarantees are specifically covered by IAS 39 and must be accounted for in accordance with that standard or IFRS 4 (see chapter 5).

When *Endeavour Limited* provides a guarantee to a bank in relation to a bank loan provided to *Tower Limited*:

- If *Tower Limited* is solvent and able to repay the loan without breaching any debt covenants, a contingent liability exists and disclosure thereof is required in the notes to the financial statements of *Endeavour Limited*;
- If *Tower Limited* has breached the debt covenants and it is probable that *Endeavour Limited* will be called upon as guarantor of the loan by the Bank, a provision should be recognised by *Endeavour Limited* for the amount likely to be paid to the Bank. This assumes that there is still uncertain 'timing or amount', otherwise the amount would be a liability.

FIGURE 4.1 Example of the difference between a provision and a contingent liability
Source: Ernst & Young (2002a).

4.6 THE RECOGNITION CRITERIA FOR PROVISIONS

The recognition criteria for provisions are the same as those for liabilities as set out in the *Framework*. Curiously, IAS 37 also includes part of the definition of a liability in its recognition criteria for provisions (part (a) of the recognition criteria below). The reason for this is most likely the desire of the standard setters to distinguish between provisions and contingent liabilities, but it is arguable whether this needs to be done via the recognition criteria, since the definitions are sufficiently clear.

Paragraph 14 of IAS 37 states that a provision should be recognised when:

> (a) an entity has a present obligation (legal or constructive) as a result of a past event;
> (b) it is probable that an outflow of resources embodying economic benefits will be required to settle the obligation; and
> (c) a reliable estimate can be made of the amount of the obligation.
>
> If these conditions are not met, no provision shall be recognised.

The concept of probability is discussed in the *Framework* and deals essentially with the likelihood of something eventuating. If it is more likely rather than less likely to eventuate, IAS 37 regards the outflow as probable. Probability is assessed for each obligation separately, unless the obligations form a group of similar obligations (such as product warranties) in which case the probability that an outflow will be required in settlement is determined by assessing the class of obligations as a whole.

Paragraphs 15 and 16 of IAS 37 discuss the concepts of a present obligation and probability, giving some useful examples:

> 15. In rare cases it is not clear whether there is a present obligation. In these cases, a past event is deemed to give rise to a present obligation if, taking account of all available evidence, it is more likely than not that a present obligation exists at the end of the reporting period.
>
> 16. In almost all cases it will be clear whether a past event has given rise to a present obligation. In rare cases, for example in a law suit, it may be disputed either whether certain events have occurred or whether those events result in a present obligation. In such a case, an entity determines whether a present obligation exists at the end of the reporting period by taking account of all available evidence, including, for example, the opinion of experts. The evidence considered includes any additional evidence provided by events after the end of the reporting period. On the basis of such evidence:
> (a) where it is more likely than not that a present obligation exists at the end of the reporting period, the entity recognises a provision (if the recognition criteria are met); and
> (b) where it is more likely that no present obligation exists at the end of the reporting period, the entity discloses a contingent liability, unless the possibility of an outflow of resources embodying economic benefits is remote [in which case no disclosure is made].

A past event that leads to a present obligation is called an obligating event. As discussed in the section on constructive obligations, for an event to be an obligating event the entity must have no realistic alternative to settling the obligation created by the event. In the case of a legal obligation this is because the settlement of the obligation can be enforced by law. In the case of a constructive obligation the event needs to create a valid expectation in other parties that the entity will discharge the obligation.

Reliable estimation is the final criterion for recognition of a provision. Although the use of estimates is a necessary part of the preparation of financial statements, in the case of provisions the uncertainty associated with reliable measurement is greater than for other liabilities. Accordingly, IAS 37 goes on to give more detailed guidance on measurement of provisions, which we will discuss later in the chapter. However, it is expected that except in very rare cases an entity will be able to determine a reliable estimate of the obligation.

Note the use of the concept of 'probability' in the recognition criteria for liabilities, including provisions, contrasted with the use of the concept of 'possibility' in determining whether or not a contingent liability should be disclosed. Paragraph 86 of IAS 37 requires contingent liabilities to be disclosed in the financial statements 'unless the possibility of an outflow in settlement is remote'. IAS 37 interprets 'probable' as meaning more likely rather than less likely. IAS 37 does not, however, provide any further guidance on what it means by 'possibility'. In plain English terms 'probability' addresses the likelihood of whether or not something will happen, whereas 'possibility' has a broader meaning — virtually anything is possible, but how probable is it? Given this distinction, we should assume that the intention of IAS 37 is that most contingent liabilities should be disclosed and that only in very rare circumstances is no disclosure appropriate.

Contingent liabilities need to be continually assessed to determine whether or not they have become actual liabilities. This is done by considering whether the recognition criteria for liabilities have been met. If it becomes probable that an outflow of economic benefits will be required for an item previously dealt with as a contingent liability, a provision is recognised in the financial statements in the period in which the change in probability occurs.

4.7 PUTTING IT ALL TOGETHER — A USEFUL DECISION TREE

In sections 4.2 through 4.6 we discussed the definitions of provisions and contingent liabilities, the recognition criteria for provisions and when a contingent liability must be disclosed. The decision tree (figure 4.2) on the opposite page summarises this discussion. The decision tree is based on Appendix B of IAS 37 but has been modified to aid understanding.

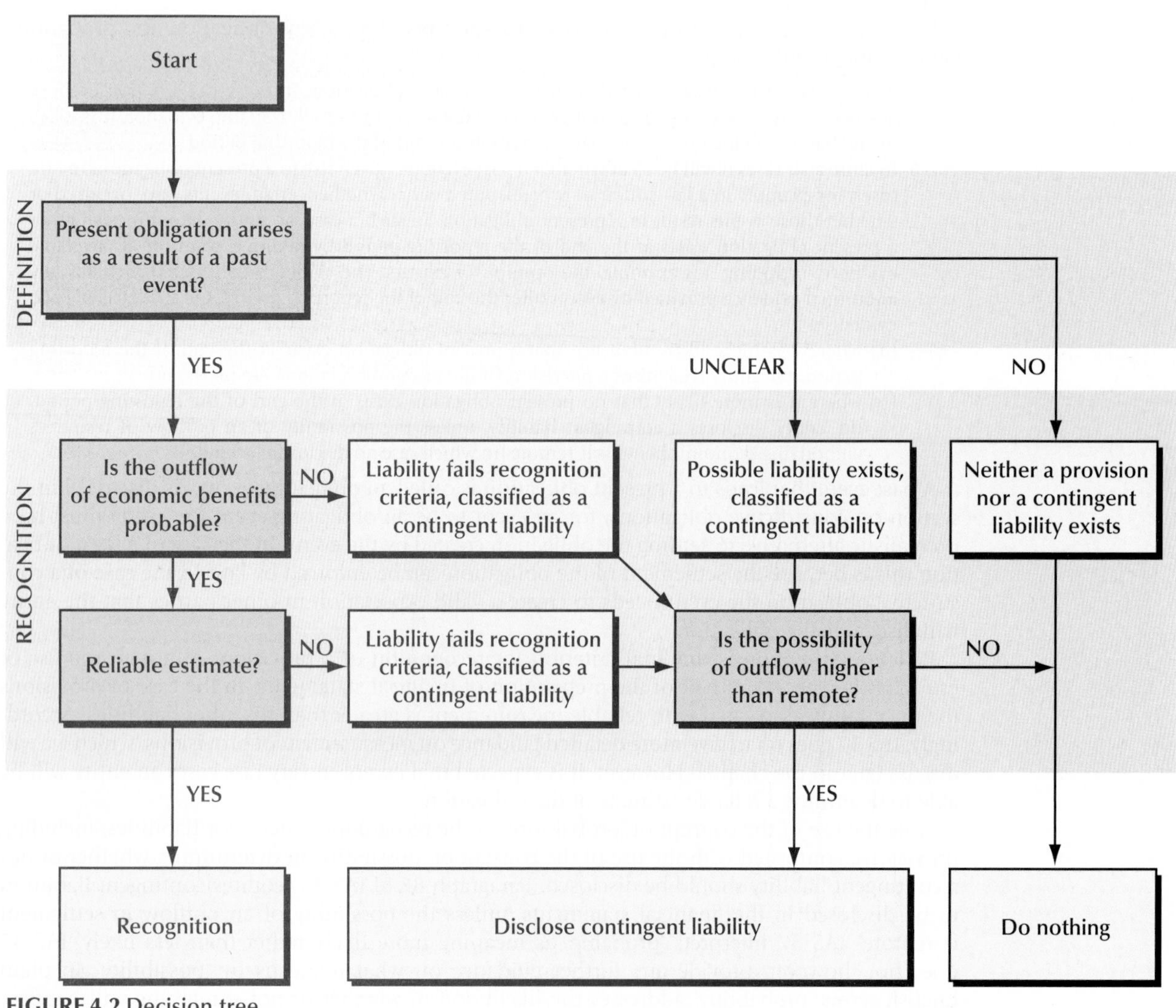

FIGURE 4.2 Decision tree
Source: Ernst & Young (2002b).

4.8 MEASUREMENT OF PROVISIONS

4.8.1 Best estimate

When measuring a provision, the amount recognised should be the *best estimate* of the consideration required to settle the present obligation at the end of the reporting period. This amount is often expressed as the amount which represents, as closely as possible, what the entity would rationally pay to settle the present obligation immediately or to provide consideration to a third party to assume it. The fact that it is difficult to measure the provision and that estimates have to be used does not mean that the provision is not reliably measurable.

Paragraphs 39 and 40 of IAS 37 address the issue of how to deal with the uncertainties surrounding the amount to be recognised as a provision:

> 39. Uncertainties surrounding the amount to be recognised as a provision are dealt with by various means according to the circumstances. Where the provision being measured involves a large population of items, the obligation is estimated by weighting all possible outcomes by their associated probabilities. The name for this statistical method of estimation is 'expected value'. The provision will therefore be different depending on whether the probability of a loss of a given amount is, for example, 60 per cent or 90 per cent. Where there is a continuous range of possible outcomes, and each point in that range is as likely as any other, the mid-point of the range is used.

Example

An entity sells goods with a warranty under which customers are covered for the cost of repairs of any manufacturing defects that become apparent within the first 6 months after purchase. If minor defects were detected in all products sold, repair costs of $1 million would result. If major defects were detected in all products sold, repair costs of $4 million would result. The entity's past experience and future expectations indicate that, for the coming year, 75% of the goods sold will have no defects, 20% of the goods sold will have minor defects and 5% of the goods sold will have major defects. In accordance with paragraph 24, an entity assesses the probability of an outflow for the warranty obligations as a whole.

The expected value of the cost of repairs is:

(75% of nil) + (20% of $1 m) + (5% of $4 m) = $400 000

> 40. Where a single obligation is being measured, the individual most likely outcome may be the best estimate of the liability. However, even in such a case, the entity considers other possible outcomes. Where other possible outcomes are either mostly higher or mostly lower than the most likely outcome, the best estimate will be a higher or lower amount. For example, if an entity has to rectify a serious fault in a major plant that it has constructed for a customer, the individual most likely outcome may be for the repair to succeed at the first attempt at a cost of $1000, but a provision for a larger amount is made if there is a significant chance that further attempts will be necessary.

The provision is measured before tax. Any tax consequences are accounted for in accordance with IAS 12 *Income Taxes*.

The need to use judgement in determining the best estimate is clearly evident. Judgement is used in assessing, inter alia:

- what the likely consideration required to settle the obligation will be
- when the consideration is likely to be settled
- whether there are various scenarios that are likely to arise
- what the probability of those various scenarios arising will be.

The distinguishing characteristic of provisions — the uncertainty relating to either the timing of settlement or the amount to be settled — is clearly illustrated in the above discussion. Because of the extent of judgement required in measuring provisions, auditors focus more on auditing provisions than on other normal liabilities such as trade creditors and accruals. This is particularly the case if a change in one of the assumptions, such as the probability of a particular scenario eventuating or the likely consideration required to settle the obligation, would have a material impact on the amount recognised as a provision and thus on the financial statements.

4.8.2 Risks and uncertainties

IAS 37 requires that the risks and uncertainties surrounding the events and circumstances should be taken into account in reaching the best estimate of a provision. Paragraph 43 states:

> Risk describes variability of outcome. A risk adjustment may increase the amount at which a liability is measured. Caution is needed in making judgements under conditions of uncertainty, so that income or assets are not overstated and expenses or liabilities are not understated. However, uncertainty does not justify the creation of excessive provisions or a deliberate overstatement of liabilities. For example, if the projected costs of a particularly adverse outcome are estimated on a prudent basis, that outcome is not then deliberately treated as more probable than is realistically the case. Care is needed to avoid duplicating adjustments for risk and uncertainty with consequent overstatement of a provision.

4.8.3 Present value

Provisions are required to be *discounted to present value* where the effect of discounting is material. IAS 37 requires that the discount rate used must be a pre-tax rate that reflects current market assessments of the time value of money and the *risks specific to the liability*. Where future cash flow estimates have been adjusted for risk, the discount rate should not reflect this risk.

In practical terms it is often difficult to determine reliably a liability-specific discount rate. Also, the higher the discount rate the lower the amount that will be recognised as a liability. This seems counter-intuitive — the higher the risk attached to the liability the lower the amount at which it is recognised. A more appropriate way to factor in risk would be to use it in assessing the probability of outcomes (as discussed in 4.8.1) and then use a risk-free rate in discounting the cash flows. Paragraph 78 of IAS 19 *Employee Benefits* states that the discount rate for long-term employee benefit obligations should be determined by reference to market yields at the end of the reporting period on high-quality corporate bonds or, where there is no deep market in such bonds, the market yield on government bonds. The currency and term of the corporate bonds or government bonds should be consistent with the currency and estimated term of the employee benefit obligations. Although there may be some debate about how to determine the risk-free rate, market yields on high-quality corporate bonds or government bonds are reasonable approximations. It is unclear why IAS 37 and IAS 19 are inconsistent, but given that IAS 19 is a more recent standard than IAS 37, we expect that IAS 37 will be modified to be consistent with IAS 19.

The following illustrative example shows the way a provision should be measured, taking into account risks and the time value of money.

ILLUSTRATIVE EXAMPLE 4.1

Measuring a provision

An entity estimates that the expected cash outflows to settle its warranty obligations at the end of the reporting period are as follows. (Note that probability of cash outflows has already been assessed similarly to the example in 4.8.1 and, accordingly, no further adjustment for risk is made.) The entity has used a discount rate based on government bonds with the same term and currency as the expected cash outflows.

Expected cash outflow	Timing	Discount rate	Present value of cash outflow
$400 000	In 1 year	6.0%	$377 358
100 000	In 2 years	6.5%	88 166
20 000	In 3 years	6.9%	16 371
Present value			481 895

4.8.4 Future events

Anticipated future events expected to affect the amount required to settle the entity's present obligation must be reflected in the amount provided, when there is reliable evidence that they will occur.

As an example, paragraph 49 of IAS 37 states:

> Expected future events may be particularly important in measuring provisions. For example, an entity may believe that the cost of cleaning up a site at the end of its life will be reduced by future changes in technology. The amount recognised reflects a reasonable expectation of technically qualified, objective observers, taking account of all available evidence as to the technology that will be available at the time of the clean-up. Thus it is appropriate to include, for example, expected cost reductions associated with increased experience in applying existing technology or the expected cost of applying existing technology to a larger or more complex clean-up operation than has previously been carried out. However, an entity does not anticipate the development of a completely new technology for cleaning up unless it is supported by sufficient objective evidence.

4.8.5 Expected disposal of assets

Gains from the expected disposal of assets must not be taken into account when measuring the amount of a provision, even if the expected disposal is closely linked to the event giving rise to the provision. Rather, when the gain on disposal is made it should be recognised at that time in accordance with the relevant international accounting standard. Therefore, it is clear that only expected cash *outflows* must be taken into account in measuring the provision. Any cash inflows are treated separately from the measurement of the provision.

4.8.6 Reimbursements

When some of the amount required to settle a provision is expected to be recovered from a third party IAS 37 requires that the recovery be recognised as an asset, but only when it is *virtually certain* that the reimbursement will be received if the entity settles the obligation. This differs from the normal asset recognition criteria, which require that the inflow of future economic benefits be *probable*. Presumably, the standard setters were concerned about an uncertain asset related to an uncertain liability, and therefore decided to make the recognition criteria stricter for these types of assets. When such an asset is recognised the amount should not exceed the amount of the provision. IAS 37 allows the income from the asset to be set off against the expense relating to the provision in the statement of comprehensive income (income statement). However, it does not mention set off in the statement of financial position (balance sheet) of the asset and the provision. One of the disclosures required, in paragraph 85(c), is the amount of any asset that has been recognised for expected reimbursements; therefore, it is reasonable to assume that IAS 37 did not intend for the provision and asset to be set off in the statement of financial position.

4.8.7 Changes in provisions and use of provisions

IAS 37 requires provisions to be reviewed at the end of each reporting period and adjusted to reflect the current best estimate. If it is no longer probable that an outflow of resources embodying economic benefits will be required to settle the obligation, the provision should be reversed.

Where discounting is used, the carrying amount of a provision increases in each period to reflect the passage of time. This increase is recognised as borrowing cost. This is similar to the way finance lease liabilities are accounted for under IAS 17 *Leases*, as shown in chapter 13.

A provision should be used only for expenditures for which the provision was originally recognised. Illustrative example 4.2 shows how a provision is accounted for where discounting is applied and where the provision is adjusted to reflect the current best climate.

ILLUSTRATIVE EXAMPLE 4.2

Accounting for a provision

Company A estimates that it will be required to pay $100 000 in 3 years time to settle a warranty obligation. The discount rate applied is 5.5%. The probability of cash outflows has been assessed in determining the $100 000.

The following table shows how the provision is accreted over the 3 years:

A. Year	B. Present value at the beginning of the year	C. Interest expense at 5.5% (B × 5.5%)	D. Cash flows	E. Present value at the end of the year (B + C – D)
1	85 161	4 683	—	89 844
2	89 844	4 942	—	94 786
3	94 786	5 214	(100 000)	—

Journal entries are as follows:

On initial recognition in year 1:			
Warranty Expense	Dr	85 161	
Warranty Provision	Cr		85 161
On recognition of interest in year 1:			
Interest Expense	Dr	4 683	
Warranty Provision	Cr		4 683
On recognition of interest in year 2:			
Interest Expense	Dr	4 942	
Warranty Provision	Cr		4 942
On recognition of interest in year 3:			
Interest Expense	Dr	5 214	
Warranty Provision	Cr		5 214
On settlement of provision, end of year 3:			
Warranty Provision	Dr	100 000	
Cash	Cr		100 000

Now assume the same facts as above except that, at the end of year 2, Company A re-estimates the amount to be paid to settle the obligation at the end of year 3 to be $90 000. The appropriate discount rate remains at 5.5%.

The present value of $90 000 at the end of year 2 is $85 306. Company A thus adjusts the provision by $9480 ($94 786–85 306) to reflect the revised estimated cash flows.

Journal entries are as follows:

Revision of estimate at end of year 2:			
Warranty Provision	Dr	9 480	
Warranty Expense (statement of comprehensive income)	Cr		9 480
On recognition of interest in year 3:			
Interest Expense	Dr	4 694	
Warranty Provision ($85 306 × 5.5% rounded)	Cr		4 694
On settlement of provision, end of year 3:			
Warranty Provision	Dr	90 000	
Cash	Cr		90 000

The re-estimated cash flows are adjusted against the warranty expense recorded in the statement of comprehensive income, while the unwinding of the discount continues to be recorded as interest expense. Any change in the discount rate used would also be adjusted against interest expense.

4.9 APPLICATION OF THE DEFINITIONS, RECOGNITION AND MEASUREMENT RULES

4.9.1 Future operating losses

IAS 37 states that provisions must not be recognised for future operating losses. Even if a sacrifice of future economic benefits is expected, a provision for future operating losses is not recognised because a past event creating a present obligation has not occurred. This is because the entity's management will generally have the ability to avoid incurring future operating losses by either disposing of or restructuring the operation in question. An expectation of future operating losses may, however, be an indicator that an asset is impaired and the requirements of IAS 36 *Impairment of Assets* should be applied.

4.9.2 Onerous contracts

An onerous contract is defined in paragraph 10 of IAS 37 as:

> a contract in which the unavoidable costs of meeting the obligations under the contract exceed the economic benefits expected to be received under it.

If an entity is a party to an onerous contract, a provision for the present obligation under the contract must be recognised. The reason these losses should be provided for is that the entity is contracted to fulfil the contract. Therefore, entry into an onerous contract gives rise to a present obligation.

Examples of onerous contracts include:

- where an electricity supplier has entered into a contract to supply electricity at a price lower than the price that it is contracted to receive it at
- where a manufacturer has entered into a supply contract at a price below the costs of production.

IAS 37 does not go into a lot of detail regarding onerous contracts and the requirements of the standard are quite vague in this area. Therefore, judgement has to be applied on a case-by-case basis to assess whether or not individual contracts qualify as onerous contracts under the standard.

For the purpose of raising a provision in respect of an onerous contract, the amount to be recognised is the least net cost of exiting the contract; that is, the lesser of:

- the cost of fulfilling the contract, and
- any compensation or penalties arising from failure to fulfil the contract.

4.9.3 Restructuring provisions

Perhaps the most controversial aspect of IAS 37 is the recognition criteria for restructuring provisions. IFRS 3 *Business Combinations* addresses restructuring provisions arising as part of a business combination, whereas IAS 37 addresses restructuring provisions arising other than as part of a business combination. Although the fundamental criteria are consistent, IFRS 3 has more prescriptive requirements than IAS 37. For ease of discussion, both types of restructuring provision are discussed here.

During the 1990s, standard setters in various jurisdictions set tougher rules on when a restructuring provision could be recognised, particularly when the provision related to the acquisition of a business. The reason for the crackdown was the tendency for companies to create restructuring provisions deliberately to avoid the recognition of an expense in future periods. The following example illustrates this point.

Rules to make it more difficult to record restructuring provisions were introduced in the United States and the United Kingdom. In the United States, the requirements for the recognition of restructuring provisions are contained primarily in Emerging Issues Task Force (EITF) Consensus EITF 94-3 and EITF 95-3. In addition, the Securities and Exchange Commission (SEC) issued a staff accounting bulletin (SAB) 100, which clarified how the SEC interprets certain aspects of the EITFs previously mentioned.

In the United Kingdom, FRS 7 *Fair Values in Acquisition Accounting* addresses the required accounting for restructuring provisions.

ILLUSTRATIVE EXAMPLE 4.3

Restructuring provisions

Assume Company A acquires Company B on 1 February 2010. The identifiable net assets of Company B are $400 million and Company A pays $500 million cash as purchase consideration. The goodwill arising on acquisition is thus $100 million. Company A then decides to create a restructuring provision of $60 million for future possible restructuring activities related to Company B. Company A records the following additional entry as part of its acquisition accounting entries:

Goodwill	Dr	60 m	
Restructuring Provision	Cr		60 m

Why does Company A have an incentive to record this entry? The entry increases the amount recorded as goodwill, and in the 1990s goodwill was required to be amortised in most jurisdictions. Why would Company A want to expose itself to future goodwill amortisation? The answer is that because the restructuring provision was recorded directly against goodwill, an expense for the restructuring will *never* be recorded. When Company A incurs the expenditure in the future, the outflows will be recorded against the provision. Company A would likely have been able to highlight goodwill amortisation as a separate item either in its statement of comprehensive income or the attached notes, and thus would have been satisfied that the amortisation expense was effectively quarantined from the rest of its reported profit. The benefit for Company A was that the restructuring expense never affected its profit, and thus the creation of the restructuring provision as part of the acquisition entries protected Company A's future profits.

IAS 37 and IAS 22 (superseded by IFRS 3) were the least prescriptive of these requirements but, when IFRS 3 *Business Combinations* superseded IAS 22, it came more into line with UK requirements.

Paragraph 70 of IAS 37 provides the following examples of events that may be considered as restructurings:

(a) sale or termination of a line of business;
(b) the closure of business locations in a country or region or the relocation of business activities from one country or region to another;
(c) changes in management structure, for example, eliminating a layer of management; and
(d) fundamental reorganisations that have a material effect on the nature and focus of the entity's operations.

In broad terms, to be able to raise a restructuring provision, three conditions need to be met. First, the entity must have a *present obligation (either legal or constructive)* to restructure such that it cannot realistically avoid going ahead with the restructuring and thus incurring the costs involved. Second, only costs that are *directly and necessarily* caused by the restructuring and *not associated with the ongoing activities* of the entity may be included in a restructuring provision. Third, if the restructuring involves the sale of an operation, no obligation is deemed to arise for the sale of an operation until the entity is committed to the sale by a *binding sale agreement*.

Each of these requirements is considered in more detail below.

Present obligation

Usually a restructuring is initiated by management and thus it is rare that a legal obligation will exist for a restructuring. IAS 37 therefore focuses on the conditions that need to be met for a constructive obligation to exist. As we saw earlier, a constructive obligation is defined in paragraph 10 as:

an obligation that derives from an entity's actions where:

(a) by an established pattern of past practice, published policies or a sufficiently specific current statement, the entity has indicated to other parties that it will accept certain responsibilities; and
(b) as a result, the entity has created a valid expectation on the part of those other parties that it will discharge those responsibilities.

In respect of restructuring provisions, paragraph 72 of IAS 37 states that a constructive obligation to restructure arises only when an entity:

(a) has a detailed formal plan for the restructuring identifying at least:
  (i) the business or part of a business concerned;
  (ii) the principal locations affected;
  (iii) the location, function, and approximate number of employees who will be compensated for terminating their services;
  (iv) the expenditures that will be undertaken; and
  (v) when the plan will be implemented; and

(b) has raised a valid expectation in those affected that it will carry out the restructuring by starting to implement that plan or announcing its main features to those affected by it.

Therefore, we see that the entity needs to have a *detailed formal plan* and must have raised a *valid expectation* in those affected. In respect of restructuring provisions arising as part of an acquisition, IAS 22 (now superseded by IFRS 3) went even further, with the following three additional requirements:

First, *at or before the date of acquisition*, the acquirer must have developed the *main features of a plan* that involves terminating or reducing the activities of the acquiree. The main features include items such as compensating employees for termination, closing facilities of the acquiree, eliminating product lines of the acquiree and terminating contracts of the acquiree that have become onerous because of the acquisition. Second, the main features of the plan must be *announced at or before the date of acquisition*, in order to meet the 'valid expectation' test in IAS 37. Third, the *detailed formal plan* required by IAS 37 must be developed by the *earlier of three months* after the date of acquisition and the date when the financial statements are authorised for issue.

IAS 22 allowed the restructuring provision to be recorded in the books of the *acquirer* (i.e. as part of the acquirer's acquisition entries), provided the criteria for recognition were met. This is in contrast to FRS 7. According to FRS 7, the identifiable assets and liabilities to be recognised should be only those of the *acquired entity* that existed at the acquisition date. FRS 7 is explicit in saying that provisions for restructuring would be recognised as identifiable liabilities only if the commitments had been made before the date of acquisition. It even goes so far as to say that only if the acquired entity was demonstrably committed to the expenditure whether or not the acquisition was completed, would it have a liability.

In October 1998 the Australian companies' regulator, the Australian Securities and Investments Commission (ASIC), issued a media release announcing that it had required St George Bank to adjust its financial statements for 1998 for a $120 million restructuring liability that had been recorded against goodwill in its 1997 financial statements. ASIC's view was that the restructuring provision could not be recognised because it did not relate to restructuring costs of the acquired entity. This was ASIC's interpretation of Urgent Issues Group (UIG) Abstract 8 *Accounting for Acquisitions — Recognition of Restructuring Costs as Liabilities* (ASIC 1998).

When the Australian Accounting Standards Board (AASB) issued its equivalent of IAS 37 (AASB 1044) in 2001, it amended the requirements of IAS 37 to reflect ASIC's view and required that the restructuring provision be a liability of the acquired entity. AASB 1044 was not very clear on this issue and it continued to be a controversial area for a number of years. Finally, in 2004, the IASB issued IFRS 3, which amended IAS 22 to require that the liability be a liability of the acquiree, recognised in accordance with IAS 37. As a result, no additional criteria are required by IFRS 3, and the three additional requirements of IAS 22 were removed.

Recording restructuring provisions

Where a provision for restructuring costs arises on the acquisition of an entity, it must be recognised as a liability in the statement of financial position of the acquiree and not in the books of the acquirer or as a consolidation entry. The provision for the restructuring costs must be taken into account by the acquirer when measuring the fair value of the net assets acquired. Illustrative example 4.4 demonstrates this principle further.

We saw above that in order to satisfy the 'valid expectation' test in IAS 37, the entity needs to have started to implement the detailed formal plan or announced the main features to those affected by it. An entity can do this in the following ways:

- By the entity having already entered into firm contracts to carry out parts of the restructuring. These contracts would be of such a nature that they effectively force the entity to carry out the restructuring. This would be the case if they contained severe penalty provisions or the costs of not fulfilling the contract were so high that it would effectively leave the entity with no alternative but to proceed.

- By starting to implement the detailed restructuring. This could include, for example, selling assets, notifying customers that supplies will be discontinued, notifying suppliers that orders will be ceasing, dismantling plant and equipment, and terminating employees' service.
- By announcing the main features of the plan to those affected by it (or their representatives). There may be a number of ways in which such an announcement could be made. It could be through written communication, meetings or discussions with the affected parties.

ILLUSTRATIVE EXAMPLE 4.4

Recording restructuring provisions

Assume Company X acquires Company Y, a manufacturing company that has a head office in the city centre and a manufacturing plant in an industrial area. As part of the acquisition plans, Company X decides to close Company Y's head office premises and move Company Y's staff to Company X's own city premises. Company Y will be paying for the office closure costs.

Assume that the cost of closing Company Y's office premises is $120 000. Company Y will record the following journal entry at the date of acquisition:

Restructuring Costs	Dr	120 000	
Restructuring Provision	Cr		120 000

In determining the fair value of the net assets acquired in Company Y (in accordance with IFRS 3), Company X will include the restructuring provision.

It is important that the communication is made in such a way that it raises a valid expectation in the affected parties such that they can be expected to act as a result of the communication, and by them doing so the entity would be left with no realistic alternative but to go ahead with the restructuring. For example, affected employees would start looking for other employment and customers would seek alternative sources of supply.

Figure 4.3 provides examples of where a present obligation does and does not arise on a restructuring as a result of an acquisition.

FIGURE 4.3 Examples of the existence of a present obligation under IFRS 3 and IAS 37

Example 1

The acquired entity has developed a detailed plan for the restructuring. Details of the plan have not been made public but, as at the date of acquisition, agreement about key features of the plan has been reached with, or information about the plan has been disclosed to, relevant third parties. These parties include employee representatives, lessors and regulatory bodies. As at the acquisition date, no elements of the plan had begun to be implemented.

A present obligation exists because the key features of the plan have been communicated to those affected and a detailed plan has been developed. The fact that parts of the plan have not begun to be implemented at the acquisition date does not negate the constructive obligation. Importantly, the *acquired entity* has the obligation.

Example 2

The acquiring entity has developed a detailed plan for the restructuring as at the date of acquisition. That plan involves the closure of a number of operating sites if the acquisition is successful and the retrenchment of all employees at those sites. As at the date of acquisition, key features of the plan have not been made public; however, employee representatives have been informed. Lessors of premises that will no longer be required have been informed of the entity's intentions, and negotiations on potential lease-termination penalty costs have commenced. Expressions of interest have been sought regarding the sale of plant and equipment that will be surplus should the acquisition proceed. Preliminary commitments have been made, and, conditional on the acquisition proceeding, agreements have been reached with third parties regarding the relocation or alternative supply of certain goods and services currently provided from the sites to be closed. The planned restructuring is such that on closure of the sites the continued employment of affected employees is not possible.

A present obligation does not exist for the *acquired entity*, so no provision is required.

Qualifying restructuring costs

The second requirement for recognition of a restructuring provision is that the provision can include only costs that are directly and necessarily caused by the restructuring and not associated with the ongoing activities of the entity (IAS 37, para. 80).

Examples of the types of costs that would be included in a restructuring provision include the costs of terminating leases and other contracts as a direct result of the restructuring; costs of operations conducted in effecting the restructuring, such as employee remuneration while they are engaged in such tasks as dismantling plant, disposing of surplus stocks and fulfilling contractual obligations; and costs of making employees redundant.

Paragraph 81 of IAS 37 specifically indicates that the types of costs excluded from provisions for restructuring would be the costs of retraining or relocating the continuing staff, marketing costs and costs related to investment in new systems and distribution networks. These types of costs relate to the future conduct of the entity and do not relate to present obligations.

These requirements relating to the types of costs that qualify as restructuring costs apply equally to internal restructurings as well as to restructurings occurring as part of an acquisition. Figure 4.4 provides examples of costs that qualify as restructuring costs and figure 4.5 provides examples of costs that *do not* qualify as restructuring costs.

Example 1

A restructuring plan includes discontinuing operations currently performed in a facility that is leased under an operating lease. A lease-cancellation penalty fee payable on terminating the lease is a restructuring cost.

Example 2

A restructuring plan includes relocating operations currently performed in a facility leased by the acquired entity to a site that is owned by the acquirer. The lessor will not release the acquired entity from the lease agreement and will not permit the acquirer or acquiree to sublease the facility. The acquirer does not intend to re-open the facility prior to the lease's expiration. The leased space provides no future benefit to the enterprise. The lease payments for the remaining non-cancellable term of the operating lease after operations cease are a restructuring cost.

FIGURE 4.4 Examples of costs that qualify as restructuring costs

Example 1

The acquired entity used to share computer resources with its previous parent company. Therefore, the restructuring plan includes activities to separate the acquired entity from its previous parent and establish independent computer resources. The costs include costs of installing a LAN, moving head office PCs, moving a call centre, moving dedicated systems and acquisitions of new software. Such costs are not restructuring costs because they are associated with the ongoing activities of the entity.

Example 2

The restructuring plan includes costs to hire outside consultants to identify future corporate goals and strategies for organisational structure. The consultants' costs are not restructuring costs because they are associated with the ongoing activities of the entity.

FIGURE 4.5 Examples of costs that do not qualify as restructuring costs

It is important to note that, although certain costs have occurred only because of restructuring (i.e. they would not have had to be incurred had the restructuring not taken place), this fact alone does not qualify them for recognition as restructuring costs. They also have to be costs that are not associated with the ongoing activities of the entity.

Binding sale agreement

The final requirement for recognition of a restructuring provision is that if the restructuring involves the sale of an operation, no obligation is deemed to arise for the sale until the entity is committed to the sale by a binding sale agreement (IAS 37, para. 78). Paragraph 79 explains:

> Even when an entity has taken a decision to sell an operation and announced that decision publicly, it cannot be committed to the sale until a purchaser has been identified and there is a binding sale agreement. Until there is a binding sale agreement, the entity will be able to change its mind and indeed will have to take another course of action if a purchaser cannot be found on acceptable terms. When the sale of an operation is envisaged as part of a restructuring, the assets of the operation are reviewed for impairment, under IAS 36 *Impairment of Assets*. When a sale is only part of a restructuring, a constructive obligation can arise for the other parts of the restructuring before a binding sale agreement exists.

4.9.4 Other applications

The examples in figures 4.6 to 4.14, sourced from IAS 37 and modified to aid understanding, illustrate other applications of the recognition requirements of IAS 37.

A manufacturer gives warranties at the time of sale to purchasers of its product. Under the terms of the contract for sale the manufacturer undertakes to make good, by repair or replacement, manufacturing defects that become apparent within three years from the date of sale. On past experience, it is probable (i.e. more likely than not) that there will be some claims under the warranties.

Present obligation as a result of a past obligating event — The obligating event is the sale of the product with a warranty, which gives rise to a legal obligation.

An outflow of resources embodying economic benefits in settlement — Probable for the warranties as a whole.

Conclusion — A provision is recognised for the best estimate of the costs of making good under the warranty products sold before the end of the reporting period.

FIGURE 4.6 Warranties
Source: IAS 37, Appendix C, Example 1.

An entity in the oil industry causes contamination but cleans up only when required to do so under the laws of the particular country in which it operates. One country in which it operates has had no legislation requiring cleaning up, and the entity has been contaminating land in that country for several years. At 31 December 2000, it is virtually certain that a draft law requiring a clean up of land already contaminated will be enacted shortly after the year end.

Present obligation as a result of a past obligating event — The obligating event is the contamination of the land (past event) which gives rise to a present obligation because of the virtual certainty of legislation requiring cleaning up.

An outflow of resources embodying economic benefits in settlement — Probable.

Conclusion — A provision is recognised for the best estimate of the costs of the clean-up.

FIGURE 4.7 Contaminated land — legislation virtually certain to be enacted
Source: IAS 37, Appendix C, Example 2A.

An entity in the oil industry causes contamination and operates in a country where there is no environmental legislation. However, the entity has a widely published environmental policy in which it undertakes to clean up all contamination that it causes. The entity has a record of honouring this policy.

Present obligation as a result of a past obligating event — The obligating event is the contamination of the land, which gives rise to a constructive obligation because the conduct of the entity has created a valid expectation on the part of those affected by it that the entity will clean up contamination.

An outflow of resources embodying economic benefits in settlement — Probable.

Conclusion — A provision is recognised for the best estimate of the costs of clean-up [the entity has a constructive obligation].

FIGURE 4.8 Contaminated land and constructive obligation
Source: IAS 37, Appendix C, Example 2B.

An entity operates an offshore oilfield where its licensing agreement requires it to remove the oil rig at the end of production and restore the seabed. Ninety per cent of the eventual costs relate to the removal of the oil rig and restoration of damage caused by building it, and 10 per cent arise through the extraction of oil. At the end of the reporting period, the rig has been constructed but no oil has been extracted.

Present obligation as a result of a past obligating event — The construction of the oil rig creates a legal obligation under the terms of the licence to remove the rig and restore the seabed and is thus an obligating event. At the end of the reporting period, however, there is no obligation to rectify the damage that will be caused by extraction of the oil.

An outflow of resources embodying economic benefits in settlement — Probable.

Conclusion — A provision is recognised for the best estimate of 90 per cent of the eventual costs that relate to the removal of the oil rig and restoration of damage caused by building it. These costs are included as part of the cost of the oil rig. The 10 per cent of costs that arise through the extraction of oil are recognised as a liability when the oil is extracted.

FIGURE 4.9 Offshore oilfield
Source: IAS 37, Appendix C, Example 3.

A retail store has a policy of refunding purchases by dissatisfied customers, even though it is under no legal obligation to do so. Its policy of making refunds is generally known.

Present obligation as a result of a past obligating event — The obligating event is the sale of the product, which gives rise to a constructive obligation because the conduct of the store has created a valid expectation on the part of its customers that it will refund purchases.

An outflow of resources embodying economic benefits in settlement — Probable. A proportion of goods are returned for refund.

Conclusion — A provision is recognised for the best estimate of the costs of refunds.

FIGURE 4.10 Refunds policy
Source: IAS 37, Appendix C, Example 4.

FIGURE 4.11 Legal requirement to fit smoke filters

Under new legislation, an entity is required to fit smoke filters to its factories by 30 June 2000. The entity has not fitted the smoke filters.

(a) At the end of the reporting period, 31 December 1999:
Present obligation as a result of a past obligating event — There is no obligation

(continued)

FIGURE 4.11 *(continued)*

because there is no obligating event either for the costs of fitting smoke filters or for fines under the legislation.

Conclusion — No provision is recognised for the cost of fitting the smoke filters.

(b) At the end of the reporting period, 31 December 2000:

Present obligation as a result of a past obligating event — There is still no obligation for the costs of fitting smoke filters because no obligating event has occurred (the fitting of the filters). However, an obligation might arise to pay fines or penalties under the legislation because the obligating event has occurred (the non-compliant operation of the factory).

An outflow of resources embodying economic benefits in settlement — Assessment of the probability of incurring fines and penalties by non-compliant operation depends on the details of the legislation and the stringency of the enforcement regime.

Conclusion — No provision is recognised for the costs of fitting smoke filters. However, a provision is recognised for the best estimate of any fines and penalties that are more likely than not to be imposed.

Source: IAS 37, Appendix C, Example 6.

An entity operates profitably from a factory that it has leased under an operating lease. During December 2000 the entity relocates its operations to a new factory. The lease on the old factory continues for the next four years. It cannot be cancelled and the factory cannot be re-let to another user.

Present obligation as a result of a past obligating event — The obligating event is the signing of the lease contract, which gives rise to a legal obligation.

An outflow of resources embodying economic benefits in settlement — When the lease becomes onerous, an outflow of resources embodying economic benefits is probable. (Until the lease becomes onerous, the entity accounts for the lease under IAS 17 *Leases*.)

Conclusion — A provision is recognised for the best estimate of the unavoidable lease payments.

FIGURE 4.12 An onerous contract
Source: IAS 37, Appendix C, Example 8.

Some assets require, in addition to routine maintenance, substantial expenditure every few years for major refits or refurbishment and the replacement of major components. IAS 16 *Property, Plant and Equipment* gives guidance on allocating expenditure on an asset to its component parts where these components have different useful lives or provide benefits in a different pattern.

A furnace has a lining that needs to be replaced every five years for technical reasons. At the end of the reporting period, the lining has been in use for three years.

Present obligation as a result of a past obligating event — There is no present obligation.

Conclusion — No provision is recognised.

The cost of replacing the lining is not recognised because, at the end of the reporting period, no obligation to replace the lining exists independently of the company's future actions — even the intention to incur the expenditure depends on the company deciding to continue operating the furnace or replace the lining. Instead of a provision being recognised, the depreciation of the lining takes account of its consumption (i.e. it is depreciated over five years). The re-lining costs incurred are capitalised with the consumption of each new lining shown by depreciation over the subsequent five years.

FIGURE 4.13 Repairs and maintenance: refurbishment costs — no legislative requirement
Source: IAS 37, Appendix C, Examples 11 and 11A.

An airline is required by law to overhaul its aircraft once every three years.

Present obligation as a result of a past obligating event — There is no present obligation.

Conclusion — No provision is recognised.

The costs of overhauling aircraft are not recognised as a provision for the same reasons as the cost of replacing the lining is not recognised as a provision in Example 11A. Even a legal requirement to overhaul does not make the costs of overhaul a liability because no obligation exists to overhaul the aircraft independently of the entity's future actions — the entity could avoid the future expenditure by its future actions, for example by selling the aircraft. Instead of a provision being recognised, the depreciation of the aircraft takes account of the future incidence of maintenance costs (i.e. an amount equivalent to the expected maintenance costs is depreciated over three years).

FIGURE 4.14 Repairs and maintenance: refurbishment costs — legislative requirement
Source: IAS 37, Appendix C, Example 11B.

It is interesting to contrast figures 4.13 and 4.14 with figures 4.7 and 4.8. In figures 4.7 and 4.8, the entity had a present obligation for the costs of clean-up or removal, which were independent of the cost and useful life of the asset in question. In addition, in those examples the entity was unable to avoid the clean-up or removal, although it could be argued that it could avoid those actions and incur any resultant fines (as in figure 4.11). In that case, provision would be made for the best estimate of the costs of non-compliance with the relevant legislation.

4.10 CONTINGENT ASSETS

Paragraph 10 of IAS 37 defines a contingent asset as:

> a possible asset that arises from past events and whose existence will be confirmed only by the occurrence or non-occurrence of one or more uncertain future events not wholly within the control of the entity.

Paragraph 31 states that an entity should *not recognise* a contingent asset. Paragraph 89 requires that a contingent asset be *disclosed* where an inflow of benefits is probable.

Note the lack of symmetry between the definition of a contingent asset and a contingent liability. The definition of a contingent liability includes both possible liabilities and liabilities that fail the recognition criteria. A contingent asset includes only possible assets. The standard setters were presumably concerned with overstatement of assets and therefore wanted to apply a more stringent test to the definition, although arguably an asset that fails the recognition criteria is more of an asset than a possible asset! Further, IAS 37 permits a contingent asset to be reclassified and recognised as an actual asset only when it has become virtually certain that an inflow of economic benefits will arise. Contrast this with the test of probability which is applied to asset recognition generally. It could be argued that IAS 37 is biased towards ensuring that contingent liabilities are disclosed in almost all circumstances and reclassified and recognised as actual liabilities as soon as they meet the liability recognition criteria. Contingent assets, however, can be disclosed only in rare circumstances and reclassified to actual assets only when they meet strict recognition criteria. This bias could be criticised as being against the IASB's own *Framework* which, although it recognises the qualitative characteristic of prudence, states that:

> the exercise of prudence does not allow, for example, . . . the deliberate understatement of assets or income, or the deliberate overstatement of liabilities or expenses, because the financial statements would not be neutral and, therefore, not have the quality of reliability (*Framework*, para. 37).

An example of a contingent asset would be the possible receipt of damages arising from a court case which, as at the end of the reporting period, has been decided in favour of the entity. The hearing to determine damages, however, will be held after the end of the reporting period. The outcome of the hearing is outside the control of the entity, but the receipt of damages is probable because the case has been decided in the entity's favour. The asset meets the definition of a contingent asset because it is possible that the entity will receive the damages and the hearing is outside its control. In addition, the contingent asset is disclosed because it is probable that the damages (the inflow of economic benefits) will flow to the entity.

4.11 DISCLOSURE

The disclosure requirements of IAS 37 are self-explanatory and are reproduced below:

84. For each class of provision, an entity shall disclose:
    (a) the carrying amount at the beginning and end of the period;
    (b) additional provisions made in the period, including increases to existing provisions;
    (c) amounts used (i.e. incurred and charged against the provision) during the period;
    (d) unused amounts reversed during the period; and
    (e) the increase during the period in the discounted amount arising from the passage of time and the effect of any change in the discount rate.

    Comparative information is not required.
85. An entity shall disclose the following for each class of provision:
    (a) a brief description of the nature of the obligation and the expected timing of any resulting outflows of economic benefits;
    (b) an indication of the uncertainties about the amount or timing of those outflows. Where necessary to provide adequate information, an entity shall disclose the major assumptions made concerning future events, as addressed in paragraph 48; and
    (c) the amount of any expected reimbursement, stating the amount of any asset that has been recognised for that expected reimbursement.
86. Unless the possibility of any outflow in settlement is remote, an entity shall disclose for each class of contingent liability at the end of the reporting period a brief description of the nature of the contingent liability and, where practicable:
    (a) an estimate of its financial effect, measured under paragraphs 36–52;
    (b) an indication of the uncertainties relating to the amount or timing of any outflow; and
    (c) the possibility of any reimbursement.
89. Where an inflow of economic benefits is probable, an entity shall disclose a brief description of the nature of the contingent assets at the end of the reporting period, and, where practicable, an estimate of their financial effect, measured using the principles set out for provisions in paragraphs 36–52.
91. Where any of the information required by paragraphs 86 and 89 is not disclosed because it is not practicable to do so, that fact shall be stated.
92. In extremely rare cases, disclosure of some or all of the information required by paragraphs 84–89 can be expected to prejudice seriously the position of the entity in a dispute with other parties on the subject matter of the provision, contingent liability or contingent asset. In such cases, an entity need not disclose the information, but shall disclose the general nature of the dispute, together with the fact that, and reason why, the information has not been disclosed.

The disclosures required for contingent liabilities and assets necessarily involve judgement and estimation. Many analysts consider the contingent liabilities note to be one of the most important notes provided by a company because it helps the analyst to make his or her own decision about the likely consequences for the company and is useful in providing an overall view of the company's exposures. Thus, the use of the exemption permitted in paragraph 92 should be treated with caution because it could be interpreted as a deliberate concealing of the company's exposures.

An example of the disclosures required by paragraph 85 is included in Appendix D of IAS 37, shown in figure 4.15.

A manufacturer gives warranties at the time of sale to purchasers of its three product lines. Under the terms of the warranty, the manufacturer undertakes to repair or replace items that fail to perform satisfactorily for two years from the date of sale. At the end of the reporting period, a provision of 60 000 has been recognised. The provision has not been discounted as the effect of discounting is not material. The following information is disclosed:

A provision of 60 000 has been recognised for expected warranty claims on products sold during the last three financial years. It is expected that the majority of this expenditure will be incurred in the next financial year, and all will be incurred within two years of the end of the reporting period.

FIGURE 4.15 Warranties
Source: IAS 37, Appendix D, Example 1.

4.12 EXPECTED FUTURE DEVELOPMENTS

In June 2005, the IASB issued an exposure draft proposing significant changes to IAS 37 as part of its program to amend IFRS 3 (see chapter 11). The exposure draft proposed amendments to the title of IAS 37 (to 'Non-financial Liabilities'), new definitions of contingencies, and new recognition and measurement criteria. The proposed changes are so far-reaching that they have attracted widespread concern by respondents to the exposure draft. At the date of updating this textbook, there is doubt as to whether the proposed changes will eventuate in their current form, and to attempt to discuss them in more detail would only confuse readers.

SUMMARY

IAS 37 deals with the recognition, measurement and presentation of provisions and contingent assets and contingent liabilities. The standard contains specific requirements regarding the recognition of restructuring provisions and onerous contracts.

The standard:

- defines provisions and specifies recognition criteria and measurement requirements for the recognition of provisions in financial statements
- defines contingent liabilities and contingent assets and prohibits their recognition in the financial statements but requires their disclosure when certain conditions are met
- requires that where provisions are measured using estimated cash flows, that the cash flows be discounted to their present value at the reporting date and specifies the discount rate to be used for this purpose
- prohibits providing for future operating losses
- defines onerous contracts and requires the estimated net loss under onerous contracts to be provided for
- specifies recognition criteria for restructuring provisions and identifies the types of costs that may be included in restructuring provisions
- requires extensive disclosures relating to provisions, recoveries, contingent liabilities and contingent assets.

Discussion questions

1. How is present value related to the concept of a liability?
2. Define (a) a contingency and (b) a contingent liability.
3. What are the characteristics of a provision?
4. Define a constructive obligation.
5. What is the key characteristic of a present obligation?
6. What are the recognition criteria for provisions?
7. At what point would a contingent liability become a provision?

STAR RATING
★ BASIC
★★ MODERATE
★★★ DIFFICULT

Exercises

Exercise 4.1 RECOGNISING A PROVISION — MEASUREMENT

★ Explain how a borrowing cost could arise as part of the measurement of a provision. Illustrate your explanation with a simple example.

Exercise 4.2 RECOGNISING A PROVISION

★ When should liabilities for each of the following items be recorded in the accounts of the business entity?

(a) Acquisition of goods by purchase on credit
(b) Salaries
(c) Annual bonus paid to management
(d) Dividends

Exercise 4.3 RECOGNISING A PROVISION

★ The government introduces a number of changes to the value added tax system. As a result of these changes, Company A, a manufacturing company, will need to retrain a large proportion of its administrative and sales workforce in order to ensure continued compliance with the new taxation regulations. At the end of the reporting period, no retraining of staff has taken place.

Required
Should Company A provide for the costs of the staff training at the end of the reporting period?

Exercise 4.4 RECOGNISING A PROVISION

★★ Company B, a listed company, provides food to function centres that host events such as weddings and engagement parties. After an engagement party held by one of Company B's customers in June 2010, 100 people became seriously ill, possibly as a result of food poisoning from products sold by Company B. Legal proceedings were commenced seeking damages from Company B, which disputed liability by claiming that the function centre was at fault for handling the food incorrectly. Up to the date of authorisation for issue of the financial statements for the year to 30 June 2010, Company B's lawyers advised that it was probable that Company B would not be found liable. However, two weeks after the financial statements were published, Company B's lawyers advised that, owing to developments in the case, it was probable that Company B would be found liable and the estimated damages would be material to the company's reported profits.

Required
Should Company B recognise a liability for damages in its financial statements at 30 June 2010? How should it deal with the information it receives two weeks after the financial statements are published?

Exercise 4.5 RESTRUCTURING COSTS

★★ A division of an acquired entity will be closed and activities discontinued. The division will operate for 1 year after the date of acquisition, after which all divisional employees will be retrenched except for the retention of some employees retained to finalise closure of the division.

Required
Which of the following costs, if any, are restructuring costs?

(a) The costs of employees (salaries and benefits) to be incurred after operations cease and that are associated with the closing of the division.

(b) The costs of leasing the factory space occupied by the division for the year after the date of acquisition.

(c) The costs of modifying the division's purchasing system to make it consistent with that of the acquirer's.

Exercise 4.6 RESTRUCTURING COSTS

★★ Company Z acquires Company Y. The restructuring plan, which satisfies the criteria for the existence of a present obligation under IAS 37 and IFRS 3, includes an advertising program to promote the new company image. The restructuring plan also includes costs to retrain and relocate existing employees of the acquired entity.

Required
Are these costs restructuring costs?

Exercise 4.7 DISTINGUISHING BETWEEN LIABILITIES, PROVISIONS AND CONTINGENT LIABILITIES

★★ Identify whether each of the following would be a liability, a provision or a contingent liability, or none of the above, in the financial statements of Company A as at the end of its reporting period of 30 June 2010. Assume that Company A's financial statements are authorised for issue on 24 August 2010.

(a) An amount of $35 000 owing to Company Z for services rendered during May 2010.
(b) Long service leave, estimated to be $500 000, owing to employees in respect of past services.
(c) Costs of $26 000 estimated to be incurred for relocating employee D from Company A's head office location to another city. The staff member will physically relocate during July 2010.
(d) Provision of $50 000 for the overhaul of a machine. The overhaul is needed every 5 years and the machine was 5 years old as at 30 June 2010.
(e) Damages awarded against Company A resulting from a court case decided on 26 June 2010. The judge has announced that the amount of damages will be set at a future date, expected to be in September 2010. Company A has received advice from its lawyers that the amount of the damages could be anything between $20 000 and $7 million.

Exercise 4.8 ★★

CONTINGENT LIABILITIES — DISCLOSURE

A customer filed a lawsuit against Company A in June 2010, for costs and damages allegedly incurred as a result of the failure of one of Company A's electrical products. The amount claimed was $3 million. Company A's lawyers have advised that the amount claimed is extortionate and that Company A has a good chance of winning the case. However, the lawyers have also advised that, if Company A loses the case, its expected costs and damages would be about $500 000.

Required
How should Company A disclose this event in its financial statements as at 30 June 2010?

Exercise 4.9 ★★

RECOGNISING A PROVISION

In each of the following scenarios, explain whether or not Company G would be required to recognise a provision.
(a) As a result of its plastics operations, Company G has contaminated the land on which it operates. There is no legal requirement to clean up the land, and Company G has no record of cleaning up land that it has contaminated.
(b) As a result of its plastics operations, Company G has contaminated the land on which it operates. There is a legal requirement to clean up the land.
(c) As a result of its plastics operations, Company G has contaminated the land on which it operates. There is no legal requirement to clean up the land, but Company G has a long record of cleaning up land that it has contaminated.

Exercise 4.10 ★★

RISK AND PRESENT VALUE OF CASH FLOWS

Using examples, explain how a liability-specific discount rate could cause the amount calculated for a provision to be lower when the risk associated with that provision is high. How could this problem be averted in practice?

Problems

Problem 4.1 ★★

MEASURING A RESTRUCTURING PROVISION

Company T's directors decided on 3 May 2010 to restructure the company's operations as follows:
- Factory Z would be closed down and put on the market for sale.
- 100 employees working in factory Z would be retrenched on 31 May 2010, and would be paid their accumulated entitlements plus three months wages.
- The remaining 20 employees working in factory Z would be transferred to factory X, which would continue operating.
- Five head-office staff would be retrenched on 30 June 2010, and would be paid their accumulated entitlements plus three months wages.

As at the end of Company T's reporting period, 30 June 2010, the following transactions and events had occurred:
- Factory Z was shut down on 31 May 2010. An offer of $4 million has been received for factory Z but there is no binding sales agreement.

- The 100 retrenched employees have left and their accumulated entitlements have been paid. However, an amount of $76 000, representing a portion of the three months wages for the retrenched employees, has still not been paid.
- Costs of $23 000 were expected to be incurred in transferring the 20 employees to their new work in factory X. The transfer is planned for 14 July 2010.
- Four of the five head-office staff who have been retrenched have had their accumulated entitlements paid, including the three months wages. However, one employee, Jerry Perry, remains in order to complete administrative tasks relating to the closure of factory Z and the transfer of staff to factory X. Jerry is expected to stay until 31 July 2010. His salary for July will be $4000 and his retrenchment package will be $13 000, all of which will be paid on the day he leaves. He estimates that he would spend 60% of his time administering the closure of factory Z, 30% on administering the transfer of staff to factory X, and the remaining 10% on general administration.

Required

Calculate the amount of the restructuring provision recognised in Company T's financial statements as at 30 June 2010, in accordance with IAS 37.

Problem 4.2 ★★

CALCULATION OF A PROVISION

In May 2010, Company A relocated employee R from Company A's head office to an office in another city. As at 30 June 2010, the end of Company A's reporting period, the costs were estimated to be $40 000. Analysis of the costs is as follows:

Costs for shipping goods	$ 3 000
Airfare	6 000
Temporary accommodation costs (May and June)	8 000
Temporary accommodation costs (July and August)	9 000
Reimbursement for lease break costs (paid in July; lease was terminated in May)	2 000
Reimbursement for cost-of-living increases (for the period 15 May 2010–15 May 2011)	12 000

Required

Calculate the provision for relocation costs for Company A's financial statements as at 30 June 2010. Assume that IAS 37 applies to this provision and that the effect of discounting is immaterial.

Problem 4.3 ★★★

RESTRUCTURING PROVISIONS ON ACQUISITION

Company A acquires Company B, effective 1 March 2010. At the date of acquisition, Company A intends to close a division of Company B. As at the date of acquisition, management has developed and the board has approved the main features of the restructuring plan and, based on available information, best estimates of the costs have been made. As at the date of acquisition, a public announcement of Company A's intentions has been made and relevant parties have been informed of the planned closure. Within a week of the acquisition being effected, management commences the process of informing unions, lessors, institutional investors and other key shareholders of the broad characteristics of its restructuring program. A detailed plan for the restructuring is developed within 3 months and implemented soon thereafter.

Required

Should Company A create a provision for restructuring as part of its acquisition accounting entries? Explain your answer. How would your answer change if all the circumstances are the same as those above except that Company A decided that, instead of closing a division of Company B, it would close down one of its own facilities?

Problem 4.4 ★★★

COMPREHENSIVE PROBLEM

ChubbyChocs Ltd, a listed company, is a manufacturer of confectionery and biscuits. The end of its reporting period is 30 June. Relevant extracts from its financial statements at 30 June 2010 are shown below.

Current liabilities		
Provisions		
Provision for warranties		$270 000
Non-current liabilities		
Provisions		
Provision for warranties		160 715
Non-current assets		
Plant and equipment		
At cost	$2 000 000	
Accumulated depreciation	600 000	
Carrying amount	1 400 000	

Plant and equipment has a useful life of 10 years and is depreciated on a straight-line basis.

Note 36 — Contingent liabilities
ChubbyChocs is engaged in litigation with various parties in relation to allergic reactions to traces of peanuts alleged to have been found in packets of fruit gums. ChubbyChocs strenuously denies the allegations and, as at the date of authorising the financial statements for issue, is unable to estimate the financial effect, if any, of any costs or damages that may be payable to the plaintiffs.

The provision for warranties at 30 June 2010 was calculated using the following assumptions (there was no balance carried forward from the prior year):

Estimated cost of repairs — products with minor defects	$1 000 000
Estimated cost of repairs — products with major defects	$6 000 000
Expected % of products sold during FY 2010 having no defects in FY 2011	80%
Expected % of products sold during FY 2010 having minor defects in FY 2011	15%
Expected % of products sold during FY 2010 having major defects in FY 2011	5%
Expected timing of settlement of warranty payments — those with minor defects	All in FY 2011
Expected timing of settlement of warranty payments — those with major defects	40% in FY 2011, 60% in FY 2012
Discount rate	6%. The effect of discounting for FY 2011 is considered to be immaterial.

During the year ended 30 June 2011, the following occurred:

1. In relation to the warranty provision of $430 715 at 30 June 2010, $200 000 was paid out of the provision. Of the amount paid, $150 000 was for products with minor defects and $50 000 was for products with major defects, all of which related to amounts that had been expected to be paid in the 2011 financial year.

2. In calculating its warranty provision for 30 June 2011, ChubbyChocs made the following adjustments to the assumptions used for the prior year:

Estimated cost of repairs — products with minor defects	No change
Estimated cost of repairs — products with major defects	$5 000 000
Expected % of products sold during FY 2011 having no defects in FY 2012	85%
Expected % of products sold during FY 2011 having minor defects in FY 2012	12%
Expected % of products sold during FY 2011 having major defects in FY 2012	3%
Expected timing of settlement of warranty payments — those with minor defects	All in FY 2012
Expected timing of settlement of warranty payments — those with major defects	20% in FY 2012, 80% in FY 2013
Discount rate	No change. The effect of discounting for FY 2012 is considered to be immaterial.

3. ChubbyChocs determined that part of its plant and equipment needed an overhaul — the conveyer belt on one of its machines would need to be replaced in about May 2012 at an estimated cost of $250 000. The carrying amount of the conveyer belt at 30 June 2010 was $140 000. Its original cost was $200 000.
4. ChubbyChocs was unsuccessful in its defence of the peanut allergy case and was ordered to pay $1 500 000 to the plaintiffs. As at 30 June 2011, ChubbyChocs had paid $800 000.
5. ChubbyChocs commenced litigation against one of its advisers for negligent advice given on the original installation of the conveyer belt referred to in (4) above. In April 2011 the court found in favour of ChubbyChocs. The hearing for damages had not been scheduled as at the date the financial statements for 2011 were authorised for issue. ChubbyChocs estimated that it would receive about $425 000.
6. ChubbyChocs signed an agreement with BankSweet to the effect that ChubbyChocs would guarantee a loan made by BankSweet to ChubbyChocs' subsidiary, CCC Ltd. CCC's loan with BankSweet was $3 200 000 as at 30 June 2011. CCC was in a strong financial position at 30 June 2011.

Required

Prepare the relevant extracts from the financial statements (including the notes) of ChubbyChocs at at 30 June 2011, in compliance with IAS 37 and related International Accounting Standards. Include comparative figures where required. Show all workings separately. Perform your workings in the following order:

(a) Calculate the warranty provision as at 30 June 2010. This should agree with the financial statements provided in the question.
(b) Calculate the warranty provision as at 30 June 2011.
(c) Calculate the movement in the warranty provision for the year.
(d) Calculate the prospective change in depreciation required as a result of the shortened useful life of the conveyer belt.
(e) Determine whether the unpaid amount owing as a result of the peanut allergy case is a liability or a provision.
(f) Determine whether the receipt of damages for the negligent advice meets the definition of an asset or a contingent asset.

(g) Determine whether the bank guarantee meets the definition of a provision or a contingent liability. (Ignore recent amendments to IAS 39 in this regard.)
(h) Prepare the financial statement disclosures.

References

ASIC 1998, *Media release 98/314*, Australian Securities and Investments Commission, October.
Ernst & Young 2002a, 'Provisions, contingent liabilities and contingent assets', *Accounting Brief*, January, Australia.
—2002b, AH 217 'Accounting for provisions', *Accounting handbook*, Australia.

DUBLIN BUSINESS SCHOOL
LIBRARY

5 Financial instruments

ACCOUNTING STANDARDS IN FOCUS

IAS 32 *Financial Instruments: Presentation*

IFRS 7 *Financial Instruments: Disclosures*

IAS 39 *Financial Instruments: Recognition and Measurement*

LEARNING OBJECTIVES

When you have studied this chapter, you should be able to:

- understand the concept of financial instruments
- understand and apply the definitions of financial assets and financial liabilities
- understand the concept of a derivative
- distinguish between equity instruments and financial liabilities
- understand the concept of a compound financial instrument
- determine the classification of revenues and expenses arising from financial instruments
- determine when financial assets and financial liabilities may be offset
- describe the main disclosure requirements of IFRS 7
- understand the scope of IAS 39
- understand the concepts of a derivative and embedded derivative
- distinguish between the four categories of financial instruments specified in IAS 39
- understand and apply the recognition criteria for financial instruments
- understand and apply the measurement criteria for each category of financial instrument
- have an overall understanding of the rules of hedge accounting set out in IAS 39 and be able to apply the rules to simple common cash flow and fair value hedges.

5.1 INTRODUCTION TO IAS 32, IFRS 7 AND IAS 39

Accounting for financial instruments has been the most controversial area in the development of the IASB's 'stable platform' of standards adopted in 2005. Indeed, the controversy surrounding IAS 39 in particular almost derailed the IASB's plans for adopting IFRSs in Europe for financial years beginning on or after 1 January 2005. As late as 30 June 2004, IAS 39 had still not been completed because changes continued to be proposed or made in response to lobbying from various European interested parties, notably the banks. The controversial aspects of the standards were largely those relating to hedge accounting.

Because IAS 32, IFRS 7 and IAS 39 are complex standards, this chapter aims to provide an overall explanation of the requirements. It emphasises those areas most commonly affecting the majority of reporting entities, and places less emphasis on specialised areas.

IAS 32 was developed before IAS 39. It sets out the definitions of financial instruments, financial assets and financial liabilities, distinguishes between financial liabilities and equity instruments, and prescribes detailed disclosures. The standard was developed separately from IAS 39 because consensus on the recognition, derecognition, measurement and hedging rules for financial instruments was difficult to achieve. Therefore the standard setters first established classification and disclosure rules, anticipating that increased disclosure by reporting entities would provide more information, not only for users, but also for the standard setters. Increased disclosure helps to provide standard setters with information that assists in developing further standards.

In 2006, IAS 32 was renamed *Financial Instruments: Presentation* and a new standard, IFRS 7 *Financial Instruments: Disclosures*, was introduced, applicable to annual periods beginning on or after 1 January 2007. IFRS 7 contains many of the disclosure requirements that were originally in IAS 32 and also introduced a number of new requirements. It also includes some of the requirements that were in IAS 30 *Disclosures in the Financial Statements of Banks and Similar Financial Institutions* and supersedes that standard.

IAS 39 was originally based largely on the similar FASB standard in the United States, Statement of Financial Accounting Standards No. 133 (SFAS 133) *Accounting for Derivative Instruments and Hedging Activities*. FASB standards have historically been rule-based rather than principle-based, and this explains why IAS 39 is considerably more rule-based than other IASB standards. As IAS 39 was amended repeatedly during 2003 and 2004, it moved further away from SFAS 133 but still reflects many of the same rules.

Each standard is addressed separately in this chapter. IAS 32, IFRS 7 and IAS 39 each contain Application Guidance, which is abbreviated in this chapter as AG. IFRS 7 and IAS 39 also contain Implementation Guidance.

5.2 IAS 32 *FINANCIAL INSTRUMENTS: PRESENTATION* AND IFRS 7 *FINANCIAL INSTRUMENTS: DISCLOSURES*

5.2.1 What is a financial instrument?

IAS 32, paragraph 11, defines a financial instrument as:

> any contract that gives rise to a financial asset of one entity and a financial liability or equity instrument of another entity.

Financial assets and financial liabilities are terms defined in IAS 32 (see section 5.2.2 of this chapter). Financial assets are defined from the perspective of the *holder* of the instrument, whereas financial liabilities and equity instruments are defined from the perspective of the *issuer* of the instrument.

An equity instrument is defined in paragraph 11 as:

> any contract that evidences a residual interest in the assets of an entity after deducting all of its liabilities.

The most common type of equity instrument is an ordinary share of a company. The holder of the shares is not entitled to any fixed return on or of its investment; instead, the holder receives the residual after all liabilities have been settled. This applies both to periodic returns (where dividends are paid after interest on liabilities has been paid) and capital returns (when a company is wound up, all liabilities are settled before shareholders are entitled to any return of their investment).

Note that the definition of a financial instrument is two-sided: the contract must always give rise to a financial asset of one party, with a corresponding financial liability or equity instrument of another party. So, for example, a contract that gives the seller of a product the right to receive cash from the purchaser creates a receivable for the seller (a financial asset) and a payable for the purchaser (a financial liability).

Financial instruments include primary instruments such as cash, receivables, investments and payables, as well as derivative financial instruments such as financial options and forward exchange contracts. Derivative financial instruments, or derivatives, are instruments that *derive* their value from another underlying item such as a share price or an interest rate. (The definition of a derivative is discussed in section 5.3.2 of this chapter.)

Financial instruments do *not* include non-financial assets such as property, plant and equipment, or non-financial liabilities such as provisions for restoration. Contracts to buy or sell non-financial items are also usually not financial instruments. Many commodity contracts fall into this category (contracts to buy or sell oil, cotton, wheat and so on). These commodity contracts are thus outside the scope of IAS 32. However, IFRS 7 requires reporting entities with commodity contracts that are within the scope of IAS 39 to follow the disclosure requirements of IFRS 7. Certain commodity contracts are, however, included within the scope of IAS 32. These include contracts to buy or sell non-financial items that can be settled net (in cash) or by exchanging financial instruments, or in which the non-financial item is readily convertible into cash. Contracts to buy or sell gold might fall into the latter category and hence might be caught by IAS 32 (IAS 32, para. 8) and IAS 39 (IAS 39, para. 5).

Note also that the definition of a financial instrument requires there to be a contractual right or obligation. Therefore liabilities or assets that are not contractual — such as income taxes that are created as a result of statutory requirements imposed by governments, or constructive obligations as defined in IAS 37 *Provisions, Contingent Liabilities and Contingent Assets* (see chapter 4) — are not financial instruments.

In addition, certain financial assets and liabilities lie outside the scope of the standard (IAS 32, para. 4). These include employee benefits accounted for under IAS 19, and investments in subsidiaries, associates and joint ventures that are accounted for under IAS 27 *Consolidated and Separate Financial Statements*, IAS 28 *Investments in Associates* and IAS 31 *Interests in Joint Ventures*.

5.2.2 Financial assets and financial liabilities

A financial asset is defined in paragraph 11 of IAS 32 as follows:

> any asset that is:
> (a) cash
> (b) an equity instrument of another entity
> (c) a contractual right:
>   (i) to receive cash or another financial asset from another entity; or
>   (ii) to exchange financial assets or financial liabilities with another entity under conditions that are potentially favourable to the entity; or
> (d) a contract that will or may be settled in the entity's own equity instruments and is:
>   (i) a non-derivative for which the entity is or may be obliged to receive a variable number of the entity's own equity instruments; or
>   (ii) a derivative that will or may be settled other than by the exchange of a fixed amount of cash or another financial asset for a fixed number of the entity's own equity instruments. For this purpose the entity's own equity instruments do not include instruments that are themselves contracts for the future receipt or delivery of the entity's own equity instruments.

Examples of common financial assets in each of the categories of the definition include:

(a) Cash — either cash on hand or the right of the depositor to obtain cash from the financial institution with whom it has deposited the cash

(b) An equity instrument of another entity — ordinary shares held in another entity, commonly known as share investments

(c) A contractual right
  (i) to receive cash or another financial asset — trade accounts receivable, notes receivable, loans receivable
  (ii) to exchange under potentially favourable conditions — an option held by the holder to purchase shares in a specified company at less than the market price.

Part (d) of the definition was added in amendments made to IAS 39 in 2003 and 2004. The amendments were made in response to issues arising from the classification of certain complex financial instruments as liabilities or equity. (Liability/equity classification is discussed in section 5.2.4 of this chapter.)

A financial liability is defined in paragraph 11 of IAS 32 as follows:

> any liability that is:
> (a) a contractual obligation:
>   (i) to deliver cash or another financial asset to another entity; or
>   (ii) to exchange financial assets or financial liabilities with another entity under conditions that are potentially unfavourable to the entity; or
> (b) a contract that will or may be settled in the entity's own equity instruments and is:
>   (i) a non-derivative for which the entity is or may be obliged to deliver a variable number of the entity's own equity instruments; or
>   (ii) a derivative that will or may be settled other than by the exchange of a fixed amount of cash or another financial asset for a fixed number of the entity's own equity instruments. For this purpose the entity's own equity instruments do not include instruments that are themselves contracts for the future receipt or delivery of the entity's own equity instruments.

Examples of common financial liabilities in each of the categories of the definition include:

(a) A contractual obligation
  (i) to deliver cash or another financial asset — trade accounts payable, notes payable, loans payable
  (ii) to exchange under potentially unfavourable conditions — an option written (i.e. issued) by the issuer to sell shares in a specified company at less than the market price.

Part (b) of the definition was added in amendments made to IAS 39 in 2003 and 2004. The amendments were made in response to issues arising from the classification of certain complex financial instruments as liabilities or equity. (Liability/equity classification is discussed in section 5.2.4 of this chapter.)

Table 5.1 contains a summary of common financial instruments.

TABLE 5.1 Summary of common financial instruments

Financial assets	Financial liabilities	Equity instruments
Cash	Bank overdraft	Ordinary shares
Accounts receivable	Accounts payable	Certain preference shares
Notes receivable	Notes payable	
Loans receivable	Loans payable	
Derivatives with potentially favourable exchange conditions	Derivatives with potentially unfavourable exchange conditions	
	Certain preference shares	

5.2.3 Demystifying derivatives

The concept of a derivative may appear daunting because there are numerous derivative financial instruments in the market that seem complex and difficult to understand. However, as already noted, fundamentally all derivatives simply *derive* their value from another underlying item such as a share price or an interest rate. Derivative financial instruments create rights and obligations that have the effect of transferring between the parties to the instrument one or more of the financial risks inherent in an underlying primary financial instrument. On inception, derivative financial instruments give one party a contractual right to exchange financial assets or financial liabilities with another party under conditions that are potentially favourable, while the other party has a contractual obligation to exchange under potentially unfavourable conditions.

Figure 5.1 provides an option contract as an example of a derivative.

An option contract

Party A buys an option that entitles it to purchase 1000 shares in Company Z at $3 a share, at any time in the next 6 months. The shares in Company Z are the *underlying* financial instruments from which the option derives its value. The option is thus the derivative financial instrument. The amount of $3 a share is called the *exercise price* of the *option*.

Party B sells the option to Party A. Party A is called the *holder* of the option, and Party B is called the *writer* of the option. Party A will usually pay an amount called a *premium* to purchase the option. The amount of the premium is less than what Party A would have to pay for the shares in Company Z.

Assume that at the date of the option contract the market price of shares in Company Z is $2.60.

The financial instrument created by this transaction is a contractual right of Party A to purchase the 1000 shares in Company Z at $3 a share (a financial asset of Party A), and a contractual obligation of Party B to sell the shares in Company Z to Party A at $3 a share (a financial liability of Party B). Party A's right is a financial asset because it has the right to exchange under potentially favourable conditions to itself. Thus, if the share price of Company Z rises above $3, Party A will exercise its option and require Party B to deliver the shares at $3 a share. Party A will have benefited from this transaction by acquiring the shares in Company Z at less than the market price. Conversely, Party B's obligation is a financial liability because it has the obligation to exchange under potentially unfavourable conditions to itself. Thus, if the shares in Company Z rise to $3.20, Party A will purchase the shares from Party B for $3000. If Party A had had to purchase the shares on the market, it would have paid $3200.

Party B may have made a loss from this transaction, depending on whether it already held the shares in Company Z, or had to go out and buy them for $3200 and then sell them to Party A for $3000, or had entered into other derivative contracts with other parties enabling it to purchase the shares at less than $3000.

What if the share price in Company Z never exceeds $2.60 over the 6-month term of the option? In this case, Party A will not exercise the option and the option will lapse. The option is termed 'out-of-the money' from Party A's perspective — it has no value to Party A because the exercise price is higher than the market price. Once the share price rises above $3, the option is termed 'in-the money'. Party A is not compelled to exercise its option, even if it is in-the-money. From Party A's perspective, it has a right to exercise the option should it so choose. However, if Party A exercises its option, Party B is then compelled to deliver the shares under its contractual obligation.

IAS 32, AG 17, notes that the nature of the holder's right and of the writer's obligation is not affected by the likelihood that the option will be exercised.

FIGURE 5.1 How an option contract works

In simple terms, parties to derivative financial instruments are taking bets on what will happen to the underlying financial instrument in the future. In the example in figure 5.1, Party A was taking a bet that the share price in Company Z would rise above $3 within 6 months, and Party B was taking a bet that it wouldn't. Party B would most likely hedge its bet by doing something to protect itself should the market price rise above $3. It could do this by entering into another derivative with another party, enabling Party B to purchase shares from that other party at $3. Often a chain of derivative financial instruments will be created in this way. Party A will probably not know anything about the chain created. (Hedging is discussed in section 5.3.6 of this chapter.)

IAS 32 does not prescribe recognition and measurement rules for derivatives; these are addressed in IAS 39. Instead, IAS 32 includes derivatives in the definition of financial instruments. Other types of derivatives include interest rate swaps, forward exchange contracts, and futures contracts.

5.2.4 Distinguishing financial liabilities from equity instruments

IAS 32 is very prescriptive in the area of distinguishing between financial liabilities and equity instruments. This area, commonly known as the debt versus equity distinction, is of great concern to many reporting entities because instruments classified as liabilities rather than equity affect:

- a company's gearing and solvency ratios
- debt covenants with financial institutions (usually a requirement that specified financial ratios of the borrower do not exceed predetermined thresholds; if they do exceed the thresholds, the financial institution has a right to require repayment of the loan)
- whether periodic payments on these instruments are treated as interest or dividends
- regulatory requirements for capital adequacy (banks and other financial institutions are required by their regulators to maintain a certain level of capital, which is calculated by reference to assets and equity).

Accordingly, reporting entities are often motivated, when raising funds, to issue instruments that are classified as equity for accounting purposes. In the years since IAS 32 was first issued, many complex instruments were devised by market participants specifically to achieve equity classification under IAS 32. Some of these instruments were liabilities in substance but were able to be classified technically as equity, notwithstanding a 'substance over form' test in IAS 32. As a result, the standard setters amended IAS 32 in 2003–04 to create specific rules designed to address these complex instruments. Unfortunately, the rules are now more complicated than the instruments themselves, so this section will address the key principles of liability versus equity classification only.

IAS 32, paragraph 15, states:

> The issuer of a financial instrument shall classify the instrument, or its component parts, on initial recognition as a financial liability, a financial asset or an equity instrument in accordance with the substance of the contractual arrangement and the definitions of a financial liability, a financial asset and an equity instrument.

To avoid any doubt, paragraph 16 goes on to repeat and clarify the definition of a financial liability. It states that an instrument shall be classified as an equity instrument if, and only if, *both* conditions (a) and (b) below are met:

(a) The instrument includes no contractual obligation:
  (i) to deliver cash or another financial asset to another entity; or
  (ii) to exchange financial assets or financial liabilities with another entity under conditions that are potentially unfavourable to the issuer.

(b) If the instrument will or may be settled in the issuer's own equity instruments, it is:
  (i) a non-derivative that includes no contractual obligation for the issuer to deliver a variable number of its own equity instruments; or
  (ii) a derivative that will be settled only by the issuer exchanging a fixed amount of cash or another financial asset for a fixed number of its own equity instruments.

Part (a) is clearly referring to the definition of a financial liability. Part (b) helps to clarify the amendments to the definitions of a financial asset and a financial liability (discussed in section 5.2.2 of this chapter). In essence, the rules in part (b) are trying to establish who bears 'equity risk' in complex transactions where an entity issues a financial instrument that will or may be settled in its own shares.

The concept of equity risk is useful for both part (b) of the test and generally in determining whether an instrument is equity or a liability. Note, however, that part (a) of the test turns only on whether or not the issuer has a contractual obligation.

Part (a) of the equity/liability test: contractual obligation

The examples in figure 5.2 apply part (a) of the equity/liability test, together with the equity risk concept.

Paragraph 17 of IAS 32 reiterates that a critical feature in differentiating a financial liability from an equity instrument is the existence of a contractual obligation of the issuer. Paragraph 18 then goes on to state that the substance of a financial instrument, rather than its legal form, governs its classification on the entity's statement of financial position. Some financial instruments, such as the preference shares in example 3 of figure 5.2, take the legal form of equity but are liabilities in substance. Other financial instruments, such as the preference shares in example 4 of figure 5.2, may combine features associated with equity instruments and those associated with financial liabilities. Sometimes the combined features result in the financial instrument being split into its component parts (see section 5.2.5 of this chapter).

FIGURE 5.2 Applying part (a) of the equity/liability test

Example 1: Ordinary shares

Company A wants to raise funds of $1 million. It does so by issuing ordinary shares to the public. The holders of those shares are exposed to equity risk (they are not entitled to any fixed return on or of their investment, and receive the residual left over after all liabilities have been settled) in respect of both periodic payments and capital returns. If there is no profit after interest on liabilities and other contractual obligations have been paid, then there are no dividends. If, on winding up, there are no assets after all liabilities have been settled, there is nothing returned to the shareholders. This is the fundamental nature of equity risk. The ordinary shares issued by Company A are equity instruments of Company A. Under part (a) of the test, Company A has no contractual obligation to its ordinary shareholders.

Company A would record the following journal entry on initial recognition:

Cash (financial asset)	Dr	1 000 000	
Ordinary Share Capital (equity)	Cr		1 000 000

Example 2: Non-cumulative, non-redeemable preference shares

Company A decides to issue preference shares instead of ordinary shares. It issues one million preference shares for $1 each. Each preference shareholder is entitled to a non-cumulative dividend of 5% annually. (A non-cumulative dividend means that, if in any year a dividend is not paid, the shareholder forfeits it.) The preference shareholders rank ahead of ordinary shareholders on the winding-up of the company. The preference shares are non-redeemable (the holders of the shares cannot get their money back).

Under part (a) of the test, Company A has no contractual obligation to the preference shareholders, either to pay dividends or to return the cash. Therefore the preference shares are equity instruments of Company A. In addition, applying the concept of equity risk reveals that the preference shareholders are exposed to equity risk, although it is lower than for the ordinary shareholders.

Company A would record the following journal entry on initial recognition:

Cash (financial asset)	Dr	1 000 000	
Preference Share Capital (equity)	Cr		1 000 000

Example 3: Cumulative, redeemable preference shares

Company A issues one million preference shares for $1 each, and each preference shareholder is entitled to a *cumulative* dividend of 5% annually. The preference shareholders rank ahead of ordinary shareholders on the winding-up of the company. The preference shares are redeemable for cash *at the option of the holder*.

Under part (a) of the test, Company A now has a contractual obligation to the preference shareholders — both in respect of dividends and to return the cash. Company A must pay the dividends and, if in any period it cannot pay, it must make up the payment with the next dividend. Furthermore, Company A must repay the money whenever the holder demands repayment. Therefore, the preference shares are financial liabilities of Company A. In addition, applying the concept of equity risk reveals that the preference shareholders are not exposed to equity risk — they are guaranteed a periodic return of 5% and they can require that their cash be returned. They bear the same risk as would a lender to the Company. A lender's risk is generally credit risk (the risk that Company A will fail to discharge its obligations) and liquidity risk (the risk that Company A will fail to raise funds to enable it to redeem the liability on demand).

(continued)

FIGURE 5.2 *(continued)*

Company A would record the following journal entry on initial recognition:

Cash (financial asset)	Dr	1 000 000	
Preference Share Liability (financial liability)	Cr		1 000 000

Example 4: Cumulative, redeemable preference shares
Company A issues one million preference shares for $1 each, and each preference shareholder is entitled to a *cumulative* dividend of 5% annually. The preference shareholders rank ahead of ordinary shareholders on the winding-up of the company. The preference shares are redeemable for cash *at the option of Company A.*

Under part (a) of the test, Company A now has a contractual obligation to the preference shareholders, but only in respect of dividends. It cannot be required to return the cash, since redemption is at its own option. In addition, applying the concept of equity risk reveals that the preference shareholders are partially exposed to equity risk — they are guaranteed a periodic return of 5% but they cannot require that their cash be returned. IAS 32, AG 25, confirms that preference shares redeemable at the option of the issuer are not financial liabilities. IAS 32, AG 26, clarifies that, when preference shares are non-redeemable, the other rights that attach to them determine the appropriate classification. It states that when distributions, whether cumulative or non-cumulative, are at the discretion of the issuer, the shares are equity instruments.

However, neither AG 25 nor AG 26 is particularly useful in helping decide what to do if the distributions are not discretionary. Is it possible for the preference share to be part liability and part equity? The answer, in theory, is yes. IAS 32 contains a section on compound financial instruments (discussed in section 5.2.5 of this chapter). In practice, though, such splitting of the instrument would be difficult to achieve. This is further complicated by having to split the 'dividend' into an interest component and a dividend component (see section 5.2.7). The discussion in AG 26 implies that cumulative dividends, on their own, would not be sufficient to cause a preference share to be classified as a liability, and that the overall substance of the arrangement must be considered. Unfortunately, it then goes on to give examples of where the distribution payments create a financial liability in substance, but says that even then the cumulative dividends do not create a liability. Therefore, in this example, the preference shares are equity instruments of Company A.

Company A would record the following journal entry on initial recognition:

Cash (financial asset)	Dr	1 000 000	
Preference Share Capital (equity)	Cr		1 000 000

Another example (added to IAS 32 in the 2003–04 revisions) of a financial instrument whose legal form may be equity but whose accounting classification is a financial liability is a puttable instrument. A puttable instrument gives the holder the right to put the instrument back to the issuer for cash or another financial asset. This is so even when the amount of cash/other financial asset is determined on the basis of an index or another amount that may increase or decrease. For example, certain mutual funds, unit trusts and partnerships provide their unit holders or members with a right to redeem their interests in the issuer at any time for cash equal to their proportionate share of the net asset value of the issuer. Traditionally, unit holder funds have been classified as equity because the legal form of their interest was equity. However, under paragraph 18 of the revised IAS 32, it is clear that these are financial liabilities. This caused a significant change to the presentation of financial statements for unit trusts. In 2007, the IASB issued an exposure draft proposing to modify the definition of a financial liability so that such puttable instruments would not automatically result in liability classification.

Paragraphs 19 and 20 of IAS 32 go on to explain that an entity has a contractual obligation to deliver cash/other financial assets notwithstanding:

- any restrictions on the entity's ability to meet its obligation (such as access to foreign currency)
- that the obligation may be conditional on the counterparty exercising its redemption right (as in example 3 of figure 5.2 — redemption is at the option of the holder and therefore could be considered to be conditional on the holder exercising its right to redeem. However, this does not negate the fact that the issuer has a contractual obligation to redeem the shares, because it cannot avoid its obligation should it be required to redeem by the holder.)
- that the financial instrument does not explicitly establish a contractual obligation to deliver cash/other financial assets. A contractual obligation may be implied in the terms and conditions of the instrument. Unfortunately, the guidance in paragraph 20 contradicts the guidance on preference shares in AG 26. AG 26 states that non-redeemable preference shares are equity instruments, notwithstanding a term that prevents ordinary share dividends from being paid if the preference share dividend is not paid, or from being paid on the issuer's expectation of profit or loss for a period. A fairly common term in certain non-redeemable preference shares is that the dividend is 'discretionary' but, if the preference dividend is not paid, then ordinary dividends cannot be paid. If these terms exist in the preference shares of highly profitable companies, one could argue under paragraph 20 of IAS 32 that the implicit terms and conditions of the preference shares require the dividend to be paid. However, AG 26 states that such conditions do not create a financial liability of the issuer.

Part (b) of the equity/liability test: settlement in the entity's own equity instruments

Paragraph 21 of IAS 32 states that a contract is not an equity instrument solely because it may result in the receipt or delivery of the entity's own equity instruments. As noted earlier in this section, such an instrument can be classified as an equity instrument under paragraph 16(b) of IAS 32 only if it is:

> (i) a non-derivative that includes no contractual obligation for the issuer to deliver a variable number of its own equity instruments; or
>
> (ii) a derivative that will be settled only by the issuer exchanging a fixed amount of cash or another financial asset for a fixed number of its own equity instruments.

Part (i) will be examined first. Assume listed Company A has an obligation to deliver to Party B as many of Company A's own ordinary shares as will equal $100 000. The number of shares that Company A will have to issue will vary depending on the market price of its own shares. If Company A's shares are each worth $1 at the date of settlement of the contract, it will have to deliver 100 000 shares. If Company A's shares are each worth 50c at the date of settlement of the contract, it will have to deliver 200 000 shares. Company A has a contractual obligation at all times to deliver $100 000 to Party B; that is, the value is fixed, and so the number of shares to be delivered will vary. Therefore, Company A's financial instrument fails the test in part (i) and the instrument is a financial liability. Applying the concept of equity risk, the *holder* of the financial instrument (Party B) is not exposed to equity risk because it will always receive $100 000 regardless of the market price of Company A's shares. A true equity risk-taker will be exposed to share price fluctuations — this reflects the residual nature of an equity risk-taker's investment.

Now examine part (ii). Assume listed Company A issues a share option to Party B that entitles Party B to buy 100 000 shares in Company A at $1 each in 3 months time. This financial instrument meets the conditions for equity classification under part (ii) because it is a derivative that will be settled by issuing a fixed number of shares for a fixed amount. Assume that, at the date of the grant of the option, Company A's share price is $1. If in 3 months time Company A's share price exceeds $1, Party B will exercise its option and Company A must issue its shares to Party B for $100 000. If, however, in 3 months time Company A's share price falls below $1, Party B will not exercise its option and Company A will not issue any shares. Applying the concept of equity risk reveals that the *holder* of the financial instrument (Party B) is exposed to equity risk because it is not guaranteed to receive $100 000 in value. Whether or not it receives $100 000 is entirely dependent on the market price of Company A's shares. As a true equity risk-taker, it is exposed to share price fluctuations; this reflects the residual nature of an equity risk-taker's investment. Party B will have paid a premium to Company A for the option. Paragraph 22 of IAS 32 states that this premium is added directly to Company A's equity, consistent with the classification of the instrument as an equity instrument.

Contingent settlement provisions and settlement options

Sometimes, when a financial instrument requires an entity to deliver cash/other financial assets, the terms of settlement are dependent on the occurrence or non-occurrence of uncertain future events that are beyond the control of both the issuer and the holder. Examples of such events include changes in a share market index, the consumer price index or the issuer's future revenues. The issuer of such an instrument does not have the unconditional right to avoid delivering the cash/other financial assets, so paragraph 25 of IAS 32 requires such instruments to be classified as financial liabilities unless they meet certain rare exceptions. For example, assume that Company A issues preference shares to Party B, the terms of which entitle Party B to redeem the preference shares for cash if Company A's revenues fall below a specified level. Because neither Company A nor Party B can control the level of Company A's revenues, the settlement provision is considered to be contingent. However, because Company A cannot avoid repaying Party B should Company A's revenues fall below the specified level, Company A does not have an unconditional right to avoid repayment. Thus the preference shares are a financial liability of Company A.

It is common for financial instruments to contain a choice of settlement. For example, preference shares may be redeemed for cash or for the issuer's ordinary shares. Sometimes the choice is the issuer's; sometimes it is the holder's. Paragraph 26 of IAS 32 requires that, when a *derivative* financial instrument gives one party a choice over how it is settled, it is a financial asset or a financial liability unless all of the settlement alternatives would result in it being an equity instrument. An example is a share option that the issuer can decide to settle net in cash or by exchanging its own shares for cash. Because not all of the settlement options would result in an equity instrument being issued, the option must be classified as a financial asset or liability. Note that the likely outcome is not taken into account; the fact that cash settlement may be required is sufficient to create a financial asset or liability.

Paragraph 26 does not address non-derivative financial instruments. Therefore, where a non-derivative financial instrument such as a preference share may be redeemed for cash or for the issuer's own ordinary shares, paragraph 26 does not apply. Instead, paragraph 16 would be applied to determine whether or not there is (a) a contractual obligation to deliver cash/other financial assets, or (b) a contractual obligation to deliver a variable number of the issuer's ordinary shares. Note that both (a) and (b) must be answered in the negative for equity classification to apply. So, for example, if the *issuer* of the preference share has the option to redeem for cash or for a variable number of its ordinary shares, the first question to ask is: does the issuer have a contractual obligation to deliver cash? If redemption is at the issuer's option, the issuer has *no* contractual obligation to redeem *at all* and therefore arguably the second question about the number of ordinary shares is irrelevant. Indeed, paragraph 16(b) asks whether or not the issuer has a contractual obligation to deliver a variable number of its own shares and, since redemption is at the issuer's option, it has no such contractual obligation, even though the number of shares that potentially will be issued is variable. Therefore, all other things being equal, the preference shares will be classified as equity. On the other hand, if redemption is at the *holder's* option, the instrument would be classified as a liability, because the issuer has a contractual obligation to deliver cash/other financial assets or ordinary shares because the holder has the right to call for redemption. This is so even if the number of ordinary shares is fixed, because the holder's right to redeem for cash means that paragraph 16(a) is met.

5.2.5 Compound financial instruments

Paragraph 28 of IAS 32 requires an issuer of a non-derivative financial instrument to determine whether it contains both a liability and an equity component. Such components must be classified separately as financial liabilities, financial assets or equity instruments.

Paragraph 29 goes on to explain that this means that an entity recognises separately the components of a financial instrument that (a) creates a financial liability of the entity, and (b) grants an option to the holder of the instrument to convert it into an equity instrument of the entity. A common example of such a financial instrument is a convertible bond or note that entitles the holder to convert the note into a fixed number of ordinary shares of the issuer. From the perspective of the *issuer*, such an instrument comprises two components: (a) a financial liability, being a contractual obligation to deliver cash/other financial assets in the form of interest payments and redemption of the note, and (b) an equity instrument, being an option issued to the holder entitling it to the right, for a specified period of time, to convert the note into a fixed number of ordinary shares of the issuer. Note that the number of shares to be issued must be fixed, otherwise the option would not meet the definition of an equity instrument under paragraph 16(b) as discussed on pages 157–8.

Classification of the liability and equity components is made on initial recognition of the financial instrument and is not revised as a result of a change in the likelihood that the conversion option may be exercised. This is because, until such time as the conversion option is either exercised or lapses, the issuer has a contractual obligation to make future payments.

How does the issuer measure the separate liability and equity components? Paragraphs 31 and 32 of IAS 32 prescribe that the financial liability must be calculated first, with the equity component by definition being the residual. The example in figure 5.3 illustrates how this is done.

Example 5: Compound financial instrument — a convertible note

Company A issues 2000 convertible notes on 1 July 2010. The notes have a 3-year term and are issued at par with a face value of $1000 per note, giving total proceeds at the date of issue of $2 million. The notes pay interest at 6% annually in arrears. The holder of each note is entitled to convert the note into 250 ordinary shares of Company A at any time up to maturity.

When the notes are issued, the prevailing market interest rate for similar debt (similar term, similar credit status of issuer and similar cash flows) without conversion options is 9%. This rate is higher than the convertible note's rate because the holder of the convertible note is prepared to accept a lower interest rate given the implicit value of its conversion option.

The issuer calculates the contractual cash flows using the market interest rate (9%) to work out the value of the holder's option, as follows:

Present value of the principal: $2 million payable in 3 years time:	$1 544 367
Present value of the interest: $120 000 ($2 million × 6%) payable annually in arrears for 3 years	303 755
Total liability component	1 848 122
Equity component (by deduction)	151 878
Proceeds of the note issue	$2 000 000

The journal entries at the date of issue are as follows:

Cash	Dr	2 000 000	
Financial Liability	Cr		1 848 122
Equity	Cr		151 878

The equity component is not remeasured (IAS 32, para. 22) and thus remains at $151 878 until the note is either converted or redeemed. If the note is converted, the remaining liability component is transferred to equity. If the note is redeemed, the equity component remains in equity despite redemption.

FIGURE 5.3 A convertible note, allocating the components between liability and equity
Source: Adapted from IAS 32, Illustrative Example 9, paras IE35–IE36.

5.2.6 Putting it all together

The liability/equity distinction rules in IAS 32 can rarely be applied in isolation. Unfortunately, IAS 32 does not contain a clear hierarchy to assist in determining which rules take precedence. Is it the substance over form rule in paragraph 15? Is it the definition rule in paragraph 15? Is it the contractual obligation rule in paragraph 16? Is it the 'settlement in own equity' rules? Is it the settlement options or contingent settlement provisions rules? Is it the components rule in paragraph 28?

Take our redeemable preference shares in example 4 of figure 5.2. Company A issued one million preference shares for $1 each, and each preference shareholder is entitled to a *cumulative* dividend of 5% annually. The preference shareholders rank ahead of ordinary shareholders on the winding-up of the company. The preference shares are redeemable for cash *at the option of Company A*. Assume that a few more terms and conditions have been added. Instead of the shares being redeemable only for cash, they are redeemable for cash or *for a fixed number of ordinary shares* at the option of Company A, at any time after 5 years. The shares also contain a conversion option, entitling the holder to convert to a fixed number of ordinary shares of Company A at any time up to 5 years. In addition, although the dividends are cumulative, they can be paid only if Company A's profit exceeds $250 000, indexed annually.

Table 5.2 helps to answer the questions, taking each set of 5 years separately.

TABLE 5.2 Applying the various liability/equity rules as a whole

Liability/equity rules	First 5 years	After 5 years
Contractual obligation to deliver cash?	No	No (issuer's option)
Contractual obligation to exchange under potentially unfavourable conditions?	No	No
Derivative or non-derivative?	Non-derivative	Non-derivative
If a non-derivative, contractual obligation to deliver shares?	Yes (holder's option to convert)	No (issuer's option to redeem)
Are shares to be delivered fixed or variable?	Fixed, therefore equity classification	Fixed
If a derivative, settled by fixed cash/fixed number of shares?	N/A	N/A
Contingent settlement provisions?	Yes — the dividends are paid only if profit targets are met[1]	Yes — the dividends are paid only if profit targets are met
If a derivative, terms of settlement options?	N/A	N/A
Compound financial instrument?	Yes — holder has the option to convert to a fixed number of ordinary shares	No
Substance over form?	Equity[2]	Equity
Classification	Equity	Equity

Notes:

1. Under paragraph 25 of IAS 32, the dividend conditions meet the contingent settlement definition and would require liability classification, but AG 26 refutes this by stating that the dividends are at the discretion of the issuer.
2. Although the instrument is a compound instrument for the first 5 years, there is no liability component because the substance of the entire instrument is equity given the other terms and conditions. This assumes that the dividend payments are discretionary. Therefore no splitting into component parts is required.

5.2.7 Interest, dividends, gains and losses

Paragraph 35 of IAS 32 requires the statement of comprehensive income classification of items relating to financial instruments to match their statement of financial position classification. Thus, statement of comprehensive income items relating to financial liabilities and financial assets are classified as income or expenses, or gains or losses. These are usually interest expense, interest income and dividend income. Distributions to holders of equity instruments are debited directly to equity. Usually these are dividends. These principles also apply to the component parts of a compound financial instrument.

Table 5.3 summarises these principles.

TABLE 5.3 Classification of revenues, expenses and equity distributions

Statement of financial position classification	Statement of comprehensive income classification	Statement of changes in equity
Equity instrument		Dividends distributed
Financial liability	Interest expense	
Financial asset	Interest income, dividend income	

The transaction costs of an equity transaction are deducted from equity, net of tax, but only to the extent to which they are incremental costs directly attributable to the equity transaction that otherwise would have been avoided (IAS 32, para. 37). Examples of such costs include registration and other regulatory fees, legal and accounting fees and stamp duties. These costs are required to be shown separately under IAS 1 *Presentation of Financial Statements.*

5.2.8 Offsetting a financial asset and a financial liability

Paragraph 42 of IAS 32 states that a financial asset and a financial liability shall be offset and the net amount presented when, and only when, an entity:

(a) currently has a legally enforceable right to set off the recognised amounts; and
(b) intends either to settle on a net basis, or to realise the asset and settle the liability simultaneously.

The underlying rationale of this requirement is that when an entity has the right to receive or pay a single net amount and intends to do so, it has effectively only a single financial asset or financial liability. Note that the right of set-off must be legally enforceable and therefore usually stems from a written contract between two parties. In rare cases, there may be an agreement between three parties allowing a debtor to apply an amount due from a third party against the amount due to a creditor. Assume, for example, that Company A owes Company B $1000, and Company Z owes Company A $1000. Company A has therefore recorded in its books the following:

Amount Receivable from Company Z	Dr	1 000	
Amount Owing to Company B	Cr		1 000

Provided there is a legal right of set-off allowing Company A to offset the amount owing to Company B against the amount owed by Company Z, the amounts may be offset in Company A's accounts. Both Company B and Company Z must be parties to this legal right of set-off with Company A.

The conditions for offsetting are strict and essentially require written legal contracts resulting in net cash settlement. Many arrangements that create 'synthetic' (manufactured) offsetting are not permitted under IAS 32. Paragraph 49 provides examples of common cases where offsetting is not permitted.

5.2.9 Disclosures

IFRS 7 contains many pages dealing with disclosures, but only relatively few 'black letter' requirements. This chapter does not address these requirements in detail, and readers are expected to have a general understanding of the requirements only.

The purpose of the disclosure requirements is to provide information to enhance understanding of the significance of financial instruments to an entity's financial position, performance and cash flows; and to assist in assessing the amounts, timing and certainty of future cash flows associated with those instruments.

Transactions in financial instruments may result in an entity assuming or transferring to another party one or more of the financial risks described in table 5.4. The purpose of the required disclosures is to assist users in assessing the extent of such risks related to financial instruments.

TABLE 5.4 Financial risks pertaining to financial instruments

Type of risk	Description
Market risk	• *Currency risk* — the risk that the value of a financial instrument will fluctuate because of changes in foreign exchange rates • *Interest rate risk* — the risk that the value of a financial instrument will fluctuate because of changes in market interest rates. For example, the issuer of a financial liability that carries a fixed rate of interest is exposed to decreases in market interest rates, such that the issuer of the liability is paying a higher rate of interest than the market rate. • *Other price risk* — the risk that the value of a financial instrument will fluctuate as a result of changes in market prices (other than those arising from interest rate risk or currency risk) Market risk embodies the potential for both loss and gain.
Credit risk	The risk that one party to a financial instrument will fail to discharge an obligation and cause the other party to incur a financial loss
Liquidity risk	The risk that an entity will encounter difficulty in meeting obligations associated with financial liabilities. This is also known as funding risk. For example, as a financial liability approaches its redemption date, the issuer may experience liquidity risk if its available financial assets are insufficient to meet its obligations.

(Illustrative examples are included in Ernst & Young's publication, *IFRS 7* Financial Instruments: Disclosures, *second edition* (2007).)

IFRS 7 applies to all entities for all types of financial instruments, other than those specifically excluded from its scope. Scope exclusions include:

- interest in subsidiaries, associates and joint ventures accounted for under IAS 27, IAS 28 or IAS 31
- employers' rights and obligations arising from employee benefit plans, to which IAS 19 *Employee Benefits* applies
- contracts for contingent consideration in a business combination (see IFRS 3 *Business Combinations*)
- insurance contracts as defined in IFRS 4 *Insurance Contracts*
- share-based payment transactions to which IFRS 2 *Share-based Payment* applies.

IFRS 7 applies to both recognised and unrecognised financial instruments. For example, loan commitments not within the scope of IAS 39 are within the scope of IFRS 7.

IFRS 7 requires disclosure of financial instruments grouped by *class*. A class of financial instrument is a lower level of aggregation than a category, such as 'available-for-sale' or 'loans and receivables' (see section 5.3). For example, government debt securities, equity securities, or asset-backed securities could all be considered classes of financial instruments (see Ernst & Young (2007)).

IFRS 7 is divided into two main sections. The first section requires disclosure of the significance of financial instruments for financial position and performance. These disclosures are grouped into:

1. the statement of financial position
2. the statement of comprehensive income
3. other disclosures.

The second section requires disclosure about the nature and extent of risks arising from financial instruments. These include both quantitative and qualitative disclosures. The risks are grouped into the three categories noted above, that is, market risk, credit risk and liquidity risk. The Application Guidance (para. B6) states that these risk disclosures shall be given either in the financial statements or incorporated by cross-reference from the financial statements to some other statement, such as a management commentary or risk report.

Examples of the types of disclosures required in each of the sections are provided in tables 5.5 and 5.6.

TABLE 5.5 Significance of financial instruments for financial position and performance

Statement of financial position	
Overall requirement	**Summary of details required**
Categories of financial assets and financial liabilities (para. 8)	• The carrying amount of specified categories, as defined in IAS 39, for example, financial assets at fair value through profit and loss, held-to-maturity investments, etc.
Financial assets or financial liabilities at fair value through profit & loss (paras. 9, 10 and 11)	• If an entity has designated loans or receivables at fair value through profit and loss, specified details are required including the maximum exposure to credit risk, the amount by which any credit derivatives or similar instruments mitigate that exposure, the amount of the change in fair value that is attributable to changes in the credit risk and the amount of the change in the fair value of any credit derivatives or similar instruments. • If an entity has designated a financial liability at fair value through profit and loss, specified details are required including the amount of the change in fair value that is attributable to changes in the credit risk and the difference between the carrying amount of the liability and the amount the entity would be contractually required to pay at maturity. An example of this would be a long-dated financial liability whose creditworthiness has deteriorated.
Reclassification (para.12)	• Disclosure is required of the amount and reason for reclassification to or from the cost or amortised cost and fair value categories (see section 5.3).
Derecognition (para.13)	• Specified disclosures are required where an entity has transferred financial assets in such a way that part or all of the financial assets do not qualify for derecognition.
Collateral (paras.14 and 15)	• Collateral given: an entity must disclose the carrying amount of financial assets it has pledged as collateral (security) for liabilities or contingent liabilities. The terms and conditions of the pledge must also be disclosed. • Collateral received: specified details must be disclosed where an entity holds collateral (of financial and non-financial assets) and is permitted to sell or repledge that collateral.
Allowance for credit losses (para.16)	• When financial assets are impaired by credit losses and the entity records the impairment in a separate account (rather than deducting the loss directly from the asset concerned), it must disclose a reconciliation of that account.
Compound financial instruments with multiple embedded derivatives (para.17)	• Disclosure is required of the existence of such features in compound financial instruments.
Defaults and breaches (paras.18 and 19)	• For loans payable, disclosure is required of any defaults during the period, the carrying amount of loans payable in default at the end of the reporting period and whether the default was remedied before the financial statements were authorised for issue.
Statement of comprehensive income	
Items of income, expense, gains or losses (para.20)	• Net gains or losses for each category of financial asset and financial liability. • Total interest income and total interest expense for financial assets or liabilities that are not at fair value through profit and loss. • Fee income and expense arising from financial assets or liabilities not at fair value through profit and loss, and from trust and other fiduciary activities. • Interest income on impaired financial assets. • The amount of any impairment loss for each class of financial asset.

It should be noted that IFRS 7 does not prescribe how statement of comprehensive income amounts are determined. For example, interest income on financial instruments carried at fair value through profit and loss may be included in total interest income or it may be included in net gains or losses for that category.

TABLE 5.6 Significance of financial instruments for other disclosures

Other disclosures	
Overall requirement	**Summary of details required**
Accounting policies (para. 21)	• Disclose relevant accounting policies. Where the accounting methods are prescribed in the relevant standards (e.g. in IAS 39) then the entity should not repeat these but rather disclose where it has applied choices available, for example, what criteria it used in designating financial assets as available-for-sale, or what criteria it used to determine whether there is objective evidence of impairment of financial assets.
Hedge accounting (paras. 22, 23 and 24)	• For each type of hedge identified in IAS 39 (i.e. fair value hedges, cash flow hedges and hedges of net investments in foreign operations), disclose a description of each type, the financial instruments designated as hedging instruments and their fair values at the reporting date and the nature of the risks being hedged. • Additional details are required for cash flow hedges, including the periods when the cash flows are expected to occur, forecast transactions not expected to occur, the ineffectiveness recognised in profit and loss and the amount recognised in and removed from equity during the period. • Additional details are required for fair value hedges: the gains or losses on the hedging instrument and on the hedged item.
Fair value (paras. 25–30)	• For each class of financial assets and liabilities, disclose the fair value of that class in a way that permits it to be compared with its carrying amount. • Disclose the methods and assumptions used in determining fair value. • If fair values are determined using valuation techniques (rather than quoted market prices) a sensitivity analysis is required. This means the entity is required to quantify the effect on profit and loss if one or more of the assumptions used, if changed, would change fair value significantly. • Other details are required in respect of gains or losses arising on initial recognition of certain financial instruments.

Table 5.7 shows the disclosure requirements for the risks arising from financial instruments.

TABLE 5.7 Nature and extent of risks arising from financial instruments

Qualitative disclosures	
Overall requirement	**Summary of details required**
For each type of risk (credit risk, liquidity risk and market risk) disclose... (para. 33)	(a) the exposures to risk and how they arise (b) the entity's objectives, policies and processes for managing the risk and the methods used to measure the risk (c) any changes in (a) or (b) from the previous period. The policies and processes an entity uses would normally include the structure and organisation of its risk management function, the policies for hedging or otherwise mitigating risks, processes for monitoring hedge effectiveness, and policies and processes for avoiding large concentrations of risk.

Quantitative disclosures	
Overall requirement	**Summary of details required**
For each type of risk (credit risk, liquidity risk and market risk) disclose... (para. 34)	(a) summary quantitative data about its exposure to that risk at the end of the reporting period. This disclosure must be based on the information provided internally to key management personnel of the entity (as defined in IAS 24 *Related Party Disclosures*) (b) the disclosures required by paragraphs 36–42 (see below) to the extent not provided in (a) (c) concentrations of risk if not apparent from (a) and (b). AG B8 states that concentrations of risk arise from financial instruments that have similar characteristics and are affected similarly by changes in economic or other conditions. For example a risk concentration may be geographic area, by industry or by currency.
Credit risk — disclose by class of financial instrument... (para. 36)	(a) the amount that best represents its maximum exposure to credit risk at the end of the reporting period without taking into account any collateral held (this amount would typically be the gross carrying amount of the asset, after deduction of any impairment losses) (b) a description of any collateral held in (a) (c) information about the credit quality of financial assets that are neither past due (past due is defined in appendix A as being when a counterparty has failed to make a payment when contractually due) or impaired (d) the carrying amount of financial assets that would otherwise be past due or impaired whose terms have been renegotiated.
Credit risk — financial assets that are either past due or impaired, disclose by class of financial instrument ... (para. 37)	(a) an analysis of the age of financial assets that are past due as at the end of the reporting period but not impaired (b) an analysis of financial assets that are individually determined to be impaired as at the end of the reporting period (c) for the amounts disclosed in (a) and (b), a description of collateral held.
Credit risk — collateral and other credit enhancements obtained (para. 38)	Specified details are required to be disclosed when an entity obtains financial or non-financial assets during the period by taking possession of collateral it holds as security.
Liquidity risk (para. 39)	(a) a maturity analysis for financial liabilities that shows the remaining contractual maturities (b) a description of how the entity manages the liquidity risk inherent in (a). An entity must use judgement to determine the appropriate time bands for a maturity analysis, that is, for when amounts fall due. For example, an entity might determine that the following time bands are appropriate: • not later than 1 month • between 1 month and 3 months • between 3 months and 6 months • later than 6 months. The Application Guidance (B14) states that the amounts disclosed in the maturity analysis must be the contractual *un*discounted cash flows. This could be problematic for liabilities that mature later than 1 year because the amounts disclosed in the note would likely not reconcile to the statement of financial position where the discounted amount would be shown. Examples of how an entity might manage liquidity risk include: • having access to undrawn loan commitments • holding readily liquid financial assets than can be sold to meet liquidity needs • having diverse funding sources.

(continued)

TABLE 5.7 *(continued)*

Overall requirement	Summary of details required
Market risk — sensitivity analysis (paras. 40 and 41)	An entity must disclose (a) for each type of market risk (i.e. currency risk, interest rate risk and other price risk) a sensitivity analysis showing how profit or loss or equity would have been affected by changes in the relevant risk variable that were reasonably possible at the end of the reporting period (b) the methods and assumptions used in preparing the sensitivity analysis (c) changes from the previous period in the methods and assumptions used. For example, if an entity has a floating interest rate (i.e. variable) liability at the end of the year, the entity would disclose the effect on interest expense for the current year if interest rates had varied by reasonably possible amounts. This effect could be disclosed as a range, for example, the entity could state that had the interest rate varied by between 0.25–0.5% then total interest expense would have increased by an amount of between $xx and $xy. If an entity prepares a sensitivity analysis that analyses the interdependencies between market risk variables (e.g. between interest rate risk and currency risk) then it need not make the disclosures in (a) but must rather disclose its own interdependent risk analysis.

5.3 IAS 39 *FINANCIAL INSTRUMENTS: RECOGNITION AND MEASUREMENT*

The stated objective of IAS 39 (see paragraph 1) is to establish principles for recognising and measuring financial assets, financial liabilities and some contracts to buy or sell non-financial items. Arguably, IAS 39 establishes rules rather than principles. Because the standard is very complex, particularly in its application to financial institutions, this chapter addresses only the more common applications of IAS 39 and aims to provide a general understanding of its requirements.

5.3.1 Scope of IAS 39

IAS 39 applies to all entities and to all types of financial instruments, with 11 exceptions set out in paragraph 2. The exceptions in themselves are complicated, so only an overview of them will be provided. The exceptions are:

1. Investments in subsidiaries, associates and joint ventures that are accounted for under IAS 27, IAS 28 and IAS 31. However, certain investments in such entities may be accounted for under IAS 39 if so permitted by IAS 27, IAS 28 and IAS 31. For example, IAS 27 permits investments in subsidiaries, associates and jointly controlled entities to be carried at cost or, under IAS 39, in the investor's own separate (not consolidated) financial statements. Also, investments in subsidiaries, associates and jointly controlled entities are measured under IFRS 5 *Non-current Assets Held for Sale and Discontinued Operations* if they are held exclusively for disposal.
2. Rights and obligations under leases to which IAS 17 *Leases* applies. However, certain lease receivables and finance lease payables are subject to the derecognition and impairment provisions of IAS 39. Also, embedded derivatives in leases are subject to IAS 39.
3. Employers' rights and obligations under employee benefit plans to which IAS 19 *Employee Benefits applies*.
4. Rights and obligations arising under insurance contracts, with certain exceptions. Insurance contracts are covered by their own standard, but contracts issued by insurers that are not insurance contracts (such as investment contracts) are covered by IAS 39. Contracts that require a payment based on climatic, geological or other physical variables are commonly used as insurance policies and payment is made based on the amount of loss to the insured entity. These contracts are caught by the standard on insurance contracts and are outside the scope of IAS 39 under this exemption. However, if the payment under the contract is *unrelated* to the insured entity's loss, then IAS 39 applies. IAS 39 also covers embedded derivatives in such contracts.
5. Financial instruments issued by the entity that meet the definition of an equity instrument in IAS 32. This applies only to the *issuer* of the equity instrument. The *holder* of such an instrument will have a financial asset that is covered by IAS 39.

6. Financial guarantee contracts, such as letters of credit, that provide for specified payments to be made to reimburse the holder of the contract for a loss it incurs because a specified debtor fails to make payment when due under a debt instrument are measured either under IFRS 4 *Insurance Contracts* or IAS 39 at the election of the issuer.
7. Contracts for contingent consideration in a business combination. This exemption applies only to the acquirer.
8. Loan commitments that cannot be settled net in cash or another financial instrument, unless the loan commitment is measured at fair value through profit or loss (see section 5.3.3 of this chapter) under IAS 39, in which case it is covered by IAS 39. Loan commitments outside the scope of IAS 39 are measured under IAS 37.
9. Contracts between an acquirer and a vendor in a business combination to buy or sell an acquiree at a future date.
10. Financial instruments to which IFRS 2 *Share-based Payment* applies.
11. Rights to payments to reimburse the entity for expenditure it is required to make to settle a liability that it recognises as a liability under IAS 37.

As discussed in section 5.2.1 of this chapter, contracts to buy or sell *non-financial* items are generally not financial instruments. Certain commodity contracts are, however, included within the scope of IAS 32. These include contracts to buy or sell non-financial items that can be settled net (in cash) or by exchanging financial instruments, or in which the non-financial item is readily convertible into cash.

Similarly, IAS 39 includes within its scope contracts to buy or sell *non*-financial items that can be settled net (in cash) or by another financial instrument, or by exchanging financial instruments. The exception to this is contracts entered into and that continue to be held for the purpose of the receipt or delivery of a non-financial item in accordance with the entity's expected purchase, sale or usage requirements (para. 5).

For example, an entity may enter into a contract to buy a machine in 2 months time for $50 000. The entity places an order and agrees to pay cash for the machine on standard credit terms after delivery. This contract is a contract for the purchase of a non-financial item and is settled *gross* in cash. The entity would not record any liability to pay for the machine until delivery of the machine because, until that time, it does not have a contractual obligation to pay the supplier since the supplier has *not* yet supplied the machine. Such a contract is outside the scope of IAS 39. However, if the entity is owed an amount of $45 000 by the supplier, and agrees to settle the purchase of the machine *net* by paying $5000 on delivery, IAS 39 catches the contract. Under IAS 39, the entity has a financial liability at the date of entering into the contract even though the machine has not yet been delivered.

The required journal entry on initial recognition of the amount owing by the supplier would be:

Amount Owed by Supplier	Dr	45 000	
Revenue (say)	Cr		45 000

At the date of entering into the contract to settle net, the journal entry would be:

Right to Receive Machine	Dr	5 000	
Financial Liability	Cr		5 000

On delivery of the machine, the journal entries would be:

Cost of Machine	Dr	45 000	
Amount Owed by Supplier	Cr		45 000
Financial liability	Dr	5 000	
Cash	Cr		5 000
Cost of Machine	Dr	5 000	
Right to Receive Machine	Cr		5 000

This accounting would be required unless the entity can prove that the contract was entered into and continues to be held for the purpose of the receipt or delivery of a non-financial item in accordance with the entity's expected purchase, sale or usage requirements. Ideally, such terms should be explicitly written into these contracts in order to avoid any doubt.

This example shows how far reaching the scope of IAS 39 is and demonstrates that it applies to contracts equally proportionately unperformed (where both parties to the contract have equal unperformed rights and obligations) unless they are specifically scoped out. Traditionally, contracts equally proportionately unperformed have not been accounted for. Common examples of such contracts are normal purchase and sale agreements, such as the purchase of the machine described above. A purchaser does not usually account for the right to receive a machine and the corresponding obligation to pay for it at the date of making a purchase order. Similarly, the supplier does not usually account for the right to receive payment for the machine, and a corresponding obligation to deliver it, at the date of receiving the purchase order. Both parties commence recognition at the date of delivery, which is the date at which the equally unperformed rights and obligations are performed. IAS 39 clearly requires accounting on a rights and obligations basis unless the contracts giving rise to those rights and obligations are scoped out of the standard — hence the scoping out of normal purchases and sales of nonfinancial items. However, as soon as the contract becomes something other than normal, with terms that embody financial assets and liabilities (as in the example above), a rights-and-obligations approach is required.

5.3.2 Derivatives and embedded derivatives

Paragraph 9 of IAS 39 defines a derivative. As explained in section 5.2.3 of this chapter, derivatives *derive* their value from another underlying item such as a share price or an interest rate. The definition requires *all* of the following three characteristics to be met:

- its value must change in response to a change in an underlying variable such as a specified interest rate, price, or foreign exchange rate
- it must require no initial net investment or an initial net investment that is smaller than would be required for other types of contracts with similar responses to changes in market factors
- it is settled at a future date.

Typical examples of derivatives are futures and forward, swap and option contracts. A typical option contract was discussed in section 5.2.3. A derivative usually has a notional amount, which is an amount of currency, a number of shares or other units specified in a contract. However, a derivative does not require the holder or writer to invest or receive the notional amount at the inception of the contract. In the example in figure 5.1, where Party A buys an option that entitles it to purchase 1000 shares in Company Z at $3 a share at any time in the next 6 months, the 1000 shares is the notional amount. However, a notional amount is not an essential feature of a derivative. For example, a contract may require a fixed payment of $2000 if a specified interest rate increases by a specified percentage. Such a contract is a derivative even though there is no notional amount (IAS 39, AG 9).

Many option contracts require a premium to be paid to the writer of the option. The premium is less than what would be required to purchase the underlying shares or other underlying financial instruments and thus option contracts meet the definition of a derivative.

Derivatives may exist on a stand-alone basis, or they may be embedded in other financial instruments. An embedded derivative is a component of a combined (or 'hybrid') instrument that also includes a non-derivative host contract, with the effect that some of the cash flows of the combined instrument vary in a way similar to a stand-alone instrument (IAS 39, para. 10). An embedded derivative cannot be contractually detached from the host contract, nor can it have a different counterparty from that of the host instrument.

For example, section 5.2.5 of this chapter showed that a common example of a compound financial instrument is a convertible bond or note that entitles the holder to convert the note into a fixed number of ordinary shares of the issuer. From the perspective of the *issuer*, such an instrument comprises two components: (a) a financial liability, being a contractual obligation to deliver cash/other financial assets in the form of interest payments and redemption of the note; and (b) an equity instrument, being an option issued to the holder entitling it to the right, for a specified period of time, to convert the note into a fixed number of ordinary shares of the *issuer*. The equity instrument is an embedded derivative. The issuer of the convertible note records the embedded derivative as an equity instrument under IAS 32 and this is specifically excluded from the scope of IAS 39 (para. 2(d)). The holder of the convertible note records the embedded derivative, being a derivative embedded in its financial asset, under IAS 39.

Paragraph 11 of IAS 39 requires an embedded derivative to be separated from the host contract if, and only if, the following three conditions are met:

- the economic characteristics and risks of the embedded derivative are *not closely related* to the economic characteristics and risks of the host contract
- a separate instrument with the same terms as the embedded derivative would meet the definition of a derivative
- the combined instrument is not measured at fair value through profit or loss. This means that a derivative embedded in a combined financial instrument measured at fair value through profit or loss is not separated, even if it could be separated. This is because the separated embedded derivative would be required to be measured at fair value through profit or loss anyway.

If an embedded derivative is separated, it is generally required to be measured at fair value. If fair value cannot be reliably measured, then the entire contract must be measured at fair value through profit or loss (IAS 39, paras. 12 and 9).

The following are examples of instruments where the economic characteristics and risks of the embedded derivative are *not closely related* to the economic characteristics and risks of the host contract:

- a put option embedded in a debt instrument that allows the holder to require the issuer to reacquire the instrument for an amount of cash that varies on the basis of the change in an equity or commodity price or index. This is because the host is a debt instrument and the variables are not related to the debt instrument
- an equity conversion feature embedded in a host convertible debt instrument (as discussed in section 5.2.5 of this chapter)
- an option to extend the remaining term to maturity of a debt instrument without a concurrent adjustment to the market rate of interest at the time of the extension
- commodity-indexed interest or principal payments embedded in a host debt instrument or insurance contract by which the amount of interest or principal is indexed to the price of the commodity (such as gold).

IAS 39, AG 30, contains other examples of such instruments. AG 33 goes on to give examples of instruments where the economic characteristics and risks of the embedded derivative *are* closely related to the economic characteristics and risks of the host contract. These examples are very prescriptive and not clearly principle-based.

5.3.3 The four categories of financial instruments

The four categories of financial instruments are set out in paragraph 9 of IAS 39. Table 5.8 summarises the requirements of paragraph 9 and provides common examples of financial instruments likely to fall into each of the four categories.

TABLE 5.8 The four categories of financial instruments

Category	Characteristics	Other requirements	Examples
A financial asset or financial liability *at fair value through profit or loss*	(a) It is classified as *held for trading*; or (b) Upon initial recognition it *is designated by the entity as at fair value through profit or loss*. Any financial asset or financial liability may be so designated, provided certain conditions are met, except for investments in equity instruments that do not have a quoted market price.	In order to be classified as held for trading, a financial asset or financial liability must be: (i) acquired or incurred principally for the purpose of selling or repurchasing it in the near term; (ii) part of a portfolio of identified financial instruments that are managed together and for which there is evidence of a recent actual pattern of short-term profit-taking; or (iii) a derivative (except for a derivative that is a financial guarantee contract or a hedging instrument).	Share portfolio held for short-term gains; forward exchange contract; interest rate swap; call option

(continued)

TABLE 5.8 *(continued)*

Category	Characteristics	Other requirements	Examples
Held-to-maturity investments	(a) Are *non-derivative* financial assets with *fixed or determinable payments and fixed maturity;* and (b) The entity has the *positive intention and ability to hold* these investments to maturity.	Excludes investments • designated as at fair value through profit or loss • designated as available-for-sale • that meet the definition of loans and receivables. Note that the ability to designate an investment as held-to-maturity relies heavily on management intent. Accordingly, IAS 39 contains a 'punishment' for managers who do not act according to their intent: if an entity sells or reclassifies more than an insignificant amount of held-to-maturity investments during the current financial year or the two preceding financial years, then the entity shall not classify any financial assets as held-to-maturity.	Commercial bill investments; government bonds; corporate bonds; converting notes (that will convert at a fixed date in future); fixed-term/maturity debentures
Loans and receivables	*Non-derivative* financial assets with *fixed or determinable payments* that are *not quoted* in an active market	Excludes loans and receivables: • designated as at fair value through profit or loss • intended to be sold in the near term, which must be classified as held-for-trading • designated as available-for-sale • those for which the holder may not recover substantially all of its initial investment, other than because of credit deterioration, which must be classified as available-for-sale.	Accounts receivable; loans to other entities; mortgage loans (financial institutions); credit card receivables
Available-for-sale financial assets	*Non-derivative financial assets* that are designated as available-for-sale and do not fall into any of the above three categories		Ordinary share investments; convertible notes; preference share investments

Note that only the first category in table 5.8 is applicable to financial assets and financial liabilities. All the other categories apply to financial assets only.

5.3.4 Recognition criteria

Paragraph 14 of IAS 39 states that an entity shall recognise a financial asset or a financial liability on its statement of financial position when, and only when, the entity becomes a party to the contractual provisions of the instrument. (This requirement to recognise rights and obligations arising under contractual agreements was discussed in section 5.3.1 of this chapter.) AG 35 provides other examples of applying the recognition criteria, as follows:

- Unconditional receivables and payables are recognised as assets or liabilities when the entity becomes a party to the contract and, as a consequence, has a legal right to receive or a legal obligation to pay cash. Normal trade debtors and trade creditors would fall into this category.

- Assets to be acquired and liabilities to be incurred under a firm commitment to purchase or sell goods or services are generally not recognised until at least one of the parties has performed under the agreement. However, this is subject to the rules set out in the scope paragraph of IAS 39 (discussed in section 5.3.1 of this chapter). Thus, if a firm commitment to buy or sell non-financial items is within the scope of IAS 39, its net fair value is recognised as an asset or liability on the commitment date.
- A forward contract within the scope of the standard is also recognised as an asset or liability at the commitment date. When an entity becomes party to a forward contract, the rights and obligations at the commitment date are often equal, so that the net fair value of the forward is zero. The example in figure 5.4 illustrates how a forward foreign exchange contract is accounted for on initial recognition.

Accounting for a forward foreign exchange contract on initial recognition

Company A enters into a forward foreign exchange contract with Company B to receive US$10 000 in 3 months time, at a forward rate of A$1.00 = US$0.70.

At the date of entering into the contract, the exchange rate (the spot rate at that date) was A$1.00 = US$0.68.

At the date of entering into the contract, Company A must recognise its rights and obligations under the contract, which are:

- a right to receive US$10 000 at the forward rate in 3 months time, which equals A$14 285
- an obligation to pay for the US$10 000 in 3 months time by delivering A$14 285.

Accordingly, Company A records the following journal entries on initial recognition:

Forward Foreign Exchange Receivable	Dr	14 285	
Forward Foreign Exchange Payable	Cr		14 285

However, because the net fair value of the contract is zero on initial recognition, no asset or liability is recognised.

FIGURE 5.4 Accounting for a forward foreign exchange contract on initial recognition

Note the following:

- Option contracts within the scope of the standard are recognised as assets or liabilities when the holder or writer becomes a party to the contract.
- Planned future transactions, no matter how likely, are not assets and liabilities because the entity has not become a party to a contract.

5.3.5 Measurement

The measurement rules in IAS 39 address:

1. initial measurement
2. subsequent measurement
3. fair value measurement considerations ('the fair value hierarchy')
4. reclassifications
5. gains and losses
6. impairment and uncollectability of financial assets.

The rules are applied distinctly to each of the four categories of financial instruments discussed in section 5.3.3 of this chapter.

1. Initial measurement

Paragraph 43 of IAS 39 requires that, on initial recognition, financial assets and financial liabilities must be measured at fair value. Fair value is defined in paragraph 9 as:

> the amount for which an asset could be exchanged, or a liability settled, between knowledgeable, willing parties in an arm's length transaction.

The concept of fair value will be discussed later in this section.

In addition, paragraph 43 requires that transaction costs directly attributable to the acquisition or issue of the financial asset or liability must be added to the fair value, except for financial assets and liabilities measured at fair value through profit or loss. Transaction costs are defined in paragraph 9 as:

> incremental costs that are directly attributable to the acquisition, issue or disposal of a financial asset or financial liability. An incremental cost is one that would not have been incurred if the entity had not acquired, issued or disposed of the financial instrument.

IAS 39, AG 13, provides further guidance. Examples of transaction costs include fees and commissions paid to agents, advisers, brokers and dealers; levies by regulatory agencies and securities exchanges; and transfer taxes and duties (such as stamp duties). Transaction costs do not include debt premiums or discounts, financing costs or internal administrative or holding costs.

The fair value of a financial instrument on initial recognition is normally the transaction price (the fair value of the consideration given or received). However, if part of the consideration given or received is for something other than the financial instrument, then the fair value must be estimated using valuation techniques. For example, if a company provides an interest-free loan to its employees, part of the consideration is given in the form of recognition of employee services or loyalty rather than for the entire loan itself. The fair value of the loan must be calculated by discounting the future cash flows using a market rate of interest for a similar loan (similar as to currency, term and credit rating). Any additional amount lent is accounted for as an expense unless it qualifies for recognition as some other type of asset. Figure 5.5 provides an example.

Initial measurement of an interest-free loan

Company Z provides interest-free loans to 10 employees for a 5-year term, payable at the end of 5 years. The total loan amount is $200 000. A market rate of interest for a similar 5-year loan is 5%. The present value of this receivable, being the future cash flows discounted at 5%, is approximately $157 000. Therefore, $43 000 is an expense to Company Z on initial recognition of the loan.

Company Z would record the following journal entries:

Loans Receivable	Dr	157 000	
Expenses	Dr	43 000	
Cash	Cr		200 000

FIGURE 5.5 Initial measurement of an interest-free loan

2. Subsequent measurement

Subsequent measurement depends on whether or not the item is a financial asset or financial liability, and on which of the categories applies.

Financial assets are measured as follows (IAS 39, para. 45):

1. 'At fair value through profit or loss' — at fair value. This includes all derivatives, other than those subject to the hedge accounting rules (see section 5.3.6 of this chapter).
2. Held-to-maturity investments — at amortised cost.
3. Loans and receivables — at amortised cost.
4. Available-for-sale financial assets — at fair value.

An exception is given for investments in equity instruments that do not have a quoted market price in an active market and whose fair value cannot be measured reliably. Such equity instruments, and any linked derivatives, must be measured at cost. Furthermore, if any of these financial assets are hedged items, they are subject to the hedge accounting measurement rules (see section 5.3.6 of this chapter).

Amortised cost is defined in paragraph 9 of IAS 39 as follows:

> the amount at which the financial asset or financial liability is measured at initial recognition minus principal repayments, plus or minus the cumulative amortisation using the effective interest method of any difference between that initial amount and the maturity amount, and minus any reduction (directly or through the use of an allowance account) for impairment or uncollectability.

The effective interest method is defined in paragraph 9 as:

> a method of calculating the amortised cost of a financial asset or a financial liability . . . and of allocating the interest income or interest expense over the relevant period.

The effective interest rate is defined in paragraph 9 as:

> the rate that exactly discounts estimated future cash payments or receipts through the expected life of the financial instrument or, when appropriate, a shorter period to the net carrying amount of the financial asset or financial liability.

The effective interest rate must be calculated considering all contractual terms of the instrument. It includes all fees, transaction costs, premiums and discounts. (A calculator with a finance function is needed to calculate the effective interest rate.)

Illustrative example 5.1 provides an example of how amortised cost is calculated.

ILLUSTRATIVE EXAMPLE 5.1

Calculation of amortised cost (based on IAS 39, Implementation Guidance B.26)

Company A purchases a debt instrument with a 5-year term for its fair value of $1000 (including transaction costs). The instrument has a principal amount of $1250 (the amount payable on redemption) and carries fixed interest of 4.7% annually. The annual cash interest income is thus $59 ($1250 × 0.047). Using a financial calculator, the effective interest rate is calculated as 10%. The debt instrument is classified as a held-to-maturity investment.

The following table sets out the cash flows and interest income for each period, using the effective interest rate of 10%:

A. Year	B. Amortised cost at beginning of year	C. Interest income ($B \times 10\%$)	D. Cash flows	E. Amortised cost at end of year ($B + C - D$)
2009	1 000	100	59	1 041
2010	1 041	104	59	1 086
2011	1 086	109	59	1 136
2012	1 136	113	59	1 190
2013	1 190	119	59 + 1 250	—

The journal entries to record this transaction on initial recognition and throughout the life of the instrument are as follows:

On initial recognition in 2009:

Held-to-Maturity Investment	Dr	1 000	
Cash	Cr		1 000

On recognition of interest in 2009:

Held-to-Maturity Investment	Dr	41	
Cash	Dr	59	
Interest Income	Cr		100

On recognition of interest in 2010:

Held-to-Maturity Investment	Dr	45	
Cash	Dr	59	
Interest Income	Cr		104

On recognition of interest in 2011:

Held-to-Maturity Investment	Dr	50	
Cash	Dr	59	
Interest Income	Cr		109

On recognition of interest in 2012:

Held-to-Maturity Investment	Dr	54	
Cash	Dr	59	
Interest Income	Cr		113

On recognition of interest in 2013:

Held-to-Maturity Investment	Dr	60	
Cash	Dr	59	
Interest Income	Cr		119

On redemption of investment in 2013:

Cash	Dr	1 250	
Held-to-Maturity Investment	Cr		1 250

Financial liabilities are measured subsequent to initial recognition at amortised cost except for those designated as 'at fair value through profit or loss', which must be measured at fair value (IAS 39, para. 47). There are four exceptions to this rule:

1. Derivative liabilities linked to investments in equity instruments that do not have a quoted market price in an active market and whose fair value cannot be measured reliably. Such linked derivatives must be measured at cost. This mirrors the exemption for derivative assets.
2. Financial liabilities arising in certain circumstances when a financial asset is transferred under the derecognition rules. These are outside the scope of this chapter.
3. Financial guarantee contracts (see section 5.3.1). These are initially measured at fair value and subsequently at the *higher* of
   (i) the amount determined in accordance with IAS 37 and
   (ii) the amount initially recognised less, where appropriate, cumulative amortisation recognised in accordance with IAS 18 *Revenue*.
   A common example of a financial guarantee contract is when a parent company guarantees the debts of its subsidiary to an external financier. The parent undertakes to pay the financier in the event that the subsidiary is unable to pay.
4. Commitments to provide a loan at a below-market interest rate. The measurement rules are the same as for (3) above.

If any of these financial liabilities are hedged items, they are subject to the hedge accounting measurement rules (see section 5.3.6 of this chapter).

Illustrative example 5.2 provides an example of a financial liability measured at amortised cost.

ILLUSTRATIVE EXAMPLE 5.2

A financial liability measured at amortised cost

Company L enters into an agreement with Company B to lend it $1 million (plus transaction costs of $25 000) on 1 July 2009. The interest to be paid is 5% for each of the first 2 years and 7% for each of the next 2 years, annually in arrears. The loan must be repaid after 4 years. The annual cash interest expense is thus $50 000 ($1 million × 0.05) for each of the first

2 years and $70 000 ($1 million × 0.07) for each of the next 2 years. Using a financial calculator, the effective interest rate is calculated as 6.67%. Company B measures the financial liability at fair value on initial recognition and subsequently at amortised cost in accordance with IAS 39, paragraphs 43 and 47.

The following table sets out the cash flows and interest expense for each period, using the effective interest rate of 6.67%:

A. Year	B. Amortised cost at beginning of year	C. Interest expense ($B \times 6.67\%$)	D. Cash flows	E. Amortised cost at end of year ($B + C - D$)
2009	975 000	65 014	50 000	990 014
2010	990 014	66 015	50 000	1 006 029
2011	1 066 029	67 083	70 000	1 003 112
2012	1 003 112	66 888	70 000 + 1 000 000	—

The journal entries to record this transaction on initial recognition and throughout the life of the instrument in the books of Company B are as follows:

On initial recognition in 2009:

Cash	Dr	975 000	
Bond – Liability	Cr		1 000 000
Bond – Liability	Dr	25 000	

On recognition of interest in 2009:

Interest Expense	Dr	65 014	
Bond – Liability	Cr		15 014
Cash	Cr		50 000

On recognition of interest in 2010:

Interest Expense	Dr	66 015	
Bond – Liability	Cr		16 015
Cash	Cr		50 000

On recognition of interest in 2011:

Interest Expense	Dr	67 083	
Bond – Liability	Cr		2 917
Cash	Cr		70 000

On recognition of interest in 2012:

Interest Expense	Dr	66 888	
Bond – Liability	Cr		3 112
Cash	Cr		70 000

On repayment of liability in 2012:

Interest Expense	Dr	0	
Bond – Liability	Dr	1 000 000	
Cash	Cr		1 000 000

3. Fair value measurement considerations

Paragraph 48 of IAS 39 refers readers to paragraphs AG 69 to AG 82 for guidance in determining fair value. These paragraphs set out what has become known as 'the fair value hierarchy', which is the order in which sources of fair value should be determined. This order is as follows:

(a) active market: quoted price
(b) no active market: valuation technique
(c) no active market: equity instruments.

(a) Active market: quoted price

A financial instrument is regarded as quoted in an active market if quoted prices are readily and regularly available from an exchange, dealer, broker, industry group, pricing service or regulatory agency; and if those prices represent actual and regularly occurring market transactions on an arm's-length basis. Examples include the Australian Securities Exchange and the Sydney Futures Exchange. The existence of a quoted price in an active market is the best evidence of fair value. Appropriate market prices are determined as shown in table 5.9.

TABLE 5.9 Determining the appropriate market price

Type of financial asset/liability	Appropriate market price
Financial asset held	Current bid price (what the market is offering to buy that asset for)
Financial liability to be issued	Current bid price
Financial asset to be acquired	Current asking price or offer price (what the market is asking to sell that asset for)
Financial liability held	Current asking price or offer price

When there is an active market but a current bid or asking price is not available, then the price of the most recent transaction provides evidence of the current fair value — so long as there has been no significant change in economic circumstances since the most recent transaction.

(b) No active market: valuation technique

If the market for a financial instrument is not active, an entity establishes fair value by using a valuation technique. Valuation techniques include:

- recent arm's-length transactions
- current fair value of another instrument that is substantially the same
- discounted cash flow analysis
- option pricing models.

The valuation technique should rely as much as possible on market inputs and as little as possible on entity-specific inputs. Inputs to valuation techniques include:

- the time value of money (interest at the basic or risk-free rate); these can be derived from observable government bond rates and are often quoted in financial publications
- credit risk (the premium over the basic interest rate for credit risk)
- foreign currency exchange rates; these are quoted daily in financial publications
- equity prices
- volatility (the expected magnitude of change in the item's price).

In applying discounted cash flow analysis, an entity should use a discount rate equal to the prevailing rate of return for a similar financial instrument. The characteristics that need to be similar are the credit quality of the instrument, the term to maturity and the currency. Short-term receivables and payables with no stated interest rate (such as trade debtors and trade creditors) may be measured at the original invoice price if the effect of discounting is immaterial.

(c) No active market: equity instruments

It was seen earlier in this section that paragraph 45 of IAS 39 provides an exception for investments in equity instruments that do not have a quoted market price in an active market and whose fair value cannot be measured reliably. Such equity instruments, and any linked derivatives, must be measured at cost. AG 80 states that such an instrument *is* regarded as being reliably measurable if (a) the variability in the range of reasonable fair value estimates is not significant, and (b) the probabilities of the various estimates within the range can be reasonably assessed and used in estimating fair value.

In all cases, fair value must be calculated on the presumption that the entity is a going concern. Fair value is not, therefore, the amount that an entity would receive or pay in a forced transaction, involuntary liquidation or distressed sale.

4. Reclassifications

IAS 39 contains various prescriptive rules on the reclassification of financial instruments. The rules are aimed at preventing inconsistent gain or loss recognition and the use of arbitrage between the categories. In summary:

- Paragraph 50 of IAS 39 states that an entity shall not reclassify a financial instrument into or out of the fair value through profit or loss category while it is held or issued.
- Held-to-maturity items can or must be reclassified to the available-for-sale category. This may occur because of a change in management's intention, or because of breaking the rules allowing held-to-maturity classification (see table 5.8).
- In rare circumstances, a financial instrument may be reclassified from a fair value measurement basis to a cost basis. These are set out in paragraph 54.

In response to the financial crisis of 2007–08, in October 2008, the IASB approved and published amendments to IAS 39 and IFRS 7 to allow reclassifications of certain financial assets (1) out of the 'fair value through profit or loss' category to either the loan and receivables, available-for-sale or held-to-maturity categories, and (2) out of the 'available-for-sale' category to the loan and receivables or held-to-maturity categories. The rationale for these amendments was that, because of the lack of liquidity in financial markets, certain financial assets that were primarily traded in active markets could no longer be so traded.

The amendments were made in response to requests by regulators to enable banks to record financial assets that are no longer traded in an active market at amortised cost. The IASB suspended its normal due process in order to make the amendments quickly as it was under intense pressure to do so.

Strict conditions need to be met in order for these new reclassifications to be made. The effective date of the amendments was 1 July 2008.

5. Gains and losses

A gain or loss arising from the change in fair value or otherwise of a financial instrument that is *not* part of a hedging relationship (see section 5.3.6 of this chapter) is recognised, in accordance with the four categories, as follows (IAS 39, para. 55):

1. 'At fair value through profit or loss' — in profit or loss.
2. Held-to-maturity investments — in profit or loss. This occurs when the asset is derecognised or impaired, and through the amortisation process.
3. Loans and receivables — in profit or loss. This occurs when the asset is derecognised or impaired, and through the amortisation process.
4. Available-for-sale financial assets — directly in equity, through the statement of changes in equity. When the financial instrument is derecognised, the cumulative amount remaining in equity is removed from equity and 'recycled' back to profit or loss. This rule is subject to four exceptions, all of which must be recognised in profit or loss:
   (a) impairment losses
   (b) foreign exchange gains and losses
   (c) interest calculated using the effective interest rate method
   (d) dividends on available-for-sale equity instruments.

6. Impairment and uncollectability of financial assets

Paragraph 58 of IAS 39 states that an entity shall assess at each balance date whether there is *objective evidence* that a financial asset is impaired. Objective evidence includes observable data about the following loss events (IAS 39, paras 58–61):

(a) significant financial difficulty of the issuer
(b) a breach of contract or default in interest or principal payments
(c) a lender granting concessions to the borrower that the lender would not otherwise consider

(d) it becoming probable that a borrower will enter bankruptcy or other financial reorganisation (such as administration)
(e) the disappearance of an active market for the financial asset because of financial difficulties
(f) observable data indicating that there is a measurable decrease in the estimated future cash flows from a group of financial assets since the original recognition of those assets. This applies mainly to large groups of receivables where companies determine whether a provision for doubtful debts is required for the group. Traditionally, entities such as banks have made a 'general provision' for impairment of a group of receivables because individual customers in that group are relatively small. IAS 39 limits the creation of such general provisions to circumstances where there are observable and directly correlating data. Such data may include, for example, an increased number of delayed payments or customers reaching their maximum credit limit in the group; national or local economic conditions that correlate with defaults on the assets within the group, such as a decrease in property prices for mortgages in the relevant area; a decrease in oil prices for loans to oil producers; or an increase in the unemployment rate in the geographical area of the borrowers
(g) in respect of investments in equity instruments, significant changes with an adverse effect that have taken place in the technological, market, economic or legal environment in which the issuer operates.

Under paragraph 60, the following events are *not*, on their own, objective evidence that a financial asset is impaired:
(a) the disappearance of an active market because an entity's financial instruments are no longer actively traded
(b) a downgrade of an entity's credit rating
(c) a decline in the fair value of a financial asset below its cost/amortised cost. For example, a decline in the fair value of an investment in a fixed-term *debt instrument* that results from an increase in the risk-free interest rate does not necessarily mean that the investment is impaired, if the investment is being held to maturity. However, a significant or prolonged decline in the fair value of an investment in an *equity instrument* below its cost is objective evidence of impairment.

Impairment losses are recognised, in accordance with the four categories, as follows (IAS 39, paras. 63–70):
(a) 'At fair value through profit or loss' — not applicable — the impairment rules do not apply to such instruments.
(b) Held-to-maturity investments — the amount of the loss is measured as the difference between the asset's carrying amount and the present value of expected future cash flows discounted at the asset's original effective interest rate. The carrying amount of the asset is reduced either directly or through use of an allowance account (traditionally termed a 'provision'). The amount of the loss must be recognised in profit or loss. An impairment loss should be reversed only if there is objective evidence of an event after the impairment was recognised, such as an improvement of the debtor's credit rating. The reversal is recognised in profit and loss. The reversal must not result in the carrying amount of the asset exceeding what the amortised cost would have been had the impairment not been recognised at the date the impairment is reversed.
(c) Loans and receivables — as for held-to-maturity investments.
(d) Available-for-sale financial assets — the cumulative loss that has been recognised directly in equity must be removed from equity and recognised in profit or loss. This includes any decline in fair value already recognised in equity plus the impairment loss. Reversals of impairment losses are permitted only for investments in *debt* instruments. The requirement for objective evidence of a reversal is the same as for categories (b) and (c) above, but there is no limit on the upward reversal because the asset is measured at fair value. Reversals of impairment losses for investments in *equity* instruments through profit or loss are not permitted. Effectively, this means that the cost of the equity investment must be reset at the impaired value, and any future upward changes in fair value must be recorded directly in equity.

Once a financial asset has been written down as a result of an impairment loss, interest income is recognised thereafter using the rate of interest used to discount the future cash flows for the purpose of measuring the impairment loss (IAS 39, AG 93).

Illustrative example 5.3 builds on illustrative example 5.1 by demonstrating the calculation of an impairment loss for a held-to-maturity investment.

ILLUSTRATIVE EXAMPLE 5.3

Impairment loss on a held-to-maturity investment

Company A purchases a debt instrument with a 5-year term for its fair value of $1000 (including transaction costs). The instrument has a principal amount of $1250 (the amount payable on redemption) and carries fixed interest of 4.7% annually. The annual cash interest income is thus $59 ($1250 × 0.047). Using a financial calculator, the effective interest rate is calculated as 10%. The debt instrument is classified as a held-to-maturity investment. During 2011, the issuer of the instrument is in financial difficulties and it becomes probable that the issuer will be put into administration by a receiver. The fair value of the instrument is estimated to be $636 at the end of 2011, calculated by discounting the expected future cash flows at 10%. No cash flows are received during 2012. At the end of 2012, the issuer is released from administration and Company A receives a letter from the receiver stating that the issuer will be able to meet all of its remaining obligations, including interest and repayment of principal.

The following table sets out the cash flows and interest income for each period, using the effective interest rate of 10%:

A. Year	B. Amortised cost at beginning of year	C. Interest income ($B \times 10\%$)	D. Cash flows	E. Amortised cost at end of year ($B + C - D$)
2009	1 000	100	59	1 041
2010	1 041	104	59	1 086
2011	1 086	109	59	1 136
2012	1 136	113	59	1 190
2013	1 190	119	59 + 1 250	—

The journal entries for 2009, 2010 and 2011 are the same as set out in illustrative example 5.1. At the end of 2011, Company A records the following journal entry:

Expense (profit and loss)	Dr	500	
Held-to-Maturity Investment	Cr		500

The asset's carrying value is now $636:

A. Year	B. Amortised cost, less impairment losses, at beginning of year	C. Interest income ($B \times 10\%$)	D. Cash flows	E. Amortised cost at end of year ($B + C - D$)
2012	636	64	—	700

During 2012, Company A records interest as 10% of $636 in accordance with IAS 39, paragraph AG 93:

Held-to-Maturity Investment	Dr	64	
Interest Income	Cr		64

At the end of 2012, Company A has objective evidence that the impairment loss has been reversed. The limit on the amount of the reversal is what the amortised cost of the asset would have been at the date of reversal had the impairment loss not been recorded. According to the first table above, this amount would have been $1190 at the end of 2012. The asset's carrying value at the end of 2012 was $700, so the reversal of the impairment loss is $490 ($1190 – $700). The journal entry is as follows:

Held-to-Maturity Investment Income (profit and loss)	Dr Cr	490	 490

The journal entries for 2013 are then the same as shown in illustrative example 5.1.

Illustrative example 5.4 shows the calculation of an impairment loss on an available-for-sale investment in a debt instrument and in an equity instrument.

ILLUSTRATIVE EXAMPLE 5.4

Impairment loss on an available-for-sale investment

Part A: In a debt instrument
Company A invests in a debt instrument on 1 July 2009. At this date, the cost and fair value of the instrument is $100 000. The instrument is classified as available-for-sale and so is measured at fair value, and changes in fair value are recorded directly in equity. The following table sets out the changes in the fair value of the debt instrument, and the nature of the change in each year:

Year	Fair value change	Nature of change
2010	($10 000)	No objective evidence of impairment
2011	($20 000)	Objective evidence of impairment
2012	$15 000	Objective evidence of reversal of impairment

The journal entries (ignoring interest income) recorded by Company A are shown below:

On initial recognition on 1 July 2009:

Available-for-Sale Investment Cash	Dr Cr	100 000	 100 000

Change in fair value for 2010:

Equity Available-for-Sale Investment	Dr Cr	10 000	 10 000

Impairment loss for 2011:

Expense (profit and loss) Available-for-Sale Investment Equity	Dr Cr Cr	30 000	 20 000 10 000

(The above entry is necessary because paragraph 67 of IAS 39 requires the cumulative loss recognised in equity to be transferred to profit and loss.)

Reversal of impairment loss in 2012:

Available-for-Sale Investment Income (profit and loss)	Dr Cr	15 000	 15 000

Part B: In an equity instrument

Assume exactly the same facts as in part A, except that the investment is in an equity instrument. All the journal entries will be the same, except for the entry in 2012, which will be as follows:

Increase in fair value in 2012 (not a reversal of an impairment loss):

Available-for-Sale Investment	Dr	15 000	
Equity	Cr		15 000

Table 5.10 summarises the measurement rules of IAS 39 discussed earlier in this section of the chapter.

TABLE 5.10 Summary of the measurement rules in IAS 39

Category of financial asset/ liability	Initial measurement	Subsequent measurement	Reclassifications	Gains and losses	Impairment
A financial asset or financial liability *at fair value through profit or loss*	Fair value	Fair value, unless a hedging instrument[1] or hedged item	Not permitted except in limited specified circumstances	Recognised in profit or loss, unless a hedging instrument[1] or hedged item	Not applicable
Held-to-maturity investments	Fair value plus transaction costs	Amortised cost, unless a hedged item	May or must be reclassified to available-for-sale	Recognised in profit or loss, unless a hedged item	Loss, recognised in profit or loss. Reversal of impairment loss permitted subject to conditions. Limit on extent of reversal.
Loans and receivables	Fair value plus transaction costs	Amortised cost, unless a hedged item	Not permitted	Recognised in profit or loss, unless a hedged item	Loss, recognised in profit or loss. Reversal of impairment loss permitted subject to conditions. Limit on extent of reversal.
Available-for-sale financial assets	Fair value plus transaction costs	Fair value, unless a hedged item	Permitted in rare circumstances	Recognised in equity, unless a hedged item. Four exceptions where gains/losses must be recognised in profit or loss. Amounts in equity are recycled to profit or loss when the asset is derecognised	Loss, recognised in profit or loss. This includes any decline in fair value already recorded in equity. Reversal of impairment loss permitted only for debt investments, subject to conditions. No limit on extent of reversal. Reversal of impairment loss through profit or loss prohibited for equity investments.
Other financial liabilities	Fair value plus transaction costs with four exceptions	Amortised cost, unless a hedged item	Not permitted	Recognised in profit or loss, unless a hedged item	Not applicable

Note:

1. This category includes derivatives that may be effective hedging instruments. The financial assets in the other categories may be hedged items (the item being hedged) but cannot be hedging instruments.

5.3.6 Hedge accounting

Entities enter into hedge arrangements for economic reasons; namely, to protect themselves from the types of risks discussed in section 5.2.9 — currency risk, fair value interest rate risk, price risk and so on. Hedge accounting generally results in a closer matching of the statement of financial position effect with the profit or loss effect, and protects the statement of comprehensive income from volatility caused by changes in fair value from period to period. The hedge accounting rules in IAS 39 are very prescriptive. They are best put into perspective by remembering that the standard is based heavily on SFAS 133, and that the standard's implicit preference is for fair value measurement so that, in order to qualify for hedge accounting, entities need to meet strict specified criteria.

Two important concepts need to be understood:

1. the hedging instrument
2. the hedged item.

The hedging instrument

Paragraph 9 of IAS 39 defines a hedging instrument as:

> a designated derivative or (for a hedge of the risk of changes in foreign currency exchange rates only) a designated non-derivative financial asset or non-derivative financial liability whose fair value or cash flows are expected to offset changes in the fair value or cash flows of a designated hedged item . . .

An instrument must meet eight essential criteria for it to be classified as a hedging instrument:

1. It must be *designated* as such. This means that management must document the details of the hedging instrument and the item it is hedging, at the inception of the hedge.
2. It *must* be a *derivative* unless criterion 3 is met.
3. It is hedging *foreign currency* exchange risk, in which case it can be a non-derivative.
4. It must be expected to *offset changes* in the fair value or cash flows of the hedged item.
5. It must be with a party *external* to the reporting entity — external to the consolidated group or individual entity being reported on (para. 73). There is one exception to this rule in respect of intragroup monetary items when certain conditions are met (para. 80).
6. It *cannot be split* into component parts, except for separating the time value and intrinsic value in an option contract, and the interest element and spot price in a forward contract (para. 74).
7. A proportion of the entire hedging instrument, such as 50% of the notional amount, may be designated as the hedging instrument. However, a hedging relationship may *not be designated for only a portion of the time* period during which the hedging instrument remains outstanding (para. 75).
8. A single hedging instrument may be designated as a hedge of more than one type of risk provided that (a) the risks hedged can be identified clearly, (b) the effectiveness of the hedge can be demonstrated, and (c) there is specific designation of the hedging instrument and different risk positions (para. 76).

Examples of hedging instruments are forward foreign currency exchange contracts, interest rate swaps and futures contracts. Written options cannot be hedging instruments of the writer because the potential exposure to loss is greater than the potential gain on the hedged item (IAS 39, AG 94), so they do not meet criterion 4.

The hedged item

IAS 39 provides the following definitions:

- a hedged item (para. 9)

  > an asset, liability, firm commitment, highly probable forecast transaction or net investment in a foreign operation that (a) exposes the entity to risk of changes in fair value or future cash flows and (b) is designated as being hedged . . .

- a forecast transaction (para. 9)

  > an uncommitted but anticipated future transaction.

  An example of a forecast transaction is expected future sales or purchases.

- a firm commitment (para. 9)

  > a binding agreement for the exchange of a specified quantity of resources at a specified price on a specified future date or dates.

  An example of a firm commitment is a purchase order to buy a machine for $50 000 in 3 months time.

Paragraph 78 of IAS 39 permits groups of assets, liabilities and so on to be the hedged item, provided they have similar risk characteristics and proportionate fair value changes (para. 83). However, under paragraph 84, a net position cannot be hedged (for example, the net of a group of similar assets and similar liabilities). Certain exceptions to this were introduced in mid 2004 to meet the concerns of financial institutions that routinely hedge net positions as part of their asset/liability management. This was one of the reasons that financial institutions were initially so opposed to the introduction of IAS 39, as it would affect their standard hedging practices.

The hedged item can be a financial item or a non-financial item. If it is a *financial item*, such as an interest-bearing investment, the risk being hedged may be only *part of the total risks* in that item, provided that effectiveness can be measured (para. 81). For example, an interest-bearing investment potentially exposes the holder to interest rate risk, credit risk and price risk. The holder may choose to hedge only the interest rate exposure, or only the credit risk, and so on. The reason for this is that the component risks of financial items can be readily identified.

Note that a held-to-maturity investment cannot be a hedged item with respect to interest rate risk or prepayment risk because, by definition, the investment must be held to maturity and thus these risks should not eventuate (para. 79). However, such an instrument may be a hedged item with respect to foreign currency risk and credit risk.

However, if the hedged item is a *non-financial item*, the risk being hedged must be the *total risks* because of the difficulty in isolating and measuring the component risks in non-financial items. The only exception to this is foreign currency risk, which may be separately hedged (para. 82).

Derivatives cannot be designated as hedged items because they are deemed held for trading and measured at fair value through profit or loss.

The conditions for hedge accounting and the three types of hedge

Hedge accounting recognises the offsetting effects on profit or loss of changes in the fair values of the hedging instrument and the hedged item. Paragraph 88 of IAS 39 sets out the five conditions that must be met in order for hedge accounting to be applied:

1. At the inception of the hedge, there must be formal *designation and documentation* of the hedging relationship and the entity's risk-management objective and strategy for undertaking the hedge. That documentation must include identification of:
   - the hedging instrument
   - the hedged item
   - the nature of the risk being hedged
   - how the entity will assess hedge effectiveness.
2. The hedge must be expected to be *highly effective* in achieving offsetting changes in fair value or cash flows attributable to the hedged risk. 'Highly effective' is elaborated on in AG 105 of IAS 39, which explains that changes must almost fully offset each other and actual results must be within a range of 80%–125%. For example, if actual results are a loss on a hedging instrument of $120 and a corresponding gain on the hedged item of $100, offset can be measured by 100/120 (being 83%) or by 120/100 (being 120%). Effectiveness is assessed, at a minimum, at the time an entity prepares its interim or annual financial statements (AG 106).
3. For cash flow hedges (discussed below), a forecast transaction that is the subject of the hedge must be highly probable and must present an exposure to variations in cash flows that could affect profit or loss. 'Highly probable' is explained further in the Implementation Guidance at F3.7 as meaning a much greater likelihood than 'more likely than not' (the meaning of 'probable').
4. The effectiveness of the hedge can be reliably measured.
5. The hedge is assessed on an ongoing basis and must be determined actually to have been highly effective throughout the financial reporting periods for which the hedge was designated.

Hedge effectiveness is defined in paragraph 9 as:

> the degree to which changes in the fair value or cash flows of the hedged item that are attributable to a hedged risk are offset by changes in the fair value or cash flows of the hedging instrument.

The three types of hedging relationships are:

- fair value hedge
- cash flow hedge

- hedge of a net investment in a foreign operation as defined in IAS 21. This is accounted for in a similar manner to cash flow hedges, but will not be discussed further in this chapter.

Note the following points:

- A fair value hedge is a hedge of the exposure to changes in fair value of an asset, liability or unrecognised firm commitment.
- A cash flow hedge is a hedge of the exposure to variability in cash flows of a recognised asset or liability, or a highly probable forecast transaction.
- Paragraph 87 of IAS 39 states that a hedge of the foreign currency risk of a firm commitment may be accounted for as either a fair value hedge or a cash flow hedge.
- A simple way of remembering the difference between the two types of hedge is that a cash flow hedge locks in future cash flows, whereas a fair value hedge does not.
- The most commonly occurring hedge transactions for average reporting entities are interest rate hedges and foreign currency hedges.

As an example of a simple cash flow hedge, assume that Company B has a borrowing with lender Bank L that carries a variable rate of interest. Company B is worried about its exposure to future increases in the variable rate of interest and decides to enter into an interest rate swap with Bank S. The borrowing is the hedged item, and the risk being hedged is interest rate risk. Under the interest rate swap, Bank S pays Company B the variable interest rate, and Company B pays Bank S a specified fixed interest rate. The interest rate swap is the hedging instrument. The net cash flows for Company B are its payments of a fixed interest rate, so it has locked in its cash flows. This is therefore a cash flow hedge, assuming all the required criteria of IAS 39 are met. Figure 5.6 illustrates this example of a simple cash flow hedge.

There is no exchange of principal in an interest rate swap — the cash flows are simply calculated using the principal as the basis for the calculation. For the example illustrated in figure 5.6, assume that the hedged item is a borrowing of \$100 000 with a variable interest rate, currently 5%. The fixed rate under the interest rate swap is 6%. For the relevant period, Company B will pay Bank L \$100 000 × 5% = \$5000. Under the swap, Company B will pay a net \$1000 (receive \$100 000 × 5% and pay \$100 000 × 6%). Thus, Company B's net cash outflow is \$5000 + \$1000 = \$6000, which is the fixed rate. Note that Bank L is not a party to the swap — it continues to receive payments from Company B under its borrowing arrangement. Company B has locked in its cash flows at \$6000, and has certainty that this is what it will pay over the term of the swap. Currently the cash flows are higher than what it would pay under a variable rate, but Company B has entered into the swap in the expectation that the variable rate will rise.

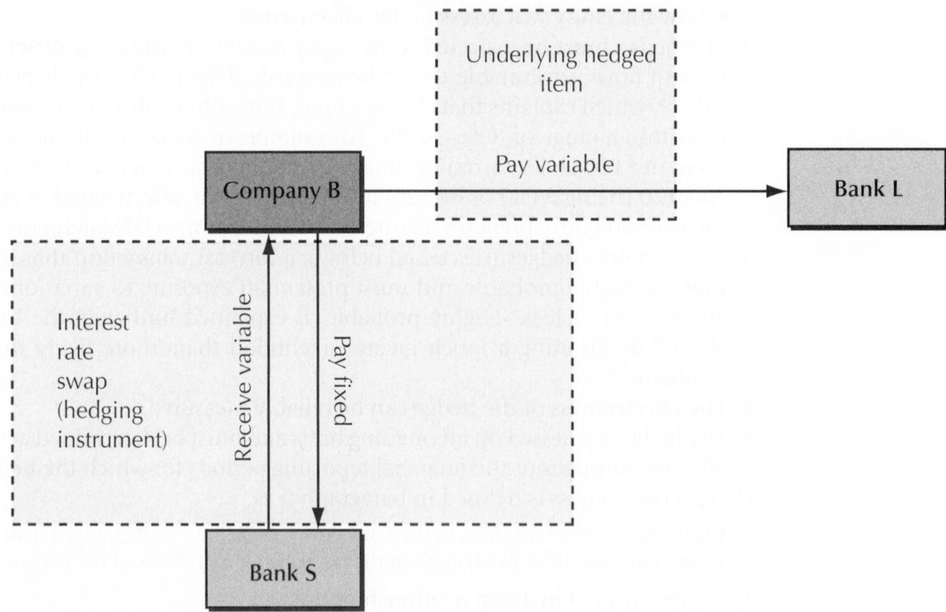

FIGURE 5.6 A simple cash flow hedge

Table 5.11 sets out the main requirements for fair value hedges and cash flow hedges.

TABLE 5.11 Summary of the main requirements of IAS 39 for fair value hedges and cash flow hedges

	Fair value hedge	Cash flow hedge
Hedged item	Fair value exposures in a recognised asset or liability or unrecognised firm commitment (para. 86)	Cash flow variability exposures in a recognised asset or liability or highly probable forecast transaction (para. 86)
Gain or loss on hedging instrument	Recognised immediately in profit and loss (para. 89)	Fully effective portion recognised directly in equity (para. 95). Ineffective portion recognised immediately in profit and loss (para. 95)
Gain or loss on hedged item	Adjust hedged item and recognise in profit and loss (para. 89). This applies even if the hedged item is otherwise measured at cost.[1] It also applies to available-for-sale investments (see exception to general rule of gain/loss recognition in section 5.3.5 of this chapter).	Not applicable because the exposure being hedged is future cash flows that are not recognised
Hedge ineffectiveness is recorded in profit or loss	Automatically, since the entire gain or loss on both the hedged item and the hedging instrument is recorded in profit and loss	Must be calculated and separated from the amount recorded in equity
Timing of recycling of hedge gains/ losses in equity to profit and loss (paras 97–100)	Not applicable	Hedge of a forecast transaction that subsequently results in the recognition of a *financial* asset or financial liability: during the periods in which said asset/ liability affects profit and loss, e.g. when the interest income or expense is recognised (para. 97) Hedge of a forecast transaction that subsequently results in the recognition of a *non-financial* asset or non-financial liability: either (a) during the periods in which said asset/liability affects profit and loss, e.g. when the depreciation expense is recognised; or (b) include immediately in the initial cost of said asset/liability (para. 98). In this case, the amount is not included in profit and loss Entities must choose between (a) or (b) as their adopted accounting policy and must apply consistently to all such transactions (para. 99)

Note:

1. If the hedged item is measured at amortised cost, then the fair value adjustment is amortised to profit or loss, using a recalculated effective interest rate (para. 92).

A simple fair value hedge is demonstrated in illustrative example 5.5.

ILLUSTRATIVE EXAMPLE 5.5

A simple fair value hedge

Company Z has an investment in an equity instrument classified as an available-for-sale investment. The cost of the investment on 1 July 2009 was $250 000. On 1 September 2009, Company Z enters into a derivative futures contract to hedge the fair value of the investment. All the conditions for hedge accounting are met, and the hedge qualifies as a fair value hedge because it is a hedge of an exposure to changes in the fair value of a recognised asset. At the next reporting date, 30 September 2009, the fair value of the investment (hedged item) was $230 000, based on quoted market bid prices. The fair value of the derivative (hedging instrument) at that date was $18 000. Company Z would record the journal entries shown below.

On initial recognition of the investment 1 July 2009:

Available-for-Sale Investment	Dr	250 000	
Cash	Cr		250 000

On entering into the futures contract 1 September 2009:
No entries because the net fair value is zero.

On remeasurement at 30 September 2009:

Expense (profit and loss)	Dr	20 000	
Available-for-Sale Investment	Cr		20 000
Futures Contract	Dr	18 000	
Income (profit and loss)	Cr		18 000

The hedge is within the effectiveness range of 85%–120% (actual range is 90%–111%), so the hedge accounting may continue. The net effect of the hedge is that Company Z records a net loss in profit and loss of $2000. The ineffective portion of the hedge ($2000) is recorded automatically in profit and loss. Note that the decline in fair value of the available-for-sale investment is recorded in profit and loss, even though the normal accounting for such investments is to recognise fair value changes directly in equity. This exception is made specifically for hedge accounting, to enable the matching effect of the hedging instrument with the hedged item in profit and loss to occur.

A cash flow hedge of a firm commitment is demonstrated in illustrative example 5.6.

ILLUSTRATIVE EXAMPLE 5.6

Cash flow hedge of a firm commitment (based on IAS 39, Implementation Guidance F.5.6)

On 30 June 2009, Company A enters into a forward exchange contract to receive foreign currency (FC) of 100 000 and deliver local currency (LC) of 109 600 on 30 June 2010. It designates the forward exchange contract as a hedging instrument in a cash flow hedge of a firm commitment to purchase a specified quantity of paper on 31 March 2010, and the resulting payable. Payment for the paper is due on 30 June 2010. All hedge accounting conditions in IAS 39 are met.

Note that a hedge of foreign currency risk in a firm commitment may be either a cash flow hedge or a fair value hedge (IAS 39, para. 87). Company A has elected to account for it as a cash flow hedge. Company A has also elected to apply IAS 39, paragraph 98(b), and adjust the cost of non-financial items acquired as a result of hedged forecast transactions.

The following table sets out the spot rate, forward rate and fair value of the forward contract at relevant dates:

Date	Spot rate	Forward rate to 30 June 2010	Fair value of forward contract
30 June 2009	1.072	1.096	—
31 December 2009	1.080	1.092	(388)[1]
31 March 2010	1.074	1.076	(1 971)
30 June 2010	1.072	—	(2 400)

Journal entries are shown below:

At 30 June 2009:

Forward Contract	Dr	LC0	
Cash	Cr		LC0
(Initial recognition of forward contract)			

On initial recognition, the forward contract has a fair value of zero (IAS 39, para. 43).

At 31 December 2009:

Equity	Dr	LC388	
Forward Contract (liability)	Cr		LC388
(Recording the change in the fair value of the forward contract)			

At 31 March 2010:

Equity	Dr	LC1 583	
Forward Contract (liability)	Cr		LC1 583
(Recording the change in the fair value of the forward contract)			
Paper (purchase price)	Dr	LC107 400	
Paper (hedging loss)	Dr	LC1 971	
Equity	Cr		LC1 971
Payable	Cr		LC107 400

The last entry recognises the purchase of the paper at the spot rate (1.074 × FC100 000), and removes the cumulative loss that has been recognised in equity and includes it in the initial measurement of the purchased paper (IAS 39, para 98(b)). The paper is thus recognised effectively at the forward rate, and the hedge has been 100% effective.

At 30 June 2010:

Payable	Dr	LC107 400	
Cash	Cr		LC107 200
Profit and Loss	Cr		LC200
(Recording settlement of the payable at the spot rate and associated exchange gain)			
Profit and Loss	Dr	LC429	
Forward Contract	Cr		LC429
(Recording loss on forward contract between 1 Apr. 10 and 30 Jun. 10)			

The forward contract has been effective in hedging the commitment and the payable up to this date. However, the loss on the contract is recognised in profit and loss because the hedge is no longer of a firm commitment but of the fair value of a recognised liability (the payable). The movement must be recorded in profit or loss because the hedge arrangement is now a fair value hedge.

Forward Contract	Dr	LC2 400	
Cash	Cr		LC2 400
(Recording net settlement of forward contract)			

If this transaction had been designated as a fair value hedge, then the entries recorded in equity for the cash flow hedge would instead be recorded as an asset or liability (IAS 39, para. 93). Paragraph 94 then requires the initial carrying amount of the asset acquired to be adjusted for the cumulative amount recognised in the statement of financial position. The adjusted journal entries would be as follows:

At 31 December 2009:

Asset	Dr	LC388	
Forward Contract (liability)	Cr		LC388
(Recording change in fair value of forward contract)			

At 31 March 2010:

Asset	Dr	LC1 583	
Forward Contract (liability)	Cr		LC1 583
(Recording change in fair value of forward contract)			
Paper (purchase price)	Dr	LC107 400	
Paper (hedging loss)	Dr	LC1 971	
Asset	Cr		LC1 971
Payable	Cr		LC107 400
(Recording purchase of paper and transferring cumulative amount recognised as an asset to the cost of the paper)			

Note:

1. This can be calculated if the applicable yield curve in the local currency is known. Assuming the rate is 6%, the fair value is calculated as follows: {([1.092 × 100 000]–109 600)/1.06(6/12)}.

Discontinuing hedge accounting

Under paragraph 91 of IAS 39, a fair value hedge must be discontinued prospectively if one of the following occurs:

(a) The hedging instrument expires or is sold, terminated or exercised.
(b) The hedge no longer meets the criteria for hedge accounting.
(c) The entity revokes the designation.

Under paragraph 101 of IAS 39, a cash flow hedge must be discontinued prospectively if one of the following occurs:

(a) The hedging instrument expires or is sold, terminated or exercised. In this case, the cumulative gain or loss that remains recognised in equity from the period when the hedge was effective should remain in equity until the forecast transaction occurs. When the transaction occurs, paragraphs 97, 98 or 100 apply.

(b) The hedge no longer meets the criteria for hedge accounting. In this case, the cumulative gain or loss that remains recognised in equity from the period when the hedge was effective should remain in equity until the forecast transaction occurs. When the transaction occurs, paragraphs 97, 98 or 100 apply.

(c) The forecast transaction is no longer expected to occur. In this case, the cumulative gain or loss that remains recognised in equity from the period when the hedge was effective should be recognised in profit or loss.

(d) The entity revokes the designation. In this case, the cumulative gain or loss that remains recognised in equity from the period when the hedge was effective should remain in equity until the forecast transaction occurs or is no longer expected to occur. When the transaction occurs, paragraphs 97, 98 or 100 apply. If the forecast transaction is no longer expected to occur, the cumulative gain or loss that remains recognised in equity from the period when the hedge was effective should be recognised in profit or loss.

The rationale behind these requirements is that hedge accounting is required for the time that the hedge was effective. If the forecast transaction occurs, then the transaction benefits from the hedge for the time that the hedge was effective. If the forecast transaction does not occur, then there is no transaction to benefit from the hedge.

SUMMARY

IAS 32 defines financial instruments, financial assets, financial liabilities and derivatives; distinguishes between financial liabilities and equity instruments. IFRS 7 prescribes disclosures. IAS 32 sets prescriptive rules for distinguishing financial liabilities from equity instruments, and for accounting for compound financial instruments that have elements of both. It requires that interest, dividends, gains and losses be accounted for consistent with the statement of financial position classification of the related financial assets and financial liabilities. It also sets prescriptive requirements for offsetting a financial asset and a financial liability.

IAS 39 requires all financial instruments including derivatives to be initially recorded at fair value. It defines an embedded derivative and establishes rules for separating an embedded derivative from the host contract. It creates four categories of financial instruments. Each category has its own rules for measurement, including initial and subsequent measurement, reclassifications, gains and losses and impairment.

IAS 39 permits hedge accounting provided that strict criteria are met. These include meeting specified conditions before hedge accounting can be applied, meeting the definition of a hedging instrument and a hedged item, and identifying which of the three types of hedge the hedge transaction meets. IAS 39 prescribes when hedge accounting must be discontinued and how the discontinuation must be accounted for. It also contains rules for the derecognition of financial instruments, but these are not addressed in this chapter.

These three standards contain more rules (and consequent exceptions to the rules) than any other IFRSs, making it difficult for preparers and users to apply the standards with confidence. Practical application of the standards, particularly IAS 39 and IFRS 7, is still in its infancy because the standards are relatively new.

Discussion questions

1. Discuss the concept of 'equity risk' and how it is useful in determining whether a financial instrument is a financial liability or an equity instrument of the issuer.
2. Discuss why the standard setters first set rules on presentation and disclosure of financial instruments before tackling recognition and measurement. Do you think the earlier creation of IAS 32 assisted in the development of IAS 39?
3. Does IAS 32 contain a clear hierarchy to be used in determining whether a financial instrument is a financial liability or an equity instrument of the issuer? Explain your answer.
4. What is the purpose of IFRS 7's disclosure requirements?
5. Describe the main risks that pertain to financial instruments.
6. Explain how a concentration of credit risk may arise for trade accounts receivable.
7. IAS 39 applies a 'rights and obligations approach' to the recognition of financial instruments. Discuss.

8. Explain what an economic hedge is. Will hedge accounting always result in the same outcome as an economic hedge?
9. Distinguish, explain and discuss the meaning of 'highly effective' and 'highly probable' in the context of the hedge accounting rules in IAS 39.

STAR RATING
★ BASIC
★★ MODERATE
★★★ DIFFICULT

Exercises

Exercise 5.1 CLASSIFICATION OF REVENUES AND EXPENSES

★ Classify the following items as statement of comprehensive income/statement of changes in equity.
(a) Dividends paid on non-redeemable preference shares
(b) Dividends paid on preference shares redeemable at the holder's option
(c) Interest paid on a 5-year, fixed interest note
(d) Interest paid on a convertible note classified as a compound instrument

Exercise 5.2 SCOPE OF IAS 32

★ Which of the following is a financial instrument (that is, a financial asset, financial liability, or equity instrument in another entity) within the scope of IAS 32? Give reasons for your answer.
(a) Cash
(b) Investment in a debt instrument
(c) Investment in a subsidiary
(d) Provision for restoration of a mine site
(e) Buildings owned by the reporting entity
(f) Forward contract entered into by a bread manufacturer to buy wheat
(g) Forward contract entered into by a gold producer to hedge the future sales of gold
(h) General sales tax payable

Exercise 5.3 SCOPE OF IAS 39

★ Which of the following is a financial instrument (that is, a financial asset, financial liability, or equity instrument in another entity) within the scope of IAS 39? Give reasons for your answer.
(a) Provision for employee benefits
(b) Deferred revenue
(c) Prepayments
(d) Forward exchange contract
(e) 3% investment in private company
(f) A percentage interest in an unincorporated joint venture
(g) A non-controlling interest in a partnership
(h) A non-controlling interest in a discretionary trust
(i) An investment in an associate
(j) A forward purchase contract for wheat to be used by the entity to make flour
(k) As for part (j), but the entity regularly settles the contracts net in cash or takes delivery of the underlying wheat and sells it shortly after making a dealer's margin
(l) Leases
(m) Trade receivables

Exercise 5.4 IMPAIRMENT

★ State whether each of the following statements is true or false.
(a) Financial assets measured 'at fair value through profit or loss' must be tested annually for impairment.
(b) A reversal of an impairment loss on a held-to-maturity investment is recognised in profit and loss.
(c) A reversal of an impairment loss on an available-for-sale investment in a debt instrument is not permitted.
(d) A reversal of an impairment loss on an available-for-sale investment in an equity instrument is not permitted.

Exercise 5.5 ★

HEDGING

State whether each of the following statements is true or false.

(a) In any hedge relationship there needs to be a hedged item and a hedging instrument.
(b) A hedging instrument must always be a derivative.
(c) A cash flow hedge locks in a reporting entity's future cash flows.
(d) A forecast transaction is an uncommitted but anticipated future transaction.
(e) In order to qualify for hedge accounting, there must be formal designation and documentation of the hedging relationship and the entity's risk-management objective and strategy for undertaking the hedge.
(f) The documentation and designation in (e) may occur at any time.

Exercise 5.6 ★★

CATEGORISING COMMON FINANCIAL INSTRUMENTS UNDER IAS 32

Categorise each of the following common financial instruments as financial assets, financial liabilities or equity instruments — of the issuer or the holder, as specified.

(a) Loans receivable (holder)
(b) Loans payable (issuer)
(c) Ordinary shares of the issuer
(d) The holder's investment in the ordinary shares in part (c)
(e) Redeemable preference shares of the issuer, redeemable at any time at the option of the holder
(f) The holder's investment in the preference shares in part (e)

Exercise 5.7 ★★

CATEGORISING COMMON FINANCIAL INSTRUMENTS UNDER IAS 39

Categorise each of the following common financial instruments in one of the four categories specified in IAS 39. Assume that the entity does not elect the 'at fair value through profit or loss category'.

(a) Loans receivable (holder)
(b) Loans payable (issuer)
(c) Ordinary shares of the issuer
(d) The holder's investment in the ordinary shares in part (c)
(e) Redeemable preference shares of the issuer, redeemable at any time at the option of the holder
(f) The holder's investment in the preference shares in part (e)

Exercise 5.8 ★★

OFFSETTING A FINANCIAL ASSET AND A FINANCIAL LIABILITY

In each of the situations below, state whether the financial asset and financial liability must be offset in the books of Company A as at 30 June 2009, and explain why.

(a) Company A owes Company B $500 000, due on 30 June 2010. Company B owes Company A $300 000, due on 30 June 2010. A legal right of set-off between the two companies is documented in writing, and the parties have indicated their intent to settle the amounts on a net basis.
(b) Company A owes Company B $500 000, due on 30 June 2010. Company B owes Company A $300 000, due on 31 March 2010. A legal right of set-off between the two companies is documented in writing, and the parties have indicated their intent to settle the amounts on a net basis whenever possible.
(c) Company A owes Company B $500 000, due on 30 June 2010. Company C owes Company A $300 000, due on 30 June 2010.
(d) Company A owes Company B $500 000, due on 30 June 2010. Company C owes Company A $500 000, due on 30 June 2010. A legal right of set-off between the three companies is documented in writing, and the parties have indicated their intent to settle the amounts on a net basis.
(e) Company A owes Company B $500 000, due on 30 June 2010. Company A has plant and equipment with a fair value of $500 000 that it pledges to Company B as collateral for the debt.

Exercise 5.9 ★★

FINANCIAL INSTRUMENTS CATEGORIES AND MEASUREMENT

Identify which of the four categories specified in IAS 39 each of the following items belongs to in the books of Company H, the holder. Also identify how each item will be measured.

(a) Forward exchange contract
(b) 5-year government bond paying interest of 5%
(c) Trade accounts receivable
(d) Trade accounts payable
(e) Mandatory converting notes paying interest of 6% (the notes must convert to a variable number of ordinary shares at the expiration of their term)
(f) Investment in a portfolio of listed shares held for capital growth
(g) Investment in a portfolio of listed shares held for short-term gains
(h) As in part (e), except that in the previous year Company H sold the majority of its held-to-maturity investments to Company Z
(i) Borrowings of $1 million, carrying a variable interest rate

Problems

Problem 5.1 ★

DISTINGUISHING FINANCIAL LIABILITIES FROM EQUITY INSTRUMENTS (1)

Company A issues 100 000 $1 convertible notes. The notes pay interest at 7%. The market rate for similar debt without the conversion option is 9%. The note is not redeemable, but it converts at the option of the holder into however many shares that will have a value of exactly $100 000.

Required
Determine whether this financial instrument should be classified as a financial liability or equity instrument of Company A. Give reasons for your answer.

Problem 5.2 ★★

DISTINGUISHING FINANCIAL LIABILITIES FROM EQUITY INSTRUMENTS (2)

Company A issues 100 000 $1 redeemable convertible notes. The notes pay interest at 5%. They convert at any time at the option of the holder into 100 000 ordinary shares. The notes are redeemable at the option of the holder for cash after 5 years. Market rates for similar notes without the conversion option are 7%.

Required
Determine whether this financial instrument should be classified as a financial liability or equity instrument of Company A. Give reasons for your answer.

Problem 5.3 ★★★

DISTINGUISHING FINANCIAL LIABILITIES FROM EQUITY INSTRUMENTS (3)

Company A issues 100 000 $1 redeemable convertible notes. The notes pay interest at 5%. They convert at any time at the option of the holder into 100 000 ordinary shares. The notes are redeemable at the option of the issuer for cash after 5 years. If after 5 years the notes have not been redeemed or converted, they cease to carry interest. Market rates for similar notes without the conversion option are 7%.

Required
Determine whether this financial instrument should be classified as a financial liability or equity instrument of Company A. Give reasons for your answer.

Problem 5.4 ★★★

DISTINGUISHING FINANCIAL LIABILITIES FROM EQUITY INSTRUMENTS (4)

Company A issues 100 000 $1 redeemable convertible notes. The notes pay interest at 5%. The notes are redeemable after 5 years at the option of the issuer for cash or for a variable number of shares (calculated according to a formula). If after 5 years the notes have not been redeemed or converted, they continue to carry interest at a new market rate to be determined at the expiration of the 5 years.

Required
Determine whether this financial instrument should be classified as a financial liability or equity instrument of Company A. Give reasons for your answer.

Problem 5.5 ★★★ DISTINGUISHING FINANCIAL LIABILITIES FROM EQUITY INSTRUMENTS (5)

Company A issues redeemable preference shares with a fixed maturity date. The shares are redeemable only on maturity at the option of the holder. The shares carry a cumulative 6% dividend.

Required
Determine whether this financial instrument should be classified as a financial liability or equity instrument of Company A. Give reasons for your answer.

Problem 5.6 ★★★ DISTINGUISHING FINANCIAL LIABILITIES FROM EQUITY INSTRUMENTS (6)

Company A issues redeemable preference shares. The shares are redeemable for cash at the option of the issuer. The shares carry a cumulative 6% dividend. In addition, the preference share dividend can be paid only if a dividend on ordinary shares is paid for the relevant period. Company A is highly profitable and has a history of paying ordinary dividends at a yield of about 4% annually without fail for the past 25 years. Company A issued the preference shares after considering various options to raise finance for building a new factory. The market interest rate for long-term debt at the time the preference shares were issued was 7%.

Required
Determine whether this financial instrument should be classified as a financial liability or equity instrument of Company A. Give reasons for your answer.

Problem 5.7 ★★★ ACCOUNTING FOR A COMPOUND FINANCIAL INSTRUMENT

The facts from example 5 of figure 5.3 are repeated below:

Company A issues 2000 convertible notes on 1 July 2009. The notes have a 3-year term and are issued at par with a face value of $1000 per note, giving total proceeds at the date of issue of $2 million. The notes pay interest at 6% annually in arrears. The holder of each note is entitled to convert the note into 250 ordinary shares of Company A at any time up to maturity.

When the notes are issued, the prevailing market interest rate for similar debt (similar term, similar credit status of issuer and similar cash flows) without conversion options is 9%. This rate is higher than the convertible note's rate because the holder of the convertible note is prepared to accept a lower interest rate given the implicit value of its conversion option.

The issuer calculates the contractual cash flows using the market interest rate (9%) to work out the value of the holder's option, as follows:

Present value of the principal: $2 million payable in 3 years time:	$1 544 367
Present value of the interest: $120 000 ($2 million × 6%) payable annually in arrears for 3 years	303 755
Total liability component	1 848 122
Equity component (by deduction)	151 878
Proceeds of the note issue	$2 000 000

Required
Prepare the journal entries to account for this transaction for each year of its term under each of the following circumstances.
(a) The holders exercise their conversion option at the expiration of the note's term.
(b) The holders do not exercise their option and the note is repaid at the end of its term.
(c) The holders exercise their option at the end of year 2.

Problem 5.8 ★★★ AMORTISED COST, JOURNAL ENTRIES

Company B issues a bond with a face value of $500 000 on 1 July 2009. Transaction costs incurred amount to $12 000. The bond pays interest at 6% per annum, in arrears. The bond must be repaid after 5 years.

Required

Prepare the journal entries to record this transaction on initial recognition and throughout the life of the bond in the books of Company B.

Problem 5.9 ★★★

EMBEDDED DERIVATIVES

Identify which of the following embedded derivatives must be separated from the relevant host contract. In each case, state also how the host contract and the embedded derivative should be measured in the books of the holder. Assume that the host instrument is not measured at fair value through profit or loss.

(a) An equity conversion feature embedded in a convertible debt instrument
(b) An embedded derivative in an interest-bearing host debt instrument, where the embedded derivative derives its value from an underlying interest rate index and can change the amount of interest that would otherwise be paid on the host debt instrument
(c) An embedded cap (upper limit) on the interest rate on a host debt instrument, where the cap is at or above the market rate of interest when the debt instrument is issued
(d) As in part (c), except that the cap is below the market rate of interest

References

Ernst & Young 2007, *IFRS 7 Financial Instruments: disclosures, second edition*.

6 Share-based payment

ACCOUNTING STANDARDS IN FOCUS

IFRS 2 *Share-based Payment*

LEARNING OBJECTIVES

When you have studied this chapter, you should be able to:

- understand the concept of a share-based payment
- distinguish between cash-settled and equity-settled share-based payment transactions
- understand and apply the accounting for equity-settled and cash-settled share-based payment transactions
- apply the requirements of IFRS 2 in respect of measuring transactions at fair value
- understand the concept of vesting
- be aware of minimum inputs to option-pricing models
- understand the concept of a share option reload feature
- apply the accounting treatment for modifications to granted equity instruments
- describe and apply the disclosure requirements of IFRS 2.

6.1 INTRODUCTION TO IFRS 2 *SHARE-BASED PAYMENT*

The purpose of this chapter is to examine share-based payments. The international accounting standard covering share-based payments is IFRS 2 *Share-based Payment*. The standard was first issued with an effective date for financial statements covering periods beginning on or after 1 January 2005. IFRS 2 has since been amended for vesting conditions and cancellations, with an effective date for these amendments of 1 January 2009. IFRS 2 was also amended by IFRS 3 *Business Combinations* as revised in 2008.

Share plans and share option plans are an increasingly common feature of remuneration for directors, senior managers and executives, and many other employees as a means of aligning employees' interests with those of the shareholders, and encouraging employee retention. The remuneration report provided by BHP Billiton in its 2008 annual report presents a rationale for engaging in share-based payment transactions with employees. It also provides examples of the types of incentives and conditions that might be incorporated into some employee share plans.

BHP Billiton's remuneration policy and structure recognises that it operates in a global environment and that corporate performance depends on the quality of its people. The overall approach and key elements embodied in BHP Billiton's remuneration policy are summarised in figure 6.1.

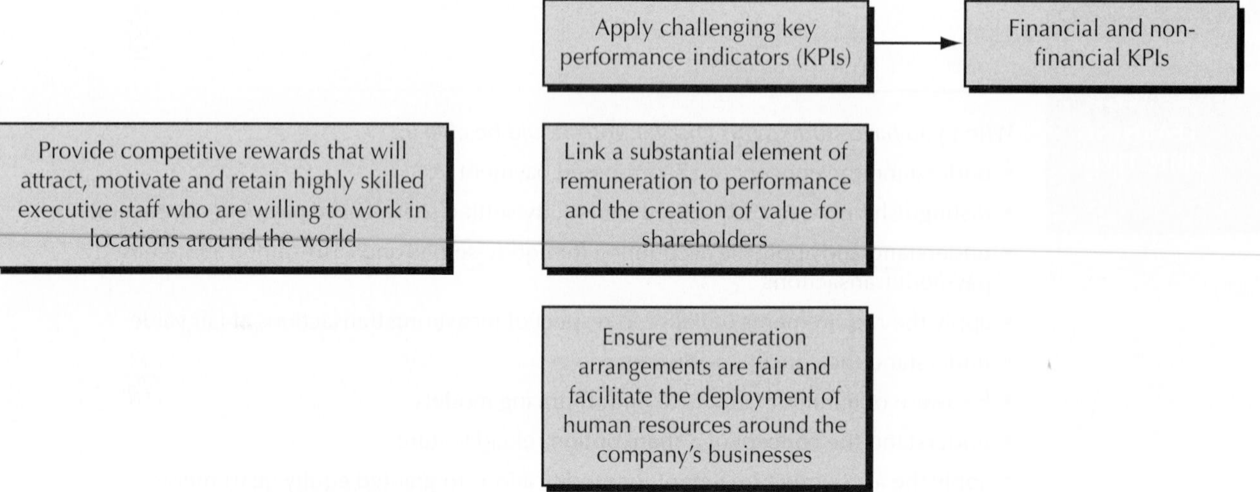

FIGURE 6.1 BHP Billiton's remuneration principles
Source: BHP Billiton (2008, p. 139).

Companies have been criticised over the size of executive remuneration, for failing to align executive incentives more closely with shareholder returns, and for using short terms (1 to 3 years) for share incentives to vest rather than longer-term incentives (5 to 10 years). A review of BHP Billiton's approach shows the inclusion of a long-term incentive component in its remuneration strategy. Companies have also been criticised for failure to disclose details of their executive performance hurdles such as return on equity rates. This lack of disclosure is usually justified on the basis of commercial sensitivity. Details of required disclosures and examples of actual disclosures are presented in section 6.6.

Some entities may also issue shares or share options to pay for the purchase of property or for professional advice or services. Before the issue of IFRS 2, there was no requirement to identify the expenses associated with this type of transaction or to measure and recognise such transactions in the financial statements of an entity. Standard setters have argued that recognising the cost of share-based payments in the financial statements of entities improves the relevance, reliability and comparability of that financial information, helps users of financial information to understand better the economic transactions affecting an entity and supports resource allocation decisions (FASB 2004).

Under IFRS 2, all such transactions with employees or other parties — whether to be settled in cash (or other assets) or equity instruments of an entity — must now be recognised in the entity's financial statements. The standard adopts the view that all share-based payment transactions ultimately lead to expense recognition, and it requires entities to reflect the effects of such transactions in profit or loss. It was generally expected that the introduction of IFRS 2 would lower the earnings of entities that are significant users of share-based payment transactions as a means of compensating their employees. Whether or not the goods or services received under share-based payment transactions are expensed immediately depends on principles for asset recognition.

BlueScope Steel Ltd, one of Australia's top 200 listed companies (by market capitalisation) applied the Australian version of IFRS 2 (AASB 2 *Share-based Payment*) from 1 January 2005. In its half-year financial statements (note 1(iv) *Share-based payments*), BlueScope Steel Ltd disclosed the measurement and accounting approaches it had taken to dealing with share-based payment transactions that vest before this date. The adverse impact of IFRS 2 (and AASB 2) on expenses is clear in the extracts from BlueScope Steel's financial statements presented in figure 6.2.

Notes to the financial statements
Interim financial report — 31 December 2005
1 Summary of significant accounting policies
(iv) Share-based payments
. . . Shares awards and rights granted before 7 November 2002 and/or vested before 1 January 2005
No expense is recognised in respect of these share awards and rights.
Shares awards and rights granted after 7 November 2002 and vested after 1 January 2005
The fair value of share awards and rights issued . . . is recognised as an employee benefit expense with a corresponding increase in equity . . .
9 Explanation of transition to Australian equivalents to IFRSs
(g) Share-based payments
. . . Upon transition to [Australian] IFRS, the Group is required to expense the fair value of share rights awarded to senior executives under the 2003 and 2004 Long Term Incentive Plans (LTIP) and any future awards. In addition, the fair value of any shares provided under the General Employee Share Plans (GESP) from 1 January 2005 onwards are required to be expensed. Under [Australian] GAAP, the shares under all these plans would have been issued at nil cost and with no expense recognised.

FIGURE 6.2 BlueScope's measurement and accounting approaches to share-based payment
Source: BlueScope Steel Ltd (2005, pp. 21, 36).

6.1.1 Scope of IFRS 2

Measurement principles and specific requirements for three forms of share-based payment transactions are dealt with in IFRS 2. The three forms of share-based payment transactions are:

1. equity-settled share-based payment transactions, in which the entity receives goods or services as consideration for equity instruments of the entity (including shares or share options)
2. cash-settled share-based payment transactions, in which the entity acquires goods or services by incurring liabilities to the supplier for amounts that are based on the value of the shares or other equity instruments of the entity
3. other transactions in which the entity receives or acquires goods or services, and the terms of the arrangement provide either the entity or the supplier (counterparty) of the goods or services with a choice of whether the transaction is settled in cash (or other assets) or by the issue of equity instruments.

The accounting treatment differs depending on the form of settlement. The three forms and the essential features of share-based payment transactions are summarised in table 6.1.

IFRS 2 does not apply to share-based payment transactions in which the entity receives or acquires goods or services as part of the net assets acquired in a business combination to which

IFRS 3 *Business Combinations* applies. This means that equity instruments issued in a business combination in exchange for control of the acquiree are not within the scope of IFRS 2. However, equity instruments granted to employees of the acquiree in their capacity as employees are within the scope of IFRS 2. Also within the scope of IFRS 2 are the cancellation, replacement or other modification of share-based payment arrangements because of a business combination or other equity restructuring. Excluded under paragraph 6 of IFRS 2 are share-based payment transactions in which the entity receives or acquires goods or services under a contract within the scope of paragraphs 8–10 of IAS 32 *Financial Instruments: Presentation* or paragraphs 5–7 of IAS 39 *Financial Instruments: Recognition and Measurement*.

TABLE 6.1 The form and features of share-based payment transactions

Form	Features
Equity-settled share-based payment	Entity receives goods or services as consideration for its own equity instruments
Cash-settled share-based payment	Entity acquires goods or services by incurring liabilities for amounts based on the value of its own equities
Other	Entity receives or acquires goods or services and the entity, or the supplier, has the choice of whether the transaction is settled in cash or equity instruments

Any transfers of an entity's equity instruments by its shareholders to parties that have supplied goods or services to the entity are considered, under paragraph 3 of IFRS 2, to be share-based payment transactions (unless the transfer is clearly for a purpose other than payment for goods or services supplied to the entity). This treatment also applies to transfers of equity instruments of the entity's parent, or equity instruments of another entity in the same group as the entity, to parties that have supplied goods or services.

A transaction with an employee in the employee's capacity as a holder of equity instruments of the entity is not regarded as within the scope of the standard (paragraph 4). If, for example, the employee is a member of a class of equity that is granted the right to acquire additional equity at a price that is less than fair value, the granting, or exercise of that right by the employee is excluded from the requirements of IFRS 2.

6.2 RECOGNITION

Paragraph 7 of IFRS 2 requires that goods or services received in a share-based payment transaction be recognised when they are received. A corresponding increase in equity must be recognised if the goods or services were received in an equity-settled share-based payment transaction, or an increase in a liability must be recognised if the goods or services were acquired in a cash-settled share-based payment transaction.

Usually an expense arises from the consumption of goods or services. For example, services are normally consumed immediately, so an expense is recognised as a service is rendered. If goods are consumed over a period of time or, in the case of inventories, sold at a later date, an expense will be recognised when the goods are consumed or sold. Sometimes it may be necessary to recognise an expense before the goods or services are consumed or sold because they do not qualify for recognition as assets. This may occur if an entity acquires goods as part of the research phase of a project. Even though the goods may not have been consumed, they will not qualify for recognition as assets under other International Financial Reporting Standards (IFRSs). When the goods or services received or acquired in a share-based payment transaction do not qualify for recognition as an asset, they must be expensed (IFRS 2, para. 8).

A share-based payment transaction would, depending on the principles for asset or liability recognition, be recognised in journal entries as shown on the next page.

Asset or Expense Equity (Recognition of an equity-settled share-based payment)	Dr Cr	XXX	 XXX
Asset or Expense Liability (Recognition of a cash-settled share-based payment)	Dr Cr	XXX	 XXX

A significant feature of IFRS 2 is the differential accounting treatment it applies to transactions settled in cash and to transactions that are equity-settled. If a share-based payment transaction is settled in cash, the general principle employed in IFRS 2 is that the goods or services received and the liability incurred are measured at the fair value of the liability. The fair value of the liability is remeasured at each reporting date and at the date of settlement, and any changes in fair value are recognised in profit or loss. For share-based payment transactions that are equity-settled, the general principal is that the goods or services received and the corresponding increase in equity are measured at the grant date at the fair value of the goods or services received. If the fair value cannot be measured reliably, the goods or services are measured indirectly by reference to the fair value of the equity instruments granted.

Under this approach a differential accounting treatment of changes in the fair value of equity instruments occurs, based on whether a transaction is classified as a liability or as equity. The fair value of transactions classified as equity is measured at grant date and subsequent value changes are ignored. In contrast, the fair value of transactions classified as liabilities (debt) are adjusted to fair value at each reporting date and the resulting profit or loss is included in income.

In the view of the AAA Committee (2004) this differential accounting treatment, based on the form of settlement, is a case of 'form over substance'. The committee has expressed a concern that it can bring with it several undesirable consequences ranging from 'transaction structuring to meet reporting goals' to 'estimate manipulation that goes uncorrected due to a lack of *truing up*' (AAA 2004, p. 66). The committee argues that items that are economically identical, such as the outflow of an entity's resources through share-based payment transactions, should be accounted for in the same way.

6.3 EQUITY-SETTLED SHARE-BASED PAYMENT TRANSACTIONS

The goods or services received in equity-settled share-based payment transactions and the corresponding increase in equity must be measured at the fair value of the goods or services unless that fair value cannot be estimated reliably (IFRS 2, para. 10). For transactions with parties other than employees, there is a rebuttable presumption in IFRS 2 (para. 13) that the fair value of goods or services can be estimated reliably. In the rare cases where the entity cannot estimate the fair value reliably, paragraph 10 requires that the goods or services and the corresponding increase in equity be measured indirectly by reference to the fair value of the equity instruments granted at the date the goods are obtained or the counterparty renders the service.

It is normally considered that the fair value of services received in transactions with employees cannot be measured reliably. Thus, the fair value of the services received from employees is measured by reference to the equity instruments granted, at grant date. In summary, under IFRS 2, equity-settled share-based payments are measured and recognised as follows:

Asset or Expense Equity (Recognition of a share-based payment in which fair value of goods or services can be reliably estimated)	Dr Cr	Fair value of goods or services received or acquired

Asset or Expense Equity (Recognition of a share-based payment where fair value of goods or services cannot be reliably estimated)	Dr Cr	Fair value of the equity instruments granted

6.3.1 Transactions in which services are received

Certain conditions may need to be satisfied before the counterparty to a share-based payment transaction becomes entitled to receive cash (or other assets) or equity instruments of the entity. When the conditions have been satisfied, the counterparty's entitlement has *vested*.

If the equity instruments vest immediately, the counterparty is not required to serve a specified period of service before becoming unconditionally entitled to those equity instruments (IFRS 2 para. 14). On grant date, the services received would be recognised in full together with the corresponding increase in equity. However, if the equity instruments do not vest until a period of service has been completed, paragraph 15 requires that the services and the corresponding increase in equity be accounted for as the services are rendered across the vesting period. This recognition approach is summarised in table 6.2.

TABLE 6.2 Vesting conditions and the recognition of services

Vesting circumstances	Treatment
Equity instrument vests immediately	Recognise the goods or services and the increase in equity on grant date
Equity instrument does not vest until the counterparty completes a period of service	Recognise the goods or services and the increase in equity as they are received across the vesting period

Source: Adapted from Parker (2005).

The granting of equity instruments in the form of share options to employees conditional on completing a 2-year period of service accounted for over the 2-year vesting period is demonstrated in illustrative example 6.1.

ILLUSTRATIVE EXAMPLE 6.1

Recognition of share options as services are rendered across the vesting period

The Ahaura Company grants 100 share options to each of its 50 employees. Each grant is conditional upon the employee working for the Ahaura Company for the next 2 years. At grant date, the fair value of each share option is estimated to be $25.

According to IFRS 2, paragraph 15(a), the Ahaura Company will recognise the following amounts during the vesting period for services received from the employees as consideration for the share options granted.

Year	Calculation	Remuneration expense for period $	Cumulative remuneration expense $
1	(100 × 50 options) × $25 × 1/2 years	62 500	62 500
2	(100 × 50 options) × $25 − $62 500	62 500	125 000

6.3.2 Transactions measured by reference to the fair value of the equity instruments granted

Determining the fair value of equity instruments granted

Paragraph 11 of IFRS 2 states that, if share-based payment transactions are with employees, it is not usually possible to measure the fair value of services received. If it is not possible to reliably estimate the value of goods or services received from other counterparties to share-based transactions, the transaction is measured by reference to the fair value of the equity instruments granted. If market prices are not available, or if the equity instruments are subject to terms and conditions that do not apply to traded equity instruments, then a valuation technique must be used to estimate what the price of the equity instruments would have been, in an arm's length transaction, on the measurement date.

While IFRS 2 (appendix B11–41) discusses the inputs to option-pricing models such as the Black–Scholes–Merton formula, the choice of model is left to the entity. The valuation technique chosen must be consistent with generally accepted valuation methodologies for pricing financial instruments. It must also account for the terms and conditions of the equity instruments (e.g. whether or not an employee is entitled to receive dividends during the vesting period), and any other factors and assumptions that knowledgeable, willing market participants would consider in setting the price. For instance, many employee share options have long lives, are usually exercisable after the vesting period and before the end of the options' life. If options are exercised early, the binomial option-pricing model might be used because such models are more versatile than the Black–Scholes model in incorporating early exercise (Saly, Jagannathan & Huddart 1999, p. 223). Option-pricing models 'typically price an option by finding a portfolio, comprised of the underlying asset and a risk-free investment, that replicates the payoffs of the option on its expiration date' (Benninga & Sarig 1997, p. 376).

Appendix B6 of IFRS 2 supplies the following list of factors that all option-pricing models take into account as a minimum:

- exercise price of the option
- life of the option
- current price of the underlying shares
- expected volatility of the share price
- dividends expected on the shares
- risk-free interest rate for the life of the option.

Expected volatility is a measure of the amount by which a price is expected to fluctuate during a period. Volatility is typically expressed in annualised terms, for example, daily, weekly or monthly price observations. Often there is likely to be a range of reasonable expectations about future volatility, dividends and exercise date behaviour. If so, an expected value should be calculated by weighting each amount within the range by its associated probability of occurrence.

Expectations about the future are generally based on experience and modified if the future is reasonably expected to differ from the past. For instance, if an entity with two distinctly different lines of business disposes of the one that was significantly less risky than the other, historical volatility may not be the best information on which to base reasonable expectations for the future. In other circumstances, historical information may not be available. For example, unlisted entities will have no historical data on share prices, and newly listed entities will have little data available.

Whether expected dividends should be taken into account when measuring the fair value of shares or options granted depends on whether the counterparty is entitled to dividends or dividend equivalents. Generally, the assumption about expected dividends is based on publicly available information.

The risk-free interest rate is the implied yield currently available on zero-coupon government issues of the country in whose currency the exercise price is expressed, with a remaining term equal to the expected term of the option being valued (IFRS 2, appendix B37). It may be necessary to use an appropriate substitute if no such government issues exist or if circumstances indicate that the implied yield on zero-coupon government issues is not representative of the risk-free interest rate (e.g. in high inflation economies).

BlueScope Steel (discussed earlier in this chapter) discloses its use of a binomial model in the determination of the grant-date fair value of share awards and rights. A relevant extract from BlueScope Steel's 2007 annual report appears in figure 6.3. BlueScope Steel provides further explanation of the inputs to the binomial option-pricing model in the remuneration report contained in its directors' report (see figure 6.4).

1 Summary of significant accounting policies
(w) Employee benefits
(iv) Share-based payments
. . . The fair value of share rights at grant date is independently determined by an external valuer using a binomial model which takes into account the exercise price, the term of the share right, the impact of dilution, the share price at grant date and expected volatility of the underlying share, the expected dividend yield and the risk free interest rate for the term of the share right.

FIGURE 6.3 BlueScope's use of option-pricing models, example 1
Source: BlueScope Steel Ltd (2008a, p. 19).

Directors' report
External valuation advice from PricewaterhouseCoopers Securities Limited has been used to determine, for accounting purposes, the value of the executive share rights at grant date for each award. The valuation has been made using an adjusted form of the Black-Scholes Option Pricing Model (BSM) that includes a Monte Carlo simulation analysis.

FIGURE 6.4 BlueScope's use of option-pricing models, example 2
Source: BlueScope Steel Ltd (2008b, p. 13).

Treatment of vesting conditions

If a grant of equity instruments is conditional on satisfying certain vesting conditions such as remaining in the entity's employment for a specified period of time, the vesting conditions are not taken into account when estimating the fair value of the equity instruments at the measurement date. Instead, vesting conditions are accounted for by adjusting the number of equity instruments included in the measurement of the transaction amount so that the amount recognised for goods or services received as consideration for the equity instrument is based on the number of equity instruments that eventually vest. On a cumulative basis, this means that if a vesting condition is not satisfied then no amount is recognised for goods or services received.

A situation where employees leave during the vesting period, and the number of equity instruments expected to vest varies, is demonstrated in illustrative example 6.2.

ILLUSTRATIVE EXAMPLE 6.2

Grant where the number of equity instruments expected to vest varies

Albury Company grants 100 share options to each of its 50 employees. Each grant is conditional on the employee working for the company for the next 3 years. The fair value of each share option is estimated to be $25. On the basis of a weighted average probability, the company estimates that 10% of its employees will leave during the 3-year period and therefore forfeit their rights to the share options.

During the year immediately following grant date (year 1) three employees leave, and at the end of year 1 the company revised its estimate of total employee departures over the full 3-year period from 10% (five employees) to 16% (eight employees). During year 2 a further two employees leave, and the company revised its estimate of total employee departures across the 3-year period down to 12% (six employees). During year 3 a further employee leaves, making a total of six (3 + 2 + 1) employees who have departed. A total of 4400 share options (44 employees × 100 options per employee) vested at the end of year 3.

Year	Calculation	Remuneration expense for period $	Cumulative remuneration expense $
1	(5 000 options × 84%) × \$25 × $\frac{1}{3}$ years	35 000	35 000
2	([5 000 options × 88%] × \$25 × $\frac{2}{3}$ years) – \$35 000	38 333	73 333
3	(4 400 options × \$25) – \$73 333	36 667	110 000

Source: Adapted from AASB 2, IG11.

In addition to continuing in employment with the entity, employees may be granted equity instruments that are conditional on the achievement of a performance condition. Where the length of the vesting period varies according to when the performance condition is satisfied, the estimated length of the vesting period at grant date is based on the most likely outcome of the performance condition (IFRS 2, para. 15(b)).

A grant of shares with a performance condition linked to the level of an entity's earnings and in which the length of the vesting period varies is demonstrated in illustrative example 6.3.

ILLUSTRATIVE EXAMPLE 6.3

Grant with a performance condition linked to earnings

At the beginning of year 1 Cambridge Company grants 100 shares to each of its 50 employees, conditional on the employee remaining in the company's employ during the 3-year vesting period. The shares have a fair value of $20 per share at grant date. No dividends are expected to be paid over the 3-year period. Additionally, the vesting conditions allow the shares to vest at the end of:

- year 1 if the company's earnings have increased by more than 18%
- year 2 if earnings have increased by more than 13% averaged across the 2-year period
- year 3 if earnings have increased by more than 10% averaged across the 3-year period.

By the end of year 1, Cambridge Company's earnings have increased by only 14% and three employees have left. The company expects that earnings will continue to increase at a similar rate in year 2 and the shares will vest at the end of year 2. It also expects that a further three employees will leave during year 2, and therefore that 44 employees will vest in 100 shares each at the end of year 2.

Year	Calculation	Remuneration expense for period $	Cumulative remuneration expense $
1	(44 employees × 100 shares) × \$20 × $\frac{1}{2}$ years	44 000	44 000

By the end of year 2 the company's earnings have increased by only 10%, resulting in an average of only 12% ([14% + 10%]/2) and so the shares do not vest. Two employees left during the year. The company expects that another two employees will leave during year 3 and that its earnings will increase by at least 6%, thereby achieving the average of 10% per year.

Year	Calculation	Remuneration expense for period $	Cumulative remuneration expense $
2	([43 employees × 100 shares] × $20 × $\frac{2}{3}$ years) – $44 000	13 333	57 333

Another three employees leave during year 3 and the company's earnings have increased by 8%, resulting in an average increase of 10.67% over the 3-year period. Therefore, the performance condition has been satisfied. The 42 remaining employees (50 – [3 + 2 + 3]) are entitled to receive 100 shares each at the end of year 3.

Year	Calculation	Remuneration expense for period $	Cumulative remuneration expense $
3	([42 employees × 100 shares] × $20) – $57 333	26 667	84 000

Source: Adapted from AASB 2, IG12.

An entity may also grant equity instruments to its employees with a performance condition and where the exercise price varies. This particular situation is demonstrated in illustrative example 6.4.

ILLUSTRATIVE EXAMPLE 6.4

Grant of equity instruments where the exercise price varies

At the beginning of year 1 Eltham Company granted 5000 share options with an exercise price of $40 to an executive, conditional upon the executive remaining with the company until the end of year 3. The exercise price drops to $30 if Eltham Company's earnings increase by an average of 10% per year over the 3-year period. On grant date the estimated fair value of the share options with an exercise price of $40 is $12 per option and, if the exercise price is $30, the estimated fair value of the options is $16 per option.

During year 1 the company's earnings increased by 12% and they are expected to continue to increase at this rate over the next 2 years. During year 2 the company's earnings increased by 13% and the company continued to expect that the earnings target would be achieved. During year 3 the company's earnings increased by only 3%. The earnings target was therefore not achieved and so the 5000 vested share options will have an exercise price of $40. The executive completed 3 years' service and so satisfied the service condition.

Year	Calculation	Remuneration expense for period $	Cumulative remuneration expense $
1	5 000 options × $16 × $\frac{1}{3}$ years	26 667	26 667
2	(5 000 options × $16 × $\frac{2}{3}$ years) – $26 667	26 666	53 333
3	(5 000 options × $12) – $53 333	6 667	60 000

Source: Adapted from AASB 2, IG12.

Because the exercise price varies depending on the outcome of a performance condition that is not a market condition, the effect of that performance condition (the possibility that the exercise price might be either $40 or $30) is not taken into account when estimating the fair value of the share options at grant date. Instead, the entity estimates the fair value of the share options at grant date and ultimately revises the transaction amount to reflect the outcome of the performance condition.

Paragraph 21 of IFRS 2 requires that market conditions (such as a target share price) be taken into account when estimating the fair value of equity instruments. The goods or services received from a counterparty who satisfies all other vesting conditions (such as remaining in service for a specified period of time) are recognised whether or not the market condition is satisfied.

A grant of equity instruments with a market condition is demonstrated in illustrative example 6.5.

ILLUSTRATIVE EXAMPLE 6.5

Grant with a market condition

At the beginning of year 1 Pakiri Company grants 5000 share options to a senior executive, conditional on that executive remaining in the company's employ until the end of year 3. The share options cannot be exercised unless the share price has increased from $15 at the beginning of year 1 to above $25 at the end of year 3. If the share price is above $25 at the end of year 3, the share options can be exercised at any time during the next 7 years (that is, by the end of year 10). The company applies an option-pricing model that takes into account the possibility that the share price will exceed $25 at the end of year 3 and the possibility that the share price will not exceed $25 at the end of year 3. It estimates the fair value of the share options with this embedded market condition to be $9 per option. The executive completes 3 years' service with the Pakiri Company.

Year	Calculation	Remuneration expense for period $	Cumulative remuneration expense $
1	5 000 options × $9 × $\frac{1}{3}$ years	15 000	15 000
2	(5 000 options × $9 × $\frac{2}{3}$ years) – $15 000	15 000	30 000
3	(5 000 options × $9) – $30 000	15 000	45 000

Source: Adapted from AASB 2, IG13.

As noted earlier, because the executive has satisfied the service condition, the company is required to recognise these amounts irrespective of the outcome of the market condition.

Treatment of non-vesting conditions

IFRS 2 was amended in 2008. The amendments clarify that vesting conditions comprise service and performance conditions only, and that other features of a share-based payment transaction are not vesting conditions.

The amendments take into account all non-vesting conditions when estimating the fair value of equity instruments granted (para. 21A, effective 1 January 2009). Under this provision, for grants of equity with non-vesting conditions, an entity must recognise the goods or services received from a counterparty that satisfies all vesting conditions that are not market conditions (such as services from an employee who remains in service for a specified period of time). This is whether or not the non-vesting conditions are satisfied.

Whether or not a condition is a non-vesting condition, or a service or performance condition, is illustrated in the flowchart in figure 6.5 on the next page.

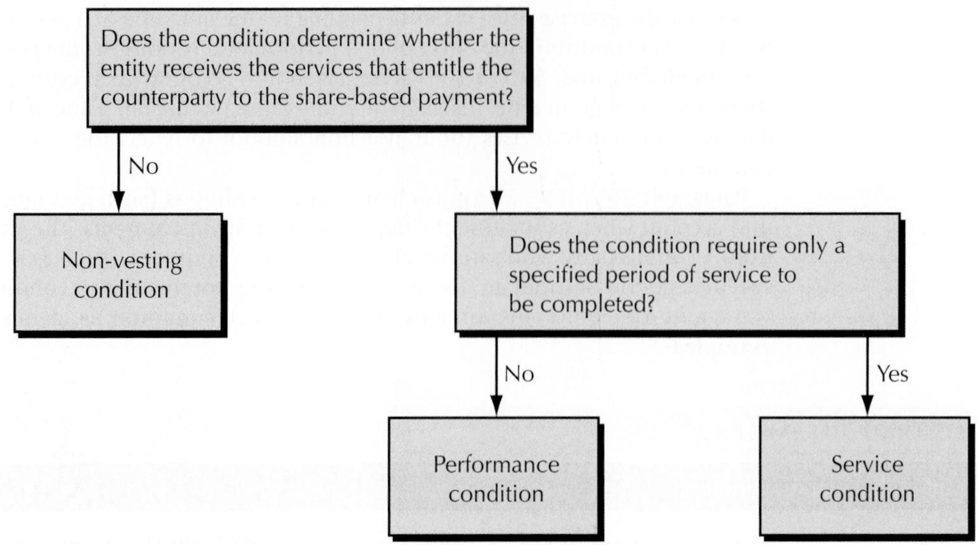

FIGURE 6.5 Distinguishing vesting and non-vesting conditions
Source: Adapted from AASB 2, IG14A.

Treatment of a reload feature

Employee share options often include features that are not found in exchange-traded options. One such feature, the reload, 'entitles the holder to automatically receive new options when the original option is exercised' (Saly, Jagannathan & Huddart 1999, p. 219). Although a reload feature can add considerably to an option's value, it is not considered feasible to value the reload feature at grant date. Under paragraph 22 of IFRS 2, a reload feature is not taken into account when estimating the fair value of the options granted at measurement date. Instead, a reload feature is accounted for as a new option grant if and when a reload option is subsequently granted.

After vesting date

Having recognised the goods or services received and a corresponding increase in equity, paragraph 23 of IFRS 2 prevents an entity from making a subsequent adjustment to total equity after vesting date. For example, if an amount is recognised for services received from an employee, it may not be reversed if the vested equity instruments are later forfeited or, in the case of share options, if the options are not subsequently exercised. This restriction applies only to total equity; it does not preclude an entity from transferring amounts from one component of equity to another.

If the fair value of the equity instruments cannot be reliably estimated

In the event that the fair value of equity instruments cannot be reliably estimated, they must instead be measured at their intrinsic value (IFRS 2, para. 24(a)). Intrinsic value is measured at the date the goods are obtained or the services rendered, at each subsequent reporting date and at the date of final settlement. Any change in intrinsic value must be recognised in profit or loss. For a grant of share options, the share-based payment arrangement is finally settled when the options are exercised or forfeited, or when they lapse. The amount to be recognised for goods or services is based on the number of equity instruments that ultimately vest or are exercised. The estimate must be revised if subsequent information indicates that the number of share options expected to vest differs from previous estimates. On vesting date, the estimate is then revised to equal the number of equity instruments that ultimately vest.

Illustrative example 6.6 provides an example of the application of the intrinsic value method of accounting for share-based payment transactions.

If share options are forfeited after vesting date or lapse at the end of the share option's life, then paragraph 24(b) of IFRS 2 requires the amount previously recognised for goods or services to be reversed.

ILLUSTRATIVE EXAMPLE 6.6

Grant of share options accounted for by applying the intrinsic value method

At the beginning of year 1, Bluff Company granted 100 share options each to its 50 employees. The share options will vest at the end of year 3 if the employees remain employed by the company at that date. The share options have a life of 5 years. The exercise price is $60, which is also Bluff Company's share price at the grant date. The company concludes that it cannot reliably estimate the fair value of the share options at the grant date.

Bluff Company's share price during years 1–5 and the number of share options exercised during years 4–5 are set out below. Share options may be exercised only at year-end.

Year	Share price at year-end	Number of share options exercised at year-end
1	63	0
2	65	0
3	75	0
4	88	2 600
5	100	1 700

A At the end of year 1 three employees have left, and the company estimates that a further seven employees will leave during years 2 and 3. Hence, only 80% of the share options are expected to vest.

Year	Calculation	Remuneration expense for period $	Cumulative remuneration expense $
A 1	(50 × 100 options × 80%) × ($63 – $60) × $\frac{1}{3}$ years	4 000	4 000

B Two employees left during year 2, and the company revises its estimate of the number of share options expected to vest to 86%.

C Two more employees leave during year 3, so there are 4300 share options vested at the end of year 3 (100 × [50 – (3 + 2 + 2)]).

Year	Calculation	Remuneration expense for period $	Cumulative remuneration expense $
B 2	(50 × 100 options × 86% × [$65 – $60] × $\frac{2}{3}$ years) – $4000	10 333	14 333
C 3	(43 × 100 options × [$75 – $60]) – $14 333	50 167	64 500

In accordance with paragraph 24 of IFRS 2, Bluff Company will recognise the following amounts in years 4 and 5:

Year	Calculation	Remuneration expense for period $	Cumulative remuneration expense $
4	(1 700 outstanding options × [$88 – $75]) + (2 600 exercised options × [$88 – $75])	55 900	120 400
5	(1 700 exercised options × [$100 – $88])	20 400	140 800*

*(1700 options × [$100 – $60]) + (2600 options × [$88 – $60])

Source: Adapted from AASB 2, IG16.

Paragraph 25 requires that if a grant of equity instruments is settled during the vesting period, the settlement must be accounted for as an acceleration of vesting, and the amount that would otherwise have been recognised for services received over the remainder of the vesting period is, instead, recognised immediately. Any payment made by the entity on settlement is accounted for as the repurchase of equity instruments (a deduction from equity). Any excess of payment amount over the intrinsic value of the equity instrument measured at repurchase date must be recognised as an expense.

6.3.3 Modifications to the terms and conditions on which equity instruments were granted

An entity might choose to modify the terms and conditions on which it granted equity instruments. For example, it might change (reprice) the exercise price of share options previously granted to employees at prices that were higher than the current price of the entity's shares; it might accelerate the vesting of share options to make the options more favourable to employees; or it might remove or alter a performance condition. If the exercise price of options is modified, the fair value of the options changes. A reduction in the exercise price would increase the fair value of share options. Irrespective of any modifications to the terms and conditions on which equity instruments are granted, paragraph 27 of IFRS 2 requires the services received, measured at the grant-date fair value of the equity instruments granted, to be recognised unless those equity instruments do not vest.

Some companies provide for retesting (repricing) to allow for the potential volatility of earnings and the cyclical nature of the market. The 2008 annual financial statements of BlueScope Steel Limited (referred to earlier in this chapter) indicate that the group has anticipated that potential volatility in its earnings could affect its share-based payments arrangements (see figure 6.6).

Directors' report
30 June 2008
Given the cyclical nature of the markets in which the Company operates, provision is generally made for limited retesting of a maximum of four retests at six monthly intervals following the initial three year performance period. This helps moderate short-term share price volatility . . . At each retest period shares only vest if they have reached the hurdles for the total period covered from the date of the initial grant.

FIGURE 6.6 Retesting (repricing) to allow for potential share price volatility, BlueScope
Source: BlueScope Steel Limited (2008b, p.13)

The incremental effects of modifications that increase the total fair value of the share-based payment arrangement, or that are otherwise beneficial to the employee, must also be recognised. The incremental fair value is the difference between the fair value of the modified equity instrument and that of the original equity instrument, both estimated at the date of modification (IFRS 2, appendix B43(a)). Similarly, if the modification increases the number of equity instruments granted, the fair value of the additional equity instruments granted, measured at the date of modification, must be included in the measurement of the amount recognised for services received.

If the modification occurs during the vesting period, the incremental fair value granted is included in the measurement of the amount recognised for services received over the period from the modification date until the date when the modified equity instruments vest, in addition to the amount based on the grant-date fair value of the original equity instruments that is recognised over the remainder of the original vesting period. If the modification occurs after the vesting date, the incremental fair value granted is recognised immediately, or over the vesting period if the employee is required to complete an additional period of service before becoming unconditionally entitled to those modified equity instruments.

The terms or conditions of the equity instruments granted may be modified in a manner that reduces the total fair value of the share-based payment arrangement or that is not otherwise beneficial to the employee. If this occurs, IFRS 2 (appendix B44) requires the services received as consideration for the equity instruments granted to be accounted for as if that modification had not occurred (that is, the decrease in fair value is not to be taken into account).

Cancellation of a grant of equity

The amendments to IFRS 2 (made in 2008, effective 1 January 2009) specified that all cancellations, whether by the entity or by other parties, should receive the same accounting treatment. IFRS 2 paragraph 28(b), as amended, requires the fair value of any liability component to be remeasured at the cancellation date. If a payment is made to settle the liability it is treated as an extinguishment of the liability.

Paragraph 28 of IFRS 2 specifies the accounting treatment if equity instruments are cancelled or settled during the vesting period. If a modification reduces the number of equity instruments granted to an employee, the reduction is to be accounted for as a cancellation of that portion of the grant. If a grant of equity instruments is cancelled during the vesting period (other than by forfeiture), the cancellation or settlement must be accounted for as an acceleration of vesting, and the amount that would otherwise have been recognised for services received over the remainder of the vesting period must be recognised immediately (IFRS 2, para. 28(a)).

If new equity instruments are granted to the employee in replacement of the cancelled instruments, the replacement equity instruments must be accounted for in the same way as a modification of the original grant (IFRS 2, para. 28(c)). The incremental fair value will be the difference between the fair value of the replacement equity instruments and the net fair value of the cancelled equity instruments at the date the replacement equity instruments are granted. The net fair value of the cancelled equity instruments is their fair value immediately before the cancellation, less the amount of any payment made to the employee on cancellation of the equity instruments that is accounted for as a deduction from equity. If new equity instruments granted are not identified as replacement equity instruments for the cancelled equity instruments, they must be accounted for as a new grant of equity instruments.

Amendments to IFRS 2 require that, from 1 January 2009, if an entity or counterparty can choose whether to meet a non-vesting condition, a failure to meet that non-vesting condition is to be treated as a cancellation (IFRS 2, para. 28A).

Illustrative example 6.7 demonstrates the accounting treatment of a cancellation when a non-vesting condition is not met by the counterparty during the vesting period.

ILLUSTRATIVE EXAMPLE 6.7

Cancellation of equity instruments when a non-vesting condition is not met

AdOil Company grants an employee, Mary Moth, the opportunity to participate in a plan in which she receives share options if she agrees to contribute to the plan 25% of her monthly salary of $400 across the next 3 years. Mary may use the accumulated savings to exercise the options at the end of the 3-year period, or take a refund of her savings at any point during this time. The estimated annual expense for this share-based payment is $150. After 18 months, Mary stops her contributions and takes a refund of her accumulated savings of $1800 ($400 × 18 × 25%).

The requirement to pay contributions to the plan is a non-vesting condition. In accordance with IFRS 2 paragraphs 28(b) and 28A, the cessation of contributions is regarded as a cancellation, and the repayment of contributions is treated as an extinguishment of the liability.

Year	Calculation	Expense $	Cash $	Liability $	Equity $
1	Salary (400 × 12 × .75)	3 600	(3 600)		
	Contribution to the plan (400 × 12 × .25)	1 200		(1 200)	
	Share-based payment	150			(150)

Year	Calculation	Expense $	Cash $	Liability $	Equity $
2	Salary (400 × 6 × .75) + (400 × 6 × 1.0)	4 200	(4 200)		
	Contribution to the plan (400 × 6 × .25)	600		(600)	
	Refund of accumulated savings		(1 800)	1 800	
	Share-based payment ([150 × 3] − 150)*	300			(300)

*Acceleration of remaining expense

Source: Adapted from AASB 2, IG15A.

Repurchases

If vested equity instruments are repurchased, IFRS 2 (para. 29) specifies that the payment made to the employee is to be accounted for as a deduction from equity. If the payment exceeds the fair value of the equity instruments repurchased, the excess is recognised as an expense.

The accounting requirements for modifications to the terms and conditions on which equity instruments were granted are summarised in table 6.3.

TABLE 6.3 Accounting requirements for modification to granted equity instruments

Modification	Accounting treatment
Modification increases the fair value of the equity instruments granted measured immediately before and after the change	*General* Include the incremental fair value granted in the amount recognised for services received *Change occurs during vesting period* In addition to the amount based on the grant-date fair value of the original equity instruments, which is recognised over the remainder of the original vesting period, include the incremental fair value in the amount recognised for services received over the period from the date of change until the date when the modified equity instruments vest *Change occurs after the vesting period* The incremental fair value granted is recognised immediately, or over the vesting period where the employee is required to complete an additional period of service before becoming unconditionally entitled to those changed equity instruments
Modification increases the number of equity instruments granted	Include the fair value of the additional equity instruments granted, measured at the date of the change, in the amount recognised for services received
Modification changes the vesting conditions in a manner that is beneficial to the employee	Take the changed vesting arrangements into account
Modification reduces the fair value of the equity instruments granted or is not otherwise beneficial to the employee	Continue to account for the services received as if that change had not occurred

Source: Adapted from e-GAAP 3/2005.

Illustrative example 6.8 demonstrates the accounting treatment of a repricing modification to the terms and conditions of share options already granted.

ILLUSTRATIVE EXAMPLE 6.8

Grant of equity instruments that are subsequently repriced

Levin Corporation grants 100 share options to each of its 50 employees, conditional upon the employee remaining in service over the next 3 years. The corporation estimates that the fair value of each option is $15. On the basis of a weighted average probability, the corporation also estimates that 10 employees will leave during the 3-year vesting period and therefore forfeit their rights to the share options.

A Four employees leave during year 1, and the corporation estimates that a further seven employees will leave during years 2 and 3. By the end of year 1 the corporation's share price has dropped, and it decides to reprice the share options. The repriced share options will vest at the end of year 3. At the date of repricing, Levin Corporation estimates that the fair value of each of the original share options is $5 and the fair value of each repriced share option is $8. The incremental value is $3 per share option, and this amount is recognised over the remaining 2 years of the vesting period along with the remuneration expense based on the original option value of $15.

Year	Calculation	Remuneration expense for period $	Cumulative remuneration expense $
A 1	(50 – 11) employees × 100 options × $15 × $\frac{1}{3}$ years	19 500	19 500

B During year 2 a further four employees leave, and the corporation estimates that another four employees will leave during year 3 to bring the total expected employee departures over the three-year vesting period to 12 employees.

Year	Calculation	Remuneration expense for period $	Cumulative remuneration expense $
B 2	([50 – 12] employees × 100 options) × ([$15 × $\frac{2}{3}$ years] + [$3 × $\frac{1}{2}$ years]) – $19 500	24 200	43 700

C A further three employees leave during year 3. For the remaining 39 employees (50 – [4 + 4 + 3]), the share options vested at the end of year 3.

Year	Calculation	Remuneration expense for period $	Cumulative remuneration expense $
C 3	([50 – 11] employees × 100 options × [$15 + $3]) – $43 700	26 500	70 200

Source: Adapted from AASB 2, IG15.

6.4 CASH-SETTLED SHARE-BASED PAYMENT TRANSACTIONS

Paragraphs 30–33 of IFRS 2 set out the requirements for share-based payment transactions in which an entity incurs a liability for goods or services received, based on the price of its own equity instruments. Such transactions are known as *cash-settled* share-based payment transactions. The fair value of the liability involved is remeasured at each reporting date and at the date of settlement, and any changes in the fair value are recognised in profit or loss for the period. In contrast, the fair value of *equity-settled* share-based payment transactions is determined at grant date, and remeasurement of the granted equity instruments at subsequent reporting dates and settlement date does not occur.

Examples of cash-settled share-based payment transactions included in paragraph 31 of IFRS 2 are share appreciation rights that might be granted to an employee as part of a remuneration package. Share appreciation rights entitle the holder to a future cash payment (rather than an equity instrument) based on increases in the share price. Another example is where an employee is granted rights to shares that are redeemable, providing the employee with a right to receive a future cash payment.

There is a presumption in IFRS 2 that the services rendered by employees in exchange for the share appreciation rights have been received. Where share appreciation rights vest immediately, the services and the associated liability must be recognised immediately. Where the share appreciation rights do not vest until the employees have completed a specified period of service, the services received and the associated liability to pay for those services are recognised as the employees render service. The liability is measured, initially and at each reporting date until settled, at the fair value of the share appreciation rights by applying an option-pricing model that takes into account the terms and conditions on which share appreciation rights were granted, and the extent to which employees have rendered service (para. 33).

Illustrative example 6.9 provides an example of the accounting treatment for cash-settled share appreciation rights.

ILLUSTRATIVE EXAMPLE 6.9

Cash-settled share appreciation rights

Brighton Company grants 100 share appreciation rights (SARs) to each of its 50 employees, conditional upon the employee not leaving the company in the next 3 years. The company estimates the fair value of the SARs at the end of each year in which a liability exists as shown below. The intrinsic values of the SARs at the date of exercise (which equal the cash paid out) at the end of years 3, 4 and 5 are also shown. All SARs held by employees remaining at the end of year 3 will vest.

Year	Fair value	Intrinsic value
1	$14.40	
2	$15.50	
3	$18.20	$15.00
4	$21.40	$20.00
5		$25.00

A During year 1 three employees leave, and the company estimates that a further six will leave during years 2 and 3.

B A further four employees leave during year 2, and the company estimates that three more employees will depart during year 3.

Year	Calculation	Expense $	Liability $
A 1	(50 – 9) employees × 100 SARs × $14.40 × $\frac{1}{3}$ years	19 680	19 680
B 2	([50 – 10] employees × 100 SARs × $15.50 × $\frac{2}{3}$ years) – $19 680	21 653	41 333

C Two employees leave during year 3.
D At the end of year 3, 15 employees have exercised their SARs.
E Another 14 employees exercise their SARs at the end of year 4.
F The remaining 12 employees exercise their SARs at the end of year 5.

Year	Calculation	Expense $	Liability $
C 3 D	([50 – 9 – 15] employees × 100 SARs × $18.20) – $41 333 15 employees × 100 SARs × $15	5 987 22 500	47 320
E 4	([26 – 14] employees × 100 SARs × $21.40) – $47 320 14 employees × 100 SARs × $20	(21 640) 28 000	25 680
F 5	(0 employees × 100 SARs × $25) – $25 680 12 employees × 100 SARs × $25	(25 680) 30 000	0
	Total	80 500	

Source: Adapted from AASB 2, IG19.

6.5 SHARE-BASED PAYMENT TRANSACTIONS WITH CASH ALTERNATIVES

Some share-based payment transactions may provide either the entity or the counterparty with the choice of having the transaction settled in cash (or other assets) or by the issue of equity instruments. If the entity has incurred a liability to settle in cash or other assets, the transaction is treated as a cash-settled share-based payment transaction. If no such liability has been incurred, paragraph 34 of IFRS 2 requires that the transaction be treated as an equity-settled share-based payment transaction. The accounting treatment is summarised in table 6.4.

TABLE 6.4 Accounting treatment of share-based payment transactions

Arrangement	Accounting treatment
A liability to settle in cash or other assets has been incurred	Cash-settled share-based payment transaction
No liability to settle in cash or other assets has been incurred	Equity-settled share-based payment transaction

Source: Adapted from e-GAAP 3/2005.

6.5.1 Share-based payment transactions where the counterparty has settlement choice

If the counterparty to a share-based payment transaction has the right to choose whether a transaction is settled in cash or equity instruments, a compound financial instrument has been created that includes a debt component and an equity component. The debt component represents the counterparty's right to demand a cash settlement, and the equity component represents the counterparty's right to demand settlement in equity instruments.

IFRS 2 (paras 35, 36) requires that transactions with employees be measured at fair value on measurement date, by taking into account the terms and conditions on which rights to cash and equity were granted. For transactions with others, in which the fair value of goods or services is measured directly, the equity component is to be measured as the difference between the fair value of the goods or services received and the fair value of the debt component at the date the goods or services are received. The fair value of the debt component must be measured before the fair value of the equity component (para. 37), allowing for the fact that the counterparty must forfeit the right to receive cash in order to receive equity instruments. The measurement of compound financial instruments with employees (and with other counterparties) is summarised in table 6.5.

TABLE 6.5 Measurement of compound financial instruments

Counterparty	Measurement approach
Employees	Measure fair value (FV) of the debt component and then FV of the equity component, at measurement date, taking into account the terms and conditions on which rights to cash or equity were granted
Parties other than employees	Equity component is the difference between FV of goods or services received and FV of the debt component, at the date the goods or services are received

The goods or services received in respect of each component of the compound financial instrument must be accounted for separately. For the debt component, the goods or services acquired and a liability to pay for those goods or services is recognised as the counterparty supplies goods or renders service, in the same manner as other cash-settled share-based payment transactions. For the equity component, the goods or services received and the increase in equity are recognised as the counterparty supplies goods or renders services, in the same manner as other equity-settled share-based payment transactions. The accounting treatment is summarised in table 6.6.

TABLE 6.6 Separate recognition of debt and equity components in compound financial instruments

Component	Recognition
Debt	Recognise goods or services acquired and the liability for payment as the counterparty supplies the goods and services
Equity	Recognise goods or services acquired and the increase in equity as the counterparty supplies the goods or services

Source: Adapted from e-GAAP 3/2005.

At settlement date, the liability must be remeasured to fair value (IFRS 2, para. 39). If equity instruments are issued rather than a settlement paid in cash, the liability must be transferred directly to equity as consideration for the equity instruments. If the counterparty elects to take a cash settlement, that payment is to be applied to settle the liability. Any equity component previously recognised must remain within equity although the issuing entity is not precluded from making a transfer within equity.

A grant of shares with a cash alternative subsequently added that provides an employee with a settlement choice is demonstrated in illustrative example 6.10.

ILLUSTRATIVE EXAMPLE 6.10

Grant of shares with a cash alternative subsequently added

At the beginning of year 1 Raglan Corporation granted 10 000 shares with a fair value of $24 per share to a senior manager, conditional on the manager remaining in the corporation's employ for 3 years. By the end of year 2 the share price had dropped to $15 per share. At that date the corporation added a cash alternative to the grant, giving the manager the right to choose whether to receive the 10 000 shares or cash equal to the value of the shares on vesting date. On vesting date the share price had dropped to $12.

Year	Calculation	Asset/expense $	Equity $	Liability $
1	10 000 shares × $24 × $\frac{1}{3}$ years	80 000	80 000	

The addition of the cash alternative at the end of year 2 created an obligation to settle in cash. The Raglan Corporation must recognise the liability to settle in cash based on the fair value of the shares at the modification date and the extent to which the specified services have been received. The liability must be remeasured at each subsequent reporting date and at the date of settlement.

Year	Calculation	Asset/expense $	Equity $	Liability $
2	(10 000 shares × $24 × $\frac{2}{3}$ years) – $80 000 10 000 shares × $15 × $\frac{2}{3}$ years	80 000	80 000 (100 000)	 100 000*

Year	Calculation	Asset/expense $	Equity $	Liability $
3	(10 000 shares × $24) – $160 000 (10 000 shares × $12) – $150 000	80 000 (30 000)	30 000	50 000* (30 000)
	Total	210 000	90 000	120 000**

* Total liability at date of modification is $150 000 ($15 × 10 000 shares).
** Total liability at date of settlement is $120 000 ($12 × 10 000 shares).

Source: Adapted from AASB 2, IG15.

An example of a share-based payment transaction in which an employee has a right to choose either a cash settlement or an equity settlement is demonstrated in illustrative example 6.11.

ILLUSTRATIVE EXAMPLE 6.11

Share-based payment transaction where employee has settlement choice

Auroa Company grants to each of its 10 senior executives a choice between receiving a cash payment equivalent to 1000 shares or receiving 1200 shares. The grant is conditional on the completion of 3 years' service with the company. If the share alternative is chosen, the shares must be held for 2 years after vesting date. At the grant date the company's share price is $25 per share. At the end of years 1, 2 and 3 the share price is $27, $28 and $30 respectively. The company does not expect to pay dividends in the next 3 years. After taking into account the effects of post-vesting transfer restrictions, the company estimates that the grant-date fair value of the share alternative is $24 per share.

The fair value of the cash alternative is $250 000 (10 × 1000 shares × $25), and the fair value of the equity alternative is $288 000 (10 × 1200 shares × $24). Therefore, the fair value of the equity component of the compound instrument is $38 000 ($288 000 – $250 000). Auroa Company will recognise the following amounts:

Year	Calculation	Asset/expense $	Equity $	Liability $
1	Liability component (10 × 1000 × $27 × $\frac{1}{3}$ years) Equity component ($38 000 × $\frac{1}{3}$ years)	90 000 12 667	 12 667	90 000
2	Liability component (10 × 1000 × $28 × $\frac{2}{3}$ years) – $90 000 Equity component ($38 000 × $\frac{1}{3}$ years)	96 667 12 667	 12 667	96 667
3	Liability component (10 × 1000 × $30) – $186 667 Equity component ($38 000 × $\frac{1}{3}$ years)	113 333 12 666	 12 666	113 333

At the end of year 3, the employees must choose whether to take the cash or shares. At settlement, the liability must be remeasured to its full value. If all employees choose the cash settlement, the liability is $300 000 (10 × 1000 × $30). If cash is paid on settlement it must be applied to settle the liability in full, with any previously recognised equity instrument remaining within equity.

Year	Calculation	Asset/expense $	Equity $	Liability $
End year 3	*Choice 1:* *Cash equivalent to 10 × 1000 shares × $30* Cash settlement of $300 000 paid Totals	 338 000	 38 000	 (300 000) 0

If the employees choose to receive shares, the liability is transferred direct to equity (IFRS 2, para. 39) as the consideration for the equity instruments that were issued. If all employees choose the equity alternative, the amount of the liability transferred to equity is $300 000.

Year	Calculation	Asset/expense $	Equity $	Liability $
End year 3	*Choice 2:* *Equity issue of 10 × 1200 shares* 12 000 shares issued Totals	 338 000	 300 000 338 000	 (300 000) 0

Source: Adapted from AASB 2, IG21.

6.5.2 Share-based payment transactions where the entity has settlement choice

Where an entity has a choice of whether to settle in cash or equity instruments, it must determine whether it has a present obligation to settle in cash. Paragraph 41 of IFRS 2 states that an entity has a present obligation to settle in cash if the choice of settlement in equity instruments has no commercial substance (perhaps the entity is legally prohibited from issuing shares), the entity has a past practice or a stated policy of settling in cash, or if it generally settles in cash whenever the counterparty asks for cash settlement. If a present obligation exists, the transaction must be accounted for as a cash-settled share-based payment transaction. If a present obligation to settle in cash does not exist, the transaction is accounted for as an equity-settled share-based payment transaction.

On settlement, if the entity elects to settle in cash, paragraph 43(a) of IFRS 2 determines that the cash payment is to be accounted for as the repurchase of an equity interest, resulting in a deduction from equity. Where there is an equity settlement, no further accounting adjustments are required. If, on settlement, the entity selects the settlement alternative with the higher fair value, at settlement date an additional expense for the excess value given must be recognised. The excess value is either the difference between the cash paid and the fair value of the equity instruments that would otherwise have been issued, or the difference between the fair value of the equity instruments issued and the amount of cash that would otherwise have been paid, whichever is applicable.

6.6 DISCLOSURES

The credit crisis of 2008 has resulted in much criticism about the inadequacy of disclosure in regard to performance hurdles and incentives used in share-based payment transactions. Corporate executives, on the other hand, complain about the onerous reporting and disclosure requirements necessary under the accounting rules. One difficulty faced by regulators is how to reduce the volume of required information yet still retain meaningful and useful disclosure.

Paragraphs 44–52 of IFRS 2 prescribe various disclosures relating to share-based payments. The objective of these disclosures is to provide significant additional information to assist financial report users to understand the nature and extent of share-based payment arrangements that existed during the reporting period. Three principles underpin the disclosures required by IFRS 2. These are that the disclosures must enable the users of the financial statements to understand:

- the nature and extent of the share-based payment arrangements (para. 44)
- how the fair value of goods or services received, or the fair value of equity instruments granted during the period, was determined (para. 46)
- the effect of share-based payment transactions on the entity's profit or loss for the period and on its financial position (para. 50).

Paragraph 45 of IFRS 2 specifies the disclosures necessary to give effect to the principle in paragraph 44 as including at least the following:

- a description of each type of share-based payment arrangement that existed at any time during the period, including the general terms and conditions of each arrangement, such as vesting requirements, the maximum term of options granted, and the methods of settlement.

An entity with substantially similar types of share-based payment arrangements may aggregate this information unless separate disclosure of each arrangement is necessary to enable users to understand the nature and extent of the arrangements.

Other specific disclosures required by paragraph 45 are the number and weighted average exercise prices of share options for options that:

- are outstanding at the beginning of the period
- are granted during the period
- are forfeited during the period
- are exercised during the period
- have expired during the period
- are outstanding at the end of the period
- are exercisable at the end of the period.

In relation to share options exercised during the period, the weighted average share price at the date of exercise must be disclosed. If the options were exercised on a regular basis throughout the period, the weighted average share price during the period may be disclosed instead. For share options outstanding at the end of the period, the range of exercise prices and weighted average remaining contractual life must be disclosed. If the range of exercise prices is wide, the outstanding options must be divided into ranges that are meaningful for assessing the number and timing of additional shares that may be issued and the cash that may be received upon exercise of those options.

If the fair value of goods or services received as consideration for equity instruments of the entity has been measured indirectly by reference to the fair value of the equity instruments granted, the following information must be disclosed (para. 47):

- the weighted average fair value of share options granted during the period, at the measurement date, and information on how the fair value was measured including:
  - the option-pricing model used and the inputs to that model including the weighted average share price, exercise price, expected volatility, option life, expected dividends, the risk-free interest rate, and any other inputs to the model including the assumptions made to incorporate the effects of expected early exercise
  - how expected volatility was determined, including an explanation of the extent to which expected volatility was based on historical volatility
  - whether, and how many, other features of the option grant (such as a market condition) were incorporated into the measurement of fair value
- for equity instruments other than share options granted during the period, the number and weighted average fair value at the measurement date, and information on how that fair value was measured, including:
  - if not measured on the basis of an observable market price, how fair value was determined
  - whether and how expected dividends were incorporated
  - whether and how any other features of the equity instruments were incorporated
- for share-based payment arrangements that were modified during the period:
  - an explanation of the modifications
  - the incremental fair value granted as a result of the modifications and information on how the incremental fair value granted was measured.

If the entity has measured the fair value of goods or services received during the period directly, it is required to disclose how that fair value was determined (e.g. at market price).

If the entity has rebutted the assumption that the fair value of goods or services received can be estimated reliably, it is required to disclose that fact (para. 49) together with an explanation of why the presumption was rebutted.

Paragraph 51 gives effect to the principle that an entity must disclose information that enables financial statement users to understand the effect of share-based payment transactions on the entity's profit or loss for the period and on its financial position. This paragraph requires disclosure of at least the following:

- the total expense recognised for the period arising from share-based payment transactions in which the goods or services received did not qualify for recognition as assets, including separate disclosure of that portion of the total expense that arises from transactions accounted for as equity-settled share-based payment transactions
- for liabilities arising from share-based payment transactions:
  - the total carrying amount at the end of the period
  - the total intrinsic value at the end of the period of liabilities for which the counterparty's right to cash or other assets had vested by the end of the period.

Finally, paragraph 52 requires the disclosure of such other additional information as may be needed to enable the users of the financial statements to understand: the nature and extent of the share-based payment arrangements; how the fair value of goods or services received, or the fair value of equity instruments granted was determined; and the effect of share-based payment transactions on the entity's profit or loss and on its financial position.

A review of the BHP Billiton Ltd 2008 annual report (discussed earlier in this chapter) shows that the remuneration report (in section 6) represents 11 pages. Appendices within this section relating to key personnel disclosures comprise five of these pages.

An extract relating to share-based payment disclosures for BlueScope Steel Ltd appears in figure 6.7.

1 Summary of significant accounting policies
(w) Employee benefits
(iv) Share-based payments
The Group provides benefits in the form of share-based payment transactions to employees . . .
There are currently three plans in place providing these share-based payment benefits:

- *The Employee Share Plan ('ESP')*
  ESP is a share awards program which, at the determination of the Board, issues eligible employees with a grant of ordinary BlueScope Steel shares . . .
- *The Long Term Incentive Plan ('LTIP')*
  LTIP is a share rights program which, at the determination of the Board, provides eligible senior managers with the right to receive ordinary BlueScope Steel shares at a later date subject to the satisfaction of certain performance criteria . . .
- *Special Share Grants and Rights*
  Special share grants and rights are awarded by the Board from time to time to meet specific or exceptional demands.

FIGURE 6.7 BlueScope's disclosure of accounting policy for share-based payments
Source: BlueScope Steel Ltd (2008a, p. 18).

Further disclosure details are provided in BlueScope's annual report. A relevant extract from the 30 June 2008 remuneration report (a section of the annual report) is provided in figure 6.8.

FIGURE 6.8 BlueScope's disclosures in relation to share-based payments

Directors' report
(b) Long Term Incentive Plan — Approach
Summary table of long term incentive plan awards

	September 2003	**September 2004**	**September 2005**	**September 2006**	**September 2007**
Grant Date	24 October 2003 (all executives excluding MD & CEO) 13 November 2003 (MD & CEO)	31 August 2004 (The grant to the MD & CEO was subject to shareholder approval at the 2004 AGM)	18 November 2005 (The grant to the MD & CEO was subject to shareholder approval at the 2005 AGM)	18 November 2006 (The grant to the MD & CEO was subject to shareholder approval at the 2006 AGM)	5 November 2007(all executives excluding MD & CEO) 14 November 2007 (MD & CEO)
Exercise Date	From 1 October 2006	From 1 September 2007	From 1 September 2008	From 1 September 2009	From 1 September 2010
Expiry Date	31 October 2008	31 October 2009	31 October 2010	31 October 2011	31 October 2012
Total Number of Share Rights Granted	3 183 800	2 306 400	1 938 100	2 310 950	1 934 845
Number of participants at Grant Date	144	201	228	206	217
Number of Current Participants	55	183	206	205	214
Exercise Price	Nil	Nil	Nil	Nil	Nil

(continued)

FIGURE 6.8 *(continued)*

	September 2003	September 2004	September 2005	September 2006	September 2007
Fair Value Estimate at Grant Date	\$9 678 752	\$11 139 912	\$7 094 170	\$11 937 799	11 468 263
Fair Value per Share Right at Grant Date	\$3.23 (24 Oct 2003) \$3.15 (13 Nov 2003)	\$5.14	\$3.89	\$5.53	\$6.37 (5 Nov 2007) \$6.42 (4 Nov 2007)
Share Rights Lapsed since Grant Date	272 345	386 941	386 671	247 580	67 310
Vesting Schedule					
TSR Hurdle — 75th–100th percentile	100%	100%	100%	100%	100%
TSR Hurdle — 51st–75th percentile	A minimum of 52% plus a further 2% for each increased percentage ranking. Any unvested Share Rights will be carried over for assessment at subsequent performance periods.				
TSR Hurdle — <51st percentile	All Share Rights will be carried over for assessment at subsequent performance periods.				
Vesting Outcome 1st Performance Period	71.42%	58%	—	—	—
Vesting Outcome 2nd Performance Period	96.84%	62.82%	—	—	—
Vesting Outcome 3rd Performance Period	100%	—	—	—	—
Vesting Outcome 4th Performance Period	—	—	—	—	—
Vesting Outcome 5th Performance Period	—	—	—	—	—

Source: BlueScope Steel Ltd (2008b, p. 14).

6.7 IASB–FASB CONVERGENCE

In February 2006, the International Accounting Standards Board (IASB) and the Financial Accounting Standards Board (FASB) (US) agreed on a convergence program. Underpinning this agreement is recognition of the need to eliminate the US GAAP (Generally Accepted Accounting Principles) reconciliation requirement for foreign groups that use IFRSs. The implementation of IFRSs should result in very positive benefits for multi-national groups as national GAAPs are swept aside and comparability between financial statements is enhanced. In turn, convergence is expected to lower the costs of raising capital, to provide better access to funding, and to result in a more efficient allocation of funding resources. The Securities and Exchange Commission (SEC) (US) has made it clear that it is not expecting complete convergence or radically new standards by the target date of 2009. Rather, the aim is to achieve a measurable progress towards convergence.

The IASB–FASB project agenda and timetable lists a range of convergence projects including IFRS 2. Amendments to IFRS 2 vesting conditions and cancellations have been actively addressed and the amended standard was released in early 2008 (effective 1 January 2009). Timing has yet to be determined on a project addressing group cash-settled share-based payment transactions (IFRS 2 and IFRIC 11).

SUMMARY

IFRS 2 deals with the recognition and measurement of share-based payment transactions. Share-based payment transactions are arrangements in which an entity receives goods or services as consideration for its own equity instruments, or acquires goods or services for amounts that are based on the price of its equity instruments. The main feature of the standard is that it requires recognition in the financial statements of the goods or services acquired or received under share-based payment arrangements, regardless of whether the form of settlement is cash or equity and regardless of whether the counterparty involved is an employee or other party.

If a share-based payment transaction is settled in cash, the general principle employed in IFRS 2 is that the goods or services received and the liability incurred are measured at the fair value of the liability. Until it is settled, the fair value of the liability is remeasured at each reporting date and at the date of settlement, and any changes in fair value are recognised in profit or loss. For transactions that are equity-settled, the general principle is that the goods or services received and the corresponding increase in equity are measured at the grant date, and at the fair value of the goods or services received. If the fair value cannot be measured reliably, the goods or services are measured indirectly by reference to the fair value of the equity instruments granted.

Another important feature of IFRS 2 is that it allows an entity to choose appropriate option-valuation models to determine fair values and to tailor those models to suit the entity's specific circumstances. Determining the fair value of options where various models may be used, and where various estimates are required, will do little to reduce ambiguity in valuation. Finally, IFRS 2 includes a lengthy set of disclosure requirements aimed at enabling financial statement users to understand the nature, extent and effect of share-based payment arrangements, and how the fair value of goods or services received or equity instruments granted was determined.

Discussion questions

1. Why do standard setters formulate rules on the measurement and recognition of share-based payment transactions?
2. What is the hierarchy, contained in IFRS 2, to be used in determining the accounting treatment for a share-based payment transaction?
3. Why are some services received in share-based payment transactions classified initially as assets rather than expenses?
4. What is the difference between equity-settled and cash-settled share-based payment transactions?
5. What is the different accounting treatment for instruments classified as debt and those classified as equity?
6. Why might market prices not be available for some equity instruments such as share options?
7. What are the factors required under IFRS 2 to be taken into account in option-pricing models?
8. When is it appropriate to use another interest rate in place of the 'risk-free' interest rate?
9. Distinguish between vesting and non-vesting conditions.
10. What is a 'reload' feature? Explain why it is not taken into account when valuing options.
11. What are the circumstances that cause a share-based payment transaction to be measured by reference to the fair value of equity instruments granted?
12. What is the difference between a debt component and an equity component that is created when a counterparty to a share-based payment transaction has settlement choice?
13. What is the definition of each of the following terms?
    (a) Vest
    (b) Reload feature
    (c) Market condition

14. Are the following statements true or false?
   (a) Goods or services received in a share-based payment transaction must be recognised when they are received.
   (b) Historical volatility provides the best basis for forming reasonable expectations of the future price of share options.
   (c) Share appreciation rights entitle the holder to a future equity instrument based on the profitability of the issuer.

STAR RATING
★ BASIC
★★ MODERATE
★★★ DIFFICULT

Exercises

Exercise 6.1 ★

SCOPE OF IFRS 2

Which of the following is a share-based payment transaction within the scope of IFRS 2? Give reasons for your answer.
(a) Goods acquired from a supplier by incurring a liability based on the market price of the goods
(b) An invoiced amount for professional advice provided to an entity, charged at an hourly rate, and to be settled in cash
(c) Services provided by an employee to be settled in equity instruments of the entity
(d) Supply of goods in return for cash or equity instruments at the discretion of the supplier
(e) Dividend payment to employees who are holders of an entity's shares

Exercise 6.2 ★

RECOGNITION PRINCIPLES

Tairua Company, a listed company, organises major sporting events. It acquires crowd control equipment in return for a liability for an amount based on the price of 1000 of its own shares.

Required
Is this a share-based payment transaction? Should Tairua Company recognise the acquisition cost as an asset or an expense? Explain.

Exercise 6.3 ★

RECOGNITION JOURNAL ENTRIES

Ohura Company received the legal title to land in exchange for the issue of 8000 of its own ordinary shares with a fair value of $5 each.

Required
Prepare an appropriate journal entry to recognise this transaction in the accounting records of Ohura Company.

Exercise 6.4 ★

CATEGORISING

An entity grants 10 000 shares to a senior manager in return for services rendered.

Required
Should the entity recognise the cost of these services as a liability or a component of equity? Explain.

Exercise 6.5 ★

EQUITY-SETTLED SHARE-BASED PAYMENT TRANSACTIONS

On 1 January 2010, Jacobs River Corporation announces a grant of 250 share options to each of its 20 senior executives. The grant is conditional on the employee continuing to work for Jacobs River Corporation for the next 3 years. The fair value of each share option is estimated to be $14. On the basis of a weighted average probability, Jacobs River Corporation estimates that 10% of its senior executives will leave during the vesting period.

Required
Prepare a schedule setting out the annual and cumulative remuneration expense to be recognised by Jacobs River Corporation for services rendered as consideration for the share options granted.

Exercise 6.6 ★

DETERMINING THE VALUE OF EQUITY INSTRUMENTS GRANTED

On 30 June 2011, the Queenstown Group granted 100 share options to each of its 20 most senior executives. As the share options are subject to certain conditions that do not apply to Queenstown's traded shares, an option-pricing model was used to determine the grant-date fair value of the options.

Required
List the factors that option-pricing models take into account.

Exercise 6.7 ★★

CASH-SETTLED SHARE-BASED PAYMENT TRANSACTIONS

An entity receives inventory from a supplier in exchange for a liability based on the price of 5000 of the entity's own shares. At the date of receiving the inventory, the entity's shares have a market value of $9.50 each.

Required
Measure the value of this transaction and prepare an appropriate journal entry to recognise it.

Exercise 6.8 ★★

MODIFICATIONS TO EQUITY-SETTLED SHARE-BASED PAYMENT TRANSACTIONS

At the beginning of year 1, the Balfour Corporation grants 50 share options to each of its 120 employees, conditional on the employee remaining in the employ of Balfour Corporation over the next 2 years. The corporation estimates that the fair value of the options on grant date is $12. On the basis of a weighted average probability, the Balfour Corporation estimates that 15% of its employees will leave during the vesting period. At the end of year 1 eight employees have left, and the Balfour Corporation estimates that a further nine will leave during year 2. By the end of year 1 the corporation's share price has dropped, and it decides to reprice the share options. It estimates that the fair value of the original share options is $7 and the fair value of the repriced share options is $10. Nine employees leave during year 2.

Required
Prepare a schedule setting out the remuneration expense to be recognised at the end of years 1 and 2.

Exercise 6.9 ★★

SHARE-BASED PAYMENT TRANSACTIONS IN WHICH THE COUNTERPARTY HAS THE SETTLEMENT CHOICE

For the following share-based payment arrangements, discuss whether they are 'debt' or 'equity' settled transactions.

(a) Entity A incurs a liability based on the price of its own share options for services received from a director of the entity.
(b) Entity A acquires property from entity B in exchange for 800 of entity A's shares.
(c) Entity A grants share options to each of its 10 senior executives in return for services to be received over the next 2 years.

Exercise 6.10 ★★★

SHARE-BASED PAYMENT WITH A NON-VESTING CONDITION

An employee is offered the opportunity to contribute 10% of his annual salary of $3000 across the next two years to a plan under which he receives share options. The employee's accumulated contributions to the plan may be used to exercise the options at the end of the 2-year period. The estimated annual expense for this share-based payment arrangement is $200.

Required
Prepare the necessary journal entry or entries to recognise this arrangement at the end of the first year.

Exercise 6.11 ★★★

SHARE-BASED PAYMENT TRANSACTIONS IN WHICH THE ENTITY HAS THE SETTLEMENT CHOICE

Marco Company grants 5000 shares with a fair value of $30 to one of its directors, conditional on that director remaining as a director for 3 years from the grant date. By the end of the first year, the share price has dropped to $23 per share. At this date the company added a cash alternative to the grant, giving the director the choice of receiving the shares or receiving cash equal to the value of the shares on vesting date. On vesting date, the share price has dropped to $18.

Required

Prepare a schedule that recognises the extent to which services have been received at the end of each year, and the obligation to settle in cash.

Exercise 6.12 ★★★

DISCLOSURE

State whether each of the following items is true or false.

(a) Information about share-based payment arrangements that are substantially the same may be aggregated.

(b) The number and weighted average exercise prices of share options outstanding at the beginning and the end of each period must be disclosed.

(c) Option-pricing models used in valuing share options must be identified.

(d) For equity instruments other than share options, it is not necessary to disclose information on how expected dividends were incorporated into the measure of fair value.

(e) The total expense arising from share-based payment transactions in which the services qualified for recognition as assets must be disclosed.

Problems

Problem 6.1 ★

ACCOUNTING FOR A GRANT WHERE THE NUMBER OF EQUITY INSTRUMENTS EXPECTED TO VEST VARIES

Waima Company grants 80 share options to each of its 200 employees. Each grant is conditional on the employee working for the company for the 3 years following the grant date. On grant date, the fair value of each share option is estimated to be $12. On the basis of a weighted average probability, the company estimates that 20% of its employees will leave during the 3-year vesting period.

During year 1, 15 employees leave and the company revises its estimate of total employee departures over the full three-year period from 20% to 22%.

Required

Prepare a schedule setting out the annual and cumulative remuneration expense for year 1.

Problem 6.2 ★

ACCOUNTING FOR A GRANT OF SHARE OPTIONS WHERE THE EXERCISE PRICE VARIES

At the beginning of 2010, Foxton Company grants 3000 employee share options with an exercise price of $45 to its newly appointed chief executive officer, conditional on the executive remaining in the company's employ for the next 3 years. The exercise price drops to $35 if Foxton Company's earnings increase by an average of 10% per year over the 3-year period. On grant date, the estimated fair value of the employee share options with an exercise price of $35 is $22 per option. If the exercise price is $45, the options have an estimated fair value of $17 each.

During 2010, Foxton Company's earnings increased by 8% and are expected to continue to increase at this rate over the next 2 years.

Required

Prepare a schedule setting out the annual remuneration expense to be recognised by Foxton Company and the cumulative remuneration expense for 2010.

Problem 6.3 ★

ACCOUNTING FOR A GRANT WITH A MARKET CONDITION

At the beginning of 2010 Toko Corporation grants 10 000 share options to a senior marketing executive, conditional on that executive remaining in the company's employ until the end of 2012. The share options cannot be exercised unless the share price has increased from $20 at the beginning of 2010 to above $30 at the end of 2012. If the share price is above $30 at the end of 2010, the share options can be exercised at any time during the following 5 years. The Toko Corporation applies a binomial option-pricing model that takes into account the possibility that the share price will exceed $30 at the end of 2012 and the possibility that the share price will not exceed $30 at the end of 2012. The fair value of the share options with this market condition is estimated to be $14 per option.

Required
Calculate the annual and cumulative remuneration expense to be recognised by Toko Corporation for 2010.

Problem 6.4 ★★

DISCLOSURE

Shannon Corporation operates a share option plan for its officers, employees and consultants for up to 10% of its outstanding shares. Under this plan, the exercise price of each option equals the closing market price of the shares on the day before the grant. Each option has a term of 5 years and vests one-third on each of the 3 years following grant date. Before this financial period, the Shannon Corporation has accounted for its share option plan on settlement date and no expense has been recognised.

Required
Prepare an appropriate memorandum outlining the disclosures that will need to be made in Shannon Corporation's financial statement following the adoption of IFRS 2.

Problem 6.5 ★★

APPLICATION OF THE INTRINSIC VALUE METHOD

At the beginning of 2010, Hawera Company grants 2000 share options to each of its 50 most senior executives. The share options have a life of 5 years and will vest at the end of year 3 if the executives remain in service until then. The exercise price is $50 and Hawera Company's share price is also $50 at the grant date. As the company's share options have characteristics significantly different from those of other traded share options, the use of option-pricing models will not provide a reliable measure of fair value at grant date.

The company's share price during years 1–3 is shown below.

Year	Share price at year-end	Estimated number of executives departing in each year	Number of executives remaining at year-end	Number of share options exercised at year-end
1	53	3	46	0
2	55	2	44	0
3	65	1	43	0

Required
Calculate the annual and cumulative remuneration expense to be recognised by Hawera Company for each of the 3 years.

Problem 6.6 ★★

ACCOUNTING FOR CASH-SETTLED SHARE-BASED PAYMENT TRANSACTIONS

Winton Corporation grants 1000 share appreciation rights (SARs) to 10 senior managers, to be taken in cash within 2 years of vesting date on condition that the managers do not leave in the next 3 years. The SARs vest at the end of year 3. Winton Corporation estimates the fair value of the SARs at the end of each year in which a liability exists as shown below. The intrinsic value of the SARs at the date of exercise at the end of year 3 is also shown.

Year	Fair value	Intrinsic value	Number of managers who exercised their SARs
1	$4.40		
2	$5.50		
3	$10.20	$9.00	4

During year 1, one employee leaves and Winton Corporation estimates that a further two will leave before the end of year 3. One employee leaves during year 2 and the corporation estimates that another employee will depart during year 3. One employee leaves during year 3. At the end of year 3, four employees exercise their SARs.

Required
Prepare a schedule setting out the expense and liability that Winton Corporation must recognise at the end of each of the first 3 years.

Problem 6.7 ★★

ACCOUNTING FOR A SHARE-BASED PAYMENT TRANSACTION WHERE THE COUNTERPARTY HAS SETTLEMENT CHOICE

Mimi Corporation operates a share plan that grants each of its 100 employees a choice between receiving a cash payment equivalent to 200 shares or receiving 300 shares. The grant is conditional on the employee completing 3 years' service with Mimi Corporation. If the share alternative is chosen, the shares must be held for 4 years after vesting date.

At grant date, Mimi Corporation's share price is $9 per share. At the end of years 1, 2 and 3, the share price is $11, $12 and $15 respectively. Mimi Corporation has no plan to issue dividends in the next 3 years. After taking into account the effect of the post-vesting transfer restriction, the Mimi Corporation estimates that the fair value of the share alternative at grant date is $8 per share. Assume that no employees leave during the vesting period.

Required
Prepare a schedule setting out the liability and equity amounts that Mimi Corporation must recognise according to IFRS 2. Show also the accounting treatment if (1) all employees choose settlement in cash, and (2) all employees choose the equity alternative.

References

AAA Financial Accounting Standards Committee 2004 (Maines, LA, Bartov, E, Beatty, AL, Botosan, CA, Fairfield, PM, Hirst, DE, Iannoconi, TE, Mallett, R, Venkatachalam, M & Vincent, L), 'Evaluation of the IASB's proposed accounting and disclosure requirements for share-based payment', *Accounting Horizons*, vol. 18, no. 1, pp. 65–76.

Benninga, SZ & Sarig, OH 1997, *Corporate finance: a valuation approach*, international edition, McGraw-Hill.

BlueScope Steel 2005, 'Directors' report', *Annual report 2005*, BlueScope Steel Limited, www.bluescopesteel.com.

— 2008a, 'Annual financial report', *Annual report 2008*, BlueScope Steel Limited, www.bluescopesteel.com.

— 2008b, 'Directors' report', *Annual report 2008*, BlueScope Steel Limited, www.bluescopesteel.com.

FASB 2004, 'FASB issues final statement on accounting for share-based payment', news release 12/16/04, Financial Accounting Standards Board, www.fasb.org.

Macquarie Group 2008, *Annual report 2008*, Macquarie Group Limited, www.macquarie.com.au.

Parker, C 2005, 'Share-based payment — new and complex IFRS equivalent standard', GAAP update no. 3/2005, April, Accountnet Pty Ltd.

Saly, PJ, Jagannathan, R & Huddart, SJ 1999, 'Valuing the reload features of executive stock options', *Accounting Horizons*, vol. 13, no. 3, pp. 219–40.

7 Income taxes

ACCOUNTING STANDARDS IN FOCUS

IAS 12 *Income Taxes*

LEARNING OBJECTIVES

When you have studied this chapter, you should be able to:

- understand the nature of income tax
- understand differences in accounting treatments and taxation treatments for a range of transactions
- explain the concept of tax-effect accounting
- calculate and account for current taxation expense
- understand the recognition requirements for current tax
- account for the payment of tax
- explain the nature of and accounting for tax losses
- calculate and account for movements in deferred taxation accounts
- understand and apply the recognition criteria for deferred tax items
- account for changes in tax rates
- account for amendments to prior year taxes
- explain the presentation requirements of IAS 12
- implement the disclosure requirements of IAS 12.

7.1 THE NATURE OF INCOME TAX

Income taxes are levied by governments on income earned by individuals and entities in order to raise money to fund the provision of government services and infrastructure. The percentage payable and the determination of taxable income are governed by income tax legislation administered by a dedicated government body, such as the Australian Taxation Office. Tax payable is normally determined annually with the lodgement of a taxation document, although some jurisdictions may require payment by instalment, with estimates of tax payable being made on a periodic basis.

This chapter analyses the accounting standard IAS 12 *Income Taxes*. According to paragraph 1 of IAS 12, the standard applies in accounting for income taxes, including all domestic and foreign taxes based on taxable profits. It also applies to withholding taxes that are payable by a subsidiary, associate or joint venture on distributions to a reporting entity. The standard does not deal with methods of accounting for government grants or investment tax credits, but it does deal with accounting for tax effects arising in respect of such transactions.

At first glance, accounting for income tax appears to be a simple matter of calculating the liability owing, recognising the liability and expense, and recording the eventual payment of the amount outstanding. Such a simplistic approach applies only if accounting profit is the same amount as taxable profit and the respective profits have been determined by the same rules. Because this is generally not the case, accounting for income taxes can be a complicated exercise; hence the need for an accounting standard.

7.2 DIFFERENCES BETWEEN ACCOUNTING PROFIT AND TAXABLE PROFIT

Accounting profit is defined in IAS 12, paragraph 5, as 'profit or loss for a period before deducting tax expense', profit or loss being the excess (or deficiency) of revenues less expenses for that period. Such revenues and expenses would be determined and recognised in accordance with accounting standards and the conceptual *Framework*. Taxable profit is defined in the same paragraph as 'the profit for a period, determined in accordance with the rules established by the taxation authorities, upon which income taxes are payable'. Taxable profit is the excess of taxable income over taxation deductions allowable against that income. Thus, accounting profit and taxable profit — because they are determined by different principles and rules — are unlikely to be the same figure in any one period. Tax expense cannot be determined by simply multiplying the accounting profit by the applicable taxation rate. Instead, accounting for income taxes involves identifying and accounting for the differences between accounting profit and taxable profit. These differences arise from a number of common transactions and may be either permanent or temporary in nature.

7.2.1 Permanent differences

Permanent differences between accounting profit and taxable profit arise when the treatment of a transaction by taxation legislation and accounting standards is such that amounts recognised as part of accounting profit are never recognised as part of taxable profit, or vice versa. In some jurisdictions, for example, entities are allowed to deduct from their taxable income more than 100% of expenditure incurred on certain research and development activities undertaken during the taxation period. As a result of this extra deduction, taxable profit for the period is lower than accounting profit, and the extra amount is never recognised as an expense for accounting purposes. Other examples of permanent differences include income never subject to taxation, and expenditure incurred by an entity that will never be an allowable deduction. Where such differences exist, taxable profit will never equal accounting profit. No accounting requirements other than disclosure exist for these permanent differences (see section 7.15 of this chapter).

7.2.2 Temporary differences

Temporary differences between accounting profit and taxable profit arise when the period in which revenues and expenses are recognised for accounting purposes is different from the period in which such revenues and expenses are treated as taxable income and allowable deductions for tax purposes. Interest revenue recognised on an accrual basis, for example, may not be taxable income until it is received as cash. Similarly, insurance paid in advance may be tax-deductible when paid but is not recognised in calculating accounting profit as an expense until a later period. The key feature of these differences is that they are temporary, because sooner or later the amount of interest revenue will equal the amount of taxable interest income, and the amount deducted against taxable income for insurance will equal the insurance expense offset against accounting revenue. However, in any one individual accounting/taxation period, these amounts will differ when calculating accounting profit and taxable profit respectively.

Differences that result in the entity paying more tax in the future (for example, when interest is received) are known as taxable temporary differences. Differences that result in the entity recovering tax via additional deductible expenses in the future (for example, when accrued expenses are paid) are known as deductible temporary differences. The existence of such temporary differences means that income tax payable that is calculated on taxable profit will vary in the current period from that based on accounting profit, but tax payments will eventually catch up. This is demonstrated in illustrative example 7.1.

ILLUSTRATIVE EXAMPLE 7.1

Reversal of temporary difference

Assume that the accounting profit of Aster Ltd for the year ended 30 June 2010 was $150 000, including $5600 in interest revenue of which only $4000 had been received in cash. The company income tax rate is 30%.

If tax is not payable on interest until it has been received in cash, the company's taxable profit will differ from its accounting profit, and a taxable temporary difference will exist in respect of the $1600 interest receivable. If accounting profit for the next year is also $150 000 and the outstanding interest is received in August 2011, tax payable for the years ending 30 June 2010 and 2011 is calculated as follows:

	2010	2011
Accounting profit	$150 000	$150 000
Interest revenue	(1 600)	1 600
Taxable profit	$148 400	$151 600
Tax payable (30%)	44 520	45 480

Note that tax of $90 000, which is equal to 30% of $300 000 (being 2 × $150 000), is paid over the 2 years. The temporary difference created in 2010 is reversed in 2011. The same process occurs with all temporary differences although it may take a number of periods for a complete reversal to occur.

Appendix A to IAS 12 gives examples of temporary differences arising from different treatments of transactions for accounting and taxation purposes, some of which are listed below. These examples are not all-inclusive, so the relevant taxation legislation for specific jurisdictions should be consulted to determine if additional differences exist.

Circumstances that give rise to taxable temporary differences

Such circumstances include the following:

1. Interest revenue is received in arrears and is included in accounting profit on a time-apportionment basis but is included in taxable profit on a cash basis.
2. Revenue from the sale of goods is included in accounting profit when goods are delivered but is included in taxable profit only when cash is collected.
3. Depreciation of an asset is accelerated for tax purposes (the taxation depreciation rate is greater than the accounting rate).

4. Development costs are capitalised and amortised to the statement of comprehensive income but are deducted in determining taxable profit in the period in which they are incurred.
5. Prepaid expenses have already been deducted on a cash basis in determining the taxable profit of the current or previous periods.
6. Depreciation of an asset is not deductible for tax purposes and no deduction will be available for tax purposes when the asset is sold or scrapped (see section 7.9 of this chapter).
7. A borrower records a loan at the proceeds received (which equal the amount due at maturity) less transaction costs, and the carrying amount of the loan is subsequently increased by amortising the transaction costs to accounting profit. The transaction costs are deducted for tax purposes in the period when the loan was first recognised.
8. A loan payable is measured on initial recognition at the amount of the net proceeds (net of transaction costs), and the transaction costs are amortised to accounting profit over the life of the loan. These transaction costs are not deductible in determining the taxable profit of future, current or prior periods (see section 7.9).
9. The liability component of a compound financial instrument (such as a convertible bond) is measured at a discount to the amount repayable on maturity, after assigning a portion of the cash proceeds to the equity component (see chapter 5 of this book). The discount is not deductible in determining taxable profit or loss.
10. Financial assets or investment property are carried at fair value, which exceeds cost, but no equivalent adjustment is made for tax purposes.
11. An entity revalues property, plant and equipment, but no equivalent adjustment is made for tax purposes.
12. The carrying amount of an asset is increased to fair value in a business combination that is an acquisition, but no equivalent adjustment is made for tax purposes.
13. Impairment of goodwill is not deductible in determining taxable profit, and the cost of the goodwill would not be deductible on disposal of the business (see section 8.9).

Temporary differences arising in circumstances 7, 8, 9 and 12 are beyond the scope of this chapter. The tax treatment of temporary differences arising from fair-value accounting and revaluation to fair value (items 10 and 11) are discussed and illustrated in section 9.6.1 of this book.

Circumstances that give rise to deductible temporary differences

Such circumstances include the following:

1. Retirement benefit costs are deducted in determining accounting profit because service is provided by the employee, but are not deducted in determining taxable profit until the entity pays either retirement benefits or contributions to a fund. Similar temporary differences arise in relation to other accrued expenses — such as product warranties, leave entitlements and interest — which are deductible on a cash basis in determining taxable profit.
2. Accumulated depreciation of an asset in the financial statements is greater than the cumulative depreciation allowed up to the end of the reporting period for tax purposes. That is, the accounting depreciation rate is greater than the allowable taxation depreciation rate.
3. The cost of inventories sold before the end of the reporting period is deducted in determining accounting profit when goods or service are delivered, but is deducted in determining taxable profit only when cash is collected.
4. The net realisable value (see chapter 8 of this book) of an item of inventory, or the recoverable amount (see chapter 9) of an item of property, plant and equipment, is less than the previous carrying amount. The entity therefore reduces the carrying amount of the asset, but that reduction is ignored for tax purposes until the asset is sold.
5. Research costs (or organisation or other start-up costs) are recognised as an expense in determining accounting profit, but are not permitted as a deduction in determining taxable profit until a later period.
6. Income is deferred in the statement of financial position but has already been included in taxable profit in current or prior periods (for example, subscriptions received in advance).
7. A government grant that is included in the statement of financial position as deferred income will not be taxable in a future period (see section 7.9 of this chapter).
8. Financial assets or investment property are carried at fair value, which is less than cost, but no equivalent adjustment is made for tax purposes. (Temporary differences arising in these circumstances are beyond the scope of this chapter.)

In summary, income tax payable in any one period is affected by differences between items used to determine accounting profit and taxable profit. Some revenue items are not taxable, have already been taxed or will not be taxed until some future period/s. Some expense items are not deductible, have already been deducted or may be deducted in some future period/s. Additionally, extra deductions for which no expense will ever be incurred may be allowable under taxation legislation. The illustrative examples, exercises and problems in this chapter assume that the revenue from selling goods and services is taxable irrespective of whether cash has been received for the sale, and that the cost of goods sold is an allowable deduction irrespective of whether cash has been paid to acquire those goods.

7.3 ACCOUNTING FOR INCOME TAXES

As the objective paragraph of IAS 12 points out:

> The principal issue in accounting for income taxes is how to account for the current and future tax consequences of:
> (a) the future recovery (settlement) of the carrying amount of assets (liabilities) that are recognised in an entity's statement of financial position; and
> (b) transactions and other events of the current period that are recognised in an entity's financial statements.

IAS 12 requires the tax consequences of transactions and other events to be accounted for in the same manner and the same period as the transactions themselves. Thus, if a transaction is recognised in profit or loss for the period, so too is the related tax payable or tax benefit. Similarly, if a transaction is adjusted directly to equity, so too is the related tax effect. Differing accounting and taxation rules (as discussed in section 7.2) mean that the actual payment (deduction) of tax relating to revenue (expense) items may take place in both current and/or future accounting periods but IAS 12, paragraph 58, requires that the total income tax expense relating to transactions is recorded in the current year irrespective of when it will be paid or deducted.

To illustrate: an entity recognises interest revenue of $21 000 for the year ended 30 June 2011. Of this amount, $15 000 has been received in cash and a receivable asset has been raised for the remaining $6000. Tax legislation regards interest revenue as taxable only when it has been received. Therefore, the entity will pay tax of $4500 ($15 000 × 30%) in the current year and tax of $1800 ($6000 × 30%) in the following year when the $6000 receivable is paid. If the entity were to record only the current tax payable amount as income tax expense, the profit for the year would be overstated by $1800 given that $6300 of the interest revenue recognised for the year (not $4500) will eventually be paid to the taxation authorities and will not be available for use by the entity. To ensure that the profit after-tax figure for the year is both relevant and reliable, IAS 12 requires the entity to record an income tax expense of $6300 for the current year in respect to the interest revenue. This tax is payable via a current liability amount of $4500 and a deferred (future) liability of $1800.

The need to recognise both current and future tax consequences of current year transactions means that each transaction has two tax effects:

1. tax payable on profit earned for the year may be reduced or increased because the transaction is not taxable or deductible in the current year
2. future tax payable may be reduced or increased when that transaction becomes taxable or deductible.

If only current tax payable is recorded as an expense, then the profit for the current year will be understated or overstated by the amount of tax or benefit to be paid or received in future years. Similarly, in the years that the tax or benefit on these transactions is paid or received, income tax expense will include amounts relating to prior periods and therefore be understated or overstated. As IAS 12 requires income tax expense to reflect all tax effects of transactions entered into during the year regardless of when the effects occur, two calculations are required at the end of the reporting period:

- the calculation of current tax liability, which determines the amount of tax payable for the period
- the calculation of movements in deferred tax effects relating to assets and liabilities recognised in the statement of financial position, which determines the net effect of deferred taxes and deductions arising from transactions during the year.

Acknowledging the current and future tax consequences of all items recognised in the statement of financial position (subject to certain exceptions) should make the information about the tax implications of an entity's operations and financial position more relevant and reliable.

7.4 CALCULATION OF CURRENT TAX

Current tax is the recognition of taxes payable to the taxation authorities in respect of a particular period. The current tax calculation involves identifying differences between accounting revenues and taxable income, and between accounting expenses and allowable deductions, for transactions during the year, as well as reversing temporary differences from prior years that occur in the current period. Accounting profit for the period is adjusted by these differences to calculate taxable profit, which is then multiplied by the current tax rate to determine current tax payable.

When selecting the tax rate to apply, the requirements of IAS 12, paragraph 46, must be considered. This paragraph states:

> Current tax liabilities (assets) for the current and prior periods shall be measured at the amount expected to be paid to (recovered from) the taxation authorities, using the tax rates (and tax laws) that have been enacted or substantively enacted by the end of the reporting period.

Therefore, if a tax rate has changed — or, in some jurisdictions, if a change has been announced — the rate applicable to the taxable profit for the period must be applied.

Identifying permanent and temporary differences in the current year's profit is a relatively simple exercise. All revenues and expenses are reviewed for amounts that are not taxable or deductible. Identifying reversals of prior year temporary differences may require referring back to prior year worksheets, transactions posted to asset and liability accounts during the current year, or reconstructions of ledger accounts. (The latter method is used in this chapter.) Such reversals include, where applicable, accrued expenses that have been paid and are now deductible, bad debts written off and now deductible, accrued revenue that has been received and is now taxable, and prepaid expenses deducted in a prior period but now included in accounting profit.

Once the differences have been isolated, there are two ways that the current tax could be determined: (1) the net differences could be adjusted against accounting profit to derive taxable profit, or (2) the gross amounts of items with differences could be added back or deducted against accounting profit. (The latter method is adopted in this chapter.) A worksheet is used to perform this reconciliation between accounting profit and taxable profit using the following formula:

Accounting profit (loss)
+ (–) accounting expenses not deductible for tax
+ (–) accounting expenses where the amount differs from deductible amounts
+ (–) taxable income where the amount differs from accounting revenue
– (+) accounting revenues not subject to taxation
– (+) accounting revenue where the amount differs from taxable income
– (+) deductible amounts where the amount differs from accounting expense
= taxable profit

The current tax rate is then applied to taxable profit to derive the current tax payable.

ILLUSTRATIVE EXAMPLE 7.2

Determination of current tax worksheet

Iris Ltd's accounting profit for the year ended 30 June 2010 was $250 450. Included in this profit were the following items of revenue and expense:

Amortisation — development project	$30 000
Impairment of goodwill expense	7 000
Depreciation — equipment (15%)	40 000

Entertainment expense	12 450
Insurance expense	24 000
Doubtful debts expense	14 000
Proceeds on sale of equipment	30 000
Carrying amount of equipment sold	36 667
Rent revenue	25 000
Annual leave expense	54 000

At 30 June 2010, the company's draft statement of financial position showed the following balances:

	30 June 2010	30 June 2009
Assets		
Cash	$ 55 000	$ 65 000
Accounts receivable	295 000	277 000
Allowance for doubtful debts	(16 000)	(18 000)
Inventories	162 000	185 000
Prepaid insurance	30 000	25 000
Rent receivable	3 500	5 500
Development project	120 000	—
Accumulated amortisation	(30 000)	—
Equipment	200 000	266 667
Accumulated depreciation	(90 000)	(80 000)
Goodwill	35 000	35 000
Accumulated impairment expense	(14 000)	(7 000)
Deferred tax asset	?	24 900
Liabilities		
Accounts payable	310 500	294 000
Provision for annual leave	61 000	65 000
Mortgage loan	100 000	150 000
Deferred tax liability	?	57 150
Current tax liability	?	12 500

Additional information

1. Taxation legislation allows Iris Ltd to deduct 125% of the $120 000 spent on development during the year.
2. Iris Ltd has capitalised development expenditure relating to a filter project and amortises the balance over the period of expected benefit (4 years).
3. The taxation depreciation rate for equipment is 20%.
4. The equipment sold on 30 June 2010 cost $66 667 when it was purchased 3 years ago.
5. Neither entertainment expenditure nor goodwill impairment expense is deductible for taxation purposes.
6. The company income tax rate is 30%.

Calculation of current tax payable

Before completing the worksheet, all differences between accounting and taxation figures must be identified:

1. Development project

There are two differences here: a permanent difference arising from the extra 25% deduction allowed by tax legislation, and a temporary difference arising from the treatment of the development costs. For accounting purposes, the $120 000 has been capitalised and will be amortised over 4 years; for tax purposes, the entire expenditure is deductible in the current year. The tax deduction for development is therefore: $150 000 (being $120 000 + [25% × $120 000]).

2. *Impairment of goodwill expense*
No deduction is allowed for impairment expense, so the taxation deduction is nil. Paragraph 21 of IAS 12 does not permit the recognition of the deferred tax liability arising from the taxable temporary difference created (see section 7.9 of this chapter). Therefore, a permanent difference exists.

3. *Depreciation expense — equipment*
Because equipment is being depreciated at a faster rate for taxation purposes, a temporary taxable difference will exist. The amount of depreciation deductible is $53 333.40 (being $266 667 × 20%).

4. *Entertainment expense*
No deduction is allowed for entertainment expenditure, so the taxation deduction is nil and there is a permanent difference between accounting profit and taxable profit.

5. *Insurance expense*
Insurance expenditure is deductible when incurred. The existence of a prepaid insurance asset account in the statement of financial position indicates that the insurance payment and insurance expense figures are different. It is therefore necessary to reconstruct the asset account to identify if any part of the expense has already been deducted for taxation purposes. This is done as follows:

Prepaid Insurance			
Balance b/d	$25 000	Balance c/d	$30 000
Insurance Paid	29 000	Insurance Expense	24 000
	54 000		54 000

The insurance paid figure of $29 000 represents the deduction allowable in determining taxable profit. The expense figure of $24 000 shows that the payment made includes $5000 for insurance cover for the next accounting period. When this amount is expensed, no deduction will be available against taxable profit.

6. *Allowance for doubtful debts*
If, under taxation legislation, no deduction is allowed for bad debts until they have been written off, the taxation amount for doubtful debts will be nil. The draft statement of financial position shows that an allowance was raised in the previous year, so any debts written off against that allowance are deductible in the current year. To determine the amount (if any) of that write-off, the ledger account is reconstructed as follows:

Allowance for Doubtful Debts			
Balance b/d	$16 000	Balance c/d	$18 000
Bad Debts Written Off	16 000	Doubtful Debts Expense	14 000
	32 000		32 000

The allowable deduction for bad debts written off is therefore $16 000.

7. *Proceeds on sale of equipment*
All this revenue is taxable, so there is no permanent or temporary difference.

8. *Carrying amount of equipment sold*
The gain or loss on the sale of equipment is different for accounting and taxation purposes, and is calculated as shown in the following table.

	Accounting	Taxation
Cost	$66 667	$66 667
Accumulated depreciation	30 000	40 000
Carrying amount	36 667	26 667
Proceeds	30 000	30 000
Gain (loss)	$ (6 667)	$ 3 333

Because the sales proceeds are recognised for both accounting and taxation purposes, the difference in the loss or gain on sale is caused by the two methods recognising different carrying amounts for the asset sold. This difference is caused by the use of different depreciation rates. When preparing the current tax worksheet, adjusting for the different carrying amounts effectively adjusts for the difference in the gain or loss on sale.

9. Rent revenue

Rent revenue is taxable when received. The presence in the statement of financial position of a rent receivable asset indicates that part of the revenue has not yet been received as cash and is not taxable in the current year. A temporary difference therefore exists in respect of rent, as demonstrated by reconstructing the ledger account:

Rent Receivable			
Balance b/d	$ 5 500	Balance c/d	$ 3 500
Rent Revenue	25 000	Cash Received	27 000
	30 500		30 500

In this instance, the cash received figure represents rent received for two different accounting periods: $5500 outstanding at the end of the prior year, and $21 500 for the current year. Thus, the taxable amount combines the reversal of last year's temporary difference and the tax payable on the current year's income. A temporary difference still exists for the $3500 rent for this year not yet received in cash.

10. Annual leave expense

Annual leave is deductible when paid in cash. The provision for annual leave indicates the existence of unpaid leave and therefore a taxation temporary difference. This is demonstrated by reconstructing the ledger account:

Provision for Annual Leave			
Balance c/d	$ 61 000	Balance b/d	$ 65 000
Leave Paid	58 000	Leave Expense	54 000
	119 000		119 000

The reconstruction reveals a payment of $58 000, which is deductible in the current year and represents a partial reversal of the temporary difference related to the opening balance. As none of the current year expense has been paid, no deduction is available this year and a further temporary difference is created.

This chapter assumes that sales revenue and cost of goods sold are taxable/deductible even when not received/paid in cash, so there are no differences with respect to the accounts receivable or accounts payable balances. If different assumptions applied, then the amounts of cash received for sales and cash paid for inventory would need to be determined in order to calculate the current tax payable.

Figure 7.1 contains the current worksheet used to calculate the current tax liability for Iris Ltd.

IRIS LTD Current Tax Worksheet for the year ended 30 June 2010		
Accounting profit		$250 450
Add:		
Amortisation of development expenditure	$ 30 000	
Impairment of goodwill expense	7 000	
Depreciation expense	40 000	
Entertainment expense	12 450	
Insurance expense	24 000	
Doubtful debts expense	14 000	
Carrying amount of equipment sold (accounting)	36 667	
Annual leave expense	54 000	
Rent received (tax)	27 000	245 117
		495 567
Deduct:		
Rent revenue (accounting)	25 000	
Carrying amount of equipment sold (tax)	26 667	
Bad debts written off	16 000	
Insurance paid	29 000	
Development costs paid	150 000	
Annual leave paid	58 000	
Depreciation of equipment for tax	53 333	(358 000)
Taxable profit		137 567
Current liability @ 30%		$ 41 270

FIGURE 7.1 Completed current tax worksheet for Iris Ltd

7.5 RECOGNITION OF CURRENT TAX

Paragraph 12 of IAS 12 states:

> Current tax for current and prior periods shall, to the extent unpaid, be recognised as a liability. If the amount already paid in respect of current and prior periods exceeds the amount due for those periods, the excess shall be recognised as an asset.

Additionally, paragraph 58 of the standard requires current tax to be recognised as income or an expense and included in the profit or loss for the period, except to the extent that the tax relates to a transaction recognised directly in equity or to a business combination. Therefore, the following journal entry is required to recognise the current tax payable for Iris Ltd at 30 June 2010:

30 June 2010			
Income Tax Expense (Current)	Dr	41 270	
Current Tax Liability	Cr		41 270
(Recognition of current tax liability)			

7.6 PAYMENT OF TAX

Taxation legislation may require taxation debts to be paid annually upon lodgement of a taxation return or at some specified time after lodgement (such as on receipt of an assessment notice, or at a set date or time). Alternatively, the taxation debt may be paid by instalment throughout the taxation year. In some jurisdictions, payments in advance relating to next year's estimated taxable profit may be required. Where one annual payment is required, the entry is:

Current Tax Liability	Dr	41 270	
Cash	Cr		41 270
(Payment of current liability)			

If payment by instalment is required, the process is a little more complicated. To pay by instalment, an estimate of taxable profit needs to be made; hence the reference in paragraph 12 of IAS 12 to amounts paid in excess of the amount due. To illustrate the process of payment by instalment, assume that Iris Ltd (from illustrative example 7.2) has to pay tax quarterly and has paid the following amounts for the first three quarters of the 2009–10 taxation year:

28 October 2009	$ 9420
28 January 2010	10 380
28 April 2010	10 750

The journal entry to record the first payment is:

Income Tax Expense	Dr	9420	
Cash	Cr		9420
(Payment of first quarterly taxation instalment)			

Similar entries are passed at 28 January 2010 and 28 April 2010. At 30 June 2010, because the tax liability has been partially paid, an adjustment is required on the current tax worksheet to determine the balance of tax owing in relation to the 2009–10 year (see below).

IRIS LTD
Current Tax Worksheet (extract)
for the year ended 30 June 2010

Taxable profit	$137 567
Tax payable @ 30%	41 270
Less Tax already paid ($9420 + $10 380 + $10 750)	(30 550)
Current tax liability	10 720

The adjusting journal entry becomes:

30 June 2010			
Income Tax Expense (Current)	Dr	10 720	
Current Tax Liability	Cr		10 720
(Recognitiion of current tax liability)			

7.7 TAX LOSSES

Tax losses are created when allowable deductions exceed taxable income. IAS 12 envisages three possible treatments for tax losses: they may be carried forward, carried back, or simply lost. Where taxation legislation allows tax losses to be carried forward and deducted against future taxable profits, the carry-forward may be either indefinite or for a limited number of years. Other restrictions — such as requiring losses to be deducted against non-taxable income on recoupment — may also apply. Carry-forward tax losses create a deductible temporary difference and therefore a deferred tax asset in that the company will pay less tax on future taxable profits. The recognition of a deferred tax asset for tax losses is discussed in detail in section 7.9.2 of this chapter.

ILLUSTRATIVE EXAMPLE 7.3

Creation and recoupment of carry-forward tax losses

The following information relates to Poppy Ltd for the year ended 30 June 2011:

Accounting loss	$ 7 600
Depreciation expense	14 700
Depreciation deductible for tax	20 300
Entertainment expense (not tax-deductible)	10 000
Income tax rate	30%

The calculation of the tax loss appears below:

POPPY LTD Current Tax Worksheet (extract) for the year ended 30 June 2011	
Accounting loss	$ (7 600)
Add:	
Depreciation expense	14 700
Entertainment expense	10 000
	17 100
Deduct:	
Depreciation deduction	(20 300)
Tax loss	(3 200)
Deferred tax asset @ 30%	$ 960

Assuming that recognition criteria are met, the adjusting journal entry is:

30 June 2011			
Deferred Tax Asset (Tax Losses)	Dr	960	
Income Tax Income	Cr		960
(Recognition of deferred tax asset from tax loss)			

If Poppy Ltd then makes a taxable profit of $23 600 for the year ending 30 June 2012, the loss is recouped as follows:

POPPY LTD Current Tax Worksheet (extract) for the year ended 30 June 2012	
Taxable profit before tax loss	$23 600
Tax loss recouped	(3 200)
Taxable profit	20 400
Current tax liability @ 30%	$ 6 120

The adjusting journal entry is:

30 June 2012			
Income Tax Expense (Current)	Dr	7 080	
Deferred Tax Asset (Tax Losses)	Cr		960
Current Tax Liability	Cr		6 120
(Recognition of current tax liability and reversal of deferred tax asset from tax loss)			

In jurisdictions where taxation legislation allows the current year's tax losses to be carried back, paragraph 13 of IAS 12 requires that: 'The benefit relating to a tax loss that can be carried back to recover current tax of a previous period shall be recognised as an asset'. Paragraph 14 further states that the recognition should take place in the period of the tax loss, because 'it is probable that the benefit will flow to the entity and the benefit can be reliably measured'.

Using the facts from illustrative example 7.3, the adjusting journal entry becomes:

30 June 2011			
Current Tax Asset	Dr	960	
Income Tax Expense	Cr		960
(Recognition of tax receivable on offset of tax loss against prior year taxable profit)			

7.8 CALCULATION OF DEFERRED TAX

As already explained, IAS 12 adopts the philosophy that the tax consequences of transactions that occur during a period should be recognised in income tax expense for that period. Where a transaction has two effects, both have to be recognised. The existence of temporary differences between accounting profit and taxable profit was identified earlier in the chapter. These temporary differences result in the carrying amounts of an entity's assets and liabilities being different from the amounts that would arise if a statement of financial position was prepared for the taxation authority. The latter are referred to as the tax base of an entity's assets and liabilities. At the end of the reporting period, a comparison of an entity's carrying amounts of assets and liabilities and their tax bases will reveal the temporary differences that exist, and adjustments will then be made to deferred assets and liabilities. (The reference to 'deferred' tax adjustments comes from the fact that assets and liabilities reflect future inflows and outflows to an entity. The deferred tax balances are related to these future flows, and hence are deferred to the future rather than affecting current tax.) For assets such as goodwill and entertainment costs payable, differences between their tax bases and carrying amounts may be caused by permanent differences. Such differences will not give rise to deferred tax adjustments.

The following steps are required to calculate deferred tax:

1. Determine the carrying amounts of items recognised in the statement of financial position and their tax bases.
2. Determine the assessable and deductible temporary differences relating to the future tax consequences of items recognised at the end of the current period.
3. Calculate and recognise the deferred tax assets and liabilities arising from these temporary differences after taking into account any relevant recognition exceptions (see section 7.8.5 of this chapter) and offset considerations (see section 7.14.1).
4. Recognise the net movement in deferred tax assets and liabilities during the period as deferred tax expense or income in profit or loss (unless an accounting standard requires recognition directly in equity or as part of a business combination).

The first three steps are carried out on a worksheet. The final step requires an adjusting journal entry.

7.8.1 Determining carrying amounts

Carrying amounts are asset and liability balances net of valuation allowances, accumulated depreciation, amortisation and impairment losses (for example, accounts receivable less allowance for doubtful debts).

7.8.2 Determining tax bases

Tax bases need to be calculated for assets and liabilities.

Tax bases of assets

The economic benefits embodied in an asset are normally taxable when recovered by an entity through the use or sale of that asset. The entity may then be able to deduct all or part of the cost or carrying amount of the asset against those taxable amounts when determining taxable profits.

Paragraph 7 of IAS 12 describes the tax base of an asset as:

> the amount that will be deductible for tax purposes against any taxable economic benefits that will flow to an entity when it recovers the carrying amount of the asset. If those economic benefits will not be taxable, the tax base of the asset is equal to its carrying amount.

The following formula can be applied to derive the tax base from the carrying amount of the asset:

Carrying amount – Future taxable amounts + Future deductible amounts = Tax base

Figure 7.2 contains examples of the calculation of tax bases for assets.

	Carrying amount	Future taxable amounts*	Future deductible amounts	Tax base
Prepayments $3000: fully deductible for tax when paid	$ 3 000	$(3 000)	$ 0	$ 0
Trade receivables less $2000 allowance for doubtful debts: sales revenue is already included in taxable profit	50 000	0	2 000	52 000
Plant and equipment costing $10 000 has a carrying value of $5400: accumulated depreciation at tax rates is $6500	5 400	(5 400)	3 500**	3 500
Loan receivable $25 000: loan repayment will have no tax consequences	25 000	0	0	25 000
Interest receivable $1000: recognised as revenue but not taxable until received	1 000	(1 000)	0	0

*Future taxable amounts are equal to carrying amounts unless economic benefits have already been included in taxable profit.
**The deductible amount represents the original cost of the asset less the accumulated depreciation based on taxation depreciation rates (being $10 000 – 6500 = 3500).

FIGURE 7.2 Calculation of the tax base of assets

The formula for calculating the tax base of an asset can be rearranged as follows:

Carrying amount – Tax base = Future taxable amounts – Future deductible amounts

In other words, a temporary difference (the difference between the carrying amount and the tax base) occurs when the future taxable amount is different from the future deductible amount.

Figure 7.2 illustrates the following situations:

- Where the future benefits are taxable, the carrying amount equals the future taxable amount. Hence, the tax base equals the future deductible amount. This can be seen in figure 7.2 for prepayments, plant and equipment, and interest receivable.
- Where there are no future taxable amounts, generally the deductible amount is zero and the tax base equals the carrying amount. In figure 7.2, this applies to the loan receivable. An exception is trade receivables where, although the future taxable amount is zero, the future deductible amount is not zero because of the existence of doubtful debts. In this case, the tax base equals the sum of the carrying amount and the future deductible amount.

Tax bases of liabilities

Liabilities, other than those relating to unearned revenue, do not create taxable amounts. Instead, settlement gives rise to deductible items.

Paragraph 8 of IAS 12 describes the tax base of a liability as:

> its carrying amount, less any amount that will be deductible for tax purposes in respect of that liability in future periods. In the case of revenue received in advance, the tax base of the resulting liability is its carrying amount, less any amount of the revenue that will not be taxable in future periods.

The following formula can be applied to derive the tax base from the carrying amount of the liability:

Carrying amount + Future taxable amounts – Future deductible amounts = Tax base

Figure 7.3 contains examples of the calculation of the tax base for liabilities.

	Carrying amount	Future taxable amounts	Future deductible amounts	Tax base
Provision for annual leave $3900: not deductible for tax until paid	$ 3 900	$ 0	$(3 900)	$ 0
Trade payables $34 000: expense already deducted from taxable income	34 000	0	0	34 000
Subscription revenue received in advance $500: taxed when received	500	(500)	0	0
Loan payable $20 000: loan repayment will have no tax consequences	20 000	0	0	20 000
Accrued expenses $6 700: deductible when paid in cash	6 700	0	(6 700)	0
Accrued penalties $700: not tax-deductible	700	0	0	700

FIGURE 7.3 Calculation of the tax base of liabilities

Figure 7.3 illustrates two situations:

- Where the carrying amount equals the future deductible amount, the tax base is zero. This applies to provisions for annual leave and accrued expenses.
- Where there is no future deductible amount, the carrying amount equals the tax base. This applies to trade payables and the loan payable.

Some items may have a tax base but are not recognised as assets and liabilities in the statement of financial position. Paragraph 9 of IAS 12 provides the example of research costs that are recognised as an expense in determining accounting profit in the period in which they are incurred but are not allowed as a deduction in determining taxable profit until a later period. Additionally, under paragraph 52 the manner in which an asset/liability is recovered/settled may affect the tax base of that asset/liability in some jurisdictions.

7.8.3 Calculating temporary differences

When the carrying amount of an asset or liability is different from its tax base, a temporary difference exists. Temporary differences effectively represent the expected net future taxable amounts arising from the recovery of assets and the settlement of liabilities at their carrying amounts. Therefore, a temporary difference cannot exist where there are no future tax consequences from the realisation or settlement of an asset or liability at its carrying value.

Taxable temporary differences

A taxable temporary difference exists when the future taxable amount of an asset or liability exceeds any future deductible amounts. This is demonstrated in illustrative example 7.4.

ILLUSTRATIVE EXAMPLE 7.4

Calculation of a taxable temporary difference

An asset, which cost 150, has an accumulated depreciation of 50.
Accumulated depreciation for tax purposes is 90 and the tax rate is 25%.

Carrying amount	= 100
Future taxable amount	= 100
Future deductible amount	= 60
Tax base	= 100 – 100 + 60
	= 60 (= 150 cost less 90 tax depreciation)

Because the future taxable amount is greater than the future deductible amount, a temporary tax difference exists. In other words, the expectation is that the entity will pay income taxes in the future, when it recovers the carrying amount of the asset, because it expects to earn 100 but receive a tax deduction of 60. The entity has a liability to pay tax on that extra 40. As the payment occurs in the future, the liability is referred to as a 'deferred tax liability'.

Source: Adapted from IAS 12, paragraph 16.

Deductible temporary differences

A deductible temporary difference exists when the future taxable amount of an asset or liability is less than any future deductible amounts. This is demonstrated in illustrative example 7.5.

ILLUSTRATIVE EXAMPLE 7.5

Calculation of a deductible temporary difference

An entity recognises a liability of 100 for accrued product warranty costs. For tax purposes, the product warranty costs will not be deductible until the entity pays claims. The tax rate is 25%.

Carrying amount	= 100
Future taxable amount	= 0
Future deductible amount	= 100
Tax base	= 100 + 0 – 100
	= 0

As the future deductible amount is greater than the future taxable amount, a deductible temporary difference exists. In other words, in settling the liability for its carrying amount, the entity will reduce its future tax profits and hence its future tax payments. The entity then has an expected benefit relating to the future tax deduction. As the benefits are to be received in the future, the asset raised is referred to as a 'deferred tax asset'.

Source: Adapted from IAS 12, paragraph 25.

7.8.4 Calculating deferred tax liabilities and deferred tax assets

Paragraphs 15 and 24 of IAS 12 require (with some exceptions) that a deferred tax liability and a deferred tax asset be recognised for all taxable temporary differences and all deductible temporary differences, and that a total be determined for taxable temporary differences and for deductible temporary differences. An appropriate tax rate can then be applied to these totals to derive the balance of deferred tax liability and deferred tax asset at the end of the period. Paragraph 47 of the standard specifies that:

> Deferred tax assets and liabilities shall be measured at the tax rates that are expected to apply to the period when the asset is realised or the liability settled, based on tax rates (and tax laws) that have been enacted or substantively enacted by the end of the reporting period.

Thus, if the tax rate is currently 30% but will rise to 32% in the next reporting period, deferred amounts should be measured at 32%. Should a change be enacted (or substantively enacted) between reporting date and the time of completion of the financial statements, no adjustment needs to be made to the tax balances recognised. However, disclosure of any material impacts should be made by note in compliance with IAS 10 *Events after the Reporting Period*.

Different tax rates may be required when temporary differences are expected to reverse in different periods and a change of tax rate is probable, or when temporary differences relate to different taxation jurisdictions. Additionally, consideration should be given to the manner in which an asset/liability is recovered/settled in jurisdictions where the manner of recovery/settlement determines the applicable tax rate (IAS 12, para. 52).

Before determining the amounts of deferred tax liabilities and deferred tax assets, consideration must be given to the recognition criteria mandated by the accounting standard. (See section 7.9 of this chapter.)

7.8.5 Excluded differences

Paragraphs 15 and 24 of IAS 12 mandate the following exceptions to the requirement that a deferred tax liability and a deferred tax asset (subject to probability assessment) be recognised for all taxable and deductible temporary differences:

(a) the initial recognition of goodwill; or
(b) goodwill for which amortisation is not deductible for tax purposes
(c) the initial recognition of an asset or liability in a transaction which:
 (i) is not a business combination; and
 (ii) at the time of the transaction, affects neither accounting profit nor taxable profit (tax loss).

Goodwill

Goodwill is the excess of the cost of the business combination over the acquirer's interest in the net fair value of the identifiable assets, liabilities and contingent liabilities (see chapter 11). In jurisdictions where impairment of goodwill is not deductible, a taxable temporary difference is created because the tax base of goodwill is always nil. IAS 12 does not permit the recognition of the deferred tax liability relating to goodwill, because goodwill is a residual amount and recognising the deferred tax amount would increase the carrying amount of goodwill (IAS 12, para. 21). In jurisdictions where goodwill can be 'depreciated' for tax purposes, a deferred tax liability may be recognised if the carrying amount of the asset remains unimpaired.

Initial recognition of an asset or liability

A temporary difference may arise on the initial recognition of an asset or liability if the carrying amount is not equal to the tax base (for example, if part or all of the cost of an asset is not deductible for tax purposes). The accounting treatment of the temporary difference depends on the nature of the transaction that created the asset or liability.

When deferred tax arises on the acquisition of an entity or business, and it has not been recognised by the acquiring or acquired entity before the acquisition, it must be recognised and taken into account in measuring the amount of goodwill or excess. Deferred tax balances are recognised if they arise from temporary differences related to assets and liabilities that have affected pre-tax accounting profit or taxable profit at or before the time of initial recognition. This most commonly occurs when items are recognised for accounting and tax purposes in different reporting periods. Examples include prepayments, deferred income and accrued expenses.

If the exception provided in paragraph 15 of IAS 12 did not exist, an entity would be allowed to recognise the deferred tax liability or asset, and adjust the carrying amount of the asset or liability by the same amount, for a transaction that was not a business combination and affected neither accounting nor taxable profits. However, the standard setters considered that: 'Such adjustments would make the financial statements less transparent' (IAS 12, para. 22(c)), and so prohibited the recognition of such deferred tax amounts. Fortunately, such items are rare and would occur only where assets have a taxable value deemed by tax laws to be different from the cost of the asset. Such deferred amounts include:

- motor vehicles acquired where the total cost is in excess of a depreciation cost limit set by tax legislation

- the 'roll over' of the tax base of assets to an acquiring entity so that future tax deductions are limited to an amount that is different from the consideration paid
- a non-taxable government grant related to an asset that is deducted from the carrying amount of the asset, but for tax purposes is not deducted from the asset's depreciable amount (its tax base).

In addition to prohibiting the recognition of deferred tax amounts on the initial recognition of the asset or liability, IAS 12 also prohibits recognition of any subsequent changes to the unrecognised deferred tax liability or asset as the asset is depreciated (para. 22(c)).

7.8.6 Deferred tax worksheet

A deferred tax worksheet is shown in illustrative example 7.6. The purpose of the deferred tax worksheet is to calculate the movements in the deferred tax asset and the deferred tax liability accounts during the current period. Determining the temporary differences relating to assets and liabilities allows the closing balances of the deferred tax accounts to be calculated. A consideration of the beginning balances and movements during the year allows the calculation of the adjustments required to achieve those closing balances. All assets and liabilities may be included in the worksheet; alternatively, only those expected to have different accounting and tax bases could be shown.

ILLUSTRATIVE EXAMPLE 7.6

Deferred tax worksheet

Using the information provided in illustrative example 7.2, the deferred tax worksheet for Iris Ltd is shown in figure 7.4.

FIGURE 7.4 Deferred tax worksheet for Iris Ltd

IRIS LTD
Deferred Tax Worksheet
as at 30 June 2010

	Carrying amount $	Future taxable amount $	Future deductible amount $	Tax base $	Taxable temporary differences $	Deductible temporary differences $
Relevant assets						
Receivables[1]	279 000	0	16 000	295 000		16 000
Prepaid insurance[2]	30 000	(30 000)	0	0	30 000	
Rent receivable[3]	3 500	(3 500)	0	0	3 500	
Development project[4]	90 000	(90 000)	0	0	90 000	
Equipment[5]	110 000	(110 000)	80 000	80 000	30 000	
Goodwill[6]	21 000	(21 000)	0	0	21 000	
Relevant liabilities						
Provision for annual leave[7]	61 000	0	(61 000)	0	—	61 000
Total temporary differences					174 500	77 000
Excluded differences[8]					(21 000)	—
Temporary differences					153 500	77 000

FIGURE 7.4 *(continued)*

	Carrying amount $	Future taxable amount $	Future deductible amount $	Tax base $	Taxable temporary differences $	Deductible temporary differences $
Deferred tax liability[9]					46 050	
Deferred tax asset[9]						23 100
Beginning balances[10]					(17 150)	(24 900)
Movement during year[11]						
Adjustment[10]					28 900 Cr	(1 800) Cr

1. The carrying amount of receivables $279 000 ($295 000 – 16 000) represents the cash that the company expects to receive after allowing for any doubtful debts. Tax on this amount has already been paid via sales revenue recognised in the current year, so the future taxable amount is zero. The allowance for doubtful debts raised as an expense in the current year is not deductible against taxable profit until the debts actually go 'bad' and are written out of the accounts receivable balance. Thus, there is a future deduction of $5000 available. The tax base for receivables is $283 000, being the total of all debts outstanding at 30 June 2010 (doubtful or otherwise). Because the future deductible amount is greater than the future taxable amount, a deductible temporary difference of $5000 exists in respect of receivables.
2. The prepaid insurance asset represents insurance monies that have been paid for insurance cover in the year ended 30 June 2011. The recovery of these benefits results in the flow of taxable economic benefits to Iris Ltd, giving a future taxable amount of $30 000. This amount was paid in the year ended 30 June 2010 and was allowed as a deduction against the taxable profit for that year. This means that no deduction is available when the $30 000 is expensed in the year ended 30 June 2011, giving a tax base for the asset of $0. As the future taxable amount exceeds the future deductible amount, a taxable temporary difference of $30 000 exists in respect of prepaid insurance.
3. The rent receivable asset represents monies to be received relating to revenue earned in the year ended 30 June 2010. The recovery of these benefits results in the flow of taxable economic benefits to Iris Ltd. Hence, a future taxable amount of $3500 exists. As this is a revenue item, no future deduction is available. The tax base is $0 because the cash received affects taxable profit in the year of receipt. As the future taxable amount exceeds the future deductible amount, a taxable temporary difference of $3500 exists in respect of the rent receivable.
4. The development project asset represents the future economic benefits expected to arise from development work undertaken in the current year. When those benefits are received, they are taxable. The total expenditure on development was deducted from taxable profit in the current year, so no future deduction is available. The tax base is $0 as the cash paid has already reduced taxable profit in the current year. As the future taxable amount exceeds the future deductible amount, a taxable temporary difference of $90 000 exists in respect of the development project.
5. The carrying amount of equipment represents the future economic benefits expected to be received from that asset over the remainder of its useful life, $110 000 ($200 000 – $90 000). When those benefits are received, they are taxable. Iris Ltd will be able to claim a deduction against those taxable benefits, but only to the extent of the carrying amount of the asset for taxation purposes. As the depreciation rate for tax purposes is greater than the accounting rate, the future deduction is only $80 000, being the original cost of $200 000 less $120 000 (that is, 3 years' accumulated depreciation at 20% per annum). As the future taxable amount exceeds the future deductible amount, a taxable temporary difference of $30 000 exists in respect of equipment.

6. The carrying amount of goodwill represents the future economic benefits expected to be received. Those benefits are taxable when received but, unlike equipment, no deduction against the benefits is available. The tax base of goodwill is $0 as taxation law does not allow a deduction for any amounts paid to acquire goodwill. As the future taxable amount exceeds the future deductible amount, a taxable temporary difference of $21 000 exists in respect of goodwill.
7. The provision for annual leave represents leave accrued by employees as at the end of the reporting period. As the leave represents future payments, there is no future taxable amount. When those payments are made, they are fully deductible against taxable profit. The tax base at 30 June 2010 is $0 because leave payments are only deductible in the year of payment. As the future deductible amount exceeds the future taxable amount, a deductible temporary difference of $61 000 exists in respect of the annual leave provision.
8. The adjustment for excluded differences recognises that IAS 12 (paras 15 and 24) has prohibited the recognition of deferred tax amounts relating to certain temporary differences (see section 7.6.5). Paragraph 15 prohibits the recognition of the taxable temporary difference relating to goodwill, so it is removed from the total temporary differences existing at 30 June 2010.
9. The deferred tax liability figure of $46 050 is the future tax payable as a result of the existence of taxable temporary differences of $153 500. The deferred tax asset figure of $23 100 is the future deductions available as a result of the existence of deductible temporary differences of $77 000. These figures represent the closing balances of the deferred tax accounts.
10. Deferred tax amounts may accumulate over time — for example, the taxable temporary difference for equipment represents 3 years differentials between accounting and taxation depreciation charges. This means that the deferred tax accounts have an opening balance representing prior year differences. If no adjustment is made for the opening balance, the deferred tax amounts are overstated. Accordingly, the opening balances are deducted from the total balances in order to determine the adjustment necessary to account for changes (additions and reversals) to deferred tax items during the current year. These adjustments are shown on the last line of the worksheet and form the basis of the adjusting journal entry for deferred tax. Positive figures are increases and negative figures are decreases in the account balances.
11. Normally, the deferred tax accounts are only adjusted at the end of each reporting period after the worksheet has been completed. Occasionally, however, adjustments are made to the deferred accounts during the year so the 'movements' line is used to adjust for such changes. Adjustments could be made for:
    - recoupment of prior year tax losses (see section 7.7)
    - a change in tax rates (see section 7.10)
    - an amendment to a prior year tax return (see section 7.11)
    - revaluation of property, plant and equipment items (see section 7.12)
    - business combinations (see section 7.13).

7.9 RECOGNITION OF DEFERRED TAX LIABILITIES AND DEFERRED TAX ASSETS

The existence of temporary taxable and deductible differences may not result in the recognition of deferred tax assets and liabilities. Paragraphs 15 and 24 of IAS 12 specify recognition criteria that must be met before recognition occurs.

7.9.1 Deferred tax liabilities

Deferred tax liabilities must be recognised for all taxable temporary differences (except as outlined below). A liability is recognised when, and only when, it is probable that an outflow of resources embodying economic benefits will result from the settlement of a present obligation, and the amount at which the settlement will take place can be measured reliably (*Framework*, para. 91). There is no need to explicitly consider the recognition criteria for a deferred tax liability, because it is always probable that resources will flow from the entity to pay the tax associated with taxable temporary differences. As the carrying amount of the asset or liability giving rise to the taxable temporary difference is recovered or settled, the temporary difference will reverse and give rise to taxable amounts in future periods.

7.9.2 Deferred tax assets

Deferred tax assets must be recognised for all deductible temporary differences (subject to certain exceptions) and from the carry forward of tax losses, but only to the extent that is it *probable* that future taxable profits will be available against which the temporary differences can be utilised.

An asset is recognised when it is probable that the future economic benefits will flow to the entity, and the asset has a cost or value that can be measured reliably (*Framework*, para. 89). According to paragraph 85 of the *Framework*, probability refers to the degree of uncertainty about whether the future economic benefits associated with the asset will flow to the entity. This probability must be assessed using the best evidence available based on the conditions at the end of the reporting period. The reversal of deductible temporary differences results in deductions against the taxable profits of future periods. Economic benefits in the form of reductions in tax payments will flow to the entity only if it earns sufficient taxable profits against which the deductions can be offset. Therefore, an entity recognises deferred tax assets only when it is probable that taxable profits will be available against which the deductible temporary differences can be utilised (IAS 12, para. 27). The realisation of a deferred tax asset would be probable where:

- there are sufficient taxable temporary differences relating to the same taxation authority and the same taxable entity that are expected to reverse in the same period as the deductible temporary differences, or in periods to which a tax loss arising from the deferred tax asset can be carried back or forward (para. 28)
- there would be taxable temporary differences arising if unrecognised increases in the fair values of assets were recognised
- it is probable that there will be other sufficient taxable profits arising in future periods against which to utilise the deductions
- other factors indicate that it is probable that the deductions can be realised.

If there are insufficient taxable temporary differences available against which to offset the deductible temporary differences, an entity can recognise a deferred tax asset only to the extent that sufficient taxable profits will be made in the future or that tax planning opportunities are available to create future taxable profits (IAS 12, para. 29). The following examples of tax planning opportunities that may be available in some jurisdictions are given in paragraph 30 of the standard:

- electing to have interest income taxed on either a received or a receivable basis
- deferring the claim for certain deductions from taxable profit
- selling, and perhaps leasing back, assets that have appreciated but for which the tax base has not been adjusted to reflect such appreciation
- selling an asset that generates non-taxable income in order to purchase another investment that generates taxable income.

A history of accounting losses, or the existence of unused tax losses, provides evidence that future taxable profits are unlikely to be available for the utilisation of deductible temporary differences. In these circumstances, the recognition of deferred tax assets would require either the existence of sufficient taxable temporary differences or convincing evidence that future taxable profits will be earned. In assessing the likelihood that tax losses will be utilised, the entity should consider whether:

- future budgets indicate that there will be sufficient taxable income derived in the foreseeable future
- the losses arise from causes that are unlikely to recur in the foreseeable future
- actions can be taken to create taxable amounts in the future
- there are existing contracts or sales backlogs that will produce taxable amounts
- there are new developments or favourable opportunities likely to give rise to taxable amounts
- there is a strong history of earnings other than those giving rise to the loss, and the loss was an aberration and not a continuing condition.

Where, on the balance of the evidence available, it is not probable that deductible temporary differences will be utilised in the future, no deferred tax asset is recognised. This probability assessment must also be applied to deferred tax assets that have previously been recognised and, if it is no longer probable that the benefits of such assets will flow to the entity, the carrying amount must be derecognised by passing the following entry:

30 June			
Income Tax Expense	Dr	XXX	
Deferred Tax Asset	Cr		XXX
(Derecognition of deferred tax assets where recovery is no longer probable)			

At the end of each reporting period, the entity should reassess the probability of recovery of all unrecognised deferred tax assets; it should recognise these assets to the extent that it is now probable that future taxable profit will allow the deduction of the temporary difference on its reversal. Changes in trading conditions, new taxation legislation, or a business combination may all contribute to improving the chance of recovering the deferred tax benefits. Paragraph 60 of IAS 12 requires that any adjustment to deferred tax be recognised in the statement of comprehensive income except to the extent that it relates to items previously charged or credited to equity.

ILLUSTRATIVE EXAMPLE 7.7

Recognition of deferred tax adjustments

Using the figures calculated in illustrative example 7.6 and assuming that the recognition criteria for deferred tax assets can be met, the adjusting journal for deferred tax movements is:

30 June 2010			
Income Tax Expense (Deferred)	Dr	30 700	
Deferred Tax Asset	Cr		1 800
Deferred Tax Liability	Cr		28 900
(Recognition of movements in deferred tax balances for the year)			

These movements can be checked back to the current worksheet as follows:

- Deferred tax assets arise in respect of doubtful debts and annual leave. In the current year, additional deductions of $2000 (doubtful debts) and $4000 (leave) are received. This indicates that more deductible temporary differences had been reversed than had been created, resulting in a decrease of $6000 in future deductions and a $1800 decrease in the deferred tax asset.
- Deferred tax liabilities arise in respect of development expenditure, equipment, insurance and rent. In the current year, additional deductions of $90 000 (development), $13 333 (depreciation) and $5000 (insurance) are offset by additional taxable amounts of $10 000 (sale of equipment) and $2000 (rent revenue), giving a net extra increase in taxable temporary differences and a $28 900 increase in the deferred tax liability.

The posting of this entry results in the deferred tax ledger accounts appearing as follows:

Deferred Tax Asset

1/7/09	Balance b/d	24 900	30/6/10	Income Tax Expense	1 800
			30/6/10	Balance c/d	23 100
		24 900			24 900
1/7/10	Balance b/d	23 100			

Deferred Tax Liability				
30/6/10 Balance c/d	46 050	1/7/09	Balance b/d	17 150
		30/6/10	Income Tax Expense	28 900
	46 050			46 050
		1/7/10	Balance b/d	46 050

If the two taxation adjusting journals — current and deferred — are combined, then the total income tax expense recorded for the year ended 2010 by Iris Ltd is:

Income tax expense (current) (see section 7.5)	$41 270
Income tax expense (deferred) (see above)	30 700
Total	$71 970

This figure represents the total tax consequences of the transactions recorded in profit and loss for the year. It can be checked in this way: The accounting profit for the year is $250 450. All items of revenue and expense are taxable or deductible with the exception of goodwill impairment and entertainment expense. The development expenditure during the year gave rise to an 'extra' deduction of $30 000 against taxable profit. If the accounting profit adjusted for these permanent differences is multiplied by the tax rate, the result represents the total tax payable above (both now and in the future):

Accounting profit	$250 450
Add Non-deductible amortisation	7 000
Add Non-deductible entertainment expense	12 450
Less Additional deduction for development	(30 000)
Taxable net profit	239 900
Tax @ 30%	$ 71 970

Thus, the income tax expense for the year has been reconciled.

7.9.3 Recognition of deferred amounts arising from investments

Where taxable or deductible temporary differences are associated with investments in subsidiaries, branches and associates, and with interests in joint ventures, the deferred tax liabilities and deferred tax assets associated with these temporary differences must be raised in accordance with paragraphs 39 and 44 of IAS 12. Temporary differences arise when the carrying amount of an investment or the interest in a joint venture differs from its tax base. Such differences may be caused by:

- the existence of undistributed profits of subsidiaries, branches, associates and joint ventures
- changes in foreign exchange rates when a parent and its subsidiary are based in different countries
- a reduction in the carrying amount of an investment in an associate to its recoverable amount.

The recognition of a deferred tax liability in relation to investments is required, by paragraph 39 of IAS 12, except where both of the following conditions are satisfied:

(a) the parent, investor or venturer is able to control the timing of the reversal of the temporary difference; and
(b) it is probable that the temporary difference will not reverse in the foreseeable future.

Because there is no definition of or discussion about the meaning of the term 'foreseeable future', managerial judgement is required to determine whether the facts and circumstances associated with a particular investment satisfy the above criteria.

As both branches and subsidiaries are 'controlled' by the parent, the first condition would always be met for such investments. However, where the temporary difference arises with respect to undistributed profits in an associate and the investor cannot control the declaration of dividends from those profits, a deferred tax liability would be recognised.

Deferred tax assets associated with investments would normally arise when the investment has been written down to the recoverable amount, or when the application of fair value or equity accounting has written it down below its tax base. The recognition of such a deferred tax asset is allowed only to the extent that the temporary difference will reverse in the foreseeable future and taxable profit will be available against which the temporary difference can be utilised (IAS 12, para. 44).

Figure 7.5 below provides a flowchart summarising the accounting for deferred tax items.

FIGURE 7.5 Accounting for deferred tax items
Source: Adapted from Deloitte Touche Tohmatsu (2001).

7.10 CHANGE OF TAX RATES

When a new tax rate is enacted (or substantively enacted), the new rate should be applied in calculating the current tax liability and adjustments to deferred tax accounts during the year. It should also be applied to the deferred amounts recognised in prior years. A journal adjustment must be passed to increase or reduce the carrying amounts of deferred tax assets and liabilities, in order to reflect the new value of future taxable or deductible amounts. Paragraph 60 of IAS 12 requires the net amount arising from the restatement of deferred tax balances to be recognised in the statement of comprehensive income, except to the extent that the deferred tax amounts relate to items previously charged or credited to equity.

ILLUSTRATIVE EXAMPLE 7.8

Change of tax rate

As at 30 June 2010, the balances of deferred tax accounts for Carnation Ltd were:

Deferred tax asset	$ 29 600
Deferred tax liability	(72 800)

In September 2010, the government reduced the company tax rate from 40 cents to 30 cents in the dollar, effective from 1 July 2010. The recorded deferred tax balances represent the tax effect of future taxable amounts and future deductible amounts at 40 cents in the dollar, so they are now overstated and must be adjusted as follows:

	Deferred tax asset	Deferred tax liability
Opening balance	$29 600	$72 800
Adjustment for change in tax rate: ([40 – 30]/40)	(7 400)	(18 200)
Restated balance	$22 200	$54 600

The adjusting journal entry is:

Deferred Tax Liability	Dr	18 200	
Deferred Tax Asset	Cr		7 400
Income Tax Expense	Cr		10 800
(Recognition of the impact of a change of tax rate on deferred tax amounts)			

7.11 AMENDED PRIOR YEAR TAX FIGURES

In taxation jurisdictions where entities self-assess their taxable profit, it is possible that the taxation authority will amend that assessment by changing the amount of taxable or deductible items. This amendment could result in the entity being liable to pay extra tax or becoming eligible for a taxation refund. Upon receipt of an amended assessment, the entity should analyse the reason for the adjustment and consider whether both current and deferred tax are affected. For example, if an entity has used an incorrect taxation depreciation rate, then the amendment to the correct rate will change both the prior year taxable profit and future taxable profits across the economic life of the depreciable asset. If only current tax for the previous year has changed, the following journal entry would be passed:

Income Tax Expense	Dr	XXX	
Current Tax Liability	Cr		XXX
(Amendment to prior year current tax on receipt of amended assessment)			

If the amendment also changes a deferred item, the new temporary difference will need to be calculated and the carry-forward balance adjusted accordingly. In the depreciation example used above, the adjustment (assuming the accounting depreciation rate is lower than the rate used to calculate taxable income) is:

Income Tax Expense	Dr	XXX	
Deferred Tax Liability	Cr		XXX
Current Tax Liability	Cr		XXX
(Amendment to prior year current tax and deferred tax liability on receipt of amended assessment)			

Any amendment to the deferred tax liability or the deferred tax asset arising from amended assessments would appear on the deferred tax worksheet as a 'movement' adjustment.

7.12 ITEMS CREDITED OR CHARGED DIRECTLY TO EQUITY

In general, the amount of current and deferred tax arising in a period must be adjusted directly to equity if it relates to an amount that is or was directly charged or directly credited to equity (IAS 12, para. 61). Examples of such items are:

- revaluation of items of property, plant and equipment to fair value (see chapter 9). At the time of revaluation, an adjustment must be made to the balance of the deferred tax liability account. For example, if an item of plant is revalued upwards from 100 to 200 and the tax rate is 30%, the entity would pass the following journal entry:

Plant	Dr	100	
Deferred Tax Liability	Cr		30
Asset Revaluation Surplus	Cr		70
(Revaluation of plant to fair value)			

- an adjustment to the opening balance of retained earnings resulting from either a change in accounting policy that is applied retrospectively or from the correction of a fundamental error
- exchange differences arising on the translation of the financial statements of a foreign entity (see chapter 26)
- amounts arising on the initial recognition of the equity component of a compound financial instrument (see chapter 5).

Where it is difficult to identify the amount of current or deferred tax relating to items charged or credited directly to equity, as may happen when graduated rates of income tax are applicable or a tax rate or rule has changed, a reasonable allocation should be made pro rata (IAS 12, para. 63).

7.13 DEFERRED TAX ARISING FROM A BUSINESS COMBINATION

The amount of deferred tax arising in relation to the acquisition of an entity or business is recognised (subject to the recognition criteria) and included as part of net assets acquired when determining the goodwill or excess arising on acquisition. (Further discussion of the determination of goodwill and excess can be found in chapter 11.) When a deferred tax asset of the acquiree not recognised at the date of a business combination is subsequently recognised by the acquirer, the resulting deferred tax income is recognised in the statement of comprehensive income. Additionally, paragraph 68 of IAS 12 requires that the amount of goodwill recognised on acquisition must be adjusted to the amount that would be recorded had the deferred tax asset been recognised on acquisition, and must recognise the reduction in the carrying amount of the goodwill as expense. The same paragraph provides an illustrative example.

7.14 PRESENTATION IN THE FINANCIAL STATEMENTS

IAS 12 specifies the way in which tax items (revenues, expenses, assets and liabilities) are to be presented in the financial statements, including the circumstances in which items can be offset.

7.14.1 Tax assets and tax liabilities

Tax assets and tax liabilities must be classified as current and non-current as required by IAS 1 *Presentation of Financial Statements* (para. 60) and presented in the statement of financial position in accordance with IAS 1, paragraphs 54(n), 54(o) and 56. Paragraph 71 of IAS 12 allows current tax assets and current tax liabilities to be offset only when the entity has a legally enforceable right to offset the amount, and intends either to settle on a net basis or to realise the asset and settle the liability simultaneously. A legal right to set off the accounts would normally exist where the accounts relate to income taxes levied by the same taxing authority.

Deferred tax assets and deferred tax liabilities can be offset only if a legally enforceable right to offset current amounts exists; and the deferred items relate to income taxes levied by the same taxing authority on the same taxable entity, or on different taxable entities which intend either to settle on a net basis or to realise the asset and settle the liability simultaneously in each future period in which significant deferred amounts will reverse (IAS 12, para. 74).

Consequently, entities operating in a single country will normally offset both current and deferred tax assets and liabilities, and show only a net current tax liability or asset and a net deferred asset or liability.

7.14.2 Tax expense

The tax expense (or income) related to profit or loss for the period is required to be presented in the statement of comprehensive income (IAS 12, para. 77).

7.15 DISCLOSURES

Paragraphs 79–82A of IAS 12 contain the required disclosures relating to income taxes. These disclosures are very detailed, and provide significant additional information about the makeup of income tax expense (or income), and both taxable and deductible temporary differences. Paragraph 79 requires the tax expense figure shown in the statement of comprehensive income to be broken down into its various components (examples of which are listed in paragraph 80), such as current tax expense and deferred tax arising from temporary differences. Paragraph 81 requires a wide range of disclosures including tax relating to equity and discontinued operations, changes in tax rates, and unrecognised deferred tax assets and liabilities.

Paragraph 81 also requires two detailed reconciliations to be prepared:

- Paragraph 81(c) requires entities to disclose 'an explanation of the relationship between tax expense (income) and accounting profit'. This essentially reconciles expected tax — accounting

profit multiplied by tax rate — to the actual tax expense recognised. The reconciliation enables financial statement users to understand why the relationship between accounting profit and income tax expense is unusual, the factors causing the variance, and factors that could affect the relationship in the future. Entities are allowed to reconcile in either or both of the following ways:
- a numerical reconciliation between tax expense and expected tax
- a numerical reconciliation between the average effective tax rate (tax expense divided by the accounting profit) and the applicable tax rate.

Irrespective of the reconciliation method used, entities must disclose the basis on which the applicable tax rate is computed.

- Paragraph 81(g) requires disclosure of the following information for deferred tax items recognised in the statement of financial position:

  in respect of each type of temporary difference, and in respect of each type of unused tax losses and unused tax credits:
  (i) the amount of the deferred tax assets and liabilities recognised in the statement of financial position for each period presented
  (ii) the amount of the deferred tax income or expense recognised in profit or loss, if this is not apparent from the changes in the amounts recognised in the statement of financial position.

  Normally, the second part of the paragraph 81(g) disclosure is required only if a change in tax rate or legislation has occurred during the year, or if some other event causes an adjustment to a deferred account during the period.

When an entity has suffered tax losses in either the current or previous period, and recognised a deferred tax asset related to those losses that is dependent on earning future taxable profits in excess of those arising on the reversal of taxable temporary differences, paragraph 82 requires disclosure of the amount of the deferred tax asset and the nature of the evidence supporting its recognition.

Paragraph 82A applies only in those jurisdictions where tax rates vary according to the quantum of profit or retained earnings distributed as dividends. In this situation, paragraph 82A requires the entity to disclose the nature and amounts (to the extent practicable) of the potential income tax consequences that would result from the payment of dividends to its shareholders.

Figure 7.6 provides an illustration of the disclosures required by IAS 12.

FIGURE 7.6 Illustrative disclosures required by IAS 12

Note 4: Income tax expense	Notes	2010 $	2009 $	IAS 12 para.
Major components of income tax expense				*79*
Current tax expense		126 600	117 600	*80(a)*
Deferred tax from origination and reversal of temporary differences		(20 250)	11 320	*80(c)*
Deferred tax relating to tax rate change		250	—	*80(d)*
Benefit from unrecognised tax loss used to reduce current tax expense		(1 500)	—	*80(e)*
Income tax expense		105 100	128 920	*80(f)*
Tax relating to items charged (credited) direct to equity				
Deferred tax relating to revaluation of land		12 500	—	*80(h)*
Reconciliation of tax expense to prima facie tax on accounting profit				*81(b)*
The applicable tax rate is the Australian company income tax rate of 30% (2009: 40%)				*81(c)(i)*

FIGURE 7.6 *(continued)*

Note 4: Income tax expense	Notes	2010 $	2009 $	IAS 12 para.
The prima facie tax on accounting profit differs from the tax expense provided in the accounts as follows:				
Accounting profit		402 000	397 000	
Prima facie tax at 30% (2009: 40%)		120 600	158 800	
Tax effect of non-deductible expenses				
Goodwill impairment		3 900	5 200	
Non-taxable revenue		(1 500)	(2 000)	
Entertainment		3 600	2 300	
		126 600	164 300	
Increase in beginning deferred taxes resulting from reduction in tax rate		250	—	
Reduction in current tax from recoupment of tax losses		(1 500)	—	
Tax effect of net movements in items giving rise to:*				
Deferred tax assets		(8 250)	3 200	
Deferred tax liabilities		(12 000)	(38 580)	
Tax expense		105 100	128 920	*81(d)*
Change in tax rate				
As of 1 July 2009, the company tax rate changed from 40% to 30%				*81(d)*
*These figures represent the net effect of movements in assets and liabilities during the year which have increased or decreased current tax. The details can be found in disclosures required by paragraph 81(g)(ii).				
Unrecognised deferred tax assets				
Tax losses in respect of which deferred tax has not been recognised as it is not probable that benefits will be received		20 000	40 000	*81(e)*
Unrecognised deferred tax liabilities				
Aggregate of temporary differences associated with investments in subsidiaries for which deferred tax liabilities have not been recognised		16 000	16 000	*81(f)*
Deferred tax assets and liabilities				
The following items have given rise to deferred tax assets:				
Accounts receivable		12 000	15 000	
Employee entitlements		24 000	22 000	
Total deferred tax assets		36 000	37 000	
The following items have given rise to deferred tax liabilities:				
Land		12 500	—	
Plant and equipment		15 000	36 000	
Total deferred tax liabilities		27 500	36 000	
Offset of deferred tax asset against liability		36 000	37 000	
Net deferred tax asset (liability)		8 500	(1 000)	*81(g)(i)*

(continued)

FIGURE 7.6 *(continued)*

Note 4: Income tax expense	Notes	2010 $	2009 $	IAS 12 para.
Deferred tax expenses (income) recognised in the statement of comprehensive income for each type of temporary difference*				
Deferred tax expense in relation to:				
Plant and equipment		(12 000)	(38 580)	
Total deferred tax expense		(12 000)	(38 580)	
Deferred tax income in relation to:				
Accounts receivable		750	1 200	
Employee entitlements		7 500	2 000	
Total deferred tax income		8 250	3 200	*81(g)(ii)*

*This disclosure is required only if the movements in deferred items cannot readily be ascertained from other disclosures made with respect to deferred assets and liabilities. This is the case in this situation because the change in tax rate adjustments has obscured the movements in deferred items.

Figure 7.7 shows the income tax notes to the financial statements of Nokia Corporation for the year ended 31 December 2007, which were prepared in accordance with International Financial Reporting Standards (IFRSs).

FIGURE 7.7 Income tax notes to the consolidated financial statements of Nokia Corporation

11. Income Taxes

EURm	2007	2006	2005
Income tax expense			
Current tax	(2 209)	(1 303)	(1 262)
Deferred tax	687	(54)	(19)
Total	(1 522)	(1 357)	(1 281)
Finland	(1 323)	(941)	(759)
Other countries	(199)	(416)	(522)
Total	(1 522)	(1 357)	(1 281)

The differences between income tax expense computed at the statutory rate in Finland of 26% and income taxes recognized in the consolidated income statement is reconciled as follows at December 31, 2007:

EURm	2007	2006	2005
Income tax expense at statutory rate	2 150	1 488	1 295
Provisions without tax benefit/expense	61	12	11
Non-taxable gain on formation of Nokia Siemens Networks[1]	(489)	0	0
Taxes for prior years	20	(24)	1
Taxes on foreign subsidiaries' profits in excess of (lower than) income taxes at statutory rates	(138)	(73)	(30)
Operating losses with no current tax benefit	15	0	0
Net increase in provisions	50	(12)	22
Change in income tax rate[2]	(114)	0	0
Deferred tax liability on undistributed earnings[3]	(37)	(3)	8
Other	4	(31)	(26)
Income tax expense	1 522	1 357	1 281

FIGURE 7.7 *(continued)*

[1]See Note 8.
[2]The change in income tax rate decreased Group tax expense primarly due to the impact of a decrease in the German statutory tax rate on deferred tax asset balances.
[3]The change in deferred tax liability on undistributed earnings mainly related to amendment of the FIN-US tax treaty, which abolished the withholding tax under certain conditions.

Income taxes include a tax benefit from received and accrued tax refunds from previous years of EUR 84 million in 2006 and EUR 48 million in 2005.

Certain of the Group companies' income tax returns for periods ranging from 2001 through 2007 are under examination by tax authorities. The Group does not believe that any significant additional taxes in excess of those already provided for will arise as a result of the examinations.

24. Deferred taxes

EURm	2007	2006
Deferred tax assets:		
Intercompany profit in inventory	**87**	34
Tax losses carried forward	**314**	41
Warranty provision	**132**	134
Other provisions	**292**	253
Depreciation differences and untaxed reserves	**367**	104
Share-based compensation	**227**	70
Other temporary differences	**134**	173
Total deferred tax assets	**1 553**	809
Deferred tax liabilities:		
Depreciation differences and untaxed reserves	**(165)**	(23)
Fair value gains/losses	**(40)**	(16)
Undistributed earnings	**(31)**	(65)
Other temporary differences[1]	**(727)**	(101)
Total deferred tax liabilities	**(963)**	(205)
Net deferred tax asset	**590**	604
The tax charged to shareholders' equity is as follows:		
Fair value and other reserves, fair value gains/losses and excess tax benefit on share-based compensation	**133**	(43)

[1]In 2007, other temporary differences included a deferred tax liability of EUR 563 million arising from purchase price allocation related to Nokia Siemens Networks.

Deferred taxes include deferred tax assets and liabilities arising from the formation of Nokia Siemens Networks at April 1, 2007. See Note 8.

At December 31, 2007, the Group had loss carry forwards, primarily attributable to foreign subsidiaries of EUR 1 403 million (EUR 143 million in 2006), most of which do not have an expiry date.

At December 31, 2007, the Group had loss carry forwards of EUR 242 million (EUR 24 million in 2006) for which no deferred tax asset was recognized due to uncertainty of utilization of these loss carry forwards. Part of these losses do not have an expiry date.

At December 31, 2007, the Group had undistributed earnings of EUR 315 million, for which no deferred tax liability was recognized as these earnings are considered permanently invested.

Source: Nokia (2007, pp. 26, 34).

SUMMARY

This chapter analyses the content of IAS 12 *Income Taxes* and provides guidance on its implementation. The principal issue in accounting for taxes is how to account for the current and future tax consequences of transactions and other events of the current period. The accounting standard requires entities to recognise (with limited exceptions) deferred tax liabilities and deferred tax-assets when the recovery or settlement of an asset or liability will result in larger or smaller tax payments than would occur if such settlement or recovery had no tax consequence. The tax consequences of transactions are to be accounted for in the same way as the transaction to which they are related. Therefore, for transactions recognised in the statement of comprehensive income, all related tax effects are also recognised in the statement of comprehensive income. Where a transaction requires a direct adjustment to equity, so do any tax effects. Deferred tax assets, particularly those relating to tax losses, are recognised only if it is probable that the entity will have sufficient taxable profit in the future against which the tax benefit can be offset. All deferred tax liabilities must be recognised in full. IAS 12 requires extensive disclosures to be made in relation to both current and deferred tax items.

Discussion questions

1. What is the main principle of tax-effect accounting as outlined in IAS 12?
2. Explain the meaning of a temporary difference as it relates to deferred tax calculations and give three examples.
3. Explain how accounting profit and taxable profit differ, and how each is treated when accounting for income taxes.
4. In tax-effect accounting, the creation of temporary differences between the carrying amount and the tax base for assets and liabilities leads to the establishment of deferred tax assets and liabilities in the accounting records. List examples of temporary differences that create:
   (a) deferred tax assets
   (b) deferred tax liabilities.
5. In IAS 12, criteria are established for the recognition of a deferred tax asset and a deferred tax liability. Identify these criteria, and discuss any differences between the criteria for assets and those for liabilities.
6. What is a 'tax loss' and how is it accounted for?
7. 'Despite the fact that deferred tax liabilities and assets are recognised in respect of certain assets and liabilities, the income tax expense (or benefit) of such items is always recognised in the current year.' Is this statement true? Discuss.
8. What action should be taken when a tax rate or tax rule changes? Why?
9. Are all temporary differences that exist at the end of the reporting period recognised as deferred tax assets or deferred tax liabilities?
10. In determining whether deferred tax assets relating to tax losses are to be recognised, what factors should be taken into consideration?

STAR RATING
★ BASIC
★★ MODERATE
★★★ DIFFICULT

Exercises

Exercise 7.1

TAX EFFECTS OF A TEMPORARY DIFFERENCE

★ The following information was extracted from the records of Protea Ltd for the year ended 30 June 2009:

PROTEA LTD
Deferred Tax Worksheet (extract)
as at 30 June 2009

	Carrying amount	Future taxable amount	Future deductible amount	Tax base	Taxable temporary differences	Deductible temporary differences
Relevant assets						
Equipment	$60 000	$(60 000)	$108 000	$108 000		$48 000

Equipment is depreciated at 25% p.a. straight-line for accounting purposes, but the allowable rate for taxation is 20% p.a.

Required

Assuming that no equipment is purchased or sold during the years ended 30 June 2010 and 30 June 2011, calculate:

(a) the accounting expense and tax deduction for each year
(b) the impact of depreciation on the taxable profit for each year
(c) the movement in the temporary difference balance for each year.

Exercise 7.2

CALCULATION OF CURRENT TAX

★ Thistle Ltd made an accounting profit before tax of $40 000 for the year ended 30 June 2011. Included in the accounting profit were the following items of revenue and expense.

Donations to political parties (non-deductible)	5 000
Depreciation — machinery (20%)	15 000
Annual leave expense	5 600
Rent revenue	12 000

For tax purposes the following applied:

Depreciation rate for machinery	25%
Annual leave paid	6 500
Rent received	10 000
Income tax rate	30%

Required

1. Calculate the current tax liability for the year ended 30 June 2011, and prepare the adjusting journal entry.
2. Explain your treatment of rent items in your answer to part 1.

Exercise 7.3

CALCULATION OF DEFERRED TAX

★ The following information was extracted from the records of Orchid Ltd for the year ended 30 June 2011:

ORCHID LTD Statement of financial position (extract) as at 30 June 2011		
Assets		
Accounts receivable	$ 25 000	
Allowance for doubtful debts	(2 000)	$23 000
Machines	100 000	
Accumulated depreciation — machines	(25 000)	75 000
Liabilities		
Interest payable		1 000

Additional information

The accumulated depreciation for tax purposes at 30 June 2011 was $50 000.
The tax rate is 30%.

Required

Prepare a deferred tax worksheet to identify the temporary differences arising in respect of the assets and liabilities in the statement of financial position, and to calculate the balance of the deferred tax liability and deferred tax asset accounts at 30 June 2011. Assume the opening balance of the deferred tax accounts was $0.

Exercise 7.4

CALCULATION OF CURRENT TAX

★ Daisy Ltd recorded an accounting profit before tax of $100 000 for the year ended 30 June 2012. Included in the accounting profit were the following items of revenue and expense.

Entertainment expenses (non-deductible)	$ 2 000
Depreciation — vehicles (10%)	17 000
Rent revenue	2 500
For tax purposes the following applied:	
Depreciation rate — vehicles	15%
Rent received	$ 3 000
Income tax rate	30%

Required

1. Use a current tax worksheet to calculate the current tax liability for the year ended 30 June 2012. Prepare the adjusting journal entry.
2. Explain the future tax effect of the adjustment made in part 1 for interest received/revenue.

Exercise 7.5

CREATION AND REVERSAL OF TEMPORARY DIFFERENCES

★★ The following are all independent situations. Prepare the journal entries for deferred tax on the creation or reversal of any temporary differences. Explain in each case the nature of the temporary difference. Assume a tax rate of 30%.

1. The entity has an allowance for doubtful debts of $10 000 at the end of the current year relating to accounts receivable of $125 000. The prior year balances for these accounts were $8 500 and $97 500 respectively. During the current year, debts worth $9 250 were written off as uncollectable.
2. The entity sold a vehicle at the end of the current year for $15 000. The vehicle cost $100 000 when purchased 3 years ago, and had a carrying amount of $25 000 when sold. The taxation depreciation rate for equipment of this type is $33\frac{1}{3}$%.
3. The entity has recognised an interest receivable asset with a beginning balance of $17 000 and an ending balance of $19 500 for the current year. During the year, interest of $127 000 was received in cash.
4. At the end of the current year, the entity has recognised a liability of $4 000 in respect of outstanding fines for non-compliance with safety legislation. Such fines are not tax-deductible.

Exercise 7.6

CREATION AND REVERSAL OF A TEMPORARY DIFFERENCE

★★ Rose Ltd purchased equipment on 1 July 2007 at a cost of $25 000. The equipment had an expected economic life of five years and was to be depreciated on a straight-line basis. The taxation depreciation rate for equipment of this type is 15% p.a. straight-line. On 30 June 2009, Rose Ltd reassessed the remaining economic life of the equipment from 3 years to 2 years, and the accounting depreciation charge was adjusted accordingly. The equipment was sold on 30 June 2010 for $15 000. The company tax rate is 30%.

Required

For each of the years ended 30 June 2008, 2009 and 2010, calculate the carrying amount and the tax base of the asset and determine the appropriate deferred tax entry. Explain your answer.

Exercise 7.7

PAYMENT OF INCOME TAX AND AMENDED ASSESSMENT

★★ Dover Ltd calculated its current tax liability at 30 June 2010 to be $57 500. This tax was paid in instalments as shown in the following table.

28 October 2009	$13 200
28 January 2010	11 600
28 April 2010	15 200
28 July 2010	17 500

On 1 November 2010, an amended assessment notice was received from the taxing authority. It disallowed a donation for $1500 claimed as a deduction, and amended the taxation depreciation rate used for vehicles from 50% to 30%. The accounting depreciation rate is 25%. As a result, further tax of $1950 was paid on 31 December 2010. The company tax rate is 30%.

Required

Prepare all journal entries necessary to record the taxation transactions for the period to 31 December 2010.

Exercise 7.8 ★★★

CALCULATION OF DEFERRED TAX, AND ADJUSTMENT ENTRY

The following information was extracted from the records of Bulb Ltd as at 30 June 2010:

Asset (liability)	Carrying amount	Tax base
Accounts receivable	$150 000	$175 000
Motor vehicles	165 000	125 000
Provision for warranty	(12 000)	0
Deposits received in advance	(15 000)	0

The depreciation rates for accounting and taxation are 15% and 25% respectively. Deposits are taxable when received, and warranty costs are deductible when paid. An allowance for doubtful debts of $25 000 has been raised against accounts receivable for accounting purposes, but such debts are deductible only when written off as uncollectable.

Required

1. Calculate the temporary differences for Bulb Ltd as at 30 June 2010. Justify your classification of each difference as either a deductible temporary difference or a taxable temporary difference.
2. Prepare the journal entry to record deferred tax for the year ended 30 June 2010 assuming no deferred items had been raised in prior years.

Problems

Problem 7.1 ★

CURRENT AND DEFERRED TAX

Myrtle Ltd has determined its accounting profit before tax for the year ended 30 June 2010 to be $256 700. Included in this profit are the items of revenue and expense shown below.

Royalty revenue (non-taxable)	$ 8 000
Proceeds on sale of building	75 000
Entertainment expense	1 700
Depreciation expense — buildings	7 600
Depreciation expense — plant	22 500
Carrying amount of building sold	70 000
Doubtful debts expense	4 100
Annual leave expense	46 000
Insurance expense	4 200
Development expense	15 000

The company's draft statement of financial position at 30 June 2010 showed the following assets and liabilities:

Assets		
Cash		$ 2 500
Accounts receivable	$ 21 500	
Less Allowance for doubtful debts	(4 100)	17 400
Inventory		31 600
Prepaid insurance		4 500
Land		75 000
Buildings	170 000	
Less Accumulated depreciation	(59 500)	110 500
Plant	150 000	
Less Accumulated depreciation	(67 500)	82 500
Deferred tax asset (opening balance)		9 600
		333 600
Liabilities		
Accounts payable		25 000
Provision for annual leave		10 000
Deferred tax liability (opening balance)		6 000
Loan		140 000
		$181 000

Additional information

(a) Quarterly income tax instalments paid during the year were:

28 October 2009	$18 000
28 January 2010	17 500
28 April 2010	18 000

with the final balance due on 28 July 2010.

(b) The tax depreciation rate for plant (which cost $150 000 3 years ago) is 20%. Depreciation on buildings is not deductible for taxation purposes.

(c) The building sold during the year had cost $100 000 when acquired 6 years ago. The company depreciates buildings at 5% p.a., straight-line. Any gain (loss) on sale of buildings is not taxable (i.e. not deductible).

(d) During the year, the following cash amounts were paid:

Annual leave	$52 000
Insurance	3 700

(e) Bad debts of $3500 were written off against the allowance for doubtful debts during the year.

(f) The $15 000 spent (and expensed) on development during the year is not deductible for tax purposes until 30 June 2011.

(g) Myrtle Ltd has tax losses amounting to $12 500 carried forward from prior years.

(h) The company tax rate is 30%.

Required

1. Determine the balance of any current and deferred tax assets and liabilities for Myrtle Ltd as at 30 June 2010.
2. Prepare any necessary journal entries.

Problem 7.2 ★

CALCULATION OF MOVEMENTS IN DEFERRED TAX ACCOUNTS

The statements of financial position of Acacia Ltd at 30 June 2011 showed the following net assets:

	2011	2010
Assets		
Cash	80 000	85 000
Inventory	170 000	155 000
Receivables	500 000	480 000
Allowance for doubtful debts	(55 000)	(40 000)
Plant	500 000	500 000
Accumulated depreciation	(260 000)	(210 000)
Deferred tax asset	?	40 500
Liabilities		
Accounts payable	290 000	260 000
Provision for long-service leave	60 000	45 000
Rent received in advance	25 000	20 000
Deferred tax liability	?	38 100

Additional information

- Accumulated depreciation of plant for tax purposes was $315 000 at 30 June 2010, and depreciation for tax purposes for the year ended 30 June 2011 amounted to $75 000.
- The tax rate is 30%.

Required

Prepare a worksheet to calculate the end of reporting period adjustment to deferred tax asset and liability accounts as at 30 June 2011, and show the necessary journal entry.

Problem 7.3 ★

CALCULATION OF CURRENT TAX LIABILITY AND ADJUSTING JOURNAL ENTRY

The profit before tax, as reported in the statement of comprehensive income of Violet for the year ended 30 June 2011, amounted to $60 000, including the following revenue and expense items:

Rent revenue	$3 000
Government grant received (non-taxable)	1 000
Bad debts expense	6 000
Depreciation of plant	5 000
Annual leave expense	3 000
Entertainment costs (non-deductible)	1 800
Depreciation of buildings (non-deductible)	800

The statement of financial position of the company at 30 June 2011 showed the following net assets.

	2011	2010
Assets		
Cash	8 000	8 500
Inventory	17 000	15 500
Receivables	50 000	48 000
Allowance for doubtful debts	(5 500)	(4 000)
Office supplies	2 500	2 200
Plant	50 000	50 000
Accumulated depreciation	(26 000)	(21 000)

(continued)

	2011	2010
Assets *(continued)*		
Buildings	30 000	30 000
Accumulated depreciation	(14 800)	(14 000)
Goodwill (net)	7 000	7 000
Deferred tax asset	?	4 050
Liabilities		
Accounts payable	29 000	26 000
Provision for long-service leave	6 000	4 500
Provision for annual leave	4 000	3 000
Rent received in advance	2 500	2 000
Deferred tax liability	?	3 150

Additional information

- Accumulated depreciation of plant for tax purposes was $31 500 at 30 June 2010, and depreciation for tax purposes for the year ended 30 June 2011 amounted to $75 000.
- The tax rate is 30%.

Required

Prepare a worksheet to calculate taxable income and the company's current tax liability as at 30 June 2011, and prepare the end of reporting period adjustment journal.

Problem 7.4 ★★

CALCULATION OF CURRENT TAX, AND PRIOR YEAR AMENDMENT

The accounting profit before tax of Jasmine Ltd for the year ended 30 June 2010 was $22 240. It included the following revenue and expense items:

Government grant (non-taxable)	$ 3 600
Proceeds from sale of plant	33 000
Carrying amount of plant sold	30 000
Entertainment expense (non-deductible)	11 100
Doubtful debts expense	8 100
Depreciation expense — plant	24 000
Insurance expense	12 900
Annual leave expense	15 400

The draft statement of financial position as at 30 June 2010 included the following assets and liabilities:

	2010	2009
Accounts receivable	$156 000	$147 500
Allowance for doubtful debts	(6 800)	(5 200)
Prepaid insurance	3 400	5 600
Plant	240 000	290 000
Accumulated depreciation — plant	(134 400)	(130 400)
Deferred tax asset	?	9 990
Provision for annual leave	14 100	9 700
Deferred tax liability	?	9 504

Additional information

- In November 2009, the company received an amended assessment for the year ended 30 June 2009 from the taxing authority. The amendment notice indicated that an amount of $4500 claimed as a deduction had been disallowed. Jasmine Ltd has not yet adjusted its accounts to reflect the amendment.

- For tax purposes, the carrying amount of plant sold was $26 000. This sale was the only movement in plant for the year.
- The tax deduction for plant depreciation was $28 800. Accumulated depreciation at 30 June 2009 for taxation purposes was $156 480.
- In the previous year, Jasmine Ltd had made a tax loss of $18 400. Jasmine Ltd recognised a deferred tax asset in respect of this loss.
- The tax rate is 30%.

Required

Show all workings.

1. Prepare the journal entry necessary to record the amendment to the prior year's taxation return.
2. Prepare the current tax worksheet and journal entry/entries to calculate and record the current tax for the year ended 30 June 2010.
3. Justify your treatment of annual leave expense in the current tax worksheet.
4. Calculate the temporary difference as at 30 June 2010 for each of the following assets. Explain how these differences arise and why you have classified them as either deductible temporary differences or taxable temporary differences:
   (a) plant
   (b) accounts receivable.

Problem 7.5 CURRENT AND DEFERRED TAX WITH TAX RATE CHANGE

★★

You have been asked by the accountant of Fennel Ltd to prepare the tax-effect accounting adjustments for the year ended 30 June 2010. Investigations revealed the following information:

(a) In September 2008, the government reduced the company tax rate from 40 cents to 30 cents in the dollar, effective from 1 July 2009.
(b) The profit for the year ended 30 June 2010 was $920 000.
(c) The assets and liabilities at 30 June were:

	2010	2009
Accounts receivable	$235 000	$ 200 000
Allowance for doubtful debts	(13 000)	(12 000)
Inventory	250 000	220 000
Land	100 000	100 000
Buildings	800 000	800 000
Accumulated depreciation — buildings	(99 000)	(70 000)
Plant	600 000	600 000
Accumulated depreciation — plant (accounting)	(190 000)	(120 000)
Development expenditure		
— costs incurred	320 000	200 000
— accumulated amortisation	(144 000)	(80 000)
Deferred tax asset	?	29 600
Goodwill (net)	–	20 000
Accounts payable	170 000	150 000
Deferred tax liability	?	72 000
Provision for long-service leave	36 000	28 000
Provision for warranty claims	32 000	34 000

(d) The company is entitled to claim a tax deduction of 125% for development expenditure in the year of expenditure. The company has adopted the accounting policy of capitalising and then amortising the expenditure over five years.

(e) Revenue for the year included:

Non-taxable income	$126 000

(f) Expenses brought to account included:

Depreciation — buildings	$ 29 000
Depreciation — plant	70 000
Impairment — goodwill (non-deductible)	20 000
Amortisation — development expenditure	64 000

(g) Accumulated depreciation on plant for tax purposes was $180 000 on 30 June 2009, and $285 000 on 30 June 2010.

(h) Bad debts of $14 000 were written off during the year, and warranty repairs to the value of $22 000 were carried out. There was no tax deduction for long-service leave in the current year.

(i) Buildings are depreciated in the accounting records but no deduction is allowed for tax purposes.

Required

1. Prepare the journal entry to account for the change in the income tax rate in September 2008.
2. Prepare the worksheets and journal entries to calculate and record the current tax liability, and any movements in deferred tax assets and liabilities in accordance with IAS 12, for the year ended 30 June 2010.

Problem 7.6 RECOGNITION OF DEFERRED TAX ASSETS

★★ Tulip Ltd incurred an accounting loss of $7 560 for the year ended 30 June 2010. The current tax calculation determined that the company had incurred a tax loss of $12 500. Taxation legislation allows such losses to be carried forward and offset against future taxable profits. The company had the following temporary differences:

	30 June 2010	30 June 2009	Expected period of reversal
Deductible temporary differences:			
Accounts receivable	$12 000	$10 000	2011
Plant and equipment	5 000	7 500	2011/2012 equally
Taxable temporary differences:			
Interest receivable	1 500	2 500	2011
Prepaid insurance	10 000	20 000	2011

At 30 June 2009, Tulip Ltd had recognised a deferred tax liability of $6750 and a deferred tax asset of $5250 with respect to temporary differences existing at that date. No adjustment has yet been made for temporary differences existing at 30 June 2010.

Required

1. Discuss the factors that Tulip Ltd should consider in determining the amount (if any) to be recognised for deferred tax assets at 30 June 2010.
2. Calculate the amount (if any) to be recognised for deferred tax assets at 30 June 2010. Justify your answer.

Problem 7.7 CURRENT AND DEFERRED TAX

★★ The accounting profit before tax for the year ended 30 June 2009 for Lily Ltd amounted to $18 500 and included:

Depreciation — motor vehicle (25%)	$ 4 500
Depreciation — equipment (20%)	20 000
Rent revenue	16 000
Royalty revenue (non-taxable)	5 000

Doubtful debts expense	2 300
Entertainment expense (non-deductible)	1 500
Proceeds on sale of equipment	19 000
Carrying amount of equipment sold	18 000
Annual leave expense	5 000

The draft statement of financial position at 30 June 2009 contained the following assets and liabilities:

	2009	2008
Assets		
Cash	$ 11 500	$ 9 500
Receivables	12 000	14 000
Allowance for doubtful debts	(3 000)	(2 500)
Inventory	19 000	21 500
Rent receivable	2 800	2 400
Motor vehicle	18 000	18 000
Accumulated depreciation — motor vehicle	(15 750)	(11 250)
Equipment	100 000	130 000
Accumulated depreciation — equipment	(60 000)	(52 000)
Deferred tax asset	?	6 450
		136 100
Liabilities		
Accounts payable	15 655	21 500
Provision for annual leave	4 500	6 000
Current tax liability	?	7 600
Deferred tax liability	?	2 745
		37 845

Additional information

- The company can claim a deduction of $15 000 (15%) for depreciation on equipment, but the motor vehicle is fully depreciated for tax purposes.
- The equipment sold during the year had been purchased for $30 000 2 years before the date of sale.
- The company tax rate is 30%.

Required

1. Determine the balance of any current and deferred tax assets and liabilities for Lily Ltd as at 30 June 2009, using appropriate worksheets. Show all workings.
2. Prepare any necessary journal entries.

Problem 7.8 ★★

DISCLOSURES

The following taxation worksheets relate to Mint Ltd's taxation adjustments for the years ending 30 June 2010 and 30 June 2011. Using these worksheets, prepare appropriate notes to the financial statements for 30 June 2011 in accordance with IAS 12 disclosure requirements.

MINT LTD Current Tax Worksheet for the year ended 30 June 2010		
Accounting profit before tax		$2 042 686
Add:		
Depreciation building — non-deductible	$108 000	
Entertainment expense — non-deductible	86 800	

(continued)

MINT LTD Current Tax Worksheet for the year ended 30 June 2010		
Add: *(continued)*		
Legal expense — non-deductible	$ 79 200	
Political donations — non-deductible	9 900	
Penalty — non-deductible	20 800	
Doubtful debts expense	123 000	
Depreciation expense — equipment	120 000	
Depreciation expense — furniture and fittings	720 000	
Depreciation expense — motor vehicles	160 000	
Annual leave expense	680 000	
Insurance expense	254 200	
Long-service leave expense	22 000	
Amortisation — patent	100 000	
Rent expense	309 600	
Interest expense	28 000	
Supplies expense	404 800	
Carrying amount of equipment sold	550 000	
Interest received for tax purposes	187 550	3 963 850
		6 006 536
Deduct:		
Interest revenue	186 050	
Political donations deductible	100	
Carrying amount of equipment sold — taxation	400 000	
Debts written off	92 300	
Depreciation — equipment (taxation)	150 000	
Depreciation — furniture and fittings (taxation)	960 000	
Depreciation — motor vehicles (taxation)	200 000	
Annual leave paid	495 000	
Interest paid	28 000	
Insurance paid	256 400	
Development expenditure — additional deduction	25 000	
Amortisation — patent (taxation)	150 000	
Supplies purchased	402 200	
Rent paid	312 500	(3 657 550)
Taxable income		2 348 986
Total tax payable (35%)		822 145
Less Tax already paid		(546 271)
Current tax liability		$ 275 874

MINT LTD Deferred Tax Worksheet at 30 June 2010						
	Carrying amount	**Future taxable amount**	**Future deductible amount**	**Tax base**	**Taxable temporary differences**	**Deductible temporary differences**
Relevant assets						
Accounts receivable (net)	$2 406 000	$ 0	$ 123 000	$2 259 000		$ 123 000
Interest receivable	18 000	(18 000)	0	0	$ 18 000	

	Carrying amount	Future taxable amount	Future deductible amount	Tax base	Taxable temporary differences	Deductible temporary differences
Relevant assets *(continued)*						
Consumable supplies	$ 118 400	$ (118 400)	$ 0	$ 0	$ 118 400	
Prepaid insurance	59 400	(59 400)	0	0	$ 59 400	
Prepaid rent	12 900	(12 900)	0	0	12 900	
Building	3 492 000	(3 492 000)	0	2 560 000	3 492 000	
Furniture and fittings	3 470 000	(3 470 000)	2 560 000	450 000	910 000	
Motor vehicles	520 000	(520 000)	450 000	150 000	70 000	
Equipment	240 000	(240 000)	150 000	50 000	90 000	
Patent	200 000	(200 000)	50 000		150 000	
Relevant liabilities						
Interest payable	7 000	0	(7 000)	0		7 000
Provision for long-service leave	220 800	0	(220 800)	0		220 800
Provision for annual leave	704 000	0	(704 000)	0		704 000
Temporary differences					4 920 700	1 054 800
Excluded differences					3 492 000	
Net temporary differences					1 428 700	1 054 800
Deferred tax liability (35%)					500 045	
Deferred tax asset (35%)						369 180
Beginning balances					(397 080)	(326 840)
Movement during year (tax rate)					49 635	40 855
Adjustment					$ 152 600	$ 83 195
					Credit	Debit

MINT LTD **Current Tax Worksheet for the year ended 30 June 2011**		
Accounting profit before tax		$1 900 591
Add:		
Depreciation building — non-deductible	$ 168 000	
Entertainment expense — non-deductible	95 600	
Legal expense — non-deductible	87 000	
Political donations — non-deductible	10 900	
Amortisation — development expenditure	40 000	
Doubtful debts expense	160 600	
Depreciation expense — equipment	135 000	
Depreciation expense — furniture and fittings	963 750	
Depreciation expense — motor vehicles	160 000	
Annual leave expense	652 000	
Insurance expense	276 300	
Long-service leave expense	48 400	
Amortisation — patent	100 000	
Rent expense	356 400	
Supplies expense	458 300	

(continued)

MINT LTD Current Tax Worksheet for the year ended 30 June 2011		
Add: (continued)		
Carrying amount of equipment sold	$ 90 000	
Interest received for tax purposes	140 650	$3 942 900
		5 843 491
Deduct:		
Interest revenue	150 650	
Political donations — deductible	100	
Carrying amount of equipment sold — taxation	37 500	
Debts written off	123 000	
Depreciation — equipment (taxation)	168 750	
Depreciation — furniture and fittings (taxation)	1 285 000	
Depreciation — motor vehicles (taxation)	200 000	
Annual leave paid	680 000	
Insurance paid	282 600	
Research and development paid (125%)	150 000	
Amortisation — patent (taxation)	50 000	
Supplies purchased	504 400	
Rent paid	358 350	(3 990 350)
Taxable income		1 853 141
Total tax payable (35%)		648 599
Less Tax already paid		(475 000)
Current tax liability		173 599

MINT LTD Deferred Tax Worksheet at 30 June 2011						
	Carrying amount	**Assessable amount**	**Deductible amount**	**Tax base**	**Taxable temporary differences**	**Deductible temporary differences**
Relevant assets						$ 160 600
Accounts receivable (net)	$2 588 400	$ 0	$ 160 600	$2 749 000		
Interest receivable	8 000	(8 000)	0	0	$ 8 000	
Consumable supplies	164 500	(164 500)	0	0	164 500	
Prepaid insurance	65 700	(65 700)	0	0	65 700	
Prepaid rent	14 850	(14 850)	0	0	14 850	
Building	6 424 000	(6 424 000)	0	0	6 424 000	
Furniture and fittings	3 406 250	(3 406 250)	2 175 000	2 175 000	1 231 250	
Motor vehicles	360 000	(360 000)	250 000	250 000	110 000	
Equipment	465 000	(465 000)	393 750	393 750	71 250	
Patent	100 000	(100 000)	0	0	100 000	
Development expenditure	80 000	(80 000)	0	0	80 000	

	Carrying amount	Assessable amount	Deductible amount	Tax base	Taxable temporary differences	Deductible temporary differences
Relevant liabilities						
Interest payable	7 000	0	(7 000	0		7 000
Provision for long-service leave	269 200	0	(269 200	0		269 200
Provision for annual leave	676 000	0	(676 000	0		676 000
Temporary differences					8 269 550	1 112 800
Excluded differences					(6 424 000)	
Net temporary differences					1 845 550	1 112 800
Deferred tax liability (35%)					645 943	
Deferred tax asset (35%)						389 480
Beginning balances					(500 045)	(369 180)
Movement during year						
Adjustment					145 898	20 300
					Credit	Debit

Problem 7.9 **CURRENT AND DEFERRED TAX WITH PRIOR YEAR LOSSES**

★★★ The accounting profit before tax of Gardenia Ltd was $175 900. It included the following revenue and expense items:

Government grant (non-taxable)	$ 3 600
Interest revenue	11 000
Long-service leave expense	7 000
Doubtful debts expense	4 200
Depreciation — plant (15% p.a., straight-line)	33 000
Rent expense	22 800
Entertainment expense (non-deductible)	3 900

The draft statement of financial position as at 30 June 2010 included the following assets and liabilities:

	2010	**2009**
Cash	$ 9 000	$ 7 500
Accounts receivable	83 000	76 800
Allowance for doubtful debts	(5 000)	(3 200)
Inventory	67 100	58 300
Interest receivable	1 000	—
Prepaid rent	2 800	2 400
Plant	220 000	220 000
Accumulated depreciation — plant	(99 000)	(66 000)
Deferred tax asset	?	30 360
Accounts payable	71 200	73 600
Provision for long-service leave	64 000	61 000
Deferred tax liability	?	720

Additional information

- The tax depreciation rate for plant is 10% p.a., straight-line.
- The tax rate is 30%.
- The company has $15 000 in tax losses carried forward from the previous year. A deferred tax asset was recognised for these losses. Taxation legislation allows such losses to be offset against future taxable profit.

Required

1. Prepare the worksheets and journal entries to calculate and record the current tax liability and the movements in deferred tax accounts for the year ended 30 June 2010.
2. Justify your treatment of the interest revenue in the current tax worksheet. Explain how and why this leads to the deferred tax consequence shown in the deferred tax worksheet.

References

Deloitte Touche Tohmatsu 2001, *Accounting for income tax: a guide to revised accounting standards AASB 1020 and AAS 3 'Income Taxes'*, Deloitte Touche Tohmatsu, Australia.

Nokia 2007, *Nokia in 2007*, Nokia Corporation, Finland, www.nokia.com.

8 Inventories

ACCOUNTING STANDARDS IN FOCUS

IAS 2 *Inventories*

LEARNING OBJECTIVES

When you have studied this chapter, you should be able to:

- understand the nature of inventories
- understand how to measure inventories
- explain what is included in the cost of inventory
- account for inventory transactions using both the periodic and the perpetual methods
- explain and apply end-of-period procedures for inventory under both periodic and perpetual methods
- explain why cost flow assumptions are required
- apply both FIFO and weighted average cost formulas
- explain the net realisable value basis of measurement
- account for adjustments to net realisable value
- account for inventory expenses
- implement the disclosure requirements of IAS 2.

8.1 THE NATURE OF INVENTORIES

For retailing and manufacturing entities inventory is the most active asset, and may make up a significant proportion of current assets. The cost of goods sold during the period is normally the largest expense of such entities.

The main accounting standard analysed in this chapter is IAS 2 *Inventories*. The standard was first issued as IAS 2 in October 1975, revised in 1993, amended in 1999 and 2000, exposed in May 2002 as a part of the *Exposure Draft of Proposed Improvements to International Accounting Standards*, and issued in its present form in 2003.

According to paragraph 2 of IAS 2, the standard applies in accounting for all inventories except work in progress arising under construction contracts (covered by IAS 11 *Construction Contracts*) and financial instruments and biological assets related to agricultural activity and agricultural produce at the point of harvest (IAS 41 *Agriculture*).

Paragraph 6 of IAS 2 defines inventories as follows:

> Inventories are assets:
> (a) held for sale in the ordinary course of business;
> (b) in the process of production for such sale; or
> (c) in the form of materials or supplies to be consumed in the production process or in the rendering of services.

Note the following points arising from this definition:

1. The assets are held for sale in the ordinary course of business. The accounting standards do not define 'ordinary', but IFRS 5 *Non-current Assets Held for Sale and Discontinued Operations* requires that non-current assets held for sale are to be distinguished from inventories. This indicates that the term 'inventories' should be applied only to those assets that are always intended for sale or use in producing saleable goods or services.
2. Accounting for assets held for use by the entity is covered by other accounting standards according to their nature. IAS 16 *Property, Plant and Equipment* covers tangible assets such as production equipment; IAS 38 *Intangible Assets* covers intangible assets such as patents.
3. Supplies or materials such as stationery would not be treated as inventories unless they are held for sale or are used in producing goods for sale.
4. IAS 16, paragraph 8, states that 'spare parts and servicing equipment are usually carried as inventory' unless those spare parts are expected to be used during more than one period, or can be used only in conjunction with an item of property, plant and equipment. This standard clearly envisages that spare parts as inventory are those items consumed regularly during the production process, such as bobbin winders on commercial sewing machines.
5. In the case of a service provider, inventories include the costs of the service for which the entity has not yet recognised the related revenue (IAS 2, para. 8).
6. The assets are current assets because they satisfy the following criteria for classification as 'current' set out in paragraph 66 of IAS 1 *Presentation of Financial Statements*:
   - it is expected to be realised in, or is intended for sale or consumption in the entity's normal operating cycle
   - it is held primarily for the purpose of being traded
   - it is expected to realise the asset within 12 months after the reporting period, or
   - the asset is cash or a cash equivalent as defined in IAS 7 *Statement of Cash Flows*.

   The operating cycle of an entity is the time between the acquisition of assets for processing and their realisation in cash or cash equivalents. In some industries, such as retailing, the operating cycle may be very short, but for others, like winemaking, the operating cycle could cover a number of years. When the entity's operating cycle is not clearly identifiable, its duration is assumed to be 12 months (IAS 1, para. 69).

To illustrate: Nokia Corporation, based in Finland, prepares its financial statements in accordance with International Financial Reporting Standards (IFRSs). The extract from Nokia's notes to the consolidated financial statements at 31 December 2005, as shown in figure 8.1, indicates what is contained in inventories.

In this chapter, accounting for inventory is considered as follows:

- initial recognition of inventory — determining the cost of inventory acquired or made
- recording of inventory transactions using either the periodic or perpetual inventory methods, including end-of-period procedures and adjustments

- assignment of costs to inventory using the FIFO or weighted average cost flow assumptions
- measurement subsequent to initial recognition — determining the amount at which the asset is reported subsequent to acquisition, including any write-down to net realisable value.

17 INVENTORIES		
	2007 EURm	2006 EURm
Raw materials, supplies and other	591	360
Work in progress	1 060	600
Finished goods	1 225	594
Total	2 876	1 554

FIGURE 8.1 Extract from the consolidated financial statements of Nokia
Source: Nokia (2007, p. 28).

8.2 INITIAL RECOGNITION OF INVENTORY

According to paragraph 9 of IAS 2: 'Inventories shall be measured at the lower of cost and net realisable value'. As the purpose of acquiring or manufacturing inventory items is to sell them at a profit, inventory will initially be recognised at cost. Two specific industry groups have been exempted from applying the lower of cost and net realisable value rule, namely:

(a) producers of agricultural and forest products, agricultural produce after harvest and minerals and mineral products, to the extent that they are measured at net realisable value in accordance with well-established practices in those industries

(b) commodity broker-traders who measure their inventories at fair value less costs to sell.

In these cases, movements in net realisable value or fair value less any selling costs incurred during the period are recognised in the statement of comprehensive income (income statement). Where inventories in these industries are measured by reference to historical cost, the lower of cost and net realisable value rule mandated by paragraph 9 would still apply.

8.3 DETERMINATION OF COST

The first step in accounting for inventory is its initial recognition at cost. IAS 2, paragraph 10, specifies three components of cost:

- costs of purchase
- costs of conversion
- other costs incurred in bringing the inventories to their present location and condition.

Costs of conversion apply only to manufacturing entities where raw materials and other supplies are purchased and then converted to other products.

8.3.1 Costs of purchase

Paragraph 11 of IAS 2 states that the costs of purchase comprise the purchase price, import duties and other taxes (other than those subsequently recoverable by the entity from the taxing authorities), transport, handling and other costs directly attributable to the acquisition of finished goods, materials and services. Trade discounts, rebates and other similar items are deducted in determining the costs of purchase.

Terms of sale

In identifying the costs of purchase, consideration must be given to the terms of sale relating to inventory items because such terms determine the treatment of transport costs associated with purchase. If goods are sold FOB (free on board) shipping point, freight costs incurred from the point of shipment are paid by the buyer, and are included in the costs of purchase. If goods are sold FOB destination, the seller pays all freight costs.

Transaction taxes

Many countries levy taxes on transactions involving the exchange of goods and services, and require entities engaging in such activities to collect and remit the tax to the government. If such a 'goods and services tax' or 'value added tax' exists, care must be taken to exclude these amounts from the costs of purchase if they are recoverable by the entity from the taxing authorities.

Trade and cash discounts

Trade discounts are reductions in selling prices granted to customers. Such discounts may be granted as an incentive to buy, as a means to quit ageing inventory or as a reward for placing large orders for goods. Because the discount reduces the purchase cost, it is deducted when determining the cost of inventory. Cash or settlement discounts are offered as incentives for early payment of amounts owing on credit sales. Credit terms appear on invoices or contracts and often take the form '2/7, n/30', which means that the buyer will receive a 2% discount if the invoice is paid within seven days of the invoice date or will get 30 days to pay without discount. Some entities may also impose an interest penalty for late payment.

Divergent accounting practices have arisen over time in respect of settlement discounts, with some countries treating the discount as a reduction in the cost of inventories and others treating the discount as revenue. This issue was settled when the International Financial Reporting Interpretations Committee (IFRIC) stated in November 2004 that 'settlement discounts should be deducted from the cost of inventories' (IASB 2004). Thus, discounts received are to be treated as a deduction from the cost of inventories rather than as discount revenue. On the other hand, rebates that specifically and genuinely refund selling expenses are not to be deducted from the cost of inventories.

Deferred payment terms

Where an item of inventory is acquired for cash or short-term credit, determination of the purchase price is relatively straightforward. One variation that may arise is that some or all of the cash payment is deferred. In this case, as noted in paragraph 18 of IAS 2, the purchase cost contains a financing element — the difference between the amount paid and a purchase on normal credit terms — which must be recognised as interest expense over the period of deferral.

8.3.2 Costs of conversion

IAS 2, paragraph 12, identifies costs of conversion as being the costs directly related to the units of production, such as direct labour, plus a systematic allocation of fixed and variable production overheads that are incurred in converting materials into finished goods. Variable overheads are indirect costs of production that vary directly with the volume of production and are allocated to each unit of production on the basis of actual use of production facilities. Fixed overheads, such as depreciation of production machinery, remain relatively constant regardless of the volume of production and are allocated to the cost of inventory on the basis of normal production capacity. Where a production process simultaneously produces one or more products, the costs of conversion must be allocated between products on a systematic and rational basis (para. 14). Costing methodologies are a managerial accounting issue and outside the scope of this book.

8.3.3 Other costs

Other costs can be included only if they are 'incurred in bringing the inventories to their present location and condition' (IAS 2, para. 15). Such costs could include specific design expenses incurred in producing goods for individual customers. IAS 23 *Borrowing Costs* allows borrowing costs such as interest to be included in the cost of inventories but only where such inventories are a qualifying asset; that is, one which takes a substantial period of time to get ready for its intended use or sale. Inventory items would rarely meet this criterion.

8.3.4 Excluded costs

The following costs are specifically listed in paragraph 16 of IAS 2 as costs that cannot be included in the cost of inventories and must be recognised as expenses when incurred:

- abnormal amounts of wasted materials, labour or other production costs
- storage costs, unless necessary in the production process before a further production stage
- administrative overheads that do not contribute to bringing inventories to their present location and condition
- selling costs.

8.3.5 Cost of inventories of a service provider

Service providers, such as cleaners, would normally measure any inventories at the cost of production. Because a service is being provided, such costs would consist primarily of labour and other personnel costs for those employees directly engaged in providing the service. The costs of supervisory personnel and directly attributable overheads may also be included, but paragraph 19 of IAS 2 prohibits the inclusion of labour and other costs relating to sales and general administrative personnel. Profit margins or non-attributable overheads that are built into the prices charged by service providers cannot be factored into the value of inventories. Such inventory assets would be recognised only for services 'in-progress' at the end of the reporting period for which the service provider has not as yet recognised any revenue (e.g. where a catering firm has provided meals for 10 days as at the end of the reporting period but bills the client on a fortnightly basis).

ILLUSTRATIVE EXAMPLE 8.1

Determination of cost

Western Ltd, an Australian company, received the following invoice from De Ferrari Garments Ltd, an Italian garment manufacturer.

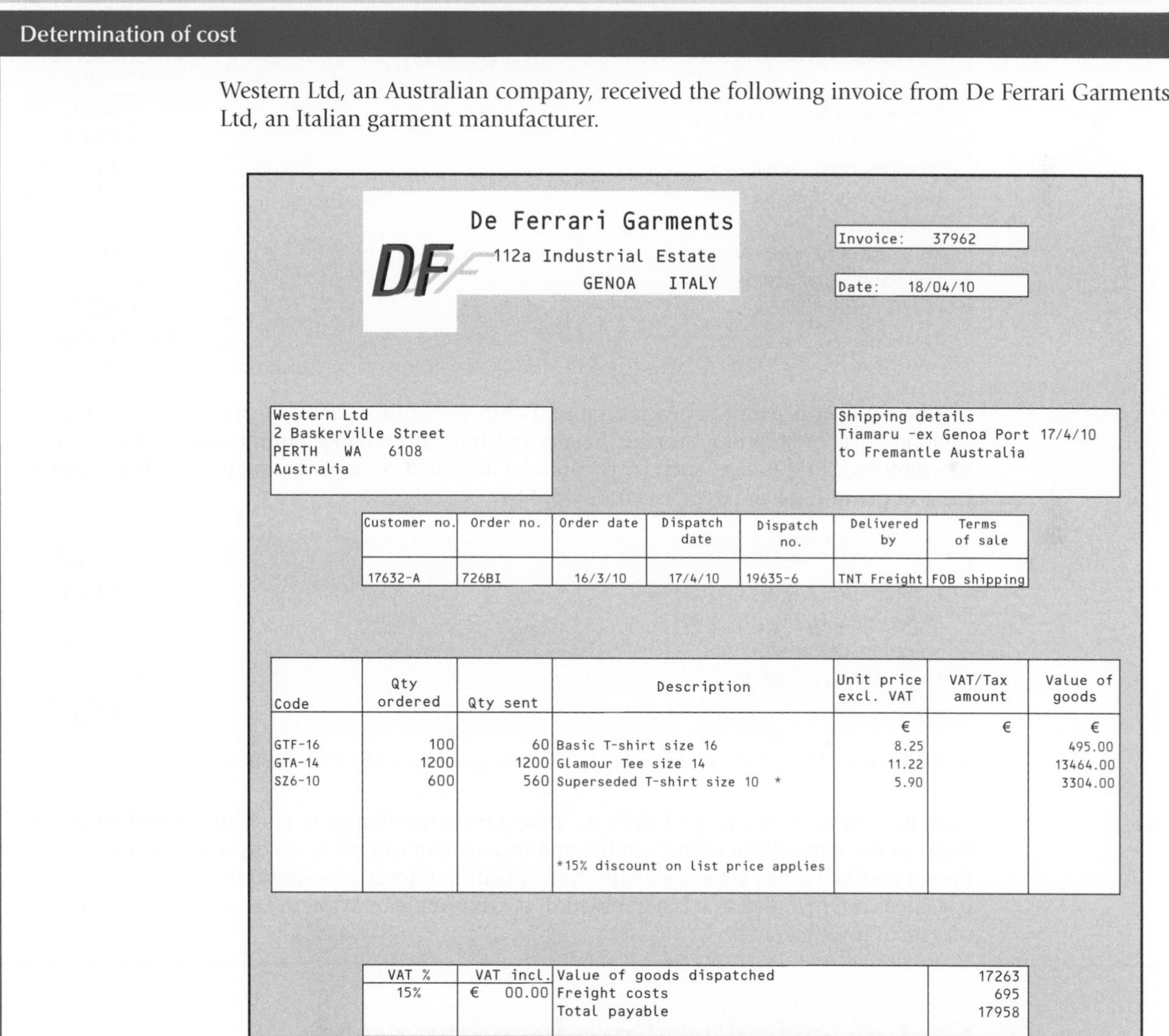

DF

De Ferrari Garments
112a Industrial Estate
GENOA ITALY

Invoice: 37962

Date: 18/04/10

Western Ltd
2 Baskerville Street
PERTH WA 6108
Australia

Shipping details
Tiamaru -ex Genoa Port 17/4/10
to Fremantle Australia

Customer no.	Order no.	Order date	Dispatch date	Dispatch no.	Delivered by	Terms of sale
17632-A	726BI	16/3/10	17/4/10	19635-6	TNT Freight	FOB shipping

Code	Qty ordered	Qty sent	Description	Unit price excl. VAT	VAT/Tax amount	Value of goods
				€	€	€
GTF-16	100	60	Basic T-shirt size 16	8.25		495.00
GTA-14	1200	1200	Glamour Tee size 14	11.22		13464.00
SZ6-10	600	560	Superseded T-shirt size 10 *	5.90		3304.00
			*15% discount on list price applies			

VAT %	VAT incl.		
15%	€ 00.00	Value of goods dispatched	17263
		Freight costs	695
		Total payable	17958

Credit terms 2/15 net 60 days

The goods arrived at Fremantle port on 29 May 2010 and were held in a bond store pending payment of import duties and taxes. After the payment of storage costs of A$145, import duty at 1.5% of the total value of goods in Australian dollars, goods and services tax (GST) of 10% and local freight charges of A$316, the goods were finally delivered to Western Ltd's warehouse on 6 June 2010. The invoice was received on 8 June and a liability of $A29 439.34 recorded using the exchange rate of A$1 = €0.61 at that date. The invoice was paid in full on 8 July by the remittance of €28 964.52 (at an exchange rate of A$1 = €0.62). Western Ltd paid A$167 to acquire the euros. Upon receipt of the goods, Western Ltd attaches its own logo to the T-shirts and repackages them for sale. The cost of this further processing is A$2.54 per T-shirt.

Problem
What is the cost of this inventory?

Solution
The cost of inventory would include the following amounts:

Purchase price	€17 263.00
Shipping costs	695.00
	€17 958.00
Conversion to Australian dollars:	
€17 958 + 0.61	29 439.34
Storage costs – bond store	145.00
Import duty ($28 300 × 1.5%)	424.50
Freight costs	316.00
Foreign exchange commission	167.00
Logo and repackaging (1820 items × $2.54)	4 622.80
Total cost	A$35 114.64

Where a cost per unit for each type of T-shirt is required, some method of allocating the 'generic' costs of shipping, storage, freight and foreign exchange commission would need to be employed. In this case, such costs could be allocated on a per garment basis. For example, the cost per unit for the Basic T-shirts would be:

	A$
Purchase price (€8.25 ÷ A$0.61)	13.52
Import duty (1.5% × $13.52)	0.20
Shipping and other costs*	0.97
Logo and repackaging	2.54
Cost per unit	$17.23

*(A$145 + 316 ÷ 167 + [€695 ÷ 0.61] = A$1767.34/1820 garments = A$0.97 per garment)

Note that the exchange gain of $474.82 arising from the change in euro–dollar exchange rates between the recognition of the liability and its payment cannot be incorporated in the calculation of cost as it is not associated with the acquisition transaction. Additionally, the GST of 10% payable is not included as it is a transaction tax receivable by Western Ltd against GST collected on sale of inventory.

8.3.6 Cost of agricultural produce harvested from biological assets

IAS 41 *Agriculture* requires inventories of agricultural produce, such as wheat and oranges, to be measured at their fair value less estimated point-of-sale costs at the point of harvest. IAS 2, paragraph 20, deems this value to be 'cost' for the purposes of applying the requirements of the inventory standard.

8.3.7 Estimating cost

Techniques for determining cost such as the standard cost method or the retail method may be used for convenience so long as the resulting values approximate cost. Manufacturing entities determine a 'standard' value of materials, direct and indirect labour and overheads for each product based on normal levels of efficiency and capacity utilisation. Adjustments are made at the end of the reporting period to account for variances between standard and actual costs. Standard costs must be regularly reviewed and amended as required. The retail method is used to measure inventories of large numbers of rapidly changing items with similar margins for which it is impractical to use other costing methods. Supermarket and department store chains most often employ this method of approximating cost. Cost is determined by reducing the sales value of the inventory by an appropriate percentage gross margin or an average percentage margin. In applying this method, care must be taken to ensure that gross margins are adjusted for goods that have been discounted below their original selling price.

8.4 ACCOUNTING FOR INVENTORY

There are two main methods of accounting for inventory: the periodic method and the perpetual method.

8.4.1 Periodic method

Under the periodic method, the amount of inventory is determined periodically (normally annually) by conducting a physical count and multiplying the number of units by a cost per unit to value the inventory on hand. This amount is then recognised as a current asset. This balance remains unchanged until the next count is taken. Purchases and returns of inventory during the reporting period are posted directly to expense accounts. Cost of goods sold during the year is determined as follows:

Opening inventory + Purchases + Freight inwards – Purchase returns
– Cash discounts received – Closing inventory = Cost of goods sold

Accounting for inventory using the periodic method is cost effective and easy to apply, but its major disadvantage is that the exact quantity and cost of inventory cannot be determined on a day-to-day basis, and this might result in lost sales or unhappy customers. Additionally, it is not possible to identify stock losses or posting errors, resulting in accounting figures that might be inaccurate or misleading.

8.4.2 Perpetual method

Under the perpetual method, inventory records are updated each time a transaction involving inventory takes place. Thus, up-to-date information about the quantity and cost of inventory on hand will always be available, enabling the entity to provide better customer service and maintain better control over this essential asset. This system is more complicated and expensive than the periodic method but, with the advent of user-friendly computerised accounting packages and point-of-sale machines linked directly to accounting records, most businesses today can afford to and do use the perpetual method.

The perpetual method requires a subsidiary ledger to be maintained, either manually or on computer, with a separate record for each inventory item detailing all movements in both quantity and cost. This subsidiary record is linked to the general ledger account for inventory, and regular reconciliations are carried out to ensure the accuracy and completeness of the accounting records. This reconciliation process is discussed in section 8.5 of this chapter.

ILLUSTRATIVE EXAMPLE 8.2

Comparing the periodic and the perpetual inventory methods

Kotka Ltd sells garden furniture settings. This example illustrates the journal entries necessary to record the normal inventory transactions that would occur during an accounting period, and the reporting of gross profit from the sale of inventory under both accounting systems.

The inventory account in the general ledger of Kotka Ltd at the beginning of the year under both methods is shown below.

Inventory			
1 July 2007	Balance b/d (10 units @ $670)	6 700	

The following transactions took place during the year:

(a) Purchased 354 settings (FOB shipping) at $670 each on credit terms of $\frac{2}{10}$, $\frac{n}{30}$ from Grimstad Pty Ltd.

(b) Sold, on credit, 352 settings for $975 each.

(c) Returned four settings to the supplier.

(d) Seven settings were returned by customers.

The journal entries necessary to record these transactions under both inventory accounting methods are shown below.

KOTKA LTD
Journal Entries

Perpetual inventory method | *Periodic inventory method*

(a) Purchased 354 settings (FOB shipping) at $670 each on credit terms of $\frac{2}{10}$, $\frac{n}{30}$ from Grimstad Pty Ltd.

	Dr	Cr		Dr	Cr
Inventory	237 180		Purchases	237 180	
A/cs Payable		237 180	A/cs Payable		237 180

(b) Sold, on credit, 352 settings for $975 each.

	Dr	Cr		Dr	Cr
A/cs Receivable	343 200		A/cs Receivable	343 200	
Sales Revenue		343 200	Sales Revenue		343 200
Cost of Goods Sold	235 840				
Inventory		235 840			

(c) Returned four settings to the supplier.

	Dr	Cr		Dr	Cr
A/cs Payable	2 680		A/cs Payable	2 680	
Inventory		2 680	Purchase Returns		2 680

(d) Seven settings were returned by customers.

	Dr	Cr		Dr	Cr
Sales Returns	6 825		Sales Returns	6 825	
A/cs Receivable		6 825	A/cs Receivable		6 825
Inventory	4 690				
Cost of Goods Sold		4 690			

Important differences to note between the two methods of accounting for inventory:

- Purchases are posted directly to the asset account under the perpetual method, and are posted to expense accounts under the periodic method.
- When goods are sold, a second entry is necessary under the perpetual method to transfer the cost of those goods from the inventory account to the expense account, cost of goods sold.
- When goods are returned to suppliers, the return is adjusted directly to inventory under the perpetual method, and is posted to a purchase returns account under the periodic method.
- When goods are returned from customers, a second journal entry is necessary under the perpetual method to transfer the cost of these goods out of the cost of goods sold account and back into the inventory account.
- Under the periodic method, freight is normally posted to a separate account. Under the perpetual method, freight is included in the cost of inventory unless the amounts are immaterial, in which case freight costs would be accumulated in a separate expense account.
- If inventory items being returned to the supplier have been paid for, an accounts receivable account would be opened pending a cash refund from the supplier.
- If sales returns have been paid for, an accounts payable entry would be raised to recognise the need to refund cash to the customer.
- Under the periodic method, cash settlement discounts would be posted to a separate ledger account. Under the perpetual method, settlement discounts would be deducted from the cost of inventory.

After posting the journal entries, the general ledger account would appear as shown below.

Perpetual inventory method

Inventory				
1/7/07	Balance b/d	6 700	Cost of Goods Sold	235 840
	A/cs Payable	237 180	A/cs Payable	2 680
	Cost of Goods Sold	4 690	Balance b/d	10 050
		248 570		248 570
	Balance c/d	10 050		

Periodic inventory method

Inventory			
1/7/07	Balance b/d	6 700	

Assuming that the physical count at the end of the reporting period found 15 settings on hand at a cost of $670 each, the gross profit earned on these would be determined as follows:

KOTKA LTD
Determination of Gross Profit

Perpetual inventory method

Sales revenue	343 200
Less Sales returns and allowances	6 825
Net sales revenue	336 375
Cost of goods sold	231 150
Gross profit	$105 225

(continued)

Periodic inventory method

Sales revenue		343 200
Less Sales returns		6 825
Net sales revenue		336 375
Cost of goods sold		
Opening inventory	6 700	
Add Purchases	237 180	
	243 880	
Less Purchase returns	2 680	
Goods available for sale	241 200	
Less Closing inventory	10 050	
Cost of goods sold		231 150
Gross profit		$105 225

Note that, in this example, the same gross profit is reported irrespective of the inventory recording method adopted. However, where adjustments are made for damaged or lost inventory, the gross profit will be different under the perpetual method.

8.5 END-OF-PERIOD ACCOUNTING

To ensure that reported figures for inventory, cost of goods sold and other expenses are accurate and complete, certain procedures must be carried out at the end of each accounting period. It is essential that good internal controls be instituted to ensure that inventory is protected from fraud or loss and that inventory figures are complete and accurate. This section examines the physical count, end-of-year cut-off and essential reconciliation procedures.

8.5.1 Physical count

Under the periodic method, inventory must be counted at the end of each accounting period to determine the value of closing inventory. Periodic counts are made under the perpetual method to verify the accuracy of recorded quantities for each inventory item, although not necessarily at the end of the reporting period, if inventory differences are historically found to be immaterial.

The way in which the physical count is conducted will depend on the type of inventory and the accounting system of the entity. Stockpiled inventory such as mineral sands may require the use of surveyors to measure quantities on hand and assay tests to determine mineral content.

The following are some steps that are generally taken to ensure the accuracy of a physical count:

- The warehouse, retail store or storage facility should be arranged so as to facilitate counting and clearly segregate non-inventory items.
- Cut-off procedures should be put in place and final numbers of important documents such as dispatch notes and invoices recorded. (Cut-off procedures are discussed in greater detail in section 8.5.2.)
- Prenumbered count sheets, tags or cards should be produced detailing inventory codes and descriptions. A supervisor should record all numbers used and account for spoiled documents to ensure that the count details are complete. Alternatively, where inventory items have bar codes, electronic scanners can be used to record the count.
- Counting should be done in teams of at least two people: one counter and one checker. All team members should sign the count records.
- Any damaged or incomplete items located during the count should be clearly listed on the count records.
- The supervisor should ensure that all goods have been counted before the count sheets are collected.

Perpetual method

Once the physical count is complete, under the perpetual method the quantities on hand are then compared to recorded quantities and all discrepancies investigated. Recording errors cause discrepancies; for example, the wrong code number or quantity might have been entered, or a transaction might not have been processed in the correct period. Alternatively, discrepancies may reveal losses of goods caused by damage or fraud. Recording errors can be corrected but the value of goods that have been lost should be written off using the following entry:

Inventory losses Inventory (Recognition of inventory losses during the period)	Dr Cr	5 000	 5 000

Unless they are immaterial, inventory losses must be disclosed separately in the notes to the financial statements (see section 8.9 of this chapter).

Periodic method

Once the count is completed, under this method the count quantities are then costed and the value of inventory brought to account. This adjustment can be done in a number of ways, but the simplest is to post the following two journal entries:

Opening Inventory (Cost of Goods Sold) Inventory (Transfer of opening balance to expense)	Dr Cr	79 600	 79 600
Inventory Closing Inventory (Cost of Goods Sold) (Recognition of final inventory balance)	Dr Cr	87 100	 87 100

Under the periodic method, inventory losses and fraud cannot be identified and recorded as a separate expense. The movement in inventory balances plus the cost of purchases is presumed to represent the cost of goods sold during the reporting period.

8.5.2 Cut-off procedures

Under both periodic and perpetual methods there is a need to ensure that, when a physical count is conducted, there is a proper cut-off of the record keeping so that the accounting records reflect the results of the physical count and include all transactions relevant to the accounting period while excluding those that belong to other periods. For all inventory transactions (sales, purchases and returns) it is possible for inventory records to be updated before transaction details are posted to the general ledger accounts. For example, goods are normally entered into inventory records when the goods are received, but accounts payable records will not record the liability until the invoice arrives because shipping documents may not record price details. Under the periodic method, there is a need to ensure a proper cut-off between the general ledger recording of goods received, shipped and returned, and the inventory counted. Under the perpetual method, there is a need to ensure that all inventory movements are properly recorded in the perpetual records, so a valid comparison is made between inventory counted and the perpetual record quantities. Further, if the perpetual method is not integrated with the general ledger, there is also a need to ensure a proper cut-off between the general ledger and the perpetual records. Thus, at the end of the reporting period it is essential that proper cut-off procedures be implemented.

The following cut-off errors could arise:

- Goods have been received into inventory, but the purchase invoice has not been processed.
- Goods have been returned to a supplier, and deleted from inventory, but the credit note has not been processed.

- Goods have been sold and dispatched to a customer, but the invoice has not been raised.
- Goods have been returned by a customer, but the credit note has not been issued.

If inventory movements have been processed before invoices and credit notes, adjusting entries are needed to bring both sides of the transaction into the same accounting period.

8.5.3 Goods in transit

Accounting for goods in transit at the end of the reporting period will depend upon the terms of trade. Where goods are purchased on an FOB shipping basis, the goods belong to the purchaser from the time they are shipped, and should be included in inventory/accounts payable at accounting date. All such purchases in transit will need to be identified and the following adjusting journal entry posted:

Goods in Transit (Inventory)	Dr	1 500	
Accounts Payable	Cr		1 500
(Recognition of inventory in transit at accounting date)			

If goods are purchased on FOB destination terms, no adjustment will be required because the goods still legally belong to the supplier.

If goods are sold on FOB destination terms, they belong to the entity until they arrive at the customer's premises. Because the sale will have been recorded in the current year, the following adjusting entries will be required to remove that sale and reinstate the inventory:

Inventory	Dr	3 000	
Cost of Goods Sold	Cr		3 000
(Reversal of sale for goods in transit at accounting date)			
Sales Revenue	Dr	4 500	
Accounts Receivable	Cr		4 500
(Reversal of sale for goods in transit at accounting date)			

8.5.4 Consignment inventory

Care must be taken in the treatment of consignment inventory. Under a consignment arrangement, an agent (the consignee) agrees to sell goods on behalf of the consignor on a commission basis. The transfer of goods to the consignee is not a legal sale/purchase transaction. Legal ownership remains with the consignor until the agent sells the goods to a third party. Steps must be taken to ensure that goods held on consignment are not included in the physical count. Equally, goods owned by the entity that are held by consignees must be added to the physical count.

8.5.5 Control account/subsidiary ledger reconciliation

This end-of-period procedure is required only under the perpetual method. The general ledger account balance must be reconciled with the total of the subsidiary ledger (manual or computerised). Recording errors and omissions will cause the reconciliation process to fail. Any material discrepancies should be investigated and corrected. This process will identify only amounts that have not been posted to both records; it cannot identify errors within the subsidiary records, such as posting a purchase to the wrong inventory item code. However, the physical count/recorded figure reconciliation will isolate these errors.

ILLUSTRATIVE EXAMPLE 8.3

End-of-period adjustments

Bob Smith, trading as Honefoss Pty Ltd, completed his first year of trading as a toy wholesaler on 30 June 2011. He is worried about his end-of-year physical and cut-off procedures.

The inventory ledger account balance at 30 June 2011, under the perpetual inventory method, was $78 700. His physical count, however, revealed the cost of inventory on hand at 30 June 2011 to be only $73 400. While Bob expected a small inventory shortfall due to breakage and petty theft, he considered this shortfall to be excessive.

Upon investigating reasons for the inventory 'shortfall', Bob discovered the following:

- Goods costing $800 were sold on credit to R Finn for $1300 on 26 June 2011 on FOB destination terms. The goods were still in transit at 30 June 2011. Honefoss Pty Ltd recorded the sale on 26 June 2011 but did not include these goods in the physical count.
- Included in the physical count were $2200 of goods held on consignment.
- Goods costing $910 were purchased on credit from Lapua Ltd on 25 June 2011 and received on 28 June 2011. The purchase was unrecorded at 30 June 2011 but the goods were included in the physical count.
- Goods costing $400 were purchased on credit from Kuovola Supplies on 23 June 2011 on FOB shipping terms. The goods were delivered to the transport company on 27 June 2011. The purchase was recorded on 27 June 2011 but, as the goods had not yet arrived, Honefoss Pty Ltd did not include these goods in the physical count.
- At 30 June 2011 Honefoss Pty Ltd had unsold goods costing $3700 out on consignment. These goods were not included in the physical count.
- Goods costing $2100 were sold on credit to Vetlonda Ltd for $3200 on 24 June 2011 on FOB shipping terms. The goods were shipped on 28 June 2011. The sale was unrecorded at 30 June 2011 and Honefoss Pty Ltd did not include these goods in the physical count.
- Goods costing $1500 had been returned to Ruovesi Garments on 30 June 2011. A credit note was received from the supplier on 5 July 2011. No payment had been made for the goods prior to their return.

These transactions and events must be analysed to determine if adjustments are required to the ledger accounts (general and subsidiary) and/or the physical count records as follows:

Workings

	Recorded balance $	Physical count $
Balance prior to adjustment	78 700	73 400
Add Goods sold, FOB destination and in transit at 30 June	800	800
Less Goods held on consignment	—	(2 200)
Add Unrecorded purchase	910	—
Add Goods purchased, FOB shipping and in transit at 30 June	—	400
Add Goods out on consignment	—	3 700
Less Unrecorded sale	(2 100)	—
Less Unrecorded purchase returns	(1 500)	—
	$76 810	$76 100

If, after all adjustments are made, the recorded balance cannot be reconciled to the physical count, the remaining discrepancy is presumed to represent inventory losses and a final adjustment is made as follows:

Adjusted balances	76 810	76 100
Inventory shortfall	(710)	—
	$76 100	$76 100

The following journal entries are necessary on 30 June 2011 to correct errors and adjust the inventory ledger accounts:

HONEFOSS PTY LTD General Journal			
2011 30 June			
Sales Revenue	Dr	1 300	
Accounts Receivable (R Finn)	Cr		1 300
(Correction of sale recorded in error)			
Inventory (Item X)	Dr	800	
Cost of Goods Sold	Cr		800
(Correction of sale recorded in error)			
Inventory (Item Y)	Dr	910	
Accounts Payable (Lapua Ltd)	Cr		910
(Correction of unrecorded purchase)			
Accounts Receivable (Vetlonda Ltd)	Dr	3 200	
Sales Revenue	Cr		3 200
(Correction of unrecorded sale)			
Cost of Goods Sold	Dr	2 100	
Inventory (Item Z)	Cr		2 100
(Correction of unrecorded sale)			
Accounts Payable (Ruovesi Garments)	Dr	1 500	
Inventory (Item W)	Cr		1 500
(Correction of unrecorded purchase return)			
Inventory Losses and Write-Downs	Dr	710	
Inventory	Cr		710
(Unexplained variance (physical/records) written off)			

8.6 ASSIGNING COSTS TO INVENTORY ON SALE

The nature of inventory held by an entity does not affect its initial recognition at cost but has a significant impact when that inventory is sold. As shown in illustrative example 8.2, under the perpetual system the cost of inventory items is transferred to a 'Cost of Goods Sold' expense account on sale, and under the periodic system a 'Cost of Goods Sold' figure is calculated at the end of the reporting period. This is an easy task if the nature of inventory is such that it is possible to clearly identify the exact inventory item that has been sold and its cost, but what if it is not possible to identify exactly the cost of the item sold? How can you measure the cost of a tonne of wheat when it is extracted from a stockpile consisting of millions of tonnes acquired at different prices over the accounting period?

IAS 2 addresses this problem by mandating two different rules for the assigning of cost to inventory items sold.

The rules differ depending on the nature of inventory held. Paragraph 23 states that:

> The cost of inventories of items that are not ordinarily interchangeable and goods or services produced and segregated for specific projects shall be assigned by using specific identification of their individual costs.

Thus, if the inventory held consists of items that can be individually identified because of their unique nature or by some other means, or cannot be individually identified but have been acquired for a specific project, then the exact cost of the item sold must be recorded as cost of goods sold expense.

Paragraph 25 states that:

> The cost of inventories, other than those dealt with in paragraph 23, shall be assigned by using the first-in, first-out (FIFO) or weighted average cost formula.

This means that, where a specific cost cannot be identified because of the nature of the item sold, then some method has to be adopted to estimate that cost. This process is known as 'assigning' cost. Most inventory items fall into this category, for example, identical items of food and clothing and bulk items like oil and minerals. There are many methods of assigning a cost to inventory items sold but IAS 2 restricts entities to a choice between two methods — FIFO and weighted average.

8.6.1 First-in, first-out (FIFO) cost formula

The FIFO formula assumes that items of inventory that were purchased or produced first are sold first, and the items remaining in inventory at the end of the period are those most recently purchased or produced (IAS 2, para. 27). Thus, more recent purchase costs are assigned to the inventory asset account, and older costs are assigned to the cost of goods sold expense account.

Consider this example: there are 515 DVD players on hand at 30 June 2011, and recent purchase invoices showed the following costs:

- 28 June 180 players at $49.00
- 15 June 325 players at $48.50
- 31 May 200 players at $47.00.

The value of ending inventory is found by starting with the most recent purchase and working backwards until all items on hand have been priced (on the assumption that it is not known when any particular DVD player was sold). The value of ending inventory would be $25 052.50 (being 180 players at $49 + 325 players at $48.50 + 10 players at $47).

Many proponents of the FIFO method argue that this method best reflects the physical movement of inventory, particularly perishable goods or those subject to changes in fashion or rapid obsolescence (as in the case of DVD players). If the oldest goods are normally sold first, then the oldest costs should be assigned to expense.

8.6.2 Weighted average cost formula

Under the weighted average cost formula, the cost of each item sold is determined from the cost of similar items purchased or produced during the period. The average may be calculated on a periodic basis (weighted average), or as each additional shipment is received (moving average).

Using a periodic basis, the cost of inventory on hand at the beginning of the period plus all inventory purchased during the year is divided by the total number of items available for sale during the period (opening quantity plus purchased quantity). This produces the cost per unit. For example: inventory on hand at 1 January 2012 was valued at $3439.78, consisting of 134 units at an average of $25.67 each. During the year the following purchases were made:

- 200 units at $27.50 = $5 500.00
- 175 units at $28.35 = $4 961.25
- 300 units at $29.10 = $8 730.00
- 120 units at $29.00 = $3 480.00.

At the end of the year, the weighted average cost of inventory would be calculated as:

$3439.78 + 5500.00 + 4961.25 + 8730.00 + 3480.00 = $26 111.03 ÷ 929 units = $28.11 per unit

Using the moving average method, the average unit cost is recalculated each time there is an inventory purchase or purchase return. This is demonstrated in illustrative example 8.4.

ILLUSTRATIVE EXAMPLE 8.4

Application of cost formulas

The following information has been extracted from the records of Savonlinna Parts about one of its products. Savonlinna Parts uses the perpetual inventory method and its reporting date is 31 December.

		No. of units	Unit cost $	Total cost $
2009				
01/01	Beginning balance	800	7.00	5 600
06/01	Purchased	300	7.05	2 115
05/02	Sold @ $12.00 per unit	1000		
19/03	Purchased	1100	7.35	8 085
24/03	Purchase returns	80	7.35	588
10/04	Sold @ $12.10 per unit	700		
22/06	Purchased	8400	7.50	63 000
31/07	Sold @ $13.25 per unit	1800		
04/08	Sales returns @ $13.25 per unit	20		
04/09	Sold @ $13.50 per unit	3500		
06/10	Purchased	500	8.00	4 000
27/11	Sold @ $15.00 per unit	3100		

Required

1. Calculate the cost of inventory on hand at 31 December 2009 and the cost of goods sold for the year ended 31 December 2009, assuming:
   (a) the FIFO cost flow assumption
   (b) the moving average cost flow assumption (round the average unit costs to the nearest cent, and round the total cost amounts to the nearest dollar).
2. Prepare the trading section of the statement of comprehensive income for the year ended 31 December 2009, assuming:
   (a) the FIFO cost flow assumption
   (b) the moving average cost flow assumption.

Part 1. (a) First-in, first-out cost formula

		Purchases			COGS			Balance[1]		
Date	Details	No. units	Unit cost	Total cost	No. units	Unit cost	Total cost	No. units	Unit cost	Total cost
01/01	Inventory balance							800	7.00	5 600
06/01	Purchases	300	7.05	2115				800 300	7.00 7.05	5 600 2 115
05/02	Sales				800 200	7.00 7.05	5 600 1 410	100	7.05	705

Date	Details	Purchases			COGS			Balance[1]		
		No. units	Unit cost	Total cost	No. units	Unit cost	Total cost	No. units	Unit cost	Total cost
19/03	Purchases	1100	7.35	8085				100 1100	7.05 7.35	705 8 085
24/03	Purchase returns	(80)	7.35	(588)				100 1020	7.05 7.35	705 7 497
10/04	Sales				100 600	7.05 7.35	705 4 410	420	7.35	3 087
22/06	Purchases	8400	7.50	63000				420 8400	7.35 7.50	3 087 63 000
31/07	Sales				420 1380	7.35 7.50	3 087 10 350	7020	7.50	52 650
04/08	Sales returns[2]				(20)	7.50	(150)	7040	7.50	52 800
04/09	Sales				3500	7.50	26 250	3540	7.50	26 550
06/10	Purchases	500	8.00	4000				3540 500	7.50 8.00	26 550 4 000
22/11	Sales				3100	7.50	23 250	440 500	7.50 8.00	3 300 4 000
				76612			74 912			

Notes: 1. As it is assumed the earliest purchases are sold first, a separate balance of each purchase at a different price must be maintained.
2. The principle of 'last-out first-in' is applied to sales returns.

Part 1. (b) Moving average cost formula

Date	Details	Purchases			COGS[2]			Balance		
		No. units	Unit cost	Total cost	No. units	Unit cost	Total cost	No. units	Unit cost[1]	Total cost
01/01	Inventory balance							800	7.00	5 600
06/01	Purchases	300	7.05	2 115				1100	7.01	7 715
05/02	Sales				1000	7.01	7 010	100	7.01	705
19/03	Purchases	1100	7.35	8 085				1200	7.33	8 790
24/03	Purchase returns	(80)	7.35	(588)				1120	7.32	8 202
10/04	Sales				700	7.32	5 124	420	7.32	3 078
22/06	Purchases	8400	7.50	63 000				8820	7.49	66 078
31/07	Sales				1800	7.49	13 482	7020	7.49	52 596
04/08	Sales returns				(20)	7.49	(150)	7040	7.49	52 746
04/09	Sales				3500	7.49	26 215	3540	7.49	26 531
06/10	Purchases	500	8.00	4 000				4040	7.56	30 531
22/11	Sales				3100	7.56	23 436	940	7.56	7 095
				76 612			75 117			

Notes: 1. The average cost per unit is recalculated each time there is a purchase or a purchase return at a different cost.
2. The 'average' cost on the date of sale is applied to calculate the 'cost of goods sold'.

Part 2.

SAVONLINNA PARTS Statement of Comprehensive Income (extract) for the year ended 31 December 2009		
	FIFO **$**	**Moving average** **$**
Sales revenue	138 070	138 070
Less Sales returns	(265)	(265)
Net sales	137 805	137 805
Less Cost of goods sold	(74 912)	(75 117)
Gross profit	$ 62 893	$ 62 688

Because the purchase price has been rising throughout the year, using the FIFO formula produces a lower cost of goods sold (higher gross profit) and a higher inventory balance than the moving average formula.

8.6.3 Which cost formula to use?

The choice of method is a matter for management judgement and depends upon the nature of the inventory, the information needs of management and financial statement users, and the cost of applying the formulas. For example, the weighted average method is easy to apply and is particularly suited to inventory where homogeneous products are mixed together, like iron ore or spring water. On the other hand, first-in, first-out may be a better reflection of the actual physical movement of goods, such as those with use-by dates where the first produced must be sold first to avoid loss due to obsolescence, spoilage or legislative restrictions. Entities with diversified operations may use both methods because they carry different types of inventory. Using diverse methods is acceptable under IAS 2, but paragraph 26 cautions that 'a difference in geographical location of inventories (or in the respective tax rules), by itself, is not sufficient to justify the use of different cost formulas'. The nature of the inventory itself should determine the choice of formula.

8.6.4 Consistent application of costing methods

Once a cost formula has been selected, management cannot randomly switch from one formula to another. Because the choice of method can have a significant impact on an entity's reported profit and asset figures, particularly in times of volatile prices, indiscriminate changes in formulas could result in the reporting of financial information that is neither comparable nor reliable. Accordingly, paragraph 13 of IAS 8 *Accounting Policies, Changes in Accounting Estimates and Errors* requires that accounting policies be consistently applied to ensure comparability of financial information. Changes in accounting policies are allowed (IAS 8, para. 14) only when required by an accounting standard or where the change results in reporting more relevant and reliable financial information. Therefore, unless the nature of inventory changes, it is unlikely that the cost formulas will change. A switch from the FIFO to the weighted average method must be disclosed in accordance with the requirements of IAS 8, in particular paragraph 19. This paragraph requires the change to be applied retrospectively, and the information disclosed as if the new accounting policy had always been applied. Hence, a change from the FIFO method to the weighted average method would require adjustments to the financial statements to show the information as if the weighted average method had always been applied. Adjustments can be taken through the opening balance of retained earnings. Comparative information would also need to be restated.

8.7 NET REALISABLE VALUE

As the measurement rule mandated by IAS 2 for inventories is the 'lower of cost and net realisable value' (para. 9), an estimate of net realisable value must be made to determine if inventory must be written down. Normally, this estimate is done before preparing the financial reports but, where management become aware during the reporting period that goods or services can no longer be sold at a price above cost, inventory values should be written down to net realisable value. The rationale for this measurement rule, according to paragraph 28 of IAS 2, is that 'assets should not be carried in excess of amounts expected to be realised from their sale or use'.

Net realisable value is the net amount that an entity expects to realise from the sale of inventory in the ordinary course of business. It is defined in paragraph 6 of IAS 2 as 'the estimated selling price in the ordinary course of business less the estimated costs of completion and the estimated costs necessary to make the sale'. Net realisable value is specific to an individual entity and is not necessarily equal to fair value less selling costs. Fair value is defined as 'the amount for which an asset could be exchanged, or a liability settled, between knowledgeable, willing parties in an arm's length transaction' (IAS 2, para. 6).

Net realisable value may fall below cost for a number of reasons including:

- a fall in selling price (e.g. fashion garments)
- physical deterioration of inventories (e.g. fruit and vegetables)
- product obsolescence (e.g. computers and electrical equipment)
- a decision, as part of an entity's marketing strategy, to manufacture and sell products for the time being at a loss (e.g. new products)
- miscalculations or other errors in purchasing or production (e.g. overstocking)
- an increase in the estimated costs of completion or the estimated costs of making the sale (e.g. air-conditioning plants).

8.7.1 Estimating net realisable value

Estimates of net realisable value must be based on the most reliable evidence available at the time the estimate is made (normally the end of the reporting period) of the amount that the inventories are expected to realise. Thus, estimates must be made of:

- expected selling price
- estimated costs of completion (if any)
- estimated selling costs.

These estimates take into consideration fluctuations of price or cost occurring after the end of the reporting period to the extent that such events confirm conditions existing at the end of the reporting period. The purpose for which inventory is held should be taken into account when reviewing net realisable values. For example, the net realisable value of inventory held to satisfy firm sales or service contracts is based on the contract price. If the sales contracts are for less than the inventory quantities held, the net realisable value of the excess is based on general selling prices. Estimated selling costs include all costs likely to be incurred in securing and filling customer orders such as advertising costs, sales personnel salaries and operating costs, and the costs of storing and shipping finished goods.

It is possible to use formulas based on predetermined criteria to initially estimate net realisable value. These formulas normally take into account, as appropriate, the age, past movements, expected future movements and estimated scrap values of the inventories. However, the results must be reviewed in the light of any special circumstances not anticipated in the formulas, such as changes in the current demand for inventories or unexpected obsolescence.

8.7.2 Materials and other supplies

IAS 2, paragraph 32, states that materials and other supplies held for use in the production of inventories are not written down below cost if the finished goods in which they will be incorporated are expected to be sold at or above cost. When the sale of finished goods is not expected to recover the costs, then materials are to be written down to net realisable value. IAS 2 suggests that the replacement cost of the materials or other supplies is probably the best measure of their net realisable value.

8.7.3 Write-down to net realisable value

Inventories are usually written down to net realisable value on an item-by-item basis. Paragraph 29 of IAS 2 states that 'it is not appropriate to write inventories down on the basis of a classification of inventory, for example, finished goods, or all the inventories in a particular industry or geographical segment'. Where it is not practical to separately evaluate the net realisable value of each item within a product line, the write-down may be applied on a group basis provided that the products have similar purposes or end uses, and are produced and marketed in the same geographical area. IAS 2 generally requires that service providers apply the measurement rule only on an item-by-item basis, as each service ordinarily has a separate selling price.

The journal entry to process the write-down would be:

Inventory Write-Down Expense Inventory (Write-down to net realisable value)	Dr Cr	800	 800

8.7.4 Reversal of prior write-down to net realisable value

If the circumstances that previously caused inventories to be written down below cost change, or if a new assessment confirms that net realisable value has increased, the amount of a previous write-down can be reversed (subject to an upper limit of the original write-down). This could occur if an item of inventory written down to net realisable value because of falling sales prices is still on hand at the end of a subsequent period and its selling price has recovered.

The journal entry to process the reversal would be:

Inventory Inventory Write-Down Expense (Write-up to revised net realisable value)	Dr Cr	800	 800

ILLUSTRATIVE EXAMPLE 8.5

Application of measurement rule

Vastervick Pty Ltd retails gardening equipment and has four main product lines: mowers, vacuum blowers, edgers and garden tools. At 30 June 2009, cost and net realisable values for each line were as shown below.

Application of lower of cost and net realisable value measurement rule

Inventory item	Quantity	Cost per unit $	NRV per unit $	Lower of cost and NRV $
Mowers	16	215.80	256.00	3 452.80
Vacuum blowers	113	62.35	60.00	6 780.00
Edgers	78	27.40	36.00	2 137.20
Garden tools	129	12.89	11.00	1 419.00
Inventory at the lower of cost and net realisable value				$13 789.00

The following journal entry would be required to adjust inventory values to net realisable value:

30 June 2009

Inventory write-down expense Inventory (Write-down to net realisable value – vacuum blowers $265.55 (113 × $2.35) and garden tools $243.81 (129 × $1.89))	Dr Cr	509.36	 509.36

8.8 RECOGNITION AS AN EXPENSE

Paragraph 34 of IAS 2 requires the following items to be recognised as expenses:

- carrying amount of inventories in the period in which the related revenue is recognised, in other words, cost of goods sold
- write-down of inventories to net realisable value and all losses
- reversals of write-downs to net realisable value.

The only exception to this rule relates to inventory items used by an entity as components in self-constructed property, plant or equipment. The cost of these items would be capitalised and recognised as an expense via depreciation.

8.9 DISCLOSURE

Paragraph 36 of IAS 2 contains the required disclosures relating to inventories. Before preparing the disclosure note, inventories on hand will need to be classified into categories because paragraph 36(b) requires 'the carrying amount in classifications appropriate to the entity' to be disclosed. Common classifications suggested in paragraph 37 are merchandise, production supplies, materials, work in progress and finished goods. Figure 8.2 provides an illustration of the disclosures required by IAS 2.

FIGURE 8.2 An example of illustrative disclosures required by IAS 2

			IAS 2 Para.
Note 1: Summary of accounting policies (extract)			
Inventories			
Inventories are valued at the lower of cost and net realisable value. Costs incurred in bringing each product to its present location and condition are accounted for as follows: • raw materials — purchase cost on a first-in, first-out basis • finished goods and work in progress — cost of direct material and labour and proportion of manufacturing overheads based on normal operating capacity • production supplies — purchase cost on a weighted average cost basis.			*36(a)*
Note 6: Inventories			
	Notes 2010 $000	2009 $000	
Inventories carried at lower of cost and net realisable value			
At cost:			*36(b)*
Raw materials	1 257	1 840	
Work in progress	649	721	
Finished goods	3 932	4 278	
Production supplies	385	316	
Total carrying amount	6 223	7 155	
Inventories carried at net realisable value			
Obsolete goods	269	174	*36(c)*
Less Costs to sell	(31)	(18)	
Total carrying amount	238	156	

(continued)

FIGURE 8.2 *(continued)*

In respect to inventory, the following items have been recognised as expenses during the period:			
Cost of sales	11 674	10 543	*36(d)*
Write-down to net realisable value	26	18	*36(e)*
Reversal of write-down[(a)]	(3)	—	*36(f)*
[(a)] A prior year write-down was reversed during the current period as a result of an increase in selling price for that inventory item.			*36(g)*
Inventory with a carrying amount of $570 000 has been pledged as security for loans to the company.			*36(h)*

SUMMARY

The purpose of this chapter is to analyse the content of IAS 2 *Inventories* and provide guidance on its implementation. The principal issue in accounting for inventories is the determination of cost and its subsequent recognition as an expense, including any write-down to net realisable value (IAS 2, *Objective*). One key decision in recognising inventory is the selection of an appropriate method for allocating costs between individual items of inventory to determine the cost of goods sold and the cost of inventory on hand. Following the initial recognition of the inventory, cost must be compared to net realisable value, and the value of inventory written down where net realisable value falls below cost. IAS 2 requires disclosures to be made in relation to the inventories held by an entity and the accounting policies adopted with respect to these assets.

Discussion questions

1. Define 'cost' as applied to the valuation of inventory.
2. What is meant by the term 'net realisable value'? Is this the same as fair value? If not, why not?
3. Explain the concept of lower of cost and net realisable value for inventory.
4. Which is more expensive to maintain: a perpetual inventory system, or a periodic inventory system? Why?
5. In what circumstances must assumptions be made in order to assign a cost to inventory items when they are sold?
6. 'Estimating the value of inventory is not sufficiently accurate to justify using such an approach. Only a full physical count can give full accuracy.' Discuss.
7. What is the difference between the first-in, first-out method and the weighted average method of assigning cost?
8. Compare and contrast the impact on the reported profit and asset value for an accounting period of the first-in, first-out method and the weighted average method.
9. Why is the lower of cost and net realisable value rule used in the accounting standard? Is it permissible to revalue inventory upwards? If so, when?
10. What impact do the terms of trade have on the determination of the quantity and value of inventory on hand where goods are in transit at the end of the reporting period?

STAR RATING
★ BASIC
★★ MODERATE
★★★ DIFFICULT

Exercises

Exercise 8.1

CONSIGNMENT OF INVENTORY

★ Arend al Ltd reported in a recent financial statement that approximately $12 million of merchandise was received on consignment. Should the company recognise this amount on its statement of financial position (balance sheet)? Explain.

Exercise 8.2

SELECTION OF COST ASSUMPTION

★ Under what circumstances would each of the following inventory cost methods be appropriate?

(a) Specific identification
(b) Last-in, first-out
(c) Average cost
(d) First-in, first-out
(e) Retail inventory

Exercise 8.3 STATEMENT OF FINANCIAL POSITION CLASSIFICATION

★ Where, if at all, should the following items be classified on a statement of financial position?

(a) Goods out on approval to customers
(b) Goods in transit that were recently purchased FOB destination
(c) Land held by a real estate firm for sale
(d) Raw materials
(e) Goods received on consignment
(f) Stationery supplies

Exercise 8.4 DISCLOSURES RELATING TO INVENTORY

★ Jokela Pty Ltd reported inventory in its statement of financial position as follows:

Inventories	$11 247 900

What additional disclosures might be necessary to present the inventory fairly?

Exercise 8.5 RECORDING INVENTORY TRANSACTIONS

★ Henry Halmstad began business on 1 March 2011. Henry balances the books at month-end and uses the periodic inventory system. Henry's transactions for March 2011 are detailed below.

01	Henry invested $16 000 cash and $10 000 office equipment into the business.
02	Purchased merchandise from B Askoy on account for $4800 on terms of 2/15, n/30.
05	Sold merchandise to S Stavanger on account for $1200 on terms of 2/10, n/30.
08	Purchased merchandise for cash, $860 on cheque no. 003.
12	Purchased merchandise from N Kurikka on account for $2000 on terms of 2/10, n/30.
14	Paid B Askoy for 2 March purchase on cheque no. 004.
15	Received $1176 from S Stavanger in payment of the account.
21	Sold merchandise to Alesund Ltd on account for $1600 on terms of 2/10, n/30.
21	Paid N Kurikka for 12 March purchase on cheque no. 005.
22	Purchased merchandise from B Kimito on account for $2400 on terms of 2/15, n/30.
23	Sold merchandise for $1300 cash.
25	Returned defective merchandise that cost $600 to B Kimito.
28	Paid salaries of $1400 on cheque no. 006.

Required

Prepare journal entries for March 2011, using the pro-forma journals provided.

Cash Receipts Journal

Date	Account	Ref.	Cash	Disc. all.	Sales	A/c rec.	Other

Cash Payments Journal								
Date	Account	Ch.	Ref.	Other	A/c pay.	Purch.	Cash	Disc. rec.

Purchases Journal				
Date	Account	Terms	Ref.	Amount

Sales Journal				
Date	Account	Terms	Ref.	Amount

General Journal				
Date	Account	Ref.	Dr	Cr

Exercise 8.6

DETERMINING INVENTORY COST AND COST OF GOODS SOLD (PERIODIC)

★ *Select the correct answer. Show any workings required and provide reasons to justify your choice.*

1. The cost of inventory on hand at 1 January 2010 was $25 000 and at 31 December 2010 was $35 000. Inventory purchases for the year amounted to $160 000, freight outwards expense was $500, and purchase returns were $1400. What was the cost of goods sold for the year ended 31 December 2010?
   (a) $148 100 (c) $149 100
   (b) $148 600 (d) $150 000
2. The following inventory information relates to K Rauma, who uses a periodic inventory system and rounds the average unit cost to the nearest dollar:
   Beginning inventory 10 units @ average cost of $25 each = $250
   January purchase 10 units @ $24 each
   July purchase 39 units @ $26 each
   October purchase 20 units @ $24 each
   Ending inventory 25 units
   What is the cost of ending inventory using the weighted average costing method?
   (a) $625 (c) $618.75
   (b) $620 (d) $610

Exercise 8.7

ASSIGNING COST (PERPETUAL)

★ *Select the correct answer. Show any workings required and provide reasons to justify your choice.*

Arvika uses the perpetual inventory method. Arvika's inventory transactions for August 2011 were as follows:

		No.	Unit cost	Total cost
01 Aug.	Beginning inventory	20	$4.00	$80.00
07 Aug.	Purchases	10	$4.20	$42.00
10 Aug.	Purchases	20	$4.30	$86.00
12 Aug.	Sales	15	?	?
16 Aug.	Purchases	20	$4.60	$92.00
20 Aug.	Sales	40	?	?
28 Aug.	Sales returns	3	?	?

1. Using this information, assume that Arvika uses the FIFO cost flow method and that the sales returns relate to the 20 August sales. The sales return should be costed back into inventory at what unit cost?
   (a) $4.00 (c) $4.30
   (b) $4.20 (d) $4.60
2. Assuming that Arvika uses the moving average cost flow method, the 12 August sales should be costed at what unit cost?
   (a) $4.16 (c) $4.06
   (b) $4.07 (d) $4.00

Exercise 8.8 ★★

END-OF-PERIOD ADJUSTMENTS

An extract from Uppsala Ltd's unadjusted trial balance as at 30 June 2010 appears below. Uppsala Ltd has a 30 June reporting date and uses the perpetual method to record inventory transactions.

	$	$
Inventory	194 400	
Sales		631 770
Sales returns	6 410	
Cost of goods sold	468 640	
Inventory losses	12 678	

Additional information

- On 24 June 2010, Uppsala Ltd recorded a $1320 credit sale of goods costing $1200. These goods, which were sold on FOB destination terms and were in transit at 30 June 2010, were included in the physical count.
- Inventory on hand at 30 June 2010 (determined via physical count) had a cost of $195 600 and a net realisable value of $194 740.

Required

1. Prepare any adjusting journal entries required on 30 June 2010.
2. Prepare the trading section of the statement of comprehensive income for the year ended 30 June 2010.

Exercise 8.9 ★★

END-OF-PERIOD ADJUSTMENTS

A physical count of inventory at 31 December 2010 revealed that Brunnsberg Pty Ltd had inventory on hand at that date with a cost of $441 000. Brunnsberg Pty Ltd uses the periodic method to record inventory transations. Inventory at 1 January 2010 was $397 000. The annual audit identified that the following items were excluded from this amount:

- Merchandise of $61 000 is held by Brunnsberg Pty Ltd on consignment. The consignor is Angelholm Ltd.
- Merchandise costing $38 000 was shipped by Brunnsberg Pty Ltd FOB destination to a customer on 31 December 2010. The customer was expected to receive the goods on 6 January 2011.
- Merchandise costing $46 000 was shipped by Brunnsberg Pty Ltd FOB shipping to a customer on 29 December 2010. The customer was scheduled to receive the goods on 2 January 2011.
- Merchandise costing $83 000 shipped by a vendor FOB destination on 31 December 2010 was received by Brunnsberg Pty Ltd on 4 January 2011.
- Merchandise costing $51 000 purchased FOB shipping was shipped by the supplier on 31 December 2010 and received by Brunnsberg Pty Ltd on 5 January 2011.

Required

1. Based on the above information, calculate the amount that should appear for inventory on Brunnsberg Pty Ltd's statement of financial position at 31 December 2010.
2. Prepare any journal entries necessary to adjust the Inventory general ledger account to the amount calculated in part 1.

Exercise 8.10 ★★

APPLYING THE LOWER OF COST AND NRV RULE

The following information relates to the inventory on hand at 30 June 2010 held by Vaasa Ltd.

Item No.	Quantity	Cost per unit $	Cost to replace $	Estimated selling price $	Cost of completion and disposal $
A1458	600	2.30	2.41	3.75	0.49
A1965	815	3.40	3.26	3.50	0.55
B6730	749	7.34	7.35	10.00	0.95
D0943	98	1.23	1.14	1.00	0.12
G8123	156	3.56	3.56	5.70	0.67
W2167	1492	6.12	6.15	7.66	0.36

Required

Calculate the value of inventory on hand at 30 June 2010 in accordance with the requirements of IAS 2.

Problems

Problem 8.1 ★

ASSIGNMENT OF COST (PERIODIC AND PERPETUAL)

Select the correct answer. Show any workings required and provide reasons to justify your choice.
Malmo Ltd's inventory transactions for April 2011 are shown below.

	Purchases			COGS			Balance		
Date	No. units	Unit cost	Total cost	No. units	Unit cost	Total cost	No. units	Unit cost	Total cost
01 April							20	$8.00	$160.00
04	90	$8.40	$756.00						
07	100	$8.60	$860.00						
10				50					
13	(20)	$8.60	($172.00)						
18				70					
21				(5)					
29				40					

1. If Malmo Ltd uses the perpetual inventory system with the moving average cost flow method, the 18 April sale would be costed at what unit cost?
   (a) $8.60
   (b) $8.46
   (c) $8.44
   (d) $8.42

2. If Malmo Ltd uses the periodic inventory system with the FIFO cost flow method, what would be the cost of goods sold for April?
   (a) $1303.00 (c) $1310.00
   (b) $1508.60 (d) $1324.00
3. If Malmo Ltd uses the perpetual inventory system with the FIFO cost flow method, the 21 April sale return (relating to the 18 April sale) would be costed at what unit cost?
   (a) $8.00 (c) $8.40
   (b) $8.60 (d) $8.50
4. If Malmo Ltd uses the periodic method with the weighted average cost flow method, what would be the value of closing inventory at 30 April 2011? (Round average cost to the nearest cent.)
   (a) $295.40 (c) $253.20
   (b) $301.00 (d) $297.50

Problem 8.2 ★★

END-OF-REPORTING-PERIOD ADJUSTMENTS

Norway Outfitters sells outdoor adventure equipment. The entity uses the perpetual inventory method to account for inventory transactions and assigns costs using the moving average method. All purchases and sales are made on FOB destination, 30-day credit terms.

At 30 June 2009, the balance of the Inventory control account in the general ledger was $248 265 after the special journal totals were posted but before the balance-date adjusting entries were prepared and posted.

A physical count showed goods worth $256 100 to be on hand. Investigations of the discrepancy between the general ledger account balance and the count total revealed the following:

- Damaged ropes worth $1200 were returned to the supplier on 29 June, but this transaction has not yet been recorded.
- During the stocktake, staff found that a box of leather gloves worth $595 had suffered water damage during a recent storm. The gloves were damaged beyond repair and so were not included in the count, but they are still recorded in the inventory records.
- Equipment worth $1500, which was sold for $2500 on 29 June, was still in transit to the customer on 30 June. The sale was recorded on 29 June and the equipment was not included in the physical count.
- An error occurred when posting the purchase journal totals for May 2009. The correct total of $25 100 was erroneously posted as $21 500.
- The physical count included goods worth $7600 that were being held on consignment for All Weather Gear Pty Ltd.
- An all-terrain kit worth $1570 was returned by a customer on 28 June. The sales return transaction was correctly journalised and posted to the ledgers, but the kit was not returned to the warehouse and therefore was not included in the physical count.

Required

Adjust and reconcile the inventory control ledger account balance to the physical account (adjusted as necessary).

Problem 8.3 ★★★

Note: Problems 8.3, 8.4 and 8.5 concern the same entity, Sweden Emporium, because the three problems have been designed so that they can be combined to form a single comprehensive problem.

ASSIGNMENT OF COST

Sweden Emporium is a gift shop situated in a small fishing village. The business carries a range of merchandise that it accounts for under the perpetual inventory method. Cost is assigned using the FIFO cost flow method. All purchases are on FOB shipping terms, with 30 days credit. The reporting date is 30 June.

The following information lists the transactions during October 2009 for one item of inventory (wall plaques):

Date	Detail	Number	Unit cost
Oct. 01	Opening balance	45	6.40
04	Purchase	50	6.50
08	Sale	60	
11	Purchase	70	6.60
14	Purchase return	10	6.60
19	Sale	70	
24	Sale return (on 19 Oct. sale)	5	
28	Purchase	40	6.70

Required
For the inventory item (wall plaques), calculate October's cost of goods sold expense and the cost of inventory on hand at 31 October 2009. Round all figures to the nearest cent.

Problem 8.4

★★★

END-OF-REPORTING-PERIOD RECONCILIATION AND NRV

Sweden Emporium is a gift shop situated in a small fishing village. The business carries a range of merchandise that it accounts for under the perpetual inventory method. Cost is assigned using the FIFO cost flow method. All purchases are on FOB shipping terms, with 30 days credit. The reporting date is 30 June.

A physical count of inventory at 30 June 2010 found inventory worth $189 650. The inventory control ledger account at that date had a balance of $193 700. Investigations of the discrepancy between these two figures revealed the following:

- An unopened carton containing posters worth $420 had not been included in the count.
- Seven large conch shells were found to be damaged beyond repair and were not recorded in the count. The shells, worth $220, are still recorded in the inventory records.
- Goods costing $590 were ordered on 27 June 2010 and delivered to the transport company by the supplier on 29 June. As the goods were in transit on 30 June, they were not included in the count. The purchase was recorded when the goods arrived at the shop on 2 July 2010.
- Sweden Emporium has a number of paintings on display in local restaurants on a consignment basis. The paintings are worth $4200 and were not included in the count.
- A brass telescope had been sold for $1200 on 30 June. As the telescope was still in the shop awaiting collection by the owner, it was included in the count. The telescope cost $950.
- Five missing dolphin statues worth $160 could not be located and are presumed to have been stolen from the shop.

Required
1. Reconcile the Inventory control ledger account balance with the physical count figure (adjust both figures as necessary).
2. Prepare any journal entries necessary to achieve the reconciliation.

Problem 8.5

★★★

END-OF-REPORTING-PERIOD RECONCILIATION AND NRV

Sweden Emporium is a gift shop situated in a small fishing village. The business carries a range of merchandise that it accounts for under the perpetual inventory method. Cost is assigned using the FIFO cost flow method. All purchases are on FOB shipping terms, with 30 days credit. The end of the reporting period is 30 June.

IAS 2 requires inventory to be recorded at the lower of cost and net realisable value. C Bligh, the owner of Sweden Emporium, assessed the net realisable value of her inventory at 30 June 2010 and concluded that the net realisable value of all items (except barometers) exceeded cost. The six barometers on hand cost $150 each, but C Bligh is of the opinion that they will need to be discounted to $90 in order to sell them.

Required
Explain what is meant by the term 'net realisable value' and detail the action C Bligh must take in respect to the wall barometers.

Problem 8.6 ★★ ALLOCATING COST (WEIGHTED AVERAGE), REPORTING GROSS PROFIT AND APPLYING THE NRV RULE

Oslo Ltd wholesales bicycles. It uses the perpetual inventory method and allocates cost to inventory on a moving average basis. The company's reporting date is 31 March. At 1 March 2011, inventory on hand consisted of 350 bicycles at $82 each and 43 bicycles at $85 each. During the month ended 31 March 2011, the following inventory transactions took place (all purchase and sales transactions are on credit):

01 March	Sold 300 bicycles for $120 each.
03	Five bicycles were returned by a customer. They had originally cost $82 each and were sold for $120 each.
09	Purchased 55 bicycles at $91 each.
10	Purchased 76 bicycles at $96 each.
15	Sold 86 bicycles for $135 each.
17	Returned one damaged bicycle to the supplier. This bicycle had been purchased on 9 March.
22	Sold 60 bicycles for $125 each.
26	Purchased 72 bicycles at $98 each.
29	Two bicycles, sold on 22 March, were returned by a customer. The bicycles were badly damaged so it was decided to write them off. They had originally cost $91 each.

Required

1. Calculate the cost of inventory on hand at 31 March 2011 and the cost of goods sold for the month of March. (Round the average unit cost to the nearest cent, and round the total cost amounts to the nearest dollar.)
2. Show the Inventory general ledger control account (in T-format) as it would appear at 31 March 2011.
3. Calculate the gross profit on sales for the month of March 2011.

Problem 8.7 ★★ ASSIGNING COST AND REPORTING GROSS PROFIT USING DIFFERENT COST METHODS

The following information has been extracted from the records of Lillehammer Trading about one of its products. Lillehammer Trading uses the perpetual inventory system and its reporting date is 30 September.

		No. of units	Unit cost $	Total cost $
2010				
01/10	Beginning balance	1 600	14.00	22 400
06/10	Purchased	600	14.10	8 460
05/11	Sold @ $24.00 per unit	2 000		
19/12	Purchased	2 200	14.70	32 340

		No. of units	Unit cost $	Total cost $
24/12	Purchase returns	160	14.70	2 352
10/01	Sold @ $24.20 per unit	1 400		
22/03	Purchased	16 800	15.00	252 000
30/04	Sold @ $26.50 per unit	3 600		
04/05	Sales returns @ $26.50 per unit	40		
04/06	Sold @ $27.00 per unit	7 000		
06/08	Purchased	1 000	16.00	16 000
27/09	Sold @ $30.00 per unit	6 200		

Required

1. Calculate the cost of inventory on hand at 30 September 2010 and the cost of goods sold for the year ended 30 September 2010, using:
   (a) the FIFO cost method
   (b) the moving average cost method (round the average unit costs to the nearest cent, and round the total cost amounts to the nearest dollar).
2. Prepare the trading section of the statement of comprehensive income for the year ended 30 September 2010, using:
   (a) the FIFO cost method
   (b) the moving average cost method.

Problem 8.8 ★★

END-OF-YEAR ADJUSTMENTS

The inventory control account balance of Johnkoping Fashions at 30 June 2010 was $221 020 using the perpetual inventory method. A physical count conducted on that day found inventory on hand worth $220 200. Net realisable value for each inventory item held for sale exceeded cost. An investigation of the discrepancy revealed the following:

- Goods worth $6600 held on consignment for Swede Accessories had been included in the physical count.
- Goods costing $1200 were purchased on credit from Vetlanda Ltd on 27 June 2010 on FOB shipping terms. The goods were shipped on 28 June 2010 but, as they had not arrived by 30 June 2010, were not included in the physical count. The purchase invoice was received and processed on 30 June 2010.
- Goods costing $2400 were sold on credit to Iceland Pty Ltd for $3900 on 28 June 2010 on FOB destination terms. The goods were still in transit on 30 June 2010. The sales invoice was raised and processed on 29 June 2010.
- Goods costing $2730 were purchased on credit (FOB destination) from Finn Handbags on 28 June 2010. The goods were received on 29 June 2010 and included in the physical count. The purchase invoice was received on 2 July 2010.
- On 30 June 2010, Johnkeping Fashions sold goods costing $6300 on credit (FOB shipping) terms to Viking Boutique for $9600. The goods were dispatched from the warehouse on 30 June 2010 but the sales invoice had not been raised at that date.
- Damaged inventory items valued at $2650 were discovered during the physical count. These items were still recorded on 30 June 2010 but were omitted from the physical count records pending their write-off.

Required

Prepare any journal entries necessary on 30 June 2010 to correct any errors and to adjust inventory.

Problem 8.9 ★★★ ALLOCATING COST (FIFO), REPORTING GROSS PROFIT AND APPLYING THE NRV RULE

Stockholm Ltd wholesales bicycles. It uses the perpetual inventory method and allocates cost to inventory on a first-in, first-out basis. The company's reporting date is 31 March. At 1 March 2010, inventory on hand consisted of 350 bicycles at $82 each and 43 bicycles at $85 each. During the month ended 31 March 2010, the following inventory transactions took place (all purchase and sales transactions are on credit):

01 March	Sold 300 bicycles for $120 each.
03	Five bicycles were returned by a customer. They had originally cost $82 each and were sold for $120 each.
09	Purchased 55 bicycles at $91 each.
10	Purchased 76 bicycles at $96 each.
15	Sold 86 bicycles for $135 each.
17	Returned one damaged bicycle to the supplier. This bicycle had been purchased on 9 March.
22	Sold 60 bicycles for $125 each.
26	Purchased 72 bicycles at $98 each.
29	Two bicycles, sold on 22 March, were returned by a customer. The bicycles were badly damaged so it was decided to write them off. They had originally cost $91 each.

Required

1. Calculate the cost of inventory on hand at 31 March 2010 and the cost of goods sold for the month of March.
2. Show the Inventory general ledger control account (in T-format) as it would appear at 31 March 2010.
3. Calculate the gross profit on sales for the month of March 2010.
4. IAS 2 requires inventories to be measured at the lower of cost and net realisable value. Identify three reasons why the net realisable value of the bicycles on hand at 31 March 2010 may be below their cost.
5. If the net realisable value is below cost, what action should Stockholm Ltd take?

Problem 8.10 ★★★ ASSIGNING COSTS AND END-OF-PERIOD ADJUSTMENTS

Lund Retailing Ltd is a food wholesaler that supplies independent grocery stores. The company operates a perpetual inventory system, with the first-in, first-out method used to assign costs to inventory items. Freight costs are not included in the calculation of unit costs. Transactions and other related information regarding two of the items (baked beans and plain flour) carried by Lund Ltd are given below for June 2010, the last month of the company's reporting period.

	Baked beans	Plain flour
Unit of packaging	Case containing 25 × 410 g cans	Box containing 12 × 4 kg bags
Inventory @ 1 June 2010	350 cases @ $19.60	625 boxes @ $38.40

	Baked beans	Plain flour
Purchases	1. 10 June: 200 cases @ $19.50 plus freight of $135 2. 19 June: 470 cases @ $19.70 per case plus freight of $210	1. 3 June: 150 boxes @ $38.45 2. 15 June: 200 boxes @ $38.45 3. 29 June: 240 boxes @ $39.00
Purchase terms	2/10, n/30, FOB shipping	n/30, FOB destination
June sales	730 cases @ $28.50	950 boxes @ 40.00
Returns and allowances	A customer returned 50 cases that had been shipped in error. The customer's account was credited for $1425.	As the June 15 purchase was unloaded, 10 boxes were discovered damaged. A credit of $384.50 was received by Lund Retailing Ltd.
Physical count at 30 June 2010	326 cases on hand	15 boxes on hand
Explanation of variance	No explanation found — assumed stolen	Boxes purchased on 29 June still in transit on 30 June
Net realisable value at 30 June 2010	$29.00 per case	$38.50 per box

Required

1. Calculate the number of units in inventory and the FIFO unit cost for baked beans and plain flour as at 30 June 2010 (show all workings).
2. Calculate the total dollar amount of the inventory for baked beans and plain flour, applying the lower of cost and net realisable rule on an item-by-item basis. Prepare any necessary journal entries (show all workings).

Problem 8.11 ★★★

ALLOCATING COST (MOVING AVERAGE), END-OF-PERIOD ADJUSTMENTS AND WRITE-DOWNS TO NRV

Part A

Mario Gothenburg uses the perpetual inventory method and special journals, balances the books at month-end and uses control accounts and subsidiary ledgers for all accounts receivable and accounts payable. All sales and purchases are made on 2/10, n/30, FOB destination terms. The moving average method is used to assign cost to inventory items.

The information below and overleaf has been extracted from Mario's books and records for May and June 2011.

		$
Inventory control ledger account balance at 31 May		20 367.30
Accounts payable control ledger account balance at 31 May		7 973.60
Inventory purchases on credit during June		11 248.90
Cash paid to trade creditors during June		15 123.40
Discount received during June		438.90
Inventory sales on credit during June		15 020.00
Inventory ledger card balances at 1 June:		
Pool filters	43 @ $232.50	9 997.50
Pool pumps	21 @ $493.80	10 369.80
		20 367.30

(continued)

The credit inventory purchases during June comprised the following:

04	5 pool pumps @ $476.10 each	2 380.50
17	3 pool pumps @ $491.30 each	1 473.90
18	12 pool filters @ $236.70 each	2 840.40
24	2 pool pumps @ $491.30	982.60
29	15 pool filters @ $238.10	3 571.50
		11 248.90

The credit inventory sales during June comprised the following:

01	1 pool pump @ $520 and 1 pool filter @ $300	820
05	18 pool filters @ $300	5 400
18	4 pool pumps @ $550	2 200
23	15 pool filters @ $330	4 950
28	5 pool filters @ $330	1 650
		15 020

Other movements in inventory during June were:

09	2 pool filters, sold 5 June (not paid for) were returned by the customer
20	3 pool filters purchased 18 June (not paid for) were returned to the supplier
26	1 pool pump, purchased 4 June (paid for) was returned to the supplier

Required

1. Prepare the perpetual inventory records for June 2011.
2. Prepare the inventory control and accounts payable control general ledger accounts (in T-format) for the month of June 2011.

Part B

At 30 June 2011, Mario conducted a physical stocktake that found 14 pool filters and 26 pool pumps on hand. An investigation of discrepancies between the inventory card balances and the physical count showed that the 15 pool filters purchased on 29 June 2011 were still in transit from the supplier's factory on 30 June 2011, and one pool pump, sold on 18 June, had been returned by a customer on 30 June. No adjustment has been made in the books for the sales return. The customer had not paid for the returned pump.

Required

Prepare any general journal entries necessary to correct the Inventory control general ledger account balance as at 30 June 2011. (Narrations are not required, but show all workings.) Do not adjust the perpetual inventory records prepared in Part A.

Part C

On 30 June 2011, Mario determined that his inventory items have the following net realisable values:

Pool filters	$232 each
Pool pumps	$546 each

Required

1. What does the term 'net realisable value' mean?
2. What sources of evidence could Mario examine to determine net realisable value?
3. What action should Mario take as at 30 June 2011 with respect to these net realisable values? Why?

References

IASB 2004, *IFRIC Update*, November, IASB.

Nokia 2007, *Nokia in 2007*, Nokia Corporation, Finland, www.nokia.com.

9 Property, plant and equipment

ACCOUNTING STANDARDS IN FOCUS

IAS 16 *Property, Plant and Equipment*

LEARNING OBJECTIVES

When you have studied this chapter, you should be able to:

- understand the nature of property, plant and equipment
- understand the recognition criteria for initial recognition of property, plant and equipment
- understand how to measure property, plant and equipment on initial recognition
- explain the alternative ways in which property, plant and equipment can be measured subsequent to initial recognition
- explain the cost model of measurement and understand the nature and calculation of depreciation
- explain the revaluation model of measurement
- understand the factors to consider when choosing which measurement model to apply
- account for derecognition
- implement the disclosure requirements of IAS 16.

9.1 THE NATURE OF PROPERTY, PLANT AND EQUIPMENT

The accounting standard analysed in this chapter is IAS 16 *Property, Plant and Equipment*. The standard was first issued by the International Accounting Standards Board (IASB) as IAS 16 in March 1982, amended on numerous occasions, exposed in May 2002 as part of the International Accounting Standard Board (IASB) project on improvements to international accounting standards (IASs), and issued in its present form in 2004. As a result of this process, the IASB has clarified selected matters and provided additional guidance. It has not reconsidered the fundamental approach to the accounting for property, plant and equipment contained in IAS 16.

According to paragraph 2 of IAS 16 the standard applies in accounting for property, plant and equipment except where another standard requires or permits a different accounting treatment. IAS 16 does not apply to property, plant and equipment classified as held for sale in accordance with IFRS 5 *Non-current Assets Held for Sale and Discontinued Operations*; biological assets related to agricultural activity as these are accounted for under IAS 41 *Agriculture*; or mineral rights and mineral reserves such as oil, gas and similar non-regenerative resources. However, IAS 16 does apply to property, plant and equipment used to develop or maintain biological assets and mineral rights and reserves.

Paragraph 6 of IAS 16 defines **property, plant and equipment** as follows:

> Property, plant and equipment are tangible items that:
> (a) are held for use in the production or supply of goods or services, for rental to others, or for administrative purposes; and
> (b) are expected to be used during more than one period.

Note the following:

- The assets are 'tangible' assets. The distinction between tangible and intangible assets is discussed in depth in chapter 10. However, a key feature of tangible assets is that they are physical assets, such as land, rather than non-physical, such as patents and trademarks.
- The assets have specific uses within an entity; namely, for use in production/supply, rental or administration. Assets that are held for sale, including land, or held for investment are not included under property, plant and equipment. Instead, assets held for sale are accounted for in accordance with IFRS 5.
- The assets are non-current assets, the expectation being that they will be used for more than one accounting period.

Property, plant and equipment may be divided into classes for disclosure purposes, a class of assets being a grouping of assets of a similar nature and use in an entity's operations. Examples of classes of property, plant and equipment are land, machinery, motor vehicles and office equipment. The notes to the statement of financial position/balance sheet of the Australian company Wesfarmers Ltd, at 30 June 2008, as shown in figure 9.1, provide an indication of what is contained in that category as well as the reasons for the movements in this category of assets.

FIGURE 9.1 Property plant and equipment of Wesfarmers Ltd

	CONSOLIDATED		PARENT	
	2008 $m	2007 $m	**2008 $m**	2007 $m
16 PROPERTY, PLANT AND EQUIPMENT				
Freehold land				
Cost	**683**	168	**1**	1
Net carrying amount	**683**	168	**1**	1
Net carrying amount at beginning of year	**168**	186	**1**	1
Additions	**162**	32	**—**	—
Transfers	**17**	5	**—**	—
Transfers to assets held for sale	**(22)**	—	**—**	—
Transfers to inventory	**(28)**	(71)	**—**	—
Disposals	**(6)**	(6)	**—**	—
Acquisitions of controlled entities	**400**	15	**—**	—
Impairment charge	**—**	4	**—**	—

FIGURE 9.1 *(continued)*

	CONSOLIDATED		PARENT	
	2008 $m	2007 $m	**2008 $m**	2007 $m
Freehold land *(continued)*				
Exchange differences	**(8)**	3	**—**	—
Net carrying amount at end of year	**683**	168	**1**	1
Buildings				
Cost	**477**	282	**3**	3
Accumulated depreciation and impairment	**(84)**	(79)	**(1)**	(1)
Net carrying amount	**393**	203	**2**	2
Net carrying amount at beginning of year	**203**	293	**2**	2
Additions	**119**	62	**—**	—
Transfers	**20**	(41)	**—**	—
Transfers to inventory	**(66)**	(104)	**—**	—
Disposals	**(1)**	(9)	**—**	—
Acquisitions of controlled entities	**129**	8	**—**	—
Depreciation expense	**(9)**	(9)	**—**	—
Exchange differences	**(2)**	3	**—**	—
Net carrying amount at end of year	**393**	203	**2**	2
Assets in course of construction included above	**3**	19	**—**	—
Leasehold improvements				
Cost	**505**	87	**2**	2
Accumulated depreciation and impairment	**(79)**	(35)	**—**	—
Net carrying amount	**426**	52	**2**	2
Net carrying amount at beginning of year	**52**	61	**2**	2
Additions	**69**	5	**—**	—
Transfers	**13**	—	**—**	—
Rehabilitation provision asset increment/ (decrement)	**—**	(13)	**—**	—
Disposals	**(5)**	—	**—**	—
Acquisitions of controlled entities	**348**	4	**—**	—
Impairment charge	**(6)**	—	**—**	—
Amortisation expense	**(45)**	(5)	**—**	—
Net carrying amount at end of year	**426**	52	**2**	2
Assets in course of construction included above	**2**	9	**—**	—
Plant vehicles and equipment				
Cost	**6476**	3366	**34**	33
Accumulated depreciation and impairment	**(1975)**	(1568)	**(12)**	(13)
Net carrying amount	**4501**	1796	**22**	20
Net carrying amount at beginning of year	**1798**	1265	**20**	20
Additions	**910**	535	**5**	2
Transfers	**(37)**	44	**—**	—
Transfers to inventory	**—**	(8)	**—**	—
Rehabilitation provision asset increment/ (decrement)	**1**	(1)	**—**	—
Disposals	**(41)**	(12)	**(1)**	—
Acquisitions of controlled entities	**2402**	156	**—**	—
Impairment charge	**(53)**	(2)	**—**	—
Depreciation expense	**(468)**	(184)	**(2)**	(2)

(continued)

FIGURE 9.1 *(continued)*

	CONSOLIDATED		PARENT	
	2008 $m	2007 $m	**2008 $m**	2007 $m
Plant vehicles and equipment *(continued)*				
Exchange differences	**(11)**	5	—	—
Net carrying amount at end of year	**4 501**	1 798	**22**	20
Assets in course of construction included above	**747**	576	**2**	1
Mineral lease and development costs				
Cost	**977**	806	—	—
Accumulated amortisation and impairment	**(381)**	(311)	—	—
Net carrying amount	**596**	495	—	—
Net carrying amount at beginning of year	**495**	591	—	—
Additions	**10**	61	—	—
Transfers	**(13)**	37	—	—
Arising on coal rebates	**183**	16	—	—
Rehabilitation provision asset increment/ (decrement)	—	(73)	—	—
Amortisation expense	**(79)**	(137)	—	—
Net carrying amount at end of year	**596**	495	—	—
Assets in course of construction included above	**1**	16	—	—
Total				
Cost	**9 118**	4 709	**40**	39
Accumulated depreciation and impairment	**(2 519)**	(1 993)	**(13)**	(14)
Net carrying amount	**6 599**	2 716	**27**	25

Source: Wesfarmers Ltd (2008, pp. 100–1).

In this chapter, accounting for property, plant and equipment is considered as follows:

- recognition of the asset — the point at which the asset is brought into the accounting records
- initial measurement of the asset — determining the initial amount at which the asset is recorded in the accounts
- measurement subsequent to initial recognition — determining the amount at which the asset is reported subsequent to acquisition, including the recording of any depreciation of the asset
- derecognition of the asset.

9.2 INITIAL RECOGNITION OF PROPERTY, PLANT AND EQUIPMENT

Paragraph 7 of IAS 16 contains the principles for recognition of property, plant and equipment:

> The cost of an item of property, plant and equipment shall be recognised as an asset if, and only if:
> (a) it is probable that future economic benefits associated with the item will flow to the entity; and
> (b) the cost of the item can be measured reliably.

This is a *general* recognition principle for property, plant and equipment. It applies to the initial recognition of an asset, when parts of that asset are replaced, and when costs are incurred in relation to that asset during its useful life. To recognise a cost as an asset, the outlay must give rise to the expectation of future economic benefits.

The criteria for recognition in paragraph 7 differ from the recognition criteria for the elements of financial statements in paragraph 83 of the *Framework*. Under the *Framework*, an asset can be recognised when the cost or value can be measured with reliability; under IAS 16, recognition can occur only if the cost can be measured reliably. Assets for which the cost cannot be reliably measured but whose initial fair value can be measured reliably cannot be recognised in the entity's records.

9.2.1 Asset versus expense

For most items of property, plant and equipment, the entity will incur some initial expenditure. One of the key problems for the entity is determining whether the outlay should be expensed or capitalised as an asset. As paragraph 7 of IAS 16 states, the elements of that decision relate to whether the entity expects there to be future economic benefits, whether the receipt of those benefits is probable, and whether the benefits will flow specifically to the entity. As noted in paragraph 90 of the *Framework*, the expensing of outlays:

> does not imply either that the intention of management in incurring expenditure was other than to generate future economic benefits for the entity or that management was misguided. The only implication is that the degree of certainty that economic benefits will flow to the entity beyond the current accounting period is insufficient to warrant the recognition of an asset.

As property, plant and equipment consists of physical assets such as land and machinery, such assets are normally traded in a market. One test of the existence of future benefits is then to determine whether there exists a market for the item in question. A problem with some assets is that once items have been acquired and installed, there is no normal market for them. However, in many cases, the expected economic benefits arise because of the use of that asset in conjunction with other assets held by the entity. At a minimum, the future benefits would be the scrap value of the item. Where the assets are intangible, such as costs associated with the generation of software, the absence of a physical asset causes more problems in terms of asset recognition. Chapter 10 discusses in detail the problems associated with the recognition of intangible assets.

9.2.2 Separate assets — components

The total property, plant and equipment of an entity may be broken down into separate assets. This is sometimes referred to as a 'components' approach to asset recognition. An entity allocates the amount initially recognised in respect of an asset to its component parts and accounts for each component separately. Paragraph 9 of IAS 16 notes that the identification of what constitutes a separate item or component of plant and equipment requires the exercise of judgement, because the standard does not prescribe the unit of measure for recognition. The key element in determining whether an asset should be further subdivided into its component parts is an analysis of what is going to happen in the future to that asset. Having identified an asset, the entity wants to recognise the expected benefits as they are consumed by the entity, with the recognition being in the period in which the benefits are received. Hence, if an asset has a number of components that have different useful lives then, in order for there to be an appropriate recognition of benefits consumed, components with different useful lives need to be identified and accounted for separately.

For example, consider an aircraft as an item of property, plant and equipment. Is it sufficient to recognise the aircraft as a single asset? An analysis of the aircraft may reveal that there are various components of the aircraft that have different useful lives. Component parts of the aircraft include the engines, the frame of the aircraft and the fittings (seats, floor coverings and so on). It may be necessary to refit the aircraft every 5 years, whereas the engines may last twice as long. Similarly, an entity that deals with the refining of metals may have a blast furnace, the lining of which needs to be changed periodically. The lining of the blast furnace therefore needs to be separated from the external structure in terms of asset recognition and subsequent accounting for the asset. Further, as noted in paragraph 9 of IAS 16, it may be appropriate to aggregate individually insignificant items (such as moulds, tools and dies) and apply the criteria to the aggregate value.

9.2.3 Generation of future benefits

Paragraph 11 of IAS 16 notes that certain assets may not of themselves generate future benefits, but instead it may be necessary for the entity itself to generate future benefits. For example, some items of property, plant and equipment may be acquired for safety or environmental reasons, such as equipment associated with the safe storage of dangerous chemicals. The entity's generation of the benefits from use of the chemicals can occur only if the safety equipment exists. Hence, even if the safety equipment does not of itself generate cash flows, its existence is necessary for the entity to be able to use chemicals within the business.

9.3 INITIAL MEASUREMENT OF PROPERTY, PLANT AND EQUIPMENT

Having established that an asset can be recognised, the entity must then assign to it a monetary amount. Paragraph 15 of IAS 16 contains the principles for initial measurement of property, plant and equipment: 'An item of property, plant and equipment that qualifies for recognition as an asset shall be measured at its cost.' Paragraph 16 specifies three components of cost, namely:

- purchase price
- directly attributable costs
- initial estimate of the costs of dismantling and removing the item or restoring the site on which it is located.

These items are considered separately in the following sections.

9.3.1 Purchase price

'Purchase price' is not defined in IAS 16, but paragraph 16(a) states that the purchase price includes import duties and non-refundable purchase taxes, and is calculated after deducting any trade discounts and rebates. The essence of what constitutes purchase price is found in the definition of cost in paragraph 6 of the standard, which states: 'Cost is the amount of cash or cash equivalents paid or the fair value of the other consideration given to acquire an asset at the time of its acquisition or construction.'

Where an item of property, plant and equipment is acquired for cash, determination of the purchase price is relatively straightforward. One variation that may arise is that some or all of the cash payment is deferred. In this case, as noted in paragraph 23 of IAS 16, the cost is the cash price equivalent at the recognition date, determined by measuring the cash payments on a present value basis (done by discounting the cash flows). Interest is then recognised as the payments are made.

More difficulties arise where the exchange involves assets other than cash. In a non-cash exchange, the acquiring entity receives a non-cash asset and in return provides a non-cash asset to the seller. In measuring the cost of the asset acquired, the question is whether the measurement should be based on the value of the asset given up by the acquirer, or by reference to the value of the asset acquired from the seller. In relation to the application of the cost principle of measurement, note the following:

1. Cost is determined by reference to the fair value of what is given up by the acquirer rather than by the fair value of the item acquired. The cost represents the sacrifice made by the acquirer. This principle is inherent in the definition of cost in paragraph 6 of IAS 16. Further, paragraph 26 states that where both the fair value of what is given up by the acquirer and the asset received are reliably measurable, then the fair value of the asset given up is used to measure the cost of the asset received, unless the fair value of the asset received is more clearly evident. 'More clearly evident' presumably relates to the cost and difficulty of determining the fair value as, in the paragraph 26 example, the fair values of both the asset received and the asset given up can be measured reliably.
2. Cost is measured by reference to fair value (paragraph 24). The term fair value is defined in paragraph 6 of the standard: 'Fair value is the amount for which an asset could be exchanged between knowledgeable, willing parties in an arm's length transaction.'

   Fair value is basically market value; in economic terms, it represents the opportunity cost of giving up an asset or assuming a liability. Note that the process of determining fair value necessarily involves judgement and estimation. The acquiring company is not actually trading the items given up in the marketplace for cash, but is trying to estimate what it would get for those items if it did so. Hence, the determination of fair value is only an estimation. A further practical problem in determining fair value is that the nature of the market in which the goods given up are normally traded may make estimation difficult. The market may be highly volatile with prices changing daily, or the market may be relatively inactive. Where no ready market exists for the goods being traded, it may be necessary to obtain a reasonable estimate of fair value by reference to a market for similar goods.

   If the acquirer gives up an asset at fair value, and the carrying amount of the asset is different from the fair value, then the entity will recognise a gain or a loss. According to paragraph 34 of IAS 1 *Presentation of Financial Statements*, gains and losses on the disposal of non-current assets are reported by deducting from the proceeds on disposal the carrying amount of the asset and related selling expenses.

Assume then that an entity acquires a piece of machinery and gives in exchange a block of land. The land is carried by the entity at original cost of $100 000 and has a fair value of $150 000. The journal entry to record the acquisition of the machinery is:

Machinery	Dr	150 000	
Proceeds on Sale of Land	Cr		150 000
(Sale of land in exchange for machinery)			
Carrying Amount of Land Sold	Dr	100 000	
Land	Cr		100 000
(Carrying amount of land sold)			

The entity then reports a gain on sale of land of $50 000.

If, instead of giving land in exchange, the entity issued shares having a fair value of $150 000, the journal entry is:

Machinery	Dr	150 000	
Share Capital	Cr		150 000
(Acquisition of machinery by issue of shares)			

Further discussion on the measurement of the fair value of equity instruments issued by the acquirer in exchange for assets is found in chapter 11.

3. Paragraph 24 of IAS 16 requires the use of fair value to measure the cost of an asset received unless the exchange transaction lacks commercial substance. Commercial substance is concerned with whether the transaction has a discernible effect on the economics of an entity. Paragraph 25 states that an exchange transaction has commercial substance if:
   (a) *the configuration (risk, timing and amount) of the cash flows of the asset received differs from the configuration of the cash flows of the asset transferred.* This would not occur if similar assets (e.g. an exchange of commodities such as oil or milk) were exchanged as would occur where, for example, suppliers exchanged inventories in various locations to fulfil demand on a timely basis in a particular location; or
   (b) *the entity-specific value of the portion of the entity's operations affected by the transaction changes as a result of the exchange.* Paragraph 6 defines **entity-specific value** as 'the present value of the cash flows an entity expects to arise from the continuing use of an asset and from its disposal at the end of its useful life or expects to incur when settling a liability'. If there is no change in the expected cash flows to the entity as a result of the exchange, as in the case of the exchange of similar items, then the transaction lacks commercial substance; and
   (c) *the difference in (a) or (b) is significant relative to the fair value of the assets exchanged.* In both (a) and (b), the change in cash flows or configuration must be material, with materiality being measured in relation to the fair value of the assets exchanged.

   Where the transaction lacks commercial substance, the asset acquired is measured at the carrying amount of the asset given up.
4. Paragraph 24 of IAS 16 also covers the situation where, in an exchange of assets, neither the fair value of the assets given up nor the fair value of the assets acquired can be measured reliably. Such situations could occur where the assets exchanged are both traded in weak markets where market transactions are infrequent. In this situation, the acquirer measures the cost of the asset acquired at the carrying amount of the asset given up.

Acquisition date

One of the problems in recording the acquisition of an item of property, plant and equipment relates to the determination of the fair values of the assets involved in the exchange. As noted above, accounting for the asset exchange requires that potentially both the fair values of the assets acquired and assets given up must be determined. However, where the markets for these assets are volatile, choosing the appropriate fair value may be difficult. This can be seen where an entity issues shares in exchange for an asset. The fair value of the shares issued may change on a daily basis. At what point in time should the fair values be measured?

Some likely dates that may be considered are:

- the date the contract to exchange the assets is signed
- the date the consideration is paid
- the date on which the assets acquired are received by the acquirer
- the date on which an offer becomes unconditional.

The advantage of these dates is that they relate to a point of time that can be determined objectively, such as the date the item of property, plant and equipment arrives at the acquirer's premises. A problem is that there may be a number of dates involved if, for example, an item of equipment arrives in stages or payment for the equipment is to be made in instalments over time.

The date on which the fair values should be measured is the date on which the acquirer *obtains control of the asset or assets acquired* — hereafter referred to as the 'acquisition date'. The definition of cost in paragraph 6 of IAS 16 refers to the 'time of its [the asset's] acquisition'. There is no specific date defined in the standard. In IFRS 3 *Business Combinations*, acquisition date is defined as 'the date on which the acquirer obtains control of the acquiree'.

The measurement of the fair value relates to the date the assets acquired are recognised in the records of the acquirer. At this date, the acquirer must be able to reliably measure the cost of the asset. Recognition of an asset requires the acquirer to have control of expected future benefits. Hence, when the item acquired becomes the asset of the acquirer (that is, when the expected benefits come under the control of the acquirer), this is the point in time when the measurements of the fair values of assets acquired and given up are made. Paragraph 23 of IAS 16 states that the cost of an item of property, plant and equipment is the cash price equivalent at the 'recognition date'. Recognition date is normally the same as acquisition date.

Acquisition of multiple assets

The above principles as stated in IAS 16 apply to the acquisition of individual items of property, plant and equipment. However, an acquisition may consist of more than one asset, such as a block of land and a number of items of machinery. The acquirer may acquire the assets as a group, paying one total amount for the bundle of assets. The cost of acquiring the bundle of assets is determined as per IAS 16, namely by measuring the fair value of what is given up by the acquirer to determine the purchase price, and adding to this any directly attributable costs. However, even if the total cost of the bundle of assets can be determined, for accounting purposes it is necessary to determine the cost of each of the separate assets as they may be in different classes, or some may be depreciable and others not. No guidance is given in this standard for determining the costs of each of the assets. However, IFRS 3 paragraph 2(b) states:

> The cost of the group shall be allocated to the individual identifiable assets and liabilities on the basis of their relative *fair values* at the date of purchase. Such a transaction or event does not give rise to goodwill.

In this situation, the cost of each asset to be recorded separately is calculated by allocating the cost of the bundle of assets over the assets acquired in proportion to the fair values of the assets acquired. To illustrate this allocation procedure, assume an entity acquired land, buildings and furniture at a total cost of \$300 000 cash. In order to separately record each asset acquired at cost, the entity determines the fair value of each asset, for example:

Land	\$ 40 000
Buildings	200 000
Furniture	80 000
	\$320 000

The total cost of \$300 000 is then allocated to each asset on the basis of these fair values as follows:

Land	\$40 000/\$320 000 × \$300 000 =	\$ 37 500
Buildings	\$200 000/\$320 000 × \$300 000 =	187 500
Furniture	\$80 000/\$320 000 × \$300 000 =	75 000
		\$300 000

The acquisition of the three assets is recorded by the entity as follows:

Land	Dr	37 500	
Buildings	Dr	187 500	
Furniture	Dr	75 000	
Cash	Cr		300 000
(Acquisition of assets for cash)			

Under IAS 16, the basic principle of recording assets acquired is to record at cost. Where a bundle of assets is acquired, the cost of the separate assets must be estimated, and the fair values of the assets acquired can be used in this process. Where the cost of the assets in total is less than the sum of the fair values of the assets acquired, a bargain purchase has been made. However, as the assets are to be recognised initially at cost, no gain is recognised on acquisition.

9.3.2 Directly attributable costs

The key feature of those costs included in the cost of acquisition is that they are directly attributable *to bringing the asset to the location and condition necessary for it to be capable of operating in the manner intended by management* (IAS 16 para. 16).

Costs to be included

Paragraph 17 of IAS 16 provides examples of directly attributable costs:

- costs of employee benefits arising directly from the construction or acquisition of the item of property, plant and equipment
- costs of site preparation
- initial delivery and handling costs
- installation and assembly costs — where buildings are acquired, associated costs could be the costs of renovation
- costs of testing whether the asset is functioning properly
- professional fees.

It can be seen that all these costs are incurred before the asset is used, and are necessary in order for the asset to be usable by the entity. Note, however, the use of the word 'necessary'. There may be costs incurred that were not necessary; for example, the entity may have incurred fines, or a concrete platform may have been placed in the wrong position and had to be destroyed and a new one put in the right place. These costs should be written off to an expense rather than being capitalised as part of the cost of the acquired asset.

A further cost that may be capitalised into the cost of an item of property, plant and equipment is that of borrowing costs. Borrowing costs, i.e. interest and other costs associated with the borrowing of funds, are accounted for under IAS 23 *Borrowing Costs*. Paragraph 8 of IAS 23 states that borrowing costs that are directly attributable to the acquisition, construction or production of a qualifying asset must be capitalised as part of the cost of the asset. (A qualifying asset is one that necessarily takes a substantial period of time to get ready for its intended use or sale, such as a building.)

Costs not to be included

Paragraphs 19 and 20 of IAS 16 contain examples of costs that should not be included in directly attributable costs:

- *costs of opening a new facility*. These costs are incurred after the item of property, plant and equipment is capable of being used; the opening ceremony, for example, does not enhance the operating ability of the asset.
- *costs of introducing a new product or service, including costs of advertising and promotional activities*. These costs do not change the location or working condition of the asset.
- *costs of conducting business in a new location or with a new class of customer* (*including costs of staff training*). Unless the asset is relocated, there is no change in the asset's ability to operate.
- *administration and other general overhead costs*. These costs are not directly attributable to the asset, but are associated generally with the operations of the entity.

- *costs incurred while an item capable of operating in the manner intended by management has yet to be brought into use or is operated at less than full capacity*. These costs are incurred because of management's decisions regarding the timing of operations rather than being attributable to getting the asset in a position for operation.
- *initial operating losses, such as those incurred while demand for the item's output builds up*. These are not incurred before the asset is ready for use.
- *costs of relocating or reorganising part or all of the entity's operations*. If a number of currently operating assets are relocated to another site, then the costs of relocation are general, and not directly attributable to the item of property, plant and equipment.

Income earned

Paragraph 17(e) of IAS 16 notes that the cost of the asset should be determined after deducting the net proceeds from selling any items produced when bringing the asset to that location and condition, such as proceeds from the sale of samples produced during the testing process. The principle here is that any flows, whether in or out, that occur before the asset is in a position to operate as management intends must be taken into account in determining the cost of the asset. The testing process is a necessary part of readying the asset for its ultimate use. Paragraph 21 provides an example of where income may be earned before the asset is ready for use but should not be included in the calculation of the cost of the asset. The example given is of income earned from the use of the construction site as a car park while there is a delay before the construction of a building. These revenues have nothing to do with the creation of the asset. They are incidental to the development activity, and should be separately recognised.

Acquisition for zero or nominal cost

An entity may acquire an asset for zero cost, or be required to pay an amount substantially different from the fair value of the asset. For example, a charitable organisation such as the Red Cross may be given a computer for no charge, or be required to pay only half price for a block of land or a building. Applying IAS 16, where there is zero cost, the entity receiving the asset would not record the asset. In the case of a heavily discounted asset, the asset would be recorded at the cost, namely the purchase price paid plus the directly attributable costs.

It is not appropriate to apply IAS 18 *Revenue* to recognise the asset at fair value and record revenue on receipt of the asset. Paragraph 1 of IAS 18 limits the application of the standard to three types of transactions, not including the acquisition of assets. However, the asset could be recognised subsequent to acquisition at fair value if the revaluation model is applied.

9.3.3 Costs of dismantling, removal or restoration

At the date the asset is initially recognised, an entity is required to estimate any costs necessary to eventually dismantle and remove an asset and restore its site. For example, when an asset such as an offshore oil platform is constructed, an entity knows that in the future it is required by law to dismantle and remove the platform in such a manner that the environment is cared for. The construction of the platform gives rise to a liability for restoration under IAS 37 *Provisions, Contingent Liabilities and Contingent Assets*. The expected costs, measured on a present value basis, are capitalised into the cost of the platform as the construction of the platform brings with it the responsibility of disposing of it. Acceptance of the liability for dismantling and removal is an essential part of bringing the asset to a position of intended use. As with directly attributable costs, the dismantling and removal costs are depreciated over the life of the asset. There may be restoration costs associated with the use of land, such as where the land is used for mining or farming. These costs are capitalised into the cost of the land at the acquisition date and, although the land is not depreciated, the restoration costs are depreciated over the period in which the benefits from use of the land are received.

As explained in paragraphs BC14 — BC15 of the Basis for Conclusions on IAS 16, because of the limited scope of the revisions undertaken during the Improvements project, the International Accounting Standards Board (IASB) concentrated on the initial estimate of the costs of dismantling, removal and restoration. Issues relating to changes in that estimate, changes in interest rates, and the emergence of obligations subsequent to the asset's acquisition are not covered in IAS 16. However, the IASB did note that, regardless of whether the obligation is incurred when the item is acquired or when it is being used, the obligation's underlying nature and its association with the asset are the same. Hence, where obligations arise because of the use of an asset, these should be included in the cost of the asset.

9.4 MEASUREMENT SUBSEQUENT TO INITIAL RECOGNITION

At the point of initial recognition of an item of property, plant and equipment, the asset is measured at cost, which is the purchase price plus directly attributable costs and removal and/or restoration costs. After this initial recognition, an entity has a choice on the measurement basis to be adopted. IAS 16 paragraph 29 recognises two possible measurement models:

- the cost model
- the revaluation model.

The choice of model is an accounting policy decision. That policy is not applied to individual assets but to an entire class of property, plant and equipment. Hence, for each class of assets, an entity must decide the measurement model to be used. Having chosen a particular measurement model for a specific class of assets, the entity may later change to the alternative basis. For example, an entity that initially chose the revaluation model may at a later date change to the cost model. In order to change from one basis to another, the principles of IAS 8 *Accounting Policies, Changes in Accounting Estimates and Errors* must be applied. Paragraph 14 of IAS 8 states:

> An entity shall change an accounting policy only if the change:
> (a) is required by an Australian Accounting Standard; or
> (b) results in the financial report providing reliable and more relevant information about the effects of transactions, other events or conditions on the entity's financial position, financial performance or cash flows.

It is part (b) that establishes the principle for change. The key is whether the change in measurement basis will make the financial statements more useful to users; in particular, will the information be more relevant and/or more reliable? In general, a change from the cost model to the revaluation model would be expected to increase the relevance of information provided because more current information is being made available. However, the change may make the information less reliable, as the determination of fair value requires estimation to occur. The entity would need to assess the overall benefit of the change in order to justify the change. In contrast, changing from the revaluation model would generally lead to a decrease in the relevance of the information. However, it may be that the determination of fair value has become so unreliable that the fair values determined have little meaning. Again, a judgement of the relative trade-offs between relevance and reliability need to be made.

Paragraph 17 of IAS 8 notes that the accounting for a change from the cost model to the revaluation model constitutes a change in accounting policy, but the accounting for such a change is done in accordance with the principles in IAS 16 rather than those in IAS 8, namely by applying the principles of the revaluation model. No such statement is made about a change from fair value back to cost. It would appear that the accounting for this is based on IAS 8, paragraph 22 in particular. This paragraph requires the change to be applied retrospectively, and the information disclosed as if the new accounting policy had always been applied. Hence, a change from the revaluation model to the cost model would require adjustments to the accounting records to show the information as if the cost model had always been applied. Adjustments can be taken through the opening balance of retained earnings. Comparative information would also need to be restated.

9.5 THE COST MODEL

Paragraph 30 of IAS 16 states: 'After recognition as an asset, an item of property, plant and equipment shall be carried at its cost less any accumulated depreciation and any accumulated impairment losses.' The cost is as described in section 9.3 of this chapter, and includes outlays incurred up to the point where the asset is at the location and in the working condition to be capable of operating in the manner intended by management. Note that this entails management determining a level of operations, a capacity of production or a use for the item of property, plant and equipment. In getting a machine to an appropriate working condition, management may need to undertake certain outlays to keep the machine running efficiently at that level. In relation to a vehicle that is needed to take a driver from point A to point B, the car needs to run efficiently and at a required safety level, without breaking down. In order for this to occur, the car needs to be regularly serviced, have tune-ups and incur any other routine checks. Costs associated with keeping the item of property, plant and equipment at the required working condition are expensed, and not added to the depreciable cost of the asset. These costs are generally referred to as repairs and maintenance.

Similar examples can be seen with other assets, such as escalators that need to be regularly maintained to ensure they achieve the basic task of moving passengers from one level to another. Most items of plant with moving parts require some form of regular maintenance. Paragraph 12 of IAS 16 notes the existence of these 'repairs and maintenance' costs, stating that these costs should not be capitalised into the cost of the asset. These costs relate to the day-to-day servicing of the asset and consist mainly of labour and consumables, but may also include the cost of small parts. Costs of repairs and maintenance are expensed as incurred.

After acquisition, management may also outlay funds refining the ability of the asset to operate. These are not outlays associated with repairs, maintenance or replacement. Examples of such expenditures relate to outlays designed to increase the remaining useful life of the asset, increase its capacity, improve the quality of the output, and adjust the asset to reduce operating costs.

A decision to capitalise these outlays requires the application of the recognition principle in paragraph 7 of IAS 16. Capitalisation requires there to be an increase in probable future economic benefits associated with the asset; that is, it should be probable that the expenditure increases the future economic benefits embodied in the asset in excess of its standard of performance assessed at the time the expenditure is made. Note the timing of the assessment process: at the time the expenditure is increased. The comparison is not with the original capacity to operate or the expected future benefits at acquisition, but with the capacity existing at the time the subsequent expenditure is incurred. Hence, if the capacity of the asset had reduced over time, expenditure to revive the asset to its original capacity would be capitalised. The assessment of capacity requires judgement, and needs to take into account matters such as the level of maintenance performed before the incurrence of the subsequent expenditure. The latter could not include the costs of any as yet unperformed maintenance work.

9.5.1 Depreciation

Under the cost model, after initial recognition, an asset continues to be recorded at its original cost. The subsequent carrying amount is determined after adjustments are made only for depreciation and impairment losses. (Impairment losses are discussed in chapter 12.) The main point of the following discussion is to determine the depreciation in relation to an item of property, plant and equipment.

In order to understand the accounting principles for depreciation, it is necessary to consider the definitions of depreciation, depreciable amount, useful life and residual value contained in paragraph 6 of IAS 16:

> *Depreciation* is the systematic allocation of the depreciable amount of an asset over its useful life.
>
> *Depreciable amount* is the cost of an asset, or other amount substituted for cost, less its residual value.
>
> The *residual value* of an asset is the estimated amount that an entity would currently obtain from disposal of the asset, after deducting the estimated costs of disposal, if the asset were already of the age and in the condition expected at the end of its useful life.
>
> *Useful life* is:
>
> (a) the period over which an asset is expected to be available for use by an entity; or
>
> (b) the number of production or similar units expected to be obtained from the asset by an entity.

Process of allocation

Depreciation is a process of allocation. Assets by definition are expected future benefits and, as noted in section 9.2, the initial recognition of an item of property, plant and equipment requires that it is probable that the future benefits will flow to the entity. On acquiring these benefits, an entity will have expectations as to the period over which these benefits are to be received and the pattern of these benefits (for example, they could be received evenly over the life of the asset). The purpose of determining the depreciation charge for the period is to measure the consumption of benefits allocable to the current period, ensuring that, over the useful life of the asset, each period will be allocated its fair share of the cost of the asset acquired. This principle is found in paragraphs 50 and 60 of IAS 16.

> 50. The depreciable amount of an asset shall be allocated on a systematic basis over its useful life.
> 60. The depreciation method used shall reflect the pattern in which the asset's future economic benefits are expected to be consumed by the entity.

It could be argued that there are two concepts of depreciation, namely:

- a process of allocation
- a change in the value of an asset.

There are at least three variables that cause a change in value of an asset over the period:

1. a reduction in value owing to the use of the asset over the period
2. an increase/decrease in the value owing to a change in the general price level
3. a change in the specific price level for this type of asset.

When depreciation is calculated as an allocation of the cost of the asset, what is being measured is variable (1) above. If an asset is measured at a revalued amount such as its fair value, and if depreciation is measured as the change in the fair value over the period, then the amount calculated will be a mixture of all the above variables. If the increase in price levels is so high that the fair value of an asset increases over the period, then there will be no depreciation calculated at all.

By describing depreciation as a process of allocation, the IASB is effectively arguing that an increase in value is not sufficient justification for not depreciating an asset. The IASB wants to consider separately the consumption of benefits and the changes in value over a period. In its 1996 discussion paper, *Measurement of Tangible Fixed Assets*, the Accounting Standards Board in the United Kingdom provided the following example (paragraph 5.15) to illustrate the difference between consumption and changes in value:

> Even where there are no general price changes, a change in the value of a tangible asset might still not reflect the consumption of economic benefits of the asset. For example, the drop in value of a new car during its first year would be unlikely to equate to the consumption of economic benefits of the car during the same period resulting from the use of the car. This difference occurs because the price change reflects the market's evaluation of the decline in economic benefits, which may differ from that made by a business. In this example the price change reflects the market's evaluation of the additional economic benefits a new car has over a second-hand car (e.g. the purchaser of a new car can specify exactly what features he wants while the purchaser of a second-hand car cannot, a new car has a known history etc.), but does not reflect the business's evaluation of the remaining economic benefits.

Under IAS 16, the depreciation charge for the period reflects the consumption of the economic benefits over the period and ignores the fall in the asset's fair value. As paragraph 52 of the standard states, depreciation is recognised even if the fair value of an asset is greater than its carrying amount (which is the amount at which an asset is recognised after deducting any accumulated depreciation and accumulated impairment losses). However, depreciation is not recognised if the asset's residual value exceeds the carrying amount.

As noted later in this chapter, where a revalued amount is used rather than cost, the depreciation charge affects current period income, and an increase in the value of the asset affects revaluation reserve. If both amounts affected income, then it would be important to determine whether it is useful to try to measure separately the two components of the change in value of the asset. If depreciation is capitalised into the cost of production, it may be argued that only the amount relating to the consumption of benefits should affect the cost of inventory produced.

Methods of depreciation

The accounting policy that an entity must adopt for depreciation is specified in paragraphs 50 and 60 of IAS 16, namely the systematic allocation of the cost or other revalued amount of an asset over its useful life in a manner that reflects the pattern in which the asset's future economic benefits are expected to be consumed. There are many methods of allocation, depending on the pattern of benefits. Paragraph 62 of the standard notes three methods:

- *Straight-line method*. This is used where the benefits are expected to be received evenly over the useful life of the asset. The depreciation charge for the period is calculated as:

$$\frac{\text{Depreciable amount}}{\text{Useful life}} = \frac{\text{Cost less residual value}}{\text{Useful life}}$$

If an item of plant had an original cost of $100 000, a residual value of $10 000, and a useful life of 4 years, the depreciation charge each year is:

$$\text{Depreciation expense p.a.} = \frac{1}{4}(\$100\,000 - \$10\,000) = \$22\,500$$

The journal entry is:

Depreciation Expense — Plant	Dr	22 500	
Accumulated Depreciation — Plant	Cr		22 500
(Depreciation on plant per annum)			

Note that both the residual value and the useful life may change during the life of the asset as expectations change.

- *Diminishing-balance method*. This method is used where the pattern of benefits is such that more benefits are received in the earlier years in the life of the asset. As the asset increases in age, the benefits each year are expected to reduce.

  It is possible to calculate a rate of depreciation that would result in the depreciable amount being written off over the useful life, with the depreciation charge each year being calculated by multiplying the rate by the carrying amount at the beginning of the year. The formula is:

$$\text{Depreciation rate} = 1 - \sqrt[n]{\frac{r}{c}}$$

where n = useful life
r = residual value
c = cost or other revalued amount

Using the same information as in the example for the straight-line method, the depreciation rate under the diminishing-balance method is:

$$\text{Depreciation rate} = 1 - \sqrt[4]{\frac{10000}{100000}} = 44\% \text{ approximately}$$

The depreciation expense each year following acquisition of the item of plant at the beginning of the first year is:

Year 1 depreciation expense =	44% × $100 000	= $44 000
Year 2 depreciation expense =	44% × $56 000	= $24 640
Year 3 depreciation expense =	44% × $31 360	= $13 798
Year 4 depreciation expense =	$13 798 – $10 000	= $ 3 798

The depreciation charge then reflects a decreasing pattern of benefits over the asset's useful life.

- *Units-of-production method*. This method is based on the expected use or output of the asset. Variables used could be production hours or production output.

  Using the above example again, assume that over the 4-year life of the asset the expected output of the asset is as follows:

Year 1	17 000 units
Year 2	15 000 units
Year 3	12 000 units
Year 4	6 000 units
	50 000 units

The depreciation expense in each of the 4 years is:

Year 1 depreciation expense =	17/50 × $90 000 =	$30 600
Year 2 depreciation expense =	15/50 × $90 000 =	$27 000
Year 3 depreciation expense =	12/50 × $90 000 =	$21 600
Year 4 depreciation expense =	6/50 × $90 000 =	$10 800
		$90 000

IAS 16 does not specify the use of any specific method of depreciation. The method chosen by an entity should be based on which method most closely reflects the expected pattern of consumption of the future economic benefits embodied in the asset.

Paragraph 61 of IAS 16 requires an entity to review the depreciation method chosen to ensure that it is providing the appropriate systematic allocation of benefits. The review process should occur at least at the end of each financial year. If there has been a change in the pattern of benefits such that the current method is inappropriate, the method should be changed to one that reflects the changed pattern of benefits. This change is not a change in an accounting policy, simply a change in accounting method. As such it is accounted for as a change in an accounting estimate, with the application of IAS 8. Under paragraph 36 of IAS 8, the change is recognised prospectively with adjustments being made to the amounts recognised in the current period and future periods as appropriate.

The depreciation method is applied from the date the asset is available for use, i.e. when it is in the location and condition necessary for it to perform as intended by management. As noted in paragraph 55 of IAS 16, depreciation continues even if the asset is temporarily idle, dependent on movements in residual value and expected useful life. However, under methods such as the units-of-production method, no depreciation is recognised where production ceases.

Useful life

Determination of useful life requires estimation on the part of management, because the way in which an item of property, plant and equipment is used and the potential for changes in the market for that item affect estimates of useful life. Paragraph 56 of IAS 16 provides the following list of factors to consider in determining useful life:

(a) the *expected usage* of the asset by the entity; this is assessed by reference to the asset's expected capacity or physical output

(b) the expected *physical wear and tear*, which depends on operational factors such as the number of work shifts for which the asset will be used and the repair and maintenance program of the entity, and the care and the maintenance of the asset while it is idle

(c) *technical or commercial obsolescence* arising from changes or improvements in pro-duction, or from a change in the market demand for the product or service output of the asset. For example, computers may be regarded as having a relatively short useful life. The actual period over which they may be expected to work is probably considerably longer than the period over which they may be considered to be technologically efficient. The useful life for depreciation purposes is related to the period over which the entity intends to use them, which is probably closer to their technological life than the period over which they would be capable of being used

(d) *legal or similar limits* on the use of the asset, such as expiry dates of related leases.

There is no necessary relationship between useful life to the entity and the economic life of the asset. Management may want to hold only relatively new assets, and a policy of replacement after specified periods of time may mean that assets are held for only a proportion of their economic lives. In other words, useful life for the purpose of calculating depreciation is defined in terms of the asset's expected usefulness to the entity. As noted earlier, the useful life of an asset covers the entire time the asset is available for use, including the time the asset is idle but available for use.

As noted in paragraph 58 of IAS 16, land is a special type of asset. Unless the land is being used for a purpose where there is a limited life imposed on the land, such as a quarry, it is assumed to have an unlimited life. Such land is not subject to depreciation. Hence, when accounting for land and buildings, these assets are dealt with separately so that buildings are made subject to depreciation. If, however, the cost of land includes the expected costs of dismantling, removal or restoration, then these costs are depreciated over the period in which the benefits from use of the land are received.

Just as the depreciation method requires a periodic review, so the useful life of an asset is subject to review. According to paragraph 51 of IAS 16, the review should occur at least at each year-end. A change in the assessment of the useful life will result in a change in the depreciation rate used. As this is a change in accounting estimate, changes are made prospectively in accordance with IAS 8 paragraph 36.

ILLUSTRATIVE EXAMPLE 9.1

Assessment of useful life

An entity is in the business of making camera lenses. The machine used in this process is very well made, and could be expected to provide a service in making the lenses currently demanded for another 20 years. As the machine is computer-driven, the efficiency of making lenses is affected by the sophistication of the computer program to define what is required in a lens. Technological advances are being made all the time, and it is thought that a new machine with advanced technology will be available within the next 5 years. The type of lens required is also a function of what cameras are considered to be in demand by consumers. Even if there is a change in technology, it is thought that cameras with the old style lens could still be marketable for another 7 years.

Required
What useful life should management use in calculating depreciation on the machine?
Solution
Three specific time periods are mentioned:

- physical life: 20 years
- technical life: 5 years
- commercial life: 7 years.

A key element in determining the appropriate life is assessing the strategy used by management in marketing its products. If management believes that to retain market share and reputation it needs to be at the cutting edge of technology, 5 years will be appropriate. If, however, the marketing strategy is aimed at the general conusmer, 7 years will be appropriate. In essence, management needs to consider at what point it expects to replace the machine.

Residual value

Note again the definition of residual value in paragraph 6 of IAS 16:

> The *residual value* of an asset is the estimated amount that the entity would currently obtain from disposal of the asset, after deducting the estimated costs of disposal, if the asset were already of the age and in the condition expected at the end of its useful life.

Residual value is an estimate based on what the entity would currently obtain from the asset's disposal; that is, what could be obtained at the time of the estimate — not at the expected date of disposal at the end of the useful life. The estimate is based on what could be obtained from disposal of similar assets that are currently, at the date of the estimate, at the end of their useful lives, and which have been used in a similar fashion to the asset being investigated. Where assets are unique, this estimation process is much more difficult than for assets that are constantly being replaced. For an asset such as a vehicle, which may have a useful life of 10 years, the residual value of a new vehicle is the net amount that could be obtained now for a 10-year-old vehicle of the same type as the one being depreciated. In many cases, the residual value will be negligible or scrap value.

This form of assessment means that the residual value will not be adjusted for expected changes in prices. Basing the residual value calculation on current prices relates to the adoption in IAS 16 of depreciation as a process of allocating economic benefits. If the residual value were adjusted for future prices, then there may be no measure of benefits consumed during the period as the residual value may exceed the carrying amount at the beginning of the period. It is also debatable whether the residual value should take into account possible technological developments. In relation to computers it may reasonably be expected that there will be such changes within a relatively short period of time, whereas with motor vehicles, trying to predict cars being powered with other than oil is more difficult. Management is not required to be a predictor of future inventions. Expectations of technological change are already built into current second-hand asset prices. Management should then take into account reasonable changes in technological development and the effect on prices. Where assets are expected to be used for the whole or the majority of their useful lives, the residual values are zero or immaterial in amount.

In paragraphs BC28 — BC29 of the Basis for Conclusions on IAS 16, the IASB raises the issue of why an entity deducts an asset's residual value from the cost of the asset for measurement of depreciation. Two reasons are proposed. First, the objective is one of precision, i.e. reducing the amount of depreciation so that it reflects the item's net cost. The second is one of economics, i.e. stopping depreciation if the entity expects the asset to increase in value by an amount greater than that by which it will diminish. The IASB did not adopt either the net cost or the economic objective completely. Expected increases in value do not override the need to depreciate an asset. An increase in the expected residual value of an asset because of past events affects the depreciable amount; expectations of future changes in residual value other than the effects of expected wear and tear will not.

Where residual values are material, an entity must, under paragraph 51 of IAS 16, review the residual value at each financial year-end. If a change is required, again the change is a change in estimate and is accounted for prospectively as an adjustment to future depreciation.

It is possible that the review of the residual value of an asset may lead to depreciation 'credits'. Consider the following situation:

Asset at cost	$100
Useful life	4 years
Depreciation method	Straight-line
Residual value at acquisition	$60

The entity would then charge depreciation at $10 p.a. If at the start of year 3 the residual value is estimated to be $90, what should the depreciation charge be in years 3 and 4?

At the end of year 2, the carrying amount of the asset is $80, being cost of $100 less 2 years depreciation of $10 p.a. At the start of year 3, there is a change in an estimate, namely to the residual value. Under IAS 8, the change in estimate must be adjusted against the current period and any future periods affected by the change. In this case, both years 3 and 4 are equally affected by the change in the estimated residual value. Hence, in both these years the entity should recognise a depreciation credit of $5 (50% of $90–$80), with a corresponding debit to accumulated depreciation. The depreciation credit reduces the entity's total depreciation expense for the period.

Components depreciation

It has been mentioned previously in this chapter that a components approach requires an entity to allocate the cost of an asset to its component parts and account for each component separately; for example, the cost of an aeroplane is allocated to such parts as the frame, the engines and the fittings. According to paragraph 43 of IAS 16, each part of an item of property, plant and equipment with a *cost that is significant* in relation to the total cost of the item must be depreciated separately. In other words, an entity is required to separate each item of property, plant and equipment into its significant parts or components, with each part or component being separately depreciated. Any remainder is also depreciated separately.

Paragraph 13 of the standard discusses the replacement or renewal of the components of an asset:

> Under the recognition principle in paragraph 7, an entity recognises in the carrying amount of an item of property, plant and equipment the cost of replacing part of such an item when that cost is incurred if the recognition criteria are met. The carrying amount of those parts that are replaced is derecognised in accordance with the derecognition provisions of this Standard (see paragraphs 67–72).

As is consistent with accounting for all separate items of property, plant and equipment, once an acquired asset is separated into the relevant components, if one of those components needs regular replacing or renewing, the component is generally accounted for as a separate asset. The replaced asset is depreciated over its useful life, and derecognised on replacement.

To illustrate the accounting for components, consider the case of a building with a roof that periodically needs replacing. If the roof is accounted for as a separate component, then the roof is accounted for as a separate asset and is depreciated separately. On replacement, paragraph 13 of IAS 16 is applied, and the carrying amount (if any) of the old roof is written off. In order for this derecognition to occur, it is necessary to know the original cost of the roof and the depreciation charged to date. The new roof is accounted for as the acquisition of a new asset, assessed under paragraph 7 and, if capitalised as an asset, subsequently depreciated. If, however, the roof is not treated as a separate component from the acquisition date of the building, then on replacement of the roof, the recognition principle in paragraph 7 and the derecognition principle in paragraph 13 also apply. An entity cannot carry both the replacement and the replaced portion as assets. Calculation of the amount to be derecognised is more difficult where no separate component is recognised because the depreciation of the building has not been separated from the depreciation of the roof.

Another example of dealing with a component of an asset arises where assets are subject to regular major inspections to ensure that they reach the requisite safety and quality requirements. Under paragraph 14 of IAS 16, such major inspections may be capitalised as a replacement component. In order for the cost of the inspection to be capitalised, the recognition criteria in paragraph 7 of the standard must be met. In particular, it must be probable that future economic benefits associated with the outlay will flow to the entity. For example, if there is a 5-year inspection of aircraft by a specific party, and this is required every 5 years in order for the plane not to be grounded, then the cost of the inspection provides benefits to the owner of the aircraft for that period of time by effectively providing a licence to continue flying. The capitalised amount is then depreciated over the relevant useful life, most probably the time until the next inspection.

Figure 9.2 contains the disclosures provided by BHP Billiton in its 2008 annual report in relation to depreciation of property, plant and equipment

Depreciation of property, plant and equipment

The carrying amounts of property, plant and equipment (including initial and any subsequent capital expenditure) are depreciated to their estimated residual value over the estimated useful lives of the specific assets concerned, or the estimated life of the associated mine or mineral lease, if shorter. Estimates of residual values and useful lives are reassessed annually and any change in estimate is taken into account in the determination of remaining depreciation charges. Depreciation commences on the date of commissioning. The major categories of property, plant and equipment are depreciated on a unit of production and/or straight-line basis using estimated lives indicated below, except that where assets are dedicated to a mine or petroleum lease the below useful lives are subject to the lesser of the asset category's useful life and the life of the mine or lease, unless the assets are readily transferable to another productive mine or lease:

- Buildings – 25 to 50 years
- Land – not depreciated
- Plant and equipment – 3 to 30 years straight-line
- Mineral rights – based on reserves on a unit of production basis
- Petroleum interests – based on the proved developed oil and gas reserves on a unit of production basis
- Capitalised exploration, evaluation and development expenditure – based on applicable reserves on a unit of production basis

FIGURE 9.2 Depreciation policy

Source: BHP Billiton (2008, p. 174).

9.6 THE REVALUATION MODEL

Use of the revaluation model of measurement is the alternative treatment to the cost model. Paragraph 31 of IAS 16 states:

> After recognition as an asset, an item of property, plant and equipment whose fair value can be measured reliably shall be carried at a revalued amount, being its fair value at the date of the revaluation less

any subsequent accumulated depreciation and subsequent accumulated impairment losses. Revaluations shall be made with sufficient regularity to ensure that the carrying amount does not differ materially from that which would be determined using fair value at the reporting date [end of the reporting period].

In relation to this paragraph, note the following points:

1. The measurement basis is fair value, defined in paragraph 6 as 'the amount for which an asset could be exchanged between knowledgeable, willing parties in an arm's length transaction'. The fair value is usually the market value of the asset. However, where there is not an active, liquid market, approximations of fair value may be made using surrogate measures such as depreciated replacement cost. It is also possible to apply market indexes of price changes to estimate fair value.
2. IAS 16 does not specify how often revaluations must take place. The principle established is that the revaluations must be of sufficient regularity such that the carrying amount of the asset does not materially differ from fair value. The frequency of revaluations depends on the nature of the assets themselves. For some assets, frequent revaluations are necessary because of continual change in the fair values owing to a volatile market. For other assets, revaluation every 3 or 5 years may be appropriate (paragraph 34). Paragraph 38 notes that assets may be revalued on a rolling basis provided that the total revaluation is completed within a short period of time, and that at no time is the total carrying amount of the class of assets materially different from fair value.
3. According to paragraph 32 of IAS 16, the fair value of land and buildings 'is usually determined from market-based evidence by appraisal normally undertaken by professionally qualified valuers'. It is then the responsibility of management to determine whether there has been sufficient change in the market for the assets held at fair value to warrant a formal appraisal by professional valuers. With items of plant and equipment, the fair value is usually their market value determined by appraisal.

Paragraph 36 of IAS 16 notes that the revaluation model is not applied to individual items of property, plant and equipment; instead, the accounting policy is applied to a class of assets. Hence, for each class of assets, management must choose whether to apply the cost model or the revaluation model.

A class of property, plant and equipment 'is a grouping of assets of a similar nature and use in an entity's operations' (IAS 16 paragraph 37). Examples of separate classes are:

- land
- land and buildings
- machinery
- ships
- aircraft
- motor vehicles
- furniture and fixtures
- office equipment (paragraph 37).

There are two purposes for requiring revaluation to be done on a class rather than on an individual asset basis. First, this limits the ability of management to 'cherry-pick' or selectively choose which assets to revalue. Second, the requirement to have all assets within the class measured on a fair value basis means that there is consistent measurement for the same type of assets in the entity.

According to paragraph 31 of IAS 16, where an asset is carried at a revalued amount, recognition of the asset should occur only when the fair value can be measured reliably. One question arising here is that, if a class of assets is being carried at fair value but there are assets within that class for which the fair value cannot be reliably measured, should those assets be written off because the recognition criteria cannot be met? The problem is that writing off these assets provides less relevant information than including the assets at cost.

The question then is whether, in order to be able to adopt the revaluation model, the fair values need to be capable of being reliably measured for all assets within the class. The problem with allowing some assets within a class to be at fair value and others at cost is that an entity can cherry-pick which assets are going to be measured at what amount. This amounts to selective revaluation. The only way to stop selective revaluation is for the standard setters to require the use of the fair value method only where all assets within the class can be reliably measured at fair value.

9.6.1 Applying the revaluation model: revaluation increments

Paragraphs 39 and 40 of IAS 16 contain the principles for applying the fair value method to revaluation increments. These paragraphs apply to individual items of property, plant and equipment. In other words, even though revaluations are done on a class-by-class basis, the accounting is done on an asset-by-asset basis.

The first part of paragraph 39 of IAS 16 states: 'If an asset's carrying amount is increased as a result of a revaluation, the increase shall be credited directly to equity under the heading of revaluation reserve.' Note that the increase is taken directly to equity, rather than being recognised in profit and loss. It is, however, disclosed as other comprehensive income. In accordance with paragraph 42 of IAS 16, the effects of any taxes on income need to be accounted for in accordance with IAS 12 *Income Taxes*. A revaluation of an asset causes a change between the tax base and the carrying amount of the asset, giving rise to a temporary difference, and a deferred tax liability needs to be raised (see paragraph 20 of IAS 12). As the increase in equity goes directly to equity, the tax effect is recognised via the revaluation reserve account; that is, this account is shown on an after-tax basis.

ILLUSTRATIVE EXAMPLE 9.2

Revaluation increments and tax effect

On 1 January 2010, an entity carries an item of land at a cost of $100 000, this amount also being the tax base of the asset. The land is revalued to $120 000. The tax rate is 30%.

The tax base of the asset is $100 000 and the new carrying amount is $120 000, giving rise to a taxable temporary difference of $20 000. A deferred tax liability of $6000 must be raised to account for the expected tax to be paid in relation to the increase in expected benefits from the asset. The asset revaluation reserve raised will be the net after-tax increase in the asset ($20 000 – $6000 = $14 000). The appropriate accounting entries on revaluation of the asset are shown in figure 9.3.

Land	Dr	20 000	
Asset Revaluation Reserve	Cr		20 000
(Revaluation of asset)			
Asset Revaluation Reserve	Dr	6 000	
Deferred Tax Liability	Cr		6 000
(Tax effect of revaluation)			

These two entries could be combined as follows:

Land	Dr	20 000	
Deferred Tax Liability	Cr		6 000
Asset Revaluation Reserve	Cr		14 000
(Revaluation of asset with associated tax effect)			

FIGURE 9.3 Journal entries for revaluation with associated tax effect

Where the item of property, plant and equipment is depreciable, there are two possible accounting treatments under paragraph 35 of IAS 16:

1. restate proportionately with the change in the gross carrying amount of the asset so that the carrying amount of the asset after revaluation equals its revalued amount; or
2. eliminate the accumulated depreciation balance against the gross carrying amount of the asset and then restate the net amount to the fair value of the asset. This method is applied in this chapter.

ILLUSTRATIVE EXAMPLE 9.3

Revaluation increments and depreciable assets

On 30 June 2009, an item of plant has a carrying amount of $42 000, being the original cost of $70 000 less accumulated depreciation of $28 000. The fair value of the asset is $50 000. The tax rate is 30%. The entries are shown in figure 9.4.

The revaluation may be done in two steps:
Step 1: Revalue the asset, disregarding the tax effect, and eliminate the accumulated depreciation.

Accumulated Depreciation	Dr	28 000	
Plant	Cr		20 000
Asset Revaluation Reserve	Cr		8 000
(Revaluation of asset)			

Step 2: Adjust for the tax effect of the revaluation.

Asset Revaluation Reserve	Dr	2 400	
Deferred Tax Liability	Cr		2 400
(Recognition of deferred tax liability as a direct adjustment against the asset revaluation surplus: 30% × $8000)			

The two entries could be *combined* as follows:

Accumulated Depreciation	Dr	28 000	
Plant	Cr		20 000
Deferred Tax Liability	Cr		2 400
Asset Revaluation Reserve	Cr		5 600
(Revaluation of asset with associated tax effect)			

FIGURE 9.4 Revaluation increment and depreciable assets

ILLUSTRATIVE EXAMPLE 9.4

Revaluation increment and the tax-effect worksheet

Assume that the depreciable asset in illustrative example 9.3 was acquired for $70 000 on 1 July 2008 to be used in the business. Depreciation rates are on a straight-line basis at 20% p.a. for accounting and 35% for tax. The tax rate is 30%.

On 30 June 2009, the carrying amount and the tax base of the asset are as follows:

	Accounting	Tax
Original cost	$70 000	$70 000
Accumulated depreciation	14 000	24 500
Net amount	56 000	45 500

Hence, the taxable temporary difference at 30 June 2009 is $10 500 ($56 000 – $45 500), with a deferred tax liability of $3150 being recognised.

On 30 June 2010, the asset has a carrying amount and tax base as follows:

	Accounting	Tax
Original cost	$70 000	$70 000
Accumulated depreciation	28 000	49 000
Net amount	42 000	21 000

Assume that on this date the asset is revalued to $50 000. The appropriate entry is:

2010				
June 30	Accumulated Depreciation	Dr	28 000	
	Plant	Cr		20 000
	Deferred Tax Liability	Cr		2 400
	Asset Revaluation Reserve	Cr		5 600
	(Revaluation of asset with associated tax effect)			

For the purpose of determining required entries for tax-effect accounting at the end of the year, the carrying amount of the asset on 30 June 2010 in the accounting records is now $50 000, but its tax base is unchanged at $21 000. This gives a taxable temporary difference of $29 000, and a total deferred tax liability of $8700 at a 30% tax rate. Since $2400 of the deferred tax liability is already recognised in the revaluation entry above, the total credit to the deferred tax liability needs to be only $6300. As the beginning deferred tax liability for the year is $3150, the adjustment required in the current year ending 30 June 2006 is $3150 ($6300–$3150). In order to recognise the adjustment to the deferred tax liability, the appropriate entry is as follows:

2010				
June 30	Income Tax Expense	Dr	3150	
	Deferred Tax Liability	Cr		3150
	(Recognition of deferred tax liability)			

The tax-effect worksheet is shown in figure 9.5.

	Carrying amount	Taxable amount	Deductible amount	Tax base	Taxable temporary differences	Deductible temporary differences
Plant	$50 000	$(50 000)	$21 000	$21 000	$29 000	
Temporary difference					29 000	
Deferred tax liability — closing balance					8 700 Dr	
Beginning balance					3 150 Cr	
Movement during the year					2 400 Cr	
Adjustment					3 150 Cr	

FIGURE 9.5 Tax-effect worksheet on revaluation of assets

Revaluation increment reversing previous revaluation decrement

The full text of paragraph 39 of IAS 16 is as follows:

> If an asset's carrying amount is increased as a result of a revaluation, the increase shall be credited directly to equity under the heading of revaluation reserve. However, the increase shall be recognised in profit or loss to the extent that it reverses a revaluation decrease of the same asset previously recognised in profit or loss.

Hence, a revaluation increment is credited to an asset revaluation reserve unless the increment reverses a revaluation decrement previously recognised as an expense. The accounting for revaluation decrements is discussed in the next section.

9.6.2 Applying the revaluation model: revaluation decrements

Paragraph 40 of IAS 16 states:

> If an asset's carrying amount is decreased as a result of a revaluation, the decrease shall be recognised in profit or loss. However, the decrease shall be debited directly to equity under the heading of revaluation reserve to the extent of any credit balance existing in the revaluation reserve in respect of that asset.

As with revaluation increments, this paragraph covers two situations: a revaluation decrement, and a revaluation decrement following a previous revaluation increment. The accounting for a revaluation decrement involves an immediate recognition of an expense in the period of the revaluation. As the change in the carrying amount of the asset directly affects income, the tax effect is dealt with in the normal workings of tax-effect accounting. Hence, no extra tax-effect entries outside those generated via the tax-effect worksheet are necessary.

ILLUSTRATIVE EXAMPLE 9.5

Revaluation decrement

Assume an item of plant has a carrying amount of $50 000, being original cost of $60 000 less accumulated depreciation of $10 000. If the asset is revalued downwards to $24 000, the appropriate journal entry is:

Accumulated Depreciation	Dr	10 000	
Expense — Downward Revaluation of Asset	Dr	26 000	
Plant	Cr		36 000
(Downward revaluation of plant)			

In relation to the tax-effect worksheet, if the carrying amount and the tax base in this example were the same immediately before the revaluation, then there would be a deductible temporary difference of $26 000. A deferred tax asset of $7800 would be raised via the tax-effect worksheet analysis at the end of the reporting period.

Decrement reversing previous revaluation increment

Where an asset revaluation reserve has been raised via a previous revaluation increment, in accounting for a subsequent revaluation decrement for the same asset, the reserve must be eliminated before any expense is recognised. In adjusting for the previous revaluation increment, both the asset revaluation reserve and the related deferred tax liability must be reversed.

ILLUSTRATIVE EXAMPLE 9.6

Decrement reversing previous increment

Assume an entity has a block of land with a carrying amount of $200 000, this having been previously revalued upwards from $100 000. The following entry was passed:

Land	Dr	100 000	
Deferred Tax Liability	Cr		30 000
Asset Revaluation Reserve	Cr		70 000
(Revaluation of plant)			

If the asset is *revalued downwards to $160 000*, the $40 000 write-down is a partial reversal of the previous upward revaluation. The adjustment is then a reduction in the deferred tax liability of

$12 000 (i.e. $40 000 × 30%), and a reduction in the asset revaluation reserve of $28 000 ($40 000[1 – 30%]). The appropriate journal entry is:

Deferred Tax Liability	Dr	12 000	
Asset Revaluation Reserve	Dr	28 000	
Land	Cr		40 000
(Downward revaluation of land)			

If the asset is *revalued downwards to $80 000*, which is a reduction of $120 000, the asset is written down to an amount $20 000 less than the original cost of the asset. The downward revaluation then requires the elimination of the deferred tax liability and the asset revaluation reserve, as well as recognition of an expense of $20 000. The appropriate entry is:

Deferred Tax Liability	Dr	30 000	
Asset Revaluation Reserve	Dr	70 000	
Expense — Downward Revaluation of Land	Dr	20 000	
Land	Cr		120 000
(Downward revaluation of land)			

The tax-effect worksheet, assuming the original revaluation increment occurred in a previous period, is shown in figure 9.6.

	Carrying amount	Taxable amount	Deductible amount	Tax base	Taxable temporary differences	Deductible temporary differences
Land	$80 000	$(80 000)	$100 000	$100 000		$ 20 000
Temporary difference						20 000
Deferred tax liability — closing balance						
Deferred tax asset — closing balance						6 000 Cr
Beginning balance					$30 000 Cr	
Movement during the year					30 000 Dr	
Adjustment						6 000 Dr

FIGURE 9.6 Tax-effect worksheet on revaluation of assets

The tax-effect worksheet shows that the entity would recognise a deferred tax asset of $6000, reflecting the fact that the carrying amount of the asset is $20 000 less than the tax base.

Net revaluation increment reversing previous revaluation decrement

Where an asset is revalued upwards, an asset revaluation reserve is credited except where the increment reverses a revaluation decrement previously recognised as an expense. In this case, the revaluation increment must be recognised as income.

ILLUSTRATIVE EXAMPLE 9.7

Revaluation increment reversing previous decrement

Assume an entity has an item of plant whose current carrying amount is $200 000 (accumulated depreciation being $20 000). The asset had cost $300 000. It was revalued downwards from a carrying amount of $270 000 to $220 000, with the following accounting entry being passed:

Expense — Downward Revaluation of Plant	Dr	50 000	
Accumulated Depreciation	Dr	30 000	
Plant	Cr		80 000
(Downward revaluation of plant)			

If the asset is now assessed as having *a fair value of $230 000*, the appropriate revaluation entry is:

Accumulated Depreciation	Dr	20 000	
Plant	Dr	10 000	
Income on Revaluation of Plant	Cr		30 000
(Upward revaluation of plant)			

If the asset is assessed as having *a fair value of $280 000*, the accounting entry recognises the increase of $80 000 as consisting partly of revenue, being the reversal of the previous $50 000 write-down, and partly of revaluation surplus. The appropriate entry is:

Accumulated Depreciation	Dr	20 000	
Plant	Dr	60 000	
Income on Revaluation of Plant	Cr		50 000
Deferred Tax Liability	Cr		9 000
Asset Revaluation Reserve	Cr		21 000
(Upward revaluation of plant)			

9.6.3 Effects of accounting on an asset-by-asset basis

If the fair value basis of measurement is chosen, IAS 16 requires it to be applied to items of property, plant and equipment on a class-by-class basis. However, in accounting for revaluation increments and decrements, the accounting is done on an individual asset basis within the class. Practising accountants and standard setters have often argued that a better accounting treatment would be to account for revaluation increments and decrements on a class-by-class basis. The rationale for this is that under IAS 16 revaluation increments (gains) are taken directly to equity, not affecting accounting profit, and revaluation decrements (losses) are recognised in profit in the period the revaluation occurs. If revaluation was done on a class-by-class basis, then it would be the net increment that would be accounted for, providing a netting of the gains and losses. Figure 9.7 illustrates this.

Assets	Carrying amount $000	Fair value $000	Increment/(decrement) $000
Plant A	1 500	2 000	500
Plant B	1 500	1 200	(300)
Total	3 000	3 200	200

FIGURE 9.7 Revaluation by asset or class of asset

Applying IAS 16, both Plant A and Plant B, being in the one class of assets, have to be revalued to fair value if the revalution model is applied to plant. However, in accounting for the movements in fair value, each asset is dealt with separately. With Plant A, as there is a revaluation increment of $500, the increment results in $350 (assuming a tax rate of 30%)

being taken directly to equity affecting an asset revaluation reserve. With Plant B, the revaluation decrement of $300 is recognised as an expense affecting current period profit. For those who argue that revaluations should be accounted for on a class-by-class basis, the net revaluation increment on plant is $200. Accounting on a class basis would result in taking $140 to an asset revaluation reserve with no effect on current period profit. The argument for the class method of accounting is that it reduces the biased effect that the IAS 16 method has on current period profit.

9.6.4 Applying the revaluation model: transfers from asset revaluation reserve

Paragraph 41 of IAS 16 covers the accounting for the asset revaluation reserve subsequent to its creation. There are two circumstances where the asset revaluation reserve may be transferred to retained earnings. Note that there is no requirement that the asset revaluation reserve must be transferred, only a specification of situations where it may be transferred. The *first* situation is where the asset is derecognised (i.e. removed from the statement of financial position, for example, by sale of the asset). In this case, the whole or part of the reserve may be transferred. The *second* situation is where an asset is being used up over its useful life, a proportion of the revaluation reserve may be transferred to retained earnings, the proportion being in relation to the depreciation on the asset. In this case, the amount of the reserve transferred would be equal to the difference between depreciation based on the original cost, and depreciation based on the revalued amount, adjusted for the tax effect relating to the reserve. This second situation is shown in illustrative example 9.8.

ILLUSTRATIVE EXAMPLE 9.8

Transferring revaluation reserve to retained earnings

Assume an item of plant is acquired for $100 000. The asset is immediately revalued to $120 000. The asset has a useful life of 10 years, and the tax rate is 30%. The revaluation entry is:

Plant	Dr	20 000	
Deferred Tax Liability	Cr		6 000
Asset Revaluation Reserve	Cr		14 000
(Revaluation of plant)			

At the end of the first year, depreciation expense of $12 000 is recorded. As the asset is being used up at 10% p.a., the entity may transfer 10% of the asset revaluation reserve to retained earnings:

Asset Revaluation Reserve	Dr	1 400	
Retained Earnings	Cr		1 400
(Transfer from asset revaluation reserve to retained earnings)			

Transfers from the asset revaluation reserve may also occur where a bonus issue of share capital is made from the asset revaluation reserve. There is no specific statement in IAS 16 in relation to the reinstatement of transfers from the asset revaluation reserve. However, as the reserve is created only via an upward revaluation of assets, it is expected that the standard setters would not allow reinstatement once transfers from the asset revaluation reserve have been made. These transfers may cause a problem if there is a downward revaluation of the asset subsequent to the transfer because, although the balance of the revaluation reserve may have changed, the related deferred tax liability has not been altered.

ILLUSTRATIVE EXAMPLE 9.9

Bonus share issue from asset revaluation reserve

Assume an entity has an item of plant that was revalued in the past from $100 000 to $200 000. The journal entry, based on a tax rate of 30%, is:

Plant	Dr	100 000	
Deferred Tax Liability	Cr		30 000
Asset Revaluation Reserve	Cr		70 000
(Revaluation of plant)			

The entity then used $30 000 of the asset revaluation reserve to issue bonus shares, leaving a balance of $40 000 in the asset revaluation reserve. The asset was subsequently written down from a carrying amount of $150 000 to $70 000, a reduction of $80 000. The appropriate journal entry for the downward revaluation is:

Asset Revaluation Reserve	Dr	40 000	
Deferred Tax Liability	Dr	24 000	
Expense — Downward Revaluation of Plant	Dr	16 000	
Accumulated Depreciation	Dr	50 000	
Plant	Cr		130 000
(Write-down of plant subsequent to upward revaluation and bonus issue)			

In relation to this entry, note the following:

- The balance of $40 000 in the asset revaluation reserve must first be used to write down the asset; the asset revaluation reserve can never be adjusted so as to have a debit balance.
- As a deferred tax liability of $30 000 was raised in relation to the upward revaluation of the asset, this must be reduced by $24 000 (30% × $80 000). The adjustment relates to the revaluation decrement grossed-up for any related recognised current tax and deferred tax.
- The balance after adjusting the asset revaluation reserve and the deferred tax liability is debited to current period expense. It arises because of the past transfer of the asset revaluation reserve to share capital.
- The balance of the deferred tax liability is $6000, representing the difference between the tax base of $100 000 and the carrying amount of $120 000.

A further problem arising from transfers from the asset revaluation reserve in situations such as a bonus issue of shares occurs where a number of assets are being revalued. IAS 16 requires the accounting for the asset revaluation reserve to be done on an asset-by-asset basis. Where there is a bonus issue from the asset revaluation reserve, the entity will have to identify which assets are being affected by the use of the asset revaluation reserve for the bonus issue. Any basis of choosing which assets are affected is purely arbitrary.

9.6.5 Applying the revaluation model: depreciation of revalued assets

Section 9.5.1 of this chapter discusses the accounting treatment for depreciation under IAS 16. As noted, the term 'depreciable amount' includes 'other amount substituted for cost'. This includes fair value. Paragraph 50 of IAS 16 notes that depreciation is a process of allocation. Hence, even though an asset is measured at fair value, depreciation is not determined simply as the change in fair value of the asset over a period. As with the cost method, depreciation for a period is calculated after considering the pattern of economic benefits relating to the asset and the residual value of the asset.

ILLUSTRATIVE EXAMPLE 9.10

Depreciation of revalued assets

Assume an entity has an item of plant that was revalued to $1000 at 30 June 2008. The asset is expected to have a remaining useful life of 5 years, with benefits being received evenly over that period. The residual value is calculated to be $100. Consider two situations.

Situation 1

At 30 June 2009, no formal revaluation occurs and the management of the entity assess that the carrying amount of the plant is not materially different from fair value.

The appropriate journal entry for the 2008–09 period is:

2009	Depreciation Expense	Dr	180	
June 30	Accumulated Depreciation	Cr		180
	(Depreciation on plant 1/5[$1000 – $100])			

The asset is reported in the statement of financial position at a carrying amount of $820, equal to a gross amount of $1000 less accumulated depreciation of $180, the carrying amount being equal to fair value.

Situation 2

At 30 June 2009, a formal revaluation occurs and the external valuers assess the fair value of the plant to be $890. Tax rate is 30%.

The appropriate journal entries for the 2008–09 period are:

2009	Depreciation Expense	Dr	180	
June 30	Accumulated Depreciation	Cr		180
	(Depreciation on plant 1/5[$1000 – $100])			
	Accumulated Depreciation	Dr	180	
	Plant	Cr		110
	Deferred Tax Liability	Cr		21
	Asset Revaluation Reserve	Cr		49
	(Revaluation of plant)			

In other words, there is a two-step process. Depreciation is allocated in accordance with normal depreciation principles. Then, as a formal revaluation occurs, the accumulated depreciation is written off and the asset revalued to fair value. The asset is reported in the statement of financial position at fair value of $890 with no associated accumulated depreciation.

It may be argued that the accounting in situation 2 is inappropriate. Whereas the depreciation charge affects the statement of comprehensive income, the revaluation of the asset goes to revaluation reserve, and is never taken to the statement of comprehensive income. The economic benefits in relation to the asset for the period are not only those achieved by consumption of the asset, but also those obtained by changes in the market value of the asset. However, these are accounted for differently under IAS 16. It could then be argued that the appropriate depreciation in situation 2 should be the change in fair value over the period, namely $110 ($1000 – $890), with the journal entry being:

Depreciation Expense	Dr	110	
Accumulated Depreciation	Cr		110
(Depreciation on plant)			

No revaluation entry is then necessary. Note, however, that this entry is not allowed under IAS 16.

Subsequent to revaluation, the entity should reassess the useful life and residual value of the revalued asset because these may change as a result of economic changes affecting the entity and its use of assets. Using the example in scenario 2, following the revaluation at 30 June 2009, assume the entity determines that the residual value is $110 and the remaining useful life is 4 years. In the 2009–10 period, the depreciation entry is:

Depreciation Expense	Dr	195	
Accumulated Depreciation	Cr		195
(Depreciation on plant $\frac{1}{4}$ [$890 – $110])			

9.7 CHOOSING BETWEEN THE COST MODEL AND THE REVALUATION MODEL

Given that IAS 16 allows entities a choice between the cost model and the revaluation model, it is of interest to consider what motivates entities to choose between the two measurement models.

Arguments relating to the choice of models generally claim that a current price (a fair value) will provide more relevant information than a past price (the original cost), and that the costs associated with continuously determining the present price reduces the incentive, on a cost–benefit basis, to move to current values. Certainly the requirement under IAS 16 to continuously adjust the carrying amounts of assets measured at fair value so that they are not materially different from current fair values provides a cost disincentive to management to adopt the revaluation model. Costs associated with adopting the revaluation model include the cost of employing valuers, annual costs associated with reviewing the carrying amounts to assess whether a revaluation is necessary, extra record-keeping costs associated with the revaluations, including accounting for the associated revaluation increments and decrements, and increased audit costs relating to the review of changing revalued amounts. In January 2002, Ernst & Young in Australia reported on entities changing valuation methods when it became a requirement in that country for entities using the fair value basis to adopt the equivalent of the current IAS 16 accounting procedures. Previously, entities could revalue assets on an irregular basis rather than keeping the fair values continuously current. Ernst & Young (2002) reported that:

- of the entities surveyed, 40% reported a change in measurement basis for one or more classes of non-current assets
- of those entities reporting a change in the measurement basis, all changed from the fair value basis to the cost basis. No entities changed from the cost basis to the fair value basis.

Ernst & Young (p. 8) argued:

> [t]he number of entities changing measurement basis to cost would appear to indicate that the costs associated with keeping the revaluations up to date at each reporting period outweighs the perceived benefits associated with improved relevance and reliability of financial information by recognising fair value adjustments.

A further factor that influences some entities' measurement choice in favour of the cost model is harmonisation with US GAAP, which does not allow the revaluation of non-current assets.

Another factor that entities have to consider when choosing their measurement bases for classes of property, plant and equipment is the effect of the model on the statement of comprehensive income. Where assets are measured on a fair value basis, the depreciation per annum is expected to be higher as the depreciable amount is higher. In the 2002 Ernst & Young study (p. 3), it was reported:

> [o]f those entities reverting to original cost as the measurement basis for a class of non-current asset, a reduction in annual depreciation expense (and therefore an increase in profit) ranging from $500 000 to $1.1 million resulted.

Besides the effect of lower depreciation, there will be the effect on the disposal of the asset. Where an asset is measured at fair value, there is expected to be an immaterial amount of profit or loss on sale as, at the time of sale, the recorded amount of the asset should be close to that of the market price. For an asset measured at cost, any gain or loss on sale will be reported in the statement of comprehensive income.

What, apart from increased relevance and reliability arguments, are the incentives for management to use the revaluation model? The effect of adopting the revaluation model is to increase the entity's assets and equities (via the revaluation reserve). Hence, entities that need to report higher amounts in these areas would consider adoption of the revaluation model. The incentives for entities to adopt fair value measures then tend to be entity-specific because the entities face pressures relating to external circumstances. Examples of such pressures are:

- Entities with debt covenants generally have constraints relating to their debt–asset ratios, such as the requirement that the debt–asset ratio must not exceed 50%. Hence, for an entity with increasing debt, adoption of the revaluation model for a class of assets that is increasing in value will ease pressures on the debt–asset ratio by increasing the asset base of the entity. This assumes that the debt covenant allows revaluations to be taken into account in measuring assets.
- An entity's reported profit figure may be under scrutiny from a specific source, such as a trade union seeking reasons to support claims for higher pay, or regulators looking at monopoly control within an industry.

Where there are pressures to report lower profits, adoption of the revaluation model provides scope for higher depreciation charges, with increases in the values of the non-current assets not affecting the statement of comprehensive income. With lower reported profits and higher asset/equity bases, any judgements made by reviewing ratios such as rates of return on assets or equity will result in the entity being seen in a less favourable light.

However, as noted above, the incentives relating to playing with profit and asset numbers tend to rely on users of the information having no knowledge of accounting rules or movements in prices within industries or sectors, or being unable to make comparisons across entities within an industry segment. One of the key elements of analysing entities within an industry is comparability of information. If all entities in the sector are applying the cost model, analysts can make their judgements by comparing the information between the entities and applying information from sources other than accounting reports, such as movements in price indexes. The entity then has less reason to incur the costs of adopting the revaluation model of measurement.

9.8 DERECOGNITION

As noted in paragraph 3 of IAS 16, the standard does not apply to non-current assets classified as held for sale and accounted for under IFRS 5. IAS 16 then deals with the disposal of non-current assets that have not previously been classified as held for sale.

Paragraph 67 of IAS 16 identifies two occasions where derecognition of an item of property, plant and equipment should occur:

- on disposal, such as the sale of the asset
- when no future economic benefits are expected, either from future use or from disposal.

When items of property, plant and equipment are sold, regardless of whether there are many or few remaining economic benefits, the selling entity will recognise a gain or loss on the asset, this being determined as the difference between the net proceeds from sale and the carrying amount of the asset at the time of sale (IAS 16 paragraph 71). In calculating the net proceeds from sale, any deferred consideration must be discounted, and the proceeds calculated at the cash price equivalent (IAS 16 paragraph 72). As the carrying amount is net of depreciation and impairment losses, it is necessary to calculate the depreciation from the beginning of the reporting period to the point of sale. Failing to do this, whether under the cost model or the revaluation model, would be out of step with the key principle established in IAS 16 that depreciation is a process of allocation and each period must bear its fair share of the cost or revalued amount of the asset.

The gain or loss on sale is included in the profit or loss for the period, with the gains not being classified as revenue. IAS 1 paragraph 29 requires only the disclosure of the gain or loss on sale, as opposed to separate disclosure of the income and the carrying amount of the asset sold.

In paragraph BC35 of the Basis of Conclusions on IAS 16, the IASB argued:

> users of financial statements would consider these gains and the proceeds from an entity's sale of goods in the course of its ordinary activities differently in their evaluation of an entity's past results and their projections of future cash flows. This is because revenue from the sale of goods is typically more likely to recur in comparable amounts than are gains from sales of items of property, plant and equipment. Accordingly, the Board concluded that an entity should not classify as revenue gains on disposals of items of property, plant and equipment.

However, in preparing a cash flow statement, proceeds from the sale of property, plant and equipment are normally shown as a cash flow from investing activities.

ILLUSTRATIVE EXAMPLE 9.11

Disposals of assets

An entity acquired an item of plant on 1 July 2007 for $100 000. The asset had an expected useful life of 10 years and a residual value of $20 000. On 1 January 2010, the entity sold the asset for $81 000.

Required

Prepare the journal entries relating to this asset in the year of sale.

Solution

At the point of sale, the depreciation on the asset must be calculated for that part of the year for which the asset was held before the sale. Hence, for the half-year before the sale, under the straight-line method, depreciation of $4000 (i.e. $0.5 \times \frac{1}{10}$ [$100 000 − $20 000]) must be charged as an expense. The entry is:

Depreciation Expense	Dr	4 000	
Accumulated Depreciation	Cr		4 000
(Depreciation charge up to point of sale)			

The gain or loss on sale is the difference between the proceeds on sale of $81 000 and the carrying amount at time of sale of $80 000 (i.e. $100 000 − 2.5[$\frac{1}{10} \times$ $80 000]), which is $1000. The required journal entries are:

Cash	Dr	81 000	
Proceeds on Disposal of Asset	Cr		81 000
(Sale of asset)			
Carrying Amount of Asset Sold	Dr	80 000	
Accumulated Depreciation	Dr	20 000	
Plant	Cr		100 000
(Carrying amount of asset sold)			

Alternatively, the gain on sale could be recognised as a net amount:

Cash	Dr	81 000	
Accumulated Depreciation	Dr	20 000	
Plant	Cr		100 000
Gain on Sale of Plant	Cr		1 000

In the above example, the asset was sold for $81 000. Assume that the asset, now referred to as plant A, was traded in for another asset, plant B. Plant B had a fair value of $280 000, with the entity making a cash payment of $202 000 as well as giving up plant A. The trade-in amount is then $78 000. The journal entries to record this transaction are:

Carrying Amount of Plant A Sold	Dr	80 000	
Accumulated Depreciation	Dr	20 000	
Plant A	Cr		100 000
(Disposal of plant A)			
Plant B	Dr	280 000	
Cash	Cr		202 000
Proceeds on Sale of Plant A	Cr		78 000
(Acquisition of plant B in exchange for cash and trade-in of plant A)			

9.9 DISCLOSURE

Paragraphs 73–79 of IAS 16 contain the required disclosures relating to property, plant and equipment. Information in paragraph 73 is required on a class-by-class basis, and paragraph 77 relates only to assets stated at revalued amounts. Paragraph 79 contains information that entities are encouraged to disclose, but are not required to do so. Figure 9.8 provides an illustration of the disclosures required by IAS 16.

FIGURE 9.8 Illustrative disclosures required by IAS 16

	IAS 16 *para.*
Note 1: Summary of accounting policies (extract) **Property, plant and equipment**	
Freehold land and buildings on freehold land are measured on a fair value basis.	*73(a)*
At the end of each reporting period, the value of each asset in these classes is reviewed to ensure that it does not differ materially from the asset's fair value at that date. Where necessary, the asset is revalued to reflect its fair value.	*77(a)*
In June 2008, revaluations were carried out by an independent valuer;	*77(b)*
since then valuations have been made internally. The basis for the assessment of fair value has been by reference to observable transactions in the property market, including an analysis of prices paid in recent market transactions for	*77(c), (d)*
similar properties. No other valuation techniques were used.	*77(a)*
All other classes of property, plant and equipment are measured at cost.	*73(a)*
Depreciation Depreciation is provided on a straight-line basis for all property, plant and equipment, other than freehold land.	*73(b)*
The useful lives of the assets are:	*73(c)*

	2010	2009
Freehold buildings	40 years	40 years
Plant and equipment	5 to 15 years	5 to 15 years

Note 10: Property, plant and equipment

	Land and buildings		**Plant and equipment**		IAS 16 *para.*
	2010	2009	**2010**	2009	
	$000	$000	**$000**	$000	
Balance at beginning of year	**1 861**	1 765	**2 840**	2 640	*73(d)*
Accumulated depreciation	**(400)**	(364)	**(732)**	(520)	
Carrying amount	**1 461**	1 401	**2 108**	2 120	
Additions	**—**	123	**755**	372	*73(e)(i)*
Disposals	**(466)**	(18)	**(181)**	(158)	*73(e)(ii)*
Acquisitions via business combinations	**739**	—	**412**	—	*73(e)(iii)*
Impairment losses	**—**	—	**(100)**	—	*73(e)(v)*
Depreciation	**(20)**	(36)	**(161)**	(212)	*73(e)(vii)*
Transfer to assets held for sale	**(438)**	—	**(890)**	—	*73(e)(ix)*
Net exchange differences	**11**	(9)	**8**	(14)	*73(e)(viii)*
Carrying amount at end of year	**1 287**	1 461	**1 951**	2 108	*73(d)*
Property, plant and equipment:					
At cost	**1 707**	1 861	**2 944**	2 840	
Accumulated depreciation and impairment losses	**(420)**	(400)	**(993)**	(732)	
Carrying amount at end of year	**1 287**	1 461	**1 951**	2 108	*73(d)*

FIGURE 9.8 *(continued)*

For the freehold land and buildings measured at fair value, the carrying amount that would have been recognised if they had been carried at cost is:			*77(e)*
	2010	2009	
	$000	$000	
Carrying amount at end of year	**942**	824	
Plant and equipment of $420 000 have been pledged as security for loans to the company.			*74(a)*
The company has entered into a contract to acquire $640 000 of plant equipment over the next two years.			*74(c)*
Activity in the revaluation reserve for land and buildings is as follows:			*77(f)*
	2010	2009	
	$000	$000	
Balance at beginning of year	**309**	303	
Revaluation reserve on land and buildings	**42**	9	
Deferred tax liability	**(13)**	(3)	
Balance at end of year	**338**	309	
There are no restrictions on the distribution of the balance of the reserve to shareholders.			

The following comprehensive illustrative examples demonstrate accounting for movements in assets, depreciation, and cost and revaluation models of measurement.

ILLUSTRATIVE EXAMPLE 9.12

Movements in assets, depreciation

Mandurah Manufacturing Ltd's post-closing trial balance at 30 June 2010 included the following balances:

Machinery control (at cost)	$244 480
Accumulated depreciation – machinery control	113 800
Fixtures (at cost; purchased 2 December 2007)	308 600
Accumulated depreciation – fixtures	134 138

The Machinery Control and Accumulated Depreciation – Machinery Control accounts are supported by subsidiary ledgers. Details of machines owned at 30 June 2010 are as follows:

Machine	Acquisition date	Cost	Estimated useful life	Estimated residual value
1	28 April 2006	$74 600	5 years	$3 800
2	4 February 2008	$82 400	5 years	4 400
3	26 March 2009	$87 480	6 years	5 400

Additional information:

(a) Mandurah Manufacturing Ltd uses the general journal for all journal entries, records depreciation to the nearest month, balances its books every 6 months, and records amounts to the nearest dollar.

(b) The company uses straight-line depreciation for machinery and reducing balance depreciation at 20% per annum for fixtures.

The following transactions and events occurred from 1 July 2010 onwards:

2010	
July 3	Exchanged items of fixtures (having a cost of $100 600; a carrying amount at exchange date of $56 872; and a fair value at exchange date of $57 140) for a used machine (Machine 4). Machine 4's fair value at exchange date was $58 000. Machine 4 originally cost $92 660 and had been depreciated by $31 790 to exchange date in the previous owner's accounts. Mandurah Manufacturing Ltd estimated Machine 4's useful life and residual value to be 3 years and $4580 respectively.
Oct. 10	Traded in Machine 2 for a new machine (Machine 5) that cost $90 740. A trade-in allowance of $40 200 was received and the balance was paid in cash. Freight charges of $280 and installation costs of $1600 were also paid in cash. Mandurah Manufacturing Ltd estimated Machine 5's useful life and residual value to be 6 years and $5500 respectively.
2011	
April 24	Overhauled Machine 3 at a cash cost of $16 910, after which Mandurah Manufacturing Ltd revised its residual value to $5600 and extended its useful life by 2 years.
May 16	Paid for scheduled repairs and maintenance on the machines of $2370.
June 30	Recorded depreciation and scrapped Machine 1.

Required

A. Prepare journal entries to record the above transactions and events.
B. Prepare the Accumulated Depreciation – Machinery Control and Accumulated Depreciation – Fixtures ledger accounts for the period 30 June 2010 to 30 June 2011.

Solution

A. *Journal entries*

Calculate the depreciation on each of the depreciable assets so that when events such as a sale occur, depreciation up to the date of the transaction can be calculated. Depreciation is calculated as:

(Cost – residual value)/expected useful life

For the three items of machinery, the depreciation per month is calculated as follows:

Machine 1 depreciation = ($74 600 – $3800)/60 months = $1180 per month
Machine 2 depreciation = ($82 400 – $4400)/60 months = $1300 per month
Machine 3 depreciation = ($87 480 – $5400)/72 months = $1140 per month

On 3 July, the company exchanges items of fixtures for a machine. After assessing that the transaction has commercial substance, the first journal entry derecognises the fixtures by eliminating both the asset account and the accumulated depreciation. The carrying amount represents the expense to be matched with the proceeds on sale to determine a gain/loss on sale.

2010				
July 3	Accumulated Depreciation – Fixtures *	Dr	43 728	
	Carrying Amount – Fixtures	Dr	56 872	
	Fixtures	Cr		100 600
	*$100 600 – $56 872			

The second journal entry recognises the acquired machine (Machine 4) at cost. Cost is measured using the fair value of the consideration given by the acquirer. As cost is the measurement used, the fair value of the machine is not relevant. Similarly, the carrying amount of the asset in the seller's records is also not relevant. The entry also records the proceeds on sale, as it is the machinery that is being received in exchange for the fixtures.

Machinery (M4)	Dr	57 140	
Proceeds on Sale – Fixtures	Cr		57 140

The depreciation per month for M4 is then calculated:

Machine 4 depreciation = ($57 140 – $4 580)/36 months = $1 460 per month

On 10 October, Machine 2 is traded in for Machine 5. Depreciation up to point of sale on Machine 2 is determined, being $1300 per month for the 3 months from July to September.

Oct. 10	Depreciation – Machinery (M2)*	Dr	3 900	
	Accumulated Depreciation – Machinery (M2)	Cr		3 900
	*$1 300 × 3 months			

Machine 2 is derecognised with the machine and related accumulated depreciation being written out of the records. The carrying amount is used to determine a gain or loss on sale.

Accumulated Depreciation – Machinery (M2)*	Dr	41 600	
Carrying Amount – Machinery (M2)**	Dr	40 800	
Machinery (M2)	Cr		82 400
*$1 300 × 32 months **$82 400 – $41 600			

Machine 5 is recorded at cost. Cost is determined as the sum of the purchase price and directly attributable costs. Purchase price is the fair value of consideration given up by the acquirer. In the absence of a fair value for Machine 2, the consideration is based on the fair value of Machine 5, namely $90 740. The directly attributable costs are the freight charges of $280 and installation costs of $1600, both being necessarily incurred to get the asset into the condition for management's intended use.

The trade-in allowance is used as the selling price of the asset, in the absence of a fair value of the asset. The cash outlay is then the sum of the balance paid to the seller of Machine 5 and the directly attributable costs.

Machinery (M5)*	Dr	92 620	
Proceeds on Sale – Machinery (M2)	Cr		40 200
Cash	Cr		52 420
*$90 740 + $280 + $1 600			

The depreciation per month for Machine 5 is then calculated:

Machine 5 depreciation = ($92 620 – $5 500)/72 months = $1 210 per month

On 24 April 2011, Machine 3 received an overhaul. This resulted in a change in the capacity of the machine, which increased the residual value and extended its useful life. Because this results in a change in the depreciation per month, depreciation based on the rate before the overhaul for the period up to the date of the overhaul is recorded.

2011 April 24	Depreciation – Machinery (M3)* Accumulated Depreciation – Machinery (M3) *$1140 × 10 months	Dr Cr	11 400	 11 400

Because the overhaul increases the expected benefits from the asset, i.e. the outlay for the overhaul results in probable future benefits, the cost of the overhaul is capitalised, increasing the overall cost of the asset.

Machinery (M3) Cash	Dr Cr	16 910	 16 910

The overhaul results in a change in expectations, so it is necessary to calculate a revised depreciation per month:

M3:	New depreciable amount = $87 480 + $16 910 – $5 600 = $98 790 Accumulated depreciation balance = $1140 × 25 months = $28 500 Carrying amount to be depreciated = $98 790 – $28 500 = $70 290 New useful life = 72 months – 25 months + 24 months = 71 months Revised depreciation = $70 290/71 months = $990 per month

Because outlays on repairs and maintenance do not lead to increased future benefits, these outlays are expensed.

May 16	Repairs and Maintenance Expense Cash	Dr Cr	2 370	 2 370

At the end of the reporting period, depreciation is accrued on all depreciable assets:

Machinery:	*M1*	$1180 × 10 months	$ 11 800
	M3	$990 × 2 months	1 980
	M4	$1460 × 12 months	17 520
	M5	$1210 × 9 months	10 890
			$ 42 190*
Fixtures:	$308 600 – $100 600		$208 000
	Less: $134 138 – $43 728		90 410
			$117 590
	20% × $117 590		$ 23 518**

June 30	Depreciation – Machinery*	Dr	42 190	
	Depreciation – Fixtures**	Dr	23 518	
	Accumulated Depreciation – Machinery	Cr		42 190
	Accumulated Depreciation – Fixtures	Cr		23 518

Machine 1 is scrapped, so the asset is derecognised by writing off the asset and related accumulated depreciation. The undepreciated amount is recognised as an expense. A residual value of $3800 was expected but not received, so the company incurs a loss of $3800.

Accumulated Depreciation – Machinery (M1)*	Dr	70 800	
Carrying Amount – Machinery (M1)**	Dr	3 800	
Machinery (M1)	Cr		74 800
*$1180 × 60 months			
**$74 600 – $70 800			

B. *Ledger accounts*

Accumulated Depreciation – Machinery Control

10/10/10	Machinery	41 600	30/6/10	Balance b/d	113 800
31/12/10	Balance c/d	76 100	10/10/10	Depreciation	3 900
		117 700			117 700
30/6/11	Machinery	70 800	31/12/10	Balance b/d	76 100
	Balance c/d	58 890	24/4/11	Depreciation	11 400
			30/6/11	Depreciation	42 190
		129 690			129 690
			30/6/11	Balance b/d	58 890

Accumulated Depreciation – Fixtures

3/7/10	Fixtures	43 728	30/6/10	Balance b/d	134 138
31/12/10	Balance c/d	90 410			
		134 138			134 138
			31/12/10	Balance b/d	90 410
30/6/11	Balance c/d	113 928	30/6/11	Depreciation	23 518
		113 928			113 928
			30/6/11	Balance b/d	113 928

ILLUSTRATIVE EXAMPLE 9.13

Cost and revaluation models of measurement

On 1 July 2009, Wollongong Ltd acquired a number of assets from Bathurst Ltd. The assets had the following fair values at that date:

Plant A	$300 000
Plant B	180 000
Furniture A	60 000
Furniture B	50 000

In exchange for these assets, Wollongong Ltd issued 200 000 shares with a fair value of $2.95 per share.

The directors of Wollongong Ltd decided to measure plant at fair value under the revaluation model and furniture at cost. The plant was considered to have a further 10-year life with benefits being received evenly over that period, whereas furniture is depreciated evenly over a 5-year period.

At 31 December 2009, Wollongong Ltd assessed the carrying amounts of its assets as follows:

- Plant A was valued at $296 000, with an expected remaining useful life of 8 years.
- Plant B was valued at $168 000, with an expected remaining useful life of 8 years.
- Furniture A's carrying amount was considered to be less than its recoverable amount.
- Furniture B's recoverable amount was assessed to be $40 000, with an expected remaining useful life of 4 years.

Appropriate entries were made at 31 December 2009 for the half-yearly accounts.

On 15 February 2010, Wollongong Ltd made a bonus issue of shares: 5600 shares fully paid to $1 per share were issued from the Plant A asset revaluation reserve.

At 30 June 2010, Wollongong Ltd assessed the carrying amounts of its assets as follows:

- Plant A was valued at $274 000.
- Plant B was valued at $161 500.
- The carrying amounts of furniture were less than their recoverable amounts.

The tax rate is 30%.

Required

Prepare the journal entries passed during the 2009–10 period in relation to the non-current assets in accordance with AASB 116 *Property, Plant and Equipment*.

Solution

The assets acquired are recorded at cost. The total cost of the assets is the fair value of the shares issued, namely $590 000 (i.e. 200 000 shares at $2.95 per share). This exactly equals the sum of the fair values of the assets acquired, hence the cost of each of the assets acquired is assumed to be equal to its fair value. If the amount were different from $590 000, say $550 000, then the cost of each asset would be determined based on the proportion of fair value to total fair value.

2009				
July 1	Plant A	Dr	300 000	
	Plant B	Dr	180 000	
	Furniture A	Dr	60 000	
	Furniture B	Dr	50 000	
	Share Capital	Cr		590 000
	(Acquisition of assets)			

At the end of each reporting period, depreciation is calculated and recorded. The next two entries record the depreciation on Plant A and Plant B after 6 months, at 31 December 2009.

Dec. 31	Depreciation Expense – Plant A	Dr	15 000	
	Accumulated Depreciation	Cr		15 000
	(Depreciation, 10% × ½ × $300 000)			
	Depreciation Expense – Plant B	Dr	9 000	
	Accumulated Depreciation	Cr		9 000
	(Depreciation, 10% × ½ × $180 000)			

Plant is measured using the revaluation model. At 31 December, the fair values of plant are assessed. In relation to Plant A, the carrying amount of the asset is $285 000 (i.e. $300 000 – $15 000). The fair value is assessed to be $296 000. There is then a revaluation increment of $11 000. This is taken directly to equity with an adjustment for the expected tax to be paid on the additional benefits being recognised. Hence 70% of the $11 000 is credited to the revaluation reserve account and 30% to the deferred tax liability account. Assets are revalued by class. However, accounting for revaluations is on an asset-by-asset basis. It is then important to associate any revaluation reserve with the asset that created that reserve.

Accumulated Depreciation – Plant A	Dr	15 000	
Plant A	Cr		4 000
Deferred Tax Liability	Cr		3 300
Asset Revaluation Reserve – Plant A	Cr		7 700
(Revaluation increment, Plant A)			

With Plant B, the carrying amount at 31 December is $171 000 (i.e. $180 000 – $9000). The fair value is assessed to be $168 000. The revaluation decrement is $3000. This amount is recognised in current period expense.

Accumulated Depreciation – Plant B	Dr	9 000	
Expense – Revaluation Decrement	Cr	3 000	
Plant B	Cr		12 000
(Revaluation decrement, Plant B)			

Furniture is measured under the cost model. Depreciation for the 6-month period is calculated based on an allocation of the cost over a 5-year period:

Depreciation Expense – Furniture A	Dr	6 000	
Accumulated Depreciation	Cr		6 000
(Depreciation, $\frac{1}{5} \times \frac{1}{2} \times \$60\,000$)			
Depreciation Expense – Furniture B	Dr	5 000	
Accumulated Depreciation	Cr		5 000
(Depreciation, $\frac{1}{5} \times \frac{1}{2} \times \$50\,000$)			

The carrying amount of Furniture B at 31 December is $45 000 (i.e. $50 000 – $5000). The recoverable amount is $40 000. The asset is written down to recoverable amount, with the write-down being added to the accumulated depreciation account, and reported as an impairment expense.

Impairment Loss – Furniture B	Dr	5 000	
Accumulated Depreciation and Impairment Losses – Furniture B	Cr		5 000
(Write-down of asset to recoverable amount)			

On 2 February 2010 the company made a bonus issue of $5600. This increased share capital, and was appropriated from the asset revaluation reserve related to Plant A. Note that revaluation increments and decrements are treated on an asset-by-asset basis, and so any transfers from revaluation reserves must be associated with specified reserves.

2010				
Feb. 15	Asset Revaluation Reserve	Dr	5 600	
	Share Capital	Cr		5 600
	(Issue of bonus shares, 5600 × $1)			

At 30 June, depreciation is recorded for plant assets based on an allocation of the fair values at 31 December 2009.

June 30	Depreciation Expense – Plant A	Dr	18 500	
	Accumulated Depreciation	Cr		18 500
	(Depreciation, $\frac{1}{8} \times \frac{1}{2} \times \$296\,000$)			

Depreciation Expense – Plant B	Dr	10 500	
Accumulated Depreciation	Cr		10 500
(Depreciation, ⅛ × ½ × $168 000)			

The fair value of Plant A is assessed to be $274 000. Since the carrying amount is $277 500 (i.e. $296 000 – $18 500), there is a revaluation decrement of $3500. Before recognising any expense on the revaluation decrement, there needs to be a reversal of the effects of any previous revaluation increment. For Plant A, at 31 December 2009, there was a revaluation increment of $11 000 which resulted in the recording of a $3300 deferred tax liability and a $7700 asset revaluation reserve. Hence, with the revaluation decrement of $3500, the normal adjustment would be to debit the deferred tax liability with $1050 (being 30% × $3500) and debit the asset revaluation reserve with $2450 (being 70% × $3500). However, because of the bonus dividend, the balance in the asset revaluation reserve for Plant A is only $2100 (i.e. $7700 – $5600). There is a deficiency of $350 in relation to the reserve.

The required journal entry then eliminates the balance of accumulated depreciation on Plant A, reduces the deferred tax liability by $1050 and writes off the total remaining balance of the asset revaluation reserve, and the deficiency on the asset revaluation reserve is recognised as per any other deficiency as a current period expense.

Accumulated Depreciation – Plant A	Dr	18 500	
Deferred Tax Liability	Dr	1 050	
Asset Revaluation Reserve	Dr	2 100	
Expense – Revaluation Decrement	Dr	350	
Plant A	Cr		22 000
(Revaluation downwards of Plant A by $3500)			

For Plant B, the carrying amount is $157 500 (i.e. $168 000 – $10 500). The fair value is $161 500. There is a revaluation increment of $4000. The accounting for this increment requires a reversal of any prior decrement. With Plant B at 31 December 2009, an expense of $3000 was recognised as a result of a revaluation decrement. The reversal of the previous decrement requires the recognition of revenue of $3000. The $1000 balance of the current increment (i.e. $4000 – $3000) is accounted for as a revaluation increment with a deferred tax liability and asset revaluation reserve being recognised. Plant B is written down from $168 000 to $161 500.

Accumulated Depreciation – Plant B	Dr	10 500	6 500
Plant B	Cr		3 000
Revenue – Revaluation Decrement Reversal	Cr		300
Deferred Tax Liability	Cr		700
Asset Revaluation Reserve	Cr		
(Revaluation of Plant B)			

Furniture at cost is depreciation for the final 6 months of the year.

Depreciation Expense – Furniture A	Dr	6 000	
Accumulated Depreciation	Cr		6 000
(Depreciation, ⅕ × ½ × $60 000)			
Depreciation Expense – Furniture B	Dr	5 000	
Accumulated Depreciation	Cr		5 000
(Depreciation, ¼ × ½ × $40 000)			

SUMMARY

'Property, plant and equipment' covers a wide range of assets such as vehicles, aircraft, all types of buildings, and specific structures such as oil and gas offshore platforms. These assets have a variety of useful lives, expected benefits, risk of receipt of benefits, movements in value over time, and expected value at point of derecognition. In some cases at derecognition, assets such as oil platforms require entities to incur costs rather than receive a residual value on sale. IAS 16, although recognising this variety, provides common principles to be applied to all items of property, plant and equipment.

Initial recognition occurs when the recognition criteria are met and assets are then recorded at cost. Subsequent to initial recognition, entities have a choice of measurement model, namely the cost model and the revaluation model. Under both measurement models, assets are subject to depreciation, this being a process of allocation and not a process of change in value. The measurement of depreciation requires judgements to be made by the accountant, including useful lives, residual values and pattern of receipt of benefits. Use of the revaluation model has additional accounting complications with revaluation increments and decrements potentially affecting asset revaluation reserve accounts, and having tax-effect consequences. Because of the judgements having to be made, IAS 16 requires extensive disclosures to be made.

Discussion questions

1. What assets constitute property, plant and equipment?
2. What are the recognition criteria for property, plant and equipment?
3. How should items of property, plant and equipment be measured at point of initial recognition, and would gifts be treated differently from acquisitions?
4. How is cost determined?
5. What choices of measurement model exist subsequent to assets being initially recognised?
6. What factors should entities consider in choosing alternative measurement models?
7. What is meant by 'depreciation expense'?
8. How is useful life determined?
9. What is meant by 'residual value' of an asset?
10. How does an entity choose between depreciation methods, for example, straight-line versus reducing-balance models?
11. What is meant by 'components depreciation'?
12. Under the revaluation model, how is a revaluation increment accounted for?
13. Under the revaluation model, how is a revaluation decrement accounted for?
14. When, and why, must tax effect be considered in accounting for revaluation increments and decrements?
15. Should accounting for revaluation increments and decrements be done on an asset-by-asset basis or on a class-of-assets basis?
16. What differences occur between asset-by-asset or class-of-asset bases in accounting for revaluation increments and decrements?
17. When should property, plant and equipment be derecognised?
18. The management of an entity has decided to use the fair value basis for the measurement of its equipment. Some of this equipment is very hard to obtain and has in fact increased in value over the current period. Management is arguing that, as there has been no decline in fair value, no depreciation should be charged on these pieces of equipment. Discuss.
19. Apollo Ltd uses tractors as a part of its operating equipment, and it applies the straight-line depreciation method to depreciate these assets. Apollo Ltd has just taken over Aphrodite Ltd, which uses similar tractors in its operations. However, Aphrodite Ltd has been using a diminishing balance method of depreciation for these tractors. The accountant in Apollo Ltd is arguing that for both entities the same depreciation method should be used for tractors. Provide arguments for and against this proposal.
20. A company is in the movie rental business. Movies are generally kept for 2 years and then either sold or destroyed. However, management wants to show increased profits, and believes that the annual depreciation charge can be lowered by keeping the movies for 3 years. Discuss.
21. A new accountant has been appointed to the firm of Athena Ltd, which owns a large number of depreciable assets. Upon analysing the firm's depreciation policy, the accountant has

implemented a new policy based on the principle that the depreciation rate for particular assets should measure the decline in the value of the assets. Discuss this policy change.

22. A new accountant has been appointed to Hades Ltd and has implemented major changes in the calculation of depreciation. As a result, some parts of the factory have much larger depreciation charges. This has incensed some operations managers who believe that, as they take particular care with the maintenance of their machines, their machines should not attract large depreciation charges that reduce the profitability of their operations and reflect badly on their management skills. The operations managers plan to meet the accountant and ask for change. How should the new accountant respond?
23. The management of Zeus Ltd has been analysing the financial reports provided by the accountant, who has been with the firm for a number of years. Management has expressed its concern over depreciation charges being made in relation to the company's equipment. In particular, it believes that the depreciation charges are not high enough in relation to the factory machines because new technology applied in that area is rapidly making the machines obsolete. Management's concern is that the machines will have to be replaced in the near future and, with the low depreciation charges, the fund will not be sufficient to pay for the replacement machines. Discuss.
24. Chaos Ltd has acquired a new building. Which of the following items should be included in the cost of the building?
    (a) Stamp duty
    (b) Real estate agent's fees
    (c) Architect's fees for drawings for internal adjustments to the building to be made before use
    (d) Interest on the bank loan to acquire the building, and an application fee to the bank to get the loan, which is secured on the building
    (e) Cost of changing the name on the building
    (f) Cost of changing the parking bays
    (g) Cost of refurbishing the lobby to the building to attract customers and make it more user friendly
25. Atlas Ltd has acquired a new machine, which it has had installed in its factory. Which of the following items should be capitalised into the cost of the building?
    (a) Labour and travel costs for managers to inspect possible new machines and for negotiating for a new machine
    (b) Freight costs and insurance to get the new machine to the factory
    (c) Costs for renovating a section of the factory, in anticipation of the new machine's arrival, to ensure that all the other parts of the factory will have easy access to the new machine
    (d) Cost of cooling equipment to assist in the efficient operation of the new machine
    (e) Costs of repairing the factory door, which was damaged by the installation of the new machine
    (f) Training costs of workers who will use the machine
26. Oceanus Ltd has acquired a new building for $500 000. It has incurred incidental costs of $10 000 in the acquisition process for legal fees, real estate agent's fees and stamp duties. Management believes that these costs should be expensed because they have not increased the value of the building and, if the building was immediately resold, these amounts would not be recouped. In other words, the fair value of the building is considered to still be $500 000. Discuss how these costs should be accounted for.

STAR RATING
★ BASIC
★★ MODERATE
★★★ DIFFICULT

Exercises

Exercise 9.1 **REVALUATION OF ASSETS**

★ In the 30 June 2009 annual report of Helios Ltd, the equipment was reported as follows:

Equipment (at cost)	$ 500 000
Accumulated depreciation	150 000
	350 000

The equipment consisted of two machines, Machine A and Machine B. Machine A had cost $300 000 and had a carrying amount of $180 000 at 30 June 2009, and Machine B had cost $200 000 and was carried at $170 000. Both machines are measured using the cost model, and depreciated on a straight-line basis over a 10-year period.

On 31 December 2009, the directors of Helios Ltd decided to change the basis of measuring the equipment from the cost model to the revaluation model. Machine A was revalued to $180 000 with an expected useful life of 6 years, and Machine B was revalued to $155 000 with an expected useful life of 5 years.

At 30 June 2010, Machine A was assessed to have a fair value of $163 000 with an expected useful life of 5 years, and Machine B's fair value was $136 500 with an expected useful life of 4 years.

The tax rate is 30%.

Required

1. Prepare the journal entries during the period 1 July 2009 to 30 June 2010 in relation to the equipment.
2. According to accounting standards, on what basis may management change the method of asset measurement, for example from cost to fair value?

Exercise 9.2 ★

REVALUATION OF ASSETS

On 30 June 2009, the statement of financial position of Uranus Ltd showed the following non-current assets after charging depreciation:

Building	$300 000	
Accumulated depreciation	(100 000)	$200 000
Motor vehicle	120 000	
Accumulated depreciation	(40 000)	80 000

The company has adopted fair value for the valuation of non-current assets. This has resulted in the recognition in previous periods of an asset revaluation reserve for the building of $14 000. On 30 June 2009, an independent valuer assessed the fair value of the building to be $160 000 and the vehicle to be $90 000. The income tax rate is 30%.

Required

1. Prepare any necessary entries to revalue the building and the vehicle as at 30 June 2009.
2. Assume that the building and vehicle had remaining useful lives of 25 years and 4 years respectively, with zero residual value. Prepare entries to record depreciation expense for the year ended 30 June 2010 using the straight-line method.

Exercise 9.3 ★★

DEPRECIATION

Acis Ltd was formed on 1 July 2007 to provide delivery services for packages to be taken between the city and the airport. On this date, the company acquired a delivery truck from Greek Trucks. The company paid cash of $50 000 to Greek Trucks, which included government charges of $600 and registration of $400. Insurance costs for the first year amounted to $1200. The truck is expected to have a useful life of 5 years. At the end of the useful life, the asset is expected to be sold for $24 000, with costs relating to the sale amounting to $400.

The company went extremely well in its first year, and the management of Acis Ltd decided at 1 July 2008 to add another vehicle, a flat-top, to the fleet. This vehicle was acquired from a liquidation auction at a cash price of $30 000. The vehicle needed some repairs for the elimination of rust (cost $2300), major servicing to the engine (cost $480) and the replacement of all tyres (cost $620). The company believed it would use the flat-top for another 2 years and then sell it. Expected selling price was $15 000, with selling costs estimated to be $400. On 1 July 2008, both vehicles were fitted out with a radio communication system at a cost per vehicle of $300. This was not expected to have any material effect on the future selling price of either vehicle. Insurance costs for the 2008–09 period were $1200 for the first vehicle and $900 for the newly acquired vehicle.

All went well for the company except that, on 1 August 2009, the flat-top that had been acquired at auction broke down. Acis Ltd thought about acquiring a new vehicle to replace this one but, after considering the costs, decided to repair the flat-top instead. The vehicle was given a major overhaul at a cost of $6500. Although this was a major expense, management believed that the company would keep the vehicle for another 2 years. The estimated selling price in 3 years time is $12 000, with selling costs estimated at $300. Insurance costs for the 2009–10 period were the same as for the previous year.

Required
Prepare the journal entries for the recording of the vehicles and the depreciation of the vehicles for each of the 3 years. The financial year ends on 30 June.

Exercise 9.4 ★★

DEPRECIATION

Eros Ltd constructed a building for use by the administration section of the company. The completion date was 1 July 2002, and the construction cost was $840 000. The company expected to remain in the building for the next 20 years, at which time the building would probably have no real salvage value and have to be demolished. It is expected that demolition costs will amount to $15 000. In December 2008, following some severe weather in the city, the roof of the administration building was considered to be in poor shape so the company decided to replace it. On 1 July 2009, a new roof was installed at a cost of $220 000. The new roof was of a different material to the old roof, which was estimated to have cost only $140 000 in the original construction, although at the time of construction it was thought that the roof would last for the 20 years that the company expected to use the building. Because the company had spent the money replacing the roof, it thought that it would delay construction of a new building, thereby extending the original life of the building from 20 years to 25 years.

Required
Discuss how you would account for the depreciation of the building and how the replacement of the roof would affect the depreciation calculations.

Exercise 9.5 ★★

DEPRECIATION CALCULATION

On 1 July 2009, Iris Airlines acquired a new aeroplane for a total cost of $10 million. A breakdown of the costs to build the aeroplane was given by the manufacturers:

Aircraft body	$3 000 000
Engines (2)	4 000 000
Fitting out of aircraft:	
Seats	1 000 000
Carpets	50 000
Electrical equipment — passenger seats	200 000
— cockpit	1 500 000
Food preparation equipment	250 000

All costs include installation and labour costs associated with the relevant part.

It is expected that the aircraft will be kept for 10 years and then sold. The main value of the aircraft at that stage is the body and the engines. The expected selling price is $2.1 million, with the body and engines retaining proportionate value.

Costs in relation to the aircraft over the next 10 years are expected to be as follows:

- *Aircraft body*. This requires an inspection every 2 years for cracks and wear and tear, at a cost of $10 000.
- *Engines*. Each engine has an expected life of 4 years before being sold for scrap. It is expected that the engines will be replaced in 2013 for $4.5 million and again in 2017 for $6 million. These engines are expected to incur annual maintenance costs of $300 000. The manufacturer has informed Iris Airlines that a new prototype engine with an extra 10% capacity should be on the market in 2015, and that existing engines could be upgraded at a cost of $1 million.

- *Fittings*. Seats are replaced every 3 years. Expected replacement costs are $1.2 million in 2012 and $1.5 million in 2018. The repair of torn seats and faulty mechanisms is expected to cost $100 000 p.a. Carpets are replaced every 5 years. They will be replaced in 2014 at an expected cost of $65 000, but will not be replaced again before the aircraft is sold in 2019. Cleaning costs amount to $10 000 p.a. The electrical equipment (such as the TV) for each seat has an annual repair cost of $15 000. It is expected that, with the improvements in technology, the equipment will be totally replaced in 2015 by substantially better equipment at a cost of $350 000. The electrical equipment in the cockpit is tested frequently at an expected annual cost of $250 000. Major upgrades to the equipment are expected every 2 years at expected costs of $250 000 (in 2008), $300 000 (in 2010), $345 000 (in 2012) and $410 000 (in 2017). The upgrades will take into effect the expected changes in technology.
- *Food preparation equipment*. This incurs annual costs for repair and maintenance of $20 000. The equipment is expected to be totally replaced in 2015.

Required

1. Discuss how the costs relating to the aircraft should be accounted for.
2. Determine the expenses recognised for the 2009–10 financial year.

Exercise 9.6 ★★ REVALUATION OF ASSETS AND TAX-EFFECT ACCOUNTING

Proteus Ltd acquired a machine on 1 July 2007 at a cost of $100 000. The machine has an expected useful life of 5 years, and the company adopts the straight-line basis of depreciation. The tax depreciation rate for this type of machine is 12.5% p.a. The company tax rate is 30%.

Proteus Ltd measures this asset at fair value. Movements in fair values are as follows:

30 June 2008	$85 000	Remaining useful life: 4 years
30 June 2009	60 000	Remaining useful life: 3 years
30 June 2010	45 000	

Owing to a change in economic conditions, Proteus Ltd sold the machine for $45 000 on 30 June 2010. The asset was revalued to fair value immediately before the sale.

Required

1. Provide the journal entries used to account for this machine over the period 2007 to 2010.
2. For each of the 3 years ended 30 June 2008, 2009 and 2010, calculate the carrying amount and the tax base of the asset, and determine the appropriate tax-effect entry in relation to the machine. Explain your answer.

Exercise 9.7 ★★ ACQUISITION AND SALE OF ASSETS, DEPRECIATION

Pan's Turf Farm owned the following items of property, plant and equipment as at 30 June 2009:

Land (at cost)		$120 000
Office building (at cost)	150 000	
Accumulated depreciation	(23 375)	126 625
Turf cutter (at cost)	65 000	
Accumulated depreciation	(42 367)	22 633
Water desalinator (at fair value)		189 000

Additional information (at 30 June 2009)

(a) The straight-line method of depreciation is used for all depreciable items of property, plant and equipment. Depreciation is charged to the nearest month and all figures are rounded to the nearest dollar.

(b) The office building was constructed on 1 April 2005. Its estimated useful life is 20 years and it has an estimated residual value of $40 000.

(c) The turf cutter was purchased on 21 January 2006, at which date it had an estimated useful life of 5 years and an estimated residual value of $3200.

(d) The water desalinator was purchased and installed on 2 July 2008 at a cost of $200 000. On 30 June 2009, the plant was revalued upwards by $7000 to its fair value on that day. Additionally, its useful life and residual value were re-estimated to 9 years and $18 000 respectively.

The following transactions occurred during the year ended 30 June 2010:

(*Note:* All payments are made in cash.)

(e) On 10 August 2009, new irrigation equipment was purchased from Pond Supplies for $37 000. On 16 August 2009, the business paid $500 to have the equipment delivered to the turf farm. Bob Digger was contracted to install and test the new system. In the course of installation, pipes worth $800 were damaged and subsequently replaced on 3 September. The irrigation system was fully operational by 19 September and Bob Digger was paid $9600 for his services. The system has an estimated useful life of 4 years and a residual value of $0.

(f) On 1 December 2009, the turf cutter was traded in on a new model worth $80 000. A trade-in allowance of $19 000 was received and the balance paid in cash. The new machine's useful life and residual value were estimated at 6 years and $5000 respectively.

(g) On 1 January 2010, the turf farm's owner Terry Clifford decided to extend the office building by adding three new offices and a meeting room. The extension work started on 2 February and was completed by 28 March at a cost of $49 000. The extension is expected to increase the useful life of the building by 4 years and increase its residual value by $5000.

(h) On 30 June 2010, depreciation expense for the year was recorded. The fair value of the water desalination plant was $165 000.

Required

(*Show all workings and round amounts to the nearest dollar.*)

Prepare general journal entries to record the transactions and events for the reporting period ended 30 June 2010. (Narrations are not required.)

Exercise 9.8 ACQUISITIONS, DISPOSALS, DEPRECIATION

★★

Notus Ltd purchased equipment on 1 July 2008 for $39 800 cash. Transport and installation costs of $4200 were paid on 5 July 2008. Useful life and residual value were estimated to be 10 years and $1800 respectively. Notus Ltd depreciates equipment using the straight-line method to the nearest month, and reports annually on 30 June. The company tax rate is 30%.

In June 2010, changes in technology caused the company to revise the estimated total life from 10 years to 5 years, and the residual value from $1800 to $1200. This revised estimate was made before recording the depreciation for the financial year ended 30 June 2010.

On 30 June 2010, the company adopted the revaluation model to account for equipment. An expert valuation was obtained showing that the equipment had a fair value of $30 000 at that date.

On 30 June 2011, depreciation for the year was charged and the equipment's carrying amount was remeasured to its fair value of $16 000.

On 30 September 2011, the equipment was sold for $8400 cash.

Required

(*Show all workings and round amounts to the nearest dollar.*)

Prepare general journal entries to record the transactions and events for the period 1 July 2008 to 30 September 2011. (Narrations are not required.)

Exercise 9.9 REVALUATION OF ASSETS

★★

On 1 July 2009, Achilles Ltd acquired two assets within the same class of plant and equipment. Information on these assets is as follows:

	Cost	Expected useful life
Machine A	$100 000	5 years
Machine B	60 000	3 years

The machines are expected to generate benefits evenly over their useful lives. The class of plant and equipment is measured using fair value.

At 30 June 2010, information about the assets is as follows:

	Fair value	Expected useful life
Machine A	$84 000	4 years
Machine B	38 000	2 years

On 1 January 2011, Machine B was sold for $29 000 cash. On the same day, Achilles Ltd acquired Machine C for $80 000 cash. Machine C has an expected useful life of 4 years. Achilles Ltd also made a bonus issue of 10 000 shares at $1 per share, using $8000 from the general reserve and $2000 from the asset revaluation reserve created as a result of measuring Machine A at fair value.

At 30 June 2011, information on the machines is as follows:

	Fair value	Expected useful life
Machine A	$61 000	3 years
Machine C	68 500	1.5 years

The income tax rate is 30%.

Required

Prepare the journal entries in the records of Achilles Ltd to record the described events over the period 1 July 2009 to 30 June 2011, assuming the ends of the reporting periods are 30 June 2010 and 30 June 2011.

Exercise 9.10 ★★

DETERMINING THE COSTS OF ASSETS

Ceyx Ltd uses many kinds of machines in its operations. It constructs some of these machines itself and acquires others from the manufacturers. The following information relates to two machines that it has recorded in the 2010–11 period. Machine A was acquired, and Machine B was constructed by Ceyx Ltd itself:

Machine A	
Cash paid for equipment, including GST of $8000	$ 88 000
Costs of transporting machine — insurance and transport	3 000
Labour costs of installation by expert fitter	5 000
Labour costs of testing equipment	4 000
Insurance costs for 2010–11	1 500
Costs of training for personnel who will use the machine	2 500
Costs of safety rails and platforms surrounding machine	6 000
Costs of water devices to keep machine cool	8 000
Costs of adjustments to machine during 2010–11 to make it operate more efficiently	7 500
Machine B	
Cost of material to construct machine, including GST of $7000	$ 77 000
Labour costs to construct machine	43 000
Allocated overhead costs — electricity, factory space etc.	22 000
Allocated interest costs of financing machine	10 000
Costs of installation	12 000
Insurance for 2010–11	2 000
Profit saved by self-construction	15 000
Safety inspection costs prior to use	4 000

Required

Determine the amount at which each of these machines should be recorded in the records of Ceyx Ltd. For items not included in the cost of the machines, note how they should be accounted for.

Exercise 9.11 ★★

CLASSIFICATION OF ACQUISITION COSTS

Dictys Ltd began operations on 1 July 2009. During the following year, the company acquired a tract of land, demolished the building on the land and built a new factory. Equipment was acquired for the factory and, in March 2010, the factory was ready. A gala opening was held on 18 March, with the local parliamentarian opening the factory. The first items were ready for sale on 25 March.

During this period, the following inflows and outflows occurred:

1. While searching for a suitable block of land, Dictys Ltd placed an option to buy with three real estate agents at a cost of $100 each. One of these blocks of land was later acquired.	
2. Payment of option fees	$300
3. Receipt of loan from bank	400 000
4. Payment to settlement agent for title search, stamp duties and settlement fees	10 000
5. Payment of arrears in rates on building on land	5 000
6. Payment for land	100 000
7. Payment for demolition of current building on land	12 000
8. Proceeds from sale of material from old building	5 500
9. Payment to architect	23 000
10. Payment to council for approval of building construction	12 000
11. Payment for safety fence around construction site	3 400
12. Payment to construction contractor for factory building	240 000
13. Payment for external driveways, parking bays and safety lighting	54 000
14. Payment of interest on loan	40 000
15. Payment for safety inspection on building	3 000
16. Payment for equipment	64 000
17. Payment of freight and insurance costs on delivery of equipment	5 600
18. Payment of installation costs on equipment	12 000
19. Payment for safety fence surrounding equipment	11 000
20. Payment for removal of safety fence	2 000
21. Payment for new fence surrounding the factory	8 000
22. Payment for advertisements in the local paper about the forthcoming factory and its benefits to the local community	500
23. Payment for opening ceremony	6 000
24. Payments to adjust equipment to more efficient operating levels subsequent to initial operation	3 300

Required

Using the information provided, determine what assets Dictys Ltd should recognise and the amounts at which they would be recorded.

Exercise 9.12 ★★

ACQUISITIONS, DISPOSALS, TRADE-INS, OVERHAULS, DEPRECIATION

Matt Midas is the owner of Gold Fishing Charters. The business's final trial balance on 30 June 2009 (end of the reporting period) included the following balances:

Processing plant (at cost, purchased 4 April 2007)	$148 650
Accumulated depreciation — processing plant	(81 274)
Charter boats	291 200
Accumulated depreciation — boats	(188 330)

The following boats were owned at 30 June 2009:

Boat	Purchase date	Cost	Estimated useful life	Estimated residual value
1	23 February 2005	$62 000	5 years	$3 000
2	9 September 2005	$66 400	5 years	$3 400
3	6 February 2006	$78 600	4 years	$3 600
4	20 April 2007	$84 200	6 years	$3 800

Additional information
Gold Fishing Charters calculates depreciation to the nearest month using straight-line depreciation for all assets except the processing plant, which is depreciated at 30% on the diminishing-value method. Amounts are recorded to the nearest dollar.

Part A
The following transactions and events occurred during the year ended 30 June 2010:

2009	
July 26	Traded in boat 1 for a new boat (Boat 5) which cost $84 100. A trade-in allowance of $8900 was received and the balance was paid in cash. Registration and stamp duty costs of $1500 were also paid in cash. Matt Midas estimated Boat 5's useful life and residual value at 6 years and $4120 respectively.
Dec. 4	Overhauled the processing plant at a cash cost of $62 660. As the modernisation significantly expanded the plant's operating capacity and efficiency, Matt Midas decided to revise the depreciation rate to 25%.
2010	
Feb. 26	Boat 3 reached the end of its useful life but no buyer could be found, so the boat was scrapped.
June 30	Recorded depreciation.

Required
Prepare general journal entries (narrations are required) to record the transactions and events for the year ended 30 June 2010.

Part B
On 26 March, Matt Midas was offered fish-finding equipment with a fair value of $9500 in exchange for Boat 2. The fish-finder originally cost its owner $26 600 and had a carrying value of $9350 at the date of offer. The fair value of Boat 2 was $9100.

Required
If Matt Midas accepts the exchange offer, what amount would the business use to record the acquisition of the fish-finding equipment? Why? Justify your answer by reference to the requirements of IAS 16 relating to the initial recognition of a property, plant and equipment item.

Exercise 9.13 ★★ ACQUISITIONS, REVALUATIONS, REPLACEMENTS, DEPRECIATION

Niobe Trading operates in a very competitive field. To maintain its market position, it purchased two new machines for cash on 1 January 2008. It had previously rented its machines. Machine A cost $40 000 and Machine B cost $100 000. Each machine was expected to have a useful life of 10 years, and residual values were estimated at $2000 for Machine A and $5000 for Machine B.

On 30 June 2009, Niobe Trading adopted the revaluation model to account for the class of machinery. The fair values of Machine A and Machine B were determined to be $32 000 and

$90 000 respectively on that date. The useful life and residual value of Machine A were reassessed to 8 years and $1500. The useful life and residual value of Machine B were reassessed to 8 years and $4000.

On 2 January 2010, extensive repairs were carried out on Machine B for $66 000 cash. Niobe Trading expected these repairs to extend Machine B's useful life by 3.5 years, and it revised Machine B's estimated residual value to $9450.

Owing to technological advances, Niobe Trading decided to replace Machine A. It traded in Machine A on 31 March 2010 for new Machine C, which cost $64 000. A $28 000 trade-in was allowed for Machine A, and the balance of Machine C's cost was paid in cash. Transport and installation costs of $950 were incurred in respect to Machine C. Machine C was expected to have a useful life of 8 years and a residual value of $8000.

Niobe Trading uses the straight-line depreciation method, recording depreciation to the nearest month and the nearest dollar. The end of its reporting period is 30 June.

On 30 June 2010, fair values were determined to be $140 000 and $65 000 for Machines B and C respectively.

Required

Prepare general journal entries to record the above transactions and the depreciation journal entries required at the end of each reporting period up to 30 June 2010. (Narrations are not required but show all workings.)

Problems

Problem 9.1 ★★★

DEPRECIATION CALCULATION

Proetus Ltd operates a factory that contains a large number of machines designed to produce knitted garments. These machines are generally depreciated at 10% p.a. on a straight-line basis. In general, machines are estimated to have a residual value on disposal of 10% of cost. At 1 July 2010, Proetus Ltd had a total of 64 machines, and the statement of financial position showed a total cost of $420 000 and accumulated depreciation of $130 000. During 2010–11, the following transactions occurred:

1. On 1 September 2010, a new machine was acquired for $15 000. This machine replaced two other machines. One of the two replaced machines was acquired on 1 July 2007 for $8200. It was traded in on the new machine, with Proetus Ltd making a cash payment of $8800 on the new machine. The second replaced machine had cost $9000 on 1 April 2008 and was sold for $7300.
2. On 1 January 2011, a machine that had cost $4000 on 1 July 2001 was retired from use and sold for scrap for $500.
3. On 1 January 2011, a machine that had been acquired on 1 January 2008 for $7000 was repaired because its motor had been damaged from overheating. The motor was replaced at a cost of $4800. It was expected that this would increase the life of the machine by an extra 2 years.
4. On 1 April 2011, Proetus Ltd fitted a new form of arm to a machine used for putting special designs onto garments. The arm cost $1200. The machine had been acquired on 1 April 2008 for $10 000. The arm can be used on a number of other machines when required and has a 15-year life. It will not be sold when any particular machine is retired, but retained for use on other machines.

Required

1. Record each of the transactions. The end of the reporting period is 30 June.
2. Determine the depreciation expense for Proetus Ltd for 2010–11.

Problem 9.2 ★★★

REVALUATION OF ASSETS AND TAX-EFFECT ACCOUNTING

For Sparta Ltd, profit before income tax for the year ended 30 June 2010 amounted to $375 000, including the expenses shown on the opposite page.

Depreciation of plant	$50 000
Goodwill impairment*	13 000
Long-service leave	40 000
Holiday pay	30 000
Doubtful debts	55 000
Entertainment*	12 000
Depreciation of furniture	5 000

*Non-deductible for taxation

The statement of financial position of Sparta Ltd at 30 June 2009 and 2010 showed the net assets of the company as follows:

Assets	**2009**	**2010**
Cash	$ 73 000	$ 82 000
Inventory	127 000	158 000
Receivables	430 000	585 000
Allowance for doubtful debts	(20 000)	(40 000)
Plant (net)	350 000	320 000
Furniture (net)	75 000	65 000
Goodwill	63 000	50 000
Deferred tax asset	21 000	?
Liabilities		
Payables	247 000	265 000
Provision for long-service leave	30 000	50 000
Provision for holiday pay	20 000	30 000
Deferred tax liability	11 250	?

Additional information

(a) Plant and furniture are different classes of assets. Both are measured at fair value. The furniture was revalued downward to $65 000 at 30 June 2010. Furniture had not previously been revalued upwards. Tax depreciation for the year ended 30 June 2010 was $7500, giving a carrying amount for tax purposes at 30 June 2010 of $55 000. The plant was revalued upwards at 30 June 2010 to $320 000. Tax depreciation on plant was $75 000, giving a carrying amount for tax purposes at 30 June 2010 of $250 000.

(b) Total bad debts written off for the 2009–10 year were $35 000.

(c) The tax rate is 30%.

Required

1. Calculate, by using worksheets, the amounts of income tax expense and current and deferred income tax assets/liabilities for the reporting period ended 30 June 2010.
2. Prepare the deferred tax asset and deferred tax liability accounts.

Problem 9.3 ★★★

COST OF ACQUISITION

Thisbe Ltd started business early in 2010. During its first 9 months, Thisbe Ltd acquired real estate for the construction of a building and other facilities. Operating equipment was purchased and installed, and the company began operating activities in October 2010. The company's accountant, who was not sure how to record some of the transactions, opened a Property ledger account and recorded debits and (credits) to this account as follows on the next page.

1. Cost of real estate purchased as a building site.	$ 170 000
2. Paid architect's fee for design of new building.	23 000
3. Paid for demolition of old building on building site purchased in (1).	28 000
4. Paid land tax on the real estate purchased as a building site in (1).	1 700
5. Paid excavation costs for the new building.	15 000
6. Made the first payment to the building contractor.	250 000
7. Paid for equipment to be installed in the new building.	148 000
8. Received from sale of salvaged materials from demolishing the old building.	(6 800)
9. Made final payment to the building contractor.	350 000
10. Paid interest on building loan during construction.	22 000
11. Paid freight on equipment purchased.	1 900
12. Paid installation costs of equipment.	4 200
13. Paid for repair of equipment damaged during installation.	2 700
Property ledger account balance	$ 1 009 700

Required

1. Prepare a schedule with the following column headings. Analyse each transaction, enter the payment or receipt in the appropriate column, and total each column.

Item no.	Land	Land improvements	Building	Manufacturing equipment	Other

2. Prepare the journal entry to close the $1 009 700 balance of the Property ledger account.

Problem 9.4 ★★★

DEPRECIATION

Rhesus Manufacturing, which started operations on 1 September 2004, is owned by Semele Ltd. Semele Ltd's accounts at 31 December 2007 included the following balances:

Machinery (at cost)	$91 000
Accumulated depreciation — machinery	48 200
Vehicles (at cost; purchased 21 November 2006)	46 800
Accumulated depreciation — vehicles	19 656
Land (at cost; purchased 25 October 2004)	81 000
Building (at cost; purchased 25 October 2004)	185 720
Accumulated depreciation — building	28 614

Details of machines owned at 31 December 2007 are as follows:

Machine	Purchase date	Cost	Useful life	Residual value
1	7 October 2004	$43 000	5 years	$2 500
2	4 February 2005	$48 400	6 years	$3 000

Additional information

(a) Semele Ltd calculates depreciation to the nearest month and balances the records at month-end. Recorded amounts are rounded to the nearest dollar, and the end of the reporting period is 31 December.

(b) Semele Ltd uses straight-line depreciation for all depreciable assets except vehicles, which are depreciated on the diminishing balance at 40% p.a.

(c) The vehicles account balance reflects the total paid for two identical delivery vehicles, each of which cost $23 400.

(d) On acquiring the land and building, Semele Ltd estimated the building's useful life and residual value at 20 years and $5000 respectively.

The following transactions occurred from 1 January 2008:

2008	
Jan. 3	Bought a new machine (Machine 3) for a cash price of $57 000. Freight charges of $442 and installation costs of $1758 were paid in cash. The useful life and residual value were estimated at 5 years and $4000 respectively.
June 22	Bought a second-hand vehicle for $15 200 cash. Repainting costs of $655 and four new tyres costing $345 were paid for in cash.
Aug. 28	Exchanged Machine 1 for office furniture that had a fair value of $12 500 at the date of exchange. The fair value of Machine 1 at the date of exchange was $11 500. The office furniture originally cost $36 000 and, to the date of exchange, had been depreciated by $24 100 in the previous owner's books. Semele Ltd estimated the office furniture's useful life and residual value at 8 years and $540 respectively.
Dec. 31	Recorded depreciation.
2009	
April 30	Paid for repairs and maintenance on the machinery at a cash cost of $928.
May 25	Sold one of the vehicles bought on 21 November 2006 for $6600 cash.
June 26	Installed a fence around the property at a cash cost of $5500. The fence has an estimated useful life of 10 years and zero residual value. (Debit the cost to a land improvements asset account.)
Dec. 31	Recorded depreciation.
2010	
Jan. 5	Overhauled Machine 2 at a cash cost of $12 000, after which Semele Ltd estimated its remaining useful life at 1 additional year and revised its residual value to $5000.
June 20	Traded in the remaining vehicle bought on 21 November 2006 for a new vehicle. A trade-in allowance of $3700 was received and $22 000 was paid in cash. Stamp duty of $500 and registration and third-party insurance of $800 were also paid for in cash.
Oct. 4	Scrapped the vehicle bought on 22 June 2008, as it had been so badly damaged in a traffic accident that it was not worthwhile repairing it.
Dec. 31	Recorded depreciation.

Required

Prepare general journal entries to record the above transactions.

Problem 9.5 ★★★

DEPRECIATION

Orion Ltd started operations on 1 October 2007. Its accounts at 30 June 2010 included the following balances:

Machinery (at cost)	$ 98 000
Accumulated depreciation — machinery	47 886
Vehicles (at cost; purchased 20 February 2008)	160 000
Accumulated depreciation — vehicles	89 440
Land (at cost; purchased 20 March 2010)	75 000
Building (at cost; purchased 20 March 2010)	290 600
Accumulated depreciation — building	3 420
Land improvements (at cost; purchased 20 March 2010)	18 000
Accumulated depreciation — land improvements	300

Details of machines owned at 30 June 2010 were:

Machine	Purchase date	Cost	Useful life	Residual value
1	2 October 2007	$25 000	4 years	$2500
2	27 December 2007	42 000	5 years	4000
3	29 July 2008	31 000	4 years	3000

Additional information

(a) Orion Ltd calculates depreciation to the nearest month and balances the records at month-end. Recorded amounts are rounded to the nearest dollar, and the end of the reporting period is 30 June.

(b) Orion Ltd uses straight-line depreciation for all depreciable assets except vehicles, which are depreciated on the diminishing balance at 30% p.a.

(c) The vehicles account balance reflects the total paid for four identical delivery vehicles, which cost $40 000 each.

(d) On acquiring the land and building, Orion Ltd estimated the building's useful life and residual value at 20 years and $17 000 respectively.

(e) The Land Improvements account balance reflects a payment of $18 000 made on 20 March 2010 for driveways and a car park. On acquiring these land improvements, Orion Ltd estimated their useful life at 15 years with no residual value.

The following transactions occurred from 1 July 2010:

2010	
Aug. 3	Purchased a new machine (Machine 4) for a cash price of $36 000. Installation costs of $1800 were also paid. Orion Ltd estimated the useful life and residual value at 5 years and $3500 respectively.
Nov. 15	Paid vehicle repairs of $600.
Dec. 30	Exchanged one of the vehicles for items of fixtures that had a fair value of $17 000 at the date of exchange. The fair value of the vehicle at the date of exchange was $16 000. The fixtures originally cost $50 000 and had been depreciated by $31 000 to the date of exchange in the previous owner's books. Orion Ltd estimated the fixtures' useful life and residual value at 5 years and $2500 respectively.
2011	
March 10	Sold Machine 1 for $5000 cash.
June 30	Recorded depreciation expense.
Sept. 20	Traded in Machine 3 for a new machine (Machine 5). A trade-in allowance of $10 000 was received for Machine 3 and $34 000 was paid in cash. Orion Ltd estimated Machine 5's useful life and residual value at 6 years and $5000 respectively.
Dec. 30	Scrapped Machine 2, as it was surplus to requirements and no buyer could be found for it.
2012	
Feb. 8	Paid $8000 to overhaul Machine 4, after which Machine 4's useful life was estimated at 2 remaining years and its residual value was revised to $5000.
June 30	Recorded depreciation expense.

Required

Prepare general journal entries to record the above transactions.

References

Accounting Standards Board 1996, *Measurement of tangible fixed assets*, discussion paper, Accounting Standards Board UK.

BHP Billiton 2008, *Annual report 2008*, BHP Billiton, www.bhpbilliton.com.

Ernst & Young 2002, *The impact of AASB 1041 'Revaluation of Non-current Assets': A survey of corporate Australia's adoption of the new standard*, Ernst & Young Australia, January.

Wesfarmers 2008, *2008 annual report*, Wesfarmers Limited, www.wesfarmers.com.au.

DUBLIN BUSINESS SCHOOL
LIBRARY

10 Intangible assets

ACCOUNTING STANDARDS IN FOCUS

IAS 38 *Intangible Assets*

LEARNING OBJECTIVES

When you have studied this chapter, you should be able to:

- understand the key characteristics of an intangible asset
- explain the criteria relating to the initial recognition of intangible assets and their measurement at point of initial recognition, distinguishing between acquired and internally generated intangibles
- explain how to measure intangibles subsequent to initial recognition, including the principles relating to the amortisation of intangibles
- explain the accounting for retirement and disposal of intangible assets
- apply the disclosure requirements of IAS 38
- discuss innovative suggestions for improving the reporting of intangible assets.

Chapter 9 discusses the accounting standards for the tangible assets of property, plant and equipment. This chapter examines the standards for intangible assets. The International Accounting Standards Board (IASB) believes it is necessary to distinguish between tangible assets (such as property, plant and equipment) and intangible assets (such as patents and brand names). In analysing the accounting for intangible assets, the question that must always be kept in mind is whether there should be any difference in the accounting treatment for tangible and intangible assets. What is it that is different about intangible assets that makes a separate accounting standard, and presumably different accounting rules, for intangible and tangible assets necessary?

Historically, it is common for entities to report all their tangible assets on the statement of financial position but be less consistent in the reporting of intangible assets. As a result, there are sometimes large differences between the market value of an entity and its recorded net assets. As Jenkins and Upton (2001, p. 4) noted:

> The problem that confronts businesses, users of business and financial reporting, standard-setters and regulators is how best to understand and communicate the difference between the value of a company (usually expressed as the market capitalisation) and the accounting book value of that company.

To assist in understanding the difference between these two numbers, Jenkins and Upton (2001, p. 5) provided the analysis shown in figure 10.1. Item 6 in this figure is not an area that accounting can directly address, although the quality of the accounting may affect the degree to which it exists. How can accounting assist in providing more information about what causes the gap between accounting book value and market capitalisation numbers? How much information should be provided about all the assets and liabilities of an entity? What should be in the financial statements and what should be in the notes to those statements? These are questions for accounting standard setters to solve.

1. Accounting book value	$xxx
2. + Market assessments of differences between accounting measurement and underlying value of recognised assets and liabilities	xxx
3. + Market assessments of the underlying value of items that meet the definition of assets and liabilities but are not recognised in financial statements (e.g. patents developed through internal research and development)	xxx
4. + Market assessments of intangible value drivers or value impairers that do not meet the definition of assets and liabilities (e.g. employee morale)	xxx
5. + Market assessments of the entity's future plans, opportunities and business risks	xxx
6. + Other factors, including puffery, pessimism and market psychology	xxx
7. Market capitalisation	$xxx

FIGURE 10.1 Differences between market capitalisation and accounting book value
Source: Jenkins and Upton (2001, p. 5). © 2001. Reproduced with the permission of CPA Australia Ltd.

The standards on accounting for intangibles are contained in IAS 38 *Intangible Assets*. In its 2004 revision, the IASB did not attempt to revisit all areas of accounting for intangibles. Its emphasis in this revision was to reflect changes as a result of decisions made in the Business Combinations project, particularly relating to accounting for intangibles acquired as part of a business combination. Hence, there still may be areas of inconsistency between accounting for intangibles obtained outside a business combination and those acquired as part of a business combination.

IAS 38 covers the accounting for all intangible assets except, as detailed in paragraphs 2 and 3, those specifically covered by another accounting standard — financial assets; and mineral rights and expenditure on exploration for, or development and extraction of, minerals, oil, natural gas and similar non-regenerative resources. Other standards that include accounting for specific intangible assets are:

- intangible assets held by an entity for sale in the ordinary course of business (IAS 2 *Inventories* and IAS 11 *Construction Contracts*)
- intangible assets arising from insurance contracts with policyholders (IAS 4 *Insurance Contracts*)
- deferred tax assets (IAS 12 *Income Taxes*)
- leases within the scope of IAS 17 *Leases*
- assets arising from employee benefits (IAS 19 *Employee Benefits*)

- goodwill acquired in a business combination (IFRS 3 *Business Combinations*)
- non-current intangible assets held for sale (IFRS 5 *Non-current Assets Held for Sale and Discontinued Operations*).

10.1 THE NATURE OF INTANGIBLE ASSETS

Paragraph 8 of IAS 38 defines an intangible asset as 'an identifiable non-monetary asset without physical substance'. Note that intangible assets are non-monetary assets; hence, assets such as receivables and cash are not intangible assets. Being assets, intangibles are resources controlled by the entity from which future economic benefits are expected to flow to the entity. Monetary assets are defined in IAS 38 as 'money held and assets to be received in fixed or determinable amounts of money'. Apart from excluding monetary assets, there are two key characteristics of intangible assets, namely:

- they are identifiable
- they lack physical substance.

The concept of intangibles used in IAS 38 is the same as that used in Statement of Financial Accounting Standards No. 142 (SFAS 142) *Goodwill and Other Intangible Assets* issued by the Financial Accounting Standards Board (FASB) in the United States in June 2001. Other writers have similar definitions. For example, Lev stated (2001, p. 5): 'An intangible asset is a claim to future benefits that does not have a physical or financial (a stock or a bond) embodiment.'

The two key characteristics of an intangible asset are now considered in detail.

10.1.1 Identifiability

The emphasis on the criterion of identifiability arose out of the Business Combinations project and the concern that, in identifying the assets and liabilities acquired, the intangible assets acquired must be distinguished from goodwill. As noted in paragraph BC8 in the Basis for Conclusions on IAS 38 *Intangible Assets*, identifiability is seen as the characteristic that conceptually distinguishes other intangible assets from goodwill. The purpose, then, is to ensure that an entity identifies and discloses its assets rather than having them subsumed into goodwill.

IAS 38 does not contain a definition of 'identifiable'. However, paragraph 12 of this standard sets down two criteria, one of which must be met for an asset to be classified as identifiable. Paragraph 12 states:

> An asset is identifiable if it either:
> (a) is separable, i.e., is capable of being separated or divided from the entity and sold, transferred, licensed, rented or exchanged, either individually or together with a related contract, identifiable asset or liability, regardless of whether the entity intends to do so; or
> (b) arises from contractual or other legal rights, regardless of whether those rights are transferable or separable from the entity or from other rights and obligations.

The criterion of separability tests whether an entity can divide an asset from other assets and deal with it as an individual asset. Not only must the asset be able to be seen as a separate item, it must be capable of being transferred to another party. Assets such as high staff morale and customer relationships may be capable of being named and discussed, and actions may be taken to adjust the levels of them within an entity, but such assets cannot be transferred to another entity. A further reason for requiring an asset to be separable before recognition is that it makes the measurability of the asset easier. Exchangeable assets will potentially have markets from which prices can be obtained, in contrast to non-exchangeable assets.

In most if not all cases, separable assets are capable of being exchanged by an entity because the entity has a *contractual or legal right* to make the exchange.

However, as noted in paragraph BC10 of the Basis for Conclusions on IAS 38:

> some contractual-legal rights establish property interests that are not readily separable from the entity as a whole. For example, under the laws of some jurisdictions some licences granted to an entity are not transferable except by sale of the entity as a whole.

The existence of the legal rights to these assets was seen as being a factor that distinguished some assets from other assets that were to be included in goodwill. Hence, separability was not seen as the only criterion for identifiability.

In his discussion of the interrelationship between tangible and intangible assets, Upton (2001, p. 61) commented: 'With control comes the ability to buy, sell, or withhold from the market — characteristics of the everyday notion of an asset.' Upton then interpreted the meaning of 'control' to require identifiability, implying that expected benefits cannot be controlled if the benefits are not separable, and the entity does not have the ability to transfer them to another entity. He also noted (p. 62):

> The definition of an asset is derived from sensible economics and everyday use of language. The more complex answer is that monetary measurement is impossible without a notion like control.

Non-physical assets cannot be recognised unless they are identifiable. The reason for this restriction is that it makes the subsequent measurement of assets easier.

Figure 10.2 contains a list of assets that could potentially meet the identifiability criteria. The list is the illustrative examples contained in the FASB's SFAS 141 (revised 2007) *Business Combinations* and the IASB's IFRS 3 *Business Combinations* (2008).

	Basis
Marketing-related intangible assets	
Trademarks, trade names, service marks, collective marks and certification marks	Contractual
Trade dress (unique colour, shape or package design)	Contractual
Newspaper mastheads	Contractual
Internet domain names	Contractual
Non-competition agreements	Contractual
Customer-related intangible assets	
Customer lists	Non-contractual
Order or production backlog	Contractual
Customer contracts and related customer relationships	Contractual
Non-contractual customer relationships	Non-contractual
Artistic-related intangible assets	
Plays, operas and ballets	Contractual
Books, magazines, newspapers and other literary works	Contractual
Musical works such as compositions, song lyrics and advertising jingles	Contractual
Pictures and photographs	Contractual
Video and audiovisual material, including motion pictures or films, music videos and television programs	Contractual
Contract-based intangible assets	
Licensing, royalty and stand-still agreements	Contractual
Advertising, construction, management, service or supply contracts	Contractual
Lease agreements (whether the acquiree is the lessee or lessor)	Contractual
Construction permits	Contractual
Franchise agreements	Contractual
Operating and broadcast rights	Contractual
Use rights such as drilling, water, air, mineral, timber cutting and route authorities	Contractual
Servicing contracts, such as mortgage servicing contracts	Contractual
Employment contracts	Contractual
Technology-based intangible assets	
Patented technology	Contractual
Computer software and mask works	Contractual
Unpatented technology	Non-contractual
Databases, including title plants	Non-contractual
Trade secrets, such as secret formulas, processes and recipes	Contractual

FIGURE 10.2 Identifiable intangible assets

Source: Illustrative examples, FASB Statement of Financial Accounting Standards No. 141 *Business Combinations* (revised 2007).

In the 1999 exposure draft (ED) to SFAS 141, the FASB provided a different list of identifiable intangible assets that might be acquired in a business combination. The list in SFAS 141 (revised), differs from the list in the 1999 ED in that the SFAS 141 (revised) list requires the application of the same identifiability criteria as in IAS 38. As a result, the following assets included in the 1999 list were excluded from the 2007 list, because they were not seen as meeting the identifiability criteria:

- customer base
- customer service capability
- presence in geographic markets or locations
- non-union status or strong labour relations
- ongoing training or recruiting programs
- outstanding credit ratings and access to capital markets
- favourable government relations.

As noted earlier, one of the problems with non-separable assets is the ability to measure them. Some assets, such as an excellent workforce and a high level of customer satisfaction, are interrelated in that very good employees will lead to high customer satisfaction. To recognise these as separate assets would raise difficulties in determining the value of one separately from the other. With the measurement of tangible assets, the emphasis is generally not on measuring the benefits from the asset, but on recording the cost of the asset. Benefits from assets are often measured at the level of a cash-generating unit rather than at the individual asset level, as is the case when determining impairment of assets (see chapter 12 of this book).

10.1.2 Lack of physical substance

Lack of physical substance is a key characteristic in the definition of an intangible asset. It is the characteristic that separates assets such as property, plant and equipment from intangible assets, in that property, plant and equipment would generally meet the criterion of identifiability.

Note at the outset that some intangible assets may be associated with a physical item, such as software contained on a computer disk. However, the asset is really the software and not the disk itself. As noted in paragraph 4 of IAS 38, judgement in some cases is required to determine which element, tangible or intangible, is most important to the classification of the asset. Use of the physical substance characteristic is interesting in that paragraph 56 of the *Framework* states:

> physical form is not essential to the existence of an asset; hence patents and copyrights, for example, are assets if future economic benefits are expected to flow from them to the entity and if they are controlled by the entity.

If physical substance is not intrinsic to the determination of assets, why then is it necessary to distinguish between physical and non-physical assets?

Many writers in the accounting literature do not agree that separating assets on a physical/non-physical basis is useful in subclassifying assets. For example:

> Indeed, once we agree that assets are future economic benefits, tangibility and even legal ownership are irrelevant for accountants; it is only some confused 'physicalist' prejudice that might persuade them otherwise (Napier & Power 1992, pp. 85–95).

> [T]he *lack of physical existence* is not of itself a satisfactory criterion for distinguishing a tangible from an intangible asset. Such assets as bank deposits, accounts receivable, and long-term investments lack physical substance, yet accountants classify them as tangible assets (Kieso & Weygandt 1992, p. 589).

There are a number of problems with defining intangible assets in terms of physical existence. The *first* problem is that it conflicts with the way in which accountants have traditionally classified assets. Non-monetary items such as investments in equity or debt instruments, leases, and deferred costs such as research and development expenditure have not generally been classified as intangible assets. Monetary items such as receivables, prepayments and deferred tax assets are similarly not classified as intangible assets.

The *second* problem relates to why accountants would want to classify assets on the basis of whether they have physical substance. There are an infinite number of ways of classifying items, such as by colour, size or shape. The choice of classification must have a purpose. Are preparers or users of accounts interested in how many assets can be touched and how many cannot be touched? It is doubtful that this is the case. In determining the appropriate criterion for classifying assets, there must be an explanation for the relevance of the classification. If useful information is the purpose of the classification, accountants' actions in practice and lack of supporting logic in the accounting literature raise doubts as to whether physical substance is the appropriate basis for classifying assets.

The *third* problem with using the physical substance criterion is the potential conflict with the *Framework* as quoted above. Based on the definition of assets as future economic benefits, all assets are intangible in that they represent a collection of perceived economic benefits. Thus, it is not the block of land or item of plant that is the asset; it is the economic benefits embodied in that physical item that constitutes the asset. A key example of this is leased assets. It is not the physical leased motor vehicle that is the asset, but the economic benefits from that physical item that constitute the asset. In relation to leased items, Stevenson (1989, p. 5) noted, 'we can quickly slip back to physical concepts of assets if we are not careful'.

The *fourth* problem with the criterion of physical substance is that tangibility is not an indication of the worth of an asset. As James (2001a) noted:

> Accounting for new-economy organisations is often problematic, because much of the value lies in intangibles: brands, customer relationships and knowledge. Spotless Services is an example. The company has maintained a relatively stable share price during a period when its tangible assets (NTA) went negative (the NTA is now positive). The reason is that Spotless's assets are mostly intangible; in recognition of this, the company no longer includes the NTA in its public accounts because, according to the company secretary, it is not relevant.

Interestingly, IAS 38 has no discussion on the characteristic of 'physical substance', yet four paragraphs are devoted to the control characteristic of an asset.

Why, then, distinguish non-physical assets? Lev (2001, p. 5) provides some answers. He defined an intangible asset as 'a claim to future benefits that does not have a physical or financial (a stock or a bond) embodiment'. He then used the terms 'intangibles', 'knowledge assets' and 'intellectual capital' interchangeably, as he saw the term 'intangibles' being used by accountants, 'knowledge assets' by economists, and 'intellectual capital' in the management and legal literature. He summarised (p. 7) intangible assets as being non-physical sources of value (claims to future benefits) generated by innovation (or discovery, relating to innovations, research and development), unique organisational designs (relating to brands, organisational structures and marketing savvy), or human resource practices (relating to unique personnel and compensation policies, recruitment successes and low turnover of employees).

The reason for distinguishing between physical and non-physical assets is that the very nature of a non-physical asset means that the accounting standards for the recognition and measurement of non-physical assets may have to be different from those for tangible assets. What are these unique characteristics and how do they cause a problem? Consider the following characteristics raised by Lev (2001):

- *Intangible assets are non-rival assets* (p. 22). They can be used at the same time for multiple purposes, such as an airline reservation system that can serve many customers. There is no opportunity cost of using the asset.
- *The assets are characterised by large fixed (sunk) costs and negligible marginal (incremental) cost* (pp. 22–3). Examples of this are the development of a headache tablet and the creation of a computer software program.
- *Many intangibles are not subject to the diminishing returns characteristic of physical assets* (p. 23). Production of more computer disks does not reduce the worth of the software asset. There may be increasing returns to scale. For example, a university may develop a software program for student enrolment that can be valuable for ongoing use by the university and may also be sold to other universities, thereby increasing the return on the original investment.
- *Intangibles may have network effects* (p. 26); that is, the value of the item increases as the number of people using the item increases. The utility of such items as a computer game (X-Box or Nintendo cube), a telephone network (Vodafone or Nokia), or a computer program (Microsoft Word or Excel spreadsheets) increases as more people use the same item.
- *Intangibles may be more difficult to manage and operate than tangible assets* (p. 32). Physical assets such as buildings are harder to steal and copy.
- *Property rights are harder to determine* (p. 33). Investments in employee training and advertising are areas where it is hard to exclude others from securing some of the benefits.
- *The relationship between the investment and the ultimate benefits is hard to track.* Are the extra sales the result of the training of employees, or because the item has become trendy?

- *The relationship between the investment and the return is skewed* (p. 39). Many investments in intangibles result in failure while some are a huge success. The investment is then often high risk. As Lev noted, a key element in intangibles is that success relies on a discovery. Investments in tangible assets tend to occur after the discovery, and alternative uses including the sale of the assets do not depend on discovery.
- *There is in general an absence of organised and competitive markets* (p. 42). Intangibles such as brand names may be sold but, given the unique nature of most intangibles, there is no active market for them. The sale of a brand name in one industry has no bearing on the potential for sale of another brand, even in the same industry. Lev (p. 47) argues that markets in intangibles lack *transparency*, so, 'details of licensing deals and alliances are generally not made public, and acquired intangibles are usually bundled with other assets'.
- *There is a high degree of uncertainty regarding the future benefits of intangible assets*. This is a general statement as there are some physical assets that also exhibit uncertainty in relation to expected benefits. As Egginton (1990, p. 194) stated:

> For example, there could be more uncertainty over the future benefits of the tangible oil and gas reserves of a section of ocean than over the future benefits of the intangible European rights to the Coca-Cola brand name.

Lev (2001, p. 47) summarised the above discussion as follows:

> Intangibles are inherently difficult to trade. Legal property rights are often hazy, contingent contracts are difficult to draw, and the cost structure of many intangibles (large sunk costs, negligible marginal costs) is not conducive to stable pricing. Accordingly, at present there are no active, organized markets in intangibles. This could soon change with the advent of Internet-based exchanges, but it will require specific enabling mechanisms, such as valuation and insurance schemes. Private trades in intangibles in the form of licensing and alliances proliferate, but they do not provide information essential for the measurement and valuation of intangibles.

Because non-physical assets have the above characteristics, they cause particular problems for accountants. The two key activities for accountants in relation to assets are the recognition and measurement of the assets. With non-physical assets, the determination of when they should be recognised (Should one wait for a point of discovery? Does an asset exist when the investment is made? Is there an asset at the point employee training occurs?), and how they should be measured (Where is the market? Can the specific benefits be isolated? Are the property rights over the expected benefits fuzzy?) is in general more difficult. Hence, the need for a specific standard on non-physical assets arises from the need for extra guidance on the recognition and measurement of those assets — not because such assets are of any greater or lesser value than physical assets. With physical assets, where there are thin markets or where the assets are of a specialised nature, the guidance in IAS 38 could be considered to be equally applicable to tangible assets.

10.1.3 Why have intangibles become important?

For quite some time, writers in the business press have noted a change in the factors that cause a company to be valuable. For example, Gottliebsen (1987, p. 6) noted a change in the composition of valuable assets in modern entities:

> Around the world, Japanese manufacturers established brands such as Sony, Toyota, Nissan, National, Honda and Mazda that have become household names. Their plans to move a vast amount of their productive capacity from Japan to the US reveal that the really fragile asset is the so-called 'tangible asset' — the bricks, mortar and plant that represented the old manufacturing capacity, now to be scrapped. The real tangible asset that endured was the brands — now to be produced for the US market from a different place.

As evidence that intangibles have been increasing in importance over time, Lev (2001, p. 9) reported the average price-to-book ratio of the Standard & Poor's (S&P) 500 companies over the period December 1977 to March 2001. Figure 10.3 on the next page shows that the mean market-to-book ratio has continuously increased over this period of time, reaching a ratio of 6:1 in March 2001. As Lev noted (p. 8), this means that of every six dollars of market value, only one dollar appears on the statement of financial position, while the remaining five dollars represent intangible assets.

Lev's arguments are supported by James (2001b), who stated that there was a growing gap between the book values of companies — a measure based mostly on tangible assets — and the market price of companies. He noted that this effect occurred not only in the United States but also in countries such as Australia:

> McKinsey estimates that in the US, the market to book value (share price versus the accounting value) for all public companies has risen from below two times in 1990 to 3.5 (it peaked at four in the bull market). This measure, called Tobin's Q, is a rough measure of the increased importance of intangible assets (because book values tend not to have accurate estimates of intangible assets such as knowledge and brands), and the rising differential suggests that intangibles are becoming more important to the value of listed companies. Stukey [the Sydney-based managing partner of consultancy McKinsey & Company] says the trend has not been as extreme in Australia, but there has been a similar increase in the gap between book value and market value. He says the Tobin's Q measure for the Australian stockmarket is now about 2.5.
>
> The Australian Stock Exchange says that, in December 1997, the average share price was 2.1 times net tangible assets. By January this year [2001], the ratio of price to net tangible assets was more than three times, a doubling of the gap between NTA and share prices in less than four years.

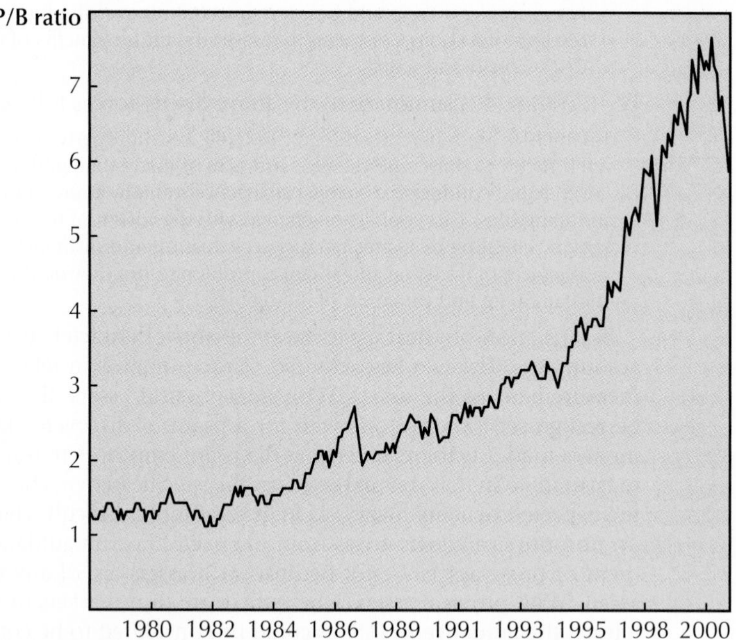

FIGURE 10.3 Average price-to-book ratio of the S&P 500 companies, December 1977 to March 2001

Source: Reproduced in Lev (2001, p. 9).

In 2007, Lloyd's Investment Blog Spot (see www.lloydsinvestment.blogspot.com) stated that the 'quintessential example of a well-known company with a high P/B [price/book] ratio is Amazon (Nasdaq: AMZN) with book value of $550 million at the end of June 2007 and current market capitalization of $35 billion, giving a strikingly high P/B of 64'. The blog also reported Boeing as having a price-to-book ratio of 13, and Apple trading at a price-to-book ratio of 9.3 compared with Microsoft at 8.7. As noted, these examples show price-to-book ratios higher than the market's average ratio of around 3. The companies quoted in the blog as having high price-to-book ratios are highly successful companies and generally leaders in their industries. However, it is also notable that these companies all rely heavily on intangible assets for their continued success with customers and in the market. In particular, they all have readily recognisable brands and rely heavily on technology for their continued success.

Looking at price-to-book ratios is seen by some writers as less than useful in making investment decisions because of the difficulties in accounting for intangible assets and the non-recognition of intangibles on the statement of financial position. For example, Cintra Scott (www.smartmoney.com) in 2001 stated:

> The very name sounds vaguely fusty. Books? Who cares about books in this digital age? And who cares about antediluvian measures like price-to-book ratios? After all, book value is mostly a reflection of

smokestack stuff: factories and oil reserves and such. It doesn't include all the stuff that supposedly really matters these days — intellectual assets like patents and trades and brands.

Because the high-tech companies that so preoccupy us these days don't have a lot of hard assets, they have low book values — which in turn means that their price-to-book ratios make them look even more absurdly expensive than their P/Es often still do.

One further example of a company with a high price-to-book ratio is the computer company DELL. As reported by Brady Willett (www.marketoracle.co.uk) in December 2007, the earnings results for DELL showed that 'the supergrowth days of the late 1990s are gone. Moreover, given that DELL's share price continues to be obscenely priced compared to book, it is also clear that shareholders still see something in DELL that I am missing? Is it really worth paying $63 billion for something that is worth $6.8 billion on paper?'

At the end of 2008 and the beginning of 2009, the global credit crunch and financial crisis had a major effect on stock prices. In the United Kingdom, the stock market left nearly a third of FTSE100 companies trading at a discount to their book value. As reported by the *Telegraph*, British Airways had a price-to-book ratio of 0.45, BHP Billiton showed 0.89 and the Royal Bank of Scotland reported 0.12. This highlights one of the difficulties in accounting for intangibles in that the measurement of these assets is more difficult than that for tangible assets.

Lev (2001, pp. 8–9) asked why intangibles are more important now than in the 1960s, 1970s and 1980s. He argued that the surge in intangibles was driven by the 'unique combination of two related economic forces' — intensified business competition and the advent of information technologies. He provided numerous examples to support his case, and the diagram in figure 10.4 illustrates his argument.

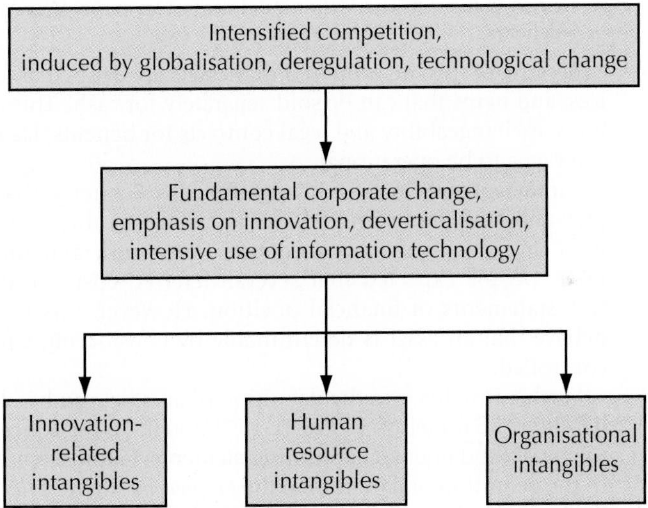

FIGURE 10.4 The ascendancy of intangibles
Source: Lev (2001, p. 18).

In support of his argument that modern entities are more dependent on their employees, Lev (2001, p. 13) quoted research published by Bhide in 2000 arguing:

> The enormous loss from employee turnover is demonstrated by the finding that 71 per cent of the firms in the Inc.500 list (a group of young, fast-growing companies) were established by persons who replicated or modified innovations developed within their former employers.

Baltes (1997, p. 7) was another who viewed a change in the world economy and believed it was more important than ever to consider accounting for 'softer' assets:

> In a decade characterized by exploding global competition, a shift from manufacturing-oriented firms to service-oriented firms and almost perpetual reengineering, more and more companies are paying far greater attention to the measurement of 'soft' or 'intangible' assets — intellectual capital, training, human resources, brand image and, most important, customer satisfaction.

The questions from an accounting perspective are whether financial reporting has experienced a similar degree of change over the same period, and whether financial statements are providing information about the variables that describe the new economy.

10.1.4 The definition of an asset and identifying intangible assets

Paragraph 49 of the *Framework* describes an asset as 'a resource controlled by the entity'. Paragraphs 13–16 of IAS 38 discuss the application of the characteristic of 'control' and the classification of certain items as intangible assets.

The crux of the debate is whether items (as noted earlier by the FASB) that probably do not meet the identifiability criterion — such as effective advertising programs, trained staff, favourable government relations and fundraising capabilities — qualify as assets. According to paragraphs 13–16 of IAS 38, items such as market and technical knowledge (paragraph 14), staff skills, specific management or technical talent (paragraph 15) and a portfolio of customers, market share, customer relationships and customer loyalty (paragraph 16) do not meet the definition of intangible assets. The key reason for excluding such items as assets is the interpretation of the term 'control' as used in the definition of an asset. According to paragraph 13 of IAS 38, control normally stems from 'legal rights that are enforceable in a court of law'. In the absence of legal rights, it is more difficult to demonstrate control.

An outspoken critic of the definition of an asset has been Walter Schuetze, former chief accountant of the Securities and Exchange Commission (SEC) in the United States and former member of the FASB. He argued (1993, p. 67): 'FASB's definition is so complex, so abstract, so open-ended, so all-inclusive, and so vague that we cannot use it to solve problems.' He further stated (2001, p. 12):

> The definition does not discriminate and help us to decide whether something or anything on the margin is an asset. That definition describes an empty box. A large empty box. A large empty box with sideboards.

Because of this, he proposed that assets are defined as 'cash, contractual claims to cash or services, and items that can be sold separately for cash'. This definition incorporates ideas of separability/exchangeability and legal contracts for benefits. He considered the concept of control to be too vague to be operational.

Samuelson (1996, p. 156) agreed with Schuetze that the definition of assets is 'too complex and ambiguous and admits too much to the category of assets'. He noted (p. 156) that, with the advent of the conceptual framework and the dropping of the matching concept, many people expected that several deferred costs would no longer appear as assets in entities' statements of financial position. However, this has not happened. Both writers did not believe that an asset is determinable by considering whether or not the expected benefits are controlled.

Further insights into the definition of an asset can be obtained by analysing the definition of a liability. As Samuelson (1996, p. 147) noted: 'In the conceptual framework of the FASB, assets are the most fundamental accounting elements. Liabilities are defined, in essence, as negative assets'. In the definition of liabilities in the *Framework*, there is no characteristic similar to control. Yet, for both asset and liability definitions, there are common characteristics of expected future benefits/outflows and existence of a past transaction. However, in determining present obligations, the mere intention to sacrifice economic benefits in the future is not sufficient to give rise to a liability. As paragraph 61 of the *Framework* states, the existence of a liability depends on the present obligation being such that:

> the economic consequences of failing to honour the obligation, for example, because of the existence of a substantial penalty, leave the entity with little, if any, discretion to avoid the outflow of resources to another party.

Although most obligations are legally enforceable because they arise from contractual or other legal rights, paragraph 60 of the *Framework* provides examples of liabilities where there are no legal contracts: 'Obligations also arise, however, from normal business practice, custom and a desire to maintain good business relations or act in an equitable manner.' For example, a provision for long-service leave and a deferred tax liability can be recognised as liabilities well before there is any legal enforceability, presumably on the grounds of past experience and/or normal business practice. Both are based on expectations of what might occur. With long-service leave provisions, provisions are based on expected retention rates because employees may change jobs before becoming eligible for payment.

Compare this with an entity that invests in its future staff by outlaying funds on training programs. The entity has invested in its staff, but it has no control over whether staff remain employed by it. Nevertheless, it has an expectation that it will receive most if not all of the benefits from the training programs. If the staff stay, the entity has control over the benefits from the increased sales that arise from the training programs. Access to the future benefits that arise from the well-trained staff who stay with the entity can be denied to other entities. Not all the expected benefits may eventuate but, if they do, they belong to the entity. In fact, if past experience indicates that the entity has a fine record of retaining staff, it can be inferred or construed from the facts in the particular situation that the benefits will flow to the entity. So, if custom and usual business practice are a guide, the benefits will flow to the entity. Although the staff could decide to go to another entity and provide it with the benefits of their training, that entity cannot argue that there are any grounds, such as normal business practice, for suggesting that this will occur. The second entity may form an expectation that the other entity's staff will change employment but there are no legal, equitable or constructive reasons for suggesting that its expectation is any more than a hope.

As noted in the Conceptual Framework Project Update on the IASB's website www.iasb.org, as of 20 May 2008, the FASB and IASB have decided to consider the following working definition of an asset:

> An *asset* of an entity is a present economic resource to which, through an enforceable right or other means, the entity has access or can limit the access of others.

An enforceable right is legally enforceable or enforceable by equivalent means, such as a professional association. This emphasis on legally enforceable rights could further narrow the recognition of resources as assets.

The debate over the 'real' assets of today's entities is heightened with the existence of Internet or dot.com entities. Some of these entities have high values but very little in non-current assets or inventory. As King and Henry (1999) noted, the value of these entities lies in their intellectual capital: 'In fact, a common saying about them is that "the assets walk out the door every night".' King and Henry did not even question whether these items were assets, being more interested in the question of reliability of measurement. They noted:

> Major banks, such as BT Commercial (part of Bankers Trust, now Deutsche Bank), have lent literally hundreds of millions of dollars to companies like Zenith, Strohs, and Florsheim with the firms' trade names and patents as collateral... Appraisals are relevant and reliable enough for America's largest banks, so they should also be relevant and reliable for individual investors.

Such difficulties in determining whether certain intangibles meet the definition of an asset caused the standard setters to introduce the further test of identifiability. By requiring identifiability for recognition of intangibles, they diffused the debate as to whether an item such as good staff relations is an asset. Regardless of whether it is an asset, it is not an intangible asset because it does not meet the identifiability criterion, and so can only be recognised, if at all, as part of goodwill. However, reducing the number of assets recognised in the financial statements because of measurement problems may also reduce the relevance of the information provided in those financial statements.

10.2 RECOGNITION AND INITIAL MEASUREMENT

IAS 38 establishes standards in relation to the recognition and initial measurement of intangible assets. In order to provide some questions to consider when analysing these standards, it is worthwhile examining some issues raised by Upton (2001). This is done in the following section.

10.2.1 Measurement and relevance issues

In his analysis of intangibles, Upton (2001, p. 53) noted that there are four criteria to consider in determining the information that should be recognised in the financial statements:

- *Definitions* — does the item meet the definition of one of the elements of financial statements?

- *Measurability* — does the item have an attribute that is measurable with sufficient reliability?
- *Relevance* — is the information about the item capable of making a difference in user decisions?
- *Reliability* — is the information representationally faithful, verifiable and neutral?

He noted further that these criteria were also subject to a cost–benefit constraint.

In this context, Upton (2001, p. 54) observed that FASB Statement No. 2 *Accounting for Research and Development* required all outlays on research and development to be charged to expense. Similarly, in IAS 38, the IASB requires all outlays on research to be expensed, and specific criteria must be met before outlays on development can be capitalised. In FASB Statement No. 2, the following reasons were given for the decision to expense outlays:

- uncertainty of future benefits
- lack of causal relationship between outlay and eventual outcome
- inability to measure future benefits
- lack of usefulness of information about capitalised costs in assessing future performance of an entity.

As Upton noted, these reasons go to the heart of the measurement and relevance issues associated with recognising items in the financial statements. He made a number of insightful comments concerning the issues of measurement and relevance, as discussed below.

Issues of measurement

Upton (2001) made the following observations:

- *Without a clear boundary, there is a risk that any measurement will double-count.* One problem in recognising and measuring intangible assets is the possibility that the same benefits are also included in the measurement of another intangible. For example, if an entity has good staff morale, this will contribute as well to a high level of customer satisfaction. Both lead to the increase in the profitability of an entity. However, measuring these two items separately creates the danger of valuing the same income stream twice. If measurements are based purely on the capitalisation of costs, this is less likely to happen.
- *Retrospective capitalisation may be a useful measure.* If all outlays on areas such as research are initially expensed, it may be useful to allow the retrospective capitalisation of these outlays when a level of success is achieved. Whether the capitalisation of all past outlays is appropriate is, however, questionable.
- *Recognition of in-process assets may be a useful measure.* When an entity outlays funds to either develop some software or find a cure for some disease, the expected results are highly uncertain. One possibility in terms of overcoming the 'expense everything' syndrome is to have a class of in-process assets, and to accumulate costs into in-process accounts. There is no doubt that some in-process information is valuable. In fact, effort expended to date is information for which other entities are willing to pay. An analogy can be made with financial options, for which there may be no value at expiration date.
- *Cross-fertilisation and multigenerational factors.* In some research programs, such as the development of medical cures, it is possible that research will never be totally wasted. The researcher may not find the desired cure for AIDS but, as a result of the research, the information discovered about blood may assist in providing solutions for other medical problems. Expensing purely because no cure for AIDS was found is being too prescriptive in relation to relating outlays to specified outcomes. Similarly, amounts may be spent on developing software that is continuously being updated. However, elements of the software in the first generation device may still be an important foundation in subsequent devices. To expense all previous outlays just because a new version of the asset is developed is again short-sighted.
- *There are two 'gaps' that frustrate attempts to recognise intangible assets.* The first is the 'time gap', which is the gap between the outlay and the determination of the outcome. The longer the gap, the more reluctant standard setters will be to allow capitalisation. The second is the 'correlation gap', which relates the expense to the eventual outcome. For example, were outlays on the AIDS cure related to the information obtained on blood clotting?

Issues of relevance

Upton (2001) also made the following observations:

- *Relevance of capitalised cost information.* An adage popular in the oil industry is 'What you spend doesn't matter. What you find does.' With many intangible assets, the level of expenditure is not proportional to the eventual worth of the outcome. To capitalise costs, then, does not indicate the potential worth of the outcome or the asset, assuming it has any.

- *Uncertainty does not mean irrelevance*. Accounting does not require certainty for information to be useful. As noted earlier, companies are willing to pay for in-process assets, even though the eventual result is uncertain. It is also true that any entity that does not spend money on developing software or finding medical cures will not produce these products. In terms of causal relationships, entities doing drug research will find drug cures even if they are not the ones originally sought. Potentially causal relationships should not be sought on individual research projects but rather on a combination of research projects.
- *Cost information may not be as relevant as fair value but may be more reliable*. One of the problems of accumulating costs is that the asset may be overstated because the level of costs does not directly relate to the level of benefits. However, the accumulation of costs is at least a reliable measure. If an entity attempts to measure the fair value of an intangible asset, even though the fair value may be more relevant the measure may be less reliable. To choose between accumulated costs and fair value is to trade off relevance and reliability. However, just because something can be measured reliably should not mean that this is what should be disclosed. The measurement attribute must be a relevant one.
- *Volatility of information*. The worth of an entity is affected by events such as a safety recall, a shift in customer tastes, or the success of rival entities and their brands. If information about these events is not disclosed and disclosure is limited to the physical assets, can users obtain a real view of what is happening to the entity? The information on these items may be volatile, but to exclude them may create a financial impression that the entity is in a constantly steady state.

As Upton noted, the determination of relevance and reliable measurement is subject to a cost–benefit test. The costs of any rules on intangibles are borne by the entities preparing the financial statements and by the auditors. The users of the financial statements also incur costs relating to keeping up with accounting rules and adapting their financial analysis models. Unfortunately, although the costs may be quantifiable, the benefits in terms of the incremental information to the users are difficult to measure. Although some research has shown that disclosure of capitalised research and development costs is useful, the benefits relative to the costs have not been empirically demonstrated.

10.2.2 Criteria for recognition and initial measurement

After determining that an asset exists and that it meets the definition of an intangible asset, the asset must meet the two criteria in paragraph 21 of IAS 38 before it can be recognised. The criteria are:

- it is *probable* that the future economic benefits attributable to the asset will flow to the entity
- the *cost* of the asset can be measured *reliably*.

These criteria are the same as those for the recognition of property, plant and equipment in IAS 16 *Property, Plant and Equipment*. If the cost of the asset cannot be reliably measured, but the fair value is determinable, an asset cannot be recognised under either IAS 16 or IAS 38 because both standards require initial measurement at cost. As noted later, this has consequences for the recognition of intangible assets that are internally generated rather than acquired, as well as causing differences in the statements of financial position of entities that internally generate assets and those that acquire assets.

In relation to the initial measurement of an intangible asset, paragraph 24 of IAS 38 states: 'An intangible asset shall be measured initially at cost.' With the reliable measurement of cost as one of the recognition criteria, this cost forms the basis for initial measurement.

10.2.3 Separate acquisition

In recognising assets acquired separately, paragraph 25 of IAS 38 notes that 'the probability recognition criterion in paragraph 21(a) is always considered to be satisfied for separately acquired intangible assets'. The standard setters argue that the price paid for the asset automatically takes into account the probability of the expected benefits being received; hence, it is unnecessary to apply a further probability test. For example, if an asset had expected cash inflows of $1000, and the probability of these inflows being received was 40%, then an acquirer would pay $400 for the asset. The standard setters argue that these benefits are now automatically probable. Further, paragraph 26 notes that the cost of a separately acquired intangible asset can usually be measured reliably. The measurement of cost may be more difficult if the exchange involves the acquirer giving up non-monetary assets rather than cash.

As with property, plant and equipment, the cost of an asset is the sum of the purchase price and the directly attributable costs (IAS 38, paragraph 27). The purchase price is measured as the fair value of what is given up by the acquirer in order to acquire the asset, and the directly attributable costs are those necessarily incurred to get the asset into the condition where it is capable of operating in the manner intended by management. (These concepts are discussed further in this book in sections 9.3.1 and 9.3.2 of chapter 9 in relation to property, plant and equipment.) The principles of accounting for separately acquired intangibles and property, plant and equipment are the same.

For not-for-profit entities, paragraph Aus24.1 requires that where an asset is acquired at no cost or for a nominal cost, the cost is its fair value as at the date of acquisition.

10.2.4 Acquisition as part of a business combination

When assets are acquired as part of a business combination, they are initially recognised at fair value in accordance with IFRS 3 *Business Combinations*. According to paragraph 33 of IAS 38, the cost of such an intangible asset is its fair value at the acquisition date. This is probably a debatable proposition, particularly if there exists a bargain purchase.

As with separately acquired assets, paragraph 33 of IAS 38 provides that, where intangible assets are acquired as part of a business combination, the effect of probability is reflected in the fair value measurement of the asset. Hence, the probability recognition criterion is automatically met. In IFRS 3 paragraph 37(c), the criterion for recognition of an intangible asset acquired in a business combination is simply that 'its fair value can be measured reliably'. As noted in paragraph BC18 of the Basis for Conclusions on IAS 38, the assumption that the probability test is automatically met conflicts with the recognition criteria for assets in the *Framework*. However, the IASB expects to revisit this inconsistency in a forthcoming concepts project.

Further, it is argued in paragraph 35 of IAS 38 that the requirement for reliability of measurement is always met as sufficient information always exists to measure reliably the fair value of the asset.

In dissenting from the issue of IAS 38, Professor Whittington (one of the IASB members) argued that the probability test in paragraph 21(a) should be applied in testing the recognition of all intangibles, stating that issues relating to the recognition criteria in the *Framework* should be resolved before having different recognition criteria for intangible assets acquired in a business combination. The justification for different criteria is presumably that there is an increased relevance of information in reporting the separate intangible assets rather than subsuming them into goodwill.

The application of these recognition requirements means that an acquirer must, in recognising separately the acquiree's intangible assets, recognise intangible assets that the acquiree has not recognised in its records, such as in-process research and development that cannot be recognised under IAS 38 as internally generated assets (discussed later in this section). As noted in paragraph 34, recognition by an acquirer of an acquiree's in-process research and development project only depends on whether the project meets the definition of an intangible asset. It can be seen that entities that acquire intangible assets in a business combination will be able, and in fact are required, to recognise intangible assets that are not separately recognisable when acquired by other means.

Paragraph 24 of IAS 38 requires intangible assets to be measured at cost initially. In a business combination, the costs of the individual assets acquired are measured by reference to the fair values of those assets. Paragraphs 39–41 discuss the measurement of these fair values. Various measures of these fair values are possible:

- *Quoted market prices in an active market*. An active market is defined in paragraph 8 as one which has all the following conditions:
  (a) the items traded within the market are homogeneous
  (b) willing buyers and sellers can normally be found at any time
  (c) prices are available to the public.

Where there is an active market, the fair value is determined by reference to quoted market prices. It is expected that active markets will be rare for intangible assets.

- *Recent transactions*. Where there is no active market, reference must be made to other sources of information, such as recent transactions in the same or similar items. One of the problems with intangible assets is that their unique nature in many cases precludes the use of information from other transactions.
- *Measurement techniques*. With the increasing importance of intangible assets, there has been a growing establishment of entities who specialise in measuring intangible assets, particularly brand names. These valuation firms measure the worth of intangible assets by using variations of present value techniques, and multiples of variables such as royalty rates. As noted in paragraph 41 of IAS 38, these methods should 'reflect current transactions and practices in the industry'.

10.2.5 Acquisition by way of a government grant

According to paragraph 44 of IAS 38, some intangible assets, such as licences to operate radio or television stations, are allocated to entities via government grants. These intangibles are accounted for in accordance with IAS 20 *Accounting for Government Grants and Disclosure of Government Assistance*, whereby an entity may choose to initially recognise both the intangible asset and the grant at fair value. If an entity does not choose to use the fair value measurement option, it will recognise the asset initially at a nominal amount plus directly attributable costs.

10.2.6 Exchanges of intangible assets

One of the problems with exchanges of intangible assets is the reliable measure of the cost of the acquired asset, particularly where comparable market transactions are infrequent. The following measures need to be considered in determining that cost:

- the fair value of the asset given up
- the fair value of the asset received, if this is more clearly evident than the fair value of the asset given up
- the carrying amount of the asset given up, when neither of the fair values can be measured reliably.

10.2.7 Internally generated goodwill

Paragraph 49 of IAS 38 states categorically that internally generated goodwill is not recognised as an asset. Hence, goodwill can be recognised only when it is acquired as part of a business combination and measured in accordance with IFRS 3 *Business Combinations*.

The reason given in paragraph 49 of IAS 38 for non-recognition is that goodwill is not identifiable; that is, it is not separable, nor does it arise from contractual or other legal rights. This argument seems strange because identifiability is the test for recognising an intangible asset separately from goodwill, rather than recognising goodwill itself. A second reason given for non-recognition, as stated in paragraph 49, is that the cost of internally generated goodwill cannot be reliably determined. The fair value of goodwill could be determined by comparing the fair value of the entity as a whole and subtracting the sum of the fair values of the identifiable net assets of the entity. However, under IAS 38, the principle for recognition is that identifiable intangible assets as well as goodwill must initially be measured at cost, not at fair value. As is discussed in more detail in the next section, this principle makes the recognition of internally generated intangibles harder than the recognition of acquired intangibles.

10.2.8 Internally generated intangible assets

Accounting for internally generated assets requires the application of a number of extra rules, potentially leaving the standard setters open to criticism for lack of consistency in the accounting for acquired intangibles versus internally generated intangibles. As Jenkins and Upton (2001, p. 6) noted, genealogy is not an essential characteristic of an asset. Therefore, the accounting should not automatically be different according to whether an asset arises from a business combination or is internally generated.

The problem from an accounting point of view with internally generated intangibles is determining at what point in time an asset should be recognised. An entity may outlay funds in an exploratory project, such as developing software to overcome a specific problem, or designing a tool for a special purpose. There is no guarantee of success at the start of the project. The program may not work or the tool may be unsatisfactory for the purpose. Should the accountant capitalise the costs from the beginning of the project, or wait until there is some indication of success? A further problem with some intangible assets such as brand names is whether the costs outlaid relate solely to increasing the worth of the brand name or simply to enhancing the overall reputation of the entity.

The standard setters' solution to the problem of when to begin capitalising costs is to classify the generation of the asset into two phases: the research phase and the development phase. These terms are defined in paragraph 8 of IAS 38 as follows:

> *Research* is original and planned investigation undertaken with the prospect of gaining new scientific or technical knowledge and understanding.
>
> *Development* is the application of research findings or other knowledge to a plan or design for the production of new or substantially improved materials, devices, products, processes, systems or services before the start of commercial production or use.

It can be seen from these definitions that the earlier stages of a project are defined as research and, at some point in time, the project moves from a research phase to a development phase. Examples of research activities are given in paragraph 56 of IAS 38, such as the search for new knowledge or for alternatives for materials, devices, products, processes, systems or services. Examples of development activities are found in paragraph 59, such as the design, construction and operation of a non-commercial pilot plant, and the design of pre-production prototypes and models. From an accounting perspective, expenditure on research is expensed when incurred (paragraph 54), and expenditure on development is capitalised as an intangible asset. It is obviously important to be able to distinguish one phase from the other.

Paragraph 57 of IAS 38 is the key paragraph in this regard. It contains a list of criteria, all of which must be met in order for a development outlay to be capitalised. In order to capitalise development outlays, an entity must be able to demonstrate all of the following:

> (a) the technical feasibility of completing the intangible asset so that it will be available for use or sale;
> (b) its intention to complete the intangible asset and use or sell it;
> (c) its ability to use or sell the intangible asset;
> (d) how the intangible asset will generate probable future economic benefits. Among other things, the entity can demonstrate the existence of a market for the output of the intangible asset or the intangible asset itself or, if it is to be used internally, the usefulness of the intangible asset;
> (e) the availability of adequate technical, financial and other resources to complete the development and to use or sell the intangible asset; and
> (f) its ability to measure reliably the expenditure attributable to the intangible asset during its development.

Given the degree of difficulty in distinguishing research activities from development activities, it seems simpler to disregard any attempt to distinguish between the two activities and just allow capitalisation when the criteria in paragraph 57 are met. In other words, for an entity to decide whether to capitalise an outlay, the decision will not be based on an application of the definitions of research and development, but rather on whether the criteria in paragraph 57 are met. If the criteria are met, it will then be decided that the project is in the development stage. The definitions of research and development are then superfluous. The recognition criteria for an internally generated intangible asset are then those contained in paragraphs 18, 21 and 57 of IAS 38.

The criteria in paragraph 57 are designed to help determine whether, in relation to a project, it is probable that there will be future benefits flowing to the entity. If there are markets for the output, the project is feasible, and the resources are available to complete the project, then it becomes probable that there will be future cash inflows. The criteria in paragraph 57 are then an elaboration — the provision of more detailed requirements — on the criteria in paragraph 18. This approach in IAS 38 provides more certainty in obtaining comparable accounting across entities than simply relying on an accounting principle that states that, if there are probable expected future benefits, an entity should capitalise the outlay.

If the criteria in paragraph 57 are all met, IAS 38 requires the intangible asset to be measured at cost. This cost is not, however, the total cost relating to the project. The amount to be capitalised is the 'sum of expenditure incurred from the date when the intangible asset first meets the recognition criteria in paragraphs 21, 22 and 57' (paragraph 65). Paragraph 71 explicitly prohibits the reinstatement of amounts previously expensed. Recognition of an asset that is not yet available for use requires an entity to subject that asset to an annual impairment test as per IAS 36 *Impairment of Assets*. Paragraphs 66–67 of IAS 38 note that the cost comprises all directly attributable costs necessary to create, produce and prepare the asset to be capable of operating in a manner intended by management, and provide examples of such costs as well as items that are not components of the cost.

In his discussion of this issue, Lev argued that the immediate expensing of all outlays distorted current and future earnings. He stated (2001, p. 124):

> Given the heightened uncertainty, it makes sense to recognize intangible investments when the uncertainty about benefits is considerably resolved.

His solution to the problem was to have a recognition principle based on the achievement of technological feasibility. He argued (p. 125):

> A major advantage of the proposed asset recognition is its allowance of managers to convey important information about the progress and success of the development program. Indiscriminate capitalization of all expenditures on intangibles does not provide such information.

It can be seen that the criteria in IAS 38 are in line with Lev's views, although the feasibility expressed in the standard require both technological and economic feasibility.

Upton (2001, p. 66) viewed the identification of such a recognition principle as 'interesting', but was still concerned that entities could manipulate the criteria to suit their ends:

> Might some managers conjure assets from thin air in an attempt to pump up the balance sheet? Might others turn a blind eye to discovered assets in an attempt to pump up future operating results (by avoiding amortization)? Both possibilities are real, and either could damage the credibility of financial reporting.

Jenkins and Upton (2001, p. 8) noted, first, that the conceptual framework does not require certainty of future benefits before the recognition of an asset and, second, that there is evidence that companies are willing to pay for in-process research and development even though the ultimate result may be uncertain. Upton's suggestion (2001, p. 66) for resolving the problem was to couple the criterion of technological feasibility with a requirement for retrospective capitalisation or value-based measurement. In either case, management would be required to establish the asset, rather than having no asset because all outlays were expensed, and subsequent periods would bear their share of the amortisation of the asset as well as recognition of the benefits.

It may seem that the use of the terms 'research' and 'development', which may be associated with such assets as patents and software development, are not applicable to all internally generated intangibles, such as brand names. However, it needs to be remembered that all intangible assets must meet the identifiability criterion, one part of which is separability, which is the capability of being separated and sold or transferred. In relation to certain assets, paragraph 63 of IAS 38 provides a major exclusion in an entity's ability to capitalise internally generated intangibles:

> Internally generated brands, mastheads, publishing titles, customer lists and items similar in substance shall not be recognised as intangible assets.

The standard setters concluded that, even though the criteria in paragraph 57(a)–(f) are met, the listed items in paragraph 63 cannot be recognised. As paragraph 64 states, the standard setters do not believe that the costs associated with developing the listed assets can be distinguished from the cost of developing the business as a whole. For example, it may be argued that funds spent on developing a brand name also enhance the overall image of the entity, and therefore the outlays cannot be solely attributable to the brand name.

The requirements under IAS 38 to recognise acquired brands only is reflected in the disclosures made by the Christian Dior Group in its 2007 financial statements, as shown in figure 10.5.

1.8 Brands, trade names and other intangible assets

Only acquired brands and trade names that are well known and individually identifiable are recorded as assets at their values calculated on their dates of acquisition.

Costs incurred in creating a new brand or developing an existing brand are expensed.

3.3 Brands and trade names

The breakdown of brands and trade names by business group is as follows:

	2007			2006	2005
(EUR millions)	**Gross**	Amortization and impairment	**Net**	Net	Net
Christian Dior Couture	**25**	—	**25**	25	25
Wines and Spirits	**2 821**	(8)	**2 813**	2 615	2 612
Fashion and Leather Goods	**3 866**	(303)	**3 563**	3 608	3 654
Perfumes and Cosmetics	**1 281**	(18)	**1 263**	1 267	1 274
Watches and Jewelry	**842**	(7)	**835**	859	887
Selective Retailing	**3 060**	(1 240)	**1 820**	2 003	2 204
Other activities	**20**	(1)	**19**	48	47
Brands and trade names	**11 915**	(1 577)	**10 338**	10 425	10 703

The brands and trade names recognized in the table above are those that the Group has acquired. As of December 31, 2007 the principal acquired brands and trade names are:

- Wines and Spirits: Hennessy, Moët, Veuve Clicquot, Krug, Château d'Yquem, Belvedere, Glenmorangie and Newton Vineyards;
- Fashion and Leather Goods: Louis Vuitton, Fendi, Celine, Loewe, Donna Karan New York, Givenchy, Kenzo, Berluti, Thomas Pink and Pucci;
- Perfumes and Cosmetics: Parfums Christian Dior, Guerlain, Parfums Givenchy, Make Up for Ever, BeneFit Cosmetics, Fresh and Acqua di Parma;
- Watches and Jewelry: TAG Heuer, Zenith, Fred and Chaumet;
- Selective Retailing: DFS Galleria, Sephora and Le Bon Marché;
- Other Activities: Investir print media publications.

These brands and trade names are recognized in the balance sheet at their value determined as of the date of their acquisition by the Group, which may be much less than their value in use or their net selling price as of the closing date for the consolidated financial statements. This is notably the case for the brands Louis Vuitton, and Christian Dior Couture, or the trade name Sephora, with the understanding that this list must not be considered as exhaustive.

Brands developed by the Group, notably Dom Pérignon champagnes, as well as the De Beers trade name developed as a joint-venture with the De Beers Group, are not capitalized in the balance sheet. Les Echos, the press publication, will be recognized as of fiscal year 2008.

FIGURE 10.5 Recognition of brands, Christian Dior Group
Source: Christian Dior Group (2007, pp. 97, 110–11).

Note that whereas the Christian Dior Group has tried to provide extensive information on its brands, the application of IAS 38 is still restrictive in allowing companies to recognise brands as assets.

The Swatch Group owns several companies that do research (Asulab, EM Microelectronic-Marin, Oscilloquartz SA), produce movements (ETA SA, F. Piguet) and produce pieces of watches (Comadur), as well as numerous watch brands, including Breguet, Blancpain, Jacquet Droz, Glashütte Original, Union Glashütte, Léon Hatot, Omega SA, Tiffany & Co., Rado, Longines, Swatch, Tissot, Calvin Klein, Certina, Mido, Pierre Balmain, Hamilton, Flik Flak and Endura. Figure 10.6 shows the company's policy on accounting for internally generated intangible assets as described in its 2007 annual report.

To assess the criteria for recognition as an intangible asset, an entity separates the generation of the internally generated intangible assets into a research phase and a development phase. Costs linked to development projects are recognized as intangible assets provided future economic benefits are anticipated. Other research and development costs are recognized as expenses. Once a product enters into commercial production, the capitalized development costs are amortized over the period of anticipated earnings. The amortization period applied does not exceed five years.

FIGURE 10.6 Accounting for internally generated intangible assets, Swatch Group
Source: Swatch Group (2007, p. 158).

The Swatch Group reported the information in figure 10.7 in its 2007 annual report in relation to its intangible assets.

(CHF million)	Capitalized development costs	Other intangible assets	Goodwill	Total
Historical cost, 1 January 2007	**27**	**159**	**226**	**412**
Translation differences		2		2
Acquisitions of subsidiaries (Note 14)		1	6	7
Additions	8	19		27
Disposals		−13		−13
Transfers	−2	2		0
Historical cost, 31 December 2007	**33**	**170**	**232**	**435**
Accumulated amortization, 1 January 2007	**−8**	**−89**	**0**	**−97**
Translation differences		−1		−1
Annual amortization	−4	−12		−16
Impairment				0
Amortization on disposals		13		13
Transfers				0
Accumulated amortization, 31 December 2007	**−12**	**−89**	**0**	**−101**
Net book value, 31 December 2007	**21**	**81**	**232**	**334**

FIGURE 10.7 Disclosure of intangible assets, Swatch Group
Source: Swatch Group (2007, p. 176).

Note that there are no disclosures in relation to brands as assets. In the financial review section of the Swatch Group's 2007 annual report, it was stated:

> A particular highlight of 2008 will be the Summer Olympic Games, which traditionally take place every four years. The highly visible presence of Omega as timekeeping and data handling partner, which will perform this role for the 23rd time in the history of the Olympic Games, will further promote awareness of the brand worldwide.

The Swatch Group owns a large number of valuable brands; yet, these are not shown as assets in the financial statements. The role of IAS 38 in achieving disclosure of relevant financial information concerning intangible assets is therefore questionable.

10.2.9 Explaining the non-recognition of internally generated assets

There are a number of problems associated with the treatment of internally generated assets versus that required for acquired intangibles. In particular, there are inconsistencies in the accounting for internally generated intangibles and intangibles acquired in a business combination. Note, in this regard:

(a) *The initial recognition of intangible assets.* IAS 38 requires intangible assets to be initially recognised at cost. However, for assets acquired in a business combination, an intangible asset can be recognised at fair value. Internally generated intangibles cannot be recognised, even if the fair value can be reliably measured. For example, outlays on research cannot be recognised as an asset. However, if an entity acquires another entity that has in-process research, an intangible asset can be recognised if the fair value can be measured reliably. Further, the research so recognised can be revalued if this class of asset is measured at fair value.

(b) *The measurement of fair value.* One of the reasons given in paragraph BCZ38(c) of the Basis for Conclusions on IAS 38 for disallowing the recognition of intangible assets is the impossibility of determining the fair value of an intangible asset reliably if no active market exists for the asset, and active markets are unlikely to exist for internally generated intangible assets. However, for intangible assets recognised in a business combination, it is assumed that fair value can be measured (reliably, it is hoped) without the existence of active markets. IAS 38 allows the use of other measurement techniques or even what an entity would have paid based on the best information available. Hence, in a business combination, the fair values of intangibles can be measured reliably using measures determined outside an active market, but these same measures cannot be used to measure the fair values of internally generated assets for asset recognition purposes. As a protection, the requirements of IAS 36 *Impairment of Assets* can be applied to both acquired and internally generated intangible assets.

(c) *Brands, mastheads, publishing titles and customer lists.* Paragraph 63 of IAS 38 prohibits the recognition of internally generated brands and items similar in substance. However, such assets can be recognised when acquired in a business combination (as well as if acquired as a separate asset). As far as the measurement of the fair value of these assets goes, the argument presented in point (b) applies — if the fair value of a brand can be determined in a business combination then it can be determined if internally generated. Further, it has been noted previously that the reason given in paragraph 64 of IAS 38 for non-recognition of internally generated brands is that the cost of these items 'cannot be distinguished from the cost of developing the business as a whole'. If this argument is true for internally generated brands, then surely it is equally true for acquired brands. How is it possible in a business combination to distinguish acquired brands from acquired goodwill? How can the cost of acquiring a brand in a business combination be distinguished from acquiring a business as a whole?

Lev (2001, pp. 85–91) believed that the non-capitalisation of internally generated intangibles is a question of politics, stating:

> The main reason for the intangibles' information failure lies, in my opinion, in the complex web of motives of the major players in the information arena: managers, auditors, and well-connected financial analysts.

He argued:

- *Managers prefer to inflate future profits.* Where major investments in research and development are written off, this is a guarantee that future revenues and earnings derived from these acquisitions will be reported unencumbered by the major expense item, the amortisation of the intangible asset. The effects on ratios such as rates of return on assets and equity are better in the future if write-offs occur now rather than periodic amortisations later.
- *Investors generally consider write-offs as one-time items, of no consequence for valuation.* A number of large hits is considered better than periodic amortisation. Investors discount the effect of one-time write-offs and cheer the improved profitability of subsequent years.
- *Immediate expensing obviates the need to provide explanations in case of failure.* Writing off assets denotes failure, and managers prefer to avoid questions and lawsuits. Further failure always attracts more attention than success.

Upton (2001, pp. 80–3) raised further arguments to support the non-recognition of intangible assets:

- *Cost and benefit.* Accounting rules involve entities in incurring costs, such as those for running analytical models, measuring fair values, and paying auditors to review the measures.
- *Lack of relevance of capitalised numbers.* Is there a sufficient link between the capitalised costs and the expected future benefits? For knowledge-based assets, the measurement of the benefits may be impossible.
- *Volatility.* Recognising intangible assets in the statement of financial position produces a subtle source of volatility in, or at least reduced control over, reported income. If intangible

assets are recognised and amortised, the amortisation continues without regard to current activity.

10.2.10 Recognition of an expense

Paragraphs 68–71 of IAS 38 cover the issue of when expenditure on an intangible asset should be expensed. However, if the previous rules in IAS 38 are followed, then the appropriate outlays are expensed when the criteria are not met. These paragraphs add nothing particularly new to the accounting for intangible assets.

Paragraph 71, however, has major import. This paragraph prohibits the recognition at a later date of past expenditure as assets. In other words, if amounts relating to research have been expensed, these amounts cannot then be capitalised, nor can appropriate adjustments to equity be made, when an intangible asset is created at the development stage. As noted earlier, Upton suggested a possible role for the retroactive capitalisation of expenses, because it forced entities to recognise and subsequently amortise their assets. Upton (2001, p. 64) also noted that retroactive capitalisation did not offer a solution to the non-capitalisation of assets such as brands, as these assets lack a series of discrete expenditures. It may be that acceptance of fair value as well as historical cost measures is necessary to solve some of these issues.

10.3 MEASUREMENT SUBSEQUENT TO INITIAL RECOGNITION

10.3.1 Measurement basis

Consistent with IAS 16, after the initial recognition of an intangible asset at cost, an entity must choose for each class of intangible asset whether to measure the assets using the *cost model* or the *revaluation model* — see paragraph 72. (These models are discussed in greater detail in chapter 9 of this book.)

Cost model

Under the cost model, the asset is recorded at the initial cost of acquisition and is then subject to amortisation (see section 10.3.3 of this chapter) and impairment testing (see chapter 12 of this book).

Revaluation model

Under the revaluation model, the asset is carried at fair value, and is subject to amortisation and impairment charges. As with property, plant and equipment, if this model is chosen, revaluations are made with sufficient regularity so that the carrying amount of the asset does not materially differ from the current fair value at the end of the reporting period.

One specification that applies to intangible assets but is not required for property, plant and equipment is how the fair value is to be measured. Under paragraph 75 of IAS 38, the fair value must be determined by reference to an active market. An active market is defined in paragraph 8 of IAS 38 as a market where items traded are homogeneous, where willing buyers and sellers can normally be found at any time, and where prices are available to the public. This means that an intangible asset acquired in a business combination and measured at fair value using some measurement technique cannot subsequently use that same measurement technique if it adopts the revaluation model. In the absence of an active market, the intangible asset would be kept at the fair value determined at the date of the business combination and accounted for by the cost basis. As paragraph 76 notes, the choice of revaluation model does not allow the recognition of intangible assets that cannot be recognised initially at cost. However, paragraph 77 allows an asset for which only part of the cost was recognised to be fully revalued to fair value.

Paragraph 78 of IAS 38 states that intangibles such as brands, newspaper mastheads, patents and trademarks cannot be measured at fair value, as there is no active market for these assets because they are unique. As with the recognition of these types of intangible assets, the standard setters have stated specifically that they can be measured only at cost.

Selection of the revaluation model requires all assets in the one class to be measured at fair value. Because of the insistence on using active markets for the measurement of fair value, the standard recognises that there will be cases where fair values cannot be determined for all assets within one class. Hence, under paragraph 81 of IAS 38, where there is no active market for an asset, the asset can be measured at cost even if the class is measured using the revaluation model. Further, if the ability to measure the asset at fair value disappears because the market for the asset no longer meets the criteria to be classified as active, the asset is carried at the latest revalued amount and effectively accounted for under the cost model. If the market again becomes active, the revaluation model can be resumed.

Accounting for intangible assets measured using the revaluation model is exactly the same as for property, plant and equipment (see chapter 9). Where there is a revaluation increment, the asset is increased and the increase is credited directly to a revaluation reserve. However, if the revaluation increment reverses a previous revaluation decrement relating to the same asset, the revaluation increase is recognised as income (IAS 38 paragraph 85). Any accumulated amortisation is eliminated at the time of revaluation.

Where there is a revaluation decrement, the decrease is recognised as an expense unless there has been a previous revaluation increment. In the latter case, the adjustment must first be made against any existing revaluation reserve before recognising an expense (IAS 38 paragraph 86). Any accumulated amortisation is eliminated at the time of the revaluation.

As with a revaluation reserve on property, plant and equipment, paragraph 87 of IAS 38 states that the revaluation reserve may be transferred to retained earnings when the reserve is realised on the retirement or disposal of the asset. Alternatively, the revaluation reserve may progressively be taken to retained earnings in proportion to the amortisation of the asset.

10.3.2 Subsequent expenditures

Paragraph 20 of IAS 38 discusses subsequent expenditures in general. It is argued in this paragraph that the unique nature of intangibles means that subsequent expenditures should be expensed rather than capitalised. Subsequent expenditures maintain expected benefits rather than increase them. Further, with many subsequent expenditures, it may be difficult to attribute them to specific intangible assets rather than to the entity as a whole. Paragraph 20 notes that with the paragraph 63 intangibles, whether acquired or internally generated, subsequent expenditures are always expensed.

Paragraph 42 provides specific guidance on subsequent expenditures relating to acquired in-process research and development projects. Effectively, the same criteria for initially recognising an asset and expensing are applied to account for subsequent expenditures. The results of this application are:

- to expense research outlays
- to expense development outlays not meeting the criteria in paragraph 57
- to add to the acquired in-process research or development project if the development expenditure satisfies the paragraph 57 criteria.

10.3.3 Amortisation of intangible assets

Useful life

A key determinant in the amortisation process for intangible assets is whether the useful life is finite or indefinite. If finite, then the asset has to be amortised over that life. If the asset has an indefinite life, then there is no annual amortisation charge. Paragraph 88 of IAS 38 states:

> An entity shall assess whether the useful life of an intangible asset is finite or indefinite and, if finite, the length of, or number of production or similar units constituting, that useful life. An intangible asset shall be regarded by the entity as having an indefinite useful life when, based on an analysis of all the relevant factors, there is no foreseeable limit to the period over which the asset is expected to generate net cash inflows for the entity.

The term 'indefinite' does not mean that the asset has an infinite life, that is, that it is going to last forever. As paragraph 91 notes, an indefinite life means that, with the proper maintenance, there is no foreseeable end to the life of the asset. Paragraph 90 provides a list of factors that should be considered in determining the useful life of the asset:

- the expected use of the asset by the entity and whether the asset could be managed efficiently by another management team

- typical product life cycles for the asset, and public information on estimates of useful lives of similar assets that are used in a similar way
- technical, technological, commercial or other types of obsolescence
- the stability of the industry, and changes in market demand
- expected actions by competitors
- the level of maintenance expenditure required and the entity's ability and intent to reach such a level
- the period of control over the asset and legal or similar limits on the use of the asset
- whether the useful life of the asset depends on the useful lives of other assets of the entity.

Paragraph 94 of IAS 38 notes that, as a general rule, assets whose lives depend on contractual or legal lives will be amortised over those lives or shorter periods in some cases. If renewal is possible, then the useful life applied can include the renewal period providing there is evidence to support renewal by the entity without significant cost.

Figure 10.8 contains two examples from those in the illustrative examples accompanying IAS 38 in relation to the assessment of useful lives.

Example: An acquired broadcasting licence that expires in 5 years
The broadcasting licence is renewable every 10 years if the entity provides at least an average level of service to its customers and complies with the relevant legislative requirements. The licence may be renewed indefinitely at little cost and has been renewed twice before the most recent acquisition. The acquiring entity intends to renew the licence indefinitely and evidence supports its ability to do so. Historically, there has been no compelling challenge to the licence renewal. The technology used in broadcasting is not expected to be replaced by another technology at any time in the foreseeable future. Therefore, the licence is expected to contribute to the entity's net cash inflows indefinitely.

The broadcasting licence would be treated as having an indefinite useful life because it is expected to contribute to the entity's net cash inflows indefinitely. Therefore, the licence would not be amortised until its useful life is determined to be finite. The licence would be tested for impairment under IAS 36 annually and whenever there is an indication that it may be impaired.

Example: An acquired trademark used to identify and distinguish a leading consumer product that has been a market-share leader for the past 8 years
The trademark has a remaining legal life of 5 years but is renewable every 10 years at little cost. The acquiring entity intends to renew the trademark continuously and evidence supports its ability to do so. An analysis of (1) product life cycles, (2) market, competitive and environmental trends, and (3) brand extension opportunities provides evidence that the trademarked product will generate net cash inflows for the acquiring entity for an indefinite period.

The trademark would be treated as having an indefinite useful life because it is expected to contribute to net cash inflows indefinitely. Therefore, the trademark would not be amortised until its useful life is determined to be finite. It would be tested for impairment under IAS 36 annually and whenever there is an indication that it may be impaired.

FIGURE 10.8 Examples of indefinite lives for intangible assets

Rather than considering the existence of an indefinite life for intangible assets, the standard setters could have set a maximum useful life such as 40 years. However, as noted in paragraph BC63 of the Basis for Conclusions on IAS 38, the IASB considers that writing standards in such a fashion would not accord with the principle that the accounting numbers should be representationally faithful. The principles in IAS 38 provide management with more discretion but allow for the provision of more relevant information. In order for an intangible asset (such as a trademark) to have an indefinite life, an entity is required to outlay funds on an annual basis to maintain the trademark. Consider in this regard the annual expenditure by soft-drink companies to maintain the value of their trademarks. The annual profit figure is then affected by these outlays. To require amortisation charges to be levied as well, when the asset is being maintained, would be to affect the statement of comprehensive income twice.

Intangible assets with finite useful lives

Paragraph 97 of IAS 38 states the principles relating to the amortisation period and choice of amortisation method. In general, the principles of amortisation are the same as those for depreciating property, plant and equipment under IAS 16. In both cases, the process involves the allocation of the depreciable amount on a systematic basis over the useful life, with the method chosen reflecting the pattern in which the expected benefits are expected to be consumed by the entity. Paragraph 98 notes that an amortisation method will rarely result in an amortisation charge that is lower than if a straight-line method had been used. Further, in accordance with paragraph 104, the amortisation period and amortisation method should be reviewed at least at the end of each annual reporting period, which is the same for property, plant and equipment.

However, IAS 38 contains a number of rules that are specific to intangible assets, presumably because of the relative uncertainty associated with intangible assets:

- Where the pattern of benefits cannot be determined reliably, the straight-line method is to be used (para. 97). This is, presumably, to bring some consistency and comparability into the calculations.
- The residual value is assumed to be zero unless there is a commitment by a third party to purchase the asset at the end of its useful life, *or* there is an active market for the asset, and:
  - residual value can be determined by reference to that market and
  - it is probable that such a market will exist at the end of the asset's useful life (para. 100).

Any changes in residual value, amortisation method or useful life are changes in accounting estimates, and accounted for prospectively with an effect on the current and future amortisation charges.

Intangible assets with indefinite useful lives

As noted earlier, where an intangible asset has an indefinite useful life, there is no amortisation charge (IAS 38, para. 107). As with finite useful lives, the useful life of an intangible that is not being amortised must be reviewed each period (para. 109). Any change from indefinite to finite useful life for an asset is treated as a change in estimate and affects the amortisation charge in current and future periods. Intangible assets with indefinite useful lives are subject to annual impairment tests (see chapter 12).

Figure 10.9 shows the disclosures provided by the Christian Dior Group in its 2007 annual report in relation to the useful lives of its intangibles, as well as the factors considered in determining those useful lives.

FIGURE 10.9 Amortisation of intangibles, Christian Dior Group

Only brands, trade names and other intangible assets with finite useful lives are amortized over their useful lives. The classification of a brand or trade name as an asset of definite or indefinite useful life is generally based on the following criteria:

- the brand or trade name's positioning in its market expressed in terms of volume of activity, international presence and notoriety;
- its expected long term profitability;
- its degree of exposure to changes in the economic environment;
- any major event within its business segment liable to compromise its future development;
- its age.

Amortizable lives of brands and trade names, depending on their estimated longevity, range from 5 to 40 years.

Amortization and any impairment expense of brands and trade names are recognized within "Other operating income and expenses".

Impairment tests are carried out for brands, trade names and other intangible assets using the methodology described in Note 1.12.

Research expenditure is not capitalized. New product development expenditure is not capitalized unless the final decision to launch the product has been taken.

Intangible assets other than brands and trade names are amortized over the following periods:

• leasehold rights	based on market conditions, generally between 100% and 200% of the lease period;
• development expenditure	3 years at most;
• software	1 to 5 years.

Source: Christian Dior Group (2007, p. 98).

10.4 RETIREMENTS AND DISPOSALS

Accounting for the retirements and disposals of intangible assets is identical to that for property, plant and equipment under IAS 16. In particular, under IAS 38:

- intangible assets are to be derecognised on disposal or when there are no expected future benefits from the asset (paragraph 112)
- gains or losses on disposal are calculated as the difference between the proceeds on disposal and the carrying amount at point of sale, with amortisation calculated up to the point of sale (paragraph 113)
- amortisation of an intangible with a finite useful life does not cease when the asset becomes temporarily idle or is retired from active use (paragraph 117).

10.5 DISCLOSURE

Paragraph 118 of IAS 38 requires disclosures for each class of intangibles, and for internally generated intangibles to be distinguished from other intangibles. Examples of separate classes are given in paragraph 119:

- brand names
- mastheads and publishing titles
- computer software
- licences and franchises
- copyrights, patents and other industrial property rights, service and operating rights
- recipes, formulas, models, designs and prototypes
- intangible assets under development.

Disclosures required by paragraph 118(a) and (b) would be contained in note 1 to the financial statements, as illustrated in figure 10.10 on the next page. Disclosures required by paragraphs 118 and 122 of IAS 38 are illustrated in figure 10.11 on the next page.

Other disclosures required, where relevant, by paragraph 118 of IAS 38 are:

- the line item in the statement of comprehensive income in which any amortisation of intangible assets is included (para. 118(d))
- increases or decreases during the period resulting from revaluations under paragraphs 75, 85 and 86 and from impairment losses recognised or reversed directly in equity (para. 118(e)(iii))
- impairment losses reversed in profit or loss during the period (para. 118(e)(v)).

Paragraph 122 of IAS 38 also requires the following disclosures, if relevant:

- for intangible assets acquired by way of a *government grant* and initially recognised at fair value (para. 122(c)):
  - the fair value initially recognised for these assets
  - their carrying amount
  - whether they are measured after recognition under the cost model or the revaluation model.
- the existence and carrying amounts of intangible assets whose *title is restricted* and the carrying amounts of intangible assets *pledged as security* for liabilities (para. 122(d)).
- the amount of *contractual commitments* for the acquisition of intangible assets (para. 122(e)).

Paragraph 124 details further disclosures where intangible assets are carried at revalued amounts. An example of this disclosure is contained in figure 10.12 (p. 389).

Note 1: Summary of significant accounting policies (extract)	IAS 38 *para. 118*
Intangible assets Intangible assets are initially recognised at cost. Intangible assets that have indefinite useful lives are tested for impairment on an annual basis. Intangible assets that have finite useful lives are amortised over those lives on a straight-line basis.	*(b)*
Patents and copyrights These have all been acquired by the company. Costs relating to these assets are capitalised and amortised on a straight-line basis over the following periods: Patent — packaging 5 years Patent — tools 10 years Copyright 10 years	*(b)*
Licence The licence relating to television broadcasting rights is determined to be indefinite.	*(a)*
Research and development Research costs are expensed as incurred. Development costs are expensed except those that it is probable will generate future economic benefits, this being determined by an analysis of factors such as technical feasibility and the existence of markets. Such costs are currently being amortised on a straight-line basis over the following periods:	*(a)*
Tool design project 5 years Water cooling project 10 years	*(b)*

FIGURE 10.10 Illustrative disclosures required by paragraph 118(a) and (b) of IAS 38

FIGURE 10.11 Illustrative disclosures required by paragraphs 118 and 122 of IAS 38

Note 11: Intangible assets — IAS 38 *para. 122*

Details about the Company's intangible assets are provided below. All intangibles are considered to have finite useful lives except for a patent held for a tool used in the manufacture of steel windmills. As this tool is able to substantially lessen the cost of manufacturing windmills, and all entities manufacturing windmills acquire the special tool from the company for use in their production process, the continued use of the tool in the manufacturing process is considered to be infinite. Hence, the patent is considered to have an indefinite life. The tool has a carrying amount of $155 000 [2009: $155 000]. *(a)*

Apart from the above, the main items constituting the intangible assets of the Company are: *(b)*

	Carrying amount		Remaining amortisation period	
	2010 $000	2009 $000	**2010** years	2009 years
Patents and copyrights				
Patent — packaging	31	45	7	8
Patent — tools	52	66	5	6
Copyright — manuals	15	24	3	4
Deferred development expenditure				
Tool design	322	312	5	6
Packaging design	95	110	3	4

FIGURE 10.11 *(continued)*

	Patents and copyrights		Deferred development expenditure		*para. 118*
	2010	2009	**2010**	2009	
	$000	$000	$000	$000	
Balance at beginning of year, at cost	576	545	592	361	*(c)*
Accumulated amortisation	276	234	166	110	
Carrying amount at beginning of year	300	311	426	251	
Additions:					*(e)(i)*
Acquisition of subsidiary	—	22	—	54	
Internal development	—	—	72	182	
Acquired separately	10	15	—	—	
Disposals	(15)	—	—	—	*(e)(ii)*
Amortisation	(38)	(32)	(52)	(44)	*(e)(vi)*
Impairment	—	(10)	—	(12)	*(e)(iv)*
Exchange differences	5	(6)	5	(5)	*(e)(vii)*
Carrying amount at end of year	262	300	451	426	
Intangible assets:					
At cost	557	576	669	592	
Accumulated amortisation	295	276	218	166	*(c)*
Carrying amount at end of year	262	300	451	426	

IAS 38
para. 124

Intangibles carried at revalued amounts

The company has recognised its Internet domain name as an intangible asset. The asset was recognised initially at cost in 2008. The revaluation model was used to measure this asset from 1 January 2009. At the end of the reporting period, 31 December 2010, the carrying amount of this asset is $52 500. If the cost method had continued to be applied, the carrying amount would have been $33 600. *(a)(i)* *(a)(ii)* *(a)(iii)*

The revaluation reserve in relation to this asset is as follows: *(b)*

	2009	**2010**
Balance at 1 January 2009	$ 48 000	$ 45 000
Increment	4 500	3 000
Balance at 31 December 2010	$ 52 500	$ 48 000

There are no restrictions on the distribution of this balance to shareholders.

The method used to value this asset is based on an analysis of sales of similar Internet domain names. There is a ready market in such names, and prices are readily available from brokers. In valuing the domain name, it is assumed that use of the Internet for marketing and communicating information to potential investors will continue to enjoy its current popularity for at least the next 10 years. *(c)*

FIGURE 10.12 Disclosures required by paragraph 124 of IAS 38

Paragraph 126 requires disclosure of the aggregate amount of research and development expenditure recognised as an expense during the period. Paragraph 128 lists disclosures that are encouraged but not required:

- a description of any fully amortised intangible asset that is still in use
- a brief description of significant intangible assets controlled by the entity but not recognised as assets because they did not meet the recognition criteria in IAS 38.

10.6 INNOVATIVE MEASURES OF INTANGIBLES

It has already been noted that there is often a large difference between the capitalised value of an entity and the net assets reported by that entity. Even with the adoption of IAS 38, the strictness of the rules relating to the recognition of internally generated intangibles means that there will not be an expansion in the recognition of intangible assets by entities. In some cases, there will be a reduction where, before the adoption of IAS 38, internally generated assets such as brand names and mastheads were recognised in the accounts. The purpose of this section is to note the existence of an ever-increasing volume of literature suggesting new ideas in reporting about the value of entities. Many of these innovative ideas are concerned with providing information about the content of the unreported assets of an entity. This section suggests that the accounting profession needs to ensure that it does not get left behind by other information professionals in the provision of information about the value of an entity and the variables that determine that value.

Figure 10.4 (p. 371) shows Lev's breakdown of intangibles into innovation-related, human resource and organisational intangibles. This analysis of the composition of intangibles has been undertaken by a number of international companies. Skandia, a company based in Sweden, issued its Intellectual Capital Prototype Report, entitled *Human Capital in Transformation,* in 1998 (see www.skandia.com). In this report, Skandia divided the market value of an entity into financial capital and intellectual capital, which was further broken down into customer capital, organisational capital and human capital. This view of the market value of an entity is reproduced in figure 10.13.

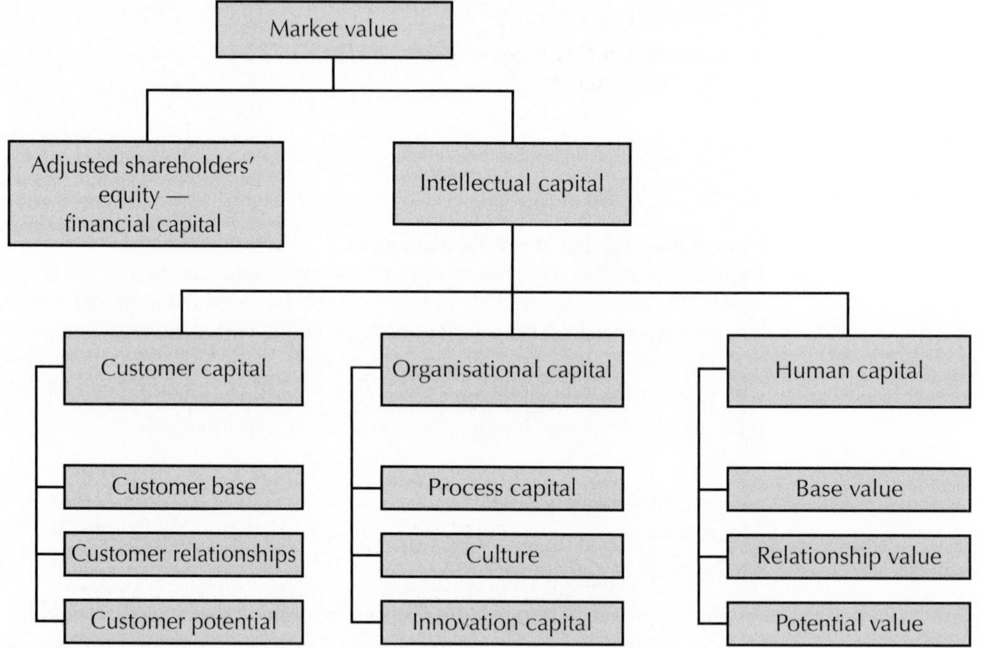

Intellectual capital consists of *human capital* and *structural capital*.

Structural capital consists of *customer capital* and *organisational capital*, i.e everything that is left once the employee goes home, such as information systems, database, IT software.

Organisational capital can be broken down into process capital (value-creating and non-value-creating processes), culture and innovation capital (intangible rights, trademarks, patents, knowledge recipes and business secrets).

Human capital can be broken down into competence, relationships and values.

FIGURE 10.13 Intellectual capital — the Skandia view
Source: Skandia (1998).

The Danish company Systematic, whose strategic business areas are mission critical systems for the defence and healthcare sectors and complex software development, has published its *Intellectual capital report* in 1999, 2000, 2002 and 2004 (see www.systematic.com). The main target groups for this report were customer groups, both present and future, employees and cooperation partners. In the 2002 report, Systematic identified four managerial challenges within knowledge management:

- partnerships with customers
- software process improvement
- recruitment and retention of employees
- competence development.

This is depicted diagrammatically in figure 10.14.

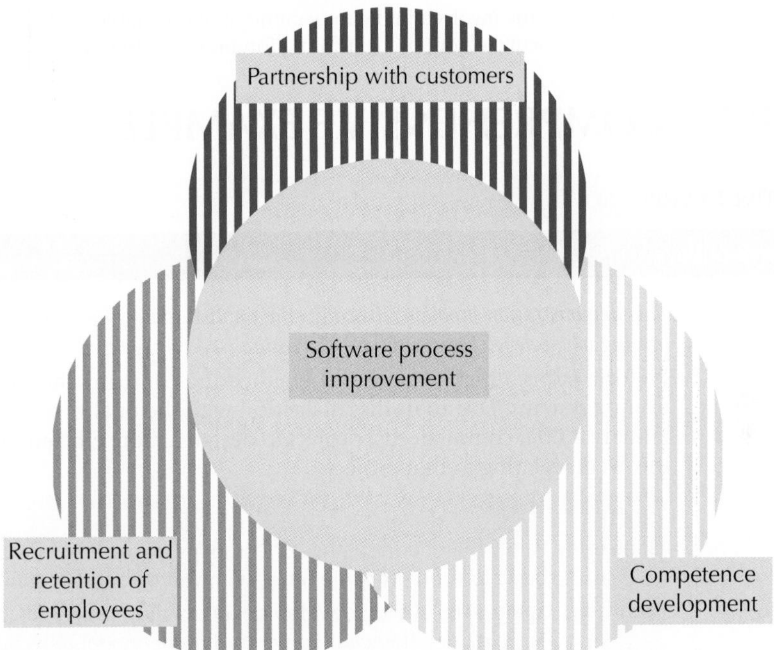

FIGURE 10.14 Management challenges — Systematic
Source: Systematic (2002, p. 10).

When analysing the reports on the intellectual capital of these organisations, the major point to consider is this: the purpose of the reports is to provide more information about variables in the organisation that management believes add value to the organisation. For example, under IAS 38, an assembled workforce is not allowed to be capitalised as an asset, even within a business combination, and funds spent on training employees must be expensed. Hence, the financial statements do not recognise any attempts by management to increase the human capital of the organisation. The question for accountants to consider is whether there are ways in which human capital can be measured, and whether the measures are sufficiently reliable (and relevant) to be included in the financial statements. There have been many attempts to measure human capital. Mayo (2001) provides an excellent summary of proposed measures in chapter 3 of his book.

Most measures are, however, not directed at including the information in financial statements. A key element in analysing the measures is to determine the variables that various authors see as important and the different ways these are measured. For example, Mayo (2001, pp. 58–60) reviewed the Balanced Scorecard approach as developed by Kaplan and Norton in 1992. He noted that, in terms of employee capabilities, three outcome measurements identified were:

- employee satisfaction
- employee retention
- employee productivity

with these being driven by the following enablers:

- staff competencies
- technology infrastructure
- the climate for action.

Such measures are not suitable for inclusion in financial statements. It is expected that, in the foreseeable future, information on aspects of capital other than financial capital will not be included in the financial statements themselves. However, companies will endeavour to plug the information gap by providing additional reports. Some accounting firms have become involved with these reports; for example, the Systematic 2004 *Intellectual capital report* was audited by Deloitte in Denmark.

In the Systematic report, the following comment was made:

> Better train people and risk they leave
> than do nothing and they stay.

Perhaps this can be adapted for the accounting profession as follows:

> Better become involved in the measurement of intangibles
> than risk being left out of the information provision business.

10.7 COMPREHENSIVE EXAMPLE

ILLUSTRATIVE EXAMPLE 10.1

Development outlays

This demonstration problem illustrates the application of the criteria in paragraph 57 of IAS 38, determining when development outlays are capitalised or expensed.

Pretoria Ltd is a highly successful engineering company that manufactures filters for airconditioning systems. Due to its dissatisfaction with the quality of the filters currently available, on 1 January 2010 it commenced a project to design a more efficient filter. The following notes record the events relating to that project:

2010	
January	Paid $145 000 in salaries of company engineers and consultants who conducted basic tests on available filters with varying modifications.
February	Spent $165 000 on developing a new filter system, including the production of a basic model. It became obvious that the model in its current form was not successful because the material in the filter was not as effective as required.
March	Acquired the fibres division of Durban Ltd for $330 000. The fair values of the tangible assets of this division were: property, plant and equipment, $180 000; inventories, $60 000. This business was acquired because one of the products it produced was a fibrous compound sold under the brand name Springbok, that Pretoria Ltd considered would be excellent for including in the filtration process. By buying the fibres division, Pretoria Ltd acquired the patent for this fibrous compound. Pretoria Ltd valued the patent at $50 000 and the brand name at $40 000, using a number of valuation techniques. The patent had a further 10-year life but was renewable on application. Further costs of $54 000 were incurred on the new filter system during March.
April	Spent a further $135 000 on revising the filtration process to incorporate the fibrous compound. By the end of April, Pretoria Ltd was convinced that it now had a viable product because preliminary tests showed that the filtration process was significantly better than any other available on the market.
May	Developed a prototype of the filtration component and proceeded to test it within a variety of models of airconditioners. The company preferred to sell the fil-tration process to current manufacturers of airconditioners if the process worked with currently available models. If this proved not possible, the company would then consider developing its own brand of airconditioners using the new fil-tration system. By the end of May, the filtration system had proved successful on all but one of the currently available commercial models. Costs incurred were $65 000.
June	Various airconditioner manufacturers were invited to demonstrations of the filtration system. Costs incurred were $25 000, including $12 000 for food and beverages for the prospective clients. The feedback from a number of the companies was that they were

prepared to enter negotiations for acquiring the filters from Pretoria Ltd. The company now believed it had a successful model and commenced planning the production of the filters. Ongoing costs of $45 000 to refine the filtration system, particularly in the light of comments by the manufacturers, were incurred in the latter part of June.

Required

Explain the accounting for the various outlays incurred by Pretoria Ltd.

Solution

The main problem in accounting for the costs is determining at what point of time costs can be capitalised. This is resolved by applying the criteria in paragraph 57 of IAS 38:

- *Technical feasibility*. At the end of April, the company believed that the filtration process was technically feasible.
- *Intention to complete and sell*. At the end of April, the company was not yet sure that the system was adaptable to currently available models of airconditioners. If it wasn't adaptable, the company would have to test whether development of its own brand of airconditioners would be a commercial proposition. Hence, it was not until the end of May that the company was convinced it could complete the project and had a product that it could sell.
- *Ability to use or sell*. By the end of May, the company had a product that it believed it had the ability to sell. Being a filter manufacturer, it knew the current costs of competing products and so could make an informed decision about the potential for the commercial sale of its own filter.
- *Existence of a market*. The market comprised the airconditioning manufacturers. By selling to the manufacturers, the company had the potential to generate probable future cash flows. This criterion was met by the end of May.
- *Availability of resources*. From the beginning of the project, the company was not short of resources, being a highly successful company in its own right.
- *Ability to measure costs reliably*. Costs are readily attributable to the project throughout its development.

On the basis of the above analysis, the criteria in paragraph 57 of IAS 38 were all met at the end of May. Therefore, costs incurred before this point are expensed, and those incurred after this point are capitalised. Hence, the following costs would be written off as incurred:

January	$ 145 000
February	165 000
March	54 000
April	135 000
May	65 000

In acquiring the fibres division from Durban Ltd, Pretoria Ltd would pass the following entry:

Property, plant and equipment	Dr	180 000	
Inventories	Dr	60 000	
Brand	Dr	40 000	
Patent	Dr	50 000	
Cash	Cr		330 000
(Acquisition of assets)			

The patent would initially be depreciated over a 10-year useful life. However, this would need to be reassessed upon application of the fibrous compound to the airconditioning filtration system. This alternative use may extend the expected useful life of the product, and hence of the patent. The brand name would be depreciated over the same useful life of the patent, because it is expected that the brand has no real value unless backed by the patent.

The company would then capitalise development costs of $45 000 in June.

The marketing costs incurred in June of $25 000 would be expensed because they are not part of the development process.

SUMMARY

Intangible assets are considered to be sufficiently different from other assets such as property, plant and equipment for the standard setters to provide a separate standard. The reason for having such a standard is that the nature of intangibles is such that there are particular measurement problems associated with these assets that require specific accounting principles to be established. IAS 38 *Intangible Assets* is concerned with the definition, recognition, measurement and disclosure of intangibles.

The characteristic of 'identifiability' is critical to the identification of intangibles, and is the same concept that arises in IFRS 3 *Business Combinations* in relation to identifiable assets, liabilities and contingent liabilities recognised by the acquirer. In considering the accounting for intangibles, it is important to consider the differences in accounting depending on the source of the intangibles. Intangible assets acquired within a business combination are easier to recognise than those internally generated by the entity. This is because within a business combination the measurement issues are limited by the amount of the cost of the combination.

Amortisation of intangibles raises particular issues in terms of the useful lives of assets. The potential to assess some intangible assets as having indefinite useful lives and hence not subject to amortisation makes the decision on what is the useful life of an asset very significant. It is important to understand how to make such a decision. Aspects of that decision process are required to be specifically disclosed.

Discussion questions

1. What are the key characteristics of an intangible asset?
2. Explain whawt is meant by 'identifiability'.
3. How do the principles for amortisation of intangible assets differ from those for depreciation of property, plant and equipment?
4. Explain what is meant by an 'active market'.
5. How is the useful life of an intangible asset determined?
6. What intangibles can never be recognised if internally generated? Why?
7. Explain the difference between 'research' and 'development'.
8. Explain when development outlays can be capitalised.
9. Explain how intangible assets are initially measured, and whether the measurement differs depending on whether the assets are acquired in a business combination or internally generated by an entity.
10. Give two ways in which it is easier to recognise intangibles that are acquired in a business combination than those that are internally generated.
11. What are the recognition criteria for intangible assets?
12. Explain why managers may prefer to expense outlays on intangibles rather than capitalise them.
13. Explain why capitalisation of outlays may not provide relevant information about the intangible assets held by an entity.
14. Explain the application of the revaluation model for intangible assets.
15. Explain the use of fair values in the accounting for intangible assets.
16. David James (2001b) stated:

    > The Australian company Health Communications Network (HCN), for example, has most of its balance sheet assets in the form of either cash or intangible assets. In its 2000–01 annual report, out of combined assets of \$49.7 million, cash assets were \$20.4 million and intangible assets were \$22.2 million. Plant and equipment were only \$1.47 million.
    >
    > This is characteristic of the shift to intangible assets, but the recent fate of HCN demonstrates some of the difficulties of ownership in the post-industrial environment. The company was the subject of a public furore when it was alleged it had plans to sell prescription information, collected from general practitioners, to undisclosed third parties, possibly pharmaceutical companies. The matter has been referred to the privacy commissioner, but the message is clear: just because a company possesses information, does not mean it can always do with it as it wishes. HCN 'owns' the information, but this does not give it the same rights of ownership as, say, ownership of plant and equipment.

    Required

    Using the information in the above quotation, discuss the characteristics of intangible assets.

17. David James (2001b) stated:

> According to its 1999–2000 annual report, Qantas had total assets of $12 billion. Intangible assets were only $25 million, around 2% of the asset base. Yet Stuckey believes the airline's intangibles are of far greater importance to the company. 'Qantas is interesting because it combines a fantastic brand — an intangible asset — with a heap of capital-intensive tangible assets — the planes they have tried to keep well utilised. They have done very well in an industry that has been a real financial under-performer internationally. They stand out as one of the best performers in that sector.'

Required

In relation to a major airline such as Qantas, discuss what intangible assets are probably not on the statement of financial position, and possible reasons for their non-recognition.

18. Nick Tabakoff (1999) stated:

> ASIC (Australian Securities and Investments Commission) may have plans to change the treatment of television licences in company accounts, as a precursor to the possible introduction of IAS 38. The commission is seeking the views of the main television networks regarding a change to the accounting rules that apply to their licences which, as intangibles, may be amortised. They have not been amortised in the past because of the view held by leading media companies that licences have an ongoing life.
>
> Some ASIC officials beg to differ — because licences need to be reapplied for and renewed every five years, they should be amortised on the grounds that they could be taken away by the Government at any time. The Seven and Nine television networks have been steadily increasing the value placed on their television licences in recent years, a practice that would almost certainly be prevented if IAS 38 was introduced.

Required

Obtain access to the most recent financial statements of your local television stations, and review their policies and accounting for television licences. Critically analyse the arguments for and against the non-amortisation of these assets.

19. Nick Tabakoff (1999) stated:

> News Corporation is far from convinced of the merits of the standard [IAS 38]. At the Australian division, News Limited, finance director and deputy chief executive Peter McCourt says: 'The reason you get standards like that is that they are prepared by people who are not really responsible to anybody. The business community gains nothing from writing off the value of intangibles over a limited time frame. If the standard comes in, the market will simply add back the amortisation.'
>
> McCourt believes the standard penalises companies that are acquisitive when it comes to intangible assets. He can see no reason for the existence of the standard. 'Who is it aimed at, who is being better informed by taking that charge? I don't think it gets you anywhere.'
>
> He is not alone in getting worked up about preventing accountants from minimising the values placed on intangibles. Even the legendary Berkshire Hathaway chief Warren Buffett has strong views on the issue. He has been quoted as saying: 'Amortisation of intangibles is rubbish. It distorts true cashflows and thus economic reality. For example, the economic earnings of Disney are much greater than reported earnings. Accounting is pushing people to do things that are nuts.'

These comments were made before the latest revisions to IAS 38.

Required

Comment on whether the current IAS 38 has resolved the issues raised in this article.

20. In the following article, Whiting and Chapman (2003) consider whether the value of rugby players, being a team's most valuable asset, should be placed on the balance sheet (statement of financial position).

Sporting glory — the great intangible

While rugby stars are heroes to many, when checking the books they become a complex intangible. Rosalind Whiting and Kyla Chapman investigate the merits of Human Resource Accounting in professional sport.

Australia, New Zealand and rugby union — a combination guaranteed to stir patriotic feelings across the Tasman! But what if we add accounting to this equation? Rugby players are the teams' most valuable assets, so should we be placing their value on the balance sheet? And if so, does it make any difference to the decisions that users of financial statements make?

(continued)

Human resource accounting in professional sport

Professional sport has been prevalent in the United Kingdom and the United States for nearly 200 years. However, professional sport arrived later to Australia and New Zealand. In particular, the Kiwis only entered this arena in 1995 when the New Zealand Rugby Football Union (NZRFU) signed the Tri Nations sponsorship deal and removed all barriers preventing rugby union players being paid for their services. Player contract expenses in New Zealand now amount to over NZ$20 million annually, according to the NZRFU.

In the United Kingdom and the United States, the professional teams' financial accounts quite often incorporate human resource accounting (HRA). HRA is basically an addition to traditional accounting, in which a value for the employees is placed on the balance sheet and is amortised over a period of time, instead of expensing costs such as professional development.

There is debate about the merits of this process and the arguments are in line with those we have been hearing about intangibles in general. More recently, there has been worldwide movement towards recognising acquired identifiable intangible assets at fair value in the financial statements. So why not include an organisation's human resources? While (thankfully) most people agree that employees are valuable, there are accounting difficulties with the concept of ownership or control of the employees (asset definition) and the reliability of measurement.

Despite these concerns, one area where HRA does have some international acceptability is in accounting for professional sport, mainly because of the measurable player transfer costs. But there is still some variability in the reporting of human resource value, ranging from the capitalisation of signing and transfer fees through to player development costs or valuations.

To the authors' knowledge, HRA is not currently practised with Australia and New Zealand's professional sports teams. The absence of transfer fees between clubs when trading players may explain this.

Decision making

Accountants are required to provide information that assists users in assessing an organisation's financial and service performance and in making decisions about providing resources to, or doing business with the firm.

The big question is whether HRA information is more useful to the decision maker than the alternative expensing treatment. Supporters of HRA argue that capitalised information is useful for strategic planning and management of employees, and provides a more accurate measure of the firm's status and total performance.

Those against HRA say it is too subjective to be useful and that it just imposes another cost on the organisation. Some detractors argue that it makes unprofitable organisations appear profitable simply because smart people work there. But those who believe in the efficiency of the market would argue that investors are not naive, and decisions would be unaffected by the way in which human resource information is presented.

Past research has shown that sophisticated users of financial information do make significantly different decisions with the different presentations. With this in mind we decided to test this outcome in New Zealand.

The New Zealand study

In June 2001, 64 members of the New Zealand professional body, the Institute of Chartered Accountants of New Zealand (ICANZ) responded to our postal questionnaire. This constituted a 20 per cent response rate from the 300 randomly selected ICANZ members.

All respondents were provided with the CEO's report, and the financial statements and notes of the fictitious Gladiator Super Twelve rugby franchise.

Half of the respondents were sent financial statements in which player training and development costs were expensed in the year that they were incurred.

The other half received an identical set of statements; however, the team was capitalised on the balance sheet.

It was stated in the notes to the accounts that the team was periodically revalued every five years, and then annual player training and development costs were capitalised and added to the valuation and subsequently amortised over a period of three years (average contract length). Respondents were asked a series of decision making questions and then the answers from the two groups (expensing and capitalising) were statistically compared.

Generally, the presentation of the human resource information made no difference to the assessments and decisions made by our respondents. They assessed financial position and performance, risk and future financial performance to be at the same level regardless of the presentation. And even when presented with an investment decision where they had to divide $100 000 between the franchise and a fixed term New Zealand bank investment, there was no difference in the levels of investment between the two groups.

In most cases respondents in the two groups gave similar reasons for their assessments.

However, when assessing current performance, the group with the expensed player development costs mainly used statement of financial performance information, whereas the group with the capitalised statements also used the statement of financial position. This suggests that they understood the nature of the information with which they were provided.

Differences in opinion

Women and men showed no overall differences in their responses. However, it was with investment experience that we uncovered some contrasting results. Most of our respondents fell into two groups, those with limited investment experience (less than one year) and those having extensive experience (five or more years).

We felt that the experienced group would more closely represent the sophisticated users as studied in previous research.

We found some differences in assessments between the experienced and the limited experience group. The groups rated financial performance and risk of the franchise differently and invested significantly different amounts in the franchise. Interestingly, members of the limited experience group rated growth as a more important reason for their investment decisions — whereas the experienced group said net profit levels were more important.

Of greater interest was whether experience level affected respondents' ability to cope with the different presentations of human resource information. In most cases it did not. However, limited experience investors did make significantly different assessments of the risk and future performance of the franchise according to the presentation of the human resource information. In these situations the limited experience expensing group acted like the experienced group of investors, whereas the limited experience capitalising group did not.

The capitalised information may have confused the less experienced investors.

In general, the users (sophisticated and unsophisticated) were unaffected in their assessments and decisions by the presentation of the human resource information. This conflicts with prior studies, which found that HRA did make a difference to decision making. This variation could be due to accountants now having a better understanding of the issues surrounding intangibles recognition and the effect of accounting method choice on financial statement numbers and ratios. Also accountants are spending less time in accounting number preparation and more time in interpretation and business advice.

However, our exercise only explored one type of decision-making process, that of an investment. Prior studies may have been of a wider nature, which could explain the differing result.

Overall, our study shows that generally accountants will make the same investment decisions regardless of whether human resource information is expensed or capitalised. If HRA is to follow the international trends emerging in intangibles reporting, then capitalised human resource information may become more prevalent. This study suggests that this won't negatively affect those accountants who provide interpretative and investment advice.

Required

Critically analyse the arguments made in the article and assess whether there should be any changes made to IAS 38 as a result.

21. In the article overleaf by Peacock (2004), it was reported that the clothing and footwear giant Pacific Brands was set to list on the stockmarket with a $1 billion + initial public offering (IPO). Patersons Securities analyst, Rob Brierley, was quoted as saying, 'The high brand awareness will certainly be its [Pacific Brand's] marketing strength.'

A history of most popular brands

Pacific Brands can trace its history back to 1893 when it began making Dunlop bicycle tyres.

Along the way, it has collected an astonishing array of brands, many remarkable stories in their own right.

Bonds, one of the company's flagship brands, was founded in 1915 by American immigrant George A. Bond who started out making hosiery and gloves in Sydney. In 1928, Bonds underwear and hosiery secured Charles Kingsford-Smith and Charles Ulm on their historic first flight across the Pacific.

King Gee workwear has been with Australians for more than 75 years, with the first overalls produced in tiny rented premises in Sydney. Its name is derived from a colloquial expression popular during the reign of King George V.

According to PacBrands' website 'King Gee' became Australian slang for a show-off. 'For example, in the 1920s someone who had a high opinion of themselves might have attracted the comment, "he's so good he thinks he's King G",' it said.

Holeproof was first made in Australia in the late 1920s when a hosiery manufacturer started turning out ladieswear under licence from the Holeproof Hosiery Company in the US. The company opened its first Australian mill in Melbourne in 1930, becoming the first manufacturer to make and market Australian-made, self-supporting socks.

Unique Corsets, later better known as bra maker Berlei, was already nearly 20 years old by then.

Founded by Fred R. Burley with a nominal capital of £10 000 in Sydney, the company set out 'to design, manufacture and sell corsets and brassieres of such perfect fit, quality and workmanship as will bring pleasure and profit to all concerned'.

Clarks shoes go back even further, to 1825, and a small sheepskin slipper business founded by Cyrus and James Clark in the small English village of Street. Sixty years later, the company was credited with creating the first shoe to follow the natural shape of the foot — 'a revolutionary concept in its time'.

Required

Given the perceived importance of the brands to the success of the IPO, discuss whether the IASB in IAS 38 has adopted too conservative an approach to the accounting for brands.

22. Ocean Catch Ltd is a leading company in the sale of frozen and canned fish produce. These products are sold under two brand names. Fish caught in southern Australian waters are sold under the brand 'Artic Fresh', which is the brand the company developed when it commenced operations and which is still used today. Fish caught in the northern oceans are sold under the brand name 'Tropical Taste', the brand developed by Seafood Feast Ltd. Ocean Catch Ltd acquired all the assets and liabilities of Seafood Feast Ltd a number of years ago when it took over that company's operations.

    Ocean Catch Ltd has always marketed itself as operating in an environmentally responsible manner, and is an advocate of sustainable fishing. The public regards it as a dolphin-friendly company as a result of its previous campaigns to ensure dolphins are not affected by tuna fishing. The marketing manager of Ocean Catch Ltd has noted the efforts of the ship, the *Princess*, to disrupt and hopefully stop the efforts of Japanese whalers in the southern oceans and the publicity that this has received. He has recommended to the board of directors that Ocean Catch Ltd strengthen its environmentally responsible image by guaranteeing to repair any damage caused to the *Princess* as a result of attempts to disrupt the Japanese whalers. He believes that this action will increase Ocean Catch Ltd's environmental reputation, adding to the company's goodwill. He has told the board that such a guarantee will have no effect on Ocean Catch Ltd's reported profitability. He has explained that, if any damage to the *Princess* occurs, Ocean Catch Ltd can capitalise the resulting repair costs to the carrying amounts of its brands, as such costs will have been incurred basically for marketing purposes. Accordingly, as the company's net asset position will increase, and there will be no effect on the statement of comprehensive income, this will be a win–win situation for everyone.

Required

The chairman of the board knows that the marketing manager is very effective at selling ideas but knows very little about accounting. The chairman has, therefore, asked you to provide him with a report advising the board on how the proposal should be accounted for under International Financial Reporting Standards and how such a proposal would affect Ocean Catch Ltd's financial statements.

23. Pics Ltd is an Australian mail-order film developer. Although the photo developing business in Australia is growing slowly, Pics Ltd has reported significant increases in sales and net income in recent years. While sales increased from $50 million in 1999 to $120 million in 2005, profit increased from $3 million to $12 million over the same period. The stock market and analysts believe that the company's future is very promising. In early 2006, the company was valued at $350 million, which was three times 2005 sales and 26 times estimated 2006 profit.

What is the secret of Pics Ltd's success? Company management and many investors attribute the company's success to its marketing flair and expertise. Instead of competing on price, Pics Ltd prefers to focus on service and innovation, including:

- Customers are offered a CD and a set of prints from the same roll of film for a set price.
- Customers are given, at no extra charge, a 'picture index' of mini-photos of the roll.
- A replacement roll is given to every customer (at no extra charge) with every development order.

As a result of such innovations, customers accept prices that are 60% above those of competitor discount film developers, and Pics Ltd maintains a gross profit margin of around 40%.

Nevertheless, some investors have doubts about the company as they are uneasy about certain accounting policies the company has adopted. For example, Pics Ltd capitalises the costs of its direct mailings to prospective customers ($4.2 million at 30 June 2005) and amortises them on a straight-line basis over 3 years. This practice is considered to be questionable as there is no guarantee that customers will be obtained and retained from direct mailings.

In addition to the mailing lists developed by in-house marketing staff, Pics Ltd purchased a customer list from a competitor for $800 000 on 4 July 2006. This list is also recognised as a non-current asset. Pics Ltd estimates that this list will generate sales for at least another 2 years, more likely another 3 years. The company also plans to add names, obtained from a phone survey conducted in August 2006, to the list. These extra names are expected to extend the list's useful life by another year.

Pics Ltd's 2005 statement of financial position also reported $7.5 million of marketing costs as non-current assets. If the company had expensed marketing costs as incurred, 2005 net income would have been $10 million instead of the reported $12 million. The concerned investors are uneasy about this capitalisation of marketing costs, as they believe that Pics Ltd's marketing practices are relatively easy to replicate. However, Pics Ltd argues that its accounting is appropriate. Marketing costs are amortised at an accelerated rate (55% in year 1, 29% in year 2, and 16% in year 3), based on 15 years' knowledge and experience of customer purchasing behaviour.

Required

Explain how Pics Ltd's costs should be accounted for under IAS 38 *Intangible Assets*, giving reasons for your answer.

STAR RATING

★ BASIC

★★ MODERATE

★★★ DIFFICULT

Exercises

Exercise 10.1

USEFUL TRADEMARK LIFE

★

X Ltd holds a trademark that is well known within consumer circles and has enabled the company to be a market leader in its area. The trademark has been held by the company for 9 years. The legal life of the trademark is 5 years, but is renewable by the company at little cost to it.

Required

Discuss how the company should determine the useful life of the trademark, noting in particular what form of evidence it should collect to justify its selection of useful life.

Exercise 10.2

ACCOUNTING FOR USEFUL LIFE

★ A company that sells DVDs by sending emails to prospective customers has acquired a customer list from another company that also markets its products in a similar fashion. The company estimates that it will generate sales from the list for a minimum of 2 years and a maximum of 3 years.

The company intends to add names to the list from answers to a questionnaire attached to each of the emails. This should extend the useful life of the list for another year.

Required

Discuss how the company should account for the cost of the customer list. If the cost is capitalised, discuss the determination of the useful life over which the asset is amortised.

Exercise 10.3

IMPORTANCE OF INTANGIBLE ASSETS

★ In its annual report, Compusoft Corporation reported £352 million of intangibles and total assets of £80 652 million. Note 8 to the report disclosed details about the entity's intangible assets, including the following breakdown:

June 30 in £ millions	Gross carrying amount	Accumulated amortisation
Contract-based	566	(382)
Technology-based	240	(131)
Marketing-based	42	(11)
Customer-related	31	(3)
	879	(527)

Required

Discuss the importance of intangible assets to computing and software companies such as Compusoft, and analyse whether there are aspects of IAS 38 that prevent such companies from disclosing more information about their intangible assets.

Exercise 10.4

RECOGNITION OF BRANDS

★ Simon Evans (2003) reported that a small Victorian wine producer was planning to raise up to $7 million and list on the Australian Securities Exchange. The report stated that Warrenmang Ltd, based in the Pyrenees region in north-west Victoria, had been set up to acquire the Warrenmang, Bazzini and Masoni business and brands. The company hoped to list on the Australian Securities Exchange in February 2004.

Required

Discuss potential problems associated with the recognition of brands by the acquiring entity.

Exercise 10.5

BRANDS AND FORMULAS

★ Wayne Upton (2001, p. 71) in his discussion of the lives of intangible assets noted that the formula for Coca-Cola has grown more valuable over time, not less, and that Sir David Tweedie, chairman of the IASB, jokes that the brand name of his favourite Scotch whisky is older than the United States of America — and, in Sir David's view, the formula for Scotch whisky has contributed more to the sum of human happiness.

Required

Outline the accounting for brands under IAS 38, and discuss the difficulties for standard setters in allowing the recognition of all brands and formulas on statements of financial position.

Exercise 10.6 ★

FINANCIAL STATEMENTS AND INTANGIBLES

Upton (2001, p. 50) notes:

> There is a popular view of financial statements that underlies and motivates many discussions of intangible assets. That popular view often sounds something like this:
>
> > If accountants got all the assets and liabilities into financial statements, and they measured all those assets and liabilities at the right amounts, stockholders' equity would equal market capitalization. Right?

Required

Comment on the truth of this 'popular view'.

Problems

Problem 10.1 ★★

RESEARCH AND DEVELOPMENT

Because of the low level of rainfall in Everest, householders find it difficult to keep their gardens and lawns sufficiently watered. As a result, many householders have installed bores that allow them to access underground water suitable for using on the garden. This is a cheaper option than incurring excess water bills by using the government-provided water system. One of the problems with much of the bore water is that its heavy iron content leaves a brown stain on paths and garden edges. This can make homes look unsightly and lower their value.

Noting this problem, Strand Laboratories believed that it should research the problem with the goal of developing a filter system that could be attached to a bore and remove the effects of the iron content in the water. This process, if developed, could be patented and filters sold through local reticulation shops.

In 2001, Strand commenced its work on the problem, resulting in August 2005 in a patent for the NoMoreIron filter process. Costs incurred in this process were as shown below.

		$000
2001–02	Research conducted to develop filter	125
2002–03	Research conducted to develop filter	132
2003–04	Design and construction of prototype	152
2004–05	Testing of models	51
2005–06	Fees for preparing patent application	12
2006–07	Research to modify design	34
2007–08	Legal fees to protect patent against cheap copies	15

Required

Discuss how the company should account for each of these outlays.

Problem 10.2 ★★

RECOGNITION OF INTANGIBLES

Makula Ltd is unsure of how to obtain computer software. Four possibilities are:

1. Purchase computer software externally, including packages for payroll and general ledger.
2. Contract to independent programmers to develop specific software for the company's own use.
3. Buy computer software to incorporate into a product that the company will develop.
4. Employ its own programmers to write software that the company will use.

Required

Discuss whether the accounting will differ depending on which method is chosen.

Problem 10.3 RESEARCH AND DEVELOPMENT

★★ Batura Laboratories Ltd manufactures and distributes a wide range of general pharmaceutical products. Selected audited data for the reporting period ended 31 December 2010 are as follows:

Gross profit	$17 600 000
Profit before income tax	1 700 000
Income tax expense	500 000
Profit for the period	1 200 000
Total assets:	
Current	7 300 000
Non-current	11 500 000

The company uses a standard mark-up on cost.

From your audit files, you ascertain that total research and development expenditure for the year amounted to $4 700 000. This amount is substantially higher than in previous years and has eroded the profitability of the company. Mr Bosch, the company's finance director, has asked for your firm's advice on whether it is acceptable accounting practice for the company to carry foward any of this expenditure to a future accounting period.

Your audit files disclose that the main reason for the significant increase in research and development costs was the introduction of a planned 5-year laboratory program to attempt to find an antidote for the common cold. Salaries and identifiable equipment costs associated with this program amounted to $2 350 000 for the current year.

The following additional items were included in research and development costs for the year:

(a) Costs to test a new tamper-proof dispenser pack for the company's major selling line (20% of sales) of antibiotic capsules — $760 000. The new packs are to be introduced in the 2011 financial year.

(b) Experimental costs to convert a line of headache powders to liquid form — $590 000. The company hopes to phase out the powder form if the tests to convert to the stronger and better handling liquid form prove successful.

(c) Quality control required by stringent company policy and by law on all items of production for the year — $750 000.

(d) Costs of a time and motion study aimed at improving production efficiency by redesigning plant layout of existing equipment — $50 000.

(e) Construction and testing of a new prototype machine for producing hypodermic needles — $200 000. Testing has been successful to date and is nearing completion. Hypodermic needles accounted for 1% of the company's sales in the current year, but it is expected that the company's market share will increase following introduction of this new machine.

Required

Respond to Mr Bosch's question for each item above.

Problem 10.4 RECOGNITION OF INTANGIBLES

★★ Muztag Ltd has recently diversified by taking over the operations of Trivor Ltd at a cost of $10 million. Trivor Ltd manufactures and sells a cleaning cloth called the 'Supaswipe', which was developed by Trivor Ltd's highly trained and innovative research staff. The unique nature of the coating used on the 'Supaswipe' has resulted in Trivor Ltd acquiring a significant share of the South African market. A recent expansion into the Equatorial African market has proved successful. As a result of the takeover, Muztag Ltd acquired the following assets:

	Fair value (at date of acquisition)
Land and buildings	$3 200 000
Production machinery	2 000 000
Inventory	1 800 000
Accounts receivable	700 000
	$7 700 000

In addition to the above, Trivor Ltd owned, but had not recognised, the following:

- trademark — 'Supaswipe'
- patent — formula for the special coating.

The research staff of Trivor Ltd have agreed to join the staff of Muztag Ltd and will continue to work on a number of projects aimed at producing specialised versions of the 'Supaswipe'.

The directors have requested your assistance in accounting for the acquisition of Trivor Ltd. In particular, they are uncertain as to the treatment of the $2.3 million discrepancy between the assets recorded by Trivor Ltd and the price paid for the company.

Required

Write to the directors outlining the alternative courses of action available in relation to the $2.3 million discrepancy. Your reply should cover the issues of asset recognition, measurement, classification and subsequent accounting treatment.

Problem 10.5 RESEARCH AND DEVELOPMENT

★★

Yamit Ltd has been involved in a project to develop an engine that runs on extracts from sugar cane. It started the project in February 2010. Between the starting date and 30 June 2010, the end of the reporting period for the company, Yamit Ltd spent $254 000 on the project. At 30 June 2010, there was no indication that the project would be commercially feasible, although the company had made significant progress and was sufficiently sure of future success that it was prepared to outlay more funds on the project.

After spending a further $120 000 during July and August, the company had built a prototype that appeared to be successful. The prototype was demonstrated to a number of engineering companies during September, and several of these companies expressed interest in the further development of the engine. Convinced that it now had a product that it would be able to sell, Yamit Ltd spent a further $65 000 during October adjusting for the problems that the engineering firms had pointed out. On 1 November, Yamit Ltd applied for a patent on the engine, incurring legal and administrative costs of $35 000. The patent had an expected useful life of 5 years, but was renewable for a further 5 years upon application.

Between November and December 2010, Yamit Ltd spent an additional amount of $82 000 on engineering and consulting costs to develop the project such that the engine was at manufacturing stage. This resulted in changes in the overall design of the engine, and costs of $5000 were incurred to add minor changes to the patent authority.

On 1 January 2011, Yamit Ltd invited tenders for the manufacture of the engine for commercial sale.

Required

Discuss how Yamit Ltd should account for these costs. Provide journal entries with an explanation of why these are the appropriate entries.

References

Baltes, M 1997, 'Measuring non-financial assets', *Wharton Alumni Magazine*, Winter, pp. 7–12.

Dior 2007, *Full annual report 2007*, Christian Dior Group, Paris, www.diorfinance.com/en.

Eccles, RG, Herz, RH, Keegan, EM & Phillips, DMH 2001, *The ValueReporting™ revolution: moving beyond the earnings game*, John Wiley, New York.

Egginton, DA 1990, 'Towards some principles for intangible asset accounting', *Accounting and Business Research*, Summer, pp. 193–205.

Evans, S 2003, 'Winery presses ahead with float', *The Australian Financial Review*, 9 December.

Gottliebsen, R 1987, 'Recognising the value of intangible assets', *Business Review Weekly*, 13 February, p. 6.

James, D 2001a, 'Intangible virtues', *Business Review Weekly, 4 May*.

— 2001b, 'Hail the "age of access"', *Business Review Weekly, 27 April*.

Jenkins, E & Upton, W 2001, 'Internally generated intangible assets: framing the discussion', *Australian Accounting Review*, vol. 11, no. 2, pp. 4–11.

Kieso, DE & Weygandt, JJ 1992, *Intermediate accounting*, 7th edn, John Wiley, New York.

King, AM & Henry, JM 1999, 'Valuing intangible assets through appraisals', *Strategic Finance*, vol. 81, no. 5, pp. 32–7.
Lev, B 2001, *Intangibles: management, measurement, and reporting*, Brookings Institution Press, Washington, DC.
Mayo, A 2001, *The human value of the enterprise*, Nicholas Brealey Publishing, London.
Napier, C & Power, M 1992, 'Professional research, lobbying and intangibles: a review essay', *Accounting and Business Research*, Winter, pp. 85–95.
Peacock, S 2004, 'A history of most popular brands', *The West Australian*, 14 February, p. 73.
Samuelson, RA 1996, 'The concept of an asset in accounting theory', *Accounting Horizons*, vol. 10, no. 3, pp. 147–57.
Schuetze, WP 1993, 'What is an asset?', *Accounting Horizons*, vol. 7, no. 3, pp. 66–70.
— 2001, 'What are assets and liabilities? Where is true north? (Accounting that my sister would understand)', *Abacus*, vol. 37, no. 1, pp. 1–25.
Swatch 2007, *Annual report 2007*, Swatch Group Ltd, Switzerland, www.swatchgroup.com/en.
Skandia 1998, *Intellectual capital prototype report*, www.skandia.com.
Stevenson, K 1989, 'The precedent in Australian thinking', paper presented at the accounting forum on off-balance-sheet structures, conducted by the Australian Accounting Research Foundation and sponsored by Coopers & Lybrand, Sydney.
Systematic 2002, *Intellectual capital report*, www.systematic.com.
Tabakoff, N 1999, 'Assets: standard deviation', *Business Review Weekly*, 21 May.
Upton, WS 2001, *Business and financial reporting, challenges from the new economy*, Financial Accounting Series No. 219-A, Financial Accounting Standards Board, Norwalk, Connecticut, USA.
Whiting, R & Chapman, K 2003, 'Sporting glory — the great intangible', *Australian CPA*, February.

11 Business combinations

ACCOUNTING STANDARDS IN FOCUS

IFRS 3 *Business Combinations*

LEARNING OBJECTIVES

When you have studied this chapter, you should be able to:

- understand the nature of a business combination and its various forms
- explain the basic steps in the acquisition method of accounting for business combinations
- account in the records of the acquirer
- recognise and measure the assets acquired and liabilities assumed in the business combination
- determine the consideration transferred
- understand the nature of and the accounting for goodwill and gain from bargain purchase
- account for shares acquired in the acquiree
- prepare the accounting records of the acquiree
- account for subsequent adjustments to the initial accounting for a business combination
- provide the disclosures required under IFRS 3.

11.1 THE NATURE OF A BUSINESS COMBINATION

The accounting standard relevant for accounting for business combinations is IFRS 3 *Business Combinations* issued by the International Accounting Standards Board (IASB) in January 2008. In reading IFRS 3, it is important to note that Appendix A contains the defined terms, while Appendix B contains application guidance — both Appendices are an integral part of IFRS 3. The IASB has also published a Basis for Conclusions on IFRS 3, but this is not an integral part of the standard.

A business combination is defined in Appendix A to IFRS 3 as:

> A transaction or other event in which an acquirer obtains control of one or more businesses.

For a business combination to occur there has to be an economic transaction between two entities. A key term in this definition is 'control'. The meaning of control is the same as in IAS 27 *Consolidated and Separate Financial Statements* and is discussed in detail in chapter 21. Control relates to the ability of an entity to determine the financial and operating policies of another entity so as to obtain benefits from the activities of that entity.

The term business is defined in Appendix A as:

> An integrated set of activities and assets that is capable of being conducted and managed for the purpose of providing a return in the form of dividends, lower costs or other economic benefits directly to investors or other owners, members or participants.

The purpose of defining a business is to distinguish between the acquisition of a group of assets — such as a number of desks, bookcases and filing cabinets — and the acquisition of an entity that is capable of producing some form of output. Accounting for a group of assets is based on standards such as IAS 16 *Property, Plant and Equipment* (see chapter 9 of this book) rather than IFRS 3. Paragraph 2(b) of IFRS 3 requires the accounting for a group of assets not constituting a business combination to be at cost, determined by reference to the relative fair values of the individual assets acquired. Fair value is defined in Appendix A to IFRS 3 as the amount for which an asset could be exchanged, or a liability settled, between knowledgeable, willing parties in an arm's length transaction.

In order to provide a return, an entity will normally consist of inputs, processes and outputs; for example, an entity will acquire raw materials which will be processed to produce finished goods that will be sold to customers. The assets of the entity, then, integrate to generate the return to the entity. Note, however, that the definition of business in IFRS 3 does not require the entity to create outputs. The definition only requires that the assets be *capable* of providing a return. Hence, an entity which is in the development stage, such as a mining operation that has not yet produced ore for sale, can still be classified as a business. It is also not necessary that the entity actually be producing outputs at the time of the acquisition, or even that the acquirer plans to use the assets in a particular fashion immediately. As long as the assets are capable of producing a return, the assets constitute a business. Note also the use of the phrase 'integrated set of activities'. As is explained in more detail later in the chapter in the analysis of the nature of goodwill, goodwill arises where there exists synergy between assets. Goodwill is defined in Appendix A to IFRS 3 as an asset representing the future economic benefits arising from assets acquired in a business combination that are not individually and separately recognised. Goodwill can only be recognised when assets are acquired as part of a business (see IFRS 3 paragraph 2(b)).

Consider the situation in figure 11.1 in which entity A acquires a mining division from entity B by issuing its shares to entity B. In this situation, entity A is considered to be the acquirer, as it obtains control of the mining business from entity B. In analysing the substance of the transaction, entity A is acquiring a business from entity B and selling shares in itself to entity B. Entity B is acquiring shares from entity A and selling a mining division to entity A. However, entity B is not undertaking a business combination. It is acquiring a single asset, shares in entity A. In contrast, entity A is acquiring a business, namely the mining division, from entity B. Both entity A and entity B are acquiring assets and giving up some form of consideration. However, only entity A is undertaking a business combination.

The combination of separate businesses requires joining the assets and liabilities of the acquirer with those acquired from the acquiree. Assuming the existence of two companies, A Ltd and B Ltd, the following general forms of business combinations are covered in this chapter:

1. A Ltd acquires all the assets and liabilities of B Ltd.
   B Ltd continues as a company, holding shares in A Ltd.

2. A Ltd acquires all the assets and liabilities of B Ltd.
   B Ltd liquidates.
3. C Ltd is formed to acquire all the assets and liabilities of A Ltd and B Ltd.
   A Ltd and B Ltd liquidate.
4. A Ltd acquires a group of net assets of B Ltd, the group of net assets constituting a business, such as a division, branch or segment, of B Ltd.
   B Ltd continues to operate as a company.

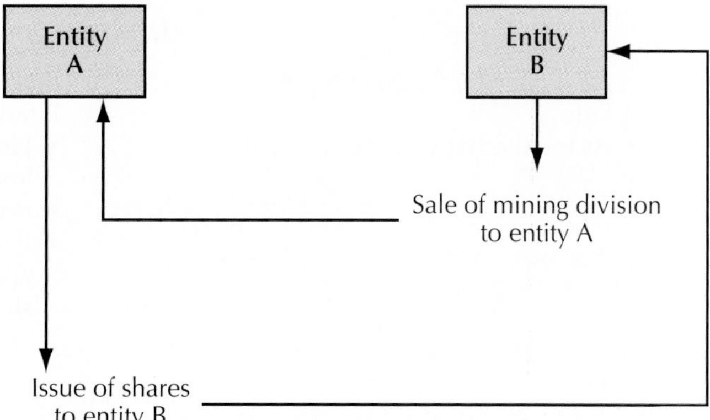

FIGURE 11.1 Identification of a business combination

Obtaining control over the net assets of another entity could be achieved by one entity acquiring the shares of another entity on the open market and, because of the quantity of shares acquired, being able to control the financial and operating policies of the other entity. Accounting for this form of business combination requires the application of the principles discussed in this chapter, but the application further involves the preparation of consolidated financial statements. Accounting for these forms of business combinations is discussed in chapters 21 to 25.

A business combination could also occur without any exchange of assets or equity between the entities involved in the exchange. For example, a business combination could occur where two entities merged under a contract. The shareholders of the two entities could agree to adjust the rights of each of their shareholdings so that they receive a specified share of the profits of both the combined entities. As a result of the contract, both entities would be under the control of a single management group. Business combinations are also not restricted to transactions involving companies. Mutual entities (see the definition in IFRS 3 Appendix A) such as credit unions and mutual insurance companies which combine together, for example to increase their market share and to lower their risk, may also have to account for the combination under IFRS 3.

There are many other forms of business combinations that can occur, such as A Ltd acquiring the assets only of B Ltd, and B Ltd paying off the liabilities and then liquidating. Alternatively, A Ltd may acquire all the assets and only some of the liabilities of B Ltd, and B Ltd pays the remaining liabilities before liquidating. The number of possible arrangements is quite large, but most situations are covered by consideration of the three alternatives in figure 11.2.

IFRS 3 applies to all business combinations except those listed in paragraph 2 of the standard, namely:

- *Where the business combination results in the formation of a joint venture.* Such a business combination is accounted for under IAS 31 *Interests in Joint Ventures*.
- *Where the business combination involves entities or businesses under common control.* According to Appendix B, such a business combination occurs where all of the combining entities or businesses ultimately are controlled by the same party or parties both before and after the combination, and where control is not transitory. This situation could arise where P Ltd owns 100% of the shares of S Ltd. The directors of P Ltd form a new entity, X Ltd, wholly owned by P Ltd, which acquires all the issued shares of S Ltd in an internal reconstruction. All the combining entities are controlled by P Ltd both before and after the reconstruction.

Alternative 1	
A Ltd acquires net assets of B Ltd A Ltd: • Receipt of assets and liabilities of B Ltd • Consideration transferred, e.g. shares, cash or other consideration	*B Ltd continues, holding shares in A Ltd* B Ltd: • Sale of assets and liabilities to A Ltd • Gain or loss on sale • Receipt of consideration transferred, e.g. shares, cash or other consideration
Alternative 2	
A Ltd acquires net assets of B Ltd A Ltd: • As for alternative 1 above, A Ltd	*B Ltd liquidates* B Ltd: • Liquidation account, including gain/loss on liquidation • Receipt of purchase consideration • Distribution of consideration to appropriate parties, including shareholders via the Shareholders' Distribution account
Alternative 3	
C Ltd formed C Ltd: • Formation of C Ltd with issue of shares • Acquisition of assets and liabilities of A Ltd and B Ltd • Payment for net assets of A Ltd and B Ltd via cash outlays or issue of shares in C Ltd	*A Ltd and B Ltd liquidate* A Ltd and B Ltd: • As for alternative 2 above, B Ltd

FIGURE 11.2 General forms of business combinations

11.2 ACCOUNTING FOR A BUSINESS COMBINATION — BASIC PRINCIPLES

The required method of accounting for a business combination under paragraph 4 of IFRS 3 is the *acquisition method*. The key steps in this method are noted in paragraph 5 of the standard:

- Identify the acquirer.
- Determine the acquisition date.
- Recognise and measure the identifiable assets acquired, the liabilities assumed, and any non-controlling interest in the acquiree.
- Recognise and measure goodwill or a gain from a bargain purchase.

The acquisition method is applied on the acquisition date, which is the date the acquirer obtains control of the acquiree. On this date, the business combination occurs. IFRS 3 also provides requirements for the subsequent measurement and accounting for assets and liabilities recognised initially at acquisition date.

11.2.1 Identifying the acquirer

Paragraph 7 of IFRS 3 states that the acquirer is the entity that obtains control of the acquiree. Paragraph 6 requires an acquirer to be identified in every business combination. It has been argued by some accountants that there are business combinations where it is impossible to identify an acquirer. For example, in its response to the Amendments ED, the Accounting Standards Board in the United Kingdom (2005, p. 8) stated:

> We have reservations about requiring the acquisition method for *all* business combinations. In certain circumstances it may not be possible to identify an acquirer and therefore the use of acquisition

accounting (which reflects acquisition of one entity by another) may not faithfully represent the business combination. We consider that 'true' mergers do occur.

Accounting for combinations achieved by contract alone was introduced in the 2007 issue of IFRS 3 — previously such combinations were excluded from the application of IFRS 3. As noted in paragraph BC79 of the IASB's Basis for Conclusions on IFRS 3, determination of an acquirer in such circumstances may be difficult as there may be no exchange of readily measurable consideration. However, difficulties in identifying an acquirer are not a sufficient reason for justifying a different accounting treatment. As explained later (see section 11.4 of this chapter), the acquisition method requires the assets and liabilities of the *acquiree* to be measured at fair value. It is then necessary in a business combination to determine which entity is the acquirer and which is the acquiree. Consider a situation where entity A enters into a business combination with entity B. If entity A were identified as the acquirer, then it would be the assets and liabilities of entity B that would be measured at fair value; whereas, if entity B were identified as the acquirer, it would be entity A's assets and liabilities that would be recorded at fair value.

In Appendix A to IFRS 3, the acquirer is defined as 'the entity that obtains control of the acquiree' while an acquiree is defined as 'the business or businesses that the acquirer obtains control of in a business combination'. The key criterion, then, in identifying an acquirer is that of control. This term is the same as that used in IAS 27 *Consolidated and Separate Financial Statements* for identifying a parent–subsidiary relation (see chapter 21 of this book), and is defined in Appendix A as 'the power to govern the financial and operating policies of an entity or business so as to obtain benefits from its activities'. In some situations, it is very easy to identify an acquirer. For example, if entity A acquires more than half the shares of entity B, then entity A will have control over entity B because its majority shareholding will give entity A more than half of the voting rights of entity B as well as control of entity B's board.

In other situations, identification of an acquirer requires judgement. Consider the situation where entity A combines with entity B. To effect the combination, a new company (entity C) is formed, which issues shares to acquire all the shares of both entities A and B. The subsequent organisation structure is as shown below:

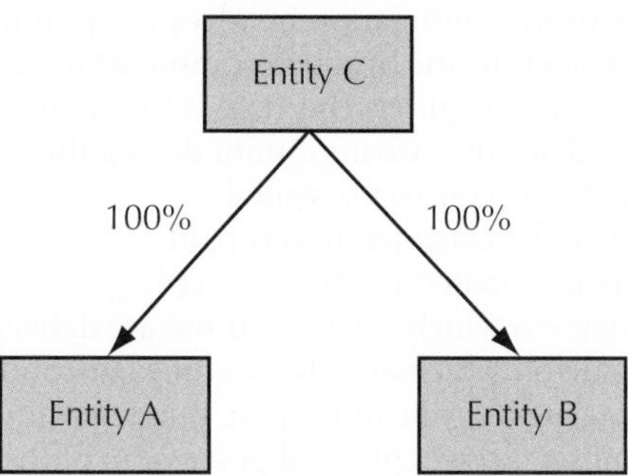

As entity C is created solely to formalise the organisation structure, it is not the acquirer although it may be considered to be the legal parent of both the other entities. As noted in paragraph B18 of Appendix B to IFRS 3, one of the entities that existed before the combination must be identified as the acquirer, as entity C is not a party to the decisions associated with the business combination, just a part of the form of the organisation structure created to facilitate the combination. As noted earlier, if entity A is identified as the acquirer, then the assets and liabilities of entity B (the acquiree) are measured at fair value at acquisition date.

Paragraphs B14–B18 of Appendix B to IFRS 3 provide some indicators to assist in assessing which entity is the acquirer:

- *What are the relative voting rights in the combined entity after the business combination?* The acquirer is usually the entity whose owners have the largest portion of the voting rights in the combined entity. As noted in paragraph B19, in a reverse acquisition, entity X may issue its shares to acquire the shares of entity Y. However, because of the greater number of X shares given to the former Y shareholders relative to those held by the shareholders in entity X before the combination, the former shareholders in entity Y may have the majority of shares in entity X and be able to determine the operating and financial policies of the combined entities.

- *Is there a large minority voting interest in the combined entity?* As discussed in chapter 21 of this book, the acquirer is usually the entity that has the largest minority voting interest in an entity that has a widely dispersed ownership.
- *What is the composition of the governing body of the combined entity?* The acquirer is usually the combining entity whose owners have the ability to elect or appoint or to remove a majority of the members of the governing body of the combined entity.
- *What is the composition of the senior management that governs the combined entity subsequent to the combination?* This is an important indicator given that the criterion for identification of an acquirer is that of control. If X and Y combine, is the senior management group of the combined entity dominated by former senior managers of X or Y?
- *What are the terms of the exchange of equity interests?* Has one of the combining entities paid a premium over the pre-combination fair value of one of the combing entities, an amount paid in order to gain control?
- *Which entity is the larger?* This could be measured by reference to the fair value of each of the combining entities, or relative revenues or profits. In a takeover, it is normally the larger company that takes over the smaller company (that is, the larger company is the acquirer). For example, if the global company Microsoft Ltd combines with Barrow Computers, a small computing company operating in only one Australian city, then it is most likely that Microsoft Ltd is the acquirer.
- *Which entity initiated the exchange?* Normally the entity that is the acquirer is the one that undertakes action to take over the acquiree.

Determining the controlling entity is the key to identification of the acquirer. However, doing so may not be straightforward in many business combinations, and the accountant might be required to make a reasoned judgement based on the circumstances.

11.2.2 Determining the acquisition date

Acquisition date is defined in Appendix A to IFRS 3 as follows:

> The date on which the acquirer obtains control of the acquiree.

A business combination involves the joining together of assets under the control of a specific entity. Therefore, the business combination occurs at the date the assets or net assets are under the control of the acquirer. This date is the acquisition date.

Other dates that are important during the process of the business combination may be:

- the date the contract is signed
- the date the consideration is paid
- a date nominated in the contract
- the date on which assets acquired are delivered to the acquirer
- the date on which an offer becomes unconditional.

These dates may be important, but determination of acquisition date does not depend on when the acquirer receives physical possession of the assets acquired, or actually pays out the consideration to the acquiree. The use of control as the key criterion to determine acquisition date ensures that the substance of the transaction determines the accounting rather than the form of the transaction. For example, assets acquired may be delivered in stages, or payments made for these assets may be made over a period of time with a number of payments being required. As noted in paragraph 9 of IFRS 3, on the closing date of the combination, the acquirer legally transfers the consideration — cash or shares — and acquires the assets and assumes the liabilities of the acquiree. However, in some cases this may not be the acquisition date.

The definition of acquisition date then relates to the point in time when the net assets of the acquiree become the net assets of the acquirer — in essence, the date on which the acquirer can recognise the net assets acquired in its own records. This approach is consistent with the *Framework* in that an asset is defined in terms of future economic benefits that are controlled by an entity.

There are four main areas where the selection of the date affects the accounting for a business combination:

- The identifiable assets acquired and liabilities assumed by the acquirer are measured at the fair value at the acquisition date. The choice of fair value is affected by the choice of the acquisition date.

- The consideration paid by the acquirer is determined as the sum of the fair values of assets given, equity issued and/or liabilities undertaken in exchange for the net assets or shares of another entity. The choice of date affects the measure of fair value. For example, in the case of shares listed on a stock exchange, the market price of these shares may fluctuate on a daily basis. The choice of the acquisition date affects the choice of which particular market price is used in calculating the fair value of shares issued by the acquirer as consideration.
- The acquirer may acquire only some of the shares of the acquiree. The owners of the balance of the shares of the acquiree are called the non-controlling interest — defined in Appendix A as the equity in a subsidiary not attributable, directly or indirectly, to a parent. This non-controlling interest is also measured at fair value at acquisition date.
- The acquirer may have previously held an equity interest in the acquiree prior to obtaining control of the acquiree. For example, entity X may have previously acquired 20% of the shares of entity Y, and now acquires the remaining 80% giving it control of entity Y. The acquisition date is the date when entity X acquired the 80% interest. The 20% share holding will be recorded as an asset in the records of entity X. At acquisition date, the fair value of this investment is measured.

The effect of determining the acquisition date is that the financial position of the combined entity at acquisition date should report the assets and liabilities of the acquiree at that date, and any profits reported as a result of the acquiree's operations within the business combination should reflect profits earned after the acquisition date.

11.3 ACCOUNTING IN THE RECORDS OF THE ACQUIRER

Where the acquirer purchases assets and assumes liabilities of another entity, it has to consider:

(a) the recognition and measurement of the identifiable assets acquired and the liabilities assumed

(b) the measurement of the consideration transferred to the acquiree

(c) the recognition and measurement of goodwill or a gain from a bargain purchase.

As noted in section 11.1, accounting for business combinations where the acquirer purchases the shares of the acquiree is covered in chapters 21 to 25. In this chapter, for such business combinations, only the recognition and measurement of the investment by the acquirer is covered (see section 11.4).

11.4 ACCOUNTING IN THE RECORDS OF THE ACQUIRER: RECOGNITION AND MEASUREMENT OF ASSETS ACQUIRED AND LIABILITIES ASSUMED

11.4.1 Recognition

Paragraph 10 of IFRS 3 states:

> As of the acquisition date, the acquirer shall recognise, separately from goodwill, the identifiable assets acquired, the liabilities assumed and any non-controlling interest in the acquiree. Recognition of identifiable assets acquired and liabilities assumed is subject to the conditions specified in paragraphs 11 and 12.

Paragraph 83 of the *Framework* specifies two recognition criteria for assets and liabilities, stating that recognition occurs if:

- it is probable that any future economic benefit will flow to or from the entity
- the item has a cost or value that can be reliably measured.

In deciding whether to recognise an asset or liability, in a business combination it is assumed that the probability test for the assets acquired and liabilities undertaken in a business combination is unnecessary and that these assets and liabilities will always be able to be measured reliably. Use of estimates simply means the measure may involve uncertainty, but does not mean the measure is unreliable.

In relation to the probability criterion, paragraph BC126 of the Basis for Conclusions on IFRS 3 states explicitly that the acquirer is required 'to recognise identifiable assets acquired and liabilities assumed regardless of the degree of probability of an inflow or outflow of economic benefits'. The assets acquired and liabilities assumed are measured at fair value. That fair value will reflect expectations about the probability of inflows or outflows of benefits. The effects of probability are then built into the measurement of the fair value, and that amount is always expected to be received for assets or paid out for liabilities. The probability criterion is then unnecessary where fair values are used as the measurement method.

In paragraphs 11 and 12 of IFRS 3, there are two conditions that have to be met prior to the recognition of assets and liabilities acquired in the business combination:

Firstly, at the acquisition date, the assets and liabilities recognised by the acquirer must meet the definitions of assets and liabilities in the *Framework*. Any expected future costs cannot be included in the calculation of assets acquired and liabilities assumed.

One area affected by this condition is the accounting for contingent liabilities. IAS 37 *Provisions, Contingent Liabilities and Contingent Assets* paragraph 10 contains the following definition of a contingent liability:

> (a) a possible obligation that arises from past events and whose existence will be confirmed only by the occurrence or non-occurrence of one or more uncertain future events not wholly within the control of the entity; or
>
> (b) a present obligation that arises from past events but is not recognised because:
>
> (i) it is not probable that an outflow of resources embodying economic benefits will be required to settle the obligation; or
>
> (ii) the amount of the obligation cannot be measured with sufficient reliability.

Note that there are two types of contingent liabilities — real liabilities (present obligations) that are not recognised because of a failure to meet the recognition criteria, and non-liabilities (possible obligations). As the contingent liabilities under (b) above are real liabilities, they are recognised by the acquirer in a business combination and measured at fair value. The requirements in terms of the recognition criteria in IAS 37 do not apply for a business combination. However, the contingent liabilities under (a) above are not real liabilities and therefore are not recognised in a business combination.

Secondly, the item acquired or assumed must be part of the business acquired rather than the result of a separate transaction. This recognition principle is an example of the application of substance over form in that the entities involved in the transaction may link another transaction with the business combination, but in substance it is a separate transaction. Paragraphs 51–52 of IFRS 3 contain examples of such transactions. One example is where the business combination transaction settles pre-existing relationships between the acquirer and the acquiree. Paragraph BC122 explains this by providing the example where a potential acquiree has a receivable for an unresolved claim against the potential acquirer. As part of the agreement to combine, the acquirer agrees to settle the claim with the acquiree, and part of the consideration transferred is for that purpose. It is then necessary to separate the two transactions and separate out of the consideration transferred the amount paid to settle the claim.

As noted in paragraph 13 of IFRS 3, a possible result of applying the principles of IFRS 3 is that there may be assets and liabilities recognised as a result of the business combination that were not recognised by the acquiree. One example of this is internally generated intangibles that were not recognised by the acquiree on the application of IAS 38 *Intangible Assets*; for example, internally generated brands would not be recognised by an acquiree but would be recognised by the acquirer. The acquirer would measure these at fair value.

In recognising the assets and liabilities, it is necessary to classify or designate them. Paragraph 15 requires that the acquirer do this on the basis of the contractual terms, economic conditions, its operating or accounting policies and other pertinent conditions that exist at acquisition date. One example of this is the classification of financial instruments, for example, as financial assets available for sale or held to maturity, or at fair value through profit or loss. One exception to this classification requirement is leases. Leases are classified as operating or finance leases in accordance with IAS 17 *Leases*.

As shown in figure 10.2 (p. 366), as a part of the illustrative examples accompanying IFRS 3, the IASB provided examples of items acquired in a business combination that would meet the definition of an intangible asset (see figure 11.3).

CLASS	BASIS
Marketing-related intangible assets	
Trademarks, trade names, service marks, collective marks and certification marks	Contractual
Trade dress (unique colour, shape or package design)	Contractual
Newspaper mastheads	Contractual
Internet domain names	Contractual
Non-competition agreements	Contractual
Customer-related intangible assets	
Customer lists	Non-contractual
Order or production backlog	Contractual
Customer contracts and the related customer relationships	Contractual
Non-contractual customer relationships	Non-contractual
Artistic-related intangible assets	
Plays, operas and ballets	Contractual
Books, magazines, newspapers and other literary works	Contractual
Musical works such as compositions, song lyrics and advertising jingles	Contractual
Pictures and photographs	Contractual
Video and audiovisual material, including motion pictures or films, music videos and television programs	Contractual
Contract-based intangible assets	
Licensing, royalty and standstill agreements	Contractual
Advertising, construction, management, service or supply contracts	Contractual
Lease agreements (whether the acquiree is the lessee or lessor)	Contractual
Construction permits	Contractual
Franchise agreements	Contractual
Operating and broadcasting rights	Contractual
Use rights such as drilling, water, air, mineral, timber-getting and route authorities	Contractual
Servicing contracts such as mortgage servicing contracts	Contractual
Employment contracts	Contractual
Technology-based intangible assets	
Patented technology	Contractual
Computer software and mask works	Contractual
Unpatented technology	Non-contractual
Databases including title plants	Non-contractual
Trade secrets such as secret formulas, processes or recipes	Contractual

FIGURE 11.3 Intangible assets, IFRS 3 illustrative examples

11.4.2 Measurement

Paragraph 18 requires an acquirer to measure the identifiable assets acquired and the liabilities assumed at their fair values on acquisition date.

Fair value is defined in Appendix A to IFRS 3 as follows:

> The amount for which an asset could be exchanged, or a liability settled, between knowledgeable, willing parties in an arm's length transaction.

Fair value is basically a market-based measure in a transaction between unrelated parties. However, the process of determining fair value necessarily involves judgement and estimation. The acquiring entity is not actually trading the items in the marketplace for cash, but is trying to estimate what the exchange price would be if it did so. Hence, the determination of fair value involves estimation.

Paragraphs 42–44 of IAS 40 *Investment Properties* discuss what 'a transaction between knowledgeable, willing parties' means:

> In this context, 'knowledgeable' means that both the willing buyer and the willing seller are reasonably informed about the nature and characteristics of the investment property, its actual and potential uses, and market conditions at the end of the reporting period. A willing buyer is motivated, but not compelled, to buy. The buyer is neither over-eager nor determined to buy at any price . . .
>
> The willing seller is motivated to sell the investment property at market terms for the best price obtainable. The factual circumstances of the actual investment property owner are not a part of this consideration because the willing seller is a hypothetical owner (e.g. a willing seller would not take into account the particular tax circumstances of the investment property owner).
>
> The definition of fair value refers to an arm's length transaction. An arm's length transaction is one between parties that do not have a particular or special relationship that makes prices of transactions uncharacteristic of market conditions. The transaction is presumed to be between unrelated parties, each acting independently.

To assist in the determination of fair value, the standard setters have developed a 'fair value hierarchy', the purpose of which is to provide a list of ways in which fair value can be measured in a business combination, in order of preference. Measurement under the fair value hierarchy is as follows:

Level 1. The estimate of fair value is to be determined by reference to *observable prices of market transactions* for identical assets or liabilities at or near the measurement date whenever that information is available.

Level 2. If Level 1 is not available, the estimate of fair value should be determined by *adjusting observable prices of market transactions for similar assets or liabilities* that occur at or near the measurement date. A similar asset or liability is one that is reasonably comparable, e.g. one having similar patterns of cash flows that can be expected to respond to changes in economic conditions in the same way as those of the item being measured. Generally, when an asset or liability is sufficiently similar to an asset or liability being measured, adjustments for any difference are objectively determinable. For example, similar assets may be identical in all respects except for location. If the only difference between two assets is their location, the fair value will equal the observable price of an identical item in a different location plus costs to ship the item to the identical location as the asset being measured.

Level 3. If neither Level 1 nor Level 2 is available, the estimate of fair value should be determined using *other valuation techniques*. Valuation techniques are to be consistent with the objective of estimating fair value, and should incorporate assumptions that marketplace participants would use whenever market-based information is available without undue cost or effort. If market-based information is not available without undue cost and effort, an entity may, as a practical expedient, use its own assumptions as inputs. However, for any valuation technique, market inputs should be maximised and use of internal estimates and assumptions minimised. For example, if an entity is aware of unique advantages or disadvantages that it possesses, such as favourable labour rates or superior processing or manufacturing technologies, it should adjust its entity-specific assumptions so that the inputs into the valuation process or model reflect those that marketplace participants would incorporate in an estimate of fair value.

This hierarchy is used in IAS 38 *Intangible Assets*, paragraphs 39–41. Paragraph 21 of this standard requires intangible assets to be initially measured at cost. In a business combination, the costs of the individual assets acquired are measured by reference to the fair values of those assets. Various measures of these fair values are possible:

- *Quoted market prices.* An active market is defined in paragraph 8 of IAS 38 as one which has all the following conditions:
  - the items traded within the market are homogeneous
  - willing buyers and sellers can normally be found at any time
  - prices are available to the public.

  Where there is an active market, the fair value is determined by reference to quoted market prices.
- *Recent transactions.* Where there is no active market, reference must be made to other sources of information, such as recent transactions in the same or similar items. One of the problems with intangible assets is that their unique nature in many cases precludes the use of information from other transactions.

- *Measurement techniques.* With the increasing importance of intangible assets, there has been a growing establishment of entities that specialise in measuring intangible assets, particularly brands. These valuation firms measure the worth of intangible assets by using variations of present value techniques, and multiples of variables such as royalty rates. As noted in paragraph 41 of IAS 38, these methods should 'reflect current transactions and practices in the industry to which the asset belongs'.

The hierarchy in IAS 38 is not substantially different from that used for assets acquired and liabilities assumed in a business combination. However, there are still issues that need to be discussed by the standard setters, such as whether the market referred to is wholesale or retail, whether it should take into account geographical markets, and whether it is the exit price or the entry price that should be considered.

Further, in Appendix A to IAS 39 *Financial Instruments: Recognition and Measurement,* paragraphs AG69–AG82 consider the measurement of fair value for financial instruments, with a hierarchy of (1) active market with quoted prices, (2) no active market and using recent market transactions, and (3) no active market and use of valuation techniques.

Figure 11.4 contains an extract from the 2006 Annual Report of Danisco Ltd, a Danish company that is one of the world's leading producers of ingredients for food and other consumer products. Danisco acquired Genencor International Inc. Ltd in 2004–05 and in its 2006 financial report provided an explanation of the fair value measurements used in accounting for this acquisition. Different techniques of measurements were used to measure the fair values of different assets.

22 Purchase of enterprises and activities

2005/06

Genencor International Inc.

The measurement of the acquired assets and liabilities was concluded in 2005/06, and the basis for their recognition and the calculation of goodwill was established. The measurement of the intangible assets was based on identification of cash generating values. Where it has been possible to relate the values directly to the earnings of the business, this has been used as the basis of the measurement. For technologies and other values not directly related to the cash flows of earnings, the measurement has been determined on the basis of replacement cost. The calculations are based on a WACC of 9%.

The fair value measurements have resulted in identification of total intangible assets of DKK 514 million and a consequent fair value adjustment against the carrying amounts of DKK 264 million. The most important identified intangible assets are patents of DKK 178 million, technology related to enzyme production of DKK 103 million, and customer contracts, licenses and other intangible assets of DKK 225 million.

The measurement of property, plant and equipment has for all major buildings and plant been based on external valuations. Production equipment and other non-current assets have primarily been measured by the company's own production engineers.

The fair value measurements have resulted in writedowns of DKK 366 million of property, plant and equipment, mainly buildings and production equipment in the USA, Belgium and Finland, which due to geographical location, wear and tear and reduced useful lives carry a lower fair value.

The fair value adjustment of deferred tax and tax payable is related to the above adjustments of intangible and tangible assets and to estimated tax liabilities associated with events before the date of acquisition.

FIGURE 11.4 Alternative measures of fair value, Danisco
Source: Danisco (2006, p. 70).

Why did the IASB choose fair value as the measurement principle? The IASB provided an answer in paragraph BC198 of the Basis for Conclusions on IFRS 3:

> In developing the measurement principle in the revised standards, the boards concluded that fair value is the most *relevant* attribute for assets acquired and liabilities assumed in a business combination. Measurement at fair value also provides information that is more *comparable* and *understandable* than measurement at cost or on the basis of allocating the total cost of an acquisition. [emphasis added]

One of the problems that may arise in measuring the assets and liabilities of the acquiree is that the initial accounting for the business combination may be incomplete by the end of the reporting period. For example, the acquisition date may be 20 June and the end of the reporting period may be 30 June. In this situation, in accordance with paragraph 45 of IFRS 3, the acquirer must report provisional amounts in its financial statements. The provisional amounts will be best estimates and will need to be adjusted to fair values when those amounts can be determined after the end of the reporting period. The measurement period in which the adjustments can be made cannot exceed one year after the acquisition date. In its acquisition in 2004–05 of Genencor Ltd, Danisco only reported provisional amounts in its 2004–05 financial statements. In its 2005–06 annual report it provided the information shown in figure 11.5.

2005/06

Danisco did not buy any enterprises in 2005/06. The opening balance sheet for acquisitions in 2004/05 was adjusted to fair value in 2005/06. The effect is shown below.

	Genencor					
DKK million	**Carrying amount prior to acquisition**	**Fair value adjustments in 2004/05**	**Preliminary opening balance at fair value at 30 April 2005**	**Fair value adjustments in 2005/06**	**Reclassifi-cation of preliminary opening balance**	**Final opening balance at fair value**
Intangible assets	—	—	—	264	250	514
Property, plant and equipment	696	—	696	(366)	—	330
Investments	101	(4)	97	1	—	98
Inventories	242	58	300	(15)	—	285
Receivables and prepayments	277	—	277	(2)	—	275
Other investments and securities	—	—	—	—	—	—
Cash and cash equivalents	551	—	551	—	—	551
Minority interests	(1)	—	(1)	—	—	(1)
Other provisions	(56)	—	(56)	(40)	—	(96)
Provisions for deferred tax	(17)	(22)	(39)	(71)	—	(110)
Financial liabilities	(106)	—	(106)	(5)	—	(111)
Non-interest-bearing debt	(136)	(78)	(214)	—	—	(214)
Corporation tax	(22)	—	(22)	19	—	(3)
Net assets	**1 529**	**(46)**	**1 483**	**(215)**	**250**	**1 518**
Goodwill on purchase of enterprises and activities			2 597	192	(250)	2 539
Adjustment of cash and cash equivalents			(551)	—	—	(551)
Cash purchase amount			**3 529**	**(23)**	**—**	**3 506**

Total fair value adjustments of acquisitions in the year	**Total fair value adjustments**	**Transferred to equity**	**Transferred to goodwill**
Genencor International Inc.	192	(90)	102
Danisco Sweeteners (Anyang) Co. Ltd	(4)	—	(4)
Rhodia Food Ingredients	30	—	30
Total	**218**	**(90)**	**128**

FIGURE 11.5 Provisional measurements of fair value, Danisco

Source: Danisco (2006, note 22, p. 69).

After the end of the reporting period, as new information and facts are gathered, the acquirer will progressively adjust the assets and liabilities acquired to fair value. This process may also result in the recognition of new assets and liabilities previously not recognised. The adjustments in assets and liabilities are recognised by means of an increase or decrease in goodwill (IFRS 3 paragraph 48).

11.5 ACCOUNTING IN THE RECORDS OF THE ACQUIRER: CONSIDERATION TRANSFERRED

Paragraph 32 of IFRS 3 states:

> The acquirer shall recognise goodwill as of the acquisition date measured as the excess of (a) over (b) below:
> (a) the aggregate of:
> (i) the consideration transferred measured in accordance with this Standard, which generally requires acquisition-date fair value (see paragraph 37);
> (ii) the amount of any non-controlling interest in the acquiree measured in accordance with this Standard; and
> (iii) in a business combination achieved in stages (see paragraphs 41 and 42), the acquisition-date fair value of the acquirer's previously held equity interest in the acquiree.
> (b) the net of the acquisition-date amounts of the identifiable assets acquired and the liabilities assumed measured in accordance with this Standard.

In relation to parts (a)(ii) and (iii) in paragraph 32, these will affect calculations only where the acquirer obtains control by acquiring shares in the acquiree. This is discussed in chapters 21–25 of this book. This means that for business combinations discussed in this chapter, goodwill is determined by comparing the consideration transferred by the acquirer with the net fair value of the identifiable assets and liabilities acquired.

According to paragraph 37, the consideration transferred:

- is measured at fair value at acquisition date
- is calculated as the sum of the acquisition-date fair values of the assets transferred by the acquirer, the liabilities incurred by the acquirer to former owners of the acquiree, and the equity interest issued by the acquirer.

In a specific exchange, the consideration transferred to the acquiree could include just one form of consideration, such as cash, but could equally well consist of a number of forms such as cash, other assets, shares and contingent consideration. These are considered in the following pages.

Cash or other monetary assets

The fair value is the amount of cash or cash equivalent dispersed. The amount is usually readily determinable. One problem that may occur arises when the settlement is deferred to a time after the acquisition date. For a deferred payment, the fair value to the acquirer is the amount the entity would have to borrow to settle the debt immediately. Hence, the discount rate used is the entity's incremental borrowing rate.

Use of cash, including a deferred payment, to acquire net assets results in the acquirer recording the following form of entry at the acquisition date:

Net assets	Dr	XXX	
Cash	Cr		XXX
Payable to Acquiree	Cr		XXX
(Acquisition of net assets with partially deferred payment)			

When the deferred payment is made to the acquiree, the interest component needs to be recognised:

Payable to Acquiree	Dr	XXX	
Interest Expense	Dr	XXX	
Cash	Cr		XXX
(Payment of deferred amount)			

Non-monetary assets

Non-monetary assets are assets such as property, plant and equipment, investments, licences and patents. As noted earlier, if active second-hand markets exist, fair values can be obtained by reference to those markets. The items sold in the market may not be exactly the same as the item being exchanged in the business combination, and an estimate of fair value for the specific item may have to be made. Where active markets do not exist, other means of valuation, including the use of expert valuers, may be used.

The acquirer is effectively selling the non-monetary asset to the acquiree. Hence, it is earning income equal to the fair value on the sale of the asset. Where the carrying amount of the asset in the records of the acquirer is different from fair value, a gain or loss on the asset is recognised at acquisition date. This principle is explained in paragraph 38 of IFRS 3: 'the acquirer shall remeasure the transferred assets or liabilities to their fair values as of the acquisition date and recognise the resulting gains or losses, if any, in profit or loss'.

Use of a non-monetary asset such as plant as part of the consideration to acquire net assets results in the acquirer recording the following entries (assume a cost of plant of $180, a carrying amount of $150 and fair value of $155):

Accumulated Depreciation	Dr	30	
Plant	Cr		25
Gain	Cr		5
(Remeasurement as part of consideration transferred in a business combination)			
Net Assets Acquired	Dr	XXX	
Plant	Cr		155
Other Consideration Payable	Cr		XXX
(Acquisition of net assets)			

The acquirer recognises a gain on the non-current asset and the asset is then included in the consideration transferred at fair value.

Equity instruments

If an acquirer issues its own shares as consideration, it needs to determine the fair value of those shares at the acquisition date. For listed entities, reference is made to the quoted prices of the shares. As noted in paragraph BC342 of the Basis for Conclusions on IFRS 3, 'equity instruments issued as consideration in a business combination should be measured at their fair values on the acquisition date'.

There has been considerable ongoing debate within the accounting community about which date should be used to measure the fair value of equity instruments issued. As noted in paragraph BC342, the IASB and the Financial Accounting Standards Board (FASB) have discussed two alternative models, namely the acquisition date model (equity instruments would be measured on the date the acquirer obtains control over the business acquired), and the agreement date model (equity instruments would be measured on the date a substantive agreement is reached between the acquirer and the target's management).

Some of the arguments raised in favour of the *agreement date model* were:

- The agreement date more effectively identifies the value of the acquired business that is negotiated between the parties to the transaction.
- Fluctuations in the price of the acquirer's equity instruments between the agreement date and the acquisition date could be due to factors unrelated to the business combination. If acquisition date is used, the consideration paid will include the effects of these factors, thus affecting the value of the net assets of the acquiree recorded.
- At the agreement date, the parties are essentially committed to the transaction such that neither party can renege on the agreements without adverse consequences. The value of the transaction should not be revalued after that date.
- The fair value at agreement date reflects the bargained exchange price between the entities involved in the exchange. Movements in the price of the acquirer's equity instruments after the agreement date will be affected by the market's reaction to the agreement. These fluctuations should not be considered in the value of the business combination transaction since they

were not specifically negotiated by the acquirer and the management of the acquiree. Further, at agreement date, there is probably some correlation between the fair value of the net assets to be received in the future and the fair value of the equity interests given as consideration. Movements in the value of the net assets and movements in the value of the equity instruments between agreement date and acquisition date are probably unrelated.

The following arguments were presented in favour of the *acquisition date model*:

- There is not a strong conceptual basis for either the acquisition date or agreement date. In this case, the simpler of the two methods should be used.
- The measurement on the acquisition date is a fairly universal concept in accounting.
- The acquisition date model values net assets or equity given up on the same date as the identifiable assets and liabilities. The agreement date model adds confusion, since the purchase consideration is valued on one date and the acquired assets and liabilities are measured on a later date.
- As the share price of the acquirer usually declines after a combination is announced, the acquisition date is less likely to require an immediate write-down of goodwill.

The IASB noted there were valid arguments for both models. It subsequently voted to support acquisition date, being the date that control passes from the acquiree to the acquirer, in the interests of convergence with the FASB. Two of the reasons given were:

- the consideration given and the assets acquired and liabilities assumed would be measured on the same date, including the residual goodwill
- the parties to a business combination are likely to take into account expected changes between the agreement date and the acquisition date in the fair value of the acquirer and the market price of the acquirer's securities issued as consideration.

Liabilities undertaken

The fair values of liabilities undertaken are best measured by the present values of expected future cash outflows. Future losses or other costs expected to be incurred as a result of the combination are not liabilities of the acquirer and are therefore not included in the calculation of the fair value of consideration paid.

Costs of issuing debt and equity instruments

In issuing equity instruments such as shares as part of the consideration paid, transaction costs such as stamp duties, professional advisers' fees, underwriting costs and brokerage fees may be incurred. As noted in paragraph 53 of IFRS 3, these costs are accounted for in accordance with IAS 32 *Financial Instruments: Disclosure and Presentation*. Paragraph 35 of IAS 32 states that these outlays should be treated as a reduction in the share capital of the entity as such costs reduce the proceeds from the equity issue, net of any related income tax benefit. Hence, if costs of $1000 are incurred in issuing shares as part of the consideration paid, the journal entry in the records of the acquirer is:

Share Capital	Dr	1 000	
Cash	Cr		1 000
(Costs of issuing equity instruments)			

Similarly, the costs of arranging and issuing financial liabilities are an integral part of the liability issue transaction. These costs are included in the initial measurement of the liability.

However, as noted in paragraph BC366, it is possible that the accounting for such costs may change in the future.

Contingent consideration

Appendix A to IFRS 3 provides the following definition of contingent consideration:

> Usually, an obligation of the acquirer to transfer additional assets or equity interests to the former owners of an acquiree as part of the exchange for control of the acquiree if specified future events occur or conditions are met. However, contingent consideration also may give the acquirer the right to the return of previously transferred consideration if specified conditions are met.

Consider two examples of contingencies. The first is where, because the future income of the acquirer is regarded as uncertain, the agreement contains a clause that requires the acquirer to provide additional consideration to the acquiree if the income of the acquirer is not equal to or exceeds a specified amount over some specified period. The second situation is where the acquirer issues shares to the acquiree and the acquiree is concerned that the issue of these shares may make the market price of the acquirer's shares decline over time. Therefore, the acquirer may offer additional cash or shares if the market price falls below a specified amount over a specified period of time.

According to paragraph 39 of IFRS 3, consistent with other measurements in transferred consideration, the acquirer shall recognise the acquisition-date fair values of contingent consideration as part of the consideration transferred.

Some respondents on the exposure draft to IFRS 3 expressed concern about the ability of preparers of financial statements to measure reliably the fair value of assets and liabilities arising from contingencies. However, as noted in paragraph BC228, standard setters believe that this measurement should be no more difficult than measuring other fair values at acquisition date. There should be sufficient information at acquisition date based upon discussions undertaken and information collected prior to acquisition date during the acquisition negotiations and process to enable fair value to be measured.

11.5.1 Acquisition-related costs

In addition to the consideration transferred by the acquirer to the acquiree, a further item to be considered in determining the cost of the business combination is the costs directly attributable to the combination, which includes costs 'such as finder's fees; advisory, legal accounting, valuation and other professional or consulting fees; [and] general administrative costs, including the costs of maintaining an internal acquisitions department;' (IFRS 3 paragraph 53).

In IAS 16 *Property, Plant and Equipment* and IAS 38 *Intangible Assets*, directly attributable costs are considered as a part of the cost of acquisition and capitalised into the cost of the asset acquired. In contrast, the acquisition-related costs associated with a business combination are accounted for as expenses in the periods in which they are incurred and the services are received. The key reasons given for this approach are provided in paragraph BC366:

- Acquisition-related costs are not part of the fair value exchange between the buyer and seller.
- They are separate transactions for which the buyer pays the fair value for the services received.
- These amounts do not generally represent assets of the acquirer at acquisition date because the benefits obtained are consumed as the services are received.

The IFRS 3 accounting for these outlays is a result of the decision to record the identifiable assets acquired and liabilities assumed at fair value. In contrast, under IAS 16 and IAS 38, the assets acquired are initially recorded at cost.

ILLUSTRATIVE EXAMPLE 11.1

Consideration transferred in a business combination

The trial balance below represents the financial position of Siena Ltd at 1 January 2011.

SIENA LTD
Trial Balance
as at 1 January 2011

	Debit	Credit
Share capital		
Preference — 6000 fully paid shares		$ 6 000
Ordinary — 30 000 fully paid shares		30 000
Retained earnings		21 500
Equipment	$42 000	
Accumulated depreciation – equipment		10 000
Inventory	18 000	
Accounts receivable	16 000	
Patents	3 500	
Debentures		4 000
Accounts payable		8 000
	$79 500	$79 500

At this date, the business of Siena Ltd is acquired by Rome Ltd, with Siena Ltd going into liquidation. The terms of acquisition are as follows:

1. Rome Ltd is to take over all the assets of Siena Ltd as well as the accounts payable of Siena Ltd.
2. Costs of liquidation of $350 are to be paid by Siena Ltd with funds supplied by Rome Ltd.
3. Preference shareholders of Siena Ltd are to receive two fully paid shares in Rome Ltd for every three shares held or, alternatively, $1 per share in cash payable at acquisition date.
4. Ordinary shareholders of Siena Ltd are to receive two fully paid ordinary shares in Rome Ltd for every share held or, alternatively, $2.50 in cash, payable half at the acquisition date and half on 31 December 2011.
5. Debenture holders of Siena Ltd are to be paid in cash out of funds provided by Rome Ltd. These debentures have a fair value of $102 per $100 debenture.
6. All shares being issued by Rome Ltd have a fair value of $1.10 per share. Holders of 3000 preference shares and 5000 ordinary shares elect to receive the cash.
7. Costs of issuing and registering the shares issued by Rome Ltd amount to $40 for the preference shares and $100 for the ordinary shares.
8. Costs associated with the business combination and incurred by Rome Ltd were $1000.

The calculation of the consideration transferred in the business combination to Rome Ltd is shown in figure 11.6. The incremental borrowing rate for Rome Ltd is 10% p.a.

Consideration transferred:

			Fair value
Cash:	Costs of liquidation	$ 350	
	Preference shareholders (3000 × $1.00)	3 000	
	Ordinary shareholders		
	– payable immediately ($\frac{1}{2}$ × 5000 × $2.50)	6 250	
		5 682	
	– payable later ($\frac{1}{2}$ × 5000 × $2.50 × 0.909091)*	4 080	$19 362
	Debentures, including premium ($4000 × 1.02)	2 200	
Shares:	Preference shareholders (2000 × $1.10)	55 000	57 200
	Ordinary shareholders (50 000 × $1.10)		$76 562
Consideration transferred			

$5682 is the cash payable in one year's time discounted at 10% p.a.

FIGURE 11.6 Consideration transferred in the business combination

In acquiring the net assets of Siena Ltd, Rome Ltd passes the journal entries shown in figure 11.7.

FIGURE 11.7 Journal entries in the acquirer's records

2011				
Jan. 1	Net Assets Acquired	Dr	76 562	
	Consideration Payable	Cr		19 362
	Share Capital — Preference	Cr		2 200
	Share Capital — Ordinary	Cr		55 000
	(Acquisition of the net assets of Siena Ltd)			
	Consideration Payable	Dr	13 680	
	Cash	Cr		13 680
	(Payment of cash consideration to Siena Ltd: $19 362 less $5682 payable later)			
	Share Capital — Ordinary	Dr	100	
	Share Capital — Preference	Dr	40	
	Cash	Cr		140
	(Share issue costs)			

(continued)

FIGURE 11.7 *(continued)*

Jan. 1 *(continued)*	Acquisition-related Expenses Cash (Acquisition-related expenses)	Dr Cr	1 000	 1 000
Dec. 31	Consideration Payable Interest Expense Cash (Balance of consideration paid)	Dr Dr Cr	5 682 568	 6 250

11.6 ACCOUNTING IN THE RECORDS OF THE ACQUIRER: GOODWILL AND GAIN FROM BARGAIN PURCHASE

11.6.1 Goodwill

As noted in section 11.5 of this chapter, for the business combinations discussed in this chapter, goodwill is the excess of the consideration transferred over the net fair value of the identifiable assets acquired and liabilities assumed.

> Goodwill = Consideration transferred
> *less*
> Acquirer's interest in the net fair value of the acquiree's identifiable assets and liabilities

Goodwill is accounted for as an asset and is defined in Appendix A to IFRS 3 as:

> An asset representing the future economic benefits arising from other assets acquired in a business combination that are not individually identified and separately recognised.

The criterion of 'being individually identified' relates to the characteristic of 'identifiability' as used in IAS 38 *Intangible Assets* to distinguish intangible assets from goodwill. Note paragraph 11 of IAS 38 in this regard:

The definition of an intangible asset requires an intangible asset to be identifiable to distinguish it from goodwill. Goodwill acquired in a business combination represents a payment made by the acquirer in anticipation of future economic benefits from assets that are not capable of being individually identified and separately recognised. The future economic benefits may result from synergy between the identifiable assets acquired or from assets that, individually, do not qualify for recognition in the financial statements but for which the acquirer is prepared to make a payment in the business combination.

In order to be identifiable, an asset must be capable of being separated or divided from the entity, or arise from contractual or other legal rights. The notion of being 'separately recognised' is also then a part of the criterion of 'identifiability'. This criterion is discussed further in chapter 10.

Goodwill is then a residual, after the acquirer's interest in the identifiable tangible assets, intangible assets, and liabilities of the acquiree is recognised.

The components of goodwill

Johnson and Petrone (1998, p. 295) identified six components of goodwill:

1. *Excess of the fair values over the book values of the acquiree's recognised assets.* In a business acquisition, as assets acquired are measured at fair value, these excesses should not exist. Subsequent to the acquisition, the acquiree's goodwill could include such excesses where assets are measured at cost.

2. *Fair values of other net assets not recognised by the acquiree.* The assets of concern here are those tangible assets which are incapable of reliable measurement by the acquiree, and non-physical assets that do not meet the identifiability criteria for intangible assets.
3. *Fair value of the 'going concern' element of the acquiree's existing business.* This represents the ability of the acquiree to earn a higher return on an assembled collection of net assets than would be expected from those net assets operating separately. This reflects synergies of the assets, as well as factors relating to market imperfections such as an ability of an entity to earn a monopoly profit, or where there are barriers to competitors entering a particular market.
4. *Fair value from combining the acquirer's and acquiree's businesses and net assets.* This stems from the synergies that result from the combination, the value of which is unique to each combination.
5. *Overvaluation of the consideration paid by the acquirer.* This relates to errors in valuing the consideration paid by the acquirer, and may arise particularly where shares are issued as consideration with differences in prices for small parcels of shares as opposed to controlling parcels of shares. There could also be overvaluation of the fair values of the assets acquired. This component could then relate to all errors in measuring the fair values in the business combination.
6. *Overpayment (or underpayment) by the acquirer.* This may occur if the price is driven up in the course of bidding; conversely, goodwill could be understated if the acquiree's net assets were obtained through a distress or fire sale.

In paragraph BC130 of the Basis for Conclusions on IFRS 3, the IASB recognised that components 1 and 2 above are not conceptually part of goodwill. Johnson and Petrone (1998, p. 295) and the IASB (paragraph BC131) recognised that components 5 and 6 in the above list also are not conceptually part of goodwill, but rather relate to measurement errors. The two components that are seen as part of goodwill are components 3 and 4, described by Johnson and Petrone (p. 296) as 'going-concern goodwill' and 'combination goodwill' respectively, with the combination of the components being referred to as 'core goodwill'. This is represented diagrammatically in figure 11.8.

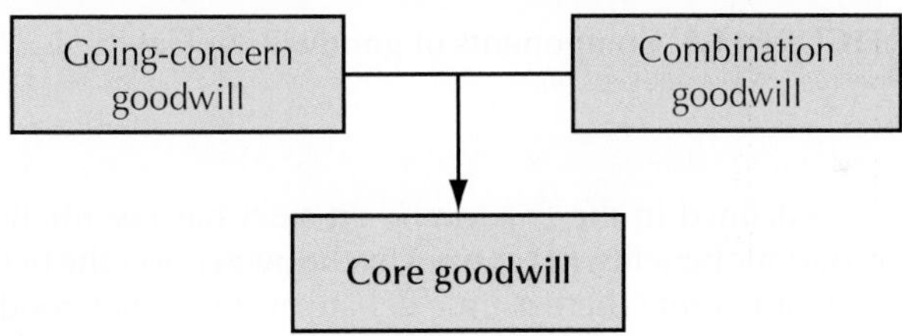

FIGURE 11.8 Core goodwill
Source: Data derived from Johnson and Petrone (1998).

It is this 'core goodwill' that the IASB is concerned with in determining how to account for goodwill. The IASB in paragraph BC137 of the Basis for Conclusions on IFRS 3 note how IFRS 3 tries to avoid subsuming the first, second and fifth components into the amount calculated as goodwill by requiring an acquirer to make every effort to:

- measure the consideration accurately (eliminating or reducing component 5)
- recognise the identifiable net assets acquired at their fair values rather than their carrying amounts (eliminating or reducing component 1)
- recognise all acquired intangible assets (reducing component 2).

Figure 11.9 on the next page contains an extract from the Nokia 2005 annual report relating to that entity's acquisition of Intellisync. Note the company's description of the items that are expected to generate goodwill.

Is goodwill an asset?

IFRS 3 accounts for goodwill as an asset. Whether core goodwill is an asset is considered in detail in Johnson and Petrone (1998, pp. 296–302) and in Miller and Islam (1988). There are many other articles in the accounting literature that discuss this issue, because it has been a source of much debate. Of the accounting standard-setting bodies that have considered the issue, the Accounting Standards Board in the United Kingdom in 1997, in its Financial

Reporting Standard 10 *Goodwill and Intangible Assets*, took the view that goodwill is not an asset (Summary, paragraph b):

> Goodwill arising on acquisition is neither an asset like other assets nor an immediate loss in value. Rather, it forms the bridge between the cost of an investment shown as an asset in the acquirer's own financial statements and the values attributed to the acquired assets and liabilities in the consolidated financial statements. Although purchased goodwill is not in itself an asset, its inclusion amongst the assets of the reporting entity, rather than as a deduction from shareholders' equity, recognises that goodwill is part of a larger asset, the investment, for which management remains accountable.

Acquisition of Intellisync

In February 2006, the Group acquired 100 percent of the outstanding common shares of Intellisync (NASDAQ: SYNC) for cash consideration of approximately EUR 368 million. Intellisync delivers wireless email and other applications over an array of devices and application platforms across carrier networks. The Group believes it is positioned to deliver the industry's most complete offering for the development, deployment and management of mobility in the enterprise and the acquisition will enhance the Group's ability to respond to customer needs in this fast growing market. Intellisync will be integrated into the Enterprise Solutions business upon acquisition and its results of operations from that date will be included in the Group's consolidated financial statements. The purchase price allocation is being performed with the assistance of a third party.

Assets acquired are expected to be EUR 51 million and liabilities EUR 17 million with a majority of the excess recognised as goodwill. The principal items that are expected to generate goodwill are the value of the synergies between Intellisync and the Group and the acquired workforce, neither of which qualifies as a separate amortizable intangible asset. None of the goodwill is expected to be deductible for tax purposes. The Group does not expect to write off any in-process R&D or dispose of any one of the acquired operations.

FIGURE 11.9 Components of goodwill, Nokia
Source: Nokia (2005, p. 34).

As defined in the *Framework*, an asset has essentially three characteristics: (1) expected future economic benefits, (2) control by the owner over the benefits, and (3) the benefits arise as the result of a past event. There is little debate over whether goodwill is a repository of expected future economic benefits, as this is evidenced by the fact that the acquirer has been prepared to pay extra consideration over and above an amount equal to the fair value of the acquiree's identifiable net assets. Similarly, the existence of the business combination is seen as a past event. The key area of debate is whether the entity has control over the benefits.

The meaning of 'control' in relation to intangibles is discussed in chapter 10 of this book. It is argued there that the IASB, because of the debates over whether items such as well-trained employees or marketing outlays are assets, introduces the identifiability criterion to ensure that the only items recognised as intangible assets are those that are separable or arise from contractual or other legal rights. Paragraph BC323 of the Basis for Conclusions on IFRS 3 recognises that goodwill arises in part because of factors such as having a well-trained workforce and loyal customers not being seen as controllable by the entity and therefore not being assets.

The problem with goodwill is that it is a unique asset. It arises as a residual. As Leo, Hoggett and Radford (1995, pp. 44–7) noted, the key difference between identifiable net assets and goodwill is measurement:

> The difference between the measurement method used for goodwill and that for measurement of all other assets of the business is whether the method involves determining the value of the business as a whole or part thereof.

The authors defined unidentifiable assets (p. 46) as those assets that meet the recognition criteria and cannot be measured without measuring the total net assets of a business entity. The existence of goodwill depends on the measurement of the entity as a whole. In recognising this, the IASB argued in paragraph BC323 of the Basis for Conclusions on IFRS 3:

> control of core goodwill is provided by means of the acquirer's power to direct the policies and management of the acquiree. Therefore, both the IASB and the FASB concluded that core goodwill meets the conceptual definition of an asset.

Accounting for goodwill

As noted earlier, goodwill is calculated as the excess of the consideration transferred in the business combination over the acquirer's interest in the net fair value of the identifiable assets acquired and liabilities assumed from the acquiree. Hence, to calculate goodwill as a part of the acquisition analysis it is necessary to calculate the consideration transferred and the net fair value of the identifiable assets acquired and liabilities assumed. A comparison of these two amounts determines the existence of goodwill. The acquirer then recognises goodwill as an asset in the same way as for all other identifiable assets acquired.

ILLUSTRATIVE EXAMPLE 11.2

Acquisition analysis

Using the figures from illustrative example 11.1, assume that Rome Ltd assesses the fair values of the identifiable assets and liabilities of Siena Ltd to be as follows:

Equipment	$ 36 000
Inventory	20 000
Accounts receivable	9 000
Patents	4 000
Furniture	6 000
Accounts payable	8 000

To determine the entries to be passed by the acquirer, prepare an acquisition analysis that compares the consideration transferred with the net fair value of the identifiable assets, liabilities and contingent liabilities acquired. The analysis for this example is shown in figure 11.10.

Acquisition analysis

Net fair value of identifiable assets acquired and liabilities assumed:

Equipment	$36 000
Inventory	20 000
Accounts receivable	9 000
Patents	4 000
Furniture	6 000
	75 000
Accounts payable	8 000
Net fair value	$67 000

Consideration transferred:

This was calculated in figure 11.6 as $76 562.

Goodwill acquired:

Net fair value acquired	= $67 000
Consideration transferred	= $76 562
Goodwill	= $76 562 − $67 000
	= $ 9 562

FIGURE 11.10 Acquisition analysis by the acquirer

The journal entries for Rome Ltd at acquisition date are as shown in figure 11.11.

Journal of Rome Ltd			
Equipment	Dr	36 000	
Inventory	Dr	20 000	
Accounts Receivable	Dr	9 000	
Patents	Dr	4 000	
Furniture	Dr	6 000	
Goodwill	Dr	9 562	
Accounts Payable	Cr		8 000
Consideration Payable	Cr		19 362
Share Capital — Preference	Cr		2 200
Share Capital — Ordinary	Cr		55 000
(Acquisition of the assets and liabilities of Siena Ltd)			
Consideration Payable	Dr	13 680	
Cash	Cr		13 680
(Payment of cash consideration)			
Acquisition-related Expenses	Dr	1 000	
Cash	Cr		1 000
(Acquisition-related costs)			
Share Capital — Ordinary	Dr	100	
Share Capital — Preference	Dr	40	
Cash	Cr		140
(Share issue costs)			
Consideration Payable	Dr	5 682	
Interest Expense	Dr	568	
Cash	Cr		6 250
(Balance of consideration payable)			

FIGURE 11.11 Journal entries of the acquirer, including recognition of goodwill

Effects of IFRS 3 on accounting for goodwill

According to paragraph BC158 of the Basis for Conclusions on IFRS 3, both the IASB and the FASB believed that the decision usefulness of financial statements would be enhanced if intangible assets acquired in a business combination were distinguished from goodwill. In its report on the application of the FASB's SFAS 141 from 2002–07, Intangible Business (see www.intangiblebusiness.com) gave many examples of US business combinations in which there was a reluctance to separate intangibles from goodwill. Two examples are shown in figures 11.12 and 11.13.

FIGURE 11.12 Separation of identifiable intangibles from goodwill 1

Walt Disney acquisition of Pixar in 2006 ($7.5 bn)

Walt Disney paid $7.5 billion for the digital animation studio, Pixar, which brought you Toy Story, Finding Nemo and other movie classics. The intangible assets, mainly trademarks and tradenames, were given a value of just $0.2 billion while goodwill was $5.6 billion. Of course, the skilled workforce of Pixar would be a key asset that Walt Disney wanted to acquire and both the US and IFRS standards on business combinations specifically exclude workforce from recognizable intangible assets. Nevertheless we do not believe that the value of other recognizable intangible assets is actually as low as that reported by Walt Disney.

FIGURE 11.12 *(continued)*

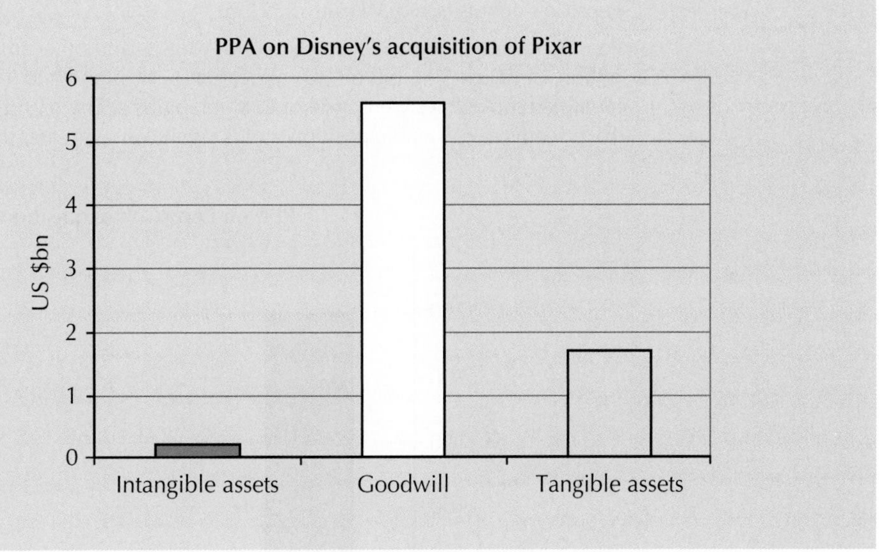

Source: Intangible Business (2007, p. 21).

Google acquisition of YouTube ($1.2 bn)

Google acquired YouTube, the internet video sharing company, in 2006 for $1.2 billion, of which $0.2 billion was allocated to intangible assets and $1.1 billion to goodwill (net tangible assets were negative). YouTube is the destination of choice for youngsters who want to share video content online. As such it depends largely on its brand name to attract subscribers. We are surprised that such a small proportion of the purchase price has been allocated to the brand. A possible conclusion from this is that the value given to the intangibles is too low or too much was paid for YouTube.

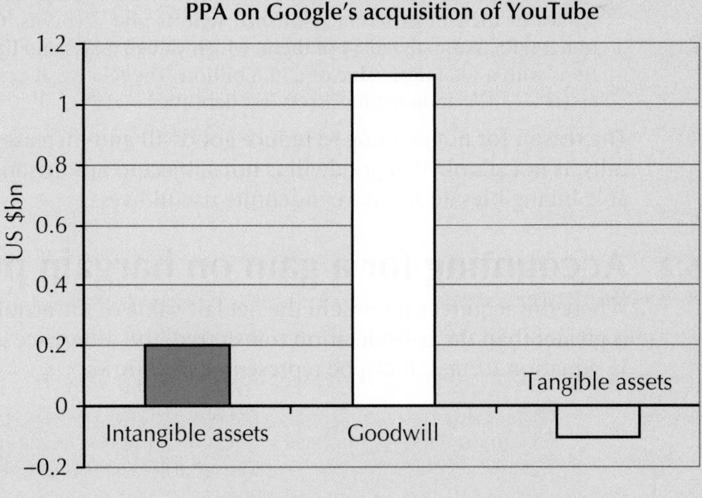

FIGURE 11.13 Separation of identifiable intangibles from goodwill 2
Source: Intangible Business (2007, p. 22).

To provide a contrast, Intangible Business showed the results of PepsiCola's acquisition of the UK snack brand Wotsits. See figure 11.14 which shows the dollars allocated to intangibles was far greater than those to goodwill.

PepsiCo's acquisition of Wotsits ($351 m)

Pepsi Cola acquired the UK snack brand, Wotsits and other smaller brands, in 2002 for $0.4 billion, of which $0.2 billion was allocated to the brand and less than $0.1 billion to goodwill. Identified intangibles were 86% of total intangibles. The brand accounting for half the acquisition price seems a reasonable position and is significantly greater than the average of 28%.

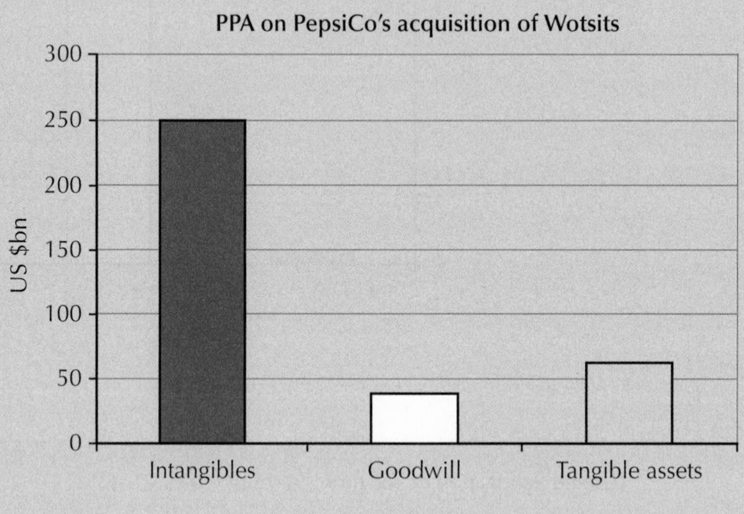

FIGURE 11.14 Separation of identifiable intangibles from goodwill 3
Source: Intangible Business (2007, p. 15).

It may be argued that the application of IFRS 3 has made a difference. However, Forbes (2007, p. 9) states:

> We analysed intangible asset values reported by the FTSE [Financial Times Stock Exchange] 100 companies in their most recent published reports and accounts. Of these companies, 89 had reported under IFRS. We analysed 84 of them, which valued assets and liabilities underlying business combinations with a total deal value of £39.8 billion. The relative allocation was goodwill — 53%; intangible assets — 30%; and tangible assets less liabilities — 17%.

The reason for not wanting to reduce goodwill and increase the recognition of intangibles, hopefully, is not simply that goodwill is not subject to amortisation under IFRS whereas most identifiable intangibles do not have indefinite useful lives.

11.6.2 Accounting for a gain on bargain purchase

Where the acquirer's interest in the net fair value of the acquiree's identifiable assets and liabilities is greater than the consideration transferred, the difference is called a gain on a bargain purchase. In equation format, it can be represented as follows:

> Gain on bargain purchase = Acquirer's interest in the net fair value of the acquiree's identifiable assets and liabilities
> *less*
> Consideration transferred

The existence of a bargain purchase is considered by the standard setters (paragraph BC371) as an anomalous transaction as parties to the business combination do not knowingly sell assets at amounts lower than their fair value. However, because the acquirer has excellent negotiation skills, or because the acquiree has made a sale for other than economic reasons or is forced to sell owing to specific circumstances such as cash flow problems, such situations do arise.

The standard setters adopt the view that most business combinations are an exchange of equal amounts, given markets in which the parties to the business combinations are informed and willing participants in the transaction. Therefore, the existence of a bargain purchase is expected to be an unusual or rare event.

Paragraph 36 of IFRS 3 requires that before a gain is recognised, the acquirer must reassess whether:

- it has correctly identified all the assets acquired and liabilities assumed
- it has correctly measured at fair value all the assets acquired and liabilities assumed
- it has correctly measured the consideration transferred.

The objective here is to ensure that all the measurements at acquisition date reflect all the information that is available at that date.

Note that one effect of recognising a bargain purchase is that there is no recognition of goodwill. A gain on bargain purchase and goodwill cannot be recognised in the same business combination.

ILLUSTRATIVE EXAMPLE 11.3

Gain on bargain purchase

Using the information regarding the consideration transferred in a business combination from illustrative examples 11.1 and 11.2, assume the fair values of the identifiable assets and liabilities of Siena Ltd are assessed to be:

Equipment	$ 45 000
Inventory	25 000
Accounts receivable	9 000
Patents	5 000
Furniture	6 000
	90 000
	8 000
Accounts payable	$ 82 000

The *acquisition analysis* now shows:

Net fair value of assets and liabilities acquired	= $82 000
Consideration transferred	= $76 562
Gain on bargain purchase	= $82 000 − $76 562
	= $ 5 438

Assuming that the reassessment process did not result in any changes to the fair values calculated, the first journal entry in Rome Ltd to record the acquisition of the net assets of Siena Ltd is:

Equipment	Dr	45 000	
Inventory	Dr	25 000	
Accounts Receivable	Dr	9 000	
Patents	Dr	5 000	
Furniture	Dr	6 000	
Accounts Payable	Cr		8 000
Consideration Payable	Cr		19 362
Share Capital — Preference	Cr		2 200
Share Capital — Ordinary	Cr		55 000
Gain (Profit and Loss)	Cr		5 438
(Acquisition of assets and liabilities acquired from Siena Ltd, and the gain on bargain purchase)			

11.7 ACCOUNTING BY THE ACQUIRER: SHARES ACQUIRED IN AN ACQUIREE

Where an entity acquires shares rather than the net assets of another entity, the acquirer records the shares acquired in accordance with paragraph 43 of IAS 39 *Financial Instruments: Recognition and Measurement*, that is, at fair value plus transaction costs. Transaction costs include fees and commissions paid to agents, advisers, brokers and dealers; levies by regulatory agencies and securities exchanges; and transfer taxes and duties, such as stamp duties. It is expected that, in the majority of cases, the fair value of the shares acquired will equal the fair value of the consideration paid. The basic form of the journal entry in the records of the acquirer is:

Shares in Acquiree	Dr	XXX	
Share Capital	Cr		XXX
Cash	Cr		XXX
(Acquisition of shares in another entity)			

ILLUSTRATIVE EXAMPLE 11.4

Acquisition of shares in an acquiree

Assume that on 1 January 2011 Rome Ltd acquired all the issued shares in Siena Ltd for $80 000, giving in exchange $10 000 cash and 20 000 shares in Rome Ltd, the latter having a fair value of $3.50 per share. Transaction costs of $500 were paid in cash. Share issue costs were $1000. The journal entries in the records of Rome Ltd at the acquisition date are as shown in figure 11.15.

Journal of Rome Ltd			
Shares in Siena Ltd	Dr	80 000	
Cash	Cr		10 000
Share Capital	Cr		70 000
(Acquisition of shares in Siena Ltd)			
Shares in Siena Ltd	Dr	500	
Cash	Cr		500
(Transaction costs)			
Share Capital	Dr	1 000	
Cash	Cr		1 000
(Costs of issuing shares to Siena Ltd)			

FIGURE 11.15 Accounting for the acquisition of shares

11.7.1 Existence of a previously held equity interest

In illustrative example 11.4, the acquirer acquired all issued shares of the acquiree in one transaction. An alternative situation could occur where the acquirer obtained its controlling interest in the acquirer by acquiring further shares and thereby adding to its previously held equity interest. For example, in illustrative example 11.4, Rome Ltd may have previously held 20% of the shares in Siena Ltd on 1 January 2011, and at that date acquired the remaining 80% of the shares of Siena Ltd. As a business combination occurs when the acquirer obtains control of the acquiree, it is on the date of the second acquisition of shares that the business combination occurs. In IFRS 3, this is referred to as a business combination achieved in stages — sometimes called a step acquisition. Obviously there may be a number of step purchases of shares in the acquiree prior to the obtaining of control.

Each of the steps prior to the date where the acquirer obtains control will be accounted for as in illustrative example 11.4; that is, the acquirer will recognise an investment in the acquiree with each step acquisition being measured at fair value.

It is also possible, of course, that the acquirer may obtain control of the acquiree without making a further step acquisition. For example, the composition of the non-controlling interest may change such that the acquirer becomes the controlling entity — see chapter 21 for further discussion on control.

The accounting for a step acquisition is given in paragraph 42 of IFRS 3:

> In a business combination achieved in stages, the acquirer shall remeasure its previously held equity interest in the acquiree at its acquisition-date fair value and recognise the resulting gain or loss, if any, in profit or loss.

Using the situation in illustrative example 11.4, but assuming that prior to acquiring 80% of the shares of Siena on 1 January 2011, Rome Ltd had acquired 20% of Siena Ltd's shares on 1 January 2010 for $10 000 and this investment had a $16 000 fair value at 1 January 2011. At 1 January 2011, Rome Ltd would then record the following entry to revalue its previously held investment in Siena Ltd:

Shares in Siena Ltd	Dr	6 000	
Gain (Profit or loss)	Cr		6 000
(Remeasurement of previously held equity interest on business combination)			

As noted in paragraph 42 of IFRS 3, where the equity interest had previously been revalued with changes in fair value being recognised in other comprehensive income, as required for financial instruments classified as available for sale, then the accounting for the amounts recognised in equity will be the same as if the equity interest was sold — in essence transferred to profit or loss. According to IAS *Presentation of Financial Statements*, paragraph 7, amounts transferred to profit or loss in the current period that were recognised in other comprehensive income in the current or previous periods are called reclassification adjustments.

11.8 ACCOUNTING IN THE RECORDS OF THE ACQUIREE

Where the acquirer purchases the acquiree's assets and liabilities, the acquiree may continue in existence or may liquidate. The acquiree accounts affected by the business combination will differ according to the actions of the acquiree.

11.8.1 Acquiree does not liquidate

In the situation where the acquiree disposes of a business, the journal entries required in the records of the acquiree are shown in figure 11.16. Under IAS 16 *Property, Plant and Equipment*, when an item of property, plant and equipment is sold, gains or losses are recognised in the statement of comprehensive income. Similarly, on the sale of a business, the acquiree recognises a gain or loss.

11.8.2 Acquiree liquidates

The entries required in the records of the acquiree when it sells *all* its net assets to the acquirer are shown in figure 11.17. The accounts of the acquiree are transferred to two accounts, the Liquidation account and the Shareholders' Distribution account.

To the *Liquidation account* are transferred:

- all assets taken over by the acquirer, including cash if relevant, as well as any assets not taken over and which have a zero value, including goodwill
- all liabilities taken over
- the expenses of liquidation if paid by the acquiree
- additional expenses to be paid by the acquiree but not previously recognised by the acquiree

- consideration from the acquirer as proceeds on sale of net assets
- all reserves, including retained earnings.

Journal of Acquiree			
Receivable from Acquirer	Dr	XXX	
Liability A	Dr	XXX	
Liability B	Dr	XXX	
Liability C	Dr	XXX	
Asset A	Cr		XXX
Asset B	Cr		XXX
Asset C	Cr		XXX
Gain on Sale of Operation*	Cr		XXX
(Sale of operation)			
**Separate proceeds on sale and carrying amounts of assets sold could be recognised — see illustrative example 11.8 for an example of the entries used.*			
Shares in Acquirer	Dr	XXX	
Cash	Dr	XXX	
Receivable from Acquirer	Cr		XXX
(Receipt of consideration from acquirer)			

FIGURE 11.16 Journal entries of acquiree on sale of business

The balance of the Liquidation account is then transferred to the Shareholders' Distribution account.

FIGURE 11.17 Journal entries of acquiree on liquidation after sale of net assets

Journal of Acquiree			
Liquidation	Dr	XXX	
Asset A	Cr		XXX
Asset B	Cr		XXX
Asset C	Cr		XXX
(Transfer of all assets acquired by acquirer, at their carrying amounts)			
Liability A	Dr	XXX	
Liability B	Dr	XXX	
Liability C	Dr	XXX	
Liquidation	Cr		XXX
(Transfer of all liabilities assumed by the acquirer)			
Liquidation	Dr	XXX	
Cash	Cr		XXX
(Liquidation and other expenses not recognised previously, if paid by the acquiree)			
Receivable from Acquirer	Dr	XXX	
Liquidation	Cr		XXX
(Consideration for net assets sold)			
Cash	Dr	XXX	
Shares in Acquirer	Dr	XXX	
Receivable from Acquirer	Cr		XXX
(Receipt of consideration)			

FIGURE 11.17 *(continued)*

Other Reserves	Dr	XXX	
Retained Earnings	Dr	XXX	
Liquidation	Cr		XXX
(Transfer of reserves)			
Liquidation	Dr	XXX	
Shareholders' Distribution	Cr		XXX
(Transfer of balance of liquidation)			
Share Capital	Dr	XXX	
Shareholders' Distribution	Cr		XXX
(Transfer of share capital)			
Shareholders' Distribution	Dr	XXX	
Cash	Cr		XXX
Shares in Acquirer	Cr		XXX
(Distribution of consideration to shareholders)			

To the *Shareholders' Distribution account* are transferred:

- the balance of share capital
- the balance of the Liquidation account
- the portion of the consideration received from the acquirer that is distributed to the shareholders. Some of the consideration received by the acquiree may be used to pay for liabilities not assumed by the acquirer, and for liquidation expenses.

ILLUSTRATIVE EXAMPLE 11.5

Entries in the acquiree's records

Using the information from illustrative example 11.1, the entries in the records of Siena Ltd are shown in figure 11.18.

FIGURE 11.18 Liquidation of acquiree

Journal of Siena Ltd			
Liquidation	Dr	69 500	
Accumulated Depreciation — Equipment	Dr	10 000	
Equipment	Cr		42 000
Inventory	Cr		18 000
Accounts Receivable	Cr		16 000
Patents	Cr		3 500
(Assets taken over)			
Accounts Payable	Dr	8 000	
Liquidation	Cr		8 000
(Liabilities taken over)			
Liquidation	Dr	350	
Liquidation Expenses Payable	Cr		350
(Liquidation expenses payable by acquiree)			
Liquidation	Dr	80	
Debenture Holders Payable	Cr		80
(Premium expense on debentures to be paid on redemption)			

(continued)

FIGURE 11.18 *(continued)*

Receivable from Rome Ltd Liquidation (Consideration receivable)	Dr Cr	76 562	 76 562
Cash Shares in Rome Ltd Receivable from Rome Ltd (Receipt of consideration from acquirer)	Dr Dr Cr	13 680 57 200	 70 880
Retained Earnings Liquidation (Transfer of retained earnings)	Dr Cr	21 500	 21 500
Liquidation Shareholders' Distribution (Balance of liquidation account transferred to shareholders' distribution)	Dr Cr	36 132	 36 132
Share Capital — Ordinary Share Capital — Preference Shareholders' Distribution (Transfer of share capital)	Dr Dr Cr	30 000 6 000	 36 000
Debentures Debenture Holders Payable (Transfer of debentures to payable account)	Dr Cr	4 000	 4 000
Liquidation Expenses Payable Debenture Holders Payable Cash (Payment of liabilities)	Dr Dr Cr	350 4 080	 4 430

Shareholders' Distribution
  Cash
  Shares in Rome Ltd
  Receivable from Rome Ltd
(Payment to shareholders)
	Dr
	Cr
	Cr
	Cr
		72 132	
			9 250
			57 200
			5 682

11.8.3 Acquirer buys only shares in the acquiree

When the acquirer buys only shares in the acquiree, there are no entries in the records of the acquiree because the transaction is between the acquirer and the shareholders of the acquiree entity. The acquiree itself is not involved.

11.9 SUBSEQUENT ADJUSTMENTS TO THE INITIAL ACCOUNTING FOR A BUSINESS COMBINATION

Three areas where adjustments need to be made subsequent to the initial accounting after acquisition date are:

- goodwill
- contingent liabilities
- contingent consideration.

Goodwill

Having recognised goodwill arising in the business combination, the subsequent accounting is directed from other accounting standards:

- goodwill is not subject to amortisation but is subject to an annual impairment test as detailed in IAS 36 *Impairment of Assets* (see chapter 12).

- goodwill cannot be revalued because IAS 38 *Intangible Assets* does not allow the recognition of internally generated goodwill.

Contingent liabilities

Having recognised any contingent liabilities of the acquiree as liabilities, the acquirer must then determine a subsequent measurement for the liability. The liability is initially recognised at fair value. Subsequent to acquisition date, according to paragraph 56 of IFRS 3, the liability is measured as the higher of:

(a) the amount that would be recognised in accordance with IAS 37; and
(b) the amount initially recognised less, if appropriate, cumulative amortisation recognised in accordance with IAS 18 *Revenue*.

Under IAS 37 paragraph 36, the liability would be measured at the best estimate of the expenditure required to settle the present obligation at the end of the reporting period. This would be used, for example, where a liability was recognised in relation to a court case. However, the IASB was also concerned about contingent liabilities such as guarantees or other financial liabilities. Under IAS 39 paragraph 47, the subsequent measurement of financial liabilities requires preparers to use the higher of the IAS 37 measurement and the amount initially recognised subject to amortisation in line with IAS 18. In order for IFRS 3 to be consistent with IAS 39, the measurement method to be used in subsequent accounting for contingent liabilities was made the same as that in IAS 39.

Contingent consideration

At acquisition date, the contingent consideration is measured at fair value, and is classified either as equity (e.g. the requirement for the acquirer to issue more shares subject to subsequent events) or as a liability (e.g. the requirement to provide more cash subject to subsequent events). Subsequent to the business combination, paragraph 54 of IFRS 3 requires the accounting for contingent consideration to be in accordance with the accounting standard that would normally apply to these accounts. However, IFRS 3 provides guidance on the measures to be used.

Where the contingent consideration is classified as equity, no remeasurement is required, and the subsequent settlement is accounted for within equity (IFRS 3 paragraph 58(a)). This means that if extra equity instruments are issued they are effectively issued for no consideration and there is no change to share capital.

Where the contingent consideration is a financial liability, it will be accounted for under IAS 39 and measured at fair value with movements being accounted for in accordance with that standard. If it is a liability not within the scope of IAS 39, it is accounted for in accordance with IAS 37. So, if there were changes in the amount of an expected cash outflow, the liability would be adjusted and an amount recognised in profit or loss.

It should be noted that the subsequent accounting for contingent consideration is to treat it as a post-acquisition event, that is, not affecting the measurements made at acquisition date. Hence, any subsequent adjustments do not affect the goodwill calculated at acquisition date.

ILLUSTRATIVE EXAMPLE 11.6

Comprehensive example

Parma Ltd's major business is in the pet food industry. It makes a number of canned pet foods, mainly for cats and dogs, as well as having a very promising line in dry dog food. It has been interested for some time in the operations of Naples Ltd, an entity that deals with the processing of grain products for a number of other industries including flour-processing, health foods and, in more recent times, the production of grain products for feeding birds. Given its interest in the pet food industry and its desire to stay as one of the leaders in this area, Parma Ltd began negotiations with Naples Ltd to acquire its birdseed product division.

Negotiations began in July 2010. After months of discussion between the relevant parties of both companies, an agreement was reached on 15 February 2011 for Parma Ltd to acquire the birdseed division. The agreement document was taken to the board of directors of Naples Ltd who ratified the agreement on 1 March 2011. The net assets were exchanged on this date.

The net assets of the birdseed division at 1 March 2011, showing the carrying amounts at that date and the fair values as estimated by Parma Ltd from documentation supplied by Naples Ltd, were as shown below.

	Carrying amount	Fair value
Plant and equipment	$160 000	$167 000
Land	70 000	75 000
Motor vehicles	30 000	32 000
Inventory	24 000	28 000
Accounts receivable	18 000	16 000
Total assets	302 000	318 000
Accounts payable	35 000	35 000
Bank overdraft	55 000	55 000
Total liabilities	90 000	90 000
Net assets	$212 000	$228 000

Details of the consideration Parma Ltd agreed to provide in exchange for the net assets of the division are described below:

- 100 000 shares in Parma Ltd — movements in the share price were as follows:

1 July 2010	$1.00
1 October 2010	1.10
1 January 2011	1.15
1 February 2011	1.30
15 February 2011	1.32
16 February 2011	1.45
1 March 2011	1.50

- Because of doubts as to whether it could sustain a share price of at least $1.50, Parma Ltd agreed to supply cash to the value of any decrease in the share price below $1.50 for the 100 000 shares issued, this guarantee of the share price lasting until 31 July. Parma Ltd believed that there was a 90% chance that the share price would remain at $1.50 or higher and a 10% chance that it would fall to $1.48.
- Cash of $40 000, half to be paid on the date of acquisition and half in one year's time.
- Supply of a patent relating to the manufacture of packing material. This has a fair value of $60 000 but has not been recognised in the records of Parma Ltd because it resulted from an internally generated research project.
- Naples Ltd was currently being sued for damages relating to a claim by a bird breeder who had bought some seed from the company, and claimed that this resulted in the death of some prime breeding pigeons. Parma Ltd agreed to pay any resulting damages in relation to the court case. The expected damages were $40 000. Lawyers estimated that there was only a 20% chance of losing the case.

Parma Ltd supplied the cash on the acquisition date as well as surrendering the patent. The shares were issued on 5 March, and the costs of issuing the shares amounted to $1000. The incremental borrowing rate for Parma Ltd is 10% p.a. Acquisition-related costs paid by Parma Ltd in relation to the acquisition amounted to $5000.

On 31 July the share price of Parma Ltd's shares was $1.52.

Required

Prepare the journal entries in the records of the acquirer.

Solution

Acquisition analysis

Net fair value of assets acquired and liabilities assumed		
Plant and equipment		$ 167 000
Land		75 000
Motor vehicles		32 000
Inventory		28 000
Accounts receivable		16 000
		318 000
Accounts payable		35 000
Bank overdraft		55 000
Provision for damages (20% × $40 000)		8 000
		98 000
		$ 220 000
Consideration transferred		
Purchase consideration:		
Shares:	100 000 × $1.50	$ 150 000
Guarantee:	10% ($1.50 – $1.48) × 100 000	200
Cash:	Payable now	20 000
	Deferred ($20 000 × 0.909091)	18 182
Patent		60 000
		$ 248 382
Goodwill ($248 382 – $220 000)		$ 28 382

The journal entries of the acquirer, Parma Ltd, are shown in figure 11.19.

Journal of Parma Ltd				
2011				
March 1	Plant and Equipment	Dr	167 000	
	Land	Dr	75 000	
	Motor Vehicles	Dr	32 000	
	Inventory	Dr	28 000	
	Accounts Receivable	Dr	16 000	
	Goodwill	Dr	28 382	
	Accounts Payable	Cr		35 000
	Bank Overdraft	Cr		55 000
	Provision for Damages	Cr		8 000
	Share Capital	Cr		150 000
	Provision for Loss in Value of Shares	Cr		200
	Cash	Cr		20 000
	Consideration Payable	Cr		18 182
	Gain on Sale of Patent	Cr		60 000
	(Acquisition of birdseed division from Naples Ltd)			
	Acquisition-related expenses	Dr	5 000	
	Cash	Cr		5 000
	(Acquisition-related costs)			
March 5	Share Capital	Dr	1 000	
	Cash	Cr		1 000
	(Costs of issuing shares)			
July 31	Provision for Loss in Value of Shares	Dr	200	
	Gain	Cr		200
	(Contingency not having to be paid)			

FIGURE 11.19 Journal entries of the acquirer

11.10 DISCLOSURE — BUSINESS COMBINATIONS

Paragraphs 59–63 of IFRS 3 contain information on disclosures required in relation to business combinations. To meet these disclosure requirements it is necessary to apply Appendix B of IFRS 3, which is an integral part of IFRS 3 containing application guidance.

Paragraph 59 requires entities to disclose information about the nature and financial effect of business combinations occurring during the current reporting period, and after the end of the reporting period but before the financial statements are authorised for issue. Paragraphs B64–B66 contain information to assist preparers to meet the disclosure objective in paragraph 59.

Note the qualitative information required to be disclosed under paragraph B64. In particular, note B64(d) which requires disclosure of the primary reasons for the business combination as well as a description of how the acquirer obtained control of the acquiree. This information should assist users to evaluate the success of the business combination and judge the ability of management to make investment decisions.

Also note that paragraph B64(e) requires disclosure of 'a qualitative description of the factors that make up goodwill recognised, such as expected synergies from combining operations of the acquiree and the acquirer, intangible assets that do not qualify for separate recognition or other factors'. Goodwill is not to be considered just a residual calculation. As explained in section 11.6.1, core goodwill can consist of elements such as combination goodwill and going-concern goodwill. An understanding of where the synergies exist will assist management in managing the earnings from goodwill as well as in any later impairment tests of goodwill (see chapter 12 for more details concerning impairment testing). Unrecognised intangible assets may also be included in goodwill (see chapter 10 for information on accounting for intangible assets in a business combination).

Paragraph 61 of IFRS 3 requires the disclosure of information to assist in the evaluation of the financial effects of adjustments recognised in the current period that relate to business combinations occurring in previous periods. Figure 11.5 (p. 416) shows disclosures made by Danisco for such adjustments. Paragraph B67 details disclosures required in meet the information objective in paragraph 61.

An example of the required disclosures is provided in figure 11.20.

FIGURE 11.20 Disclosures required by Parma Ltd under IFRS 3

26. Business combinations		**IFRS 3** para.
Acquisition of division from Naples Ltd During the current reporting period, the company acquired the birdseed division of Naples Ltd. The acquisition date was 1 March 2011. The company has not had to dispose of any operations as a result of this combination. The primary reason for the business combination was to gain synergies in terms of the sales outlets for products sold by both entities.		*B64(a)* *B64(b)* *B64(d)*
The consideration transferred to Naples Ltd was $250 380. The components of the cost were		*B64(f)*
Shares in the company	$150 000	
Cash	46 380	
Patent for packaging	50 000	
Guarantee relating to the maintenance of the company's share price	4 000	*B64(g)(i)*
The contingent consideration — the guarantee — was measured at acquisition date at $4000 being based on an analysis of probable movements in share prices and budgeted information on future sales. The company issued 100 000 shares, determining a fair value of $1.50 based on the current market price of the company at 1 March 2011 as reported by the stock exchange.		*B64(g)(ii)* *B64(f)(iv)*

FIGURE 11.20 *(continued)*

The assets acquired and liabilities assumed from Naples Ltd were as at 1 March 2011:	*B67(i)*

	Carrying amount	Fair value
Plant and equipment	$160 000	$167 000
Land	70 000	75 000
Motor vehicles	30 000	32 000
Inventory	24 000	28 000
Accounts receivable	18 000	16 000
	302 000	318 000
Accounts payable	35 000	35 000
Bank overdraft	55 000	55 000
	90 000	90 000
Contingent liability acquired	8 000	8 000
		98 000
Net assets acquired		$220 000

Goodwill of $30 380 was recognised in the acquisition, the extra consideration being paid due to the excellent reputation and customer following relating to the quality of the birdseed products.	*B64(e)*
An adjustment of $2000 was made to the fair value of the plant and equipment and goodwill subsequent to the acquisition due to the provisional nature of the fair value of some of the specialised equipment determined at acquisition date.	*B67(a)*
The contingent liability acquired related to a court case involving a claim from a customer that certain bird food was of poor quality. If the court case were lost, which is not expected, the damages could be $40 000. A present obligation is regarded as existing at the end of the reporting period.	*B64(j)*
Subsequent to the end of the reporting period, the provision in relation to the company's guarantee in relation to maintenance of the share price expired. No extra payment was required, as the share price had been maintained.	*B64(g)(iii)*
Acquisition-related costs amounted to $10 000, all of which was recognised as an expense against the line item 'operating expenses'. Share issue costs of $5000 were treated as a reduction in share capital.	*B64(m)*
Acquisition of shares in Milan Ltd On 1 August 2010, the company acquired 100% of the shares in Milan Ltd, a company involved mainly in manufacturing bird cages, for $100 000. The primary reason for acquiring the company was to expand the variety of products sold to customers in the same industry. The consideration paid was cash.	*B64(a),(b),(c)* *B64(d)* *B64(f)*
The assets and liabilities of Milan Ltd at acquisition date were:	*B64(i)*

	Carrying amount	Fair value
Plant and equipment	$ 82 000	$ 88 000
Vehicles	22 000	20 000
Cash	12 000	12 000
Accounts receivable	8 000	7 000
	124 000	127 000
Accounts payable	32 000	32 000
Net assets	$ 92 000	$ 95 000

Goodwill of $5000 was acquired, attributable to a quality, well-trained workforce.	*B64(e)*

(continued)

FIGURE 11.20 *(continued)*

The consolidated revenue for the consolidated group is \$952 000. If the business combinations occurring during the year had occurred on 1 July 2010 instead of during the year, it is estimated that consolidated revenue would have been \$985 000. The consolidated profit under the same assumption would have been \$322 000 instead of \$299 000.	*B64(q)*

27. Goodwill

	2011	2010	
Gross amount at beginning of period	\$20 600	\$19 600	*B67(d)(i)*
Accumulated impairment losses	500	300	
	20 100	19 300	
Goodwill acquired	35 380	3 000	*B67(d)(ii)*
	55 480	22 300	
Adjustments — tax assets recognised	—	2 000	*B67(d)(iii)*
		20 300	
Impairment losses for current period	—	200	*B67(d)(iv)*
Carrying amount at end of period	\$55 480	\$20 100	
Consisting of:			*B67(d)(viii)*
Gross amount at end of period	\$55 980	\$20 600	
Accumulated impairment losses	500	500	
	\$55 480	\$20 100	

Figure 11.21 contains the disclosures provided by the Western Australian company Wesfarmers in its 2008 annual report concerning its business combinations.

FIGURE 11.21 Disclosures of business combinations, Wesfarmers

27 BUSINESS COMBINATIONS

Acquisitions

During the period, Wesfarmers completed several acquisitions the most significant being:

On 23 November 2007, Wesfarmers Limited through its controlled entity Wesfarmers Retail Holdings Pty Ltd, acquired, through a scheme of Arrangement ("the Scheme"), 89.4% of the voting shares of the Coles group Limited ("Coles group"), a publicly listed company and its subsidiaries. Combined with the initial interest of 10.6% purchased in April 2007 at a total cost of \$2077 million, Wesfarmers held 100% of the voting shares in Coles group on 23 November 2007.

Coles group is based in Australia and operates retail businesses in Australia and New Zealand. The Scheme consideration consisted of 152.6 million Wesfarmers ordinary shares, 152.6 million Wesfarmers partially protected shares and \$4328 million in cash. The cost of the acquisition totalled \$19307 million.

The provisional fair value of identifiable assets and liabilities recognized on acquisitions of Coles group has decreased \$238 million compared to the fair value amounts previously reported. This reduction is due largely to a decrease in plant and equipment and an increase in provisions recognized an acquisition. The reduction in the fair value of identifiable assets and liabilities results in a corresponding increase to goodwill recognized on acquisition. At 30 June 2008, the acquisition accounting balances are provisional due to ongoing work finalizing valuations and tax related matters which may impact acquisition accounting entries.

On 1 September 2007, the Group's chemicals and fertilizers subsidiary, CSBP Limited, acquired 100% of Australian Vinyls Corporation, a privately owned company, which is the only manufacturer of poly vinyl chloride in the Australian market. The cost of the acquisition totalled \$142 million.

Acquisition *(continued)*

Details of the provisional fair value of identifiable assets of the Coles group and the Group's other acquisitions as at the date of acquisitions are:

	Consolidated	
	Recognised on acquisition $m	Book carrying value $m
Assets		
Cash and cash equivalents	505	505
Trade and other receivables	525	551
Inventories	3 662	3659
Investment in associate	8	8
Property, plant and equipment	3 279	3443
Investment property	6	8
Intangible assets	4 295	709
Assets held for sale	40	26
Deferred tax assets	378	458
Other assets	53	53
	12 751	9420
Liabilities		
Trade and other payables	3 305	3297
Interest bearing borrowings	2 013	2079
Provisions	1 543	1070
Other liabilities	223	277
	7 084	6723
Fair value of identifiable net assets	5 667	2697
Goodwill arising on acquisition	13 846	
	19 513	
Cost of the combinations		
Cash paid to shareholders	6 604	
Shares issued to shareholders	12 733	
Costs associated with the acquisitions	176	
	19 513	
Cash outflow on acquisitions		
Net cash acquired — operating accounts	502	
Net cash acquired — broking trust accounts	3	
Cash paid for initial holding in Coles group (in prior reporting period)	2 077	
Cash paid	(6 780)	
Net cash outflow	(4 198)	

From the date of acuquisition, the Coles group and other acquisitions contributed $475 million to the net profit after tax of the Group.

If the combinations had taken place at the beginning of the period, the revenue from continuing operations for the Group would have been $49 427 million. It is considered impracticable to obtain robust normalised pre-acquisition resuits from 1 July 2007 due to the differences in reporting periods and the timing of accounting period and adjustments recognised by the Coles group prior to acquisition.

The goodwill of $13 846 million arising on consolidation includes goodwill attributable to the Coles group acquisition of $13 801 million and is attributable to various factors, including the ability to provide improved products and services to customers, the value of growth opportunities and inseparable intangible assets.

Source: Wesfarmers (2008, pp. 114–5)

11.11 COMPREHENSIVE EXAMPLES

ILLUSTRATIVE EXAMPLE 11.7

Acquisition analyses

On 1 January 2010, Trevally Ltd concluded agreements to take over the operations of Mackerel Ltd and to acquire the rest of the shares of Perch Ltd. The statements of financial position of the three companies as at that date were:

	Trevally Ltd	Mackerel Ltd	Perch Ltd
Cash	$ 20 000	$ 1 000	$ 12 500
Accounts receivable	35 000	19 000	30 000
Inventory	52 000	26 500	40 000
Property, plant and equipment (net)	280 500	149 500	107 500
Shares in Perch Ltd (15 000 shares)	19 000	—	—
Debentures in Hangi Ltd	45 000	18 000	—
	$451 500	$214 000	$190 000
Accounts payable	$ 78 000	$ 76 000	$ 27 500
Loan payable	—	40 000	—
$10 debentures — nominal value	—	—	50 000
Share capital — issued at $1	300 000	80 000	70 000
Retained earnings	73 500	18 000	42 500
	$451 500	$214 000	$190 000

Mackerel Ltd included in the notes to its accounts a contingent liability relating to a guarantee for a loan. Although a present obligation existed, a liability was not recognised by Mackerel Ltd because of the difficulty of measuring the ultimate amount to be paid.

The details of the acquisition agreements are as follows:

Mackerel Ltd

Trevally Ltd is to acquire all the assets (except cash) and all the liabilities of Mackerel Ltd. In exchange, for every four shares in Mackerel Ltd shareholders are to receive three shares in Trevally Ltd *and* $1.00 in cash. Each share in Trevally Ltd has a fair value of $1.80. Trevally Ltd is to pay additional cash to Mackerel Ltd to cover the total liquidation expenses of Mackerel Ltd which are expected to amount to $6000. The cash already held by Mackerel Ltd is to go towards the liquidation costs. The assets of Mackerel Ltd are all recorded in Mackerel Ltd's records at cost (depreciated if applicable). The fair values of Mackerel Ltd's assets are:

Receivables	$ 17 500
Inventory	32 000
Property, plant and equipment	165 500
Debentures in Hangi Ltd	19 000

Mackerel Ltd had been undertaking research into new manufacturing machinery, and had expensed a total of $10 000 research costs. Trevally Ltd determined that the fair value of this in-process research was $2000 at acquisition date. The contingent liability relating to the guarantee was considered to have a fair value of $1500.

External accounting advice and valuers fees amounted to $3000.

Perch Ltd

Trevally Ltd is to acquire the remaining issued capital of Perch Ltd. In exchange, the shareholders in Perch Ltd are to receive four shares in Trevally Ltd for every five shares held in Perch Ltd. The shares already held in Perch Ltd are valued at $21 600, and have been accounted for as available-for-sale financial instruments with $5000 having been recognised in other comprehensive income since the shares were acquired.

The legal costs incurred by Trevally Ltd in issuing its shares to Mackerel Ltd and Perch Ltd amounted to $1300 and $800 respectively.

Required

Prepare the acquisition analyses and journal entries necessary to record the acquisition of both Mackerel Ltd and Perch Ltd in the records of Trevally Ltd.

Solution

Prepare acquisition analyses and journal entries

The first step is to analyse the nature of the business combination, in particular what happens to each entity involved in the transactions. In this example, Trevally Ltd is the acquirer. It acquires assets and liabilities of Mackerel Ltd, probably with the latter entity going into liquidation. With Perch Ltd, Trevally Ltd acquires only shares in that entity; hence, the transaction is between Trevally Ltd and the shareholders of Perch Ltd and not with Perch Ltd.

Considering the combination between Trevally Ltd and Mackerel Ltd, the first step is to prepare an acquisition analysis. This involves looking at the two sides of the transaction, determining the fair value of the identifiable assets and liabilities acquired and calculating the consideration transferred. The difference between these two amounts will be goodwill or gain on bargain purchase.

1. *Acquisition analysis — Trevally Ltd and Mackerel Ltd*

Trevally Ltd acquired all the assets except cash, and assumed all the liabilities of Mackerel Ltd. These assets and liabilities are now measured at fair value.

Accounts receivable	$ 17 500
Inventory	32 000
Property, plant and equipment	165 500
Debentures in Hangi Ltd	19 000
Deferred research	2 000
	236 000
Contingent liability	1 500
Loan payable	40 000
Accounts payable	76 000
	117 500
Net fair value	118 500

Consideration transferred

The consideration transferred is the purchase consideration payable to Mackerel Ltd and is measured as the sum of the fair values of shares issued, liabilities undertaken and assets given up by the acquirer. In this example, Trevally Ltd issues shares and gives up cash. The share price is the fair value of the shares at the acquisition date.

Consideration transferred				
Shares:	Share capital of Mackerel Ltd	$80 000		
	Shares issued by Trevally Ltd (3/4)	60 000	× $1.80	$108 000
Cash:	80 000/4 × $1.00	20 000		
	Liquidation costs	6 000		
Less:	Held by Mackerel Ltd	(1 000)		25 000
Consideration transferred				$133 000

The consideration transferred is then compared with the net fair value of the identifiable assets and liabilities acquired to determine whether goodwill or a gain arises. In this case the consideration transferred is greater, hence, goodwill has been acquired.

Goodwill = $133 000 – $118 500 = $14 500

2. *Acquisition analysis — Trevally Ltd and Perch Ltd*

In this situation, Trevally Ltd acquires the shares in the acquiree rather than the actual assets and liabilities. Note that Trevally Ltd can gain control over the net assets of another entity by either buying the actual net assets or by acquiring a controlling interest in the entity that holds those net assets. The acquisition of the shares as an asset is not a business combination. However, by acquiring the shares, a business combination may have occurred, and as is shown in chapter 14, a set of consolidated financial statements is prepared for the combined businesses and the principles of AASB 3 are applied in that process.

Cost of shares acquired	
Share capital of Perch Ltd	$ 70 000
Already held by Trevally Ltd	15 000
To acquire	$ 55 000
Trevally Ltd to issue 55 000 × 4/5 × $1.80 =	$ 79 200

The shares already held by Trevally Ltd in Perch Ltd are recorded at $19 000 at acquisition date. The fair value is $21 600. The investment is revalued at acquisition date to fair value, and the difference between these two amounts, $2600, is recorded as a gain. Further, the $5000 already recognised in other comprehensive income is transferred from equity to income.

The general journal entries can then be read from the acquisition analysis. Note that when shares are issued the relevant account is 'Share Capital'.

TREVALLY LTD
General Journal

Accounts Receivable	Dr	17 500	
Inventory	Dr	32 000	
Property, Plant and Equipment	Dr	165 500	
Debentures in Hangi Ltd	Dr	19 000	
Deferred Research	Dr	2 000	
Goodwill	Dr	14 500	
Accounts Payable	Cr		76 000
Loan Payable	Cr		40 000
Provision for Guarantee	Cr		1 500
Share Capital	Cr		108 000
Payable to Mackerel Ltd	Cr		25 000
(Acquisition of net assets of Mackerel Ltd)			
Payable to Mackerel Ltd	Dr	25 000	
Cash	Cr		25 000
(Payment of consideration transferred)			
Acquisition-related Expenses	Dr	3000	
Cash	Cr		3000
(Acquisition-related costs)			
Shares in Perch Ltd	Dr	2 600	
Gain on revaluation of investment	Cr		2 600
(Revaluation of investment to fair value)			
Investments Valuation Reserve	Dr	5 000	
Transferred gain on financial instruments	Cr		5 000
(Transfer of gains on available-for-sale investments from other comprehensive income to income)			
Shares in Perch Ltd	Dr	79 200	
Share Capital	Cr		79 200
(Purchase of remaining shares in Perch Ltd)			
Share Capital	Dr	2 100	
Cash	Cr		2 100
(Share issue costs incurred)			

Note that the costs of share issue reduce the Share Capital account which shows the net proceeds from share issues.

ILLUSTRATIVE EXAMPLE 11.8

Acquisition and liquidation

On 1 July 2011, Barramundi Ltd and Bay Ltd sign an agreement whereby the operations of Bay Ltd are to be taken over by Barramundi Ltd. Bay Ltd will liquidate after the transfer is complete. The statements of financial position of the two companies on that day were as shown below.

	Barramundi Ltd	Bay Ltd
Cash	$ 50 000	$ 20 000
Accounts receivable	75 000	56 000
Inventory	46 000	29 000
Land	65 000	—
Plant and equipment	180 000	167 000
Accumulated depreciation – plant and equipment	(60 000)	(40 000)
Patents	10 000	—
Shares in Cape Ltd	—	26 000
Debentures in Brett Ltd (nominal value)	10 000	—
	$376 000	$258 000
Accounts payable	$ 62 000	$ 31 000
Mortgage loan	75 000	21 500
10% debentures (face value)	100 000	30 000
Contributed equity:		
Ordinary shares of $1, fully paid	100 000	—
A class shares of $2, fully paid	—	40 000
B class shares of $1, fully paid		60 000
Retained earnings	39 000	75 500
	$376 000	$258 000

Barramundi Ltd is to acquire all the assets of Bay Ltd (except for cash). The assets of Bay Ltd are recorded at their fair values except for:

	Carrying amount	Fair value
Inventory	$ 29 000	$ 39 200
Plant and equipment	127 000	155 000
Shares in Cape Ltd	26 000	22 500

In exchange, the A class shareholders of Bay Ltd are to receive one 7% debenture in Barramundi Ltd, redeemable on 1 July 2012, for every share held in Bay Ltd. The fair value of each debenture is $3.50. Barramundi Ltd will also provide one of its patents to be held jointly by the A class shareholders of Bay Ltd and for which they will receive future royalties. The patent is carried at $4000 in the records of Barramundi Ltd, but is considered to have a fair value of $5000.

The B class shareholders of Bay Ltd are to receive two shares in Barramundi Ltd for every three shares held in Bay Ltd. The fair value of each Barramundi Ltd share is $2.70. Costs to issue these shares amount to $900. Additionally, Barramundi Ltd is to provide Bay Ltd with sufficient cash, additional to that already held, to enable Bay Ltd to pay its liabilities. The outstanding debentures are to be redeemed at a 10% premium. Annual leave entitlements of $16 200 outstanding at 1 July 2011 and expected liquidation costs of $5000 have not been recognised by Bay Ltd. Costs incurred in arranging the business combination amounted to $1600.

Required

1. Prepare the journal entries in the records of Barramundi Ltd to record the acquisition of Bay Ltd.
2. Prepare the Liquidation, Liquidator's Cash and Shareholders' Distribution ledger accounts in the records of Bay Ltd.

Solution

1. Prepare the journal entries of Barramundi Ltd

The nature of the transaction in this question is that the acquirer, Barramundi Ltd, is acquiring the operations (assets and liabilities) of Bay Ltd with the acquiree going into liquidation.

The first step is to prepare the acquisition analysis, which is a comparison of the fair value of the identifiable assets and liabilities acquired with the consideration transferred.

Acquisition analysis — Barramundi Ltd and Bay Ltd

Note that all the assets acquired and the liabilities assumed by the acquirer are measured at fair value.

Accounts receivable	$ 56 000
Inventory	39 200
Plant and equipment	155 000
Shares in Cape Ltd	22 500
	$272 700

Consideration transferred

The consideration transferred is measured by calculating the fair value of the assets given up, liabilities undertaken and shares issued by the acquirer. In this example, the acquirer issues shares and debentures in itself, gives up a patent and provides cash.

Purchase consideration			
Shareholders			
Debentures:	A shares of Bay Ltd	20 000	
	Debentures in Barramundi (1/1)	20 000 × $3.50	$ 70 000
Shares:	B shares of Bay Ltd	60 000	
	Shares in Barramundi (2/3)	40 000 × $2.70	108 000
Patent			5 000
Creditors		30 000	
Cash:	Debentures issued	$ 3 000	
	Plus premium (10%)	33 000	
	Accounts payable	31 000	
	Mortgage loan	21 500	
	Liquidation costs	5 000	
	Annual leave	16 200	
	Total cash required	106 700	
	Less: Already held	(20 000)	86 700
Total consideration transferred			$269 700

Because the total consideration transferred is less than the net fair value of the identifiable assets and liabilities acquired, the acquirer has to assess the measurements undertaken in the acquisition analysis. Having been assured that all relevant assets and liabilities have been included and that the fair values are reliable, the difference is then accounted for as a bargain purchase, and is included in current period income.

Gain on bargain purchase [$272 700 – $269 700]	$3 000

The general journal entries can then be read from the acquisition analysis. Note that when shares are issued the relevant account is 'Share Capital'.

In relation to the patent, prior to accounting for the business combination, the acquirer remeasures the asset to fair value.

BARRAMUNDI LTD General Journal			
Patent	Dr	1000	
Gain	Cr		1000
(Remeasurement to fair value as part of consideration transferred on business combination)			
Accounts Receivable	Dr	56 000	
Inventory	Dr	39 200	
Property, Plant and Equipment	Dr	155 000	
Shares in Cape Ltd	Dr	22 500	
Payable to Bay Ltd	Cr		156 700
Share Capital	Cr		108 000
Patent	Cr		5 000
Gain on bargain purchase	Cr		3 000
(Acquisition of Bay Ltd)			
Payable to Bay Ltd	Dr	156 700	
7% Debentures	Cr		70 000
Cash	Cr		86 700
(Payment of consideration)			
Acquisition-related expenses	Dr	1 600	
Cash	Cr		1600
(Acquisition-related costs)			
Share Capital	Dr	900	
Cash	Cr		900
(Payment of share issue costs)			

Note that the costs of share issue reduce the share capital issued with the Share Capital account then showing the net proceeds from share issues.

2. *Prepare the ledger accounts of Bay Ltd*

The Liquidation account effectively records the sale of the assets and the receipt of the purchase consideration.

- All items being sold by the acquiree — whether assets or a package of assets and liabilities — are taken at their carrying amount to the Liquidation account.
- Any amounts arising during the liquidation process and not previously recorded by the acquiree are also taken to the Liquidation account. In this example, there are three such items: premium on debentures, annual leave payable and liquidation costs. The relevant amounts are debited to the Liquidation account and liabilities are raised in relation to these items.
- Any reserves recognised by the acquiree — in this example it is retained earnings — are taken to the Liquidation account.
- The purchase consideration is credited to the Liquidation account, with the recognition of assets received, namely cash, patent, shares in Barramundi Ltd and debentures in Barramundi Ltd.

The balance of the Liquidation account is transferred to the Shareholders' Distribution account.

Liquidation			
Receivables	56 000	Retained Earnings	75 500
Inventory	29 000	Accumulated Depreciation	40 000
Plant and Equipment	167 000	Receivable from Barramundi Ltd	269 700
Shares in Cape Ltd	26 000		
Debentures – Premium	3 000		
Annual Leave Payable	16 200		
Liquidation Costs Payable	5 000		
Shareholders' Distribution	83 000		
	385 200		385 200

The cash received via the purchase consideration and the balance originally held by the acquiree is used to pay the liabilities of the acquiree, including liabilities such as liquidation costs payable raised during the liquidation process.

Liquidator's Cash			
Opening balance	20 000	Accounts Payable	31 000
Receivable from Barramundi Ltd	86 700	Debentures	33 000
		Mortgage Loan	21 500
		Liquidation Costs Payable	5 000
		Annual Leave Payable	16 200
	106 700		106 700

The capital balances of the acquiree, in this example the capital relating to both A and B shares issued by the acquiree, are taken to the credit side of the Shareholders' Distribution account. The assets to be distributed to the former shareholders of the acquiree are transferred to the debit side of the account. In this case they consist of the debentures and shares in Barramundi Ltd and the patent, all these having been received as part of the purchase consideration from the acquirer. The account balances when the balance transferred from the Liquidation account is included. At this stage, all accounts of the acquiree are closed.

Shareholders' Distribution			
Debentures in Barramundi Ltd	70 000	Share Capital – A Shares	40 000
Shares in Barramundi Ltd	108 000	Share Capital – B Shares	60 000
Patent	5 000	Liquidation	83 000
	183 000		183 000

SUMMARY

IFRS 3 was issued in March 2008 on completion of a major project on business combinations undertaken by the IASB. IFRS 3 specifies accounting standards that have implications not only for the exchanges of assets between entities but also for the accounting for subsidiaries and associated entities. The standard specifies how an acquirer accounts for the assets and liabilities acquired as well as the measurement of the consideration transferred. In making these calculations, the acquirer must determine the acquisition date as all fair value measurements are made at acquisition date. The standard interacts with other standards such as IAS 38 *Intangible Assets* and IAS 37 *Provisions, Contingent Liabilities and Contingent Assets* because the acquirer has to recognise intangible assets and liabilities acquired in a business combination. The nature and calculation of goodwill is also covered in this accounting standard, as is the treatment of a gain on a bargain purchase.

Entities commonly trade with each other, exchanging one set of assets for another. When a grouping of assets constitutes a business, the accounting for the exchange transaction is determined by IFRS 3. IFRS 3 requires the application of the acquisition method under which the accountant must be able to identify which of the entities involved in the combination is the acquirer. The identifiable assets and liabilities acquired are measured at fair value.

Goodwill or the gain on a bargain purchase is determined as a residual which, for the business combinations considered in this chapter, is generally determined by comparing the consideration transferred and the net fair value of the identifiable assets and liabilities acquired. Where the acquirer acquires the shares in the acquiree and where the acquirer already holds some shares in the acquiree at the acquisition date, the determination of goodwill is more involved. Understanding the nature of goodwill is essential to understanding how to account for it. With the existence of the accounting standard on impairment of assets, goodwill is not required to be amortised. Where a bargain purchase arises, the gain is recognised in current period income.

Discussion questions

1. What is meant by a 'business combination'?
2. Discuss the importance of identifying the acquisition date.
3. What is meant by 'contingent consideration' and how is it accounted for?
4. Explain the key components of 'core' goodwill.
5. What recognition criteria are applied to assets and liabilities acquired in a business combination?
6. How is an acquirer identified?
7. Explain the key steps in the acquisition method.
8. How is the consideration transferred calculated?
9. If an acquiree liquidates, what are the key accounts raised by the acquiree and which accounts are transferred to these accounts?
10. How is fair value determined?
11. How is a gain on bargain purchase accounted for?
12. Why is it important to identify an acquirer in a business combination?
13. Lecee Ltd has recently undertaken a business combination with Lodi Ltd. At the start of negotiations, Lecee Ltd owned 30% of the shares of Lodi Ltd. The current discussions between the two entities concerned Lecee Ltd's acquisition of the remaining 70% of shares of Lodi Ltd. The negotiations began on 1 January 2010 and enough shareholders in Lodi Ltd agreed to the deal by 30 September 2010. The purchase agreement was for shareholders in Lodi Ltd to receive in exchange shares in Lecee Ltd. Over the negotiation period, the share price of Lecee Ltd shares reached a low of $5.40 and a high of $6.20.

    The accountant for Lecee Ltd, Mr Spencer, knows that IFRS 3 has to be applied in accounting for business combinations. However, he is confused as to how to account for the original 30% investment in Lodi Ltd, what share price to use to account for the issue of Lecee Ltd's shares, and how the varying dates such as the date of exchange and acquisition date will affect the accounting for the business combination.

    Required
    Provide Mr Spencer with advice on the issues that are confusing him.

14. Genoa Ltd has acquired a major manufacturing division from Florence Ltd. The accountant, Ms Ball, has shown the board of directors of Genoa Ltd the financial information regarding the acquisition. Ms Ball calculated a residual amount of $45 000 to be reported as goodwill in the accounts. The directors are not sure whether they want to record goodwill on Genoa Ltd's statement of financial position. Some directors are not sure what goodwill is or why the company has bought it. Other directors even query whether goodwill is an asset, with some being concerned with future effects on the statement of comprehensive income.

    Required
    Prepare a report for Ms Ball to present to the directors to help them understand the nature of goodwill and how to account for it.

15. Enna Ltd has been negotiating with Foggia Ltd for several months, and agreements have finally been reached for the two companies to combine. In considering the accounting for the combined entities, management realises that, in applying IFRS 3, an acquirer must be identified. However, there is debate among the accounting staff as to which entity is the acquirer.

    Required
    1. What factors/indicators should management consider in determining which entity is the acquirer?
    2. Why is it necessary to identify an acquirer? In particular, what differences in accounting would arise if Enna Ltd or Foggia Ltd were identified as the acquirer?

16. Como Ltd has acquired all the net assets of Latina Ltd with the latter going into liquidation. Both companies operate in the area of testing and manufacturing pharmaceutical products. One of the main reasons that Como Ltd sought to acquire Latina Ltd was that the latter company had an impressive record in the development of drugs for the cure of some mosquito-related diseases. Latina Ltd employed a number of scientists who were considered to be international experts in their area and at the leading edge of research in their field. Much of the recent work undertaken by these scientists was classified for accounting purposes as research, and as per IAS 38 *Intangible Assets* was expensed by Latina Ltd. However, in deciding what it would pay to take over Latina Ltd, Como Ltd had paid a sizeable amount of money for the ongoing research being undertaken by Latina Ltd as it was expected that it would be successful eventually.

The accountant for Como Ltd, Mr Basket, has suggested that the amount paid by Como Ltd for this research should be shown as goodwill in the company's statement of financial position. However, the directors of the company do not believe that this faithfully represents the true nature of the assets acquired in the business combination, and want to recognise an asset separately from goodwill. Mr Basket believes that this will not be in accordance with IAS 38.

Required

Provide the directors with advice on the accounting for the aforementioned transaction.

17. One of the responsibilities of the Group Accountant for Bari Ltd, Ms Bluff, is to explain the accounting principles applied by the company in preparing the annual report to the company's Board of Directors. Having analysed IFRS 3, Ms Bluff is puzzled by the requirement in paragraph 53 of IFRS 3 that any acquisition-related costs such as fees for lawyers and valuers should be expensed. Ms Bluff has analysed other accounting standards such as IAS 16 *Property, Plant and Equipment* and notes that under this standard such costs are capitalised into the cost of any property, plant and equipment acquired. She therefore believes that to expense such costs in accounting for a business combination would not be consistent with accounting for acquisitions of other assets.

Further, Ms Bluff believes that to expense such costs would result in a loss being reported in the statement of comprehensive income in the period the business combination occurs. She is not sure how she will explain to the board of directors that the company makes a loss every time it enters a business combination. She believes the directors will wonder why the company enters into business combinations if immediate losses occur — surely losses indicate that bad decisions have been made by the company.

Required

Prepare a report for Ms Bluff on how she should explain the accounting for acquisition-related costs to the board of directors.

STAR RATING
★ BASIC
★★ MODERATE
★★★ DIFFICULT

Exercises

Exercise 11.1 ★

ACCOUNTING BY THE ACQUIRER

On 1 July 2010, Asti Ltd acquired the following assets and liabilities from Ascoli Ltd:

	Carrying amount	Fair value
Land	$300 000	$350 000
Plant (cost $400 000)	280 000	290 000
Inventory	80 000	85 000
Cash	15 000	15 000
Accounts payable	(20 000)	(20 000)
Loans	(80 000)	(80 000)

In exchange for these assets and liabilities, Asti Ltd issued 100 000 shares that had been issued for $1.20 per share but at 1 July 2010 had a fair value of $6.50 per share.

Required

1. Prepare the journal entries in the records of Asti Ltd to account for the acquisition of the assets and liabilities of Ascoli Ltd.
2. Prepare the journal entries assuming that the fair value of Asti Ltd shares was $6 per share.

Exercise 11.2 ACCOUNTING BY AN ACQUIRER

★ Padova Ltd acquired all the assets and liabilities of Prato Ltd on 1 July 2011. At this date, the assets and liabilities of Prato Ltd consisted of:

	Carrying amount	Fair value
Current assets	$1 000 000	$ 980 000
Non-current assets	4 000 000	4 220 000
	5 000 000	5 200 000
Liabilities	500 000	500 000
	$4 500 000	$4 700 000
Share capital — 100 000 shares	$3 000 000	
Reserves	1 500 000	
	$4 500 000	

In exchange for these net assets, Padova Ltd agreed to:

- issue 10 Light Ltd shares for every Prato Ltd share — Padova Ltd shares were considered to have a fair value of $10 per share; costs of share issue were $500
- transfer a patent to the former shareholders of Prato Ltd — the patent was carried in the records of Padova Ltd at $350 000 but was considered to have a fair value of $1 million
- pay $5.20 per share in cash to each of the former shareholders of Prato Ltd.

Padova Ltd incurred $10 000 in costs associated with the acquisition of these net assets.

Required

1. Prepare an acquisition analysis in relation to this acquisition.
2. Prepare the journal entries in Padova Ltd to record the acquisition.

Exercise 11.3 ACQUISITION OF SHARES IN ACQUIREE

★ On 1 January 2011, Arezzo Ltd acquired all the issued shares of Ascoli Ltd. At this date the equity of Ascoli Ltd consisted of:

Share capital — 100 000 shares issued at $5 per share	$ 500 000
General reserve	200 000
Asset revaluation surplus	100 000
Retained earnings	50 000

In exchange for these shares, Arezzo Ltd agreed to pay the former shareholders of Ascoli Ltd two shares in Arezzo Ltd, these having a fair value of $4 per share, plus $1.50 cash for each share held in Ascoli Ltd. The costs of issuing the shares were $800.

Required

Prepare the journal entries in the records of Arezzo Ltd to record these events.

Exercise 11.4 ACCOUNTING BY AN ACQUIRER

★ Venice Ltd acquired the assets and liabilities of Verona Ltd on 1 July 2011. These net assets measured at fair value consisted of:

Equipment	$50 000
Land	80 000
Trucks	40 000
Current assets	10 000
Current liabilities	(16 000)

Required

Prepare the journal entries in Venice Ltd to record this business combination assuming that, to acquire these net assets, Venice Ltd:

1. issued 100 000 shares at $1.80 per share
2. issued 100 000 shares at $1.60 per share.

Exercise 11.5 LIQUIDATION OF THE ACQUIREE

★ Trento Ltd acquired all the net assets of Turin Ltd, giving in exchange 100 000 shares, these having a fair value of $2.80 per share, and $50 000 cash.

At the acquisition date, the statement of financial position of Turin Ltd was as follows:

Cash	$ 10 000
Accounts receivable	20 000
Land	80 000
Plant	240 000
Vehicles	50 000
	$400 000
Accounts payable	$ 40 000
Loans	60 000
	$100 000
Share capital	$200 000
General reserve	40 000
Retained earnings	$ 60 000
	$300 000

Costs of liquidation amounted to $1000.

Required

Prepare the journal entries to liquidate Trento Ltd.

Exercise 11.6 DETERMINING THE FAIR VALUE OF EQUITY ISSUED BY THE ACQUIRER

★ On 1 December 2011, Terni Ltd acquired all the assets and liabilities of Aosta Ltd, with Terni Ltd issuing 100 000 shares to acquire these net assets. The fair values of Aosta Ltd's assets and liabilities at this date were:

Cash	$ 50 000
Furniture and fittings	20 000
Accounts receivable	5 000
Plant	125 000
Accounts payable	15 000
Current tax liability	8 000
Annual leave payable	2 000

The financial year for Terni Ltd is January to December.

Required

1. Prepare the journal entries for Terni Ltd to record the business combination at 1 December 2011, assuming the fair value of each Terni Ltd share at acquisition date is $1.90. Prepare any note disclosures for Terni Ltd at 31 December 2011 in relation to the business combination.
2. Assume the fair value of each Terni Ltd share at acquisition date is $1.90. At acquisition date, the acquirer could only determine a provisional fair value for the plant. On 1 March 2012, Terni Ltd received the final value from the independent appraisal, the fair value at acquisition date being $131 000. Assuming the plant had a further 5-year life from the acquisition date, explain how Terni Ltd will account for the business combination both at acquisition date and in the financial statements for 2012.
3. Prepare the journal entries for Terni Ltd to record the business combination at 1 December 2011, assuming the fair value of each Terni Ltd share at acquisition date is $1.70.

Exercise 11.7 DETERMINING THE FAIR VALUE OF EQUITY ISSUED BY THE ACQUIRER

★ The following are the statements of financial position at 30 September 2010 of Novara Ltd and Matera Ltd.

Novara Ltd

Share capital — 80 000 shares	$ 80 000	Non-current assets (at valuation less depreciation)	$ 190 000
Asset revaluation reserve	140 000	Current assets	148 000
General reserve	60 000		
Retained earnings	30 000		
Creditors and provisions	28 000		
	$ 338 000		$ 338 000

Matera Ltd

Share capital — 60 000 shares	$ 60 000	Non-current assets (at cost less depreciation)	$ 50 000
General reserve	20 000	Current assets	65 000
Retained earnings	25 000		
Creditors and provisions	10 000		
	$ 115 000		$ 115 000

Additional information

(a) During September the shares of the companies were selling on the stock exchange at or near the following prices:

Novara Ltd $5.80 Matera Ltd $1.80

(b) On 30 September the directors of Novara Ltd made an offer to the shareholders of Matera Ltd to acquire their shares on the basis of one fully paid share at $1 in Novara Ltd for every two fully paid shares at $1 in Matera Ltd.

The offer was open for 1 month and was contingent upon being accepted by the holders of at least 75% of Matera Ltd's capital.

(c) Immediately after the announcement, Novara Ltd's shares rose in price on the stock exchange to $6.20 and the shares of Matera Ltd rose to $3. The shares of both companies stayed at or close to this price throughout October.

(d) By the end of October, holders of 90% of Matera Ltd shares accepted the Novara Ltd offer and the latter company proceeds to acquire these shares on the agreed basis.

(e) By mid-November, Novara Ltd shares dropped in price on the stock exchange to $5.50.

(f) Costs of issuing and registering shares issued by Novara Ltd amounted to $2000.

Required

1. Give the journal entries necessary to record the transactions. (Show clearly to which company particular entries relate.)
2. State briefly why you selected the value adopted in recording the acquisition, and whether you consider there is any acceptable alternative recording value.
3. Show the statement of financial position of Novara Ltd after the entries have been recorded.

Exercise 11.8 ★★

LIQUIDATION OF ACQUIREE, ACCOUNTING BY ACQUIRER

Abruzzo Ltd, a supplier of snooker equipment, agreed to acquire the business of a rival firm, Lazio Ltd, taking over all assets and liabilities as at 1 June 2010.

The price agreed on was $60 000, payable $20 000 in cash and the balance by the issue to the selling company of 16 000 fully paid shares in Abruzzo Ltd, these shares having a fair value of $2.50 per share.

The trial balances of the two companies as at 1 June 2010 were as follows:

	Abruzzo Ltd		Lazio Ltd	
	Dr	Cr	Dr	Cr
Share capital		$ 100 000		$ 90 000
Retained earnings		12 000	$ 24 000	
Accounts payable		2 000		20 000
Cash	$ 30 000		—	
Plant (net)	50 000		30 000	
Inventory	14 000		26 000	
Accounts receivable	8 000		20 000	
Government bonds	12 000		—	
Goodwill	—		10 000	
	$114 000	$114 000	$110 000	$110 000

All the identifiable net assets of Lazio Ltd were recorded by Lazio Ltd at fair value except for the inventory, which was considered to be worth $28 000 (assume no tax effect). The plant had an expected remaining life of 5 years.

The business combination was completed and Lazio Ltd went into liquidation. Costs of liquidation amounted to $1000. Abruzzo Ltd incurred incidental costs of $500 in relation to the acquisition. Costs of issuing shares in Abruzzo Ltd were $400.

Required

1. Show the Liquidation account and the Shareholders' Distribution account in the records of Lazio Ltd.
2. Prepare the journal entries in the records of Abruzzo Ltd to record the business combination.
3. Show the statement of financial position of Abruzzo Ltd after completion of the business combination.
4. On 31 July 2010, Abruzzo Ltd became aware that there had been an error in measuring the fair value of the plant at 1 June 2010. It had in fact a fair value at that date of $36 000. Explain how Abruzzo Ltd is required to adjust for that error. Abruzzo Ltd's reporting period ends on 30 June.

Exercise 11.9 ★★

CONSIDERATION TRANSFERRED

On 1 September 2009, the directors of Umbria Ltd approached the directors of Sicily Ltd with the following proposal for the acquisition of the issued shares of Sicily Ltd, conditional on acceptance by 90% of the shareholders of Sicily Ltd by 30 November 2009:

- Two fully paid ordinary shares in Umbria Ltd plus $3.10 cash for every preference share in Sicily Ltd, payable at acquisition date.
- Three fully paid ordinary shares in Umbria Ltd plus $1.20 cash for every ordinary share in Sicily Ltd. Half the cash is payable at acquisition, and the other half in one year's time.

By 30 November, 90% of the ordinary shareholders and all of the preference shareholders of Sicily Ltd had accepted the offer. The directors of Umbria Ltd decided *not* to acquire the remaining ordinary shares. Share transfer forms covering the transfer were dated 30 November 2009, and showed a price per Umbria Ltd ordinary share of $4.20. Umbria Ltd's incremental borrowing rate is 8% p.a.

The statement of financial position of Sicily Ltd at 30 November 2009 was as shown on the next page.

SICILY LTD Statement of Financial Position as at 30 November 2009		
Current assets		$120 000
Non-current assets:		
Land and buildings	$203 000	
Plant and equipment	168 000	
Less: Accumulated depreciation	(45 000)	
Shares in other companies listed on stock exchange at cost (market $190 000)	30 000	
Government bonds, at cost	50 000	
Total non-current assets		406 000
Total assets		526 000
Current liabilities		30 000
Net assets		$496 000
Equity		
Share capital		
80 000 ordinary shares fully paid	$160 000	
50 000 6% preference shares fully paid	100 000	$260 000
Retained earnings		236 000
Total equity		$496 000

Umbria Ltd then appointed a new board of directors of Sicily Ltd. This board took office on 1 December 2009 and immediately:

- revalued the asset Shares in Other Companies to its market value (assume no tax effect)
- used the surplus so created to make a bonus issue of $32 000 to ordinary shareholders, each shareholder being allocated two ordinary shares for every ten ordinary shares held.

Required

Prepare all journal entries (in general form) to record the above transactions in the records of (a) Umbria Ltd and (b) Sicily Ltd.

Exercise 11.10 ★★

LIQUIDATION OF ACQUIREE, ACCOUNTING BY ACQUIRER

Salerno Ltd is seeking to expand its share of the widgets market and has negotiated to take over the operations of Savona Ltd on 1 January 2011. The statements of financial position of the two companies as at 31 December 2010 were as follows:

		Salerno Ltd	Savona Ltd
Cash		$ 23 000	$ 12 000
Accounts receivable		25 000	34 700
Inventory		35 500	27 600
Freehold land		150 000	100 000
Buildings (net)		60 000	30 000
Plant and equipment (net)		65 000	46 000
Goodwill		25 000	2 000
		$383 500	$252 300
Accounts payable		$ 56 000	$ 43 500
Mortgage loan		50 000	40 000
Debentures		100 000	50 000
Share capital	— 100 000 shares	100 000	—
	— 60 000 shares	—	60 000
Other reserves		28 500	26 800
Retained earnings		49 000	32 000
		$383 500	$252 300

Salerno Ltd is to acquire all the assets, except cash, of Savona Ltd. The assets of Savona Ltd are all recorded at fair value except:

	Fair value
Inventory	$ 39 000
Freehold land	130 000
Buildings	40 000

In exchange, Salerno Ltd is to provide sufficient extra cash to allow Savona Ltd to repay all of its outstanding debts and its liquidation costs of $2400, plus two fully paid shares in Salerno Ltd for every three shares held in Savona Ltd. The fair value of a share in Salerno Ltd is $3.20. An investigation by the liquidator of Savona Ltd reveals that at 31 December 2010 the following debts were outstanding but had not been recorded:

Accounts payable	$1600
Mortgage interest	4000

The debentures issued by Savona Ltd are to be redeemed at a 5% premium. Costs of issuing the shares were $1200.

Required

1. Prepare the acquisition analysis and journal entries to record the business combination in the records of Salerno Ltd.
2. Prepare the Liquidation, Liquidator's Cash, and Shareholders' Distribution accounts for Savona Ltd.

Exercise 11.11 ★★

ACCOUNTING FOR BUSINESS COMBINATION BY ACQUIRER, LIQUIDATION ACCOUNTS OF ACQUIREE

On 1 July 2010, two companies — Tuscany Ltd and Calabria Ltd — sign an agreement whereby the operations of Calabria Ltd are to be taken over by Tuscany Ltd. Calabria Ltd is to liquidate after the transfer is complete. The statements of financial position of the two companies on that day were as follows:

	Tuscany Ltd	Calabria Ltd
Cash	$ 50 000	$ 20 000
Accounts receivable	75 000	56 000
Inventory	56 000	29 000
Land	65 000	—
Plant and equipment	180 000	167 000
Accumulated depreciation — plant and equipment	(60 000)	(40 000)
Shares in Catania Ltd	—	26 000
Debentures in Caserta Ltd (face value)	10 000	—
	$376 000	$258 000
Accounts payable	$ 62 000	$ 31 000
Mortgage loan	75 000	21 500
10% debentures (face value)	100 000	30 000
Share capital:		
Ordinary shares of $1, fully paid	100 000	—
A class shares of $2, fully paid	—	40 000
B class shares of $1, fully paid	—	60 000
Retained earnings	39 000	75 500
	$376 000	$258 000

Acquisition of Calabria Ltd

Tuscany Ltd is to acquire all of the assets of Calabria Ltd (except for cash). The assets of Calabria Ltd are recorded at their fair values except for the following:

	Carrying amount	Fair value
Inventory	$ 29 000	$ 39 200
Plant and equipment	127 000	140 000
Shares in Catania Ltd	26 000	22 500

In exchange, the A class shareholders of Calabria Ltd are to receive one 7% debenture in Tuscany Ltd, redeemable on 1 July 2012, for every share held in Calabria Ltd. The fair value of each debenture is $3.50. The B class shareholders of Calabria Ltd are to receive two shares in Tuscany Ltd for every three shares held in Calabria Ltd. The fair value of each Tuscany Ltd share is $2.70. Costs to issue these shares will amount to $900.

Additionally, Tuscany Ltd is to provide Calabria Ltd with sufficient cash, additional to that already held, to enable Calabria Ltd to pay its liabilities. The outstanding debentures are to be redeemed at a 10% premium. Annual leave entitlements of $16 200 outstanding at 1 July 2010 and expected liquidation costs of $5000 have not been recognised by Calabria Ltd. Costs to transport and install Calabria Ltd's assets at Tuscany Ltd's premises will be $1600.

Required

1. Prepare the acquisition analysis and journal entries in the books of Tuscany Ltd to record the acquisition of Calabria Ltd.
2. Prepare the Liquidation, Liquidator's Cash, and Shareholders' Distribution ledger accounts in the records of Calabria Ltd.

Exercise 11.12 ★★

ACCOUNTING FOR BUSINESS COMBINATION BY ACQUIRER, JOURNAL ENTRIES FOR LIQUIDATION OF ACQUIREE

Veneto Ltd and Molise Ltd are small family-owned companies engaged in vegetable growing and distribution. The Spencer family owns the shares in Molise Ltd and the Rokocoko family own the shares in Veneto Ltd. The head of the Spencer family wishes to retire but his two sons are not interested in carrying on the family business. Accordingly, on 1 July 2011, Veneto Ltd is to take over the operations of Molise Ltd, which will then liquidate. Veneto Ltd is asset-rich but has limited overdraft facilities so the following arrangement has been made.

Veneto Ltd is to acquire all of the assets, except cash, delivery trucks and motor vehicles, of Molise Ltd and will assume all of the liabilities except accounts payable. In return, Veneto Ltd is to give the shareholders of Molise Ltd a block of vacant land, two delivery vehicles and sufficient additional cash to enable the company to pay off the accounts payable and the liquidation costs of $1500. The land and vehicles had the following values at 30 June 2011:

	Carrying amount	Fair value
Freehold land	$50 000	$120 000
Delivery trucks	30 000	28 000

On the liquidation of Molise Ltd, Mr Spencer is to receive the land and the motor vehicles and his two sons are to receive the delivery trucks.

The statements of financial position of the two companies as at 30 June 2011 were as follows:

	Veneto Ltd	Molise Ltd
Cash	$ 3 500	$ 2 000
Accounts receivable	25 000	15 000
Freehold land	250 000	100 000
Buildings (net)	25 000	30 000
Cultivation equipment (net)	65 000	46 000
Irrigation equipment	16 000	22 000

(continued)

	Veneto Ltd	Molise Ltd
Delivery trucks	45 000	36 000
Motor vehicles	25 000	32 000
	$454 500	$283 000
Accounts payable	$ 26 000	$ 23 500
Loan – Bank of Italy	150 000	80 000
Loan – Trevally Bros	35 000	35 000
Loan – Long Cloud	70 000	52 500
Share capital — 100 000 shares	100 000	—
— 60 000 shares	—	60 000
Reserves	28 500	—
Retained earnings	45 000	32 000
	$454 500	$283 000

All the assets of Molise Ltd are recorded at fair value, with the exception of:

	Fair value
Freehold land	$120 000
Buildings	40 000
Cultivation equipment	40 000
Motor vehicle	34 000

Required

1. Prepare the acquisition analysis and the journal entries to record the acquisition of Molise Ltd's operations in the records of Veneto Ltd.
2. Prepare the journal entries to record the liquidation of Molise Ltd.
3. Prepare the statement of financial position of Veneto Ltd after the business combination, including any notes relating to the business combination.

Exercise 11.13 ★★

ACCOUNTING FOR BUSINESS COMBINATION BY ACQUIRER

Varese Ltd and Udine Ltd are two family-owned flax-producing companies in Italy. Varese Ltd is owned by the Wood family and the Bradbury family owns Udine Ltd. The Wood family has only one son and he is engaged to be married to the daughter of the Bradbury family. Because the son is currently managing Udine Ltd, it is proposed that, after the wedding, he should manage both companies. As a result, it is agreed by the two families that Varese Ltd should take over the net assets of Udine Ltd.

The statement of financial position of Udine Ltd immediately before the takeover is as follows:

	Carrying amount	Fair value
Cash	$ 20 000	$ 20 000
Accounts receivable	140 000	125 000
Land	620 000	840 000
Buildings (net)	530 000	550 000
Farm equipment (net)	360 000	364 000
Irrigation equipment (net)	220 000	225 000
Vehicles (net)	160 000	172 000
	$2 050 000	
Accounts payable	$ 80 000	80 000
Loan — Trevally Bank	480 000	480 000
Share capital	670 000	
Retained earnings	820 000	
	$2 050 000	

The takeover agreement specified the following details:

- Varese Ltd is to acquire all the assets of Udine Ltd except for cash, and one of the vehicles (having a carrying amount of $45 000 and a fair value of $48 000), and assume all the liabilities except for the loan from the Trevally Bank. Udine Ltd is then to go into liquidation. The vehicle is to be transferred to Mr and Mrs Bradbury.
- Varese Ltd is to supply sufficient cash to enable the debt to the Trevally Bank to be paid off and to cover the liquidation costs of $5500. It will also give $150 000 to be distributed to Mr and Mrs Bradbury to help pay the costs of the wedding.
- Varese Ltd is also to give a piece of its own prime land to Udine Ltd to be distributed to Mr and Mrs Bradbury, this eventually being available to be given to any offspring of the forthcoming marriage. The piece of land in question has a carrying amount of $80 000 and a fair value of $220 000.
- Varese Ltd is to issue 100 000 shares, these having a fair value of $14 per share, to be distributed via Udine Ltd to the soon to-be-married-daughter of Mr and Mrs Bradbury, who is currently a shareholder in Udine Ltd.

The takeover proceeded as per the agreement, with Varese Ltd incurring incidental acquisition costs of $25 000 and $18 000 share issue costs.

Required

Prepare the acquisition analysis and the journal entries to record the acquisition of Udine Ltd in the records of Varese Ltd.

Problems

Problem 11.1

★★★

ACCOUNTING FOR A BUSINESS COMBINATION BY BOTH THE ACQUIRER AND THE ACQUIREE

Vercelli Ltd was finding difficulty in raising finance for expansion. Chieti Ltd was interested in achieving economies by marketing a wider range of products.

The following shows the financial positions of the companies at 30 June 2010.

	Vercelli Ltd	Chieti Ltd
Share capital		
40 000 shares	$ 40 000	
90 000 shares		$ 90 000
Retained earnings	12 000	30 000
	52 000	120 000
Liabilities:		
Debentures (secured by floating charge)	20 000	—
Accounts payable	42 000	12 000
	62 000	12 000
Total equity and liabilities	$114 000	$132 000
Assets:		
Cash	$ 12 000	$ 24 000
Accounts receivable	18 000	20 000
Inventory (at cost)	43 000	47 000
Land and buildings (at cost)	23 000	19 000
Plant and machinery (at cost)	52 000	41 000
Accumulated depreciation on plant and machinery	(34 000)	(19 000)
Total assets	$114 000	$132 000

It was agreed that it would be mutually advantageous for Vercelli Ltd to specialise in manufacturing, and for marketing, purchasing and promotion to be handled by Chieti Ltd. Accordingly, Chieti Ltd sold *part* of its assets to Vercelli Ltd on 1 July 2010, the identifiable assets acquired having the following fair values:

Inventory $22 000 (cost $15 000)
Land and buildings $34 000 (carrying amount $10 000)
Plant and machinery $27 000 (cost $38 000, accumulated depreciation $18 000)

The acquisition was satisfied by the issue of 40 000 'A' ordinary shares (fully paid) in Vercelli Ltd.

Required

1. Show the journal entries to record the above transactions in the records of Vercelli Ltd:
   (a) if the fair value of the 'A' ordinary shares of Vercelli Ltd was $2 per share
   (b) if the fair value of the 'A' ordinary shares of Vercelli Ltd was $2.20 per share. (Assume the assets acquired constitute a business entity.)
2. Show the journal entries in the records of Chieti Ltd under (1) and (2) in requirement A above.
3. Show the statement of financial position of Vercelli Ltd after the transactions, assuming the fair value of Vercelli's Ltd's 'A' ordinary shares was $2.20 per share. Provide the notes to the financial statements relating to the business combinations.

Problem 11.2 ACCOUNTING FOR ACQUISITIONS OF A BUSINESS AND SHARES IN ANOTHER ENTITY

★★★

Biella Ltd is seeking to expand its share of the pet care market and has negotiated to acquire the operations of Cuneo Ltd and the shares of Ferrara Ltd.

At 1 July 2010, the trial balances of the three companies were:

	Biella Ltd	Cuneo Ltd	Ferrara Ltd
Cash	$145 000	$ 5 200	$ 84 000
Accounts receivable	34 000	21 300	12 000
Inventory	56 000	30 000	25 400
Shares in listed companies	16 000	22 000	7 000
Land and buildings (net)	70 000	40 000	36 000
Plant and equipment (net)	130 000	105 000	25 000
Goodwill (net)	6 000	5 000	5 600
	$457 000	$228 500	$ 195 000
Accounts payable	$ 65 000	$ 40 000	$ 29 000
Bank overdraft	0	0	1 500
Debentures	50 000	0	100 000
Mortgage loan	100 000	30 000	0
Contributed equity:			
Ordinary shares of $1, fully paid	200 000	150 000	60 000
Other reserves	15 000	6 500	2 500
Retained earnings (30/6/10)	27 000	2 000	2 000
	$457 000	$228 500	$ 195 000

Cuneo Ltd

Biella Ltd is to acquire all assets (except cash and shares in listed companies) of Cuneo Ltd. Acquisition-related costs are expected to be $7600. The net assets of Cuneo Ltd are recorded at fair value except for the following:

	Carrying amount	Fair value
Inventory	$ 30 000	$ 26 000
Land and buildings	40 000	80 000
Shares in listed companies	22 000	18 000
Accounts payable	(40 000)	(49 100)
Accrued leave	0	(29 700)

In exchange, the shareholders of Cuneo Ltd are to receive, for every three Cuneo Ltd shares held, one Biella Ltd share worth $2.50 each. Costs to issue these shares are $950. Additionally, Biella Ltd will transfer to Cuneo Ltd its 'Shares in Listed Companies' asset, which has a fair value of $15 000. These shares, together with those already owned by Cuneo Ltd, will be sold and the proceeds distributed to the Cuneo Ltd shareholders. Assume that the shares were sold for their fair values.

Biella Ltd will also give Cuneo Ltd sufficient additional cash to enable Cuneo Ltd to pay all its creditors. Cuneo Ltd will then liquidate. Liquidation costs are estimated to be $8700.

Ferrara Ltd

Biella Ltd is to acquire all the issued shares of Ferrara Ltd. In exchange, the shareholders of Ferrara Ltd are to receive one Biella Ltd share, worth $2.50, and $1.50 cash for every two Ferrara Ltd shares held.

Required

1. Prepare the acquisition analysis and journal entries to record the acquisitions in the records of Biella Ltd.
2. Prepare the Liquidation account and Shareholders' Distribution account for *Cuneo* Ltd.
3. Explain in detail why, if *Cuneo* Ltd has recorded a goodwill asset of $5000, Biella Ltd calculates the goodwill acquired via an acquisition analysis. Why does Biella Ltd not determine a fair value for the goodwill asset and record that figure as it has done for other assets acquired from *Cuneo* Ltd?
4. If Biella Ltd subsequently receives a dividend cheque for $1500 from *Ferrara* Ltd, paid from retained earnings earned before its acquisition of the shares in *Ferrara* Ltd, how should Biella Ltd account for that cheque? Why?
5. Shortly after the business combination, the liquidator of *Cuneo* Ltd receives a valid claim of $25 000 from a creditor. As Biella Ltd has agreed to provide sufficient cash to pay all the liabilities of *Cuneo* Ltd at acquisition date, the liquidator requests and receives a cheque for $25 000 from Biella Ltd. How should Biella Ltd record this payment? Why?

Problem 11.3 ★★★ ACQUISITION OF TWO BUSINESSES

Livorno Ltd is a manufacturer of specialised industrial machinery seeking to diversify its operations. After protracted negotiations, the directors decided to purchase the assets and liabilities of Laspezia Ltd and the spare parts retail division of Lucca Ltd.

At 30 June 2011 the statements of financial position of the three entities were as follows:

	Livorno Ltd	Laspezia Ltd	Lucca Ltd
Land and buildings (net)	$ 60 000	$ 25 000	$ 40 000
Plant and machinery (net)	100 000	36 000	76 000
Office equipment (net)	16 000	4 000	6 000
Shares in listed companies	24 000	15 000	20 800
Debentures in listed companies	20 000	—	—
Accounts receivable	35 000	26 000	42 000
Inventory	150 000	54 000	30 200
Cash	59 000	11 000	9 000
Goodwill	—	7 000	—
	$464 000	$178 000	$224 000
Accounts payable	26 000	14 000	27 000
Current tax liability	21 000	6 000	7 000
Provision for leave	36 000	10 000	17 500
Bank loan	83 000	16 000	43 500
Debentures	60 000	50 000	—
Share capital (issued at $1, fully paid)	200 000	60 000	90 000
Retained earnings	38 000	22 000	39 000
	$464 000	$178 000	$224 000

The acquisition agreement details are as follows:

Laspezia Ltd

Livorno Ltd is to acquire all the assets (other than cash) and liabilities (other than debentures, provisions and tax liabilities) of Laspezia Ltd for the following purchase consideration:

- Shareholders in Laspezia Ltd are to receive three shares in Livorno Ltd, credited as fully paid, in exchange for every four shares held. The shares in Livorno Ltd are to be issued at their fair value of $3 per share. Costs of share issue amounted to $2000.

- Livorno Ltd is to provide sufficient cash which, when added to the cash already held, will enable Laspezia Ltd to pay out the current tax liability and provision for leave, to redeem the debentures at a premium of 5%, and to pay its liquidation expenses of $2500.

The fair values of the assets and liabilities of Laspezia Ltd are equal to their carrying amounts with the exception of the following:

	Fair value
Land and buildings	$60 000
Plant and machinery	50 000

Incidental costs associated with the acquisition amount to $2500.

Lucca Ltd

Livorna Ltd is to acquire the spare parts retail business of Lucca Ltd. The following information is available concerning that business, relative to the whole of Lucca Ltd:

	Total amount	Spare parts division	
	Carrying amount	Carrying amount	Fair value
Land and buildings (net)	$40 000	$20 000	$30 000
Plant and machinery (net)	76 000	32 000	34 500
Office equipment (net)	6 000	2 000	2 500
Accounts receivable	42 000	21 000	20 000
Inventory	30 200	12 000	12 000
Accounts payable	27 000	14 000	14 000
Provision for leave	17 500	7 000	7 000

The divisional net assets are to be acquired for $10 000 cash, plus 11 000 ordinary shares in Livorno Ltd issued at their fair value of $3, plus the land and buildings that have been purchased from Laspezia Ltd.

Incidental costs associated with the acquisition are $1000.

Required

1. Prepare the acquisition analysis for the acquisition transactions of Livorno Ltd.
2. Prepare the liquidation account for Laspezia Ltd.
3. Prepare the journal entries for the acquisition transactions in the records of Livorno Ltd and Lucca Ltd.

REFERENCES

Accounting Standards Board UK 2005, Letter of comment (no. 130) on *Exposure Draft of Proposed Amendments to IFRS 3 Business Combinations*, 28 October, www.fasb.org.

Danisco 2006, *Annual report 2005/06*, Danisco Corporation, Denmark, www.danisco.com.

Intangible Business 2007, *SFAS141: The first 5 years*, Intangible Business, London, www.intangiblebusiness.com.

Johnson, LT & Petrone, KR 1998, 'Is goodwill an asset?', *Accounting Horizons*, vol. 12, no. 3, pp. 293–303.

Leo, KJ, Hoggett, JR & Radford, J 1995, *Accounting for identifiable intangibles and goodwill*, Australian Society of Certified Practising Accountants, Melbourne.

Miller, M & Islam, A 1988, *The definition and recognition of assets*, Accounting Theory Monograph No. 7, Australian Accounting Research Foundation, Melbourne.

Nokia 2006, *Nokia in 2005*, Nokia Corporation, Finland, www.nokia.com.

Wesfarmers 2008, *2008 annual report*, Wesfarmers Limited, www.wesfarmers.com.au.

12 Impairment of assets

ACCOUNTING STANDARDS IN FOCUS

IAS 36 *Impairment of Assets*

LEARNING OBJECTIVES

When you have studied this chapter you should be able to:

- understand the purpose of the impairment test for assets
- understand when to undertake an impairment test
- explain how to undertake an impairment test for an individual asset
- identify a cash-generating unit, and account for an impairment loss for a cash-generating unit — not including goodwill
- account for the impairment of goodwill
- account for reversals of impairment losses
- apply the disclosure requirements of IAS 36.

12.1 INTRODUCTION TO IAS 36

Chapters 9 and 10 discuss the measurement and recognition criteria for property, plant and equipment, and intangibles. These assets are measured at cost or revalued amount and, for each asset, the cost or revalued amount is allocated over its useful life. The exception is where intangible assets have indefinite useful lives, in which case no amortisation is charged. In the statement of financial position/balance sheet at the end of a reporting period, the assets are reported at cost or revalued amount less the accumulated depreciation/amortisation. Because there are many judgements in the depreciation/amortisation process — estimates of useful life, residual values and the pattern of benefits — the question to be asked at the end of the reporting period is whether the carrying amounts of the assets in the statement of financial position overstate the worth of the assets. In other words, can an entity expect to recover in future periods the carrying amounts of an entity's assets? Recovery can be from future use of the asset and/or from the eventual disposal of the asset. If an entity does not expect to recover the carrying amount of an asset, the entity has an impairment loss in relation to that asset. Paragraph 6 of IAS 36 *Impairment of Assets* defines an impairment loss as follows:

> An impairment loss is the amount by which the carrying amount of an asset or a cash-generating unit exceeds its recoverable amount.

This chapter examines the impairment test for assets. The accounting standard covering impairment is IAS 36 *Impairment of Assets*. The standard was issued initially by the International Accounting Standards Board (IASB) as IAS 36 in July 1998, amended on numerous occasions, exposed for further amendment in December 2002, and issued in its present form in 2004.

Under IAS 36, an entity is required to conduct impairment tests for its assets to see whether it has incurred any impairment losses. The purpose of the impairment test is to ensure that assets are not carried at amounts that exceed their recoverable amounts or, more simply, that assets are not overstated.

Key questions in relation to the impairment test are:

- How does the test work?
- Is the test the same for all assets?
- Should the test apply to individual assets or to groups of assets? If to groups, which groups?
- Is the accounting treatment the same for assets measured at cost and for those measured at revalued amount?
- When should the test be carried out? Should it be done annually? every 3 years? or some other time?
- Can the results of the impairment test be reversed; that is, if an asset is written down because it is impaired, can later events lead to the reversal of that write-down?

12.1.1 Scope of IAS 36

Paragraph 2 of IAS 36 notes that the standard does not apply to all assets; that is, not all assets are subject to impairment testing. Assets to which IAS 36 does not apply are:

- inventories — IAS 2 *Inventories*
- assets arising from construction contracts — IAS 11 *Construction Contracts*
- deferred tax assets — IAS 12 *Income Taxes*
- assets arising from employee benefits — IAS 19 *Employee Benefits*
- financial assets — IAS 39 *Financial Instruments: Recognition and Measurement*
- investment properties measured at fair value — IAS 40 *Investment Property*
- biological assets measured at fair value less estimated point-of-sale costs — IAS 41 *Agriculture*
- deferred acquisition costs and intangible assets relating to insurance contracts — IFRS 4 *Insurance Contracts*
- non-current assets or disposal groups classified as held for sale — IFRS 5 *Non-current Assets Held for Sale and Discontinued Operations*.

The accounting standards listed contain the principles for recognition and measurement of the particular assets covered by those standards. Note that in some of these standards the assets are required to be recorded at fair value, or fair value less costs to sell. Where assets are recorded at fair value, there is no need to test for recoverability of the carrying amount of the asset. Under IAS 2, inventory is recorded at the lower of cost and net realisable value. As net realisable value is defined in terms of estimated selling price, IAS 2 has an inbuilt impairment test requiring inventory to be written down when the cost is effectively greater than the recoverable amount.

12.2 WHEN TO UNDERTAKE AN IMPAIRMENT TEST

As noted earlier, the purpose of the impairment test is to ensure that disclosed assets do not have carrying amounts in excess of their recoverable amounts. However, under IAS 36 it is not necessary at the end of each reporting period to test each asset in order to determine whether it is impaired. The only assets that need to be tested at the end of the reporting period are those where there is any *indication* that an asset may be impaired (see paragraph 9 of IAS 36). An entity therefore must determine by looking at various sources of information whether there is sufficient evidence to suspect that an asset may be impaired. If there is no such evidence, then an entity can assume that impairment has not occurred.

For most assets, the need for an impairment test can be assessed by analysing sources of evidence. However, there are some assets for which an impairment test *must* be undertaken every year. Paragraph 10 identifies these assets:

- intangible assets with indefinite useful lives
- intangible assets not yet available for use
- goodwill acquired in a business combination.

The reason for singling out these assets for automatic impairment testing is that the carrying amounts of these assets are considered to be more uncertain than those of other assets. For intangible assets with indefinite useful lives, there is no annual amortisation charge, and hence no ongoing reduction in the carrying amounts of the assets. As the assets are not being reduced via amortisation, it is considered essential that the carrying amounts be tested against the recoverable amounts. Goodwill is calculated as a residual amount when a business combination occurs. (This is discussed in more detail later in this chapter.) Goodwill is also not subject to annual amortisation; instead, it is subject to an annual impairment test. However, impairment testing does not absolve management from being aware of events that may cause impairment to occur within an accounting period and accounting for such impairments as they occur.

Another important reason for remeasuring assets and testing for impairment relates to the concept of depreciation adopted by the IASB. As noted in chapter 9, depreciation is viewed as a process of allocation rather than as a valuation process, even when an asset is measured at a revalued amount. Hence, the carrying amount of an asset reflects the unallocated measure of the asset rather than the benefits to be derived from the asset in the future. The impairment test relates to the assessment of recoverability of the asset, which is not a feature of the depreciation allocation process.

12.2.1 Collecting evidence of impairment

The purpose of the impairment test is to determine whether the carrying amount of an asset exceeds its recoverable amount. The evidence of impairment relates to variables that may support the belief that the asset under investigation is not worth as much as it was previously. The indicators noted in IAS 36 are only the minimum that an entity's management should look at. Management should take into account the nature and use of a specific asset and determine the factors that may indicate deterioration in the asset's worth. The minimum indicators listed in IAS 36 are described in two groups: external sources of information, and internal sources of information.

External sources of information

Paragraph 12 of IAS 36 lists four sources of information relating to the external environment in which the entity operates:

1. *Market value*. Has the asset's market value declined more than would normally be expected during the period? This may occur for many reasons relating to changes in expectations concerning the operation of the entity. For example, there may have been a significant reduction in the entity's sales when new products or technologies that the entity planned to introduce within a certain timeframe are not introduced within that timeframe. Further, there may have been movements in key personnel that affect the productivity of the entity itself and bring increased pressure from competitors who employed those people.

2. *Entity's environment/market.* Have significant adverse changes occurred or will they occur in the technological, market, economic or legal environment in which the entity operates, or in the market to which the asset is dedicated? For example, a competitor may have developed a product or technology that is likely to cause or has caused a significant and permanent reduction in the entity's market share.
3. *Interest rates.* Have market interest rates or market rates of return increased during the period, with potential changes in the interest rate used in assessing an entity's present value of future cash flows?
4. *Market capitalisation.* Is the carrying amount of the net assets of the entity greater than the market capitalisation of the entity?

Internal sources of information

Paragraph 12 of IAS 36 lists three sources of information based on events within the entity itself:

1. *Obsolescence or physical damage.* Does an analysis of the asset reveal physical damage or obsolescence?
2. *Changed use within the entity.* Is the asset expected to be used differently within the entity? For example, the asset may become idle; there may be a restructure in the entity that changes the use of the asset; there may be plans to sell the asset; or the useful life of an intangible may be changed from indefinite to finite.
3. *Economic performance of the asset.* Do internal reports indicate that the economic performance of the asset is worse than expected? Evidence of this consists of:
   - actual cash flows for maintenance or operating the asset may be significantly higher than expected
   - actual cash inflows or profits may be lower than expected
   - expected cash flows for maintenance of operations may have increased, or expected profits may be lower.

In analysing the information from the above sources, paragraph 15 of IAS 36 notes that materiality must be taken into account. If, in previous analyses, the carrying amount of an asset was significantly lower than the asset's recoverable amount, minor movements in the factors listed above may cause the recoverable amount to be closer to the carrying amount but not large enough to expect the carrying amount to be greater than the recoverable amount. For example, if short-term interest rates changed, this may not be expected to affect long-term interest rates.

In its notes to the 2007 consolidated financial statements, Nokia provided details of the factors that trigger an impairment review for the entity (see figure 12.1).

Assessment of the recoverability of long-lived and intangible assets and goodwill

For the purposes of impairment testing, goodwill is allocated to cash-generating units that are expected to benefit from the synergies of the acquisition in which the goodwill arose.

The Group assesses the carrying value of goodwill annually, or more frequently if events or changes in circumstances indicate that such carrying value may not be recoverable. The Group assesses the carrying value of identifiable intangible assets and long-lived assets if events or changes in circumstances indicate that such carrying value may not be recoverable. Factors that trigger an impairment review include underperformance relative to historical or projected future results, significant changes in the manner of the use of the acquired assets or the strategy for the overall business and significant negative industry or economic trends.

FIGURE 12.1 Indicators of impairment for Nokia
Source: Nokia (2007, p. 13).

12.3 IMPAIRMENT TEST FOR AN INDIVIDUAL ASSET

The impairment test involves comparing the carrying amount of an asset with its recoverable amount. To understand the nature of this test, it is necessary to understand a number of definitions given in paragraph 6 of IAS 36:

> The **recoverable amount** of an asset or a cash-generating unit is the higher of its fair value less costs to sell and its value in use.
>
> **Fair value less costs to sell** is the amount obtainable from the sale of an asset or cash-generating unit in an arm's length transaction between knowledgeable, willing parties, less the costs of disposal.

Costs of disposal are incremental costs directly attributable to the disposal of an asset or cash-generating unit, excluding finance costs and income tax expense.

Value in use is the present value of the future cash flows expected to be derived from an asset or cash-generating unit.

Note the phrase 'an asset or cash-generating unit' in the above definitions. The discussion in this section focuses on an individual asset, and it is assumed that, for the asset being tested for impairment, there are specific cash flows that can be associated with the asset. Cash-generating units are discussed in section 12.4.

From the definition of recoverable amount, there are two possible amounts against which the carrying amount can be tested for impairment: (1) fair value less costs to sell and (2) value in use. Although the definition of recoverable amount refers to the 'higher' of these two amounts, an impairment occurs if the carrying amount exceeds recoverable amount (paragraph 8). However, it is not always necessary to measure both amounts when testing for impairment. If either one of these amounts is greater than carrying amount, the asset is not impaired (paragraph 19). Where there are active markets, determining fair value less costs to sell is probably easier than calculating value in use. However, where the carrying amount exceeds the fair value less costs to sell, it is necessary to calculate the value in use. Figure 12.2 is a diagrammatic representation of the impairment test.

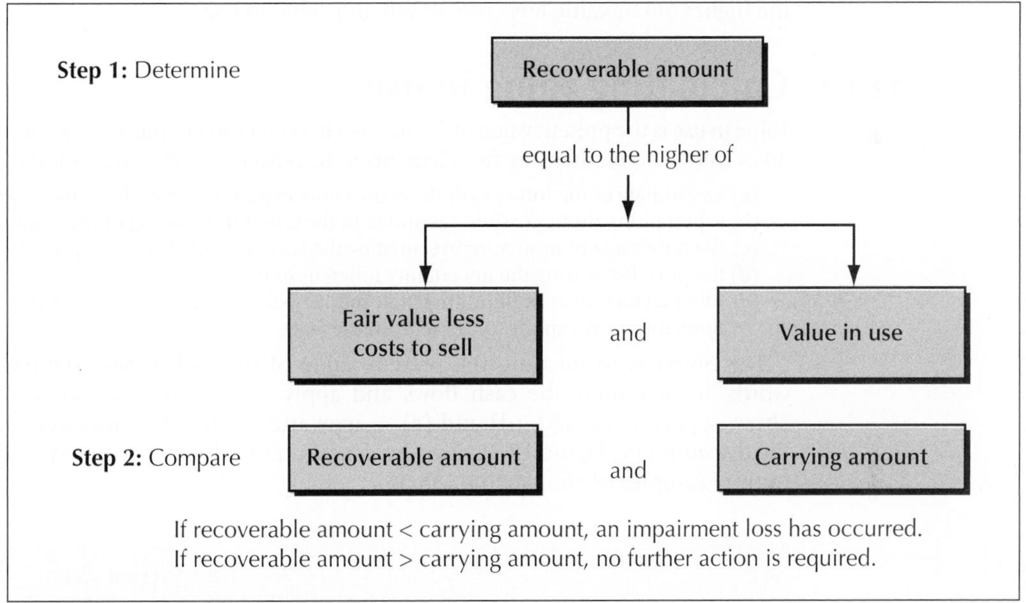

FIGURE 12.2 The impairment test

In calculating either fair value less costs to sell or value in use, paragraph 23 of IAS 36 notes that in 'some cases, estimates, averages and computational shortcuts may provide reasonable approximations', rather than an entity having to perform in-depth calculations annually. It is also possible to use the most recent detailed calculation of recoverable amount made in a preceding year (paragraph 24) in the case of an intangible asset with an indefinite useful life. The latter is possible if *all* the following criteria are met:

- for the intangible asset, if tested as part of a cash-generating unit (see section 12.4 of this chapter), the other assets and liabilities in the unit have not changed significantly
- in the preceding year's calculation, the difference between the carrying amount and recoverable amount was substantial
- an analysis of all evidence relating to events affecting the asset suggests that the likelihood of the recoverable amount being less than carrying amount is remote.

12.3.1 Calculating fair value less costs to sell

There are two parts to the determination of fair value less costs to sell, namely *fair value* and *costs of disposal*. Where there is an active market, the fair value is the market price. If the market is not active, a fair value may be determined by observing evidence such as amounts paid in recent sales transactions. The fair value reflects what the entity could obtain from the sale of the asset to knowledgeable, willing buyers.

Paragraph 28 of IAS 36 provides the following examples of costs of disposal: legal costs, stamp duty and similar transaction taxes, costs of removing the asset, and direct incremental costs to bring the asset into condition for sale. The costs must be directly associated with either the sale of the asset or getting the asset ready for sale. Any costs arising after the sale of the asset, even if arising as a result of the sale, are not regarded as costs of disposal.

Paragraph 5 of IAS 36 provides guidance where an asset is measured under the alternative accounting treatment in IAS 16, namely at a revalued amount (i.e. fair value). Fair value as a measure does not include a consideration of disposal costs. Hence, if an asset's fair value is equal to its market value, the difference between fair value and fair value less costs to sell is the disposal costs of the asset. If the disposal costs are immaterial, then there is no significant difference between fair value and fair value less costs to sell. Therefore, where an asset is measured at fair value, revaluation decrements are not distinguishable from impairment losses. If the disposal costs are material, then fair value less costs to sell is less than the carrying amount (i.e. fair value). The asset's value in use would then need to be calculated to determine whether it was less than fair value. If so, the asset is impaired and must be written down to recoverable amount, which is the higher of fair value less costs to sell and value in use.

12.3.2 Calculating value in use

Value in use is the present value of future cash flows relating to the asset being measured. As paragraph 30 of IAS 36 notes, there are five elements to be reflected in the calculation of the value in use:

(a) an estimate of the future cash flows the entity expects to derive from the asset;
(b) expectations about possible variations in the amount or timing of those future cash flows;
(c) the time value of money, represented by the current market risk-free rate of interest;
(d) the price for bearing the uncertainty inherent in the asset;
(e) other factors, such as illiquidity, that market participants would reflect in pricing the future cash flows the entity expects to derive from the asset.

The object is to measure the present value of the cash flows relating to the asset, in other words, to determine the cash flows and apply a discount rate. Some of the elements noted above — particularly (b), (d) and (e) — may affect either the measurement of the cash flows or the discount rate. Figure 12.3 shows a calculation of value in use based on Example 2 in the Illustrative Examples accompanying IAS 36.

Year	Long-term growth rates	Future cash flows	Present value factor at 15% discount rate	Discounted future cash flows
2009		$ 230*	0.869 57	$ 200
2010		253*	0.756 14	191
2011		273*	0.657 52	180
2012		290*	0.571 75	166
2013		304*	0.497 18	151
2014	3%	313**	0.432 33	135
2015	–2%	307**	0.375 94	115
2016	–6%	289**	0.326 90	94
2017	–15%	245**	0.284 26	70
2018	–25%	184**	0.247 19	45
2019	–67%	61**	0.214 94	13
Value in use				$1360

*Based on management's best estimate of net cash flow projections.
**Based on an extrapolation from preceding year cash flow using declining growth rates.

FIGURE 12.3 Calculation of value in use

As can be seen from figure 12.3, the calculation of value in use requires the estimation of future cash flows and a discount rate applied to these future cash flows.

Determining future cash flows

Paragraphs 33–54 of IAS 36 provide guidance in measuring future cash flows. Some important guidelines are:

- Cash flow projections should be based on *management's best estimate* of the range of economic conditions that will exist over the remaining useful life of the asset. These should be tempered by an analysis of past cash flows and management's success in the past in predicting future cash flows accurately. Where external evidence is available, this should be given greater weight than simple reliance on management's expectations.
- Cash flow projections should be based on the most recent *financial budgets and forecasts*. These projections should cover a maximum period of 5 years unless a longer period can be justified. For most entities, a detailed analysis of future operations rarely extends beyond 5 years.
- For years after the 5-year budget projection, reliance should be placed on a steady or declining *growth rate*, unless there are specific reasons for predicting an increasing growth rate. In cases where an entity is doing particularly well, expectations of competitors entering the industry must be taken into consideration. The growth rate used should not exceed the long-term growth rate for the products, industries or country in which the entity operates. See figure 12.3 for an example of this.
- The cash inflows should include those from *continuing use* of the asset over its expected useful life as well as those expected to be received on *disposal* of the asset. Further, any cash *outflows* necessary to achieve the projected inflows must be taken into account. This may be particularly applicable at the time of the asset's disposal, where outlays are incurred to prepare the asset for disposal.
- Projected cash flows must be estimated for the asset in its *current* condition (paragraph 44). Where there is an expected restructuring of the entity in future periods, or where there are possibilities for improving or enhancing the performance of the asset by subsequent expenditure, projections of cash flows will not take these possible events into consideration. In the Illustrative Examples accompanying IAS 36, Examples 5 and 6 demonstrate how cash flows are determined when restructuring and capital expenditure are made to enhance performance. In both cases, if the value in use is being determined at 2010, and the restructuring/capital expenditure will not occur until 2014, the value in use at 2010 is determined by excluding the cash inflows/outflows relating to these future events. Once the entity is committed to the restructure, for example in 2012, the value in use calculated at that date could include the benefits from the restructure, such benefits being an increase in the expected cash flows. In the example of capital expenditure, using an aircraft as an example, management may include in its 2010 budget capital expenditure for 2013 that is necessary to renew the operating capacity of the aircraft. However, the value in use at 2010 excludes expected renewal costs and subsequent benefits. When the capital expenditure is incurred in 2013, the increased benefits from the capital expenditure can be included in the calculation in order to determine the value in use at the end of that period. Day-to-day servicing costs are included in the outflows used to measure value in use, as are the costs of major inspections.
- Cash flows relating to *financing activities* or *income tax* are not included in the calculations of future cash flows. As the discount rate is based on a pre-tax basis, the future cash flows must also be on a pre-tax basis.
- In assessing cash flows from *disposal*, the expected disposal price will take into account specific future price increases/decreases, and be based on an analysis of prices prevailing at the date of the estimate for similar assets in conditions similar to those expected for the asset under consideration at the end of its useful life.
- Appendix A to IAS 36, described as an 'integral part of the standard', contains guidance on the use of present value techniques in measuring value in use. In paragraph A2, two approaches to calculating present value are noted. The first is the 'traditional' approach. It adjusts for expectations about possible variations in cash flow, the price for bearing uncertainty, and other factors used in pricing the asset by making the adjustments in the discount rate. The second is the 'expected cash flow' approach. It makes adjustments for these variables in arriving at risk-adjusted expected cash flows. The expected cash flows are based on consideration of all

possible cash flows rather than just the most likely cash flow. Paragraph A7 provides the example of a situation where the possible cash flows and their related probabilities are:

	Cash flow	Probability	Expected cash flow
Cash flow 1	$100	10%	$ 10
Cash flow 2	200	60%	120
Cash flow 3	300	30%	90
Expected cash flow			$220

It is also possible for the expected cash flow to take into account probabilities of being received in different years. As noted in paragraph A7, a cash flow of $1000 may be received in 1 year, 2 years or 3 years, with probabilities of 10%, 60% and 30% respectively:

	Present value	Probability	Expected cash flow
$1000 in 1 year at 5%	$952.38	10%	$ 95.24
$1000 in 2 years at 5%	907.03	60%	544.22
$1000 in 3 years at 5%	863.84	30%	259.15
Expected present value			$898.61

A further refinement could be to apply different discount rates for different future periods where value in use is sensitive to a difference in risk for different periods or to the term structure of interest rates (paragraph A8):

	Present value	Probability	Expected cash flow
$1000 in 1 year at 5%	$952.38	10%	$ 95.24
$1000 in 2 years at 5.25%	902.73	60%	541.64
$1000 in 3 years at 5.5%	851.61	30%	255.48
Expected present value			$892.36

Undertaking this level of detail in measuring the expected cash flows must always be subject to a cost–benefit constraint (paragraph A12).

Paragraph A6 notes that there are further disadvantages with using the traditional approach because it relies on finding an interest rate that is commensurate with the risk. This requires isolating an asset existing in the market that has similar characteristics to the one being measured, and being able to observe the discount rate. The expected cash flow approach does not rely on finding such an asset but incorporates variations in risk and cash flows into the calculations of the expected cash flows. A range of possible outcomes is then built into the model, reducing the reliance on a single most likely outcome.

Determining the discount rate

Paragraph 55 of IAS 36 notes that the discount rate should:

- reflect the time value of money
- reflect the risks specific to the asset for which the future cash flow estimates have not been adjusted.

The rate may be determined by viewing rates used for similar assets in the market, or from the weighted average cost of capital of a listed entity that has a single asset, or portfolio of assets, similar to the asset under review (paragraph 56).

Paragraph A3 of Appendix A notes that a general principle in choosing a discount rate is that the interest rate 'should reflect assumptions that are consistent with those inherent in the estimated cash flows'. Not to do so could lead to double counting. The example given in paragraph A3(a) to illustrate this is as follows:

> For example, a discount rate of 12 per cent might be applied to contractual cash flows of a loan receivable. That rate reflects expectations about future defaults from loans with particular characteristics.

That same 12 per cent rate should not be used to discount expected cash flows because those cash flows already reflect assumptions about future defaults.

Further advice contained in paragraphs A15–A21 of Appendix A includes the following:

- As a starting point in choosing a discount rate, an entity may consider the current rates affecting it, such as the entity's weighted cost of capital, the entity's incremental borrowing rate and other market borrowing rates.
- The rate must reflect specific risks affecting the entity, with consideration being given to risks such as country risk, currency risk and price risk.
- The way the entity is financed as a whole, and the way the entity specifically financed the acquisition of the asset in question, should not affect the determination of the discount rate.

Figure 12.4 contains information provided in note 17 to the financial statements in the 2008 annual report of Wesfarmers Ltd. Note in particular the information provided about the calculation of the recoverable amount using value-in-use calculations.

FIGURE 12.4 Calculation of value in use for Wesfarmers Ltd

IDENTIFIABLE INTANGIBLE ASSETS AND GOODWILL

Key assumptions used in impairment calculations

The recoverable amount of the cash generating units have been determined based on using cash flow projections based on business corporate plans approved by senior management covering a five year period. Where a value in use methodology has been used, these plans have been adjusted to exclude the costs and benefits of expansion capital, and have been prepared in the understanding that many actual outcomes will differ from assumptions used in the calculations. Cash flows beyond the five year period are extrapolated using the estimated growth rates, which are based on management estimates taking into account past historical performance and expected long term operating conditions. The growth rates do not exceed the long term average growth rate for the business in which the cash generating unit operates. Discount rates are based on a risk-free rate (using the 10-year swap rate) plus risk weightings for various risks or the weighted average cost of capital where appropriate. Other assumptions are consistent with external sources of information and use consistent and conservative estimates for such variables as terminal cash flow multiples. Outlined below are the assumptions used in fair value less costs to sell calculations for divisions with significant goodwill balances.

The impairment calculations have been prepared for the purpose of ensuring that the cash generating units' carrying amounts do not exceed their recoverable amount and do not purport to be a market valuation of the relevant business operations.

Management believes that any reasonably possible change in the key assumptions would not cause the carrying amount of any cash generating units to exceed their recoverable amount, other than where outlined below.

	CONSOLIDATED	
	2008	2007
Key assumptions used in fair value less costs to sell calculations		
Coles		
Discount rate	9.2%	N/A
Growth rate beyond five year financial plan	3.2%	N/A
Perpetuity factor for calculation of terminal value (1/(discount rate – growth rate))	16.7	N/A

For the Coles division, possible changes in key assumptions could cause the carrying value of the division to exceed its recoverable amount. The recoverable amount for the Coles division currently exceeds its carrying value by $991 million. This excess in recoverable amount could be reduced should changes in the following key assumptions occur:

i. Trading conditions — The cash flows are based on the forecast improved operating and financial performance of the Coles division which have been derived from the 2008 Wesfarmers Board approved Corporate Plan. Although the timing of the cash flows arising from this improvement are influenced by retail conditions in the short to medium term, Wesfarmers believes that the magnitude of improvements in the long term cash flows will be

(continued)

FIGURE 12.4 *(continued)*

less impacted. This view is based on the likely longer term trends in the business (i.e. steadily increasing market demand) and the inherent value of the network, especially once the network has been revitalised. Notwithstanding this, should such an improvement not occur, the impact on the cash flows could result in a reduction of the recoverable amount to below the carrying value.

ii. Discount rate — The discount rate for the Coles division has been determined with reference to the prevailing risk-free and borrowing rates. Consequently should these rates increase, the discount rate would also increase. An increase in the discount rate of over 0.4% would result in a reduction of the recoverable amount to below the carrying value.

Target		
Discount rate	**10.5%**	N/A
Growth rate beyond five year financial plan	**3.2%**	N/A
Perpetuity factor for calculation of terminal value (1/(discount rate – growth rate))	**13.7**	N/A

Other key assumptions include retail sales and trade sales inflation rates (which are based on past experience) and the programme for store upgrades (which are based on management projections).

Source: Wesfarmers (2008, p. 104).

12.3.3 Recognition and measurement of an impairment loss for an individual asset

Paragraphs 58–64 of IAS 36 provide the principles for recognition and measurement of an impairment loss for an individual asset. If the recoverable amount of an asset is less than its carrying amount, an impairment loss occurs, and the asset must be written down from its carrying amount to the recoverable amount.

Where an asset is measured using the *cost model*, according to paragraph 60 of IAS 36 an impairment loss is recognised immediately in profit or loss. In relation to the other side of the accounting entry to the loss, reference should be made to paragraph 73(d) of IAS 16 *Property, Plant and Equipment*. According to this paragraph, for items of property, plant and equipment 'the gross carrying amount and the accumulated depreciation (aggregated with accumulated impairment losses) at the beginning and end of the period' should be disclosed. When impairment occurs, there is no need to write off any existing accumulated depreciation or create a separate accumulated impairment account. The impairment write-down can be included in accumulated depreciation, preferably referred to as 'Accumulated Depreciation and Impairment Losses'.

Hence, if an asset having a carrying amount of $100 (original cost $160) has a recoverable amount of $90, the appropriate journal entry to account for the impairment loss is:

Impairment Loss	Dr	10	
Accumulated Depreciation and Impairment Losses	Cr		10
(Impairment loss on asset)			

Where an asset is measured using the *revaluation model* (i.e. at fair value), according to paragraph 60 of IAS 36 any impairment loss is treated as a revaluation decrement and accounted for as set out in IAS 16. If an asset at the end of an accounting period has a carrying amount of $100, being previously calculated as fair value of $120 less accumulated depreciation of $20, and the asset's recoverable amount (and possibly its fair value) at the end of the period is determined to be $90, the accounting entry is:

Accumulated Depreciation	Dr	20	
Revaluation Write-down	Dr	10	
Asset	Cr		30
(Write-down of asset)			

If the revalued asset had a previous revaluation increment of $20, giving rise to a revaluation surplus of $14 and a deferred tax liability (using a tax rate of 30%) of $6, then the entry to write the asset down to a recoverable amount of $90 requires an adjustment directly against the revaluation reserve:

Accumulated Depreciation	Dr	20	
Asset Revaluation Reserve	Dr	7	
Deferred Tax Liability	Dr	3	
Asset	Cr		30
(Write-down of asset to recoverable amount)			

Regardless of whether the cost model or the revaluation model is used, once the impairment loss is recognised, any subsequent depreciation/amortisation is based on the new recoverable amount. In accordance with paragraph 63 of IAS 36, the depreciation charge is that necessary to allocate the asset's revised carrying amount (the recoverable amount) less its residual value (if any) on a systematic basis over its remaining useful life. Consider the example of the asset recorded at cost of $160 less accumulated depreciation of $60 and having a recoverable amount of $90. The impairment loss of $10 is recognised, the remaining useful life of the asset is assessed (assume 3 years, with equal benefits each year), and the residual value is determined (assume zero). Hence, in the year following recognition of the impairment loss, depreciation of $30 (i.e. $\frac{1}{3} \times \$90$) is recognised.

It is possible that the recoverable amount is negative owing to large expected future cash outflows relating to the asset, so the impairment loss could be greater than the carrying amount of the asset. According to paragraph 62 of IAS 16, a liability for the excess should be raised only if another standard requires it.

Figure 12.5 contains information disclosed in note 8 to the 2006 financial statements of Nokia Ltd relating to the impairment of specific assets of that company.

2006, EURm	Mobile Phones	Multimedia	Enterprise Solutions	Networks	Common Group Functions	Group
Impairment of available-for-sale investments	—	—	—	—	18	18
Impairment of other intangible assets	33	—	—	—	—	33
Total, net	33	—	—	—	18	51
2005, EURm						
Impairment of available-for-sale investments	—	—	—	—	30	30
Total, net	—	—	—	—	30	30
2004, EURm						
Impairment of available-for-sale investments	—	—	—	—	11	11
Impairment of capitalized development costs	—	—	—	115	—	115
Total, net	—	—	—	115	11	126

During 2006, the Group's investment in certain equity securities held as non-current available-for-sale suffered a permanent decline in fair value resulting in an impairment charge of EUR 18 million (EUR 30 million in 2005, EUR 11 million in 2004) relating to non-current available-for-sale investments.

In connection with the restructuring of its CDMA business, the Group recorded an impairment charge of EUR 33 million during 2006 related to an acquired CDMA license. The impaired CDMA license was included in Mobile Phones business group.

During 2004, the Group recorded an impairment charge of EUR 65 million of capitalized development costs due to the abandonment of FlexiGateway and Horizontal Technology modules. In addition, an impairment charge of EUR 50 million was recorded on WCDMA radio access network program due to changes in market outlook. The impairment loss was determined as the difference between the carrying amount of the asset and its recoverable amount. The recoverable amount for WCDMA radio access network was derived from the discounted cash flow projections, which cover the estimated life of the WCDMA radio access network current technology, using a pre-tax discount rate of 15%. The impaired technologies were part of the Networks business group.

FIGURE 12.5 Impairment of assets for Nokia
Source: Nokia (2006, p. 23).

12.4 CASH-GENERATING UNITS — EXCLUDING GOODWILL

The discussion in section 12.3 focuses on individual assets and whether they have been impaired. The impairment test in such cases involves the determination of recoverable amount, and this requires the measurement of fair value less costs to sell and value in use of the asset being tested for impairment. However, for some assets, fair value less costs to sell may be determinable, because the asset is separable and a market for that asset exists, but it may be impossible to determine the value in use. Value in use requires determining the expected cash flows to be received from an asset.

Some assets do not individually generate cash flows because the cash flows generated are the result of a combination of several assets. For example, a motor vehicle used by a manager does not by itself generate cash flows. Similarly, a machine in a factory works in conjunction with the rest of the assets in the factory to produce inventory which, when sold, creates cash inflows for an entity. For such assets, if the carrying amount exceeds the fair value less costs to sell, some other measure relating to value in use must be used. Figure 12.6 reproduces an example provided in IAS 36 paragraph 67.

> Example
>
> A mining entity owns a private railway to support its mining activities. The private railway could be sold only for scrap value and it does not generate cash inflows that are largely independent of the cash inflows from the other assets of the mine.
>
> *It is not possible to estimate the recoverable amount of the private railway because its value in use cannot be determined and is probably different from scrap value. Therefore, the entity estimates the recoverable amount of the cash-generating unit to which the private railway belongs, that is, the mine as a whole.*

FIGURE 12.6 Cash flows and individual assets

The private railway described in figure 12.6 'could be sold only for scrap value', but this information is unimportant in determining the cash-generating unit. Even if the railway could be sold for a reasonable amount of money, the answer to what constitutes the cash-generating unit is the same. The key question is whether the cash flows expected to be received by the entity as a whole can be allocated to the various parts of the entity. The railway by itself does not generate cash flows; the cash flows are generated by the combination of the mine and the railway. Hence, the railway is not a separate cash-generating unit. Because the railway is being used by the mining entity, there are no expected cash flows from disposal of the railway, so any consideration of the proceeds on sale of the railway is irrelevant.

Paragraph 66 of IAS 36 requires that, where there is any indication an asset may be impaired, if possible the recoverable amount should be estimated for the individual asset. However, if this is not possible, the entity should 'determine the recoverable amount of the cash-generating unit to which the asset belongs'. In other words, the impairment test is applied to a cash-generating unit rather than to an individual asset. Paragraph 6 contains the following definition of a cash-generating unit:

> A cash-generating unit is the smallest identifiable group of assets that generates cash inflows from continuing use that are largely independent of the cash inflows from other assets or groups of assets.

12.4.1 Identifying a cash-generating unit

The identification of a cash-generating unit requires judgement. As is stated in the definition, the key is to determine the 'smallest identifiable group of assets', and this group must create 'independent' cash flows from continuing use. Guidelines given in paragraphs 67–73 of IAS 36 include the following:

- Consider how management monitors the entity's operations, such as by product lines, businesses, individual locations, districts or regional areas.
- Consider how management makes decisions about continuing or disposing of the entity's assets and operations.
- If an active market exists for the output of a group of assets, this group constitutes a cash-generating unit.

- Even if some of the output of a group is used internally, if the output could be sold externally, then these prices can be used to measure the value in use of the group of assets.
- Cash-generating units should be identified consistently from period to period for the same group of assets.

Figure 12.7 contains examples adapted from those in the Illustrative Examples (accompanying IAS 36) relating to the identification of cash-generating units.

A. Retail store chain

Cool Surf City Store belongs to a retail store chain, Cool Surf Enterprises, which sells clothing under the Cool Surf brand. City Store makes all its retail purchases through Cool Surf Enterprises' purchasing centre. Pricing, marketing, advertising and human resource policies (except for hiring City Store's cashiers and salespeople) are decided by Cool Surf Enterprises. Cool Surf Enterprises also owns five other stores in the same city as Cool Surf City Store and 20 other stores in other cities. All stores are managed in the same way. Is Cool Surf City Store a cash-generating unit?

Analysis

- *An entity should consider whether internal management reporting is organised to measure performance on a store-by-store basis, and whether the business is run on a store-by-store profit basis, or on a region/city basis.*
- *All Cool Surf Enterprises' stores are in different suburbs, and probably have different customer bases. So, although City Store is managed at a corporate level, it generates cash inflows that are largely independent of those of other Cool Surf stores. Therefore, it is likely that the City Store is a cash-generating unit.*

B. Magazine titles

A publisher owns 150 magazine titles of which 70 were acquired and 80 were self-created. The price paid for a purchased magazine title is recognised as an intangible asset. The costs of creating magazine titles and maintaining existing titles are recognised as an expense as incurred. Cash inflows from direct sales and advertising are identifiable for each magazine title. Titles are managed by customer segments. The level of advertising income for a magazine title depends on the range of titles in the customer segment to which the magazine title relates. Management has a policy of abandoning old titles before the end of their economic lives and replacing them immediately with new titles for the same customer segment. Does an individual magazine title represent a separate cash-generating unit?

Analysis

- *It is likely that the recoverable amount of an individual magazine title can be assessed. Even though the level of advertising income for a title is influenced, to a certain extent, by the other titles in the customer segment, cash inflows from direct sales and advertising are identifiable for each title. In addition, although titles are managed by customer segments, decisions to abandon titles are made on an individual title basis.*
- *It is likely that individual magazine titles generate cash inflows that are largely independent of each other and that each magazine title is a separate cash-generating unit.*

C. Building half-rented to others and half-occupied for own use

Biscuits Ltd is a manufacturing company. It owns a headquarters building that used to be fully occupied for internal use. After downsizing, half the building is now used internally and half is rented to third parties. The lease agreement with the tenant is for 5 years. Is the building a cash-generating unit?

Analysis

- *The main purpose of the building is to serve as a corporate asset, supporting Biscuits Ltd's manufacturing activities. The building as a whole cannot be considered to generate cash inflows that are largely independent of the biscuit-making activities. It is likely that the cash-generating unit for the building is Biscuits Ltd as a whole.*
- *The building is not held as an investment. Therefore, it would not be appropriate to determine the value in use of the building based on projections of future market-related rents.*

FIGURE 12.7 Identifying cash-generating units

One of the problems with using a cash-generating unit is that the identification of a particular unit within an entity is arbitrary. It requires judgement on the part of management, and the factors used in the determination will vary from entity to entity. There is no question of comparability between entities, because the cash-generating unit is used for internal accounting purposes and not external reporting disclosures. However, there is the issue of whether management will select cash-generating units with an eye to which assets may decrease in value, and ensure that such assets are included in units in which other assets increase in value.

One alternative to the cash-generating unit is the segment concept as in IFRS 8 *Operating Segments*. Although determination of segments is also arbitrary, an accounting standard covers the identification of segments, which should improve the comparability across entities, and the identified segments are reported to the public. Note, however, that IAS 36 allows a segment to be used as the cash-generating unit only if the segment equates to the smallest identifiable group of assets that generate independent cash flows. For example, in the notes to its 2008 financial statements, Wesfarmers reported the company allocated goodwill to its cash-generating units as shown in figure 12.8:

	CONSOLIDATED	
	2008 $M	2007 $M
Allocation of goodwill to cash generating units		
Carrying amount of goodwill		
Energy	**312**	312
Home improvement and office supplies		
– Bunnings	**846**	846
– Officeworks	**813**	—
Industrial and safety	**455**	450
Insurance	**945**	958
Coles	**10 241**	—
Kmart	**328**	—
Target	**2 443**	—
Resources	**—**	—
Other	**4**	2
	16 387	2 568

FIGURE 12.8 Allocation of goodwill to CGUs of Wesfarmers
Source: Wesfarmers (2008, p. 103).

12.4.2 Impairment loss for a cash-generating unit — excluding goodwill

An impairment loss occurs when the carrying amount of the assets of a cash-generating unit exceed their recoverable amount.

Determining the impairment loss

In determining the carrying amount of the assets, all those assets that are directly attributable to the cash-generating unit and that contribute to generating the cash flows used in measuring recoverable amount must be included. There must be consistency between what is being measured for recoverable amount — namely cash flows relating to a group of assets — and the measurement of the carrying amount of those assets.

The principles for determining the recoverable amount of a cash-generating unit are the same as those described for an individual asset in section 12.3 of this chapter. However, note that paragraph 76(b) of IAS 36 requires that the carrying amount of a cash-generating unit does not include the carrying amount of any recognised liability. This is because, as stated in paragraph 43(b), the calculation of the future cash flows of the cash-generating unit does not include cash outflows that relate to obligations that have been recognised as liabilities, such as payables and provisions.

Accounting for an impairment loss in a cash-generating unit

If an impairment loss is recognised in a cash-generating unit that has not recorded any goodwill, paragraph 104 of IAS 36 states that the impairment loss should be allocated to reduce the carrying amount of the assets of the unit by allocating the impairment loss on a pro rata basis based on the carrying amount of each asset in the unit. The reduction in each carrying amount relates to each specific asset, and should be treated as an impairment of each asset, even though the impairment loss was based on an analysis of a cash-generating unit. The loss is accounted for in the same way as that for an individual asset as described in section 12.3, with losses relating to an asset measured at cost being recognised immediately in profit or loss.

Paragraph 105 of IAS 36 places some restrictions on an entity's ability to write down assets as a result of the allocation of the impairment loss across the carrying amounts of the assets of the cash-generating unit. For each asset, the carrying amount should not be reduced below the highest of:

(a) its fair value less costs to sell (if determinable);
(b) its value in use (if determinable); and
(c) zero.

If there is an amount of impairment loss allocated to an asset, but a part of it would reduce the asset below, say, its fair value less costs to sell, then that part is allocated across the other assets in the cash-generating unit on a pro rata basis (see illustrative example 12.1). However, as paragraph 106 notes, if the recoverable amount of each of the assets cannot be estimated without undue costs or effort, then an arbitrary allocation of the impairment loss between the assets of the unit will suffice because all the assets of a cash-generating unit work together.

ILLUSTRATIVE EXAMPLE 12.1

Impairment of a cash-generating unit

A cash-generating unit has been assessed for impairment and it has been determined that the unit has incurred an impairment loss of $12 000. The carrying amounts of the assets and the allocation of the impairment loss on a proportional basis are as shown below.

	Carrying amount	Proportion	Allocation of impairment loss	Net carrying amount
Buildings	$ 500 000	5/12	$ 5 000	$ 495 000
Equipment	300 000	3/12	3 000	297 000
Land	250 000	2.5/12	2 500	247 500
Fittings	150 000	1.5/12	1 500	148 500
	$ 1 200 000		$ 12 000	

However, if the fair value less costs to sell of the buildings was $497 000, then this is the maximum to which these assets could be reduced. Hence, the balance of the allocated impairment loss to buildings of $2000 (i.e. $5000 – [$500 000 – $497 000]) has to be allocated across the other assets:

	Carrying amount	Proportion	Allocation of impairment loss	Net carrying amount
Buildings				$ 497 000
Equipment	$297 000	297/693	$ 857	296 143
Land	247 500	247.5/693	714	246 786
Fittings	148 500	148.5/693	429	148 071
	$693 000		$2000	

The journal entry to reflect the recognition of the impairment loss is:

Impairment Loss	Dr	12 000	
Accumulated Depreciation and Impairment Losses – Buildings	Cr		3000
Accumulated Depreciation and Impairment Losses – Equipment	Cr		3857
Land	Cr		3214
Accumulated Depreciation and Impairment Losses – Fittings	Cr		1929

Corporate assets

One problem that arises when dividing an entity into separate cash-generating units is dealing with corporate assets. Corporate assets, such as the headquarters building or the information technology support centre, are integral to all cash-generating units generating cash flows but do not by themselves independently generate cash flows. Paragraph 102 of IAS 36 sets out how corporate assets should be dealt with in determining impairment losses for an entity:

Step 1: If any corporate assets can be allocated on a reasonable and consistent basis to cash-generating units, then this should be done. Each unit is then, where appropriate, tested for an impairment loss. Where a loss occurs in a cash-generating unit, the loss is allocated pro rata across the assets including the portion of the corporate asset allocated to the unit.

Step 2: If some corporate assets cannot be allocated across the cash-generating units, the entity:

- compares the carrying amount of each unit being tested (excluding the unallocated corporate asset) with its recoverable amount and recognises any impairment loss by allocating the loss across the assets of the unit
- identifies the smallest cash-generating unit that includes the unit under review and to which a portion of the unallocated corporate asset can be allocated on a reasonable and consistent basis
- compares the carrying amount of the larger cash-generating unit, including the portion of the corporate asset, with its allocated amount. Any impairment loss is then allocated across the assets of the larger cash-generating unit.

Figure 12.9 contains an example of an allocation of corporate assets based on Example 8 of the Illustrative Examples accompanying IAS 36.

FIGURE 12.9 Allocation of corporate assets

An entity has three cash-generating units, A, B and C. As a result of adverse changes in the technological environment, impairment tests are conducted on each of the cash-generating units. At the end of 2010, the carrying amounts of A, B and C are $100, $150 and $200 respectively.

There are two corporate assets: the headquarters building carried at $150, and a research centre that has a carrying amount of $50. The relative carrying amounts of the cash-generating units are a reasonable indication of the proportion of the headquarters building devoted to each cash-generating unit. However, the carrying amount of the research centre cannot be allocated on a reasonable basis to the individual cash-generating units.

The remaining estimated useful life of cash-generating unit A is 10 years, and the remaining useful lives of B and C and the headquarters are 20 years. The headquarters are depreciated on a straight-line basis.

The *first step* is to allocate that part of the corporate assets to the individual cash-generating units where it can be done in a reasonable manner. In this example, this can be done for the headquarters building but not for the research centre. The allocation of the headquarters building has to be done on a weighted allocation basis because the useful lives of the units differ:

End of 2010	A	B	C	Total
Carrying amount	100	150	200	450
Useful life	10 years	20 years	20 years	
Weighting based on useful life	1	2	2	
Carrying amount after weighting	100	300	400	800
Pro rata allocation of building	12%	38%	50%	100%
	(100/800)	(300/800)	(400/800)	
Allocation of the carrying amount of building	19	56	75	150
Carrying amount after allocation of building	119	206	275	600

FIGURE 12.9 *(continued)*

For each cash-generating unit, the carrying amount of the assets is compared with the recoverable amount. After calculating the present value of the expected cash flows for each unit as well as the entity as a whole, the recoverable amounts were determined to be:

A	$199
B	164
C	271
Entity	720

It is assumed that the entity as a whole has a recoverable amount greater than the sum of that for the individual units. Impairment losses can now be determined for each individual unit:

	A	B	C
Carrying amount	119	206	275
Recoverable amount	199	164	271
Impairment loss	0	42	4

The impairment losses are allocated across the assets of units B and C in proportion to their carrying amounts, including the allocated headquarters building:

	B		C	
To headquarters building	12	[42 × 56/206]	1	[4 × 75/275]
To other assets	30	[42 × 150/206]	3	[4 × 200/275]
	42		4	

The headquarters building is therefore to be written down from 150 to 137.

The *second step* is to deal with the research centre that could not be allocated in a reasonable manner across the units. This requires identifying the smallest cash-generating unit that includes the research centre. In this case, it is the entity as a whole. This unit is then tested for impairment:

	A	B	C	Building	Research centre	Entity
Carrying amount	100	150	200	150	50	650
Impairment loss	—	30	3	13	—	46
	100	120	197	137	50	604
Recoverable amount						720

The entity therefore has not incurred an impairment loss, because its recoverable amount is greater than its carrying amount. There is no need for a further write-down of the assets of the entity.

12.5 CASH-GENERATING UNITS AND GOODWILL

In accounting for impairment losses for cash-generating units, one of the assets that may be recorded by an entity is goodwill. IAS 36 contains specific requirements for accounting for goodwill and how its existence affects the allocation of impairment losses across the assets of a cash-generating unit.

Goodwill is recognised only when it is acquired in a business combination. As discussed in chapter 10, IAS 38 *Intangible Assets* does not allow the recognition of internally generated goodwill, or the revaluation of any acquired goodwill. In accounting for a business combination, goodwill is calculated as a residual, involving calculation of variables including the consideration transferred and the net fair value of the identifiable assets and liabilities acquired. (See chapter 11 for more information on business combinations.) Goodwill then consists of those assets that cannot be individually identified or separately recognised.

Goodwill is an accumulation of assets, and may arise from synergy between the assets in the combined businesses or from assets that individually do not qualify for recognition. The assets that constitute goodwill increase the wealth of the entity and add to the expected future cash flows of the entity. However, for specific assets to be included in goodwill, either the cash flows associated with the specific assets cannot be reliably measured or the cash flows are earned in conjunction with other assets. Hence, it is not possible to determine a fair value less costs to sell for goodwill, or to identify a set of cash flows that relates specifically to goodwill.

Accounting for goodwill acquired in a business combination is specified in paragraph 32 of IFRS 3 *Business Combinations*. The acquirer measures goodwill acquired in a business combination at cost less any accumulated impairment losses. Goodwill is not subject to amortisation. Instead, the acquirer tests the carrying amount of goodwill annually in accordance with IAS 36.

When a business combination occurs, and goodwill is calculated as part of accounting for that combination, the goodwill acquired is allocated to one or more cash-generating units (IAS 36 paragraph 80). Even though goodwill was acquired in relation to the entity as a whole, the cash flow earning capacity of goodwill must be allocated across the cash-generating units. The aim is to allocate all assets, whether corporate assets or goodwill, to the cash-generating units so they can be associated with the cash flows received by those units.

When deciding which units should have goodwill allocated to them, consideration should be given to how internal management monitors the goodwill. According to paragraph 80, the goodwill should be allocated to the *lowest level* at which management monitors the goodwill. When the business combination occurred, the acquirer would have analysed the earning capacity of the entity it proposed to acquire, and would have equated aspects of goodwill to various cash-generating units. It is possible that the allocation of goodwill would be made to each of the segments identified by management under the application of paragraph 80(b) of IAS 36, which states that each unit or group of units to which the goodwill is so allocated shall not be larger than an operating segment as defined in paragraph 5 of IFRS 8 *Operating Segments*. An operating segment is identified on the basis of internal reports that are regularly reviewed by the entity's chief operating decision maker in order to allocate resources to the segment and assess its performance.

In its response to the Financial Accounting Standards Board (FASB) in the United States in relation to the board's deliberations on the impairment testing of goodwill, as reported in the FASB Summary of Comment Letters, Technology Network suggested that goodwill should be tested at the enterprise level in all cases, or at least that option should be permitted:

> Many acquisitions are integrated into existing businesses for internal reporting purposes with many companies recording the goodwill at an operating or business unit level. However, over time, successful acquisitions frequently (and hopefully) create synergies with other internal reporting units and throughout an enterprise.
>
> The only way to ensure that this value is captured may be to perform impairment testing at the enterprise level. While we recognize that the Board has rejected such an approach, we believe that testing at the enterprise level would be appropriate in limited circumstances. For example, in the software industry, the acquired goodwill frequently becomes so integrated into the company's entire product line that it essentially becomes a new company platform. Thus, we do not believe there should be any firm rule prohibiting enterprise level testing. It should be allowed in appropriate circumstances.

The IASB (paragraph BC139 of the Basis for Conclusions on IAS 36) considered this argument and rejected impairment testing of goodwill at the level of the entity itself. It saw the important link as being the level at which goodwill is tested, with the level of internal reporting reflecting the management and reporting of goodwill that occurs within the entity itself.

As noted in paragraph BC139, the IASB was concerned that entities did not resort to testing the goodwill at the level of the entity itself. It stated:

> There should be a link between the level at which goodwill is tested for impairment and the level of internal reporting that reflects the way an entity manages its operations and with which the goodwill naturally would be associated.

In that sense, the allocation of goodwill should not be an arbitrary process. As noted in paragraph 82 of IAS 36, developing additional reporting systems should not normally be necessary.

Under IFRS 3, there is an allowance for a provisional initial accounting for the business combination. Paragraph 84 of IAS 36 therefore provides, consistent with IFRS 3, that where the allocation of goodwill cannot be completed before the end of the annual period in which the business combination occurred, the initial allocation is to be completed before the end of the first annual period beginning after the acquisition date.

12.5.1 Impairment testing of goodwill

A cash-generating unit that has goodwill allocated to it must be tested for impairment *annually* or more frequently if there is an indication the unit may be impaired (IAS 36 paragraph 90). As with other impairment tests, this involves comparing the carrying amount of the unit's assets, including goodwill, with the recoverable amount of the unit's assets.

Recoverable amount exceeds carrying amount

If the recoverable amount exceeds the carrying amount, there is no impairment loss. In particular, there is no impairment of goodwill. The goodwill balance remains unadjusted; that is, it is not reduced due to impairment loss.

Note that this test is not a robust test of the amount of goodwill recorded by the unit. Under this test, the goodwill is protected or 'cushioned' against impairment by:

- *internally generated goodwill:* the benefits relating to the acquired goodwill may have been received by the entity, but unrecognised internally generated goodwill may exist in the entity. The internally generated goodwill may have arisen subsequent to the business combination, or could consist of that existing in the acquirer itself prior to the business combination.
- *unrecognised identifiable net assets:* intangibles may exist which do not meet the recognition criteria under IAS 38 *Intangible Assets*. These are not included in the measure of the carrying amount of the assets of the cash-generating unit, yet the cash flows generated by these assets increase the recoverable amount of the unit.
- *excess value over carrying amount of recognised assets:* the impairment test uses the carrying amount of the unit's recognised assets. If the fair values of these assets are greater than their carrying amounts, the extra benefits relating to these assets increase the recoverable amount of the unit.

The IASB recognises that the above test provides a cushion against recognising impairment losses for goodwill. In paragraph BC135 of the Basis for Conclusions on IAS 36, it notes that the carrying amount of goodwill will always be shielded from impairment by internally generated goodwill. The impairment test for goodwill is at best ensuring that the carrying amount of goodwill is recoverable from cash flows generated by both acquired and internally generated goodwill. Such a cushion works, of course, only if the recoverable amount is being maintained; that is, if the value of the assets both identifiable and unidentifiable are being maintained by the entity. If the assets of the unit are being well managed then, in most cases, the goodwill of the unit is also being maintained. The test is then a screening mechanism. However, one advantage of the screening test is that it significantly reduces the cost of applying an impairment test, particularly in comparison to other tests that require a remeasurement of goodwill by measuring the net fair values of the identifiable assets and liabilities of the unit on an annual basis.

Figure 12.10 is an extract from the notes to the 2007 statement of financial position of the Swatch Group, explaining how the company conducted its impairment tests for goodwill.

FIGURE 12.10 Impairment testing for goodwill for the Swatch Group

Goodwill impairment testing

Goodwill is allocated to the Group's cash-generating units (CGUs), which correspond to the profit centers for the segment "Watches & Jewelry" and the reportable segments for the business segments "Production" and "Electronic Systems".

A segment-level summary of the goodwill allocation is presented below:

(CHF million)	31.12.2007	31.12.2006
Watches & Jewelry	155	154
Production	32	27
Electronic Systems	45	45
Total	**232**	**226**

(continued)

FIGURE 12.10 *(continued)*

The recoverable amount of a cash-generating unit is determined based on value-in-use calculations. These calculations use cash flow projections based on financial budgets approved by management covering a five-year period. Cash flows beyond the five-year period are extrapolated using a steady growth rate. The discount rates used are derived from a capital asset pricing model using data from Swiss capital markets and reflect specific risks relating to the relevant segments. This is then adjusted to a pre-tax rate.

Ranges of key assumptions used

	2007			2006		
	Watches & Jewelry	**Production**	**Electronic Systems**	Watches & Jewelry	Production	Electronic Systems
Estimated growth rate beyond five-year period	1%	1%	0.5%	0%–1%	1%	1%
Expected gross margin	56%–68%	27%–32%	35%–40%	56%–68%	27%–29%	35%–39%
Pre-tax discount rate	6.5%	7.4%	7.6%	7.0%	8.8%	9.6%

No impairment charge for goodwill had to be recorded in 2007. Management believes that any reasonably possible change in any of the key assumptions would not cause the carrying value of goodwill to exceed the recoverable amount.

Source: Swatch (2007, p. 177).

Carrying amount exceeds recoverable amount

If the carrying amount exceeds the recoverable amount, there is an impairment loss, and this loss is recognised in accordance with paragraph 104 of IAS 36. This paragraph states that the impairment loss must be allocated to reduce the carrying amount of the assets of the unit, or group of units, in the following order:

- firstly, to reduce the carrying amount of any goodwill allocated to the cash-generating unit
- then, to the other assets of the unit pro rata on the basis of the carrying amount of each asset in the unit.

These reductions in carrying amounts are treated as impairment losses on the individual assets of the unit and recognised as any other impairment losses on assets.

However, paragraph 105 of IAS 36 provides some restrictions on the write-downs to individual assets:

> In allocating an impairment loss in accordance with paragraph 104, an entity shall not reduce the carrying amount of an asset below the highest of:
> (a) its fair value less costs to sell (if determinable);
> (b) its value in use (if determinable); and
> (c) zero.
> The amount of the impairment loss that would otherwise have been allocated to the asset shall be allocated pro rata to the other assets of the unit (group of units).

Figure 12.11 is an example of accounting for an impairment loss for a cash-generating unit that contains goodwill. It is adapted from Illustrative Example 2 accompanying IAS 36.

FIGURE 12.11 Accounting for impairment loss in a cash-generating unit with allocated goodwill

At the end of 2010, entity T acquired entity M for $10 000. M has manufacturing plants in three countries. Each of these plants is considered to be a cash-generating unit. The goodwill recognised on the acquisition is allocated to these three units on a reasonable and consistent basis:

End of 2010	**Allocation of purchase price**	**Fair value of identifiable assets**	**Goodwill**
Activities in Country A	$ 3 000	$2000	$1000
Activities in Country B	2 000	1500	500
Activities in Country C	5 000	3500	1500
Total	$10 000	$7000	$3000

FIGURE 12.11 *(continued)*

Because goodwill has been allocated to each of the cash-generating units, each unit must be tested for impairment annually. For the years ending 2010 and 2011, the recoverable amount of each unit exceeded the carrying amount and hence the activities in each country as well as the goodwill allocated to these activities are regarded as not impaired.

At the beginning of 2012, a new government is elected in Country A and, as a result of government policies relating to export restrictions, there are concerns about the recoverability of the assets in Country A. The carrying amounts of assets in the Country A cash-generating unit at this point are:

Beginning of 2012	Goodwill	Identifiable assets	Total
Cost	$1000	$2000	$3000
Accumulated depreciation (12-year life)	—	167	167
Carrying amount	$1000	$1833	$2833

The recoverable amount of the Country A cash-generating unit is calculated as $1360, based on a value-in-use calculation. As the total carrying amount of the assets in this unit amount to $2833, there is an impairment loss of $1473 (i.e. $2833 – $1360).

The impairment loss is first allocated to the goodwill, writing it down to zero. The balance of the impairment loss ($473) is then allocated across the carrying amounts of the identifiable assets of the Country A cash-generating unit on a pro rata basis:

Beginning of 2012	Goodwill	Identifiable assets	Total
Cost	$1000	$2000	$3000
Accumulated depreciation (12-year life)	—	167	167
Carrying amount	1000	1833	2833
Impairment loss	1000	473	1473
Carrying amount after impairment loss	$ 0	$1360	$1360

The journal entries to record the allocation of the impairment loss are:

Impairment Loss – Goodwill	Dr	1000	
Goodwill	Cr		1000
(Impairment loss)			
Impairment Loss	Dr	473	
Accumulated Depreciation and Impairment Losses – Plant and Equipment	Cr		XXX
Land	Cr		XXX
(Allocation of impairment loss to assets on a pro rata basis)			

There has been much controversy over the goodwill impairment test. In fact, three IASB members dissented on the issue of IAS 36, mainly over aspects of this test.

The advantage of the procedure used in IAS 36 is that it is not complex or costly, leading to a belief that the benefits outweigh the costs — see paragraph BC170 of the Basis for Conclusions on IAS 36.

The criticism of the test is that it *does not measure whether goodwill has been impaired.* Using the example in figure 12.11, although there is an impairment loss of $1473, there is no subsequent test to determine whether the goodwill has been impaired or whether some of the identifiable assets have been impaired. The method arbitrarily allocates the impairment loss firstly to goodwill — it assumes goodwill has been impaired. In the exposure draft to IAS 36, the impairment test suggested was a two-step approach, the second step of which is outlined in figure 12.12.

Once an impairment loss is determined, the *second step* requires three actions:

Action 1: Calculate the implied value of goodwill

The implied value of goodwill is calculated as follows:

Recoverable amount of the cash-generating unit	*less*	net fair value of the identifiable assets, liabilities, and contingent liabilities the entity would recognise if it acquired the cash-generating unit in a business combination on the date of the impairment test excluding any identifiable asset acquired in a business combination but not recognised separately from goodwill at the acquisition date.

Note that this measure of implied goodwill reduces the cushions. The assets and liabilities measured are not just those recorded by the entity, but those that would be recognised in an acquisition at the date the impairment test is made. Implied goodwill is, then, not protected by unrecognised identifiable assets because, under IFRS 3, these can be recognised in a business combination. Nor is it protected by excess values of the recognised assets because these assets are now measured at fair value rather than at carrying amount. If the object of the second step of the impairment test is to measure the current value of goodwill, then failing to exclude these other assets means the implied value of goodwill would consist of 'real' goodwill and identifiable assets.

The goodwill figure is still cushioned by internally generated goodwill, but it is not possible to distinguish between acquired goodwill and internally generated goodwill. There also does not seem any point in doing so because, if the purpose of the impairment test is to ensure that assets are not overstated, then whether the goodwill is 'old acquired' or 'new internally generated' does not matter. The question is whether at the time of the impairment test the unit has the carrying amount of goodwill as shown in the accounts.

Action 2: Compare the carrying amount of goodwill with the implied value of goodwill

If the carrying amount is *less than* the implied value, goodwill is not impaired, and no impairment loss needs to be recognised for goodwill. The impairment loss on the cash-generating unit then relates to the other assets of the unit. If the carrying amount is *greater than* the implied value, an impairment loss for goodwill has occurred and would be recognised immediately in profit or loss.

Action 3: Allocate the balance (if any) of the impairment loss to the other assets of the unit on a pro rata basis according to the carrying amount of each asset in the unit

The accounting for the balance of the impairment loss is the same as for an impairment loss in a cash-generating unit where there is no goodwill.

Using the same example as in figure 12.11, having determined the impairment loss of $1473, the implied value of goodwill in Country A is then measured. The net fair value of the identifiable assets it would recognise if entity T acquired the Country A cash-generating unit at the date of the impairment test is calculated to be $1000. Hence, the implied value of goodwill is $360 (i.e. $1360 – $1000).

As the carrying amount of the goodwill of $1000 exceeds the implied value of $360, there is an impairment loss for goodwill of $640. The total impairment loss is $1473, so the balance of the impairment loss of $833 ($1473 – $640) is allocated across the carrying amounts of the identifiable assets of the Country A cash-generating unit:

Beginning of 2009	**Goodwill**	**Identifiable assets**	**Total**
Cost	$1000	$2000	$3000
Accumulated depreciation (12-year life)	—	167	167
Carrying amount	1000	1833	2833
Impairment loss	640	833	1473
Carrying amount after impairment loss	$ 360	$1000	$1360

FIGURE 12.12 **Impairment loss in a cash-generating unit with allocated goodwill — the three actions of the second step**

Note in figure 12.12 that the process endeavours to measure the goodwill of the cash-generating unit, something IAS 36 does not do. The problem with the two-step process is that the calculation of the implied value for goodwill requires determining the fair values of the assets, liabilities and contingent liabilities of the cash-generating unit. This is seen by the IASB (paragraph BC166 of the Basis for Conclusions on IAS 36) as costly and impracticable. The field tests conducted by the IASB led it to change from the two-step method to the one-step method. An example of one company's opinion of the costliness of the approach is found in the comments of the Dow Chemical Company in its submission to the FASB on goodwill impairment, as reported in the Summary of Comment letters. The Dow Chemical Company's comments were considered by the FASB to be representative of the majority of comments on this issue:

> The mechanics of the impairment test will be cost prohibitive to undertake. The Board cannot seriously expect companies to regularly estimate the fair value of its assets and liabilities in attempting to calculate the implied fair value of goodwill. Our experience with obtaining such appraisals in the context of business acquisitions has led us to believe that any benefit from such precise impairment measurements is far outweighed by the prohibitive costs of retaining and regularly engaging outside valuation experts whose opinions can vary widely in their professional assessment. As a practical and cost-effective alternative, we strongly recommend the use of *book values* of reported assets for this purpose.

Timing of impairment tests

As noted earlier, goodwill has to be tested for impairment annually. However, the test does not have to occur at the end of the reporting period. As paragraph 96 of IAS 36 notes, the test may be performed at any time during the year, provided it is performed at the same time every year. According to paragraph BC171 of the Basis for Conclusions on IAS 36, this measure was allowed as a means of reducing the costs of applying the test. However, if a business combination has occurred in the current period, and an allocation has been made to one or more cash-generating units, all units to which goodwill has been allocated must be tested for impairment before the end of that year — see paragraph 96 of IAS 36 in this regard.

It is also not necessary for all cash-generating units to be tested for impairment at the same time. If there are two units being tested for impairment, one being a smaller cash-generating unit within a larger unit and the larger unit contains an allocation of goodwill, it is necessary to test the smaller unit for impairment first. This ensures that, if necessary, the assets of the smaller unit are adjusted before the testing of the larger unit. Similarly, if the assets of a cash-generating unit containing goodwill are being tested at the same time as the unit, then the assets must be tested first.

One of the reasons for requiring annual testing for both goodwill and intangibles with an indefinite life, apart from the uncertainty of measuring these assets, relates to the depreciation concept adopted by the standard setters, discussed in chapter 9 of this book. Depreciation is seen as a 'process of allocation'. Hence, to have assets such as goodwill and indefinite life intangibles permanently on the records with no allocation to accounting periods seems to depart from the allocation process and to move to a valuation concept. The IASB (paragraph BC121 of the Basis for Conclusions on IAS 36) noted that 'non-amortisation of an intangible asset increases the reliance that must be placed on impairment reviews of that asset to ensure that its carrying amount does not exceed its recoverable amount'. However, in accordance with paragraph 10(a) for indefinite life intangibles and paragraph 96 for goodwill, both may be tested at any time during the year, provided the test is performed at the same time every year. It must also be remembered that, as stated in paragraph BC122 of the Basis for Conclusions on IAS 36, annual testing is not a substitute for management being aware of events or changing circumstances that may indicate possible impairment and the need for additional testing.

Other impairment issues relating to goodwill

IAS 36 raises a number of other issues that need to be considered in accounting for the impairment of goodwill within a cash-generating unit:

- *Disposal of an operation within a cash-generating unit.* Where the cash-generating unit has a number of distinct operations and goodwill has been allocated to the unit, if one of the operations is disposed of, it is necessary to consider whether any of the goodwill relates to the operation disposed of. If it does, the amount of goodwill is measured on the basis of the relative values of the operation disposed of and the portion of the cash-generating unit retained, unless the entity can demonstrate that some other method better reflects the goodwill associated with the operation disposed of. In calculating the gain or loss on disposal of the operation, the allocated portion of the goodwill is included in the carrying amount of the assets sold (paragraph 86).

For example, if part of a cash-generating unit was sold for $200 and the recoverable amount of the remaining part of the unit is $600, then it is assumed that 25% (200/[200 + 600]) of the goodwill has been sold and is included in the carrying amount of the operation disposed of.

- *Reorganisation of the entity.* Where an entity containing a number of cash-generating units restructures, changing the composition of the cash-generating units, and where goodwill has been allocated to the original units, paragraph 87 requires the reallocation of the goodwill to the new units. The allocation is done on a relative value basis similar to that used where a cash-generating unit is disposed of, again unless the entity can demonstrate that some other method better reflects the goodwill associated with the operation disposed of.

12.6 REVERSAL OF AN IMPAIRMENT LOSS

An impairment loss is recognised after an entity analyses the future prospects of an individual asset or a cash-generating unit. Subsequent to an impairment loss occurring because of doubts about the performance of assets, it is possible for circumstances to change such that, when the recoverable amount of the assets increases, consideration can be given to a reversal of a past impairment loss. Paragraph 110 of IAS 36 requires an entity to assess *at the end of each reporting period* whether there are indications that an impairment loss recognised in previous periods may not exist or may have decreased. If such indications exist, the entity should estimate the recoverable amount of the asset or unit.

Similar to the assessment of whether there is an indication of an impairment loss, an entity needs to look at internal and external evidence to determine the existence of evidence for a reversal of the previous loss. Paragraph 111 of IAS 36 requires an entity to assess specific internal and external sources of information. These indicators are effectively the same as those for assessing the existence of a loss except that the indicators for a reversal relate to improvements in the entity's prospects. The indicators noted in paragraph 111 are (with italics added):

External sources of information

(a) the asset's market value has *increased* significantly during the period;

(b) significant changes with a *favourable effect* on the entity have taken place during the period, or will take place in the near future, in the technological, market, economic or legal environment in which the entity operates or in the market to which the asset is dedicated;

(c) market interest rates or other market rates of return on investments have *decreased* during the period, and those decreases are likely to affect the discount rate used in calculating the asset's value in use and increase the asset's recoverable amount materially;

Internal sources of information

(d) significant changes with a *favourable effect* on the entity have taken place during the period, or are expected to take place in the near future, in the extent to which, or manner in which, the asset is used or is expected to be used. These changes include capital expenditure incurred during the period to improve or enhance an asset in excess of its standard of performance assessed immediately before the expenditure is made or a commitment to discontinue or restructure the operation to which the asset belongs; and

(e) evidence is available from internal reporting that indicates that the economic performance of the asset is, or will be, *better* than expected.

It is possible, as envisaged by paragraph 113 of IAS 36, that a review of the evidence will not result in a reversal of a previous impairment loss, but instead may lead to changes in the depreciation/amortisation measure of an asset. The review may lead to changes in expectations about useful life, residual value, and the pattern of benefits to be received.

If the evidence is such that there is a change in the estimates in relation to an asset (and only if there has been a change in the estimates), a reversal of impairment loss can be recognised. The reversal process requires the recognition of an increase in the carrying amount of the asset to its recoverable amount.

The ability to recognise a reversal of an impairment loss and the accounting for that reversal depend on whether the reversal relates to an individual asset, a cash-generating unit or goodwill.

12.6.1 Reversal of an impairment loss — individual asset

Where the recoverable amount is greater than the carrying amount of an individual asset (other than goodwill), the reversal of a previous impairment loss requires adjusting the carrying amount of the asset to recoverable amount. In determining the amount by which the carrying amount is to be adjusted, one limitation, as outlined in paragraph 117 of IAS 36, is that the carrying amount cannot be increased to an amount in excess of the carrying amount that would have been determined had no impairment loss been recognised. Hence, for a depreciable asset, if there were changes made to the useful life, residual value or pattern of benefits as a result of the impairment loss in the previous period, then there needs to be a calculation of carrying amount using the depreciation variables applied before the impairment loss to determine what the carrying amount would have been if there had been no impairment loss. This latter amount is the maximum to which the actual carrying amount can be increased.

If the individual asset is recorded under the *cost model*, then the increase in the carrying amount is recognised immediately in profit or loss:

Accumulated Depreciation/Amortisation and Impairment Losses	Dr	XXX	
Income – Impairment Loss Reversal	Cr		XXX
(Reversal of impairment loss)			

After the reversal of the impairment loss and the adjustment of the asset to its new carrying amount, in accordance with paragraph 121 of IAS 36 the depreciation/amortisation charge must be adjusted so that the revised carrying amount, less any residual value, is allocated across the remaining useful life on a systematic basis.

12.6.2 Reversal of an impairment loss — cash-generating unit

If the reversal of the impairment loss relates to a cash-generating unit, in accordance with paragraph 122 of IAS 36 the reversal of the impairment loss is allocated pro rata to the assets of the unit, except for goodwill, with the carrying amounts of those assets. These reversals will then relate to the specific assets of the cash-generating unit and will be accounted for as detailed above for individual assets. In relation to those individual assets, the carrying amount of an asset cannot, as per paragraph 123 of IAS 36 be increased above the lower of its recoverable amount (if determinable) and the carrying amount that would have been determined had no impairment loss been recognised for the asset in previous periods.

If the situation envisaged in paragraph 123 occurs, then the amount of impairment loss reversal that cannot be allocated to an individual asset is then allocated on a pro rata basis to the other assets of the cash-generating unit, except for goodwill.

12.6.3 Reversal of an impairment loss — goodwill

Paragraph 124 of IAS 36 states that an impairment loss recognised for goodwill is *not* to be reversed in a later period. The reasons for this decision by the standard setters are detailed in paragraphs BC187–BC191 of the Basis for Conclusions on IAS 36.

The key principle driving the accounting for goodwill in a reversal of impairment loss situation is that established in IAS 38 *Intangibles*, namely that internally generated goodwill cannot be recognised. Where there is a reversal of an impairment loss, in order to be able to allocate some of the reversal amount to goodwill it would be necessary to establish that the old acquired goodwill still existed, rather than the increase in goodwill being recognition of internally generated goodwill. Because of the nature of goodwill, it is not possible to determine how much of any goodwill existing in an entity is remaining acquired goodwill or goodwill internally generated since the acquisition. To allow an impairment reversal to increase the carrying amount of goodwill is potentially allowing the recognition of internally generated goodwill, or, as described in paragraph BC190, 'backdoor' capitalisation of internally generated goodwill — hence the prohibition in IAS 36.

Some IASB members saw a potential inconsistency with disallowing the reinstatement of goodwill based on the grounds of non-recognition of internally generated goodwill and the allowance in IAS 36 of internally generated goodwill to act as a cushion to recognition of an impairment loss on goodwill. The standard setters, however, concluded that to shield or cushion an impairment loss is not as bad as direct recognition of internally generated goodwill in a reversal situation. However, there is probably some truth in the accusation that inconsistent accounting is allowed because the entity that has acquired goodwill is effectively allowed to recognise internally generated goodwill via the cushion effect in the impairment test, while at the same time those entities that have not acquired goodwill are not allowed to recognise internally generated goodwill.

An example of a reversal of a previous period impairment loss within a cash-generating unit to which goodwill has been allocated is given in figure 12.13. This example is adapted from Example 4 of the Illustrative Examples accompanying IAS 36.

This example uses the situation in figure 12.11 in which the Country A cash-generating unit incurred an impairment loss and the assets and goodwill were written down by $473 and $1000 respectively.

In 2013, the business situation improves in Country A and government policies change. As a result, management re-estimates the recoverable amount of the Country A cash-generating unit, determining the recoverable amount to be $1910. This amount is compared with the carrying amount of the unit:

Beginning of 2012	**Goodwill**	**Identifiable assets**	**Total**
Historical cost	$ 1000	$2000	$ 3000
Accumulated depreciation	—	(167)	(167)
Impairment loss	(1000)	(473)	(1473)
Carrying amount	$ 0	$1360	$ 1360
End of 2013			
Additional depreciation (2 years at new rate): $1360/11 × 2	—	(247)	(247)
Carrying amount	$ 0	$1113	$ 1113
Recoverable amount			1910
Excess of recoverable amount over carrying amount			$ 797

As the excess of $797 cannot be allocated to goodwill, the question is whether the whole amount can be recognised as a reversal of impairment loss. The impairment reversal cannot exceed the carrying amount that would have been determined had no impairment loss been recognised. The carrying amount of the identifiable assets at 2013 if there had been no impairment loss is as follows (note that the depreciation rate before the impairment was straight-line over 12 years, whereas the rate has been adjusted after the impairment loss as a result of expected changes in the pattern of benefits of the assets):

End of 2013	**Identifiable assets**
Historical cost	$2000
Accumulated depreciation ($\frac{3}{12}$ × $2000)	500
Depreciated historical cost	1500
Actual carrying amount	
Difference	$1113
	387

Hence, the maximum impairment loss reversal is $387. This amount is recognised immediately in profit or loss as income.

FIGURE 12.13 Accounting for the reversal of an impairment loss

12.7 DISCLOSURE

Paragraph 126 of IAS 36 requires the following disclosures for each class of assets:

(a) the amount of impairment losses recognised in profit or loss during the period and the line item(s) of the statement of comprehensive income in which those impairment losses are included;
(b) the amount of reversals of impairment losses recognised in profit or loss during the period and the line item(s) of the statement of comprehensive income in which those impairment losses are reversed;
(c) the amount of impairment losses on revalued assets recognised directly in equity during the period; and
(d) the amount of reversals of impairment losses on revalued assets recognised directly in equity during the period.

As noted in chapter 9 of this book, paragraph 73(e) of IAS 16 *Property, Plant and Equipment* requires, in relation to the reconciliation of the carrying amount at the beginning and end of the period for each class of property, plant and equipment, disclosure of:

- increases or decreases during the period resulting from impairment losses recognised or reversed directly in equity
- impairment losses recognised in profit or loss during the period
- impairment losses reversed in profit or loss during the period.

Similar disclosures are required for intangibles under paragraph 118 of IAS 38 *Intangible Assets* for each class of intangible asset.

As paragraph 128 of IAS 36 states, the disclosures required by paragraph 126 may be presented or included in a reconciliation of the carrying amount of assets at the beginning and end of the period. (Such disclosures were illustrated in chapter 9.) For parts (a) and (b) of paragraph 126, disclosure is required of the relevant line item(s) used. If these were included in other expenses or other income then information relating to impairment losses or reversals would be required in the note to the statement of comprehensive income relating to these line items in the statement of comprehensive income. For example, the note to other expenses may be as shown in figure 12.14.

NOTE 5: Expenses			IAS 36 *para.*
Other operating expenses			
	2008	2007	
	\$000	\$000	
Amortisation of intangibles	521	435	
Impairment losses:			
Plant and equipment	100	—	*126(a)*
Land and buildings	—	—	
Trade receivables	52	21	
Patents	64	—	

FIGURE 12.14 Disclosures required by paragraph 126(a) of IAS 36

Paragraph 129 of IAS 36 details information to be disclosed for each reportable segment where an entity applies IFRS 8 *Operating Segments*.

Disclosures required by paragraph 130 of IAS 36 are illustrated in figure 12.15 on the next page. If impairment losses relate to items of property, plant and equipment, such a note can be included in the note detailing disclosures of property, plant and equipment. Disclosures concerning impairment losses for a cash-generating unit may be provided in a separate note, or if applicable attached to the segment report. In figure 12.15, an impairment note is used because the information is given for both individual assets as well as a cash-generating unit.

Paragraph 133 of IAS 36 requires disclosures in relation to any goodwill that has not been allocated to a cash-generating unit at the end of the reporting period. In particular, an entity must disclose the amount of the unallocated goodwill and the reasons that amount has not been allocated to the cash-generating units in the entity.

14. Impairment	IAS 36 *para. 130*
The company incurred an impairment loss of $10 000 in relation to property	*(b)*
held by the entity for future expansion, the item being written down to	*(c)(i)*
recoverable amount due to the pending closure of the plant. The value of the	*(a)*
property was reduced due to there being environmental concerns over future development in that area.	
Impairment losses were also recognised in the current period in relation to	*(d)(i)*
the pet food division. This division is one of the company's cash-generating units as well as being a reportable segment of the company. The reason for the write-	
downs was the expected fall in future cash flows due to increased competition	*(a)*
in the area, particularly given the lowering of government restrictions on	
imported products. The recoverable amount of the cash-generating unit is based	*(e)*
on a value-in-use calculation. The discount rate used in the calculation of value	*(g)*
in use was 10%, compared with the 11% rate used for a previous value-in-use	
calculation made in 2005. There has been no change in the aggregation of	*(d)(iii)*
assets in the cash-generating unit since 2010. The impairment loss amounted to	*(b)*
$2 600 000 and was allocated as follows:	*(d)(ii)*

Land and buildings	$ 500 000
Leasehood improvements	420 000
Plant and equipment	310 000
Leased plant and equipment	—
Patents and licences	480 000
Research and development	370 000
Goodwill	520 000
	$2 600 000

FIGURE 12.15 Disclosures required by paragraph 130 of IAS 36

Because the calculation of recoverable amount requires assumptions and estimates relating to future cash flows, IAS 36 requires disclosures relating to the calculation of recoverable amount. Paragraph 132 encourages, but does not require, disclosure of *key assumptions* used to determine the recoverable amounts of assets or cash-generating units.

Paragraph 134 of IAS 36 requires disclosures about the *estimates* used to measure the recoverable amount of a cash-generating unit when goodwill or an intangible asset with an indefinite life is included in the carrying amount of the unit, and the carrying amount of goodwill or intangible assets with indefinite useful lives allocated to that unit is *significant* in comparison with the entity's total carrying amount of goodwill or intangible assets with indefinite useful lives. Where the carrying amount of goodwill or intangible assets is not significant for a unit, paragraph 135 requires that fact to be disclosed. If, for a number of such units, the recoverable amounts are based on the same key assumptions and the aggregate carrying amount of goodwill or intangible assets with indefinite lives is significant in comparison to the total for the entity, paragraph 135 requires similar, but not as extensive, disclosures to those in paragraph 134.

Example 9 of the Illustrative Examples accompanying IAS 36 provides illustrative disclosures about such cash-generating units. Figures 12.16 and 12.17 are based on this example, with references made to the appropriate part of paragraphs 134 and 135 which require that disclosure. Figure 12.16 contains the information about entity M for which the disclosures are made.

FIGURE 12.16 Background information for entity M

Entity M is a multinational manufacturing firm that uses geographical segments as its main format for reporting segment information. M's three reportable segments based on that format are Europe, North America and Asia. Goodwill has been allocated for impairment testing purposes to three individual cash-generating units — two in Europe (units A and B) and one in North America (unit C) — and to one group of cash-generating units (comprising operation XYZ in Asia).

FIGURE 12.16 *(continued)*

M acquired unit C, a manufacturing operation in North America, in December 2010. Unlike M's other North American operations, C operates in an industry with high margins and high growth rates, and with the benefit of a 10-year patent on its main product. The patent was granted to C just before M's acquisition of C. As part of accounting for the acquisition of C, M recognised, in addition to the patent, goodwill of $3000 and a brand name of $1000. M's management has determined that the brand name has an indefinite useful life. M has no other intangible assets with indefinite useful lives.

During the year ending 31 December 2011, M determines that there is no impairment of any of its cash-generating units containing goodwill or intangible assets with indefinite useful lives. The recoverable amounts of those units, including unit C, are determined on the basis of value-in-use calculations. XYZ has determined that the recoverable amount calculations are most sensitive to changes in the following assumptions:

European units containing goodwill	North American units containing goodwill (excluding unit C)	Unit C
Gross margin during the budget period (4 years)	Five-year government bond rate during the budget period (5 years)	Gross margin during the budget period (5 years)
Market share during the budget period	Market share during the budget period	Market share during the budget period
Euro/dollar exchange rate during the budget period	Raw material price inflation during the budget period	Raw material price inflation during the budget period
Growth rate used to extrapolate cash flows beyond the budget period	Growth rate used to extrapolate cash flows beyond the budget period	Growth rate used to extrapolate cash flows beyond the budget period

Figure 12.17 contains the disclosures required for Entity M by paragraph 134 of IAS 36.

FIGURE 12.17 Disclosures required by paragraphs 134 and 135 of IAS 36

15. Impairment: goodwill and intangible assets	**IAS 36** *Para.*
Goodwill has been allocated for impairment testing purposes to three individual cash-generating units — two in Europe (units A and B) and one in North America (unit C) — and to one group of cash-generating units (operation XYZ) in Asia. The carrying amount of goodwill allocated to unit C and operation XYZ is significant in comparison with the total carrying amount of goodwill, but the carrying amount of goodwill allocated to each of units A and B is not. Nevertheless, the recoverable amounts of units A and B are based on some of the same key assumptions, and the aggregate carrying amount of goodwill allocated to those units is significant. Unit C also has an intangible asset with an indefinite useful life for which the carrying amount is significant in comparison with the entity's total carrying amount of such assets.	*135*
Operation XYZ	
The carrying amount of goodwill allocated to this cash-generating unit is $1200. The recoverable amount of operation XYZ has been determined based on a value-in-use calculation. The recoverable amount calculations are most sensitive to changes in the following assumptions:	*134* *(a)* *(c)*
• gross margin during the budget period (5 years) • Japanese yen/dollar exchange rate during the budget period • market share during the budget period • growth rate used to extrapolate cash flows beyond the budget period.	*(d)(i)*

(continued)

FIGURE 12.17 *(continued)*

Management relies on past experience as well as reference to published market indicators and economists' forecasts to determine the values assigned to these key assumptions.	*(d)(ii)*
The calculation of recoverable amount uses cash flow projections based on financial budgets approved by management covering a 5-year period, and a discount rate of 8.4%.	*(d)(iii)* *(d)(v)*
Cash flows beyond that 5-year period have been extrapolated using a steady 6.3% growth rate. This growth rate does not exceed the long-term average growth rate for the market in which XYZ operates. Management believes that any reasonably possible change in the key assumptions on which XYZ's recoverable amount is based would not cause XYZ's carrying amount to exceed its recoverable amount.	*(d)(iv)* *(f)*
Unit C	
The carrying amount of goodwill allocated to this unit is $1200.	*(a)*
The unit has an intangible asset, being the brand name *Chanell*, which has a carrying amount of $1000.	*(b)*
The recoverable amount of unit C has been determined on a value-in-use calculation. That calculation is most sensitive to changes in the following assumptions:	*(c)* *(d)(i)*
• 5-year government bond rate during the budget period (5 years) • raw materials price inflation during the budget period • market share during the budget period • growth rate used to extrapolate cash flows beyond the budget period.	
Management relies on past experience as well as reference to published market indicators and economists' forecasts to determine the values assigned to these key assumptions.	*(d)(ii)*
The calculation uses cash flow projections based on financial budgets approved by management covering a 5-year period, and a discount rate of 8.4%.	*(d)(iii)* *(d)(v)*
Cash flows beyond that 5-year period have been extrapolated using a steady 6.3% growth rate. This growth rate does not exceed the long-term average growth rate for the market in which XYZ operates. Management believes that any reasonably possible change in the key assumptions on which XYZ's recoverable amount is based would not cause XYZ's carrying amount to exceed its recoverable amount.	*(d)(iv)*
Units A and B	
Units A and B have an aggregate carrying amount of goodwill of $700 allocated to them.	*135* *(a)*
The recoverable amounts of units A and B have been determined on the basis of value-in-use calculations. Those units produce complementary products and their recoverable amounts are based on some of the same key assumptions. These assumptions are:	
• gross margin during the budget period (4 years) • raw materials price inflation during the budget period • market share during the budget period • growth rate used to extrapolate cash flows beyond the budget period.	*(c)*
Management relies on past experience as well as reference to published market indicators and economists' forecasts to determine the values assigned to these key assumptions.	*(d)*
Management believes that any reasonably possible change in any of these key assumptions would not cause the aggregate carrying amount of A and B to exceed the aggregate recoverable amount of those units.	*(e)*

In the example used in figures 12.16 and 12.17, the recoverable amount is based on value in use. Similar information is required to be disclosed if recoverable amount is based on fair value less costs to sell — see paragraph 134(e) of IAS 36 for details.

Illustrative examples 12.2 and 12.3 are comprehensive examples that demonstrate the accounting for impairment losses with and without corporate assets.

ILLUSTRATIVE EXAMPLE 12.2

Impairment losses, no corporate assets

Magenta Ltd has two divisions, Turquoise and Pink, each of which is a separate cash-generating unit (CGU). Magenta Ltd adopts a decentralised management approach whereby unit managers are expected to operate their units. However, there is one corporate asset, the information technology network, which is centrally controlled and provides a computer network to the company as a whole. The information technology network is not a depreciable asset.

At 30 June 2010 the net assets of each division, including its allocated share of the information technology network, were as follows:

	Turquoise	Pink
Information technology (IT) network	$ 284 000	$ 116 000
Land	450 000	290 000
Plant (20% p.a. straight-line depreciation)	1 310 000	960 000
Accumulated depreciation (plant)	(917 000)	(384 000)
Goodwill	46 000	32 000
Patent (10% straight-line amortisation)	210 000	255 000
Accumulated amortisation (patent)	(21 000)	(102 000)
Cash	20 000	12 000
Inventory	120 000	80 000
Receivables	34 000	40 000
	1 536 000	1 299 000
Liabilities	(276 000)	(189 000)
Net assets	$1 260 000	$1 110 000

Additional information as at 30 June 2010:

- Turquoise land had a fair value less costs to sell of $437 000.
- Pink patent had a carrying amount below fair value less costs to sell.
- Pink plant had a fair value less costs to sell of $540 000.
- Receivables were considered to be collectable.
- The IT network is not depreciated, as it is assumed to have an indefinite life.

Magenta Ltd's management undertook impairment testing at 30 June 2010 and determined the recoverable amount of each cash-generating unit to be: $1 430 000 for Turquoise and $1 215 000 for Pink.

Required

Prepare any journal entries necessary to record the results of the impairment testing for each of the CGUs.

Solution

The first step is to determine whether either CGU has an impairment loss. This is done by comparing the carrying amount of the assets of each CGU with the recoverable amount of these assets. Note that it is the carrying amount of the *assets* not the net assets that is used — the test is for the impairment of assets, not net assets.

	Turquoise	Pink
Carrying amount of assets	$1 536 000	$1 299 000
Recoverable amount	1 430 000	1 215 000
Impairment loss	$ (106 000)	$ (84 000)

As a result of the comparison, both CGUs have suffered impairment losses.

For each CGU, the impairment loss is used to write off any goodwill and then to allocate any balance across the other assets in proportion to their carrying amounts.

Turquoise CGU

Turquoise has goodwill of $46 000. Therefore, the first step is to write off goodwill of $46 000.

The second step is to allocate the remaining impairment loss of $60 000 (i.e. $106 000–$46 000).

Note that although all the assets are included in the calculation to determine whether the CGU has incurred an impairment loss, the allocation of that loss is only to those assets that will be written down as a result of the allocation process. Cash and receivables are not written down as they are recorded at amounts equal to fair value. The inventory is recorded under IAS 2 at the lower of cost and net realisable value, and as such is excluded from the impairment test write-down under IAS 36. The allocation of the balance of the impairment loss is done on a pro rata basis, in proportion to the assets' carrying amounts.

	Carrying amount	Proportion	Allocation of loss	Adjusted carrying amount
IT network	$ 284 000	284/1316	$12 948	$271 052
Land	450 000	450/1316	20 517	429 483
Plant	393 000	393/1316	17 918	375 082
Patent	189 000	189/1316	8 617	180 383
	$1 316 000		$60 000	

After the initial allocation across the assets, a check has to be made on the amount of each write-down as IAS 36 places limitations on the amount to which assets can be written down. Paragraph 105 of IAS 36 states that for each asset the carrying amount should not be reduced below the highest of the following:

- its fair value less costs to sell
- its value in use
- zero.

In this example, the land has a fair value less costs to sell of $437 000. Hence it cannot be written down to $429 483 as per the above allocation table. Only $13 000 (to write the asset down from $450 000 to $437 000) of the impairment loss can be allocated to it. Therefore, the remaining $7517 allocated loss (i.e. $20 517 – $13 000) must be allocated to the other assets. This allocation is based on the adjusted carrying amounts, the right-hand column of the table above.

	Carrying amount	Proportion	Allocation of loss	Adjusted carrying amount
IT Network	$271 052	271 052/826 517	$2 465	$268 587
Plant	375 082	375 082/826 517	3 411	371 671
Patent	180 383	180 383/826 517	1 641	178 742
	$826 517		$7 517	

The impairment loss for each asset is then based, where relevant, on the accumulation of both allocations. With non-depreciable assets such as land, the asset is simply written down, whereas with depreciable assets such as plant, the account increased is the accumulated depreciation and impairment losses account.

The journal entry for Turquoise:

Impairment Loss	Dr	106 000	
Goodwill	Cr		46 000
Land	Cr		13 000
IT Network*	Cr		15 413
Accumulated Depreciation and Impairment Losses – Plant**	Cr		21 329
Accumulated Depreciation and Impairment Losses – Patent***	Cr		10 258

*$12 948 + $2 465
**$17 918 + $3 411
***$8 617 + $1 641

Pink CGU

As with the Turquoise CGU, the impairment loss is used to write off the goodwill balance, $32 000, and then the balance of the impairment loss, $52 000 (i.e. $84 000 – $32 000), is allocated across the remaining assets, except for cash, receivables and inventory. Further, as the patent's carrying amount is below fair value less costs to sell, no impairment loss can be allocated to it.

	Carrying amount	Proportion	Allocation of loss	Adjusted carrying amount
IT network	$116 000	116/982	$ 6 143	$109 857
Land	290 000	290/982	15 356	274 644
Plant	576 000	576/982	30 501	545 499
	$982 000		$ 52 000	

Because the plant has a fair value less costs to sell of $540 000 and this is below the adjusted carrying amount of $545 499, the full impairment loss of $30 501 can be allocated to it.

The journal entry for Pink is:

Impairment Loss	Dr	84 000	
Goodwill	Cr		32 000
IT Network	Cr		6 143
Land	Cr		15 356
Accumulated Depreciation and Impairment Losses – Plant	Cr		30 501

ILLUSTRATIVE EXAMPLE 12.3

Impairment losses, corporate asset

Puce Ltd has three CGUs, a head office and a research facility. The carrying amounts of the assets and their recoverable amounts are as follows:

	Unit A	Unit B	Unit C	Head office	Research facility	Puce Ltd
Carrying amount	$100	$150	$200	$150	$50	$650
Recoverable amount	129	164	271			584

The assets of the head office are allocable to the three units as follows:

- Unit A: $19
- Unit B: $56
- Unit C: $75

The assets of the research facility cannot be reasonably allocated to the CGUs.

Required

Assuming all assets can be adjusted for impairment, prepare the journal entry relating to any impairment of the assets of Puce Ltd.

Solution

For each unit there needs to be a comparison between the carrying amounts of the assets of the units and their recoverable amounts to determine which, if any, of the CGUs is impaired. As the asset of the head office can be allocated to each of the units, the carrying amounts of each of the units must then include the allocated part of the head office.

Calculation of impairment losses for units

	Unit A	Unit B	Unit C
Carrying amount	$119	$206	$275
Recoverable amount	129	164	271
Impairment loss	—	42	4

Because the assets of Unit A are not impaired, no write-down is necessary. For Units B and C, the impairment losses must be allocated to the assets of the units. The allocation is in proportion to the carrying amounts of the assets.

Allocation of impairment loss

	Unit B		Unit C	
To head office	$12	[42 × 56/206]	$1	[4 × 75/275]
To other assets	30	[42 × 150/206]	3	[4 × 200/275]
	42		4	

In relation to the research centre, the assets of the centre cannot be allocated to the units, so the impairment test is based on the smallest CGU that contains the research centre, which in this case is the entity as a whole, Puce Ltd. For this calculation, the carrying amounts of the assets of the units as well as the head office are reduced by the impairment losses already allocated. The total assets of Puce Ltd consist of all the assets of the entity.

Impairment testing for CGU as a whole

	Unit A	Unit B	Unit C	Head office	Research centre	Puce Ltd
Carrying amount	100	150	200	150	50	650
Impairment loss	—	30	3	13	—	46
Net	**100**	**120**	**197**	**137**	**50**	**604**
Recoverable amount						**584**
Impairment loss						20

Because the carrying amount of the assets of Puce Ltd is less than the recoverable amount of the entity, the entity has incurred an impairment loss. This loss is allocated across all the assets of the entity in proportion to their carrying amounts.

Allocation of impairment loss

	Carrying amount	Proportion	Allocation of loss	Adjusted carrying amount
Unit A	$100	100/604 × 20	$ 3	$ 97
Unit B	120	120/604 × 20	4	116
Unit C	197	197/604 × 20	6	191
Head office	137	137/604 × 20	5	132
Research centre	50	50/604 × 20	2	48
	$604		$20	

Journal entry for impairment loss

The journal entry for the impairment loss recognises the reduction in each of the assets. As the composition of the assets is not detailed in this question, the credit adjustments are made against the asset accounts. They could also have been made against an accumulated depreciation and impairment losses account. Obviously if the composition of each of the assets of each unit had been given, the impairment loss would have been allocated to specific assets rather than assets as a total category as in the solution here.

Impairment Loss	Dr	66	
Assets – Unit A	Cr		3
Assets – Unit B	Cr		34
Assets – Unit C	Cr		9
Assets – Head Office	Cr		18
Assets – Research Facility	Cr		2

SUMMARY

It is important that users of financial statements can rely on the information provided. In particular they need to be assured that the assets in the statement of financial position are not stated at amounts greater than an entity could expect to recover from those assets. It needs to be recognised that an entity can obtain cash flows from two sources in relation to any asset: (1) by using the asset or (2) by selling the asset. One of these involves an ongoing use of the asset whereas the other relates to an immediate sale of the asset. Any test of the carrying amounts of assets against their recoverable amounts must take both sources of cash flows into account.

For an entity to conduct an impairment test, there must be indications of impairment. Entities then need to continuously obtain information about factors that may indicate that assets are impaired. These sources of information may consist of an analysis of economic factors external to the organisation, such as actions of competitors, or economic factors within the entity itself, such as the performance of the entity's property, plant and equipment over time. When there are indications of impairment, an entity conducts an impairment test, comparing the carrying amounts of relevant assets and their recoverable amounts. The latter involves measurement of value in use and fair value less costs to sell.

In many cases, single assets do not produce cash flows for the entity. Instead, the assets of the entity are allocated to units, called cash-generating units, as each unit produces independent cash flows for an entity. In such cases, impairment tests are conducted on the cash-generating units, rather than on individual assets. Where an impairment loss occurs, the loss must be allocated across the assets of the unit, with goodwill being the first asset affected. Where corporate assets, such as research facilities exist, it may be necessary to combine a number of cash-generating units together in order to test for impairment of the corporate asset.

Having written down assets as a result of impairment tests, entities may see potential improvement in the recoverable amounts of assets by observing the same indicators used for detecting impairment losses. In such cases, where the recoverable amounts of assets have increased, impairment losses may be reversed, subject to constraints. Impairment losses relating to goodwill, however, can never be reversed.

Discussion questions

1. What is an impairment test?
2. Why is an impairment test considered necessary?
3. When should an entity conduct an impairment test?
4. What are some external indicators of impairment.
5. What are some internal indicators of impairment?
6. What is meant by recoverable amount?
7. How is an impairment loss calculated in relation to a single asset accounted for?
8. What are the limits to which an asset can be written down in relation to impairment losses?

9. What is a cash-generating unit?
10. How are impairment losses accounted for in relation to cash-generating units?
11. Are there limits in adjusting assets within a cash-generating unit when impairment losses occur?
12. How is goodwill tested for impairment?
13. What is a corporate asset?
14. How are corporate assets tested for impairment?
15. When can an entity reverse past impairment losses?
16. What are the steps involved in reversing an impairment loss?
17. Fresh Milk Ltd owns a large number of dairy farms in Queensland. It has a number of factories that are used to produce milk products that are then sent to other factories to be converted into milk-based products such as yoghurt and custard. In applying IAS 36 *Impairment of Assets*, the accountant for Fresh Milk Ltd is concerned about correctly identifying the cash-generating units (CGUs) for the company, and has sought your advice on such questions as to whether the milk production section is a separate CGU even though the company does not sell milk directly to other parties, or whether it should be included in the milk-based products CGU.

    Required
    Write a report to the accountant of Fresh Milk Ltd, including the following:
    1. Define a CGU.
    2. Explain why impairment testing requires the use of CGUs, rather than being based on single assets.
    3. Explain the factors that the accountant should consider in determining the CGUs for Fresh Milk Ltd.

18. At 30 June 2010, Cyan Ltd is considering undertaking an impairment test. Having only recently adopted the international accounting standards, the management of Cyan Ltd seeks your advice in relation to this test under IAS 36 *Impairment of Assets*.

    Required
    Write a report to management, specifically explaining:
    1. the purpose of the impairment test
    2. how the existence of goodwill will affect the impairment test
    3. the basic steps to be followed in applying the impairment test.

19. In setting up its systems to apply IAS 36 *Impairment of Assets*, management of Khaki Ltd wants to know how often the company needs to apply an impairment test on its assets, and what information it needs to generate to determine whether a test is needed.

    Required
    Prepare a response to management.

20. The Taupe City Council contracts out the bus routes in Taupe to various subcontractors based on a tender arrangement. Some routes, such as the Express to City routes, are profitable, while others, such as those collecting schoolchildren from remote areas, are unprofitable. As a result, the city council requires tenderers to take a package of routes, some profitable, some less so. The Red Bus Company has won the contract to operate its buses with a package of five separate routes, one of which operates at a significant loss. Specific buses are allocated by the Red Bus Company to each route, and cash flows can be isolated to each route because drivers and takings are specific to each route.

    Required
    Discuss the determination of cash-generating units for the Red Bus Company.

21. Read the comments made by the European Financial Reporting Advisory Group (EFRAG) in its response, dated 4 April 2003 (pp. 4–5), to the IASB on the proposed amendments to IAS 36.

Impairment test

The proposed impairment test does not distinguish between acquired goodwill and pre-existing goodwill of the acquirer nor between acquired goodwill and goodwill internally generated after the combination. This results in 'cushions', so avoiding recognition of real impairment losses of goodwill in certain situations when the impairment test is performed. We believe that this undermines the reliability of the information obtained.

The Board claims that there seems to be no alternative design for the impairment test to avoid this. This may be true for the replacement of acquired goodwill by self-generated goodwill of the acquired business but we believe a stronger effort should be made to eliminate the cushion provided by the pre-acquisition self-generated goodwill of the acquirer. The current UK accounting standard FRS 11 *Impairment of Fixed Assets and Goodwill* attempts to make such a distinction.

We urge the Board to delete the second step of the impairment test (paragraph 86). We believe that the second step, which measures the amount of goodwill impairment by comparing its carrying amount with its implied value, is costly and does not improve the quality of the information.

In our view it suffices to allocate the identified impairment firstly to goodwill and then to intangible assets with indefinite useful lives that are part of the cash-generating unit and any remainder to other assets on a pro rata basis.

Required

Evaluate the comments made by EFRAG.

22. Read the following comments made by Deloitte Touche Tohmatsu (4 April 2003, p. 7) on the proposed amendments to IAS 36:

We agree with the conclusion that goodwill acquired in a business combination should be recognised as an asset. With regard to the accounting for goodwill after initial recognition, we generally agree with the Board's proposal. However, we note that there may be circumstances where goodwill has a finite life. For example, this may be the case when an entity has a specified life. In certain jurisdictions such as the People's Republic of China (the PRC), foreign investment is made by means of certain legal structures that expire after a specified number of years. At the end of the agreed period, the assets will revert to the PRC partner. In such circumstances, any goodwill will have an implied value of zero at the end of the entity's life.

Consequently, we believe that, in accounting for goodwill after initial recognition, there should be a rebuttable presumption that goodwill has an indefinite life and, therefore, accounted for at cost less any accumulated impairment losses. However, in those cases where that presumption is rebutted and sufficient persuasive evidence exists indicating that goodwill has a finite life, we believe that a method of systematic amortisation is preferable to 'impairment only' accounting. In such cases, we believe that goodwill, consistently with other intangible assets that have a finite life, should be amortised and tested for impairment when an indicator exists. The impairment test applied to goodwill with a definite life should be the same test as goodwill with an indefinite life.

Required

Evaluate the comments made by Deloitte Touche Tohmatsu.

23. Burger Queen is a chain of fast-food restaurants — most reasonably sized towns in the country have a Burger Queen outlet. The key claim to fame of the Burger Queen restaurants is that their fried chips are extra crunchy. Also, to ensure that there is a consistent standard of food and service across the country, the management of the chain of restaurants conducts spot checks on restaurants. Failure to provide the high standard expected by Burger Queen management can mean that the franchise to a particular location can be taken away from the franchisee. Burger Queen management is responsible for the television advertising across the country as well as the marketing program, including the special deals that may be available at any particular time.

Each restaurant is responsible for its own sales, cooking of food, training of staff, and general matters such as cleanliness of the store. However, all material used in the making of the burgers and other items sold are provided at a given cost from the central management, which can thereby control the quality and the price.

Required

Identify the cash-generating unit(s) in this scenario. Give reasons for your conclusions.

24. Marla Macalister is in the business of making rubber tubing that comes in all sorts of sizes and shapes. Marla has established three factories in the north, south and east parts of the city. Each factory has a large machine that can be adjusted to produce all the varieties of tubing that Marla sells. Each machine is capable of producing around 100 000 metres of tubing a week, depending on diameter and shape. Marla's current sales amount to about 250 000 metres a week. Each factory is never worked to full capacity. However, sales are sufficiently high that Marla cannot afford to shut one of the factories.

In order to satisfy customer demand as quickly as possible, all orders are directed to Marla, who allocates the jobs to the various factories depending on the current workload of each factory. This also ensures that efficient runs of particular types of tubing can be done at the same time. Each factory is managed individually in terms of maintenance of the machines, the hiring of labour and the packaging and delivery of the finished product.

Required

Identify the cash-generating unit(s) in this scenario. Give reasons for your conclusions.

25. Fad Furniture Ltd has three separate operating divisions. The first, the timber division, is in charge of producing milled timber. This division manages a number of timber plantations and timber mills from which the finished timber is produced. The majority of the timber is sold, at an internal transfer price, to the second area of operations in Fad Furniture, the parts division. Any excess timber is sold to external parties. The parts division is responsible for turning the timber into parts for the making of timber furniture, both indoor and outdoor. These parts are suitable only for the manufacture of the furniture produced by Fad Furniture. The parts are then transferred at internal transfer prices to the third area of operations, the furniture division. This division assembles the furniture and delivers it to the various outlets that retail Fad Furniture's products.

Required

1. Identify the cash-generating unit(s) in this scenario, giving reasons for your conclusions.
2. Would the determination of the cash-generating units be affected if the parts division was also responsible for kit furniture, where the parts are made available to customers for self-assembly?

26. Management is assessing the future cash flows in relation to an entity's assets, and considers that there are two possible scenarios for future cash flows. The first, for which there is a 70% probability of occurrence, would provide future cash flows of $5 million. The second, which has a probability of occurrence of 30%, would provide future cash flows of $8 million. Management has decided that the calculation of value in use should be based on the most likely scenario, namely the one that will produce cash flows of $5 million.

Required

Evaluate management's decision.

27. Gold Enterprises Ltd acquired a building in which to conduct its operations at a cost of $10 million. The building generates no cash flows on its own and is considered a part of the cash-generating unit, which is the firm as a whole. Since the building was acquired, the value of inner-city properties has declined owing to an overabundance of office space and the downturn in the economy. The company would receive only $8 million dollars if it decided to sell the building now. However, the company believes the building is serving its purpose and the profits are high, so there is no current intention of selling the building.

Required

Discuss whether the building should be written down to $8 million. Provide any journal entries necessary.

28. Brown Ltd acquired a network facility for its administration section on 1 July 2008. The network facility cost $550 000 and was depreciated using a straight-line method over a

5-year period, with a residual value of $50 000. On 30 June 2010, the company assessed the current market value of the facility given that there was an active market for such facilities as many companies used a similar network. The value was determined to be $300 000.

Required

Discuss whether the network facility asset is impaired and whether it should be written down to $300 000. Provide any journal entries necessary.

STAR RATING

★ BASIC

★★ MODERATE

★★★ DIFFICULT

Exercises

Exercise 12.1

IMPAIRMENT LOSS

★ Bronze Ltd has determined that its fine china division is a cash-generating unit. The carrying amounts of the assets at 30 June 2009 are as follows:

Factory	$210 000
Land	150 000
Equipment	120 000
Inventory	60 000

Bronze Ltd calculated the value in use of the division to be $510 000.

Required

Provide the journal entry(ies) for the impairment loss, assuming that the fair value less costs to sell of the land are (a) $140 000 and (b) $145 000.

Exercise 12.2

IMPAIRMENT LOSS, GOODWILL

★ On 1 January 2008, Silver Ltd acquired all the assets and liabilities of Emerald Ltd. Emerald Ltd has a number of operating divisions, including one whose major industry is the manufacture of toy trains, particularly those of historical significance. The toy trains division is regarded as a cash-generating unit. In paying $2 million for the net assets of Emerald Ltd, Silver Ltd calculated that it had acquired goodwill of $240 000. The goodwill was allocated to each of the divisions, and the assets and liabilities acquired measured at fair value at acquisition date.

At 31 December 2010, the carrying amounts of the assets of the toy train division were:

Factory	$250 000
Inventory	150 000
Brand — 'Froggy'	50 000
Goodwill	50 000

There is a declining interest in toy trains because of the aggressive marketing of computer-based toys, so the management of Silver Ltd measured the value in use of the toy train division at 31 December 2010, determining it to be $423 000.

Required

Prepare the journal entries to account for the impairment loss at 31 December 2010.

Exercise 12.3

IMPAIRMENT LOSS, GOODWILL, PARTLY OWNED SUBSIDIARY

★ Olive Ltd acquired 60% of the issued shares of Claret Ltd on 1 January 2010 for $426 000. At this date, the net fair value of the identifiable assets and liabilities of Claret Ltd was $660 000.

At 31 December 2010, the tangible assets and liabilities of Claret Ltd as included in the consolidated financial statements of Olive Ltd were as follows:

Property, plant and equipment	$ 863 000
Accumulated depreciation	(120 000)
	743 000
Inventory	55 000
Cash	22 000
	820 000
Liabilities	(50 000)
	$ 770 000

Goodwill had not been written down over the year.

In conducting an impairment test on Claret Ltd as a cash-generating unit, Olive Ltd assessed the recoverable amount of Claret Ltd to be $800 000.

Required

1. Explain how the impairment loss in relation to Claret Ltd should be allocated. Prepare journal entry(ies) in relation to the assets of Claret Ltd at 31 December 2010 as a result of the impairment test.
2. Explain the accounting for the impairment (if any) if the recoverable amount was $860 000.

Exercise 12.4 IMPAIRMENT LOSS FOR A CASH-GENERATING UNIT, REVERSAL OF IMPAIRMENT LOSS

★★ One of the cash-generating units of Lemon Ltd is associated with the manufacture of wine barrels. At 30 June 2009, Lemon Ltd believed, based on an analysis of economic indicators, that the assets of the unit were impaired. The carrying amounts of the assets and liabilities of the unit at 30 June 2009 were:

Buildings	$ 420 000
Accumulated depreciation – buildings*	(180 000)
Factory machinery	220 000
Accumulated depreciation – machinery**	(40 000)
Goodwill	15 000
Inventory	80 000
Receivables	40 000
Allowance for doubtful debts	(5 000)
Cash	20 000
Accounts payable	30 000
Loans	20 000

*Depreciated at $60 000 p.a.
**Depreciated at $45 000 p.a.

Lemon Ltd determined the value in use of the unit to be $535 000. The receivables were considered to be collectable, except those considered doubtful. The company allocated the impairment loss in accordance with IAS 36.

During the 2009–10 period, Lemon Ltd increased the depreciation charge on buildings to $65 000 p.a., and to $50 000 p.a. for factory machinery. The inventory on hand at 1 July 2009 was sold by the end of the year. At 30 June 2010, Lemon Ltd, because of a return in the market to the use of traditional barrels for wines and an increase in wine production, assessed the recoverable amount of the cash-generating unit to be $30 000 greater than the carrying amount of the unit. As a result, Lemon Ltd recognised a reversal of the impairment loss.

Required

1. Prepare the journal entries for Lemon Ltd at 30 June 2009 and 2010.
2. What differences would arise in relation to the answer in requirement A if the recoverable amount at 30 June 2010 was $20 000 greater than the carrying amount of the unit?
3. If the recoverable amount of the buildings at 30 June 2010 was $175 000, how would this change the answer to requirement B?

Exercise 12.5 ★★

ALLOCATION OF CORPORATE ASSETS

Rose Ltd has three cash-generating units, Amber Division, Purple Division and Cerise Division. The head office is in the city, and the infrastructure for the divisions is located outside the city centre. Because of the potential for the company to have problems of an environmental nature or in relation to social justice, particularly with its mix of employees, Rose Ltd has recently established a social responsibility centre (SRC), which interacts with the divisions, generating information and statistics for the production of a triple-bottom-line social responsibility report.

At 30 June 2010, the net assets relating to each of the divisions as well as the headquarters section and the SRC were as follows:

	Amber Division	Purple Division	Cerise Division	Head office	SRC
Land	$ 120 000	$ 140 000	$ 80 000	$10 000	$ 5 000
Plant and equipment	420 000	310 000	270 000	40 000	15 000
Accumulated depreciation	(120 000)	(100 000)	(80 000)	(5 000)	(4 000)
Inventories	150 000	110 000	100 000	0	0
Accounts receivable	90 000	80 000	50 000	0	0
	660 000	540 000	420 000	45 000	16 000
Liabilities	60 000	50 000	50 000	0	0
Net assets	$ 600 000	$ 490 000	$370 000	$45 000	$16 000

Rose Ltd believes that the corporation's headquarters supplies approximately equal service to the three divisions, and an immaterial amount to the SRC. Because the SRC has been established only recently, it is not possible at this stage to allocate the assets of the SRC to the three divisions. Economic indicators suggest that the company's assets may have been impaired, so management has determined the value in use of each of the divisions — the head office and the SRC do not generate cash inflows. The value in use of the three divisions were calculated to be:

Amber Division	$720 000
Purple Division	500 000
Cerise Division	400 000

Required

Determine how Rose Ltd should account for any impairment loss to the entity.

Exercise 12.6 ★★

ALLOCATION OF CORPORATE ASSETS AND GOODWILL

Cherry Ltd acquired all the assets and liabilities of Hazel Ltd on 1 January 2010. Hazel Ltd's activities were run through three separate businesses, namely the Sandstone Unit, the Sapphire Unit and the Silverton Unit. These units are separate cash-generating units. Cherry Ltd allowed unit managers to effectively operate each of the units, but certain central activities were run through the corporate office. Each unit was allocated a share of the goodwill acquired, as well as a share of the corporate office.

At 31 December 2010, the assets allocated to each unit were as follows:

	Sandstone	Sapphire	Silverton
Factory	$ 820	$ 750	$ 460
Accumulated depreciation	(420)	(380)	(340)
Land	200*	300**	150*
Equipment	300	410	560
Accumulated depreciation	(60)	(320)	(310)
Inventory	120	80	100*
Goodwill	40	50	30
Corporate property	200	150	120

* These assets have carrying amounts less than fair value less costs to sell.
** This asset has a fair value less costs to sell of $293.

Cherry Ltd determined the value in use of each of the business units at 31 December 2010:

Sandstone	$1 170
Sapphire	900
Silverton	800

Required
Determine how Cherry Ltd should allocate any impairment loss at 31 December 2010.

Exercise 12.7 ★★

IMPAIRMENT, TWO CASH-GENERATING UNITS

Blue Ltd has two divisions, Jade and White. Each of these is regarded as a separate cash-generating unit.

At 31 December 2009, the carrying amounts of the assets of the two divisions were:

	Jade	White
Plant	$1 500	$1 200
Accumulated depreciation	(650)	(375)
Patent	240	
Inventory	54	75
Receivables	75	82
Goodwill	25	20

The receivables were regarded as collectable, and the inventory's fair value less costs to sell was equal to its carrying amount. The patent had a fair value less costs to sell of $220. The plant at Jade was depreciated at $300 p.a., and that at White was depreciated at $250 p.a.

Blue Ltd undertook impairment testing at 31 December 2009, and determined the value in use of the two divisions to be:

Jade	$1 044
White	990

As a result, management increased the depreciation of the Jade plant from $300 to $350 p.a. for the year 2009.

By 31 December 2010, the performance in both divisions had improved, and the carrying amounts of the assets of both divisions and their recoverable amounts were as follows:

	Jade	White
Carrying amount	$1 322	$1 433
Recoverable amount	1 502	1 520

Required
Determine how Blue Ltd should account for the results of the impairment tests at both 31 December 2009 and 31 December 2010.

Exercise 12.8 ★★

CORPORATE ASSETS

Black Ltd recently conducted an impairment test on the company. It determined that it had two cash-generating units, Division One and Division Two. Both divisions were considered to be impaired, with Division One having an impairment loss of $25 000 and Division Two having an impairment loss of $30 000. These losses were allocated to the assets of the divisions in accordance with IAS 36 *Impairment of Assets*, with the assets and liabilities of the divisions after the allocation being recorded as follows:

	Division One	Division Two
Cash	$ 5 000	$ 8 000
Inventory	30 000	40 000
Receivables	20 000	8 000
Plant	320 000	300 000
Accumulated depreciation	(120 000)	(120 000)
	Division One	**Division Two**
Land	80 000	50 000
Buildings	110 000	100 000
Accumulated depreciation	(40 000)	(60 000)
Furniture & fittings	40 000	30 000
Accumulated depreciation	(15 000)	(10 000)
Total assets	430 000	346 000
Provisions	20 000	40 000
Borrowings	30 000	66 000
Total liabilities	50 000	106 000
Net assets	$ 380 000	$ 240 000

Black Ltd also recorded goodwill of $14 000 (net of accumulated impairment losses of $12 000) and had corporate assets consisting of a head office building carried at $150 000 (net of depreciation of $50 000) and furniture and fittings of $80 000 (net of depreciation of $20 000).

Black Ltd determined that the value in use of the entity's assets was $950 000.

The management of Black Ltd then completed the accounting for impairment losses. The receivables in both divisions were considered to be collectable.

Required

Prepare a table of the assets and liabilities of Black Ltd, using the headings 'Division One', 'Division Two' and 'Corporate', after the completion of accounting for impairment losses.

Exercise 12.9 ★★

CORPORATE ASSET

Fiery Ltd is a company that is operated through two divisions, namely Green Ltd and Dragon Ltd. These divisions were regarded as separate cash-generating units. The assets of the two divisions at 30 June 2009 were as follows:

	Green Ltd	Dragon Ltd
Land	$100 000	$ 64 000
Plant	280 000	145 000
Accumulated depreciation	(60 000)	(30 000)
Equipment	160 000	220 000
Accumulated depreciation	(40 000)	(20 000)
Inventory	60 000	36 000
Goodwill	200 000	15 000
	$520 000	$430 000

Fiery Ltd had a corporate headquarters carried at an amount of $100 000. This asset could not be allocated on a reasonable basis to the cash-generating units.

At 30 June 2009 there were indications that the assets of the company may be impaired. The company calculated the recoverable amounts to be as follows:

Fiery Ltd	$973 000
Green Ltd	$478 000
Dragon Ltd	$420 000

The inventory had fair values less costs to sell greater than the current carrying amounts. The land held by Green Ltd had fair value less costs to sell of $97 000.

Required
Prepare the journal entries at 30 June 2009 to record the accounting for the impairment losses.

Exercise 12.10 ★★

REVERSAL OF IMPAIRMENT LOSSES

At 30 June 2009, Yellow Ltd reported the following assets:

Land	$ 50 000
Plant	250 000
Accumulated depreciation	(50 000)
Goodwill	8 000
Inventory	40 000
Cash	2 000

All assets are measured using the cost model.

At 30 June 2009, the recoverable amount of the entity, considered to be a single cash-generating unit, was $272 000.

For the period ending 30 June 2010, the depreciation charge on plant was $18 400. If the plant had not been impaired the charge would have been $25 000.

At 30 June 2010, the recoverable amount of the entity was calculated to be $13 000 greater than the carrying amount of the assets of the entity. As a result, Yellow Ltd recognised a reversal of the previous year's impairment loss.

Required
Prepare the journal entries relating to impairment at 30 June 2009 and 2010.

Problems

Problem 12.1 ★★★

ALLOCATION OF CORPORATE ASSET AND GOODWILL

Indigo Ltd has two cash-generating units, Division One and Division Two. At 30 June 2010, the net assets of the two divisions were as follows:

	Division One	Division Two
Cash	$ 12 000	$ 8 000
Inventory	30 000	40 000
Receivables	20 000	8 000
Plant	320 000	0
Accumulated depreciation (Plant)	(120 000)	0
Land	90 000	150 000
Buildings	110 000	140 000
Accumulated depreciation (Buildings)	(40 000)	(60 000)
Furniture & fittings	0	30 000
Accumulated depreciation (Furniture & fittings)	0	(10 000)
Total assets	422 000	306 000
Provisions	20 000	40 000
Borrowings	30 000	66 000
Total liabilities	50 000	106 000
Net assets	$372 000	$200 000

Additional information regarding the divisions' assets:

- the receivables of both divisions were considered to be collectable
- Division Two's land had a fair value less costs to sell of $135 000 at 30 June 2010.

At 30 June 2010 Indigo Ltd also had the following corporate assets, which Perth's management decided to allocate equally to the two divisions:

- goodwill of $14 000
- a head office building with a carrying amount of $160 000 (net of $50 000 accumulated depreciation).

Indigo Ltd's management conducted impairment testing on the company's assets at 30 June 2010 and determined that Division One's value in use was $415 000 and Division Two's value in use was $310 000.

Required

Prepare the journal entries required at 30 June 2010 to account for any impairment losses.

Problem 12.2 ★★★

CORPORATE ASSETS, ALLOCATED AND UNALLOCATED

Orange Ltd has three divisions, Green, Navy and Ruby, which operate independently of each other to produce milk products. The company has a headquarters and a research centre located in Aqua, with the divisions located throughout Australia. The research centre interacts with all the divisions to assist in the improvement of the manufacturing process and the quality of the products manufactured by the entity.

There is not as yet any basis on which to determine how the work of the research centre will be allocated to each of the three divisions, as this will depend on priorities of the company overall and issues that arise in each division. The company headquarters provides approximately equal services to each of the divisions, but an immaterial amount to the research centre.

Neither the headquarters nor the research centre generates cash inflows.

On 30 June 2010, the net assets of Orange Ltd were as follows:

	Green	Navy	Ruby	Head office	Research centre
Land	440 000	280 000	160 000	110 000	67 000
Plant & equipment	840 000	620 000	540 000	80 000	45 000
Accumulated depreciation	(240 000)	(200 000)	(160 000)	(10 000)	(12 000)
Inventories	240 000	180 000	140 000	0	0
Accounts receivable	120 000	100 000	60 000	0	0
	1 400 000	980 000	740 000	180 000	100 000
Liabilities	120 000	100 000	100 000	0	0
Net assets	1 280 000	880 000	640 000	180 000	100 000

Management of Orange Ltd believes there are economic indicators to suggest that the company's assets may have been impaired. Accordingly, they have had value in use assessed for each of the divisions:

Green	$1 550 000
Navy	1 000 000
Ruby	750 000

The land held by Green Ltd was measured at fair value using the revaluation model because of the specialised nature of the land. At 30 June 2010, the fair value was $440 000. The land held by Navy Ltd was measured at cost, and had a fair value less costs to sell of $270 264 at 30 June 2010.

Required

Determine how Orange Ltd should account for any impairment of the entity. Justify your decisions and complete any required journal entries.

Problem 12.3 IMPAIRMENT LOSS

★★★ Cherry Ltd prepared the following draft statement of financial position at 30 June 2010:

Cash	$ 5 000	Share capital	$1 000 000
Receivables	15 000	Retained earnings	280 000
Land (at fair value 1/7/09)	160 000	General reserve	120 000
Company headquarters	1 000 000		1 400 000
Accumulated depreciation	(180 000)	Long-term loans	400 000
Factories	1 790 000	Provisions	40 000
Accumulated depreciation	(910 000)	Other liabilities	160 000
Goodwill	60 000		600 000
Accumulated impairment losses	(40 000)		
Intangibles	150 000		
Accumulated amortisation	(50 000)		
Total assets	2 000 000	Equity and liabilities	2 000 000

At the end of the reporting period, after undertaking an analysis, management determined that it was probable that the assets of the entity were impaired. Management conducted an impairment test, determining that the recoverable amount for the entity's assets was $1 820 000. The whole entity was regarded as a cash-generating unit.

Land is measured by Cherry Ltd at fair value, while all other assets are accounted for by the cost model. At 30 June 2010, the fair value of the land was determined to be $150 000. The land had previously been revalued upwards by $20 000. The tax rate is 30%.

Required

(*Show all workings.*)

1. Prepare the journal entries required on 30 June 2010 in relation to the measurement of the assets of Cherry Ltd.
2. Assume that, as the result of the allocation of the impairment loss, the factories were to be written down to $800 000. If the fair value less costs to sell of the factories was determined to be $750 000, outline the adjustments, if any, that would need to be made to the journal entries you prepared in part A of this question, and explain why adjustments are or are not required.

References

Deloitte Touche Tohmatsu 2003, Comments of Deloitte Touche Tohmatsu on Exposure Draft 3 *Business Combinations*, 4 April, p. 7, www.iasplus.com.

European Financial Reporting Advisory Group 2003, Comments of EFRAG on Exposure Draft 3 *Business Combinations*, 4 April, p. 10, www.iasplus.com.

FASB 2003, Summary of Comment Letters, Exposure Draft (Revised) *Business Combinations and Intangible Assets — Accounting for Goodwill*, www.iasb.org.

Nokia 2007, *Nokia in 2007*, Nokia Corporation, Finland, www.nokia.com.

— 2006, *Nokia in 2006*, Nokia Corporation, Finland, www.nokia.com.

Wesfarmers 2008, *2008 annual report*, Wesfarmers Limited, www.wesfarmers.com.au.

13 Leases

ACCOUNTING STANDARDS IN FOCUS

IAS 17 *Leases*

LEARNING OBJECTIVES

When you have studied this chapter, you should be able to:

- discuss the characteristics of a lease
- explain the difference between a finance lease and an operating lease
- understand and apply the guidance necessary to classify leases
- discuss the incentives to misclassify leases
- account for finance leases from the perspective of a lessee
- account for finance leases from the perspective of a lessor
- account for finance leases by manufacturer or dealer lessors
- account for operating leases from the perspective of both lessors and lessees
- recognise and account for sale and leaseback transactions
- discuss possible future changes to lease accounting.

The rapid growth of leasing as a means of gaining access to the economic benefits embodied in assets during the 1970s led to a concern among standard setters worldwide that the credibility of financial reports was compromised by extensive use of such 'off-balance-sheet' arrangements. Accordingly, the 1980s saw the issue of leasing standards by both international and national standard-setting bodies. These standards adopted similar accounting treatments based on the premise that, when a lease transfers substantially all of the risks and rewards incidental to ownership to the lessee, that lease is in substance equivalent to the acquisition of an asset on credit by the lessee, and to a sale or financing by the lessor. The mandatory recognition of the asset/liability relating to the lease is justified by two arguments.

First, IAS 17 paragraph 21 states:

> Although the legal form of a lease agreement is that the lessee may acquire no legal title to the leased asset, in the case of finance leases the substance and financial reality are that the lessee acquires the economic benefits of the use of the leased asset for the major part of its economic life in return for entering into an obligation to pay for that right an amount approximating, at the inception of the lease, the fair value of the asset and the related finance charge.

Second, paragraph 22 states:

> If such lease transactions are not reflected in the lessee's balance sheet [statement of financial position], the economic resources and the level of obligations of an entity are understated, thereby distorting financial ratios.

Interestingly, these justifications for the recognition of lease assets and liabilities make no reference to the *Framework* definitions and recognition criteria, but concentrate on the substance of the exchange of benefits and the reliability of financial information. This rationale seems to view the lease transaction as the quasi-purchase of an asset, in the sense that it records the acquisition of an asset even though no transfer of legal title takes place.

Apart from some minor amendments, these standards remained substantially unchanged until 1996. Concern that this accounting treatment was not compatible with the conceptual frameworks developed during the 1980s led to the publication in 1996 of a G4+1 special report authored by Warren McGregor and entitled *Accounting for leases: a new approach — recognition by lessees of assets and liabilities arising under lease contracts*. (G4+1 was a grouping of national accounting regulators. Initial membership consisted of standard setters from the United States, Canada, Australia and Great Britain, with the '+1' component being an IASB representative.) In preparing the 'stable platform' of accounting standards in 2004, the IASB made no major changes to IAS 17 *Leases*. The Joint International Working Group on Leasing was set up on 19 July 2006 as a combined project of the IASB and the US Financial Accounting Standards Board to review the current accounting standard.

13.1 WHAT IS A LEASE?

Paragraph 4 of IAS 17 defines a lease as:

> an agreement whereby the lessor conveys to the lessee in return for a payment or series of payments the right to use an asset for an agreed period of time.

Thus, under a lease agreement the lessee acquires, not the asset itself, but the *right* to use the asset for a set time. Leased assets range from physical assets such as land, plant and vehicles, through to intangible assets such as patents, copyright and mineral rights. Lease agreements may also result in the eventual transfer of ownership from lessor to lessee. For example, under a hire purchase agreement, the lessee will use the asset while paying for its acquisition. The agreed period of time may vary from a short period, such as the daily hire of a motor vehicle, to a longer period, such as the rental of office space by a company. The key feature of leases is the existence of an asset owned by one party (the lessor) but used, for some or all of its economic life, by another party (the lessee).

Service agreements relating to the provision of services, such as cleaning or maintenance, between two parties are not regarded as leases because the contract does not involve the use of an asset. These agreements are regarded as executory contracts; that is, both parties are still to perform to an equal degree the actions required by the contract. Thus, each party is regarded as having a right and obligation to participate in a future exchange or, alternatively, to compensate or be compensated for the consequences of not doing so. A cleaning contract entitles an entity to receive cleaning services on a regular basis and creates an obligation to pay for those services after they have been received. The key issue is the performance of the service. Until the cleaning services are delivered, the contract is merely an exchange of promises, not of future economic benefits. The existence of a non-cancellable service agreement or one that includes significant penalties for non-performance may, however, result in the service recipient acquiring control over future economic benefits (the right to receive cleaning services) that are likely to be delivered and can be reliably measured — in other words, an asset.

Accounting for leases is complicated by the fact that there are two parties involved — the lessor and the lessee.

13.1.1 Scope of application of IAS 17

Paragraph 2 of IAS 17 excludes the following types of leases from the scope of the accounting standard:

- lease agreements to explore for or use minerals, oil, natural gas and similar non-regenerative resources
- licensing agreements for such items as motion picture films, video recordings, plays, manuscripts, patents and copyrights.

No explanation is given for the exclusion of resource exploitation rights and licensing agreements, which means that the standard applies only to leases for assets with physical substance. Ironically, paragraph 3 states that the standard 'applies to agreements that transfer the right to use assets'. An agreement allowing a licensee to use a patented process provides future economic benefits to that licensee and meets the *Framework*'s definition of an asset in just the same way as a motor vehicle lease. The exclusion of these agreements from the scope of the standard is difficult to justify. Presumably, the expectation is that accounting standards on extractive industries, self-generating and renewable assets and intangibles will deal with leases of this type.

Additionally, paragraph 2 of IAS 17 prescribes that the standard must not be applied as the basis of measurement for leased investment properties or leased biological assets, because the measurement rules for such assets are contained in IAS 40 *Investment Property* and IAS 41 *Agriculture* respectively.

13.2 CLASSIFICATION OF LEASES

Paragraph 8 of IAS 17 requires both lessees and lessors to classify each lease arrangement as either an *operating lease* or a *finance lease* and to make this classification at the inception of the lease (paragraph 13), which is defined in paragraph 4 as 'the earlier of the date of the lease agreement and the date of commitment by the parties to the principal provisions of the lease'. This classification process is vitally important because the accounting treatment and disclosures prescribed by the standard for each type of lease differ significantly.

IAS 17 paragraph 4 defines a finance lease as:

> a lease that transfers substantially all the risks and rewards incidental to ownership of an asset. Title may or may not eventually be transferred.

An operating lease is simply defined as:

> a lease other than a finance lease.

The key criterion of a finance lease is the transfer of substantially all the risks and rewards without a transfer of ownership. The classification process therefore consists of three steps. Firstly, the potential rewards and potential risks associated with the asset must be identified. Secondly, the lease agreement must be analysed to determine what rewards and risks are transferred from the lessor to the lessee. Thirdly, an assessment must be made as to whether the risks and rewards associated with the asset have been substantially passed to the lessee.

The *risks* of ownership include:

- unsatisfactory performance, with the asset unable to provide benefits or service at the expected level or quality
- obsolescence, particularly with regard to the development of more technically advanced items
- idle capacity
- decline in residual value or losses on eventual sale of the asset
- uninsured damage and condemnation of the asset.

The *rewards* include:

- any benefits obtained from using the asset to provide benefit or service to the entity
- appreciation in residual value or gains on the eventual sale of the asset.

The risks and rewards relating to movements in realisable value are the most difficult to transfer without transferring the title. If the leased asset is to be returned to the lessor, then the risk of an adverse movement in realisable value has not been transferred unless the lessee guarantees some or all of the value of the asset at the end of the lease term.

IAS 17 does not define the term 'substantially' or prescribe classification criteria. This is left as a judgement call. By omitting quantitative examples, the IASB has placed the classification decision back in the hands of managers, who must decide what is 'substantial' for their entity and particular circumstances. The disadvantage of this approach is that similar or even identical lease agreements may be classified differently because of varying interpretations of what the terms 'major part' and 'substantially all' mean.

13.3 CLASSIFICATION GUIDANCE

To help account preparers in the classification process, paragraphs 10 and 11 of IAS 17 provide the following series of situations that individually or in combination would normally lead to a lease transaction being classified as a finance lease:

- The lease transfers ownership of the asset by the end of the lease term.
- The lessee has the option to purchase the asset at a price that is expected to be sufficiently lower than the fair value at the date the option becomes exercisable for it to be reasonably certain that the option will be exercised.
- The lease term is for the major part of the economic life of the asset even if title is not transferred.
- At the inception of the lease, the present value of the minimum lease payments amounts to substantially all of the fair value of the leased asset.
- The leased assets are of such a specialised nature that only the lessee can use them without major modification.
- If the lessee can cancel the lease, the lessor's losses associated with the cancellation are borne by the lessee.
- Gains or losses from the fluctuation in the fair value of the residual accrue to the lessee.
- The lessee has the ability to continue the lease for a secondary period at a rental that is substantially less than market rent.

Note that these pointers are guidelines in assessing whether substantially all the risks and rewards are transferred. Each pointer then relates to some measure of risk or reward.

For the purpose of analysis, the guidelines have been restated as five main questions, as represented in figure 13.1, to aid in classifying lease arrangements as either operating leases or finance leases.

Therefore when classifying leases, managers will need to examine three main conditions of the lease agreement:

- cancellability of the lease
- extent of the asset's economic life transferred to the lessee
- present value of minimum lease payments.

13.3.1 Cancellability of the lease

A non-cancellable lease locks both parties into the agreement and ensures that the exchange of risks and rewards will occur. A lease from which both or either party could walk away at any time may result in only a limited transfer of risks and rewards. However, the application

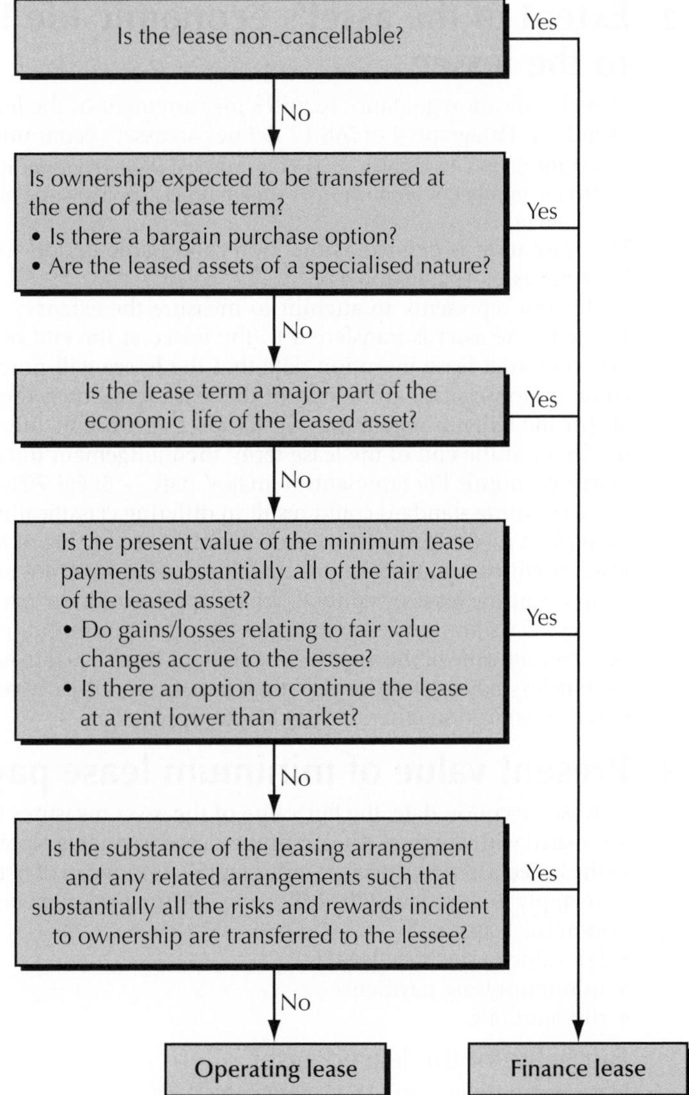

FIGURE 13.1 Guidelines for classifying a lease

of this classification guidance is not a simple cancellable/non-cancellable choice. The definition of a non-cancellable lease provided in paragraph 4 of IAS 17 introduces shades of grey into the equation by deeming cancellable leases with the following characteristics to be 'non-cancellable':

- leases that can be cancelled only upon the occurrence of some remote contingency
- leases that can be cancelled only with the permission of the lessor
- leases where the lessee, upon cancellation, is committed to enter into a further lease for the same or equivalent asset with the same lessor
- leases that provide that the lessee, upon cancellation, incurs a penalty large enough to discourage cancellation in normal circumstances.

A careful examination of the lease agreement is necessary to ensure that cancellable leases are correctly designated.

It would appear that the standard setters have based the assessment of the probability that future risks and rewards have been transferred on whether or not a lease can be cancelled. That is, if a lease can be cancelled at any time without penalty, then there is no certainty that the transfer will be completed.

13.3.2 Extent of the asset's economic life transferred to the lessee

This classification guidance requires measurement of the lease term against the asset's economic useful life. Paragraph 4 of IAS 17 defines an asset's economic life as either:

(a) the period over which an asset is expected to be economically usable by one or more users; or
(b) the number of production or similar units expected to be obtained from the asset by one or more users.

The lease term is defined as the 'non-cancellable period for which the lessee has contracted to lease the asset' (paragraph 4).

This test represents an attempt to measure the extent of the transfer of rewards to the lessee. If title to the asset is transferred to the lessee at the end of the lease, or if there is a reasonable expectation at lease inception date that the lessee will purchase the asset (via a favourable purchase option clause) at the end of the lease term, then the lessee effectively holds the asset for all (or the balance remaining) of the asset's economic life. Where the asset is to be returned to the lessor at the end of the lease term, then judgement must be applied. What percentage of the asset's economic life represents a 'major' part — 60%? 70%? 80%? The lack of clear guidance in the accounting standard could result in differing classifications of similar lease arrangements. For example, a 6-year lease of an asset with an economic life of 8 years could be classified as a finance lease by entity A on the grounds that the lease term is 74% of the asset's economic life, but treated as an operating lease by entity B, which applies an 85% 'cut off'.

These classification criteria assume that the consumption pattern of economic benefits across the economic life of the asset will be straight-line (equal in each year). However, some assets, such as vehicles, may provide more of their benefits in the early years of their economic lives, so a time-based classification criterion may not be appropriate.

13.3.3 Present value of minimum lease payments

At lease inception date, the fair value of the asset measures the present value of the total benefits associated with the asset. The minimum lease payments represent payments for benefits transferred to the lessee. This test therefore indicates the proportion of benefits being paid for by the lessee.

To apply this guidance, the following information must be gathered or determined at the inception of the lease:

- fair value of the leased asset
- minimum lease payments
- discount rate.

Fair value of the leased asset

Fair value is defined in IAS 17 paragraph 4 as:

> The amount for which an asset could be exchanged or a liability settled between knowledgeable, willing parties in an arm's length transaction.

The fair value is normally a market price. However, if the lease relates to specialised equipment constructed or obtained for the lease contract, a fair value may be difficult to obtain. The fair value is regarded as representing the future rewards available to the user of the asset, discounted by the market to allow for the risk that the rewards will not eventuate and for changes in the purchasing power of money over time.

Minimum lease payments

The definition of minimum lease payments contained in paragraph 4 of the standard can be expressed as follows:

Minimum lease payments =	(i)	Payments over the lease term
	+ (ii)	Guaranteed residual value
	+ (iii)	Bargain purchase option
	− (iv)	Contingent rent
	− (v)	Reimbursement of costs paid by the lessor

(i) The lease payments are simply the total amounts payable under the lease agreement.
(ii) The guaranteed residual value is that part of the residual value of the leased asset guaranteed by the lessee or a third party related to the lessee (paragraph 4). The lessor will estimate the

residual value of the leased asset at the end of the lease term based on market conditions at the inception of the lease, and the lessee will guarantee that, when the asset is returned to the lessor, it will realise at least that amount. The guarantee may range from 1% to 100% of the residual value and is a matter for negotiation between lessor and lessee. If the guarantee is provided by a party related to the lessor rather than the lessee, that part of the residual value is regarded, for the purposes of IAS 17, as unguaranteed. Where a lessee guarantees some or all of the residual value of the asset, the lessor has transferred risks associated with movements in the residual value to the lessee.

(iii) A bargain purchase option is a clause in the lease agreement allowing the lessee to purchase the asset at the end of the lease for a preset amount, significantly less than the expected residual value at the end of the lease term; hence, the 'bargain' description. In paragraph 4 of IAS 17, within the definition of minimum lease payments, the option price is described as one:

> that is expected to be sufficiently lower than the fair value at the date the option becomes exercisable for it to be reasonably certain, at the inception of the lease, that the option will be exercised.

Together, amounts (i), (ii) and (iii) above represent the maximum possible payment the lessee is legally obliged to make under the lease agreement, assuming that the guaranteed amount must be paid in full or the purchase option will be exercised.

(iv) Scheduled lease payments may be increased or decreased during the lease term by the occurrence of events specified in the lease agreement. Additional payments arising from such changes are called contingent rent. For example, an agreement to lease a photocopier may specify an additional charge where the number of copies made in a month exceed 100 000; or a motor vehicle lease charge may be decreased if the vehicle is driven only on sealed metropolitan roads. These charges/reductions relate to the use of the leased asset but, as the occurrence of the contingent event is uncertain at lease inception date, they are ignored when calculating the minimum lease payments.

(v) Lease payments may include two components: a charge for using the asset, and a charge to *reimburse the lessor for operating expenses* paid on behalf of the lessee. These operating amounts include insurance, maintenance, consumable supplies, replacement parts and rates. These costs are given the generic title executory costs in this chapter. Amounts paid to reimburse such costs are excluded from minimum lease payments because they do not relate to the value of the asset transferred between lessor and lessee. Payments for such items give rise to equally unperformed contracts.

Discount rate

The minimum lease payments are discounted to present value by applying an appropriate discount rate. Discounting is not necessary if the lease contains a bargain purchase option or a 100% guaranteed residual value because, in both cases, the present value of the minimum lease payments will equal the fair value of the leased asset. Hence, a complete transfer of risks and rewards is deemed to have taken place.

To discount the minimum lease payments, the lessee/lessor will need to ascertain the interest rate implicit in the lease. This is defined in paragraph 4 of IAS 17 as:

> the discount rate that, at the inception of the lease, causes the aggregate present value of:
> (a) the minimum lease payments; and
> (b) the unguaranteed residual value
> to be equal to the sum of:
> (c) the fair value of the leased asset, and
> (d) any initial direct costs of the lessor.

Initial direct costs (IDC) are incremental costs that are directly attributable to negotiating and arranging a lease, except for such costs incurred by manufacturer or dealer lessors (paragraph 4). Examples include commission and legal fees and internal costs, but exclude general overheads such as those incurred by a sales and marketing team (paragraph 38). Initial direct costs incurred by a manufacturer/dealer lessor are excluded from the definition of initial direct costs (paragraph 38) because, according to paragraph 46, the costs of negotiating and arranging a finance lease are 'mainly related to earning the manufacturer's or dealer's selling profit'. How the IASB reached this conclusion is hard to understand. Thus, for the purposes of determining the interest rate implicit in the lease, any initial direct costs incurred by a lessee or a manufacturer/dealer lessor are ignored.

The interest rate implicit in the lease is determined at the inception date of the lease, and this may differ from the commencement date of the lease term, which is a date set by the agreement.

This may lead to the use of a distorted discount rate if the inception date of the lease differs from the commencement of the lease term, as this is the date from which the lessee is entitled to exercise its right to use the leased asset and presumably the date from which the lessee is entitled to receive the lease payments. As (a) and (b) from the paragraph 4 definition equal the future economic rewards obtainable from the asset, the interest rate is that used by the market to determine the fair value. From this comes the notion that the rate is implicit in the terms of the agreement.

If it is not possible to determine the fair value of the asset at the inception of the lease or the residual value at the end of the lease term, then the interest rate implicit in the lease cannot be calculated. In this situation, paragraph 20 of IAS 17 states that the lessee's (rather than the lessor's) incremental borrowing rate should be used to discount the minimum lease payments. The incremental borrowing rate is the rate of interest the lessee would have to pay on a similar lease or, if this is not determinable, the rate that (at the inception of the lease) the lessee would incur to borrow over a similar term, and with a similar security, the funds necessary to purchase the asset (paragraph 4).

Substantial transfer?

The present value of the minimum lease payments can be determined as a percentage of the fair value of the leased asset and a judgement made as to whether this represents the transfer of 'substantially all' of the fair value of the asset from the lessor to the lessee. Again, a lack of quantitative guidelines may result in the inconsistent classification of similar lease arrangements.

ILLUSTRATIVE EXAMPLE 13.1

Classification of a lease agreement

On 30 June 2009, Bahamas Ltd leased a vehicle to Canary Ltd. Bahamas Ltd had purchased the vehicle on that day for its fair value of $89 721. The lease agreement, which cost Bahamas Ltd $1457 to have drawn up, contained the following:

Lease term	4 years
Annual payment, payable in advance on 30 June each year	$23 900
Economic life of vehicle	6 years
Estimated residual value at end of lease term	$15 000
Residual value guaranteed by lessee	$7 500

The lease is cancellable, but cancellation will incur a monetary penalty equivalent to 2 years rental payments. Included in the annual payment is an amount of $1900 to cover reimbursement for the costs of insurance and maintenance paid by the lessor. The directors of Canary Ltd have indicated that they intend to return the asset to Black Ltd at the end of the lease term.

IAS 17 requires the lease to be classified as either a finance lease or an operating lease, based on the extent to which the risks and rewards associated with the vehicle have been effectively transferred from Bahamas Ltd to Canary Ltd.

Is the lease non-cancellable?

The lease agreement is cancellable, but a significant monetary penalty equal to 2 years rental payments will apply. This meets part (d) of the definition of non-cancellable in IAS 17 paragraph 4. Therefore, the lease is deemed to be non-cancellable.

Is ownership expected to be transferred at the end of the lease term?

The expectation is that the asset will be returned to the lessor.

Is the lease term a major part of the economic life of the leased asset?

The lease term is 4 years, which is only 60% of the asset's economic life of 6 years. If expected benefits were receivable evenly over the asset's useful life, it would be doubtful that the lease arrangement is not for the major part of the asset's life.

Is the present value of the minimum lease payments substantially all of the fair value of the leased asset?

Minimum lease payments

The minimum lease payments consist of:

- lease payments net of cost reimbursement — there is an immediate payment of $22 000 (being $23 900 – $1900) and four subsequent payments of $22 000

- contingent rental — which does not arise in this example
- guaranteed residual value — an amount of $7500 is guaranteed at the end of the fourth year.

The unguaranteed residual value is $7500.

Interest rate implicit in the lease

The discount rate is the rate that discounts the minimum lease payments and the unguaranteed residual value to the aggregate of the asset's fair value and any initial indirect costs of the lessor. In this example, the discount rate is the rate that discounts the lessee rental payments and the residual value to $91 178, which is the sum of the asset's fair value at 1 July 2009 of $89 721 and the initial direct costs of $1457 incurred by the lessor. This rate is found by trial and error using present value tables or a financial calculator.

The implicit interest rate in this example is 7%, that is:

Present value = $22 000 + ($22 000 × 2.6243 [T_2 7% 3*y*]) + ($15 000 × 0.7629 [$T_1$ 7% 4*y*])
= $22 000 + $57 735 + $11 443
= $91 178
where *T* = present value table
y = years

Note the following:

- As the first payment is made at the inception of the lease, it is not discounted.
- The discount factor used is an annuity factor based on three equal payments of $22 000 for the next 3 years at 7%.
- The discount factor used is based on a single payment of $15 000 (the residual value) at the end of the lease term in 4 years time at a rate of 7%. The $15 000 comprises $7500 guaranteed by the lessee plus the unguaranteed balance of $7500.

The present value is equal to the fair value (FV) plus initial direct costs (IDC), so the interest rate implicit in the lease is 7%.

Present value of minimum lease payments (PV of MLP)

PV of MLP = $22 000 + ($22 000 × 2.6243 [T_2 7% 3*y*]) + ($7 500 × 0.7629 [$T_1$ 7% 4*y*])
= $22 000 + $57 735 + $5 722
= $85 457

FV + IDC = $91 178

PV/(FV + IDC) = ($85 457/$91 178) × 100%
= 93.7%

Therefore, at a 93.7% level, the present value of the minimum lease payments is considered to be substantially all of the fair value of the leased asset.

Classification of the lease

Application of the guidelines provides mixed signals. The key criterion in classifying leases is whether substantially all the risks and rewards incident to ownership have been transferred. This requires an overall analysis of the situation, but insufficient information is given in the example to do this. The different signals coming from the lease term test and the present value test may be due to the fact that the majority of the rewards will be transferred in the early stages of the life of the asset, as with motor vehicles. This is reflected in the relatively low residual value at the end of the lease term. These mixed signals demonstrate that the guidelines must be used for guidance only and not treated as specific criteria that must be met.

Further, an analysis of the substance of the lease arrangement must be undertaken to ensure that it is not just the form of the lease agreement that is being accounted for (see section 13.5 of this chapter for more details).

Given no extra information, it is concluded that the lease agreement should be classified as a finance lease because substantially all the risks and rewards incident to ownership have been passed to the lessee.

13.4 SUBSTANCE OVER FORM: INCENTIVES TO MISCLASSIFY LEASES

The classification of lease arrangements as either finance leases or operating leases determines the accounting treatment of transactions associated with the lease. For finance leases, the lessee recognises an asset and liability at the inception of the lease. The leased asset is subsequently depreciated and the liability is reduced through rental payments. An annual interest charge is recognised in respect of the liability. For operating leases, the lessee treats rental payments as expenses.

These divergent accounting treatments provide an incentive to managers to classify lease arrangements as operating leases. Finance leases may have the following adverse impacts on a lessee entity's financial statements or on decisions made by users of those statements.

- The capitalisation of the leased asset increases the value of reported non-current assets and reduces the return on assets ratio.
- Recognition of the present value of future lease payments as a liability increases reported current and non-current liabilities. This adversely affects debt–equity ratios and liquidity–solvency ratios, such as the current ratio (current assets/current liabilities). Reporting increased liabilities may result in entities breaching debt covenants, thereby causing debts to become due and payable immediately.
- Subsequent depreciation and interest expenses may exceed rental payments and result in lower profits being reported in the early years of the lease.
- Depreciation and interest expenses are not deductible for tax purposes, so additional liabilities may have to be recognised under IAS 12 *Income Taxes* when these expenses are less than the deduction for rental payments.
- More onerous disclosure requirements are prescribed for finance leases.

The ability to manipulate gearing ratios and thereby possibly reduce the cost of capital or increase the availability of finance for an entity is the most significant reward of keeping financing arrangements off the statement of financial position by classifying them as operating leases. As a result, since the release of IAS 17, the leasing industry has been geared towards promoting lease structures or arrangements that meet the guidelines for classification as operating leases. As noted in paragraph 21 of IAS 17, classification and the subsequent accounting must be based on substance and financial reality and not merely legal form. Hence, after considering the guidelines, which concentrate on the form of the lease agreement, the process of classifying a lease must include an analysis of the substance of the lease arrangement.

Features of lease arrangements that can be manipulated include the lease term (in particular, using short terms with options to renew), residual values, economic life estimates and bargain price options.

McGregor (1996, appendix 2, pp. 33–4) gives the following examples of finance leases structured as operating leases:

- *Novated motor vehicle leases*. Under this arrangement, employees enter into finance lease arrangements with a lessor finance company to finance motor vehicles. The employer and employee then enter into a sublease. When the ultimate risk rests with the employee, the arrangement is an operating lease. However, if the employer assumes the risk by, for example, guaranteeing the lease payments, the lease may be in substance a finance lease.
- *Rolling stock sale and leaseback*. In Australia, public sector entities have entered into offshore sale and leaseback arrangements in respect of public transport. Typically, the leases are for periods of 4 to 7 years with options for renewal, and are classified as operating leases. Assets involved include suburban trains, locomotives, light rail vehicles and buses. The unique rail gauges and other user-specific characteristics of this type of equipment make it unlikely that it would find a ready secondary market at the expiration of the lease term, and therefore underline the implausibility of any contention that the leases would not be renewed.
- *Private funding of public infrastructure*. Such funding arrangements often involve the establishment of a special-purpose company by a financier to raise private sector finance by the issue of debt securities for the construction of buildings such as police stations and courthouses. Apart from special-purpose fitting out, the buildings are of a generic type for which alternative uses would therefore be readily available. The buildings are then leased to a government

department or other public sector operator. The leases are invariably classified as operating leases by the government department or other public sector operator. An integral feature of most of these arrangements is that the government guarantees the debt securities, thereby ensuring that the bondholders are fully indemnified. Often the government also agrees to a pricing structure that ensures that capital as well as all other costs of the project will be recouped by the investor. Therefore, the risks and rewards of ownership are effectively transferred to the lessee (the government).

- *Separate arrangements for bargain purchase options or guaranteed residual values*. Some leases have been structured to include bargain purchase options or guaranteed residual values that are not specified directly as part of the lease agreements. For example, a bargain purchase option may be specified in an agreement completely separate from the lease agreement itself, and may be portrayed as unrelated to the lease agreement. Alternatively, a trust may be interposed between the lessor and lessee, with the lessee subscribing for units in the trust that are to be drawn against in the event of a shortfall in residual value. In these situations, the very existence of these arrangements may be difficult to detect and, even if detected, may be claimed to be unrelated to the lease and therefore not relevant to the lease classification process.

Shanahan (1989) described another scheme using an interposed entity. Under this arrangement, the lessor leases the asset to the interposed entity, which is owned 50/50 by the lessor and lessee, in the form of a finance lease. The interposed entity then subleases the asset to the ultimate lessee via a series of short-term operating leases, with options to renew. The lessor normally holds a 'put' option, whereby the lessor can force the lessee to buy its share of the interposed entity should the lessee fail to renew the operating lease. The lessee would then control the interposed entity and must consolidate its accounts (including the finance lease) with those of the lessee.

Tolling agreements (a non-lease) may also be used whereby the lessee has no right to use the leased equipment, but pays a toll to the lessor for provision of an asset *and* an operator for the asset. As the lessor's operator uses the asset, it is argued by those not wanting to recognise lease assets and liabilities that no lease as defined by IAS 17 exists.

The fact that managers can circumvent the requirements of the accounting standard and keep leases off the statement of financial position by using such contrivances means that the comparability and usefulness of financial reports is considerably diminished. As McGregor (1996, p. 3) points out:

> standards which do not require the recognition of assets and liabilities in respect of rights and obligations arising under certain financing arrangements have become a motivating factor in the selection of that type of financing arrangement over other forms of arrangement.

All the arrangements described above are finance leases in substance, and a strict application of the IAS 17 definition of a finance lease should result in the classification of the arrangement as a finance lease. However, the notion of what is substantial is capable of a wide range of interpretations, and the lack of clear quantitative guidance in the accounting standard may allow unethical managers to manipulate the lease classification process.

13.4.1 Interpretation 127

In December 2001, the Standing Interpretations Committee (SIC) of the IASB issued SIC 27 *Evaluating the Substance of Transactions Involving the Legal Form of a Lease* in an attempt to provide authoritative guidance to assist in the classification decision. SIC 27 requires that a series of transactions that includes a lease should be accounted for as a single transaction 'when the overall economic effect cannot be understood without reference to the series of transactions as a whole' (paragraph 3). This merely reiterates the 'substance over form' approach adopted by IAS 17. However, paragraph 5 of SIC 27 also provides the following indicators of arrangements that do not in substance involve a lease:

> (a) an entity retains all the risks and rewards incident to ownership of an underlying asset and enjoys substantially the same rights to its use as before the arrangement;
> (b) the primary reason for the arrangement is to achieve a particular tax result, and not to convey the right to use an asset; and
> (c) an option is included on terms that make its exercise almost certain (e.g. a put option that is exercisable at a price sufficiently higher than the expected fair value when it becomes exercisable).

Thus, the interpretation clearly details transactions that are *not* leases but does little to assist the classification of leases as either financing or operating, other than to state in paragraph 14:

> When an entity does not control the assets that will be used to satisfy the lease payment obligations, and is not obligated to pay the lease payments, it does not recognise the assets and lease payment obligations, because the definitions of an asset and a liability have not been met.

13.4.2 Interpretation 4

To further assist account preparers, the IASB issued IFRIC Interpretation 4 *Determining Whether an Arrangement Contains a Lease* in December 2004 (amended in November 2006). This interpretation was issued to assist account preparers in determining whether arrangements that are *not* in the legal form of a lease may in fact convey the right to use an item for an agreed period of time in return for a series of payments, and should therefore be treated as a lease for accounting purposes. Such arrangements may include:

- outsourcing arrangements
- arrangements in the telecommunications industry where suppliers of network capacity enter into contracts to provide purchases with rights to capacity
- take-or-pay contracts in which purchasers must make specified payments irrespective of whether they take delivery of services or products
- service concession arrangements where a supplier provides the use of an item of infrastructure to a purchaser.

The assessment of whether an arrangement contains a lease must be done at the inception of the arrangement using the information available at that time. If the provisions of the arrangement are subsequently changed, a reassessment will be made. Using the definition of a lease as an agreement whereby the lessor conveys to the lessee the right to use an asset for an agreed period of time in return for a payment or series of payments (IAS 17, paragraph 4), two criteria were developed to identify the lease component within an arrangement. These are stated in Interpretation 4, paragraph 6:

> (a) fulfilment of the arrangement is dependent on the use of a specific asset or assets (the asset); and
> (b) the arrangement conveys a right to use the asset.

Interpretation 4 uses an illustrative example of a purchaser who enters into a take-or-pay arrangement with an industrial gas supplier. If that supplier provides the gas from a plant that is built on the purchaser's premises and used solely to provide gas under the arrangement then, applying the above criteria, this lease is a 'de facto' lease of the gas plant.

If an arrangement does contain a lease component, then that part of the arrangement must be segregated and accounted for in accordance with IAS 17. This would require classification as an operating or financing lease at the inception of the arrangement. Payments made under the arrangement would need to be separated into lease payments and payments for other services on the basis of their relative fair values (Interpretation 4, paragraph 13).

13.5 ACCOUNTING FOR FINANCE LEASES BY LESSEES

Once an arrangement has been classified as a finance lease, the asset and liability arising from it must be determined and recognised in the accounts.

13.5.1 Initial recognition

When a lease has been classified as a finance lease, paragraph 20 of IAS 17 requires the lessee to recognise, at the commencement of the lease term, an asset and a liability, each determined at the inception of the lease, equal in amount to the fair value of the leased property or, if lower, the present value of the minimum lease payments. The form of the entry is:

Lease Asset	Dr	PV of MLP	
Lease Liability	Cr		PV of MLP

The commencement of the lease term is the date from which the lessee is entitled to exercise its right to use the leased asset, and may be the same date as the inception of the lease or a later date. If not already determined as part of the classification process, the value of the asset or liability needs to be calculated at the inception of the lease by reference to the terms of the lease agreement. If the lessee incurs initial direct costs associated with the negotiation and securing of the lease arrangements then, according to paragraph 24 of IAS 17, these costs are added to the amount recognised as an asset. The journal entry is:

Lease Asset	Dr	PV of MLP + IDC	
Lease Liability	Cr		PV of MLP
Cash	Cr		IDC

13.5.2 Subsequent measurement

After initial recognition, IAS 17 prescribes differing accounting treatments for the lease asset and the lease liability.

Leased assets

Paragraph 27 of IAS 17 states:

> The depreciation policy for depreciable leased assets shall be consistent with that for depreciable assets that are owned, and the depreciation recognised shall be calculated in accordance with IAS 16 *Property, Plant and Equipment* and IAS 38 *Intangible Assets*.

Depreciable assets are those whose future benefits are expected to expire over time or by use. The asset is depreciated over its useful life in a pattern reflecting the consumption or loss of the rewards embodied in the asset. The length of a leased asset's useful life depends on whether or not ownership of the asset will transfer at the end of the lease term. If the asset is to be returned to the lessor, then its useful life is the lease term. If ownership is reasonably certain to transfer to the lessee, then its useful life is its economic life or remainder thereof. Additionally, to determine whether a leased asset has become impaired, the lessee must apply IAS 36 (see chapter 12).

Lease liability

Because lease payments are made over the lease term, paragraph 25 of IAS 17 requires the payments to be divided into the following components:

- reduction of the lease liability
- interest expense incurred
- reimbursement of lessor costs
- payment of contingent rent.

The second two are easily determined by reference to the lease agreement, but the first two need to be calculated. The lease liability recognised at the commencement of the lease term represents the present value of future lease payments relating to the use of the asset. This present value is determined by applying the interest rate implicit in the lease. Thus, the interest expense can be obtained by applying the same rate to the outstanding lease liability at the beginning of the payment period. A payments schedule can be used to determine the interest expense and the reduction in the liability over the lease period.

Accounting for the reimbursement of lessor costs and contingent rent

Paragraph 25 of IAS 17 requires contingent rent to be recognised as an expense of the year in which it is incurred. The accounting standard is silent about the component of lease payments that represents a reimbursement of costs incurred by the lessor. However, as the cost of such items is effectively borne by the lessee, the payment should be recognised as an expense. Consideration must be given to the pattern of consumption relating to those expenses and normal prepayment and accrual rules apply.

ILLUSTRATIVE EXAMPLE 13.2

Accounting for finance leases by lessees

Using the facts from illustrative example 13.1, the lease payments schedule prepared by Canary Ltd, based on annual payments of $22 000 for the vehicle and an interest rate of 7%, would be:

CANARY LTD Lease Payments Schedule				
	Minimum lease payments[a]	Interest expense[b]	Reduction in liability[c]	Balance of liability[d]
30 June 2009[e]				$85 457[f]
30 June 2009	$22 000	—	$22 000	63 457
30 June 2010	22 000	$ 4 442	17 558	45 899
30 June 2011	22 000	3 213	18 787	27 112
30 June 2012	22 000	1 898	20 102	7 010
30 June 2013	7 500	490	7 010	—
	$95 500	$10 043	$85 457	

(a) Four annual payments of $22 000 payable in advance on 30 June of each year, plus a guaranteed residual value of $7500 on the last day of the lease.
(b) Interest expense = balance of liability each year multiplied by 7%. No interest expense is incurred in the first year because payment is made at the commencement of the lease.
(c) Reduction in liability = minimum lease payments less interest expense. The total of this column must equal the initial liability, which may require rounding the final interest expense figure.
(d) The balance is reduced each year by the amount in column 3.
(e) At lease inception.
(f) Initial liability = present value of minimum lease payments. As the present value of minimum lease payments is less than the fair value of the asset, paragraph 20 of IAS 17 requires the lower amount to be recognised.

The payment schedule is used to prepare lease journal entries and disclosure notes each year. The journal entries recorded by Canary Ltd for the 4 years of the lease in accordance with IAS 17 are:

CANARY LTD General Journal			
Year ended 30 June 2009			
30 June 2009:			
Leased Vehicle	Dr	85 457	
Lease Liability	Cr		85 457
(Initial recording of lease asset/liability)			
Lease Liability	Dr	22 000	
Prepaid Executory Costs*	Dr	1 900	
Cash	Cr		23 900
(First lease payment)			
*Executory costs have been capitalised because the insurance and maintenance benefits will not be received until the next reporting period.			
Year ended 30 June 2010			
1 July 2009:			
Executory Costs	Dr	1 900	
Prepaid Executory Costs	Cr		1 900
(Reversal of prepayment)			

30 June 2010:			
Lease Liability	Dr	17 558	
Interest Expense	Dr	4 442	
Prepaid Executory Costs	Dr	1 900	
Cash	Cr		23 900
(Second lease payment)			
Depreciation Expense	Dr	19 489	
Accumulated Depreciation	Cr		19 489
(Depreciation charge for the period [$85 457 – $7500]/4)*			

*Because the asset will be returned at the end of the lease term, the useful life is the lease term of 4 years and the depreciable amount is the cost less the guaranteed residual value.

Year ended 30 June 2011			
1 July 2010:			
Executory Costs	Dr	1 900	
Prepaid Executory Costs	Cr		1 900
(Reversal of prepayment)			
30 June 2011:			
Lease Liability	Dr	18 787	
Interest Expense	Dr	3 213	
Prepaid Executory Costs	Dr	1 900	
Cash	Cr		23 900
(Third lease payment)			
Depreciation Expense	Dr	19 489	
Accumulated Depreciation	Cr		19 489
(Depreciation charge for the period [$85 457 – $7500]/4)			
Year ended 30 June 2012			
1 July 2011:			
Executory Costs	Dr	1 900	
Prepaid Executory Costs	Cr		1 900
(Reversal of prepayment)			
30 June 2012:			
Lease Liability	Dr	20 102	
Interest Expense	Dr	1 898	
Prepaid Executory Costs	Dr	1 900	
Cash	Cr		23 900
(Fourth lease payment)			
Depreciation Expense	Dr	19 489	
Accumulated Depreciation	Cr		19 489
(Depreciation charge for the period [$85 457 – $7500]/4)			
Year ended 30 June 2013			
1 July 2012:			
Executory Costs	Dr	1 900	
Prepaid Executory Costs	Cr		1 900
(Reversal of prepayment)			
30 June 2013:			
Lease Liability	Dr	7 010	
Interest Expense	Dr	490	
Leased Vehicle*	Cr		7 500
(Return of leased vehicle)			

Depreciation Expense Accumulated Depreciation (Depreciation charge for the period [$85 457 – $7500]/4)	Dr Cr	19 490	 19 490
Accumulated Depreciation Leased Vehicle (Fully depreciated asset written off)	Dr Cr	77 957	 77 957

*The final 'payment' is the return of the asset at its guaranteed residual value. If the asset is being purchased, this entry will record a cash payment. Another entry will then be required to reclassify the undepreciated balance of the asset from a 'leased' asset to an 'owned' asset.

13.5.3 Disclosures required

Paragraph 31 of IAS 17 requires that, in addition to meeting the requirements of IAS 32 *Financial Instruments: Disclosure and Presentation*, the following information must be disclosed by lessees:

- the carrying amount of each class of leased asset as at the end of the reporting period
- a reconciliation between the total future minimum lease payments at the end of the reporting period and their present value
- the total of future minimum lease payments at the end of the reporting period and their present value for each of the following periods:
  - not later than 1 year
  - later than 1 year and not later than 5 years
  - later than 5 years
- contingent rents recognised as an expense in the period
- the total of future minimum sublease payments expected to be received under non-cancellable subleases at the end of the reporting period
- a general description of the lessee's material leasing arrangements.

Future minimum lease payments include all future amounts payable under the lease agreement less reimbursements of the lessor's costs and any known contingent rents. This reconciliation provides some information about future cash flows to financial statement users.

Figure 13.2 shows the leasing accounting policy disclosures and extracts from the provisions and commitments notes to the financial statements of Qantas Ltd for the year ended 30 June 2008.

FIGURE 13.2 Note extracts from Qantas Ltd annual report 30 June 2008

1. Statement of significant accounting policies
(P) Property, Plant and Equipment
Leased and Hire Purchase Assets

Leased assets under which the Qantas Group assumes substantially all the risks and benefits of ownership are classified as finance leases. Other leases are classified as operating leases.

Linked transactions involving the legal form of a lease are accounted for as one transaction when a series of transactions are negotiated as one or take place concurrently or in sequence and cannot be understood economically alone.

Finance leases are capitalised. A lease asset and a lease liability equal to the present value of the minimum lease payments and guaranteed residual value are recorded at the inception of the lease. Any gains and losses arising under sale and leaseback arrangements are deferred and amortised over the lease term where the sale is not at fair value. Capitalised leased assets are amortised on a straight-line basis over the period in which benefits are expected to arise from the use of those assets. Lease payments are allocated between the reduction in the principal component of the lease liability and the interest element.

The interest element is charged to the Income Statement over the lease term so as to produce a constant periodic rate of interest on the remaining balance of the lease liability.

Fully prepaid leases are classified in the Balance Sheet as hire purchase assets, to recognise that the financing structures impose certain obligations, commitments and/or restrictions on the Qantas Group, which differentiate these aircraft from owned assets.

FIGURE 13.2 *(continued)*

Leases are deemed to be non-cancellable if significant financial penalties associated with termination are anticipated.

Operating Leases

Rental payments under operating leases are charged to the Income Statement on a straight-line basis over the period of the lease.

With respect to any premises rented under long-term operating leases, which are subject to sub-tenancy agreements, provision is made for any shortfall between primary payments to the head lessor less any recoveries from sub-tenants. These provisions are determined on a discounted cash flow basis, using a rate reflecting the cost of funds.

22. Provisions

	Qantas Group		Qantas	
	2008 $M	2007 $M	**2008 $M**	2007 $M
Make good on leased assets				
The Qantas Group has leases that require the asset to be returned to the lessor in certain condition. A provision has been raised for the present value of the future expected cost at lease expiry.				
Balance as at 1 July	**33.7**	17.5	**26.6**	12.8
Provisions made	**7.9**	16.2	**3.0**	13.8
Balance as at 30 June	**41.6**	33.7	**29.6**	26.6

27. Commitments

(A) Finance lease and hire purchase commitments

	Qantas Group		Qantas	
	2008 $M	2007 $M	**2008 $M**	2007 $M
Included in the Financial Statements as finance lease and hire purchase liabilities are the present values of future rentals of the following:				
Aircraft and engines	**606.0**	1 058.1	**1 984.9**	2 651.9
Computer and communications equipment	**—**	0.4	**—**	—
	606.0	1 058.5	**1 984.9**	2 651.9
Payable				
Not later than one year	**83.7**	458.2	**336.4**	710.6
Later than one year but not later than five years	**271.9**	375.4	**1 346.2**	1 474.1
Later than five years	**354.7**	400.8	**693.2**	983.6
Less: future lease and hire purchase finance charges	**710.3**	1 234.4	**2 375.8**	3 168.3
	104.3	175.9	**390.9**	516.4
	606.0	1 058.5	**1 984.9**	2 651.9
Finance lease and hire purchase liabilities provided for the Financial Statements				
Current liability (refer Note 21)				
– controlled entities	**—**	—	**176.7**	174.0
– other parties	**66.8**	483.2	**66.8**	483.2
Non-current liability (refer Note 21)				
– controlled entities	**—**	—	**1 202.2**	1 419.4
– other parties	**539.2**	575.3	**539.2**	575.3
	606.0	1 058.5	**1 984.9**	2 651.9

FIGURE 13.2 *(continued)*

The Qantas Group leases aircraft and plant and equipment under finance leases with expiry dates between one and 17 years. Most finance leases contain purchase options exercisable at the end of the lease term. The Qantas Group has the right to negotiate extensions on most leases.

(B) Operating lease and rental commitments

	Qantas Group		Qantas	
As lessee	**2008 $M**	2007 $M	**2008 $M**	2007 $M
Future net operating lease and rental commitments not provided for in the Financial Statements	**4 417.1**	3 322.9	**1 802.9**	1 759.6
Payable				
Not later than one year	**697.1**	568.4	**378.3**	370.7
Later than one year but not later than five years	**2 388.4**	1 677.9	**929.3**	833.9
Later than five years	**1 332.4**	1 085.8	**496.0**	562.8
	4 417.9	3 332.1	**1 803.6**	1 767.4
Less: provision for potential under recovery of rentals on unused premises available for sub-lease (included in onerous contract provision)	**0.8**	9.2	**0.7**	7.8
	4 417.1	3 322.9	**1 802.9**	1 759.6
Operating lease commitments represent:				
Cancellable operating leases	**1 055.8**	991.8	**1 028.5**	974.0
Non-cancellable operating leases:				
– Aircraft leases	**3 361.3**	2 331.1	**774.3**	785.6
	4 417.1	3 322.9	**1 802.9**	1 759.6
Non-cancellable operating lease commitments, excluding unguaranteed residual payments, not provided for in the Financial Statements:				
Not later than one year	**488.2**	391.0	**183.2**	200.5
Later than one year but not later than five years	**1 965.9**	1 287.0	**519.8**	453.3
Later than five years	**907.2**	653.1	**71.2**	131.8
	3 361.3	2 331.1	**774.3**	785.6

The Qantas Group leases aircraft, buildings and plant and equipment under operating leases with expiry dates between one and 35 years. The Qantas Group has the right to negotiate extensions on most leases.

As lessor				
Receivable				
Not later than one year	**11.7**	10.7	**6.2**	4.7
Later than one year but not later than five years	**46.8**	46.8	**25.0**	18.7
Later than five years	**67.5**	76.5	**36.0**	28.6
	126.0	134.0	**67.2**	52.0

Qantas leases out freighter aircraft under long-term operating leases with rentals received monthly.

Source: Qantas (2008, pp. 84,113,121–2).

Figure 13.3 provides an illustration of the disclosures required by IAS 17, and is based on the figures used in illustrative example 13.2.

	IAS 17 *para.*
Note 1: Summary of accounting policies (extract) **Leasing** Leases are classified as finance leases whenever the terms of the lease transfer substantially all the risks and rewards of ownership to the lessee. All other leases are classified as operating leases. *The entity as a lessee* Assets held under finance leases are recognised as assets of the entity at their fair value at the date of acquisition or, if lower, at the present value of the minimum lease payments. The corresponding liability to the lessor is included in the statement of financial position as a finance lease liability. Lease payments are apportioned between finance charges and reduction of the lease liability to achieve a constant rate of interest on the remaining balance of the liability. Finance charges are charged directly against income unless they are directly attributable to qualifying assets, in which case they are capitalised in accordance with the entity's general policy on borrowing costs.	*31(e)*
Note 16: Property, plant and equipment (extract) The carrying amount of the entity's plant and equipment includes an amount of $46 479 (2010: $65 968) relating to leased assets.	
Note 36: Finance lease liabilities	*31(b)*

	Minimum lease payments 2011	PV of payments 2011	Minimum lease payments 2010	PV of payments 2010
Amounts payable under finance leases:				
Within 1 year	22 000	20 102	22 000	18 787
After 1 year but not more than 5 years	7 500	7 010	29 500	27 112
Total minimum lease payments	29 500	27 112	51 500	45 899
Less: Finance charges	(2 388)		(5 601)	
Present value of minimum lease payments	27 112		45 899	

In respect of finance leases, the following item has been recognised as an expense during the period: *31(c)*

	2011	2010
Contingent rent	1 200	0

FIGURE 13.3 Illustrative disclosures required by IAS 17 for lessees of finance leases

13.6 ACCOUNTING FOR FINANCE LEASES BY LESSORS

When a lease is classified as a finance lease, the lessor will need to 'derecognise' the leased asset and record a lease receivable.

13.6.1 Initial recognition

In theory, the classification process required by IAS 17 should result in identical classifications by both lessors and lessee. In reality, differing circumstances may result in the same lease being classified differently; for example, where the lessor benefits from a residual value guarantee provided by a party unrelated to the lessee (paragraph 9).

Paragraph 36 of IAS 17 requires the lessor to recognise assets held under a finance lease in its statement of financial position and present them as a receivable at an amount equal to the net investment in the lease. The net investment in the lease is defined in paragraph 4 as the gross investment in the lease discounted at the interest rate implicit in the lease, with the gross investment being equal to:

(a) the minimum lease payments receivable by the lessor under a finance lease; and
(b) any unguaranteed residual value accruing to the lessor.

This value would normally equate to the fair value of the asset at the inception of the lease. Initial direct costs, except those incurred by manufacturer or dealer lessors, are included in the initial measurement of the finance lease receivable and reduce the amount of interest revenue recognised over the lease term. The definition of interest rate implicit in the lease automatically includes initial direct costs in the finance lease receivable, so there is no need to add them separately (paragraph 38). Lessees are required to recognise assets and liabilities associated with finance leases at the commencement of the lease term but no date for recognition is specified for lessors; presumably, it would be the same date.

The recognition of the fair value of the leased asset as a receivable raises an interesting issue in that the 'receivable', for those leases with no purchase option, has both a monetary component (the rent payments) and non-monetary component (the return of the asset). The problem with this 'combination asset' is that IAS 32 requires specific disclosures to be made for the rent part of the receivable, which is a financial asset as defined by that standard, but does not require disclosures with respect to the non-monetary component. Additionally, these components are subject to different risks, and recording both as an ostensible financial asset may mislead financial statements users.

13.6.2 Subsequent measurement

As the lease payments are received from the lessee over the lease term, the receipts need to be analysed into the following components:

- reduction of the lease receivable
- interest revenue earned
- reimbursement of costs paid on behalf of the lessee
- receipt of contingent rent.

The latter two are easily determined by reference to the lease agreement, but the first two need to be calculated in a similar fashion to that used by the lessor. The lease receivable recognised at the commencement of the lease term represents the present value of future lease payments relating to the use of the asset. This present value is determined by applying the interest rate implicit in the lease. Thus, the interest revenue can be obtained by applying the same rate to the outstanding lease receivable at the beginning of the payment period. A receipts schedule can be used to determine the interest revenue and the reduction in the receivable over the lease period.

13.6.3 Accounting for executory costs and contingent rentals

IAS 17 is silent on the treatment of contingent rent and the reimbursements of costs incurred on behalf of the lessee. However, as these receipts meet the definition of income in the *Framework*, contingent rents should be recognised as revenue in the period they were earned, and reimbursements should be recorded as revenue in the same period in which the related expenses are incurred.

ILLUSTRATIVE EXAMPLE 13.3

Accounting for finance leases by lessors

On 30 June 2009, Bahamas Ltd leased a vehicle to Canary Ltd. Bahamas Ltd had purchased the vehicle on that day for its fair value of $89 721. The lease agreement, which cost Bahamas Ltd $1457 to have drawn up, contained the following:

Lease term	4 years
Annual payment, payable in advance on 30 June each year	$23 900
Economic life of vehicle	6 years

Estimated residual value at end of economic life	$2 000
Estimated residual value at end of lease term	$15 000
Residual value guaranteed by lessee	$7 500

The lease is cancellable, but cancellation will incur a monetary penalty equivalent to 2 years rental payments. Included in the annual payment is an amount of $1900 to cover reimbursement for the costs of insurance and maintenance paid by the lessor. The directors of Canary Ltd have indicated that they will return the asset to Bahamas Ltd at the end of the lease term.

Classification of the lease by the lessor

Bahamas Ltd would apply IAS 17 guidelines and classify the lease as a finance lease. See illustrative example 13.1 for workings.

The lease receipts schedule based on annual payments of $22 000 for the vehicle and an interest rate implicit in the lease of 7% shows:

BAHAMAS LTD
Lease Receipts Schedule

	Minimum lease receipts[(a)]	Interest revenue[(b)]	Reduction in receivable[(c)]	Balance of receivable[(d)]
30 June 2009				$91 178[(e)]
30 June 2009	$ 22 000	—	$22 000	69 178
30 June 2010	22 000	$ 4 842	17 158	52 020
30 June 2011	22 000	3 641	18 359	33 661
30 June 2012	22 000	2 356	19 644	14 017
30 June 2013	15 000	983	14 017	—
	$103 000	$11 822	$91 178	

(a) Four annual receipts of $22 000 payable in advance on 30 June of each year, plus a residual value of $15 000 (of which $7500 is guaranteed by the lessee) on the last day of the lease.
(b) Interest revenue = balance of receivable each year multiplied by 7%. No interest revenue is earned in the first year because the payment is received at the inception of the lease.
(c) Reduction in receivable = minimum lease receipts less interest revenue. The total of this column must equal the initial receivable, which may require rounding the final interest revenue figure.
(d) The balance is reduced each year by the amount in column 3.
(e) Initial receivable = fair value of $89 721 plus initial direct costs of $1457. This figure equals the present value of minimum lease payments receivable and the present value of the unguaranteed residual value.

The lease receipts schedule is used to prepare lease journal entries and disclosure notes each year, as shown below:

BAHAMAS LTD
General Journal

Year ended 30 June 2009			
30 June 2009:			
Vehicle	Dr	89 721	
Cash	Cr		89 721
(Purchase of motor vehicle)			
Lease Receivable	Dr	89 721	
Vehicle	Cr		89 721
(Lease of vehicle to Canary Ltd)			

Lease Receivable	Dr	1 457	
Cash	Cr		1 457
(Payment of initial direct costs)			
Cash	Dr	23 900	
Lease Receivable	Cr		22 000
Reimbursement in advance*	Cr		1 900
(Receipt of first lease payment)			

*The reimbursement of executory cost has been carried forward to 2010, when Bahamas Ltd will pay the costs.

Year ended 30 June 2010			
1 July 2009:			
Reimbursement in Advance	Dr	1 900	
Reimbursement Revenue	Cr		1 900
(Reversal of accrual)			
30 June 2010:			
Insurance and Maintenance	Dr	1 900	
Cash	Cr		1 900
(Payment of costs on behalf of lessee)			
Cash	Dr	23 900	
Lease Receivable	Cr		17 158
Interest Revenue	Cr		4 842
Reimbursement in Advance	Cr		1 900
(Receipt of second lease payment)			
Year ended 30 June 2011			
1 July 2011:			
Reimbursement in Advance	Dr	1 900	
Reimbursement Revenue	Cr		1 900
(Reversal of accrual)			
30 June 2011:			
Insurance and Maintenance	Dr	1 900	
Cash	Cr		1 900
(Payment of costs on behalf of lessee)			
Cash	Dr	23 900	
Lease Receivable	Cr		18 359
Interest Revenue	Cr		3 641
Reimbursement in Advance	Cr		1 900
(Receipt of third lease payment)			
Year ended 30 June 2012			
1 July 2011:			
Reimbursement in Advance	Dr	1 900	
Reimbursement Revenue	Cr		1 900
(Reversal of accrual)			
30 June 2012:			
Insurance and Maintenance	Dr	1 900	
Cash	Cr		1 900
(Payment of costs on behalf of lessee)			
Cash	Dr	23 900	
Lease Receivable	Cr		19 644
Interest Revenue	Cr		2 356
Reimbursement in Advance	Cr		1 900
(Receipt of fourth lease payment)			

Year ended 30 June 2013			
1 July 2012:			
Reimbursement in Advance	Dr	1 900	
Reimbursement Revenue	Cr		1 900
(Reversal of accrual)			
30 June 2013:			
Insurance and Maintenance	Dr	1 900	
Cash	Cr		1 900
(Payment of costs on behalf of lessee)			
Vehicle	Dr	15 000	
Interest Revenue	Cr		983
Lease Receivable	Cr		14 017
(Return of vehicle at end of lease)			

13.6.4 The initial direct costs anomaly

The inclusion (by the standard setters) of initial direct costs incurred by lessors in the definition of the interest rate implicit in the lease creates an interest rate differential between lessee and lessor where a lease agreement transfers all of the risks and rewards related to an asset.

To illustrate: consider the same situation as described in illustrative example 13.3 but increasing the guaranteed residual value to \$15 000 (100% of the residual), which effectively transfers all of the benefits of the vehicle from Bahamas Ltd to Canary Ltd. The present value of the minimum lease payments would then be:

PV of MLP = \$22 000 + (\$22 000 × 2.6243 [T_2 7% 3*y*]) + (\$15 000 × 0.7629 [T_1 7% 4*y*])
= \$22 000 + \$57 735 + \$11 443
= \$91 178

This figure equals the fair value of the asset, \$89 721, plus the initial direct costs incurred by the lessor of \$1457.

However, paragraph 20 of IAS 17 requires lessees to recognise, at the inception of the lease, an asset and a liability equal to the fair value of the leased asset or, if *lower*, the present value of the minimum lease payments. As the present value of the minimum lease payments using the 7% interest rate implicit in the lease is *higher* than the asset's fair value, it cannot be recognised by the lessee even though it would be recognised by the lessor. The lessee, Canary Ltd, can only recognise a lease asset and liability of \$89 721, and must recalculate the interest rate implicit in the lease in order to determine interest expense charges over the lease term.

The interest rate that discounts the lease payments to \$89 721 is 8%, so Canary Ltd will calculate its interest at 8% and Bahamas Ltd will calculate its interest revenue at 7%. The difference represents the recovery of the initial direct costs by Bahamas Ltd via the lease payments received.

13.6.5 Disclosures required

Paragraph 47 of IAS 17 requires that, in addition to disclosures required by IAS 32, the following information must be disclosed separately in the financial statements in respect of finance leases:

- a reconciliation between the gross investment in the lease and the present value of the minimum lease payments at the end of the reporting period
- the gross investment in the lease and the present value of minimum lease payments receivable at the end of the reporting period, for each of the following periods:
  - not later than 1 year
  - later than 1 year and not later than 5 years
  - later than 5 years

- unearned finance income
- the unguaranteed residual values accruing to the benefit of the lessor
- the accumulated allowance for uncollectable minimum lease payments receivable
- contingent rents recognised as income in the period
- a general description of the lessor's material leasing arrangements.

Figure 13.4 provides an illustration of the disclosures required by IAS 17. The information used in this figure is derived from the Bahamas Ltd lease shown in illustrative example 13.3.

					IAS 17 *para.*
Note 1: Summary of accounting policies (extract) **Leasing** Leases are classified as finance leases whenever the terms of the lease transfer substantially all the risks and rewards of ownership to the lessee. All other leases are classified as operating leases. *The entity as a lessor* Amounts due from lessees under finance leases are recorded as a receivable at the amount of the entity's net investment in the leases. Finance lease income is allocated to accounting periods, so as to reflect a constant periodic rate of return on the entity's net investment outstanding in respect of the leases.					*47(f)*
Note 36: Finance lease receivables					
	Investment in lease 2011	**PV of receivables 2011**	**Investment in lease 2010**	**PV of receivables 2010**	
Amounts payable under finance leases:					*47(a)*
Within 1 year	22 000	19 644	22 000	18 359	
After 1 year but not more than 5 years	15 000	14 017	37 000	33 661	
Total minimum lease payments receivable	37 000	33 661	59 000	52 020	
Less: Unearned finance income	(3 339)		(6 980)		*47(b)*
Present value of minimum lease payments	33 661		52 020		
Unguaranteed residual values of assets leased under finance leases at the end of the reporting period are estimated at $7500 (2010: $7500)					*47(c)*
In respect of finance leases, contingent rents amounting to $1200 (2010: nil) were recognised as income during the period.					*47(e)*

FIGURE 13.4 Illustrative disclosures required by IAS 17 for lessors of finance leases

13.7 ACCOUNTING FOR FINANCE LEASES BY MANUFACTURER OR DEALER LESSORS

When manufacturers or dealers offer customers the choice of either buying or leasing an asset, a lease arrangement gives rise to two types of income:

- profit or loss equivalent to the outright sale of the asset being leased
- finance income over the lease term.

Accounting for the lease is identical to that required by non-manufacturer/dealer lessors except for an initial entry to recognise profit or loss and the fact that initial direct costs are not included in the lease receivable amount.

IAS 17 paragraph 42 requires manufacturer and dealer lessors to recognise selling profit or loss at the commencement of the lease, in accordance with the policy followed by the entity for outright sales. Where artificially low interest rates have been offered to entice the customer to enter the lease, the selling profit recorded must be restricted to that which would apply if a market rate of interest had been charged.

Hence, as well as recognising the lease receivable, the manufacturer or dealer records the profit or loss on sale (at market interest rates) at the commencement of the lease. The sales revenue recognised is equal to the fair value of the asset or, if lower, the minimum lease payments calculated at a market rate of interest. The cost of sale expense is the cost or carrying amount of the leased property less the present value of any unguaranteed residual value. Sales revenue less cost of sales expense equals selling profit or loss. Additionally, paragraph 42 of IAS 17 requires the initial direct costs incurred by the manufacturer or dealer in negotiating and arranging the lease to be recognised as an expense when the profit is recognised. Such costs are regarded as part of earning the profit on sale rather than a cost of leasing (paragraph 46).

ILLUSTRATIVE EXAMPLE 13.4

Calculating and recognising profit on sale with initial direct costs

Falkland Ltd manufactures specialised moulding machinery for both sale and lease. On 1 July 2009, Falkland leased a machine to Barbados Ltd, incurring $1500 in costs to negotiate, prepare and execute the lease document. The machine cost Falkland Ltd $195 000 to manufacture, and its fair value at the inception of the lease was $212 515. The interest rate implicit in the lease is 10%, which is in line with current market rates. Under the terms of the lease, Barbados Ltd has guaranteed $25 000 of the asset's expected residual value of $37 000 at the end of the 5-year lease term.

After classifying the lease as a finance lease, Falkland Ltd passes the following entries on 1 July 2009:

Lease Receivable[a]	Dr	212 515	
Sales Revenue[b]	Cr		205 063
Cost of Sales[c]	Dr	187 548	
Inventory[d]	Cr		195 000
(Initial recognition of lease receivable and recording sale of machine)			
Lease Costs	Dr	1 500	
Cash	Cr		1 500
(Payment of initial direct costs)			

Notes

(a) The lease receivable represents the net investment in the lease and is equal to the fair value of the leased machine.

(b) Sales revenue represents the present value of the minimum lease payments, which in this situation is less than the fair value of the asset due to the existence of an unguaranteed residual value.

(c) Cost of sales represents the cost of the leased machine ($195 000) less the present value of the unguaranteed residual value ($12 000 × 0.620 921 = $7452).

(d) Inventory is reduced by the cost of the leased machine.

13.8 ACCOUNTING FOR OPERATING LEASES

Operating leases are those where substantially all the risks and rewards incident to ownership remain with the lessor. IAS 17 requires such arrangements to be treated as rental agreements, with all payments treated as income or expense by the respective parties.

13.8.1 Accounting treatment

Lessees

Paragraph 33 of IAS 17 requires the lessee to recognise lease payments as an expense on a straight-line basis over the lease term unless another systematic basis is more representative of the time pattern of the user's benefit.

Lessors

Lease receipts

Paragraph 50 of IAS 17 requires lessors to account for receipts from operating leases as income on a straight-line basis over the lease term unless another systematic basis is more representative of the time pattern in which the benefit derived from the leased asset is diminished.

Initial direct costs

Any initial direct costs incurred by lessors in negotiating operating leases are to be added to the carrying amount of the leased asset and recognised as an expense over the lease term on the same basis as the lease income (IAS 17 paragraph 52). The initial direct costs are then capitalised into a deferred costs account and disclosed as follows:

Asset	$XXX
Less: Acccumulated depreciation	XXX
	XXX
Plus: Initial direct costs	XXX
	XXX

Because the IAS 17 definition of initial direct costs excludes costs incurred by manufacturers and dealers in negotiating and executing a lease, paragraph 52 applies only to costs incurred by non-dealer/manufacturer lessors.

Depreciation of leased assets

Paragraph 49 of IAS 17 requires the leased asset to be presented in the statement of financial position according to the nature of the asset. According to paragraph 53, depreciation of assets provided under operating leases should be consistent with the lessor's normal depreciation policy for similar assets, and should be calculated in accordance with IAS 16 and IAS 38.

ILLUSTRATIVE EXAMPLE 13.5

Accounting for operating leases

On 1 July 2009, Bioko Ltd leased a bobcat from Greenland Ltd. The bobcat cost Greenland Ltd $35 966 on that same day. The finance lease agreement, which cost Greenland Ltd $381 to have drawn up, contained the following:

Lease term	3 years
Estimated economic life of the bobcat	10 years
The lease is cancellable	
Annual rental payment, in arrears (commencing 30/6/10)	$3 900
Residual value at end of the lease term	$24 500
Residual guaranteed by Bioko Ltd	$0
Interest rate implicit in lease	6%

IAS 17 requires the lease to be classified as either a finance lease or an operating lease based on the extent to which the risks and rewards associated with the vehicle have been effectively transferred between Bioko Ltd and Greenland Ltd.

Is the lease non-cancellable?

The lease agreement is cancellable; either party can walk away from the arrangement without penalty.

Is ownership expected to be transferred at the end of the lease term?
Bioko Ltd expects to return the bobcat to Greenland Ltd.

Is the lease term a major part of the economic life of the leased asset?
The lease term is 3 years, which is only 30% of the bobcat's economic life of 10 years. Therefore, it would appear that the lease arrangement is not for the major part of the asset's life.

Is the present value of the minimum lease payments substantially all of the fair value of the leased asset?

Minimum lease payments
The minimum lease payments consist of three payments, in arrears, of $3900. There are no contingent rentals, executory costs or guaranteed residual value.

Present value of minimum lease payments

PV of MLP = \$3 900 × 2.6730 [3 years T_2 6%]
= \$10 425
PV/FV = \$10 425/\$35 966
= 29%

Is the substance of the transaction such that substantially all the risks and rewards incident to ownership have been transferred?
The shortness of the lease term compared with the asset's economic life indicates that it is, in substance, an operating lease.

Classification of the lease
On the basis of the evidence available, there has not been an effective transfer of substantially all the risks and rewards associated with the bobcat to the lessee. Hence, the lease should be classified and accounted for as an *operating lease.*

Journal entries
The following journal entries would be passed in the books of both the lessor and the lessee for the year ended 30 June 2010:

BIOKO LTD General Journal			
30 June 2010:			
Lease Expense	Dr	3 900	
Cash	Cr		3 900
(Payment of first year's rental)			

GREENLAND LTD General Journal			
1 July 2009:			
Plant and Equipment	Dr	35 966	
Cash	Cr		35 966
(Purchase of bobcat)			
Deferred Initial Direct Costs – Plant and Equipment	Dr	381	
Cash	Cr		381
(Initial direct costs incurred for lease)			
30 June 2010:			
Cash	Dr	3 900	
Lease Income	Cr		3 900
(Receipt of first year's rental)			

Lease Expense	Dr	127	
Deferred Initial Direct Costs – Plant and Equipment	Cr		127
(Recognition of initial direct cost: $381/3 years)			
Depreciation Expense	Dr	3 597	
Accumulated Depreciation	Cr		3 597
(Depreciation charge for the period: $35 966/10)			

13.8.2 Disclosures required

Lessees

Paragraph 35 of IAS 17 requires lessees, in addition to meeting the requirements of IAS 32, to disclose the following information in respect of operating leases:

(a) the total of future minimum lease payments under non-cancellable operating leases for each of the following periods:
  (i) not later than one year;
  (ii) later than one year and not later than five years;
  (iii) later than five years.
(b) the total of future minimum sublease payments expected to be received under non-cancellable subleases at the reporting date [end of the reporting period].
(c) lease and sublease payments recognised as an expense in the period, with separate amounts for minimum lease payments, contingent rents, and sublease payments.
(d) a general description of the lessee's significant leasing arrangements . . .

The key feature of these disclosures is the identification of future commitments with respect to those operating leases which are non-cancellable. This information allows users of financial statements to factor in lease expenses against expected future profits, and alerts potential creditors to the fact that some future cash flows are not available to service new liabilities.

Figure 13.5 provides an illustration of the disclosures required by IAS 17.

			IAS 17 *para.*
Note 1: Summary of accounting policies (extract) **Leasing** Leases are classified as finance leases whenever the terms of the lease transfer substantially all the risks and rewards of ownership to the lessee. All other leases are classified as operating leases. *The entity as a lessee* Rentals payable under operating leases are charged to income on a straight-line basis over the term of the relevant lease.			*35(d)*
Note 43: Operating lease arrangements Minimum lease payments recorded as expense amounted to $167 500 (2008: $152 100) for the period.			*35(c)*
Future minimum lease payments under non-cancellable operating leases are as follows:			
	2009	**2008**	
Within 1 year	70 000	51 700	*35(a)*
After 1 year but not more than 5 years	115 500	100 000	
More than 5 years	76 200	64 800	
	261 700	216 500	

FIGURE 13.5 Illustrative disclosures required by IAS 17 for lessees of operating leases

Lessors

Paragraph 56 of IAS 17 requires lessors to make the following disclosures, in addition to those required by IAS 32, with respect to operating leases:

(a) the future minimum lease payments under non-cancellable operating leases in the aggregate and for each of the following periods:
 (i) not later than one year;
 (ii) later than one year and not later than five years;
 (iii) later than five years;
(b) total contingent rents recognised as income in the period; and
(c) a general description of the lessor's leasing arrangements.

Figure 13.6 provides an illustration of the disclosures required by IAS 17.

			IAS 17 *para.*
Note 1: Summary of accounting policies (extract) **Leasing** Leases are classified as finance leases whenever the terms of the lease transfer substantially all the risks and rewards of ownership to the lessee. All other leases are classified as operating leases. *The entity as a lessor* Rental income from operating leases is recognised on a straight-line basis over the term of the relevant lease.			*56(c)*
Note 43: Operating lease arrangements Future minimum lease payments receivable under non-cancellable operating leases are as follows:			
	2009	**2008**	
Within 1 year	81 000	60 200	*56(a)*
After 1 year but not more than 5 years	317 900	324 000	
More than 5 years	153 900	228 800	
	552 800	613 000	
Contingent rent income amounting to $15 600 (2008: nil) was recognised during the period.			*56(b)*

FIGURE 13.6 Illustrative disclosures required by IAS 17 for lessors of operating leases

13.8.3 Accounting for lease incentives

In order to induce prospective lessees to enter into non-cancellable operating leases, lessors may offer lease incentives such as rent-free periods, upfront cash payments or contributions towards lessee expenses such as fit-out or removal costs. However attractive these incentives appear, it is unlikely that they are truly free because the lessor will structure the rental payments so as to recover the costs of the incentives over the lease term. Thus, rental payments will be higher than for leases that do not offer incentives.

IAS 17 is silent about incentives, and deals only with accounting for the rental payments made under the operating lease agreement. As a result, SIC 15 *Operating Leases — Incentives* was issued in December 1998 to provide guidance on accounting for incentives by both lessors and lessees. Paragraph 3 of this interpretation requires that all incentives associated with an operating lease should be regarded as part of the net consideration agreed for the use of the leased asset, irrespective of the nature or form of the incentive or the timing of the lease payments.

- For lessors — the aggregate cost of the incentives is treated as a reduction in rental income over the lease term on a straight-line basis.

- For lessees — the aggregate benefit of incentives is treated as a reduction in rental expense over the lease term on a straight-line basis.

In both cases, another systematic basis can be used if it better represents the diminishment of the leased asset.

ILLUSTRATIVE EXAMPLE 13.6

Accounting for lease incentives

As an incentive to enter a 4-year operating lease for a warehouse, Florida Ltd receives an upfront cash payment of $600 upon signing an agreement to pay Iceland Ltd an annual rental of $11 150.

Florida Ltd will make the following journal entries with respect to the lease incentive:

At inception of the lease			
Cash	Dr	600	
Incentive from Lessor	Cr		600
(Recognition of liability to lessor)			
Payment entry (year 1)			
Lease Expense	Dr	11 000	
Incentive from Lessor*	Dr	150	
Cash	Cr		11 150
(Record payment of rent and reduction in liability)			
*Being 600/4.			

Iceland Ltd will make the following journal entries with respect to the lease incentive:

At inception of the lease			
Incentive to lessee	Dr	600	
Cash	Cr		600
(Recognition of receivable)			
Receipt entry (year 1)			
Cash	Dr	11 150	
Incentive to lessee*	Cr		150
Rent income	Cr		11 000
(Record receipt of rent and reduction in receivable)			
*Being 600/4.			

This broad-brush approach assumes that all incentives are the same, but a number of issues need to be resolved:

- the need to distinguish between 'capital' incentives such as property fit-outs, particularly in the retail industry, and 'cash' incentives such as rent-free periods
- the need to distinguish between property fit-outs that became part of the structure of a leased property and were owned by the lessor, and fit-outs that were owned by the lessee
- the difficulty of determining in practice whether market rentals were being paid by major tenants who had received incentives to lease space in a property
- the need to exclude incentives provided to achieve a desired tenancy mix aimed at improving rentals under future leases of the property.

To date, these matters have not been considered by the IASB.

13.9 ACCOUNTING FOR SALE AND LEASEBACK TRANSACTIONS

A 'sale and leaseback' is a lease transaction that creates an accounting problem for lessees. Effectively, this type of arrangement involves the sale of an asset that is then leased back from the purchaser for all or part of its remaining economic life. Hence, the original owner becomes the lessee but the asset itself does not move. In substance, the lessee gives up legal ownership but still retains control over some or all of the asset's future economic benefits via the lease agreement. Generally, the asset is sold at a price equal to or greater than its fair value, and is leased back for lease payments sufficient to repay the purchaser for the cash invested plus a reasonable return. Therefore, the lease payment and the sale price are usually interdependent because they are negotiated as a package (IAS 17 paragraph 58).

Entities normally enter into sale and leaseback arrangements to generate immediate cash flows while still retaining the use of the asset. Such arrangements are particularly attractive where the fair value of an asset is considerably higher than its carrying amount, or where a large amount of capital is tied up in property and plant.

The major accounting issue revolves around the sale rather than the lease component of the transaction. The lease is classified and accounted for in exactly the same fashion as normal lease transactions, but accounting for the sale transaction differs according to whether the lease is classified as a finance lease or an operating lease.

13.9.1 Finance leases

According to IAS 17 paragraph 59:

> If a sale and leaseback transaction results in a finance lease, any excess of sales proceeds over the carrying amount shall not be immediately recognised as income by a seller-lessee. Instead, it shall be deferred and amortised over the lease term.

This accounting treatment is justified on the basis that the leaseback of the asset negates the sale transaction. In other words, there was a finance agreement between the lessor and the lessee — not a sale — with the asset used as security. Paragraph 60 of IAS 17 states that for this reason 'it is not appropriate to regard an excess of sales proceeds over the carrying amount as income'. The accounting standard provides no guidance on how the deferred income is to be classified in the statement of financial position. In this chapter, any deferred income is recognised separately and classified as 'other' liabilities on the statement of financial position. Amortisation is on a straight-line basis over the lease term.

ILLUSTRATIVE EXAMPLE 13.7

Sale and leaseback

In an attempt to alleviate its liquidity problems, Faroe Ltd entered into an agreement on 1 July 2009 to sell its processing plant to Brazil Ltd for $3.5 million (which is the fair value of the plant). At the date of sale, the plant had a carrying amount of $2.75 million. Brazil Ltd immediately leased the processing plant back to Faroe Ltd. The terms of the lease agreement were:

Lease term	6 years
Economic life of plant	8 years
Annual rental payment, in arrears (commencing 30/6/10)	$700 000
Residual value of plant at end of lease term (fully guaranteed)	$500 000
Interest rate implicit in the lease	10%

The lease is non-cancellable. The annual rental payment includes $35 000 to reimburse the lessor for maintenance costs incurred on behalf of the lessee.

Accounting for the sale of the processing plant

Step 1 — Classify the leaseback

Faroe Ltd must determine whether the leaseback has resulted in the company retaining substantially all of the risks and rewards associated with the processing plant, even though legal title has passed to Brazil Ltd, before classifying the lease as a finance lease in accordance with IAS 17 requirements.

Based on the following evidence, both lessor and lessee should conclude that the lease should be classified as a *finance lease*:

- the lease is non-cancellable
- ownership is not expected to be transferred at the end of the lease term
- the lease term is a major part of the economic life of the leased asset
- the present value of the minimum lease payments is substantially all of the fair value of the leased asset. It was calculated as follows:

PV of MLP	= ($665 000 × 4.3553) + ($500 000 × 0.5645)
	= $2 896 275 + $282 250
	= $3 178 525
PV/FV	= $3 178 525/$3 500 000
	90.8%

Step 2 — Record the 'sale' transaction

This illustrative example shows only those journal entries relating to the sale of the processing plant to Brazil Ltd. The lease is recorded as shown in illustrative example 13.2.

FAROE LTD General Journal			
Year ended 30 June 2010			
1 July 2009:			
Cash	Dr	3 500 000	
Deferred Gain on Sale	Cr		750 000
Processing Plant	Cr		2 750 000
(Sale of plant under sale and leaseback agreement)			
30 June 2010:			
Deferred Gain on Sale	Dr	125 000	
Gain on Sale of Leased Plant	Cr		125 000
(Amortisation of deferred gain: $750 000/6)			

The deferred gain is recognised as income on a straight-line basis over the lease term.

13.9.2 Operating leases

All operating leases are accounted for in the same way regardless of whether a sale and leaseback transaction is involved. The only accounting issue involves the initial recognition of the sale transaction.

The accounting treatment of the gain or loss on sale is determined by the relationship between the sale price of the asset and the asset's fair value on the date of sale. Essentially, a gain or loss on sale can be recognised immediately only when it equates to the gain or loss that would have been earned on a sale at fair value. Excess or reduced gains or losses are to be deferred and amortised over the lease term. Table 13.1 is part of the Implementation Guidance to IAS 17, and sets out the alternative treatments as required by paragraphs 61–63 of the standard.

TABLE 13.1 Alternative treatments of gain or loss on sale

	Carrying amount equal to fair value	Carrying amount less than fair value	Carrying amount above fair value
Sale price at fair value (paragraph 61)			
Profit	No profit	Recognise profit immediately	Not applicable
Loss	No loss	Not applicable	Recognise loss immediately
Sale price below fair value (paragraph 61)			
Profit	No profit	Recognise profit immediately	No profit (note 1)
Loss not compensated for *by future lease payments at below market price*	Recognise loss immediately	Recognise loss immediately	(note 1)
Loss compensated for by future lease payments at below market price	Defer and amortise loss	Defer and amortise loss	(note 1)
Sale price above fair value (paragraph 61)			
Profit	Defer and amortise profit	Defer and amortise excess of selling price over fair value Recognise any excess of fair value over carrying amount immediately (note 3)	Defer and amortise profit (note 2)
Loss	No loss	No loss	(note 1)

Notes

1. These parts of the table represent circumstances dealt with in paragraph 63 of the standard. Paragraph 63 requires the carrying amount of an asset to be written down to fair value where it is subject to a sale and leaseback. This therefore results in a carrying amount equal to fair value.
2. Profit is the difference between the fair value and sale price because the carrying amount would have been written down to fair value in accordance with paragraph 63.
3. The excess profit (the excess of selling price over fair value) is deferred and amortised over the period for which the asset is expected to be used. Any excess of fair value over the carrying amount is recognised immediately.

Source: Adapted from IAS 17 Implementation Guidance, pp. 28–9.

13.9.3 Disclosures required

Sale and leaseback transactions are subject to the same disclosure requirements prescribed for lessees and lessors in relation to both operating and finance leases. Unique or unusual provisions of the agreement should be disclosed as part of the required description of material leasing arrangements. Additionally, sale and leaseback transactions may fall under the separate disclosure criteria in IAS 1 *Presentation of Financial Statements* with respect to gains or losses on the sale of assets.

13.9.4 Deferral and amortisation — some theoretical concerns

The accounting treatment prescribed by IAS 17 paragraphs 59 and 61 relating to any gain or loss on the sale of an asset in a sale and leaseback transaction may result in the deferral of such gains or losses and their amortisation over the lease term. The *Framework* does not support this accounting treatment, because it results in reporting debit and credit balances in the statement of financial position that do not meet the definitions of assets and liabilities. In illustrative example 13.7,

Faroe Ltd records a 'deferred gain' of $750 000 on 1 July 2009, but is this a liability? The *Framework* in paragraph 49 defines a liability as:

> a present obligation of the entity arising from past events, the settlement of which is expected to result in an outflow from the entity of resources embodying economic benefits.

The $750 000 credit balance recorded by the lessee certainly arises from a past event — the sale of the asset — but, as there is no future outflow in respect of this amount, it should not be classified and reported as a liability. Income is defined in paragraph 70 of the *Framework* as follows:

> Income is increases in economic benefits during the accounting period in the form of inflows or enhancements of assets or decreases of liabilities that result in increases in equity, other than those relating to contributions from equity participants.

The sale of its asset by Faroe Ltd provides a cash inflow of $3.5 million and the loss of $2.75 million in future benefits, resulting in a net increase in equity of $750 000. This transaction clearly gives rise to income. The accounting treatment prescribed by IAS 17 paragraphs 59 and 61 results in entities incorrectly reporting income as liabilities, or expenses as assets. Accordingly, the profit reported in the statement of comprehensive income will be incorrect, as will the total asset and liability figures reported on the statement of financial position. This 'error' situation will continue throughout the lease term as the 'deferred credit' or 'deferred debit' balances are amortised to profit and loss. Again, the rationale for this accounting treatment seems to be based on the notion that a lease is a quasi-sale transaction. There can be only one 'sale' recorded for a finance leaseback, and only a 'real' profit recorded for an operating leaseback. The reality, of course, is that the two transactions should be treated independently and recorded in accordance with the *Framework*.

13.10 PROPOSALS TO CHANGE THE LEASING STANDARD

In July 2006, as a result of the agreement between the IASB and the Financial Accounting Standards Board (FASB) to converge accounting standards, a joint working party was formed between the two bodies to propose a new accounting standard on leases. The aims of the project were stated as:

- to produce an improved accounting standard that faithfully reports the economics of leasing transactions
- to develop a principles-based standard
- to produce a converged standard that can be applied internationally.

As noted in the information provided for observers at the IASB meeting in July 2008, the main concerns about the current IAS 17 were:

- the dividing line between finance and operating leases is hard to define in a principled way
- any dividing line means that similar transactions are accounted for differently
- obligations under non-cancellable leases are little different from borrowings, but for operating leases are not recognised as liabilities
- assets used in the business that are held under operating leases are not shown on the statement of financial position, thereby overstating return on assets
- leases are scoped out of the financial instruments standards, leading to inconsistencies between leases and similar transactions
- lessor accounting is based on a deferral and matching model that is inconsistent with the direction the revenue recognition project is likely to take.

At the July 2008 meeting of the IASB, the IASB staff presented to the board a revised project plan for leases (see the meeting summaries and observer notes tab under the leases project on the current projects page of the IASB website www.iasb.org). The project plan envisaged a new accounting standard on leases being issued in 2011. The key issues discussed at the meeting were:

- the scope of the project and whether to include or exclude lessor accounting
- options to extend or terminate a lease
- contingent rentals
- the initial and subsequent measurement of a lessee's right-of-use asset and obligation to make rental payments
- whether to retain the requirements to classify leases as operating or finance leases.

Two key decisions made by the IASB at the July meeting were:

1. *To defer the development of a new accounting model for lessors*: because lessor accounting raises additional issues such as revenue recognition, the IASB does not believe that a standard can be issued in 2011 if both lessee and lessor accounting need to be resolved. Deferring the development of a new lessor accounting model may result in a lack of symmetry between lessee and lessor accounting, but the IASB believes that the benefits of an improvement to lessee accounting, particularly in relation to the recognition of assets and liabilities arising from operating leases, outweighs the costs of having a different accounting model for lessees and lessors.
2. *To apply the present finance lease model to all leases*: currently leases are classified into finance and operating leases. The IASB staff produced five reasons why the requirement to classify leases should be removed:
   (a) All leases give rise to a right to use the leased item that meets the definition of an asset; a single conceptual model to account for all leases is preferable.
   (b) The removal of classification would result in a simpler accounting standard.
   (c) Classification is a difficult process, often resulting in similar transactions being accounted for differently. Removal of classification would result in similar transactions being accounted for in the same way.
   (d) Retaining the classification may result in inconsistencies in how the minimum lease payments are determined for classification purposes. For example, contingent rentals may be included for finance leases but not operating leases.
   (e) Any differences between current accounting requirements for finance leases and any new model developed for operating leases are unlikely to justify the additional complexity of a classification requirement.

Some tentative decisions made by the IASB were:

- to develop a new approach for *contingent lease payments* using a probability-weighted best estimate of the rentals payable
- that a lessee should *initially measure* both its right-to-use asset and its lease obligation at the present value of the lease payments
- that a lessee should *discount* the lease payments using the lessee's incremental rate for secured borrowing instead of the interest rate implicit in the lease
- that, on subsequent measurement, a lessee should *amortise* the right-to-use asset over the shorter of the lease term and the economic life of the leased asset based upon the pattern of consumption of economic benefits embodied in the asset.

Accounting for leases by most countries is very comparable, in that most countries require the application of principles similar to those in IAS 17. However, it is also recognised that the accounting principles applied are flawed. Hopefully, completion of the joint project between the IASB and the FASB will result in the issue of a principles-based accounting standard that provides relevant information on lease transactions.

13.11 COMPREHENSIVE EXAMPLE

ILLUSTRATIVE EXAMPLE 13.8

Manufacturer lessor

On 1 July 2008, Pebble Ltd leased a photocopier from Staats Ltd, a company that manufactures, retails and leases copiers. The photocopier had cost Staats Ltd $30 000 to make but had a fair value on 1 July 2008 of $35 080. The lease agreement contained the following provisions:

Lease term	3 years
Annual payment, payable in advance on 1 July each year	$14 500
Economic life of the copier	4 years
Estimated residual value at the end of the lease term when the copier is returned to Staats Ltd	$3 000
Residual value guaranteed by Pebble Ltd	$1 500
Interest rate implicit in the lease	10%
The lease is cancellable, provided another lease is immediately entered into.	

The annual payment included an amount of $2500 p.a. to reimburse Staats Ltd for the cost of paper and toner supplied to Pebble Ltd. Staats Ltd's solicitor prepared the lease agreement for a fee of $1365.

On 30 June 2011, at the end of the lease term, Pebble Ltd returned the copier to Staats Ltd, which sold the copier for $3000.

Required

Part A

A. Classify the lease for both the lessor and the lessee. Justify your answer.

B. Prepare the following:
  1. *for the lessee:* the lease payment schedule and the journal entries for the year ended 30 June 2011 only
  2. *for the lessor:* the lease receipts schedule and the journal entries for the year ended 30 June 2009 only.

Part B

Assume that the lease term is for 2 years, payments are $12 000 immediately and a further $12 000 in 12 months time, and no residual value has been guaranteed by Pebble Ltd on return of the asset to Staats Ltd.

A. Classify the lease for both the lessor and the lessee. Justify your answer.

B. Prepare the journal entries for both lessor and lessee for the year ended 30 June 2009 only.

Solution to Part A

A. *Classify the lease.*

1. Determine whether the lessor is a financier or a manufacturer/dealer. This is essential as it changes the accounting treatment for initial direct costs paid by the lessor and the definition of the interest rate implicit in the lease.

   Staats Ltd is a manufacturer lessor. Accordingly, the initial direct costs are treated as part of cost of sales and are not included in calculating the interest rate implicit in the lease.

2. Examine the terms of the lease agreement to determine whether substantially all of the risks and rewards associated with ownership of the copier have been transferred to the lessee.
   (a) *Is the lease non-cancellable?* The lease is cancellable provided that another lease is immediately entered into. Such an arrangement is deemed to be non-cancellable under part (c) of the definition of a 'non-cancellable lease' in IAS 17 paragraph 4.
   (b) *Is ownership expected to be transferred at the end of the lease term?* No, the copier will be returned to the lessor at the end of the lease term, but the lessee has partially guaranteed its residual value at that date.
   (c) *Is the lease term for all or a major part of the asset's economic life?* The lease term at 3 years is 75% of the copier's economic life. This represents a major part of that economic life.
   (d) *Is the present value of the minimum lease payments equal to substantially all of the fair value of the asset at the inception of the lease? (Minimum lease payments are the payments over the lease term that the lessee is required to make excluding contingent rent and executory costs together with any guaranteed residual value.)* Annual payments of $14 500 are required but included in these is an amount of $2500 p.a. to cover operational costs paid by the lessor. Thus, the minimum lease payments for the copier are one payment of $12 000 immediately, two future payments of $12 000 and a guaranteed residual value of $1500.

Interest rate implicit in the lease

The interest rate which discounts the minimum lease payments and the unguaranteed residual value of $1500 to the aggregate of the fair value of the copier ($35 080) at the inception of the lease is 10%.

Applying the discount rate to the minimum lease payments, we find the present value to be 97%, which is substantially all of the fair value of the copier.

$$
\begin{aligned}
\text{PV of MLP} &= \$12\,000 + (\$12\,000 \times 1.7355\ [T_2\ 10\%\ 2y]) + (\$1\,500 \times 0.7513\ [T_1\ 10\%\ 3y]) \\
&= \$12\,000 + \$20\,826 + \$1\,127 \\
&= \$33\,953/35\,080 = 96.8\%
\end{aligned}
$$

Given the above, both companies will classify the transaction as a finance lease.

B. 1. *Prepare a lease payments schedule and journal entries for the lessee for the year ended 30 June 2011 only.*

PEBBLE LTD (Lessee)
Lease Payments Schedule

	MLP	Interest expense	Reduction in liability	Balance of liability
1 July 2008				$33 953[a]
1 July 2008	$12 000	—[b]	$12 000	21 953[c]
1 July 2009	12 000	$2195[d]	9 805[e]	12 148
1 July 2010	12 000	1215	10 785	1 363
30 June 2011	1 500	137	1 363	—
	$37 500	$3547	$33 953	

(a) The lower of PV of MLP and fair value of the copier as required by IAS 17 paragraph 20.
(b) Because the first payment is made immediately it is not discounted.
(c) The balance is reduced as each lease payment is made.
(d) Equals the balance of the liability $21 953 × 10%, the interest rate implicit in the lease.
(e) The payment must be split into interest expense and reduction of the lease liability as per IAS 17 paragraph 25.

PEBBLE LTD
Journal Entries
for year ended 30 June 2011

2010				
July 1	Lease Liability	Dr	10 785	
	Interest Payable	Dr	1 215	
	Executory Costs	Dr	2 500	
	Cash	Cr		14 500
	(Recording the third and final lease payment)			
2011				
June 30	Depreciation Expense	Dr	10 817	
	Accumulated Depreciation	Cr		10 817
	(Recognition of the depreciation of the leased asset for the year as per paragraph 27 [$33 953 – $1 500/3])			
	Lease Liability	Dr	1 363	
	Interest Expense	Dr	137	
	Accumulated Depreciation	Dr	32 453	
	Leased Asset	Cr		33 953
	(Return of the copier at the end of the lease term)			

B. 2. *Prepare a lease receipts schedule and journal entries for the lessor for the year ended 30 June 2009 only.*

STAATS LTD (Lessor)
Lease Receipts Schedule

	MLR	Interest revenue	Reduction in receivable	Balance of receivable
1 July 2008				$35 080[a]
1 July 2008	$12 000	—[b]	$12 000	23 080[c]
1 July 2009	12 000	$2 308[d]	9 692[e]	13 388
1 July 2010	12 000	1 339	10 661	2 727
30 June 2011	3 000	273	2 727	—
	$39 000	$3 920	$35 080	

(a) Net investment in the lease = fair value of the copier as required by IAS 17 paragraph 36.
(b) Because the first receipt occurs immediately it is not discounted.
(c) The balance is reduced as each lease receipt is recorded.
(d) Equals the balance of the receivable $23 080 × 10%, the interest rate implicit in the lease.
(e) The receipt must be split into interest revenue and reduction of the lease receivable as per IAS 17 paragraph 37.

Because Staats Ltd is a manufacturer lessor, the first journal entry must record the profit or loss on sale of the asset as required by IAS 17 paragraph 42.

STAATS LTD
Journal Entries
for year ended 30 June 2009

2008				
July 1	Lease Receivable	Dr	35 080	
	Sales Revenue*	Cr		33 953
	Cost of Sales**	Dr	28 873	
	Inventory	Cr		30 000
	(Recognition of lease receivable and recording sale of copier)			
	*PV of MLP **Cost less PV of unguaranteed residual ($1 500 × 0.7513)			
	Lease Costs	Dr	1 365	
	Cash	Cr		1 365
	(Payment of initial direct costs)			
	Cash	Dr	14 500	
	Lease Receivable	Cr		12 000
	Reimbursement Revenue	Cr		2 500
	(Receipt of first payment)			
2009				
June 30	Paper and Toner Expense	Dr	2 500	
	Cash	Cr		2 500
	(Payment of executory costs)			
	Interest Receivable	Dr	2 308	
	Interest Revenue	Cr		2 308
	(Interest expense accrual)			

Solution to Part B

A. *Classify the lease.*

1. Determine whether the lessor is a financier or a manufacturer/dealer. This is essential as it changes the accounting treatment for initial direct costs paid by the lessor and also the definition of the interest rate implicit in the lease.

Staats Ltd is a manufacturer lessor. Accordingly, the initial direct costs are treated as part of cost of sales and are not included in calculating the interest rate implicit in the lease.

2. Examine the terms of the lease agreement to determine whether substantially all the risks and rewards associated with ownership of the copier have been transferred to the lessee.
   (a) *Is the lease non-cancellable?* The lease is cancellable provided that another lease is immediately entered into. Such an arrangement is deemed to be non-cancellable under part (c) of the definition of a 'non-cancellable lease' in IAS 17 paragraph 4.
   (b) *Is ownership expected to be transferred at the end of the lease term?* No, the copier will be returned to the lessor at the end of the lease term.
   (c) *Is the lease term for all or a major part of the asset's economic life?* The lease term at 2 years is 50% of the copier's economic life. At this level, it does not represent a major part of that economic life.
   (d) *Is the present value of the minimum lease payments equal to substantially all of the fair value of the asset at the inception of the lease? (Minimum lease payments are the payments over the lease term that the lessee is required to make excluding contingent rent and executory costs together with any guaranteed residual value.)* Annual payments of \$14 500 are required but included in these is an amount of \$2500 p.a. to cover operational costs paid by the lessor. Thus, the minimum lease payments for the copier are one payment of \$12 000 immediately and one payment of \$12 000 next year.

Interest rate implicit in the lease

The interest rate which discounts the minimum lease payments and the unguaranteed residual value of \$1500 to the aggregate of the fair value of the copier (\$35 080) at the inception of the lease is 10%.

Applying the discount rate to the minimum lease payments, we find the present value is 65%, and not substantially all of the fair value of the copier.

$$\begin{aligned}\text{PV of MLP} &= \$12\,000 + (\$12\,000 \times 0.9091\ [T_1\ 10\%\ 1y])\\ &= \$12\,000 + \$10\,909\\ &= \$22\,909/35\,080 = 65.3\%\end{aligned}$$

Given the above, both companies will classify the transaction as an operating lease.

B. *Prepare the journal entries for both lessor and lessee for the year ended 30 June 2009 only.*

PEBBLE LTD (Lessee)
Journal Entries
for year ended 30 June 2009

2008				
July 1	Rent Expense	Dr	12 000	
	Cash	Cr		12 000
	(Recording the first lease payment)			

STAATS LTD (Lessor)
Journal Entries
for year ended 30 June 2009

2008				
July 1	Cash	Dr	12 000	
	Rental Income	Cr		12 000
	(Recording the first lease receipt)			
2009				
June 30	Depreciation Expense – Copier	Dr	7 500	
	Accumulated Depreciation	Cr		7 500
	(Depreciation on copier for the year [\$30 000/4])			

ILLUSTRATIVE EXAMPLE 13.9

Financier lessor

On 30 June 2009, Bravo Ltd leased a vehicle to Saunders Ltd. Bravo Ltd had purchased the vehicle on that day for its fair value of $89 721. The lease agreement, which cost Bravo Ltd $1457 to have drawn up, contained the following provisions:

Lease term	4 years
Annual payment, payable in advance on 30 June each year	$23 900
Economic life of vehicle	6 years
Estimated residual value at end of economic life	$2 000
Estimated residual value at end of lease term	$15 000
Residual value guaranteed by lessee	$15 000
Interest rate implicit in the lease	7%

The lease is cancellable, but cancellation will incur a monetary penalty equivalent to 2 years rental payments. Included in the annual payment is an amount of $1900 to cover reimbursement for the costs of insurance and maintenance paid by the lessor. The directors of Saunders Ltd have indicated that they are interested in acquiring the asset at the end of the lease.

Required

A. Explain why both Saunders Ltd and Bravo Ltd classify the above transaction as a finance lease.

B. Prepare the following for the lessor, Bravo Ltd:
   1. the lease receipts schedule (show all workings)
   2. the journal entries for the year ended 30 June 2009 and 30 June 2010.

C. Prepare the following for the lessee, Saunders Ltd:
   1. the lease payments schedule (show all workings)
   2. the journal entries for the year ended 30 June 2009 and 30 June 2010.

Solution

A. *Classify the lease.*

1. Determine whether the lessor is a financier or a manufacturer/dealer. This is essential as it changes the accounting treatment for initial direct costs paid by the lessor and the definition of the interest rate implicit in the lease.

   Bravo Ltd is a financier lessor. Accordingly, the initial direct costs are treated as part of the lease receivable and are included in calculating the interest rate implicit in the lease.

2. Examine the terms of the lease agreement to determine whether substantially all of the risks and rewards associated with ownership of the copier have been transferred to the lessee.
   (a) *Is the lease non-cancellable?* The lease is cancellable, but cancellation will incur a monetary penalty equivalent to 2 years rental payments. Such an arrangement is deemed to be non-cancellable under part (d) of the definition of a 'non-cancellable lease' in IAS 17 paragraph 4.
   (b) *Is ownership expected to be transferred at the end of the lease term?* Yes, the directors of Saunders Ltd have indicated that they are interested in acquiring the asset at the end of the lease term. Additionally, they have guaranteed all of its residual value at that date.
   (c) *Is the lease term for all or a major part of the asset's economic life?* The lease term at 4 years is 67% of the copier's economic life. At this level, the lease term is not a major part of that economic life.
   (d) *Is the present value of the minimum lease payments equal to substantially all of the fair value of the asset at the inception of the lease? (Minimum lease payments are the payments over the lease term that the lessee is required to make excluding contingent rent and executory costs together with any guaranteed residual value.)* Annual payments of $23 600 are required but included in these is an amount of $1900 p.a. to cover operational costs paid by the lessor. Thus, the minimum lease payments for the copier are one payment of $22 000 immediately, three future payments of $22 000, and a guaranteed residual value of $15 000.

Interest rate implicit in the lease

The interest rate, which discounts the minimum lease payments and the unguaranteed residual value of $1500 to the aggregate of the fair value of the vehicle ($89 721) and the initial direct costs incurred by Bravo Ltd ($1457) at the inception of the lease, is 7% as shown below:

$22 000 + ($22 000 × 2.6243 [T_2 7% 3y]) + ($15 000 × 0.7629 [$T_1$ 7% 4y])
= $22 000 + $57 735 + $11 443
= $89 721 (fair value) + $1457 (initial direct costs) = $91 178

Therefore 7% is the interest rate implicit in the lease.

Since the lessee has guaranteed all of the residual value at the end of the lease term, substantially all the risks and rewards relating to the vehicle have been transferred to the lessee.

Given the above, both companies have classified the transaction as a finance lease.

B. 1. *Prepare the lease receipts schedule for the lessor, Bravo Ltd.*

BRAVO LTD
Lease Receipts Schedule

	MLR	Interest revenue	Reduction in receivable	Balance of receivable
30 June 2009				$91 178
30 June 2009	$ 22 000	—	$22 000	69 178
30 June 2010	22 000	$ 4 842	17 158	52 020
30 June 2011	22 000	3 641	18 359	33 661
30 June 2012	22 000	2 356	19 644	14 017
30 June 2013	15 000	983	14 017	—
	$103 000	$11 822	$91 178	

B. 2. *Prepare the journal entries for Bravo Ltd for years ended 30 June 2009 and 30 June 2010.*
Since Bravo Ltd is a financier lessor, the initial direct costs are included in the lease receivable.

BRAVO LTD
Journal Entries
for years ended 30 June 2009 and 2010

Year ending 2009			
Vehicle	Dr	89 721	
Cash	Cr		89 721
(Purchase of vehicle to be leased)			
Lease Receivable	Dr	89 721	
Vehicle	Cr		89 721
Cash	Cr		1 457
(Lease of vehicle and payment of initial direct costs)			
Cash	Dr	23 900	
Lease Receivable	Cr		22 000
Unearned Executory Revenue	Cr		1 900
(Receipt of first payment)			

Year ending 2010			
Insurance and Maintenance	Dr	1 900	
Cash	Cr		1 900
(Costs paid on behalf of lessee)			
Unearned Executory Revenue	Dr	1 900	
Reimbursement Revenue	Cr		1 900
(Transfer of reimbursement revenue)			
Cash	Dr	23 900	
Interest Revenue	Cr		4 842
Lease Receivable	Cr		17 158
Unearned Executory Revenue	Cr		1 900
(Receipt of second payment)			

C. 1. *Prepare the lease payments schedule for the lessee, Saunders Ltd.*
Paragraph 20 of IAS 17 requires the lessee to record a lease liability measured at the lower of fair value of the leased asset and the PV of MLP at the inception of the lease. In this situation, the PV of MLP discounted at the 7% interest rate used by the lessor is greater than fair value, hence the lessee must recalculate the interest rate based on the fair value of the asset as below:

$\$22\,000 + (\$22\,000 \times 2.5771\ [T_2\ 8\%\ 3y]) + (\$15\,000 \times 0.7350\ [T_1\ 8\%\ 4y])$
$= \$22\,000 + \$56\,696 + \$11\,025$
$= \$89\,721$ (fair value)

Therefore 8% is the interest rate implicit in the lease for the lessee.

SAUNDERS LTD
Lease Payments Schedule

	MLP	Interest expense	Reduction in liability	Balance of liability
30 June 2009				$89 721
30 June 2009	$ 22 000	—	$22 000	67 721
30 June 2010	22 000	$ 5 418	16 582	51 139
30 June 2011	22 000	4 091	17 909	33 230
30 June 2012	22 000	2 658	19 342	13 888
30 June 2013	15 000	1 112	13 888	—
	$103 000	$13 279	$89 721	

C. 2. *Prepare the journal entries for Saunders Ltd for the years ended 30 June 2009 and 2010.*

SAUNDERS LTD
Journal Entries
for years ended 30 June 2009 and 2010

Year ending 2009			
Leased Vehicle	Dr	89 721	
Lease Liability	Cr		89 721
(Recognition of lease)			
Lease Liability	Dr	22 000	
Prepaid Executory Costs	Dr	1 900	
Cash	Cr		23 900
(First lease payment)			

Year ending 2010			
Executory Costs	Dr	1 900	
Prepaid Executory Costs	Cr		1 900
(Executory costs expired during the year)			
Depreciation Expense	Dr	14 620	
Accumulated Depreciation	Cr		14 620
(Depreciation of leased asset for the year $89 721 – 2 000/6 (use economic life as ownership may be transferred))			
Lease Liability	Dr	16 582	
Interest Expense	Dr	5 418	
Prepaid Executory Costs	Dr	1 900	
Cash	Cr		23 900
(Second lease payment)			

SUMMARY

Leases are arrangements whereby the right to use an asset is transferred to a lessee but ownership is retained by the lessor. By definition, finance leases transfer substantially all of the risks and rewards incidental to ownership from the lessor to the lessee. Operating leases do not. All leases must be classified as either operating leases or finance leases at the inception of the lease.

For finance leases, lessees must record a lease asset and a lease liability measured at the lower of the fair value of the leased property and the present value of the minimum lease payments. The asset is subsequently depreciated over the lease term or its economic life if ownership is to be transferred at the end of the lease. The liability is reduced as lease payments are made.

For finance leases, lessors must transfer their net investment in the lease to a receivable account which is subsequently reduced by lease receipts and the eventual return of the asset at the end of the lease. Manufacturer and dealer lessors must also record a profit or loss on sale of the asset at the beginning of the lease term.

Operating leases are treated as a rental arrangement with lessors recording rental revenue and lessees recording rental expense over the term of the lease.

Some of the accounting treatments required by IAS 17, notably those relating to sale and leaseback arrangements, create assets and liabilities which are not in accordance with the *Framework*'s definitions. Accordingly, the IASB is reviewing the accounting standard with a view to removing such anomalies.

Discussion questions

1. Leases are classified on the basis of 'substance over form'. What does this criterion mean and how does it relate to the capitalisation of finance leases?
2. What are 'minimum lease payments'?
3. If a lease agreement states that 'the lessee guarantees a residual value, at the end of the lease term, of $20 000', what does this mean?
4. What is meant by 'the interest rate implicit in a lease'?
5. Where a lessor incurs initial direct costs in establishing a lease agreement, how are these costs to be accounted for by the lessor?
6. Identify three possible adverse effects on a lessee entity's financial statements arising from the classification of a lease arrangement as a finance lease.
7. How, according to IAS 17 requirements, are finance leases to be accounted for by lessees?
8. How, according to IAS 17 requirements, are finance leases to be accounted for by lessors?
9. How does the accounting treatment for a finance lease change if the lessor is a manufacturer/dealer lessor?

10. How, according to IAS 17 requirements, are operating leases accounted for by lessees?
11. How, according to IAS 17 requirements, are operating leases to be accounted for by lessors?
12. In the context of operating leases, what are lease incentives and how are they accounted for?
13. Explain how a profit made by a lessee on a sale and leaseback transaction is to be accounted for.
14. 'The accounting treatment required by IAS 17 paragraph 59 is not in accordance with the *Framework*.' Discuss.
15. What changes to accounting for leases are proposed in future versions of the standard?
16. For the following arrangements, discuss whether they are 'in substance' lease transactions, and thus fall under the ambit of IAS 17.
    1. Entity A leases an asset to Entity B, and obtains a non-recourse loan from a financial institution using the lease rentals and asset as collateral. Entity A sells the asset subject to the lease and the loan to a trustee, and leases the same asset back.
    2. Entity A enters into an arrangement to buy petroleum products from Entity B. The products are produced in a refinery built and operated by Entity B on a site owned by Entity A. Although Entity B could provide the products from other refineries which it owns, it is not practical to do so. Entity B retains the right to sell products produced by the refinery to other customers but there is only a remote possibility that it will do so. The arrangement requires Entity A to make both fixed unavoidable payments and variable payments based on input costs at a target level of efficiency to Entity B.
    3. Entity A leases an asset to Entity B for its entire economic life and leases the same asset back under the same terms and conditions as the original lease. The two entities have a legally enforceable right to set off the amounts owing to one another, and an intention to settle these amounts on a net basis.
    4. Entity A enters into a non-cancellable 4-year lease with Entity B for an asset with an expected economic life of 10 years. Entity A has an option to renew the lease for a further 4 years at the end of the lease term. At the conclusion of the lease arrangement, the asset will revert back to Entity B. In a separate agreement, Entity B is granted a put option to sell the asset to Entity A should its market value at the end of the lease be less than the residual value.
17. Hebrides Ltd is a company involved in a diverse range of activities involving power generation, machinery retailing and agriculture. The accounting policy note attached to the 2010 financial statements included the following under the heading 'Leases':

    During the year the company entered into a refinancing arrangement which involved the sale of the Lilac Mountain power station under a sale and leaseback arrangement. The difference between the carrying amount of the power station and its original cost has been included in profit and disclosed as a gain on sale of a non-current asset. Sales proceeds in excess of the original cost have been treated as deferred income in the statement of financial position. The amount of deferred income will be systematically amortised over the term of the lease.

    The power station is a unique asset in that the licence to generate power from that station is held by Hebrides Ltd and cannot be transferred. The leaseback period is for the remaining 20 years economic life of the power station and Hebrides Ltd has guaranteed its expected residual value at that time of $55 000.

    Required
    1. Does the Hebrides Ltd sale and leaseback arrangement involve a finance lease or an operating lease? Justify your choice.
    2. Critically evaluate the accounting treatment adopted by Hebrides Ltd with respect to the sale and leaseback agreement. Refer, where necessary, to relevant sections of IAS 17.
    3. Compare the resulting deferred income account with the *Framework*'s definitions of and recognition criteria for the elements of financial statements.
18. Shetland Ltd runs a successful chain of fashion boutiques, but has been experiencing significant cash flow problems. The directors are examining a proposal made by an accounting consultant that all the shops currently owned by the company be sold and either leased back or the businesses moved to alternative leased shops. The directors are keen on the plan but are puzzled by the consultant's insistence that all lease agreements for the shops be 'operating' rather than 'finance' leases.

Required

1. Explain the difference between a finance lease and an operating lease.
2. Explain, by reference to the requirements of IAS 17, why the consultant prefers operating to finance leases.
3. Describe three disadvantages to the company of entering into finance lease agreements.

19. Read the following article written by Cathy Bolt that appeared in *The West Australian*, 17 February 2007.

> **Bunnings to sell, lease back $200m of stores**
> Buoyed by the strength of the retail property market, Wesfarmers yesterday put a package of 11 of its Bunnings hardware warehouse stores on the block on a sale-and-leaseback basis in a move expected to raise more than $200 million.
>
> Over the past decade, it has become standard practice for Bunnings to offload its retail warehouses to external landlords once they are fully developed but the latest sales campaign puts an unprecedented number on the market at once.
>
> Bunnings Warehouse Property Trust, set up by Wesfarmers in 1998 to remove the real estate underlying its expanding hardware empire from its balance sheet, confirmed yesterday it would be among the bidders for the portfolio, which would deliver a big step-up in its existing portfolio of 51 Bunnings warehouses, around a third of the retailer's Australasian big-box network.
>
> But investment bank Grant Samuel, appointed to manage the sale process, said it expected competition to be very high.
>
> The portfolio is six properties in Australia — Belconnen in the ACT, Penrith and Nowra in NSW, Nerang and Stafford in Queensland and Box Hill in Victoria — and five in New Zealand at Whangarei, Rotorua, Palmerston North, Hamilton and Nae Nae.
>
> The initial lease terms are for 12 years followed by two five-year options. Bunnings managing director John Gillam said it had been encouraged by a trend over the past 18 months for investment grade properties bundled together to be keenly sought. Since the initial 20 properties were put into the Bunnings Warehouse Property Trust, the biggest number sold at once was three to Valad Property in 2005.
>
> The most recent was a property in North Belmont, NSW, bought by BWPT for $10.85 million on an initial yield of 6.95 per cent rising to 7.2 per cent in March.

Required

1. Discuss whether the set up of the Bunning Warehouse Property Trust would achieve the stated aim of removing the real estate from Wesfarmer's balance sheet (statement of financial position).
2. Outline how the trust should account for the leaseback given the lease terms outlined in the article. Support your answer by reference to the requirements of IAS 17.

STAR RATING
★ BASIC
★★ MODERATE
★★★ DIFFICULT

Exercises

Exercise 13.1 ★

LEASE CLASSIFICATION AND DETERMINATION OF INTEREST RATES

This exercise contains four multiple-choice questions. Select the correct answer and show any workings required.

1. Gough Ltd sells land that originally cost $150 000 to Rockall Ltd for $230 000 when the land's fair value is $215 000, and then enters into a cancellable lease agreement to use the land for 2 years at an annual rental of $2000. In the current year, how much profit would Gough Ltd record on the sale of the land?
   (a) $15 000
   (b) $80 000
   (c) $65 000
   (d) Nil

2. Using the information from part 1 above, how would Rockall Ltd record the annual cash received from Gough Ltd?
   (a) As rental revenue
   (b) As a reduction of the lease receivable
   (c) As rental expense
   (d) As interest revenue and a reduction of the lease receivable
3. On 1 July 2009, Madeira Ltd leases a machine with a fair value of $109 445 to Lynns Ltd for 5 years at an annual rental (in advance) of $25 000, and Lynns Ltd guarantees in full the estimated residual value of $15 000 on return of the asset. What would be the interest rate implicit in the lease?
   (a) 10%
   (b) 12%
   (c) 9%
   (d) 14%
4. Using the information from part 3, how would Lynns Ltd classify the lease?
   (a) As an operating lease
   (b) As a finance lease
   (c) As a sale and leaseback
   (d) As a lease incentive

Exercise 13.2 LEASE INCENTIVES

★ As an incentive to enter a non-cancellable operating lease for office premises for 10 years, the lessor has offered the lessee a rent-free period of 2 years. Rental payments under the lease beginning in year 3 are $5000 p.a.

Required

Prepare journal entries to account for the lease payment in year 3 of the lease in the records of both the lessor and the lessee.

Exercise 13.3 FINANCE LEASE

★ If a lease has been capitalised as a finance lease, identify two circumstances in which the lease receivable raised by the lessor will differ from the lease asset raised by the lessee.

Exercise 13.4 FINANCE LEASE — LESSOR

★ On 1 July 2007, Jane Plum decided she needed a new car. She went to the local car yard, Helena Ltd, run by Fred Peach. Jane discussed the price of a new Roadster Special with Fred, and they agreed on a price of $37 000. As Helena Ltd had acquired the vehicle from the manufacturer for $30 000, Fred was pleased with the deal. On learning that Jane wanted to lease the vehicle, Fred agreed to arrange for Pierre Ltd, a local finance company, to set up the lease agreement. Helena Ltd then sold the car to Pierre Ltd for $37 000.

Pierre Ltd wrote a lease agreement, incurring initial direct costs of $1410 as a result. The lease agreement contained the following provisions:

Initial payment on 1 July 2007	$13 000
Payments on 1 July 2008 and 1 July 2009	$13 000
Guaranteed residual value at 30 June 2010	$10 000
Implicit interest rate in the lease	6%
The lease is non-cancellable.	

Pierre Ltd agreed to pay for the insurance and maintenance of the vehicle, the latter to be carried out by Helena Ltd at regular intervals. The cost of these services is valued at $3000 p.a.

The vehicle had an expected useful life of 4 years. The expected residual value of the vehicle at 30 June 2010 was $12 000.

Costs of maintenance and insurance incurred by Pierre Ltd over the years ended 30 June 2008 to 30 June 2010 were $2810, $3020 and $2750 respectively. At 30 June 2010, Jane returned the vehicle to Pierre Ltd, which sold the car for $9000 on 5 July 2010 and invoiced Jane for the appropriate balance. Jane subsequently paid the debt on 13 July 2010.

Required

1. Assuming the lease is classified as a finance lease, prepare the journal entries in the books of Pierre Ltd in relation to the lease from 1 July 2007 to 31 July 2010.
2. In relation to finance leases, explain why the balance of the asset account raised by the lessee at the inception of the lease may differ from the balance of the receivable asset raised by the lessor.

Exercise 13.5

LEASE CLASSIFICATION; ACCOUNTING BY LESSEE

★ On 1 July 2010, Akilia Ltd leased a plastic-moulding machine from Warming Ltd. The machine cost Warming $130 000 to manufacture and had a fair value of $154 109 on 1 July 2010. The lease agreement contained the following provisions:

Lease term	4 years
Annual rental payment, in advance on 1 July each year	$41 500
Residual value at end of the lease term	$15 000
Residual guaranteed by lessee	nil
Interest rate implicit in lease	8%
The lease is cancellable only with the permission of the lessor.	

The expected useful life of the machine is 6 years. Akilia Ltd intends to return the machine to the lessor at the end of the lease term. Included in the annual rental payment is an amount of $1500 to cover the costs of maintenance and insurance paid for by the lessor.

Required

1. Classify the lease for both lessee and lessor based on the guidance provided in IAS 17. Justify your answer.
2. Prepare (1) the lease schedules for the lessee (show all workings), and (2) the journal entries in the books of the lessee for the year ended 30 June 2011.

Exercise 13.6

LEASE CLASSIFICATION; ACCOUNTING BY LESSOR

★ Use the information contained in question 13.5 to complete the following:

1. Classify the lease for both lessee and lessor based on the guidance provided in IAS 17. Justify your answer.
2. Prepare (1) the lease schedules for the lessor (show all workings) and (2) the journal entries in the books of the lessor for the year ended 30 June 2009.

Exercise 13.7

ACCOUNTING BY LESSEE AND LESSOR

★ On 1 July 2009, Sao Ltd leased a processing plant to Tome Ltd. The plant was purchased by Sao Ltd on 1 July 2009 for its fair value of $467 112. The lease agreement contained the following provisions:

Lease term	3 years
Economic life of plant	5 years
Annual rental payment, in arrears (commencing 30/6/2010)	$150 000
Residual value at end of the lease term	$90 000
Residual guaranteed by lessee	$60 000
Interest rate implicit in lease	7%
The lease is cancellable only with the permission of the lessor.	

Tome Ltd intends to return the processing plant to the lessor at the end of the lease term. The lease has been classified as a finance lease by both the lessee and the lessor.

Required

1. Prepare:
   (a) the lease payment schedule for the lessee (show all workings)
   (b) the journal entries in the records of the lessee for the year ended 30 June 2011.
2. Prepare:
   (a) the lease receipt schedule for the lessor (show all workings)
   (b) the journal entries in the records of the lessor for the year ended 30 June 2011.

Exercise 13.8 FINANCE LEASE — LESSEE

★★ Trindase Ltd prepares the following lease payments schedule for the lease of a machine from Martim Ltd. The machine has an economic life of 6 years. The lease agreement requires four annual payments of $33 000, and the machine will be returned to Martim Ltd at the end of the lease term. The lease payments schedule is:

	MLP	Interest expense (10%)	Reduction in liability	Balance of liability
1 July 2009				$98 512
1 July 2010	$ 30 000	$ 9 851	$20 149	78 363
1 July 2011	30 000	7 836	22 164	56 199
1 July 2012	30 000	5 620	24 380	31 819
1 July 2013	35 000	3 181	31 819	—
	$125 000	$26 488	$98 512	

The following five multiple-choice questions relate to the information provided above. Select the correct answer and show any workings required.

1. In its notes to the accounts at 30 June 2011, Trindase Ltd would disclose future lease payments of what amount?
   (a) $95 000
   (b) $65 000
   (c) $99 000
   (d) $104 000
2. For the year ended 30 June 2010, what would Trindase Ltd record in relation to the lease?
   (a) An interest payable of $26 488
   (b) An interest payable of $nil
   (c) An interest payable of $9851
   (d) An interest payable of $7836
3. How much annual depreciation expense would Trindase Ltd record?
   (a) $24 628
   (b) $16 419
   (c) $15 585
   (d) $23 378
4. If Martim Ltd (the lessor) records a lease receivable of $102 327, the variance between this receivable and the liability of $98 512 recorded by Trindase Ltd could be due to what?
   (a) Initial direct costs paid by Martim Ltd
   (b) An unguaranteed residual value
   (c) Both of the above
   (d) Neither of the above
5. Assume that the 1 July 2010 lease payment included an additional amount of $3000 for exceeding a limit for machine usage hours specified in the lease agreement. Trindase Ltd would account for this charge by recognising it as what?
   (a) An expense and disclosing the amount in the notes (if material)
   (b) Additional executory costs
   (c) Revenue
   (d) A reduction in the lease liability

Exercise 13.9 LEASE CLASSIFICATION

★★ Burgundy Ltd manufactures specialised moulding machinery for both sale and lease. On 1 July 2009, Burgundy Ltd leased a machine to Claret Ltd. The machine being leased cost Burgundy Ltd $195 000 to make and its fair value at 1 July 2009 is considered to be $212 515. The terms of the lease are as follows:

The lease term is for 5 years, starting on	1 July 2009
Annual lease payment, payable on 30 June each year	$57 500
Estimated useful life of machine (scrap value $2500)	8 years
Estimated residual value of machine at end of lease term	$37 000
Residual value guaranteed by Claret Ltd	$25 000
Interest rate implicit in the lease	10%
The annual lease payment includes an amount of $7500 to cover annual maintenance and insurance costs.	
Claret Ltd may cancel the lease but only with the permission of the lessor.	
Claret Ltd intends to lease a new machine at the end of the lease term.	

Required

Classify the lease for both Burgundy Ltd and Claret Ltd. Justify your answer.

Exercise 13.10 LEASE SCHEDULES AND JOURNAL ENTRIES (YEAR 1)

★★ On 1 July 2009, Sea Ltd leased a crane from Island Ltd. The crane cost Island Ltd $120 307, considered to be its fair value on that same day. The finance lease agreement contained the following provisions:

The lease term is for 3 years, starting on	1 July 2009
The lease is non-cancellable	
Annual lease payment, payable on 30 June each year	$39 000
Estimated useful life of crane	4 years
Estimated residual value of crane at end of lease term	$22 000
Residual value guaranteed by Sea Ltd	$16 000
Interest rate implicit in the lease	7%
The lease was classified as a finance lease by both Sea Ltd and Island Ltd at 1 July 2009.	

Required

1. Prepare the lease schedules for both the lessee and the lessor.
2. Prepare the journal entries in the records of the lessee only for the year ended 30 June 2010.

Exercise 13.11 FINANCE LEASE — LESSEE (INCLUDING DISCLOSURES)

★★ Long Ltd decided to lease from Beach Ltd a motor vehicle that had a fair value at 30 June 2009 of $38 960. The lease agreement contained the following provisions:

Lease term (non-cancellable)	3 years
Annual rental payments (commencing 30/6/09)	$11 200
Guaranteed residual value (expected fair value at end of lease term)	$12 000
Extra rental per annum if the car is used outside the metropolitan area	$1 000

The expected useful life of the vehicle is 5 years. At the end of the 3-year lease term, the car was returned to the lessor, which sold it for $10 000. The annual rental payments include an amount of $1200 to cover the cost of maintenance and insurance arranged and paid for by the lessor. The car was used outside the metropolitan area in the 2010–11 year. The lease is considered to be a finance lease.

Required

1. Prepare the journal entries for Long Ltd from 30 June 2009 to 30 June 2012.
2. Prepare the relevant disclosures required under IAS 17 for the years ending 30 June 2010 and 30 June 2011.
3. How would your answer to requirement A change if the guaranteed residual value was only $10 000, and the expected fair value at the end of the lease term was $12 000?

Exercise 13.12 ★★

SALES AND LEASEBACK

Mount Ltd is asset rich but cash poor. In an attempt to alleviate its liquidity problems, it entered into an agreement on 1 July 2010 to sell its processing plant to Desert Ltd for $467 100. At the date of sale, the plant had a carrying amount of $400 000 and a future useful life of 5 years. Desert Ltd immediately leased the processing plant back to Mount Ltd. The terms of the lease agreement were:

Lease term	3 years
Economic life of plant	5 years
Annual rental payment, in arrears (commencing 30/6/11)	$165 000
Residual value of plant at end of lease term	$90 000
Residual value guaranteed by Mount Ltd	$60 000
Interest rate implicit in the lease	6%
The lease is cancellable, but only with the permission of the lessor.	

At the end of the lease term, the plant is to be returned to Desert Ltd. In setting up the lease agreement Desert Ltd incurred $9414 in legal fees and stamp duty costs. The annual rental payment includes $15 000 to reimburse the lessor for maintenance costs incurred on behalf of the lessee.

Required

1. Classify the lease for both lessor and lessee. Justify your answer.
2. Prepare a lease payments schedule and the journal entries in the records of Mount Ltd for the year ending 30 June 2011. Show all workings.
3. Prepare a lease receipts schedule and the journal entries in the records of Desert Ltd for the year ending 30 June 2011. Show all workings.
4. Explain how and why your answers to requirements A and B would change if the lease agreement could be cancelled at any time without penalty.
5. Explain how and why your answer to requirements A, B and C would change if the processing plant had been manufactured by Desert Ltd at a cost of $400 000.

Problems

Problem 13.1 ★★★

LEASE CLASSIFICATION; ACCOUNTING AND DISCLOSURES

Martha Ltd has entered into an agreement to lease a D9 bulldozer to Vinyard Ltd. The lease agreement details are as follows:

Length of lease	5 years
Commencement date	1 July 2010
Annual lease payment, payable 30 June each year commencing 30 June 2011	$8 000
Fair value of the bulldozer at 1 July 2010	$34 797
Estimated economic life of the bulldozer	8 years
Estimated residual value of the plant at the end of its economic life	$2 000
Residual value at the end of the lease term, of which 50% is guaranteed by Vinyard Ltd	$7 200
Interest rate implicit in the lease	9%

The lease is cancellable, but a penalty equal to 50% of the total lease payments is payable on cancellation. Vinyard Ltd does not intend to buy the bulldozer at the end of the lease term. Martha Ltd incurred $1000 to negotiate and execute the lease agreement. Martha Ltd purchased the bulldozer for $34 797 just before the inception of the lease.

Required

1. State how both companies should classify the lease. Give reasons for your answer.
2. Prepare a schedule of lease payments for Vinyard Ltd.
3. Prepare a schedule of lease receipts for Martha Ltd.
4. Prepare journal entries to record the lease transactions for the year ended 30 June 2011 in the records of both companies.
5. Prepare an appropriate note to the financial statements of both companies as at 30 June 2011.

Problem 13.2 FINANCE LEASE WITH GRV AND LEASEBACK VARIATIONS

★★★

On 1 July 2010, Nantucket Ltd acquired an item of plant for $31 864. On the same date, Nantucket Ltd entered into a lease agreement with Rhode Ltd in relation to the asset. According to the lease agreement, Rhode Ltd agreed to pay $12 000 immediately, with a further two payments of $12 000 on 1 July 2011 and 1 July 2012.

At 30 June 2013, the asset is to be returned to the lessor and its residual value is expected to be $6000. Rhode Ltd has agreed to guarantee the expected residual value at 30 June 2013. All insurance and maintenance costs are to be paid by Nantucket Ltd and are expected to amount to $2000 p.a. The costs of preparing the lease agreement amounted to $360. The interest rate implicit in the lease is 9%. The lease is classified as a finance lease. Plant is depreciable on a straight-line basis.

Required

1. Prepare a schedule of lease receipts for Nantucket Ltd and the journal entries for the year ended 30 June 2011.
2. Prepare a schedule of lease payments for Rhode Ltd and the journal entries for the year ended 30 June 2011.
3. Assume that Rhode Ltd guaranteed a residual value of only $4000. Prepare a lease schedule for both Nantucket Ltd and Rhode Ltd.
4. Instead of acquiring the plant for $31 864, assume that Nantucket Ltd manufactured the plant at a cost of $29 500 before entering into the lease agreement with Rhode Ltd. Prepare a schedule of lease receipts for Nantucket Ltd and the journal entries for the year ended 30 June 2011.
5. Assume that Rhode Ltd manufactured the plant itself at a cost of $29 500 and sold the plant to Nantucket Ltd for $31 864. Rhode Ltd then leased it back under the original terms of the finance lease, with Rhode Ltd guaranteeing a residual value of $4000. Prepare a lease schedule for both Nantucket Ltd and Rhode Ltd for the year ended 30 June 2011.

Problem 13.3 FINANCE LEASE — MANUFACTURER LESSOR

★★★

Bioko Ltd manufactures specialised moulding machinery for both sale and lease. On 1 July 2007, Bioko Ltd leased a machine to Jason Ltd, incurring $1500 in costs to prepare and execute the lease document. The machine being leased cost Bioko Ltd $195 000 to make and its fair value at 1 July 2007 is considered to be $212 515. The terms of the lease agreement are as follows:

Lease term commencing on 1 July 2007	5 years
Annual lease payment commencing on 1 July 2008	$57 500
Estimated useful life of machine (scrap value $2500)	8 years
Estimated residual value of machine at end of lease term	$37 000
Residual value guaranteed by Jason Ltd	$25 000
Interest rate implicit in the lease	10%
The lease is classified as a finance lease.	

The annual lease payment includes an amount of $7500 to cover annual maintenance and insurance costs. Actual executory costs for each of the 5 years were:

2007–08	$7 200
2008–09	7 700
2009–10	7 800
2010–11	7 100
2011–12	7 000

Jason Ltd may cancel the lease but will incur a penalty equivalent to 2 years' payments if it does so. Jason Ltd intends to lease a new machine at the end of the lease term. The end of the reporting period for both companies is 30 June.

Required

1. Prepare a schedule of lease receipts for Bioko Ltd.
2. Prepare the general journal entries to record the lease transactions for the year ended 30 June 2008 in the records of Bioko Ltd.

Problem 13.4 FINANCE LEASE — LESSEE AND LESSOR

★★★

On 1 July 2007, Scilly Ltd acquired a new car. The manager of Scilly Ltd, Jack Scilly, went to the local car yard, Ireland Autos, and discussed the price of a new Racer Special with John Ireland. Jack and John agreed on a price of $37 876. As Ireland Autos had acquired the vehicle from the manufacturer for $32 000, John was pleased with the deal. On discussing the financial arrangements in relation to the car, Jack decided that a lease arrangement was the most suitable. John agreed to arrange for Staten Ltd, a local finance company, to set up the lease agreement. Ireland Autos then sold the car to Staten Ltd for $37 876.

Staten Ltd wrote a lease agreement, incurring initial direct costs of $534 in the process. The lease agreement contained the following clauses:

Initial payment on 1 July 2007	$13 000
Interest rate implicit in the lease	$13 000
Payments on 1 July 2008 and 1 July 2009	6%

The lease agreement also specified for Staten Ltd to pay for the insurance and maintenance of the vehicle, the latter to be carried out by Ireland Autos at regular intervals. A cost of $3000 per annum was included in the lease payments to cover these services.

Jack was concerned that the lease be considered an operating lease for accounting purposes. To achieve this, the lease agreement was worded as follows:

- The lease was cancellable by Scilly Ltd at any stage. However, if the lease was cancelled, Scilly Ltd agreed to lease, on similar terms, another car from Staten Ltd.
- Scilly Ltd was not required to guarantee the payment of any residual value. At the end of the lease term, 30 June 2010, or if cancelled earlier, the car would automatically revert to the lessor with no payments being required from Scilly Ltd.

The vehicle had an expected economic life of 6 years. The expected fair value of the vehicle at 30 June 2010 was $12 000. Because of concern over the residual value, Paul Staten required Jack to sign another contractual arrangement separate from the lease agreement which gave Staten Ltd the right to sell the car to Scilly Ltd if the fair value of the car at the end of the lease term was less than $10 000.

Costs of maintenance and insurance paid by Staten Ltd to Ireland Autos over the years ended 30 June 2008 to 30 June 2010 were $2810, $3020 and $2750.

At 30 June 2010, Jack returned the vehicle to Staten Ltd. The fair value of the car was determined by to be $9000. Staten Ltd invoked the second agreement. With the consent of Scilly, Staten Ltd sold the car to Ireland Autos for a price of $9000 on 5 July 2010, and invoiced Scilly Ltd for $1000. Scilly Ltd subsequently paid this amount on 13 July 2010.

Required

Assuming the lease is classified as a finance lease, prepare:

1. a schedule of lease payments for Scilly Ltd
2. journal entries in the records of Scilly Ltd for the years ending 30 June 2008, 30 June 2010 and 30 June 2011
3. a schedule of lease receipts for Staten Ltd
4. journal entries in the records of Staten Ltd for the years ending 30 June 2008, 30 June 2010 and 30 June 2011.

References

Accounting Standards Board UK 1999, *Leases: implementation of a new approach*, discussion paper prepared for the IASC, ASB Publications, Central Milton Keynes, UK.

IASB 2005, *Project report*, International Accounting Standards Board UK, www.iasb.org.

McGregor, W 1996, *Accounting for leases: a new approach — recognition by lessees of assets and liabilities arising under lease contracts*, FASB, July. Quoted material sourced from this publication.

Qantas 2008, *Annual report 2008*, Qantas Airways Limited, www.qantas.com.au.

Shanahan, J 1989, '$1 plus $1 equals a million-dollar lease', *Australian Business*, 14 June, pp. 79–80.

14 Accounting for mineral resources

ACCOUNTING STANDARDS IN FOCUS

IFRS 6 *Exploration for and Evaluation of Mineral Resources*

LEARNING OBJECTIVES

When you have studied this chapter, you should be able to:

- understand the background behind the issuance of IFRS 6
- understand the scope of IFRS 6
- understand the range of industry accounting policies applied to the recognition of exploration and evaluation assets
- explain how to measure exploration and evaluation assets
- understand the impairment procedures applicable to exploration and evaluation assets
- implement the presentation and disclosure requirements of IFRS 6
- discuss the possible future developments related to the accounting for the extractive industries.

14.1 INTRODUCTION TO IFRS 6 *EXPLORATION FOR AND EVALUATION OF MINERAL RESOURCES*

IFRS 6 *Exploration and Evaluation of Mineral Resources* was issued by the IASB in December 2004. Historically, the IASB has tended to avoid industry-specific standard setting. However, the extractive industries, which include industries involved in the seeking, finding and extracting of minerals, oil and gas, represent a significant economic contributor to the global economy and, due to the unique accounting issues faced by these industries, are routinely excluded from the scope of many IFRSs.

In November 2000, the IASB's predecessor, the International Accounting Standards Committee (IASC), published an issues paper, *Extractive Industries Issues Paper,* that was meant to be the first step in the process of developing a comprehensive IFRS for the extractive industries. However, the economic strength of entities in the extractive industries also gives them significant political influence and, as a result, they tend to be very effective lobbyists. This, along with the reformation of the IASC into the IASB, resulted in the issuance of IFRS 6, which merely grandfathers current industry practice.

The issuance of IFRS 6 was, and still remains, a much debated political exercise. Some would say IFRS 6 reflects the significant influence the various extractive industries' lobby groups exert. Others would say it was merely issued because something was needed in time for the 2005 wave of IFRS adopters, given the extra time that development of comprehensive guidance would likely have required. The effort to develop such comprehensive guidance continues even today, as discussed in section 14.7 of this chapter.

14.2 SCOPE OF IFRS 6

The scope of IFRS 6 is specifically limited to accounting for exploration and evaluation (E&E) expenditures incurred by an entity in connection with the 'exploration for and evaluation of mineral resources', which the standard defines as 'the search for mineral resources, including minerals, oil, natural gas and similar non-regenerative resources after the entity has obtained legal rights to explore in a specific area, as well as the determination of the technical feasibility and commercial viability of extracting the mineral resource'.

The IASB deliberately decided not to expand the scope of IFRS 6 to avoid pre-empting the outcome of its extractive activities project, as well as to avoid any significant delay in the issuance of E&E expenditure guidance, which would have resulted from an expanded scope. Therefore, the accounting policies applicable under IFRSs for other aspects of the extractive industries activities should be determined in accordance with paragraphs 7 to 12 of IAS 8 *Accounting Policies, Changes in Accounting Estimates and Errors*. As explained in chapter 17, that means:

1. If a transaction, other event or condition is specifically covered by an existing IFRS, that standard should be applied in determining the appropriate accounting policy. For example, the acquisition of equipment to be used in the extraction of mineral resources is not covered by IFRS 6 because that extraction occurs after the technical feasibility and commercial viability of extracting that mineral resource is demonstrated in the first place. However, acquisition of property, plant and equipment is addressed by IAS 16 *Property, Plant and Equipment* so IAS 16 should be applied in arriving at the accounting policy to apply to the acquisition of that plant and equipment.
2. If there is no specific IFRS that applies to a transaction, other event or condition, the entity's management must apply its judgement in determining an appropriate accounting policy to result in information that is:
   a. relevant to the economic decision-making needs of users; and
   b. reliable, in that the financial report:
      i. represents faithfully the financial position, financial performance and cash flows of the entity;
      ii. reflects the economic substance of transactions, other events and conditions, and not merely the legal form;
      iii. is neutral, that is, free from bias;

iv. is prudent; and
v. is complete in all material respects.

3. In applying this judgement, management should consider the requirements and guidance in IFRSs dealing with similar and related issues, followed by the definitions, recognition criteria and measurement concepts for assets, liabilities, income and expenses in the *Framework for the Preparation and Presentation of Financial Statements* (the *Framework*).
4. Management may also consider the most recent pronouncements of other standard-setting bodies that use a similar conceptual framework to develop accounting standards, other accounting literature and accepted industry practices, to the extent that these do not conflict with IFRSs or the *Framework*.

The difficulty for entities in the extractive industries is that mineral resources are excluded from the scope of a number of standards including:

- IAS 2 *Inventories*
- IAS 16 *Property, Plant and Equipment*
- IAS 17 *Leases*
- IAS 18 *Revenue*
- IAS 38 *Intangible Assets*
- IAS 40 *Investment Properties*
- IFRIC Interpretation 4 *Determining whether an Arrangement contains a Lease.*

This is further complicated by the fact that these scope exclusions are not complete. For example, IAS 16 does not apply to 'the recognition and measurement of exploration and evaluation assets' (i.e. they are covered by IFRS 6) or 'mineral rights and mineral reserves such as oil, natural gas and similar non-regenerative resources'. However, it does apply to property, plant and equipment used to develop or maintain E&E assets, mineral rights and mineral reserves. IFRS 6 at least addresses the accounting for one significant activity undertaken at some stage by all entities in the extractive industries: exploration and evaluation.

Figure 14.1 illustrates the scope of IFRS 6.

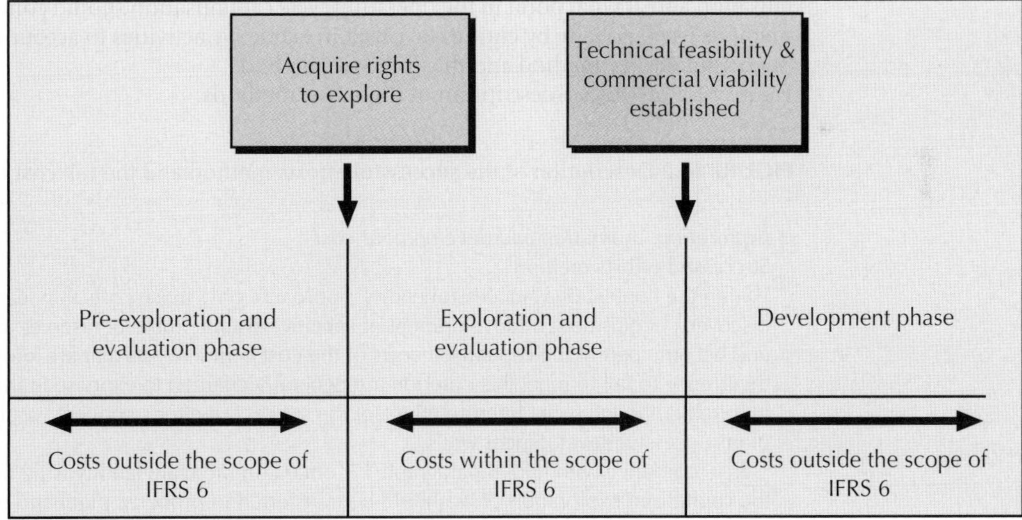

FIGURE 14.1 Scope of IFRS 6

As figure 14.1 shows, entities engaged in the exploration for and evaluation of mineral resources should not apply IFRS 6 to expenditures incurred before the E&E phase (i.e. before the rights to explore the area have been obtained) or after the E&E phase (i.e. after the technical feasibility and commercial viability of extracting the resource are demonstrable). Rather, in these phases, management must apply appropriate judgement in determining which accounting policies should apply to such costs by considering the requirements of other IFRSs or the *Framework*.

14.3 RECOGNITION OF EXPLORATION AND EVALUATION ASSETS

14.3.1 Application of previous accounting policies

E&E assets are merely those E&E expenditures that have been capitalised as assets in accordance with the entity's accounting policy. In line with the IASB's objective of minimising disruptions caused by the adoption of IFRSs by entities involved in E&E activities, IFRS 6 provides a temporary exemption from application of the hierarchy in paragraphs 11 and 12 of IAS 8 to E&E assets and instead only requires the application of paragraph 10 of IAS 8. This means that management must apply their judgement as set out in item (2) of section 14.2 but are not required to consider items (3) and (4) in applying that judgement.

This temporary exemption has the effect of allowing the accounting practices that existed prior to the issuance of IFRS 6 to continue to the extent they meet the requirements of item (2). This means that the entity's accounting policy for recognition of E&E assets need not be fully compliant with the *Framework* and, as a result, some costs may be capitalised earlier than would normally be allowed under the *Framework*. For example, when an entity obtains the rights to explore an area, costs incurred to undertake such exploration (e.g. equipment rental, engineering costs, contractor fees) would not normally meet the asset definition and recognition criteria contained in the *Framework* until the existence of probable future economic benefits have been established (i.e. until the entity has established the existence of mineral resources in the area and confirmed the probability of being able to economically benefit from those resources). However, under IFRS 6, if an entity previously had a policy of capitalising such costs, they are allowed to continue with that policy. This means entities will show more assets and less costs as a result of the application of IFRS 6 than they otherwise would be able to under the *Framework*.

The main issue in accounting for E&E expenditures is whether such expenditures should be expensed as incurred or capitalised and, if they are capitalised, which costs qualify for such capitalisation and at what point in the operating cycle capitalisation should commence. Two common methods used globally by entities involved in extractive activities to account for E&E costs are the 'successful efforts' method and the 'full cost' method.

Figure 14.2 provides a description of these two methods.

FIGURE 14.2 Description of the successful efforts method and the full cost method

Exploration, evaluation and development costs

Successful efforts method

Within the context of a 'successful efforts' approach, only those costs that lead directly to the discovery, acquisition, or development of specific, discrete mineral reserves are capitalised and become part of the capitalised costs of the cost centre. Costs that are known at the time of incurrence to fail to meet this criterion are generally charged to expense in the period they are incurred, although some interpretations of the successful efforts concept would capitalise the cost of unsuccessful development wells.

In accordance with IFRS 6 paragraph 17, once commercial viability is demonstrated the capitalised exploration costs should be transferred to property, plant and equipment or intangibles, as appropriate after being assessed for impairment. If commercial viability is uncertain or not immediately obvious then costs can remain capitalised while a company is still actively engaged in the exploration effort. If the exploration effort has ceased, but there is potential for future benefits, although this is subject to factors outside of this particular exploration effort, the exploration phase is over. The capitalised exploration costs should then be tested for impairment and reclassified into PP&E or Intangible assets.

Other methods of accounting for exploration, evaluation and development costs

Full cost method

The full cost method under most national GAAPs requires that all costs incurred in prospecting, acquiring mineral interests, exploration, appraisal, development, and construction are accumulated in large cost centres. For example, costs may be accumulated for each individual

FIGURE 14.2 *(continued)*

country, for groups of countries, or for the entire world. However, IFRS 6 does not permit application of the full cost method outside the Exploration and Evaluation phase.

There are several other areas in which application of the full cost method under IFRS is restricted because:

- while the full cost method under most national GAAPs requires application of some form of 'ceiling test', IFRS 6 requires — when impairment indicators are present — an impairment test in accordance with IAS 36 to be performed;
- IFRS 6 requires exploration and evaluation assets to be classified as tangible or intangible assets according to the nature of the assets. In other words, even when an entity accounts for Exploration and Evaluation costs in relatively large pools, it will still need to distinguish between tangible and intangible assets; and
- once the technical feasibility and commercial viability of extracting mineral resources are demonstrable, IFRS 6 requires exploration and evaluation assets to be tested for impairment under IAS 36, reclassified in the balance sheet [statement of financial position] and accounted for under IAS 16 or IAS 38. That means that it is not possible to account for successful and unsuccessful projects within one cost centre or pool.

For these reasons it is not possible to apply the full cost method of accounting under IFRS without making very significant modifications in the application of the method. An entity might want to use the full cost method as its starting point in developing its accounting policy for the Exploration and Evaluation assets under IFRS. However, it will rarely be appropriate to describe the resulting accounting policy as a 'full cost method' because key elements of the full cost method are not permitted under IFRS.

Source: Ernst & Young, *Good Petroleum (International) Limited* (2008, p. 17).

Reproduced in figures 14.3 and 14.4 are the accounting policies from the 2007 financial statements of Xstrata plc (a mining company) and Royal Dutch Shell plc (an oil and gas company), two international companies in the extractive industries. The figures illustrate the accounting policies the companies apply to their E&E expenditure.

6. Principal Accounting Policies

Exploration and evaluation expenditure

Exploration and evaluation expenditure relates to costs incurred on the exploration and evaluation of potential mineral reserves and resources and includes costs such as exploratory drilling and sample testing and the costs of pre-feasibility studies. Exploration and evaluation expenditure for each area of interest, other than that acquired from the purchase of another mining company, is carried forward as an asset provided that one of the following conditions is met:

- such costs are expected to be recouped in full through successful development and exploration of the area of interest or alternatively, by its sale; or
- exploration and evaluation activities in the area of interest have not yet reached a stage which permits a reasonable assessment of the existence or otherwise of economically recoverable reserves, and active and significant operations in relation to the area are continuing, or planned for the future.

Purchased exploration and evaluation assets are recognised as assets at their cost of acquisition or at fair value if purchased as part of a business combination.

An impairment review is performed, either individually or at the cash-generating unit level, when there are indicators that the carrying amount of the assets may exceed their recoverable amounts. To the extent that this occurs, the excess is fully provided against, in the financial year in which this is determined. Exploration and evaluation assets are reassessed on a regular basis and these costs are carried forward provided that at least one of the conditions outlined above is met. Expenditure is transferred to mine development assets or capital work in progress once the work completed to date supports the future development of the property and such development receives appropriate approvals.

FIGURE 14.3 Example of E&E expenditure accounting policy for Xstrata plc, a mining company
Source: Xstrata (2007, p. 149).

2. Accounting Policies
Exploration Costs
Shell follows the successful efforts method of accounting for oil and natural gas exploration costs. Exploration costs are charged to income when incurred, except that exploratory drilling costs are included in property, plant and equipment, pending determination of proved reserves. Exploration wells that are more than 12 months old are expensed unless (a) proved reserves are booked, or (b) (i) they have found commercially producible quantities of reserves, and (ii) they are subject to further exploration or appraisal activity in that either drilling of additional exploratory wells is under way or firmly planned for the near future or other activities are being undertaken to sufficiently progress the assessing of reserves and the economic and operating viability of the project.

FIGURE 14.4 Example of E&E expenditure accounting policy for Royal Dutch Shell, an oil and gas company
Source: Royal Dutch Shell (2007, p. 118).

14.3.2 Summary of cost methods used in extractive industries

So far, we have discussed the full cost method and the successful efforts method. The IASC's *Extractive Industries Issues Paper*, also mentions the appropriation method, although use of this method tends to be limited to small mining companies in South Africa. Table 14.1 compares and contrasts these four methods (note that hybrids of these methods are also used) based on the descriptions and discussion in the IASC's paper.

TABLE 14.1 A comparison of E&E historical cost measurement accounting methods

	Area of interest	Successful efforts	Full cost	Appropriation
Description	E&E costs are capitalised on an area of interest basis and if the area of interest is not found to contain commercial reserves, the costs are written off.	E&E costs are not capitalised unless they are expected to lead to finding, acquiring, and developing mineral reserves. If the expectation is not borne out, the costs are written off.	E&E costs are capitalised using a larger cost centre than an area of interest such as a country or even a group of countries.	This is similar to the successful efforts method except that the accounting subsequent to the E&E phase differs (i.e. no depreciation and expensing of all ongoing capital expenditure to maintain production capacity). This method is mainly used by companies with only one mine.
Pros	• Defines the asset for which costs are accumulated because the area is the objective of the costs expended • Reflects the way in which operations are carried out	• Reflects the traditional concept of an asset • Reflects the volatility inherent in E&E activities • Is consistent with the matching concept (i.e. matching of costs to related income) • Better reflects management's successes or failures in its E&E activities	• Reflects the way in which operations are carried out • Is consistent with the matching concept (i.e. matching of costs to related income) • Is similar to absorption costing for manufactured inventories • Avoids distortions of reported earnings	• Recognises that shareholders' funds are invested in a wasting asset • Is well suited to mines that are prone to excessive volatility in relation to the quality and price of their products

TABLE 14.1 *(continued)*

	Area of interest	Successful efforts	Full cost	Appropriation
Cons	• Defers costs as assets for some activities known to be unsuccessful • Fails to recognise that management makes its plans and allocates resources to its E&E activities on an entity-wide basis	• Can give a false impression of success in finding new reserves in the income statement due to decisions to expand or curtail E&E activities • Can be used to 'manage earnings' • Can understate assets and net income of a growing company with a successful and increasing exploration program • Assesses success or failure too early in a project • Fails to recognise that management makes its plans and allocates resources to its E&E activities on an entity-wide basis	• Is inconsistent with the traditional concept of an asset • Delays loss recognition • Impedes measurement of the efficiency and effectiveness of the company's E&E activities	• Is inconsistent with historical cost accounting • Is inconsistent with the going concern concept • Reports debt payments as a deduction after arriving at net profit rather than recognising interest as an expense • Is only suitable for companies with one mine • Does not provide useful information and can be confusing to investors

14.4 MEASUREMENT OF EXPLORATION AND EVALUATION ASSETS

14.4.1 Initial recognition

Regardless of the method used, E&E assets must initially be measured at cost. This raises the question of what types of E&E expenditures qualify for capitalisation as E&E assets. Paragraph 9 of IFRS 6 provides the following guidance:

> An entity shall determine an accounting policy specifying which expenditures are recognised as exploration and evaluation assets and apply the policy consistently. In making this determination, an entity considers the degree to which the expenditure can be associated with finding specific mineral resources. The following are examples of expenditures that might be included in the initial measurement of exploration and evaluation assets (the list is not exhaustive):
> (a) acquisition of rights to explore;
> (b) topographical, geological, geochemical and geophysical studies;
> (c) exploratory drilling;
> (d) trenching;
> (e) sampling; and
> (f) activities in relation to evaluating the technical feasibility and commercial viability of extracting a mineral resource.

IFRS 6 also indicates that costs related to activities undertaken prior to commencement of E&E activities, which is presumed to be before the entity has obtained the legal rights to explore a specific area, and costs incurred for the development of mineral resources after the E&E phase, are not covered by the standard and therefore should be accounted for in accordance with other applicable IFRSs and the *Framework*. In practice, this usually results in the immediate expensing of costs incurred prior to obtaining exploration licences and the treatment of development costs as intangible assets accounted for under IAS 38 *Intangible Assets*.

14.4.2 Obligations for removal and restoration

Obligations for removal and restoration incurred as a result of E&E activities are recognised in accordance with IAS 37 *Provisions, Contingent Liabilities and Contingent Assets* (see chapter 4). This means if an entity has an obligation to restore an area of interest damaged by its E&E activities in that area, it must recognise a liability for that restoration as the related damage is incurred. This is a complex and highly judgemental process because of the significant degree of estimation involved and the impact of laws and regulations applicable to each area of interest. Also, if mineral resources are found as a result of the E&E activities undertaken and the area is developed into a producing asset, the remediation will not occur until those resources are exhausted and production ceases, which could be a long period of time.

In practice, any damage caused to a site during the E&E phase is usually immaterial compared with the damage caused during construction of production facilities after confirmation of the existence and ability to extract commercial quantities of mineral resources in the area. Therefore, most of the liability for removal and restoration tends to be recognised during this production construction period, which is after the E&E phase covered by IFRS 6.

Figure 14.5 provides an example of a typical accounting policy for restoration obligations.

FIGURE 14.5 Example of a typical accounting policy for restoration obligations

1 Principal accounting policies

(k) Provisions for close down and restoration and for environmental clean up costs

Close down and restoration costs include the dismantling and demolition of infrastructure and the removal of residual materials and remediation of disturbed areas. Estimated close down and restoration costs are provided for in the accounting period when the obligation arising from the related disturbance occurs, whether this occurs during the mine development or during the production phase, based on the net present value of estimated future costs. Provisions for close down and restoration costs do not include any additional obligations which are expected to arise from future disturbance. The costs are estimated on the basis of a closure plan. The cost estimates are updated annually during the life of the operation to reflect known developments, eg revisions to cost estimates and to the estimated lives of operations, and are subject to formal review at regular intervals.

Close down and restoration costs are a normal consequence of mining, and the majority of close down and restoration expenditure is incurred at the end of the life of the mine. Although the ultimate cost to be incurred is uncertain, the Group's businesses estimate their respective costs based on feasibility and engineering studies using current restoration standards and techniques.

The amortisation or 'unwinding' of the discount applied in establishing the net present value of provisions is charged to the income statement in each accounting period. The amortisation of the discount is shown as a financing cost, rather than as an operating cost.

The initial closure provision together with other movements in the provisions for close down and restoration costs, including those resulting from new disturbance, updated cost estimates, changes to the estimated lives of operations and revisions to discount rates are capitalised within property, plant and equipment. These costs are then depreciated over the lives of the assets to which they relate.

Where rehabilitation is conducted systematically over the life of the operation, rather than at the time of closure, provision is made for the estimated outstanding continuous rehabilitation work at each balance sheet date and the cost is charged to the income statement.

Provision is made for the estimated present value of the costs of environmental clean up obligations outstanding at the balance sheet date. These costs are charged to the income statement. Movements in the environmental clean up provisions are presented as an operating cost, except for the unwind of the discount which is shown as a financing cost. Remediation procedures may commence soon after the time the disturbance, remediation process and estimated remediation costs become known, but can continue for many years depending on the nature of the disturbance and the remediation techniques.

As noted above, the ultimate cost of environmental remediation is uncertain and cost estimates can vary in response to many factors including changes to the relevant legal requirements, the emergence of new restoration techniques or experience at other mine sites. The expected timing

FIGURE 14.5 *(continued)*

of expenditure can also change, for example in response to changes in ore reserves or production rates. As a result there could be significant adjustments to the provision for close down and restoration and environmental clean up, which would affect future financial results.

Source: Rio Tinto (2007, pp. 11–12).

Illustrative example 14.1 explains the journal entries for recording a restoration obligation. Figures 4.7, 4.8 and 4.9 in chapter 4 provide examples of the application of IAS 37 in the extractive industries (the impact of discounting the liability has been ignored for simplicity).

ILLUSTRATIVE EXAMPLE 14.1

Recording restoration obligations

A mining company has obtained a new lease over a specific area it is conducting E&E activities in. One of the conditions of the lease is that the area must be returned to its original state at the end of the lease. During the financial year, the company estimates that its E&E activities have resulted in damage to the environment that would cost $65 000 to repair. Therefore, the company would record the following journal entry:

E&E Asset	Dr	65 000	
Provision for Restoration	Cr		65 000
(Recognition of provision for restoration arising from E&E activities)			

14.4.3 Subsequent measurement

Subsequent to initial recognition, E&E assets must be measured using the cost model or the revaluation model. The implications of using the revaluation model will differ depending on the extent to which the components of E&E assets are classified as property, plant and equipment under IAS 16 or intangible assets under IAS 38. The classification issue is discussed further in section 14.6.1.

The revaluation model in IAS 38 requires the existence of an active market, which is discussed in chapter 10, whereas the revaluation model in IAS 16 only requires that fair value be reliably measurable, which is discussed in chapter 9.

Note that regardless of which model is selected, cost or revaluation, it must be applied consistently to all E&E assets.

14.4.4 Changes in accounting policies

Paragraph 13 of IFRS 6 allows an entity to change its accounting policies related to E&E costs on the condition that the change 'makes the financial report more relevant to the economic decision-making needs of users and no less reliable, or more reliable and no less relevant to those needs'. In assessing the relevance and reliability of the change, entities are directed to the criteria in IAS 8, although they are not expected to fully comply with those criteria. An example of an acceptable change in accounting policy following this guidance would be a change from the full cost method to the successful efforts method.

14.5 IMPAIRMENT

14.5.1 Recognition and measurement

E&E assets must be tested for impairment in accordance with IAS 36 *Impairment of Assets* using an indicators approach, subject to the exception explained in section 14.5.2. This means that if facts and circumstances indicate that the book values of E&E assets might exceed their recoverable amounts, the entity is required to calculate those recoverable amounts in order to confirm the existence of any impairment. In the absence of any indication of impairment, no further work is required.

IFRS 6 provides a listing of indicators specific to E&E assets that should be considered, rather than the general indicators of impairment set out in IAS 36, which are discussed in section 12.2 of chapter 12. The list in IFRS 6 is not exhaustive, although it does represent the minimum an entity should consider, and includes:

- whether the exploration rights for the specific area have expired or are expected to expire in the near future and there is no expectation of renewal
- where there is no budget or plan for the incurrence of further substantial E&E expenditure in the specific area
- where the entity has decided to discontinue E&E activities in the specific area on the basis that such activities have not led to the discovery of commercially viable quantities of mineral resources — see figure 14.6 for example
- where the entity has established that the book value of the E&E asset is unlikely to be recovered in full from successful development or sale of the specific area — see figure 14.6 for example.

With respect to expiry of exploration rights, the term 'near future' is generally accepted to mean 12 months from the end of the reporting period.

Other impairment indicators not listed in IFRS 6 might include changes in market prices of the applicable mineral resources, adverse regulatory or taxation changes, liquidity restrictions affecting access to funding for E&E activities, civil unrest affecting access to the specific area, and natural disasters causing damage or restricting access to the specific area.

An example of the reasons for impairment of E&E assets as disclosed by BP plc is provided in figure 14.6.

FIGURE 14.6 Example of disclosure of reason for impairment of E&E assets

10 Impairment and losses on sale of businesses and fixed assets

		$ million	
	2007	2006	2005
Impairment losses			
Exploration and Production	**292**	137	266
Refining and Marketing	**1186**	155	93
Gas, Power and Renewables	**40**	100	—
Other businesses and corporate	**43**	69	59
	1561	461	418
Impairment reversals			
Exploration and Production	**(237)**	(340)	—
	(237)	(340)	—
Loss on sale of fixed assets			
Exploration and Production	**42**	195	39
Refining and Marketing	**313**	228	64
Other businesses and corporate	**—**	5	6
	355	428	109
Loss on remeasurement to fair value less costs to sell on disposal of Innovene operations	**—**	184	481
Innovene operations	**1679**	733	1118
	—	(184)	(650)
Continuing operations	**1679**	549	468

Impairment

In assessing whether a write-down is required in the carrying value of a potentially impaired asset, its carrying value is compared with its recoverable amount. The recoverable amount is the higher of the asset's fair value less costs to sell and value in use. Given the nature of the group's activities, information on the fair value of an asset is usually difficult to obtain unless negotiations with potential purchasers are taking place. Consequently, unless indicated otherwise, the recoverable amount used in assessing the impairment charges described below is value in use. The group generally estimates value in use using a discounted cash flow model. The future cash flows are usually adjusted for risks specific to the asset and discounted using a pre-tax discount rate of 11% (2006 10% and 2005 10%). This discount rate is derived from the group's post-tax weighted average cost of capital. In some cases the group's pre-tax discount rate may be adjusted to account for political risk in the country where the asset is located.

Exploration and Production

During 2007, the Exploration and Production segment recognized impairment losses of $292 million. The main elements were a charge of $112 million relating to the cancellation of the DF1 project in Scotland, a $103 million partner loan write-off as a result of unsuccessful drilling in the West Shmidt licence block in Sakhalin and a $52 million write-off of the Whitney Canyon gas plant in US Lower 48 driven by management's decision to abandon this facility. In addition, there were several individually insignificant impairment charges, triggered by downward reserves revisions, amounting to $25 million in total.

These charges were largely offset by reversals of previously recognized impairment charges amounting to $237 million. Of this total, $208 million resulted from a reassessment of the decommissioning liability for damaged platforms in the Gulf of Mexico Shelf. The remaining $29 million related to other individually insignificant impairment reversals, resulting from favourable revisions to the estimates used in determining the assets' recoverable amounts.

During 2006, Exploration and Production recognized a net gain on impairment. The main element was a $340 million credit for reversals of previously booked impairments relating to the UK North Sea, US Lower 48 and China. These reversals resulted from a positive change in the estimates used to determine the assets' recoverable amount since the impairment losses were recognized. This was partially offset by impairment losses totalling $137 million. The major element was a charge of $109 million against intangible assets relating to properties in Alaska. The trigger for the impairment test was the decision of the Alaska Department of Natural Resources to terminate the Point Thompson Unit Agreement. We are defending our right through the appeal process. The remaining $28 million relates to other individually insignificant impairments, the impairment tests for which were triggered by downward reserves revisions and increased tax burden.

During 2005, Exploration and Production recognized total charges of $266 million for impairment in respect of producing oil and gas properties. The major element of this was a charge of $226 million relating to fields in the Shelf and Coastal areas of the Gulf of Mexico. The triggers for the impairment tests were primarily the effect of Hurricane Rita, which extensively damaged certain offshore and onshore production facilities, leading to repair costs and higher estimates of the eventual cost of decommissioning the production facilities and, in addition, reduced estimates of the quantities of hydrocarbons recoverable from some of these fields. The recoverable amount was based on management's estimate of fair value less costs to sell consistent with recent transactions in the area. The remainder related to fields in the UK North Sea, which were tested for impairment following a review of the economic performance of these assets.

Source: BP plc (2007, p. 121).

Illustrative example 14.2 explains the journal entries for recording an impairment charge for an E&E asset.

ILLUSTRATIVE EXAMPLE 14.2

Recording an impairment charge for an E&E asset

An oil and gas company has determined that although one of its areas (Area A) contains mineral reserves it would currently be cost prohibitive to extract them effectively. The E&E asset in relation to that area has a carrying value of $275 000 at the end of the reporting period.

Therefore, the company would record the following journal entry:

Impairment Expense	Dr	275 000	
Provision for E&E Asset Impairment — Area A	Cr		275 000
(Recognition of provision for impairment related to Area A)			

14.5.2 Identification of cash-generating units

In determining the level at which to assess E&E assets for impairment, entities are required to determine an accounting policy for allocating those E&E assets to cash-generating units or groups of cash-generating units. The concept of a cash-generating unit is discussed in chapter 12. Further, IFRS 6 requires that each cash-generating unit or group of cash-generating units to which an E&E asset is allocated must not be larger than a segment based on the entity's primary or secondary reporting format under IAS 14 *Segment Reporting* or larger than an operating segment under IFRS 8 *Operating Segments*. IAS 14 and IFRS 8 are discussed in chapter 20. As a result, the level at which an E&E asset is tested for impairment may consist of one or more cash-generating units. Those cash-generating units may contain a mix of E&E assets and other assets.

It is important to note that although an impairment loss on an E&E asset is reversible under IAS 36, in practice, sometimes an E&E asset is completely derecognised when an impairment is recognised because no further future economic benefits are expected. See illustrative example 14.3.

ILLUSTRATIVE EXAMPLE 14.3

Reversal of impairment losses on E&E assets

Company A is an oil and gas company, which has determined that its exploration activity in a specific area, accounted for as a separate cash-generating unit, did not result in the discovery of any oil and gas resources. As a result, the company recognises an impairment of that area and derecognises all related E&E assets in that area.

Alternatively, Company B is also an oil and gas company, which has discovered a significant quantity of oil and gas resources in a specific area, but these are located in a complex reservoir. As a result, the company determines that, at present, the costs of extraction of the resources do not justify the construction of the required infrastructure. Nevertheless, Company B's management believes that it is possible the required infrastructure will be constructed in the future given the pace of technology and the possibility of development of more cost-effective extraction methods. As Company B's management has no current intention of further exploration activity in that area, the company recognises an impairment of the related E&E assets; however, as there are expectations of possible future economic benefits, it does not derecognise those assets.

The implication of the above is that Company A cannot reverse the impairment as the E&E asset no longer exists while Company B could reverse the impairment should extraction of the discovered resources become viable.

Source: Adapted from Example 39.3, Ernst & Young, International GAAP (2008).

14.6 PRESENTATION AND DISCLOSURE

14.6.1 Classification

IFRS 6 does not specify whether E&E assets are tangible or intangible assets; however, it does require an assessment of the nature of E&E assets to determine how they should be classified. For example, the standard notes that drilling rights are treated as intangible assets while vehicles and drilling rigs are treated as tangible assets.

Table 14.2 illustrates the typical components of E&E assets classified between tangible and intangible assets based on generally accepted industry practice.

TABLE 14.2 Typical components of E&E assets classified as tangible versus intangible assets

Tangible	Intangible
– Vehicles and drilling rigs – Costs of replacing major parts of equipment used in E&E activities – Costs of major inspections of equipment used in E&E activities	– Acquisition of rights to explore (e.g. drilling rights and exploration licences) – Topographical, geological, geochemical and geophysical study costs – Deferred costs associated with consumables (e.g. materials and fuel used, contractor payments, employee remuneration)

As table 14.2 shows, the majority of E&E assets are classified as intangible assets and, as a result, they are measured using the cost model because of the restrictive requirements associated with use of the IAS 38 revaluation model as discussed in section 10.3 of chapter 10. Note that even though equipment used in E&E activities is classified as a tangible asset, the consumption of that equipment, which is reflected through depreciation charges, may qualify for capitalisation as part of an intangible E&E asset if that equipment is being consumed in the E&E activities associated with development of that intangible E&E asset. This is illustrated in illustrative example 14.4.

ILLUSTRATIVE EXAMPLE 14.4

Consumption of tangible E&E asset in development of intangible E&E asset

Company A is a mining company, which acquires a drilling rig to be used for drilling of core samples for the purpose of analysis as part of its E&E activities in a new area (Area X) it has recently acquired the rights to explore. The following transactions occurred during 2008–09.

- The rig is acquired at a cost of $140 000 on 1 July 2008 and is capitalised as a tangible E&E asset with an estimated useful life of 14 years.
- During Company's A financial year ending 30 June 2009, the drilling rig is used solely for the purposes of drilling core samples in Area X, as expected.
- Depreciation attributable to that drilling rig for the year ended 30 June 2009 is calculated as follows: $140 000/14 = $10 000.

The $10 000 of depreciation on the drilling rig has therefore been consumed as part of the development of the intangible E&E asset associated with Area X. These transactions would result in the following journal entries:

Equipment	Dr	140 000	
Cash	Cr		140 000
(Acquisition of drilling rig for cash)			
Intangible E&E asset — Area X	Dr	10 000	
Accumulated Depreciation — Equipment	Cr		10 000
(Recognition of consumption of equipment in development of intangible E&E asset)			

14.6.2 Depreciation methods

Illustrative example 14.4 reflects use of the straight-line method to depreciate the E&E equipment. As explained in paragraph 62 of IAS 16, this method results in a constant charge over the equipment's useful life if its residual value does not change. Therefore, the straight-line method is appropriate if the economic benefits embodied in the asset are expected to be consumed evenly over the useful life of the asset. However, in the extractive industries, many items of property, plant and equipment are depreciated using the unit-of-production method, which results in a charge based on the expected use or output of the asset. 'The underlying principle of the unit-of-production method is that capitalised costs associated with a cost centre are incurred to find and develop the commercially producible reserves in that cost centre, so that each unit produced from the centre is assigned an equal amount of cost'. (IASC Issues Paper, *Extractive Industries Issues Paper*, IASC, November 2000, para. 7.19). So the straight-line method allocates an equal amount of cost to each year while the unit-of-production method allocates an equal amount of cost to each unit produced. By its very nature, the unit-of-production method would therefore result in no depreciation being recognised during the E&E phase because production would not have commenced.

In practice, items of plant and equipment used in extractive-industry activities that have an expected useful life shorter than the time expected to be necessary to extract all of the mineral resources in the area they are being used in are depreciated on a straight-line basis over the period they are expected to be used. The straight-line method is seen as easier to apply than the unit-of-production method, and as not necessarily giving a materially different result where production (i.e. extraction and processing of the mineral resource) is relatively stable year-on-year.

Alternatively, items of plant and equipment used in extractive activities with longer lives are often depreciated using the unit-of-production method. This method, although not as simple as the straight-line method, is particularly useful for areas where production is expected to vary significantly over the life of the field or mine development.

Figure 14.7 shows to which assets Woodside Petroleum Ltd applies the unit-of-production method.

(h) Depreciation and amortisation

Oil and gas properties and other plant and equipment are depreciated to their estimated residual values at rates based on their expected useful life. The major categories of assets are depreciated as follows:

Category	Method	Estimated useful lives (years)
Oil and gas properties		
Land and buildings	Straight line over useful life	40
Transferred exploration and evaluation assets and off-shore plant and equipment	Units-of-production basis over proved plus probable reserves	5–50
On-shore plant and equipment	Straight line over the lesser of useful life and the life of proved plus probable reserves	40
Marine vessels	Straight line over useful life	10–40
Other plant and equipment	Straight line over useful life	5–15

FIGURE 14.7 Example of the different depreciation methods applied to different classes of assets
Source: Woodside Petroleum Ltd (2007, p. 69).

14.6.3 Reclassification

Once the technical feasibility and commercial viability of extracting a mineral resource has been established for a particular area, IFRS 6 requires that the related E&E asset be tested for impairment and then reclassified and accounted for under IAS 16 or IAS 38 as appropriate. If no resources are found as a result of the E&E activities in a specific area, the E&E assets related to that area would be impaired and therefore written off or fully provided for (see illustrative example 14.1).

The technical feasibility and commercial viability of extracting a mineral resource is normally considered to be established once an entity has confirmed the existence of 'economically recoverable reserves', which IFRS 6 defines as 'the estimated quantity of product in an area of interest that can be expected to be profitably extracted, processed and sold under current and foreseeable economic conditions'. Costs incurred after this stage are specifically scoped out of IFRS 6, IAS 16 and IAS 38, although they are generally viewed as costs associated with development of an internal project and accounted for by analogy to IAS 38, or costs associated with construction of an asset and accounted for by analogy to IAS 16. Figure 14.8 provides an example of a typical accounting policy applied by a mining company to costs incurred once the existence of economically recoverable reserves has been confirmed.

Development expenditure
When proved reserves are determined and development is sanctioned, capitalised exploration and evaluation expenditure is reclassified as 'Assets under construction', and is disclosed as a component of property, plant and equipment. All subsequent development expenditure is capitalised and classified as 'Assets under construction'. Development expenditure is net of proceeds from the sale of ore extracted during the development phase. On completion of development, all assets included in 'Assets under construction' are reclassified as either 'Plant and equipment' or 'Other mineral assets'.

FIGURE 14.8 Example of accounting policy for development expenditure as applied by a mining company
Source: BHP Billiton Ltd (2008, p. 173).

14.6.4 Disclosure

Paragraphs 23–25 of IFRS 6 contain the required disclosures relating to E&E costs, which are aimed at identifying and explaining the amounts recognised in an entity's financial statements arising from its E&E activities. Such disclosures include:

- accounting policies applicable to E&E costs and E&E assets
- the amounts of assets, liabilities, income, expenses, operating cash flows and investing cash flows related to E&E activities.

Further, the disclosure requirements of IAS 16 or IAS 38 must also be applied depending on whether E&E assets have been classified as tangible or intangible assets respectively.

Examples of some of the disclosures have been provided throughout this chapter; however, illustrative example 14.5 provides a comprehensive illustration of all disclosures required by IFRS 6.

ILLUSTRATIVE EXAMPLE 14.5

Illustrative disclosures required by IFRS 6

Relevant note to the financial statements	**IFRS 6** Para.
Note 1: Summary of accounting policies (extract) **Exploration and evaluation expenditures** Exploration and evaluation expenditures include those expenditures incurred in connection with the search for mineral resources after the Group has obtained legal rights to explore in a specific area but before the technical feasibility and commercial viability of extracting a mineral resource are demonstrable. These expenditures normally include those associated with the following activities: • topographical, geological, geochemical and geophysical studies • exploratory drilling, trenching and sampling • evaluating the technical feasibility and commercial viability of extracting a mineral resource such as surveying transportation and infrastructure requirements and conducting market and finance studies. Costs associated with the acquisition of rights to explore in a specific area are capitalised and amortised over the term of the rights. General and administrative costs not related directly to exploration and evaluation operational activities in a specific area of interest are recognised in profit or loss as incurred. An area of interest is an individual geological area that is considered to constitute a favourable environment for the presence of a mineral resource, or has been proved to contain a mineral resource.	23, 24(a)

Relevant note to the financial statements			IFRS 6 Para.
All other exploration and evaluation expenditures (including amortisation of capitalised exploration rights) are recognised in profit or loss as incurred, except when both of the following conditions with respect to a specific area of interest are met, in which case such costs are capitalised as an exploration and evaluation asset: • the rights to tenure of the area of interest are current • the expenditures are expected to be recouped through successful development and exploitation of the area of interest or by its sale, or alternatively, at the end of the reporting period, exploration and evaluation activities in the area of interest have not reached a stage that permits a reasonable assessment of the existence or otherwise of economically recoverable reserves, and active and significant operations in, or in relation to, the area of interest are continuing. Economically recoverable reserves refer to the estimated quantity of product in an area of interest that can be expected to be profitably extracted, processed and sold under current and foreseeable economic conditions. Assets recognised in accordance with the above conditions are assessed at the end of each reporting period to ensure that such conditions continue to be met. Expenditure that is not expected to be recouped is recognised in profit or loss. Exploration and evaluation assets are classified as a separate class of intangible assets, which are measured at cost less accumulated impairment charges and are not depreciated as they are not yet available for use. Exploration and evaluation assets are assessed for impairment when facts and circumstances suggest that their carrying amounts may exceed their recoverable amounts. If any indication of impairment exists, an impairment assessment is performed for each area of interest in conjunction with the group of operating assets to which the exploration and evaluation assets are associated.			
Note 3: Income and expenses	**2010 $'000**	**2009 $'000**	23, 24(b)
Profit before tax includes the following items of income and (expense):			
Impairment of exploration and evaluation assets (a)	(146)	(87)	
Reversal of previously impaired exploration and evaluation assets (b)	25	—	
(a) The Group's rights to explore one of its areas of interest expired during the current reporting period and the local authority responsible for granting such rights has declined renewal of those rights on the basis that the area contains habitat considered vital to support an endangered species and no significant mineral reserves have been identified to-date. As a result, the Group has fully provided for the exploration and evaluation assets associated with this area of interest. The impairment charge is included in exploration and evaluation expenses.			
(b) During 2009, the Group recognised an impairment charge associated with one of its smaller areas of interest on the basis that the mineral reserves identified in that area to date would not have been adequate to recoup the costs capitalised. However, during the current reporting period further unexpected findings in that area have confirmed that such costs would in fact be recoverable.			

Note 5: Exploration and evaluation assets	2010 $'000	2009 $'000	23, 24(b), 25
Opening balance	2134	1993	
Costs capitalised during the period	229	256	
Impairment charges	(146)	(87)	
Reversal of impairment charges	25	—	
Transferred to oil and gas properties	(37)	(28)	
Closing balance	2195	2134	
Recoverability of the carrying amount of the exploration and evaluation assets is dependent on successful development and commercial exploitation, or alternatively, sale of the respective areas of interest.			

14.7 FUTURE DEVELOPMENTS

14.7.1 IASB project

In 1998, the International Accounting Standards Committee (IASC), the predecessor organisation of the IASB, created a Steering Committee to deal with financial reporting in the extractive industries. This resulted in the release of an issues paper *Extractive Industries Issues Paper* in 2000. The project was put on hold as the IASB did not believe it could complete it in time for the 2005 adoption of IFRSs by many parts of the world. As previously discussed, IFRS 6 was released by the IASB as an interim measure pending completion of a comprehensive project dealing with the accounting for extractive activities.

The comprehensive project recommenced in 2004, the overall scope of which is summarised in table 14.3 below.

TABLE 14.3 Summary of scope of IASB's extractive activities project

Issue	Comments
Define reserves and resources	May involve use of existing definitions or development of new definitions identifying the main features for the purposes of recognition and/or disclosure of reserves and resources.
Identify the reserves and resources that would meet the criteria for recognition as an asset	To be based on the asset definition and recognition criteria contained in the *Framework*.
How to measure reserves and resources recognised as an asset on initial recognition	Alternatives include: • historical cost (i.e. using successful efforts, area of interest, full cost or another method) • fair value • other current value basis.
Subsequent measurement of reserves and resources recognised as assets	Including remeasurement, impairment and amortisation.
Whether to expense or capitalise costs incurred prior to recognition of reserves and resources as assets	Could involve expensing all or partial capitalisation.
Disclosure requirements for reserves and resources	See section 14.7.2 for discussion of US developments in this area.
Other issues	Focused on other issues arising from implementation of IFRS in the extractive industries.

One of the main issues in accounting for extractive activities, which has a direct impact on selection of the measurement model, is determining the 'unit of account' (i.e. the level at which to separately account for assets). Illustrative example 14.6 shows how the unit of account can impact the accounting.

ILLUSTRATIVE EXAMPLE 14.6

Unit of account selection

An oil and gas company concludes, based on a number of exploration wells, that mineral reserves are present. However, it needs to drill a number of delineation wells (used to define the boundaries of a reservoir) to determine the amount of reserves present in the area of interest. The first delineation well drilled is a dry hole (i.e. it contains no reserves).

There are two ways of looking at the cost of drilling this dry hole:

- it provides important information about the extent of the mineral reserves present in the area of interest and should therefore be capitalised as part of that area of interest, or
- it will not produce oil in the future and therefore in the absence of future economic benefits related to that specific dry hole, the costs should be expensed immediately.

As the above shows, treating the unit of account as the area of interest would result in a very different accounting outcome from treating it as each individual well.

Source: Adapted from Example 39.4, Ernst & Young, International GAAP (2008).

Discussions by the IASB to date indicate it is likely the unit of account that would apply during the E&E phase would initially be defined by the exploration rights held. This is basically equivalent to an area of interest model as the unit of account would be the area of interest to which each right to explore, which is usually in the legal form of a licence, relates. However, over time that unit of account would naturally contract to the specific areas within the initial area to which E&E activities are particularly focused. Then, if and when an area results in development of a mine or well, the unit of account would likely be each mine or well assuming they produce largely independent cash flows (similar to the cash-generating unit concept in IAS 36). Even then each unit of account may well be componentised as is required for property, plant and equipment by IAS 16.

14.7.2 US SEC reporting requirements

The US Securities and Exchange Commission (SEC) has published a revised rule relating to its oil and gas reserves estimation and disclosure requirements with the objective of increasing transparency of reserve disclosures and maximising comparability among oil and gas companies. The changes are effective no earlier than 2010.

Included in these proposals is a revised definition of oil and gas reserves which are 'the estimated remaining quantities of oil and gas and related substances anticipated to be economically producible, as of a given date, by application of development projects to known accumulations. In addition, there must exist, or there must be a reasonable expectation that there will exist, the legal right to produce or a revenue interest in the production of oil and gas, installed means of delivering oil and gas or related substances to market, and all permits and financing required to implement the project.

The proposed rule issued in advance of the final revised rule also made reference to the IASB's extractive activities project, including the fact that it involves determining a definition of oil and gas reserves, and notes that although the SEC staff intends to monitor the IASB's progress, the IASB may establish guidelines that differ from the SEC estimation and disclosure requirements, which would make it more difficult for investors to compare non-US entities with US SEC registrants. Both the timing of the issue of this revised rule and this comment by the SEC staff would tend to indicate that the SEC has no intention of converging its requirements with that of the IASB should they end up differing. That is not to say that the IASB won't consider the SEC guidance in drawing its conclusions though. Only time will tell.

SUMMARY

The purpose of this chapter is to analyse the content of IFRS 6 *Exploration for and Evaluation of Mineral Resources* and provide guidance on its implementation. The principal issues in the financial reporting for E&E expenditures are the recognition and measurement of E&E assets, assessment of impairment of E&E assets, and determining appropriate disclosures to identify and explain the amounts in the entity's financial statements arising from the exploration for and evaluation of mineral resources (Objective, IFRS 6). The key issues in recognising and initially measuring the asset are in determining when capitalisation of costs related to E&E activities should commence and identifying which elements of that cost should be capitalised. After the initial recognition of the asset, a decision has to be made about whether to apply the cost model or the revaluation model. If the revaluation model is applied, a further decision has to be made about whether the IAS 16 *Property, Plant and Equipment* or the IAS 38 *Intangible Assets* revaluation model should apply, consistent with the classification of the asset as tangible or intangible. Regardless of which measurement basis is used, the asset must be assessed for impairment when impairment indicators are present in accordance with IAS 36 *Impairment of Assets.* In performing an impairment test for E&E assets, a decision has to be made about the level at which the test should be applied, this being limited to a level no larger than an operating segment as defined in IFRS 8 (see chapter 20). IFRS 6 requires specific disclosures to be made in relation to the accounting policies for E&E assets and the amounts recognised in the financial statements related to E&E activities. In addition, for E&E assets classified as tangible assets and for E&E assets classified as intangible assets, the disclosures required by IAS 16 and IAS 38 respectively must also be provided.

Discussion questions

1. Which expenditures is the scope of IFRS 6 limited to?
2. Discuss the complexities and considerations an entity involved in the extractive industries faces in determining the accounting policies to apply to expenditures it incurs that are outside of the scope of IFRS 6.
3. Discuss what entities need to consider if they want to change their accounting policies applicable to E&E costs.
4. Explain how the area of interest method of accounting for E&E expenditure compares to the successful efforts method.
5. Discuss the possible challenges in applying the revaluation models under IAS 16 or IAS 38 to E&E assets.
6. Discuss the impact of the unit of account on impairment testing of E&E assets.
7. Discuss the possible future developments related to the accounting for extractive activities.

STAR RATING
★ BASIC
★★ MODERATE
★★★ DIFFICULT

Exercises

Exercise 14.1 ★★

ELEMENTS OF COST OF E&E ASSETS

Exploration plc has acquired a licence to explore a new area and its accounting policy is to fully capitalise all of its E&E expenditures. During the period, costs have been incurred in relation to the following:

(a) the acquisition of speculative seismic data in relation to the areas to be used to determine whether to apply for an exploration licence for that area
(b) labour costs of engineers to analyse that seismic data obtained
(c) the exploration licence fee
(d) legal costs associated with obtaining the exploration licence
(e) labour costs for engineers to carry out topographical, geological, geochemical and geophysical studies on the area after obtaining the exploration licence
(f) payroll-related costs for that labour
(g) contractors fees for exploratory drilling
(h) hire of drilling equipment.

Required

Which of the above items should be capitalised into the E&E asset?

Exercise 14.2 OBLIGATIONS FOR REMOVAL AND RESTORATION

★ The management of Mining plc is concerned that the E&E activities it has commenced in a specific area will cause significant damage to the surrounding environment and the government of the country where the area is located has attached strict conditions to the exploration licence for that area. Those conditions require that Mining plc return the environment to its original condition.

Required
What are the implications of the above for Mining plc's financial statements?

Exercise 14.3 IMPAIRMENT OF E&E ASSETS

★ During the year ended 30 June 2010, the management of Gas Ltd has been analysing its engineering reports for a specific area, which indicate that sample drilling has not resulted in any findings that confirm the existence of oil and gas in that area. As a result, Gas Ltd is reluctant to invest any further funds in exploring the area. An E&E asset with a carrying value of $1.2 million exists in relation to that area as at 30 June 2010.

Required
What is the impact of this decision on Gas Ltd's financial statements as at 30 June 2010?

Exercise 14.4 APPLICATION OF THE REVALUATION MODEL

★★ Resource plc classifies its E&E assets as intangible assets. A new accountant has just been employed and has suggested that Resource plc should change its accounting policy for E&E assets from its existing cost model to the fair value model under IAS 38 because it would provide more relevant information.

Required
What might prevent Resource plc from being able to make this change in accounting policy?

Exercise 14.5 SPECIFYING THE LEVEL AT WHICH E&E ASSETS ARE ASSESSED FOR IMPAIRMENT

★★★ E&E activity in one of Minerals Ltd's areas has not reached a stage that permits a reasonable assessment of the existence of economically recoverable reserves. The exploration licence for that area is still current and Minerals Ltd intends to continue E&E activities in that area. One of the wells drilled by Minerals Ltd in that area during the period did not result in the finding of any mineral reserves. However, other wells drilled in the area have resulted in mineral reserve findings.

Required
What alternatives does Minerals Ltd have for determining the level at which to assess its E&E assets for impairment in that area?

Exercise 14.6 CHANGE IN ACCOUNTING POLICY

★★ Sandy Oil plc is a company involved in the search for, production of and sale of oil and gas resources. The company has been following an accounting policy of expensing all of its E&E costs as incurred since adoption of IFRS 6. However, it has noted that its most significant competitor follows a policy of capitalising such costs on an area of interest basis. This makes the competitor's net profit look better in some years than Sandy Oil plc's net profit.

Required
Discuss whether Sandy Oil plc can change its accounting policy to capitalise all of its E&E costs to match its competitor's accounting policy.

Problems

Problem 14.1 RECOGNITION OF E&E ASSETS

★★ Digging Ltd has incurred the following costs during the period in relation to a specific area. Its accounting policy is to capitalise all E&E costs.

Cash paid to acquire seismic study from government who is selling exploration rights for the area (GST exempt)	$ 3 000
Cash paid to acquire exploration rights for the area from government (GST exempt)	10 000
Cash paid to acquire fencing materials to mark out the area of interest, including GST of $80	880
Contractor fees for labour to set up the fencing, including GST of $50	550
Contractor fees for exploratory drilling, including GST of $2500	27 500
Hire of drilling equipment for contractor use, including GST of $500	5 500
Salary of project manager hired specifically to manage E&E activities in the area	60 000
Stationery and other office supplies used by the project manager, including GST of $30	330
Mining Ltd non-executive directors' fees paid during the period	160 000

Required

Determine the amount of the E&E asset to be capitalised by Digging Ltd in relation to the area.

Problem 14.2 ★★★

MEASUREMENT OF E&E ASSETS

During the year ended 30 June 2011, Reserves plc explored four different areas and spent $100 000 in each. The results of E&E activities suggested that Areas A, B and C may contain mineral reserves so the company acquired leases over these three areas. The leases cost $140 000, $220 000 and $180 000 respectively.

During the year ended 30 June 2012, Reserves plc commenced a drilling program to evaluate Areas A, B and C. Seven exploratory wells were drilled, four in Area A, two in Area B and one in Area C at a cost of $120 000 each. The five wells drilled in Area A did not result in any mineral resource findings (i.e. they were dry holes). The two wells drilled in Area B indicated that the company had discovered economically recoverable reserves. Management was uncertain about the likelihood of finding economically recoverable reserves for the well in Area C as some mineral reserves were found but not enough to be considered economically recoverable at this stage. Therefore Reserves plc decided to continue E&E activities in Area C as of 30 June 2012. Area A was abandoned, and, after incurring costs of $50 000 to confirm the technical feasibility and commercial viability of extracting the mineral resources, development of Area B commenced.

During the year ended 30 June 2013, to evaluate the area further, three more wells were drilled in Area B. Of these, two were dry. Each well cost $140 000. The successful wells in Area B were developed for a total cost of $300 000. Expenditure on additional plant and equipment related to development was $325 000. After further dry wells costing $175 000 were drilled in Area C, management concluded that Area C did not contain any commercially viable quantities of mineral resources, so it was abandoned.

These costs are summarised as follows:

Costs incurred for each area of interest

		A	B	C	D	Total
30/06/2011	Exploration	100 000	100 000	100 000	100 000	400 000
	Leases	140 000	220 000	180 000	—	550 000
30/06/2012	Dry wells	600 000	—	—	—	600 000
	Other wells	—	240 000	120 000	—	360 000
	Technical feasibility/ commercial viability costs	—	50 000	—	—	50 000
30/06/2013	Dry wells	—	280 000	175 000	—	455 000
	Other wells	—	140 000	—	—	140 000
	Development	—	300 000	—	—	300 000
	PPE	—	325 000	—	—	325 000
Total		850 000	1 655 000	575 000	100 000	3 180 000

Required

Determine what expenses would be recognised in profit or loss versus capitalised as an asset related to each area for each financial year assuming Reserves plc:

(a) expenses all of its E&E costs as incurred

(b) applies the full cost method

(c) applies the successful efforts method.

References

BHP Billiton 2008, *2008 annual report*, BHP Billiton Limited, www.bhpbilliton.com.

BP 2007, *Annual report and accounts 2007*, BP plc, UK, www.bp.com.

Ernst & Young 2008a, *Good Petroleum (International) Limited, International GAAP illustrative financial statements*, www.ey.com/global.

– 2008b, *International GAAP 2008: Generally Accepted Accounting Practice under International Financial Reporting Standards*, John Wiley, New York.

IASC 2000, *Extractive Industries Issues Paper*, International Accounting Standards Committee, November.

Rio Tinto 2007, *2007 annual report*, Rio Tinto Limited, www.riotinto.com.

Royal Dutch Shell 2007, *Annual report and Form 20-F for the year ended December 31 2007*, Royal Dutch Shell plc, The Netherlands, www.shell.com.

Securities and Exchange Commission 2008, *Modernization of the oil and gas reporting requirements proposed rule*, United States, www.sec.gov.

Woodside 2007, *Annual report 2007*, Woodside Petroleum Ltd, www.woodside.com.au.

Xstrata 2007, *Annual report 2007*, Xstrata plc, London, www.xstrata.com.

15 Employee benefits

ACCOUNTING STANDARDS IN FOCUS

IAS 19 *Employee Benefits*

LEARNING OBJECTIVES

When you have studied this chapter, you should be able to:

- understand the rationale for accounting for employee benefits
- prepare journal entries to account for short-term liabilities for employee benefits, such as wages and salaries, sick leave and annual leave
- contrast defined benefit and defined contribution post-employment benefit plans
- prepare entries to account for expenses, assets and liabilities arising from defined contribution post-employment plans
- prepare entries to record expenses, assets and liabilities arising from defined benefit post-employment benefit plans
- explain how to measure and record other long-term liabilities for post-employment benefits, such as long service leave
- explain when a liability should be recognised for termination benefits.

15.1 INTRODUCTION TO ACCOUNTING FOR EMPLOYEE BENEFITS

Employee benefits typically constitute a significant component of an entity's expenses, particularly in the services sector. Employees are remunerated for the services they provide. In addition to regular wages, which may be paid weekly, fortnightly or monthly, employment agreements often provide for entitlements to be paid, such as sick leave, annual leave, long service leave and contributions for post-employment benefits, often referred to as superannuation plans or pension plans. While the measurement of short-term liabilities for employee benefits, such as sick leave and annual leave, is relatively straightforward, the measurement of long-term liabilities, such as long service leave, is more complex because it requires estimation and present value calculations. As well as the above entitlements, we will also consider in this chapter the two major types of post-employment plans: defined benefit plans and defined contribution plans.

15.2 SCOPE AND PURPOSE OF IAS 19

IAS 19 *Employee Benefits* applies to all employee benefits except those to which IFRS 2 *Share-based Payment* applies. Employee benefits arise from formal agreements, which are often referred to as workplace agreements, between an entity and its individual employees. Alternatively, employee benefits may arise from agreements between an entity and groups of employees or their representatives. These agreements are often referred to as enterprise bargaining agreements. Employee benefits also include requirements specified by legislation or industry arrangements for employers to contribute to an industry, state or national plan. Informal practices that generate a constructive obligation, such as payment of annual bonuses, also fall within the scope of employee benefits under IAS 19. Share-based employee benefits are beyond the scope of IAS 19. Chapter 6 considers share-based payments, including share-based employee remuneration.

The purpose of IAS 19 is to prescribe the measurement and recognition of expenses and liabilities for employee benefits arising from services provided by employees. Liabilities arise when employees provide services in exchange for benefits to be provided later by the employer. Accounting for employee benefits is complicated because some benefits may be provided many years after employees have provided services. The measurement of liabilities for employee benefits is made more difficult because the payment of some employee benefits for past services may be conditional upon the continuation of employment.

15.3 DEFINING EMPLOYEE BENEFITS

Paragraph 7 of IAS 19 defines employee benefits as:

> all forms of consideration given by an entity in exchange for services rendered by employees.

Employee benefits are usually paid to employees but the term also includes amounts paid to their dependants or to other parties.

Wages, salaries and other employee benefits are usually recognised as expenses. However, the costs of employee benefits may be allocated to assets in accordance with other accounting standards. For example, the cost of labour used in the manufacture of inventory is included in the cost of inventory in accordance with IAS 2 *Inventories*. The cost of an internally generated intangible asset recognised in accordance with IAS 38 *Intangible Assets*, such as the development of a new production process, includes the cost of employee benefits for staff, such as engineers, employed in generating the new production process.

15.4 SHORT-TERM EMPLOYEE BENEFITS

Short-term employee benefits include wages, salaries, bonuses and profit-sharing arrangements. They also include various forms of paid leave entitlements for which employees may be eligible. Sick leave and annual leave are common forms of paid leave entitlements. IAS 19 refers to various forms of leave entitlements as compensated absences.

Short-term employee benefits also include non-monetary benefits, which are often referred to as 'fringe benefits'. Non-monetary benefits include the provision of health insurance, housing and motor vehicles. An entity may offer non-monetary benefits to attract staff. For example, a mining company may provide housing to employees where there are no major towns located near its mining sites. Non-monetary benefits may also arise from salary sacrifice arrangements, otherwise referred to as salary packaging. A salary sacrifice arrangement involves the employee electing to forgo some of his or her salary or wages in return for other benefits, such as a motor vehicle, provided by the employee.

15.4.1 Payroll

The subsystem for regular recording and payment of employee benefits is referred to as the payroll. The payroll involves:

- recording the amount of wages or salaries for the pay period
- updating personnel records for the appointment of new employees
- updating personnel records for the termination of employment contracts
- calculating the amount to be paid to each employee, net of deductions
- remitting payment of net wages or salaries to employees
- remitting payment of deductions to various external parties, and
- complying with regulatory requirements, such as reporting to taxation authorities.

Businesses may process several payrolls. For example, a business may process a payroll each fortnight for employees who are paid on a fortnightly basis and process a separate monthly payroll for managers paid on a monthly basis.

In return for providing services to the employer, employees regularly receive benefits, or remuneration, in the form of wages or salaries. Employers are typically required to deduct income tax from employees' wages and salaries. Thus the employee receives a payment that is net of tax, and the employer subsequently pays the amount of income tax to the taxation authority.

Employers may offer a service of deducting other amounts from employees' wages and salaries and paying other parties on their behalf. For example, the employer may deduct union membership fees from employees' wages and make payments to the various unions on behalf of the employees. Similarly, the employer may deduct health insurance premiums from the employees' wages, and remit payments to the various health insurance funds that its employees have joined.

Payments made on behalf of an employee from amounts deducted from the employee's wages or salaries form part of the entity's wages and salaries expense. As these amounts are typically remitted in the month following the payment of wages and salaries, they represent a short-term liability for employee benefits at the end of each month.

Paragraph 10 of IAS 19 requires short-term employee benefits for services rendered during the period to be recognised as a liability after deducting any amounts already paid. Short-term liabilities for employee benefits must be measured at the nominal (undiscounted) amount that the entity expects to pay.

15.4.2 Accounting for the payroll

The following illustrative example demonstrates accounting for the payroll, including deductions from employees' remuneration, the remittance of payroll deductions and the measurement of resulting liabilities at the end of the period.

ILLUSTRATIVE EXAMPLE 15.1

Accounting for the payroll

Amberg Ltd pays its managers on a monthly basis. All of Amberg Ltd's salaries are recognised as expenses. Amberg Ltd's employees can elect to have their monthly health insurance premiums deducted from their salaries and paid to their health insurance fund on their behalf. The company provides a similar service for the payment of union membership fees. Amberg Ltd also operates a giving scheme under which employees can elect to have donations to nominated charities deducted from their salaries and wages and remitted on their behalf to the selected charities. Figure 15.1 summarises the managerial payrolls for May and June 2010.

	$	May 2010 $	$	June 2010 $
Gross payroll for the month		2 400 000		2 500 000
Deductions payable to:				
Taxation authority	530 000		600 000	
Total Care Health Fund	40 000		40 000	
National Health Fund	20 000		20 000	
UNICEF	3 000		3 000	
National Heart Research Fund	4 000		4 000	
Union fees	12 000		12 500	
Total deductions for the month		609 000		679 500
Net salaries paid		1 791 000		1 820 500

FIGURE 15.1 Summary of Amberg Ltd's payroll

Each time the monthly payroll is processed, the cost of the salaries is charged to expense accounts and a liability is accrued for the gross wages payable. Payments of net wages and salaries and remittance of payroll deductions to taxation authorities and other parties reduce the payroll liability account.

The managerial payroll is processed on the second Monday of the month and net salaries are paid to employees on the following Tuesday. During May, managers earned salaries of $2.4 million. After deducting amounts for income tax, union membership fees, contributions to health funds and donations, Amberg Ltd paid its managers a net amount of $1 791 000 during May. All of the deductions are paid to the various external bodies in the following month. Health insurance deductions and union subscriptions are remitted on the first Friday of the following month. Thus, the deductions for health insurance and union subscriptions for the May payroll are remitted on Friday 4 June. Income tax withheld is remitted on the 15th of the following month. Deductions for donations are paid on the 16th of the following month.

The balance of Amberg Ltd's Accrued Payroll account at 1 June 2010 is $609 000, being the deductions from employees' salaries for income tax, health insurance premiums, union fees and donations for May 2010. These amounts are paid during June 2010.

During June 2010, Amberg Ltd's employees earned gross salaries of $2.5 million. Employees actually received $1 820 500, being the net wages and salaries after deductions for income tax, health insurance premiums, union fees and donations to charities. In total, $679 500 was deducted from managers' salaries for June 2010. This amount is a liability at the end of June 2010. The amounts deducted from employees' salaries during June 2010 are remitted during July 2010.

The journal entries to record Amberg Ltd's payroll and remittances for June 2010 are as follows:

June 4	Accrued Payroll	Dr	40 000	
	Bank	Cr		40 000
	(Payment of May payroll deductions for Total Health Care Fund)			
	Accrued Payroll	Dr	20 000	
	Bank	Cr		20 000
	(Payment of May payroll deductions for National Health Fund)			
	Accrued Payroll	Dr	12 000	
	Bank	Cr		12 000
	(Payment of May payroll deductions for union fees)			
June 14	Salaries Expense	Dr	2 500 000	
	Accrued Payroll	Cr		2 500 000
	(Managerial payroll for June)			

June 15	Accrued Payroll Bank (Payment of net salaries for June)	Dr Cr	1 820 500	 1 820 500
	Accrued Payroll Bank (Payment of May payroll deductions for withheld income tax)	Dr Cr	530 000	 530 000
June 16	Accrued Payroll Bank (Payment of May payroll deductions for UNICEF)	Dr Cr	3 000	 3 000
	Accrued Payroll Bank (Payment of May payroll deductions for National Heart Research Fund)	Dr Cr	4 000	 4 000

15.4.3 Accrual of wages and salaries

The end of the payroll period often differs from the end of the reporting period because payrolls are usually determined on a weekly or fortnightly basis. Accordingly, it is usually necessary to recognise an expense and a liability for employee benefits for the business days between the last payroll period and the end of the reporting period. This is demonstrated in illustrative example 15.2.

ILLUSTRATIVE EXAMPLE 15.2

Accrual of wages and salaries

Bergen Ltd pays its employees on a fortnightly basis. The last payroll in the year ended 30 June 2010 was for the fortnight (10 working days) ended 18 June 2010. As this was a Friday, there were 8 business days between the end of the final payroll period and the end of the reporting period. Assuming the cost of employee benefits for the remaining 8 days was $1 million, Bergen Ltd would record the following accrual:

Wages and Salaries Expense Accrued Wages and Salaries (Accrual of wages and salaries)	Dr Cr	1 000 000	 1 000 000

The accrued wages and salaries is a liability for short-term employee benefits. Paragraph 19 of IAS 19 requires accrued short-term employee benefits to be measured at nominal value, i.e., the amount expected to be paid to settle the obligation.

15.4.4 Short-term compensated absences

Employees may be entitled to be paid during certain absences, such as annual recreational leave or short periods of illness. Some entities also offer other forms of paid leave, including maternity leave, parental leave, carers' leave and bereavement leave. Entitlements to short-term compensated absences are those entitlements that are expected to be settled within 12 months after the end of the reporting period.

Short-term compensated absences may be either accumulating or non-accumulating. Non-accumulating compensated absences are leave entitlements that the employee may not carry forward to a future period. For example, an employment agreement may provide for 5 days of paid, non-cumulative sick leave. If the employee does not take sick leave during the year, the unused leave lapses, that is, it does not carry forward to an increased entitlement in the following year.

Accumulating compensated absences are leave entitlements that the employee may carry forward to a future period if unused in the current period. For example, an employment agreement may provide for 20 days of paid annual leave. If the employee only takes 15 days of annual leave during the year, the remaining 5 days may be carried forward and taken in the following year.

Accumulating compensated absences may be vesting or non-vesting. If accumulating compensated absences are vesting, the employee is entitled to cash settlement for unused leave. If accumulating compensated absences are non-vesting, the employee has no entitlement to cash settlement of unused leave. For example, an employment contract may provide for cumulative annual leave of 20 days, vesting to a maximum of 30 days, and non-vesting cumulative sick leave of 10 days per annum. After 2 years, the employee would have been entitled to take 40 days of annual leave and 20 days of sick leave, but if the employee resigned after 2 years of employment, during which no annual leave or sick leave had been taken, the termination settlement would include payment for 30 days' unused annual leave (the maximum allowed by the employment agreement). There would be no cash settlement of the unused sick leave because it was non-vesting.

Paragraph 11 of IAS 19 requires expected short-term accumulating compensated absences to be recognised when the employee renders services that increase the entitlement. For example, if its employees are entitled to 2 weeks of cumulative sick leave for every year of service, the entity is required to accrue the sick leave throughout the year, to the extent that future settlement is expected. If the leave is cumulative but non-vesting, it is possible that there will not be a future settlement. The sick leave might remain unused when the employment contract is terminated. However, the sick leave must still be accrued throughout the period of employment because an obligation arises when the employee provides services that give rise to the leave entitlement. If the leave is non-vesting, it is necessary to estimate the amount of accumulated compensated absence that the entity expects to pay in the short term.

For non-accumulating short-term compensated absences, paragraph 19 requires the entity to recognise the employee benefit when the absence occurs. A liability is not recognised for unused non-accumulating leave entitlements because the employee is not entitled to carry them forward to a future period.

The alternative forms of short-term compensated absences and the corresponding recognition and measurement requirements are depicted in figure 15.2.

Accumulation	Vesting/non-vesting	Recognition	Liability measurement
Accumulating — employee may carry forward unused entitlement	Vesting — employee is entitled to cash settlement of unused leave	Recognised as employee provides services giving rise to entitlement	Nominal, amount expected to be paid, i.e. total vested accumulated leave
	Non-vesting — no cash settlement of unused leave	Recognised as employee provides services giving rise to entitlement	Nominal, amount expected to be paid, requires estimation of amount that will be used
Non-accumulating — unused entitlement lapses each period		Recognised when absences occur	No liability is recognised

FIGURE 15.2 Short-term compensated absences

The following illustrative examples demonstrate accounting for short-term compensated absences. First, illustrative example 15.3 demonstrates accounting for annual leave.

ILLUSTRATIVE EXAMPLE 15.3

Accounting for annual leave

Cham Ltd has four employees in its Bavarian branch. Each employee is entitled to 20 days of paid recreational leave per annum, referred to as annual leave (AL). A loading of 17.5% is paid when annual leave is taken. At 1 July 2009 the balance of the provision for annual leave was $5264. After annual leave taken during the year had been recorded, the provision had a debit balance of $2100 in the trial balance at 30 June 2010 before end-of-period adjustments. All annual leave accumulated at 30 June 2010 is expected to be paid by 30 June 2011. The following information is obtained from the payroll records for the year ended 30 June 2010:

Employee	Wage per day	AL 1 July 2009 in days	Increase in entitlement in days	AL taken in days
East	$120	10	20	16
North	$160	7	20	16
South	$180	8	20	14
West	$ 90	8	20	24

A liability must be recognised for accumulated annual leave at 30 June 2010. This is measured as the amount that is expected to be paid. As annual leave is vesting, all accumulated leave is expected to be paid. The first step in measuring the liability is to calculate the number of days of accumulated annual leave for each employee at 30 June 2010. Although this calculation would normally be performed by payroll software, we will calculate manually the number of days to enhance your understanding of the process. The next step is to multiply the number of days of accumulated annual leave by each employee's daily wage, increased by 17.5% for the annual leave loading.

Employee	AL 1 July 2009 in days	Increase in entitlement in days	AL taken in days	Accumulated AL 30 June 2010	Liability for AL 30 June 2010 $
East	10	20	16	14	1 974
North	7	20	16	11	2 068
South	8	20	14	14	2 961
West	8	20	24	4	423
					7 426

The calculation of accumulated annual leave in days and the resultant liability are as follows:

East: 10 + 20 − 16 = 14 days × $120 per day × 117.5% = $1 974
North: 7 + 20 − 16 = 11 days × $160 per day × 117.5% = $2 068
South: 8 + 20 − 14 = 14 days × $180 per day × 117.5% = $2 961
West: 8 + 20 − 24 = 4 days × $90 per day × 117.5% = $423

The above calculations show that a liability of $7426 should be recognised for annual leave at 30 June 2010. After recording annul leave taken during the year, the unadjusted trial balance shows a debit balance of $2100 for the provision for annual leave. Thus, a journal entry is required to record an increase of $9526.

Wages and Salaries Expense	Dr	9 526	
Provision for Annual Leave	Cr		9 526
(Accrual of liability for annual leave)			

In illustrative example 15.3, an annual adjustment was made to the provision for annual leave. Some entities make accruals for annual leave more frequently to facilitate more comprehensive internal reporting to management. This is easily achieved with electronic accounting systems or payroll software.

Accounting for accumulating sick leave is demonstrated in illustrative example 15.4. In this illustration, the accumulating sick leave is non-vesting.

ILLUSTRATIVE EXAMPLE 15.4

Accounting for accumulating sick leave

Diez Ltd has 10 employees who are each paid $500 per week for a 5-day working week (i.e. $100 per day). Employees are entitled to 5 days of accumulating non-vesting sick leave each year. At 1 July 2009, the accumulated sick leave brought forward from the previous year was 10 days in total. During the year ended 30 June 2010, employees took 35 days of paid sick leave and 10 days of unpaid sick leave. One employee resigned at the beginning of the year. At the time of her resignation she had accumulated 5 days of sick leave. It is estimated that 60% of the unused sick leave will be taken during the following year and that the remaining 40% will not be taken at all.

After recording sick leave taken during the year, the unadjusted trial balance shows that the balance of the provision for sick leave at 30 June 2010 is $3000 Dr.

The following table is constructed to assist in calculating the amount of the provision for sick leave that Diez Ltd should recognise at 30 June 2010:

		Sick leave		% of leave expected to be taken		
No. of employees	Base pay/day $	Balance b/d 1 July 2009 Days	Accumulated in 2010 Days	Taken or lapsed Days	Within 12 months %	After 1 year %
10	100	10	50	40	60	0

The 10 employees who were employed for all of the year ended 30 June 2010 became entitled to 5 days of sick leave during the year. Thus the total increase in entitlement during the year is 50 days. During the year, 35 days of paid sick leave were taken and 5 days of sick leave entitlement lapsed because an employee with 5 days' accumulated sick leave resigned without having used her entitlement. Thus, the aggregate sick leave entitlement reduced by 40 days during the year.

The amount of the liability at 30 June 2010 is measured by first calculating the number of days of accumulated sick leave entitlement at 30 June 2010.

	Days
Brought forward July 2009	10
Increase in entitlement for services provided in the current year	50
Sick leave entitlement taken or lapsed during the year	(40)
Sick leave carried forward 30 June 2010	20

The number of days of accumulated sick leave at the end of the reporting period is multiplied by the proportion of days expected to be taken, in this case, 60%. This amount, 12 days, is then multiplied by the current rate of pay per day:

20 days × 60% × $100 per day = $1 200

Thus a provision for sick leave of $1200 Cr should be recognised at 30 June 2010.

The unadjusted balance of the provision for sick leave is $3000 Dr. Accordingly, the provision must be increased by $4200 as follows:

Wages and Salaries Expense	Dr	4200	
Provision for Sick Leave	Cr		4200
(Accrual of liability for sick leave)			

For simplicity, the accrual adjustment to recognise sick leave is made at the end of the year in this example. Many companies make such adjustments throughout the year to provide more complete internal reporting to management. This is facilitated by payroll software that automates the calculation of accumulated entitlements.

15.4.5 Profit-sharing and bonus plans

Employers may offer profit-sharing arrangements and bonuses to their employees. Bonuses may be determined as a lump-sum amount or based on accounting or market-based measures of performance. Many large companies use bonuses in management incentive schemes. The bonus forms part of a management remuneration package designed to align the interests of the manager with the interests of the entity or its equity holders. Figure 15.3 shows several extracts that explain the structure of remuneration paid to members of BHP Billiton's Group Management Committee (GMC). The management remuneration packages include incentive-based components that are based on key performance indicators, thus rewarding management for achievement.

6.3.1 Key principles of our remuneration policy
The remuneration paid and payable to members of the GMC (including executive Directors) in respect of FY2008 is disclosed in this Report. It comprises *fixed and at risk* components.

6.3.3 Fixed remuneration
Fixed remuneration is made up of base salary, retirement and other benefits. It represents approximately 28 per cent of the individual's remuneration package (based on target performance and using Expected Values for share awards).

Base salary is targeted at industry average levels for comparable roles in global companies of similar complexity and size. Market data are used to benchmark salary levels and to inform decisions on base salary changes. Base salaries are set by reference to the scope and nature of the individual's performance and experience, and are reviewed each year.

6.3.4 At risk remuneration
At risk remuneration is geared to Group performance and is made up of short-term and long-term incentives. It represents approximately 72 per cent of the individual's remuneration package (based on target performance and using Expected Values for share awards).

FIGURE 15.3 BHP Billiton remuneration report (extract)
Source: BHP (2008, p. 140).

Paragraph 17 of IAS 19 requires an entity to recognise the expected cost of profit-sharing arrangements and bonus plans if:

(a) the entity has a present legal or constructive obligation to make such payments as a result of past events; and
(b) a reliable estimate of the obligation can be made.
A present obligation exists when, and only when, the entity has no realistic alternative but to make the payments.

Although the entity may have no legal obligation to pay the bonus, a constructive obligation arises if the entity has a well-established practice of paying the bonus and it has no realistic alternative but to pay the bonus. For instance, non-payment may be harmful to the entity's relations with its employees.

Liabilities for short-term profit-sharing arrangements and bonuses are measured at the nominal (i.e. undiscounted) amount that the entity expects to pay. Thus, if payment under a profit-sharing arrangement is subject to the employee still being employed when the payment is due, the amount recognised as a liability is reduced by the amount that will go unpaid due to staff turnover. For example, assume an entity has a profit-sharing arrangement in which it is obligated to pay 1% of profit for the period to employees and the amount becomes payable 3 months after the end of the reporting period. Based on staff turnover in prior years, the entity estimates that only 95% of employees will be eligible to receive a share of profit 3 months after the end of the reporting period. Accordingly, the amount of the liability that should be recognised for the profit-sharing scheme is equal to 0.95% of the entity's profit for the period. In this simple example it is assumed the bonus is distributed equally among employees.

15.5 POST-EMPLOYMENT BENEFITS

In many countries, employment benefits can include amounts that are not paid until after the employee retires. These are referred to as post-employment benefits. Where post-employment benefits involve significant obligations, it is common (and in some countries compulsory) for employers to contribute to a post-employment benefit plan for employees. For example, in Australia, it is compulsory for most private sector employers to contribute to a superannuation plan for employees.

Post-employment benefit plans are defined in paragraph 7 of IAS 19 as:

> formal or informal arrangements under which an entity provides post-employment benefits for one or more employees.

Post-employment benefit plans are also referred to as superannuation plans, employee retirement plans and pension plans. The employer makes payments to a fund. The fund, which is a separate entity, invests the contributions and provides post-employment benefits to the employees, who are the members of the fund. The two types of post-employment benefit plans are defined benefit plans and defined contribution plans, including multi-employer plans.

Paragraph 7 of IAS 19 refers to defined contribution post-employment plans as those for which the employer pays fixed contributions into a fund. The contributions are normally based on the wages and salaries paid to employees. The amount received by employees on retirement is dependent upon the level of contributions and the return earned by the fund on its investments. The employer has no legal or constructive obligation to make further contributions if the fund does not hold sufficient assets to pay all benefits relating to employees' past service when they retire.

In paragraph 7 of IAS 19, defined benefit post-employment plans are defined as post-employment plans other than defined contribution plans. If a post-employment plan is not classified as a defined contribution plan, by default, it is a defined benefit plan. Critical to the definition of a defined contribution post-employment benefit plan is the absence of an obligation for the employer to make further payments if the fund is unable to pay all the benefits accruing to members for their past service. Thus, defined benefit post-employment plans are those in which the employer has some obligation to pay further contributions to enable the fund to pay members' benefits. In a defined benefit post-employment plan, the benefit received by the member on retirement is determined by a formula reflecting their years of service and level of remuneration. It is not dependent upon the performance of the fund. If the performance of the fund is insufficient to pay members' post-employment benefits, the employer, who is the sponsor of the fund, has an obligation to make additional payments to the fund. Similarly, if the fund achieves higher returns than are required to pay members' post-employment benefits, the employer may be able to take a 'contribution holiday'.

Most private sector (and many public sector) post-employment benefit plans are defined contribution plans. Employers often prefer defined contribution plans because there is no risk of liability for further contributions if the fund fails to earn an adequate return.

IAS 19 prescribes accounting treatment for contributions to post-employment benefit funds and assets and liabilities arising from post-employment benefit plans from the perspective of the employer. It does not prescribe accounting requirements for the post-employment benefit fund. In Australia, the preparation and presentation of financial statements by post-employment benefit funds is prescribed by AAS 25 *Financial Reporting by Superannuation Plans*.

15.5.1 Accounting for defined contribution post-employment plans

As described above, entities that participate in defined contribution post-employment plans make payments to a post-employment benefit fund, such as a superannuation fund. The amount is determined as a percentage of remuneration paid to employees who are members of the fund. Contributions payable to defined contribution funds are recognised in the period the employee renders services. The contributions payable during the period are recognised as expenses unless another standard permits the cost of employment benefits to be allocated to the carrying amount of an asset, such as internally constructed plant in accordance with IAS 16 *Property, Plant and Equipment*.

If the amount paid to the defined contribution fund by the entity during the year is less than the amount payable in relation to services rendered by employees, a liability for unpaid contributions must be recognised at the end of the period. The liability is measured at the undiscounted amount payable to the extent that contributions are due within 12 months after the reporting period. Paragraph 45 of IAS 19 requires discounting of liabilities for contributions to defined contribution plans that are due more than 12 months after the reporting period in which the employee provides the related services. The discount rate used to discount a post-employment benefit obligation is determined by reference to market yields on high quality corporate bonds in accordance with IAS 19 paragraph 78. If the obligation is to be settled in a country that does not have a deep market in high quality corporate bonds, the market yield on government bonds must be used.

If the amount paid to the defined contribution fund by the entity during the year is greater than the amount of contributions payable in relation to services rendered by employees, the entity recognises an asset to the extent that it is entitled to a refund or reduction in future contributions.

ILLUSTRATIVE EXAMPLE 15.5

Accounting for defined contribution post-employment plans

Ellrich Ltd provides a defined contribution superannuation plan for its employees. Under the plan, Ellrich Ltd is required to contribute 8% of gross wages, salaries and bonuses payable for services rendered by employees. Ellrich Ltd makes monthly payments of $25 000 to the superannuation plan. Ellrich Ltd's annual reporting period ends on 30 June. If the amount paid to the superannuation fund during the financial year is less than 8% of gross wages, salaries and bonuses for that year, Ellrich Ltd must pay the outstanding contributions by 30 September of the following financial year. If the amount paid during the financial year is more than 8% of the gross wages, salaries and bonuses for the year, the excess contributions are deducted from amounts payable in the following year.

Ellrich Ltd's employee benefits for the year ended 30 June 2010 comprise:

	$
Gross wages and salaries	3 900 000
Gross annual bonuses	100 000
	4 000 000

The deficit in Ellrich Ltd's superannuation contributions for the year ended 30 June 2010 is determined as follows:

	$
Contributions payable:	
8% × gross wages, salaries and bonuses	320 000
Contributions paid during 2010:	
$25 000 × 12	300 000
Superannuation contribution payable	20 000

Ellrich Ltd must recognise a liability for the unpaid superannuation contributions. The liability is not discounted because it is a short-term liability for employee benefits. Ellrich Ltd would record the following entry for 30 June 2010:

Wages and Salaries Expense	Dr	20 000	
Superannuation Payable	Cr		20 000
(Accrual of liability for unpaid superannuation contributions)			

15.5.2 Accounting for defined benefit post-employment plans

As described in section 15.5, the employer pays contributions to a fund, which is a separate entity from the employer. The fund accumulates assets through contributions and returns on investments. The accumulated assets are used to pay post-employment benefits to members (retired employees). The return on investments held by the superannuation fund comprises dividend and interest income and changes in the fair value of investments. The benefits paid to members are a function of their remuneration levels while employed and the number of years of service. If there is a shortfall in the fund's capacity to pay benefits to members, the trustee of the fund may require the employer to make additional contributions. Thus, the employer bears the risk of the fund being unable to pay benefits.

The view adopted in IAS 19 is that the employer has an obligation for the accrued benefits of the defined benefit post-employment benefit plan and that the obligation is reduced by the assets of the plan. The assets of the plan are not controlled by the employer because they cannot be used for its benefit; the assets of the plan are only used directly and indirectly to pay post-employment benefits to the members of the plan. The accrued benefits are the estimated retirement benefits payable to members of the plan as a result of services provided in the current and prior period. Under the net asset capitalisation method, the employer recognises a liability to the extent that the present value of accrued benefits exceeds the plan assets. Conversely, an asset is recognised to the extent that the plan assets exceed the accrued benefits.

IAS 19, paragraph 7 defines the present value of a defined benefit obligation as:

> the present value, without deducting any plan assets, of expected future payments required to settle the obligation resulting from employee service in the current or prior periods.

The defined benefit obligation, also referred to as the accrued liability, increases with the period of service of the employees covered by the plan and the level of the employees' remuneration. Obligations to pay pensions during employees' lives or that of his/her eligible dependants further complicate the measurement of accrued benefits because the total payment is dependent upon the mortality rate of the employees and their eligible beneficiaries. Further, the present value of the accrued benefits increases as the expected settlement time approaches because the expected settlement is discounted over a shorter period of time.

Companies often rely on actuarial assessments to estimate the defined benefit obligation and the level of investment required to enable the fund to pay accrued benefits as and when they fall due. Actuaries apply mathematical, statistical, economic and financial analysis to assess risks associated with contracts, such as insurance contracts and superannuation funds. They also provide financial planning advice, on matters such as the level of investment needed to generate sufficient future cash flows to meet the expected obligations as and when they fall due. Some companies employ their own actuaries, while many others engage actuaries as professional consultants. Actuarial estimates rely on assumptions. For example, the estimation of the level of required contributions depends upon assumptions about the rate of return that the fund will earn on the investment of plan assets.

There is ongoing debate as to how an employer should account for post-employment benefits, including pension funds, and the adequacy of disclosures in corporate financial statements. For further reading on research in this area refer to Gallery (2003) and Gordon (2005).

The International Accounting Standards Board issued a discussion paper in 2008 outlining the board's preliminary views on amendments to IAS 19. After consideration of responses to the discussion paper, the IASB plans to issue an exposure draft of a revised standard on accounting for employee benefits. In this section, we will consider alternative approaches to the recognition and measurement of assets and liabilities arising from defined benefit post-employment plans. The first of these approaches is the net capitalisation method.

Net capitalisation method

ILLUSTRATIVE EXAMPLE 15.6

Net capitalisation method

Freiberg Ltd has a defined benefit superannuation plan for its senior staff. The following information is available for the Freiberg DB Super Fund:

	30 June 2010 $	30 June 2009 $
Present value of accrued benefits	5 700 000	4 900 000
Fair value of plan assets	5 400 000	4 500 000
Net obligation (surplus)	300 000	400 000

During the year ended 30 June 2010 Freiberg Ltd's contributions to the Freiberg DB Super Fund were $450 000.

The journal entries to record Freiberg Ltd's superannuation contributions and superannuation liability for the year ended 30 June 2010 are as follows:

Summary entry	Superannuation Liability Bank (Payment of contributions to Freiberg DB Super Fund)	Dr Cr	450 000	 450 000
June 30	Superannuation Expenses Superannuation Liability (Net capitalisation of defined benefit superannuation plan)	Dr Cr	350 000	 350 000

The payment of contributions would occur regularly throughout the year. For brevity, these entries are recorded as a summary entry in the journal above. In applying the net capitalisation method, Freiberg Ltd must recognise a liability of $400 000 at 30 June 2009. The contributions paid during 30 June 2010 reduce the liability, resulting in a debit balance of $50 000 ($400 000 Cr – $450 000 Dr) prior to the entry to recognise the liability at 30 June 2010. Accordingly, the superannuation liability account must be increased by $350 000 on 30 June 2010.

The net capitalisation method can result in large gains and losses being recognised in profit or loss due to changes in the surplus or deficit of the fair value of plan assets over the present value of accrued benefits. For instance, the present value of the defined benefit obligation increases if employee retention is greater than the amount assumed in the previous actuarial estimate, resulting in a deficit in the superannuation fund. Similarly, an unexpected decline in the return on investment of plan assets may cause the plan assets to grow at a slower rate than the present value of the defined benefit obligation, giving rise to an increase in the superannuation liability recognised by the employer. The net capitalisation method is unpopular with some preparers of financial statements who would prefer less volatility of earnings. IAS 19 adopts the partial capitalisation method, which has the effect of smoothing profit and leaving part of the net superannuation asset or liability off-balance sheet.

Partial capitalisation method

The partial capitalisation method does not require all the defined benefit obligation and the fair value of plan assets to be reflected in the net asset or net liability recognised by the employer. To understand the partial capitalisation method, it is necessary to identify the various components of the change in the present value of the defined benefit obligation as well as actuarial gains or losses, because the components are accounted for differently.

The present value of the defined benefit obligation is increased by current service costs, past service cost and interest cost. Paragraph 7 of IAS 19 defines these terms as follows:

> *Current service cost* is the increase in the present value of a defined benefit obligation resulting from employee service in the current period.
>
> *Past service cost* is the increase in the present value of the defined benefit obligation for employee service in prior periods, resulting in the current period from the introduction of, or changes to, post-employment benefits or other long-term employee benefits. Past service cost may be either positive (where benefits are introduced or improved) or negative (where existing benefits are reduced).
>
> *Interest cost* is the increase during a period in the present value of a defined benefit obligation which arises because the benefits are one period closer to settlement.
>
> *Actuarial gains and losses* comprise
>
> (a) experience adjustments (the effects of differences between the previous actuarial assumptions and what has actually occurred); and
>
> (b) the effects of changes in actuarial assumptions.

Experience adjustments in relation to plan assets refer to differences between the expected return on plan assets and the actual return achieved. Experience adjustments in relation to the defined benefit obligation refer to differences between the actual results and previous actuarial estimates used to measure the defined benefit obligation. An example is the difference between the estimated employee turnover for the year and the actual employee turnover during the year. An example of a change in an actuarial assumption is a change in the discount rate used to determine the present value of the obligation.

Under the partial capitalisation method adopted by IAS 19, only the current service cost and the interest cost are recognised in the period in which they arise. Past service costs are amortised on a straight-line basis over the average period until they become vested. Paragraph 92 requires the immediate recognition of past service costs to the extent that the change in defined benefits is immediately vested. The amortisation of past service costs (if positive) results in an increase in expenses and an increase in the superannuation liability. The unamortised portion of past service costs is off-balance sheet.

Current service costs and interest costs increase the defined benefit obligation and superannuation expense for the period. The return on investment on plan assets increases plan assets, thus reducing the net liability. Thus, the return on investment reduces the superannuation expense and reduces the net superannuation liability recognised by the employer. However, paragraph 105 requires the expected return on plan assets, rather than the actual return, to be used to determine superannuation expense. The difference between the expected return and the actual return on plan assets during the period is an actuarial gain or loss.

Corridor method

IAS 19 allows the corridor method for the recognition of actuarial gains and losses. Under the corridor method, a portion of actuarial gains or losses must be recognised if the net cumulative unrecognised actuarial gains and losses at the end of the previous reporting period exceeded the greater of (paragraph 92):

> (a) 10% of the present value of the defined benefit obligation at that date (before deducting plan assets); and
>
> (b) 10% of the fair value of any plan assets at that date.

Accumulated actuarial gains or losses within the corridor are not recognised. To the extent that the surplus or deficit in the defined benefit plan relates to accumulated actuarial gains or losses within the corridor, it remains off-balance sheet.

If accumulated actuarial gains or losses exceed the 10% corridor defined in paragraph 92, a portion of the excess over the 10% corridor must be recognised. The portion of the excess that must be recognised is determined as the excess divided by the average expected remaining work life of the members of the plan.

Illustrative example 15.7 demonstrates the application of the corridor method to the recognition of actuarial gains and losses. While more accelerated approaches to the recognition of actuarial gains and losses are permitted by IAS 19, it is useful to consider the corridor approach because it reflects the most income smoothing and deferred recognition of actuarial gains and losses permitted by IAS 19, and thus provides a point of comparison for alternative approaches, such as the net capitalisation approach.

ILLUSTRATIVE EXAMPLE 15.7

Recognition of actuarial gains and losses using the corridor method

During the year ended 30 June 2009, Genthin Ltd's defined benefit superannuation plan incurred large unexpected losses on investments as a result of the global financial crisis. Thus, actuarial losses arose because actual returns earned from the investment of plan assets were significantly less than expected returns.

The following information pertains to Genthin Ltd's defined benefit superannuation plan as at 30 June:

	2009 $	2008 $
Present value of the defined benefit obligation	10 000 000	9 000 000
Fair value of plan assets	7 000 000	7 200 000
Net obligation (surplus)	3 000 000	1 800 000
Accumulated actuarial losses	1 200 000	150 000
	Years	**Years**
Average expected remaining work life of members	10	11

Recognition of actuarial loss in 2009

To determine whether any portion of the accumulated actuarial losses should be recognised during the year ended 30 June 2009, we must compare the amount of the accumulated actuarial losses at 30 June 2008 with 10% of the greater of the present value of the defined benefit obligation and the fair value of plan assets at that date. The workings are based on the present value of the defined benefit obligation because it is greater than the fair value of plan assets.

10% × $9 000 000 = $900 000

The accumulated actuarial losses at 30 June 2008 are only $150 000. As this is less than 10% of the present value of the defined benefit obligation, none of the accumulated actuarial losses is recognised in 2009.

Recognition of actuarial loss in 2010

The present value of the defined benefit obligation exceeds the fair value of plan assets at 30 June 2009. Accordingly the present value of the defined benefit obligation is used to determine the corridor within which the accumulated actuarial losses are not recognised.

	$
Accumulated actuarial losses at 30 June 2009	1 200 000
Corridor — 10% × $10 000 000	1 000 000
Actuarial losses in excess of corridor	200 000
Amortisation during 2010 ($200 000/10 years average expected remaining work life of members)	20 000

Thus, an expense of $20 000 is recognised for the amortisation of the recognisable accumulated actuarial losses as follows:

30 June 2010	Superannuation Expenses	Dr	20 000	
	Superannuation Liability	Cr		20 000
	(Amortisation of accumulated actuarial losses)			

Figure 15.4 summarises the components of defined benefit post-employment plans and their accounting treatment under the partial capitalisation method adopted by IAS 19.

	Accounting treatment	IAS 19 *para.*
Interest costs	Increase in expenses* and post-employment benefit liability	*61*
Current service costs	Increase in expenses and post-employment benefit liability	*61*
Past service costs	Deferred off-balance sheet; amortised, increasing expenses and post-employment benefit liability over the average remaining period until they become vested	*61, 96*
Expected return on plan assets	Decrease in expenses and post-employment benefit liability	*105*
Accumulated actuarial gains and losses within corridor of 10% of the fair value of plan assets or the present value of the defined benefit obligation, whichever is the greater	Not required to be recognised	*92*
Accumulated actuarial gains and losses outside corridor of 10% of the fair value of plan assets or 10% of the present value of the defined benefit obligation, whichever is the greater	Deferred off-balance sheet; amortised as change in expenses and post-employment benefit liability over the average expected remaining working life of members	*92, 93*

*The costs of employee benefits for post-employment benefits are included in the cost of assets if required by another accounting standard.

FIGURE 15.4 Summary of components of defined benefit post-employment plans

Paragraph 93 permits entities to adopt a systematic method of amortising actuarial gains and losses that results in faster recognition than would occur through straight-line amortisation over the average expected remaining working life of members. If an accelerated amortisation policy is adopted in accordance with paragraph 93 it must be applied consistently to both accumulated actuarial gains and accumulated actuarial losses.

Paragraph 93 of IAS 19 also permits recognition of all actuarial gains and losses in the period in which they are incurred. That is, an entity may choose to recognise actuarial gains and losses that are within the corridor of 10% of the greater of the fair value of plan assets and the present value of the defined benefit obligation. If an entity adopts a policy of full recognition of actuarial gains and losses, it may also choose to classify the actuarial gains and losses in other comprehensive income. Paragraph 93A permits actuarial gains or losses recognised in the period in which they are incurred to be classified as other comprehensive income, provided that the classification is applied to:

- all defined benefit plans sponsored by the entity, and
- all actuarial gains and losses.

Classification of actuarial gains and losses as components of other comprehensive income shields reported profit from the volatility that would arise from the recognition of actuarial gains and losses.

ILLUSTRATIVE EXAMPLE 15.8

Accounting for a defined benefit plan

Hofheim Ltd has a defined benefit superannuation plan for its senior managers. The following information is available for Hofheim DB Superannuation Fund for the year ended 30 June 2010:

Discount rate at 1 July 2009	7%
Expected rate of return on plan assets at 1 July 2009	9%
Average expected remaining working lives of employees at 1 July 2009	10 years
Net superannuation asset recognised by Hofheim Ltd at 30 June 2009	$4 000 000

Members of the plan are entitled to 10% of their average salary for every year of service. Hofheim Ltd revised its defined benefits on 1 July 2009 and increased the entitlement to 11% of average salary. The increase in the defined benefit obligation is a past service cost to the extent the increase relates to services rendered before 1 July 2009. The revision to the defined benefit plan results in an increase in the defined benefit obligation of $5 million on 1 July 2009. Thus, the past service cost is $5 million, as shown in the second row of the table below. The average remaining period until the additional benefits become vested is 5 years from 1 July 2009.

All employee benefits costs are recognised as expenses because the company is not subject to requirements in other standards to include employee benefits in the cost of assets.

The accumulated actuarial losses at 30 June 2009 were $3 million, most of which arose during that year. Hofheim Ltd applies the corridor approach and amortises the excess accumulated actuarial gains and losses on a straight-line basis over the average expected remaining working lives of employees.

Changes in the present value of Hofheim DB Superannuation Fund and other items relating to the plan for the year ended 30 June 2010 are as follows:

	$'000
Present value of the defined benefit obligation at 30 June 2009	28 000
Past service cost (present value of increase in defined benefits at 1 July 2009)	5 000
Present value of the defined benefit obligation at 1 July 2009	33 000
Interest cost (7% of defined benefit obligation at 1 July 2009)	2 310
Current service cost	4 000
Benefits paid by the fund during the year	(3 000)
Actuarial (gain) or loss on obligation (in current period)[1]	190
Present value of defined benefit obligation at 30 June 2010	36 500
Fair value of plan assets at 1 July 2009	29 000
Expected return on plan assets (9% x plan assets at 1 July 2009)	2 610
Contributions paid to the fund during the year	4 800
Benefits paid by the fund during the year	(3 000)
Actuarial gain (loss) on plan assets[2]	(210)
Fair value of plan assets at 30 June 2010[3]	33 200

Notes

1. The actuarial gain or loss on the defined benefit obligation in the current period reflects the change in the defined benefit obligation that is not explained by interest cost, current service costs or benefits paid. It may relate to changes in the discount rate or actuarial assumptions, such as staff turnover rates, used to estimate the extent to which benefits become vested.
2. The actuarial gain or loss on the plan assets is the difference between the expected return on the plan assets and the actual return.
3. The fair value of plan assets is derived from valuations performed by Hope & Moore Valuers as at 30 June 2010.

The present value of the defined benefit obligation at 1 July 2009 is $33 million, including the increase in the defined benefit obligation arising from past service.

The present value of the obligation is increased by the interest cost, which reflects the unwinding of the discount as the period to settlement of the obligation is reduced. The present value of the defined benefit obligation at 1 July 2009 is $33 000. This reflects the future cash flows discounting at a rate of 7% per annum. Accordingly, the interest cost for the year ended 30 June 2010 is 7% × $33 million.

The current service cost is given as $4 million. This estimation information would be based on actuarial advice and provided by the manager of the superannuation fund.

Benefits paid during the year are $3 million, and refer to payments that the fund has made to members retiring during the year. Note that benefits paid by the superannuation fund reduce both the defined benefit obligation and the plan assets.

The net superannuation asset recognised by Hofheim Ltd at 30 June 2009 can be reconciled to the surplus of the superannuation fund as follows:

	$'000
Present value of defined benefit obligation at 30 June 2009	28 000
Fair value of plan assets	(29 000)
Net obligation (surplus) of superannuation fund	(1 000)
Unamortised actuarial losses	(3 000)
Net superannuation asset recognised by Hofheim Ltd at 30 June 2009	(4 000)

The information shown above is used to prepare the journal entries to account for Hofheim Ltd's superannuation asset in accordance with IAS 19. The payment of contributions during the period increases the net superannuation asset. The interest cost and current service cost increase the defined benefit obligation. The expected return on investment of plan assets increases the net asset. The entries to account for these components of the change in the superannuation asset are as follows:

Summary entry	Superannuation Asset Bank (Payment of superannuation contributions)	Dr Cr	4 800 000	 4 800 000
30 June 2010	Superannuation Expenses Superannuation Asset (Interest cost $2 310 000 and current service cost $4 000 000 less expected return on plan assets $2 610 000)	Dr Cr	3 700 000	 3 700 000

The next step is to determine the portion of past service costs that must be recognised in the current period. The amount of amortisation of past service costs is calculated as:

Past service costs

Average remaining period until past service costs become vested

$$= \frac{\$5\,000\,000}{5 \text{ years}}$$

= $1 000 000 for the year ended 30 June 2010

The amortisation of past service costs is recorded by the following journal entry:

30 June 2010	Superannuation Expenses Superannuation Asset (Amortisation of past service costs)	Dr Cr	1 000 000	 1 000 000

Thus, at 30 June 2010, unamortised past service costs were $4 million (total past service costs, $5 million, less amount amortised to date, $1 million).

The final step is to determine the portion, if any, of accumulated actuarial gains or losses to be amortised in the current period. Recall that the amount recognised in the current period is the amortisation of the accumulated actuarial gains or losses at the end of the previous period. Thus, to determine the amount to be recognised as an expense and a decrease in the net superannuation asset for the year ended 30 June 2010 we must compare the accumulated actuarial losses at 30 June 2009 with the limits of the corridor at 30 June 2009. The fair value of plan assets is used to determine the corridor because it exceeds the present value of the defined benefit obligation at 30 June 2009.

	$
Accumulated actuarial losses at 30 June 2009	3 000 000
Corridor — 10% × $29 000 000	(2 900 000)
Actuarial losses in excess of corridor	100 000
Amortisation during 2010 ($100 000/10 years average expected remaining work life of members)	10 000

The journal entry to record the amortisation of accumulated actuarial losses is:

30 June 2010	Superannuation Expenses	Dr	10 000	
	Superannuation Asset	Cr		10 000
	(Amortisation of accumulated actuarial losses)			

Accumulated unamortised actuarial losses at 30 June 2010 can be determined as follows:

	$'000
Unamortised accumulated actuarial losses at 30 June 2009	3 000
Amortisation during 2010	(10)
Actuarial losses for the year ended 30 June 2010:	
Actuarial loss on obligation	190
Actuarial loss on plan assets	210
Unamortised accumulated actuarial losses at 30 June 2010	3 390

The Superannuation Asset general ledger account shows the changes in the net asset during the year ended 30 June 2010.

Superannuation Asset					
1/7/09	Balance b/d	4 000 000	30/6/10	Superannuation Expense (interest cost, current service cost, expected returns)	3 700 000
30/6/10	Bank (contributions)	4 800 000	30/6/10	Superannuation Expense (past service cost)	1 000 000
			30/6/10	Superannuation Expense	10 000
			30/6/10	Balance c/d	4 090 000
		8 800 000			8 800 000

The net superannuation asset recognised by Hofheim Ltd at 30 June 2010 can be reconciled to the deficit of the superannuation fund as follows:

	$'000
Present value of defined benefit obligation	36 500
Fair value of plan assets	(33 200)
Net obligation (surplus) of superannuation fund	3 300
Unamortised past service costs	(4 000)
Unamortised actuarial losses	(3 390)
Net superannuation asset recognised by Hofheim Ltd at 30 June 2010	(4 090)

Although the superannuation fund is in deficit, Hofheim Ltd reports a superannuation surplus because unamortised past service costs obligations and unamortised actuarial losses are off-balance sheet.

15.6 OTHER LONG-TERM EMPLOYEE BENEFITS

Long-term employee benefits are benefits for services provided in the current period that will not be paid until more than 12 months after the end of the period. Post-employment benefits were considered in section 15.5. This section considers long-term employee benefits that are provided to employees during the period of their employment. A common form of long-term employee benefits is long service leave, which is a compensated absence after the employee has provided a long period of service, such as 3 months of paid leave after 10 years of continuous employment.

Long service leave accrues to employees as they provide service to the entity. The principle adopted by IAS 19 is that an obligation arises for long service leave when the employees provide services to the employer, even though the employees may have no legal entitlement to the leave. Thus, a liability is recognised for long service leave as it accrues. Long service leave payments reduce the long service leave liability.

Paragraph 128 requires the liability for long-term employee benefits to be measured as the net of:

(a) the present value of the defined benefit obligation at the reporting date (see paragraph 64);
(b) minus the fair value at the reporting date of plan assets (if any) out of which the obligations are to be settled directly (see paragraphs 102–104).

In some countries, such as Australia, it is extremely unusual to establish plan assets to provide for the payment of long service leave benefits to employees. Thus, the accounting treatment for long service leave benefits is usually confined to the recognition of the present value of the obligation referred to in part (a) of paragraph 128.

The standard adopts the projected unit credit method. This means that the obligation for long-term employee benefits is measured by calculating the present value of the expected future payments that will result from employee services provided to date. The measurement of the present value of the obligation for long service leave payments is complicated by the need to make several estimates. These include estimation of when the leave will be taken, projected salary levels, and the proportion of employees who will continue in the entity's employment long enough to become entitled to long service leave. Actuarial advice is often used in the measurement of long service leave obligations.

The steps involved in the measurement of a liability for long service leave are as follows:

Step 1 Estimate the number of employees who are expected to become eligible for long service leave. The probability that employees will become eligible for long service leave generally increases with the period of employment. For example, if an entity provides long service leave after 10 years of employment, the probability that employees who have already been working for the entity for 7 years will continue in employment for another 3 years is very high, as the closer proximity to long service leave entitlement provides an incentive to employees to stay with their current employer. Thus, the proportion of employees who are expected to become eligible for long service leave is usually calculated separately for employees with different levels of prior service.

Step 2 Estimate the projected wages and salaries at the time that long service leave is expected to be paid. This step involves the application of expected inflation rates or other cost adjustment rates over the remaining period before long service leave is paid. Applying an estimated inflation rate:

Projected salaries = current salaries × $(1 + \text{inflation rate})^n$
where n = number of years until long service leave is expected to be paid.

For example, for employees who have 3 years remaining before long service leave is expected to be paid, current salaries are projected over a period of 3 years.

Step 3 Determine the accumulated benefit. The projected unit credit is determined as the proportion of projected long service leave attributable to services that have already been provided by the employee.

The accumulated benefit is calculated as:

$$\frac{\text{Years of employment}}{\text{Years required for LSL}} \times \frac{\text{weeks of paid leave}}{52} \times \text{projected salaries}$$

Step 4 Measure the present value of the accumulated benefit. The accumulated benefit is discounted at a rate determined by reference to market yields on high quality corporate bonds, in accordance with paragraph 78. If the country in which the long service leave entitlement will be paid does not have a deep market in high quality corporate bonds, the government bond rate is used.

$$\text{Present value} = \frac{\text{accumulated benefit}}{(1 + i)^n}$$

where i is the interest rate on high quality corporate bonds maturing n years later.

The liability for long service leave is a provision. After determining the amount of the obligation for long service leave at the end of the period, following steps 1 to 4 above, the provision is increased or decreased as required.

Illustrative example 15.9 demonstrates the measurement of the obligation for long service leave, applying the projected unit credit method in accordance with IAS 19, and the entries to account for changes in the provision for long service leave.

ILLUSTRATIVE EXAMPLE 15.9

Accounting for long service leave

Ilsenburg Ltd commenced operations on 1 July 2009 and had 150 employees. Average salaries were \$60 000 per annum for the year. Ilsenburg Ltd accounts for all recognised employee costs as expenses. Employees are entitled to 13 weeks of long service leave after 10 years of employment. The following information is based on advice received from actuarial consultants at 30 June 2010:

Number of years unit credit	1 year
Number of years until long service leave is expected to be paid	9 years
Probability that long service leave will be taken (proportion of employees expected to stay long enough to become entitled to long service leave)	50%
Expected increase in salaries (based on inflation)	2% per annum
Yield on 9-year high quality corporate bonds at 30/6/2010	10%

The discount rate is determined using 9-year bonds because the long service leave is expected to be paid 9 years after the end of the reporting period.

Step 1 Estimate the number of employees who are expected to become eligible for long service leave.

$$50\% \times 150 \text{ employees} = 75 \text{ employees}$$

Step 2 Estimate the projected salaries.

$$= \text{Salary} \times (1 + \text{inflation rate})^n$$
$$= \$60\,000 \times 75 \text{ employees} \times (1 + 0.02)^9 = \$5\,377\,917$$

The current salary is inflated over nine years because employees are expected to take long service leave 9 years after the end of the reporting period.

Step 3 Determine the accumulated benefit.

$$= \frac{\text{Years of employment}}{\text{Years required for LSL}} \times \frac{\text{weeks of paid leave}}{52} \times \text{projected salaries}$$
$$= \frac{1}{10} \times \frac{13}{52} \times \$5\,377\,917 = \$134\,448$$

Step 4 Measure the present value of the accumulated benefit.

$$= \frac{\text{Accumulated benefit}}{(1+i)^n}$$
$$= \frac{\$134448}{(1+0.1)^9} \text{[or \$134 448} \times 0.4241 \text{ from present value tables]}$$
$$= \$57\,019$$

The change in the provision for long service leave is recorded by the following journal entry:

30 June 2010	Long Service Leave Expense Provision for Long Service Leave (Increase in provision for long service leave)	Dr Cr	57 019	 57 019

Note there was no beginning of period provision for long service leave as this is the first year.

During the following year, Ilsenburg Ltd's 150 employees continued to work for the company. Average salaries increased to $68 000 per annum for the year. The following information is based on advice received from actuarial consultants at 30 June 2011:

Number of years unit credit	2 years
Number of years until long service leave is expected to be paid	8 years
Probability that LSL will be taken (proportion of employees expected to stay long enough to be entitled)	55%
Expected increase in salaries (based on inflation)	2% per annum
Yield on 8-year high quality corporate bonds 30/6/2011	9%

The discount rate is determined using 8-year bonds because the long service leave is expected to be paid 8 years after the end of the reporting period.

Step 1 Estimate the number of employees who are expected to become eligible for long service leave.

55% × 150 employees = 82.5 employees

Step 2 Estimate the projected salaries.

$$= \text{Salary} \times (1 + \text{inflation rate})^n$$
$$= \$68\,000 \times 82.5 \text{ employees} \times (1 + 0.02)^8 = \$6\,573\,009$$

The current salary is inflated over 8 years because employees are expected to take long service leave 8 years after the end of the reporting period.

Step 3 Determine the accumulated benefit.

$$= \frac{\text{Years of employment}}{\text{Years required for LSL}} \times \frac{\text{weeks of paid leave}}{52} \times \text{projected salaries}$$
$$= \frac{2}{10} \times \frac{13}{52} \times \$6\,573\,009 = \$328\,650$$

Step 4 Measure the present value of the accumulated benefit.

$$= \frac{\text{Accumulated benefit}}{(1+i)^n}$$
$$= \frac{\$328650}{(1+0.09)^8} \text{ [or } \$328\,650 \times 0.50187 \text{ from present value tables]}$$
$$= \$164\,939$$

The increase in the long service leave can be calculated as $164 939 less $57 019 because there have been no long service leave payments during the year to reduce the provision from the amount recognised at the end of the previous year. The change in the provision for long service leave is recorded by the following journal entry:

30 June 2011	Long Service Leave Expense Provision for Long Service Leave (Increase in provision for long service leave)	Dr Cr	107 920	 107 920

The increase in the provision for long service leave during 2011 can be attributed to several factors:

- An increase in unit credit accumulated by employees. In the first year, the employees' accumulation was 10% of the leave, but, by the end of the second year, 20% had been accumulated because the employees had completed 2 of the 10 years of service required to become eligible for long service leave.
- The interest cost, being the increase in the present value arising from discounting the future cash flows over a shorter period.
- An increase in projected salaries resulting from an increase in remuneration. That is, salaries increased beyond the projected 2% during 2011.
- A reduction in the interest rate used from 10% at 30 June 2010 to 9% at 30 June 2011.

15.7 TERMINATION BENEFITS

When an employee is retrenched or made redundant, the employer may be obliged to pay termination benefits. For example, a downturn in the economy may cause a manufacturer to reduce the scale of its operations, resulting in some portion of the entity's workforce being made redundant. Paragraph 7 of IAS 19 refers to termination benefits as employee benefits that are payable as a result of either:

(a) an entity's decision to terminate an employee's employment before the normal retirement date; or

(b) an employee's decision to accept voluntary redundancy in exchange for those benefits.

Thus, termination benefits can be distinguished from other forms of employee benefits because the obligation to pay termination benefits arises from the termination of an employment contract, rather than from past services provided by the employee. Although the obligation arises from a decision to terminate employment, the extent of past services provided by each employee is usually a factor in determining the amount of the payment.

The decision to undertake a redundancy program is not sufficient for the recognition of a liability for termination benefits. Merely deciding to undertake a redundancy program does not create an obligation to a third party and does not, therefore, meet the definition of a liability in accordance with the *Framework*.

Paragraph 133 of IAS 19 requires an entity to recognise an expense and a liability for termination benefits when, and only when, the entity is demonstrably committed to either:

(a) terminate the employment of an employee or group of employees before the normal retirement date; or

(b) provide termination benefits as a result of an offer made in order to encourage voluntary redundancy.

Paragraph 134 elaborates on the term 'demonstrably committed', specifying that an entity does not become demonstrably committed until it has a detailed formal plan for the termination of employment without any realistic possibility of withdrawing. The minimum requirements for the detailed plan include the location, function and approximate number of employees whose services are to be terminated, the benefits payable for each job classification or function, and the time at which the plan is scheduled for implementation.

ILLUSTRATIVE EXAMPLE 15.10

Termination benefits

During June 2009, the board of directors of Jarmen Ltd approved a plan to outsource its data processing operations. The closure of the data processing operations is expected to result in the retrenchment of 180 employees throughout Australia and New Zealand. The chief financial officer provided an estimate of redundancy costs of A$1.2 million. The board expected that it would take at least 6 months to select a contractor for outsourcing the data processing and that it would take a further 3 months for training before internal data processing operations could be discontinued.

During May 2010, redundancy packages were negotiated with trade union representatives. Data processing operations were to be transferred to an external service provider in India on 1 October 2010.

The management of Jarmen Ltd is wondering when it should to recognise an expense and liability for the redundancy payments.

2009

Jarmen Ltd must recognise a liability for termination benefits when (and only when) it becomes demonstrably committed to a detailed redundancy plan in accordance with paragraph 133 of IAS 19. There is some evidence of a plan existing by June 2009 because management had specified the location (Australia and New Zealand) and function (data processing) of the employees becoming redundant, and estimated their number at 180. The termination benefit payable for each job specification is likely to have formed the basis of the estimated redundancy costs of $1.2 million. However, until Jarmen Ltd has identified an alternative source of data processing, it will not be able to decide on a time at which the redundancy plan should be implemented. Thus the plan does not constitute a formal detailed plan in accordance with paragraph 134 of IAS 19. Further, although the decision to discontinue the internal data processing operation had been made by Jarmen Ltd's board of directors, there is no obligation to another party. The company is not demonstrably committed to the redundancy plan. Therefore, Jarmen Ltd should not recognise an expense and liability for termination benefits in association with the planned closure of its data processing operations at 30 June 2009 in accordance with IAS 19.

2010

By June 2010, the company had completed the formal detailed redundancy plan by specifying when it is to be implemented. The negotiations with unions over the amount of redundancy payments and entering into a contract with an external provider demonstrably commit the company to the redundancy plan. Accordingly, Jarmen Ltd should recognise an expense and a liability for termination benefits in association with the planned closure of its data processing operations in its financial statements for the period ended 30 June 2010 in accordance with IAS 19.

SUMMARY

Employee benefit costs are a significant expense for most reporting entities. Accounting for employee benefits is complicated by the diversity of arrangements for remuneration for services provided by employees. This area of accounting is further complicated by the different methods prescribed by IAS 19 to account for various forms and categories of employee benefits. Liabilities for short-term employee benefits, such a salaries, wages, sick leave, annual leave and bonuses payable within 12 months after the reporting period, are measured at the undiscounted amount that the entity expects to pay. The long-term component of employee benefits, such as bonuses payable more than 12 months after the reporting period, are measured at fair value. Long-term liabilities for defined benefits, such as long service leave, are measured at the present value of the defined benefit obligations less the fair value of plan assets, if any, out of which the obligation is to be settled. The obligation for long service leave is measured using the projected unit credit method. IAS 19 also prescribes accounting treatment for post-employment benefit plans. Accounting for defined contribution post-employment plans is relatively straightforward: a liability is recognised by the entity for contributions payable for the period in excess of contributions paid. Conversely, an asset is recognised if contributions paid exceed the contributions payable, to the extent that the entity expects the excess contributions to be refunded or deducted from future contributions. For defined benefit post-employment plans, IAS 19 adopts the partial capitalisation method. While current service costs and interest costs are recognised as incurred, past service costs are off-balance sheet and amortised over the average expected period until the benefits become vested. The corridor method is permitted for actuarial gains and losses, such that recognition of accumulated actuarial gains and losses within the limits of the corridor is not required. Further, to the extent that accumulated actuarial gains or losses fall outside the limits of the corridor, they may be amortised over the average expected remaining working life of members of the fund.

Discussion questions

1. What is a compensated absence? Provide an example.
2. What is the difference between accumulating and non-accumulating sick leave? How does the recognition of accumulating sick leave differ from the recognition of non-accumulating sick leave?
3. What is the difference between vesting and non-vesting sick leave? How does the recognition of vesting sick leave differ from the recognition of non-vesting sick leave?
4. Explain how a defined contribution superannuation plan differs from a defined benefit superannuation plan.
5. During October 2008 there was a sudden global decline in the price of equity securities and credit securities. Many superannuation funds made negative returns on investments during this period. How would this event affect the wealth of employees and employers? Consider

both defined benefit and defined contribution superannuation funds in your answer to this question.

6. Explain how an entity should account for its contribution to a defined contribution superannuation plan in accordance with IAS 19.
7. IAS 19 adopts the partial capitalisation method to account for defined benefit post-employment plans. How does this approach differ from the net capitalisation method?
8. In relation to defined benefit post-employment plans, paragraph 49 of IAS 19 states, '... the entity is, in substance, underwriting the actuarial and investment risks associated with the plan'. Critically evaluate whether the partial capitalisation approach adopted by IAS 19 reflects the economic substance of an entity's exposure to a defined benefit post-employment plan.
9. Identify and discuss the assumptions involved in the measurement of a provision for long service leave.
10. What is the projected unit credit method of measuring and recognising an obligation for long-term employee benefits?
11. The board of directors of Ilsenburg Ltd met in June 2010 and decided to close down a branch of the company's operations when the lease expired in the following February. The chief financial officer advised that termination benefits of $2.0 million are likely to be paid. Should the company recognise a liability for termination benefits in its financial statements for the year ended June 2010? Explain why or why not.

STAR RATING
★ BASIC
★★ MODERATE
★★★ DIFFICULT

Exercises

Exercise 15.1 ★

ACCOUNTING FOR THE PAYROLL

Konz Ltd pays its employees on a monthly basis. The payroll is processed on the 6th day of the month and payable on the 7th day of the month. Gross salaries for July were $500 000, from which $125 000 was deducted in tax. All of Konz Ltd's salaries are accounted for as expenses. Deductions for health insurance were $10 000. Payments for health insurance and employee withheld income taxes are due on the 15th day of the following month.

Required

1. Prepare all journal entries to the record the July payroll, the payment of July salaries and the remittance of deductions.
2. Calculate the balance of the Accrued Payroll account at the end of July.

Exercise 15.2 ★

ACCRUAL OF WAGES AND SALARIES

Linden Ltd has a weekly payroll of $125 000. The last payroll processed before the end of the annual reporting period was for the week ended Friday 24 June. Employees do not work during weekends.

Required

Prepare a journal entry to accrue the weekly payroll as at 30 June.

Exercise 15.3 ★

ACCOUNTING FOR SICK LEAVE

Mansfeld Ltd has 100 employees who each earn a gross wage of $150 per day. In an attempt to reduce absenteeism, Mansfeld Ltd introduced a new workplace agreement providing all employees with entitlement to 5 days of non-vesting, accumulating sick leave per annum, effective from 1 July 2009. Under the previous workplace agreement, all sick leave was non-cumulative. During the year ended 30 June 2010, 300 days of paid sick leave were taken by employees. It is estimated that 60% of unused sick leave will be taken during the year ended 30 June 2011 and that 40% will not be taken at all.

Required

Prepare a journal entry to recognised Mansfeld Ltd's liability, if any, for sick leave at 30 June 2010.

Exercise 15.4

ACCOUNTING FOR SICK LEAVE

★ Nabburg Ltd has 200 employees who each earn a gross wage of $140 per day. Nabburg Ltd provides 5 days' paid non-accumulating sick leave for each employee per annum. During the year, 150 days' paid sick leave and 20 days' unpaid sick leave were taken. Staff turnover is negligible.

Required
Calculate the employee benefits expense for sick leave during the year and the amount that should be recognised as a liability, if any, for sick leave at the end of the year.

Exercise 15.5

ACCOUNTING FOR ANNUAL LEAVE

★ Ortrand Ltd provides employees with 4 weeks (20 days) of annual leave for each year of service. The annual leave is accumulating and vesting up to a maximum of 6 weeks. Thus, all employees take their annual leave within 6 months after the end of each reporting period so that it does not lapse. Ortrand Ltd pays a loading of 17.5% on annual leave; that is, employees are paid an additional 17.5% of their regular wage while taking annual leave. Refer to the following extract from Ortrand Ltd's payroll records for the year ended 30 June 2010:

Employee	Wage/day	AL 1 July 2009 Days	Increase in entitlement Days	AL taken Days
Chand	$160	5	20	15
Kim	$120	3	20	16
Smith	$150	2	20	14
Zhou	$100	4	20	17

Required
Calculate the amount of annual leave that should be accrued for each employee.

Exercise 15.6

ACCOUNTING FOR PROFIT-SHARING ARRANGEMENTS

★ Parchim Ltd has a profit-sharing arrangement in which 1% of profit for the period is payable to employees, paid 3 months after the end of the reporting period. Employees' entitlements under the profit-sharing arrangement are subject to their continued employment at the time the payment is made. Based on past staff turnover levels, it is expected that 95% of the share of profit will be paid. Parchim Ltd's profit for the period was $70 million.

Required
Prepare a journal entry to record Parchim Ltd's liability for employee benefits arising from the profit-sharing arrangement at the end of the reporting period.

Exercise 15.7

ACCOUNTING FOR LONG SERVICE LEAVE

★ Rain Ltd provides long service leave entitlement of 13 weeks of paid leave after 10 years of continuous employment. The provision for long service leave had a credit balance of $140 000 at 30 June 2009. During the year ended 30 June 2010, long service leave of $25 000 was paid. At the end of the year, the present value of the defined benefit obligation for long service leave was $150 000.

Required
Prepare all journal entries in relation to long service leave for the year ended 30 June 2010.

Exercise 15.8

ACCOUNTING FOR DEFINED CONTRIBUTION SUPERANNUATION PLANS

★ Sassenberg Ltd provides a defined contribution superannuation fund for its employees. The company pays contributions equivalent to 10% of annual wages and salaries. Contributions of $50 000 per month were paid for the year ended 30 June 2010. Actual wages and salaries were $7 million. Three months after the reporting period, there is a settlement of the difference between the amount paid and the annual amount payable determined with reference to Sassenberg Ltd's audited payroll information. The settlement at 30 September involves either an additional contribution payment by Sassenberg Ltd or a refund of excess contributions paid.

Required

Prepare all journal entries required during June 2010 for Sassenberg Ltd's payment of, and liability for, superannuation contributions.

Exercise 15.9

ACCOUNTING FOR DEFINED BENEFIT SUPERANNUATION PLANS

★★

Tessin Ltd provides a defined benefit superannuation plan for its managers. At 30 June 2010, the present value of the defined benefit obligation was $13.5 million and the fair value of plan assets was $14 million. The change in accumulated actuarial losses during the year was as follows:

	$
Accumulated unamortised actuarial losses at 1 July 2010	1 100 000
Actuarial loss on the defined benefit obligation	500 000
Actuarial loss on plan assets	600 000
Amortisation of actuarial losses	0
Accumulated actuarial losses	2 200 000

The average expected remaining work life of members at 30 June 2010 is 8 years.

Required

Calculate the minimum amount, if any, of the accumulated actuarial losses that must be amortised during the year ended 30 June 2011 in accordance with IAS 19.

Exercise 15.10

ACCOUNTING FOR DEFINED BENEFIT SUPERANNUATION PLANS

★★

Which of the following items are components of the superannuation expense in relation to a defined benefit fund in accordance with the partial capitalisation method permitted by IAS 19?

(a) current service cost
(b) past service cost incurred during the period
(c) interest cost
(d) actual return on plan assets
(e) expected return on plan assets
(f) current period actuarial gains in relation to the defined benefit obligation
(g) current period actuarial losses in relation to the defined benefit obligation
(h) current period actuarial gains in relation to the assets of the plan
(i) current period actuarial losses in relation to the assets of the plan
(j) amortisation of past service costs
(k) contributions paid
(l) amortisation of accumulated actuarial gains
(m) amortisation of accumulated actuarial losses
(n) benefits paid.

Problems

Problem 15.1

ACCOUNTING FOR THE PAYROLL AND ACCRUAL OF WAGES AND SALARIES

★

Vacha Ltd pays its employees on a fortnightly basis. All employee benefits are recognised as expenses. The following information is provided for its July and August payrolls:

	July		August	
	$	$	$	$
Fortnightly payroll		580 000 720 000		700 000 600 000

	July		August	
	$	$	$	$
Gross payroll for the month		1 300 000		1 300 000
Deductions payable to:				
Taxation authority	250 000		245 000	
Health Fund	20 000		20 000	
Community Charity	4 000		4 000	
Union fees	6 500		6 500	
Total deductions for the month		280 500		275 500
Net wages and salaries paid				
14 July, 11 August	458 775		553 230	
28 July, 25 August	560 725	1 019 500	471 270	1 024 500
		1 300 000		1 300 000

The two fortnightly payrolls in August were for the fortnight ended Friday 7 August and Friday 21 August. The payrolls were processed and paid on the following Monday and Tuesday respectively. Payroll deductions are remitted as follows:

Health fund deductions	3rd day of the following month
Union fees	3rd day of the following month
Taxation authority	15th day of the following month
Community charity	21st day of the following month

Required

1. Prepare all journal entries to account for the August payroll and all payments relating to employee benefits during August.
2. Prepare a journal entry to accrue wages for the remaining days in August not included in the final August payroll. Use the same level of remuneration as per the final payroll for August.

Problem 15.2 ACCOUNTING FOR ANNUAL LEAVE

★ Wadern Ltd provides 4 weeks (20 days) of accumulating vested annual leave for each year of service. The company policy is that annual leave must be taken within 6 months of the end of the period in which it accrues. Annual leave is paid at the base salary rate (which excludes commissions, bonuses and overtime). A 17.5% loading is applied to annual leave payments.

The following summary data is derived from Wadern Ltd's payroll records for the year ended 30 June 2010. Base pay rates have increased during the year. The amounts shown are applicable at 30 June 2010.

		Annual leave		
Employee category	Base pay/day $	Balance b/d 1 July 2009 Days	Accumulated during year Days	Taken during year Days
Managers	400	100	200	260
Sales staff	200	150	600	590
Office workers	100	120	400	370
Other	80	60	200	210

Additional information

After leave taken during the year had been recorded, Wadern Ltd's trial balance revealed that the provision for annual leave had a debit balance of $230 000 at 30 June 2010.

Required
Prepare journal entries to account for the liability for annual leave at 30 June 2010.

Problem 15.3

ACCOUNTING FOR SICK LEAVE

★ Xanten Ltd opened a call centre on 1 July 2009. The company provides 1 week (5 days) of sick leave entitlement for the employees working at the call centre. The following information has been obtained from Xanten Ltd's payroll records and actuarial assessments for the year ended 30 June 2010. The column headed 'Term. in 2010' indicates the leave entitlement arising from service of employees whose employment was terminated during the year. The actuary has estimated the percentage of unused leave that would be taken within 12 months if Xanten Ltd allowed leave to accumulate. Due to high staff turnover, the remaining leave would lapse (or be settled in cash, if vesting) within 1 year after the end of the reporting period.

Employee category	Base pay/day $	Current service Days	Leave taken in 2010 Days	Term. in 2010 Days	Estimated leave used 2011 %	Estimated termination 2011 %
Supervisors	100	30	20	3	90	10
Operators	80	500	400	60	70	30

Required
Calculate the employee benefits expense for sick leave for the year and the amount that should be recognised as a liability for sick leave assuming that sick leave entitlements are:
(a) non-accumulating
(b) accumulating and non-vesting
(c) accumulating and vesting.

Problem 15.4

ACCOUNTING FOR SICK LEAVE

★★ Zossen Ltd provides 1 week (5 days) of accumulating non-vesting sick leave for each year of service. Sick leave is paid at the base pay rate, which does not include commissions, bonuses and overtime. The proportion of accumulated sick leave that will be taken is estimated for each category of employees due to differences in staff turnover rates. The following summary data is derived from Zossen Ltd's payroll records for the year ended 30 June 2010:

		Sick leave			% of leave expected to be taken		
Employee category	Base pay/day $	Balance b/d 1 July 2009 Days	Leave from current Days	Taken or lapsed Days	Within 12 months %	1 year later %	2 years later %
Managers	450	120	50	10	8	6	5
Consultants	300	110	100	90	75	10	0
Clerical staff	100	80	100	70	65	8	0

Additional information
The yield on high quality corporate bonds at 30 June 2010 is 7% for one-year bonds and 8% for two-year bonds. After leave taken during the year had been recorded Zossen Ltd's trial balance at 30 June 2010 revealed the provision for sick leave had a credit balance of $4 000.

Required
1. Prepare journal entries to account for the liability for sick leave at 30 June 2010.
2. State how much of the provision should be classified as non-current liability.

Problem 15.5

ACCOUNTING FOR BONUSES AND DEFINED CONTRIBUTION SUPERANNUATION PLANS

★★ Arnstein Ltd contributes to a defined contribution superannuation plan for its employees. Contributions have been established as 10% of wages and salaries, including bonuses, actually paid during the year. Contributions based on budgeted payroll costs were set at $100 000 per month. There is annual net settlement of superannuation contributions payable or refundable based on actual audited payroll information. The net settlement occurs on 30 September for the preceding year ended 30 June.

Managers are entitled to a bonus calculated at 5% of their base salary if Arnstein Ltd's profit before tax (excluding the bonus) is more than 20% of market capitalisation of the company at the beginning of the year. The profit target was achieved in 2009 and 2010. The bonus is payable 6 months after the end of the reporting period, provided the manager has remained in the company's employment.

	2010 $	2009 $
Managerial salaries expense	4 500 000	4 000 000
Other salaries and wages	8 000 000	7 800 000
	12 500 000	11 800 000
Accrued wages and salaries	300 000	250 000
Accrued managerial bonuses	?	400 000

At 30 June 2009, Arnstein Ltd correctly anticipated that all managers would be eligible for the bonus because staff turnover among managers had been very low. However, by 30 June 2010, the company had moved to new premises and one manager, with a salary of $800 000, indicated that the additional travel was causing him to reconsider his position. The directors estimated that there was a 50% probability that the manager would resign by 31 December 2010, and an 80% probability that he would resign by 30 June 2011.

Required

1. Prepare the journal entry to record the contribution to the superannuation plan for June 2010.
2. Prepare a journal entry to record the liability, if any, arising from with the bonus plan at 30 June 2010.
3. Prepare a journal entry to account for the superannuation asset or liability, if any, at 30 June 2010.

Problem 15.6

★★

ACCOUNTING FOR LONG SERVICE LEAVE

Bonn Ltd provides long service leave for its retail staff. Long service leave entitlement is determined as 13 weeks of paid leave for 10 years of continued service. The following information is obtained from Bonn Ltd's payroll records and actuarial reports for its retail staff at 30 June 2010:

Unit credit (years)	No. of employees	% expected to become entitled	Annual salary per employee	No. of years until vesting	Yield on HQ corporate bonds
1	60	20%	$25 000	9	10%
2	50	30%	$25 000	8	9%
3	30	45%	$25 000	7	9%
4	24	55%	$25 000	6	9%

Additional information

- The estimated annual increase in retail wages is 1% per annum for the next 10 years, reflecting expected inflation.
- The provision for long service leave for retail staff at 30 June 2009 was $27 000.
- No employees were eligible to take long service leave during the year ended 30 June 2010.

Required

Prepare the journal entry to account for Bonn Ltd's provision for long service leave at 30 June 2010.

Problem 15.7 ACCOUNTING FOR LONG SERVICE LEAVE

★★★ Cottbus Ltd provides credit services. Cottbus Ltd provides the employees with long service leave entitlements of 13 weeks of paid leave for every 10 years of continuous service. As the company has only been operating for 5 years, no employees have become entitled to long service leave. However, the company recognises a provision for long service leave using the unit credit approach required by IAS 19. The following information is obtained from Cottbus Ltd's payroll records and actuarial reports for the non-managerial staff of its debt collection business at 30 June 2010:

Unit credit (years)	No. of employees	% expected to become entitled	Average annual salary	No. of years until vesting	Yield on govt. corporate bonds
1	100	16%	$40 000	9	6%
2	60	25%	$42 000	8	6%
3	40	35%	$44 100	7	5%
4	32	50%	$46 300	6	5%
5	25	65%	$48 600	5	5%

Additional information

- The estimated annual increase in retail wages is 5% per annum for the next 10 years, reflecting Cottbus Ltd's policy of increasing salaries of its debt collection staff for each year of additional experience.
- At 30 June 2009, the provision for long service leave for non-managerial debt collection staff was $85 000.

Required

Prepare the journal entry to account for Cottbus Ltd's provision for long service leave at 30 June 2010 in relation to the non-managerial employees of the company's debt collection business.

Problem 15.8 ACCOUNTING FOR DEFINED BENEFIT SUPERANNUATION PLANS

★★★ Dahlen Ltd provides a defined benefit superannuation plan for its managers. The following information is available in relation to the plan:

	2010 $
Present value of the defined benefit obligation 1 July 2009	10 000 000
Interest cost	?
Current service cost	?
Benefits paid	(1 200 000)
Actuarial gains incurred in the current period	(100 000)
Present value of the defined benefit obligation 30 June 2010	10 750 000
Fair value of plan assets at 1 July 2009	9 500 000
Expected return on plan assets	975 000
Contributions paid to the fund during the year	1 000 000
Benefits paid by the fund during the year	(1 200 000)
Actuarial gain (loss) on plan assets	?
Fair value of plan assets at 30 June 2010	10 047 500

Additional information

- There are no past service costs included in the measurement of the present value of defined benefits.
- The interest rate used to measure the present value of defined benefits at 30 June 2009 was 9%.

- The unamortised balance of accumulated actuarial losses was $700 000 at 1 July 2009. The average expected remaining working life of members of the fund was 10 years at 30 June 2009 and 30 June 2010.
- Dahlen Ltd applies the corridor method and amortises accumulated gains or losses beyond the limits of the corridor over the maximum period permitted by IAS 19.

Required

1. Calculate the interest cost, current service cost and actuarial gain or loss on plan assets for the year ended 30 June 2010.
2. Determine whether Dahlen Ltd is required to amortise a portion of the accumulated actuarial loss during the year ended 30 June 2010.
3. Calculate the superannuation expense for the year ended 30 June 2010.
4. Calculate the net superannuation asset or liability recognised by Dahlen Ltd at 30 June 2010.

Problem 15.9 ★★★

ACCOUNTING FOR DEFINED BENEFIT SUPERANNUATION PLANS

Some years ago, Erkner Ltd established a defined benefit superannuation plan for its employees. The company has since introduced a defined contribution plan, which all new staff join when commencing employment with Erkner Ltd. Although the defined benefit plan is now closed to new recruits, the fund continues to provide for employees who have been with the company for a long time. The following actuarial report has been received for the defined benefit plan:

	2010	2009
Present value of the defined benefit obligation 1 July 2009	$20 000 000	
Interest cost	2 000 000	
Current service cost	800 000	
Benefits paid	(2 100 000)	
Actuarial loss incurred during the period	100 000	
Present value of the defined benefit obligation 30 June 2010	$20 800 000	$20 000 000
Fair value of plan assets at 1 July 2009	$19 000 000	
Expected return on plan assets	2 280 000	
Contributions paid to the fund during the year	1 000 000	
Benefits paid by the fund during the year	(2 100 000)	
Actuarial loss on plan assets during the period	(50 000)	
Fair value of plan assets at 30 June 2010	$20 130 000	$19 000 000
Unamortised accumulated actuarial losses (net)		$ 1 950 000
Average expected remaining working life of members	5 years	5.5 years

Additional information

Erkner Ltd applies the corridor method and amortises accumulated gains or losses beyond the limits of the corridor over the maximum period permitted by IAS 19.

Required

1. Prepare all journal entries to account for the defined benefit superannuation plan in the books of Erkner Ltd for the year ended 30 June 2010.
2. Calculate the portion of accumulated actuarial losses, if any, that should be amortised as superannuation expenses in the year ended 30 June 2011.

References

BHP Billiton 2008, *Annual Report 2008*, BHP Billiton, www.bhpbilliton.com.

Gallery, N 2003, 'Are superannuation disclosures in company financial reports useful?', *Australian Accounting Review*, Vol. 13:2, pp. 60–72.

Gordon, I 2005, 'Accrual accounting catches up with employers sponsoring defined benefit plans', *Financial Reporting, Regulation and Governance*, Vol. 4:1, www.cbs.curtin.edu.au.

IASB 2008, *Discussion paper: preliminary views on amendments to IAS 19* Employee Benefits, www.iasb.org.

16 Agriculture

ACCOUNTING STANDARDS IN FOCUS

IAS 41 *Agriculture*

LEARNING OBJECTIVES

When you have studied this chapter, you should be able to:

- understand and explain the background to the development of IAS 41
- distinguish between agricultural activities, agricultural produce and biological assets
- understand and explain the different accounting treatment required before and after harvest
- explain the recognition criteria for biological assets and agricultural produce
- describe the meaning of 'fair value' when applied to biological assets and agricultural products
- understand and explain the practical implications of measuring these assets at fair value
- apply the recognition and measurement requirements of IAS 41 to a simple statement of comprehensive income and statement of financial position
- understand the interaction between IAS 41 and IAS 20 *Accounting for Government Grants and Disclosure of Government Assistance*
- understand the interaction between IAS 41 and IAS 16 *Property, Plant and Equipment,* IAS 17 *Leases* and IAS 40 *Investment Property*
- describe the disclosure requirements of IAS 41
- understand and interpret the disclosures made by companies applying the standard.

16.1 INTRODUCTION TO IAS 41

IAS 41 was issued by the International Accounting Standards Committee (IASC) in February 2001 and was confirmed as being included in the core set of standards to be issued by the International Accounting Standards Board (IASB) in April 2001. (Refer to chapter 1 for the history of and distinction between the IASC and IASB.) The IASC's project on agriculture commenced in 1994. The IASC had decided to develop a separate standard on agriculture because, although it generally developed standards that are relevant to all businesses, it regarded agriculture as an industry with a particular need for its own standard. This was for a number of reasons; one of the main ones being that diversity in accounting for agricultural activity had arisen because:

- of the specific exclusion of assets related to agricultural activity from other standards (such as IAS 2 *Inventories*, IAS 16 *Property, Plant and Equipment*, IAS 18 *Revenue* and IAS 40 *Investment Property*)
- accounting guidelines for agricultural activity developed by national standard setters had, in general, been piecemeal (with the exception of Australia and New Zealand who had developed and applied a standard on 'Self-Generating and Regenerating Assets' or 'SGARAs')
- the nature of agricultural activity had created uncertainty or conflicts when applying traditional accounting models (IAS 41, Basis for Conclusions para. B1–B7).

The IASC also regarded agriculture as an emerging industry that was seeking to attract capital from investors and this increased the need to develop standards for general purpose financial statements of the entities involved (IAS 41, Basis for Conclusions para. B1–B7).

IAS 41 was a controversial standard when it was first issued, mainly because of the requirement to measure assets related to agricultural activity at fair value, with movements in fair value being taken to the statement of comprehensive income as gains or losses. To this day, companies applying the standard indicate their implicit disagreement with this requirement; for example, by highlighting the fair value movements separately in their statements of comprehensive income so that users can clearly see and understand the impact on reported profit. We will look at some examples of this later in the chapter.

16.2 SCOPE AND DEFINITIONS

16.2.1 Scope

IAS 41 applies to the accounting for the following when they relate to agricultural activity:

1. biological assets
2. agricultural produce
3. government grants.

The standard does not apply to land or intangible assets related to agricultural activity (IAS 41, para. 2). Land related to agricultural activity is recognised and measured by applying either IAS 16 or IAS 40, whichever is appropriate in the circumstances. So, for example, if the land meets the definition of an investment property it is measured using either the fair value model or the cost model — an accounting policy choice permitted by IAS 40. Note that 'investment property' is defined in IAS 40 as 'property (land or a building — or part of a building — or both) held (by the owner or by the lessee under a finance lease) to earn rentals or for capital appreciation or both, rather than for (a) use in the production or supply of goods or services or for administrative purposes; or (b) sale in the ordinary course of business'. If the land does *not* meet the definition of an investment property then it must be recognised and measured by applying IAS 16 (see chapter 9 for further explanation). IAS 16 allows an accounting policy choice between the cost model and the revaluation model. The cost model under IAS 40 is the same as that under IAS 16. However, the fair value model under IAS 40 differs from the revaluation model under IAS 16, essentially in that fair value movements are taken to the statement of comprehensive income under IAS 40; whereas, under IAS 16 they are taken to equity (usually to an asset revaluation reserve). Also, IAS 16 requires revalued assets to be depreciated, although this does not apply to land.

The impact of the accounting policy choice in respect of land is discussed further in section 16.7.

Intangible assets related to agricultural activity are accounted for under IAS 38 *Intangible Assets* (see chapter 10 for further explanation).

16.2.2 Key definitions

IAS 41, paragraph 5 contains the following important definitions:

> **Agricultural activity** is the management by an entity of the biological transformation of biological assets for sale, into agricultural produce, or into additional biological assets.
> **Agricultural produce** is the harvested product of the entity's biological assets.
> **A biological asset** is a living animal or plant.
> **Biological transformation** comprises the processes of growth, degeneration, production and procreation that cause qualitative or quantitative changes in a biological asset.
> **Harvest** is the detachment of produce from a biological asset or the cessation of a biological asset's life processes.

Agricultural activity covers a diverse range of activities. However, IAS 41, paragraph 6 states that there are three common features that exist within this diversity:

(a) *Capability to change:* Living plants and animals are capable of biological transformation;
(b) *Management of change:* Management facilitates biological transformation. For example management of a vineyard or orchard by providing nutrients, water and protection from pests facilitates the growth of the vines and trees. This can be distinguished from unmanaged biological change such as the growth of fishes in the ocean. Thus ocean fishing is not an agricultural activity;
(c) *Measurement of change:* The change in quality (for example ripeness, protein content or fibre strength) or quantity (for example weight, cubic metres or diameter) brought about by biological transformation is measured and monitored as a routine management function.

16.2.3 The harvest distinction

There is a very important distinction between agricultural produce, which is the harvested product of the entity's biological assets, and products that result from processing after harvest. IAS 41 only applies to the harvested product *at the point of harvest*. Thereafter, IAS 2, or another applicable standard is applied.

The standard includes examples to illustrate the difference between biological assets, agricultural produce and products that are the result of processing after harvest. Table 16.1 is based on paragraph 4 of IAS 41, modified to aid understanding.

TABLE 16.1 Distinction between biological assets, agricultural produce and products that are a result of processing after harvest

Biological assets (IAS 41 applies)	Agricultural produce (IAS 41 applies)	Products that are a result of processing after harvest (generally IAS 2 applies)
Sheep	Wool	Yarn, carpet, clothing
Trees in a plantation forest	Logs	Lumber, furniture
Plants	Cotton	Thread, clothing
	Harvested cane	Sugar
Dairy cattle	Milk	Cheese
Pigs	Carcass	Sausages
Bushes	Leaf	Tea
Vines	Grapes	Wine
Fruit trees	Picked fruit	Processed fruit e.g. tinned fruit

One of the initial criticisms of IAS 41 was that it requires assets for which there is often not an active or ready market to be measured at fair value, while those assets for which there is an active and ready market are measured at cost under IAS 2. For example, it can be difficult to determine a fair value for immature trees in a plantation because there may not be an active or ready market for trees before they are fully grown. In contrast, there would be a much more easily identifiable market value for lumber or furniture, yet this is measured at cost under IAS 2. The IASB rejected criticisms of the fair value model for biological assets and agricultural produce but conceded by permitting an exemption when fair value can not be reliably measured (IAS 41, Basis for Conclusions para. B13–B21). This is discussed further in section 16.4.2.

Some respondents to the exposure draft that preceded IAS 41 also commented that in some cases processing after harvest was akin to biological transformation (e.g. wine production from grapes and cheese production from milk) and therefore there should not be a distinction at the harvest point. While acknowledging this issue, the IASB considered that it would be difficult to differentiate these circumstances from other manufacturing processes. The IASB also decided not to include a revision of IAS 2 as part of its process of approving IAS 41 (IAS 41, Basis for Conclusions para. B9–B11).

16.3 THE RECOGNITION CRITERIA FOR BIOLOGICAL ASSETS AND AGRICULTURAL PRODUCE

16.3.1 The recognition criteria

Paragraph 10 of IAS 41 states that an entity shall recognise a biological asset or agricultural produce when, and only when:

(a) The entity controls the asset as a result of past events;
(b) It is probable that future economic benefits associated with the asset will flow to the entity; and
(c) The fair value or cost can be measured reliably.

Note that (a) repeats one of the essential characteristics of the *definition* of an asset in the *Framework* (control) while (b) and (c) repeat the recognition criteria in the *Framework*.

16.3.2 The problem with 'control'

The issue of control can be problematic in the agricultural industry where leases or management agreements are involved. For example, a vineyard may be owned by one entity but managed by another. Because the definition of 'agricultural activity' talks about 'the management' by an entity of the biological transformation of biological assets it is possible to confuse management with control. Therefore, it is important to distinguish between these two concepts.

Illustrative example 16.1 demonstrates the distinction between management and control.

ILLUSTRATIVE EXAMPLE 16.1

Distinguishing management from control of biological assets and agricultural produce

Company A owns Vineyard X. Company A invests in many vineyards and so appoints Manager M to manage Vineyard X. Manager M is responsible for all the operations of the vineyard including daily care, regular maintenance, harvesting of the grapes and storage of the grapes after harvest. The grapes are then sent to be processed into wine by Winemaker W.

Manager M and Winemaker W are not related parties of Company A. Company A pays Manager M a management fee for its services. The fee includes reimbursement of all costs incurred by Manager M plus an agreed margin. Company A pays Winemaker W a production fee for its services. The fee includes reimbursement of all costs incurred by Winemaker W plus an agreed margin.

All sales and marketing of the bottled wine is managed by Distributor D. Distributor D is not a related party of Company A. Company A pays Distributor D a fee for its services. The fee includes reimbursement of all costs incurred by Distributor D plus an agreed margin.

Who controls the biological asset (the vines)? Company A or Manager M?

Who controls the agricultural produce (the grapes)? Company A, Manager M, Winemaker W or Distributor D?

Unfortunately control is not defined in the *Framework* and is used throughout IFRSs without consistency. Sometimes control refers to the power to govern so as to obtain benefits from an entity (IAS 27, see chapter 21). Sometimes it refers to the exposure to risks as well as benefits and the residual risks of an entity (SIC-12 *Consolidation — Special Purpose Entities*). In IAS 17 *Leases* the concept of control of an asset is linked to who has the risks and rewards incidental to ownership (even though this concept is not referred to as 'control'). In IAS 39 *Financial Instruments: Recognition and Measurement* (see chapter 5) there is a distinction between risks and rewards of ownership of an asset and control of that asset. Control in this case is referred to in terms of the entity's ability to sell the asset. If the entity is able to sell the asset then IAS 39 regards the entity as having control of the asset. In IAS 39 it is possible to *not* have the risks and rewards of ownership of an asset but still control it (para. 23). In IFRIC 4 *Determining Whether an Arrangement Contains a Lease* the concept of *control of the use* of an asset is central. This is because a lease is defined as a *right of use* of an asset. IFRIC 4 contains conditions that must be met in order for an entity to control the right of use of an asset. These include the ability to operate the asset while obtaining more than a significant amount of output from the asset; or the ability to control physical access to the asset while obtaining more than a significant amount of output from the asset. Note, however, that these conditions will indicate whether or not the arrangement *is a lease* (i.e. whether a right of use has been given to an entity). Whether the lease transfers the risks and rewards of ownership of the asset to the entity (i.e. whether it is a finance lease or an operating lease) is a second question. Then we have to go back to IAS 17, which appears to equate risks and rewards of ownership with control!

To make the question of control of the biological asset in this example simpler, let's assume that control in this case means both the legal ownership of the asset (i.e. the ability to sell or pledge the asset) as well as the exposure to the risks and rewards of ownership of the asset.

What are the key rewards of the vines and grapes? These would be the growth of the vines so as to produce grapes and the revenues to be earned by either selling the grapes at a profit or by processing them into wine to sell at a profit.

Who benefits from these rewards? Manager M, Winemaker W and Distributor D each have a share in these rewards because they are paid a margin by Company A. This means that they recover their costs but also benefit from increases in value of the vines and grapes via the margin paid to them by Company A. However, because this margin is agreed upfront it is a fixed margin. This means that Company A benefits from any increases in value over and above the recovery of costs plus the fixed margin. Manager M, Winemaker W and Distributor D do not share in these excess profits because their return is fixed.

What are the key risks in the vines and grapes? These would be the risks of disease, drought, and so on such that the vines fail to grow and produce grapes of adequate quality. This in turn would result in an inability to sell the produce of the vines either at all or the generation of lower returns than expected or needed to remain profitable. There are also market risks such as a glut of wine on the market causing prices to fall.

Who bears these risks? The majority of these risks are borne by Company A because — as we saw above — each of Manager M, Winemaker W and Distributor D is entitled to a fixed return even if there are no profits. This means that Company A bears all of the downside risk in the vines and the grapes. It must pay the management fee, production fee and distribution fee even if there is no return from the vines, grapes or wine.

Who controls the vines and the grapes? While Manager M manages the daily operations of the vineyard it does so on behalf of Company A. Similarly, Winemaker W makes the wine on behalf of Company A, and Distributor D sells the wine on behalf of Company A. Thus, Company A has the ability to sell or pledge the vines and the grapes even though, practically, the sale of the grapes is effected by Manager M on behalf of Company A. These entities all act as agents of Company A.

So we can conclude that Company A controls the biological assets and agricultural produce under paragraph 10 of IAS 41. Therefore, Company A should recognise these assets (assuming the other requirements of paragraph 10 are met).

However, the agricultural activity as defined in paragraph 5 of IAS 41 is carried out by Manager M. It is the entity that manages the transformation of the vines into grapes. Does this mean that Manager M applies IAS 41 while Company A does not? Since we have concluded that Company A controls the biological assets and agricultural produce, these assets must be recognised by Company A. If Manager M were to apply IAS 41 it would apply the standard to nothing since it does not control the assets in question. Therefore, it is arguably reasonable to conclude that Manager M conducts the agricultural activity on behalf of Company A, and thus Company A should apply IAS 41. This argument could be attacked on the basis of applying the recognition criteria of the standard before the scope section. It is further complicated by the interaction with IAS 17 and IAS 40 (refer section 16.7).

16.4 MEASUREMENT AT FAIR VALUE

16.4.1 Measurement requirement

Paragraph 12 of IAS 41 states that:

> A biological asset shall be measured on initial recognition and at the end of each reporting period at its fair value less estimated point-of-sale costs, except for the case described in paragraph 30 where the fair value cannot be measured reliably.

Paragraph 13 of IAS 41 states that:

> Agricultural produce harvested from an entity's biological assets shall be measured at its fair value less estimated point-of-sale costs at the point of harvest. Such measurement is the cost at that date when applying IAS 2 *Inventories* or another applicable Standard.

'Fair value' is defined in paragraph 8 as:

> The amount for which an asset could be exchanged, or a liability settled, between knowledgeable, willing parties in an arm's length transaction.

Point-of-sale costs include commissions to brokers and dealers, levies by regulatory agencies and commodity exchanges and transfer taxes and duties. Point-of-sale costs exclude transport and other costs necessary to get assets to a market. However, such transport costs are included in determining fair value (IAS 41, Basis for Conclusions para. B22).

16.4.2 Arguments for and against the use of fair value

When IAS 41 was first proposed as E65, the requirement to use fair value as the measurement basis was controversial. The arguments for and against the use of fair value are summarised in table 16.2 (IAS 41, Basis for Conclusions para. B14–B21).

TABLE 16.2 Arguments for and against the use of fair value for measuring biological assets

	Case for Fair Value	Case against Fair Value
Biological transformation has a direct relationship to changes in expectations of future economic benefits to the entity	✓	
The relationship between cost incurrence and future economic benefits is weak particularly for biological assets that take a long time to mature	✓	
Relevance	✓ (many biological assets are traded in active markets; long production cycles mean that the change in asset value is more relevant than a period-end measure of costs incurred)	✓ (market prices at the end of the reporting period may not bear a close relationship to the prices at which the assets will be sold)
Reliability	✓ (active markets provide reliable information; allocation of costs is arbitrary when there are joint products and joint costs)	✓ (cost of historic transactions is more reliable and objective; market prices are often volatile and cyclical; active markets may not exist, particularly during periods of growth of assets that have a long growth period)

	Case for Fair Value	Case against Fair Value
Comparability and Understandability	✓ (different sources of animals and plants — home grown or purchased — should not be measured differently, which would be the outcome under an historic cost model)	✓ (reporting of unrealised gains and losses is not useful to users)

The Board decided to proceed with the requirement to use fair value, but was persuaded by the arguments that fair value may not always be able to be measured reliably where market prices are not available and alternative estimates of fair value are determined to be clearly unreliable. This resulted in the exception in paragraph 30 which states:

> There is a presumption that fair value can be measured reliably for a biological asset. However, that presumption can be rebutted only on initial recognition for a biological asset for which market-determined prices or values are not available and for which alternative estimates of fair value are determined to be clearly unreliable. In such a case, that biological asset shall be measured at its cost less any accumulated depreciation and any accumulated impairment losses. Once the fair value of such a biological asset becomes reliably measurable, an entity shall measure it at its fair value less estimated point-of-sale costs.

It is important to note that this exception can only be applied on initial recognition of the asset. So, for example, in Australia where a similar standard to IAS 41 was being applied prior to the adoption of IFRSs, companies had already recognised their biological assets and were measuring them at fair value. They could not avail themselves of the exception in paragraph 30 because the assets had already been recognised.

In addition, the exception applies only to biological assets, not to agricultural produce. IAS 41 takes the view that the fair value of agricultural produce at the point of harvest can always be measured reliably (para. 32).

16.4.3 How to apply the fair value measurement requirement

The board also included guidance in the standard on how to apply the fair value measurement requirement (paragraphs 15–25):

- Biological assets or agricultural assets may be grouped according to significant attributes such as age or quality (e.g. all 'A' grade cattle may be grouped and a fair value determined for that group).
- Contract prices are not necessarily relevant because they may not represent the current market. For example, a company may enter into a contract to sell its cotton in 6 months time at a set price (known as a forward price). This forward price would not normally be the same as the current market price (known as the spot price). IAS 41 requires the spot price to be used for determining fair value even if a forward contract has been entered into.
- If an active market exists, the quoted price in that market should be used. If an entity has access to two different markets, the entity uses the most relevant one; that is, the one it expects to use. For example, if an entity can sell its produce either at the farm gate or at auction it must select which of the two it expects to use.
- If an active market does *not* exist, an entity uses one or more of the following:
  (a) the most recent transaction price provided that there has not been a significant change in economic circumstances between the date of the transaction and the end of the reporting period;
  (b) market prices for similar assets with adjustments to reflect differences;
  (c) sector benchmarks such as the value of an orchard expressed per export tray, bushel or hectare.
- Where market prices do not exist for the biological asset in its present condition, an entity uses the present value of expected net cash flows from the asset discounted at a current market-determined pre-tax rate. Note that the objective of this calculation is to determine the fair value of the asset in its *present* condition. This requirement means that any increases in value from future biological transformation must be excluded (para. 21). In 2007, the IFRIC received a

request to clarify this requirement because entities said they were having difficulty in applying the requirement to exclude future biological transformation. For example, how does an entity estimate future cash flows from an immature forest if it cannot assume the forest will continue to grow and generate future cash flows in its fully mature state? In practice, entities may need to work out the cash flows from a biological asset in its mature state and work backwards to then calculate the cash flows from the asset in its immature state. The IFRIC referred the matter to the IASB for clarification. In its *IASB Update* and related Observer Notes in March 2008, the IASB issued a proposed amendment to IAS 41 to clarify that future biological transformation may be taken into account by a buyer of an immature biological asset because the buyer would assess the potential for the asset to reach maturity in determining how much to pay for the asset in its immature state. In addition, the IASB proposed to amend the standard to use the phrase 'biological transformation or harvest' where appropriate to clarify that a harvested asset is not the same as a growing asset. Therefore, a market value for a growing asset may be calculated based on its potential to continue to grow and be harvested, taking into account risk factors regarding the potential growth of the asset. This is illustrated in illustrative example 16.3.

- When estimating cash flows, an entity does not include any cash flows for financing the assets, taxation, or reestablishing biological assets after harvest. Variations in expected cash flows are taken into account in either the discount rate or the expected cash flows, but not in both (otherwise the effect of the possible variations would be double counted).
- Cost may sometimes approximate fair value, particularly when:
  1. little biological transformation has taken place since initial cost incurrence (e.g. fruit tree seedlings planted immediately prior to the end of a reporting period), or
  2. the impact of the biological transformation on price is not expected to be material (e.g. the initial period of growth in a 30-year pine production cycle).
- Where biological assets are attached to land and there is no separate market for the assets without the land, the entity may use information regarding the combined assets to determine the fair value of the biological assets. For example, the fair value of the raw land may be deducted from the fair value of the combined assets to arrive at the fair value of the biological assets.

Illustrative example 16.2 illustrates the calculation of fair value where there is an active market.

ILLUSTRATIVE EXAMPLE 16.2

Calculating fair value

Company A owns dairy cattle. The market value of cattle is calculated by reference to the litres of milk able to be produced and the lactation rate of the cows. Cattle are regularly sold at auction. Costs incurred to transport the cattle to auction are $500 per truck. The normal capacity of a truck is approximately 200 cattle.

Company A has determined that, based on latest auction prices close to the end of the reporting period, a mature cow's market value is 5000 litres × lactation rate (0.5) × price of milk (0.35$) = $850 and a heifer's market value is 2000 litres × 0.5 × $0.35 = $350.

At the end of the reporting period, Company A had 1000 mature cows and 400 heifers.

Transport costs are included in determining fair value in accordance with paragraph B22 of IAS 41. The approximate cost per cow is $\frac{500}{200}$ = $2.50. Thus the market value for each cow is $850 – $2.50 = $847.50. The market value for each heifer is $350 – $2.50 = $347.50. The fair value as at the end of the reporting period is thus:

1000 × 847.50 =	$847 500
400 × 347.50 =	$139 000
	$986 500

Illustrative example 16.3 illustrates the calculation of fair value where there is not an active market.

ILLUSTRATIVE EXAMPLE 16.3

Calculation of fair value where there is no active market

Company A owns and manages an orchard that produces apples. In 2010 Company A spent $450 000 establishing the orchard, as follows:

Cost of the land	$350 000
Cost of the seedlings	$ 30 000
Plant and equipment (estimated useful life of 10 years)	$ 50 000
Fertilisers, feed and other costs	$ 10 000
Salaries and wages	$ 10 000

During 2011 and 2012, Company A incurred further costs as follows:

Salaries and wages	$20 000
Fertilisers, feed and spraying costs	$ 5 000

At the end of 2012, the trees were 3 years old and Company A expected its first harvest in 2014. Company A expects the orchard to have a life of 30 years from the date of first harvest. In Company A's jurisdiction there is no active market for immature apple trees. How would Company A determine the fair value of the orchard as at the end of 2012?

In accordance with paragraph 18 of IAS 41, Company A would need to determine whether there is:
(a) a recent transaction price, or
(b) market prices for similar assets, or
(c) sector benchmarks.

Assume that Company A cannot find any of these three for the orchard in its present condition. It would then need to calculate the present value of expected net cash flows in accordance with paragraph 20 of IAS 41.

Company A determines that once the orchard starts producing apples it expects annual cash inflows from sales of the apples as follows:

2014	$ 50 000
2015	$ 90 000
2016	$150 000
2017	$200 000
2018 and onwards	$200 000

Company A also expects to pay annual salaries, wages and other operating costs of $40 000 from 2014. During 2013, it expects to pay $25 000 for these costs. Company A determines that the appropriate discount rate to use is 6% up until and including 2018 and 15% for the years thereafter to take account of the increased risk that the estimated cash flows may not eventuate as predicted. Point-of-sale costs are estimated to be 1% of sales. The calculation of the present value of expected net cash flows *as at the end of 2012* is as follows:

Year ended	Cash inflows $	Cash outflows $	Net cash flows $	Present value at 6% (15% from 2019) $
2013	—	25 000	(25 000)	(23 585)
2014	50 000	40 000 + 500	9 500	8 482

(continued)

Year ended	Cash inflows $	Cash outflows $	Net cash flows $	Present value at 6% (15% from 2019) $
2015	90 000	40 000 + 900	49 100	41 260
2016	150 000	40 000 + 1500	108 500	86 111
2017	200 000	40 000 + 2000	158 000	117 910
2018	200 000	40 000 + 2000	158 000	111 268
2019–34	200 000	40 000 + 2000	158 000	443 443

The net present value of expected net cash flows is thus $784 889. This is the fair value of the orchard in its present condition, taking into account the risk that future cash flows may not occur as planned in the higher discount rate applied to the 26 years beyond 2018.

Note the establishment costs are not included in this calculation. The costs of establishing the orchard must be accounted for under the relevant accounting standards such as IAS 16 and IAS 40. The land would be recorded as an asset under either IAS 16 or IAS 40. The plant and equipment would be recorded as an asset under IAS 16 and depreciated over 10 years. The other establishment costs would be expensed unless Company A could justify recording the costs as an asset under IAS 38. Salaries and wages and other operating costs are unlikely to meet the requirements for recognition as an asset under IAS 38. The cost of the seedlings — which are not intangible assets — could qualify for recognition as an asset under the *Framework* because they are the basis from which the future cash flows generated by the mature trees derive. This question is not addressed in IAS 41. It is clear that the *cost* of the seedlings cannot be included in the fair value of the orchard because the fair value measurement method does not allow a mixture of cost and fair value estimates. However, it is possible for the costs to be recorded as a separate asset and amortised over the life of the orchard. If this is done then care must be taken to ensure that the *value* of the seedlings is not taken into account again in determining the fair value of the biological asset.

The following would be the journal entries for years 2010, 2011 and 2012, assuming that the land is recorded at cost under IAS 16, the plant and equipment is recorded at cost under IAS 16 and amortised over its useful life, the seedlings are recorded as an asset and amortised over the life of the orchard and all other costs are expensed. Also assume that all amounts are paid for in cash.

Journal entries 2010			
Land	Dr	350 000	
Cash	Cr		350 000
(To record the acquisition of the land)			
Plant & Equipment	Dr	50 000	
Cash	Cr		50 000
(To record the acquisition of plant and equipment)			
Seedlings Asset	Dr	30 000	
Cash	Cr		30 000
(To record the acquisition of the seedlings)			
Operating Expenses	Dr	20 000	
Cash	Cr		20 000
(To record operating expenses)			
Depreciation expense	Dr	5 000	
Accumulated Depreciation	Cr		5 000
(To record 1 year's depreciation of the plant and equipment)			

Depreciation Expense	Dr	1 000	
Accumulated Depreciation	Cr		1 000
(To record 1 year's depreciation of the seedlings asset)			
Journal entries 2011			
Operating Expenses	Dr	25 000	
Cash	Cr		25 000
(To record operating expenses)			
Depreciation Expense	Dr	5 000	
Accumulated Depreciation	Cr		5 000
(To record 1 year's depreciation of the plant and equipment)			
Depreciation Expense	Dr	1 000	
Accumulated Depreciation	Cr		1 000
(To record 1 year's depreciation of the seedlings asset)			
Journal entries 2012			
Operating Expenses	Dr	25 000	
Cash	Cr		25 000
(To record operating expenses)			
Depreciation Expense	Dr	5 000	
Accumulated Depreciation	Cr		5 000
(To record 1 year's depreciation of the plant and equipment)			
Depreciation Expense	Dr	1 000	
Accumulated Depreciation	Cr		1 000
(To record 1 year's depreciation of the seedlings asset)			
Biological Asset — Orchard	Dr	784 889	
Profit & Loss	Cr		784 889
(To record the fair value of the orchard on initial recognition)			

The gain on initial recognition of a biological asset is discussed further in section 16.4.4.

What is clear from this example is that when the orchard is established, the company will show a loss in its statement of comprehensive income (in years 2010 and 2011), but as soon as the orchard is recognised at its fair value a large gain is recognised. There is no concept of 'matching' the establishment costs with the fair value movements under IAS 41.

16.4.4 Gains and losses

Paragraph 26 of IAS 41 states that:

> A gain or loss arising on initial recognition of a biological asset at fair value less estimated point-of-sale costs and from a change in fair value less estimated point-of-sale costs of a biological asset shall be included in profit or loss for the period in which it arises.

Paragraph 28 of IAS 41 contains a similar requirement for agricultural produce except that it does not refer to a change in fair value of agricultural produce. This is because agricultural produce is recognised and measured only at the point of harvest (see IAS 41, para. 1(b) and 13) and this amount becomes its cost for ongoing measurement under IAS 2 or another applicable standard. Thus, there is no remeasurement to fair value of agricultural produce whereas biological assets are remeasured to fair value at the end of each reporting period.

How do gains or losses on initial recognition (sometimes referred to as 'day one profits/losses') arise? Illustrative example 16.4 explains how this may occur.

ILLUSTRATIVE EXAMPLE 16.4

Gains or losses on initial recognition of biological assets and agricultural produce

In the case of biological assets, a loss may arise on initial recognition because point-of-sale costs (which are deducted in arriving at fair value) may exceed the fair value. A profit may arise on initial recognition when, for example, an animal is born. For example, say the fair value of a newborn calf is $50. On initial recognition of the newborn animal, the journal entry would be as follows:

Biological Asset	Dr	50	
Profit & Loss	Cr		50
(To record the acquisition of the newborn calf)			

In the case of agricultural produce a gain or loss on initial recognition may arise as a result of harvesting. For example, say the fair value of a tonne of grapes is $20 and the fair value of the related vines is $100 at the date of harvest. On initial recognition of the grapes, the following journal entries are required:

Profit & Loss	Dr	20	
Biological Asset	Cr		20
(To remeasure the vines to fair value — removing the fair value of the grapes)			
Agricultural Produce	Dr	20	
Profit & Loss	Cr		20
(To recognise the grapes at fair value)			

A change in fair value of a biological asset is recorded as a gain or loss at the end of each reporting period. Illustrative example 16.5 illustrates the relevant journal entries.

ILLUSTRATIVE EXAMPLE 16.5

Recording a change in fair value of a biological asset

Assume that as at the end of the reporting period, 30 June 2011, the fair value of Company A's vineyard was $2 500 000. As at 30 June 2012, Company A determines the following:

Fair value of the grapes harvested at 31 March 2012	500 000
Estimated point-of-sale costs of the grapes	10 000
Estimated point-of-sale costs of the vines	20 000
Fair value of the vines as at 31 March 2012, prior to harvest	3 100 000

Company A determines that there is no change in fair value of the vines between 31 March 2012 and 30 June 2012 and so uses the valuation as at 31 March for the purposes of the end of reporting period valuation.

The fair value of the vines less estimated point of sale costs as at 30 June 2012 is calculated as follows:

$3 100 000 less $500 000 (fair value of the harvested grapes)
less $20 000 (point-of-sale costs) = $2 580 000

The change in fair value of the vines is therefore $2 580 000 less $2 500 000 = $80 000.

The fair value of the grapes as at 30 June 2012 is calculated as follows:

$500 000 less $10 000 (point-of-sale costs) = $490 000.

The journal entries as at 30 June 2012 are as follows:

Biological Asset — Vines	Dr	80 000	
Profit & Loss	Cr		80 000
(To record the change in fair value of the vines)			
Agricultural Produce — Grapes	Dr	490 000	
Profit & Loss	Cr		490 000
(To record the grapes at fair value)			

16.5 PRACTICAL IMPLEMENTATION ISSUES WITH THE USE OF FAIR VALUE

Determining fair value in the agricultural industry creates some practical difficulties, particularly in the case of immature biological assets such as young trees in a forest or young salmon in a salmon farm.

16.5.1 A fishy story

During 2005 and 2006, as IAS 41 was first being implemented in Europe, there was controversy in the salmon farming industry over the measurement of immature salmon. A practice was emerging of measuring live immature salmon at cost on the basis that fair value could not be reliably measured. The regulator intervened and required that the *live* immature salmon be measured at fair value on the basis that there was an active market for *slaughtered* immature salmon and that the fair value should be determined in accordance with paragraph 18(b) of IAS 41; that is, on the basis of similar assets. The regulator stated that since there was an active market for slaughtered immature salmon this should be the basis used for measuring the fair value of live immature salmon.

The text of the decision as reported by the Committee of European Securities Regulators (CESR) is reproduced in figure 16.1.

FIGURE 16.1 Extract from Committee of European Securities Regulators' decision on IAS 41

Decision ref.EECS/0407–11: Accounting for biological assets
Financial year end: 31 December 2005/Interim Financial Satements
Category of issue: Biological assets, fair value
Standard involved: IAS 41
Date of the decision: 14 February 2006
Description of the issuer's accounting treatment
The issuer measured live farmed salmon with a weight exceeding 4 kg (3,3 kg slaughtered head-on gutted) at their fair value, while more immature salmon was measured at cost. The fair value of mature salmon exceeding 4 kg was determined by using the observed prices in an active market of slaughtered salmon, classified as a similar asset according to IAS 41

(continued)

FIGURE 16.1 *(continued)*

Paragraph 18 b. Based on an overall assessment, the issuer considered alternative estimates (incl. present value of future net cash-flows) of the fair value of live immature farmed salmon (< 4 kg) to be clearly unreliable, and hence accounted for these biological assets at cost according to IAS 41 paragraph 30.

The enforcement decision

The enforcer found that there existed observable market prices for similar assets (IAS 41 paragraph 18 b), also for salmon weighing less than 4kg. Hence, such biological assets should be accounted for at fair value and not cost.

Rationale for the enforcement decision

Farming salmon from egg to mature fish takes on average approximately 3 years. There are two main stages of growth; from egg to smolt (approx. 100 grams) and from smolt to mature fish, each stage taking approximately 15–18 months. In some markets there may be some turnover of live smolt, but as a rule farmed salmon is slaughtered before it is sold. The national production and sale in 2004 was approx 54,000 tonnes of farmed salmon. Industry organizations publish weekly price reports, summarizing trades of slaughtered and gutted superior quality salmon specified by weight classes (1–2 kg, 2–3 kg, 3–4 kg, 4–5 kg, 5–6 kg, 7+, head-on-gutted slaughter weight). Approximately 20–30% of all salmon sold weigh less than 4 kg. These markets for salmon weighing less than 4 kg are not scrap markets, but markets where superior quality salmon is sold for human consumption.

The enforcer was of the view that slaughtered salmon which is sold whole and gutted is, in an accounting sense, to be considered as a similar asset to live salmon, according to IAS 41, paragraph 18 b. This also applies to so-called immature farmed salmon. In the absence of observable prices in an active market for live farmed salmon, fair value of live farmed salmon should be determined based on observable prices in an active market for the same category of slaughtered salmon (IAS 41 paragraph 15 and IAS 41 paragraph 18 b). The alternative method of estimating fair value as the present value of future net cash flows, cf. IAS 41 paragraph 20, should not be used when market determined prices or values as mentioned in IAS 41 paragraph 17 and 18 are available.

Active markets satisfying the criteria in IAS 41 paragraph 8 exist for the trading of such slaughtered salmon. The sizes of slaughtered salmon for which willing buyers and sellers normally can be found at any time, can vary from market to market. According to IAS 41 paragraph 9, the fair value of biological assets should be based on its present location and condition, including its weight and quality at the balance sheet date. Hence live salmon should be valued based on observable prices in an active market of slaughtered salmon in the weight class (taking into account adjustments for conversion from live weight to slaughter weight) in which the salmon would be sold if it were slaughtered at the balance sheet date.

Follow up

The decision was appealed to the Ministry of Finance. The Ministry of Finance upheld the decision of the enforcer, with some adjustments and additions. Most significantly, the final ruling upholds the enforcer's decision that slaughtered salmon which is sold whole and gutted is in an accounting sense to be considered as a similar asset of live salmon, according to IAS 41 paragraph 18 b and that this also applies to so-called immature farmed salmon. Hence, the observable prices of slaughtered salmon shall be used as a basis for determining the fair value of live immature salmon. The key amendment to the decision made by the Ministry of Finance is that it added certain comments relating to how the term "adjustments to reflect differences" in IAS 41 paragraph 18 b was to be applied. The adjustments should reflect the differences between the price of slaughtered immature salmon and the hypothetical market price in an active market for live immature salmon. These adjustments should be consistent with the assessments that would be expected to be made by market participants to set the price of live salmon in an arms length transaction, given its present location and condition.

The Ministry of Finance ruling was made with effect from the 4th quarter 2006 financial reporting and forward. Comparative financial information relating to prior accounting periods was to be revised accordingly.

Source: The Committee of European Securities Regulators. Extract from EECS database of enforcement decisions. April 2007, Ref: 07–120.

It is interesting to observe the nature of disclosures made by companies applying the fair value requirements of IAS 41 in these circumstances. For example, Lighthouse Caledonia ASA, a Scottish company, reported the following (see figure 16.2) in its 2007 annual report:

FIGURE 16.2 Disclosures illustrating IAS 41 practical implementation

Note 15 — Biological Assets

Book value of biological assets	**2007**	**2006**
Book value of live fish	27 227.0	31 895.4
Book value of smolt	2 779.1	2 687.5
Total book value of biological assets	**30 006.1**	**34 582.9**

Reconciliation of changes in book value of live fish	**2007**	**2006**
Book value 01.01	31 895.4	20 543.5
Book value in Fjord Seafood Scotland when acquired	—	5 298.9
Increase due to purchases	38 792.6	33 914.7
Gain/loss from change in fair value	(1 607.5)	1 105.9
Fair value (excess of cost) on biomass acquired and harvested	(462.0)	(1 192.6)
Write-down fish in sea in period	(1 779.1)	(460.0)
Decreases due to sales	(39 612.4)	(31 342.0)
Book value in Marine Harvest sites when acquired	—	4 027.1
Book value of live fish at year end	**27 227.0**	**31 895.4**

Fair value adjustments on biological assets in the balance sheet	**2007**	**2006**
Lighthouse Caledonia Ltd	936.3	2 971.1
Fjord Seafood Scotland	897.8	470.4
Sites taken over from Marine Harvest Scotland	—	462.0
Total fair value adjustment in the balance sheet	**1 834.1**	**3 903.5**

Fair value adjustments on biological assets in the profit & loss statement	**2007**	**2006**
Lighthouse Caledonia Ltd	(2 496.9)	635.4
Fair value adjustment on biomass in Fjord Seafood Scotland when consolidated	—	(1 192.6)
Fjord Seafood Scotland after consolidation	427.4	470.5
Total change in fair value on biological assets in the profit and loss statement	**(2 069.5)**	**(86.7)**

Volumes of biomass (in tonnes)	**2007**	**2006**
Volume of biomass harvested during the year in Lighthouse Caledonia Ltd (Gwt)	19 648	15 582
Volume of biomass harvested during the year in Fjord Seafood Scotland (Gwt)	3 034	3 688
Volume of biomass in the sea at year-end Lighthouse Caledonia Ltd (Lwt)	10 199	11 591

(continued)

FIGURE 16.2 *(continued)*

Volumes of biomass (in tonnes)	2007	2006
Volume of biomass in the sea at year-end Fjord Seafood Scotland (Lwt)	5 531	3 433
Volume of biomass in the sea at year-end Marine Harvest sites (Lwt) (consolidated in to Lighthouse Caledonia Ltd for 2007)	—	2 023
Total volume of biomass in the sea at year-end (Lwt)	15 730	17 047

Valuation of Biological Assets

IAS 41 require that biomass being accounted for at estimated fair value net of sales costs and harvesting costs.

According to the understanding of IAS 41 in Norway (FSA) the valuation should aim to establish an estimated market price at closing date that would have occurred in a (non-existing) active market for live immature fish. A model has been established to calculate a fair value on the biomass based on observed market prices, which are then adjusted to reflect that the observed prices are not prices for live fish. The calculated value of the biomass will vary from period to period during the year depending of the volume and the nature of the biomass.

Where no external market price exists/is quoted the valuation can be based on internal achieved prices and this has been done in Scotland. The prices are reduced for harvesting costs and freight costs to market, to arrive at a net value for the farmer. The valuation reflects expected quality grading. In the accounts the change in estimated fair value is charged to the profit and loss account on a monthly basis, and in the accounts these adjustments are reported separated (own line) from the related cost of the biomass when harvested.

About the valuation model

The valuation is based on biomass in sea for each location. The specification of biomass include total number of fish, estimated average weight and biological cost for the biomass. In the calculation the value is estimated by setting a value for the total kilo of biomass. Number of kilo biomass is multiplied by a value per kilo which reflect the actual value. For the fish that are not saleable the price in the calculation is adjusted to include only part of the estimated earning. The earning is estimated based on normal costs related to the fish and observed prices. The valuation take into consideration that not all the fish are of the same quality.

Significant assumptions for determining fair value of live fish

The estimate of fair value of biomass will always contain uncertain assumptions, even though the company has built substantial expertise in assessing these factors. The volume of biomass is in itself an estimate that is based on the smolt put to sea, the estimated growth from the smolt stage, estimated mortality based on observed mortality in the period etc. Based on experience some mortality will occur during harvest and this is reflected in the calculation. The quality of the fish is difficult to assess prior to harvesting, and the estimates of quality is quite uncertain. Each individual fish in the sea grows independently from the other fish, and even in a situation with good estimates of the average weight of the fish there will be considerable variance in quality and weight of the fish actually in the cage.

The price assumption is very important for the valuation. A biomass in sea of 15 730 tons will change its value with GBP 793.66 k if the price changes with GBP 10 p.

Source: Lighthouse Caledonia ASA (2007, pp. 44–5).

The above extract highlights a few key points:

1. The company has disclosed separately the 'live fish' and the 'smolt'. Smolt is immature live salmon.
2. The company makes the point that it has to refer to a 'non-existing' active market for live immature fish and that it has had to make adjustments to observed market prices to arrive at a fair value for the live immature fish. The company is complying with the CESR determination referred to above, but some incredulity with the decision is implicit in the disclosures!
3. The company discloses the significant assumptions used in determining the fair value of live fish. This is in accordance with paragraph 47 of IAS 41.

16.5.2 Measuring the fair value of vineyards and grapes

Figure 16.3 shows the disclosure by Foster's Group in its 2008 annual report illustrating how the group has determined the fair value of its vineyards and grapes.

FIGURE 16.3 Disclosure of fair value of vineyards and grapes

Note 16 – Agricultural Assets

	Consolidated	
	2008	**2007**
	$m	**$m**
Agricultural assets	291.6	335.1

Agricultural assets mainly comprise grape vines, with a minor holding of olive trees.

Foster's has total vineyard resources of over 15 021 hectares (2007: 15 972 hectares). These vineyards provide the Group with access to some of Australia's highest quality super premium fruit from regions such as the Barossa Valley in central South Australia, Coonawarra in south-eastern South Australia and the Hunter Valley in New South Wales. Other Australia vineyards are also located in the Clare Valley, Eden Valley, Great Western, Heathcote, Langhorne Creek, the Limestone Coast, McLaren Vale, Margaret River, Mornington Peninsula, Mudgee, Murray Valley, Padthaway, Robe, and the Yarra Valley. The Group also holds vineyards in North America (mainly Napa Valley and Sonoma County), Italy, France and New Zealand.

The geographic spread of the vineyard holdings not only provides Foster's with a diversity of premium fruit styles, but also reduces viticultural risk.

Of the total land area under vine around 1872 hectares (2007: 1500 hectares) is under lease arrangements. The Group also has around 7 hectares (2007: 7 hectares) of olive groves in the Tuscany region of Italy.

During the fiscal year Foster's owned and leased vineyards yielded 120 500 tonnes of grapes (2007: 95 000 tonnes). Northern Hemisphere harvest of vines normally occurs in September – October, with Southern hemisphere harvest around March – April.

Vines and grapes are measured at fair value, less estimated point-of-sale costs, with changes in fair value included in the income statement in the period in which it arises. The fair value of acquired vines is determined with reference to independent valuations of vineyards and the market price of purchased vines (rootlings). Subsequent movements in the fair value of vines is determined through operational reviews of the vineyard portfolio which identify, where applicable, any factors affecting the long term viability and value of the vines. The fair value of harvested grapes is determined with reference to the weighted district average of grape prices for each region for the current vintage. Annual prices for grapes will vary with the grade quality of grapes produced in each particular region.

The measurement basis for vines and grapes as prescribed by AASB 141 'Agriculture' has resulted in a net loss before tax of $22.9 million (2007: loss before tax of $38.0 million) comprising a decrement in vines valuation of $24.8 million (2007: nil) partly offset by a gain on grape valuation of $1.9 million (2007: loss of $38.0 million).

Reconciliations

Reconciliations of the carrying amount of agricultural assets at the beginning and end of the current and previous year are set out below.

	Consolidated	
	2008	**2007**
	$m	**$m**
Consolidated		
carrying amount at start of year	335.1	354.1
acquisitions	1.2	5.1

(continued)

FIGURE 16.3 *(continued)*

	2008 $m	2007 $m
Consolidated *(continued)*		
disposals	**(0.4)**	(2.1)
fair value decrement	**(24.8)**	—
assets classified as held for sale	**2.4**	(6.7)
transfers to property, plant and equipment	**(4.7)**	—
foreign exchange	**(17.2)**	(15.3)
carrying amount at end of year	**291.6**	335.1

Source: Foster's Group Limited (2008, p. 72).

16.5.3 Disclosure practices

It is common for companies applying IAS 41 to separately disclose the fair value movements attributable to agricultural assets, either in the statement of comprehensive income or in the notes, and in information reported outside the financial statements to investors such as in 'investor packs' or 'financial commentaries'. This is because companies want to highlight the fair value movements as being separate from other forms of income. To some extent, the separate disclosure also reflects the implicit disagreement with the requirements of the standard, particularly where it is difficult to measure fair value.

The extract in figure 16.4 from Foster's Group 2008 annual report illustrates this point.

FIGURE 16.4 Separate disclosure of fair value movements attributable to agricultural assets

Group Financial Review Financial Commentary 12 Months to 30 June	**2008 Reported $m**	**2007 Reported $m**	**2007 Constant Currency $m**	**Reported %**	**Change Constant Currency %**
Net sales revenue[1]	**4 372.7**	4 555.2	4 376.8	(4.0)	(0.1)
– Australia, Asia and Pacific	**948.4**	870.0	877.1	9.0	8.1
– Americas	**150.8**	254.2	191.2	(40.7)	(21.1)
– Europe, Middle East and Africa	**87.3**	82.2	74.9	6.2	16.6
– Corporate	**(47.6)**	(51.5)	(51.2)	7.6	7.0
EBITS[1]	**1 138.9**	1 154.9	1 092.0	(1.4)	4.3
SGARA	**1.9**	(38.1)	(38.2)	105.0	105.0
EBIT	**1 140.8**	1 116.8	1 053.8	2.1	8.3
Net finance costs	**(144.7)**	(187.1)	(166.8)	22.7	13.2
Continuing net profit before tax	**996.1**	929.7	887.0	7.1	12.3
Tax[1]	**(279.3)**	(260.7)	(248.7)	(7.1)	(12.3)
Continuing net profit after tax	**716.8**	669.0	638.3	7.1	12.3
Minority Interests	**(5.8)**	(3.7)	(3.7)	(56.8)	(56.8)
Continuing net profit after tax and minority interests (before significant items)	**711.0**	665.3	634.6	6.9	12.0
Discontinued operations trading result after tax[1]	**3.6**	23.4	23.5	(84.6)	(84.7)

FIGURE 16.4 *(continued)*

12 Months to 30 June	2008 Reported $m	2007 Reported $m	2007 Constant Currency $m	Reported %	Change Constant Currency %
Net profit after tax (before significant items)	**714.6**	688.7	658.1	3.8	8.6
Continuing operations significant items (net of tax)	**(605.8)**	107.8	107.8		
Discontinued operations significant items[1] (net of tax)	**2.9**	169.7	174.9		
Net profit after tax attributable to members of Foster's Group Limited	**111.7**	966.2	940.8	(88.4)	(88.1)
Net profit after tax (before significant items & SGARA)	**713.2**	716.1	685.6	(0.4	4.0
EPS (before significant items & SGARA)	**36.8**	35 .6	34.1	3.4)	7.9
Reported EPS	**5.8**	48.0	46.7	(87.9)	(87.6)
Average shares (number — million)	**1938.3**	2013.5	2013.5		

1 Refer reconciliation to the Income Statement on page 34.
Exchange rates: average exchange rates used for profi t and loss purposes in 2008 are: $A1 = $US 0.8960 (2007: $A1 = $US 0.7866), $A1 = GBP 0.4473 (2007: $A1 = GBP 0.4066). Period end exchange rates used for balance sheet items in 2008 are: $A1 = $US 0.9617 (2007: $A1 = $US 0.8466), $A1 = GBP 0.4822 (2007: $A1 = GBP 0.4229).
Constant currency: Throughout this report constant currency assumes current and prior earnings of self-sustaining foreign operations are translated and cross border transactions are transacted at current year exchange rates.
SGARA: Australian Accounting standard AASB141 "Agriculture"

Reconciliation to the Income Statement

12 Months to 30 June	Reference	2008 Reported $m	2007 Reported $m
Net Sales Revenue (NSR)	Commentary — page 33	**4372.7**	4555.2
Other Revenue		**185.8**	205.0
Total Revenue	Income statement — page 42	**4558.5**	4760.2
EBITS	Commentary — page 33	**1138.9**	1154.9
SGARA		**1.9**	(38.1)
EBIT		**1140.8**	1116.8
Significant items before tax		**(730.4)**	96.7
Profit from continuing operations before tax and finance costs	Income statement — page 42	**410.4**	1213.5
Tax	Commentary — page 33	**(279.3)**	(260.7)
Significant items — tax		**124.6**	11.1
Income tax expense relating to continuing operations	Income statement — page 42	**(154.7)**	(249.6)
Discontinued operations trading result after tax	Commentary — page 33	**3.6**	23.4
Discontinued operations significant items after tax		**2.9**	169.7
Net profit from discontinued operations	Income statement — page 42	**6.5**	193.1
Net profit after tax before significant Items and SGARA	Commentary — page 33	**713.2**	716.1

(continued)

FIGURE 16.4 *(continued)*

12 Months to 30 June	Reference	2008 Reported $m	2007 Reported $m
Continuing operations significant items after tax		(605.8)	107.8
Discontinued operations significant items after tax		2.9	169.7
SGARA post tax		1.4	(27.4)
Net profit attributable to members of Foster's Group Limited	Income statement — page 42	111.7	966.2

Source: Foster's Group Limited (2008, pp. 33–4).

16.6 GOVERNMENT GRANTS

Sometimes entities may receive government grants in respect of agricultural activity. IAS 41 prescribes how these should be accounted for where biological assets are measured at fair value, distinguishing between conditional and unconditional government grants.

1. Unconditional government grants are recognised as income when the grant becomes receivable (para. 34).
2. Conditional government grants are recognised as income when the conditions attaching to the grant are met (para. 35).

Note that if biological assets are not measured at fair value (i.e. where the exemption in paragraph 30 applies) then IAS 20 applies. IAS 20 allows various choices in the accounting for government grants, including deferral of the revenue and permitting the grant to be offset against the cost of the asset. These approaches are not permitted for biological assets measured at fair value under IAS 41.

Illustrative example 16.6 demonstrates how conditional and unconditional government grants are accounted for when biological assets are measured at fair value.

ILLUSTRATIVE EXAMPLE 16.6

Conditional and unconditional government grants

Company B engages in agricultural activities and measures its biological assets at fair value in accordance with IAS 41. In 2010, Company B received two grants from the government. Grant A, of $10 000, was notified to the company on 7 January 2010 and had no conditions attaching to it. The grant was received on 14 March 2010. Grant B, of $50 000, was notified to the company on 31 January 2010. Grant B had the following condition attached to it: 'Company B must continue to operate its agricultural activities in the Zone Z Area until at least 31 January 2018. If Company B discontinues all or part of its operations in the Zone Z Area before that date then Company B shall immediately repay Grant B in full'. Grant B was received on 14 April 2010.

The end of Company B's reporting period is 30 June. The journal entries for Company B for the year ended 30 June 2010 would be as follows:

Receivables	Dr	10 000	
Income	Cr		10 000
(To recognise the unconditional Grant A when it became receivable on 7 January)			
Cash	Dr	10 000	
Receivables	Cr		10 000
(To recognise receipt of the cash on 14 March)			
Cash	Dr	50 000	
Performance Obligation	Cr		50 000
(To recognise the cash received on 14 April and the corresponding obligation to comply with the conditions of Grant B)			

Grant B is thus recorded as a liability until such time as the conditions are met. Note that if the conditions attaching to Grant B permitted Company B to retain some of the grant based on the passing of time (e.g. by means of a formula), then Company B would be able to recognise the grant as income over the period of time.

16.7 THE INTERACTION BETWEEN IAS 41 AND IAS 16, IAS 40 AND IAS 17

As noted in section 16.2.1, IAS 41 does not apply to land related to agricultural activity. Rather, an entity follows IAS 16 or IAS 40, depending on the circumstances. If the land meets the definition of an investment property (see section 16.2.1) it is measured using either the cost model or the fair value model under IAS 40. Thus, land related to agricultural activity that is an investment property may either be measured (i) at cost and tested for impairment under IAS 16, or (ii) at fair value with changes in fair value being taken through profit or loss. However, the agricultural assets attaching to that land (e.g. orchards, forests or vineyards) must be measured at fair value under IAS 41. Further, if the land does not meet the definition of an investment property it must be accounted for under IAS 16. IAS 16 also allows a choice between the cost method and the revaluation method. Under the revaluation method, changes in fair value are generally taken to equity rather than through profit or loss.

Table 16. 3 summarises the accounting choices available.

TABLE 16.3 Accounting policy choices available in respect of land related to agricultural activity

	Land that is an investment property (IAS 40)		Land that is not an investment property (IAS 16)	
Accounting policy choice	Cost model	Fair value model	Cost model	Revaluation model
Increase in fair value over cost	Not recorded	Recorded through profit or loss	Not recorded	Recorded through equity
Decrease in fair value	Recorded through profit or loss if it is an impairment	Recorded through profit or loss as part of the fair value measurement	Recorded through profit or loss if it is an impairment	Recorded through equity to the extent available with remainder through profit or loss

The related agricultural assets must be measured at fair value in accordance with IAS 41. The accounting policy choices for land mean that an entity could have a mixed measurement basis for its agricultural activities, with inconsistencies between the treatment of the land and the biological assets growing on the land.

The IASB considered this issue and commented as follows in the basis for conclusions (paras. 56–7):

> Some argue that land attached to biological assets related to agricultural activity should also be measured at its fair value. They argue that fair value measurement of land results in consistency of measurement with the fair value measurement of biological assets. They also argue that it is sometimes difficult to measure the fair value of such biological assets separately from the land since an active market often exists for the combined assets (that is, land and biological assets; for example, trees in a plantation forest).
>
> The Board rejected this approach, primarily because requiring the fair value measurement of land related to agricultural activity would be inconsistent with IAS 16.

In addition, the interaction between IAS 40 and IAS 17 *Leases* poses further complications. When IAS 41 was issued, an amendment was made to IAS 17 to clarify that IAS 17 should not be applied to the measurement by:

1. lessees of biological assets held under finance leases (IAS 17, para. 2(c)), and
2. lessors of biological assets leased out under operating leases (IAS 17, para. 2(d)).

While the recognition and measurement requirements of IAS 41 apply, the disclosure requirements of both IAS 41 and IAS 17 apply (IAS 41, para. B82 (n)). This means that in these situations the lessee or lessor (as appropriate) must apply IAS 41 rather than IAS 17. So, for example, if a lessee leases a vineyard under a finance lease, then the vineyard is accounted for as a biological asset of the lessee under IAS 41. The lessee would thus record the vineyard as its own asset and measure it at fair value. The lease liability would be recorded as a borrowing. The requirements are summarised in table 16.4.

TABLE 16.4 Lessees and lessors — application of IAS 41 and IAS 17

	Finance Lease		Operating Lease	
	Lessee	Lessor	Lessee	Lessor
Biological assets	Assets recorded and measured under IAS 41	Does not record biological assets — applies IAS 17	Does not record biological assets — applies IAS 17	Assets recorded and measured under IAS 41
Lease receivable	N/A	Recorded under IAS 17	N/A	N/A
Lease liability	Recorded as a borrowing to finance the biological asset	N/A	N/A	N/A
Disclosures	Made under both IAS 41 and IAS 17	Made under both IAS 41 and IAS 17	Made under both IAS 41 and IAS 17	Made under both IAS 41 and IAS 17

Let us now return to the facts of illustrative example 16.1 and overlay this with the requirements in respect of leased assets.

Assume the same facts as in illustrative example 16.1 except that Manager M is a lessee under a finance lease, in addition to managing the vineyard. If this were the case, Manager M would record the vineyard as its own asset because it has assumed substantially all of the risks and rewards of the vineyard under the finance lease. The question of control versus management does not arise in this case because Manager M both manages the vineyard and 'controls' the assets under the finance lease (refer to the discussion in illustrative example 16.1). Therefore, the biological assets are recorded by Manager M and measured under IAS 41, while Company A would be the lessor and record a finance lease receivable under IAS 17.

16.8 DISCLOSURE REQUIREMENTS

Paragraphs 40 through 57 set out the disclosure requirements of IAS 41. These are divided into three sections:

1. general;
2. additional disclosures for biological assets where fair value cannot be measured reliably; and
3. government grants.

The requirements are summarised overleaf. Students should refer to the standard for full details.

16.8.1 General disclosures

These are contained in paragraphs 40–53 and include the following:

- aggregate gain or loss on initial recognition (biological assets and agricultural produce) and as a result of fair value movements (biological assets)
- description of each group of biological assets (groups may be determined based on consumable (e.g. crops) versus bearer (e.g. fruit trees) biological assets or based on mature versus immature biological assets, or both)
- description of the nature of activities involving each group of biological assets
- non-financial measures or estimates of the physical quantities of biological assets at the end of the period and output of agricultural produce during the period
- methods and assumptions applied in determining the fair value of each group of agricultural produce at the point of harvest and each group of biological assets
- fair value of agricultural produce harvested during the period, at the point of harvest
- details of biological assets whose title is restricted or which has been pledged as security, commitments for the development or acquisition of biological assets and financial risk management strategies related to agricultural activity
- reconciliation of the changes in the carrying amount of biological assets between the beginning and end of the current period. Note 3 of Example 1 of IAS 41 illustrates this reconciliation.

Entities are also encouraged, but not required, to disclose separately the fair value changes attributable to physical changes and price changes. Example 2 of IAS 41 illustrates these disclosures.

Example 1 of IAS 41 illustrates the general disclosure requirements.

16. 8.2 Additional disclosures for biological assets where fair value cannot be measured reliably

These additional disclosures are contained in paragraphs 54–56 and include the following:

- a description of the biological assets, an explanation of why fair value cannot be measured reliably, the range of estimates within which fair value is likely to lie, the depreciation method and rates/useful lives used, the gross carrying amount and accumulated depreciation at the beginning and end of the period
- gain or loss on disposal, impairment losses and depreciation — shown separately in the reconciliation required under 'General' disclosures
- specified details if the fair value becomes reliably measurable during the period.

16.8.3 Government grants

Paragraph 57 requires disclosure of the nature and extent of government grants recognised, unfulfilled conditions and other contingencies attaching to government grants and significant decreases expected in the level of government grants.

16.9 PREPARING FINANCIAL STATEMENTS WHEN APPLYING IAS 41

Illustrative example 16. 7 shows how a company would present its statement of comprehensive income and statement of financial position when applying IAS 41.

ILLUSTRATIVE EXAMPLE 16.7

Preparing a statement of comprehensive income and statement of financial position under IAS 41

Company A owns dairy cattle and has an end of reporting period date of 30 June.

At 1 July 2010, Company A had 900 cows and 200 heifers, with a fair value (less point-of-sale costs) of $800 per cow and $320 per heifer.

During the year ended 30 June 2011 the following occurred:

1. 200 new cows were purchased at $810 each
2. 50 heifers matured into cows
3. 5 heifers died
4. 100 cows were sold for $830 each
5. Salaries and other operating costs were $60 000.

Company A owns the farmland, which was purchased for $1.5 million. The land is measured at cost under IAS 16. As at 30 June 2011 the market value of the land was assessed at $5.6 million.

Company A also has plant and equipment which was purchased for $1 000 000 and is depreciated over its expected useful life of 10 years. As at 1 July 2010, the plant and equipment was 2 years old.

As at 30 June 2011, the fair value (less point-of-sale costs) is determined as $850 per cow and $350 per heifer. Company A has determined that these are the appropriate fair values to use for the purposes of transfers and deaths of heifers.

The price change between a heifer and a cow at the time of maturity during the year was estimated to be $500.

During the year, Company A produced milk with a fair value less point-of-sale costs of $500 000.

Workings

1. Reconciliation of movements in livestock

	Cows	Fair value	Heifers	Fair value
Balance as at 1 July 2010	900	$720 000	200	$64 000
Purchases	200	162 000	—	
Sales	(100)	(83 000)	—	
Transfer to cows	50	17 500	(50)	(17 500)
Deaths			(5)	(1 750)
Balance as at 30 June 2011	1 050	892 500	145	50 750
Increase in fair value				
• attributable to physical change		25 000		
• attributable to price change		51 000		6 000

2. Reconciliation of movements in fair value — cows

Physical balance (assuming FIFO)	Change in fair value	Total
Opening balance 900 @ $800		
Sold 100@ $830	100 @ $30	$ 3 000
Balance 800 @ $800		
Year end 800 @ $850	800 @ $50	$40 000
Purchased 200 @ $810		
Year end 200 @ $850	200 @ $40	$ 8 000
Total attributable to fair value changes		$51 000
Heifers 50 @ $350		
Year end 50 @ $850	50 @ $500	$25 000 (all attributable to physical change)

3. Reconciliation of movements in fair value — heifers

Physical balance (assuming FIFO)	Change in fair value	Total
Opening balance 200 @ $320		
Transfer 50 @ $350	50 @ $30	1 500
Balance 150 @ $320		
Year end 150 @ $350	150 @ $30	4 500
Total attributable to fair value changes		6 000
Died 5 @ $350	5 @ $350 (all value lost)	(1 750)
Total		4 250

4. Property, plant & equipment

Land measured at cost, no impairment as market value exceeds carrying amount as at 30 June 2011.

Plant and equipment	
Cost	$1 000 000
Accumulated depreciation as at 1 July 2010	(200 000)
Balance as at 1 July 2010	800 000
Annual depreciation	100 000
Balance as at 30 June 2010:	
Land	1 500 000
Plant & Equipment	800 000
Total	2 300 000
Balance as at 30 June 2011:	
Land	1 500 000
Plant & Equipment	700 000
Total	2 200 000

COMPANY A
Statement of Comprehensive Income (Extract)
for the year ended 30 June 2011

Fair Value of milk produced	$500 000
Net gains arising from changes in fair value less estimated point-of-sale costs of dairy livestock (note y)	80 250
Deprecation expense	(100 000)
Other operating expenses	(60 000)
Profit from operations	420 250
Income tax expense	XX
Profit after income tax	XX

COMPANY A
Statement of Financial Position (Extract)
as at 30 June 2011

	2011	2010
Assets		
Non-current assets		
Dairy livestock — immature	$ 50 750	$ 64 000
Dairy livestock — mature	892 500	720 000
Subtotal — biological assets	943 250	784 000
Property, plant & equipment	2 200 000	2 300 000

Note y

Biological assets

Reconciliation of carrying amounts of dairy livestock	
Carrying amount at 1 July 2010	$784 000
Increases due to purchases	162 000
Increase in fair value less point-of-sale costs	
— attributable to price changes	57 000
— attributable to physical changes	25 000
Total increase in fair value less point-of-sale costs	82 000

(continued)

Biological assets *(continued)*

Decreases due to deaths	(1 750)
Net increase in fair value	80 250
Decreases due to sales	(83 000)
Carrying amount as at 30 June 2011	943 250

SUMMARY

IAS 41 was a controversial standard when it was first issued, mainly because of its requirement to measure assets related to agricultural activity at fair value, with movements in fair value being taken to the statement of comprehensive income as gains or losses. To this day, companies applying the standard indicate their implicit disagreement with this requirement, for example, by highlighting the fair value movements separately in their statements of comprehensive income so that users can clearly see and understand the impact on reported profit. The IASB rejected criticisms of the fair value model for biological assets and agricultural produce but conceded by permitting an exemption when fair value can not be reliably measured. The board also included guidance in the standard on how to apply the fair value measurement requirement.

IAS 41 distinguishes between biological assets, agricultural produce and products that are the result of processing after harvest, and prescribes different accounting treatments for each category. The interaction between IAS 41 and IAS 16, IAS 17 and IAS 40 is very important to understand and apply, particularly since, in the agricultural industry, it is common to find different parties involved in owning, leasing and managing agricultural assets.

Discussion questions

1. Why do you think IAS 41 was a controversial standard when it was issued?
2. Explain why the concept of 'control' is problematic when applying the recognition criteria of IAS 41.
3. What are the arguments for and against the use of fair value as the measurement basis for biological assets and agricultural produce? Why do you think the IASB settled on requiring fair value?
4. How is the risk that future cash flows pertaining to biological assets may not eventuate as predicted, taken into account when determining the fair value of a biological asset using the present value of net cash flows method?
5. How does a gain or loss on initial recognition of a biological asset or agricultural produce arise?
6. Why is agricultural produce not remeasured to fair value during a reporting period?
7. Discuss the requirement of paragraph 18(b) of IAS 41 in the context of the CESR ruling in respect of immature salmon.

STAR RATING
★ BASIC
★★ MODERATE
★★★ DIFFICULT

Exercises

Exercise 16.1 ★

AGRICULTURAL ACTIVITY — DEFINITIONS

State which of the following meets the definition of 'agricultural activity' in IAS 41. Give reasons for your answer:

1. pig farming
2. ocean fishing
3. clearing forests to create farmland
4. salmon farming
5. managing vineyards.

Exercise 16.2 ★

AGRICULTURAL ACTIVITY — DEFINITIONS

State whether the following are (a) biological assets, (b) agricultural produce or (c) products that are as a result of processing after harvest:

1. living pigs
2. living sheep

3. pigs' carcasses
4. pork sausages
5. trees growing in a plantation forest
6. furniture
7. olive trees
8. olives
9. olive oil
10. vines growing in a vineyard.

Exercise 16.3 ★

AGRICULTURAL ACTIVITY — MEASUREMENT

For each of the items in exercise 16.2 state whether they would be measured (a) at fair value under IAS 41 or (b) at the lower of cost and net realisable value under IAS 2:

1. living pigs
2. living sheep
3. pigs' carcasses
4. pork sausages
5. trees growing in a plantation forest
6. furniture
7. olive trees
8. olives
9. olive oil
10. vines growing in a vineyard.

Exercise 16.4 ★★

FAIR VALUE DETERMINATION

Which of the following is included in determining the fair value of a biological asset that does not have an active market and which has a 5-year production cycle?

1. Revenue from sale in 5 years time
2. Costs of growing for 5 years
3. Financing costs on borrowings taken out to fund the growing costs
4. Taxation on taxable income generated from sale in 5 years time
5. Discount rate that reflects expected variability in cash flows.

Exercise 16.5 ★

FAIR VALUE DETERMINATION

Company A owns a plantation forest. As at the end of the reporting period the fair value of the plantation forest including the land was $2.5 million. Company A needs to determine the fair value of the trees excluding the land to comply with IAS 41 at the end of its reporting period. How does Company A determine the fair value of the trees?

Exercise 16.6 ★★

DISCLOSURE OF BIOLOGICAL ASSETS

State whether each of the following is true or false:

1. Companies applying IAS 41 must disclose separately the fair value (less estimated point-of-sale costs) of mature and immature biological assets.
2. A lessee of an orchard that is classified as a finance lease must measure the orchard (excluding the land) at fair value (less estimated point-of-sale costs) in its financial statements.
3. A vineyard planted on land classified as an investment property by the owner must be recognised and measured as part of that investment property.
4. A lessor of an orchard that is classified as a finance lease must measure the orchard (excluding the land) at fair value in its financial statements.
5. An entity availing itself of the exemption in paragraph 30 of IAS 41 for a particular biological asset must apply IAS 20 if it receives a government grant in respect of that asset.
6. If agricultural produce cannot be reliably measured then it may be accounted for at cost under paragraph 30 of IAS 41.

Exercise 16.7 ★★★

ACCOUNTING FOR A GOVERNMENT GRANT

Company Z engages in agricultural activities and measures its biological assets at fair value in accordance with IAS 41. In 2010 Company Z received a grant of $250 000 from the government. The grant was notified to the company on 31 March 2010. The terms and conditions of the grant were as follows.

> This grant is effective from 1 July 2010. Company Z must continue to employ staff from Area A in its agricultural activities until at least 30 June 2015. If Company Z ceases to employ staff from Area A before that date then Company Z shall immediately repay the grant. The amount to be repaid shall be calculated according to the following formula:
>
> $$A = B - (C \times D)$$
>
> Where:
> A = amount to be repaid
> B = amount of initial grant
> C = number of years the company has employed staff in Area A
> D = $50 000.

The end of Company Z's reporting period is 30 June. The grant was received on 15 April 2010.

Required
Prepare the journal entries to account for the grant by Company Z for the years ended 30 June 2010 and 30 June 2011, assuming Company Z complies with the conditions of the grant.

Problems

Problem 16.1 ★★

ACCOUNTING FOR LAND RELATING TO AGRICULTURAL ACTIVITY

Company C entered into a lease agreement in respect of a vineyard with Company L on 1 January 2006. The lease was classified as a finance lease as it transferred substantially all the risks and rewards of the vineyard to Company C. The lease was for a period of 10 years, with annual lease payments of $212 000. The vineyard was established on land owned by Company L and was recorded as a biological asset at fair value in the books of Company L prior to the lease agreement. The land is classified as an investment property by Company L, using the fair value model under IAS 40. Company C engaged Manager M to manage the vineyard on its behalf.

Company L acquired the land for $5 million in 2000. As at 31 December 2006 the fair value of the land was independently assessed to be $14 million ($13 million as at 31 December 2005).

The fair value of the minimum lease payments under the finance lease was $2 million as at 1 January 2006. This was determined to be substantially the same as the fair value of the vineyard as at that date. Company L determined that the amount of finance lease income for the year ended 31 December 2006 was $12 000.

The fair value of the vineyard was independently assessed to be $2.6 million as at 31 December 2006.

Company C paid Manager M $245 000 to manage the vineyard for the year ended 31 December 2006.

The end of the reporting period for Company C, Company L and Manager M is 31 December.

Required
Prepare the journal entries to record the above transactions in the books of each of Company C, Company L and Manager M for the year ended 31 December 2006.

Problem 16.2 ★★★

PREPARATION OF FINANCIAL STATEMENTS APPLYING IAS 41

Company S owns sheep and the end of its reporting period is 30 June. The sheep are held to produce wool.

At 1 July 2010, Company S had 1000 sheep and 200 lambs, with a fair value (less point-of-sale costs) of $200 per sheep and $50 per lamb.

During the year ended 30 June 2011 the following occurred:

1. 100 new sheep were purchased at $210 each
2. 20 lambs matured into sheep
3. 3 lambs died
4. 15 lambs were born
5. 100 sheep were sold for $240 each
6. Salaries and other operating costs were $34 000.

Company S owns the farmland which was purchased for $1.5 million. The land is measured at fair value using the revaluation model under IAS 16. As at 30 June 2011, the fair value of the land was assessed at $5.6 million ($4.7 million as at 30 June 2010).

Company S also has plant and equipment which was purchased for $1 million and is depreciated over its expected useful life of 10 years. As at 1 July 2010, the plant and equipment was 2 years old.

As at 30 June 2011, the fair value (less point-of-sale costs) is determined as $250 per sheep and $55 per lamb. Company S has determined that these are the appropriate fair values to use for the purposes of transfers, births and deaths of lambs.

The price change between a lamb and a sheep at the time of maturity during the year was estimated to be $195.

During the year Company S produced wool with a fair value less point-of-sale costs of $387 000.

Required

Prepare the relevant extracts from the statement of comprehensive income and statement of financial performance and the reconciliation required by paragraph 50 of IAS 41 for Company S in accordance with IAS 41 for the year ended 30 June 2011. Show all workings.

References

Committee of European Securities Regulators 2007, *Extract from EECS's database of enforcement decisions*, Ref: 07–120.

Foster's 2008, *Annual report 2008*, Foster's Group Limited, www.fosters.com.au.

IASB 2008, *IASB update*, March, www.iasb.org.

Lighthouse Caledonia 2007, *Annual report and accounts 2007*, Lighthouse Caledonia ASA, Scotland, www.lighthousecaledonia.com.

Part 3

Disclosure

17 Principles of disclosure — IAS 1, IAS 8 and IAS 10

ACCOUNTING STANDARDS IN FOCUS

International: **IAS 1** *Presentation of Financial Statements*
IAS 8 *Accounting Policies, Changes in Accounting Estimates and Errors*
IAS 10 *Events after the Reporting Period*

LEARNING OBJECTIVES

When you have studied this chapter, you should be able to:

- explain the purpose of financial statements
- describe the main components of financial statements
- understand the overall considerations that are applied in the presentation of financial statements
- understand the requirements of IAS 8 regarding the selection and application of accounting policies
- distinguish between changes in accounting policies, changes in accounting estimates and errors
- apply the requirements of IAS 8 in respect of changes in accounting policies, changes in accounting estimates and errors
- apply the disclosure requirements of IAS 10
- distinguish between adjusting and non-adjusting events after the reporting period.

17.1 INTRODUCTION TO IAS 1, IAS 8 AND IAS 10

IAS 1 *Presentation of Financial Statements*, IAS 8 *Accounting Policies, Changes in Accounting Estimates and Errors* and IAS 10 *Events after the Reporting Period* are largely disclosure standards, although IAS 8 and IAS 10 also contain certain measurement requirements. These standards deal with fundamental disclosures and considerations that underpin financial statement presentation.

The overall principles and other considerations relating to the presentation of financial statements contained in IAS 1 are addressed in this chapter. Detailed matters relating to the presentation of a statement of financial position, statement of comprehensive income, statement of changes in equity and notes are considered in chapter 18. The requirements for the presentation of a statement of cash flows are outlined in chapter 19. IAS 8 and IAS 10 are addressed separately in this chapter.

17.2 IAS 1 *PRESENTATION OF FINANCIAL STATEMENTS*

17.2.1 Purpose of financial statements

Financial statements are a structured presentation of the financial position and financial performance of an entity. The statement about the financial position of an entity is shown at a point in time — known as the reporting date or balance date — and is referred to as a statement of financial position in IAS 1. The statements about the financial performance of an entity are shown for a specified period of time (usually one financial year) or an interim period such as a half-year. They are referred to as a 'statement of comprehensive income' and 'statement of cash flows' in IAS 1, showing the historic profit or loss and comprehensive income, and historic cash flows, respectively, for the period presented.

IAS 1 does not prescribe *who* must prepare financial statements. This is dealt with to some extent in the IASB *Framework* (refer to chapter 1 of this book) that sets out the objective of financial statements and defines general purpose financial statements. However, the requirement to *prepare* financial statements usually stems from a country's legislative environment and from individual entities' constitutions. For example, in Australia the Corporations Act requires most companies to prepare financial statements, with certain exceptions for small private companies. In addition, non-corporate entities such as partnerships and trusts usually have a constitution or other enabling legislation that requires the preparation of financial statements. The relevant legislation or constitution will also specify *when* the entity must prepare its financial statements. This is usually for an annual reporting period or, for certain entities such as listed entities, an interim period as well. IAS 1, paragraph 36, states that financial statements shall be presented at least annually.

Whether or not those financial statements are *general purpose* financial statements depends on users' needs. Paragraph 7 of IAS 1 states that general purpose financial statements are those intended to meet the needs of users who are not in a position to demand reports that are tailored to their particular information needs. In Australia, an entity with users dependent upon general purpose financial statements is referred to as a reporting entity in Statement of Accounting Concepts 1 issued by the AASB. The reporting entity concept plays an important role in Australia's differential reporting regime. For most Australian Accounting Standards, a company that is required by legislation to prepare financial statements is only required to apply the standards if they are also a reporting entity. In the course of a joint project with the US Financial Accounting Standards Board (FASB), the IASB issued *Discussion Paper: Preliminary Views on an Improved Conceptual Framework for Financial Reporting: The Reporting Entity* in 2008. However, the IASB uses the term to refer to various boundaries that might constitute the entity, rather than as a basis for differential reporting.

The IASB *Framework* is concerned with financial statements prepared to meet the common information needs of a wide range of users, including investors, creditors and others. According to the *Framework*, if users cannot command financial information tailored to their individual needs, then the financial statements required of an entity must be *general purpose* financial statements. This means that entities (such as listed entities and many public companies) with large and varied groups of users (such as shareholders, creditors and employees) must prepare general purpose financial statements, and these general purpose financial statements must comply with the accounting standards of the IASB.

Paragraph 9 of IAS 1 states that the objective of general purpose financial statements is to provide information about the financial position, financial performance and cash flows of an entity that is useful to a wide range of users in making economic decisions. Financial statements also show the results of management's stewardship of the resources entrusted to it. IAS 1 states that, to meet this objective, financial information should provide information about an entity's:

- assets
- liabilities
- equity
- income and expenses, including gains and losses
- other changes in equity
- cash flows.

17.2.2 The components of financial statements

IAS 1 requires that a complete set of financial statements include the following:

- a statement of financial position
- a statement of comprehensive income
- a statement of changes in equity
- a statement of cash flows
- notes, comprising a summary of significant accounting policies and other explanatory notes.

'Notes' are defined in paragraph 7 of IAS 1 as follows:

> *Notes* contain information in addition to that presented in the statement of financial position, statement of comprehensive income, separate income statement (if presented), statement of changes in equity and statement of cash flows. Notes provide narrative descriptions or disaggregations of items presented in those statements and information about items that do not qualify for recognition in those statements.

While IAS 1 refers to the statements as a 'statement of financial position', a 'statement of comprehensive income', a 'statement of changes in equity' and a 'statement of cash flows', reporting entities may use other labels when presenting financial statements in accordance with IAS 1. For example, an entity may choose to label its statement of financial position as a 'balance sheet'.

Entities often present other information, such as certain financial ratios or a narrative review of operations by management or the directors. These reports are sometimes referred to as 'management discussion and analysis'. In some jurisdictions, entities are obliged under corporations legislation to prepare a 'directors' report' that covers, among other matters, commentary on the results of operations and financial position of the entity. In addition, some entities voluntarily prepare environmental and other reports. This other information is reported outside the financial statements and is not within the scope of International Financial Reporting Standards (IFRSs).

17.2.3 Overall considerations in the presentation of financial statements

IAS 1 sets out eight overall principles that need to be applied in the presentation of financial statements. These requirements are intended to ensure that the financial statements of an entity are a faithful presentation of its financial position, financial performance and cash flows.

1. Fair presentation and compliance with IFRSs

Paragraph 15 of IAS 1 states that financial statements shall present fairly the financial position, financial performance and cash flows of an entity. It goes on to define 'fair presentation' as follows:

> Fair presentation requires the faithful representation of the effects of transactions, other events and conditions in accordance with the definitions and recognition criteria for assets, liabilities, income and expenses set out in the *Framework*. The application of IFRSs, with additional disclosure when necessary, is presumed to result in financial statements that achieve a fair presentation.

Paragraph 16 of IAS 1 requires an entity presenting financial statements that are compliant with IFRSs to make an explicit and unreserved statement of such compliance in the notes to the financial statements. Such financial statements must comply with all the requirements of the IFRSs.

The last sentence of paragraph 16 is very significant. There is an assumption that full compliance with IFRSs will result in fair presentation. This also includes selecting and applying accounting policies in accordance with IAS 8; presenting information in a manner that provides relevant, reliable, comparable and understandable information (refer to chapter 1 of this book for the discussion of these qualitative characteristics of financial information); and providing additional disclosures to those specified by IFRSs, where necessary.

Paragraph 19 of IAS 1 says that, in extremely rare circumstances, management may depart from IFRSs. This is allowed only if two conditions are met:

- management concludes that compliance with a requirement in a standard or interpretation would be so misleading that it would conflict with the objective of financial statements set out in the *Framework*
- the relevant regulatory framework requires, or otherwise does not prohibit, such a departure.

Note that IFRSs include IASB standards as well as interpretations of these standards issued by the International Financial Reporting Interpretations Committee (IFRIC).

Paragraph 24 of IAS 1 explains that an item of information would be in conflict with the objective of financial statements if it did not represent faithfully the transactions, other events and conditions that it either purports to represent or could reasonably be expected to represent. Consequently, it would be likely to influence economic decisions made by users of financial statements. The paragraph establishes a rebuttable assumption that if other entities in similar circumstances apply the requirement of the standard, then the entity's compliance would not be so misleading that it would contradict the objective of financial statements in the *Framework*. Hence, when assessing whether non-compliance is supportable, management must assess whether the entity's circumstances differ from those of other entities that comply with the requirement.

Paragraphs 20–22 of IAS 1 address the disclosure requirements when an entity makes such a departure. In such circumstances, the entity must disclose (paragraph 20):

(a) that management has concluded that the financial statements present fairly the entity's financial position, financial performance and cash flows;
(b) that it has complied with applicable IFRSs, except that it has departed from a particular requirement to achieve fair presentation;
(c) the title of the IFRS from which the entity has departed, the nature of the departure, including the treatment that the IFRS would require, the reason why that treatment would be so misleading in the circumstances that it would conflict with the objective of financial statements set out in the *Framework*, and the treatment adopted; and
(d) for each period presented, the financial effect of the departure on each item in the financial statements that would have been reported in complying with the requirement.

Paragraph 21 of IAS 1 further requires that if a departure in a prior period affects the amounts recognised in the financial statements for the current period, the disclosures set out in (c) and (d) above are to be made.

For example, if a company had departed from the requirements of IAS 38 in a prior period by not amortising an intangible asset with a finite useful life, both assets and amortisation expense in subsequent periods would be affected.

In regulatory environments such as Australia where the regulatory framework prohibits the departure from the requirements of a standard or an interpretation, even in circumstances where compliance is considered to be so misleading that it would conflict with the objective of financial statements set out in the *Framework*, paragraph 23 of IAS 1 requires the following disclosures:

(a) the title of the IFRS in question, the nature of the requirement, and the reason why management has concluded that complying with that requirement is so misleading in the circumstances that it conflicts with the objective of financial statements set out in the *Framework*; and
(b) for each period presented, the adjustments to each item in the financial statements that management has concluded would be necessary to achieve fair presentation.

The ability to depart from an accounting standard in the circumstances envisaged by paragraph 19 has commonly been termed the 'true and fair view override', and has been the subject of much debate in the accounting profession. In Australia, for example, the regulatory environment does not permit a company to depart from accounting standards, and paragraph 19 does not appear in AASB 101, the Australian equivalent of IAS 1. However, Australian company legislation in the past did permit a true and fair view override. The override was removed in 1991 following concerns that companies were abusing the legislation, for example, to justify the use of questionable accounting policies that result in higher profit figures than would have been attained by applying the relevant accounting standard. This point illustrates the difficulty with paragraph 19 of IAS 1 — it is open to abuse because it allows for a subjective determination of what 'presents fairly' means. If the presumption that compliance with IFRSs results in fair presentation was applied, it would remove this area of subjectivity because all entities would then have to interpret the meaning of 'presents fairly' under the same framework.

Paragraph 19 also presents difficulties for auditors and users. Consider the examples shown in figure 17.1 of what could occur if paragraph 19 was retained.

Example 1

Company A and Company B have the same auditor, audit firm C. Company A and Company B operate in the same industry (retail of consumer products) in the same country. Both companies routinely use leases as a means of obtaining their distribution and operating facilities. Company A applies IAS 17 *Leases* and capitalises all leases that meet the definition of a finance lease. Company B decides that, although its leases meet the definition of a finance lease under IAS 17, capitalisation of these leases would not result in fair presentation under paragraph 19 of IAS 1. Accordingly, Company B departs from IAS 17.

Audit firm C must now decide whether it agrees with Company A or with Company B, since it is auditing both companies who have different interpretations of 'presents fairly' in exactly the same circumstances. If audit firm C agrees with Company A, then it would have to qualify its audit opinion on the financial statements of Company B on the basis that Company B has departed from IAS 17 and IAS 1. If audit firm C agrees with Company B, then it would have to qualify its audit opinion on the financial statements of Company A on the basis that Company A has, in complying with IAS 17, departed from IAS 1!

Example 2

Company A and Company B have different auditors. Audit firm X audits Company A and audit firm Z audits Company B. Company A and Company B operate in the same industry (retail of consumer products) in the same country. Both companies routinely use leases as a means of obtaining their distribution and operating facilities. Company A applies IAS 17 *Leases* and capitalises all leases that meet the definition of a finance lease. Company B decides that, although its leases meet the definition of a finance lease under IAS 17, capitalisation of these leases would not result in fair presentation under paragraph 19 of IAS 1. Accordingly, Company B departs from IAS 17.

Audit firm X agrees with Company A's interpretation of IAS 17 and IAS 1, and signs an unqualified audit opinion on the financial statements of Company A. Audit firm Z agrees with Company B and signs an unqualified audit opinion on the financial statements of Company B.

Ms Green is a shareholder of both companies. She reads the disclosures made by Company B in accordance with IAS 1 and the audit opinion of audit firm Z, and understands that Company B has departed from IAS 17 in order to provide a fair presentation of its financial statements, and that audit firm Z agrees with Company B because the audit report is unqualified. Ms Green then reads the financial statements of Company A and, because she cannot find any disclosure of a departure from IAS 17, correctly concludes that Company A has fully complied with IAS 17. Ms Green is confused, however, because she knows that both companies are very similar. She rings her financial adviser, who is similarly confused. They ring a student of external financial reporting, who explains the objective of financial reporting. Ms Green and her financial adviser explain the situation with Company A and Company B to the student. All three are now confused, because the objective of financial reporting seems not to have been met — they are unable to confidently make economic decisions about either company.

FIGURE 17.1 Examples of the difficulties of the subjective test of 'presents fairly'

Although the examples given in figure 17.1 might be considered extreme, they illustrate the practical difficulties in applying paragraph 17 of IAS 1. The requirements of IFRSs are unlikely to be perfect in all contexts. Nonetheless, it can be argued that it is better for financial statement users to know that a consistent framework has been applied by companies, and to be able to rely on that consistency in making their economic decisions, instead of having to deal with the uncertainty and inconsistency caused by the 'true and fair view override'.

2. Going concern

Paragraph 25 of IAS 1 states that financial statements shall be prepared on a going concern basis unless management intends to either liquidate the entity or cease trading, or has no realistic alternative but to do so. The IASB *Framework* sets out a similar underlying assumption. When management is aware of any material uncertainties that cast doubt upon the entity's ability to continue as a going concern, those uncertainties must be disclosed. When financial statements are not prepared on a going concern basis, that fact must be disclosed, together with the basis on which the financial statements are prepared and the reason why the entity is not regarded as a going concern. An example of this is where an entity has been placed in receivership and it is anticipated that liquidation will follow. In such circumstances, the financial statements would be prepared on a 'liquidation' basis, which means that assets and liabilities are measured at the amounts expected to be received or settled on liquidation. In the case of assets, this will often be a 'fire-sale' value rather than a fair market value; in the case of liabilities, some creditors may forgive the company's debts. It is more common for a company (and its auditors) to disclose uncertainty regarding the going concern assumption than to prepare the financial statements on a liquidation basis.

3. Accrual basis of accounting

Financial statements, except for the statement of cash flows, must be prepared using the accrual basis of accounting. This is discussed further in the IASB *Framework* (see chapter 1 of this book).

4. Consistency of presentation

Paragraph 45 of IAS 1 requires that the presentation and classification of items in the financial statements shall be retained from one period to the next unless:

> (a) it is apparent, following a significant change in the nature of the entity's operations or a review of its financial statements, that another presentation or classification would be more appropriate having regard to the criteria for the selection and application of accounting policies in IAS 8; or
> (b) an IFRS requires a change in presentation.

When such a change is made, the comparative information must also be reclassified. For example, an entity may present its assets and liabilities in current and non-current classifications, in accordance with paragraph 60 of IAS 1. However, paragraph 60 allows an entity to present its assets and liabilities in order of liquidity where this presentation is more reliable and relevant. Financial institutions, such as banks, typically present items on the statement of financial position in order of liquidity. If an entity begins to function like a financial institution after a change in the nature of its operations, it would be able to reclassify its assets and liabilities from the current/non-current presentation to the liquidity presentation, in accordance with paragraph 45.

5. Materiality and aggregation

Paragraph 7 of IAS 1 defines 'material' as follows:

> Omissions or misstatements of items are material if they could, individually or collectively, influence the economic decisions that users make on the basis of the financial statements. Materiality depends on the size and nature of the omission or misstatement judged in the surrounding circumstances. The size or nature of the item, or a combination of both, could be the determining factor.

Paragraph 29 states that each material class of similar items must be presented separately in the financial statements. Items of a dissimilar nature or function must be presented separately unless they are immaterial.

Financial statements result from processing large volumes of transactions that are then aggregated into classes according to their nature or function. These classes form the line items on the statement of financial position, statement of comprehensive income, statement of changes in equity, and statement of cash flows. IAS 1 specifies the minimum line items to be so presented; this is discussed in chapter 18.

6. Offsetting

IAS 1, paragraph 32, states that assets and liabilities, and income and expenses, shall not be offset unless required or permitted by a standard or interpretation. IAS 32 *Financial Instruments: Disclosure and Presentation* defines a right of set-off in respect of *financial* assets and liabilities (this is discussed further in chapter 5 of this book). Essentially, for items to be offset under IAS 32, there must be a *legal right* of set-off. This means that there must be a legal agreement documenting the right of the parties to settle amounts owed to/from each other on a net basis. IAS 1 is not as prescriptive in relation to other *non-financial* items. Rather, it implies that offsetting is undesirable unless it reflects the substance of transactions or events (para. 33). Paragraphs 34 and 35 then go on to identify situations where offsetting would be appropriate. These include the following:

- gains and losses on the disposal of non-current assets should be reported net, instead of separately reporting the gross proceeds as income and the cost of the asset disposed of as an expense

- expenditure related to a provision recognised in accordance with IAS 37 (see chapter 4) may be offset against an amount reimbursed under a contractual arrangement with a third party
- gains and losses arising from a group of similar transactions, such as gains and losses arising from foreign exchange or from financial instruments held for trading, should be reported net unless they are material. This means that a net gain or loss may be reported, rather than separately reporting the gains and the losses. However, a gain or loss must be reported separately if it is material.

Because IAS 1 is not prescriptive about offsetting, this will be an area of judgement and subjectivity. Interestingly, in Australia prior to its adoption of IFRSs, gains and losses on the disposal of non-current assets were not permitted to be reported net, because Australia had a *gross* definition of revenue that did not permit revenue to be determined on a net basis. Thus, the revenue would include the proceeds on disposal, and expenses would include the cost of the disposed asset.

7. Frequency of reporting

Financial statements must be prepared at least annually. If an entity's reporting period changes, the length of the reporting period will be greater or less than a year in the period of the change. For example, if an entity with a reporting period ending on 30 September changed its reporting period to end on 30 June, the first financial statements it prepares for the period ending 30 June would only cover a nine-month period. When this occurs, paragraph 36 of IAS 1 requires the entity to disclose the reason for the longer or shorter reporting period and the fact that the amounts presented in the financial statements are not entirely comparable.

8. Comparative information

IAS 1, paragraph 38, requires the disclosure of comparative information in respect of the previous period for all amounts reported in the financial statements. This extends to narrative information where the comparative narrative information remains relevant. An example of this would be details of a contingent liability, where the development of the issue over time is relevant to users. In addition, IAS 1 requires that when the presentation or classification of items in the financial statements is amended, comparative amounts should be reclassified. This excludes changes in accounting policies or corrections of errors, which are dealt with in IAS 8 (and addressed later in this chapter).

17.2.4 Structure and content of financial statements: general requirements

The financial statements must be identified clearly and distinguished from other information in the same published document. For example, a company generally prepares an annual report that contains details of the company's operations during the year, a chairman's review and so on. This information is usually glossy and colourful, with the financial statements appended at the back in a less colourful style. As a result, it is usually quite clear where the financial statements are, but IAS 1 still requires them to be clearly identified as financial statements.

Other general requirements (IAS 1, paragraphs 49–51) are:

- each component of the financial statements must be identified clearly (statement of financial position, statement of comprehensive income and so on)
- disclosure must be made of:
  - the name of the reporting entity and any change in that name from the preceding reporting date
  - whether the financial statements cover an individual entity or a group of entities
  - the reporting period or the date of the end of the reporting covered by the financial statements, whichever is appropriate to that component of the financial statements (the date of the end of the reporting period is appropriate for the statement of financial position, and the reporting period is appropriate to statements that report on flows such as the statement of comprehensive income)
  - the presentation currency, as defined in IAS 21 *The Effects of Changes in Foreign Exchange Rates*
  - the level of rounding used in presenting amounts in the financial statements

Paragraph 138 of IAS 1 requires an entity to disclose the following information in the notes (if it is not disclosed elsewhere in the financial statements):

> (a) the domicile and legal form of the entity, its country of incorporation and the address of its registered office (or principal place of business, if different from the registered office);

(b) a description of the nature of the entity's operations and its principal activities; and
(c) the name of the parent and the ultimate parent of the group.

17.3 IAS 8 *ACCOUNTING POLICIES, CHANGES IN ACCOUNTING ESTIMATES AND ERRORS*

The objective of IAS 8 is to prescribe the criteria for selecting and changing accounting policies, together with associated disclosures. IAS 8 is especially relevant where there is no specific standard or interpretation dealing with a particular transaction or event, and the entity must therefore decide on its own how to account for such a transaction or event.

17.3.1 Selecting and applying accounting policies

IAS 8, paragraph 5, defines 'accounting policies' as:

> the specific principles, bases, conventions, rules and practices applied by an entity in preparing and presenting financial statements.

IFRSs prescribe accounting policies for certain topics, transactions or events. IAS 8 deals with areas where there are no accounting standards, and sets out the principles that entities must apply in selecting appropriate accounting policies. Paragraph 10 of IAS 8 specifies that where there is no standard dealing with a particular transaction, preparers should use judgement in developing and applying accounting policies so that the resulting information is:

(a) relevant to the economic decision-making needs of users; and
(b) reliable, in that the financial statements:
  (i) represent faithfully the financial position, financial performance and cash flows of the entity;
  (ii) reflect the economic substance of transactions, other events and conditions, and not merely the legal form;
  (iii) are neutral, i.e. free from bias;
  (iv) are prudent; and
  (v) are complete in all material respects.

The concept of substance over form is particularly important. This is an area revealed as a weakness in the rule-based approach to standard setting used by the United States and implicated in some of the corporate collapses in that country in 2001 and 2002. Transactions that were, in substance, financing transactions were accounted for as sales, applying very literal interpretations of the US rules. Applying the principle of substance over form should result in transactions being accounted for appropriately. The accounting treatment of finance leases provides an example of applying the principle of substance over form. While the form of the transaction is a lease, its economic substance is comparable to the purchase of the leased property, combined with a loan payable by instalments. Accordingly, in applying the principle of substance over form, IAS 17 requires finance leases to be capitalised by recognising the leased property as an asset, and the corresponding obligation arising from the lease as a liability.

Paragraphs 11 and 12 of IAS 8 go on to explain what is commonly termed the 'hierarchy' of relevant sources of information to be used by management in selecting and applying accounting policies:

> 11. In making the judgement described in paragraph 10, management shall refer to, and consider the applicability of, the following sources in descending order:
> (a) the requirements and guidance in IFRSs dealing with similar and related issues; and
> (b) the definitions, recognition criteria and measurement concepts for assets, liabilities, income and expenses in the *Framework*.
>
> 12. In making the judgement described in paragraph 10, management may also consider the most recent pronouncements of other standard setting bodies that use a similar conceptual framework to develop accounting standards, other accounting literature and accepted industry practices, to the extent that these do not conflict with the sources in paragraph 11.

In the United States there are numerous detailed rules on how to account for specific transactions. In contrast, the IFRSs are generally principle-based standards and do not specify how to account for each and every type of transaction. An entity may find detailed guidance on how to account for a specific transaction in the rules of the US Emerging Issues Task Force (EITF), for example, but it may apply that EITF rule only if it is consistent with the IASB standards and the *Framework*.

Paragraph 13 of IAS 8 requires that an entity must apply accounting policies consistently for similar transactions, events or conditions unless otherwise required by an accounting standard.

17.3.2 Distinguishing between accounting policies, accounting estimates and errors

Accounting for a change in accounting policy is not a straightforward exercise. IAS 8 contains detailed measurement and disclosure requirements for changes in accounting policies as well as for changes in accounting estimates. It also specifies how errors must be accounted for. Before dealing with changes in these items, it is necessary to differentiate between them.

The term *accounting policy* refers to principles or conventions applied in preparing the financial statements, such as using the straight-line method of depreciation for property, plant and equipment. By contrast, an accounting *estimate* is a judgement applied in determining the carrying amount of an item in the financial statements such as an estimate of the useful life of a depreciable asset. The use of reasonable estimates is an essential part of the process of preparing financial statements because many elements of the financial statements — such as provisions for warranties — cannot be calculated with precision. So, for example, an entity's accounting *policy* in respect of warranties may be that it always makes a provision for warranty claims based on history, the volume of sales and the length of outstanding warranty periods. The *calculation* of the amount of the warranty provision is then an accounting *estimate* that applies this accounting policy.

An 'error' is an omission or misstatement in the financial statements. Errors may arise from mathematical mistakes, mistakes in applying accounting policies, oversights or misinterpretations of facts, and fraud (IAS 8, para. 5). For example, assume Company C owns a building from which it derives rental income. In testing for impairment, Company C measures the value in use of the building by discounting future rental income. The amount of rental income should be reduced by any waivers of rent allowed to tenants such as rent-free periods offered to new tenants. Assume that in measuring the value in use in a prior period, the cash inflows foregone from rent-free periods were added to annual rentals, instead of being deducted, and that this resulted in an overstated carrying amount of the building. When the overstatement of the asset is discovered in a subsequent period, it would be necessary to correct the prior-period amount. The misstatement would be classified as an error in the prior-period financial statements because it results from a mistake in the application of information that was available at the time. In contrast, if, in hindsight, the building was found to have been overstated because the estimated rental growth rates used in a prior period were too high, the subsequent restatement of the carrying amount of the building would be treated as a change of accounting estimate.

17.3.3 Changes in accounting policies

IAS 8, paragraph 14, specifies only two circumstances in which an entity is permitted to change an accounting policy. These are:

- if the change is *required* by an IFRS; or
- if the change, *made voluntarily*, results in the financial statements providing reliable and more relevant information about the effects of transactions, other events or conditions on the entity's financial position, financial performance or cash flows.

However, the initial application of a policy to revalue assets in accordance with IAS 16 *Property, Plant and Equipment* or IAS 38 *Intangible Assets* must be accounted for as a revaluation in accordance with those standards and not as a change in accounting policy under IAS 8. Note that this applies to the *initial* application of a revaluation policy only. IAS 8 would apply if an entity initially chooses the revaluation method under IAS 16 or IAS 38, and then changes to the cost method at a later date.

Where an entity changes an accounting policy because it is required to do so, it must account for that change as set out in the specific transitional provisions of the relevant accounting standard requiring the change. If the accounting standard does not specify how to account for the change, then the change must be applied *retrospectively*. Retrospective application is also required for all voluntary changes in accounting policy (IAS 8, para. 19). Retrospective application means applying a new accounting policy to transactions, other events and conditions as if that policy had always been applied (para. 5). When an entity applies the change retrospectively, the entity must adjust the *opening* balance of each affected component of equity for the earliest prior period presented, and the other comparative amounts disclosed for each prior period must be presented as if the new accounting policy had always been applied (para. 22).

Illustrative example 17.1 shows how to apply a change in accounting policy retrospectively.

ILLUSTRATIVE EXAMPLE 17.1

Applying a change in accounting policy retrospectively

During 2010, Company A changed its accounting policy for training costs in order to comply with IAS 38. Previously, Company A had capitalised certain training costs. Under IAS 38, it cannot capitalise training costs and, according to the transitional provisions of the standard, it must apply the change in accounting policy retrospectively.

During 2009, Company A had capitalised training costs of $6000. In periods before 2009, it had capitalised training costs of $12 000. In 2010, it incurred training costs of $4500.

Company A's statement of comprehensive income for 2009 reported profit of $49 000 after income taxes of $21 000. Its statement of comprehensive income for 2010 reported profit of $56 000 after income taxes of $24 000. The training costs of $4500 were expensed in 2010.

Company A's retained earnings were $600 000 at the beginning of 2009 and $649 000 at the end of 2009. It had $100 000 in share capital throughout 2009 and 2010, representing 100 000 ordinary shares, and there were no other reserves.

Company A's tax rate was 30% for both periods. Its reporting period ends on 30 June.

Applying the change in accounting policy retrospectively, Company A's statement of comprehensive income for 2010, with comparative figures, shows the following:

	2010 $	2009 (restated) $
Profit before income taxes	80 000	64 000[1]
Less Income taxes	24 000	19 200[2]
Profit for the period	56 000	44 800
other items of comprehensive income	—	—
comprehensive income	56 000	44 800

Company A's statement of changes in equity is as follows:

	Share capital $	Retained earnings $	Total $
Balance at 30 June 2008 as previously reported	100 000	600 000	700 000
Change in accounting policy for capitalisation of training costs		(8 400)[3]	(8 400)
Balance at 30 June 2008 as restated	100 000	591 600	691 600
Comprehensive income for the year ended 30 June 2009 (restated)		44 800	44 800
Balance at 30 June 2009	100 000	636 400	736 400
Comprehensive for the year ended 30 June 2010		56 000	56 000
Balance at 30 June 2010	100 000	692 400	792 400

Notes:

1. Being $70 000 – $6000
2. Being $21 000 – $6000 × 30%
3. Being $12 000 × (1–30%)

Paragraphs 23–25 of IAS 8 deal with circumstances where retrospective application of a change in accounting policy is impracticable and thus cannot be applied. 'Impracticable' in the context of IAS 8 means that 'the entity cannot apply it after making every reasonable effort to do so' (para. 5). For example, the retrospective application of an accounting policy would be impracticable if it required assumptions about what management's intent might have been at a prior point in time. Hindsight is not used when applying a new accounting policy retrospectively. For example, an asset measured on the fair value basis retrospectively should be measured at the fair value as at the date of the retrospective adjustment and should not take into account subsequent events. When it is impracticable for an entity to apply a new accounting policy retrospectively because it cannot determine the cumulative effect of applying the policy to all prior periods, the entity should apply the new policy prospectively from the start of the earliest period practicable. This may be the current period.

Extensive disclosures are required when an entity changes its accounting policy. These are separated between mandatary changes and voluntary changes, as follows:

> 28. When initial application of an IFRS has an effect on the current period or any prior period, would have such an effect except that it is impracticable to determine the amount of the adjustment, or might have an effect on future periods, an entity shall disclose:
> (a) the title of the IFRS;
> (b) when applicable, that the change in accounting policy is made in accordance with its transitional provisions;
> (c) the nature of the change in accounting policy;
> (d) when applicable, a description of the transitional provisions;
> (e) when applicable, the transitional provisions that might have an effect on future periods;
> (f) for the current period and each prior period presented, to the extent practicable, the amount of the adjustment:
> (i) for each financial statement line item affected; and
> (ii) if IAS 33 *Earnings per Share* applies to the entity, for basic and diluted earnings per share;
> (g) the amount of the adjustment relating to periods before those presented, to the extent practicable; and
> (h) if retrospective application required by paragraph 19(a) or (b) is impracticable for a particular prior period, or for periods before those presented, the circumstances that led to the existence of that condition and a description of how and from when the change in accounting policy has been applied.
>
> Financial statements of subsequent periods need not repeat these disclosures.
>
> 29. When a voluntary change in accounting policy has an effect on the current period or any prior period, would have an effect on that period except that it is impracticable to determine the amount of the adjustment, or might have an effect on future periods, an entity shall disclose:
> (a) the nature of the change in accounting policy;
> (b) the reasons why applying the new accounting policy provides reliable and more relevant information;
> (c) for the current period and each prior period presented, to the extent practicable, the amount of the adjustment:
> (i) for each financial statement line item affected; and
> (ii) if IAS 33 applies to the entity, for basic and diluted earnings per share;
> (d) the amount of the adjustment relating to periods before those presented, to the extent practicable; and
> (e) if retrospective application is impracticable for a particular prior period, or for periods before those presented, the circumstances that led to the existence of that condition and a description of how and from when the change in accounting policy has been applied.
>
> Financial statements of subsequent periods need not repeat these disclosures.

IAS 1, paragraph 106(b), also requires that the statement of changes in equity disclose the effects of changes in accounting policies and the correction of errors for each component of equity.

Following on from illustrative example 17.1, illustrative example 17.2 shows the additional disclosures required.

17.3.4 Changes in accounting estimates

As discussed in section 17.3.2, an accounting estimate is a judgement applied in determining the carrying amount of an item in the financial statements. An estimate may need revision if changes occur in the circumstances on which the estimate was based, or as a result of new information

ILLUSTRATIVE EXAMPLE 17.2

Additional disclosures for the change in accounting policy shown in illustrative example 17.1

For the year ended 30 June 2010, Company A applied IAS 38 *Intangible Assets* for the first time. As a result, certain training expenses that had been capitalised in the past were expensed. In accordance with the transitional provisions of IAS 38, the change in accounting policy was applied retrospectively. The comparative financial statements for 2009 have been restated. The effect of the change for each line item affected is tabulated below:

	Effect on 2009 $
(Decrease) in profit before tax	(6 000)
Decrease in income tax expense	1 800
(Decrease) in profit for the period	(4 200)
(Decrease) in comprehensive income	(4 200)
(Decrease) in intangible assets	(6 000)
Decrease in deferred tax liabilities	1 800
(Decrease) in retained earnings as at 30 June 2009	(12 600)[1]

	Effect on periods prior to 2009 $
(Decrease) in profit for the period	(8 400)[2]
(Decrease) in comprehensive income	(8 400)
(Decrease) in intangible assets	(12 000)
Decrease in deferred tax liabilities	3 600

Adjusted basic and diluted earnings per share for 2009 were 44.8 cents. Reported earnings per share for 2009 was 49 cents.

Notes:

1. Per illustrative example 17.1, original closing retained earnings were $649 000 and adjusted closing retained earnings were $636 400. The difference is $12 600.
2. This amount has been adjusted against opening retained earnings at 1 July 2008.

or more experience. Paragraph 36 of IAS 8 requires that a change in estimate be accounted for *prospectively*. Paragraph 5 explains that prospective application means:

- applying the new accounting estimate to transactions or events occurring after the date the estimate is changed; and
- recognising the effect of the change in the current and future periods affected by the change.

Paragraph 37 of IAS 8 goes on to state that if the change in estimate affects assets, liabilities or equity, then the carrying amounts of those items shall be adjusted in the period of the change. Paragraphs 39 and 40 contain the disclosure requirements for a change in an accounting estimate:

> 39. An entity shall disclose the nature and amount of a change in an accounting estimate that has an effect in the current period or is expected to have an effect in future periods, except for the disclosure of the effect on future periods when it is impracticable to estimate that effect.
> 40. If the amount of the effect in future periods is not disclosed because estimating it is impracticable, an entity shall disclose that fact.

Illustrative example 17.3 demonstrates accounting for a change in accounting estimate, and the relevant disclosures.

ILLUSTRATIVE EXAMPLE 17.3

Accounting for a change in accounting estimate, and relevant disclosures

Company Z has historically depreciated its factory plant and equipment over 15 years. In 2010, Company Z's directors determined that, due to technological developments in its industry, the factory plant and equipment should be depreciated over a shorter period: 10 years. Company Z's reporting period ends on 30 June.

As at 1 July 2009, the balance of factory plant and equipment was as follows:

	$
Cost	150 000
Accumulated depreciation	(40 000)
Carrying amount	110 000

For the year ended 30 June 2010, Company Z's depreciation expense will be $18 333. This is calculated as $110 000/6 (being the carrying amount of the asset at the date of the change in estimate, divided by the remaining useful life). Since the total useful life is reassessed to 10 years, and four years have already elapsed, the remaining useful life is six years.

Extract from Company Z's financial statements for the year ended 30 June 2010:
Company Z has historically depreciated its factory plant and equipment over 15 years. As at 1 July 2009, the company's directors determined that, due to technological developments in its industry, the factory plant and equipment should be depreciated over a shorter period, being 10 years. The effect of the change in accounting estimate in the current period is an increase in depreciation expense and accumulated depreciation of $8333. In future periods, annual depreciation expense will be $18 333.

17.3.5 Correction of errors

As discussed in section 17.3.2, an 'error' is an omission or misstatement in the financial statements. Errors may arise from mathematical mistakes, mistakes in applying accounting policies, oversights or misinterpretations of facts, and fraud (IAS 8, para. 5). If an error is discovered in a subsequent period, paragraph 42 states that the error must be corrected retrospectively by:

- restating the comparative amounts for the prior period/s presented in which the error occurred; or
- if the error occurred before the earliest prior period presented, restating the opening balances of assets, liabilities and equity for the earliest prior period presented.

As with changes in accounting policy, retrospective restatement is required unless it is impracticable to do so (paras 43–45). Similar disclosures are required for correction of errors as for changes in accounting policy (para. 49).

In practice, a change in accounting policy occurs more often than the correction of an error. Remember that the error must be material to the financial statements (IAS 8, paras 5 and 6), materiality being defined according to whether or not the omission or misstatement could influence the economic decisions of users. Materiality depends on the size and the nature of the item. If an error is material, the company and its auditors will usually suffer embarrassment, reputation damage or even litigation as a result of the restatement.

17.4 IAS 10 *EVENTS AFTER THE REPORTING PERIOD*

The objective of IAS 10 is to prescribe when an entity should adjust its financial statements for events after the reporting period, and what disclosures the entity should make about events after the reporting period.

IAS 10, paragraph 3, defines an *event after the reporting period* as one that occurs after the end of the reporting period but before the date on which the financial statements are authorised for issue. An event after the reporting period may be favourable or unfavourable. Paragraph 3 categorises events after the reporting period as being either adjusting events of non-adjusting events. An adjusting event is one that provides further evidence of conditions that existed at the end of the reporting period, and can include an event that indicates that the going concern assumption may be inappropriate. A non-adjusting event after the reporting period is one that indicates conditions that arose after the end of the reporting period, such as the unintended destruction of property that existed at the end of the reporting period.

Usually the date at which financial statements are authorised for issue is the date on which the directors or other governing body formally approve the financial statements for issue to shareholders and/or other users. The fact that subsequent ratification by the shareholders at an annual meeting is required does not mean that the date of authorisation for issue is at that later ratification date.

17.4.1 Adjusting events after the reporting period

Paragraph 8 of IAS 10 requires an entity to adjust the amounts recognised in its financial statements to reflect adjusting events after the reporting period. Examples of adjusting events after the reporting period include the following:

- The receipt of information after the reporting period indicates that an asset was impaired as at the end of the reporting period. This may occur, for example, if a trade receivable recorded at the end of the reporting period is shown to be irrecoverable because of the insolvency of the customer that occurs after the reporting period.
- The sale of inventories after the reporting period may give evidence of their net realisable value at the end of the reporting period.
- The settlement after the reporting period of a court case confirms that the entity had a present obligation at the end of the reporting period. The entity adjusts any previously recognised provision related to this court case in accordance with IAS 37 *Provisions, Contingent Liabilities and Contingent Assets* or recognises a new provision. (See chapter 4 of this book for further details.)

Illustrative example 17.4 shows how an adjusting event after the reporting period is accounted for.

ILLUSTRATIVE EXAMPLE 17.4

Accounting for an adjusting event after the reporting period

Company B is a retailer with a reporting period that ends on 30 June. In its financial statements for the year ended 30 June 2010, Company B included revenue and a receivable of $35 000 in respect of a large customer, Company R. On 31 July 2010, before the financial statements were authorised for issue, Company B was advised by the liquidator of Company R that Company R was insolvent and would be unable to repay the full amount owed to Company B. The liquidator advised Company B in writing that she would be paying all of Company R's creditors 10 cents in the dollar for every dollar owed. The liquidator estimated that the amount would be paid in November 2010. Company B's financial statements were authorised for issue by the directors on 25 August 2010.

In accordance with IAS 8, the insolvency of Company R is an adjusting event after the reporting period because it provides further evidence of the amount recognised as at 30 June 2010. Because the liquidator has confirmed in writing that $3500 will be paid in settlement, Company B will adjust the receivable from $35 000 to $3500 as follows:

Expenses	Dr	31 500	
Receivables	Cr		31 500
(Impairment of receivable)			

Company B will need to reassess the carrying amount of this receivable at the end of the reporting period. If, at the end of the next reporting period, the liquidator has not settled the amount, Company B may need to write off the receivable or, at a minimum, transfer it to non-current receivables, depending on the evidence available to support recoverability of the amount.

17.4.2 Non-adjusting events after the reporting period

Paragraph 10 of IAS 10 states that an entity shall not adjust the amounts recognised in its financial statements to reflect non-adjusting events after the reporting period. Examples of non-adjusting events include:

- a major business combination after the reporting period
- the destruction of property by fire after the reporting period
- the issuance of new share capital after the reporting period
- commencing major litigation arising solely out of events that occurred after the reporting period.

Although these events are not adjusted for, paragraph 21 of IAS 10 requires the following disclosure:

> If non-adjusting events after the reporting period are material, non-disclosure could influence the economic decisions of users taken on the basis of the financial statements. Accordingly, an entity shall disclose the following for each material category of non-adjusting event after the reporting period:
> (a) the nature of the event; and
> (b) an estimate of its financial effect, or a statement that such an estimate cannot be made.

Paragraph 11 of IAS 10 refers to a controversial area of accounting for events after the reporting period. It states that a decline in the market value of investments between the end of the reporting period and the date when the financial statements are authorised for issue is a non-adjusting event, because the decline in market value does not normally relate to the condition of the investments at the end of the reporting period but instead reflects circumstances that have arisen subsequently. However, it could just as easily be argued that the same applies in the case of the receivables referred to in paragraph 9(b)(i) of IAS 10, regarding the insolvency of a debtor after the reporting period. IAS 10 paragraph 9(b)(i) states that this would constitute an adjusting event because the insolvency confirms that a loss existed at the end of the reporting period. This is not necessarily true because the debtor may well have been solvent at the end of the reporting period. However, the critical issue here is the amount and uncertainty of the future cash flows arising from the receivable, not whether the debtor was insolvent at the end of the reporting period. There may have been some concerns about collectibility at the end of the reporting period. The additional information about the debtor's insolvency provides further evidence that it was impaired and enable a better assessment of the extent of impairment.

The same applies to example 9(b)(ii) of IAS 10, regarding the sale of inventories after the reporting period. The issue is what are the *conditions* referred to in paragraph 3. Are they (1) subsequent events that provide further evidence about the *measurement* of items such as receivables, investments and inventories which existed at the end of the reporting period, even if the evidence in relation to measurement occurred after the reporting period; or (2) must the evidence in relation to measurement have existed at the end of the reporting period? It is submitted that (1) is the correct interpretation, which is applied in the examples in paragraph 9. Again, the sale of inventories may provide evidence of net realisable value that existed but was unknown at the end of the reporting period. However, for assets, such as investments in securities that are traded in an active market, the market value at the reporting date would have been observable. Thus, the position taken in paragraph 11 is that the change in market value of the securities observed after the reporting period is indicative of conditions that arose after the reporting period, and, as such, it is a non-adjusting event after the reporting period.

17.4.3 Other disclosures

IAS 10 also requires other disclosures, namely:

- disclosure of the date the financial statements were authorised for issue (para. 17)
- updating disclosure about conditions at the end of the reporting period (para. 19).

SUMMARY

IAS 1 *Presentation of Financial Statements*, IAS 8 *Accounting Policies, Changes in Accounting Estimates and Errors* and IAS 10 *Events after the Reporting Period* are largely disclosure standards, although IAS 8 and IAS 10 also contain certain measurement requirements. These standards deal with fundamental disclosures and considerations that underpin financial statement presentation.

IAS 1 prescribes the components of financial statements, overall considerations to be applied in the preparation of financial statements, and the structure and content of financial statements. IAS 8 distinguishes between accounting policies, accounting estimates and errors, and prescribes different requirements for each, particularly when there is a change. Any change in accounting policy must be applied retrospectively. Any change in an accounting estimate must be recognised prospectively. A correction of an error must be recognised, wherever possible, in the period when the error occurred.

IAS 10 distinguishes between two types of events after the reporting period — adjusting and non-adjusting. Adjusting events must be recognised in the financial statements, whereas non-adjusting events must be disclosed only.

Discussion questions

1. Discuss the eight overall considerations to be applied in the presentation of financial statements. Of these, which are more subjective? Explain your answer.
2. Why is it important for entities to disclose the measurement bases used in preparing the financial statements?
3. Explain the difference between retrospective application of a change in accounting policy and prospective application of a change in accounting estimate. Why do you think the standard setters require prospective application of a change in accounting estimate?
4. Explain the difference between adjusting and non-adjusting events after the reporting period. Give examples to illustrate your answer.
5. What comprises a complete set of financial statements in accordance with IAS 1?
6. What is the difference between an accounting policy and an accounting estimate?

STAR RATING
★ BASIC
★★ MODERATE
★★★ DIFFICULT

Exercises

Exercise 17.1 ★

FAIR PRESENTATION

Under what circumstances can an entity depart from IFRSs? Are these circumstances expected to be common or rare? Explain your answer.

Exercise 17.2 ★

FAIR PRESENTATION

Both Company A and Company B are manufacturers of plastic pipes. Company A complies with all IFRSs. Company B wishes to depart from IAS 39 in respect of hedge accounting, on the basis that compliance with the hedge accounting rules would result in Company B's reported profit being misleading. Both Company A and Company B operate in a country whose regulatory framework permits departures from IFRSs. Must Company B have regard to Company A's accounting policies in making its decision to depart from IAS 39?

Exercise 17.3 ★

CONSISTENCY, MATERIALITY AND AGGREGATION

State whether each of the following statements is true or false:

(a) A material item is determined solely on the basis of its size.
(b) A class of assets or liabilities is determined by reference to items of a similar nature or function.
(c) Inventories and trade accounts receivable may be aggregated in the statement of financial position.
(d) Cash and cash equivalents may be aggregated in the statement of financial position.

Exercise 17.4 ★★

MATERIALITY, OFFSETTING

Company A is a retailer that imports about 30% of its goods. The following foreign exchange gains and losses were recognised during the year:

	Loss $m	Gain $m
Foreign currency borrowings with Bank L	50	
Forward exchange contracts used as hedging instruments		1
Forward exchange contracts not used as hedges	3	
Foreign currency borrowings with Bank S		10

Required

Identify which of the above gains and losses are permitted to be offset in Company A's financial statements. Assume that materiality has been determined as $5 million for profit and loss purposes.

Exercise 17.5

ACCOUNTING POLICIES, ACCOUNTING ESTIMATES

★★

State whether each of the following is an accounting policy or an accounting estimate for Company A:

(a) The useful life of depreciable plant is determined as being six years.

(b) Company A's management determines that it will provide for all invoices in transit as at the end of the reporting period.

(c) Company A determines that it will calculate its warranty provision using past experience of defective products.

(d) The current year's warranty provision is calculated by providing for 1% of current year sales, based on last year's warranty claimed amounting to 1% of sales.

Exercise 17.6

ACCOUNTING POLICIES, ACCOUNTING ESTIMATES, ERRORS

★★

State whether the following changes should be accounted for retrospectively or prospectively:

(a) A change in accounting policy made voluntarily.

(b) A change in accounting policy required by an accounting standard.

(c) A change in an accounting estimate.

(d) An immaterial error discovered in the current year, relating to a transaction recorded two years ago.

(e) A material error discovered in the current year, relating to a transaction recorded two years ago. Management determines that retrospective application would cause undue cost and effort.

(f) A change in accounting policy required by an accounting standard. Retrospective application of that standard would require assumptions about what management's intent would have been in the relevant period(s).

Exercise 17.7

ADJUSTING/NON-ADJUSTING POST-BALANCE DATE EVENTS

★★★

State whether each of the following would be an adjusting or non-adjusting event after the reporting period in the financial statements of Company N. The financial statements of Company N are authorised for issue on 12 August 2010, and the end of the reporting period is 30 June 2010.

(a) At 30 June, Company N had recorded $40 000 owed by Company P, which is due on 31 August. On 16 July, a receiver was appointed to Company P. The receiver informed Company N that the $40 000 would be paid in full by 30 September 2010.

(b) On 24 July, Company N issued a corporate bond of $1 million, paying interest of 5% semi-annually in arrears.

(c) Company N measures its investments in listed shares as held-for-trading at fair value through profit or loss in accordance with IAS 39. As at 30 June, these investments were recorded at the market value at that date, which was $500 000. During the period leading up to 12 August 2010, there was a steady decline in the market values of all the shares in the portfolio, and at 12 August 2010 the fair value of the investments had fallen to $400 000.

(d) Company A had reported a contingent liability at 30 June 2010 in respect of a court case in which Company A was the defendant. The case was not heard until the first week of August. On 11 August, the judge handed down her decision, against Company A. The judge determined that Company A was liable to pay damages and costs totalling $3 million.

(e) As in part (d), except that the damages and costs awarded against Company A were $50 million, leading Company A to place itself into voluntary liquidation.

Problems

Problem 17.1

CHANGE IN ACCOUNTING ESTIMATE

★★

Company H has historically depreciated its administration buildings over 15 years. In 2010, Company H's directors reviewed the depreciation rates for similar buildings used in its industry.

Consequently, they decided that the buildings should be depreciated over a longer period, being 20 years. Company H's reporting period ends on 30 June.

As at 1 July 2009, the balance of administration buildings was as follows:

	$
Cost	5 000 000
Accumulated depreciation	(1 666 667)
Carrying amount	3 333 333

Required

Prepare the note describing Company H's change in accounting estimate for the year ended 30 June 2010, including comparative figures, in accordance with IAS 8. Show all workings.

Problem 17.2 ★★★ CHANGE IN ACCOUNTING POLICY — COMPREHENSIVE PROBLEM

During 2010, Company A changed its accounting policy for measuring property assets. Until 30 June 2009, Company A had been applying the cost model under IAS 16 *Property, Plant and Equipment*. On 1 July 2009, the company's directors determined that the revaluation model would be more relevant and reliable, given that the fair value of the properties could be measured reliably.

Company A had been depreciating the property over its useful life of 20 years. There was no change to the estimate of useful life when the change in accounting policy was made.

Relevant balances in Company A's financial statements were as follows:

	30 June 2010 $	30 June 2009 $
Property assets — at cost	6 000 000	6 000 000
Accumulated depreciation	(1 500 000)	(1 200 000)
Carrying amount	4 500 000	4 800 000
Retained earnings	67 000 000	64 000 000
Share capital	40 000 000	40 000 000

Additional information

- Company A's statement of comprehensive income for 2009 reported a profit of $3 million after income taxes of $1 285 714.
- Company A's statement of comprehensive income for 2010 reported a profit of $3.5 million, after income taxes of $1.5 million and before the application of the change in accounting policy.
- The fair value of the property assets was determined by an independent valuer to be $7 800 000 as at 30 June 2009, and $6 800 000 as at 30 June 2008. No reliable measure could be determined for earlier periods. There was no change in fair value as at 30 June 2010.
- Company A's tax rate was 30% for both periods. Its reporting period ends on 30 June, and it includes one year's comparative figures in its financial statements.

Required

Prepare the note disclosing the change in accounting policy for Company A's financial statements for the year ended 30 June 2010. Include a full statement of changes in equity. Show comparative figures and all workings. Break down your workings as follows:

1. Calculate the age of the asset.
2. Calculate the increase in the carrying amount of the asset (from depreciated cost to revalued amount).

3. Calculate the revised depreciation of the asset, based on the new carrying amount and the remaining life of the asset.
4. Prepare the note disclosure in accordance with IAS 8.
5. Note that the change in the asset revaluation reserve is a component of comprehensive income but is not included in profit for the period.

18 Presentation of financial statements

ACCOUNTING STANDARDS IN FOCUS

IAS 1 *Presentation of Financial Statements*

LEARNING OBJECTIVES

When you have studied this chapter, you should be able to:

- understand the purpose of a statement of financial position and its limitations
- understand and apply the requirements for the classification of terms reported in the statement of financial position
- understand and apply the requirements for the presentation of information in the statement of financial position or in the notes
- understand the purpose of a statement of comprehensive income and its limitations
- understand and apply the requirements for the presentation of information in the statement of comprehensive income or in the notes
- understand the purpose of a statement of changes in equity
- understand and apply the requirements for the presentation of information in the statement of changes in equity or in the notes
- understand and apply the requirements relating to the notes to financial statements.

18.1 PRESENTATION OF FINANCIAL STATEMENTS

The overall principles and other considerations relating to the presentation of financial statements as contained in IAS 1 *Presentation of Financial Statements* are addressed in chapter 17. This chapter deals with detailed matters relating to the presentation of a statement of financial position (balance sheet), statement of comprehensive income (income statement), statement of changes in equity and notes. IAS 1 prescribes the structure and minimum content of these statements and notes. Other International Financial Reporting Standards (IFRSs) mandate disclosures relating to specific financial statement elements and transactions and events, as well as their recognition and measurement. Specific required disclosures relevant to the topics of the various chapters of this book are outlined in those chapters.

18.2 SCOPE

IAS 1 applies to all general purpose financial statements prepared and presented in accordance with IFRSs, except that its requirements relating to the structure and content of financial statements are not applicable to condensed interim financial statements. The structure and content requirements of condensed interim financial statements are contained in IAS 34 *Interim Financial Reporting*. The requirements of IAS 1 that deal with the frequency of reporting, comparative information and consistency of presentation also do not apply to condensed interim financial statements. The requirements of IAS 1 apply to the separate financial statements of entities, as well as consolidated financial statements, which are required to be prepared under IAS 27 *Consolidated and Separate Financial Statements.*

Paragraph 5 of IAS 1 explains that the terminology used in IAS 1 is suitable for profit-oriented entities, including public sector business entities. However, if IAS 1 is applied to entities with not-for-profit activities in the private or public sectors there may be a need to amend the descriptions used for particular line items in the financial statements and for the financial statements themselves.

18.3 STATEMENT OF FINANCIAL POSITION

18.3.1 The purpose of a statement of financial position

A major purpose of financial statements is to provide information about an entity's financial position. The statement of financial position of an entity is the prime source of information about the entity's financial position because it summarises the elements directly related to the measurement of financial position: an entity's assets, liabilities and equity. It thus provides the basic information for evaluating an entity's capital structure and analysing its liquidity, solvency and financial flexibility. It also provides a basis for computing rates of return (e.g. return on total assets and equity and measures of solvency and liquidity).

However, the view of an entity's financial position presented by the statement of financial position is by no means perfect and is often criticised by some commentators as being of limited value. These limitations primarily arise from:

- the optional measurement of certain assets at historical cost or depreciated historical cost rather than at a current value (refer to chapter 9 for further details)
- the mandatory omission of intangible self-generated assets from the statement of financial position as a result of the recognition and measurement requirements of IAS 38 *Intangible Assets*. Significant examples include successful research expenditure, brand names and mastheads (refer to chapter 10 for further details)
- financial engineering that frequently leads to off-balance-sheet rights and obligations. A significant example is that the rights and obligations pertaining to non-cancellable operating leases are not recognised on the statement of financial position (refer to chapter 13 for further details).

Because of these limitations the statement of financial position should be read in conjunction with the notes to the financial statements.

18.3.2 Statement of financial position classifications

The statement of financial position presents a structured summary of the assets, liabilities and equity of an entity. Assets and liabilities are classified in a manner that facilitates the evaluation of an entity's financial structure and its liquidity, solvency and financial flexibility. Consequently, assets and liabilities are classified according to their function in the operations of the entity concerned and their liquidity and financial flexibility characteristics.

Paragraph 60 of IAS 1 requires an entity to classify assets and liabilities as current or non-current in its statement of financial position, except when a presentation based on liquidity is considered to provide more relevant and reliable information. When that exception arises, all assets and liabilities are required to be presented broadly in order of liquidity.

The current/non-current classification is ordinarily considered to be more relevant when an entity has a clearly identifiable operating cycle. This is because it distinguishes between those assets and liabilities that are expected to circulate within the entity's operating cycle and those used in the entity's long-term operations. The typical cycle operates from cash, purchase of inventory (in the case of a manufacturer, production) and then receivables through sales of inventory and finally back to cash through collection of the receivables. The average time of the operating cycle varies with the nature of the operations making up the cycle and may extend beyond 12 months. Industries where long operating cycles may exist include construction, agriculture (such as plantation development) and property development.

Figure 18.1 shows the assets classified as current in the consolidated balance sheet of BHP Billiton at 30 June 2008, while figure 18.2 shows the liabilities classified as current.

	Notes	2008 US$M	2007 Restated US$M
Current assets			
Cash and cash equivalents	30	4 237	2 449
Trade and other receivables	11	9 801	6 239
Other financial assets	12	2 054	1 059
Inventories	13	4 971	3 744
Other		498	265
Total current assets		21 561	13 756

FIGURE 18.1 Current assets of BHP Billiton at 30 June 2008
Source: BHP Billiton (2008, p. 167).

	Notes	2008 US$M	2007 Restated US$M
Current liabilities			
Trade and other payables	17	6 774	5 137
Interest bearing liabilities	18	3 461	1 640
Other financial liabilities	19	2 088	655
Current tax payable		2 022	2 193
Provisions	20	1 596	1 383
Deferred income		418	299
Total current liabilities		16 359	11 307

FIGURE 18.2 Current liabilities of BHP Billiton at 30 June 2008
Source: BHP Billiton (2008, p. 167).

Paragraph 63 of IAS 1 explains that for entities such as financial institutions a presentation based broadly on order of liquidity is usually considered to be more relevant than a current/non-current presentation. This is because such entities do not supply goods or services within a clearly identifiable operating cycle.

Figure 18.3 shows Dresdner Bank's consolidated balance sheet as at 31 December 2007, in which the assets and liabilities of the group are presented in order of liquidity.

Assets	Note	31/12/2007 €m	31/12/2006 €m	Change €m	Change %
Cash funds	12	6 643	5 191	1 452	28.0
Trading assets	13	159 700	176 854	(17 154)	(9.7)
Financial assets designated at fair value	14	8 648	5 954	2 694	45.2
Loans and advances to banks	15	113 200	145 339	(32 139)	(22.1)
Loans and advances to customers	16	188 211	196 775	(8 564)	(4.4)
Loan impairment allowances	18	(762)	(980)	218	(22.2)
Financial investments	19	13 718	15 948	(2 230)	(14.0)
Equity-accounted investments	19	565	468	97	20.7
Property and equipment	20	1 265	1 359	(94)	(6.9)
Intangible assets	21	445	432	13	3.0
Deferred tax assets	31	1 912	1 978	(66)	(3.3)
Other assets	22	6 664	5 579	1 085	19.4
Total assets		**500 209**	**554 897**	**(54 688)**	**(9.9)**

Liabilities and equity	Note	31/12/2007 €m	31/12/2006 €m	Change €m	Change %
Trading liabilities	24	119 026	115 044	3 982	3.5
Financial liabilities designated at fair value	25	2 309	937	1 372	>+100.0
Liabilities to banks	26	128 149	168 847	(40 698)	(24.1)
Liabilities to customers	27	185 372	191 322	(5 950)	(3.1)
Securitised liabilities	28	34 633	45 970	(11 337)	(24.7)
Provisions	29	3 109	3 456	(347)	(10.0)
Deferred tax liabilities	31	107	86	21	24.4
Other liabilities	32	7 145	6 583	562	8.5
Subordinated liabilities	33	6 267	6 192	75	1.2
Profit-participation certificates	34	1 686	2 262	(576)	(25.5)
Equity	35	12 406	14 198	(1 792)	(12.6)
– Equity attributable to shareholder of parent		10 587	12 219	(1 632)	(13.4)
– Subscribed capital		1 503	1 503	—	—
– Capital reserves		6 383	6 383	—	—
– Retained earnings		3 138	2 759	379	13.7
– Treasury shares		(1 150)	—	(1 150)	—
– Translation reserve		(622)	(478)	(144)	30.1
– Cumulative remeasurement gains/losses on financial instruments		1 335	1 751	(416)	(23.8)
– Distributable profit		0	301	(301)	(100.0)
– Minority interests		1 819	1 979	(160)	(8.1)
Total liabilities and equity		**500 209**	**554 897**	**(54 688)**	**(9.9)**

FIGURE 18.3 Balance sheet of Dresdner Bank Group at 31 December 2007
Source: Dresdner Bank (2007, p. 103).

Where an entity has diverse operations, paragraph 64 of IAS 1 permits the use of both methods of presentation for the relevant assets and liabilities when this provides more relevant and reliable information.

For entities that are required to present their statement of financial position in a format that classifies assets and liabilities as current and non-current, paragraphs 66 and 69 of IAS 1 specify when assets and liabilities should be classified as current. By default, if assets and liabilities are not classified as current, they are classified as non-current by entities adopting that presentation format.

In accordance with IAS 1:

> 66. An entity shall classify an asset as current when:
> (a) it expects to realise the asset, or intends to sell or consume it, in its normal operating cycle;
> (b) it holds the asset primarily for the purpose of trading;
> (c) it expects to realise the asset within twelve months after the reporting period; or
> (d) the asset is cash or a cash equivalent (as defined in IAS 7) unless the asset is restricted from being exchanged or used to settle a liability for at least twelve months after the reporting period.
>
> An entity shall classify all other assets as non-current.
>
> 69. An entity shall classify a liability as current when:
> (a) it expects to settle the liability in its normal operating cycle;
> (b) it holds the liability primarily for the purpose of trading;
> (c) the liability is due to be settled within twelve months after the end of the reporting period; or
> (d) the entity does not have an unconditional right to defer settlement of the liability for at least twelve months after the reporting period.
>
> An entity shall classify all other liabilities as non-current.

Figure 18.4 shows the assets classified as non-current assets in the consolidated balance sheet of BHP Billiton at 30 June 2008, while figure 18.5 shows the liabilities classified as non-current.

	Notes	**2008 US$M**	2007 Restated US$M
Non-current assets			
Trade and other receivables	11	**720**	642
Other financial assets	12	**1 448**	899
Inventories	13	**232**	166
Property, plant and equipment	15	**47 332**	42 261
Intangible assets	16	**625**	713
Deferred tax assets	8	**3 486**	2 832
Other		**485**	135
Total non-current assets		**54 328**	47 648

FIGURE 18.4 Non-current assets of BHP Billiton at 30 June 2008
Source: BHP Billiton (2008, p. 167).

	Notes	**2008 US$M**	2007 Restated US$M
Non-current liabilities			
Trade and other payables	17	**138**	140
Interest bearing liabilities	18	**9 234**	10 780
Other financial liabilities	19	**1 260**	595
Deferred tax liabilities	8	**3 116**	2 260
Provisions	20	**6 251**	5 859
Deferred income		**488**	545
Total non-current liabilities		**20 487**	20 179

FIGURE 18.5 Non-current liabilities of BHP Billiton at 30 June 2008
Source: BHP Billiton (2008, p. 167).

Under these classifications, current assets may include inventories and receivables that are expected to be sold, consumed or realised as part of the normal operating cycle beyond 12 months after the reporting period. Similarly, current liabilities may include payables that are expected to be settled after more than 12 months after the reporting period. Because of these possibilities paragraph 61 of IAS 1 requires that irrespective of whether assets and liabilities are classified on the current/non-current basis or in order of liquidity:

> . . . an entity shall disclose the amount expected to be recovered or settled after more than twelve months for each asset and liability line item that combines amounts expected to be recovered or settled:
> (a) no more than twelve months after the reporting period, and
> (b) more than twelve months after the reporting period.

For example, note 39 to the 2007 consolidated financial statements of Dresdner Bank reports that the total loans and advances to customers of €188 211 million includes €68 062 million that matures more than 12 months after the reporting period. A further breakdown is provided for each 1-year maturity band (e.g. '>2 years–3 years') for each year up to 'more than five years'.

The criteria for classifying liabilities as current or non-current are based solely on the conditions existing at the end of the reporting period. Paragraph 72 of IAS 1 clarifies that financial liabilities that are due to be settled within 12 months after the reporting period are classified as current liabilities; this is even if an agreement to refinance or to reschedule payments on a long-term basis is completed after the reporting period and before the financial statements are authorised for issue. Consistent with this approach, paragraph 73 explains that if an entity expects and has the discretion to refinance or roll over an obligation for at least 12 months after the reporting period under an existing loan facility (i.e. one entered into before the end of the reporting period), the obligation is classified as non-current, even if it would otherwise be due within a shorter period. Similarly, paragraph 74 explains that if an entity breaches an undertaking under a long-term loan agreement during the reporting period with the effect that the loan is repayable on demand, the loan is classified as current. However, the loan should be classified as non-current if the lender agrees by the end of the reporting period to waive the right to demand immediate repayment for at least 12 months after the reporting period. If such an agreement is made after the reporting period but before the accounts are authorised for issue (i.e. an event occurring after the reporting period) it does not change the required classification of the loan as current.

The classification of liabilities as current or non-current is a particularly important issue for calculating summary indicators for assessing an entity's solvency. For example, an entity's current ratio (current assets to current liabilities) is often used as an indicator of solvency. Financiers, in setting the terms of borrowings, may also use it — some financiers will require that an entity not fall below a certain ratio of current assets to current liabilities. This is known as a 'negative pledge'. If the entity falls below that ratio then the financier has the right to demand repayment of the borrowing. These factors then affect the going concern assumption discussed in chapter 17.

18.3.3 Information required to be presented in the statement of financial position

IAS 1 does not prescribe a standard format that must be adopted for the statement of financial position. Rather, it prescribes a list of items that are considered to be sufficiently different in nature or function to warrant presentation in the statement of financial position as separate line items. These items are set forth in paragraph 54 and are:

(a) property, plant and equipment;
(b) investment property;
(c) intangible assets;
(d) financial assets (excluding amounts under (e), (h) and (i));
(e) investments accounted for using the equity method;
(f) biological assets;
(g) inventories;
(h) trade and other receivables;
(i) cash and cash equivalents;
(j) the total of assets classified as held for sale and assets included in disposal groups classified as held for sale in accordance with IFRS 5 *Non-current Assets Held for Sale and Discontinued Operations;*
(k) trade and other payables;
(l) provisions;

(m) financial liabilities (excluding amounts shown under (k) and (l));
(n) liabilities and assets for current tax, as defined in IAS 12 *Income Taxes*;
(o) deferred tax liabilities and deferred tax assets, as defined in IAS 12;
(p) liabilities included in disposal groups classified as held for sale in accordance with IFRS 5;
(q) non-controlling interests, presented within equity; and
(r) issued capital and reserves attributable to owners of the parent.

Figure 18.6 shows the disclosures made in the BHP Billiton consolidated balance sheet at 30 June 2008 concerning the issued capital and reserves attributable to equity holders of the parent and non-controlling interests, referred to as 'minority interests' at the time of issue of the report.

	Notes	2008 US$M	2007 Restated US$M
EQUITY			
Share capital — BHP Billiton Limited	21	**1 227**	1 221
Share capital — BHP Billiton Plc	21	**1 116**	1 183
Treasury shares held	21	**(514)**	(1 457)
Reserves	22	**750**	991
Retained earnings	23	**35 756**	27 729
Total equity attributable to members of BHP Billiton Group		**38 335**	29 667
Minority interests	24	**708**	251
Total equity	24	**39 043**	29 918

FIGURE 18.6 Equity of BHP Billiton at 30 June 2008
Source: BHP Billiton (2008, p. 167).

Paragraph 55 of IAS 1 requires additional line items, headings and subtotals to be presented in the statement of financial position when their inclusion is relevant to an understanding of the entity's financial position. Paragraph 58 explains that the judgement on whether additional items should be separately presented is based on an assessment of:

(a) the nature and liquidity of assets;
(b) the function of assets within the entity; and
(c) the amounts, nature and timing of liabilities.

18.3.4 Information required to be presented in the statement of financial position or in the notes

To provide greater transparency and enhance the understandability of the statement of financial position, paragraph 77 of IAS 1 requires the subclassification of line items to be reported either in the statement or in the notes. For example, an entity might provide subclassification of intangible assets as brand names, licences and patents.

In some cases, the subclassifications are governed by a specific IFRS. For example, IAS 2 requires the total carrying amount of inventories to be broken down into classifications appropriate to the entity (refer to chapter 8). Such classifications may include merchandise, production supplies, materials, work in progress and finished goods. IAS 16 requires items of property, plant and equipment to be disaggregated into classes (refer to chapter 9). Entities typically separately report land and buildings from plant and equipment. Other examples are outlined in the other chapters included in part 2 of this book.

Figure 18.7 shows the subclassifications of inventories reported in note 13 to the 2008 consolidated financial statements of BHP Billiton.

BHP Billiton subclassifies its inventory as raw materials, work in progress and finished goods. Within each of those three subclassifications, the amount carried at cost and the amount recognised at net realisable value is identified.

		2008 US$M	2007 US$M
Current			
Raw materials and consumables	— at net realisable value[a]	16	67
	— at cost	1433	874
		1449	941
Work in progress	— at net realisable value[a]	5	4
	— at cost	1617	1056
		1622	1060
Finished goods	— at net realisable value[a]	1	7
	— at cost	1899	1736
		1900	1743
Total current inventories		4971	3744
Non-current			
Raw materials and consumables	— at cost	55	58
Work in progress	— at cost	171	100
Finished goods	— at cost	6	8
Total non-current inventories		232	166

(a) US$24 million of inventory write-downs were recognised during the year (2007: US$16 million; 2006: US$6 million). Inventory write-downs of US$7 million made in previous periods were reversed during the year (2007: US$21 million; 2006: US$19 million).

FIGURE 18.7 Inventories of BHP Billiton at 30 June 2008
Source: BHP Billiton (2008, p. 191).

Paragraph 78 of IAS 1 explains that subclassifications of line items in the statement of financial position are also dependent on the size, nature and function of the amounts involved and that judgement about the need for subclassifications should have regard to the same factors previously outlined when judging whether additional line items should be presented in the statement of financial position (refer to section 18.3.3).

Other typical subclassifications include the disaggregation of:

(a) receivables between amounts receivable from trade customers, receivables from related parties, prepayments and other amounts
(b) provisions into those for employee benefits, restructuring provisions, warranty provisions and other items
(c) issued capital and reserves into share capital, reserves and retained earnings.

Figure 18.8 shows the subclassifications of trade and other receivables reported in note 11 of the 2008 consolidated financial statements of BHP Billiton.

In addition, paragraph 79 of IAS 1 requires an entity to disclose the following, either in the statement of financial position or in the notes:

(a) for each class of share capital:
  (i) the number of shares authorised;
  (ii) the number of shares issued and fully paid, and issued but not fully paid;
  (iii) par value per share, or that the shares have no par value;
  (iv) a reconciliation of the number of shares outstanding at the beginning and at the end of the period;
  (v) the rights, preferences and restrictions attaching to that class including restrictions on the distribution of dividends and the repayment of capital;
  (vi) shares in the entity held by the entity or by its subsidiaries or associates; and
  (vii) shares reserved for issue under options and contracts for the sale of shares, including the terms and amounts; and
(b) a description of the nature and purpose of each reserve within equity.

	2008 US$M	2007 US$M
Current		
Trade receivables	8050	4837
Provision for doubtful debts	(49)	(10)
Total trade receivables	8001	4827
Employee Share Plan loans [(a)]	3	3
Other sundry receivables	1799	1410
Provision for doubtful debts	(2)	(1)
Total sundry receivables	1800	1412
Total current receivables	9801	6239
Non-current		
Employee Share Plan loans [(a)]	21	39
Other sundry receivables	699	603
Total non-current receivables	720	642

(a) Under the terms of the BHP Billiton Limited Employee Share Plan, shares have been issued to employees for subscription at market price less a discount not exceeding 10 per cent. Interest free employee loans are full recourse and are available to fund the purchase of such shares for a period of up to 20 years, repayable by application of dividends or an equivalent amount.

FIGURE 18.8 Trade and other receivables of BHP Billiton at 30 June 2008
Source: BHP Billiton (2008, p. 190).

18.3.5 Illustrative statement of financial position

The IASB issues implementation guidance to accompany IFRSs. While not forming part of the standard, part 1 of the IAS 1 Implementation Guidance (IAS 1 IG) includes illustrative examples of the presentation of financial statements. The illustrative example of a statement of financial position in the IAS 1 IG is presented in figure 18.9. Figure 18.10 shows the consolidated balance sheet of Nokia Corporation at 31 December 2007 prepared in accordance with IFRSs.

FIGURE 18.9 Illustrative statement of financial position

XYZ Group — Statement of financial position as at 31 December 20X7 (in thousands of currency units)

	31 Dec 20X7	31 Dec 20X6
ASSETS		
Non-current assets		
Property, plant and equipment	350 700	360 020
Goodwill	80 800	91 200
Other intangible assets	227 470	227 470
Investments in associates	100 150	110 770
Available-for-sale financial assets	142 500	156 000
	901 620	945 460
Current assets		
Inventories	135 230	132 500
Trade receivables	91 600	110 800
Other current assets	25 650	12 540
Cash and cash equivalents	312 400	322 900
	564 880	578 740
Total assets	1 466 500	1 524 200

(continued)

FIGURE 18.9 *(continued)*

	31 Dec 20X7	31 Dec 20X6
EQUITY AND LIABILITIES		
Equity attributable to owners of the parent		
Share capital	650 000	600 000
Retained earnings	243 500	161 700
Other components of equity	10 200	21 200
	903 700	782 900
Non-controlling interests	70 050	48 600
Total equity	973 750	831 500
Non-current liabilities		
Long-term borrowings	120 000	160 000
Deferred tax	28 800	26 040
Long-term provisions	28 850	52 240
Total non-current liabilities	177 650	238 280
Current liabilities		
Trade and other payables	115 100	187 620
Short-term borrowings	150 000	200 000
Current portion of long-term borrowings	10 000	20 000
Current tax payable	35 000	42 000
Short-term provisions	5 000	4 800
Total current liabilities	315 100	454 420
Total liabilities	492 750	692 700
Total equity and liabilities	1 466 500	1 524 200

Source: IASB IAS 1 IG (2008, pp. 945–6).

FIGURE 18.10 Consolidated balance sheet of Nokia Corporation at 31 December 2007

December 31	Notes	**2007 EURm**	2006 EURm
ASSETS			
Non-current assets			
Capitalized development costs	12	378	251
Goodwill	12	1 384	532
Other intangible assets	12	2 358	298
Property, plant and equipment	13	1 912	1 602
Investments in associated companies	14	325	224
Available-for-sale investments	15	341	288
Deferred tax assets	24	1 553	809
Long-term loans receivable	16,25	10	19
Other non-current assets		44	8
		8 305	4 031
Current assets			
Inventories	17,19	2 876	1 554
Accounts receivable, net of allowances for doubtful accounts (2007: EUR 332 million, 2006: EUR 212 million)	19,35	11 200	5 888
Prepaid expenses and accrued income	18	3 070	2 496
Current portion of long-term loans receivable	35	156	—
Other financial assets		239	111
Available-for-sale investments, liquid assets	15,35	4 903	5 012

FIGURE 18.10 *(continued)*

December 31	Notes	2007 EURm	2006 EURm
Current assets *(continued)*			
Available-for-sale investments, cash equivalents	15,32,35	4 725	2 046
Bank and cash	32,35	2 125	1 479
		29 294	18 586
Total assets		37 599	22 617
SHAREHOLDERS' EQUITY AND LIABILITIES			
Capital and reserves attributable to equity holders of the parent			
Share capital	21	246	246
Share issue premium		644	2 707
Treasury shares, at cost		(3 146)	(2 060)
Translation differences		(163)	(34)
Fair value and other reserves	20	23	(14)
Reserve for invested non-restricted equity		3 299	—
Retained earnings		13 870	11 123
		14 773	11 968
Minority interests		2 565	92
Total equity		17 338	12 060
Non-current liabilities			
Long-term interest-bearing liabilities	23,35	203	69
Deferred tax liabilities	24	963	205
Other long-term liabilities		119	122
		1 285	396
Current liabilities			
Current portion of long-term loans	35	173	—
Short-term borrowings	35	898	247
Accounts payable	35	7 074	3 732
Accrued expenses	25	7 114	3 796
Provisions	27	3 717	2 386
		18 976	10 161
Total shareholders' equity and liabilities		37 599	22 617

Source: Nokia (2007, p. 9).

18.4 STATEMENT OF COMPREHENSIVE INCOME

18.4.1 The purpose of a statement of comprehensive income

As explained in chapter 1, the statement of comprehensive income is the prime source for information about an entity's financial performance. Paragraph 81 of IAS 1 requires all items of income and expense recognised in a period to be included in a single statement of comprehensive income, or in two separate statements, comprising a separate income statement reporting components of profit or loss, and a second statement commencing with profit or loss and reporting other components of comprehensive income. The statement of comprehensive income summarises the elements used to measure profit or loss for the period as well as all gains or losses recognised directly in equity during the period. Thus the statement of comprehensive income reports on all non-owner transactions and valuation adjustments affecting net assets during the period. Profit or loss is the most common measure of an entity's performance. It is used in the determination of other summary indicators, such as earnings per share and rates of return on total assets or equity. However, an assessment of the full financial performance of an entity requires consideration of not only the items of income and expense included in the determination of profit or loss for the period, but also of the gains and losses recognised directly in equity.

The statement of comprehensive income can also be used to assist to predict an entity's future performance and future cash flows. This is particularly the case if there is appropriate disclosure of unusual items of income and expense that will assist a user in judging the quality of an entity's performance — in terms of the likely future sustainability of the reported profit or loss. The ability to identify likely non-recurring items of income or expense is of particular significance in making this judgement.

However, like the view of an entity's financial position presented by the statement of financial position, the view of an entity's performance presented by the statement of comprehensive income is by no means perfect. The statement has its limitations that primarily arise from:

- the mandatory expensing of expenditure relating to intangible self-generated assets as required by IAS 38 (refer to chapter 10)
- deliberate earnings management through the making of biased judgements relating to the measurement of items of income or expense, such as impairment and restructuring losses, with the objective of smoothing earnings or projecting an image of earnings growth.

While the statement of comprehensive income incorporates all income, expenses and losses, a distinction is made between profit or loss for the period and other components of comprehensive income. As outlined above, profit or loss is reported in a separate statement or as a subtotal within a single statement of comprehensive income. However, the distinction between amounts recognised in profit or loss and as other components of comprehensive income is dependent upon prescriptions of accounting standards and accounting policy choices, rather than being driven by conceptual differences. For example, IAS 16 requires asset revaluation losses to be recognised in profit or loss, unless reversing a previous revaluation gain. However, IAS 16 requires asset revaluation gains to be recognised directly in equity, unless reversing a previous revaluation loss (refer to chapter 9). Accordingly, a revaluation loss would be reported in profit or loss while a revaluation gain would be reported below the profit line as an other component of comprehensive income.

18.4.2 Information required to be presented in the statement of comprehensive income

As for the statement of financial position, IAS 1 does not prescribe a standard format for the statement of comprehensive income. Rather, it prescribes line items that are considered to be of sufficient importance to the reporting of the performance of an entity to warrant their presentation in the statement of comprehensive income. These items are set forth in paragraph 82 of IAS 1 and comprise:

(a) revenue;
(b) finance costs;
(c) share of profit or loss of associates and joint ventures accounted for using the equity method;
(d) tax expense;
(e) a single amount comprising the total of (i) the post-tax profit or loss of discontinued operations and (ii) the post-tax gain or loss recognised on the measurement to fair value less costs to sell or on the disposal of the assets or disposal group(s) constituting the discontinued operation;
(f) profit or loss;
(g) each component of other comprehensive income classified by nature (excluding amounts in (h));
(h) share of the other comprehensive income of associates and joint ventures accounted for using the equity method; and
(i) total comprehensive income.

The components of other comprehensive income referred to in item (g) include:

- changes in the fair value of available-for-sale investments recognised directly in equity in accordance with IAS 39 (see chapter 5)
- cash flow hedges deferred in equity in accordance with IAS 39 (see chapter 5)
- asset revaluation gains recognised in accordance with IAS 16 (see chapter 9)
- foreign currency gains and losses on translation of the financial statements of net investments in foreign operations recognised directly in equity in accordance with IAS 21 (see chapter 26), and
- actuarial gains and losses deferred in equity in accordance with IAS 19 (see chapter 15).

The share of comprehensive income of associates and joint ventures accounted for using the equity method refers to the investor's proportionate share of gains and losses recognised directly in equity, such as an asset revaluation, recognised by an associate or joint venture entity (see chapters 27 and 28).

Items (a)–(f) may be reported in a separate income statement if the two-statement alternative is adopted for reporting on comprehensive income.

Paragraph 83 of IAS 1 requires disclosure of the following items as allocations of profit or loss for the period in the statement of comprehensive income:

(a) profit or loss for the period attributable to:
  (i) non-controlling interests; and
  (ii) owners of the parent; and
(b) total comprehensive income for the period attributable to:
  (i) non-controlling interests; and
  (ii) owners of the parent.

Alternatively, this information may be reported in the separate income statement if the two-statement alternative is adopted for reporting comprehensive income.

Further, paragraph 85 of IAS 1 requires additional line items, headings and subtotals to be presented in the statement of comprehensive income or separate income statement when such presentation is relevant to an understanding of the entity's financial performance.

Paragraph 86 of IAS 1 explains that 'an entity includes additional line items in the statement of comprehensive income and in the separate income statement (if presented), and it amends the descriptions used and the ordering of items when this is necessary to explain the elements of financial performance.' Paragraph 86 further explains that the factors to be considered in making judgements concerning the inclusion of additional line items include the materiality and the nature and function of the components of income and expense. Such disclosures may assist users' understanding of the entity's performance and predictions about future earnings and cash flow because items may vary in the frequency and extent to which they recur. An item of income or expense is said to be recurring if the amount in one period influences the amount in a future period or if it is relevant to forecasting future earnings.

However, paragraph 87 of IAS 1 specifically prohibits the presentation of any items of income and expense as 'extraordinary items' either in the statement of comprehensive income or in the notes. This prohibition was inserted in IAS 1 following the IASB's decision to eliminate the concept of extraordinary items from IAS 8. IAS 8 previously defined 'extraordinary items' as 'income or expenses that arise from events or transactions that are clearly distinct from the ordinary activities of the enterprise and therefore are not expected to recur frequently or regularly'. In amending IAS 8 and prohibiting the presentation of 'extraordinary items', the IASB concluded that items previously treated as extraordinary items resulted from the normal business risks faced by an entity and do not warrant presentation in a separate component of the statement of comprehensive income.

In the past, accounting standards have also classified items as 'abnormal' items depending on whether they were large or unusual. As with extraordinary items, this classification has been eliminated. The classification of items as abnormal or extraordinary allowed entities to report variations of their profit or loss for the period — for example, 'profit before abnormal items' or 'profit before extraordinary items'. Unfortunately the distinctions tended to be abused such that a profit figure was made to look better by reporting it before a large abnormal or extraordinary expense. Now that abnormal and extraordinary items have been eliminated, this practice should disappear. However, there is nothing in IAS 1 to prevent an entity from creating as many subtotals as it wishes. Thus, it could report a profit before and after any line item such as depreciation or impairment losses.

18.4.3 Information required to be presented in the statement of comprehensive income or in the notes

To enhance the understandability of the statement of comprehensive income, paragraph 97 of IAS 1 requires the separate disclosure of the nature and amount of material items of income and expense. Paragraph 98 of IAS 1 explains that the circumstances that would give rise to the separate disclosure of items of income and expense include:

(a) write-downs of inventories to net realisable value or of property, plant and equipment to recoverable amount, as well as reversals of such write-downs;

(b) restructurings of the activities of an entity and reversals of any provisions for the costs of restructuring;
(c) disposals of items of property, plant and equipment;
(d) disposals of investments;
(e) discontinued operations;
(f) litigation settlements; and
(g) other reversals of provisions.

Disclosure of these items is particularly important to users of the statement of comprehensive income wishing to predict the likely future sustainability of the reported profit or loss.

Paragraph 99 of IAS 1 requires an entity to present an analysis of expenses classified either by their nature (e.g. purchases of material, transport costs, employee benefits, depreciation and advertising costs) or their function within the entity (e.g. costs of sales, costs of distribution and administrative activities), whichever provides the more relevant and reliable information. Paragraph 100 encourages, but does not require, the presentation of this expense analysis in the separate income statement or statement of comprehensive income.

Figure 18.11 shows an example of a classification using the nature of expense method provided in paragraph 102 of IAS 1.

Revenue		X
Other income		X
Changes in inventories of finished goods and work in progress	X	
Raw materials and consumables used	X	
Employee benefits expense	X	
Depreciation and amortisation expense	X	
Other expenses	X	
Total expenses		(X)
Profit before income tax		X

FIGURE 18.11 Example of classification of expenses by nature
Source: IAS 1 *Presentation of Financial Statements*, paragraph 102.

Figure 18.12 shows an example of a classification using the function of expense method provided in paragraph 103 of IAS 1.

Revenue	X
Cost of sales	(X)
Gross profit	X
Other income	X
Distribution costs	(X)
Administrative expenses	(X)
Other expenses	(X)
Profit before income tax	X

FIGURE 18.12 Example of classification of expenses by function
Source: IAS 1 *Presentation of Financial Statements*, paragraph 103.

If the classification of expenses by function method is used, additional information on the nature of expenses, including depreciation and amortisation expense and employee benefits expense, must be disclosed. Paragraph 105 of IAS 1 explains that this additional information is required because it is useful in predicting future cash flows.

18.4.4 Illustrative statement of comprehensive income

The guidance on implementing IAS 1 that accompanies, but is not part of, IAS 1 includes illustrative statements of comprehensive income. These illustrative statements, along with references to IAS 1, are presented in figures 18.13 and 18.14.

The single statement presentation of the statement of comprehensive income is illustrated in figure 18.13. The analysis of expenses classified by function is presented in the statement of comprehensive income, as encouraged by paragraph 100 of IAS 1, rather than in the notes. Figure 18.14 illustrates the presentation of the statement of comprehensive income in two statements: a separate income statement and a statement displaying other components of comprehensive income. The analysis of expenses classified by nature is presented in the separate income statement, rather than in the notes.

Figure 18.15 shows the consolidated income statement and the consolidated statement of recognised income and expense of BHP Billiton for the year ended 30 June 2008. While these financial statements were prepared before the requirement to present a statement of comprehensive income, they are comparable to the presentation of financial statements prescribed by IAS 1 for annual reporting periods commencing on or after 1 January 2009. In its financial statements, BHP Billiton elected to present a separate statement of recognised income and expense to report on gains and losses recognised directly in equity. Together with the income statement, this is comparable to the presentation of the statement of comprehensive income in two statements. The first section of figure 18.15 shows a statement labelled 'consolidated income statement'. This statement is equivalent to the separate income statement, which displays components of profit or loss. The second section of figure 18.15 shows BHP Billiton's consolidated statement of recognised income and expense, which commences with profit after taxation and shows gains and losses recognised directly in equity.

FIGURE 18.13 Illustrative statement of comprehensive income using the single-statement format with classification of expenses by function

XYZ Group — Statement of comprehensive income
for the year ended 31 December 20X7
(in thousands of currency units)

	20X7	20X6
Revenue	390 000	355 000
Cost of sales	(245 000)	(230 000)
Gross profit	145 000	125 000
Other income	20 667	11 300
Distribution costs	(9 000)	(8 700)
Administrative expenses	(20 000)	(21 000)
Other expenses	(2 100)	(1 200)
Finance costs	(8 000)	(7 500)
Share of profit of associates[1]	35 100	30 100
Profit before tax	161 667	128 000
Income tax expense	(40 417)	(32 000)
Profit for the year from continuing operations	121 250	96 000
Loss for the year from discontinued operations	—	(30 500)
PROFIT FOR THE YEAR	121 250	65 500
Other comprehensive income:		
Exchange differences on translating foreign operations[2]	5 334	10 667
Available-for-sale financial assets[2]	(24 000)	26 667
Cash flow hedges[2]	667	4 000
Gains on property revaluation	933	3 367
Actuarial gains (losses) on defined benefit pension plans	(667)	1 333
Share of other comprehensive income of associates[3]	400	(700)
Income tax relating to components of other comprehensive income[4]	4 667	(9 334)
Other comprehensive income for the year, net of tax	(14 000)	28 000
TOTAL COMPREHENSIVE INCOME FOR THE YEAR	107 250	93 500

(continued)

FIGURE 18.13 *(continued)*

	20X7	20X6
Profit attributable to:		
Owners of the parent	97 000	52 400
Non-controlling interests	24 250	13 100
	121 250	65 500
Total comprehensive income attributable to:		
Owners of the parent	85 800	74 800
Non-controlling interests	21 450	18 700
	107 250	93 500

1 This means the share of associates' profit attributable to owners of the associates, i.e. it is after tax and non-controlling interests in the associates.
2 This illustrates the aggregated presentation, with disclosure of the current year gain or loss and reclassification adjustment presented in the notes. Alternatively, a gross presentation can be used.
3 This means the share of associates' other comprehensive income attributable to owners of the associates, i.e. it is after tax and non-controlling interests in the associates.
4 The income tax relating to each component of other comprehensive income is disclosed in the notes.

Source: IASB IAS 1 IG (2008, pp. 947–8).

FIGURE 18.14 Illustrative statement of comprehensive income using the two-statement format with classification of expenses by nature

XYZ Group — Income statement
for the year ended 31 December 20X7
(in thousands of currency units)

	20X7	20X6
Revenue	390 000	355 000
Other income	20 667	11 300
Changes in inventories of finished goods and work in progress	(115 100)	(107 900)
Work performed by the entity and capitalised	16 000	15 000
Raw material and consumables used	(96 000)	(92 000)
Employee benefits expense	(45 000)	(43 000)
Depreciation and amortisation expense	(19 000)	(17 000)
Impairment of property, plant and equipment	(4 000)	—
Other expenses	(6 000)	(5 500)
Finance costs	(15 000)	(18 000)
Share of profit of associates[5]	35 100	30 100
Profit before tax	161 667	128 000
Income tax expense	(40 417)	(32 000)
Profit for the year from continuing operations	121 250	96 000
Loss for the year from discontinued operations	—	(30 500)
PROFIT FOR THE YEAR	121 250	65 500
Profit attributable to:		
Owners of the parent	97 000	52 400
Non-controlling interests	24 250	13 100
	121 250	65 500
Earnings per share (in currency units):		
Basic and diluted	0.46	0.30

5 This means the share of associates' profit attributable to owners of the associates, i.e. it is after tax and non-controlling interests in the associates.

FIGURE 18.14 *(continued)*

XYZ Group — Statement of comprehensive income for the year ended 31 December 20X7 (in thousands of currency units)		
	20X7	**20X6**
Profit for the year		
Other comprehensive income:	121 250	65 500
Exchange differences on translating foreign operations	5 334	10 667
Available-for-sale financial assets	(24 000)	26 667
Cash flow hedges	(667)	(4 000)
Gains on property revaluation	933	3 367
Actuarial gains (losses) on defined benefit pension plans	(667)	1 333
Share of other comprehensive income of associates[6]	400	(700)
Income tax relating to components of other comprehensive income[7]	4 667	(9 334)
Other comprehensive income for the year, net of tax	(14 000)	28 000
TOTAL COMPREHENSIVE INCOME FOR THE YEAR	107 250	93 500
Total comprehensive income attributable to:		
Owners of the parent	85 800	74 800
Non-controlling interests	21 450	18 700
	107 250	93 500

6 This means the share of associates' other comprehensive income attributable to owners of the associates, i.e. it is after tax and non-controlling interests in the associates.
7 The income tax relating to each component of other comprehensive income is disclosed in the notes.

Source: IASB IAS 1 IG (2008, pp. 949–50).

FIGURE 18.15 Components of profit and other components of comprehensive income

	Notes	**2008 US$M**	2007 Restated[(a)] US$M	2006 Restated[(a)] US$M
Revenue				
Group production		**51 918**	41 271	34 139
Third party products	2	**7 555**	6 202	4 960
Revenue	2	**59 473**	47 473	39 099
Other income	3	**648**	621	1 229
Expenses excluding net finance costs	4	**(35 976)**	(28 370)	(24 612)
Profit from operations		**24 145**	19 724	15 716
Comprising:				
Group production	2	**24 529**	19 650	15 605
Third party products	2	**(384)**	74	111
	2	**24 145**	19 724	15 716
Financial income	6	**293**	264	222
Financial expenses	6	**(955)**	(776)	(822)
Net finance costs	6	**(662)**	(512)	(600)
Profit before taxation		**23 483**	19 212	15 116
Income tax expense	8	**(6 798)**	(5 305)	(4 122)
Royalty related taxation (net of income tax benefit)	8	**(723)**	(411)	(460)
Total taxation expense	8	**(7 521)**	(5 716)	(4 582)

(continued)

FIGURE 18.15 *(continued)*

	Notes	2008 US$M	2007 Restated[(a)] US$M	2006 Restated[(a)] US$M
Profit after taxation		15 962	13 496	10 534
Profit attributable to minority interests		572	80	84
Profit attributable to members of BHP Billiton Group		15 390	13 416	10 450
Earnings per ordinary share (basic) (US cents)	9	275.3	229.5	173.2
Earnings per ordinary share (diluted) (US cents)	9	275.1	229.0	172.4
Dividends per ordinary share — paid during the period (US cents)	10	56.0	38.5	32.0
Dividends per ordinary share — declared in respect of the period (US cents)	10	70.0	47.0	36.0
Profit after taxation		15 962	13 496	10 534
Amounts recognised directly in equity				
Actuarial (losses)/gains on pension and medical schemes		(96)	79	111
Available for sale investments:				
Valuation (losses)/gains taken to equity		(76)	147	(1)
Cash flow hedges:				
Losses taken to equity		(383)	(50)	(27)
Losses transferred to the income statement		73	—	—
Gains transferred to the initial carrying amount of hedged items		(190)	(88)	(25)
Exchange fluctuations on translation of foreign operations		(21)	12	(1)
Tax on items recognised directly in, or transferred from, equity		306	82	4
Total amounts recognised directly in equity		(387)	182	61
Total recognised income and expense		15 575	13 678	10 595
Attributable to minority interests	24	571	82	84
Attributable to members of BHP Billiton Group	24	15 004	13 596	10 511

(a) Comparative periods have been restated as described in note 1.

Source: BHP Billiton (2008, pp. 165–6).

Note that in figure 18.15 earnings per share is disclosed pursuant to the requirements of IAS 33 *Earnings per Share.*

18.5 STATEMENT OF CHANGES IN EQUITY

18.5.1 The purpose of a statement of changes in equity

The changes in equity during a period comprise comprehensive income and the effect of any transactions with owners as owners, such as contributions of capital and payment of dividends. Further, the beginning of period amount of retained earnings may be affected by the effects of retrospective application of a change in accounting policy or correction of prior period errors recognised in accordance with IAS 8 (refer chapter 17).

The purpose of the statement of changes in equity is to report transactions with equity holders, such as new share issues and the payment of dividends, and the effect of any retrospective adjustments to beginning-of-period components of equity.

18.5.2 Information required to be reported in the statement of changes in equity

Paragraph 106 of IAS 1 requires the following information to be presented in the statement of changes in equity:

(a) total comprehensive income for the period, showing separately the total amounts attributable to owners of the parent and to non-controlling interests;
(b) for each component of equity, the effects of retrospective application or retrospective restatement recognised in accordance with IAS 8; and
(c) [deleted by the IASB]
(d) for each component of equity, a reconciliation between the carrying amount at the beginning and the end of the period, separately disclosing changes resulting from:
  (i) profit or loss;
  (ii) each item of other comprehensive income; and
  (iii) transactions with owners in their capacity as owners, showing separately contributions by and distributions to owners and changes in ownership interests in subsidiaries that do not result in a loss of control.

The total comprehensive income for the period includes profit (loss) for the period, which increases (decreases) retained earnings. Other components of comprehensive income are recognised directly in equity and thus affect other components of equity. For example, a gain on revaluing assets, net of its tax effect, increases the asset revaluation reserve.

The statement of changes in equity is usually presented in a tabular format. The various components of equity, such as share capital, retained earnings and revaluation reserve, are listed in separate columns. The opening balance, current period movements and closing balance are shown in different rows. As for the other financial statements, comparative amounts are required to be reported in the statement of changes in equity. The comparative figures are usually presented in a separate table from the current period figures.

18.5.3 Information to be presented in the statement of changes in equity or in the notes

Paragraph 107 of IAS 1 requires the presentation of the amount of dividends recognised as distributions to owners during the period and the amount of dividends per share for the period either in the statement of changes in equity or in the notes.

18.5.4 Illustrative statements of changes in equity

The guidance on implementing IAS 1 that accompanies, but is not part of, IAS 1 provides an illustrative statement of changes in equity, which is shown in figure 18.16. This example illustrates the reconciliation of the movements in each element of equity attributable to the equity holders of the parent and the non-controlling interests and total equity for the current and the prior year.

FIGURE 18.16 Illustrative statement of changes in equity

XYZ Group — Statement of changes in equity for the year ended 31 December 20X7
(in thousands of currency units)

	Share capital	Retained earnings	Translation of foreign operations	Available-for-sale financial assets	Cash flow hedges	Revaluation surplus	Total	Non-controlling interests	Total equity
Balance at 1 January 20X6	600 000	118 100	(4 000)	1 600	2 000	—	717 700	29 800	747 500
Changes in accounting policy	—	400	—	—	—	—	400	100	500
Restated balance	600 000	118 500	(4 000)	1 600	2 000	—	718 100	29 900	748 000

(continued)

FIGURE 18.16 *(continued)*

	Share capital	Retained earnings	Translation of foreign operations	Available-for-sale financial assets	Cash flow hedges	Revaluation surplus	Total	Non-controlling interests	Total equity
Changes in equity for 20X6									
Dividends	—	(10 000)	—	—	—	—	(10 000)	—	(10 000)
Total comprehensive income for the year[11]	—	53 200	6 400	16 000	(2 400)	1 600	74 800	18 700	93 500
Balance at 31 December 20X6	600 000	161 700	2 400	17 600	(400)	1 600	782 900	48 600	831 500
Changes in equity for 20X7									
Issue of share capital	50 000	—	—	—	—	—	50 000	—	50 000
Dividends	—	(15 000)	—	—	—	—	(15 000)	—	(15 000)
Total comprehensive income for the year[12]	—	96 600	3 200	(14 400)	(400)	800	85 800	21 450	107 250
Transfer to retained earnings	—	200	—	—	—	200	—	—	—
Balance at 31 December 20X7	650 000	243 500	5 600	3 200	(800)	2 200	903 700	70 050	973 750

11 The amount included in retained earnings for 20X6 of 53 200 represents profit attributable to owners of the parent of 52 400 plus actuarial gains on defined benefit pension plans of 800 (1333, less tax 333, less non-controlling interests 200). The amount included in the translation, available-for-sale and cash flow hedge reserves represent other comprehensive income for each component, net of tax and non-controlling interests, eg other comprehensive income related to available-for-sale financial assets for 20X6 of 16 000 is 26 667, less tax 6667, less non-controlling interests 4000. The amount included in the revaluation surplus of 1600 represents the share of other comprehensive income of associates of (700) plus gains on property revaluation of 2300 (3367, less tax 667, less non-controlling interests 400). Other comprehensive income of associates relates solely to gains or losses on property revaluation.

12 The amount included in retained earnings for 20X7 of 96 600 represents profit attributable to owners of the parent of 97 000 plus actuarial losses on defined benefit pension plans of 400 (667, less tax 167, less non-controlling interests 100). The amount included in the translation, available-for-sale and cash flow hedge reserves represent other comprehensive income for each component, net of tax and non-controlling interests, eg other comprehensive income related to the translation of foreign operations for 20X7 of 3200 is 5334, less tax 1334, less non-controlling interests 800. The amount included in the revaluation surplus of 800 represents the share of other comprehensive income of associates of 400 plus gains on property revaluation of 400 (933, less tax 333, less non-controlling interests 200). Other comprehensive income of associates relates solely to gains or losses on property revaluation.

Source: IASB IAS 1 IG (2008, p. 953).

18.6 STATEMENT OF CASH FLOWS

IAS 7 *Statement of Cash Flows* sets out the requirements for the presentation of the statement of cash flows and related disclosures. These requirements and disclosures are outlined in chapter 19.

18.7 NOTES

Notes are an integral part of the financial statements. Their purpose is to enhance the understandability of the statement of financial position, statement of comprehensive income, statement of cash flows and statement of changes in equity. As far as practicable, each item in these statements is cross-referenced to any related information in the notes (IAS 1, para. 113).

In relation to compliance with accounting standards, IAS 1 require that the notes disclose:

- a statement of compliance with IFRSs (para. 16) if applicable
- in rare circumstances where an entity has departed from the requirements of IFRSs (which could only arise because compliance would be so misleading that it would conflict with the objectives of financial statements) a statement that management has concluded that the financial statements fairly present the financial position, financial performance and cash flows, particulars of the departure including the title of the standard with which the entity has not complied and why compliance would be misleading, and the financial effect of the departure for each item affected, for each period presented (para. 20) (for further discussion of this requirement see chapter 17).

As discussed in this chapter, IAS 1 allows some information to be presented either in the notes or in the financial statement, such as the statement of financial position and the statement of comprehensive income. This section considers other information that is required to be disclosed in the notes, including the basis of preparation of the financial statements, specific accounting policies used, sources of information uncertainty, information about capital and other disclosures.

18.7.1 Disclosure of accounting policies and sources of estimation uncertainty

IAS 1 requires significant accounting policies to be summarised in the notes to the financial statements. The summary of accounting policies is normally presented as the first note and usually commences with a statement about compliance with IFRSs. Specifically, paragraph 117 of IAS 1 requires disclosure in the notes of the measurement basis or bases used and other accounting policies that are relevant to understanding the financial statements. The measurement basis an entity uses will significantly affect users' analyses. For example, the historical cost basis has a distorting effect on comparison of trends in summary performance indicators such as return on investment. This occurs because depreciation and amortisation reduce the carrying amount of total assets, resulting in an increase in return on investment without any increase in profit or reduction in the actual assets used to generate the return.

In deciding whether to disclose particulars of an accounting policy, managers must consider its relevance in assisting users to understand how transactions and events have been reported in the financial statements. In some cases, disclosure is prescribed by other IFRSs. This is usually the case where a standard allows a choice of accounting policy. For example, IAS 16, which allows a choice of cost or fair value for measuring property, plant and equipment subsequent to initial recognition, requires disclosure of the measurement basis used to determine the gross carrying amount for each class of property, plant and equipment (para. 73 (a)) (see chapter 9). Other examples of alternative accounting policies permitted by IFRSs include:

- the use of the equity method or proportionate consolidation to account for an interest in a jointly controlled entity (see chapter 28)
- the different accounting policies for recognising financial instruments arising from alternative classifications of certain financial assets at fair value through profit or loss (if held for trading investments), held-to-maturity investments, or available-for-sale financial assets (see chapter 5).

An entity also must disclose information about the assumptions concerning the future, and other major sources of estimation uncertainty at the end of the reporting period, that have a significant risk of causing material adjustments to the carrying amounts of assets and liabilities within the next financial year (e.g. assumptions about growth rates used in performing significant asset impairment tests) (para. 125).

IAS 1 also requires disclosure of other judgements management has made in the process of applying the entity's accounting policies that have the most significant effect on the amounts recognised in the financial statements (e.g. whether financial assets are held-to-maturity investments, whether a lease is a finance or operating lease and whether sales of goods are, in substance, financing arrangements) (para. 122 and 123).

Figure 18.17 contains extracts from note 1 to the 2008 consolidated financial statements of BHP Billiton. Note 1 describes the accounting principles used by the group in preparing its financial statements, including matters such as the basis of preparation and the alternative bases of measurement.

FIGURE 18.17 Note 1 accounting policies of BHP Billiton at 30 June 2008 (extract)

Basis of preparation

This general purpose financial report for the year ended 30 June 2008 has been prepared in accordance with the requirements of the UK Companies Act 1985 and Australian Corporations Act 2001 and with:

- Australian Accounting Standards, being Australian equivalents to International Financial Reporting Standards as issued by the Australian Accounting Standards Board (AASB) and interpretations effective as of 30 June 2008
- International Financial Reporting Standards and interpretations as adopted by the European Union (EU) effective as of 30 June 2008
- International Financial Reporting Standards and interpretations as issued by the International Accounting Standards Board effective as of 30 June 2008
- those standards and interpretations adopted early for each applicable reporting period as described below

The above standards and interpretations are collectively referred to as 'IFRS' in this report.

The principal standards that have been adopted for the first time in these financial statements are:

- IFRS 7/AASB 7 'Financial Instruments: Disclosures'. IFRS 7/AASB 7 modifies the basis and details of disclosures concerning financial instruments, but does not impact the recognition or measurement of financial instruments
- Amendment to IAS 1/AASB 101 'Presentation of Financial Statements'. This amendment requires new disclosures concerning the objectives, policies and processes for managing capital
- AASB 2007–4 'Amendments to Australian Accounting Standards arising from ED 151 and Other Amendments'. AASB 2007–4 reinstates optional accounting treatments permitted by IFRS that were not initially available under Australian Accounting Standards. Refer 'Change in accounting policy' below for the impact of the adoption of AASB 2007–4 on the financial statements.

Basis of measurement

The financial report is drawn up on the basis of historical cost principles, except for derivative financial instruments and certain other financial assets which are carried at fair value.

Currency of presentation

All amounts are expressed in millions of US dollars, unless otherwise stated, consistent with the predominant functional currency of the Group's operations.

Change in accounting policy

The accounting policies have been consistently applied by all entities included in the Group consolidated financial report and are consistent with those applied in all prior years presented, except for the impact of adopting AASB 2007–4 'Amendments to Australian Accounting Standards arising from ED 151 and Other Amendments'. AASB 2007–4 reinstates optional accounting treatments permitted by IFRS that were not initially available under Australian Accounting Standards. The principal impacts of AASB 2007–4 are described below.

Proportionate consolidation

As permitted by AASB 2007–4 'Amendments to Australian Accounting Standards arising from ED 151 and Other Amendments' and IAS 31 'Interests in Joint Ventures', the Group has adopted the policy of recognising its proportionate interests in the assets, liabilities, revenues and expenses of jointly controlled entities within each applicable line item of the financial statements. All such

FIGURE 18.17 *(continued)*

interests were previously recognised using the equity method. The Group believes the change in policy to proportionate consolidation of jointly controlled entities provides more relevant information about the financial performance and financial position of the Group.

Following this change in policy, comparative information has been restated for all periods included in these financial statements, with the impact summarised below. There was no impact on profit after taxation, profit attributable to members of the Group, total equity or the Group's earnings per share in the current or comparative periods.

Intangible assets

Amounts paid for the acquisition of identifiable intangible assets, such as software and licences, are capitalised at the fair value of consideration paid and are recorded at cost less accumulated amortisation and impairment charges. Identifiable intangible assets with a finite life are amortised on a straight-line basis over their expected useful life, which is typically no greater than eight years. The Group has no identifiable intangible assets for which the expected useful life is indefinite.

Property, plant and equipment

Property, plant and equipment is recorded at cost less accumulated depreciation and impairment charges. Some assets acquired prior to 1 July 1998 are measured at deemed cost, being the revalued amount of the asset immediately prior to that date. Subsequent to 1 July 1998, the cost regime was applied to all assets. Cost is the fair value of consideration given to acquire the asset at the time of its acquisition or construction and includes the direct cost of bringing the asset to the location and condition necessary for operation and the direct cost of dismantling and removing the asset. Disposals are taken to account in the income statement. Where the disposal involves the sale or abandonment of a significant business (or all of the assets associated with such a business) the gain or loss is disclosed as an exceptional item.

Source: BHP Billiton (2008, pp. 169, 170, 172, 173).

18.7.2 Capital

Paragraph 134 of IAS 1 requires disclosure of information that enables users of financial statements to evaluate the entity's management of capital. This requirement encompasses qualitative information about objectives, policies and processes, including a description of what is managed as capital, the nature of any externally imposed capital requirements, whether the entity has complied with externally imposed requirements, and, if the entity has not complied with external requirements, the implications of non-compliance.

Quantitative disclosures are also required, including summary data of what is managed as capital. This may differ from reported equity because an entity may exclude some components of equity, such as deferred amounts pertaining to cash flow hedges, from what is managed as capital, while including some items that are classified as liabilities, such as subordinated debt.

The standard adopts a management perspective by focusing on how capital is viewed by management, rather than prescribing specific definitions of capital for the purposes of the disclosures. The entity is required to base its capital disclosures on the information provided internally to key management personnel (para. 136).

18.7.3 Other disclosures

IAS 1 prescribes other disclosures, including certain information about dividends and corporate details, such as the legal structure.

Dividends may be proposed or declared (i.e. approved by the appropriate authorising body such as the directors) before the directors or other governing body approve the issue of the financial statements. Unless the dividends are declared before the end of the reporting period they cannot be recognised. In accordance with IAS 10 *Events after the Reporting Period*, dividends that have not been recognised as a liability in the financial statements but which have been proposed or declared before the authorisation of the issue of the financial statements must be disclosed in the notes to the financial statements. Paragraph 137(a) of IAS 1 requires the disclosure to include the amount of the dividends that have been proposed or declared but not recognised, and the related amount of the dividend per share. The amount of any cumulative preference dividends that have not been recognised as liabilities must be disclosed in accordance with paragraph 137(b).

IAS 1 also requires disclosure of certain non-financial information. The prescribed disclosures include (para. 138):

- the legal form of the entity such as whether it is a company or a trust
- the country of incorporation
- the address of the registered office or the principal place of business (if different from the registered office)
- a description of the nature of the entity's operations and its principal activities
- the name of the parent and the ultimate parent of the group.

Other notes are then normally presented in the following order:

(a) supporting information for items presented in the statement of financial position, statement of comprehensive income, statement of changes in equity and statement of cash flows, in the order in which each statement and each line is presented; and

(b) other disclosures that do not appear in the financial statements, including:

- contingent liabilities (refer to chapter 4)
- unrecognised contractual commitments, including commitments under operating leases (refer to chapter 13)
- non-financial disclosures, such as an entity's risk management objectives and policies (refer to chapter 5).

Figure 18.18 shows the disclosure of contingent liabilities made in note 27 to the 2008 consolidated financial statements of BHP Billiton.

27. Contingent liabilities

Contingent liabilities at balance date, not otherwise provided for in the financial report, are categorised as arising from:

	2008 US$M	2007 US$M
Jointly controlled entities		
Bank guarantees[b]	—	1
Other[a]	535	416
	535	417
Subsidiaries and jointly controlled assets (including guarantees)		
Bank guarantees[b]	1	1
Performance guarantees[b]	—	25
Other[a]	327	296
	328	322
Total contingent liabilities	863	739

(a) Other contingent liabilities relate predominantly to actual or potential litigation of the Group for which amounts are reasonably estimable but the liability is not probable and therefore the Group has not provided for such amounts in these financial statements. The amounts relate to a number of actions against the Group, none of which are individually significant. Additionally, there are a number of legal claims or potential claims against the Group, the outcome of which cannot be foreseen at present, and for which no amounts have been included in the table above.

(b) The Group has entered into various counter-indemnities of bank and performance guarantees related to its own future performance in the normal course of business.

FIGURE 18.18 Contingent liabilities of BHP Billiton at 30 June 2008

Source: BHP Billiton (2008, p. 216).

SUMMARY

IAS 1 *Presentation of Financial Statements* is a disclosure standard that prescribes the structure and content of general purpose financial statements, other than condensed interim financial statements. It prescribes various matters that are intended to ensure that the financial statements, which comprise a statement of financial position, statement of comprehensive income, statement of cash flows, statement of changes in equity and notes, faithfully present the financial position, financial performance and cash flows of an entity. These matters include various items that must be presented in the financial statements and other matters that may or must be presented in the notes. All such disclosures are designed to ensure the understandability of the financial statements by users of the financial statements in their economic decision making.`

Discussion questions

1. What is the purpose of a statement of financial position?
2. What are the major limitations of a statement of financial position as a source of information for users of financial statements?
3. Under what circumstances are assets and liabilities ordinarily classified broadly in order of liquidity rather than on a current/non-current classification?
4. Can an asset that is not realisable within 12 months ever be classified as a current asset? If so, under what circumstances?
5. What is meant by classification of expenses by nature or function?
6. What is the objective of a statement of changes in equity?
7. Does the separate identification of profit and other components of comprehensive income provide a meaningful distinction between the effects of different types of non-owner transactions and events?
8. Why is a summary of accounting policies important to ensuring the understandability of financial statements to users of general purpose financial statements?
9. What are some of the more important judgements made that can lead to estimation uncertainty at the end of the reporting period? What disclosures are required in the notes in regard to such matters?
10. What disclosures are required in the notes in regard to accounting policy judgements?

STAR RATING

★ BASIC

★★ MODERATE

★★★ DIFFICULT

Exercises

Exercise 18.1 ★

CLASSIFICATION OF ITEMS IN THE STATEMENT OF FINANCIAL POSITION

The general ledger trial balance of Ella Limited includes the following accounts that are reported in the statement of financial position:

(a) Trade receivables
(b) Work in progress
(c) Trade creditors
(d) Prepayments
(e) Property
(f) Goodwill
(g) Debentures payable
(h) Preference share capital
(i) Unearned revenue
(j) Accrued salaries
(k) Trading securities held
(l) Share capital

Required

Assume you are the accountant responsible for preparing the statement of financial position of Ella Limited for consideration by the company's directors. In which caption and classification on the statement of financial position would you include each of the above accounts? You should assume that assets and liabilities are classified into current and non-current categories and use the minimum line items permitted under IAS 1. If you need additional information to finalise your decision as to the appropriate classification or caption, indicate what information you require.

Exercise 18.2 CURRENT ASSET AND LIABILITY CLASSIFICATIONS

★ The general ledger trial balance of Emily Ltd at 30 June 2010 includes the following asset and liability accounts:

(a) Dividends payable	$ 25 000
(b) Trade receivables	100 000
(c) Accounts payable	85 000
(d) Prepayments	12 000
(e) Inventory of finished goods	120 000
(f) Allowance for doubtful debts	5 000
(g) Cash	10 000
(h) Accrued liabilities	20 000
(i) Inventory of raw materials	60 000
(j) Loan repayable 31 October 2010	50 000
(k) Bank overdraft	75 000
(l) Current tax payable	30 000

The bank overdraft is not payable on demand, but is subject to annual review by the bank and may become due and payable.

Required

Assume you are the accountant of Emily Ltd responsible for the preparation of the statement of financial position of the company at 30 June 2010. Assume the company classifies assets and liabilities using a current/non-current basis. Prepare the current assets and current liabilities sections of the statement of financial position, using the minimum line items permitted under IAS 1.

Exercise 18.3 STATEMENT OF COMPREHENSIVE INCOME

★ The general ledger trial balance of Mia Ltd includes the following accounts at 30 June 2010:

(a) Sales revenue	$1 200 000
(b) Interest income	24 000
(c) Gain on sale of plant	5 000
(d) Valuation gain on trading investments	20 000
(e) Dividends revenue	5 000
(f) Cost of sales	840 000
(g) Finance expenses	18 000
(h) Selling and distribution expenses	76 000
(i) Administrative expenses	35 000
(j) Income tax expense	85 000

Additional information

- The loss on valuation of available-for-sale investments recognised directly in equity was $1000 net of tax.
- Mia Ltd uses the single statement format for the statement of comprehensive income.

Required

Assume you are the accountant of Mia Ltd, responsible for the preparation of the statement of comprehensive income of the company for the year ended 30 June 2010. The company classifies expenses by function. Prepare the statement of comprehensive income of Mia Ltd, showing the analysis of expenses in the statement of comprehensive income.

Exercise 18.4 STATEMENT OF CHANGES IN EQUITY

★ The shareholders' equity section of the statement of financial position of Chloe Ltd at 30 June 2010 is as follows.

	2010	2009
Share capital	$ 200 000	$ 160 000
General reserve	50 000	40 000
Revaluation reserve	74 000	60 000
Retained earnings	170 000	160 000
	$ 494 000	$ 420 000

Additional information

- Chloe Ltd issued 16 000 shares at $2.50 each on 31 May 2010 for cash.
- A transfer of $10 000 was made from retained earnings to the general reserve.
- Comprehensive income for the year was $144 000, including a revaluation gain of $14 000 net of tax.
- Dividends for the year comprised: interim dividend $50 000; final dividend provided $60 000.

Required

Prepare the statement of changes in equity of Chloe Ltd for the year ended 30 June 2010 in accordance with IAS 1.

Exercise 18.5 CURRENT ASSET CLASSIFICATIONS

★ The general ledger trial balance of Charlotte Ltd includes the following asset and liability accounts at 30 June 2010:

(a) Inventory	$ 100 000
(b) Trade receivables	120 000
(c) Prepaid insurance	8 000
(d) Listed investments held for trading purposes at fair value	20 000
(e) Available-for-sale investments	80 000
(f) Cash	30 000
(g) Deferred tax asset	15 000

Additional information

Charlotte Ltd's available-for-sale investments are held as part of a long-term investment strategy.

Required

Assume you are the accountant of Charlotte Ltd responsible for the preparation of the statement of financial position of the company at 30 June 2010. Assume the company classifies assets and liabilities using a current/non-current basis. Prepare the current asset section of the statement of financial position, using the minimum line items permitted under IAS 1.

Exercise 18.6 STATEMENT OF COMPREHENSIVE INCOME

★ The general ledger trial balance of Isabella Ltd includes the following accounts at 30 June 2010:

(a) Sales revenue	$950 000
(b) Interest revenue	25 000
(c) Gain on sale of plant and equipment	10 000
(d) Cost of goods sold	600 000
(e) Finance expenses	15 000
(f) Selling and distribution costs	50 000
(g) Administrative expenses	30 000
(h) Income tax expense	75 000

Additional information

- A revaluation gain of $20 000 net of tax was recognised for available-for-sale investments held during 2010. No available-for-sale investments were sold during the year.
- Isabella Ltd uses the single statement format for the statement of comprehensive income.

Required

Assume you are the accountant of Isabella Ltd responsible for the preparation of the statement of comprehensive income of the company for the year ended 30 June 2010. Assume the company classifies expenses by function. Prepare the statement of comprehensive income of Isabella Ltd, showing the analysis of expenses in the statement.

Exercise 18.7

★★

STATEMENT OF COMPREHENSIVE INCOME

The general ledger trial balance of Olivia Ltd includes the following accounts at 30 June 2010:

(a) Sales revenue	$ 975 000
(b) Interest income	20 000
(c) Share of profit of associates	15 000
(d) Gain on sale of available-for-sale investments	10 000
(e) Decrease in inventories of finished goods	25 000
(f) Raw materials and consumables used	350 000
(g) Employee benefit expenses	150 000
(h) Loss on translation of foreign operations (nil tax effect)	30 000
(i) Depreciation of property, plant and equipment	45 000
(j) Impairment loss on property	80 000
(k) Finance costs	35 000
(l) Other expenses	45 000
(m) Income tax expense	75 000

Additional information

- Available-for-sale (AFS) investments are revalued regularly, with changes in fair value recognised directly in equity. When an AFS financial asset is sold, the accumulated amount recognised in equity for the asset is recognised in profit or loss. Movements in the AFS reserve during the year ended 30 June 2010 comprised:
  - gross revaluation increments recognised $44 000 (related deferred income tax $14 000)
  - gross transfers on sale of AFS investments $10 000 gain (related income tax $3000).
- Olivia Ltd uses the single statement format for the statement of comprehensive income.

Required

Assume you are the accountant of Oliva Ltd responsible for the preparation of the statement of comprehensive income of the company for the year ended 30 June 2010. Assume the company classifies expenses by nature. Prepare the statement of comprehensive income of Oliva Ltd, showing the analysis of expenses in the statement.

Exercise 18.8

★★

STATEMENT OF CHANGES IN EQUITY

The shareholders' section of the statement of financial position of Sophie Ltd at 30 June 2010 was as follows:

	2010	2009	2008
Share capital	$ 300 000	$ 180 000	$ 180 000
Available-for-sale investments revaluation reserve	60 000	40 000	40 000
Retained earnings	210 000	180 000	100 000
	$570 000	$ 400 000	$ 320 000

Additional information

- During the year ended 30 June 2010 an error was detected in the financial statements for the year ended 30 June 2009. The reported profit of $130 000 for 2009 had been overstated in error by $50 000 (net of tax of $20 000). There were no other items of comprehensive income during 2009 and no dividends were paid during 2009. The comparative figures in the equity section of the statement of financial position shown above have already been restated to correct the error.
- Comprehensive income for the year ended 30 June 2010 $160 000, comprising profit $140 000 and other comprehensive income $20 000.
- During 2010 dividends declared amounted to $110 000 (dividends subject to dividend reinvestment scheme $30 000).

Required
Prepare the statement of changes in equity of Sophie Ltd for the year ended 30 June 2010 and comparative amounts for 2009 in accordance with IAS 1.

Exercise 18.9
★★

Consider the following items for Sienna Ltd at 30 June 2010:
(a) contingent liabilities
(b) the effect on retained earnings of the correction of a prior period error
(c) cash and cash equivalents
(d) capital contributed during the year
(e) revaluation gain on land (not reversing any previous revaluation)
(f) judgements that management has made in classifying financial assets
(g) income tax expense
(h) provisions.

Required
State whether each item is reported:
1. in the statement of financial position
2. in profit or loss in the statement of comprehensive income
3. as other comprehensive income in the statement of comprehensive income
4. in the statement of changes in equity
5. in the notes to the financial statements.

Exercise 18.10
★★

Consider the following items for Lily Ltd at 30 June 2010:
(a) loss on revaluation of available-for-sale investments
(b) finance expenses
(c) aggregate amount of dividends declared and paid during the year
(d) revaluation loss on building (not reversing any previous revaluation)
(e) allowance for doubtful debts
(f) transfer from retained earnings to general reserve
(g) contractual commitments under an operating lease
(h) deferred tax liability.

Required
State whether each item is reported:
1. in the statement of financial position
2. in profit or loss in the statement of comprehensive income
3. as other comprehensive income in the statement of comprehensive income
4. in the statement of changes in equity
5. in the notes to the financial statements.

Problems

Problem 18.1
★

PREPARATION OF A STATEMENT OF FINANCIAL POSITION

The summarised general ledger trial balance of Ava Ltd, a manufacturing company, includes the following accounts at 30 June 2010:

	Dr	Cr
Cash	$ 117 000	
Trade debtors	1 163 000	
Allowance for doubtful debts		$ 50 000
Sundry debtors	270 000	
Prepayments	94 000	
Sundry loans (current)	20 000	
Raw materials	493 000	

(continued)

	Dr	Cr
Finished goods	695 000	
Investments in unlisted companies (at cost)	30 000	
Land (at cost)	234 000	
Buildings (at cost)	687 000	
Accumulated depreciation — buildings		80 000
Plant and equipment (at cost)	6 329 000	
Accumulated depreciation — plant and equipment		3 036 000
Goodwill	2 425 000	
Brand names	40 000	
Patents	25 000	
Deferred tax asset	189 000	
Trade creditors		1 078 000
Sundry creditors and accruals		568 000
Bank overdrafts		115 000
Bank loans		1 848 000
Other loans		646 000
Current tax payable		74 000
Provision for employee benefits		222 000
Dividends payable		100 000
Provision for warranty		20 000
Share capital		3 459 000
Retained earnings		1 515 000
	$12 811 000	$12 811 000

Additional information

- The bank overdraft is subject to annual review, which may result in repayment of the balance outstanding.
- Bank loans include loans repayable within 1 year $620 000.
- Other loans outstanding are repayable within 1 year.
- Provision for employee benefits includes $143 000 payable within 1 year.
- Provision for warranty is in respect of a 6-month warranty given over certain goods sold.
- The investment in unlisted companies are long-term investments.

Required

Prepare the statement of financial position of Ava Ltd at 30 June 2010 in accordance with IAS 1, using the captions that a listed company is likely to use.

Problem 18.2

PREPARATION OF A STATEMENT OF FINANCIAL POSITION

★ The summarised general ledger trial balance of Jessica Ltd, a manufacturing company, includes the following accounts at 30 June 2010:

	Dr	Cr
Cash	$ 175 000	
Deposits, at call	36 000	
Trade debtors	1 744 000	
Allowance for doubtful debts		$80 000
Sundry debtors	320 000	
Prepayments	141 000	
Raw materials	490 000	
Work in progress	151 000	
Finished goods	1 042 000	
Investments in listed companies (available for sale)	52 000	

	Dr	Cr
Land, at valuation	250 000	
Buildings, at cost	1 030 000	
Accumulated depreciation — buildings		120 000
Plant and equipment	8 275 000	
Accumulated depreciation — plant and equipment		3 726 000
Leased assets	775 000	
Accumulated depreciation — leased assets		310 000
Goodwill	3 200 000	
Accumulated impairment — goodwill		670 000
Patents	110 000	
Trade creditors		1 617 000
Sundry creditors and accruals		715 000
Bank overdrafts		350 000
Bank loans		2 215 000
Debentures		675 000
Other loans		575 000
Lease liabilities		350 000
Current tax payable		152 000
Deferred tax liability		420 000
Provision for employment benefits		275 000
Provision for restructuring		412 000
Provision for warranty		42 000
Share capital		3 500 000
Investments revaluation reserve		25 000
Land revaluation reserve		81 000
Retained earnings		1 481 000
	$17 791 000	$17 791 000

Additional information

- Bank loans and other loans are all repayable beyond 1 year.
- $300 000 of the debentures is repayable within 1 year.
- Lease liabilities include $125 000 repayable within 1 year.
- Investments in other companies are long-term investments.
- Provision for employment benefits includes $192 000 payable within 1 year.
- The planned restructuring is intended to be completed within 1 year.
- Provision for warranty includes $20 000 estimated to be incurred beyond 1 year.

Required

Prepare the statement of financial position of Jessica Ltd at 30 June 2010 in accordance with IAS 1, using the captions that a listed entity is likely to use.

Problem 18.3 PREPARATION OF A STATEMENT OF FINANCIAL POSITION

★ The summarised general ledger trial balance of Hannah Ltd, an investment company, includes the following accounts at 30 June 2010:

	Dr	Cr
Cash at bank	$ 7 000	
Deposits at call	112 869	
Dividends receivable	15 693	

(continued)

	Dr	Cr
Interest receivable	478	
Outstanding settlements receivable	4 900	
Trading securities	68 455	
Listed securities (available for sale)	1 880 472	
Deferred tax asset	655	
Outstanding settlements payable		$ 10 253
Interest payable		280
Other payables		83
Current tax payable		242
Provision for employee benefits		752
Deferred tax liability		56 414
Share capital		1 368 024
Revaluation reserve — investments		376 090
Retained earnings		278 384
	$2 090 522	$2 090 522

Additional information

- Provision for employee benefits includes $525 payable within 1 year.
- Available-for-sale listed securities are held as long-term investments
- The deferred tax asset and deferred tax liability do not satisfy the criteria for offsetting in accordance with IAS 12.

Required

Prepare the statement of financial position of Hannah Ltd at 30 June 2010 in accordance with IAS 1, using the captions that a listed company is likely to use.

Problem 18.4

PREPARATION OF A STATEMENT OF COMPREHENSIVE INCOME

★ The general ledger trial balance of Grace Ltd, a medical manufacturing and research company, includes the following accounts at 30 June 2010.

	Dr	Cr
Sales revenue		$1 300 000
Interest income		2 000
Gain on sale of plant		26 000
Rental income		2 000
Royalties		10 000
Other revenue		1 000
Cost of sales	$820 000	
Interest on borrowings	33 000	
Sundry borrowing costs	1 000	
Research costs	51 000	
Advertising	25 000	
Sales staff salaries	97 000	
Commission on sales	7 000	
Freight out	32 000	
Shipping supplies	16 000	
Depreciation on sales equipment	5 000	
Administrative salaries	72 000	
Legal and professional fees	13 000	
Office rent expense	30 000	
Insurance expense	14 000	

	Dr	Cr
Depreciation of office equipment	16 000	
Stationery and supplies	5 000	
Miscellaneous expenses	2 000	
Income tax expense	31 000	

Additional information

- Land was revalued by $100 000 during the year ended 30 June 2010. The related tax was $30 000.
- Grace Ltd uses the single statement format for the statement of comprehensive income.

Required

Prepare the statement of comprehensive income of Grace Ltd for the year ended 30 June 2010, using a functional classification of expenses in accordance with IAS 1.

Problem 18.5

★

PREPARATION OF A STATEMENT OF COMPREHENSIVE INCOME

The general ledger trial balance of Amelia Ltd, an investment company, includes the following revenue and expense items for the year ended 30 June 2010:

	Dr	Cr
Dividends from investments		$920 000
Distributions from trusts		70 000
Interest on deposits		70 000
Income from bank bills		10 000
Income from dealing in securities and derivatives (held for trading purposes)		40 000
Loss on credit derivatives (held for trading)	$60 000	
Other income		10 000
Interest expense	10 000	
Administrative staff costs	30 000	
Sundry administrative costs	40 000	
Income tax expense	30 000	

Additional information

- The revaluation gain for available-for-sale investments held during the year ended 30 June 2010 was $70 000. The related tax was $21 000.
- No available-for-sale investments were sold during the year ended 30 June 2010.
- Amelia Ltd uses the single statement format for the statement of comprehensive income.

Required

Prepare the statement of comprehensive income of Amelia Ltd for the year ended 30 June 2010, using a functional classification of expenses in accordance with IAS 1.

Problem 18.6

★★

PREPARATION OF A STATEMENT OF FINANCIAL POSITION AND STATEMENT OF COMPREHENSIVE INCOME

The summarised general ledger trial balance of Ruby Ltd, a distributor of goods, for the year ended 30 June 2010 is detailed below:

	Dr	Cr
Sales of goods		$7 360 000
Share of profits of associates		36 000
Rent received		9 000
Other income		6 000

(continued)

	Dr	Cr
Cost of goods sold	$ 4 978 000	
Distribution expenses	143 000	
Sales and marketing expenses	1 367 000	
Administration expenses	420 000	
Interest expense	74 000	
Other borrowing expenses	6 000	
Income tax expense	141 000	
Cash at bank	20 000	
Cash on deposits, at call	150 000	
Trade debtors	740 000	
Allowance for doubtful debts		24 000
Other debtors	154 000	
Employee share plan loans	260 000	
Raw materials	53 000	
Finished goods	1 190 000	
Investment in associates	375 000	
Land and buildings	426 000	
Accumulated depreciation — land and buildings		61 000
Plant and equipment	2 100 000	
Accumulated depreciation — plant and equipment		940 000
Available-for-sale investments	60 000	
Goodwill	1 450 000	
Bank loans		111 000
Other loans		810 000
Trade creditors		820 000
Employee benefit provisions		153 000
Provision for restructuring		62 000
Current tax payable		30 000
Provision for warranty		40 000
Deferred tax liability		100 000
Issued capital		2 920 000
Retained earnings, 1 July 2009		760 000
Dividends paid	150 000	
Available-for-sale revaluation reserve		15 000
	$14 257 000	$14 257 000

Additional information

- Employee share plan loans receivable include $50 000 due within 1 year.
- $25 000 of bank loans is repayable within 1 year.
- $400 000 of other loans is repayable within 1 year.
- Employee benefit provisions include $110 000 payable within 1 year.
- The planned restructuring is intended to be fully implemented within 1 year.
- Provision for warranty is in respect of a 6-month warranty on certain goods sold.
- The available-for-sale investments were acquired during the current year and were revalued by $23 000 at the end of the reporting period. The related income tax was $8000.
- The available-for-sale investments are held as part of a long-term investment strategy.
- Ruby Ltd uses the single statement format for the statement of comprehensive income and classifies expenses by function.

Required

Prepare the statement of financial position and statement of comprehensive income of Ruby Ltd for the year ended 30 June 2010 in accordance with IAS 1, using statement captions that a listed company is likely to use.

Problem 18.7 ★★★ PREPARATION OF A STATEMENT OF FINANCIAL POSITION, STATEMENT OF COMPREHENSIVE INCOME AND STATEMENT OF CHANGES IN EQUITY

The summarised general ledger trial balance of Georgia Ltd, a manufacturing company, for the year ended 30 June 2010 is detailed below:

	Dr	Cr
Sales of goods		$4 469 000
Interest income		6 000
Cost of goods sold	$2 987 000	
Distribution expenses	86 000	
Sales and marketing expenses	820 000	
Administration expenses	252 000	
Interest expense	44 000	
Other borrowing expenses	4 000	
Income tax expense	85 000	
Cash on hand	4 000	
Cash on deposit, at call	150 000	
Bank overdraft		50 000
Trade debtors	450 000	
Allowance for doubtful debts		14 000
Other debtors	93 000	
Raw materials	188 000	
Finished goods	714 000	
Listed investments (available for sale)	225 000	
Land and buildings	257 000	
Accumulated depreciation — buildings		36 000
Plant and equipment	1 260 000	
Accumulated depreciation — plant and equipment		564 000
Patents	45 000	
Goodwill	870 000	
Bank loans		66 000
Other loans		570 000
Trade creditors		510 000
Employee benefit provisions		93 000
Warranty provision		37 000
Current tax payable		25 000
Deferred tax liability		135 000
Retained earnings, 30 June 2009		326 000
Dividends paid	150 000	
Land revaluation reserve		50 000
Investments revaluation reserve		42 000
Share capital		1 691 000
	$8 684 000	$8 684 000

Additional information

- Share issues during 2010 were $120 000.
- Share capital was $1 541 000 at 30 June 2009.
- Of the $150 000 dividend, $30 000 was reinvested as part of a dividend reinvestment plan.
- The balances of the land revaluation reserve and the investments revaluation reserve at 30 June 2009 were $15 000 credit and $35 000 credit respectively.
- The following revaluations were recognised during the year ended 30 June 2010: land revalued upward by $50 000 (related income tax $15 000) and available-for-sale investments revalued upward by $10 000 (related income tax $3000).

- Georgia Ltd uses the single statement format for the statement of comprehensive income and classifies expenses by function.
- The available-for-sale investments are held as part of a long-term investment strategy.
- $30 000 of bank loans is repayable within 1 year.
- $110 000 of other loans is repayable within 1 year.
- Employee benefit provisions include $62 000 payable within 1 year.
- The warranty provision is in respect of a 9-month warranty given on certain goods sold.
- The bank overdraft facility is subject to annual review and could be withdrawn.

Required

Prepare the statement of financial position, statement of comprehensive income and statement of changes in equity of Georgia Ltd for the year ended 30 June 2010 in accordance with the requirements of IAS 1, using statement captions that a listed company is likely to use.

Problem 18.8

★★★

PREPARATION OF A STATEMENT OF FINANCIAL POSITION, STATEMENT OF COMPREHENSIVE INCOME AND STATEMENT OF CHANGES IN EQUITY

The summarised general ledger trial balance of Emma Ltd, a manufacturing company, for the year ended 30 June 2010 is detailed below:

	Dr	Cr
Sales of goods		$5 000 000
Interest income		22 000
Sundry income		25 000
Change in inventory of work in progress	$ 125 000	
Change in inventory of finished goods		60 000
Raw materials used	2 200 000	
Employee benefit expense	950 000	
Depreciation expense	226 000	
Impairment of patent	25 000	
Rental expense	70 000	
Advertising expense	142 000	
Insurance expense	45 000	
Freight out expense	133 000	
Doubtful debts expense	10 000	
Interest expense	30 000	
Other expenses	8 000	
Income tax expense	320 000	
Cash	4 000	
Cash on deposit, at call	120 000	
Bank overdraft		40 000
Trade debtors	495 000	
Allowance for doubtful debts		18 000
Other debtors	27 000	
Raw materials	320 000	
Finished goods	385 000	
Land	94 000	
Buildings	220 000	
Accumulated depreciation — land and buildings		52 000
Plant and equipment	1 380 000	
Accumulated depreciation — plant and equipment		320 000
Patents	90 000	
Goodwill	620 000	
Bank loans		92 000
Other loans		450 000
Trade creditors		452 000

	Dr	Cr
Employee benefit provisions		120 000
Current tax payable		35 000
Deferred tax liability		140 000
Retained earnings, 30 June 2009		310 000
Dividends paid	210 000	
Share capital		1 137 000
Dividends reinvested		41 000
Deferred cash flow hedge	65 000	
	$8 314 000	$8 314 000

Additional information

- $20 000 of bank loans is repayable within 1 year.
- $90 000 other loans is repayable within 1 year.
- The bank overdraft facility is subject to review every 6 months. The bank may demand repayment within one month of an unfavourable review.
- Emma Ltd uses the single statement format for the statement of comprehensive income and classifies expenses by nature.

Required

Prepare the statement of financial position, statement of comprehensive income and statement of changes in equity of Emma Ltd for the year ended 30 June 2010 in accordance with the requirements of IAS 1, using statement captions that a listed company is likely to use.

References

BHP Billiton 2008, *2008 annual report*, BHP Billiton Limited, www.bhpbilliton.com.

Dresdner Bank Corporation 2007, *Annual report*, Frankfurt am Main, www.dresdner-bank.com.

Nokia 2007, *Nokia in 2007*, Nokia Corporation, Finland, www.nokia.com.

19 Statement of cash flows

ACCOUNTING STANDARDS IN FOCUS

IAS 7 *Statement of Cash Flows*

LEARNING OBJECTIVES

When you have studied this chapter, you should be able to:

- explain the purposes of a statement of cash flows and its usefulness
- explain the definition of cash and cash equivalents
- explain the classification of cash flow activities and classify cash inflows and outflows into operating, investing and financing activities
- contrast the direct and indirect methods of presenting net cash flows from operating activities
- prepare a statement of cash flows
- identify other disclosures required or encouraged by IAS 7
- use a worksheet to prepare a statement of cash flows with more complex transactions.

19.1 INTRODUCTION TO IAS 7

As explained in chapter 2, ultimately, all investors, creditors and other capital providers to an entity want to get cash out of their investment. Consequently, information about an entity's receipts and payments is of fundamental importance to such users of financial statements. The statement of cash flows provides this information by reporting cash inflows and outflows classified into operating, investing and financing activities, and the net movement in cash and cash equivalents during the period.

19.2 SCOPE OF IAS 7

IAS 7 *Statement of Cash Flows* requires that a statement of cash flows be prepared in accordance with the requirements of the standard, and be presented as an integral part of an entity's financial statements for each period for which financial statements are presented.

19.3 PURPOSES OF A STATEMENT OF CASH FLOWS

The overall purpose of a statement of cash flows is to present information about the historical changes in cash and cash equivalents of an entity during the period classified by operating, investing and financing activities. This information is particularly useful to investors, creditors and other users of financial statements to assist in:

- evaluating an entity's ability to generate cash and cash equivalents, and the timing and certainty of their generation
- evaluating an entity's financial structure (including liquidity and solvency) and its ability to meet its obligations and to pay dividends
- understanding the reasons for the difference between profit or loss for a period and the net cash flow from operating activities (the reasons for the differences are often helpful in evaluating the quality of earnings of an entity)
- comparing the operating performance of different entities, because net operating cash flows reported in the statement of cash flows are unaffected by different accounting choices and judgements under accrual accounting used in determining the profit or loss of an entity
- enabling the development of models to assess and compare the present value of the future cash flows of different entities.

19.4 DEFINING CASH AND CASH EQUIVALENTS

Paragraph 6 of IAS 7 defines cash and cash equivalents as follows:

> Cash comprises cash on hand and demand deposits.
>
> Cash equivalents are short-term, highly liquid investments that are readily convertible to known amounts of cash and which are subject to an insignificant risk of changes in value.

Paragraph 7 of IAS 7 explains that cash equivalents are held for the purpose of meeting short-term cash commitments, and not for investment or other purposes. Since a cash-equivalent investment must by definition be readily convertible to cash and have an insignificant risk of changing in value, an investment will qualify as a cash equivalent only if it has a short maturity (usually three months or less). Examples of cash and cash equivalents include cash on hand, cash at bank, short-term money market securities and 90-day term deposits. Equity investments will not qualify unless they are cash equivalents such as preferred shares acquired shortly before their specified maturity date.

Bank borrowings are ordinarily classified as a financing activity, except for bank overdrafts that are repayable on demand and which form an integral part of an entity's cash management. Such overdrafts may fluctuate from being overdrawn to being positive.

The statement of cash flows reports on changes in aggregate cash and cash equivalents. Therefore, movements between items classified as cash and cash equivalents, such as a transfer from cash at bank to a 90-day term deposit, are not reported in the statement of cash flows.

19.5 CLASSIFYING CASH FLOW ACTIVITIES

As stated earlier, cash flow activities are reported in the statement of cash flows classified into operating, investing and financing activities. Paragraph 6 of IAS 7 defines these activities as follows:

> **Operating activities** are the principal revenue-producing activities of the entity and other activities that are not investing or financing activities.
>
> **Investing activities** are the acquisition and disposal of long-term assets and other investments not included in cash equivalents.
>
> **Financing activities** are activities that result in changes in the size and composition of the contributed equity and borrowings of the entity.

Figure 19.1 classifies the typical cash receipts and payments of an entity between operating, investing and financing activities.

Operating activities
- Cash inflows from:
  - Sale of goods
  - Rendering of services
  - Royalties, fees, commissions
  - Interest received (may be investing)
  - Dividends received (may be investing)
- Cash outflows to:
  - Suppliers for goods and services
  - Employees
  - Government for income tax and other taxes
  - Lenders for interest (may be financing)

Investing activities
- Cash inflows from:
  - Sale of property, plant and equipment
  - Sale of intangibles
  - Sale of shares and debt instruments of other entities
  - Repayment of loans to other parties
- Cash outflows to:
  - Acquire property, plant and equipment
  - Acquire intangibles
  - Acquire shares and debt instruments of other entities
  - Lend money to other entities

Financing activities
- Cash inflows from:
  - Issuing shares and other equity instruments
  - Issuing debentures, unsecured notes and other borrowings
- Cash outflows to:
  - Buy back shares
  - Repay debentures, unsecured notes and other borrowings
  - Pay dividends to shareholders (may be operating)

FIGURE 19.1 Typical cash receipts and payments classified by activity

19.5.1 Classifying interest and dividends received and paid

IAS 7 does not prescribe how interest and dividends received and paid should be classified. Rather, paragraph 31 of IAS 7 requires cash flows from interest and dividends received and paid to be disclosed separately and classified in a consistent manner from period to period as operating, investing or financing activities. Paragraph 33 of IAS 7 explains that interest paid and interest and dividends received are usually classified as operating cash flows for a financial institution, but there is no consensus on the classification of these cash flows for other entities. This is because interest paid and interest and dividends received may be classified as operating cash flows — they may be viewed as entering into the determination of profit or loss — or as financing cash flows (for interest paid) and investing cash flows (for interest and dividends received), being viewed as the costs of financing or the returns on investments respectively.

19.5.2 Classifying taxes on income

Paragraph 35 of IAS 7 requires that income tax paid be separately disclosed in the statement of cash flows and classified as cash flows from operating activities, unless it can be specifically identified with financing or investing activities. Paragraph 36 of IAS 7 explains that, while the tax expense may be readily identifiable with investing or financing activities, the related tax flows are often impracticable to identify and may arise in a different period from the cash flows of the underlying transaction. For this reason, taxes paid are usually classified as cash flows from operating activities.

19.6 FORMAT OF THE STATEMENT OF CASH FLOWS

The general format of a statement of cash flows follows the three cash flow activities. Cash flows from operating activities are presented first, followed by cash flows from investing activities and then those from financing activities. The resultant net increase or decrease in cash and cash equivalents during the period is then used to report the movement in cash and cash equivalents from the balance at the beginning of the period to the balance at the end of the period.

A typical format of a statement of cash flows is presented in figure 19.2.

Statement of Cash Flows for the year ended 31 December ...		
Cash flows from operating activities		
Cash receipts from customers	$XXX	
Cash paid to suppliers and employees	(XXX)	
Cash generated from operations	XXX	
Interest received	XXX	
Interest paid	(XXX)	
Income taxes paid	(XXX)	
Net cash from operating activities		XXX
Cash flows from investing activities		
Acquisition of subsidiary, net of cash acquired	(XXX)	
Purchase of property and plant	(XXX)	
Proceeds from sale of plant	XXX	
Net cash used in investing activities		(XXX)
Cash flows from financing activities		
Proceeds from share issue	XXX	
Proceeds from borrowings	XXX	
Payment of borrowings	(XXX)	
Dividends paid	(XXX)	
Net cash from financing activities		XXX
Net increase in cash and cash equivalents		XXX
Cash and cash equivalents at beginning of year		XXX
Cash and cash equivalents at end of year		XXX

FIGURE 19.2 Typical format of a statement of cash flows using the direct method of reporting cash flows from operating activities

19.6.1 Reporting cash flows from operating activities

Paragraph 18 of IAS 7 provides that cash flows from operating activities may be reported using one of two methods:

- the *direct method* — whereby major classes of gross cash receipts and gross cash payments are disclosed, or
- the *indirect method* — whereby profit or loss is adjusted for the effects of transactions of a non-cash nature, any deferrals or accruals of past or future operating cash receipts or payments, and items of income or expense associated with investing or financing cash flows.

The direct method is encouraged.

The typical format of a statement of cash flows illustrated in figure 19.2 uses the direct method. Figure 19.3 illustrates the typical format of the indirect method of reporting cash flows from operating activities.

As can be seen in figure 19.3, depreciation expense is added back to profit in calculating cash flows from operating activities. This is because depreciation expense reduces profit but has no effect on cash flows. The loss on the sale of investment is added back to profit because it reduces profit but does not affect cash flows from operating activities. Conversely, a gain on the disposal of equipment would be deducted from profit in calculating cash flows from operations. The related cash flow (i.e. the cash proceeds on the sale of the equipment) is included in cash flows from investing activities.

Statement of Cash Flows for the year ended 31 December ...	
Profit before tax	$XXX
Adjustments for:	
Depreciation	XXX
Foreign exchange loss	XXX
Loss on sale of equipment	XXX
Interest income	(XXX)
Interest expense	XXX
Increase in trade and other receivables	(XXX)
Decrease in inventories	XXX
Increase in accounts payable	XXX
Decrease in accrued liabilities	(XXX)
Cash generated from operations	XXX
Interest received	XXX
Interest paid	(XXX)
Income taxes paid	(XXX)
Net cash from operating activities	XXX

FIGURE 19.3 Typical format for the indirect method of reporting cash flows from operating activities

Profit is adjusted for the difference between an amount recognised in profit and the corresponding operating cash flows, such as the change in receivables. This process is explained in more detail in section 19.7. Note that in applying the indirect method, an adjustment is made for the total amount of interest income, rather than for the difference between interest income measured on an accrual basis and the amount of interest received. This is because paragraph 31 of IAS 7 requires disclosure of interest received in the statement of cash flows, irrespective of whether cash flows from operating activities are presented using the direct method or the indirect method. Similarly, dividends received and interest paid must be disclosed separately in the statement of cash flows.

19.6.2 Reporting cash flows from investing and financing activities

Paragraph 21 of IAS 7 requires separate reporting of the major classes of gross cash receipts and gross cash payments arising from investing and financing activities, except for certain cash flows (outlined in the following section) that may be reported on a net basis.

19.6.3 Reporting cash flows on a net basis

Paragraph 22 of IAS 7 provides that cash flows arising from the following operating, investing or financing activities may be reported on a net basis:

(a) cash receipts and payments on behalf of customers when the cash flows reflect the activities of the customer rather than those of the entity; and
(b) cash receipts and payments for items in which the turnover is quick, the amounts are large, and the maturities are short.

Examples of cash receipts and payments covered by paragraph 22(a) are the acceptance and repayment of a bank's demand deposits, funds held for customers by an investment entity, and rents collected on behalf of and paid over to the owners of properties. Examples of cash receipts and payments referred to in paragraph 22(b) are principal amounts relating to credit card customers, and the purchase and sale of investments and other short-term borrowings (usually those that have a maturity period of three months or less).

Paragraph 24 of IAS 7 provides that cash flows arising from each of the following activities of a financial institution may be reported on a net basis:

(a) cash receipts and payments for the acceptance and repayment of deposits with a fixed maturity date;

(b) the placement of deposits with and withdrawal of deposits from other financial institutions; and
(c) cash advances and loans made to customers and the repayment of those advances and loans.

For instance, assume an entity finances some of its operations with a 90-day bill acceptance facility with its bank. This means that the entity writes commercial bills, giving rise to a contractual obligation to pay the face value of the bill. The bank accepts the bill and pays the entity a discounted amount, with the difference being interest effectively paid by the entity. Thus, the entity is borrowing the discounted amount of the bill and repaying the face value, which is the sum of the amount borrowed and interest. The entity will have cash inflows from financing activities each time a commercial bill is accepted by the bank and cash outflows from financing activities each time one of its commercial bills matures. Paragraph 22(b) permits the entity to offset the cash received for the 90-day bills against the repayment on maturity, such that only the net movement in the level of borrowing is reported. However, if the entity finances its operations through 180-day bills, it would have to report the related cash receipts and payments on a gross basis because this would not be a short-term borrowing as referred to in paragraphs 22 and 23.

19.7 PREPARING A STATEMENT OF CASH FLOWS

Unlike the statement of financial position and statement of comprehensive income, the statement of cash flows is not prepared from an entity's general ledger trial balance. Preparation requires information to be compiled concerning the cash inflows and cash outflows of the relevant entity over the period covered by the statement. It is possible to compile the required information through a detailed analysis and summary of the cash records of the entity over the period. Ordinarily, though, a statement of cash flows is prepared by using comparative statements of financial position to determine the net amount of changes in assets, liabilities and equities over the period. The comparative statements of financial position are supplemented by various statement of comprehensive income data and additional information extracted from the accounting records of the entity to enable certain cash receipts and payments to be fully identified. This method of preparation is demonstrated in simplified form using the information presented in figure 19.4 (below and opposite). The same method can be used to prepare a consolidated statement of cash flows for a group of entities.

Paris Ltd
Statement of Comprehensive Income
for the year ended 31 December 2010

Revenue		
Sales revenue		$800 000
Interest income		5 000
Gain on sale of plant		4 000
		809 000
Expenses		
Cost of goods sold	$480 000	
Wages and salaries expense	120 000	
Depreciation – plant and equipment	25 000	
Interest expense	4 000	
Other expenses	76 000	705 000
Profit before tax		104 000
Income tax expense		30 000
Profit for the year		74 000
Other comprehensive income		
Gain on available-for-sale investments	2 000	
Income tax	(600)	
Other comprehensive income net of tax		1 400
Total comprehensive income for the year		$ 75 400

Paris Ltd Comparative Statements of Financial Position as at:			
	31 December 2009	31 December 2010	Increase (decrease)
Cash at bank	$ 60 000	$ 56 550	$ (3 450)
Accounts receivable	70 000	79 000	9 000
Inventory	65 000	70 000	5 000
Prepayments	8 000	9 500	1 500
Interest receivable	150	100	(50)
Plant[A]	150 000	165 000	15 000
Investments (AFS)	12 000	14 000	2 000
Intangibles[B]	—	15 000	15 000
	$365 150	$409 150	
Accounts payable	42 000	45 000	3 000
Wages and salaries payable	4 000	5 000	1 000
Accrued interest	—	200	200
Other expenses payable	3 000	1 800	(1 200)
Current tax payable	14 000	16 000	2 000
Deferred tax liability	5 000	8 600	3 600
Long-term borrowings[C]	60 000	70 000	10 000
Share capital	200 000	200 000	—
Retained earnings[D]	37 150	61 150	24 000
AFS Reserve	—	1 400	1400
	$365 150	$409 150	

Additional information extracted from the company's records:

A Plant that had a carrying amount of $10 000 was sold for $14 000 cash. New equipment purchased for cash amounted to $50 000.
B Intangibles ($15 000) were acquired for cash.
C A borrowing of $10 000 was made during the year and received in cash.
D Dividends paid in cash were $50 000.

FIGURE 19.4 Financial statements and additional accounting information of Paris Ltd

19.7.1 Cash flows from operating activities

Ascertaining the net cash flows from operating activities is the first step in preparing a statement of cash flows. The process used varies according to whether the direct or the indirect method of disclosure is used. The recommended direct method of preparation is demonstrated first.

Determining cash receipts from customers

The starting point for determining how much cash was received from customers is the sales revenue reported in the statement of comprehensive income. However, this figure reflects sales made by the entity during the period irrespective of whether the customers have paid for their purchases. Credit sales are recorded by a debit to accounts receivable and a credit to sales revenue. On the other hand, cash received from customers includes sales made in the previous period that are not collected in cash until the current period, and excludes sales made in the current period for which customers have not paid by the end of the period. Hence, cash received from customers (assuming there have been no bad debts written off or settlement discounts given) equals:

Sales revenue + Beginning accounts receivable – Ending accounts receivable

Using the Paris Ltd information from figure 19.4, receipts from customers is determined as follows:

	Sales revenue	$800 000
+	Beginning accounts receivable	70 000
	Cash collectable from customers	870 000
–	Ending accounts receivable	(79 000)
	Receipts from customers	$791 000

The entity may offer settlement discounts to customers for prompt or early payment of their accounts. Settlement discounts are accounted for as a non-cash expense (discount allowed) in profit or loss and a reduction in accounts receivable. Thus, settlement discounts allowed reduce the amount of cash collected from customers and must be adjusted for in calculating cash receipts from customers. Similarly, adjustment would be necessary for bad debts written off if the entity used the direct write-off method of accounting for uncollectable debts. Calculation of cash receipts from customers under the allowance method of accounting for uncollectable debts is considered later in this chapter.

The logic of this calculation is apparent from the following summarised Accounts Receivable account in the general ledger for the year:

Accounts Receivable			
Opening balance	70 000	Bad debts Expense	—
Sales Revenue	800 000	Discount Allowed	—
		Cash receipts	791 000
		Closing balance	79 000
	870 000		870 000

The above summarised general ledger account can be reconstructed from the statement of financial position including comparative amounts (the opening and closing balances) and statement of comprehensive income (bad debts expense, discount allowed and sales revenue). The cash receipts amount is then determined as the 'plug' figure (balancing item) in the Accounts Receivable account.

The above approach may be simplified by working with the change in receivables over the period. Under this approach, cash received from customers (assuming there are no bad debts written off or discounts allowed) equals:

Sales revenue – Increase in accounts receivable
or
+ Decrease in accounts receivable

Thus, cash received from customers for Paris Ltd can alternatively be determined as:

$800 000 – $9000 = $791 000

Determining interest received

A similar approach is used to determine interest received, which equals:

Interest revenue – Increase in interest receivable
or
+ Decrease in interest receivable

Thus, Paris Ltd's interest received is:

$$\$5000 + \$50 = \$5050$$

Determining cash paid to suppliers and employees

Payments to suppliers may comprise purchases of inventory and payments for services. However, not all inventory purchased during the year is reflected in profit or loss as cost of goods sold, because cost of goods sold includes beginning inventory and excludes ending inventory. Purchases of inventory made during the period equals:

Cost of goods sold – Beginning inventory + Ending inventory

Alternatively, this could be expressed as:

Cost of goods sold + Increase in inventory
or
– Decrease in inventory

Using a similar approach to that outlined for cash receipts from customers, it is then necessary to adjust for accounts payable at the beginning and end of the period to arrive at cash paid to suppliers for purchases of inventory. Thus, cash paid to suppliers of inventories is calculated as:

Purchases of inventories + Beginning accounts payable – Ending accounts payable

Alternatively, this could be expressed as:

Purchases of inventory + Decrease in accounts payable
or
– Increase in accounts payable

As shown in figure 19.4, Paris Ltd's comparative statements of financial position report an increase in inventory of $5000 and in accounts payable of $3000. Hence, cash paid to suppliers for purchases is calculated as follows:

	Cost of goods sold	$480 000
+	Increase in inventory	5 000
	Purchases for year	485 000
–	Increase in accounts payable	(3 000)
	Payments to suppliers for purchases of inventory	$482 000

If the entity receives a discount from its suppliers for prompt or early payment of accounts payable the settlement discount received is accounted for as discount revenue and a reduction in accounts payable. Thus, settlement discounts reduce the amount of cash paid to suppliers and must be deducted in calculating cash paid to suppliers.

The logic of the previous calculations incorporating adjustment for discount received is apparent from the following summarised inventory and accounts payable (for inventory) accounts in the general ledger for the year:

Inventory			
Opening balance	65 000	Cost of Goods Sold	480 000
Purchases	485 000	Closing balance	70 000
	550 000		550 000

Accounts Payable			
Discount Received	—	Opening balance	42 000
Cash payments	482 000	Purchases	485 000
Closing balance	45 000		
	527 000		527 000

The above summarised general ledger accounts can be reconstructed from the information contained in the comparative statements of financial position (the opening and closing balances) and the statement of comprehensive income (cost of goods sold). The purchases amount is then determined by the difference in the Inventory account and inserted in the Accounts Payable account. The amount of cash payments can then be determined as the 'plug' figure in reconciling the Accounts Payable account.

A similar approach is taken to determine the amount of payments made to suppliers for services and to employees. Adjustments must be made to the relevant expenses recognised in profit or loss for changes in the beginning and ending amounts of prepayments and relevant accounts payable and accrued liabilities. Thus, payments to suppliers for services is calculated as follows:

Expenses charged in profit or loss	–	Beginning prepayments
	+	Ending prepayments
	+	Beginning accounts payable/accruals
	–	Ending accounts payable/accruals

Alternatively, this could be expressed as:

Expenses charged in profit or loss	+	Increase in prepayments or
	–	Decrease in prepayments
	+	Decrease in accounts payable/accruals or
	–	Increase in accounts payable accounts

Paris Ltd's comparative statements of financial position show:

Increase in prepayments	$1 500
Increase in wages and salaries payable	1 000
Decrease in other expenses payable	(1 200)

Thus cash paid to suppliers of services is calculated as follows:

Other expenses	$76 000
+ Increase in prepayments	1 500
+ Decrease in other expenses payable	1 200
Payments to suppliers of services	$78 700

Similarly, cash paid to employees is calculated as follows:

Wages and salaries expense	$120 000
– Increase in wages and salaries payable	1 000
Payments to employees	$119 000

Using the previous calculations, total payments to suppliers and employees to be reported in the statement of cash flows comprises:

Payments to suppliers for purchases	$482 000
Payments to suppliers for services	78 700
Payments to employees	119 000
Total payments to suppliers and employees	$679 700

Determining interest paid

Using the same approach as for other expenses, Paris Ltd's interest paid is determined as follows:

Interest expense	$4 000
– Increase in accrued interest	200
Interest paid	$3 800

Determining income tax paid

The determination of income tax paid can be complicated by movements in the current and deferred tax accounts that are not reflected in the income tax expense recognised in profit or loss. For example, as explained in chapter 7, deferred tax may arise from a revaluation of property, plant and equipment that causes a difference between the book value and tax base of those assets, thereby resulting in a charge for income tax being made to the revaluation reserve account. Taxes may also be charged to other equity accounts such as the Available-For-Sale Investments Revaluation. As a result, it is often simpler to reconstruct the Deferred Tax Liability account to determine the allocation of income tax expense.

Deferred Tax Liability			
		Opening balance	5 000
		Tax effect recognised in equity	600
Closing balance	8 600	Income Tax Expense	3 000
	8 600		8 600

The above summarised general ledger account can be reconstructed from the comparative statements of financial position (opening and closing balances) and the statement of comprehensive income (tax effect recognised directly in equity). The income tax expense is the deferred component of income tax expense, that is, the amount of income tax expense pertaining to the movement in deferred tax balances.

The movement in the Deferred Tax Liability account for Paris Ltd can be summarised as follows:

Beginning balance	$5 000
+ Tax recognised directly in equity	600
+ Income tax expense (deferred component)	3 000
Ending balance	$8 600

The current component of income tax expense can then be calculated by deducting the deferred component of income tax expense from the total income tax expense recognised in profit or loss. The current component of income tax expense for Paris Ltd can be calculated as follows:

Income tax expense	$30 000
Deferred component of income tax expense	(3 000)
Current component of income tax expense	$27 000

To illustrate, the movement in Paris Ltd's Current Tax Payable account may be summarised as follows:

Beginning balance	$14 000
+ Income tax expense	27 000
– Income tax paid	25 000
Ending balance	$16 000

For Paris Ltd, the amount of income tax paid consists of the final balance in respect of the previous year's current tax payable, and instalments (e.g. quarterly) in respect of the current year. The income tax expense may include an adjustment for any under- or over-accrual for current tax payable at the beginning of the period.

Summarising cash flows from operating activities

Using the direct method, the cash flows from the operating activities section of Paris Ltd's statement of cash flows for the year are presented in figure 19.5.

Paris Ltd
Statement of Cash Flows (extract)
for the year ended 31 December 2010

Cash flows from operating activities	
Cash receipts from customers	$ 791 000
Cash paid to suppliers and employees	(679 700)
Cash generated from operations	111 300
Interest received	*5 050
Interest paid	**(3 800)
Income taxes paid	(25 000)
Net cash from operating activities	$ 87 550

* May be classified as investing
** May be classified as financing

FIGURE 19.5 Cash flows from operating activities (direct method)

The presentation of Paris Ltd's cash flows from operating activities under the indirect method is shown in figure 19.6. In this illustration, wages and salaries payable and other expenses payable are combined as one line item.

Paris Ltd
Statement of Cash Flows (extract)
for the year ended 31 December 2010

Cash flows from operating activities	
Profit before tax	$ 104 000
Adjustment for:	
Depreciation	25 000
Interest income	(5 000)
Gain on sale of plant	(4 000)
Interest expense	4 000
Increase in accounts receivable	(9 000)
Increase in inventory	(5 000)
Increase in prepayments	(1 500)
Increase in accounts payable	3 000
Decrease in other payables	(200)
Cash generated from operations	111 300
Interest received	*5 050
Interest paid	**(3 800)
Income taxes paid	(25 000)
Net cash from operating activities	$ 87 550

* May be classified as investing
** May be classified as financing

FIGURE 19.6 Cash flows from operating activities (indirect method)

19.7.2 Cash flows from investing activities

Determining cash flows from investing activities requires identifying cash inflows and outflows relating to the acquisition and disposal of long-term assets and other investments not included in cash equivalents.

The comparative statements of financial position of Paris Ltd in figure 19.4 show that plant has increased by $15 000, investments by $2000 and intangibles by $15 000. To determine the cash flows relating to these increases, it is necessary to analyse the underlying transactions.

The plant reported in the statement of financial position is net of accumulated depreciation. The net increase in plant reflects the recording of acquisitions, disposals and depreciation. Using the data provided, the analysis of the plant movement (which is net of accumulated depreciation) is as follows:

Beginning balance	$150 000
Acquisitions	50 000
Disposals	(10 000)
Depreciation for year	(25 000)
Ending balance	$165 000

The additional information provided in figure 19.4 states that the acquisitions were made for cash during the period, so no adjustment is necessary for year-end payables. Assuming that there were no outstanding payables for plant purchases at the beginning of the year, the cash flow for plant acquisitions for the year is $50 000 (note A in figure 19.4). (If payables for plant purchases were outstanding at the beginning of the period, the amount would need to be included in plant purchases paid during the period.)

The gain or loss on disposal of plant is the difference between the carrying amount and the proceeds on the sale of plant. Thus, the proceeds on sale of plant can be calculated as:

Net book value of plant disposed	+	Gain on disposal of plant
		or
	−	Loss on disposal of plant

For Paris Ltd, the calculation is as follows:

$10 000 + 4000 = $14 000

However, the proceeds from the sale of plant equals the cash inflow for the year only if there are no receivables outstanding arising from the sale of plant at either the beginning or end of the year. If receivables exist, the cash inflow is determined using the approach that was previously outlined for sales revenue and interest receivable. For simplicity, it is assumed that Paris Ltd had no receivables outstanding, at the beginning or end of the year, arising from the sale of plant.

Issues similar to those outlined for the acquisition of plant arise in respect of investments and intangibles. The comparative statements of financial position for Paris Ltd show that the movement in intangibles equals the additional cash acquisitions made during the period, as detailed in the additional information presented in figure 19.4. Note, however, that the movement in intangibles equals the cash outflows for the year only if it is assumed that there were no related accounts payable at the beginning or end of the year that were settled during the year. If payables exist, the cash outflow is determined using the approach that was previously outlined for cash paid to suppliers and employees.

Investments increased by $2000 during the year, as shown in the comparative statements of financial position. This increase relates to the gain on revaluation of available-for-sale investments reported in the statement of comprehensive income. Thus the movement in investments does not affect cash flows from investing activities. Using the above information, the cash flows from investing activities reported in Paris Ltd's statement of cash flows for 2010 is presented in figure 19.7.

Paris Ltd Statement of Cash Flows (extract) for the year ended 31 December 2010	
Cash flows from investing activities	
Purchase of intangibles	$(15 000)
Purchase of plant	(50 000)
Proceeds from sale of plant	14 000
Net cash used in investing activities	$(51 000)

FIGURE 19.7 Cash flows from investing activities

19.7.3 Cash flows from financing activities

Determining cash flows from financing activities requires identifying cash flows that resulted in changes in the size and composition of contributed equity and borrowings.

The additional information (C) in figure 19.4 confirms that the increase in borrowings of $10 000 derived from the comparative statements of financial position of Paris Ltd arose from an additional borrowing. It would normally be necessary to analyse the net movement in borrowings in order to identify whether the movement reflects repayments and additional borrowings, and whether any new borrowings arose from non-cash transactions.

Share capital is unchanged at $200 000. The movement in retained earnings of $24 000 reflects:

Profit for the period	$74 000	
Dividends (paid in cash)	50 000	(D in figure 19.4)
Net movement	$24 000	

Using the previous information, the financing cash flow section of Paris Ltd's statement of cash flows for 2010 is presented in figure 19.8.

Paris Ltd Statement of Cash Flows (extract) for the year ended 31 December 2010	
Cash flows from financing activities	
Proceeds from borrowings	$ 10 000
Dividends paid	*(50 000)
Net cash used in financing activities	$(40 000)

*Dividends paid may be classified as an operating cash flow.

FIGURE 19.8 Cash flows from financing activities

All that remains to complete the statement of cash flows for Paris Ltd is the determination of the net increase or decrease for the period in cash held, and to use this total to reconcile cash at the beginning and end of the year.

The complete statement of cash flows for Paris Ltd (using the direct method for reporting cash flows from operating activities) is shown in figure 19.9.

The balance of cash at year-end of $56 550 shown in figure 19.9 agrees with the cash at bank balance shown in the statement of financial position at 31 December 2010 in figure 19.4. There are no cash equivalents such as short-term deposits or a bank overdraft. The components of cash and cash equivalents must be disclosed and reconciled to amounts reported in the statement of financial position. The reconciliation provides better transparency of how items are reported in the financial statements. For example, cash and cash equivalents may comprise cash, short-term deposits and an overdraft. The end-of-period amount of cash and cash equivalents reported in the statement of cash flows may differ from that reported in the statement of financial position because the cash and short-term deposits are reported as current assets while the overdraft is a liability. In addition, paragraph 48 requires an entity to disclose the amount of significant cash and cash-equivalent balances held that are not available for general use, for example, as a result of exchange controls that may affect the general availability of the cash held by a foreign subsidiary in the case of a consolidated statement of cash flows.

Paris Ltd Statement of Cash Flows for the year ended 31 December 2010		
Cash flows from operating activities		
Cash receipts from customers	$ 791 000	
Cash paid to suppliers and employees	(679 700)	
Cash generated from operations	111 300	
Interest received	5 050	
Interest paid	(3 800)	
Income taxes paid	(25 000)	
Net cash from operating activities		$ 87 550
Cash flows from investing activities		
Purchase of intangibles	$ (15 000)	
Purchase of plant	(50 000)	
Proceeds from sale of plant	14 000	
Net cash used in investing activities		(51 000)
Cash flows from financing activities		
Proceeds from borrowings	$ 10 000	
Dividends paid	(50 000)	
Net cash used in financing activities		(40 000)
Net decrease in cash and cash equivalents		(3 450)
Cash and cash equivalents at beginning of year		60 000
Cash and cash equivalents at end of year		$ 56 550

FIGURE 19.9 Complete statement of cash flows of Paris Ltd

19.8 OTHER DISCLOSURES

Additional information is often necessary to obtain a complete picture of the change in an entity's financial position, because not all transactions are simple cash transactions. Significant changes can result from the acquisition or disposal of subsidiaries or other business units, or from transactions that do not involve current cash flows.

19.8.1 Acquisitions and disposals of subsidiaries and other business units

Part 4 of this book deals with the financial reporting of consolidated groups of entities. When a parent entity acquires an operating entity, or disposes of an existing subsidiary, a comparative consolidated statement of financial position of the group before and after the acquisition or disposal will frequently disclose significant changes in the assets and liabilities arising from the acquisition or disposal. Financial statement users need to be aware of such changes in order to understand the change in financial position of the consolidated group, so IAS 7 specifies additional reporting requirements relating to the acquisitions and disposals of subsidiaries and other business units. They are as follows:

39. The aggregate cash flows arising from acquisitions and from disposals of subsidiaries or other business units shall be presented separately and classified as investing activities.
40. An entity shall disclose, in aggregate, in respect of both acquisitions and disposals of subsidiaries or other business units during the period each of the following:
    (a) the total purchase or disposal consideration;
    (b) the portion of the purchase or disposal consideration discharged by means of cash and cash equivalents;

(c) the amount of cash and cash equivalents in the subsidiary or business unit acquired or disposed of;
(d) the amount of the assets and liabilities other than cash or cash equivalents in the subsidiary or business unit acquired or disposed of, summarised by each major category.

Separate presentation of the cash flow effects of acquisitions and disposals of subsidiaries and other business units is required. The cash flow effects of disposals are not deducted from those of acquisitions. The aggregate amount of the cash paid (received) as purchase (sale) consideration is reported in the statement of cash flows net of cash equivalents acquired (disposed of).

For example, assume Blois Ltd acquired Chartres Ltd during the period at a cost of $1.5 million paid in cash and that Chartres Ltd held cash and cash equivalents of $0.1 million at the time of the acquisition. The net cash flow arising from the acquisition reported in the consolidated statement of cash flows for the period would be $1.4 million. This would be reported as a cash outflow from investing activities.

19.8.2 Non-cash transactions

Not all investing or financing transactions involve current cash flows, although such transactions may significantly affect the financial structure of the entity. However, such transactions need to be understood in order to comprehend the change in financial position of an entity. Examples include:

- acquisition of assets by means of a finance lease or by assuming other liabilities
- acquisition of assets or an entity by means of an equity issue
- conversion of debt to equity and preference shares to ordinary shares
- refinancing of long-term debt
- payment of dividends through a share reinvestment scheme.

In regard to non-cash transactions, paragraph 43 of IAS 7 states:

> Investing and financing transactions that do not require the use of cash or cash equivalents shall be excluded from a statement of cash flows. Such transactions shall be disclosed elsewhere in the financial statements in a way that provides all the relevant information about these investing and financing activities.

19.8.3 Disclosures that are encouraged but not required

Paragraph 50 of IAS 7 encourages, but does not require, additional information that may be relevant to users in understanding the financial position and liquidity of an entity. They are as follows:

(a) the amount of undrawn borrowing facilities that may be available for future operating activities and to settle capital commitments, indicating any restrictions on the use of these facilities;
(b) the aggregate amounts of the cash flows from each of operating, investing and financing activities related to interests in joint ventures reported using proportionate consolidation;
(c) the aggregate amount of cash flows that represent increases in operating capacity separately from those cash flows that are required to maintain operating capacity; and
(d) the amount of the cash flows arising from the operating, investing and financing activities of each reportable segment (see IFRS 8 *Operating segments*).

Chapter 28 of this book provides an outline of proportionate consolidation of interests in joint ventures referred to in paragraph 50(b) of the standard. Chapter 20 deals with segment reporting referred to in paragraph 50(d).

19.9 COMPREHENSIVE EXAMPLE

The example in this section demonstrates a more complex statement of cash flows prepared using a worksheet. Figure 19.10 presents the financial statements of Amiens Ltd, and the worksheet is shown in figure 19.11. An explanation of the reconciling adjustments follows the worksheet. The indirect method is used to present cash flows from operating activities.

The worksheet commences with further information about items reported in the financial statements, such as the components of income tax expense and the composition of accounts payable at the beginning and end of the year. The body of the worksheet lists the items reported in the comparative statements of financial position and shows how the movement in each item is used in the calculation of items reported in the statement of cash flows. This is followed by an explanation in section 19.9.1 of each item reported in the statement of cash flows, commencing with the items shown in the operating activities section of the statement.

Amiens Ltd
Comparative Statements of Financial Position as at:

	31 December 2009	31 December 2010	Increase (decrease)
Cash	$ 60 000	$ 69 800	$ 9 800
Short-term deposits	120 000	140 000	20 000
Accounts receivable, net	140 000	190 000	50 000
Inventory	130 000	155 000	25 000
Prepayments	16 000	19 000	3 000
Interest receivable	300	200	(100)
Investment in associate	40 000	45 000	5 000
Land	80 000	120 000	40 000
Plant	300 000	420 000	120 000
Accumulated depreciation	(50 000)	(65 000)	(15 000)
Intangibles	90 000	60 000	(30 000)
	$926 300	$ 1 154 000	$227 700
Accounts payable	84 000	90 000	6 000
Accrued liabilities	14 000	12 000	(2 000)
Current tax payable	28 000	32 000	4 000
Deferred tax liability	20 000	25 000	5 000
Borrowings	120 000	180 000	60 000
Share capital	600 000	680 000	80 000
Retained earnings	60 300	135 000	74 700
	$926 300	$1 154 000	$227 700

Amiens Ltd
Statement of Comprehensive Income
for the year ended 31 December 2010

Revenue		
Sales revenue		$1 600 000
Interest		10 000
Share of profits of associate		10 000
Gain on sale of plant		8 000
		$1 628 000
Expenses		
Cost of goods sold	$960 000	
Wages and salaries	240 000	
Depreciation – plant	40 000	
Impairment – intangibles	30 000	
Interest	12 000	
Doubtful debts	8 000	
Other expenses	132 000	1 422 000
Profit before tax		206 000
Income tax expense		(65 000)
Profit for the year		141 000
Other comprehensive income		—
Total comprehensive income		$ 141 000

FIGURE 19.10 Financial statements of Amiens Ltd

FIGURE 19.11 Statement of cash flows worksheet

Other information used in worksheet:		
(a) Changes in equity:	**Share capital**	**Retained earnings**
Balance at 31 December 2009	$600 000	$ 60 300
Profit for the year	—	141 000
Dividends – cash	—	(36 300)
– reinvested under dividend scheme	30 000	(30 000)
Cash share issue	50 000	—
Balance at 31 December 2010	$680 000	$135 000
(b) Investment in associate (equity method)		
Balance at 31 December 2009		$ 40 000
Share of profit of associate		10 000
Dividend received		(5 000)
Balance at 31 December 2010		$ 45 000
(c) Land		
Additional land acquired		$ 40 000
Finance provided by vendor		(35 000)
Cash paid		$ 5 000
(d) Plant		
Acquisitions		$180 000
Cash paid		171 000
Accounts payable outstanding at year-end		9 000
		$180 000
Disposals – cost		60 000
Accumulated depreciation		(25 000)
Proceeds received in cash		43 000
(e) Intangibles		
There were no acquisitions or disposals.		
Impairment write-down		$ 30 000
(f) Accounts payable comprises:	**2009**	**2010**
Purchase of inventory	$ 49 000	$ 56 000
Purchase of plant	15 000	9 000
Other purchases	20 000	25 000
	$ 84 000	$ 90 000
(g) Accrued liabilities comprises accruals for:		
Interest	$ 1 200	$ 2 100
Wages, salaries and other expenses	12 800	9 900
	$ 14 000	$ 12 000
(h) Borrowings of $60 000		
Increase reflects:		
Land vendor finance		$ 35 000
Additional cash borrowing		25 000
		$ 60 000

FIGURE 19.11 *(continued)*

(i) Income tax expense comprises:	
Currently payable	$ 60 000
Movement in deferred tax	5 000
	$ 65 000
(j) Movement in current tax payable:	
Balance at 31 December 2009	$ 28 000
Income tax expense	60 000
Payments made	(56 000)
Balance at 31 December 2010	$ 32 000

Amiens Ltd
Statement of Cash Flows Worksheet
for year ended 31 December 2010

	Balance 31.12.09	Reconciling items Debits		Reconciling items Credits		Balance 31.12.10
Cash	$ 60 000	(26)	$9 800			$ 69 800
Short-term deposits	120 000	(27)	20 000			140 000
Accounts receivable, net	140 000	(2)	50 000			190 000
Interest receivable	300			(13)	100	200
Inventory	130 000	(3)	25 000			155 000
Prepayments	16 000	(4)	3 000			19 000
Investment in associate	40 000	(7)	5 000			45 000
Land	80 000	(18)	5 000			
		(19)	35 000			120 000
Plant	300 000	(9)	8 000	(21)	43 000	
		(19)	180 000	(22)	25 000	420 000
Accumulated depreciation	(50 000)	(22)	25 000	(10)	40 000	(65 000)
Intangibles	90 000			(11)	30 000	60 000
	$926 300					$1 154 000
Accounts payable	84 000	(20)	6 000	(5)	12 000	90 000
Accrued liabilities	14 000	(6)	2 900	(14)	900	12 000
Current tax payable	28 000			(16)	4 000	32 000
Deferred tax liability	20 000			(17)	5 000	25 000
Borrowings	120 000			(19)	35 000	
				(22)	25 000	180 000
Share capital	600 000			(23)	50 000	
				(24)	30 000	680 000
Retained earnings	60 300	(15)	65 000	(1)	206 000	
		(24)	30 000			
		(25)	36 300			135 000
	$926 300					$1 154 000
Cash flow statement data						
Operating activities						
Profit before tax		(1)	$206 000			$ 206 000
Increase in accounts receivable				(2)	$50 000	(50 000)
Increase in inventory				(3)	25 000	(25 000)
Increase in prepayments				(4)	3 000	(3 000)
Increase in accounts payable		(5)	12 000			12 000
Decrease in accrued liabilities				(6)	2 900	(2 900)
Share of profits of associate				(7)	10 000	(10 000)

(continued)

FIGURE 19.11 *(continued)*

	Balance 31.12.09	Reconciling items		Balance 31.12.10
		Debits	Credits	
Interest income			(8) 10 000	(10 000)
Gain on sale of plant			(9) 8 000	(8 000)
Depreciation – plant		(10) $ 40 000		40 000
Impairment – intangibles		(11) 30 000		30 000
Interest expense		(12) 12 000		12 000
Cash generated from operations		300 000	108 900	191 100
Interest received		(8) 10 000		
		(13) 100		10 100
Dividend received from associate		(7) 5 000		5 000
Interest paid		(14) 900	(12) 12 000	(11 100)
Income tax paid		(16) 4 000		
		(17) 5 000	(15) 65 000	(56 000)
Net cash from operating activities		325 000	185 900	139 100
Investing activities				
Purchase of land			(18) 5 000	(5 000)
Purchase of plant			(19) 180 000	
			(20) 6 000	(186 000)
Proceeds from sale of plant		(21) 43 000		43 000
Net cash used in investing activities		43 000	191 000	(148 000)
Financing activities				
Proceeds from borrowings		(22) 25 000		25 000
Proceeds from share issue		(23) 50 000		50 000
Payment of cash dividends			(25) 36 300	(36 300)
Net cash flows from financing activities		75 000	36 300	38 700
Net increase in cash and cash equivalents		443 000	413 200	$ 29 800
Increase in cash			(26) 9 800	
Increase in short-term deposits			(27) 20 000	
		$443 000	$ 443 000	

19.9.1 Explanation of reconciling adjustments in worksheet

Explanations of the reconciling adjustments made in compiling the statement of cash flows data in figure 19.11 are below.

A — Profit before tax

When using the indirect method of presenting cash flows from operating activities, the profit before tax of $206 000 is the starting point. Accordingly, an adjustment (1) is made to retained earnings to reflect the profit before tax for the year, and a separate adjustment (15) is made for income tax expense.

B — Increase in net accounts receivable

The net increase in accounts receivable of $50 000 is a movement that did not result in cash flows for the period. It must therefore be deducted from profit before tax (adjustment 2). Because the indirect method is being used, there is no need to include separate adjustments for bad debts written off, changes in any provision for doubtful debts or discounts allowed. Such adjustments are necessary to determine cash flows from customers only under the direct method.

C — Increase in inventory

The increase in inventory of $25 000 results in an operating cash outflow subject to any increase funded through an increase in accounts payable (adjustment 3).

D — Prepayments

The increase in prepayments is an operating cash outflow during the period that is not reflected in profit before tax (adjustment 4).

E — Accounts payable

Accounts payable comprise:

	2009	2010	Increase (decrease)	
Amount arising from the:				
Purchase of inventory and services	$69 000	$81 000	$12 000	(Adjustment 5)
Purchase of plant	15 000	9 000	(6 000)	(Adjustment 20)
	$84 000	$90 000	$ 6 000	

The increase in accounts payable arising from the purchase of inventory and services does not involve an operating cash outflow for the period. In this example, it partly offsets the increase in inventory reflected in adjustment 3.

The reduction in accounts payable arising from the purchase of plant of $6000 increases the cash outflow for the purchase of plant (adjustment 20).

F — Accrued liabilities

Accrued liabilities comprise:

	2009	2010	Increase (decrease)
Amount arising from:			
Accrued interest	$ 1 200	$ 2 100	$ 900
Other	12 800	9 900	(2 900)
	$14 000	$12 000	$(2 000)

The reduction in other accrued liabilities increases the operating cash outflows for the year and is reflected in adjustment 6. The increase in accrued interest payable does not involve a cash flow and is reflected in adjustment 14.

G — Share of profits of associate

The investment in associate (accounted for under the equity method) increased by $5000, comprising the share of profits of the associate of $10 000, net of a dividend received of $5000. The $10 000 share of profits is excluded from cash generated from operations and the $5000 dividend received is included in net cash from operating activities. The $5000 net increase in the investment does not represent a cash flow and this is reflected in the $10 000 adjustment, net of the $5000 dividend (adjustment 7).

H — Interest income

Interest income is initially transferred out of profit before tax in order to arrive at cash generated from operations (adjustment 8), and is then increased by the reduction in interest receivable of $100 (adjustment 13) to arrive at the interest cash inflow. Alternatively, the interest cash inflow could be classified as an investing activity.

I — Gain on sale of plant

Note that the accumulated depreciation for the plant sold is transferred to the plant account and that the gross proceeds from the sale of the plant are shown as a credit adjustment. These transfers are consistent with the following journal entries:

Accumulated Depreciation	Dr	25 000	
Plant	Cr		25 000
(Closing accumulated depreciation against the plant account on disposal of the plant)			

The carrying amount of the plant sold is $35 000.

Cash	Dr	43 000	
Plant	Cr		35 000
Gain on Disposal	Cr		8 000
(Disposal of plant)			

Plant is reduced by $35 000, being the net effect of the credit to plant for the cash proceeds from the sale $43 000 (Cr), and debit against plant for the gain on disposal of $8000 (Dr).

Gain on disposal of plant of $8000 is not a cash inflow, so it is deducted from profit before tax in arriving at net cash from operating activities (adjustment 9). A separate adjustment is made for the proceeds from sale of plant of $43 000 as an investing cash flow. The reduction in plant for the amount of plant sold, $60 000, comprises the following adjustments:

Proceeds	$43 000	(Adjustment 21)
– Gain on sale	(8 000)	(Adjustment 9)
+ Accumulated depreciation	25 000	(Adjustment 22)
Cost of plant sold	$60 000	

J — Depreciation of plant and impairment of intangibles

Both of these expenses in the statement of comprehensive income do not constitute cash flows in the current period, so they are added back in arriving at net cash from operating activities (depreciation adjustment 10 of $40 000 and impairment adjustment 11 of $30 000).

K — Interest expense

Interest expense is initially transferred out of profit before tax in order to arrive at cash generated from operations (adjustment 12). It is then reduced by the increase in accrued interest $900 (adjustment 14), to arrive at the interest cash outflow. The calculation is shown above in explanation F. Alternatively, the interest cash outflow could be classified as a financing activity.

L — Income tax paid

Income tax expense of $65 000 (adjustment 15) is reduced by the increase in current tax payable of $4000 (adjustment 16) and the increase in deferred income tax of $5000 (adjustment 17) to determine the income tax cash outflow of $56 000. In this example, there are no tax charges — such as on revaluation or translation reserve increments — made directly to equity accounts. This is evident because there are no components of other comprehensive income reported in the statement of comprehensive income.

M — Purchase of land and plant

Additional land was acquired at a cost of $40 000, with $35 000 being financed by the vendor. Adjustment 18 records the cash outflow of $5000 and adjustment 19 records the non-cash component of $35 000. The other side of the adjustment is made to borrowings.

Plant acquisitions for the year are $180 000 (adjustment 19). This amount is increased by the reduction in plant accounts payable of $6000 (adjustment 20); this is discussed in explanation E above.

N — Proceeds from borrowings

The cash proceeds from borrowings of $25 000 comprise the gross increase in borrowings of $60 000 ($180 000 – $120 000) reduced by the $35 000 of land vendor finance (adjustment 19); this is discussed in explanation M above.

O — Proceeds from share issue and payment of cash dividends

To determine the proceeds from share issue (adjustment 23), the increase in share capital of $80 000 ($680 000 – $600 000) is reduced by the $30 000 of reinvested dividends (adjustment 24) because these dividends did not involve a cash inflow. Similarly, cash flows from financing activities include only the $36 300 of dividends paid in cash (adjustment 25).

P — Increase in cash and short-term deposits

Short-term deposits are considered to be cash equivalents. Therefore, the increase is included in the net increase in cash and cash equivalents for the period of $29 800 (adjustments 26 and 27).

Figure 19.12 contains Amiens Ltd's statement of cash flows for the year ended 31 December 2010 (without prior year comparatives).

FIGURE 19.12 Statement of cash flows of Amiens Ltd

Amiens Ltd Statement of Cash Flows for year ended 31 December 2010		
Cash flows from operating activities		
Profit before tax	$ 206 000	
Adjustments for:		
Depreciation	40 000	
Impairment of intangibles	30 000	
Gain on sale of plant	(8 000)	
Share of profits of associate	(10 000)	
Interest income	(10 000)	
Interest expense	12 000	
Increase in receivables	(50 000)	
Increase in inventory	(25 000)	
Increase in prepayments	(3 000)	
Increase in accounts payables	12 000	
Decrease in accrued liabilities	(2 900)	
Cash generated from operations	191 100	
Interest received	10 100	
Dividend received from associate	5 000	
Interest paid	(11 100)	
Income taxes paid	(56 000)	
Net cash from operating activities		$ 139 100
Cash flows from investing activities		
Purchase of land (Note A)	(5 000)	
Purchase of plant	(186 000)	
Proceeds from sale of plant	43 000	
Net cash used in investing activities		(148 000)
Cash flow from financing activities		
Proceeds from borrowings	25 000	
Proceeds from share issue (Note B)	50 000	
Dividends paid (Note B)	(36 300)	
Net cash from financing activities		38 700
Net increase in cash and cash equivalents		29 800
Cash and cash equivalents at beginning of year (Note C)		180 000
Cash and cash equivalents at end of year (Note C)		$ 209 800

Notes:

A Land

During the year, land at a cost of $40 000 was acquired by means of vendor finance of $35 000 and a cash payment of $5000.

(continued)

FIGURE 19.12 *(continued)*

B Dividends
During the year, shareholders elected to reinvest dividends amounting to $30 000 under the company's dividend share reinvestment scheme. (This information will be reported in the company's statement of changes in equity, so a cross-reference to that statement may be used instead of this note.)

C Cash and cash equivalents
Cash and cash equivalents included in the statement of cash flows comprise the following amounts reported in the statements of financial position:

	2010	2009
Cash	$ 69 800	$ 60 000
Short-term deposits	140 000	120 000
	$209 800	$180 000

If the direct method of presenting operating cash flows is used, the cash receipts from customers and cash paid to suppliers and employees can be determined by reconstructing the relevant general ledger accounts or by using the equations previously given. For the purposes of this example, it is assumed that net accounts receivable comprises:

	2009	2010
Accounts receivable	$160 000	$215 000
Allowance for doubtful debts	(20 000)	(25 000)
	$140 000	$190 000

It is further assumed that bad debts of $3000 were deducted from the allowance for doubtful debts and the remaining allowance for doubtful debts was increased by a charge to profit or loss of $8000 (refer to the statement of comprehensive income).

As demonstrated previously, the summarised general ledger accounts can be reconstructed from the statements of financial position and supplementary information (opening and closing balances), and statement of comprehensive income and supplementary information (bad debts and sales). The cash receipts amount is then determined as the balancing figure.

The reconstructed Accounts Receivable and Allowance for Doubtful Debts general ledger accounts would appear as follows:

Accounts Receivable			
Opening balance	160 000	Bad Debts Write-Off	3 000
Sales Revenue	1 600 000	Cash received	1 542 000
		Closing balance	215 000
	1 760 000		1 760 000

Allowance for Doubtful Debts			
Bad Debts Write-Off	3 000	Opening balance	20 000
Closing balance	25 000	Doubtful Debts Expense	8 000
	28 000		28 000

Cash paid to suppliers of inventory can be determined by reconstructing the relevant general ledger accounts. The purchases amount is determined as the difference between the opening and closing balances (obtained from the statements of financial position) and cost of goods sold (obtained from the statement of comprehensive income). The determined amount of purchases is then recorded in the Accounts Payable (for inventory) account to calculate the cash payments to suppliers of inventory. This is shown as follows:

Inventory			
Opening balance	130 000	Cost of Goods Sold	960 000
Purchases	985 000	Closing balance	155 000
	1 115 000		1 115 000

Accounts Payable — Inventory Purchases			
Cash payments	978 000	Opening balance	49 000
Closing balance	56 000	Purchases	985 000
	1 034 000		1 034 000

Cash paid to other suppliers and employees can be similarly determined or found by using the equations previously given. Cash payments to other suppliers and employees comprise:

Wages and salaries	$240 000
Other expenses	132 000
	372 000
Prepayments increase	3 000
Increase (decrease) in accounts payable (worksheet note F)	(5 000)
Accruals liabilities	2 900
Total payments to employees and other suppliers of services	$372 900

Using the above calculations, total payments to suppliers and employees comprise:

Payments for:	
Inventory	$ 978 000
Service providers	372 900
	$1 350 900

Using the above calculations, cash flows from operating activities presented under the direct method are shown in figure 19.13.

Cash flow from operating activities:	
Cash received from customers	$ 1 542 000
Cash payments to suppliers and employees	(1 350 900)
Cash generated from operations	191 100
Interest received	10 100
Dividend received from associate	5 000
Interest paid	(11 100)
Income taxes paid	(56 000)
Net cash from operating activities	$ 139 100

FIGURE 19.13 Cash flows from operating activities using the direct method

19.10 EXTRACTS FROM FINANCIAL REPORTS

Figure 19.14 shows the information disclosed by BHP Billiton in its consolidated cash flow statement (statement of cash flows) and related notes for the year ended 30 June 2008. The notes include an extract from note 1 Accounting policies, providing a statement about the choice of the indirect method of presenting operating cash flows, and note 30, which reconciles cash and cash equivalents reported in the cash flow statement (statement of cash flows) to cash and cash equivalents reported in the balance sheet (statement of financial position). Further information is also provided about exploration and evaluation expenditure.

FIGURE 19.14 BHP Billiton consolidated cash flow statement and related notes for 2008

CONSOLIDATED CASH FLOW STATEMENT
for the year ended 30 June 2008

	Notes	**2008 US$M**	2007 Restated[(a)] US$M	2006 Restated[(a)] US$M
Operating activities				
Profit before taxation		**23 483**	19 212	15 116
Adjustments for:				
Depreciation and amortisation expense		**3 612**	2 754	2 613
Exploration and evaluation expense (excluding impairment)		**859**	539	566

(continued)

FIGURE 19.14 *(continued)*

	Notes	**2008 US$M**	2007 Restated[(a)] US$M	2006 Restated[(a)] US$M
Net gain on sale of non-current assets		**(129)**	(101)	(600)
Impairments of property, plant and equipment, investments and intangibles		**274**	305	163
Employee share awards expense		**97**	72	61
Financial income and expenses		**662**	512	600
Other		**(629)**	(382)	32
Changes in assets and liabilities:				
Trade and other receivables		**(4 787)**	(1282)	(1 226)
Inventories		**(1 313)**	(732)	(427)
Net financial assets and liabilities		**512**	26	(58)
Trade and other payables		**1 661**	462	(52)
Provisions and other liabilities		**1 188**	589	(520)
Cash generated from operations		**25 490**	21 974	16 268
Dividends received		**51**	38	27
Interest received		**169**	139	132
Interest paid		**(799)**	(633)	(590)
Income tax paid		**(5 867)**	(5 007)	(3 853)
Royalty related taxation paid		**(885)**	(554)	(659)
Net operating cash flows		**18 159**	15 957	11 325
Investing activities				
Purchases of property, plant and equipment		**(7 558)**	(7 129)	(5 876)
Exploration expenditure (including amounts expensed)		**(1 350)**	(805)	(771)
Purchase of intangibles		**(16)**	(18)	—
Purchases of financial assets		**(166)**	(38)	(65)
Purchases of, or increased investment in, subsidiaries, operations and jointly controlled entities, net of their cash		**(154)**	(701)	(531)
Cash outflows from investing activities		**(9 244)**	(8 691)	(7 243)
Proceeds from sale of property, plant and equipment		**43**	77	103
Proceeds from sale of financial assets		**59**	98	153
Proceeds from sale or partial sale of subsidiaries, operations and jointly controlled entities, net of their cash		**78**	203	844
Net investing cash flows		**(9 064)**	(8 313)	(6 143)
Financing activities				
Proceeds from ordinary share issues		**24**	22	34
Proceeds from interest bearing liabilities		**9 478**	7 395	6 273
Repayment of interest bearing liabilities		**(10 228)**	(5 781)	(7 518)
Purchase of shares by Employee Share Ownership Plan Trusts		**(250)**	(165)	(187)
Share buy back – BHP Billiton Limited		**—**	(2 824)	(1 619)
Share buy back – BHP Billiton Plc		**(3 115)**	(2 917)	(409)
Dividends paid		**(3 135)**	(2 271)	(1 936)
Dividends paid to minority interests		**(115)**	(68)	(190)
Net financing cash flows		**(7 341)**	(6 609)	(5 552)
Net increase/(decrease) in cash and cash equivalents		**1 754**	1 035	(370)
Cash and cash equivalents, net of overdrafts, at beginning of year		**2 398**	1 351	1 720
Effect of foreign currency exchange rate changes on cash and cash equivalents		**21**	12	1
Cash and cash equivalents, net of overdrafts, at end of year	30	**4 173**	2 398	1 351

The accompanying notes form part of these financial statements.
(a) Comparative periods have been restated as described in note 1.

FIGURE 19.14 *(continued)*

Note 1. Accounting policies (extract)

Cash flow presentation

The Group has also elected to adopt the indirect method of cash flow presentation as permitted by AASB 2007–4 'Amendments to Australian Accounting Standards arising from ED 151 and Other Amendments' and IAS 7 'Cash Flow Statements'. The Group believes this change in presentation more effectively conveys the relationship between its financial performance and operating cash flows.

Note 30. Notes to the consolidated cash flow statement

Cash and cash equivalents

For the purpose of the consolidated cash flow statement, cash equivalents include highly liquid investments that are readily convertible to cash and with a maturity of less than 90 days, bank overdrafts and interest bearing liabilities at call.

	2008 US$M	2007 US$M	2006 US$M
Cash and cash equivalents comprise:			
Cash assets [(a)]			
Cash	**1734**	846	707
Short-term deposits	**2503**	1603	660
Total cash and cash equivalents	**4237**	2449	1367
Bank overdrafts and short-term borrowings – refer to note 18	**(64)**	(51)	(16)
Total cash and cash equivalents, net of overdrafts	**4173**	2398	1351

(a) Cash and cash equivalents include US$591 million (2007: US$325 million; 2006: US$297 million) which is restricted by legal or contractual arrangements.

Exploration and evaluation expenditure

Exploration and evaluation expenditure (excluding impairments) is classified as an investing activity as described in IAS 7/AASB 107 'Cash Flow Statements' and is therefore a reconciling item between profit after taxation and net operating cash flows. Exploration and evaluation expenditure classified as investing activities in the cash flow statement is reconciled as follows:

	2008 US$M	2007 US$M	2006 US$M
Expensed in the income statement (excluding impairments)	**859**	539	566
Capitalised in property, plant and equipment	**491**	266	205
Cash outflow from investing activities	**1350**	805	771

Significant non-cash transactions

Non-cash transactions of US$211 million (2007: US$6 million; 2006: US$ nil) represent assets acquired under finance leases.

Standby arrangements and unused credit facilities

	Facility available 2008 US$M	**Used 2008 US$M**	**Unused 2008 US$M**	Facility available 2007 US$M	Used 2007 US$M	Unused 2007 US$M
Acquisition finance facility	**55 000**	—	**55 000**	—	—	—
Revolving credit facilities	**3 000**	—	**3 000**	3 000	—	3 000
Other facilities	**60**	—	**60**	58	—	58
Total financing facilities	**58 060**	—	**58 060**	3 058	—	3 058

(continued)

FIGURE 19.14 *(continued)*

Details of major standby and support arrangements are as follows:

Acquisition finance facility

On 5 February 2008, the Group entered into a multi-currency term and revolving facility and subscription agreement to, among other things, meet potential funding requirements in relation to our offer to acquire Rio Tinto. The facility agreement provides for four debt facilities in an aggregate amount of US$55 billion as follows:

- a US$20 billion term loan facility with a term of 364 days, which may be extended (at our election) for a further 12 months and thereafter up to US$10 billion may be extended for a further six months (at our election) subject to payment of an extension fee;
- a US$15 billion term loan facility with a term of three years;
- a US$12.5 billion term loan facility with a term of five years; and
- a US$7.5 billion revolving facility with a term of five years incorporating Euro and US dollar swing line facilities.

Revolving credit facility

The multi-currency revolving credit facility is available for general corporate purposes and matures in October 2011.

Other facilities

Other bank facilities are arranged with a number of banks with the general terms and conditions agreed on a periodic basis.

Disposal of subsidiaries and operations

The Group disposed of the following subsidiaries and operations during the year ended:

30 June 2008

- Optimum Colliery operations
- Elouera coal mine

30 June 2007

- The Group's 45.5 per cent interest in the Valesul joint venture
- Interest in Cascade and Chinook oil and gas prospects
- Southern Cross Fertilisers
- The Group's interest in the Typhoon facility and associated oil fields in the Gulf of Mexico
- The Group's interest in Australian coal bed methane assets
- Koornfontein coal business

30 June 2006

- The Group's 50 per cent interest in the Wonderkop joint venture
- Zululand Anthracite Collieries operations
- The Group's interest in Green Canyon 10 and 60 oil fields in the Gulf of Mexico
- DMS Powders business
- Tintaya copper mine

The carrying value of assets and liabilities disposed are as follows:

	2008 US$M	2007 US$M	2006 US$M
Carrying amount of assets and liabilities of entities disposed:			
Cash and cash equivalents	—	—	5
Trade and other receivables	**14**	54	7
Inventories	**20**	51	63
Other current assets	—	11	—
Property, plant and equipment	**223**	192	377
Intangible assets	—	24	—
Trade and other payables	**(107)**	(45)	(26)
Provisions	**(304)**	(94)	(110)
Net identifiable (liabilities)/assets	**(154)**	193	316

FIGURE 19.14 *(continued)*

	2008 US$M	2007 US$M	2006 US$M
Net consideration – Cash	**38**	203	849
– Intangible received	**—**	12	—
– Deferred (payable)/consideration	**(126)**	40	37
– Deferred settlement of intercompany balance	**—**	—	(40)
Total net consideration (paid)/received	**(88)**	255	846

Source: BHP Billiton (2008, pp. 168, 171, 221–2).

SUMMARY

IAS 7 *Statement of Cash Flows* is a disclosure standard requiring the presentation of a statement of cash flows as an integral part of an entity's financial statements. The statement of cash flows is particularly useful to investors, lenders and others when evaluating an entity's ability to generate cash and cash equivalents, and to meet its obligations and pay dividends. The statement is required to report cash flows classified into operating, investing and financing activities, as well as the net movement in cash and cash equivalents during the period. Net cash flows from operating activities may be presented using either the direct or the indirect method of presentation. IAS 7 requires additional information to be presented elsewhere in the financial statements concerning investing and financing activities that do not involve cash flows and are therefore excluded from a statement of cash flows. The standard also requires additional disclosures relating to the acquisitions and disposals of subsidiaries and other business units.

Discussion questions

1. What is the purpose of a statement of cash flows?
2. How might a statement of cash flows be used?
3. What is the meaning of 'cash equivalent'?
4. Explain the required classifications of cash flows under IAS 7.
5. What sources of information are usually required to prepare a statement of cash flows?
6. Explain the differences between the presentation of cash flows from operating activities under the direct method and their presentation under the indirect method. Do you consider one method to be more useful than the other? Why?
7. The statement of cash flows is said to be of assistance in evaluating the financial strength of an entity, yet the statement can exclude significant non-cash transactions that can materially affect the financial strength of an entity. How does IAS 7 seek to overcome this issue?
8. An entity may report significant profits over a number of successive years and still experience negative net cash flows from its operating activities. How can this happen?
9. An entity may report significant accounting losses over a number of successive years and still report positive net cash flows from operating activities over the same period. How can this happen?
10. What supplementary disclosures are required when a consolidated statement of cash flows is being prepared for a group that has acquired or disposed of a subsidiary?

STAR RATING
★ BASIC
★★ MODERATE
★★★ DIFFICULT

Exercises

Exercise 19.1 CASH RECEIVED FROM CUSTOMERS

★

At 30 June 2009, Biarritz Ltd had net accounts receivable of $180 000. At 30 June 2010, accounts receivable were $220 000 and sales for the year amounted to $1 800 000. Doubtful debts expense was $5000 for the year. Discount allowed was $3000 for the year.

Required
Calculate cash received from customers by Biarritz Ltd for the year ended 30 June 2010.

Exercise 19.2

★

CASH PAYMENTS TO SUPPLIERS

Calais Ltd had the following balances:

	30 June 2009	30 June 2010
Inventory	$170 000	$210 000
Accounts payable for inventory purchases	51 000	65 000

Cost of goods sold was $1 700 000 for the year ended 30 June 2010.

Required
Calculate cash payments to suppliers for the year ended 30 June 2010.

Exercise 19.3

★

CASH RECEIVED FROM CUSTOMERS

At 30 June 2009, Dijon Ltd had accounts receivable of $200 000. At 30 June 2010, accounts receivable were $240 000 and sales for the year amounted to $2 100 000. Bad debts amounting to $50 000 had been written off during the year, and discounts of $17 000 had been allowed in respect of payments from customers made within prescribed credit terms. Dijon Ltd did not have an allowance for doubtful debts in either year.

Required
Calculate cash received from customers for the year ended 30 June 2010.

Exercise 19.4

★

INVESTING CASH FLOWS

The following information has been compiled from the accounting records of Evreux Ltd for the year ended 30 June 2010:

Purchase of land, with the vendor financing $100 000 for 2 years	$350 000
Purchase of plant	250 000
Sale of plant:	
Book value	50 000
Cash proceeds	42 000

Required
Determine the amount of investing net cash outflows Evreux Ltd would report in its statement of cash flows for the year ended 30 June 2010.

Exercise 19.5

★

INVESTING CASH FLOWS

The following information has been compiled from the accounting records of Foix Ltd for the year ended 30 June 2010:

Dividends — paid	$200 000
— share reinvestment scheme	120 000
Additional cash borrowing	300 000
Issue of shares — cash	340 000
— dividend reinvestment	120 000

Required

Determine the amount of net cash from financing activities Foix Ltd would report in its statement of cash flows for the year ended 30 June 2010.

Exercise 19.6 ★★

NET INVESTING CASH FLOWS

The statement of financial position of Gap Ltd at 30 June 2010 recorded the following non-current assets:

	30 June 2009	30 June 2010
Land, at independent valuation	$100 000	$120 000
Plant, at cost	70 000	85 000
Accumulated depreciation	(20 000)	(28 000)
Available-for-sale listed investments, at fair value	30 000	40 000
Goodwill	25 000	20 000
Land revaluation reserve	20 000	34 000
Investments revaluation reserve	5 000	11 000
Additional information		
Impairment of goodwill	—	5 000

- There were no acquisitions or disposals of land.
- There were no disposals of plant or investments.
- The land revaluation reserve increment is net of deferred tax of $6000.
- The investments revaluation reserve increment for the year is net of deferred tax of $2000.

Required

Prepare the investing section of the statement of cash flows for Gap Ltd for the year ended 30 June 2010.

Exercise 19.7 

NET FINANCING CASH FLOWS

The following information has been extracted from the accounting records of Laval Ltd:

	30 June 2009	30 June 2010
Borrowings	$100 000	$200 000
Share capital	200 000	250 000
Property revaluation reserve	50 000	60 000
Retained earnings	75 000	95 000

Additional information

- Borrowings of $20 000 were repaid during the year to 30 June 2010. New borrowings include $80 000 vendor finance arising on the acquisition of a property.
- The increase in share capital includes $30 000 arising from the company's dividend reinvestment scheme.
- The movement in retained earnings comprises profit for the year $90 000, net of dividends $70 000.
- There were no dividends payable reported in the statement of financial position at either 30 June 2009 or 30 June 2010.

Required

Prepare the financing section of the statement of cash flows for Laval Ltd for the year ended 30 June 2010.

Exercise 19.8 ★★★

CASH RECEIPTS FROM CUSTOMERS AND CASH PAID TO SUPPLIERS AND EMPLOYEES

The accounting records of Marseille Ltd recorded the following information:

	30 June 2009	30 June 2010
Accounts receivable	$40 000	$ 50 000
Inventories	32 000	34 000
Prepaid expenses	1 000	3 000
Accounts payable for inventory purchased	15 000	16 000
Employee liabilities	5 000	5 500
Other accruals (including accrued interest: 2009 – $700; 2010 – $850)	4 000	3 800
Sales revenue		600 000
Cost of goods sold		480 000
Expenses (including $5000 depreciation and $2000 interest)		75 000

Required

1. Calculate the amount of cash received from customers during the year ended 30 June 2010.
2. Calculate the amount of cash paid to suppliers and employees during the year ended 30 June 2010.

Problems

Problem 19.1 ★

PREPARATION OF A STATEMENT OF CASH FLOWS

A summarised comparative statement of financial position of Nantes Ltd is presented below:

	30 June 2009	30 June 2010
Cash	$ 40 000	$ 55 000
Trade receivables	92 000	140 000
Investments	35 000	30 000
Plant	130 000	180 000
Accumulated depreciation	(45 000)	(60 000)
	$252 000	$345 000
Trade accounts payable	$ 75 000	$ 95 000
Deferred tax liability		3 000
Share capital	100 000	150 000
Retained earnings	77 000	90 000
Investment revaluation reserve	—	7 000
	$252 000	$345 000

Additional information

- An investment was sold for $15 000. There was no gain to be transferred from the investment revaluation reserve.
- There were no disposals of plant.
- The profit for the year was $60 000, after income tax expense of $30 000.
- A dividend of $47 000 was paid during the year.
- The only item of other comprehensive income was a revaluation of available-for-sale investments.

Required

Using the indirect method of presenting cash flows from operating activities, prepare a statement of cash flows in accordance with IAS 7 for the year ended 30 June 2010.

Problem 19.2 PREPARATION OF A STATEMENT OF CASH FLOWS

★ A summarised comparative statement of financial position of Orleans Ltd is presented below:

	30 June 2009	30 June 2010
Cash	$ 20 000	$ 91 000
Trade accounts receivable	65 000	90 000
Inventory	58 000	62 000
Prepayments	10 000	12 000
Land	80 000	90 000
Plant	280 000	320 000
Accumulated depreciation	(60 000)	(92 000)
	$453 000	$573 000
Accounts payable	$ 45 000	$ 48 000
Borrowings	160 000	200 000
Share capital	200 000	230 000
Retained earnings	48 000	95 000
	$453 000	$573 000

Additional information

- There were no disposals of land or plant during the year.
- A $30 000 borrowing was settled through the issue of ordinary shares. There were no other borrowing repayments.
- Profit for the year was $120 000, interest expense was $14 000, and income tax expense was $41 000. There were no items of other comprehensive income.
- A $73 000 dividend was paid during the year.
- Sales revenue for the year was $300 000. There was no other revenue.

Required

1. Using the indirect method of presenting cash flows from operating activities, prepare a statement of cash flows in accordance with IAS 7 for the year ended 30 June 2010.
2. Prepare the operating section of the statement of cash flows using the direct method.

Problem 19.3 PRESENTATION OF A STATEMENT OF CASH FLOWS

★ A summarised comparative statement of financial position of Poitiers Ltd is presented below, together with the statement of comprehensive income for the year ended 30 June 2010:

	30 June 2009	30 June 2010
Cash	$ 30 000	$ 68 000
Trade receivables	46 000	70 000
Inventory	30 000	32 000
Investments	35 000	40 000
Plant	125 000	150 000
Accumulated depreciation	(23 000)	(35 000)
	$243 000	$325 000
Accounts payable	$ 39 000	$ 43 000
Accrued interest	3 000	5 000
Current tax payable	10 000	12 000
Deferred tax liability	—	1 500
Borrowings	60 000	100 000
Share capital	100 000	100 000
Retained earnings	31 000	60 000
Investment revaluation reserve	—	3 500
	$243 000	$325 000

Statement of Comprehensive Income for the year ended 30 June 2010	
Sales	$700 000
Cost of sales	483 000
Gross profit	217 000
Distribution costs	62 000
Administration costs	74 000
Interest	6 000
Profit before tax	75 000
Income tax expense	23 000
Profit for the year	52 000
Other comprehensive income	
Gain on revaluation of investments (net of tax)	3500
Total comprehensive income	$ 55 500

Additional information

- There were no disposals of investments or plant during the year.
- A dividend of $23 000 was paid during the year.
- The deferred tax liability is in relation to investments.

Required

Using the direct method of presenting cash flows from operating activities, prepare a statement of cash flows in accordance with IAS 7 for the year ended 30 June 2010.

Problem 19.4 ★★

PREPARATION OF A STATEMENT OF CASH FLOWS

A summarised comparative statement of financial position of Rennes Ltd is presented below:

	30 June 2009	30 June 2010
Cash	$ 96 000	$ 49 000
Accounts receivable (net)	147 000	163 000
Prepayments	20 000	15 000
Inventory	60 000	104 000
Land	40 000	40 000
Plant	368 000	420 000
Accumulated depreciation	(45 000)	(70 000)
Deferred tax asset	20 000	24 000
	$706 000	$745 000
Accounts payable	$140 000	$152 000
Accrued liabilities	36 000	42 000
Current tax payable	24 000	31 000
Dividend payable	56 000	50 000
Borrowings	73 000	75 000
Share capital	335 000	345 000
Retained earnings	42 000	50 000
	$706 000	$745 000

Additional information

- Plant additions amounted to $72 000. Plant with a carrying amount value of $15 000 (cost $20 000, accumulated depreciation $5000) was sold for $22 000. The proceeds were outstanding at 30 June 2010.
- Accounts payable at 30 June 2009 include $34 000 arising from the acquisition of plant.
- Accrued liabilities include accrued interest of $3000 at 30 June 2009 and $4000 at 30 June 2010.
- The share capital increase of $10 000 arose from the reinvestment of dividends.

- The profit for the year was $92 000, after interest expense of $6000 and income tax expense of $46 000. There were no other components of comprehensive income.
- Dividends declared out of profits for the year were: interim dividend $34 000, final dividend $50 000.

Required

Using the indirect method of presenting cash flows from operating activities, prepare a statement of cash flows in accordance with IAS 7 for the year ended 30 June 2010.

Problem 19.5 PREPARATION OF A STATEMENT OF CASH FLOWS

★★ A summarised comparative statement of financial position of Strasbourg Ltd is presented below, together with an statement of comprehensive income for the year ended 30 June 2010.

	30 June 2009	30 June 2010
Cash	$ 45 000	$ 35 000
Trade receivables	69 000	105 000
Allowance for doubtful debts	(3 000)	(6 000)
Inventory	45 000	67 000
Available-for-sale investments	53 000	60 000
Plant	187 000	225 000
Accumulated depreciation	(35 000)	(53 000)
	$361 000	$433 000
Accounts payable	$ 65 000	$ 75 000
Accrued interest	5 000	7 000
Current tax payable	15 000	18 000
Deferred tax	30 000	37 000
Borrowings	80 000	100 000
Share capital	100 000	100 000
Investment revaluation reserve	2 000	7 000
Retained earnings	64 000	89 000
	$361 000	$433 000

Statement of Comprehensive Income
for the year ended 30 June 2010

Sales	$1 035 000
Cost of sales	(774 000)
Gross profit	261 000
Distribution costs	(76 000)
Administration costs	(96 000)
Interest expense	(7 000)
Profit before tax	82 000
Income tax expense	(24 000)
Profit for the year	58 000
Other comprehensive income	
Gain on revaluation of investment (net of tax)	5 000
Total comprehensive income	$ 63 000

Additional information

- The movement in the allowance for doubtful debts for the year comprises:

Balance at 30 June 2009	$ 3 000
Charge for year	5 000
Bad debts written off	(2 000)
Balance at 30 June 2010	6 000

- Available-for-sale investments are valued at fair value, with increments/decrements being recognised in the investment revaluation reserve until investments are sold.
- There were no disposals of plant during the year.
- A dividend of $33 000 was paid during the year.
- There were no acquisitions or disposals of investments during the year.

Required

1. Using the direct method of presenting cash flows from operating activities, prepare a statement of cash flows in accordance with IAS 7 for the year ended 30 June 2010.
2. Prepare the operating activities section of the statement of cash flows using the indirect method of presentations.

Problem 19.6 ★★

PREPARATION OF A STATEMENT OF CASH FLOWS

A comparative statement of financial position of Tovlon Ltd is presented below:

	30 June 2009	30 June 2010
Cash	$120 000	$ 218 000
Trade receivables	184 000	204 000
Inventory	100 000	160 000
Land (at valuation)	50 000	62 000
Plant	460 000	520 000
Accumulated depreciation	(90 000)	(120 000)
	$824 000	$1 044 000
Accounts payable	$150 000	$ 155 000
Accrued interest	12 000	16 000
Other accrued liabilities	45 000	43 000
Current tax payable	30 000	34 000
Provision for employee benefits	38 000	42 000
Dividend payable	—	60 000
Borrowings	95 000	105 000
Deferred tax liability	58 000	39 000
Share capital	350 000	380 000
Revaluation reserve	12 000	20 000
Retained earnings	34 000	150 000
	$824 000	$1 044 000

Statement of Comprehensive Income
for the year ended 30 June 2010

Sales	$3 580 000
Cost of sales	(2 864 000)
Gross profit	716 000
Gain on sale of plant	16 000
Dividend income	4 000
Distribution costs	(185 000)
Administrative costs	(160 000)
Interest expense	(8 000)
Other costs	(40 000)
Profit before tax	343 000
Income tax expense	(103 000)
Profit for the year	240 000
Other comprehensive income	
Gain on asset revaluation (net of tax)	8 000
Total comprehensive income	$ 248 000

Additional information

- The land revaluation reserve increment for the year is net of deferred tax of $4000.
- Plant with a carrying amount of $60 000 (cost $85 000, accumulated depreciation $25 000) was sold for $76 000.
- Accounts payable at 30 June 2010 include $22 000 in respect of plant acquisitions.
- There were borrowing repayments of $30 000 during the year.
- The increase in share capital of $30 000 arose from the company's dividend reinvestment scheme.
- Dividends declared out of profits for the year were: interim dividend $64 000, final dividend $60 000.

Required

Using the direct method of presenting cash flows from operating activities, prepare a statement of cash flows in accordance with IAS 7 for the year ended 30 June 2010.

Problem 19.7

PREPARING STATEMENT OF CASH FLOW INFORMATION

★★ The statement of comprehensive income and comparative statements of financial position of Valence Ltd are as follows:

Valence Ltd
Statement of Financial Position as at 31 December

	2009	2010
Current assets		
Deposits at call	$ 19 000	$ 30 000
Accounts receivable	340 000	320 000
Allowance for doubtful debts	(19 000)	(15 000)
Inventory	654 000	670 000
Prepayments	52 000	55 000
	$1 046 000	$1 060 000
Non-current assets		
Land	$ 400 000	$ 400 000
Buildings	1 175 000	1 850 000
Accumulated depreciation – buildings	(200 000)	(235 000)
Plant	850 000	940 000
Accumulated depreciation – plant	(375 000)	(452 000)
	1 850 000	2 503 000
Total assets	$2 896 000	$3 563 000
Current liabilities		
Bank overdraft	$ 140 000	$ 49 000
Accounts payable	553 000	570 000
Interest payable	25 000	30 000
Final dividend payable	205 000	230 000
Current tax payable	70 000	77 000
	993 000	956 000
Non-current liabilities		
Borrowings	900 000	1 300 000
Deferred tax liability	12 000	16 000
	912 000	1 316 000
Total liabilities	1 905 000	2 272 000
Equity		
Share capital	800 000	1 000 000
Retained earnings	191 000	291 000
	991 000	1 291 000
Total liabilities and equity	$2 896 000	$3 563 000

Valence Ltd Statement of Comprehensive Income for the year ended 31 December 2010	
Sales	$ 8 550 000
Less Cost of sales	4 517 000
Gross profit	4 033 000
Gain on sale of plant	18 000
	4 051 000
Distribution costs	(1 635 000)
Administration costs	(1 566 000)
Interest	(70 000)
Profit before tax	780 000
Income tax expense	(250 000)
Profit for the period	530 000
Other comprehensive income	—
Total comprehensive income	$ 530 000

The following additional information has been extracted from the accounting records of Valence Ltd:

1. Movement in allowance for doubtful debts:		
Balance 31 December 2009	$ 19 000	
Charge for year	7 000	
Bad debts written off	(11 000)	
Balance 31 December 2010	$ 15 000	
2. Building additions were completed. There were no disposals.		
3. The movement in plant and accumulated depreciation on plant comprised:	**Cost**	**Accumulated depreciation**
Balance 31 December 2009	$ 850 000	$ 375 000
Additions – cash	160 000	—
Disposals	(70 000)	(50 000)
Depreciation	—	127 000
Balance 31 December 2010	$ 940 000	$ 452 000
4. There was no outstanding interest payable at year-end.		
5. Income tax expense comprised:		
Income tax currently payable	$ 246 000	
Deferred income tax	4 000	
	$ 250 000	
6. Additional cash borrowings	$ 400 000	
7. Movement in equity	**Share capital**	**Retained earnings**
Balance 31 December 2009	$ 800 000	$ 191 000
Additional shares issued for cash	200 000	—
Profit for the period	—	530 000
Interim dividend – cash	—	(200 000)
Final dividend payable		(230 000)
Balance 31 December 2010	$1 000 000	$ 291 000

Required

1. Prepare a summary of cash flows from operating activities using the indirect method of presentation.

2. Prepare a summary of cash flows from investing activities.
3. Prepare a summary of cash flows from financing activities.
4. Prepare a summary of cash flows from operating activities using the direct method of presentation.

Problem 19.8 ★★★

PREPARING A STATEMENT OF CASH FLOWS WITH NOTES

The statement of comprehensive income and comparative statements of financial position of Arras Ltd were as follows:

Arras Ltd Statements of Financial Position as at 31 December		
	2009	**2010**
Current assets		
Cash at bank	$ 46 000	$ 52 000
Cash deposits (30-day)	40 000	70 000
Accounts receivable	110 000	117 000
Allowance for doubtful debts	(12 000)	(16 000)
Interest receivable	2 000	3 000
Inventory	294 000	320 000
Prepayments	13 000	9 000
	493 000	555 000
Non-current assets		
Land	100 000	140 000
Plant	600 000	700 000
Accumulated depreciation	(140 000)	(180 000)
Investments in associate	80 000	92 000
Brand names	120 000	90 000
	760 000	842 000
Total assets	$1 253 000	$1 397 000
Current liabilities		
Accounts payable	$ 180 000	$ 196 000
Accrued liabilities	85 000	92 000
Current tax payable	40 000	43 000
Current portion of long-term borrowings	20 000	20 000
	325 000	351 000
Non-current liabilities		
Borrowings	98 000	$ 138 000
Deferred tax liability	35 000	40 000
Provision for employee benefits	40 000	43 000
	173 000	221 000
Total liabilities	498 000	572 000
Equity		
Share capital	500 000	530 000
Retained earnings	255 000	295 000
	755 000	825 000
Total liabilities and equity	$1 253 000	$1 397 000

Arras Ltd Statement of Comprehensive Income for the year ended 31 December 2010	
Sales	$1 780 000
Cost of sales	(1 030 000)
Gross profit	750 000
Interest	2 000
Share of profits of associate	20 000
Gain on sale of plant	8 000
Total income	780 000
Expenses	
Salaries and wages	352 000
Depreciation	50 000
Discount allowed	8 000
Doubtful debts	6 000
Interest	21 000
Other (including impairment of brand names $30 000)	186 000
	623 000
Profit before tax	157 000
Income tax expense	(47 000)
Profit for the period	110 000
Other comprehensive income	—
Total comprehensive income	$ 110 000

The following additional information has been extracted from the accounting records of Arras Ltd:

1. 30-day cash deposits are used in the course of the daily cash management of the company.	
2. Movement in allowance for doubtful debts:	
Balance 31 December 2009	$ 12 000
Charge for year	6 000
Bad debts written off	(2 000)
Balance 31 December 2010	$ 16 000
3. Land	
Additional cash purchase	$ 40 000
4. Plant	
Purchases for year (including $50 000 purchase financed by vendor)	$150 000
5. Disposals	
Cost of disposals	$ 50 000
Accumulated depreciation	(10 000)
6. Investments in associate	
Share of profit	$ 20 000
Dividends received	8 000
7. Accounts payable	
Includes amounts owing in respect of plant purchases:	
31 December 2009	$ 12 000
31 December 2010	18 000

8. Accrued liabilities
Includes accrued interest payable:

31 December 2009	$ 4 000
31 December 2010	5 000

9. Income tax expense comprises:

Current tax payable	$ 42 000
Deferred tax	5 000
Income tax expense	$ 47 000

10. Dividends paid
Under a dividend reinvestment share scheme, shareholders have the right to receive additional shares in lieu of cash dividends. Dividends paid comprised:

Dividends paid in cash during the year	$ 40 000
Dividends reinvested	30 000
Total dividends	$ 70 000

Required

1. Using the direct method of presenting cash flows from operating activities, prepare a statement of cash flows in accordance with IAS 7 for the year ended 31 December 2010.
2. Prepare a summary of cash flows from operating activities using the indirect method of presentation in accordance with IAS 7.
3. Prepare any notes to the statement of cash flows that you consider are required under IAS 7.

Reference

BHP Billiton 2008, *Annual report 2008*, BHP Billiton, www.bhpbilliton.com.

20 Operating segments

ACCOUNTING STANDARDS IN FOCUS

IAS 14 *Segment Reporting*

IFRS 8 *Operating Segments*

LEARNING OBJECTIVES

When you have studied this chapter, you should be able to:

- understand the objectives of financial reporting by segments
- distinguish between a business segment and a geographical segment
- determine an entity's primary and secondary segment reporting formats
- identify an entity's reportable segments
- understand and apply the requirements for segment accounting policies, including the allocation of assets, liabilities, revenues and expenses to segments
- understand and apply the disclosure requirements of IAS 14
- Identify the main differences between IAS 14 and IFRS 8.

20.1 INTRODUCTION TO IAS 14

IAS 14 *Segment Reporting* is primarily a disclosure standard and is particularly relevant for large organisations that operate in different geographic locations and/or in diverse businesses.

20.2 SCOPE

IAS 14 applies to entities whose equity or debt securities are publicly traded (i.e. entities listed on an authorised securities exchange such as the Australian Securities Exchange or the London Stock Exchange) and by entities that are in the process of listing.

If an entity voluntarily chooses to disclose segment information then it must fully comply with IAS 14. This may be the case, for example, where a large public company that is not listed, but has a large number of dependent users such as a number of minority shareholders, employees and creditors, elects to provide segment information. However, voluntary segment disclosures are not expected to be common, for reasons discussed in section 20.3.

Where the entity presents both consolidated financial statements and parent entity financial statements in a single financial report, then segment information need be presented only on the basis of the consolidated financial statements.

20.3 OBJECTIVES OF FINANCIAL REPORTING BY SEGMENTS

Many entities operate in different geographical areas or provide products or services that are subject to differing rates of profitability, opportunities for growth, future prospects and risks. Information about an entity's geographical and business segments is relevant to assessing the risks and returns of a diversified or multinational entity where often that information cannot be determined from aggregated data. Therefore, segment information is regarded as necessary to help users of financial statements:

- better understand the entity's past performance
- better assess the entity's risks and returns
- make more informed judgements about the entity as a whole.

As we saw in 20.2, IAS 14 applies only to listed entities. Many securities analysts rely on the segment disclosures to help them assess not only an entity's past performance but also to help them predict future performance. Analysts use these assessments to determine an entity's share price. Segment disclosures are widely regarded as some of the most useful disclosures in financial reports because of the extent to which they disaggregate financial information into meaningful and often revealing groupings. For example, an entity may appear profitable on a consolidated basis, but segment disclosures may reveal that one part of the business is performing poorly while another part is performing well. The part that is performing poorly may be significant to the entity as a whole and over time continued poor performance by that part (or segment) may cause the entire entity's performance to suffer. This is the kind of information that impacts an entity's share price because analysts frequently look at predicted future cash flows in making their share price determinations.

On the other hand, preparers of financial reports may not wish to reveal too much information on a disaggregated basis to their competitors. Some may consider IAS 14's disclosure requirements to be too revealing. For example, a user can determine an entity's profit margin by segment when reading the segment disclosures. This is a key reason why it is unlikely that entities would volunteer to disclose segment information (see section 20.2). Another reason is that it is often a time-consuming exercise to prepare the segment disclosures.

20.4 BUSINESS AND GEOGRAPHICAL SEGMENTS

20.4.1 Definitions

Paragraph 9 of IAS 14 defines business and geographical segments as follows:

> A *business segment* is a distinguishable component of an entity that is engaged in providing an individual product or service or a group of related products or services and that is subject to risks and

returns that are different from those of other business segments. Factors that shall be considered in determining whether products and services are related include:
(a) the nature of the products or services;
(b) the nature of the production processes;
(c) the type or class of customer for the products or services;
(d) the methods used to distribute the products or provide the services; and
(e) if applicable, the nature of the regulatory environment, for example, banking, insurance, or public utilities.

A *geographical segment* is a distinguishable component of an entity that is engaged in providing products or services within a particular economic environment and that is subject to risks and returns that are different from those of components operating in other economic environments. Factors that shall be considered in identifying geographical segments include:
(a) similarity of economic and political conditions;
(b) relationships between operations in different geographical areas;
(c) proximity of operations;
(d) special risks associated with operations in a particular area;
(e) exchange control regulations; and
(f) the underlying currency risks.

The predominant sources of risks affect how most entities are organised and managed. Therefore, IAS 14 (para. 27) states that an entity's organisational structure and internal financial reporting system should normally be the basis for identifying its segments. The risks and returns of an entity are influenced both by the geographical *location of its operations* (where its products are produced or where its service delivery activities are based) and also by the *location of its markets* (where its products are sold or services are rendered). The definition (para. 13) allows geographical segments to be based on either:

(a) the location of an entity's production or service facilities and other assets; or
(b) the location of its markets and customers.

Determining the composition of a business or geographical segment involves a certain amount of judgement. In making that judgement, entities should take into account the objective of reporting financial information by segment (as discussed in section 20.3) and the qualitative characteristics of financial statements as identified in the Framework (see chapter 1). Those qualitative characteristics include:

- the relevance, reliability and comparability over time of financial information that is reported about an entity's different groups of products and services and about its operations in particular geographical areas; and
- the usefulness of that information for assessing the risks and returns of the entity as a whole.

Illustrative example 20.1 provides examples of business segments and geographical segments.

ILLUSTRATIVE EXAMPLE 20.1

Examples of business segments and geographical segments

Diversified manufacturing Company A

Company A is a listed diversified manufacturing company. It produces most of its products in Australia and its markets are also mainly in Australia. It has three main product lines: wine, water heaters and olive oil. Each of these product lines has different production processes, markets and distribution processes. Company A is organised into three business units: wine, water heaters and olive oil. Each business unit reports separate financial and operational information to the chief executive officer (CEO) and chief financial officer (CFO). The results of all three business units are then aggregated to form the consolidated financial information. In preparing its financial statements in accordance with IAS 14, Company A identifies three business segments: wine, water heaters and olive oil. It has only one geographical segment: Australia.

Manufacturing Company B

Company B is a listed manufacturing company. It produces most of its products in Australia but it exports 70% of these products to Japan. It has only one main product line: grain-fed beef. Company B is organised into two business units: local and export. Each business unit reports separate financial and operational information to the chief executive officer (CEO) and chief financial officer (CFO). The results of the two business units are then aggregated to form the consolidated financial information. In preparing its financial statements in accordance with IAS 14, Company B identifies two geographical segments: Australia and Japan. It has only one business segment: grain-fed beef.

20.5 PRIMARY AND SECONDARY SEGMENT REPORTING FORMATS

20.5.1 Determining primary and secondary segment reporting formats

Illustrative example 20.1 provided some simple examples of business and geographical segments. Often, however, an entity will operate and/or have markets in different geographical locations as well as having different types of products and services. Therefore, an entity will often have both geographical segments and business segments. It is not always easy to delineate clearly business segments and geographical segments. However, IAS 14 requires an entity to determine which type of segment — business or geographical — will be its primary segment reporting format. The disclosures required for the primary segment format are extensive (IAS 14, paras 50–67) whereas the disclosures required for the secondary segment format are limited (IAS 14, paras 69–72).

Paragraph 26 of IAS 14 states:

> The dominant source and nature of an entity's risks and returns shall govern whether its primary segment reporting format will be business segments or geographical segments. If the entity's risks and rates of return are affected predominantly by differences in the products and services it produces, its primary format for reporting segment information shall be business segments, with secondary information reported geographically. Similarly, if the entity's risks and rates of return are affected predominantly by the fact that it operates in different countries or other geographical areas, its primary format for reporting segment information shall be geographical segments, with secondary information reported for groups of related products and services.

As noted earlier, IAS 14 requires that an entity's organisational structure and its internal financial reporting system should normally be the basis for identifying its segments (IAS 14, para 27). However, paragraph 27 goes on to say that:

> (a) if an entity's risks and rates of return are strongly affected both by differences in the products and services it produces and by differences in the geographical areas in which it operates, as evidenced by a 'matrix approach' to managing the company and to reporting internally to the board of directors and the chief executive officer, then the entity shall use business segments as its primary segment reporting format and geographical segments as its secondary reporting format; and
>
> (b) if an entity's internal organisational and management structure and its system of internal financial reporting to the board of directors and the chief executive officer are based neither on individual products or services or on groups of related products/services nor on geography, the directors and management of the entity shall determine whether the entity's risks and returns are related more to the products and services it produces or more to the geographical areas in which it operates and, as a consequence, shall choose either business segments or geographical segments as the entity's primary segment reporting format, with the other as its secondary reporting format.

For most entities, the predominant source of risks and returns determines how the entity is organised and managed. An entity's organisational and management structure and its internal financial reporting system normally provide the best evidence of the entity's predominant source of risks and returns for purposes of its segment reporting. Therefore, except in rare circumstances, an entity will report segment information in its financial statements on the same basis as it reports internally to top management. Its predominant source of risks and returns becomes its primary segment reporting format. Its secondary source of risks and returns becomes its secondary segment reporting format. Subparagraph 27(a) recognises, however, that some companies use a matrix approach for internal reporting. In such circumstances IAS 14 requires the company to select business segments as its primary format. This is aimed at enhancing comparability in financial reporting between different companies.

In some cases, an entity's internal reporting may have developed along lines unrelated either to differences in the types of products and services it produces or to the geographical areas in which it operates. For instance, internal reporting may be organised solely by legal entity, resulting in internal segments composed of groups of unrelated products and services. In those cases, the internally reported segment data will not meet the objective of IAS 14. Accordingly, paragraph 27(b) requires the directors and management of the entity to determine whether the entity's risks and returns are more product or service driven or geographically driven, and to choose either business segments or geographical segments as the entity's primary basis of segment reporting. Again, the objective is to achieve a reasonable degree of comparability with other entities, enhance comprehensibility of the resulting information and meet the needs of users for information about product or service-related and geographically related risks and returns. Paragraph 32 of IAS 14 explains how an entity should determine its segments in these circumstances, as follows:

(a) if one or more of the segments reported internally to the directors and management is a business segment or a geographical segment based on the factors in the definitions in paragraph 9 but others are not, subparagraph (b) below shall be applied only to those internal segments that do not meet the definitions in paragraph 9 (that is, an internally reported segment that meets the definition shall not be further segmented);
(b) for those segments reported internally to the directors and management that do not satisfy the definitions in paragraph 9, management of the entity shall look to the next lower level of internal segmentation that reports information along product and service lines or geographical lines, as appropriate under the definitions in paragraph 9; and
(c) if such an internally reported lower-level segment meets the definition of business segment or geographical segment based on the factors in paragraph 9, the criteria in paragraphs 34 and 35 for identifying reportable segments shall be applied to that segment.

Paragraphs 34 and 35 of IAS 14 deal with reportable segments, which are discussed in section 20.6.

Building on illustrative example 20.1, the following illustrative example shows how the companies would determine their primary and secondary segments.

ILLUSTRATIVE EXAMPLE 20.2

Primary and secondary segments

Diversified manufacturing Company A

Company A is a listed diversified manufacturing company. It produces most of its products in Australia and its markets are also mainly in Australia. It has three main product lines: wine, water heaters and olive oil. Each of these product lines has different production processes, markets and distribution processes. Company A is organised into three business units: wine, water heaters and olive oil. Each business unit reports separate financial and operational information to the chief executive officer (CEO) and chief financial officer (CFO). The results of all three business units are then aggregated to form the consolidated financial information. In preparing its financial statements in accordance with IAS 14, company A identifies three business segments: wine, water heaters and olive oil. It has only one geographical segment: Australia. Because Company A's risks and rates of return are affected predominantly by differences in the products and services it produces, its primary format for reporting segment information should be business segments, with secondary information reported geographically.

Manufacturing Company B

Company B is a listed manufacturing company. It produces most of its products in Australia but it exports 70% of these products to Japan. It has only one main product line: grain-fed beef. Company B is organised into two business units: local and export. Each business unit reports separate financial and operational information to the chief executive officer (CEO) and chief financial officer (CFO). The results of the two business units are then aggregated to form the consolidated financial information. In preparing its financial statements in accordance with IAS 14, Company B identifies two geographical segments: Australia and Japan. It has only one business segment: grain-fed beef. Because Company B's risks and rates of return are affected predominantly by the fact that it operates in different countries, its primary format for reporting segment information should be geographical segments, with secondary information reported for its business segment.

In both of the above examples, the companies' predominant source of risks and returns determines their organisational and management structure and internal financial reporting. Therefore, their internal reporting structure is appropriate for segment reporting under IAS 14.

The following example illustrates the circumstances envisaged in IAS 14 paragraphs 27(b) and 32.

Diversified manufacturing Company C

Company C is a listed diversified manufacturing company. It produces most of its products in Australia and its markets are also mainly in Australia. It has three main product lines: beer, picture frames and office workstation accessories. Each of these product lines has different production processes, markets and distribution processes. Company C is organised into two business units: beer and other entities. The beer business unit reports separate financial and operational information to the chief executive officer (CEO) and chief financial officer (CFO). The other entities business unit is divided into six legal entities, each of which reports separate financial and operational information to the CEO and CFO. The reporting by the six legal entities does not reflect Company C's predominant sources of risks and returns from the picture frames and office workstation accessories products. The results of the two business units are then aggregated to form the consolidated financial information. In preparing its financial statements in accordance with IAS 14, Company C identifies three business segments: beer, picture frames and office workstation accessories. In doing so, it will need to determine the reported segment information for the picture frames and office workstation accessories business segments by further analysing and rearranging the information presented by the six legal entities. It has only one geographical segment: Australia. Because Company C's risks and rates of return are affected predominantly by differences in the products and services it produces, its primary format for reporting segment information should be business segments, with secondary information reported geographically.

20.6 IDENTIFYING AN ENTITY'S REPORTABLE SEGMENTS

20.6.1 Definition of a reportable segment

Paragraph 9 of IAS 14 defines a reportable segment as follows:

> A reportable segment is a business segment or a geographical segment identified based on the foregoing definitions for which segment information is required to be disclosed by this Standard.

This is not a very helpful definition. Paragraphs 34 through 43 go into detail about how an entity should determine its reportable segments. The requirements are complex and are best understood by reference to the decision tree included as appendix A to the standard and reproduced in figure 20.1.

For ease of reference, the requirements of paragraphs 34 through 43 are reproduced below:

34. Two or more internally reported business segments or geographical segments that are substantially similar may be combined as a single business segment or geographical segment. Two or more business segments or geographical segments are substantially similar only if:
    (a) they exhibit similar long-term financial performance; and
    (b) they are similar in all of the factors in the appropriate definition in paragraph 9.
35. A business segment or geographical segment shall be identified as a reportable segment if a majority of its revenue is earned from sales to external customers and:
    (a) its revenue from sales to external customers and from transactions with other segments is 10 per cent or more of the total revenue, external and internal, of all segments; or
    (b) its segment result, whether profit or loss, is 10 per cent or more of the combined result of all segments in profit or the combined result of all segments in loss, whichever is the greater in absolute amount; or
    (c) its assets are 10 per cent or more of the total assets of all segments.
36. If an internally reported segment is below all of the thresholds of significance in paragraph 35:
    (a) that segment may be designated as a reportable segment despite its size;
    (b) if not designated as a reportable segment despite its size, that segment may be combined into a separately reportable segment with one or more other similar internally reported segment(s) that are also below all of the thresholds of significance in paragraph 35 (two or more business segments or geographical segments are similar if they share a majority of the factors in the appropriate definition in paragraph 9); and
    (c) if that segment is not separately reported or combined, it shall be included as an unallocated reconciling item.

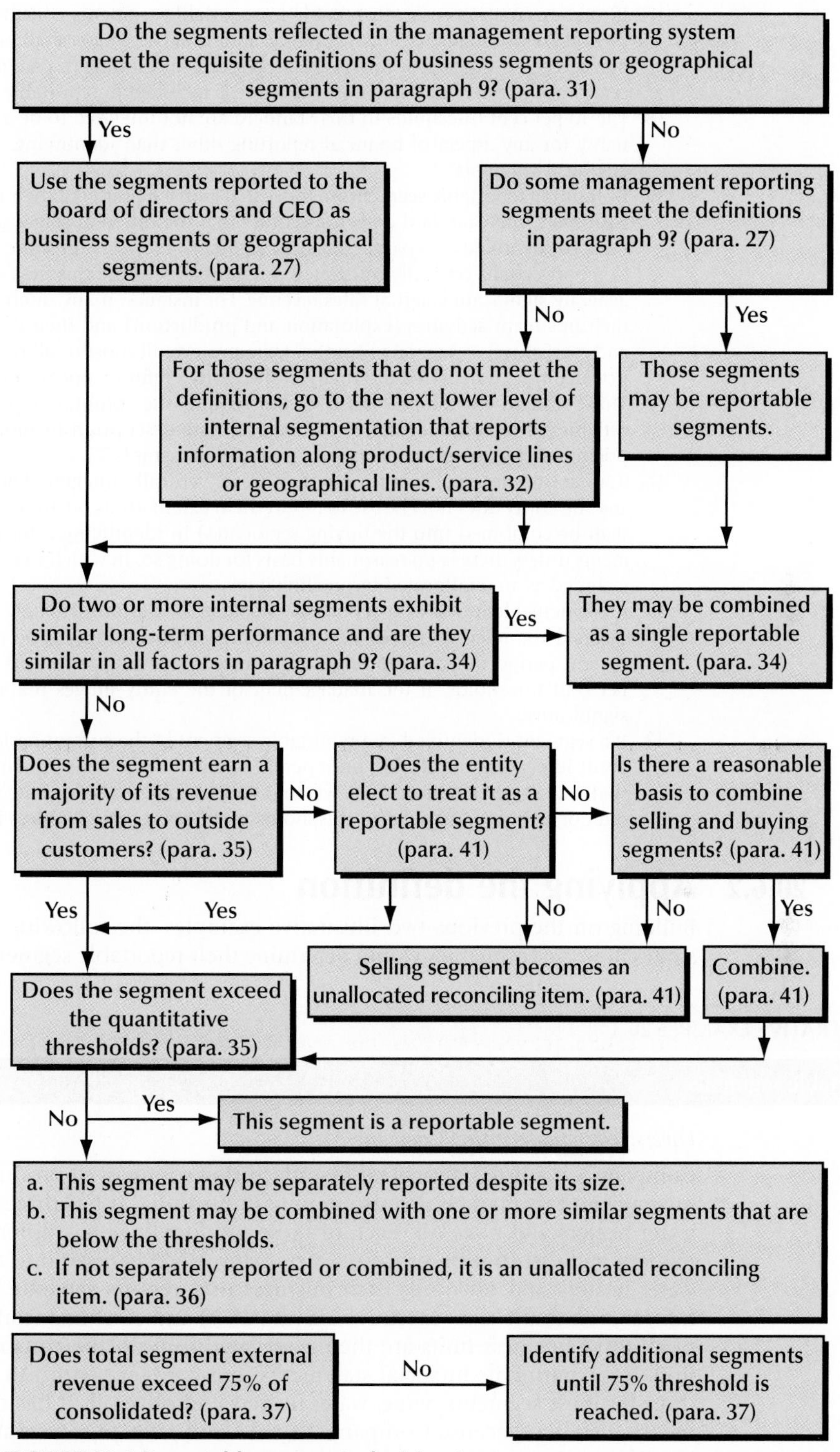

FIGURE 20.1 Reportable segments decision tree
Source: IAS 14 *Segment Reporting,* Appendix A.

37. If total external revenue attributable to reportable segments constitutes less than 75 per cent of the total consolidated or entity revenue, additional segments shall be identified as reportable segments, even if they do not meet the 10 per cent thresholds in paragraph 35, until at least 75 per cent of total consolidated or entity revenue is included in reportable segments.
38. The 10 per cent thresholds in this Standard are not intended to be a guide for determining materiality for any aspect of financial reporting other than identifying reportable business and geographical segments.
39. By limiting reportable segments to those that earn a majority of their revenue from sales to external customers, this Standard does not require that the different stages of vertically integrated operations be identified as separate business segments. However, in some industries, current practice is to report certain vertically integrated activities as separate business segments even if they do not generate significant external sales revenue. For instance, many international oil companies report their upstream activities (exploration and production) and their downstream activities (refining and marketing) as separate business segments even if most or all of the upstream product (crude petroleum) is transferred internally to the entity's refining operation.
40. This Standard encourages, but does not require, the voluntary reporting of vertically integrated activities as separate segments, with appropriate description including disclosure of the basis of pricing inter-segment transfers as required by paragraph 75.
41. If an entity's internal reporting system treats vertically integrated activities as separate segments and the entity does not choose to report them externally as business segments, the selling segment shall be combined into the buying segment(s) in identifying externally reportable business segments unless there is no reasonable basis for doing so, in which case the selling segment would be included as an unallocated reconciling item.
42. A segment identified as a reportable segment in the immediately preceding period because it satisfied the relevant 10 per cent thresholds shall continue to be a reportable segment for the current period notwithstanding that its revenue, result, and assets all no longer exceed the 10 per cent thresholds, if the management of the entity judges the segment to be of continuing significance.
43. If a segment is identified as a reportable segment in the current period because it satisfies the relevant 10 per cent thresholds, prior period segment data that is presented for comparative purposes shall be restated to reflect the newly reportable segment as a separate segment, even if that segment did not satisfy the 10 per cent thresholds in the prior period, unless it is impracticable to do so.

20.6.2 Applying the definition

Building on the previous two illustrative examples, the following illustrative example demonstrates how the companies would determine their reportable segments.

ILLUSTRATIVE EXAMPLE 20.3

Reportable segments

Diversified manufacturing Company A

Company A is a listed diversified manufacturing company. It produces most of its products in Australia and its markets are also mainly in Australia. It has three main product lines: wine, water heaters and olive oil. Each of these product lines has different production processes, markets and distribution processes. Company A is organised into three business units: wine, water heaters and olive oil. Each business unit reports separate financial and operational information to the chief executive officer (CEO) and chief financial officer (CFO). The results of all three business units are then aggregated to form the consolidated financial information. In preparing its financial statements in accordance with IAS 14, Company A identifies three business segments: wine, water heaters and olive oil. It has only one geographical segment: Australia. Because Company A's risks and rates of return are affected predominantly by differences in the products and services it produces, its primary format for reporting segment information should be business segments, with secondary information reported geographically.

Now Company A must determine its reportable segments. None of the business segments is substantially similar (per IAS 14, para. 34) and so they cannot be combined. The following additional information is provided: all three business units earn most of their revenue from external customers. Total consolidated revenue of Company A is $253 million.

	Wine $	Water heaters $	Olive oil $	All segments $
Revenue	150m	90m	10m	250m
Segment result (profit)	14m	5m	1m	20m
Assets	500m	200m	100m	800m

All three segments are reportable segments because each earns a majority of its revenues from external customers and each equals or exceeds at least one of the 10% thresholds set out in paragraph 35. Wine and water heaters exceed all three and olive oil exceeds only the assets threshold. Because total external revenue attributable to the reportable segments exceeds 75% of total consolidated revenue, there is no requirement to identify additional segments in accordance with paragraph 37.

Manufacturing Company B

Company B is a listed manufacturing company. It produces most of its products in Australia but it exports 70% of these products to Japan. It has only one main product line: grain-fed beef. Company B is organised into two business units: local and export. Each business unit reports separate financial and operational information to the chief executive officer (CEO) and chief financial officer (CFO). The results of the two business units are then aggregated to form the consolidated financial information. In preparing its financial statements in accordance with IAS 14, Company B identifies two geographical segments: Australia and Japan. It has only one business segment: grain-fed beef. Because Company B's risks and rates of return are affected predominantly by the fact that it operates in different countries, its primary format for reporting segment information should be geographical segments, with secondary information reported for its business segment.

Now Company B must determine its reportable segments. Neither of the geographical segments is substantially similar (per IAS 14, para 34) and so they cannot be combined. The following additional information is provided: each business unit earns a majority of its revenues from external customers. Total consolidated revenue of Company B is $750 million.

	Export $	Local $	All segments $
Revenue	490m	210m	700m
Segment result (profit)	80m	20m	100m
Assets	800m	200m	1 000m

Each geographical segment is a reportable segment because each earns a majority of its revenues from external customers and each equals or exceeds at least one of the 10% thresholds set out in paragraph 35. In fact, each exceeds all three of the thresholds. Because total external revenue attributable to the reportable segments exceeds 75% of total consolidated revenue, there is no requirement to identify additional segments in accordance with paragraph 37.

Diversified manufacturing Company C

Company C is a listed diversified manufacturing company. It produces most of its products in Australia and its markets are also mainly in Australia. It has three main product lines: beer, picture frames and office workstation accessories. Each of these product lines has different production processes, markets and distribution processes. Company C is organised internally into two business units: beer and other entities. The beer business unit reports separate financial and operational information to the chief executive officer (CEO) and chief financial officer (CFO). The other entities business unit is divided into six legal entities, each of which reports separate financial and operational information to the CEO and CFO. The reporting by the six legal entities does not reflect Company C's predominant sources of risks and returns from the picture frames and office workstation accessories products. The results of the two business units are then aggregated to form the consolidated financial information. In preparing its financial statements in accordance with IAS 14, Company C identifies three business segments: beer, picture frames and office workstation accessories. In doing so, it needs to determine the reported segment information for the picture frames and office workstation accessories business segments by further analysing and rearranging the information presented by the six legal entities. It has only one geographical segment: Australia. Because Company C's risks and rates of return are affected predominantly by differences in the products and services it produces, its primary format for reporting segment information should be business segments, with secondary information reported geographically.

Now Company C must determine its reportable segments. None of the business segments is substantially similar (per IAS 14, para. 34) and so they cannot be combined. The following additional information is provided: all three business units earn a majority of their revenues from external customers. Total consolidated revenue of Company C is $250 million.

	Beer $	Picture frames $	Office accessories $	All segments $
Revenue	150m	90m	10m	250m
Segment result (profit)	14m	5m	1m	20m
Assets	600m	150m	50m	800m

Only the beer and picture frames segments are reportable segments because each earns a majority of its revenues from external customers and each equals or exceeds at least one of the 10% thresholds set out in paragraph 35. In fact each exceeds all three of the thresholds. Office accessories is not a reportable segment because, although it earns a majority of its revenues from external customers, it does not equal or exceed any of the thresholds in paragraph 35. Company C may elect to designate office accessories as a reportable segment despite its size or include it as an unallocated reconciling item in the segment disclosures (IAS 14, para 36). Because total external revenue attributable to the reportable segments exceeds 75% of total consolidated revenue (it equals total consolidated revenue), there is no requirement to identify additional segments in accordance with paragraph 37.

20.7 SEGMENT ACCOUNTING POLICIES

20.7.1 Accounting policies and allocation of amounts to segments

Paragraph 44 of IAS 14 requires that segment information be prepared in conformity with the accounting policies adopted for preparing and presenting the financial statements of the consolidated group or entity.

This does not mean, however, that the consolidated or entity accounting policies are to be applied to reportable segments as if the segments were separate stand-alone reporting entities. A detailed calculation done in applying a particular accounting policy at the entity-wide level may be allocated to segments if there is a reasonable basis for doing so. Pension and other employee benefit calculations, for example, often are done for an entity as a whole, but the entity-wide figures may be allocated to segments based on salary and demographic data for the segments.

IAS 14 paragraph 47 states that assets that are jointly used by two or more segments should be allocated to segments if, and only if, their related revenues and expenses are also allocated to those segments.

At this point it is necessary to consider the definitions of segment assets, liabilities, revenues and expenses: They are defined in paragraph 16 of IAS 14 as follows:

> *Segment revenue* is revenue reported in the entity's statement of comprehensive income [income statement] that is directly attributable to a segment and the relevant portion of entity revenue that can be allocated on a reasonable basis to a segment, whether from sales to external customers or from transactions with other segments of the same entity. Segment revenue does not include:
>
> (a) [deleted; this used to refer to 'extraordinary items', which are no longer permitted under IFRSs]
>
> (b) interest or dividend income, including interest earned on advances or loans to other segments, unless the segment's operations are primarily of a financial nature; or

(c) gains on sales of investments or gains on extinguishment of debt unless the segment's operations are primarily of a financial nature.

Segment revenue includes an entity's share of profits or losses of associates, joint ventures, or other investments accounted for under the equity method only if those items are included in consolidated or total entity revenue.

Segment revenue includes a joint venturer's share of the revenue of a jointly controlled entity that is accounted for by proportionate consolidation in accordance with IAS 31, *Investments in Joint Ventures*.

Segment expense is expense resulting from the operating activities of a segment that is directly attributable to the segment and the relevant portion of an expense that can be allocated on a reasonable basis to the segment, including expenses relating to sales to external customers and expenses relating to transactions with other segments of the same entity. Segment expense does not include:

(a) [deleted]
(b) interest, including interest incurred on advances or loans from other segments, unless the segment's operations are primarily of a financial nature;
(c) losses on sales of investments or losses on extinguishment of debt unless the segment's operations are primarily of a financial nature;
(d) an entity's share of losses of associates, joint ventures, or other investments accounted for under the equity method;
(e) income tax expense; or
(f) general administrative expenses, head-office expenses, and other expenses that arise at the entity level and relate to the entity as a whole. However, costs are sometimes incurred at the entity level on behalf of a segment. Such costs are segment expenses if they relate to the segment's operating activities and they can be directly attributed or allocated to the segment on a reasonable basis.

Segment expense includes a joint venturer's share of the expenses of a jointly controlled entity that is accounted for by proportionate consolidation in accordance with IAS 31.

For a segment's operations that are primarily of a financial nature, interest income and interest expense may be reported as a single net amount for segment reporting purposes only if those items are netted in the consolidated or entity financial statements.

Segment result is segment revenue less segment expense. Segment result is determined before any adjustments for minority interest.

Segment assets are those operating assets that are employed by a segment in its operating activities and that either are directly attributable to the segment or can be allocated to the segment on a reasonable basis.

If a segment's segment result includes interest or dividend income, its segment assets include the related receivables, loans, investments, or other income-producing assets.

Segment assets do not include income tax assets.

Segment assets include investments accounted for under the equity method only if the profit or loss from such investments is included in segment revenue. Segment assets include a joint venturer's share of the operating assets of a jointly controlled entity that is accounted for by proportionate consolidation in accordance with IAS 31.

Segment assets are determined after deducting related allowances that are reported as direct offsets in the entity's statement of finacial position [balance sheet].

Segment liabilities are those operating liabilities that result from the operating activities of a segment and that either are directly attributable to the segment or can be allocated to the segment on a reasonable basis.

If a segment's segment result includes interest expense, its segment liabilities include the related interest-bearing liabilities.

Segment liabilities include a joint venturer's share of the liabilities of a jointly controlled entity that is accounted for by proportionate consolidation in accordance with IAS 31.

Segment liabilities do not include income tax liabilities.

Segment accounting policies are the accounting policies adopted for preparing and presenting the financial statements of the consolidated group or entity as well as those accounting policies that relate specifically to segment reporting.

The way in which asset, liability, revenue and expense items are allocated to segments depends on such factors as the nature of those items, the activities conducted by the segment and the relative autonomy of that segment. Paragraph 48 of IAS 14 states that it is not possible or appropriate to specify a single basis of allocation that should be adopted by all entities. Nor is it appropriate to force allocation of entity asset, liability, revenue and expense items that relate jointly to two or more segments if the only basis for making those allocations is arbitrary or difficult to understand.

At the same time, the definitions of segment revenue, expense, assets and liabilities are interrelated, and the resulting allocations should be consistent. Therefore, jointly used assets are allocated to segments if, and only if, their related revenues and expenses are also allocated to those segments. For example, an asset is included in segment assets if, and only if, the related depreciation or amortisation is deducted in measuring segment result. Segment assets do not include assets used for general entity or head-office purposes. These are disclosed as 'unallocated' head-office or corporate assets. Examples include income tax assets and buildings used for head-office administration only.

Similarly, the liabilities of segments whose operations are not primarily of a financial nature do not include borrowings and similar liabilities because segment result represents an operating, rather than a net-of-financing, profit or loss. Further, because debt is often issued at the head-office level on an entity-wide basis, it is often not possible to directly attribute, or reasonably allocate, the interest-bearing liability to the segment. Therefore these liabilities are disclosed as 'unallocated' head-office or corporate liabilities.

Measurements of segment assets and liabilities include adjustments to the prior carrying amounts of the identifiable segment assets and segment liabilities of a company acquired in a business combination, even if those adjustments are made only for the purpose of preparing consolidated financial statements and are not recorded in either the parent's or the subsidiary's separate financial statements. Similarly, if property, plant and equipment have been revalued subsequent to acquisition in accordance with the revaluation model in IAS 16, then measurements of segment assets reflect those revaluations (para. 21). Segment assets include goodwill that is directly attributable to a segment or that can be allocated to a segment on a reasonable basis, and segment expense includes any related impairment losses.

However, segment revenue, expense, assets and liabilities are determined before intragroup balances and intragroup transactions are eliminated as part of the consolidation process, except to the extent that such intragroup balances and transactions are between group entities within a single segment. Eliminations made on consolidation will be disclosed in a separate column as part of the reconciliation between the segment information and the consolidated information (see section 20.8 on disclosures).

While the accounting policies used in preparing and presenting the financial statements of the entity as a whole are also the fundamental segment accounting policies, segment accounting policies also include policies that relate specifically to segment reporting. These include identification of segments, method of pricing inter-segment transfers, and basis for allocating revenues and expenses to segments.

Note that, in relation to the determination of segment result, extraordinary items are no longer permitted under IAS 1 *Presentation of Financial Statements*.

Building on illustrative example 20.3, the following illustrative example shows how diversified manufacturing company A will determine its segment revenue, expense, assets and liabilities.

ILLUSTRATIVE EXAMPLE 20.4

Applying the requirements

Determining segment revenue, expense, assets and liabilities

The following financial information is provided for diversified manufacturing Company A for the year ended 30 June 2010:

	Wine $	Water heaters $	Olive oil $	All segments $
Segment revenue	150m	90m	10m	250m
Segment result (profit)	14m	5m	1m	20m
Segment assets	500m	200m	100m	800m

Total consolidated revenue of Company A is $253 million. Total consolidated profit — after income tax expense of $5 million, interest income of $1 million and a gain on disposal of investments of $2 million — is $8 million. Total consolidated liabilities of Company A are $200 million. These include borrowings of $150 million. Related interest expense is $10 million. $40 million of liabilities are trade creditors and other payables directly attributable to the wine segment. $10 million of liabilities are trade creditors and other payables directly attributable to the water heaters segment. All assets and related depreciation have been allocated to the business segments.

The allocation of segment revenue, expense, assets and liabilities is determined as follows:

	Wine $	Water heaters $	Olive oil $	Unallocated $	Consolidated $
Revenue	150m	90m	10m	3m (interest income and gain on disposal of investments)	253m
Segment result (profit)	14m	5m	1m	3m revenue and 15m expenses (interest expense and income tax expense)	8m
Assets	500m	200m	100m	—	800m
Liabilities	40m	10m	—	150m (borrowings — not allocated because the segments' operations are not primarily of a financial nature)	200m

This example also shows that before an entity can determine its reportable segments (as demonstrated in illustrative example 20.3) it needs first to calculate correctly the segment allocations and unallocated amounts.

20.8 DISCLOSURES

20.8.1 Outline of disclosure requirements

Paragraphs 50–67 of IAS 14 specify the disclosures required for reportable segments for an entity's *primary* segment reporting format. Paragraphs 68–72 identify the disclosures required for an entity's *secondary* reporting format. Paragraphs 74–83 address several other segment disclosure matters.

Appendix C to IAS 14 summarises the required disclosures and is quoted in figure 20.2 for ease of reference. You should refer to the detail in each relevant paragraph in IAS 14 when reviewing this table. Note also the 10% thresholds for secondary segment disclosures set out in paragraphs 69 through 71.

FIGURE 20.2 Appendix C to IAS 14: Summary of required disclosure

APPENDIX C
Summary of required disclosure

The appendix is illustrative only and does not form part of the standards. Its purpose is to summarise the disclosures required by paragraphs 49–83 for each of the three possible primary segment reporting formats.

[¶ xx] refers to paragraph xx in the Standard.

Primary format is business segments	Primary format is geographical segments by location of assets	Primary format is geographical segments by location of customers
Required primary disclosures:	*Required primary disclosures:*	*Required primary disclosures:*
Revenue from external customers by business segment [¶ 51]	Revenue from external customers by location of assets [¶ 51]	Revenue from external customers by location of customers [¶ 51]
Revenue from transactions with other segments by business segment [¶ 51]	Revenue from transactions with other segments by location of assets [¶ 51]	Revenue from transactions with other segments by location of customers [¶ 51]

(continued)

FIGURE 20.2 *(continued)*

Primary format is business segments	Primary format is geographical segments by location of assets	Primary format is geographical segments by location of customers
Segment result by business segment [¶52]	Segment result by location of assets [¶52]	Segment result by location of customers [¶52]
Carrying amount of segment assets by business segment [¶55]	Carrying amount of segment assets by location of assets [¶55]	Carrying amount of segment assets by location of customers [¶55]
Segment liabilities by business segment [¶56]	Segment liabilities by location of assets [¶56]	Segment liabilities by location of customers [¶56]
Cost to acquire property, plant, equipment and intangibles by business segment [¶57]	Cost to acquire property, plant, equipment and intangibles by location of assets [¶57]	Cost to acquire property, plant, equipment and intangibles by location of customers [¶57]
Depreciation and amortisation expense by business segment [¶58]	Depreciation and amortisation expense by location of assets [¶58]	Depreciation and amortisation expense by location of customers [¶58]
Non-cash expenses other than depreciation and amortisation by business segment [¶61]	Non-cash expenses other than depreciation and amortisation by location of assets [¶61]	Non-cash expenses other than depreciation and amortisation by location of customers [¶61]
Share of profit or loss of [¶64] and investment in [¶66] equity method associates or joint ventures by business segment (if substantially all within a single business segment)	Share of profit or loss of [¶64] and investment in [¶66] equity method associates or joint ventures by location of assets (if substantially all within a single business segment)	Share of profit or loss of [¶64] and investment in [¶66] equity method associates or joint ventures by location of customers (if substantially all within a single business segment)
Reconciliation of revenue, result, assets and liabilities by business segment [¶67]	Reconciliation of revenue, result, assets and liabilities [¶67]	Reconciliation of revenue, result, assets and liabilities [¶67]
Required secondary disclosures:	*Required secondary disclosures:*	*Required secondary disclosures:*
Revenue from external customers by location of customers [¶69]	Revenue from external customers by business segment [¶70]	Revenue from external customers by business segment [¶70]
Carrying amount of segment assets by location of assets [¶69]	Carrying amount of segment assets by business segment [¶70]	Carrying amount of segment assets by business segment [¶70]
Cost to acquire property, plant, equipment and intangibles by location of assets [¶69]	Cost to acquire property, plant, equipment and intangibles by business segment [¶70]	Cost to acquire property, plant, equipment and intangibles by business segment [¶70]
	Revenue from external customers by geographical customers if different from location of assets [¶71]	
		Carrying amount of segment assets by location of assets if different from location of customers [¶72]
		Cost to acquire property, plant, equipment and intangibles by location of assets if different from location of customers [¶72]
Other required disclosures:	*Other required disclosures:*	*Other required disclosures:*
Revenue for any business or geographical segment whose external revenue is more than 10% of entity revenue but that is not a reportable segment because a majority of its revenue is from internal transfers [¶74]	Revenue for any business or geographical segment whose external revenue is more than 10% of entity revenue but that is not a reportable segment because a majority of its revenue is from internal transfers [¶74]	Revenue for any business or geographical segment whose external revenue is more than 10% of entity revenue but that is not a reportable segment because a majority of its revenue is from internal transfers [¶74]

FIGURE 20.2 *(continued)*

Primary format is business segments	Primary format is geographical segments by location of assets	Primary format is geographical segments by location of customers
Basis of pricing inter-segment transfers and any change therein [¶75]	Basis of pricing inter-segment transfers and any change therein [¶75]	Basis of pricing inter-segment transfers and any change therein [¶75]
Changes in segment accounting policies [¶76]	Changes in segment accounting policies [¶76]	Changes in segment accounting policies [¶76]
Types of products and services in each business segment [¶81]	Types of products and services in each business segment [¶81]	Types of products and services in each business segment [¶81]
Composition of each geographical segment [¶81]	Composition of each geographical segment [¶81]	Composition of each geographical segment [¶81]

Source: IAS 14 *Segment Reporting*, Appendix C.

Appendix B to IAS 14 also provides a useful illustration of the required disclosures.

20.8.2 Additional disclosures that are encouraged but not required

IAS 14 contains a number of paragraphs encouraging, but not requiring, additional information. They are as follows:

> 53. If an entity can compute segment net profit or loss or some other measure of segment profitability other than segment result without arbitrary allocations, reporting of such amount(s) is encouraged in addition to segment result, appropriately described. If that measure is prepared on a basis other than the accounting policies adopted for the consolidated or entity financial statements, the entity will include in its financial statements a clear description of the basis of measurement.

IAS 14 states that an example of a measure of segment performance above segment result on the statement of comprehensive income is gross margin on sales. Examples of measures of segment performance below segment result on the statement of comprehensive income are profit or loss from ordinary activities (either before or after income taxes) and net profit or loss.

> 59. An entity is encouraged, but not required to disclose the nature and amount of any items of segment revenue and segment expense that are of such size, nature, or incidence that their disclosure is relevant to explain the performance of each reportable segment for the period.

IAS 1 states that when items of income or expense are material their nature and amount shall be disclosed separately. Paragraph 59 of IAS 14 is not intended to change the classification of any such items or to change the measurement of such items. The disclosure encouraged by that paragraph, however, does change the level at which the significance of such items is evaluated for disclosure purposes from the entity level to the segment level.

> 63. An entity that provides the segment cash flow disclosures that are encouraged by IAS 7 need not also disclose depreciation and amortisation expense pursuant to paragraph 58 or non-cash expenses pursuant to paragraph 61.

IAS 7 *Statement of Cash Flows* notes that disclosing cash flow information for each reportable industry and geographical segment is relevant to understanding the entity's overall financial position, liquidity and cash flows. IAS 7 encourages the disclosure of such information. IAS 14 therefore also encourages the segment cash flow disclosures that are encouraged by IAS 7.

It is not common for entities to provide these 'encouraged' disclosures for a number of reasons, including competitive disadvantage (revealing too much information to competitors), cost of compiling the additional information and the arbitrary nature of more detailed segment allocations.

20.8.3 Comparative information

IAS 14, paragraph 76 states:

> Changes in accounting policies adopted for segment reporting that have a material effect on segment information shall be disclosed, and prior period segment information presented for comparative purposes shall be restated unless it is impracticable to do so. Such disclosure shall include a description

of the nature of the change, the reasons for the change, the fact that comparative information has been restated or that it is impracticable to do so, and the financial effect of the change, if it is reasonably determinable. If an entity changes the identification of its segments and it does not restate prior period segment information on the new basis because it is impracticable to do so, then for the purpose of comparison the entity shall report segment data for both the old and the new bases of segmentation in the year in which it changes the identification of its segments.

Changes in accounting policies adopted at the entity level that affect segment information are dealt with in accordance with IAS 8 *Accounting Policies, Changes in Accounting Estimates and Errors*. Essentially, IAS 8 requires that a change in accounting policy should be applied retrospectively and that prior period information be restated unless it is impracticable to do. IAS 1 defines 'impracticable' as follows:

> Applying a requirement is impracticable when the entity cannot apply it after making every reasonable effort to do so.

Therefore, it is not sufficient for an entity to argue that it will take too much time or that it will incur too great a cost to restate comparative information. It is only if the entity cannot recalculate the information on a reasonable basis after making every effort to do so that it can say that it is impracticable. This requirement is particularly relevant for large organisations that frequently change their business segments; for example, as a result of internal changes in the way that the segments report to the CEO. Every time an internal reorganisation occurs, resulting in a change of business segments, restatement of comparative information using the new basis of segmentation is required.

20.8.4 Extracts from companies' financial reports

Some extracts from companies' recent financial reports are reproduced in figures 20.3–20.6. They are useful in understanding how companies in different industries produce segment information to meet users' needs.

FIGURE 20.3 Segment information from Queensland Cotton Holdings Ltd annual report 2007

4. SEGMENT REPORTING

Segment information is presented in respect of the consolidated entity's business and geographical segments. The primary format, business segments, is based on the consolidated entity's management and internal reporting structure.

Segment results, assets and liabilities include items directly attributable to a segment as well as those that can be allocated on a reasonable basis. Unallocated items mainly comprise income-earning assets and revenue, interest-bearing loans, borrowings and expenses, and corporate assets and expenses. Inter-segment pricing is determined on an arm's length basis.

Segment capital expenditure is the total cost incurred during the year to acquire segment assets that are expected to be used for more than one period.

Business Segments

The consolidated entity comprises the following main business segments, based on the consolidated entity's management reporting system:

- Ginning services.
- Marketing of cotton.

Included in Other are the following non-reportable segments:

- Distribution and sale of chemicals, fertilisers and planting seed.
- Sale of pulse seed.
- Warehousing services.
- Provision of grower loans.

Geographical Segments

In presenting information on the basis of geographical segments, segment revenue, results and assets is based on the geographical location of the assets. The consolidated entity's geographical segments reported are Australia, United States of America and Brazil.

FIGURE 20.3 *(continued)*

PRIMARY REPORTING BUSINESS SEGMENTS	GINNING SERVICES		MARKETING OF COTTON		OTHER		TOTAL	
	2007 $'000	2006 $'000	2007 $'000	2006 $'000	2007 $'000	2006 $'000	2007 $'000	2006 $'000
REVENUE								
External segment revenue	109 012	113 179	396 969	493 150	65 450	78 569	571 431	684 898
TOTAL REVENUE							**571 431**	**684 898**
RESULTS								
Segment result	3 635	8 120	20 777	22 012	(5 704)	(5 088)	18 708	25 044
Unallocated corporate expenses							(8 966)	(6 078)
Profit from ordinary activities before income tax							9 742	18 966
Income tax expense							(2 993)	(5 915)
NET PROFIT							**6 749**	**13 051**
Acquisition of property, plant and equipment and intangible assets	10 904	35 762	484	799	1 818	2 682	13 206	39 243
Depreciation and amortisation	(6 853)	(7 506)	(639)	(831)	(2 250)	(1 496)	(9 747)	(9 833)
Non-cash gains/(expenses) other than depreciation and amortisation	(253)	(1 019)	3 318	7 909	478	727	3 543	7 617
Share of net profits of partnerships accounted for using the equity method included in segment results	51	156	—	—	—	—	51	156
Carrying value of equity accounted investments included in segment assets	887	1 205	—	—	—	—	887	1 205
Impairment losses on property, plant and equipment	(2 089)	(1 790)	—	(30)	(94)	28	(2 183)	1 792

(continued)

FIGURE 20.3 *(continued)*

	GINNING SERVICES		MARKETING OF COTTON		OTHER		TOTAL	
	2007 $'000	2006 $'000	2007 $'000	2006 $'000	2007 $'000	2006 $'000	2007 $'000	2006 $'000
ASSETS								
Segment assets	154 112	158 096	80 734	96 875	73 503	93 041	308 349	348 012
Unallocated corporate assets							10 257	14 551
CONSOLIDATED TOTAL ASSETS							**318 606**	**362 563**

LIABILITIES								
Segment liabilities	11 495	12 509	18 942	26 110	17 799	25 851	48 236	64 470
Unallocated corporate liabilities							126 281	154 140
CONSOLIDATED TOTAL LIABILITIES							**174 517**	**218 610**

SECONDARY REPORTING GEOGRAPHICAL SEGMENTS	SEGMENT REVENUES FROM EXTERNAL CUSTOMERS		CARRYING AMOUNT OF SEGMENT ASSETS		ACQUISITIONS OF PROPERTY PLANT & EQUIPMENT & INTANGIBLES	
	2007 $'000	2006 $'000	2007 $'000	2006 $'000	2007 $'000	2006 $'000
Australia	357 236	439 061	217 718	209 245	8 341	37 585
United States	174 867	181 103	87 853	136 818	4 792	1 658
Brazil	39 328	64 734	2 778	1 949	73	—
TOTAL	**571 431**	**684 898**	**308 349**	**348 012**	**13 206**	**39 243**

EXTERNAL SEGMENT REVENUE BY LOCATION OF CUSTOMER	2007 $'000	2006 $'000
Australia	124 533	181 173
China	117 068	151 934
Indonesia	74 890	73 913
United States	57 387	71 503
Korea	49 737	46 559
Japan	41 826	39 897
Thailand	33 882	41 652
Other sales to external customers	72 108	78 267
TOTAL SEGMENT REVENUE	**571 431**	**684 898**

Source: Queensland Cotton Holdings (2007, pp. 37–9).

FIGURE 20.4 Segment information from ANZ Banking Group financial report 2008

36: Segment Analysis

For management purposes the Group is organised into four major business segments being Personal, Institutional, Asia Pacific and New Zealand Business. An expanded description of the principal activities for each of the business segments is contained in the Glossary on pages 188 to 190.

A summarised description of each business segment is shown below:

Personal	Provides:	• Rural Commercial & Agribusiness Products, Small Business Banking Products, Banking Products, Consumer Finance, Investment and Insurance Products, Mortgages and other (including the branch network) in Australia; and • Vehicle and equipment finance, rental services and fixed and at call investments.
Institutional	Provides:	• A full range of financial services to the Group's business banking, corporate and institutional customers including Corporate Finance, Business Banking, Markets and Working Capital. Institutional has a major presence in Australia and New Zealand and also has operations in Asia, Europe and the United States.
Asia Pacific	Provides:	• Personal and private banking business in Asia. • A portfolio of strategic retail partnerships in Asia. • Trade finance, relationship lending, markets and corporate finance businesses in Asia. • Retail banking services in the Pacific region.
New Zealand Businesses	Provides:	• A full range of banking services for personal, small business and corporate customers in New Zealand. • Including ANZ Retail, NBNZ Retail, Corporate and Commercial Banking, Investment Insurance Products, Private Banking, Rural Banking and Central Support.

As the composition of segments was amended during the year, September 2007 comparatives have been adjusted to be consistent with the 2008 segment definitions.

BUSINESS SEGMENT ANALYSIS[1,2]

Consolidated Year ended 30 September 2008	**Personal $m**	**Institutional $m**	**Asia Pacific $m**	**New Zealand Businesses $m**	**Other[3] $m**	**Less: Institutional Asia Pacific[4] $m**	**Consolidated total $m**
External interest income	13 444	11 753	1 124	6 668	365	(750)	32 604
External interest expense	(4 262)	(8 002)	(802)	(4 361)	(7 836)	509	(24 754)
Adjust for intersegment interest	(5 758)	(1 492)	158	(663)	7 684	71	—
Net interest income	3 424	2 259	480	1 644	213	(170)	7 850
Other external operating income	1 481	1 074	413	487	714	(221)	3 948
Share of net profit of equity accounted investments	—	(3)	146	19	199	—	361
Segment revenue	4 905	3 330	1 039	2 150	1 126	(391)	12 159
Other external expenses	(2 020)	(1 231)	(428)	(1 031)	(1 078)	92	(5 696)
Net intersegment (income)/expenses	(329)	(261)	(42)	4	579	49	—
Operating expenses	(2 349)	(1 492)	(470)	(1 027)	(499)	141	(5 696)
Provision for credit impairment	(437)	(1 218)	(64)	(240)	(9)	20	(1 948)

(continued)

FIGURE 20.4 *(continued)*

Consolidated Year ended 30 September 2008	Personal $m	Institutional $m	Asia Pacific $m	New Zealand Businesses $m	Other[3] $m	Less: Institutional Asia Pacific[4] $m	Consolidated total $m
Segment result	2 119	620	505	883	618	(230)	4 515
Income tax expense	(634)	(91)	(86)	(283)	(151)	57	(1 188)
Minority interests	—	(3)	(6)	—	—	1	(8)
Profit after income tax attributable to shareholders of the company	1 485	526	413	600	467	(172)	3 319
Capital expenditure	15	57	43	40	404	—	559
Non-Cash Expenses							
Depreciation & amortisation	(115)	(42)	(20)	(37)	(117)	1	(330)
Equity-settled share-based payment expenses	(20)	(33)	(7)	(11)	(13)	—	(84)
Provision for credit impairment	(437)	(1 218)	(64)	(240)	(9)	20	(1 948)
Credit risk on derivatives[5]	—	(721)	—	—	—	—	(721)
Provisions for employee entitlements	(32)	(21)	(2)	(59)	(20)	—	(134)
Provision for restructuring	(9)	(6)	(1)	(1)	(164)	—	(181)
Financial Position							
Total external assets[6]	167 744	207 776	31 977	76 125	10 410	(23 463)	470 569
Share of associate and joint venture companies	16	465	2 209	196	1 639	(150)	4 375
Total external liabilities[7]	80 738	175 264	30 172	67 682	111 170	(20 862)	444 164
Goodwill	264	6	61	20	2 713	—	3 064
Intangibles	308	205	44	38	82	—	677

1 Results are equity standardised.
2 Intersegment transfers are accounted for and determined on an arm's length or cost recovery basis.
3 Includes INGA, Group Centre and significant items. Also includes the London headquartered project finance and certain structured finance transactions that ANZ has exited as part of its de-risking strategy.
4 Institutional Asia Pacific is included in both the Institutional business segment and the Asia Pacific business segment consistent with how this business is internally managed. Segment information for Institutional Asia Pacific therefore needs to be deducted to tie back to a consolidated total for Group.
5 This charge arose from changes to the credit worthiness of counterparties to our structured credit intermediation trades, defaults on customer derivative exposures and changes in counterparty credit ratings on the remainder of our derivatives portfolio.
6 Excludes deferred tax assets.
7 Excludes income tax liabilities.

BUSINESS SEGMENT ANALYSIS[1,2]

Consolidated Year ended 30 September 2007	Personal $m	Institutional $m	Asia Pacific $m	New Zealand Businesses $m	Other[3] $m	Less Institutional Asia Pacific[4] $m	Consolidated total $m
External interest income	10 811	9 062	844	5 811	212	(530)	26 210
External interest expense	(3 196)	(6 396)	(643)	(3 539)	(5 491)	357	(18 908)
Adjust for intersegment interest	(4 503)	(682)	146	(614)	5 573	80	—
Net interest income	3 112	1 984	347	1 658	294	(93)	7 302
Other external operating income	1 322	1 465	299	488	369	(164)	3 779
Share of net profit of equity accounted investments	4	16	66	20	153	—	259
Segment revenue	4 438	3 465	712	2 166	816	(257)	11 340
Other external expenses	(1 839)	(1 086)	(285)	(1 035)	(762)	54	(4 953)
Net intersegment (income)/expenses	(311)	(249)	(37)	(1)	561	37	—

FIGURE 20.4 *(continued)*

Consolidated Year ended 30 September 2007	Personal $m	Institutional $m	Asia Pacific $m	New Zealand Businesses $m	Other[3] $m	Less Institutional Asia Pacific[4] $m	Consolidated total $m
Operating expenses	(2 150)	(1 335)	(322)	(1 036)	(201)	91	(4 953)
Provision for credit impairment	(386)	(24)	(42)	(69)	(2)	1	(522)
Segment result	1 902	2 106	348	1 061	613	(165)	5 865
Income tax expense	(571)	(621)	(73)	(341)	(111)	39	(1 678)
Minority interests	(1)	(3)	(4)	—	—	1	(7)
Profit after income tax attributable to shareholders of the company	1 330	1 482	271	720	502	(125)	4 180
Capital expenditure	43	26	26	36	282	—	413
Non-Cash Expenses							
Depreciation & amortisation	(124)	(39)	(17)	(40)	(96)	1	(315)
Equity-settled share-based payment expenses	(19)	(24)	(4)	(11)	(4)	—	(62)
Provision for credit impairment	(386)	(24)	(42)	(69)	(2)	1	(522)
Credit risk on derivatives[5]	—	(45)	—	—	—	—	(45)
Provisions for employee entitlements	(25)	(17)	(1)	(56)	(22)	—	(121)
Provision for restructuring	(6)	(9)	1	—	(9)	—	(23)
Financial Position							
Total external assets[6]	150 403	157 503	16 998	70 602	8 370	(11 216)	392 660
Share of associate and joint venture companies	16	177	1 557	181	1 499	—	3 430
Total external liabilities[7]	72 516	143 628	16 672	58 509	87 792	(9 155)	369 962
Goodwill	264	4	57	20	2 781	—	3 126
Intangibles	312	141	11	22	65	—	551

1 Results are equity standardised.
2 Intersegment transfers are accounted for and determined on an arm's length or cost recovery basis.
3 Includes INGA, Group Centre and significant items. Also includes the London headquartered project finance and certain structured finance transactions that ANZ has exited as part of its de-risking strategy.
4 Institutional Asia Pacific is included in both the institutional business segment and the Asia Pacific business segment consistent with how this business is internally managed. Segment information for Institutional Asia Pacific therefore needs to be deducted to tie back to a consolidated total for Group.
5 This charge arose from changes to the credit worthiness of counterparties to our structured credit intermediation trades, defaults on customer derivative exposures and changes in counterparty credit ratings on the remainder of our derivatives portfolio.
6 Excludes deferred tax assets.
7 Excludes income tax liabilities.

The following analysis details financial information by geographic location.

GEOGRAPHIC SEGMENT ANALYSIS[1,2]

	2008		2007	
Consolidated	**$m**	**%**	**$m**	**%**
Income				
Australia	25 033	68%	20 134	66%
New Zealand	9 110	25%	8 092	27%
Overseas Markets	2 770	7%	2 021	7%
	36 913	100%	30 247	100%
Total assets[3]				
Australia	321 705	69%	272 968	70%
New Zealand	100 270	21%	91 193	23%
Overseas Markets	48 594	10%	28 499	7%
	470 569	100%	392 660	100%

(continued)

FIGURE 20.4 *(continued)*

	2008		2007	
Consolidated	**$m**	**%**	**$m**	**%**
Capital Expenditure				
Australia	460	82%	326	79%
New Zealand	40	7%	36	9%
Overseas Markets	59	11%	51	12%
	559	100%	413	100%

1 Intersegment transfers are accounted for and determined on an arm's length or cost recovery basis.
2 The geographic segments represent the locations in which the transaction was booked.
3 Excludes deferred tax assets.

Source: ANZ (2008, pp. 148–51).

FIGURE 20.5 Segment information from Wesfarmers Ltd annual report 2008

3 SEGMENT INFORMATION

The Group's primary reporting format is business segments as the Group's risks and rates of return are affected predominantly by differences in the products and services provided. The operating businesses are organised and managed separately according to the nature of the products and services provided, with each segment representing a strategic business unit that offers different products and serves different markets. The Group operations are substantially in one material geographical segment only, being Australia, and therefore a secondary reporting format is not provided.

Transfer prices between business segments are set at an arm's length basis in a manner similar to transactions with third parties. Segment revenue, segment expense and segment result include transfers between business segments. Those transfers are eliminated on consolidation where material.

The business segments are as follows:

Coles
Supermarket, liquor, convenience and Coles property businesses, and previously unallocated Coles retail support costs.

Home improvement and office supplies
Retail of building materials and home and garden improvement products;
Servicing project builders and the housing industry; and
Office supplies products.

Resources
Coal mining and development; and
Coal marketing to both domestic and export markets.

Insurance
Supplier of specialist rural and small business regional insurance;
Supplier of general insurance through broking intermediaries; and
Supplier of insurance broking services.

Kmart
Retail of apparel and general merchandise.

Target
Retail of apparel and general merchandise.

Industrial and safety distribution
Supplier and distributor of maintenance, repair and operating (MRO) products; and
Specialised supplier and distributor of industrial safety products and services.

Energy
National marketing and distribution of LPG;
LPG extraction for domestic and export markets;
Manufacture and marketing of industrial gases and equipment; and
Electricity supply to mining operations and regional centres.

Chemicals and fertilisers
Manufacture and marketing of chemicals for industry, mining and mineral processing; and
Manufacture and marketing of broadacre and horticultural fertilisers.

FIGURE 20.5 *(continued)*

Other

Forest products: non-controlling interest in Wespine Pty Ltd, which manufactures products to service the wholesale timber market in Australia.

Property: includes a non-controlling interest in Bunnings Warehouse Property Trust, which acquires and builds properties suitable for retail property development and investment:

Investment banking: non-controlling interest in Gresham Partners Group Limited, which is an investment bank providing financial advisory and investment management services; and

Private equity investment: commitments to, and interests in, Gresham Private Equity Funds which are closed-end private equity funds targeting larger size private equity transactions in the areas of management buy-outs, expansion capital and corporate restructuring.

Revenue and earnings of various divisions are affected by seasonality and cyclicality as follows:

- Home improvement and office supplies, Coles, Kmart and Target - earnings are typically greater in the December half of the financial year due to the impact on the retail business of the Christmas holiday shopping period;
- Resources — the majority of the entity's export coal contracts are subject to price review each April, and depending upon the movement in prevailing coal prices this can result in significant changes in revenue and earnings in the last quarter of the financial year through to the third quarter of the following year; and
- Chemicals and fertilisers - earnings are typically much greater in the June half of the financial year due to the impact of the Western Australian winter season break on fertiliser sales.

	COLES		HOME IMPROVEMENT AND OFFICE SUPPLIES		RESOURCES*		INSURANCE		KMART	
	2008 $m	2007 $m	**2008 $m**	2007 $m	**2008 $m**	2007 $m	**2008 $m**	2007 $m	**2008 $m**	2007 $m
Segment revenue	**16 876**	—	**6 160**	4 939	**1 311**	1 134	**1 649**	1 410	**2 454**	—
Segment result										
Earnings before interest, tax, depreciation, amortisation (EBITDA) and corporate overheads	**714**	—	**700**	586	**571**	520	**160**	144	**145**	—
Depreciation and amortisation	**(240)**	—	**(75)**	(58)	**(148)**	(182)	**(28)**	(24)	**(31)**	—
Earnings before interest, tax (EBIT) and corporate overheads	**474**	—	**625**	528	**423**	338	**132**	120	**114**	—
Finance costs										
Corporate overheads										
Profit before income tax expense										
Income tax expense										
Profit attributable to members of the parent										
Assets and liabilities										
Segment assets	**18 476**	—	**3 905**	2 399	**1 595**	1 285	**3 304**	3 199	**1 593**	—
Investments in associates	**14**	—	**—**				**17**	27	**—**	—
Tax assets										
Total assets										

(continued)

FIGURE 20.5 *(continued)*

	2008 $m	2007 $m	**2008 $m**	2007 $m	**2008 $m**	2007 $m	**2008 $m**	2007 $m	**2008 $m**	2007 $m
Segment liabilities	**3 061**	—	**598**	424	**522**	325	**2 001**	1 973	**486**	—
Tax liabilities										—
interest bearing liabilities										
Total liabilities										
Other segment information										
Capital expenditure	**351**	—	**302**	196	**146**	178	**18**	15	**41**	—
Share of net profit or loss of associates included in EBIT	—	—	—	—	—	—	**1**	1	—	—
Non-cash expenses other than depreciation and amortisation	**194**	—	**105**	76	**40**	14	**56**	15	**49**	—

*Was previously known as Coal Division.
The above results for the former Coles group businesses are for the period from the date of acquisition on 23 November 2007 to 30 June 2008.

TARGET		INDUSTRIAL AND SAFETY		ENERGY		CHEMICALS AND FERTILISERS		OTHER		CONSOLIDATED	
2008 $m	2007 $m	**2008 $m**	2007 $m	**2008 $m**	2007 $m	**2008 $m**	2007 $m	**2008 $m**	2007 $m	**2008 $m**	2007 $m
2 198	—	**1 309**	1 208	**565**	463	**997**	592	**65**	8	**33 584**	9 754
256	—	**141**	128	**128**	104	**172**	138	**(2)**	97	**2 985**	1 717
(33)	—	**(11)**	(13)	**(38)**	(29)	**(48)**	(37)	**(2)**	(2)	**(654)**	(345)
223	—	**130**	115	**90**	75	**124**	101	**(4)**	95	**2 331**	1 372
										(800)	(200)
										(88)	(67)
										1 443	1 105
										(393)	(319)
										1 050	786
3 911	—	**982**	930	**904**	819	**1 219**	747	**562**	2 308	**36 451**	11 687
—	—	—	—	**3**	10	**68**	60	**363**	292	**465**	389
										390	—
										37 306	12 076
423	—	**192**	172	**107**	104	**263**	127	**310**	83	**7 963**	3 208
										236	242
										9 517	5 123
										17 716	8 573
60	—	**20**	26	**118**	78	**252**	199	**5**	3	**1 313**	695
—	—	—	—	**4**	6	**8**	8	**27**	68	**40**	83
31	—	**23**	17	**6**	6	**3**	3	**8**	6	**515**	137

Source: Wesfarmers (2008, pp. 87–9).

20.9 A NEW STANDARD — IFRS 8 *OPERATING SEGMENTS*

20.9.1 Overview

In January 2006, the IASB issued ED 8 *Operating Segments,* which it proposed as a replacement to IAS 14. The ED was part of the IASB's program for achieving convergence with standards issued by the US Financial Accounting Standards Board (FASB) and essentially adopted the requirements of the FASB Statement of Financial Accounting Standards No. 131 (SFAS 131) *Disclosures about Segments of an Enterprise and Related Information.* The major change from IAS 14 is the adoption of the management approach to identifying segments as the only acceptable approach. ED 8 was finally issued as a new standard, IFRS 8 *Operating Segments,* in November 2006. IFRS 8 is applicable for annual reporting periods beginning on or after 1 January 2009, with early adoption permitted. Where standards are issued with a long time allowed for implementation and with early adoption permitted, there will be a number of years during which some companies will apply the old standard and others will apply the new standard. Accordingly, this section provides an overview of the main differences between IAS 14 and IFRS 8 and reviews the financial statements of a company that early adopted IFRS 8.

20.9.2 Main differences between IAS 14 and IFRS 8

Table 20.1 analyses the main differences between IAS 14 and IFRS 8.

TABLE 20.1 Main differences between IAS 14 and IFRS 8

Requirement	IAS 14	IFRS 8
Basis for identification of segments	Segments are identified based on the predominant sources of risks and returns. This may result in either a business or geographic basis for segment identification. Where this does not coincide with the basis on which the entity reports internally to senior management, the internally reported segment information is *not* used as the basis for external financial reporting. Rather, the internally reported information must be rearranged to meet the requirements of IAS 14. (IAS 14, paras. 27 and 32).	Segments (called operating segments) *must* be determined based on the way information is reported internally to the chief operating decision maker (CODM) (IFRS 8, para. 5). This may not coincide with the way information is reported externally and therefore may not agree with the entity's statement of comprehensive income and statement of financial position. Where this is the case, IFRS 8 requires reconciliations to be provided between the segment information (which will usually be in a note to the financial statements) and the statement of comprehensive income and statement of financial position (IFRS 8, para. 28). Commentators on ED 8 were concerned that comparability between different companies is likely to be reduced as a result of IFRS 8's focus on internal reporting versus IAS 14's focus on sources of risks and rewards (see section 20.9.3). The reconciliation requirements in IFRS 8 are expected to counter some of the potential lack of comparability between segment reporting of different entities.
Primary and secondary segments	IAS 14 requires an entity to identify primary and secondary segments (IAS 14, para. 26).	IFRS 8 does not refer to primary or secondary segments.
Revenues from third parties as the basis for identifying reportable segments	IAS 14 requires that a business or geographical segment be identified as a reportable segment if a majority of its revenue	IFRS 8 does not distinguish between revenues and expenses from transactions with third parties and those from transactions *within the group* for the

(continued)

TABLE 20.1 *(continued)*

Requirement	IAS 14	IFRS 8
	is earned from sales to *external* customers and certain other conditions are met (IAS 14, para. 35).	purposes of identifying operating segments (IFRS 8, para. 5). Therefore, in an entity with internal vertically integrated businesses, it is possible that such internal businesses might be identified as operating segments under IFRS 8. Under IAS 14, such internal businesses would not qualify as reportable segments.
Definitions of information to be reported for each reportable segment	IAS 14 defines 'segment revenue', 'segment expense', 'segment result', 'segment assets' and 'segment liabilities' (IAS 14, para. 16). This ensures consistency in the determination of amounts that are disclosed by different companies.	IFRS 8 requires disclosure of 'a measure' of profit or loss and total assets for each reportable segment and 'a measure' of liabilities for each reportable segment if such an amount is regularly provided to the CODM (IFRS 8, para. 23). These amounts are not defined in IFRS 8. Thus, different judgements will likely be made by different entities based on what and how information is internally reported, potentially reducing comparability between entities. To counter this concern, IFRS 8 requires entities to explain how they measure segment profit or loss, segment assets and segment liabilities for each reportable segment (IFRS 8, para. 27).
Conformity with the entity's accounting policies for preparing its financial statements	IAS 14 requires that segment information be prepared in conformity with the entity's accounting policies for preparing and presenting its financial statements (IAS 14, para. 44).	IFRS 8 requires that the amount of each segment item reported shall be the measure reported to the CODM for the purposes of making decisions about allocating resources to the segment and assessing its performance, even if this information is not prepared in accordance with the entity's IFRS accounting policies (IFRS 8, para. 25). The reconciliations required by paragraph 28 (see above) are designed to allow users to assess the differences between management's determination of segment measures and the accounting policies used in the financial statements. Note, however, that this is only required on an overall basis, not on a segment-by-segment basis.
Disclosures	IAS 14 specifies the disclosures required for each reportable segment (IAS 14, paras. 50–83). Therefore, all entities are required to report the same line items for each of their reportable segments.	IFRS 8 requires that 'a measure' of segment profit or loss and segment assets be disclosed for each reportable segment. Other items, such as liabilities, interest revenue, interest expense, depreciation and amortisation, revenues from external customers, inter-segment revenue and so on, are only required to be disclosed if they are provided to the CODM for that reportable segment (IFRS 8, paras. 23 and 24). Therefore, the line items reported for each reportable segment will likely differ, not only between companies, but also within companies.
Reliance on major customers	IAS 14 requires disclosure of revenue from external customers (IAS 14, paras. 51, 69 and 70) but not about reliance on major customers.	IFRS 8 requires that, if revenues from transactions with a *single* external customer amount to 10% or more of the entity's revenues, certain information be disclosed about the entity's reliance on that single customer (IFRS 8, para. 34).

20.9.3 A controversial standard

In Europe, the replacement of IAS 14 with IFRS 8 was highly controversial. The European Parliament is required to endorse all IASB standards and IFRIC interpretations in order for the standards and interpretations to come into effect. The European Financial Reporting Advisory Group (EFRAG) reviews the proposed standards and makes its recommendations to the European Commission as to whether or not the parliament should endorse the standards and interpretations. When ED 8 was issued, concern was expressed by many commentators to both the IASB and EFRAG about the management approach. After the IASB issued IFRS 8, the European Commission sought further feedback, by means of a questionnaire, on whether or not the European Parliament should endorse IFRS 8. The questions focused on the management approach, the lack of mandatory disclosure requirements and whether these were perceived as positive or negative by commentators.

A paper prepared and presented by Nicolas Véron, Research Fellow at Bruegel (a European think tank created to contribute to the quality of economic policymaking in Europe) argued that IFRS 8 should not be endorsed. The paper argues that the success of IFRS thus far can be attributed both to market (investor) demand and to European Union (EU) leadership and that convergence with US GAAP 'is far from universally accepted as an appropriate framework for setting the current standard-setting agenda'. The paper contends that 'segment information is one of the most vital aspects of financial reporting for investors and other users' and is also inherently divisive between preparers of financial statements on the one hand, who want to control the information, and users on the other, who want it to be specifically objective. The risks and rewards approach to identifying segments (see section 20.5.1) arguably meets the needs of users while the management approach arguably meets the needs of preparers, although both approaches may be consistent (as envisaged by IAS 14). The paper argues that the discretion permitted by IFRS 8 in determining the content of segment profit or loss and segment assets and in making or not making certain disclosures (e.g. disclosure of liabilities, statement of comprehensive income line items and geographical information) contrasts with IAS 14's prescribed measurement and disclosure requirements, favouring preparers over users. The paper quotes from various respondents' letters to the IASB, particularly those of analysts, who did not support changing IAS 14 and moving to a standard based on SFAS 131, because they regarded SFAS 131 as inferior to IAS 14.

It is also notable that two IASB board members dissented from the issuance of IFRS 8 (refer the Dissenting Opinion in IFRS 8) because of the lack of definition of segment profit or loss and because IFRS 8 does not require consistent attribution of assets and profit or loss to segments. In addition, these board members also believed that the changes from IAS 14 were not justified by the need for convergence with US GAAP because IAS 14 is a disclosure standard and therefore does not affect the reconciliation of IFRS amounts to US GAAP.

The preparer's viewpoint is argued, for example, in the submission by the Association of German Banks to the European Commission's questionnaire referred to above. This letter argues that IFRS 8 should be endorsed and that the information provided under the management approach will be more relevant and reliable because it will, inter alia, enable investors to evaluate the entity on the same basis as that used by management in its decision making and that any concerns about understandability are addressed by IFRS 8's reconciliation requirements.

Despite the objections, IFRS 8 was finally endorsed by the European Parliament in November 2007. In its endorsement resolution, the European Parliament stated that the IASB should carry out a review of the new standard 2 years after its implementation. Further, the parliament's requirement that the European Commission 'follow closely the application of IFRS 8 and (to) report back to Parliament no later than 2011, inter alia regarding reporting of geographical segments, segment profit or loss, and use of non-IFRS measures; underlines that if the Commission discovers deficiencies in the application of IFRS 8 it has a duty to rectify such deficiencies'.

The message from the European Parliament to European companies is therefore that entities will be watched closely to determine whether they are taking advantage of IFRS 8's discretionary approach in order to control reported information. Only time will tell whether concerns about the approach eventuate.

In Australia, IFRS 8 was issued as AASB 8 by the Australian Accounting Standards Board in February 2007, with little fanfare, although Australian commentators had expressed similar concerns about the management approach and the US GAAP convergence issue discussed above.

20.9.4 Requirements of IFRS 8

The following is an overview of the requirements of IFRS 8, with emphasis on the areas of difference from IAS 14.

Core principle

Paragraph 1 of IFRS 8 sets out the standard's core principle:

> An entity shall disclose information to enable users of its financial statements to evaluate the nature and financial effects of the business activities in which it engages and the economic environments in which it operates.

Scope

IFRS 8 applies to the financial statements of entities 'whose debt or equity instruments are traded in a public market' or 'that files, or is in the process of filing, its financial statements with a securities commission or other regulatory organisation for the purpose of issuing any class of instruments in a public market' (IFRS 8, para. 2). This is a similar scope to IAS 14.

Where financial statements contain both consolidated financial statements and the parent's separate financial statements, segment information is required only for the consolidated financial statements (IFRS 8, para. 4).

Identifying operating segments

An operating segment is defined in IFRS 8, paragraph 5 as:

> A component of an entity:
> (a) that engages in business activities from which it may earn revenues and incur expenses (including revenues and expenses relating to transactions with other components of the same entity);
> (b) whose operating results are regularly reviewed by the entity's chief operating decision maker to make decisions about resources to be allocated to the segment and assess its performance; and
> (c) for which discrete financial information is available.

The CODM identifies a function, not necessarily a manager with a specific title. That function may be a group of people, for example, an executive committee. Generally, an operating segment has a segment manager who is directly accountable to the CODM. As with the CODM, the term 'segment manager' identifies a function, not necessarily a manager with a specific title. A single manager may be the segment manager for more than one operating segment and the CODM may also be the segment manager for one or more operating segments. When an entity has a matrix structure, for example, with some managers responsible for different product and service lines and other managers responsible for specific geographic areas, and the CODM regularly reviews the operating results for both sets of components, the entity uses the core principle (see above) to determine its operating segments (IFRS 8, para. 10).

As discussed in section 20.9.2, this approach to identifying segments is completely different from the 'sources of risks and rewards' approach in IAS 14.

Figure 20.6 (opposite) summarises the key decision points in identifying operating segments.

The following examples illustrate the steps in identifying operating segments.

ILLUSTRATIVE EXAMPLE 20.5

Identifying operating segments under IFRS 8 — the four steps

Company A has a chief executive officer (CEO), a chief operating officer (COO) and an executive committee comprising the CEO, COO and the heads (general managers) of three business units — units X, Y and Z. Every month, financial information is presented to the executive committee for each of business units X, Y and Z and for Company A as a whole in order to assess the performance of each business unit and of the company as a whole. Units X, Y and Z each generate revenue and incur expenses from their business activities. Unit Y derives the majority of its revenue from Unit Z. Corporate headquarter costs that are not allocated to units X, Y or Z are also reported separately each month to the executive committee in order to determine the results for Company A as a whole.

Step 1: Who is the CODM?

In this case, the CODM is likely to be the executive committee, since it is this group that regularly reviews the operating results of all business units and the company as a whole. However, if the

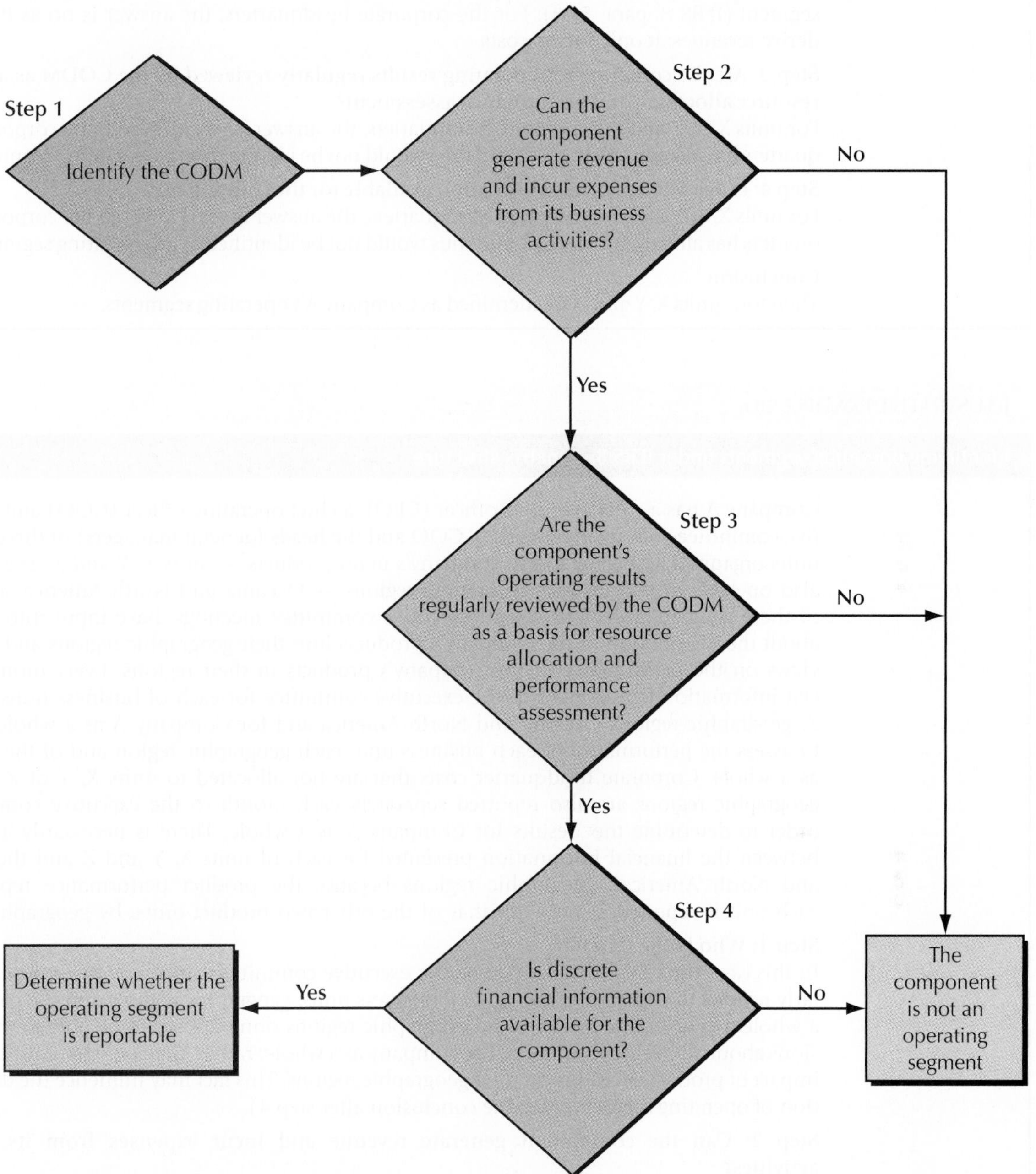

FIGURE 20.6 Identifying operating segments under IFRS 8
Source: Ernst & Young (2007, p. 4). © 2009 EYGM Limited. All rights reserved.

business unit heads only join the committee meetings to report on their specific business unit and then leave the meeting, and the CEO and COO were the only people who review all the business units and the company as a whole, and the ones who make made resource allocation decisions, for example, about changing the structure of the business units, then the CODM would be the CEO and COO. In practice, this would not make any difference to the identification of the operating segments (see step 2).

Step 2: Can the component generate revenue and incur expenses from its business activities? For units X, Y and Z, the answer is clearly yes. For Unit Y, the answer is also yes — even though its revenue is derived internally this does not prevent it from being identified as an operating segment (IFRS 8, para. 5(a)). For the corporate headquarters, the answer is no as it does not derive revenues; it only incurs costs.

Step 3: Are the component's operating results regularly reviewed by the CODM as a basis for resource allocation and performance assessment?
For units X, Y, Z and the corporate headquarters, the answer is yes. However, the corporate headquarters has already failed step 2 and thus would not be identified as an operating segment.

Step 4: Is discrete financial information available for the component?
For units X, Y, Z and the corporate headquarters, the answer is yes. However, the corporate headquarters has already failed step 2 and thus would not be identified as an operating segment.

Conclusion
Therefore, units X, Y and Z are identified as Company A's operating segments.

ILLUSTRATIVE EXAMPLE 20.6

Identifying operating segments under IFRS 8 — matrix structure

Company A has a chief executive officer (CEO), a chief operating officer (COO) and an executive committee comprising the CEO, COO and the heads (general managers) of three business units organised according to the company's main products — units X, Y and Z. The company also operates in two distinct geographic regions — Oceania and North America. The heads of these geographic regions attend executive committee meetings, have input into decisions about the distribution of the company's products into their geographic regions and give their views on the performance of the company's products in their regions. Every month, financial information is presented to the executive committee for each of business units X, Y and Z, geographic regions Oceania and North America and for Company A as a whole in order to assess the performance of each business unit, each geographic region and of the company as a whole. Corporate headquarter costs that are not allocated to units X, Y or Z or to the geographic regions are also reported separately each month to the executive committee in order to determine the results for Company A as a whole. There is necessarily an overlap between the financial information presented for each of units X, Y and Z and the Oceania and North American geographic regions because the product performance reported for each unit is reported again, with that of the other two product units, by geographic region.

Step 1: Who is the CODM?
In this case, the CODM is likely to be the executive committee, since it is the group that regularly reviews the operating results of all business units, geographic regions and the company as a whole. However, the heads of the geographic regions don't appear to be able to make decisions about all business units and the company as a whole; rather, they only have input into the impact of product decisions on their geographic regions. This fact may influence the determination of operating segments (see the conclusion after step 4).

Step 2: Can the component generate revenue and incur expenses from its business activities?
For units X, Y and Z, the answer is clearly yes. For the geographic regions, the answer is also yes, even though the revenues are generated from deployment of the products from units X, Y and Z in the regions. For the corporate headquarters, the answer is no as it does not derive revenues; it only incurs costs.

Step 3: Are the component's operating results regularly reviewed by the CODM as a basis for resource allocation and performance assessment?
For units X, Y, Z, the geographic regions and the corporate headquarters, the answer is yes. However, the corporate headquarters has already failed step 2 and thus would not be identified as an operating segment.

Step 4: Is discrete financial information available for the component?
For units X, Y, Z, the geographic regions and the corporate headquarters, the answer is yes. However, the corporate headquarters has already failed step 2 and thus would not be identified as an operating segment.

Conclusion

This leaves the entity potentially having two sets of operating segments — units X, Y and Z, and geographic regions Oceania and North America. It is in this situation that IFRS 8, paragraph 10 directs the entity to the core principle of the standard to decide which set will best 'enable users of its financial statements to evaluate the nature and financial effects of the business activities in which it engages and the economic environments in which it operates'. In this situation, management must exercise judgement. Arguably, in this case, identifying units X,Y and Z as the operating segments best reflects the core principle because the organisation of the company along product lines seems to be dominant over the organisation by geographic lines (as reflected in the slightly lower impact on decision-making by the geographic region heads).

Identifying reporting segments

IFRS 8, paragraph 11 states that an entity shall report separately information about each operating segment that:

(a) has been identified as an operating segment in accordance with the four steps discussed above, or results from aggregating two or more of those segments in accordance with paragraph 12; and

(b) exceeds the quantitative thresholds in paragraph 13. These quantitative thresholds are the same as those in IAS 14, i.e. an entity shall report separately information about an operating segment that meets ANY of the following:

  (i) its reported revenue is 10% or more of the combined revenue of all operating segments (revenue includes both external and internal revenue);

  (ii) the absolute amount of its reported profit or loss is 10% or more of the greater of (1) the combined reported profit of all operating segments that reported a profit and (2) the combined reported loss of all operating segments that reported a loss;

  (iii) its assets are 10% or more of the combined assets of all operating segments.

If management believes that information about an operating segment would be useful to users, it may treat that segment as a reportable segment even if the quantitative thresholds are not met (IFRS 8, para. 13). This is similar to IAS 14 (para. 36).

The aggregation criteria in paragraph 12 are also similar to those in IAS 14. That is, two or more operating segments may be aggregated into a single operating segment if aggregation is consistent with the core principle of the standard, the segments have similar economic characteristics and the segments are similar in each of the following respects:

1. the nature of the products and services;
2. the nature of the production processes;
3. the type or class of customer for their products and services;
4. the methods used to distribute their products or provide their services; and
5. if applicable, the nature of the regulatory environment.

An entity may combine operating segments that do not meet the quantitative thresholds to produce a reportable segment only if the segments have similar economic characteristics and meet the aggregation criteria of paragraph 12 (IFRS 8, para. 14). This is similar to IAS 14 (para. 36).

Paragraph 15 of IFRS 8 contains the same requirement as IAS 14, paragraph 37 in respect of identifying operating segments until at least 75% of the entity's revenue is included in reportable segments. Importantly, revenue here is *external* revenue.

Paragraph 16 of IFRS 8 contains a similar requirement to IAS 14, paragraph 36 in respect of non-reportable segments. However, IFRS 8 specifically states that business activities and operating segments that are not reportable must be disclosed as 'all other segments' and not as reconciling items, whereas IAS 14 states that they should be disclosed as unallocated reconciling items.

As noted in section 20.9.2, IFRS 8 does not distinguish between revenues and expenses from transactions with third parties and those from transactions *within the group* for the purposes of identifying operating segments (IFRS 8, para. 5). Therefore, in an entity with internal vertically integrated businesses, it is possible that such internal businesses might be identified as operating segments under IFRS 8. Under IAS 14, such internal businesses would not qualify as reportable segments, although IAS 14 permits an entity to make voluntary disclosures about vertically integrated segments (IAS 14, paras. 39–41).

IFRS 8 provides additional guidance to entities regarding the maximum number of reportable segments — indicating that 10 is a reasonable maximum (IFRS 8, para. 19).

Figure 20.7 on the next page summarises the key decision points in identifying reporting segments, and continues from figure 20.6.

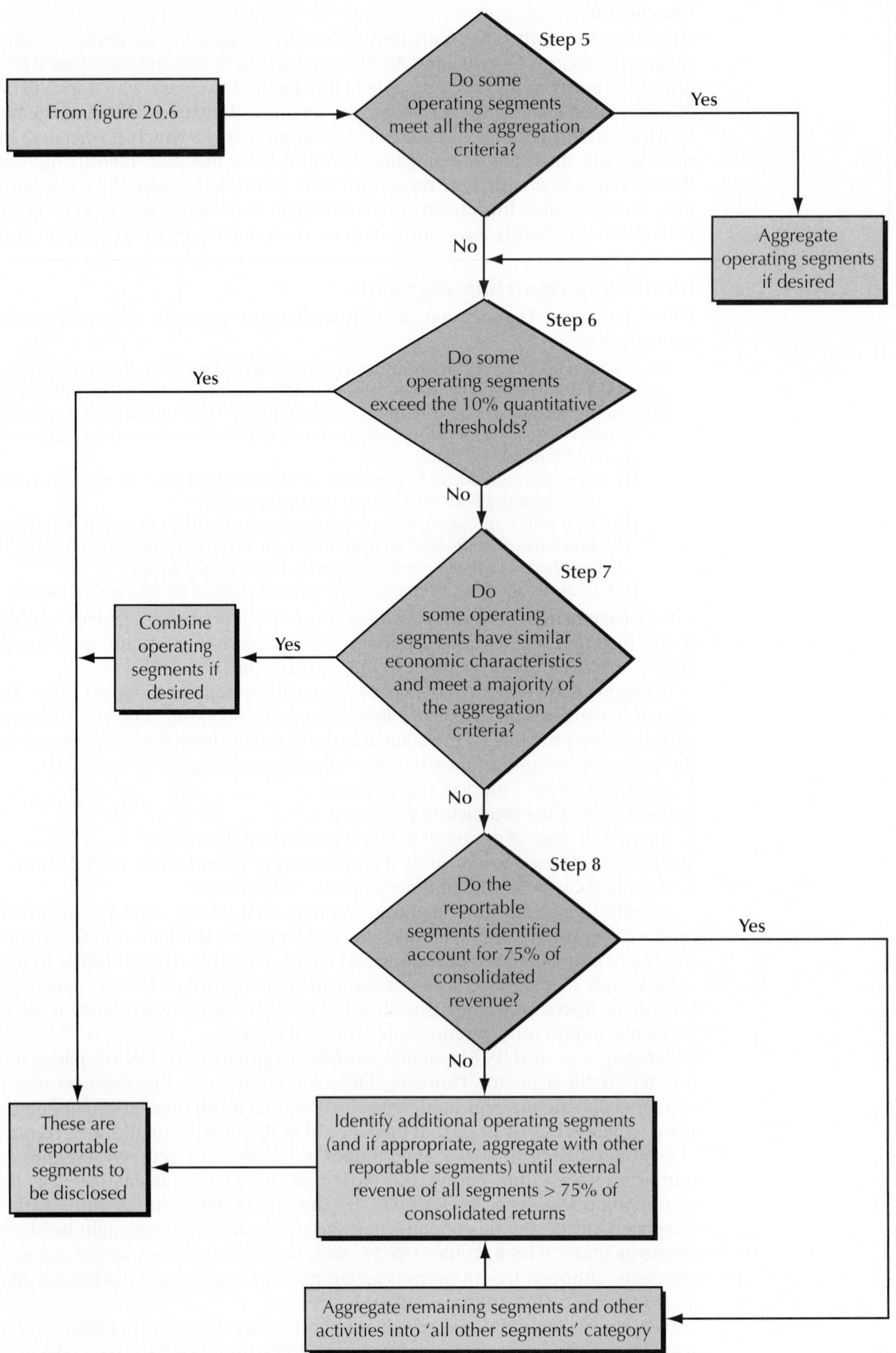

FIGURE 20.7 Identifying reporting segments under IFRS 8

Source: Ernst & Young (2007, p. 8).

Building on illustrative example 20.6, the following example illustrates how Company A identifies its reporting segments under IFRS 8.

ILLUSTRATIVE EXAMPLE 20.7

Identifying reporting segments under IFRS 8

Company A has identified units X, Y and Z as operating segments (see illustrative example 20.6). The following additional information is provided:

	Unit X $'000	Unit Y $'000	Unit Z $'000	Total operating segments $'000	Corporate headquarters $'000	Other businesses $'000	Total Company A (consolidated) $'000
Revenue	200	100 (80 earned from Unit Z)	400	700	—	230	850
Profit/ (loss)	50	30 (10 earned from Unit Z)	100	180	(25)	20	165
Assets	800	300	950	2 050	250	200	2 500

Management has determined that units X, Y and Z do not meet the aggregation criteria of IFRS 8. Unit Z has no inventory on hand at year-end in respect of purchases from unit Y.

Quantitative thresholds: note that the quantitative thresholds are in respect of the *totals for the operating segments* not the total for Company A (IFRS 8, para. 13):

	Revenue % of total	Profit % of total	Assets % of total
Unit X	29%	28%	39%
Unit Y	14%	17%	15%
Unit Z	57%	55%	46%

Therefore, all three units meet all three of the quantitative thresholds. (Note that only one threshold needs to be met). Thus, all three units are reportable segments.

The next question is whether the reportable segments account for 75% of consolidated revenue. This test is applied to the *external* revenues of the segments (IFRS 8, para. 15). Total consolidated revenue (after inter-segment eliminations) is $850 000. Total external operating segment revenue is: Unit X: $200 000; Unit Y: $20 000 and Unit Z: $400 000, giving a total of $620 000. This constitutes 73% of total consolidated revenue, which is below the 75% requirement. Therefore, additional operating segments need to be identified. Management will need to further analyse the 'other businesses' and identify another reportable segment from that component.

Disclosure

As discussed in section 20.9.2, the approach to disclosure is a key point of difference between IFRS 8 and IAS 14. While IAS 14 is prescriptive, IFRS 8 sets out a general approach to disclosure and largely allows management to determine what is disclosed and how the amounts disclosed are measured.

The general principle of disclosure is set out in paragraph 20 of IFRS 8, which is, in effect, a restatement of the core principle of the standard:

> An entity shall disclose information to enable users of its financial statements to evaluate the nature and financial effects of the business activities in which it engages and the economic environments in which it operates.

To give effect to this principle, paragraph 21 requires an entity to disclose:

(a) general information as described in paragraph 22;
(b) information about reported segment profit or loss, segment assets, segment liabilities and the basis of measurement as set out in paragraphs 23–27; and
(c) reconciliations of the totals of segment revenues, reported segment profit or loss, segment assets, segment liabilities and other material segment items to corresponding entity amounts as described in paragraph 28.

General information

An entity must disclose:
(a) factors used to identify the entity's reportable segments, including the basis of organisation, and
(b) types of products or services from which each reportable segment derives its revenues.

In complying with (a), for example, management would disclose whether it identified operating segments based on products or services, or geographic regions and whether segments have been aggregated.

Information about profit or loss, assets and liabilities

Paragraph 23 states that an entity shall report 'a measure' of *profit or loss* and *total assets* for each reportable segment. This measure is that which is reported to the CODM for the purposes of making decisions about allocating resources to the segment and assessing its performance (IFRS 8, para. 25). In other words, whatever the CODM uses to measure and assess the operating segment is what is disclosed under IFRS 8. This extends to the allocation of amounts of profit or loss and assets and liabilities to segments. If the CODM uses information based on amounts that are allocated to segments, then those amounts should be allocated for the purposes of disclosing 'a measure'. If the CODM does not use that information, the amounts should not be allocated. This is in contrast to the prescriptive rules in IAS 14 about allocating amounts to segments.

The requirement to report a measure of profit or loss and segment assets is the only prescribed disclosure in IFRS 8 in respect of statement of comprehensive income and statement of financial position items. The remainder of paragraph 23 is more discretionary:

A measure of *segment liabilities* is required to be reported only if such an amount is regularly reported to the CODM.

In respect of segment profit or loss, certain line items are also required to be disclosed only if these items are included in the measure of segment profit or loss reported to the CODM, or are otherwise regularly provided to the CODM:
(a) revenues from external customers
(b) inter-segment revenues
(c) interest revenue
(d) interest expense
(e) depreciation and amortisation
(f) material items of income and expense disclosed in accordance with paragraph 86 of IAS 1
(g) the entity's interest in the profit or loss of associates and joint ventures accounted for by the equity method
(h) income tax expense or income
(i) material non-cash items other than depreciation and amortisation (IFRS 8, para. 23).

Interest revenue and interest expense may be reported on a net basis only if a majority of the segment's revenues are from interest and the CODM relies primarily on net interest revenue to assess the performance of the segment.

In respect of segment assets, certain line items are also required to be disclosed only if these items are included in the measure of segment assets reported to the CODM, or are otherwise regularly provided to the CODM:
(a) the amount of investment in associates and joint ventures accounted for by the equity method
(b) the amounts of additions to non-current assets (with certain exceptions) (IFRS 8, para. 24).

Measurement

Because management has discretion about measurement, IFRS 8 requires disclosure of how the entity has determined the measures of profit or loss, assets and, if applicable, liabilities, for each reportable segment (IFRS 8, para. 27). This includes:
(a) the basis of accounting for any transactions between reportable segments

(b) the nature of any differences between the measurements of the reportable segments' profits or losses and the entity's profit or loss before income taxes and discontinued operations (i.e. the profit or loss reported in the statement of comprehensive income in accordance with IFRSs). For example, if the CODM uses concepts such as 'cash profit' for measuring the segment profit or loss, the entity would need to disclose how 'cash profit' is determined and how it differs from the IFRS measure of profit. This could include, for example, the fact that the CODM determines 'cash profit' to be profit or loss before fair value movements, depreciation and amortisation, and impairment charges

(c) the nature of any differences between the measurements of the reportable segments' assets and the entity's assets. For example, this could include accounting policies and policies for allocation of jointly used assets

(d) the nature of any differences between the measurements of the reportable segments' liabilities and the entity's liabilities. For example, this could include accounting policies and policies for allocation of jointly utilised liabilities

(e) the nature of any changes from prior periods in the measurement methods used to determine reported segment profit or loss and the effect, if any, of those changes on the measure of segment profit or loss. For example, if the CODM decides to change the measure of segment profit or loss used from one that excludes fair value movements to one that includes fair value movements, this fact would need to be disclosed together with the impact on reported segment profit or loss

(f) the nature and effect of any asymmetrical allocations to reportable segments. For example, an entity might allocate depreciation expense to a segment without allocating the related depreciable assets to that segment.

Reconciliations

An entity is required to provide reconciliations of all of the following:

(a) the total of the reportable segments' revenues to the entity's revenue. In illustrative example 20.7, ignoring the identification of additional segments to meet the 75% threshold, this would be a reconciliation of total operating segments' revenues of $700 000 to Company A's revenue of $850 000

(b) the total of the reportable segments' measures of profit or loss to the entity's profit or loss before income tax and discontinued operations (or, if items such as income tax are allocated to segments, to profit or loss after income tax). In illustrative example 20.7, ignoring the identification of additional segments to meet the 75% threshold, this would be a reconciliation of total operating segments' profit of $180 000 to Company A's profit of $165 000

(c) the total of the reportable segments' assets to the entity's assets. In illustrative example 20.7, ignoring the identification of additional segments to meet the 75% threshold, this would be a reconciliation of total operating segments' assets of $2.05 million to Company A's assets of $2.5 million

(d) the total of the reportable segments' liabilities to the entity's liabilities if segment liabilities are reported under paragraph 23

(e) the total of the reportable segments' amounts for every other material item of information disclosed to the corresponding amount for the entity. This would include, for example, the line items disclosed under paragraphs 23 and 24, if the amount disclosed differs from that disclosed in the entity's statement of comprehensive income or statement of financial position.

All material reconciling items must be separately identified and described. For example, in illustrative example 20.7, assuming the amounts are material, the entity would need to disclose its reconciliation of total reportable segments' profit to Company A's profit as follows:

	$'000
Total reportable segments' profit:	180
Less: inter-segment profit	(10)
Less: corporate headquarter costs not allocated to reportable segments	(25)
Add: profit from other businesses not identified as reportable segments	20
Total Company A profit	165

Entity-wide disclosures

The following disclosures apply to all entities subject to IFRS 8, including those that have only one reportable segment (unless the information is already provided as part of the reportable segment information).

- Information about products and services: revenues from external customers for *each product or service* or each group of similar products or services. In this case, the amount of revenues must be based on the financial information used to produce the entity's financial statements, not based on amounts reported to the CODM. If the information is not available and the cost to develop it would be excessive, the entity need not disclose the information but it must state this fact (IFRS 8, para. 32). This requirement is potentially onerous in that it is possible that one reportable segment includes numerous products and/or services. IAS 14 does not have a similar disclosure requirement — it requires disclosure of revenues from external customers by business or geographic segment (IAS 14, para. 51).
- Information about geographical areas: revenues from external customers and non-current assets (i) attributed to/located in the entity's country of domicile and (ii) attributed to/located in foreign countries. If revenues or non-current assets attributed to/located in an individual foreign country are material, those revenues/assets shall be disclosed separately. The entity must also disclose the basis for attributing revenues from external customers to individual countries. In this case, as in paragraph 32, the amount of revenues and assets must be based on the financial information used to produce the entity's financial statements. If the information is not available and the cost to develop it would be excessive then the entity need not disclose the information but it must state this fact (IFRS 8, para. 33). IAS 14 contains similar, but not identical, disclosure requirements (IAS 14, para. 69).
- Information about major customers: if revenues from transactions with a single external customer amount to 10% or more of an entity's revenues, disclose that fact, the total amount of revenues from each such customer, and the segment or segments reporting the revenues. The identity of the customer or customers does not have to be disclosed. IAS 14 does not have a similar disclosure requirement (see section 20.9.2).

Comparative information

There are a few circumstances in which comparative information is required to be restated or otherwise taken into account.

(a) If an operating segment was a reportable segment for the immediately preceding prior period but is not for the current period, and management decides that the segment is of continuing significance, information about that segment must continue to be reported in the current period (IFRS 8, para. 17).

(b) If an operating segment becomes a reportable segment for the current period, comparative information must be restated to reflect the newly reportable segment, even if that segment did not meet the criteria for reportability in the prior period. This is required unless the information is not available and the cost to develop it would be excessive (IFRS 8, para. 18).

(c) If management changes its measure of segment profit or loss, paragraph 27(e) requires disclosure of the nature and effect of that change, as discussed above. The standard does not specify whether comparative information must be restated in this circumstance. However, applying the principles of IAS 8 *Accounting Policies, Changes in Accounting Estimates and Errors* and the general principle apparent in IFRS 8 in respect of consistency of comparative information, one would expect the comparative information to be restated in this circumstance.

(d) If an entity changes the structure of its internal organisation in a manner that causes the composition of its reportable segments to change, the corresponding information for prior periods, including interim periods, must be restated. This applies unless the information is not available and the cost to develop it would be excessive (IFRS 8, para. 29). Note that in this case the exemption from restatement applies to each individual item of disclosure. This could result in restatement of some items and not of others.

(e) If an entity changes the structure of its internal organisation in a manner that causes the composition of its reportable segments to change and the corresponding information for prior periods is *not* restated, the entity must disclose the segment information for the current period on both the old and the new basis. This applies unless the information is not available and the cost to develop it would be excessive (IFRS 8, para. 30).

(f) On transition to the new standard (i.e. when the entity first applies IFRS 8), comparative information must be restated unless the information is not available and the cost to develop it would be excessive.

Note the repeated use of the phrase 'unless the information is not available and the cost to develop it would be excessive' in the above exemptions and other exemptions within the standard. This phrase is consistent with that used in SFAS 131 and differs from the term 'impracticable', which is used in IAS 14 and in IAS 1 *Presentation of Financial Statements*. Arguably the phrase is more precise than 'impracticable'. It is also notable that IFRS 8 contains more exemptions from disclosure than IAS 14 does: IAS 14 provides an 'impracticability' exemption only for restatement of comparative information (IAS 14, para. 76) and on transition (IAS 14, para. 84), whereas IFRS 8 provides exemptions from the entity-wide disclosures as well as for restatement of comparatives.

20.9.5 Case study — early adopter of IFRS 8

Telstra Corporation Limited early adopted AASB 8, the Australian equivalent of IFRS 8, in its 2008 financial statements. Note 2(c) of the financial statements stated:

> AASB 8: "Operating Segments" was approved by the AASB in February 2007 and replaces AASB 114: "Segment Reporting". We have elected to early adopt and apply this standard in our financial report for the year ended 30 June 2008.

Figure 20.8 shows the segment information as provided in the 2007 financial statements in accordance with IAS 14 and then as provided, with the 2007 information restated, in the 2008 financial statements in accordance with AASB 8. The 2008 and 2007 income statements and 2008 statement of financial position are also shown for reconciliation purposes.

FIGURE 20.8 Segment information under IAS 14 compared with under AASB 8, Telstra

2007
Notes to the Financial Statements

5. Segment information

We report our segment information on the basis of business segments as our risks and returns are affected predominantly by differences in the products and services we provide through those segments.

Our internal management reporting structure drives how our Company is organised and managed. This internal structure provides the initial basis for determining our business segments.

Our business segments are predominantly distinguishable by the different type of customers we deliver our key products and services to. Our customer facing business segments service different customer types. Other reportable business segments are also aligned with our specific customer or business needs. These segments provide operational support services or product support services to our customer facing business segments, or service other telecommunication carriers. Our "Other" segment consists of various business units that do not qualify as business segments in their own right and which service a variety of customer or business needs.

The main adjustments from our internal management reporting structure to our reported business segments are in relation to certain offshore operations. For internal reporting purposes, our TelstraClear group (TelstraClear) and our CSL New World Mobility group (CSL New World) are business units in their own right, with TelstraClear managed by our Telstra Enterprise and Government business unit. Also, the International Head Office group is included as part of our Strategic Marketing business unit. These offshore operations are reported as part of a segment we have called Telstra International for segment reporting purposes.

For the purposes of the applicable accounting standard, we consider that the risks and returns of these offshore operations differ from those of our local operations and as a result we have grouped these operations into the Telstra International business segment.

Business segments

Our business segments during fiscal 2007 are substantially consistent with their structure in the prior year. We have restated all our comparative information to reflect our current reporting position as if all our business segments and segment accounting policies existed in fiscal 2006.

For segment reporting purposes, the Telstra Group is organised into the following business segments:

(continued)

FIGURE 20.8 *(continued)*

Telstra Consumer Marketing and Channels (TC&C) is responsible for:
- the provision of the full range of telecommunication products, services and communication solutions to consumers; and
- leading the mass market channels including inbound and outbound call centres, Telstra Shops and Telstra Dealers.

Telstra Business (TB) is responsible for:
- the provision of the full range of telecommunication products and services, communication solutions, and information and communication technology services to small to medium enterprises.

Telstra Enterprise and Government (TE&G) is responsible for:
- the provision of the full range of telecommunication products and services, communication solutions, and information and communication technology services to corporate and government customers; and
- the provision of global communication solutions to multi-national corporations through our interests in the United Kingdom, Asia and North America.

Telstra Wholesale (TW) is responsible for:
- the provision of a wide range of telecommunication products and services delivered over our networks and associated support systems to non-Telstra branded carriers, carriage service providers, Internet service providers, system integrators and application service providers.

Sensis is responsible for:
- the management and growth of the advertising and directories business, including printed publications, voice and directory services and online products and services; and
- the provision of China's largest online real estate, home furnishings and home improvements portal through the investment in SouFun.

Telstra International (Tint.) consists of the following offshore business operations:
- CSL New World is a 76.4% owned subsidiary in Hong Kong responsible for providing full mobile services including handset sales, voice and data products;
- International Head Office Group is responsible for our Asia-Pacific investments; and
- TelstraClear is our New Zealand subsidiary that provides full telecommunications services to the New Zealand market.

Telstra Operations (TO) is responsible for:
- co-ordination and execution for our company's multi-year business improvement and transformation program;
- leading the identification, analysis, validation, development and implementation of product, technology and information technology strategies for both the network infrastructure and customer solutions of our Company;
- overall planning, design, specification of standards, commissioning and decommissioning of our communication networks;
- construction of infrastructure for our Company's fixed, mobile, Internet protocol (IP) and data networks;
- operation and maintenance, including activation and restoration of these networks;
- supply and delivery of information technology solutions to support our products, services and customer support function;
- the development and lifecycle management of products and services over the networks, as well as application platforms and the online environment; and
- operational support functions for our Company, including procurement, billing, credit management and property management.

Telstra Country Wide (TCW) is responsible for:
- the local management and control of providing telecommunication products, services and solutions to all consumer customers, except those in Sydney and Melbourne, and small business, enterprise and some government customers outside the mainland state capital cities, in outer metropolitan areas, and in Tasmania and the Northern Territory.

Telstra BigPond is responsible for:
- the management and control of our consumer retail Internet products, contact centres, and online and mobile content services.

Telstra Media is responsible for:
- the management of our investment in the FOXTEL partnerships; and
- the development and management of the hybrid fibre coaxial (HFC) cable network.

(continued)

FIGURE 20.8 *(continued)*

Strategic Marketing is responsible for:
- the co-ordination and delivery of strategy and marketing activities across our Company and market segments.

Corporate areas include:
- Legal Services — provides legal services across the Company;
- Public Policy and Communications — responsible for managing our relationships and positioning with key groups such as our customers, the media, governments, community groups and staff. It also has responsibility for regulatory positioning and negotiation;
- Finance and Administration — encompasses the functions of corporate planning, accounting and administration, treasury, risk management and assurance, investor relations and the office of the company secretary. It also includes providing financial support to all business units and financial management of the majority of the Telstra Entity fixed assets (including network assets) through the Asset Accounting Group; and
- Human Resources — encompasses talent management, organisational development, human resource operations, health, safety and environment, as well as workplace relations and remuneration.

In our segment financial results, the "Other" segment consists of various business units that do not qualify as reportable segments in their own right. These include:
- Telstra Country Wide;
- Telstra BigPond;
- Telstra Media;
- Strategic Marketing; and
- our corporate areas,

Segment financial results

For segment reporting purposes, we have reallocated certain items between the respective business segments pursuant to the definitions of segment revenues, segment expenses, segment assets and segment liabilities contained in the applicable accounting standard, where a reasonable allocation basis exists.

There are certain items that are not reallocated to alternative segments due to the management accountability framework and internal reporting system. These items are reported within the same segment as for internal management reporting. As a result, our segment revenues, segment expenses, segment assets and segment liabilities do not reflect actual operating results achieved for our business segments in certain circumstances.

The following narrative further explains our segment results for those individual items that have not been reallocated:
- sales revenue associated with mobile handsets for TC&C, TB and TE&G are mainly allocated to the TC&C segment. Ongoing prepaid and postpaid mobile revenues derived from our mobile usage is recorded in TC&C, TB and TE&G depending on the type of customer serviced. In addition, the majority of goods and services purchased associated with our mobile revenues are allocated to the TC&C segment. As a result, the TC&C segment also holds segment assets and segment liabilities related to those revenues and expenses recorded in TC&C;
- trade debtors in relation to the mobile repayment option on mobile handsets sold by our dealers are allocated totally to TC&C;
- revenue received in advance in relation to installation and connection fees is allocated totally to TC&C; and
- revenue derived from our BigPond® Internet products and its related segment assets are recorded in the customer facing business segments of TC&C, TB and TE&G. Certain distribution costs in relation to these products are recognised in these three business segments. Telstra Operations recognise certain expenses in relation to the installation and running of the broadband cable network. The related segment assets are managed by the Asset Accounting Group. In accordance with our application of the business segment definition in relation to customer type, we have not reallocated these items to the Telstra BigPond business segment.

Segment assets and liabilities

Segment assets and segment liabilities form part of the operating activities of a segment and can be allocated directly to that segment.

The Asset Accounting Group performs a company wide function in relation to the financial management of certain assets. These assets are accounted for at the corporate level (aggregated in the "Other" segment) and not allocated across segments.

(continued)

FIGURE 20.8 *(continued)*

The "Other" segment also includes balances that do not meet the definition of segment assets and segment liabilities for our reportable business segments. As a result, borrowings and income tax assets and liabilities are recorded as reconciling items within the "Other" segment.

Inter-segment transfers

We account for all transactions between entities within the Telstra Group, including international transactions between Australian and non-Australian businesses, at market value. For segment reporting purposes, transfer pricing is not used within the Company. As such the inter-segment revenue line purely relates to intercompany revenue.

The Asset Accounting Group does not allocate depreciation expense related to the use of assets owned at the corporate level to other business segments.

Telstra Group										
Year ended 30 June 2007	**TC&C $m**	**TB $m**	**TE&G $m**	**TW $m**	**Sensis $m**	**Tint. $m**	**TO $m**	**Other[(a)] $m**	**Elimina-tions $m**	**Total $m**
Revenue from external customers	9 509	3 241	4 465	2 657	1 968	1 574	192	103	—	23 709
Add inter-segment revenue	—	—	64	300	—	32	51	5	(452)	—
Total segment revenue	9 509	3 241	4 529	2 957	1 968	1 606	243	108	(452)	23 709
Segment result	5 593	2 592	2 572	2 867	749	52	(3 915)	(4 830)	45	5 725
Share of equity accounted net (losses)/profits	—	—	(6)	—	(1)	—	—	—	—	(7)
Less net gain on sale of investments	—	—	43	—	4	9	2	3	—	61
Earnings before interest and income tax expense (EBIT)	5 593	2 592	2 609	2 867	752	61	(3 913)	(4 827)	45	5 779
Segment result has been calculated after charging/(crediting) the following non cash expenses:										
Impairment losses	182	8	7	6	143	21	14	14	—	395
Reversal of impairment losses	—	(1)	—	(1)	—	—	(4)	—	—	(6)
Depreciation and amortisation	—	—	51	—	130	325	61	3 515	—	4 082
Other significant non cash expenses	24	10	21	4	1	—	142	64	—	266
Non current segment assets acquired –accrual basis (excluding acquisition of investments)	13	5	59	9	226	195	5 361	11	—	5 879
As at 30 June 2007 **Segment assets**	1 599	394	1 649	365	2 188	3 645	4 090	24 124	(179)	37 875
Segment assets include:										
Trade and other receivables	1 315	390	915	362	725	340	104	101	(171)	4 081
Investments accounted for using the equity method	—	—	12	—	3	1	—	—	—	16
Segment liabilities	1 227	182	631	274	691	558	2 899	19 005	(172)	25 295

(a) Revenue for the "Other" segment relates primarily to our revenue earned by Telstra Media from reselling FOXTEL[†] pay television services to our customers and for services provided to FOXTEL. The Asset Accounting Group is the main contributor to the segment result for this segment, which is primarily depreciation and amortisation charges.

Segment assets for the "Other" segment includes the Telstra Entity fixed assets (including network assets) managed through the centralised Asset Accounting Group. Segment liabilities includes income tax liabilities and borrowings, which have been reallocated from the reportable business segment in accordance with the applicable accounting standard.

(continued)

FIGURE 20.8 *(continued)*

Telstra Group										
Year ended 30 June 2006	**TC&C $m**	**TB $m**	**TE&G $m**	**TW $m**	**Sensis $m**	**Tint. $m**	**TO $m**	**Other[(a)] $m**	**Eliminations $m**	**Total $m**
Revenue from external customers	8 879	3 163	4 474	2 610	1 825	1 450	226	107	—	22 734
Add inter-segment revenue	—	—	57	292	10	31	81	9	(480)	—
Total segment revenue	8 879	3 163	4 531	2 902	1 835	1 481	307	116	(480)	22 734
Segment result	5 634	2 541	2 632	2 694	864	86	(4 173)	(4 877)	29	5 430
Share of equity accounted net (losses)/profits	—	—	—	—	(1)	12	—	(6)	—	5
Less net gain on sale of investments	—	—	4	—	—	58	—	—	—	62
Earnings before interest and income tax expense (EBIT)	5 634	2 541	2 636	2 694	863	156	(4173)	(4 883)	29	5 497
Segment result has been calculated after charging/(crediting) the following non cash expenses:										
Impairment losses	134	14	6	—	13	11	140	33	—	351
Reversal of impairment losses	—	—	—	(17)	—	—	(5)	—	—	(22)
Depreciation and amortisation	—	—	58	—	91	298	48	3 583	—	4 078
Other significant non cash expenses	25	4	20	5	1	3	144	8	—	210
Non current segment assets acquired — accrual basis (excluding acquisition of investments)	11	—	54	23	96	224	4 058	5	—	4 471
As at 30 June 2006										
Segment assets	1 420	372	1 812	450	1 886	3 817	3 315	23 331	(179)	36 224
Segment assets include:										
Trade and other receivables	1 226	372	839	444	693	323	89	57	(176)	3 867
Investments accounted for using the equity method	—	—	19	—	3	1	—	—	—	23
Segment liabilities	1 263	166	608	241	673	615	2 587	17 414	(177)	23 390

(a) Revenue for the "Other" segment relates primarily to our revenue earned by Telstra Media from reselling FOXTEL[†] pay television services and for services provided to FOXTEL. The Asset Accounting Group is the main contributor to the segment result for this segment, which is primarily depreciation and amortisation charges.

Segment assets for the "Other" segment includes the Telstra Entity fixed assets (including network assets) managed through the centralised Asset Accounting Group. Segment liabilities excludes income tax liabilities and borrowings, which are included as part of the "Other" segment.

	Telstra Group	
	Year ended 30 June	
	2007 $m	2006 $m
Information about our geographic operations[(i)]		
Segment revenue from external customers		
Australian customers	**21 729**	20 976
International customers	**1 980**	1 758
	23 709	22 734

(continued)

FIGURE 20.8 *(continued)*

	2007 $m	2006 $m
Carrying amount of segment assets		
Australian customers	33 503	32 043
International customers	4 372	4 181
	37 875	36 224
Non current segment assets acquired-accrual basis (excluding acquisition of investments)		
Located in Australia	5 684	4 247
Located in international countries	195	224
	5 879	4 471

(i) Our geographical operations are split between our Australian and international operations. Our international operations include the business of our international business segment (primarily businesses in Hong Kong and New Zealand), the SouFun business which is part of our Sensis segment, and our international business that serves multinational customers in the TE&G segment. No individual geographical area forms a significant part of our operations apart from our Australian operations.

2008
Notes to the Financial Statements
5. Segment information

We have elected to early adopt AASB 8: "Operating Segments" for the year ended 30 June 2008 (refer to note 2.1(c)). Comparative segment information has been restated in accordance with AASB 8.

Business segments

Under AASB 8 we report our segment information on the same basis as our internal management reporting structure, which drives how our company is organised and managed. This is different to prior reporting periods where certain adjustments and reallocations were made to our internal structure for segment reporting purposes, pursuant to the definitions of segment revenues and segment expenses contained in the previous accounting standard.

As a result of the adoption of AASB 8, the following changes have been made to the identification of our reportable segments for the year ended 30 June 2008:

- CSL New World Mobility group (CSL NW) and TelstraClear group (TClear), previously aggregated under "Telstra International", are now reported separately; and
- The International Head Office previously included in "Telstra International" now forms part of Strategic Marketing to reflect internal accountability. As such there is no longer a separate "Telstra International" segment.

The Telstra Group is organised into the following business segments for internal management reporting purposes:

Telstra Consumer Marketing and Channels (TC&C) is responsible for:

- the provision of the full range of telecommunication products, services and communication solutions to consumers; and
- leading the mass market channels including inbound and outbound call centres, Telstra Shops and Telstra Dealers.

Telstra Business (TB) is responsible for:

- the provision of the full range of telecommunication products and services, communication solutions, and information and communication technology services to small to medium enterprises.

Telstra Enterprise and Government (TE&G) is responsible for:

- the provision of the full range of telecommunication products and services, communication solutions, and information and communication technology services to corporate and government customers; and
- the provision of global communication solutions to multi-national corporations through our interests in the United Kingdom, Asia and North America.

(continued)

FIGURE 20.8 *(continued)*

Telstra Operations (TO) is responsible for;

- co-ordination and execution of our company's multi-year business improvement and transformation program;
- leading the identification, analysis, validation, development and implementation of product, technology and information technology strategies for both the network infrastructure and customer solutions of our Company;
- overall planning, design, specification of standards, commissioning and decommissioning of our communication networks;
- construction of infrastructure for our Company's fixed, mobile, Internet protocol (IP) and data networks;
- operation and maintenance, including activation and restoration of these networks;
- supply and delivery of information technology solutions to support our products, services and customer support function;
- the development and lifecycle management of products and services over the networks, as well as application platforms and the online environment; and
- operational support functions for our Company, including procurement and property management.

Telstra Wholesale (TW) is responsible for:

- the provision of a wide range of telecommunication products and services delivered over our networks and associated support systems to non-Telstra branded carriers, carriage service providers, Internet service providers, system integrators and application service providers.

Sensis is responsible for:

- the management and growth of the advertising and directories business, including printed publications, voice and directory services, location and publishing products, and online products and services;
- the provision of China's largest online real estate, home furnishings and home improvements portal through the investment in SouFun; and
- the provision of automotive and digital device internet businesses in China through our recent acquisitions of 55% of Norstar Media and Autohome/PCPop.

CSL New World (CSL NW) is our 76.4% owned subsidiary in Hong Kong responsible for:

- providing full mobile services including handset sales, voice and data products to the Hong Kong market.

TelstraClear (TClear) is our New Zealand subsidiary responsible for:

- providing full telecommunications services to the New Zealand market.

Telstra Country Wide (TCW) is responsible for:

- the local management and control of providing telecommunication products, services and solutions to all consumer customers, except those in Sydney and Melbourne, and small business, enterprise and some government customers outside the mainland state capital cities, in outer metropolitan areas, and in Tasmania and the Northern Territory.

Telstra BigPond is responsible for:

- the management and control of our retail Internet products, contact centres, and online and mobile content services.

Telstra Media is responsible for:

- the management of our investment in the FOXTEL partnerships; and
- the development and management of the hybrid fibre coaxial (HFC) cable network.

Strategic Marketing is responsible for:

- the co-ordination and delivery of strategy and marketing activities across our Company and market segments.

Corporate areas include:

- Legal Services – provides legal services across the Company;

(continued)

FIGURE 20.8 *(continued)*

- Public Policy and Communications – responsible for managing our relationships and positioning with key groups such as our customers, the media, governments, community groups and staff. It also has responsibility for regulatory positioning and negotiation;
- Finance and Administration – encompasses the functions of corporate planning, accounting and administration, treasury, risk management and assurance, investor relations and the office of the company secretary. It also includes providing financial support to all business units and financial management of the majority of the Telstra Entity fixed assets (including network assets) through the Asset Accounting Group; and
- Human Resources – encompasses talent management, organisational development, human resource operations, health, safety and environment, as well as workplace relations and remuneration.

In our segment financial results, the "Other" category consists of various business units that do not qualify as reportable segments in their own right. These include:
- Telstra Country Wide;
- Telstra BigPond;
- Telstra Media;
- Strategic Marketing; and
- our Corporate areas.

Revenue for the "Other" segment relates primarily to our revenue earned by Telstra Media from providing access to our HFC network and other services to FOXTEL. The Asset Accounting Group is the main contributor to the segment result for this segment, which is primarily depreciation and amortisation charges.

Segment assets for the "Other" segment includes the Telstra Entity fixed assets (including network assets) managed through the centralised Asset Accounting Group.

Segment results and segment assets

The measurement of segment results has also changed with the adoption of AASB 8 to be in line with the basis of information presented to management for internal management reporting purposes. The performance of each segment is measured based on their "underlying EBIT contribution" to the Telstra Group. EBIT contribution excludes the effects of all inter-segment balances and transactions. As such only transactions external to the Telstra Group are reported. Furthermore, certain items of income and expense are excluded from the segment results to show a measure of underlying performance. These items are separately disclosed in the reconciliation of total reportable segments to Telstra Group reported EBIT in the financial statements.

Certain items are recorded by our corporate areas, rather than being allocated to each segment. These items include the following:
- the Telstra Entity fixed assets (including network assets) are managed centrally. The resulting depreciation and amortisation is also recorded centrally;
- the adjustment to defer our basic access installation and connection fee revenues and costs in accordance with our accounting policy. Instead our reportable segments record these amounts upfront;
- redundancy expenses for the Telstra Entity; and
- doubtful debt expenses for the Telstra Entity.

In addition, the following narrative further explains how some items are allocated and managed, and as a result how they are reflected in our segment results and segment assets:
- sales revenue associated with mobile handsets for TC&C, TB and TE&G are mainly allocated to the TC&C segment along with the associated goods and services purchased. Ongoing prepaid and postpaid mobile revenues derived from our mobile usage is recorded in TC&C, TB and TE&G depending on the type of customer serviced;
- revenue derived from our BigPond Internet products and its related segment assets are recorded in the customer facing business segments of TC&C, TB and TE&G. Certain distribution costs in relation to these products are recognised in these three business segments. Telstra Operations recognise certain expenses in relation to the installation and running of the broadband cable network; and
- revenue derived from our TCW customers is recorded in our TC&C, TB and TE&G segments. Direct costs associated with this revenue is also recorded in TC&C, TB and TE&G.

(continued)

FIGURE 20.8 *(continued)*

Telstra Group										
Year ended 30 June 2008	**TC&C $m**	**TB $m**	**TE&G $m**	**TO $m**	**TW $m**	**Sensis $m**	**CSL NW $m**	**TClear $m**	**All Other $m**	**Total $m**
Revenue from external customers	9 971	3 640	4 623	123	2 512	2 127	917	562	223	24 698
Other income	59	16	1	14	1	—	—	—	44	135
Total income	10 030	3 656	4 624	137	2 513	2 127	917	562	267	24 833
Labour expenses	386	201	675	1 421	72	459	77	98	769	4 158
Goods and services purchased	2 533	693	977	74	17	172	416	272	27	5 181
Other expenses	690	138	188	2 573	27	402	165	85	974	5 242
Share of equity accounted losses	—	—	—	—	—	—	—	—	1	1
Depreciation and amortisation	—	—	41	67	—	150	246	127	3 559	4 190
EBIT contribution	6 421	2 624	2 743	(3 998)	2 397	944	13	(20)	(5 063)	6 061
Total assets as at 30 June 2008	1 548	446	1 591	3 886	376	2 559	1 873	1 099	24 543	37 921

Telstra Group										
Year ended 30 June 2007	**TC&C $m**	**TB $m**	**TE&G $m**	**TO $m**	**TW $m**	**Sensis $m**	**CSLNW $m**	**TClear $m**	**All Other $m**	**Total $m**
Revenue from external customers	9 398	3 352	4 464	133	2 631	1 968	1 000	573	190	23 709
Other income	123	9	2	17	14	2	—	—	14	181
Total income	9 521	3 361	4 466	150	2 645	1 970	1 000	573	204	23 890
Labour expenses	380	168	759	1 465	73	379	81	101	611	4 017
Goods and services purchased	2 578	657	937	70	(24)	182	458	294	(1)	5 151
Other expenses	598	115	183	2 440	30	350	181	108	800	4 805
Share of equity accounted losses	—	—	6	—	—	1	—	—	—	7
Depreciation and amortisation	—	—	51	61	—	131	196	129	3 514	4 082
EBIT contribution	5 965	2 421	2 530	(3 886)	2 566	927	84	(59)	(4 720)	5 828
Total assets as at 30 June 2007	1 513	411	1 637	3 721	413	2 185	2 154	1 324	24 479	37 837

A reconciliation of EBIT contribution for reportable segments to Telstra Group EBIT is provided below:

		Telstra Group	
		Year ended 30 June	
	Note	**2008 $m**	2007 $m
EBIT contribution for reportable segments		**11 124**	10 548
All other		**(5 063)**	(4 720)
Total all segments		**6 061**	5 828

(continued)

FIGURE 20.8 *(continued)*

	Note	2008 $m	2007 $m
Amounts excluded from underlying results:			
– distribution from FOXTEL[(a)]	6	130	—
– net gain on disposal of non current assets	6	38	69
– impairment in value of other intangibles[(b)]	7	—	(118)
– impairment in value of investments	7	(5)	—
– other		2	—
Telstra Group EBIT (reported)		6 226	5 779

(a) The $130 million distribution received from FOXTEL during the period has been recorded as revenue in the income statement.

(b) In the prior year, we recognised an impairment charge of $110 million in relation to Trading Post mastheads. This impairment is attributable to the Sensis segment.

	Telstra Group	
	Year ended 30 June	
	2008 $m	2007 $m
Information about our geographic operations[(c)]		
Revenue from external customers		
Australian customers	22 884	21 729
International customers	1 944	1 980
	24 828	23 709
Carrying amount of non–current assets[(d)]		
Located in Australia	28 574	27 863
Located in international countries	3 207	3 609
	31 781	31 472

(c) Our geographical operations are split between our Australian and international operations. Our international operations include CSL New World (Hong Kong), TelstraClear (New Zealand), the SouFun, Norstar Media and Autohome/PCPop businesses in China which are part of our Sensis segment, and our international business, including Telstra Europe (UK), that serves multi–national customers in the TE&G segment. No individual geographical area forms a significant part of our operations apart from our Australian operations.

(d) The carrying amount of our segment non–current assets excludes derivative financial assets, defined benefit assets and deferred tax assets.

	Telstra Group	
	Year ended 30 June	
	2008 $m	2007 $m
Information about our products and services		
PSTN	6 666	6 887
Other fixed telephony	2 283	2 276
Mobiles	6 376	5 657

(continued)

FIGURE 20.8 *(continued)*

	2008 $m	2007 $m
Internet	2 486	1 939
IP and data access	1 745	1 630
Business services and applications	1 049	1 059
Pay TV bundling	426	344
Advertising and directories	2 116	1 954
CSL New World	917	1 000
TelstraClear	562	573
Offshore services revenue	346	348
Other minor items	250	261
Elimination for wireless broadband (e)	(565)	(255)
Other revenue	171	36
Total revenue	24 828	23 709

(e) Elimination of $565 million of revenue (2007: $255 million) relating to wireless broadband services and data packs recorded within both Mobiles and Internet revenue.

Income Statement					
for the year ended 30 June 2008		**Telstra Group**		**Telstra Entity**	
		Year ended 30 June		**Year ended 30 June**	
	Note	**2008 $m**	2007 $m	**2008 $m**	2007 $m
Income					
Revenue (excluding finance income)	6	24 828	23 709	21 758	20 662
Other income	6	174	251	135	201
		25 002	23 960	21 893	20 863
Expenses					
Labour		4 158	4 017	3 248	3 074
Goods and services purchased		5 181	5 151	3 680	3 634
Other expenses	7	5 246	4 924	4 892	4 517
		14 585	14 092	11 820	11 225
Share of net loss from jointly controlled and associated entities	26	1	7	—	—
		14 586	14 099	11 820	11 225
Earnings before interest, income tax expense, depreciation and amortisation (EBITDA)		10 416	9 861	10 073	9 638
Depreciation and amortisation	7	4 190	4 082	3 621	3 588
Earnings before interest and income tax expense (EBIT)		6 226	5 779	6 452	6 050
Finance income	6	72	57	60	47
Finance costs	7	1 158	1 144	1 152	1 147
Net finance costs		1 086	1 087	1 092	1 100

(continued)

FIGURE 20.8 *(continued)*

	Note	Telstra Group Year ended 30 June 2008 $m	2007 $m	Telstra Entity Year ended 30 June 2008 $m	2007 $m
Profit before income tax expense		**5 140**	4 692	**5 360**	4 950
Income tax expense	9	**1 429**	1 417	**1 543**	1 512
Profit for the year		**3 711**	3 275	**3 817**	3 438
Attributable to:					
Equity holders of Telstra Entity		**3 692**	3 253		
Minority interests		**19**	22		
		3 711	3 275		
Earnings per share (cents per share)		**cents**	cents		
Basic	3	**29.9**	26.3		
Diluted	3	**29.8**	26.2		

The notes following the financial statements form part of the financial report.

Statement of Financial Position
as at 30 June 2008

	Note	Telstra Group As at 30 June 2008 $m	2007 $m	Telstra Entity As at 30 June 2008 $m	2007 $m
Current assets					
Cash and cash equivalents	20	**899**	823	**542**	546
Trade and other receivables	10	**3 952**	3 853	**3 502**	3 391
Inventories	11	**309**	318	**264**	261
Derivative financial assets	18	**54**	41	**54**	41
Prepayments		**299**	266	**234**	204
Total current assets		**5 513**	5 301	**4 596**	4 443
Non current assets					
Trade and other receivables	10	**198**	190	**318**	273
Inventories	11	**12**	17	**12**	17
Investments – accounted for using the equity method	12	**14**	16	**12**	12
Investments – other	12	**1**	3	**5 461**	5 890
Property, plant and equipment	13	**24 311**	24 607	**22 665**	22 723
Intangible assets	14	**7 245**	6 639	**3 738**	3 098
Deferred tax assets	9	**1**	1	**—**	—
Derivative financial assets	18	**444**	249	**444**	249
Defined benefit assets	24	**182**	814	**161**	784
Total non current assets		**32 408**	32 536	**32 811**	33 046
Total assets		**37 921**	37 837	**37 407**	37 489
Current liabilities					
Trade and other payables	15	**3 930**	4 221	**3 420**	3 871
Provisions	16	**535**	614	**457**	555
Borrowings	18	**2 055**	2 743	**2 484**	3 616

(continued)

FIGURE 20.8 *(continued)*

	Note	Telstra Group As at 30 June 2008 $m	2007 $m	Telstra Entity As at 30 June 2008 $m	2007 $m
Derivative financial liabilities	18	82	177	82	177
Current tax liabilities		264	449	222	413
Revenue received in advance		1 257	1 192	972	930
Total current liabilities		8 123	9 396	7 637	9 562
Non current liabilities					
Trade and other payables	15	181	195	56	58
Provisions	16	776	834	739	787
Borrowings	18	13 444	11 619	13 419	11 590
Derivative financial liabilities	18	1 222	1 328	1 222	1 328
Deferred tax liabilities	9	1 575	1 513	1 734	1 643
Revenue received in advance		355	372	355	368
Total non current liabilities		17 553	15 861	17 525	15 774
Total liabilities		25 676	25 257	25 162	25 336
Net assets		12 245	12 580	12 245	12 153
Equity					
Share capital	17	5 534	5 611	5 534	5 611
Reserves		(410)	(258)	358	232
Retained profits		6 893	6 976	6 353	6 310
Equity available to Telstra Entity shareholders		12 017	12 329	12 245	12 153
Minority interests		228	251	—	—
Total equity		12 245	12 580	12 245	12 153

Income Statement for the year ended 30 June 2007	Note	Telstra Group Year ended 30 June 2007 $m	2006 $m	Telstra Entity Year ended 30 June 2007 $m	2006 $m
Income					
Revenue (excluding finance income)	6	23 709	22 734	20 662	20 447
Other income	6	251	328	201	163
		23 960	23 062	20 863	20 610
Expenses					
Labour	7	4 017	4 364	3 074	3 483
Goods and services purchased	7	5 151	4 701	3 634	3 276
Other expenses	7	4 924	4 427	4 517	4 562
		14 092	13 492	11 225	11 321
Share of net loss/(gain) from jointly controlled and associated entities	30	7	(5)	—	—
		14 099	13 487	11 225	11 321

(continued)

		Telstra Group		Telstra Entity	
		Year ended 30 June		Year ended 30 June	
		2007	2006	**2007**	2006
	Note	**$m**	$m	**$m**	$m
Earnings before interest, income tax expense, depreciation and amortisation (EBITDA)		**9 861**	9 575	**9 638**	9 289
Depreciation and amortisation	7	**4 082**	4 078	**3 588**	3 648
Earnings before interest and income tax expense (EBIT)		**5 779**	5 497	**6 050**	5 641
Finance income	6	**57**	74	**47**	71
Finance costs	7	**1 144**	1 007	**1 147**	990
Net finance costs		**1 087**	933	**1 100**	919
Profit before income tax expense		**4 692**	4 564	**4 950**	4 722
Income tax expense	9	**1 417**	1 381	**1 512**	1 483
Profit for the year		**3 275**	3 183	**3 438**	3 239
Attributable to:					
Equity holders of Telstra Entity		**3 253**	3 183		
Minority interest		**22**	—		
		3 275	3 183		
Earnings per share (cents per share)		**cents**	cents		
Basic	3	**26.3**	25.7		
Diluted	3	**26.2**	25.7		

The notes following the financial statements form part of the financial report.

Source: Telstra (2008, pp. 102, 104, 126–9; 2007, pp. 114, 137–41).

The key differences between Telstra's 2007 segment information (as originally reported in 2007 in accordance with IAS 14) and its 2008 segment information as reported in 2008 are as follows:

(a) Identification of segments
In 2008, note 5, under the heading 'Business segments', explains how segment information is now reported on the same basis as Telstra's internal management reporting structure, and that adjustments and reallocations are no longer required as they were under IAS 14. This has resulted in the separate reporting of CSL New World Mobility group (CSL NW) and Telstra-Clear group (TClear), which were previously aggregated under 'Telstra International'. In addition, the International Head Office primarily included in 'Telstra International' now forms part of Strategic Marketing to reflect internal accountability. ('Strategic Marketing' is not a separately reportable segment.) As a result, there is no longer a separate 'Telstra International' segment.

(b) Measurement of segment results and segment assets
In 2008, the measurement basis is described as being based on 'underlying EBIT contribution' to the Telstra Group. EBIT contribution excludes the effects of all inter-segment balances and transactions. The measurement basis is that used by management for internal reporting purposes. In 2007, in accordance with IAS 14, segment results, assets and liabilities were measured in accordance with the prescribed requirements of the standard.

(c) Items disclosed and format of the disclosures
In 2008, the format of the disclosures and the items disclosed are very different from 2007 — where a prescribed format was followed. The format used in 2008 reflects the items disclosed to management for internal reporting purposes and thus provides a useful clue to users as to

what information management regards as important. The format is also simpler and easier to follow than the 2007 format. However, in both cases, the information reported in respect of performance is either directly (2008) or indirectly (2007) EBIT (earnings before interest and tax). Certain items prescribed by IAS 14 (e.g. significant non-cash expenses) were reported in 2007 but not in 2008, primarily because they are not regularly provided to the CODM (in accordance with IFRS 8, para. 23). The same applies to segment liabilities, which were reported in 2007 but not in 2008.

(d) Reconciliations

As required by IFRS 8, the 2008 segment information includes reconciliations of segment EBIT to Telstra Group EBIT reported in accordance with IFRSs in Telstra's income statement. The reconciliation shows the items that were excluded from the segment EBIT, including net gains on disposal of non-current assets, impairment losses and a distribution from FOXTEL. These items appear to relate to investments and intangibles that, according to management, do not give a measure of underlying segment performance. Note that there is no reconciliation of total assets as these agree directly to the statement of financial position.

(e) Information about products and services (revenue)

This is disclosed in 2008 in accordance with IFRS 8; whereas, it was not disclosed in 2007 (in accordance with IAS 14). It reconciles to the total amount of revenue in the 2008 income statement.

Which set of information do you think is more useful — that disclosed in 2007 or that disclosed in 2008?

SUMMARY

IAS 14 *Segment Reporting* is primarily a disclosure standard and is particularly relevant for large organisations that operate in different geographical locations and/or in diverse businesses. Information about an entity's geographical and business segments is relevant to assessing the risks and returns of a diversified or multinational entity where often that information cannot be determined from aggregated data. IAS 14 requires that an entity should determine which type of segment — business or geographical — is its primary segment reporting format. The disclosures required for the primary segment format are extensive whereas the disclosures required for the secondary segment format are limited.

Determining the composition of a business or geographical segment involves a certain amount of judgement. In making that judgement, entities should take into account the objective of reporting financial information by segment and the qualitative characteristics of financial statements as identified in the *Framework*. Similarly, allocating revenues, expenses, assets and liabilities to segments on a reasonable basis involves judgement. The allocations must be based on whether the items relate to the particular segment's operations, can be directly attributed to that segment or can be reasonably allocated to that segment.

In January 2006, the IASB issued ED 8 *Operating Segments*, which it proposed as a replacement to IAS 14. The ED was part of the IASB's program for achieving convergence with standards issued by the FASB in the United States and essentially adopted the requirements of the FASB Statement of Financial Accounting Standards No. 131 (SFAS 131) *Disclosures about Segments of an Enterprise and Related Information*. The major changes from IAS 14 are the adoption of the management approach to identifying segments and the lack of prescription in respect of segment disclosures. ED 8 was finally issued as a new standard, IFRS 8 *Operating Segments*, in November 2006. IFRS 8 is applicable for annual reporting periods beginning on or after 1 January 2009, with early adoption permitted. Where standards are issued with a long time allowed for implementation and with early adoption permitted, there will be a number of years during which some companies will apply the old standard and others will apply the new standard.

In Europe, the replacement of IAS 14 with IFRS 8 was highly controversial. Concern was expressed by many commentators about the management approach and the lack of mandatory disclosure requirements. Those in favour of the management approach argued that the information provided under that approach will be more relevant and reliable because it will, inter alia, enable investors to evaluate the company on the same basis as that used by management in its decision making and that any concerns about understandability are addressed by IFRS 8's reconciliation requirements. Those against the management approach argued that management will take advantage of the discretion provided in IFRS 8 in order to control the information provided to users. Only time will tell whether concerns about the approach eventuate.

Discussion questions

1. Segment disclosures are widely regarded as some of the most useful disclosures in financial reports because of the extent to which they disaggregate financial information into meaningful and often revealing groupings. Discuss this assertion by reference to the objectives of financial reporting by segments.
2. IAS 14 contains a number of paragraphs encouraging, but not requiring, additional information to be disclosed. Do you think many reporting entities would voluntarily provide these disclosures? Explain your answer.
3. Discuss the meaning of 'impracticable' in the context of paragraph 76 of IAS 14. What reasons could a reporting entity validly give for not restating comparative segment information?
4. IAS 14 states that it is not possible or appropriate to specify a single basis of allocation of assets, liabilities, revenues and expenses to segments that should be adopted by all entities. Explain the main factors that an entity should consider in determining how to allocate amounts to segments.
5. The underlying rationale for the identification of segments espoused in IAS 14 is that business or geographical segments should reflect the entity's different groupings of risks and rewards, either by product or service or by location. Further, IAS 14 asserts that for most entities the predominant source of risks and returns determines how the entity is organised and managed. Discuss this rationale.
6. Discuss the extracts from companies' segment notes provided in section 20.8.4. What are the similarities and differences between the companies' disclosures? What do the disclosures indicate about the relative performance of segments within companies?
7. Discuss the main differences between IAS 14 and IFRS 8.

STAR RATING
★ BASIC
★★ MODERATE
★★★ DIFFICULT

Exercises

Exercise 20.1 DEFINING GEOGRAPHICAL SEGMENTS

★ IAS 14 states that a geographical segment can be defined by reference either to location of assets or location of customers.

Required

Explain, by way of example, how an entity's location of assets could differ from its location of customers.

Exercise 20.2 IDENTIFYING PRIMARY AND SECONDARY SEGMENTS

★ Company B is a listed manufacturing company. It produces most of its products in Australia but exports 90% of these products to the United States, Canada and Germany. It has only one main product line: scientific equipment. Company B is organised internally into two main business units: local and export. The export business unit is in turn divided into two sub-units: North America and Germany (North America includes Canada). Each business unit reports separate financial and operational information to the chief executive officer (CEO) and chief financial officer (CFO). The results of the two business units are then aggregated to form the consolidated financial information. Details of the geographical groups are as follows:

	United States	Canada	Germany	Australia
Economic and political conditions	Stable	Stable. Closely related to US environment	Stable	Stable
Relationships between operations	Closely linked to Canadian operations	Closely linked to US operations	Self-sustaining	Self-sustaining

	United States	Canada	Germany	Australia
Proximity of operations	Closely linked to Canadian operations	Closely linked to US operations	Not close to other operations	Not close to other operations
Special risks	None	None	Stricter regulations	Small market
Exchange control regulations	None	None	None	None
Currency risks	Low	Low to medium	Low	Low to medium

Required
Identify Company B's primary and secondary segment reporting formats in accordance with IAS 14.

Exercise 20.3

IDENTIFYING BUSINESS AND GEOGRAPHICAL SEGMENTS

★★ Using the information from exercise 20.2, identify Company B's business and geographical segments.

Exercise 20.4

IDENTIFYING REPORTABLE SEGMENTS

★★ Company A is a listed diversified retail company. Its stores are located mainly in Australia. It has three main types of stores: general department stores, liquor stores and specialist toy stores. Each of these stores has different products, customer types and distribution processes. In accordance with IAS 14, Company A has identified three business segments: general department stores, liquor stores and specialist toy stores.

All three business units earn most of their revenue from external customers. Total consolidated revenue of company A is $600 million.

	General department stores $m	Liquor stores $m	Toy stores $m	All segments $m
Revenue	400	100	50	550
Segment result (profit)	15	7	4	26
Assets	900	200	100	1200

Required
Identify Company A's reportable segments in accordance with IAS 14. Explain your answer.

Exercise 20.5

ANALYSING THE INFORMATION PROVIDED

★★ Using the information provided about Company A in exercise 20.4, analyse the relative profitability of the three business segments.

Exercise 20.6

DISCLOSURES

★★ Company X has three reportable segments A, B and C. It also has another segment, D, which is not classified as a reportable segment because it earns a majority of its revenue from sales to segments A and C. However, D's sales to external customers amount to 13% of Company X's total sales to external customers.

Required
What, if anything, must Company X disclose about segment D in accordance with IAS 14?

Exercise 20.7 ★★

SEGMENT ASSETS, LIABILITIES, REVENUES AND EXPENSES

Company X, a listed manufacturing company, has two reportable segments, A and B. Both A and B are manufacturing segments.

Required

For each item listed, state whether or not it would be allocated to the reportable segments, identify the segments to which it would be allocated and explain why it would or would not be allocated in accordance with IAS 14.

1. Interest income
2. Dividend income
3. Share of profits from investments in equity-method associates attributable to segment A
4. Interest expense
5. Losses on sales of investments
6. Income tax expense
7. Payables and trade creditors attributable to segment B
8. Costs incurred at head-office level on behalf of segment A in relation to operating costs of segment A
9. Outside equity interest in Company X's profit
10. Depreciation of equipment attributable to segment B

Problems

Problem 20.1 ★★

REPORTABLE SEGMENTS, ALLOCATING AMOUNTS TO SEGMENTS

Company A is a listed diversified retail company. Its stores are located mainly in Australia. It has three main types of stores: general department stores, liquor stores and specialist toy stores. Each of these stores has different products, customer types and distribution processes. In accordance with IAS 14, Company A has identified three business segments: general department stores, liquor stores and specialist toy stores.

For the year ended 30 June 2009 each business unit reported the following financial information to Company A's CFO:

	General department stores $m	Liquor stores $m	Toy stores $m	All segments $m
Revenue	400	100	50	550
Segment result (profit)	15	7	4	26
Assets	900	200	100	1200

All three business units earn a majority of their revenue from external customers. Total consolidated revenue of Company A for the year ended 30 June 2009 is $800 million. Included in general department stores' revenue is $50 million of revenue from toy stores. As at balance date toy stores owed general department stores $45 million. This amount is included in general department stores' assets. Within the general department stores business unit there are five different legal entities including legal entities Y and Z. As at 30 June 2009 legal entity Z owed $23 million to legal entity Y. These amounts have not been eliminated in determining the assets of the general department stores segment.

Required

State whether the following statements are true or false. Give reasons for your answers.

1. Company A has three reportable segments.
2. The revenue figure that should be used by the general department stores segment for the purposes of determining whether or not it is a reportable segment is $350 million.

3. When Company A discloses segment liabilities in accordance with IAS 14, the toy stores segment liabilities should include the $45 million owed to general department stores.
4. The assets figure that should be used by the general department stores segment for the purposes of determining whether or not it is a reportable segment is $900 million.
5. The assets figure that should be used by the general department stores segment for the purposes of determining whether or not it is a reportable segment is $855 million.
6. The assets figure that should be used by the general department stores segment for the purposes of determining whether or not it is a reportable segment is $832 million.
7. The assets figure that should be used by the general department stores segment for the purposes of determining whether or not it is a reportable segment is $877 million.

Problem 20.2

IDENTIFYING BUSINESS AND GEOGREAPHICAL SEGMENTS

★★

Company A is a listed diversified manufacturing company. It produces most of its products in Australia and its markets are also mainly in Australia. It produces four types of products and services as follows:

	Home furniture	Office furniture	Interior design services	Soft furnishings
Nature of product/ service	Timber tables, chairs, beds	Metal and plastic workstations and chairs	Advice on interior design	Curtains, cushions and bed linen
Production process	Mainly handmade, labour intensive, specialised machinery for timber products	Mainly machine-made, specialised machinery for metal and plastic products	None, labour intensive	Mainly handmade, labour intensive
Type of customer	Families, high income, aged 35–55 years	Corporate customers — company purchasing officers, no specific age group	Mainly females, high income, over age 35	Mainly females, high income, over age 35
Distribution process	Distributed through selected furniture stores and own home furniture outlets	Distributed through own specialised office furniture outlets	Distributed through own home furniture outlets	Distributed through own home furniture outlets
Regulatory environment	Not highly regulated	Specialised regulations	Not highly regulated	Not highly regulated

Company A is organised internally into three business units: manufacturing home furniture, manufacturing office furniture and stores. Stores include own home furniture outlets, own office furniture outlets and interior design. Manufacturing home furniture includes soft furnishings. Each business unit reports separate financial and operational information to the chief executive officer (CEO) and chief financial officer (CFO).

Required

Identify Company A's business segments and geographical segments in accordance with IAS 14.

Problem 20.3

COMPREHENSIVE PROBLEM

★★★

Company A is a diversified financial institution. It provides three main types of services: banking, funds management and life insurance. Each of these services provides different products, serves different types of customer and has different distribution processes. Its operations are located mainly in Australia, although 12% of revenues from external customers are from bank branches in New Zealand. Company A is divided into three business units that report separately to top management. The business units are banking, funds management and life insurance. In accordance with IAS 14, Company A has identified three business segments: banking, funds management and life insurance.

All three business units earn a majority of their revenues from external customers. The following financial information was reported to the company's CEO by each business unit for the year ended 30 June 2009:

	Banking $m	Funds management $m	Life insurance $m	All segments $m
Revenue — external sales	850 (all interest income)	90 (fees and commissions)	10 (premium income and other fees)	950
Segment result (profit before amortisation, depreciation and income tax expense)	130	16	1	147
Segment assets	12 750	630	100	13 480

For the year ended 30 June 2009, the total consolidated revenue of Company A is $984 million. Company A owns three properties with a total written-down value at 30 June 2009 of $300 million. One of the properties, with a written-down value of $220 million, is the corporate head office, where administration for the entire company is performed. The other two properties are large regional bank branches. Customers visiting those branches purchase mainly banking services but the company's full range of services may be provided at any bank branch office. The company's CFO has determined that these bank branch properties should be allocated to all three segments in proportion to the revenues generated by each business segment. Depreciation on the corporate head office property for the year was $4.4 million. Depreciation on the bank branch properties for the year was $1.6 million. During the year Company A sold an investment property, realising a gain of $34 million. The investment property had not been allocated to any of the business segments in prior years.

The banking segment's assets are mainly loan receivables. A provision for doubtful debts of $630 million has been deducted in determining that segment's assets. During the year the provision was increased by $30 million. The banking segment's result also includes a share of profits from an associated entity of $2 million. The investment in the associated entity, carried at 30 June 2009 at $25 million, is included in the banking segment's assets because it is part of that segment's operations.

As at 30 June 2009, Company A has $200 million of goodwill (written-down value) that it has not allocated to any of the business segments because there was no reasonable basis to do so. Goodwill amortisation for the year ended 30 June 2009 is $20 million.

For the year ended 30 June 2009, company A's total consolidated profit, after income tax expense of $36 million, is $85 million.

Total consolidated liabilities of Company A at 30 June 2009 are $11 250 million. These include borrowings and deposits of $11 000 million that relate to the banking segment's operations and are directly attributable to that segment. Related interest expense for the year ended 30 June 2009 is $400 million. Creditors and policyholder liabilities that relate to the funds management and life insurance segments' operations and are directly attributable to those segments are $200 million and $50 million respectively. There is no related interest expense. A payable of $35 million from the life insurance segment to the wealth management segment was eliminated in calculating total consolidated liabilities of Company A as at 30 June 2009. The related receivable is not included in the segment assets figure in the table shown above.

Other information

- Only 2% of Company A's total assets are located in New Zealand.
- There were no inter-segment sales during the year.
- The products and services offered by each business segment are as follows:
  - banking: provides a full range of banking services for consumers and corporate customers
  - funds management: provides wealth creation, management and protection products and services to consumers
  - life insurance: provides life insurance policies and other protection products to consumers.
- There are no other internally reported segments.

Required

Prepare the segment disclosures note for Company A for the year ended 30 June 2009 in accordance with IAS 14. Ignore comparative figures and show all workings. Perform your workings in the following order:

1. Identify the business segments and geographic segments.
2. Determine the primary segment reporting format.
3. Determine which segments are reportable segments.
4. Allocate relevant assets, liabilities, revenues and expenses to the reportable segments. In doing so, specifically consider:
   (a) the corporate head office and related depreciation
   (b) the regional bank branch properties and related depreciation
   (c) the gain on sale of investment properties
   (d) the investment in the associated entity and related share of profits
   (e) goodwill and related amortisation
   (f) interest income and interest expense.
5. Identify which segment assets, liabilities, revenues and expenses require separate disclosure, including amounts to be disclosed or eliminated on consolidation.
6. Calculate consolidated profit after tax.
7. Prepare the required segment disclosures.

References

ANZ Bank 2008, *2008 annual report*, Australia and New Zealand Banking Group Limited, www.anz.com.au.

Bundesverband Deutscher Banken 2007, *Endorsement of IFRS 8 operating segments — analysis of potential impacts, response from the Association of German Banks*, 28 June.

Ernst & Young 2007, *IFRS 8 Operating Segments: implementation guidance*.

European Parliament 2007, Document B6–0437/2007, *Motion for a resolution*, 7 November, www.europarl.europa.eu.

Queensland Cotton 2007, *Annual report 07*, Queensland Cotton Holdings Ltd, www.qcotton.com.au.

Telstra Corporation 2008, *Annual report 2008*, Telstra Corporation Limited, www.telstra.com.au.

- 2007, *Annual report 2007*, Telstra Corporation Limited, www.telstra.com.au.

Véron, N 2007, *EU adoption of the IFRS 8 standard on operating segments*, presented to the Economic and Monetary Affairs Committee of the European Parliament, 19 September.

Wesfarmers Ltd 2008, *2008 annual report*, Wesfarmers Limited, www.wesfarmers.com.au.

Part 4

Economic entities

21 Controlled entities: the consolidation method

ACCOUNTING STANDARDS IN FOCUS

IFRS 3 *Business Combinations*
IAS 27 *Consolidated and Separate Financial Statements*

LEARNING OBJECTIVES

When you have studied this chapter, you should be able to:

- understand the nature and various forms of controlled entities
- explain how the consolidation method is applied
- explain the key components of the term 'control' as used in determining a parent–subsidiary relationship
- discuss which entities should prepare consolidated financial statements
- explain the interrelationship between a parent and an acquirer in a business combination
- understand the alternative concepts of consolidation
- explain the differences in report format between single entities and consolidated entities.

The purpose of this chapter is to discuss the preparation of a single set of financial statements, referred to as the consolidated financial statements, for a number of entities that are managed as a single economic entity and, in particular, a group of entities that are under the control of one of those entities. The preparation of consolidated financial statements involves combining the financial statements of the individual entities so that they show the financial position and performance of the group of entities, presented as if they were a single economic entity.

As well as analysing the form that consolidated financial statements might take, this chapter also considers the concept of control as the criterion for consolidation, that is, as the key characteristic that determines the existence of which entities' financial statements should be combined. In section 21.1 a number of combinations of entities for which consolidated financial statements could be prepared are considered. However, the concentration of the chapter, and the following four chapters in this book, is on the particular situation where one entity, the parent, controls another entity, the subsidiary, and the preparation of the consolidated financial statements for such a group of entities.

The accounting standards mainly used in this chapter are IFRS 3 *Business Combinations* and IAS 27 *Consolidated and Separate Financial Statements*, both issued in March 2008. The latter standard deals only with the preparation of consolidated financial statements for parent–subsidiary situations. In this chapter, reference is also made to exposure draft ED 10 *Consolidated Financial Statements* issued by the IASB in December 2008, with comments to be received by March 2009.

21.1 FORMS OF CONTROLLED ENTITIES

Appendix A to IFRS 3 contains the following definition of a business combination:

> A transaction or other event in which an acquirer obtains control of one or more businesses.

A business combination thus involves the formation of an entity that consists of a number of separate entities that together form a combined entity, with users of financial information requiring information about that entity as a whole. Some examples of such business combinations are given below.

21.1.1 Acquisition of shares in another entity

Entity A may acquire all or part of the issued shares of another entity. For example, as shown in figure 21.1, Entity A may acquire 80% of the issued shares of Entity B. Entity A will record an investment in Entity B, and the giving up of some form of consideration such as cash, or shares, in Entity A itself. As the transaction is between Entity A and the shareholders in Entity B, there are no accounting entries in Entity B in relation to this transaction.

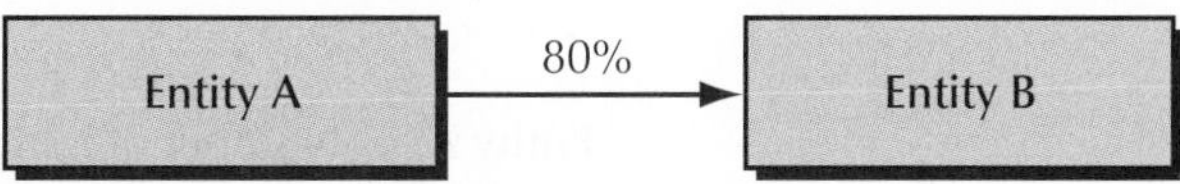

FIGURE 21.1 Acquisition of shares in another entity

Depending on the percentage of shares held in Entity B, as well as other factors, Entity A may have the ability to control the decision making in relation to Entity B. The two entities may then operate as a combined entity, with the wealth of the shareholders in Entity A dependent on the capacity of both entities to generate profits. The shareholders in Entity A are then interested in the combined financial performance and financial position of the two entities.

As is discussed in more detail later in this chapter, where Entity A controls the operations of Entity B, the business combination results in the formation of a parent–subsidiary relationship; that is, Entity A is regarded as the parent, with Entity B as its subsidiary. The application of IFRS 3 and IAS 27 requires the preparation of a special set of financial statements — the consolidated financial statements — to report the economic performance and position of the two entities as a combined entity.

21.1.2 Formation of a new entity to acquire the shares of two other entities

A variation on the first example is where, instead of Entity A acquiring the shares of Entity B, after negotiation the two entities agree to the formation of a new entity, Entity C. Entity C acquires all the shares of the other two entities, as in figure 21.2.

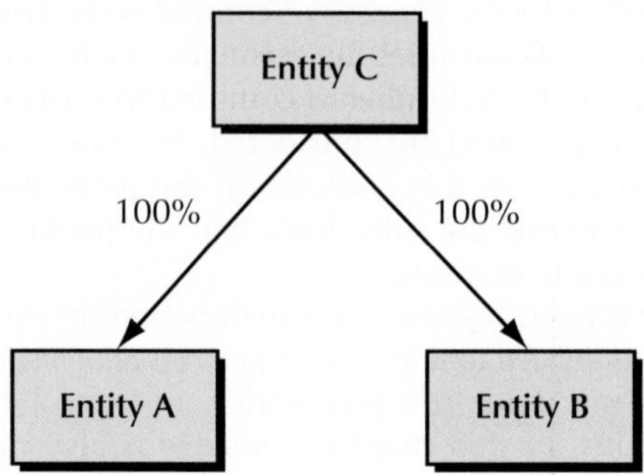

FIGURE 21.2 Formation of new entity

The shareholders in Entity A and Entity B receive shares in Entity C in exchange for their shares in the other entities. The business combination has resulted in the three entities being brought together into one entity, as Entity C now controls the operations of both Entity A and Entity B. The shareholders in Entity C are then interested in the combined entity, which consists of all three entities. Their information needs are better met by the production of a set of consolidated financial statements showing the financial position and performance of the combined entities as a single entity.

21.1.3 Dual-listed entities

A 'dual-listed' structure involves the formation of a contractual arrangement between two entities under which the activities of both entities are brought together, managed and operated on a unified basis as if they were a single entity while retaining their separate legal entities, tax residencies and stock exchange listings. An example of such a structure is that between the Australian company BHP Ltd and the UK company Billiton Plc.

Details of that structure and the subsequent accounting are contained in note 1 of the 2008 BHP Billiton annual report (see www.bhpbilliton.com).

Figure 21.3 diagrammatically illustrates dual-listed entities. For example, Entity A may be a listed entity in Australia and Entity B may be a listed entity in Hong Kong. Assume the following information:

Entity A:	Number of issued shares	100
	Value per share	$1
Entity B	Number of issued shares	100
	Value per share	$3

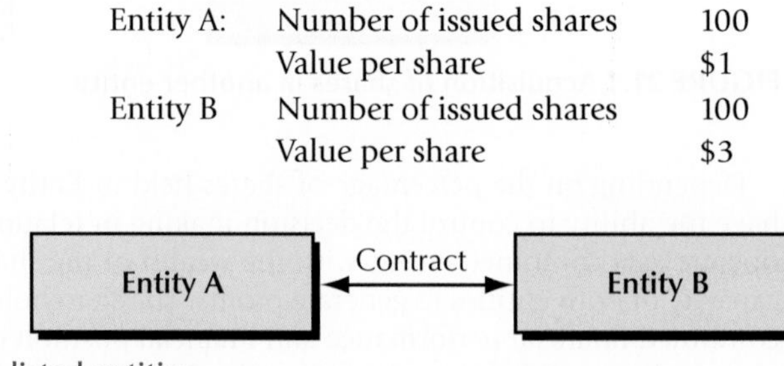

FIGURE 21.3 Dual-listed entities

The two entities could agree to an arrangement whereby each entity retains its own listing, and the shareholders in each entity retain their ownership in their respective entities, but there is a sharing of rights between the shareholder groups such that the shareholders have an economic interest in the combined assets of both entities. In this example, Entity B could issue 200 bonus shares so that the number of shares issued increases to 300 to reflect the fact that Entity B is three times as valuable as Entity A. The rights of shares in both Entity A and Entity B are changed so that they are entitled to a 1/400 interest per share in the combined wealth of both entities. The two entities are managed on a unified basis, with shareholders of both companies being able to vote on substantial issues affecting their combined interests, such as the appointment of directors. The shareholders in both entities are interested in the preparation of a set of financial statements about the combined entities rather than just the individual entities themselves.

The common feature of the above business combinations is the interest of users of financial statements in the financial performance and position of the combined entities rather than the individual entities. These financial statements are the consolidated financial statements because they are prepared by adding together the financial statements of the individual entities within the business combination. A key question to be covered later in this chapter concerns which entities should be required to prepare consolidated financial statements. In other words, what is the concept or criterion that provides the basis for consolidation?

21.2 APPLYING THE CONSOLIDATION METHOD

Although there are a number of situations (as shown in section 21.1) where business combinations may usefully apply the consolidation process to prepare a set of consolidated financial statements for the combined entities, the only accounting standard in Australia that currently requires the application of the consolidation method is IAS 27. IAS 27 applies to situations as depicted in figures 21.1 and 21.2, specifically where parent and subsidiary entities exist. Paragraph 4 of IAS 27 contains the following definitions:

> **Consolidated financial statements** are the financial statements of a group presented as those of a single economic entity.
> A **group** is a parent and all its subsidiaries.
> A **parent** is an entity that has one or more subsidiaries.
> A **subsidiary** is an entity, including an unincorporated entity such as a partnership, that is controlled by another entity (known as the parent).

In figure 21.1, Entity A is the parent and Entity B is the subsidiary, assuming that, because of its 80% holding in Entity B, Entity A is able to control Entity B (the meaning of 'control' is discussed in section 21.3). Entity A and Entity B as a combined unit, or economic entity, are referred to as a group. The consolidated financial statements are then the financial statements of the group, and the process of preparing the consolidated financial statements is referred to as consolidation.

Paragraph 18 of IAS 27 states that in preparing the consolidated financial statements, 'the financial statements of the parent and its subsidiaries [are combined] line by line by adding together like items of assets, liabilities, equity, income and expenses'. For example, assuming that at the end of a specified reporting period Entity A and Entity B both report cash balances in the financial statements for their individual legal entities, the cash for the group, as reported in the consolidated financial statements, is determined by adding the cash balances of the parent and the subsidiary:

	Entity A + Entity B	=	Group (consolidated financial statements)
Cash	$50 000 + $20 000	=	$70 000

This aggregation process is subject to a number of adjustments, which are covered in detail in the following chapters. These adjustments are necessary because of intragroup shareholdings and transactions between entities within the group. However, at this stage, the process of consolidation should be seen as simply a process of aggregation of the financial statements of all the entities in the group. Note that the consolidation process does not involve making adjustments to the individual financial statements or the accounts of the entities in the group. The consolidated financial statements are an additional set of financial statements and, as demonstrated in chapter 22, are prepared using a worksheet or spreadsheet to facilitate the addition and adjustment process.

The consolidated financial statements consist of a consolidated statement of financial position, consolidated statement of comprehensive income, consolidated statement of changes in equity, and a consolidated statement of cash flows. The format of these statements is as presented in chapters 17 and 19.

It is important to understand that the preparation of the consolidated financial statements does not necessarily overcome the need or requirement to prepare financial statements for the individual entities within the group. The consolidated financial statements are required in addition to the individual financial statements. The need for the individual financial statements depends on legal requirements within a specific jurisdiction, and the need to provide information to users of financial statements. For example, in Australia, paragraph Aus6.1 requires the preparation and presentation of both consolidated financial statements and separate financial statements in a set of general purpose financial statements.

21.3 CONTROL AS THE CRITERION FOR CONSOLIDATION

In paragraph 4 of IAS 27, a subsidiary is defined as an entity that is *controlled* by another entity, the parent. The criterion for identifying a parent–subsidiary relationship, and hence the basis for consolidation, is control. The determination of whether one entity controls another is then crucial to the determination of which entities should prepare consolidated financial statements.

Although IAS 27 contains a definition of control, and provides some discussion on the meaning of the term, there is still much disagreement over what constitutes control. The standard setters are currently debating the definition of control, but as of 2008 have not yet agreed on any change to the definition in IAS 27. To help in understanding the debate, as well as giving an insight into the application of IAS 27, extensive references are made in this chapter to the debate in the Financial Accounting Standards Board (FASB) in the United States, as this reflects many aspects of the debate occurring in the IASB.

Paragraph 4 of IAS 27 contains the following definition of control:

> Control is the power to govern the financial and operating policies of an entity so as to obtain benefits from its activities.

Note that there are two parts to this definition of control:

- the ability to direct the financial and operating policies of another entity (*the power criterion*)
- the ability to obtain benefits from the other entity (*the benefit criterion*).

In February 1999, the FASB issued an exposure draft *Consolidated Financial Statements: Purpose and Policy* (hereafter referred to as the FASB ED). The FASB ED was very controversial and, as reported in the 28 February 2001 edition of the FASB *Status Report*, 'at this time, there is not sufficient Board member support to proceed with either a final statement on consolidation policy, or an exposure draft on entities with specific limits on their powers (SPEs)'. However, the concepts in the FASB ED are not dissimilar from those in IAS 27, and give insight into the meaning of terms used in IAS 27. In the FASB ED, control is defined as follows:

> The ability of an entity to direct the policies and management that guide the ongoing activities of another entity so as to increase its benefits and limit its losses from that other entity's activities. For purposes of consolidated statements, control involves decision-making ability that is not shared with others.

This definition also relies on the power criterion and the benefit criterion used in the IAS 27 definition. However, it also emphasises a link between these two criteria, in that the ability to control another entity should be such as to allow the controller to use that power to increase its benefits and limit its losses from the subsidiary's activities. This dimension effectively requires that the benefits relate to the use of the power, rather than being independent of the power. In the use of the words 'so as' in the definition of control in IAS 27, this same dimension is inherent in that definition.

Appendix A of ED 10 contains the following definition of 'control of an entity':

> The power of a reporting entity to direct the activities of another entity to generate returns for the reporting entity.

This definition contains both the elements of power and benefits. The power must enable the reporting entity to affect the benefits it receives from the other entity. ED 10 uses the term 'returns' rather than 'benefits', as the latter may imply only positive returns. As noted in paragraph BC42 of the Basis for Conclusions on ED 10, the definition of control includes three components: power, returns, and the link between power and returns.

21.3.1 Power to govern the financial and operating policies of an entity

The IASB uses the term 'power to govern' whereas the FASB uses 'ability to direct'. There is no difference between the two terms, as both refer to an entity's *capacity* to control. In ED 10, the term 'power to direct' is used (e.g. see para. 4).

One of the key elements of the debate on the meaning of control is the distinction between the notion of 'capacity to control' and that of 'actual control'. Capacity to control does not require the holder to actually exercise control. Similarly, an entity that is actually controlling another may not have the capacity to control.

These are several factors to consider in determining the existence of capacity to control.

Passive vs active control

The entity having the power to govern, or the capacity to control, may not be actively involved in the management of the controlled entity; the controller may play a passive role. However, in situations where another party is actively formulating the policies of a subsidiary, in order for another entity to be the controlling entity, it must have the ability to change or modify those policy decisions if the need for change is seen to exist. The existence of actual control (i.e. determining the actual policies of the subsidiary) often signals the existence of capacity to control, but the two are not necessarily coexistent.

Non-shared control

Regardless of whether the control is passive or active, there can be only one controlling entity; there cannot be two or more entities that share the control. It is possible that one entity may delegate control to another entity, but the first entity has the capacity to control even if it is the delegated party that actually controls the subsidiary.

In the FASB ED, the FASB argued (paragraph 11) that the parent's ability to control a subsidiary is an exclusionary power. The decision-making ability cannot be shared and the parent must be able to:

- direct the use of and access to another entity's assets, generally by having the power to set the policies that guide how those assets are used in ongoing activities
- hold the management of that other entity accountable for the conduct of its ongoing activities, including the use of that entity's assets, generally by having the power to select, terminate and determine the compensation of the management responsible for carrying out the directives of the parent.

However, as the FASB ED noted (paragraph 12), this does not mean that the parent must be able to make any decision it likes in relation to another entity, as the parent will be constrained by 'laws, regulations, corporate charters, shareholder and partnership agreements, debt covenants, and other agreements that impose limits to protect the interests of noncontrolling investors, creditors, and others'. These are protective rights and do not affect the ability of one entity to control another.

Level of share ownership

Paragraph 13 of IAS 27 states that control is presumed to exist when the parent owns, directly or indirectly through subsidiaries, more than half of the voting power of an entity. Hence, where the parent owns more than 50% of the shares of another entity, it is expected that the latter is a subsidiary of the former.

Ownership of shares normally provides voting rights that enable the holder of the majority of shares to dominate the appointment of directors or an entity's governing board. As paragraph 13 of IAS 27 states, control exists (when the parent owns half or less of the voting power of an entity) where there is:

> (a) power to appoint or remove the majority of the members of the board of directors or equivalent governing body and control of the entity is by that board or body; or

(b) power to cast the majority of votes at meetings of the board of directors or equivalent governing body and control of the entity is by that board or body.

There is no debate about the existence of control where the parent has a majority shareholding in the subsidiary. However, where the ownership interest is less than 50% or is based on possible future actions, there is less consensus about whether control exists. As the FASB noted in its 2001 *Status Report*:

> Several FASB Board members are concerned about the appropriateness of determining that nonshared decision-making ability can exist based on the anticipated nonaction by other holders of voting rights.

Control under IAS 27 is *non-shared* control. A distinction needs to be made between non-shared control and what can be described as 'unilateral control'. Unilateral control means that the controlling party does not depend on the support of others to exercise control, which is the case where the parent owns more than 50% of the shares of the subsidiary. Where the holding is less than 50%, the parent has a non-shared or dominant control. This is not control in a legal sense as with unilateral control, but is control that is achieved both because of its own actions and because of the actions (or inactions) of other parties. This form of control is referred to by the FASB (see figure 21.4 for an example) as 'effective control', and appears to be the form adopted by IAS 27.

In determining the existence of effective control it is necessary to examine the actions of other parties. In particular, factors to assess include:

- *The existence of contracts.* Paragraph 13 of IAS 27 identifies two circumstances where control exists because of the existence of contracts:

  (a) power over more than half of the voting rights by virtue of an agreement with other investors;
  (b) power to govern the financial and operating policies of the entity under a statute or an agreement.

The contract or agreement may take many forms; however, a contract may cover a limited time period. Control will then exist only while the contract is current.

- *Size of the voting interest.* Although all shareholders may attend general meetings and vote in matters relating to governance of an entity, it is rare for this to occur. If, therefore, only 60% of the eligible votes are cast at a general meeting and an entity has more than a 30% interest in that entity, it can cast the majority of votes at that meeting. It then has effective control of the entity.
- *Dispersion of other shareholders.* Shareholders can be dispersed geographically as well as in numbers of shares held. The annual general meeting may be held in Sydney, Australia, but the majority of shareholders may live in South-East Asia. The probability of these shareholders attending the general meeting is then lessened by location.

  Further, even if all the shareholders live in Sydney, if they hold small parcels of shares then the probability of attendance at general meetings is reduced. For example, if the number of shares issued by the subsidiary is 1000, the shareholders will be more dispersed if there are 1000 shareholders with one share each than if there are four shareholders with 250 shares each. However, assuming the prospective parent has a 40% interest, it is not clear where the cut-off point is between lack of control where there are two other shareholders with 30% each and having control where there are 60 other shareholders with 1% each.
- *Level of disorganisation or apathy of the remaining shareholders.* This factor is affected by the dispersion of the shareholders, and reflected in their attendance at general meetings. Holders of small parcels of shares are often not organised into forming voting blocks. Shareholders with environmental or ethical concerns may be less apathetic about the actions of the entity and its management policies, and may form voting blocks.

Figure 21.4 is an abbreviated version of an example given in paragraphs 87–94 of the FASB ED to illustrate the application of the concept of control where the parent has less than 50% of the shareholding in a subsidiary. In the example, the ownership by Company A of shares in Company B reduces over time from 100% to 60% to 45% and finally to 35%. The question is whether Company A retains control of Company B as its shareholding decreases. The FASB argues in this example that control is maintained even at the 35% level, applying factors such as those discussed earlier.

Company A, a cement manufacturer, acquired all of the voting shares of Company B, a rug manufacturer, as part of a diversification program.

Several years later, Company A decided as part of its corporate strategy to commit capital resources only to its primary line of business, and was unwilling to support the projected growth of Company B. Company A caused Company B to issue additional shares in an initial public offering, resulting in a reduction in Company A's ownership interest in Company B from 100% to 60%.

Shortly after the offering, the newly issued shares are widely held, no other party having more than 3% of Company B's outstanding shares. Both before and after the initial public offering, Company A's shareholding represents a majority interest in Company B, which leads to a presumption of control in the absence of evidence to the contrary (FASB ED, paragraph 18(a)). Moreover, there is no evidence that demonstrates that Company A, through its 60% interest, no longer has the ability to dominate the nomination and selection of the members of the board of Company B.

Five years later, to raise additional capital needed to finance the growth of Company B, Company A causes Company B to issue additional shares, which reduces Company A's ownership of outstanding shares to 45%. At this time, Company A's 45% holding is the largest block of shares held by any single party, and the remaining shares outstanding continue to be widely held — no other party holds more than 3% of the outstanding shares. Ten days after the public offering, Company A is able, through the board of directors of Company B, to cause the renomination of all of its choices for the 11 board members of Company B.

During the preceding 5 years, about 80% of the eligible rights to vote in an election of the board of directors of Company B were cast at any given annual meeting of Company B. The percentage of votes cast in each of the past 5 years is as follows (the last being the most recent): 76, 81, 82, 79 and 82. Company A voted all of its shares each year, but only about half of the other eligible votes were cast in each of those years.

In this case, Company A no longer has legal control of Company B but, based on the facts, effective control has not been lost. Company A still has the ability to dominate the process of nominating and electing the members of the board of Company B, which is based mainly on two factors: Company A's large minority holding and the wide dispersion of the remaining shares.

About 2 years later, another issue of Company B's shares reduces Company A's holdings to 35%, and the voting patterns and all other facts remain constant. Company A's 35% holding is now less than half of the 80% of votes typically cast in past elections and may still be nearly half of the votes cast in future elections.

In this case, Company A's ability to maintain control becomes questionable. However, assurance of an entity's ability to maintain its control is not a condition for consolidation. Rather, the assessment is based on whether an entity has a current ability to control another entity. In this case, based on the facts and the weight of evidence, the 35% voting interest, the strong ties to the directors of Company B and the continuing success of Company B's operations under its control, collectively give Company A the ability to dominate the nomination and election of Company B's board of directors. In this case, there is no evidence that demonstrates that control of Company B has been lost.

FIGURE 21.4 Controlling partially owned entities

However, it is the assessment of the non-action of others in determining the existence of control that caused some FASB board members to be concerned, particularly because of the subjectivity of assessing the reasons for the shareholders' actions. Do the non-voting shareholders not vote because they are happy with the management ability of Company A as opposed to their being apathetic? Would they be willing to combine to outvote Company A if the latter's decisions were considered untenable? The success of Company B's operations under the control of Company A is a further measure of the potential for generally passive shareholders to be sufficiently concerned to cast a vote at the next general meeting. While shareholders see positive results, they are less likely to react against Company A. When the company is performing poorly, the interest of shareholders increases as well as their willingness to become involved. Poor performance with resultant lowering of share price may also result in a current or new shareholder acquiring a large block of shares and changing the voting mix at general meetings.

A number of problems arise in applying the concept of effective control. First, there is the question of temporary control. Where the parent holds more than 50% of the shares of the subsidiary, there is no danger of a change in the identity of the parent. However, if the identification of the parent is based on factors that may change over time, the process becomes difficult. For example, the percentage of votes cast at general meetings may historically be 70%, but in a particular year it may be 50%. A shareholder with 30% of the voting power has control in the latter circumstance but not in the former. This control may, however, last for only a year until the next general meeting.

Second, the ability of an entity to control another may be affected by relationships with other parties. For example, a holder of 40% of the voting power may be 'friendly' with the holder of another 11% of the votes. This friendly relationship could include a financial institution that has invested in the holder of the 40% votes and plans to vote with that party to increase its potential for repayment of loans. However, business relationships and loyalties are not always permanent.

Third, a minority holder that did not have control may, due to changing circumstances, find itself with the capacity to control. For example, a holder of a 30% block of shares may not have had control because the remaining shares were tightly held by a small number of parties. However, if one or more of these parties sold their shares in small lots, the minority holder could have the controlling parcel of shares. Regardless of whether this shareholder wanted to exercise that control or not, he or she has the capacity to control and is the parent.

The theoretical question is whether in these circumstances an entity really controls in its own right or in fact has control that is shared with the other shareholders, as control is affected by their actions. The practical question relates to how to determine control in changing circumstances. Is it sufficient to rely on *usual circumstances* — such as the average attendance at general meetings — or the *probability* of how other shareholders will act?

21.3.2 Potential voting rights

Paragraphs 14–15 of IAS 27 discuss the issue of potential voting rights. For example, an entity may have share call options or convertible instruments which, if exercised or converted, give the entity voting power over the financial and operating policies of another entity. There are two types of convertible voting rights that need to be considered:

- potential voting rights that are currently exercisable or convertible
- potential voting rights that cannot be exercised or converted until a future date or until the occurrence of a future event.

The second circumstance does not influence the current assessment of capacity to control and hence such potential voting rights are not considered in assessing the existence of control. In relation to a situation where at the end of the reporting period the holder of an instrument has the capacity to exercise the instrument and obtain the power to govern the financial and operating policies of another entity, then that entity is a parent of the other entity.

It may be argued that control should be based on the actual situation at the end of the reporting period and, as the holder of the convertible instrument has not exercised the instrument, the actual situation is that the holder is not yet in control. In other words, it would require an action on the part of the holder to have a current capacity to control. However, as stated previously in this chapter, control exists even when the holder is passive. A holder of 51% of the shares of another entity is the parent of that entity even if the holder does not attend general meetings or participate in determination of the directors of the entity.

The implementation guidance to IAS 27 provides a number of illustrative examples to help determine when potential voting rights should be taken into consideration in the assessment of the existence of control.

21.3.3 Ability to obtain benefits from the other entity's activities

The second part of the IAS 27 definition of control is concerned with a parent's ability to use that power to obtain benefits from the activities of its subsidiary.

This characteristic of control acts to exclude such parties as trustees and those with fiduciary relationships with the subsidiary. These parties may be able to direct certain activities of the subsidiary but, apart from fees for service, the activities do not lead to increased or decreased benefits to these parties.

Apart from the obvious benefits in terms of dividends relating to the holding of an ownership interest, there are other benefits that can accrue to the controlling entity. Paragraph 38 of the FASB ED lists some of these:

- benefits from structuring transactions with a subsidiary to obtain necessary and scarce raw materials on a priority basis, at strategic locations, or at reduced costs of delivery
- benefits from gaining access to the subsidiary's distribution network, patents, or proprietary production techniques
- benefits from combining certain functions of the parent and subsidiary to create economies of scale in, for example, costs of management, employee benefits, or insurance
- benefits from denying or regulating access to a subsidiary's assets by its non-controlling investors, creditors, competitors and others.

The FASB argued (paragraph 217) that 'because of the stewardship responsibilities and risks associated with being in control of an entity, the Board believes that an entity rarely acquires control of another entity without obtaining significant opportunities to benefit from that control'. No entity wants to control another entity for purely altruistic reasons.

In March 2002, the Accounting Standards Board (ASB) in the United Kingdom, in a draft paper on consolidation policy, provided some principles to be used in applying a control-based consolidation policy, particularly in relation to linking controlling policies with benefits to be accrued from their application:

> *The commercial outcomes for each party should be assessed:* Arrangements between entities should be assessed from a perspective that makes commercial sense for each of the entities involved. This perspective requires that, at the outset at least, no entity should expect benefit without exposure to commensurate risk and no entity should be exposed to risks without expecting commensurate benefit.
>
> *Control requires both the ability to direct and to benefit:* Control has two aspects: the ability to direct the operating and financial policies and the ability to benefit or suffer from that direction.
>
> *The ability to benefit and the exposure to risk assume particular importance where policies of direction are pre-determined:* Where through pre-determination or otherwise, there is no real present choice of financial and operating policies, the ability to direct becomes irrelevant in deciding issues of control. Decisions on consolidation then depend on the nature of the ability to benefit of the different entities involved and their exposure to the risks inherent in those benefits.

The philosophy being expressed in these principles is that there is an association between benefits and risk, and one of the risks relates to taking control of another entity. Identification of the controlling entity should, therefore, be helped by an analysis of which entities are bearing the risks in relation to another entity, and which entities are likely to benefit from their association with that entity. Importantly, the ability to be able to vary the amount of benefits or to affect the generation of benefits is also important in identifying who is in control.

The third principle noted by the ASB relates to the situation where a parent may set up a special-purpose entity in which it has a small shareholding and the majority shareholding might be held by the party which finances the activities of the special-purpose entity. However, the entity is set up such that the operating and financial policies are virtually fixed (see figure 21.5 on the next page for a case example). In this case, as the ASB noted, the determination of the parent focuses on the ability to benefit and the exposure to risk rather than the ability to determine policies of the special-purpose entity. Company J does not control the board of directors of Company X. However, there are not many decisions left for Company X to make as the product and dealers are all predetermined. In terms of benefits, the investor group receives a return on the entity as the inventory is sold. However, Company J receives a greater range of benefits as Company X is acting as a sales agent for its boats. Company X still runs all the risks in relation to production of the boats and disposing of any unsold boats, and receives the major benefits from the sale of the boats via the fee for services. Company J is then the parent of Company X.

Paragraph 12 of ED 10 notes that when assessing control, a reporting entity shall consider power and returns together, and how the reporting entity can use its power to affect the returns. Appendix A of ED 10 contains the following definition of 'returns from involvement with an entity':

> Returns that vary with the activities of an entity and can be positive or negative.

Company J, a public company, is a boat manufacturer specialising in sailboats for private use. Company J, with the assistance of an investment banker and in conjunction with an independent investor group, created Company X.

The business purpose of Company X is to purchase all Company J's luxury line sailboats on completion of production. The investor group contributed \$600 000 and Company J contributed \$400 000 to capitalise Company X. The investor group will own 60% of the voting interest in Company X, with Company J having the remaining 40% voting interest. Company X is governed by a board of directors and consists of ten directors, six appointed by the investor group and four appointed by Company J. All significant business decisions must be approved by 60% of the board, except for decisions relating to liquidation, issue of additional debt or equity capital and changes to the size of the board of directors, these decisions requiring approval by 80% of the board.

Company X's operations consist of acquiring 100% of Company J's luxury line sailboats at cost of production. Company X may, at its option, return any unsold inventory to Company J after one year at cost. Company X is allowed to enter into other transactions with unrelated parties, but the investor group and Company J have agreed that Company X will not enter into such transactions. Company J has an agreement with Company X to maintain relationships with its dealer network. Company J will provide all necessary post-production storage facilities, arrange for shipment to dealers, provide incentive plans to dealers and provide manufacturer's warranties. Apart from inventory, Company X will not have any substantive assets.

Company J receives a fee for services provided to Company X equal to the revenue from sales after deducting the cost of sales, financing fees and a facilitation fee paid to the investor group.

FIGURE 21.5 Special purpose entity

Source: Adapted from a case written by the FASB as part of its testing of the FASB ED.

In paragraphs BC52–BC57 of the Basis for Conclusions on ED 10, the IASB made the following points:

- The reason for including the ability to benefit, rather than simply defining control as a synonym of power, is to exclude situations in which an entity might have power over another entity but only as a trustee or agent.
- The returns accruing to a controlling entity must vary according to the activities of the controlled entity. The board's assumption is that the entity that receives the greatest returns from another entity is likely to have the greatest power over that entity. However, the proportion of returns accruing to an entity need not be directly correlated with the amount of power to direct activities.
- Power and returns must be linked. If one entity has power over another but not the ability to benefit from that power, it would be unlikely that the two entities represent a circumscribed area of business activity of interest to equity investors.

21.3.4 Dissimilar activities

In determining the existence of a parent–subsidiary relationship, the fact that the parent is involved in totally different activities from the subsidiary is not sufficient to exclude the subsidiary from consolidation. Some have argued that if, for example, the parent's activities are in mining while the subsidiary's are in retailing clothing that the consolidated financial statements will lack meaning. However, the criterion for consolidation is control. As the parent has control of the assets of the subsidiary, regardless of the activities of the entities within the group, consolidated financial statements are necessary for performance measurement and assessment of economic responsibility of the management of the parent. In this regard paragraph 17 of IAS 27 states:

> A subsidiary is not excluded from consolidation because its business activities are dissimilar from those of the other entities within the group. Relevant information is provided by consolidating such subsidiaries and disclosing additional information in the consolidated financial statements about the different business activities of subsidiaries. For example, the disclosures required by IFRS 8 *Operating Segments* help to explain the significance of different business activities within the group.

21.3.5 Alternatives to control

In the Discussion Memorandum written by Paul Pacter and issued in 1991 by the FASB before determining the exposure draft on consolidation policy and procedures, the FASB requested comments on three possible conditions for consolidation:

- a parent's level of ownership in another entity, even if not controlled by the parent
- control of an entity by a parent without a specified level of ownership or
- control and a level of ownership as two separate and necessary conditions.

As reported in paragraph 203 of the FASB ED, nearly all respondents agreed that control is a necessary condition, rejecting ownership without control. However, a majority of respondents supported the third possibility listed above — namely, that both control and a significant level of ownership should be required for determining the existence of a parent–subsidiary relationship. Most of the respondents suggested an ownership level of 50% or more.

The FASB rejected the advice of the respondents, giving a number of reasons (paragraphs 215–218):

- *There is no link between ownership and control.* The level of ownership does not affect whether a parent controls a subsidiary. An entity can direct the use of the assets of another entity regardless of the level of its direct ownership interest. An analogy can be drawn with the definition of an asset in the IASB *Framework*. There is no requirement in the definition of an asset for an entity to have ownership in order to have an asset; the requirement is that an entity must control the benefits expected to flow from the resource.
- *Stewardship responsibilities.* If an entity is in control of another entity it has a responsibility to be accountable for management of all assets and liabilities under its command.
- *Reporting of risks and benefits.* There are risks associated with controlling an entity, and an entity rarely acquires control of another entity without obtaining significant opportunities to benefit from that control.
- *Not to require consolidation for entities where there is less than 50% ownership would be a significant step backwards in the evolution of consolidated financial statements.* The historical development of consolidation has been to move from a legalistic position of greater than 50% ownership to a more conceptual position of control. To revert to reliance on ownership percentages is to move backwards in terms of conceptual accounting.

21.3.6 Reasons for consolidation

Given the amount of debate on the criterion of consolidation, is there any potential solution to the problem? It seems that there has to be a compromise between those who want unilateral control, which equates to control with greater than 50% ownership, and those who prefer effective control. The choice of the criterion for consolidation must be based on the reasons for requiring consolidation, i.e. the reasons for requiring the preparation of consolidated financial statements.

A key purpose for all financial reporting is the discharge of accountability. Entities that are responsible or accountable for managing a pool of resources, being the recipients of economic benefits and responsible for paying economic benefits, are generally required to report on their activities, and are held accountable for their management of those activities. Those who are in control of resources are accountable for their use. The definition of control should reflect this aspect of accountability.

The FASB, in its arguments against the use of a joint ownership–control criterion, placed emphasis on the need to consider the qualitative characteristics of accounting information. The requirement to prepare consolidated financial statements must then be associated with the need for that information:

- In paragraph 179 of the FASB ED, it is argued that the consolidated financial statements must *represent as faithfully* as possible the financial position, financial performance and cash flows of a parent and its subsidiaries. These statements must then show all the elements under the control of the parent.
- The consolidated financial statements must provide the information that is *relevant* to the users of those statements. Which entities should be combined with the parent to provide the information needed by users to make their economic decisions?
- The information must be *understandable* to the users, providing information exceeding that provided in the separate financial statements of the entities in the group.

- The information must increase the ability of the users to *compare* the position and performance of the group with other entities that are organised differently such as by the use of divisions and branches.

This emphasis on user needs leads to a consideration of the role of a reporting entity, as the key feature of a reporting entity is the existence of users who are dependent on a set of financial statements to make their economic decisions.

21.3.7 Users of consolidated financial statements

Consider the situation in figure 21.6 where Entity A acquires all the shares of Entity B, the combined entities thus forming a group.

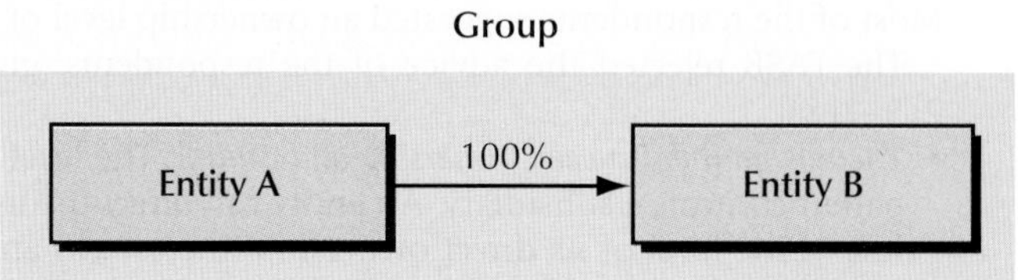

FIGURE 21.6 Combined entities

The law may require each of the individual entities to prepare financial reports about each separate entity, but there may be users of financial information who want information about the group (i.e. the combination of the two legal entities). For example, as Entity A owns all the shares of Entity B, the wealth of the shareholders of Entity A depends on the combined performance of both A and B. The combined businesses then become a reporting entity as there are users of financial information who want a financial report on the combined entities A and B.

Who are the users?

Paragraph 9 of the *Framework* identifies seven user groups that are important in determining the existence of a reporting entity:

1. investors
2. employees
3. lenders
4. suppliers and other trade creditors
5. customers
6. governments and their agencies
7. the public.

These users can be classified into the following three groups:

- resource providers: shareholders, employees, suppliers and lenders
- recipients of goods and services: customers
- parties having a review or oversight function: governments, regulatory agencies, unions and the media.

The problem with this classification is that there is no potential user group excluded. All people or entities, regardless of the strength of their link with an entity, can effectively fit within the 'users' category. The difficulty of having such a broad category of users is twofold. First, for an entity's management to attempt to isolate the existence of dependent users, to have to analyse the position with respect to such a broad grouping is very time-consuming and costly. Second, the breadth of the grouping introduces many parties that have tenuous relationships with an entity, such as environmental groups.

Some users are more dependent than others on the financial information publicly provided by an entity. There are user groups who, because of their relationship with an entity, are not dependent on the issue of general purpose financial statements to obtain information about an entity. For example, lenders such as banks often have the capacity to require entities to supply required information, and the entities are willing to do so in order to obtain loans at lower interest rates than if the information were not supplied. The banks are not, then, dependent users. In Statement of Accounting Concepts (SAC) 1 *Definition of the Reporting Entity* issued by the Australian Accounting Research Foundation in Australia in 1990 and adopted by the Australian

Accounting Standards Boards as a part of its conceptual framework, a number of factors were given in paragraphs 19–22 to help identify dependent users:

- *Separation of management from economic interest*. The further the owners are removed from the management of the entity, the more likely it is that the owners will be dependent on the supply of information about the entity.
- *Economic or political importance/influence*. An entity could be economically and politically important for many reasons (e.g. it is involved in a strategic industry such as defence, or in oil and gas production; it is a major employer in a particular part of the country; it is involved in environmentally sensitive areas; it enjoys monopoly privileges or tariff protection). Entities that have dominant positions or privileges will always attract interested parties and potentially dependent users.
- *Financial characteristics*. Characteristics to consider include the amount of debt, number of employees, size of profit, value of sales and value of assets. Users will be attracted to particular characteristics based on their interest in the entity. Investors will be interested in investment, employees in long-term employment and the survival of the entity, suppliers in long-term markets and solvency, and customers in solvency and profitability affecting worth of warranties and after-sales service.

To illustrate the needs of users for information, consider the economic entity structure in figure 21.7.

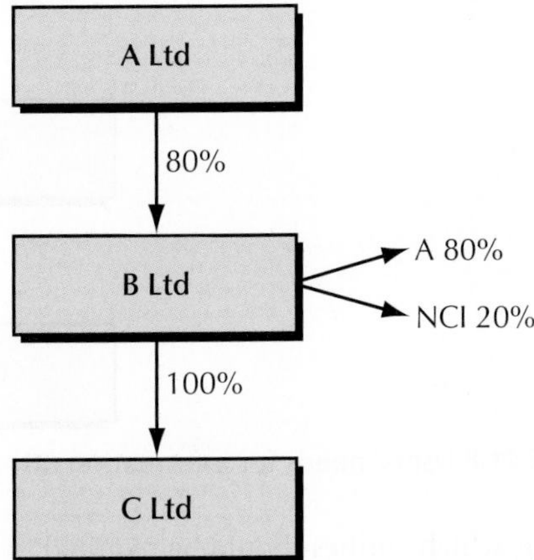

FIGURE 21.7 Users' needs for information (1)

Assume A Ltd owns 80% of the issued shares of B Ltd, while B Ltd owns all the issued shares of C Ltd. Note that the ownership interest in B Ltd consists of two parties: the parent interest, A Ltd, of 80% and the non-controlling interest (NCI) of 20%. The non-controlling shareholders in an entity are the shareholders other than the parent. Paragraph 4 of IAS 27 defines the non-controlling interest (NCI) as the equity in a subsidiary not attributable, directly or indirectly, to a parent. The question is, in figure 21.7 which users have a need for information about a combined entity?

- It is possible that there are users who require information about each of the individual entities A Ltd, B Ltd and C Ltd. Resource providers such as employees and creditors and recipients of goods and services such as customers would be interested in the financial performance and position of each of the entities as a separate unit. From a shareholder perspective, it is possible that information about A Ltd alone is not important as the shareholders in A Ltd are more concerned with a report about the combination of entities A Ltd, B Ltd and C Ltd than about the individual performance of A Ltd.
- Users would probably also require information about the combined group of A Ltd, B Ltd and C Ltd. The wealth and earning capacity of the owners of A Ltd depends on the performance not only of A Ltd but also of B Ltd and C Ltd, given the investment that A Ltd has in these entities.
- It is also possible that information about the group of B Ltd and C Ltd would be required by some users. As A Ltd owns only 80% of the shares of B Ltd, there is a non-controlling interest holding in B Ltd of 20%. The non-controlling interest in B Ltd has no financial interest in A Ltd and would be concerned only with the financial performance of the combined grouping of B Ltd and C Ltd.

There are therefore five possible groupings of entities or individual entities in figure 21.7 that would be of interest to some users.

If the structure in figure 21.7 were changed to that in figure 21.8 such that A Ltd now owns all the issued shares of B Ltd, would there be any change in the number of entities of interest to users? The possible change is whether information about the group of B Ltd and C Ltd would still be of interest to users. Considering shareholders as a possible user group, there are no shareholders who are interested in the group of B Ltd and C Ltd. The shareholders in A Ltd are still interested in the combination of A Ltd, B Ltd and C Ltd. For the group of B Ltd and C Ltd to be of interest, interested parties other than shareholders would need to be identified. As far as lenders are concerned, they are often able to demand special-purpose reports and do not qualify as users interested in general purpose financial statements. Further, lenders are often associated with individual entities rather than groups because of the nature of the lending contract. One possible scenario where lenders would be interested in the economic entity of B Ltd and C Ltd would be where a lender to C Ltd has its loan guaranteed by B Ltd. The probability of the lender having the loan repaid then depends on the combined resources of B Ltd and C Ltd.

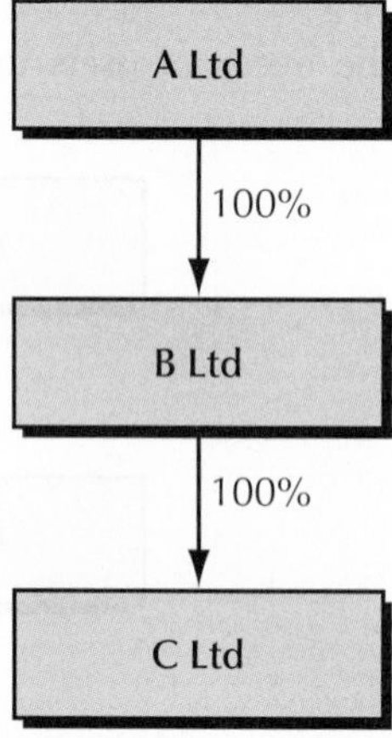

FIGURE 21.8 Users' needs for information (2)

Hence, which entities should be required to prepare consolidated financial statements requires an analysis of the needs of users for information.

21.3.8 Control and users' needs

An analysis of the needs of users for information should help standard setters to determine the definition of control for consolidation purposes, in that the appropriate definition should lead to the financial statements required by the dependent users. Consider the following situations:

1. Assume A Ltd owns 45% of B Ltd, but adopts a passive position, making no effort to control B Ltd. Control is held by another entity, C Ltd, which holds 40% of B Ltd. Hence, A Ltd has the capacity to control but C Ltd actually controls B Ltd on a day-to-day basis. Who should prepare consolidated financial statements — A Ltd or C Ltd? Who is responsible or accountable for the use of the resources of B Ltd — A Ltd or C Ltd? The answer lies in considering the needs of users for information. Do the users want consolidated financial statements about A Ltd + B Ltd and/or C Ltd + B Ltd?
2. If A Ltd owns 40% of B Ltd and there are two other shareholders in B Ltd each holding 30%, it is generally argued that A Ltd does not have the capacity to control B Ltd. Consider the case where A Ltd actually controls B Ltd because the other two investors are passive investors, or have high regard for A Ltd's managerial expertise. A Ltd is then actually controlling the policies of both A Ltd and B Ltd, but does not have the capacity to control. Should A Ltd prepare consolidated financial statements for A Ltd + B Ltd? Analysis of user needs should help determine whether there is a need for such a set of financial statements.

As the standard setters are currently debating the definition of control for consolidation purposes, it is possible that changes will be made to IAS 27 in the future.

21.4 PRESENTATION OF CONSOLIDATED FINANCIAL STATEMENTS

Paragraph 9 of IAS 27 details which entities are required to prepare consolidated financial statements. It states:

> A parent, other than a parent described in paragraph 10 shall present consolidated financial statements in which it consolidates its investments in subsidiaries in accordance with this Standard.

Hence, all parents, other than the paragraph 10 exceptions, are responsible for the preparation of consolidated financial statements.

Paragraph 10 contains the list of parents exempted from the preparation of consolidated financial statements. It states:

> A parent need not present consolidated financial statements if and only if:
> (a) the parent is itself a wholly-owned subsidiary, or is a partially-owned subsidiary of another entity and its other owners, including those not otherwise entitled to vote, have been informed about, and do not object to, the parent not presenting consolidated financial statements;
> (b) the parent's debt or equity instruments are not traded in a public market (a domestic or foreign stock exchange or an over-the-counter market, including local and regional markets);
> (c) the parent did not file, nor is it in the process of filing, its financial statements with a securities commission or other regulatory organisation for the purpose of issuing any class of instruments in a public market; and
> (d) the ultimate or any intermediate parent of the parent produces consolidated financial statements available for public use that comply with International Financial Reporting Standards.

Consider the group structure in figure 21.8. A Ltd is required under paragraph 9 to prepare consolidated financial statements combining the financial statements of the parent entity A Ltd and its subsidiaries B Ltd and C Ltd. B Ltd is also a parent entity with C Ltd being its subsidiary. Is B Ltd also required to prepare consolidated financial statements? If B Ltd meets the requirements of paragraph 10, it does not have to prepare consolidated financial statements:

- Is B Ltd itself a wholly owned subsidiary? In figure 21.8, B Ltd is itself a wholly owned subsidiary. Even in the group structure in figure 21.7 where A Ltd has only an 80% interest in B Ltd, B Ltd may be exempted from preparing consolidated financial statements if, in accordance with paragraph 10(a), B Ltd can persuade its other owners, the 20% non-controlling interest, not to object to not presenting consolidated financial statements.
- Are the debt and equity instruments of B Ltd traded in a public market? In figure 21.8, where B Ltd is a wholly owned subsidiary, it would be unlikely that its shares would be traded in a public market.
- Has B Ltd filed its financial reports with a regulatory agency for the purpose of issuing any class of instruments in a public market?
- Has A Ltd produced consolidated financial statements complying with international financial reporting standards?

Note that IAS 27 distinguishes between 'separate financial statements' and 'consolidated financial statements'. Separate financial statements are defined in paragraph 4 of IAS 27:

> Separate financial statements are those presented by a parent, an investor in an associate or a venturer in a jointly controlled entity, in which the investments are accounted for on the basis of the direct equity interest rather than on the basis of the reported results and net assets of the investees.

In figure 21.8, A Ltd will prepare its own financial statements which contain its investment in B Ltd as an asset, recorded in accordance with IAS 39 *Financial Instruments: Recognition and Measurement*. According to paragraph 6 of IAS 27, A Ltd is not required to append its own financial statements to its consolidated financial statements.

IAS 27 does not allow a parent to exclude any subsidiary from the consolidated financial statements. Paragraph 12 of IAS 27 requires that the consolidated financial statements include *all* subsidiaries of the parent.

IAS 27 specifically notes some areas where exclusions of subsidiaries from consolidation are *not* permitted, namely, where:

- the business activities of a subsidiary are different from those of other subsidiaries (paragraph 17)

- the investor is not a company, such as a trust, partnership, a mutual fund or a venture capital organisation (paragraph 16).

Similarly, exclusions from consolidation do not exist where:

- there is a large non-controlling interest
- there are severe long-term restrictions that impair the ability to transfer funds to the parent.

21.5 PARENT ENTITIES AND IDENTIFICATION OF AN ACQUIRER

As noted in chapter 11, accounting for a business combination under the acquisition method requires the identification of an acquirer. The acquirer is the combining entity that obtains control of the other combining entities or businesses. Hence, as the criterion for identification of a parent–subsidiary relationship is control, it is expected that when a business combination is formed by the creation of a parent–subsidiary relationship, the parent will be identified as the acquirer. However, there are a number of situations where the parent entity is not the acquiring entity.

In paragraph B19 of Appendix B to IFRS 3, a distinction is made between the *legal acquirer/acquiree* and the *accounting acquirer/acquiree*. The parent entity is usually the legal acquirer as it issues its equity interests as consideration in the combination transaction, with the subsidiaries being the legal acquirees. However, the accounting acquirer is determined based on which entity in the subsequent business combination is the controlling entity.

21.5.1 Formation of a new entity

Consider the situation in figure 21.9 in which A Ltd and B Ltd combine by the formation of a new entity, C Ltd, which acquires all the shares of both of these entities with the issue of shares in C Ltd. C Ltd controls both A Ltd and B Ltd.

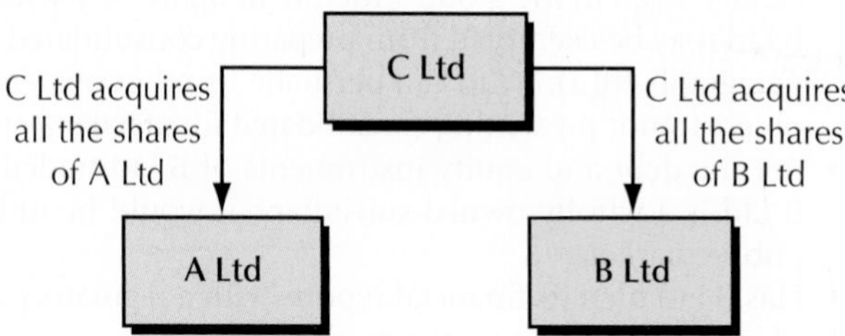

FIGURE 21.9 Identification of an acquirer where new entity formed

Paragraph B18 of IFRS 3 states: 'If a new entity is formed to issue equity interests to effect a business combination, one of the combining entities that existed before the business combination shall be identified as the acquirer by applying the guidance in paragraphs B13–B17.' In other words, even though C Ltd is acquiring the shares of both A Ltd and B Ltd, it is not to be considered the accounting acquirer; either A Ltd or B Ltd must be considered to be the accounting acquirer. Deciding which entity is the acquirer involves a consideration of such factors as which of the combining entities initiated the combination, and whether the assets and revenues of one of the combining entities significantly exceed those of the others (see chapter 25 for a more detailed discussion). The reasons for this decision by the IASB are given in paragraphs BC98–BC101 of the Basis for Conclusions on IFRS 3.

The key reason for the IASB's decision is in paragraph BC100. The argument is that the new entity, C Ltd, may have no economic substance, and the accounting result for the combination of the three entities should be the same if A Ltd simply combined with B Ltd without the formation of C Ltd. It is argued in paragraph BC100 that to account otherwise would 'impair both the comparability and the reliability of the information'.

However, the problem that then arises in the scenario in figure 21.9 is that a choice has to be made: is A Ltd or B Ltd the acquirer? In deciding on which entity is the acquirer, paragraphs

B14–B18 of Appendix B to IFRS 3 provide some indicators to consider in situations where it may be difficult to identify an acquirer. The entity likely to be the acquirer is the one:

- that has a significantly greater fair value
- that gives up the cash or other assets, in the case where equity instruments are exchanged for cash or other assets
- whose management is able to dominate the business combination.

21.5.2 Reverse acquisitions

A further situation considered in paragraphs B19–B27 of IFRS 3 is the 'reverse acquisition' form of business combination. Consider the situation in figure 21.10.

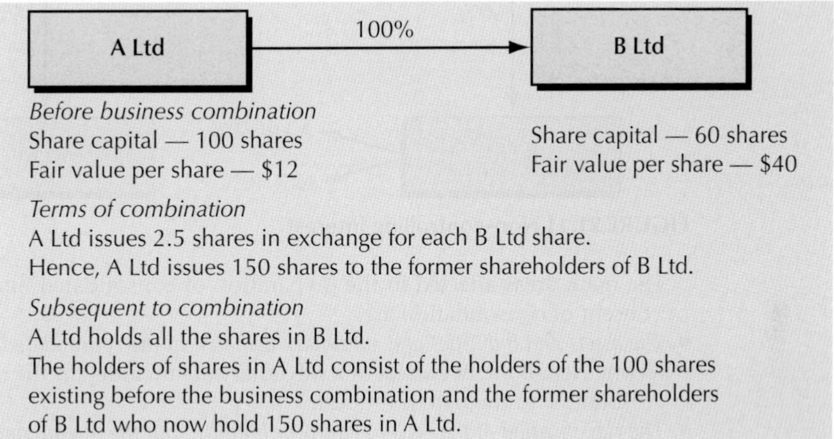

FIGURE 21.10 Reverse acquisition

A Ltd acquired all the shares in B Ltd, and A Ltd can therefore legally control the financial and operating policies of B Ltd. However, an analysis of the shareholding in A Ltd shows that the former shareholders of B Ltd hold 60% (i.e. 150/250) of the shares of A Ltd. Some people argue that the substance of the business combination is that B Ltd has really taken over A Ltd because the former shareholders of B Ltd are in control. Paragraph BC96 of the Basis for Conclusions on IFRS 3 provides a further example of a reverse acquisition:

> The IASB also observed that in some reverse acquisitions, the acquirer may be the entity whose equity interests have been acquired and the acquiree is the issuing entity. For example, a private entity might arrange to have itself 'acquired' by a smaller public entity through an exchange of equity interests as a means of obtaining a stock exchange listing. As part of the agreement, the directors of the public entity resign and are replaced by directors appointed by the private entity and its former owners. The IASB observed that in such circumstances, the private entity, which is the legal subsidiary, has the power to govern the financial and operating policies of the combined entity so as to obtain benefits from its activities. Treating the legal subsidiary as the acquirer in such circumstances is thus consistent with applying the control concept for identifying the acquirer.

The problem with the reverse acquisitions argument is that it relies on an analysis of which *shareholders* control the decision making; i.e. the acquiring entity is the one whose *owners* control the combined entity and who have the power to govern the financial and operating policies of the entity so as to obtain benefits from its activities.

The accounting for reverse acquisitions is covered in chapter 22.

21.6 CONCEPTS OF CONSOLIDATION

Having decided on the criterion for consolidation, and hence the definitions of 'parent' and 'subsidiary', the standard setters decided on the choice of a concept of consolidation. The accounting literature makes reference to many concepts of consolidation, the most common being the proprietary concept, the parent entity concept and the entity concept.

Differences in consolidation arise under these concepts only if the parent does not own all the equity in a subsidiary, in other words if a non-controlling interest (NCI) exists. An NCI is defined in paragraph 4 of IAS 27 as the equity in a subsidiary not attributable, directly or indirectly, to a parent.

In figure 21.11, it can be seen that in B Ltd the parent (A Ltd) has an ownership interest of 60% and there is an NCI of 40%. Similarly in Y Ltd there is a parent interest of 35% and an NCI of 65%. The meaning and measurement of the NCI are discussed in more detail in chapter 24.

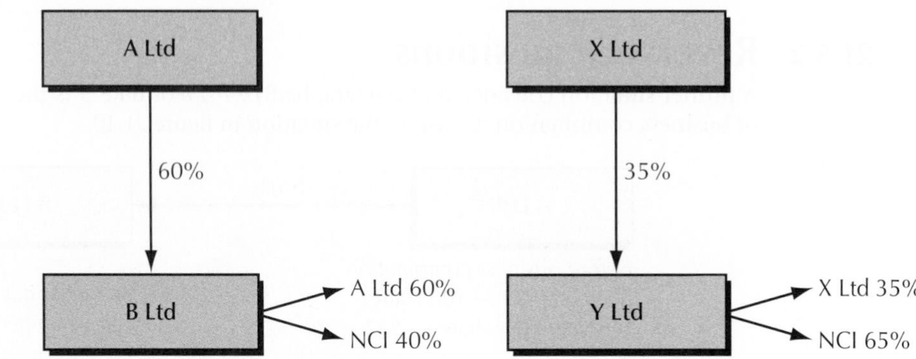

FIGURE 21.11 Non-controlling interest

The main areas affected in the preparation of consolidated financial statements by the choice of concept of consolidation are:

- *The assets and liabilities of a subsidiary included in the consolidated financial statements.* This relates to whether all the net assets of a subsidiary are included in the consolidated group or just those attributable to the parent interest.
- *The classification of the NCI as equity or liability, and the measurement of the NCI.* The consolidated assets consist of the sum of the assets of the parent and those of the subsidiaries. The choice of concept affects the amount shown as total consolidated liabilities and equity, since the choice of concept affects the category into which the NCI is placed as well as the calculation of the amount of the NCI.
- *The adjustments for the effects of transactions within the group.* The consolidated financial statements show the performance and financial position of the group in its dealings with parties external to the group. Where, for example, profits are made by one part of the group, such as a subsidiary, in selling inventory to another part of the group, such as the parent, the effects of these transactions must be eliminated with adjustments being made to the profits recorded by the subsidiary. The choice of concept affects whether all the profit on such transactions is adjusted for or whether only part of the profit is eliminated.

No specific concept of consolidation is explicitly recognised in IAS 27. However, the accounting treatments adopted in IAS 27 are consistent with the adoption of the entity concept of consolidation. In this chapter, only a brief outline of the alternative concepts of consolidation is given. A more detailed analysis can be found in Leo (1987) and Pacter (1991).

21.6.1 Entity concept of consolidation

Under the entity concept of consolidation:

- the group consists of the assets and liabilities of the parent as well as all the assets and liabilities of the subsidiaries
- the NCI is classified as an equity holder or contributor of capital to the group in the same capacity as the equity holders/owners of the parent.

Diagrammatically, the group under the entity concept is as shown in figure 21.12.

The implications of adopting the entity concept of consolidation for the preparation of the consolidated financial statements are as follows:

- Where there are transactions between members of the group, the effects of these transactions are adjusted in full, as required by paragraph 20 of IAS 27 (see chapter 23 for a detailed discussion). This accords with the view that the consolidated financial statements should show the results of transactions between the group and entities external to the group. The adjustments are then unaffected by the extent of the parent's ownership interest in the subsidiary.

- Because the NCI is classified as a contributor of equity to the group, it is disclosed in the equity section of the consolidated financial statements, as per paragraph 54(q) of IAS 1 *Presentation of Financial Statements* and paragraph 27 of IAS 27.
- Because of the classification of the NCI as equity, its measurement is based on a share of consolidated equity and not on a share of the recorded equity of the subsidiary in which the NCI ownership interest is held (discussed in more detail in chapter 24).

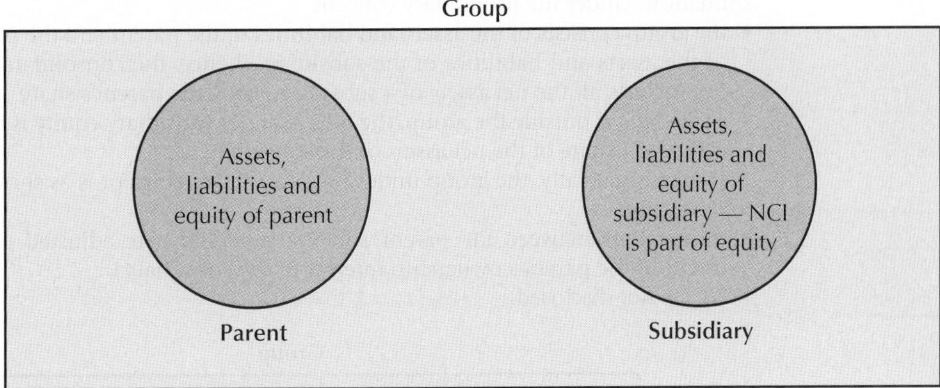

FIGURE 21.12 Group under the entity concept

21.6.2 Parent entity concept of consolidation

Under the parent entity concept:

- the consolidated group consists of the assets and liabilities of the parent and all the assets and liabilities of the subsidiaries
- the NCI is classified as a liability.

Diagrammatically, the group under the parent entity concept is as shown in figure 21.13.

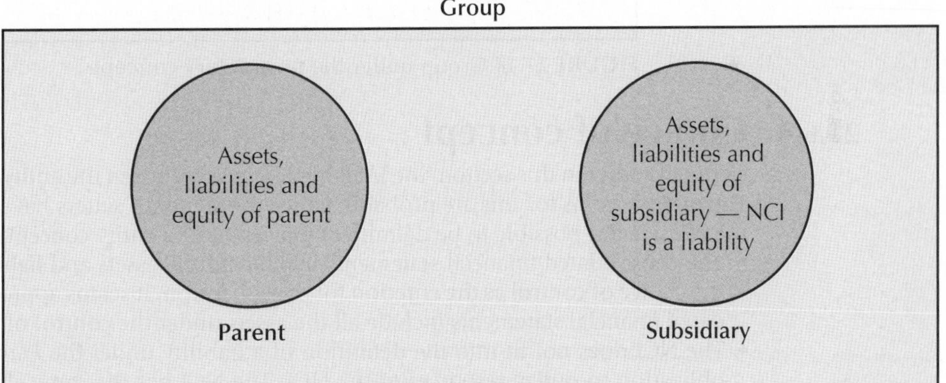

FIGURE 21.13 Group under the parent entity concept

Under this concept:

- Adjustments for transactions within the group involve both partial (i.e. to the extent of the parent's interest in the subsidiary) and total elimination procedures. Only the parent's share of the intragroup profit is eliminated where the subsidiary is the selling entity, but all the profit is eliminated where the parent is the seller. The rationale for this is based on the classification of the NCI as a liability, and the need to increase the share of the NCI when the subsidiary makes a profit on transacting with the parent. The justification is based on the need to report accurately the liability to the NCI.
- The NCI is reported in the liability section of the consolidated statement of financial position.
- The NCI is calculated as its proportionate share of the recorded equity of the subsidiary, with no adjustments for transactions within the group.

The focus of the parent entity concept is on the parent's owners as the main user group. All controlled assets and liabilities are included in the consolidated financial statements, but the claim by the parent's owners is net of the liability claim of the NCI.

21.6.3 Proprietary concept of consolidation

The proprietary concept is sometimes referred to as proportional consolidation or pro rata consolidation. Under the proprietary concept:

- the group consists of the assets and liabilities of the parent and the parent's proportional share of the assets and liabilities of the subsidiary; hence, the consolidated financial statements do not include all the net assets of a subsidiary, only the parent's share
- as the NCI is outside the group, the NCI share of subsidiary equity is not disclosed, and neither is the NCI share of the net assets of the subsidiary.

Diagrammatically, the group under the proprietary concept is as shown in figure 21.14. Under this concept:

- transactions between the parent and the subsidiary are adjusted proportionally (i.e. to the extent of the parent's ownership interest in the subsidiary)
- NCI is not disclosed.

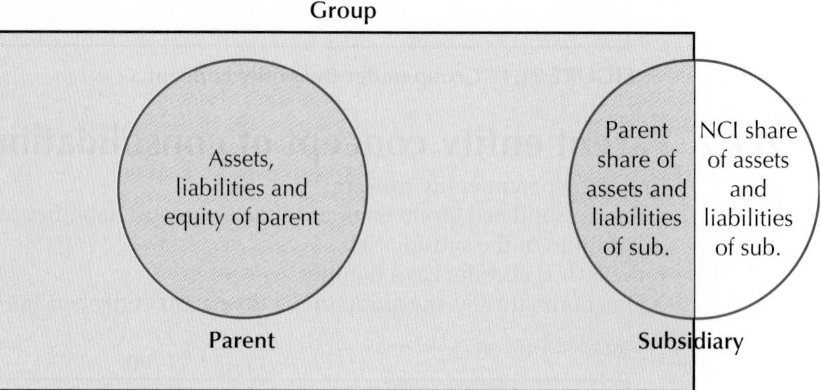

FIGURE 21.14 Group under the proprietary concept

21.6.4 Choice of concept

As noted earlier in this section, the IASB has effectively chosen the entity concept of consolidation. The main reasons for this are probably (since the standard setters have not stated any reasons in IAS 27, it is not possible to be definitive) that under the entity concept:

- The consolidated financial statements include all the assets and liabilities of the group. Given the choice of control as the criterion for consolidation, it seems appropriate that all the consolidated financial statements include all the assets under the control of the parent.
- The NCI does not fit into the definition of a liability under the *Framework*. The group has no obligation to outlay resources to the NCI. The NCI has the same claim on the net assets of a subsidiary as does the parent. The NCI does not have a priority claim, which is normally the case with liability claims. In the Basis for Conclusions on IAS 27, the IASB made the following comments in relation to the NCI:

> BC30. The Board decided to amend this requirement to require minority (non-controlling) interests to be presented in the consolidated balance sheet [statement of financial position] within equity, separately from the equity of the shareholders' of the parent. The Board concluded that a minority (non-controlling) interest is not a liability of a group because it does not meet the definition of a liability in the *Framework for the Preparation and Presentation of Financial Statements*.
>
> BC31. Paragraph 49(b) of the *Framework* states that a liability is a present obligation of the entity arising from past events, the settlement of which is expected to result in an outflow from the entity of resources embodying economic benefits. Paragraph 60 of the *Framework* further indicates that an essential characteristic of a liability is that the entity has a present obligation and that an obligation is a duty or responsibility to act or perform in a particular way. The Board noted that the existence of a minority (non-controlling) interest in the net assets of a subsidiary

does not give rise to a present obligation of the group, the settlement of which is expected to result in an outflow of economic benefits from the group.

BC32. Rather, the Board noted that a minority (non-controlling) interest represents the residual interest in the net assets of those subsidiaries held by some of the shareholders of the subsidiaries within the group, and therefore meet the *Framework*'s definition of equity. Paragraph 49(c) of the *Framework* states that equity is the residual interest in the assets of the entity after deducting all its liabilities.

One of the members of the IASB, Tatsumi Yamada, dissented on the issue of IAS 27 subsequent to the exposure draft in 2005. In his dissenting opinion, Mr Yamada argued that the IASB is taking the entity view without giving enough consideration to the fundamental issues of what information should be provided in the consolidated financial statements, and to whom the information is being provided. This requires an in-depth analysis of the objectives of consolidation. Since the issue of IAS 27, there has been more debate on the choice of concept. This debate is outlined below.

In July 2006, the IASB issued a discussion paper (DP) *Preliminary Views on an Improved Conceptual Framework for Financial Reporting: The Objective of Financial Reporting and Qualitative Characteristics of Decision-useful Financial Reporting Information.* One of the issues raised in this document was the range of users to be considered in financial reporting. In the Basis for Conclusions on the DP paragraphs BC1.9–BC1.13, reasons were given for adopting a wide range of users, including the adoption of the viewpoint of the entire consolidated group rather than just the perspective of the parent entity. Paragraph BC1.10 states:

> The boards decided to retain the focus on a wide range of users because it is more consistent with the objective of providing information that is useful for resource allocation decisions by investors, creditors, and other users than a narrower focus on existing ordinary shareholders would be.

Adoption of a wide range of users led the IASB to also adopt the entity perspective. Paragraph OB10 of the DP states:

> Accordingly, financial reports reflect the perspective of the entity rather than only the perspective of the entity's owners (existing ordinary shareholders or ordinary shareholders of the parent entity in consolidated financial statements) or any other single group of users. However, adopting the entity perspective as the basic perspective underlying financial reporting does not preclude also including in financial reports information that is primarily directed to the entity's owners or to another group of users. For example, financial reports include *earnings per (ordinary) share,* which may be of interest largely to holders and potential purchasers of those shares.

This was elaborated on in paragraph BC1.11 of the Basis for Conclusions:

> The boards also concluded that the entity perspective is consistent with the focus on a wide range of users because it views the effects of transactions and other events from the perspective of the entire entity rather than only a part of it (in consolidated financial statements, that part would be the parent entity).

In its summary of the 179 comment letters received by the IASB and FASB on the discussion paper (see www.iasb.org) the following statements were made:

- Nearly all respondents who commented on the entity perspective proposed in the DP stated that the issue should not be prejudged until it has been deliberated fully.
- Many respondents said that the issue of the entity versus the proprietary approach should be considered as part of Phase D of the project Reporting Entity which concerns the definitions and boundaries of the reporting entity.
- Many respondents disagreed with the boards' decision to adopt the entity perspective as the basic perspective underlying financial reports.
- Respondents disagreed with the boards' reason for choosing the entity perspective, as the entity perspective is consistent with a wide range of users while a proprietary approach is more consistent with the DP approach which has a focus on a primary interest group consisting of current and potential investors and creditors.

However, in subsequent discussions by the boards, as reported in the Project Update as of 18 March 2008 (see www.iasb.org), they have made the following decisions:

- The entity perspective should be adopted as proposed in the preliminary views. The boards agreed that adopting the entity perspective is intended to convey that an entity, not its owners and others having an interest in it, is the object of general purpose financial reporting.
- The entity perspective involves reporting on the entity's resources (assets), the claims (liabilities and equity) on the entity's resources, and the changes in those resources.

Some of this debate seems to have been the cause of dissension amongst IASB members on the classification of NCI. In the published dissent on the 2008 amendments to IAS 27, paragraph DO6 states:

> Messrs Danjou, Gélard and Yamada agree that, in conformity with the *Framework for the Preparation and Presentation of Financial Statements*, non-controlling interests should be presented within the group's equity, because they are not liabilities. However, they believe that until the debates over the objectives of consolidated financial statements (i.e. what information should be provided and to whom) and the definition of the reporting entity have been settled at the conceptual level, transactions between the parent and non-controlling interests should not be accounted for in the same manner as transactions in which the parent entity acquires its own shares and reduces its equity. In their view, non-controlling interests cannot be considered equivalent to the ordinary ownership interests of the owners of the parent. The owners of the parent and the holders of the non-controlling interests in a subsidiary do not share the same risks and rewards in relation to the group's operations and net assets because ownership interests in a subsidiary share only the risks and rewards associated with that subsidiary.

In May 2008, the IASB issued the exposure draft (ED) *An improved Conceptual Framework for Financial Reporting: Chapter 1: The Objective of Financial Reporting. Chapter 2: Qualitative Characteristics and Constraints of Decision-Useful Financial Reporting Information*, based upon deliberations subsequent to the DP. As proposed in the DP, the ED recommended the adoption of the entity perspective.

In the Basis for Conclusions to the ED, the IASB argued in paragraph BC1.12 that, 'Under the entity perspective... the reporting entity is deemed to have substance of its own, separate from that of its owners. Economic resources provided by capital providers become resources of the entity and cease to be resources of the capital providers'. In contrast, as per paragraph BC1.1.3, 'under the proprietary perspective... the reporting entity does not have substance of its own separately from that of its proprietors or owners. The resources of equity capital providers remain their resources and do not become resources of an entity because the entity does not exist separately from its owners'.

The IASB believed that the proprietary perspective did not reflect a realistic view of financial reporting, stating in BC1.1.5 that 'the entity perspective is more consistent with the fact that the majority of today's business entities engaged in financial reporting have substance distinct from that of its capital providers'.

A key question now is what are the implications for financial reporting of adopting the entity perspective? How will this affect the rest of the conceptual framework project? The IASB tried to answer these questions in paragraph BC1.16:

> Although the boards decided to adopt the entity perspective as it pertains to the objective of financial reporting, they have not yet considered all the possible implications of that decision on future phases of the framework. The boards have not yet considered the effect that adopting the entity perspective in Chapter 1 will have on phases that have yet to be deliberated, and therefore have not yet decided whether there are implications for decisions to be made in those phases. Those decisions will be made when the boards deliberate those phases.

21.7 FORMAT OF CONSOLIDATED FINANCIAL STATEMENTS

The format of the consolidated financial statements is the same as that for single entities, as per IAS 1 *Presentation of Financial Statements* (discussed in chapter 17). The only additional requirements are in relationship to the disclosure of the NCI.

Paragraph 27 of IAS 27 states:

> Non-controlling interests shall be presented in the consolidated statement of financial position within equity, separately from the equity of the owners of the parent.

These disclosures link with that in IAS 1. According to paragraph 83 of IAS 1:

> An entity shall disclose the following items in the statement of comprehensive income as allocations of profit or loss for the period:
>
> (a) profit or loss for the period attributable to
>
> (i) non-controlling interest; and
>
> (ii) owners of the parent; and

(b) total comprehensive income for the period attributable to:
 (i) non-controlling interest; and
 (ii) owners of the parent

Figure 21.15 demonstrates this form of disclosure.

Consolidated Statement of Comprehensive Income (extract)
for the year ended 30 June 2010

	2010 $000	2009 $000
Profit before tax	X	X
Income tax expense	X	X
Profit for the year	X	X
Other comprehensive income		
Available-for-sale financial assets	X	X
Gains on property revaluation	X	X
Income tax relating to components of other comprehensive income	X	X
Other comprehensive income for the year, net of tax	X	X
TOTAL COMPREHENSIVE INCOME FOR THE YEAR	XX	XX
Profit attributable to:		
Owners of the parent	X	X
Non-controlling interests	X	X
	X	X
Total comprehensive income attributable to:		
Owners of the parent	X	X
Non-controlling interests	X	X
	X	X

FIGURE 21.15 Illustrative disclosures of NCI in the consolidated statement of comprehensive income

In the consolidated statement of changes in equity, IAS 1 paragraph 106 requires the disclosure of:

(c) total comprehensive income for the period . . . showing separately the total amounts attributable to owners of the parent and to non-controlling interests.

There are various formats for the statement of changes in equity. However, the format illustrated in the Implementation Guidance on IFRS 1 is shown in figure 21.16.

Consolidated Statement of Changes in Equity (extract)
for the year ended 30 June 2010

	Attributable to owners of the parent					Non-controlling interests	Total equity
	Share capital	Available-for-sale financial assets	Revaluation surplus	Retained earnings	Total		
Balance at 1 July 2009	X	X	X	X	X	X	X
Profit for the period				X	X	X	X

FIGURE 21.16 Illustrative disclosures of NCI in the consolidated statement of changes in equity

Note that the information required by paragraph 106(a) could be provided as shown in figure 21.17.

Consolidated Statement of Changes in Equity (extract) for the year ended 30 June 2010		
	Consolidated $000	**Parent** $000
Total comprehensive income for the year	X	X
Attributable to:		
Owners of the parent	X	X
Non-controlling interests	X	X
	X	X

FIGURE 21.17 Illustrative disclosures of NCI in the consolidated statement of changes in equity

In relation to the information required by paragraph 106(d) concerning movements in the equity accounts, only the consolidated figures are required. However, it is expected that most entities will disclose both a consolidated and a parent column as in figure 21.17.

Paragraph 54 of IAS 1 states:

> As a minimum, the statement of financial position shall include line items that present the following amounts:
>
> . . .
>
> (q) non-controlling interests, presented within equity; and
> (r) issued capital and reserves attributable to owners of the parent.

Figure 21.18 illustrates this disclosure in the consolidated statement of financial position.

Consolidated Statement of Financial Position (extract) as at 30 June 2010		
	2010 $000	**2009** $000
EQUITY AND LIABILITIES		
Equity attributable to owners of the parent		
Share capital	X	X
Other components of equity	X	X
Retained earnings	X	X
	X	X
Non-controlling interests	X	X
Total equity	X	X

FIGURE 21.18 Illustrative disclosures of NCI in the consolidated statement of financial position

21.7.1 Other disclosures required by IAS 27

Paragraph 41(a)–(d) of IAS 27 requires the following disclosures in the consolidated financial statements:

> (a) the nature of the relationship between the parent and a subsidiary when the parent does not own, directly or indirectly through subsidiaries, more than half of the voting power;
> (b) the reasons why the ownership, directly or indirectly through subsidiaries, of more than half of the voting or potential voting power of an investee does not constitute control;
> (c) the end of the reporting period of the financial statements of a subsidiary when such financial statements are used to prepare consolidated financial statements and are as of a date or for a period that is different from that of the parent's financial statements, and the reason for using a different date or period; and

(d) the nature and extent of any significant restrictions (e.g. resulting from borrowing arrangements or regulatory requirements) on the ability of subsidiaries to transfer funds to the parent in the form of cash dividends or to repay loans or advances.

Where, in accordance with paragraph 10 of IAS 27, an entity elects not to prepare consolidated financial statements, paragraph 42 requires the following disclosures in the separate financial statements of the parent:

(a) the fact that the financial statements are separate financial statements; that the exemption from consolidation has been used; the name and country of incorporation or residence of the entity whose consolidated financial statements that comply with International Financial Reporting Standards have been produced for public use; and the address where those consolidated financial statements are obtainable;
(b) a list of significant investments in subsidiaries, jointly controlled entities and associates, including the name, country of incorporation or residence, proportion of ownership interest and, if different, proportion of voting power held; and
(c) a description of the method used to account for the investments listed under (b).

Other than those parent entities applying paragraph 10, in the separate financial statements of a parent the following disclosures are required by paragraph 43 of IAS 27:

(a) the fact that the statements are separate financial statements and the reasons why those statements are prepared if not required by law;
(b) a list of significant investments in subsidiaries, jointly controlled entities and associates, including the name, country of incorporation or residence, proportion of ownership interest and, if different, proportion of voting power held; and
(c) a description of the method used to account for the investments listed under (b);

and shall identify the financial statements prepared in accordance with paragraph 9 of this Standard, IAS 28 and IAS 31 to which they relate.

SUMMARY

Where entities form relationships with other entities, accounting standards often require additional disclosure so that users of financial statements can understand the economic substance of the entities involved. Some entities are classified as joint ventures, others as associates and others as subsidiaries. Where an entity is classified as a subsidiary of another, the parent, the accounting standards establish principles for the preparation of consolidated financial statements. These statements are in addition to those prepared for either the parent or a subsidiary as separate legal entities. The consolidated financial statements are prepared by adding the financial statements of a parent and each of its subsidiaries, with adjustments being made in this process.

An important decision is the determination of whether the relationship between two entities is such as to be classified as a parent–subsidiary relationship. The existence of this relationship is determined by whether one entity has the capacity to control another. The existence of control requires the assessment of the power an entity has to determine the financial and operating policies of another, and whether that power provides benefits to the controlling entity. This analysis requires the accountant to exercise judgement in analysing the specific relationships between entities, since the existence of control is not simply a matter of determining whether an entity owns a majority of shares in another.

In general, parent entities are responsible for the preparation of the consolidated financial statements. However, IAS 27 exempts parent entities that meet specified criteria from the preparation of these statements.

The consolidated financial statements prepared under IAS 27 are prepared using the entity concept of consolidation. This choice of concept has an effect where the subsidiary is not wholly owned by the parent. Application of this concept affects such things as the net assets to be included in the consolidated financial statements, the measurement and classification of a non-controlling interest, and the adjustments made for the effects of intragroup transactions.

Discussion questions

1. What is a subsidiary?
2. What is meant by the term 'control'?
3. Why should control be the key criterion for consolidation?

4. For what purposes are the consolidated financial statements prepared?
5. What factors could be considered in determining when one entity controls another?
6. Are potential voting rights considered when deciding if one entity controls another?
7. Is the non-controlling interest classified as a liability or as equity?
8. What is meant by the entity concept? How does the choice of this concept affect the preparation of consolidated financial statements?
9. What is meant by the parent entity concept? How does the choice of this concept affect the preparation of consolidated financial statements?
10. Has the IASB chosen the parent entity or the entity concept of consolidation? Why?
11. Where should the non-controlling interest be disclosed in the consolidated statement of financial position?
12. Which users of financial statements would be interested in consolidated financial statements rather than just the financial statements of the entities within a group?
13. Are only those entities in which another entity owns more than 50% of the issued shares classified as subsidiaries?
14. What benefits could be sought by an entity that obtains control over another entity?
15. Singapore Ltd establishes Peru Ltd for the sole purpose of developing a new product to be manufactured and marketed by Singapore Ltd. Singapore Ltd engages Mr Smith to lead the team to develop the new product. Mr Smith is named Managing Director of Peru Ltd at an annual salary of $100 000, $10 000 of which is advanced to Mr Smith by Peru Ltd at the time Peru Ltd is established. Mr Smith invests $10 000 in the project and receives all of Peru Ltd's initial issue of ten shares of voting ordinary shares.

    Singapore Ltd transfers $500 000 to Peru Ltd in exchange for 7%, 10-year debentures convertible at any time into 500 shares of Peru Ltd voting ordinary shares. Peru Ltd has enough shares authorised to fulfil its obligation if Singapore Ltd converts its debentures into voting ordinary shares.

    The constitution of Peru Ltd provides certain powers for the holders of voting common shares and the holders of securities convertible into voting ordinary shares that require a majority of each class voting separately. These include:

    (a) the power to amend the corporate purpose of Peru Ltd, and
    (b) the power to authorise and issue voting shares of securities convertible into voting shares.

    At the time Peru Ltd is established, there are no known economic legal impediments to Singapore Ltd converting the debt.

    Required
    Discuss whether Peru Ltd is a subsidiary of Singapore Ltd.

    Source: Adapted from Case V issued by the FASB as a part of its Consolidations project.

16. Canada Ltd is a production company that produces movies and television shows. It also owns cable television systems that broadcast its movies and television shows. Canada Ltd transferred to Chile Ltd its cable assets and the shares in its previously owned and recently acquired cable television systems, which broadcast Canada Ltd's movies. Chile Ltd assumed approximately $200 million in debt related to certain of the companies it acquired in the transaction. After the transfer date, Chile Ltd acquired additional cable television systems, incurring approximately $2 billion of debt, none of which was guaranteed by Canada Ltd.

    Chile Ltd was initially established as a wholly owned subsidiary of Canada Ltd. Several months after the transfer, Chile Ltd issued ordinary shares in an initial public offering, raising nearly $1 billion in cash and reducing Canada Ltd's interest in Chile Ltd to 41%. The remaining 59% of Chile Ltd's voting interest is widely held.

    The managing director of Chile Ltd was formerly manager of broadcast operations for Canada Ltd. Half the directors of Chile Ltd are or were executive officers of Canada Ltd.

    Chile Ltd and its subsidiaries have entered individually into broadcast contracts with Canada Ltd, pursuant to which Chile Ltd and its cable system subsidiaries must purchase 90% of their television shows from Canada Ltd at payment terms, and other terms and conditions of supply as determined from time to time by Canada Ltd. That agreement gives Chile Ltd and its cable television system subsidiaries the exclusive right to broadcast Canada Ltd's movies and television shows in specific geographic areas containing approximately 45% of the country's population. Chile Ltd and its cable television subsidiaries determine the advertising rates charged to their broadcast advertisers.

Under its agreement with Canada Ltd, Chile Ltd has limited rights to engage in businesses other than the sale of Canada Ltd's movies and television shows. In its most recent financial year, approximately 90% of Chile Ltd's sales were Canada Ltd movies and television shows. Canada Ltd provides promotional and marketing services and consultation to the cable television systems that broadcast its movies and television shows. Chile Ltd rents office space from Canada Ltd in its headquarters facility through a renewable lease agreement, which will expire in 5 years.

Required

1. Should Canada Ltd consolidate Chile Ltd? Why?
2. If Canada Ltd had not established Chile Ltd but had instead purchased 41% of Chile Ltd's voting shares on the open market, does this change your answer to requirement A? Why?

Source: Adapted from Case III issued by the FASB as a part of its Consolidations project.

17. Palau Ltd and India Ltd own 80% and 20% respectively of the ordinary shares that carry voting rights at a general meeting of shareholders of Cook Islands Ltd. Palau Ltd sells half of its interest to Kobe Ltd and buys call options from Kobe Ltd that are exercisable at any time at a premium to the market price when issued, and if exercised would give Palau Ltd its original 80% ownership interest and voting rights. At 30 June 2010, the options are out of the money.

Required

Discuss whether Palau Ltd is the parent of Cook Islands Ltd.

Source: Adapted from the Implementation Guidance to IAS 27.

18. Brunei Ltd, Burma Ltd and Bhutan Ltd each own one-third of the ordinary shares that carry voting rights at a general meeting of shareholders of Comoros Ltd. Brunei Ltd, Burma Ltd and Bhutan Ltd each have the right to appoint two directors to the board of Comoros Ltd. Brunei Ltd also owns call options that are exercisable at a fixed price at any time and, if exercised, would give it all the voting rights in Comoros Ltd. The management of Brunei Ltd does not intend to exercise the call options, even if Burma Ltd and Bhutan Ltd do not vote in the same manner as Brunei Ltd.

Required

Discuss whether Comoros Ltd is a subsidiary of any of the other entities.

Source: Adapted from the Implementation Guidance to IAS 27.

19. Vanuatu Ltd and Vietnam Ltd own 55% and 45% respectively of the ordinary shares that carry voting rights at a general meeting of shareholders of Tonga Ltd. Vietnam Ltd also holds debt instruments that are convertible into ordinary shares of Tonga Ltd. The debt can be converted at a substantial price, in comparison with Vietnam Ltd's net assets, at any time, and if converted would require Vietnam Ltd to borrow additional funds to make the payment. If the debt were to be converted, Vietnam Ltd would hold 70% of the voting rights and Vanuatu Ltd's interest would reduce to 30%. Given the effect of increasing its debt on its debt–equity ratio, Vietnam Ltd does not believe that it has the financial ability to enter into conversion of the debt.

Required

Discuss whether Vietnam Ltd is a parent of Tonga Ltd.

Source: Adapted from the Implementation Guidance to IAS 27.

20. Thailand Ltd has acquired, during the current year, the following investments in the shares issued by other companies:

Tuvala Ltd	$120 000 (40% of issued capital)
Tonga Ltd	$117 000 (35% of issued capital)

Thailand Ltd is unsure how to account for these investments and has asked you, as the auditor, for some professional advice.

Specifically, Thailand Ltd is concerned that it may need to prepare consolidated financial statements under IAS 27. To help you, the company has provided the following information about the two investee companies:

Tuvala Ltd

- The remaining shares in Tuvala Ltd are owned by a diverse group of investors who each hold a small parcel of shares.
- Historically, only a small number of the shareholders attend the general meetings or question the actions of the directors.
- Thailand Ltd has nominated three new directors and expects that they will be appointed at the next annual general meeting. The current board of directors has five members.

Tonga Ltd

- The remaining shares in Tonga Ltd are owned by a small group of investors who each own approximately 15% of the issued shares. One of these shareholders is Tuvala Ltd, which owns 17%.
- The shareholders take a keen interest in the running of the company and attend all meetings.
- Two of the shareholders, including Tuvala Ltd, already have representatives on the board of directors who have indicated their intention of nominating for re-election.

Required

1. Advise Thailand Ltd as to whether, under IAS 27, it controls Tuvala Ltd and/or Tonga Ltd. Support your conclusion.
2. Would your conclusion be different if the remaining shares in Tuvala Ltd were owned by three institutional investors each holding 20%? If so, why?

21. Russia Ltd owns 40% of the shares of Samoa Ltd, and holds the only substantial block of shares in that entity, no other party owning more than 3% of the shares. The annual general meeting of Samoa Ltd is to be held in a month's time. Two situations that may arise are:

- Russia Ltd will be able to elect a majority of Samoa Ltd's board of directors as a result of exercising its votes as the largest holder of shares. As only 75% of shareholders voted in the previous year's annual meeting, Russia Ltd may have the majority of the votes that are cast at the meeting.
- By obtaining the proxies of other shareholders and, after meeting with other shareholders who normally attend general meetings of Samoa Ltd, by convincing these shareholders to vote with it, Russia Ltd may obtain the necessary votes to have its nominees elected as directors of the board of Samoa Ltd, regardless of the attendance at the general meeting.

Required

Discuss the potential for Samoa Ltd being classified as a subsidiary of Russia Ltd.

22. On 1 March 2010, Napal Ltd acquired 40% of the voting shares of Pakistan Ltd. Under the company's constitution, each share is entitled to one vote. On the basis of past experience, only 65% of the eligible votes are typically cast at the annual general meetings of Pakistan Ltd. No other shareholder holds a major block of shares in Pakistan Ltd.

The financial year of Pakistan Ltd ends on 30 June each year. The directors of Napal Ltd argue that they are not required under IAS 27 to include Pakistan Ltd as a subsidiary in Napal Ltd's consolidated financial statements at 30 June 2010 as there is no conclusive evidence that Napal Ltd can control the financial and operating policies of Pakistan Ltd. The auditors of Napal Ltd disagree, referring specifically to past years' voting figures.

Required

Provide a report to Napal Ltd on whether it should regard Pakistan Ltd as a subsidiary in its preparation of consolidated financial statements at 30 June 2010.

23. IAS 27 implicitly adopts the entity concept of consolidation. In his dissenting opinion to the issue of IAS 27 in 2004, Mr Yamada argued that the IASB was taking the entity concept without giving enough consideration to the objectives of consolidated financial statements.

Required

1. What are the main objectives of preparing consolidated financial statements?

2. How would the choice of objectives affect the adoption of particular concepts of consolidation?

24. Japan Ltd has 37% of the voting interest in Maldives Ltd. An investment bank with which Japan has business relationships holds a 15% voting interest. Because of the closeness of the business relationship with the bank, Japan Ltd believes it can rely on the bank's support to ensure it cannot be outvoted at general meetings of Maldives Ltd.

Required
Given that there is no guarantee that the bank will always support Japan Ltd, particularly if there is a potential for economic loss, discuss whether Japan Ltd is a parent of Maldives Ltd.

25. Some have argued that the criteria for consolidation should be control plus significant risks and rewards of ownership or economic benefits. These parties argue that the consolidated financial statements are not meaningful if they include subsidiaries in which the parent's level of benefits is less than 50% or is not significant.

Required
Discuss:
(a) the place of a benefits criterion in the definition of control
(b) possible benefits that could occur as a result of obtaining control of another entity
(c) the need to place a specified level of benefits in the definition of control.

References

Leo, KJ 1987, *Consolidated financial statements*, Discussion Paper No. 11, Australian Accounting Research Foundation, Melbourne.

Pacter, P 1991, *Consolidation policy and procedures*, Discussion Memorandum, Financial Accounting Standards Board, Norwalk CT.

22 Consolidation: wholly owned subsidiaries

ACCOUNTING STANDARDS IN FOCUS

IFRS 3 *Business Combinations*

IAS 27 *Consolidated and Separate Financial Statements*

LEARNING OBJECTIVES

When you have studied this chapter, you should be able to:

- understand the nature of the group covered in this chapter, and the initial adjustments required in the consolidation worksheet
- explain how a consolidation worksheet is used
- prepare an acquisition analysis for the parent's acquisition in a subsidiary
- prepare the worksheet entries at the acquisition date, being the business combination valuation entries and the pre-acquisition entries
- prepare the worksheet entries in periods subsequent to the acquisition date, adjusting for movements in assets and liabilities since acquisition date and dividends from pre-acquisition equity
- prepare the worksheet entries where the subsidiary revalues its assets at acquisition date
- prepare the disclosures required by IFRS 3 and IAS 27
- explain the consolidation procedures for a reverse acquisition.

22.1 THE CONSOLIDATION PROCESS

This chapter discusses the preparation of consolidated financial statements. As stated in paragraph 18 of IAS 27 *Consolidated and Separate Financial Statements*, consolidated financial statements are the result of combining the financial statements of a parent and all its subsidiaries. (The determination of whether an entity is a parent or a subsidiary is discussed in chapter 21 of this book.) The two accounting standards mainly used in this chapter are IAS 27 and IFRS 3 *Business Combinations*. Chapter 11 of this book contains the accounting principles relevant for business combinations. An in-depth understanding of that chapter is essential to the preparation of consolidated financial statements because the parent's acquisition of shares in a subsidiary is simply one form of a business combination.

In IFRS 3 Appendix A, 'acquisition date' is defined as the date on which the acquirer effectively obtains control of the acquiree. As discussed in chapter 11, both the fair values of the identifiable assets and liabilities of the subsidiary and the consideration transferred are measured at the acquisition date. In this chapter, the only combinations considered are those where the parent acquires its controlling interest in a subsidiary and, as a result, owns all the issued shares of the subsidiary — the subsidiary is then a wholly owned subsidiary. This may occur by the parent buying all the shares in a subsidiary in one transaction, or by the parent acquiring the controlling interest after having previously acquired shares in the subsidiary.

Note, however, as discussed in chapter 21, control of a subsidiary does not necessarily involve the parent acquiring shares in a subsidiary. The consolidated financial statements of a parent and its subsidiaries include information about a subsidiary from the date the parent obtains control of the subsidiary, that is, from the acquisition date. A subsidiary continues to be included in the parent's consolidated financial statements until the parent no longer controls that entity, that is, until the date of disposal of the subsidiary.

Before undertaking the consolidation process, it may be necessary to make adjustments in relation to the content of the financial statements of the subsidiary:

- If the end of a subsidiary's reporting period does not coincide with the end of the parent's reporting period, adjustments must be made for the effects of significant transactions and events that occur between those dates, with additional financial statements being prepared where it is practicable to do so (IAS 27 para. 22). In most cases where there are different dates, the subsidiary will prepare adjusted financial statements as at the end of the parent's reporting period, so that adjustments are not necessary on consolidation. Where the preparation of adjusted financial statements is unduly costly, the financial statements of the subsidiary prepared at a different date from the parent may be used, subject to adjustments for significant transactions. However, as paragraph 23 states, for this to be a viable option, the difference between the ends of the reporting periods can be no longer than 3 months. Further, the length of the reporting periods, as well as any difference between the ends of the reporting periods, must be the same from period to period.
- The consolidated financial statements are to be prepared using uniform accounting policies for like transactions and other events in similar circumstances (IAS 27 para. 24). Where different policies are used, adjustments are made so that like transactions are accounted for under a uniform policy in the consolidated financial statements.

The preparation of the consolidated financial statements involves adding together the financial statements of the parent and its subsidiaries. As a part of this summation process, a number of adjustments are made, these being expressed in the form of journal entries:

- As required by IFRS 3, at the acquisition date the acquirer must recognise the identifiable assets and liabilities of the subsidiary at fair value. Adjusting the carrying amounts of the subsidiary's assets and liabilities to fair value and recognising any identifiable assets acquired and liabilities assumed as a part of the business combination but not recorded by the subsidiary is a part of the consolidation process. The entries used to make these adjustments are referred to in this chapter as the *business combination valuation entries*. As noted in section 22.2 of this chapter, these adjusting entries are generally not made in the records of the subsidiary itself but in a consolidation worksheet.
- Where the parent has an ownership interest (i.e. owns shares) in a subsidiary, adjusting entries are made, referred to in this chapter as the *pre-acquisition entries*. As noted in paragraph 18(a) of IAS 27, this involves eliminating the carrying amount of the parent's investment

in each subsidiary and the parent's portion of pre-acquisition equity in each subsidiary. The name of these entries is derived from the fact that the equity of the subsidiary at the acquisition date is referred to as pre-acquisition equity, and it is this equity that is being eliminated. These entries are also made in the consolidation worksheet and not in the records of the subsidiary.
- The third set of adjustments to be made is for transactions between the entities within the group subsequent to the acquisition date, including events such as sales of inventory or non-current assets. These intragroup transactions are referred to in IAS 27 paragraph 20, and adjustments for these transactions are discussed in detail in chapter 23 of this book.

In this chapter, the group under discussion is one where:
- there are only two entities within the group: one parent and one subsidiary (see figure 22.1)
- both entities have share capital
- the parent owns all the issued shares of the subsidiary, that is, the subsidiary is wholly owned (partially owned subsidiaries, where it is necessary to account for the non-controlling interest, are covered in chapter 24 of this book)
- there are no intragroup transactions between the parent and its subsidiary after the acquisition date.

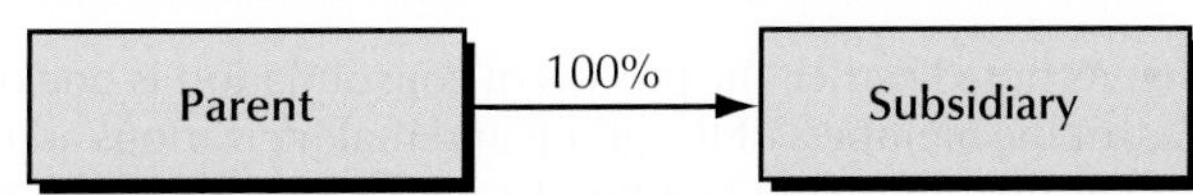

FIGURE 22.1 A wholly owned group

22.2 CONSOLIDATION WORKSHEETS

The consolidated financial statements are prepared by adding together the financial statements of the parent and the subsidiary. It is the *financial statements* of the parent and the subsidiary, rather than the underlying accounts, which are added together. There are no consolidated ledger accounts. The financial statements that are added together are the statements of financial position, statements of comprehensive income and statements of changes in equity prepared by the management of the parent and the subsidiary. Consolidated statements of cash flows must also be prepared, but these are not covered in this book.

To facilitate the addition process, particularly where there are a number of subsidiaries, as well as to make the necessary valuation and pre-acquisition entry adjustments, a worksheet or computer spreadsheet is often used. From the worksheet, the external statements are prepared — the consolidated statement of financial position, statement of comprehensive income and statement of changes in equity.

The format for the worksheet is presented in figure 22.2, which contains the information used for the consolidation of the parent, P Ltd, and the subsidiary, S Ltd.

Financial statements	Parent P Ltd	Subsidiary S Ltd		Adjustments Dr	Adjustments Cr		Consolidation
Retained earnings	25 000	12 000	1	5 000			32 000
Share capital	30 000	15 000	1	15 000			30 000
	55 000	27 000					62 000
Shares in S Ltd	20 000	—			20 000	1	—
Other assets	35 000	27 000					62 000
	55 000	27 000		20 000	20 000		62 000

FIGURE 22.2 Consolidation worksheet — basic format

Note the following points about the worksheet:

- Column 1 contains the names of the accounts, as the financial statements are combined on a line-by-line basis.
- Columns 2 and 3 contain the internal financial statements of the parent, P Ltd, and its subsidiary, S Ltd. These statements are obtained from the separate legal entities. The number of columns is expanded if there are more subsidiaries within the group.
- The next four columns, headed 'Adjustments', are used to make the adjustments required in the consolidation process. These include adjustments for valuations at acquisition date, pre-acquisition equity, and intragroup transactions such as sales of inventory between the parent and subsidiary. The adjustments, written in the form of journal entries, are recorded on the worksheet. Where there are many adjustments, each journal entry should be numbered so that it is clear which items are being affected by a particular adjustment entry. In figure 22.2 there is only one worksheet entry, hence the number '1' is entered against each adjustment item. The worksheet adjustment entry is:

(1) Retained earnings (opening balance)	Dr	5 000	
Share capital	Dr	15 000	
Shares in S Ltd	Cr		20 000

- As noted earlier, the process of consolidation is one of adding together the financial statements of the members of the group and making various adjustments. Hence, figures for each line item in the right-hand column, headed 'Consolidation', arise through addition and subtraction as you proceed horizontally across the worksheet. For example, for share capital:

$30 000 + $15 000 − $15 000 = $30 000

  The figures in the right-hand column provide the information for the preparation of the consolidated financial statements of P Ltd and S Ltd.
- In the 'Consolidation' column, the totals and subtotals are the result of adding the preceding items in that column rather than totalling items across the rows. For example, the total consolidated equity of $62 000 is determined by adding the retained earnings balance of $32 000 and the share capital balance of $30 000, both these balances appearing in the 'Consolidation' column. It is from this column that the information for preparing the consolidated statement of comprehensive income, statement of changes in equity and statement of financial position is obtained. These statements will not include all the line items in the consolidation worksheet. However, information for the notes to these statements is also obtained from line items in the worksheet.

In preparing the consolidated financial statements, *no* adjustments are made in the accounting records of the individual entities that constitute the group. The adjustment entries recorded in the columns of the worksheet do not affect the accounts of the individual entities. They are recorded in a separate consolidation journal, not in the journals of any of the member entities, and are then recorded on the consolidation worksheet. Hence, where consolidated financial statements are prepared over a number of years, a particular entry (such as a pre-acquisition entry) needs to be made every time a consolidation worksheet is prepared, because the entry never affects the actual financial statements of the individual entities.

22.3 THE ACQUISITION ANALYSIS

As noted in chapter 11 of this book, the parent records its investment in the subsidiary based upon the consideration transferred, often the equity shares of the parent. However, as noted in paragraph 33 of IFRS 3, where the business combination occurs by the parent exchanging its equity interests for the equity interests of the former owners of the subsidiary, the acquisition-date fair values of the acquiree's equity interests may be more reliably measurable than the acquisition-date fair values of the acquirer's equity interests. In that case, fair value of the acquiree's equity interests will be used in subsequent calculations.

At acquisition date, an acquisition analysis is undertaken to determine if there has been any goodwill acquired, or whether a bargain purchase has occurred. Paragraph 32 of IFRS 3 sets out the measurement of goodwill:

The acquirer shall recognise goodwill as of the acquisition date measured as the excess of (a) over (b) below:

(a) the aggregate of:
   (i) the consideration transferred measured in accordance with this Standard, which generally requires acquisition-date fair value (see paragraph 37);
   (ii) the amount of any non-controlling interest in the acquiree measured in accordance with this Standard; and
   (iii) in a business combination achieved in stages (see paragraphs 41 and 42), the acquisition-date fair value of the acquirer's previously held equity interest in the acquiree.

(b) the net of the acquisition-date amounts of the identifiable assets acquired and the liabilities assumed measured in accordance with this Standard.

In this chapter, because the parent acquires all the shares in the subsidiary, there is no effect due to (a)(ii). However due to (a)(iii), the acquisition analysis is affected by whether at acquisition date the parent has previously acquired any shares or other equity interests in the subsidiary.

22.3.1 Parent has no previously held equity interest in the subsidiary

In this case, the parent acquires all the shares of the subsidiary at acquisition date in one transaction. In terms of paragraph 32 of IFRS 3, goodwill arises when the consideration transferred [32(a)(i)] is greater than the net fair value of the identifiable assets and liabilities acquired 32[(b)]. Where the reverse occurs, income from a bargain purchase is recognised.

An acquisition analysis is conducted at acquisition date because it is necessary to recognise the identifiable assets and liabilities of the subsidiary at fair value, and to determine whether there has been an acquisition of goodwill or a gain. As noted in chapter 11, this may give rise to the recognition of assets and liabilities that are not recognised in the records of the subsidiary; for example, the business combination may give rise to intangibles that were not capable of being recognised in the subsidiary's records such as internally generated brands.

The first step in the consolidation process is to undertake the above acquisition analysis in order to obtain the information necessary for making both the business combination valuation and pre-acquisition entry adjustments for the consolidation worksheet. Consider the example in figure 22.3 on the next page.

The analysis at acquisition date consists of comparing the fair value of the consideration transferred and the net fair value of the identifiable assets and liabilities of the subsidiary at acquisition date. The net fair value of the subsidiary could be calculated by revaluing the assets and liabilities of the subsidiary from the carrying amounts to fair values, remembering that under IAS 12 *Income Taxes* where there is a difference between the carrying amount and the tax base caused by the revaluation, the tax effect of such a difference has to be recognised. However, in calculating the net fair value of the subsidiary, because particular information is required to prepare the valuation and pre-acquisition entries, the calculation is done by adding the recorded equity of the subsidiary (which represents the recorded net assets of the subsidiary) and the differences between the carrying amounts of the assets and liabilities and their fair values, adjusted for tax. The book equity of the subsidiary in figure 22.3 consists of:

$300 000 capital + $140 000 retained earnings

The equity relating to the differences in fair value and carrying amounts for assets and liabilities recorded by Sub Ltd — as well as for assets and liabilities not recognised by the subsidiary but recognised as being acquired as part of the business combination — is referred to in this chapter as the *business combination valuation reserve* (BCVR). This reserve is not an account recognised in the subsidiary's records, but it is recognised in the consolidation process as part of the business combination. For example, for land there is a difference of $20 000 in the fair value carrying amount and, on revaluation of the land to fair value, a business combination valuation reserve of $14 000, that is, $20 000(1 – 30%), is raised.

On 1 July 2010, Parent Ltd acquired all the issued share capital of Sub Ltd, giving in exchange 100 000 shares in Parent Ltd, these having a fair value of $5 per share. At acquisition date, the statements of financial position of Parent Ltd and Sub Ltd, and the fair values of Sub Ltd's assets and liabilities, were as follows:

	Parent Ltd	Sub Ltd	
	Carrying amount	Carrying amount	Fair value
EQUITY AND LIABILITIES			
Equity			
Share capital	$550 000	$300 000	
Retained earnings	350 000	140 000	
Total equity	900 000	440 000	
Liabilities			
Provisions	30 000	60 000	$ 60 000
Payables	27 000	34 000	34 000
Tax liabilities	10 000	6 000	6 000
Total liabilities	67 000	100 000	
Total equity and liabilities	$967 000	$540 000	
ASSETS			
Land	$120 000	$150 000	170 000
Equipment	620 000	480 000	330 000
Accumulated depreciation	(380 000)	(170 000)	
Shares in Sub Ltd	500 000		
Inventory	92 000	75 000	80 000
Cash	15 000	5 000	5 000
Total assets	$967 000	$540 000	

At acquisition date, Sub Ltd has an unrecorded patent with a fair value of $20 000, and a contingent liability with a fair value of $15 000. This contingent liability relates to a loan guarantee made by Sub Ltd which did not recognise a liability in its records because it did not consider it could reliably measure the liability. The tax rate is 30%.

FIGURE 22.3 Information at acquisition date

The acquisition analysis, including the determination of the goodwill of the subsidiary, is as shown in figure 22.4.

At 1 July 2010:

Net fair value of identifiable assets and liabilities of Sub Ltd	= $300 000 + $140 000 (recorded equity)
	+ ($170 000 – $150 000)(1 – 30%) (BCVR – land)
	+ ($330 000 – $310 000)(1 – 30%) (BCVR – equipment)
	+ ($80 000 – $75 000)(1 – 30%) (BCVR – inventory)
	+ $20 000(1 – 30%) (BCVR – patent)
	– $15 000(1 – 30%) (BCVR – provision for guarantee)
	= $475 000
Consideration transferred	= 100 000 × $5
	= $500 000
Goodwill	= $500 000 – $475 000
	= $25 000

FIGURE 22.4 Acquisition analysis — no previously held equity interests

The information from the completed acquisition analysis is used to prepare the adjustment entries for the consolidation worksheet. These entries are the business combination valuation entries and the pre-acquisition entries.

In this book, it is assumed that the tax base of the subsidiary's assets and liabilities is unchanged as a result of the parent's acquisition of the subsidiary. In some jurisdictions, where the group becomes the taxable entity, there is a change in the tax base to the fair value amounts. In this case, no tax effect would be recognised in relation to the assets and liabilities acquired.

22.3.2 Parent has previously held equity interest in the subsidiary

The situation used in figure 22.3 will be used here with the only difference being that on 1 July 2010 Parent Ltd acquires 80% [240 000 shares] of the shares in Sub Ltd, giving in exchange 80 000 shares in Parent Ltd, these having a fair value of $5 per share. Parent Ltd had previously acquired the other 20% [60 000] shares of Sub Ltd for $75 000. At 1 July 2010, this investment in Sub Ltd was recorded at $92 000. The investment was classified as available-for-sale financial instruments and measured at fair value, with $12 000 having previously been recognised in other comprehensive income. At 1 July 2010, these shares had a fair value of $100 000.

In accordance with IFRS 3, paragraph 12, Parent Ltd revalues the previously held investment to fair value, recognising the increment in current income, as well as transferring the amounts previously recognised in other comprehensive income to current income as a reclassification adjustment. The journal entries in Parent Ltd at acquisition date, both for the previously held investment as well as the acquisition of the remaining shares in Sub Ltd are as follows:

Shares in Sub Ltd	Dr	8 000	
Income	Cr		8 000
(Revaluation to fair value)			
Available-for-sale investments reserve	Dr	12 000	
Income	Cr		12 000
(Reclassification adjustment — available-for-sale financial instruments — on investment becoming a subsidiary)			
Shares in Sub Ltd	Dr	400 000	
Share Capital	Cr		400 000
(Acquisition of shares in Sub Ltd: 80 000 at $5 per share)			

The acquisition analysis is shown in figure 22.5.

At 1 July 2010:

Net fair value of identifiable assets and liabilities of Sub Ltd	= $300 000 + $140 000 (recorded equity)
	+ ($170 000 – $150 000)(1 – 30%) (BCVR – land)
	+ ($330 000 – $310 000)(1 – 30%) (BCVR – equipment)
	+ ($80 000 – $75 000)(1 – 30%) (BCVR – inventory)
	+ $20 000(1 – 30%) (BCVR – patent)
	– $15 000(1 – 30%) (BCVR – provision for guarantee)
	= $475 000
Consideration transferred	= 80 000 × $5
	= $400 000
Fair value of previously held equity interests	= $100 000
Aggregate investment	= $400 000 + $100 000
	= $500 000
Goodwill	= $500 000 – $475 000
	= $25 000

FIGURE 22.5 Acquisition analysis — previously held equity interests

As a result of the numbers used in this example, the goodwill number is the same as that shown in figure 22.4. There are no subsequent effects on the consolidation process because the parent had previously held an investment in the subsidiary.

22.4 WORKSHEET ENTRIES AT THE ACQUISITION DATE

As noted earlier, the consolidation process does not result in any entries being made in the actual records of either the parent or the subsidiary. The adjustment entries are made in the consolidation worksheet. Hence, adjustment entries need to be passed in each worksheet prepared, and these entries change over time. In this section, the adjustment entries that would be passed in a consolidation worksheet prepared *immediately after the acquisition date* are analysed.

22.4.1 Business combination valuation entries

In figure 22.3, there are three identifiable assets recognised by the subsidiary whose fair values differ from their carrying amounts at acquisition date, as well as an intangible asset and a contingent liability recognised as part of the business combination. The entries for the business combination valuations are done in the consolidation worksheet rather than in the records of the subsidiary (see section 22.6 for a discussion on making these adjustments in the records of the subsidiary itself). The identifiable assets and liabilities that require adjustment to fair value can be easily identified by reference to the acquisition analyses in figures 22.4 and 22.5, namely land, equipment, inventory, patent and the unrecorded guarantee. Goodwill also has to be recognised on consolidation. These differences are all recognised using business combination valuation entries.

Consolidation worksheet adjustment entries for each of these assets and the unrecorded liability are given in figure 22.6. Note that the goodwill adjustment does not give rise to a deferred tax asset or liability as it is assumed that this is an excluded difference under IAS 12. The total balance of the business combination valuation reserve is \$60 000. The adjustments to assets and liabilities at acquisition date could be achieved by one adjustment entry, giving a net balance to the business combination valuation reserve. However, in order to keep track of movements in that reserve as assets are depreciated or sold, liabilities paid or goodwill impaired, it is practical to prepare a valuation entry for each component of the valuation process. The valuation entries are passed in the adjustment columns of the worksheet, which is illustrated in section 22.4.3.

Business combination valuation entries			
(1) Land	Dr	20 000	
Deferred Tax Liability	Cr		6 000
Business Combination Valuation Reserve	Cr		14 000
(2) Accumulated Depreciation – Equipment	Dr	170 000	
Equipment	Cr		150 000
Deferred Tax Liability	Cr		6 000
Business Combination Valuation Reserve	Cr		14 000
(3) Inventory	Dr	5 000	
Deferred Tax Liability	Cr		1 500
Business Combination Valuation Reserve	Cr		3 500
(4) Patent	Dr	20 000	
Deferred Tax Liability	Cr		6 000
Business Combination Valuation Reserve	Cr		14 000
(5) Business Combination Valuation Reserve	Dr	10 500	
Deferred Tax Asset	Dr	4 500	
Provision for Loan Guarantee	Cr		15 000
(6) Goodwill	Dr	25 000	
Business Combination Valuation Reserve	Cr		25 000

FIGURE 22.6 Business combination valuation entries at acquisition date

22.4.2 Pre-acquisition entries

As noted in paragraph 22(a) of IAS 27, the pre-acquisition entries are required to eliminate the carrying amount of the parent's investment in the subsidiary and the parent's portion of pre-acquisition equity. The pre-acquisition entries, then, involve three areas:

- The investment account Shares in Subsidiary, as shown in the financial statements of the parent.
- The equity of the subsidiary at the acquisition date (i.e. the pre-acquisition equity). The pre-acquisition equity is not just the equity recorded by the subsidiary but includes the business combination valuation reserve recognised on consolidation via the valuation entries. Because the accounts containing pre-acquisition equity may change over time as a result of bonus dividends and reserve transfers, more than one pre-acquisition entry may be required in a particular year.
- Recognition of goodwill. Note that paragraph 21 of IAS 12 *Income Taxes* states that there is no recognition of a deferred tax liability in relation to goodwill because goodwill is a residual, and the recognition of a deferred tax liability would increase its carrying amount.

Using the example in figure 22.3, and reading the information from the acquisition analysis in figure 22.4 (including the business combination valuation reserve for the revalued assets including goodwill and the contingent liability), the pre-acquisition entry at acquisition date is as shown in figure 22.7. The pre-acquisition entry in this figure is numbered (7) because there were six previous valuation entries.

Pre-acquisition entry			
(7) Retained Earnings (1/7/10)	Dr	140 000	
Share Capital	Dr	300 000	
Business Combination Valuation Reserve	Dr	60 000	
Shares in Sub Ltd	Cr		500 000

FIGURE 22.7 Pre-acquisition entry at acquisition date

The pre-acquisition entry is necessary to avoid overstating the equity and net assets of the group. To illustrate, consider the information in figure 22.3 relating to Parent Ltd's acquisition of the shares of Sub Ltd. Having acquired the shares in Sub Ltd, Parent Ltd records the asset 'Shares in Sub Ltd' at $500 000. This asset represents the actual net assets of Sub Ltd; that is, the ownership of the shares gives Parent Ltd the right to the net assets of Sub Ltd. To include both the asset 'Shares in Sub Ltd' and the net assets of Sub Ltd in the consolidated statement of financial position would double-count the assets of the group, because the investment account is simply the right to the other assets. On consolidation, the investment account is therefore eliminated and, in its place, the net assets of the subsidiary are included in the consolidated statement of financial position.

Similarly, to include both the equity of the parent and the equity of the subsidiary in the consolidated statement of financial position would double-count the equity of the group. In the example, Parent Ltd has equity of $900 000, which is represented by its net assets including the investment in the subsidiary. Because the investment in the subsidiary is the same as the net assets of the subsidiary, the equity of the parent effectively relates to the net assets of the subsidiary. To include in the consolidated statement of financial position the equity of the subsidiary at acquisition date as well as the equity of the parent would double-count equity in relation to the net assets of the subsidiary.

22.4.3 Consolidation worksheet

Figure 22.8 contains the consolidation worksheet prepared at acquisition date, with adjustments being made for business combination valuation and pre-acquisition entries. The right-hand column reflects the consolidated statement of financial position, showing the position of the group. In relation to the figures in this column, note the following:

- In relation to the three equity accounts — share capital, business combination valuation reserve and retained earnings — only the parent's balances are carried into the consolidated statement of financial position. At acquisition date, all the equity of the subsidiary is pre-acquisition and eliminated.

- With the business combination valuation reserve, the valuation entry establishes the reserve, and the pre-acquisition entry eliminates it because it is by nature pre-acquisition equity.
- The assets of the subsidiary are carried forward into the consolidated statement of financial position at fair value.
- The debit and credit adjustment columns each total $755 000. This means that the adjusting journal entries have equal debits and credits, which is essential if the statement of financial position is to balance.

			Adjustments				
Financial statements	**Parent Ltd**	**Sub Ltd**		**Dr**	**Cr**		**Consolidation**
Retained earnings	350 000	140 000	7	140 000			350 000
Share capital	550 000	300 000	7	300 000			550 000
Business combination			5	10 500	14 000	1	—
valuation reserve			7	60 000	14 000	2	
					3 500	3	
					14 000	4	
					25 000	6	
	900 000	440 000					900 000
Provisions	30 000	60 000			15 000	5	105 000
Payables	27 000	34 000					61 000
Tax liabilities (net of tax assets)	10 000	6 000	5	4 500	6 000	1	31 000
					6 000	2	
					1 500	3	
	—	—			6 000	4	
	67 000	100 000					197 000
Total equity and liabilities	967 000	540 000					1 097 000
Cash	15 000	5 000					20 000
Land	120 000	150 000	1	20 000			290 000
Equipment	620 000	480 000			150 000	2	950 000
Accumulated depreciation	(380 000)	(170 000)	2	170 000			(380 000)
Shares in Sub Ltd	500 000	—			500 000	7	—
Inventory	92 000	75 000	3	5 000			172 000
Patent	—	—	4	20 000			20 000
Goodwill	—	—	6	25 000			25 000
Total assets	967 000	540 000		755 000	755 000		1 097 000

FIGURE 22.8 Consolidation worksheet at acquisition date

22.4.4 Subsidiary has recorded goodwill at acquisition date

In the example used in section 22.4.3, at acquisition date the subsidiary did not have any recorded goodwill. Consider the situation where the assets recorded by the subsidiary at acquisition date are the same as in figure 22.3 except that now there is recorded goodwill, as follows:

	Sub Ltd	
	Carrying amount	**Fair value**
Cash	$ 5 000	$ 5 000
Land	150 000	170 000
Equipment	480 000	330 000
Accumulated depreciation	(170 000)	
Goodwill	**10 000**	
Inventory	75 000	80 000
	$ 550 000	

Assume that the retained earnings balance is now $150 000 rather than $140 000. The acquisition analysis, assuming no previously held equity interests by the parent, is then as follows:

Net fair value of identifiable assets and liabilities of Sub Ltd	= $300 000 + $150 000 (equity) + ($170 000 − $150 000)(1 − 30%) (BCVR − land) + ($330 000 − $310 000)(1 − 30%) (BCVR − equipment) + ($80 000 − $75 000)(1 − 30%) (BCVR − inventory) + $20 000(1 − 30%) (BCVR − patent) − $15 000(1 − 30%) (BCVR − guarantee) **− $10 000 (goodwill)**
	= $475 000
	= 100 000 × $5
Consideration transferred	= $500 000
Goodwill	= $500 000 − $475 000
	= $25 000
Recorded goodwill	**= $10 000**
Unrecorded goodwill	**= $15 000**

Note that, since the first calculation of the acquisition analysis relates to the fair value of the *identifiable* assets, the goodwill of the subsidiary (i.e. the unidentifiable assets) must be subtracted. Further, it is necessary to calculate the additional goodwill not recorded by the subsidiary, this being the amount recognised on consolidation. The amount of goodwill recognised in the business combination valuation entry is $15 000:

(6) Goodwill	Dr	15 000	
Business Combination Valuation Reserve	Cr		15 000

The pre-acquisition entry is:

(7) Retained Earnings (1/7/10)	Dr	150 000	
Share Capital	Dr	300 000	
Business Combination Valuation Reserve	Dr	50 000	
Shares in Sub Ltd	Cr		500 000

The line item for goodwill in the consolidation worksheet would show:

Financial statements	Parent Ltd	Sub Ltd		Adjustments Dr		Adjustments Cr	Consolidation
Goodwill	—	10 000	6	15 000			25 000

The consolidated statement of financial position thus shows the total acquired goodwill of the subsidiary.

22.4.5 Subsidiary has recorded dividends at acquisition date

Using the information in figure 22.3, assume that one of the payables at acquisition date is a dividend payable of $10 000. The parent can acquire the shares in the subsidiary on a *cum div.* or an *ex div.* basis.

If the shares are acquired on a *cum div. basis*, then the parent acquires the right to the dividend declared at acquisition date. In this case, if Parent Ltd pays $500 000 for the shares in Sub Ltd, then the entry it passes to record the business combination is:

Shares in Sub Ltd	Dr	490 000	
Dividend Receivable	Dr	10 000	
Share Capital	Cr		500 000

In other words, the parent acquires two assets — the investment in the subsidiary and the dividend receivable. In calculating the goodwill in the subsidiary, using the information in figure 22.3 the acquisition analysis is:

Net fair value of identifiable assets and liabilities of Sub Ltd	= $300 000 + $140 000 (equity)
	+ ($170 000 – $150 000)(1 – 30%) (BCVR – land)
	+ ($330 000 – $310 000)(1 – 30%) (BCVR – equipment)
	+ ($80 000 – $75 000)(1 – 30%) (BCVR – inventory)
	+ $20 000(1 – 30%) (BCVR – patent)
	– $15 000(1 – 30%) (BCVR – guarantee)
	= $475 000
Consideration transferred	**= (100 000 × $5) – $10 000 (dividend receivable)**
	= $490 000
Goodwill	= $490 000 – $475 000
	= $15 000

In other words, the fair value of the consideration paid must be that for the investment in the subsidiary, excluding the amount paid for the dividend receivable. The pre-acquisition entry is:

(7) Retained Earnings (1/7/10)	Dr	140 000	
Share Capital	Dr	300 000	
Business Combination Valuation Reserve	Dr	50 000	
Shares in Sub Ltd	Cr		490 000

A further consolidation worksheet entry is also required:

Dividend Payable	Dr	10 000	
Dividend Receivable	Cr		10 000

This entry is necessary so that the consolidated statement of financial position shows only the assets and liabilities of the group, that is, only those benefits receivable from and obligations payable to entities external to the group. In relation to the dividend receivable recorded by Parent Ltd, this is not an asset of the group, because that entity does not expect to receive dividends from a party external to it. Similarly, the dividend payable recorded by the subsidiary is not a liability of the group. That dividend will be paid within the group, not to entities outside the group.

22.4.6 Gain on bargain purchase

In figure 22.3, Parent Ltd paid $500 000 for the shares in Sub Ltd. Consider the situation where Parent Ltd paid $470 000 for these shares. The acquisition analysis is as shown in figure 22.9 opposite.

As the net fair value of the identifiable assets and liabilities of the subsidiary is greater than the consideration transferred, in accordance with paragraph 36 of IFRS 3 the acquirer must firstly reassess the identification and measurement of the subsidiary's identifiable assets and liabilities as well as the measurement of the consideration transferred. The expectation under IFRS 3 is that the excess of the net fair value over the consideration transferred is usually the result of measurement errors rather than being a real gain to the acquirer. However, having confirmed the identification and measurement of both amounts paid and net assets acquired, if an excess still exists, under paragraph 34 it is recognised immediately in profit as a gain on bargain purchase.

Net fair value of identifiable assets and liabilities of Sub Ltd	= $300 000 + $140 000 (equity)
	+ ($170 000 − $150 000)(1 − 30%) (BCVR − land)
	+ ($330 000 − $310 000)(1 − 30%) (BCVR − equipment)
	+ ($80 000 − $75 000)(1 − 30%) (BCVR − inventory)
	+ $20 000(1 − 30%) (BCVR − patent)
	− $15 000(1 − 30%) (BCVR − guarantee)
	= $475 000
Consideration transferred	= $470 000
Gain on bargain purchase	= $475 000 − $470 000
	= $5000

FIGURE 22.9 Gain on bargain purchase

Existence of a gain on bargain purchase has no effect on the business combination valuation entries unless, as discussed in section 22.4.4, the subsidiary has previously recorded goodwill. In that case, a business combination revaluation entry crediting goodwill and debiting business combination valuation reserve for the amount of goodwill recorded by the subsidiary would be required.

The pre-acquisition entry for the situation in figure 22.9 is as shown in figure 22.10.

Pre-acquisition entry			
(7) Retained Earnings (1/7/10)	Dr	140 000	
Share Capital	Dr	300 000	
Business Combination Valuation Reserve	Dr	35 000	
Excess	Cr		5 000
Shares in Sub Ltd	Cr		470 000

FIGURE 22.10 Pre-acquisition entry at acquisition date — gain on bargain purchase

22.5 WORKSHEET ENTRIES SUBSEQUENT TO THE ACQUISITION DATE

At acquisition date, the business combination valuation entries result in the economic entity recognising assets and liabilities not recorded by the subsidiaries. Subsequently, changes in these assets and liabilities occur as assets are depreciated or sold, liabilities paid and goodwill impaired. Movements in pre-acquisition equity also occur as dividends are paid or declared and transfers are made within equity.

22.5.1 Business combination valuation entries

In the example used in figure 22.3, there were five items for which valuation entries were made — land, equipment, inventory, patent and the guarantee. In this section, a 3-year time period subsequent to the acquisition date, 1 July 2010, is analysed (giving an end of reporting period of 30 June 2013) with the following events occurring:

- the land is sold in the 2012–13 period
- the equipment is depreciated on a straight-line basis over a 5-year period
- the inventory on hand at 1 July 2010 is all sold by 30 June 2011, the end of the first year
- the patent has an indefinite life, and is tested for impairment annually, with an impairment loss of $5000 recognised in the 2011–12 period
- the liability for the guarantee results in a payment of $10 000 in June 2011, with no further liability existing
- goodwill is written down by $5000 in the 2011–12 period as a result of an impairment test.

Each of the assets will now be analysed separately with the consolidation worksheet subsequently shown for the 2012–13 period.

Land

At acquisition date, 1 July 2010, the business combination valuation entry is:

Land	Dr	20 000	
Deferred Tax Liability	Cr		6 000
Business Combination Valuation Reserve	Cr		14 000

At *30 June 2011*, because the land is still on hand, the same valuation entry is made in the consolidation worksheet used to prepare the consolidated financial statements at that date. It is assumed in this period that the asset is not held for sale and is recorded at cost.

Assume in the *2011–12 financial period* that the land is classified as held for sale and is accounted for under IFRS 5 *Non-current Assets Held for Sale and Discontinued Operations*. The land is then recorded at the lower of its carrying amount and fair value less costs to sell. Assuming the carrying amount is the lower value, then the business combination valuation entry in the consolidation worksheet prepared at 30 June 2012 is the same as that for 30 June 2011.

Assume in the *2012–13 financial period* that the land is sold for $200 000, with $1000 costs to sell incurred. Sub Ltd will record a gain on sale of $49 000 (i.e. $200 000 – $150 000 – $1000). From the group's perspective, the gain on sale is only $29 000 (i.e. $200 000 – $170 000 – $1000). Hence, on consolidation, an adjustment to reduce the recorded gain by $20 000 is required. The factor causing the difference in gain on sale is the carrying amount of the land sold. The cost of the land is greater to the group than to the subsidiary. As the asset has been sold, the deferred tax liability is reversed, with an adjustment being made to income tax expense. Assuming the subsidiary records both proceeds on sale and carrying amount of land sold, the valuation entry at 30 June 2012 is:

Carrying Amount of Land Sold	Dr	20 000	
Income Tax Expense	Cr		6 000
Business Combination Valuation Reserve	Cr		14 000

Alternatively, if the subsidiary's financial statements show a gain on sale:

Gain on Sale of Land	Dr	20 000	
Income Tax Expense	Cr		6 000
Business Combination Valuation Reserve	Cr		14 000

In subsequent periods, the valuation entry is:

Retained Earnings (opening balance)	Dr	14 000	
Business Combination Valuation Reserve	Cr		14 000

This entry has no effect on total equity. It reflects the fact that whereas the subsidiary recognised the increase in worth of the land in retained earnings, the group recognised the increased value in the business combination valuation reserve. Where revalued assets are derecognised, as noted in paragraph 41 of IAS 16 *Property, Plant and Equipment*, it is usual business practice to transfer the revaluation reserve to retained earnings. If this principle is applied on consolidation, then the business combination valuation entries in the year of sale of the land are:

Carrying Amount of Land Sold/Gain on Sale	Dr	20 000	
Income Tax Expense	Cr		6 000
Business Combination Valuation Reserve	Cr		14 000
Business Combination Valuation Reserve	Dr	14 000	
Transfer from Business Combination Valuation Reserve	Cr		14 000

These two entries can be simplified into one entry:

Carrying Amount of Land Sold/Gain on Sale	Dr	20 000	
Income Tax Expense	Cr		6 000
Transfer from Business Combination Valuation Reserve	Cr		14 000

Because this entry has no effect on retained earnings, no consolidation worksheet entries are required in subsequent periods.

Equipment

The business combination valuation entry at 1 July 2010 is:

Accumulated Depreciation – Equipment	Dr	170 000	
Equipment	Cr		150 000
Deferred Tax Liability	Cr		6 000
Business Combination Valuation Reserve	Cr		14 000

The asset is depreciated on a straight-line basis evenly over a 5-year period at 20% p.a. Because the asset is recognised on consolidation at an amount that is $20 000 greater than that recognised in the records of the subsidiary, the depreciation expense to the group must also be greater. The difference in depreciation reflects the extra amount paid for the equipment by the group. The adjustment for depreciation results in changes to the carrying amount of the asset. Differences between the tax base and the carrying amount are reflected in the deferred tax liability. As the asset is recovered by use, the deferred tax liability recognised at acquisition date is progressively reversed, with the movement being in proportion to depreciation charges — in this case 20% p.a. The adjustments for depreciation and the related tax effects are recognised in the consolidation worksheet valuation entries in the periods subsequent to acquisition date.

The business combination valuation entries for equipment at 30 June 2011 are:

Accumulated Depreciation – Equipment	Dr	170 000	
Equipment	Cr		150 000
Deferred Tax Liability	Cr		6 000
Business Combination Valuation Reserve	Cr		14 000
Depreciation Expense	Dr	4 000	
Accumulated Depreciation	Cr		4 000
(20% × $20 000 p.a.)			
Deferred Tax Liability	Dr	1 200	
Income Tax Expense	Cr		1 200
(20% × $6000, or 30% × $4000 p.a.)			

Note that the first entry is the same as that made at acquisition date, with the other two entries reflecting subsequent depreciation and tax-effect changes.

The valuation entries at 30 June 2013 reflect the need to adjust for 3 years depreciation (i.e. for two previous periods and a current period):

Accumulated Depreciation – Equipment	Dr	170 000	
Equipment	Cr		150 000
Deferred Tax Liability	Cr		6 000
Business Combination Valuation Reserve	Cr		14 000
Depreciation Expense	Dr	4 000	
Retained Earnings (1/7/12)	Dr	8 000	
Accumulated Depreciation	Cr		12 000
(20% × $20 000 p.a.)			

Deferred Tax Liability	Dr	3 600	
Income Tax Expense	Cr		1 200
Retained Earnings (1/7/12)	Cr		2 400
(20% × $6000, or 30% × $4000 p.a.)			

The equipment is fully depreciated by 30 June 2015. In that year, the valuation entries for equipment are:

Accumulated Depreciation – Equipment	Dr	170 000	
Equipment	Cr		150 000
Deferred Tax Liability	Cr		6 000
Business Combination Valuation Reserve	Cr		14 000
Depreciation Expense	Dr	4 000	
Retained Earnings (1/7/14)	Dr	16 000	
Accumulated Depreciation	Cr		20 000
(20% × $20 000 p.a.)			
Deferred Tax Liability	Dr	6 000	
Income Tax Expense	Cr		1 200
Retained Earnings (1/7/14)	Cr		4 800
(20% × $6000, or 30% × $4000 p.a.)			

Since the equipment is fully consumed and then derecognised, a further entry is required:

Equipment	Dr	150 000	
Accumulated Depreciation – Equipment	Cr		150 000

These entries could be combined as follows:

Depreciation Expense	Dr	4 000	
Income Tax Expense	Cr		1 200
Retained Earnings (1/7/14)	Dr	11 200	
Business Combination Valuation Reserve	Cr		14 000

As with the land example, and because the asset is derecognised at 30 June 2015, the credit could be made to Transfer from Business Combination Valuation Reserve instead of to Business Combination Valuation Reserve. Consequently, there would be no need for any valuation adjustment entries for equipment in subsequent periods.

Inventory

The valuation entry for inventory at acquisition date, 1 July 2010, is:

Inventory	Dr	5 000	
Deferred Tax Liability	Cr		1 500
Business Combination Valuation Reserve	Cr		3 500

The key event affecting the subsequent accounting for inventory is the sale of the inventory by the subsidiary. Assume the inventory is sold in the 2010–11 period for $90 000. The subsidiary records cost of sales at the carrying amount of $75 000, whereas the cost to the group is $80 000. In the consolidation worksheet, instead of the $5000 adjustment to inventory, a $5000 adjustment to cost of sales is required. As the inventory is sold, the deferred tax liability is reversed. As with land and equipment, the business combination valuation reserve is transferred to retained earnings because the asset is derecognised.

The valuation entry at 30 June 2011 is then:

Cost of Sales	Dr	5 000	
Income Tax Expense	Cr		1 500
Transfer from Business Combination Valuation Reserve	Cr		3 500

Because this entry has a zero effect on closing retained earnings, no consolidation worksheet entry is required in subsequent years.

In relation to the sale of inventory, a comparison of what is recorded by Sub Ltd and what is shown in the consolidated financial statements at 30 June 2011 is as follows:

	Sub Ltd	Consolidation	
Sales	$90 000	$90 000	
Cost of sales	75 000	80 000	(75 000 + 5 000)
Profit before income tax	15 000	10 000	
Income tax expense	4 500	3 000	(4 500 – 1 500)
Profit	$10 500	$ 7 000	

If at 30 June 2011 only 80% of the inventory had been sold, then the valuation entry must reflect adjustments both to cost of sales and ending inventory. The consolidation worksheet valuation entries, reflecting the 80% sold and the 20% still on hand, are:

Cost of Sales	Dr	4 000	
Income Tax Expense	Cr		1 200
Transfer from Business Combination Valuation Reserve	Cr		2 800
[This entry has no effect on the consolidation worksheets of subsequent periods.]			
Inventory	Dr	1 000	
Deferred Tax Liability	Cr		300
Business Combination Valuation Reserve	Cr		700

Assuming the inventory is all sold by 30 June 2012, the valuation entry in the consolidation worksheet prepared at that date is:

Cost of Sales	Dr	1 000	
Income Tax Expense	Cr		300
Transfer from Business Combination Valuation Reserve	Cr		700

Patent

The business combination valuation entry at acquisition date, 1 July 2010, is:

Patent	Dr	20 000	
Deferred Tax Liability	Cr		6 000
Business Combination Valuation Reserve	Cr		14 000

This entry is used in each year that the patent continues to have an indefinite life. A change occurs only if there is an impairment loss. In this example, an impairment loss of $5000 occurs in the 2011–12 period. The business combination valuation entries at 30 June 2012 are:

Patent	Dr	20 000	
Deferred Tax Liability	Cr		6 000
Business Combination Valuation Reserve	Cr		14 000

Impairment Loss	Dr	5 000	
Accumulated Impairment Losses	Cr		5 000
Deferred Tax Liability	Dr	1 500	
Income Tax Expense	Cr		1 500

The entries at 30 June 2013 are:

Patent	Dr	20 000	
Deferred Tax Liability	Cr		6 000
Business Combination Valuation Reserve	Cr		14 000
Retained Earnings (1/7/12)	Dr	3 500	
Deferred Tax Liability	Dr	1 500	
Accumulated Impairment Losses	Cr		5 000

Liability — Provision for Loan Guarantee

The business combination valuation entry at 1 July 2010 is:

Business Combination Valuation Reserve	Dr	10 500	
Deferred Tax Asset	Dr	4 500	
Provision for Loan Guarantee	Cr		15 000

If the liability is paid or derecognised, the above entry changes. In this example, a payment of $10 000 is made during the first year in relation to the liability. The subsidiary records an expense of $10 000. Since there is no expense to the group, it must be eliminated on consolidation. Instead, a gain of $5000 is recognised by the group as the liability of $15 000 is settled for $10 000. The business combination valuation entry at 30 June 2011 is:

Transfer from Business Combination Valuation Reserve	Dr	10 500	
Income Tax Expense	Dr	4 500	
Expense	Cr		10 000
Gain on De-recognition of Loan Guarantee	Cr		5 000

No entry is required on 30 June 2013.

Goodwill

Impairment tests for goodwill are undertaken annually. Goodwill is written down by $5000 in the 2011–12 period as a result of an impairment test. In the consolidation worksheet prepared at 30 June 2012, the business combination valuation entry will recognise the $25 000 goodwill acquired. However, a further entry is required to recognise the impairment of the goodwill:

Impairment Expense	Dr	5 000	
Accumulated Impairment Losses	Cr		5 000

The entries at 30 June 2013 are:

Goodwill	Dr	25 000	
Business Combination Valuation Reserve	Cr		25 000
Retained Earnings (1/7/12)	Dr	5 000	
Accumulated Impairment Losses	Cr		5 000

Business combination valuation entries at 30 June 2013

The valuation entries for all assets at 30 June 2013 are as shown in figure 22.11.

(1) Carrying Amount of Land Sold/Gain on Sale	Dr	20 000	
Income Tax Expense	Cr		6 000
Transfer from Business Combination Valuation Reserve	Cr		14 000
(2) Accumulated Depreciation – Equipment	Dr	170 000	
Equipment	Cr		150 000
Deferred Tax Liability	Cr		6 000
Business Combination Valuation Reserve	Cr		14 000
Depreciation Expense	Dr	4 000	
Retained Earnings (1/7/12)	Dr	8 000	
Accumulated Depreciation	Cr		12 000
(20% × $20 000 p.a.)			
Deferred Tax Liability	Dr	3 600	
Income Tax Expense	Cr		1 200
Retained Earnings (1/7/12)	Cr		2 400
(20% × $6 000, or 30% × $4 000 p.a.)			
(3) Patent	Dr	20 000	
Deferred Tax Liability	Cr		6 000
Business Combination Valuation Reserve	Cr		14 000
Retained Earnings (1/7/12)	Dr	3 500	
Deferred Tax Liability	Dr	1 500	
Accumulated Impairment Losses	Cr		5 000
(4) Goodwill	Dr	25 000	
Business Combination Valuation Reserve	Cr		25 000
Retained Earnings (1/7/12)	Dr	5 000	
Accumulated Impairment Losses	Cr		5 000

FIGURE 22.11 Business combination valuation entries at 30 June 2013

22.5.2 Pre-acquisition entries

The pre-acquisition entry at acquisition date, relating to the example in figure 22.3, is:

Retained Earnings (1/7/10)	Dr	140 000	
Share Capital	Dr	300 000	
Business Combination Valuation Reserve	Dr	60 000	
Shares in Sub Ltd	Cr		500 000

There are three events that can cause a change in this entry after acquisition date:

- transfers from business combination valuation reserve, as undertaken in the consolidation worksheet valuation entries
- bonus dividends paid from pre-acquisition equity
- transfers to and from pre-acquisition retained earnings and other reserves.

In any particular year, some of these events will have occurred in previous periods, and some will occur in the current period. The pre-acquisition entries for the current period consist of the combined pre-acquisition entry at the beginning of the current period — that is, the pre-acquisition entry at the acquisition date adjusted for the effects of all pre-acquisition equity changes up to the beginning of the current period — and entries relating to changes in pre-acquisition equity in the current period.

Changes in business combination valuation entries

For the items affected by business combination valuation adjustments, three changes since acquisition date have affected the pre-acquisition entry. Two of these occurred in the year ending 30 June 2011:

- the sale of inventory on hand at acquisition date
- the payment and write-off of the loan guarantee liability.

In both cases, the adjustment was made to Transfer from Business Combination Valuation Reserve in the business combination valuation entries at 30 June 2011.

This transfer affects the pre-acquisition entry because the valuation reserves are created in the valuation entries and, being part of pre-acquisition equity, are eliminated in the pre-acquisition entry — see, for example, the worksheet in figure 22.8. If the valuation entry gives rise to a *transfer from* the business combination valuation reserve, instead of a business combination valuation reserve, then the adjustment in the pre-acquisition entry must also be made to the transfer account. This is done by adding another entry to the pre-acquisition entry in the year of transfer (see below). The need to make an extra adjustment in the pre-acquisition entry should be obvious from viewing the valuation entries. It is only if there is, or has been in previous periods, a transfer in the valuation entries that this flows through to the pre-acquisition entry.

The pre-acquisition entries at *30 June 2011* affected by the sale of inventory and the payment of the loan guarantee liability are then:

Retained Earnings (1/7/10)	Dr	140 000	
Share Capital	Dr	300 000	
Business Combination Valuation Reserve	Dr	60 000	
Shares in Sub Ltd	Cr		500 000
Business Combination Valuation Reserve	Dr	7 000	
Transfer from Business Combination Valuation Reserve	Cr		7 000
($3500 inventory and $(10 500) loan guarantee liability)			

In the consolidation worksheet at *30 June 2012*, assuming no other transfers or events, the pre-acquisition entry is the combination of the two entries from the previous period's worksheet:

Retained Earnings (1/7/11)*	Dr	133 000	
Share Capital	Dr	300 000	
Business Combination Valuation Reserve**	Dr	67 000	
Shares in Sub Ltd	Cr		500 000
*$140 000 + $3500 (inventory) – $10 500 (loan guarantee)			
**$60 000 – $3500 (inventory) + $10 500 (loan guarantee)			

In the 2012–13 period — the current period — pre-acquisition balances are affected by the sale of the land. As can be seen from the valuation entry for land in section 22.5.1, in the current period there is a transfer from the business combination valuation reserve to retained earnings of $14 000. This requires the following entry to be included in the pre-acquisition entries for the current period:

Transfer from Business Combination Valuation Reserve	Dr	14 000	
Business Combination Valuation Reserve	Cr		14 000

In summary, the pre-acquisition entries to be passed in the consolidation worksheet at 30 June 2013 are as shown in figure 22.12. These are affected by the sale of inventory and payment of the loan guarantee in 2010–11, the impairment of goodwill in 2011–12 and the sale of land in 2012–13.

(5) Retained Earnings (1/7/12)*	Dr	133 000	
Share Capital	Dr	300 000	
Business Combination Valuation Reserve**	Dr	67 000	
Shares in Sub Ltd	Cr		500 000
*$140 000 + $3500 (inventory) – $10 500 (loan guarantee)			
**$60 000 – $3500 (inventory) + $10 500 (loan guarantee)			
Transfer from Business Combination Valuation Reserve	Dr	14 000	
Business Combination Valuation Reserve	Cr		14 000

FIGURE 22.12 Pre-acquisition entries at 30 June 2013

Figure 22.13 shows the consolidation worksheet at 30 June 2013 containing the adjustment entries from figures 22.11 and 22.12.

FIGURE 22.13 Consolidation worksheet at 30 June 2013

Financial statements	Parent Ltd	Sub Ltd	Adjustments				Consolidation
				Dr	Cr		
Revenues	120 000	95 000					215 000
Expenses	85 000	72 000	2	4 000			161 000
	35 000	23 000					54 000
Gain on sale of non-current assets	15 000	31 000	1	20 000			26 000
Profit before tax	50 000	54 000					80 000
Income tax expense	15 000	21 000			6 000	1	
					1 200	2	28 800
Profit for the period	35 000	33 000					51 200
Retained earnings (1/7/12)	420 000	220 000	2	8 000	2 400	2	
			3	5 000			
			4	5 000			
			5	133 000			491 400
Transfer from business combination valuation reserve	—	—	5	14 000	14 000	1	—
Retained earnings (30/6/13)	455 000	253 000					542 600
Share capital	550 000	300 000	5	300 000			550 000
Business combination valuation reserve	—		5	67 000	14 000	2	
					14 000	3	
					25 000	4	
					14 000	5	—
	1 005 000	553 000					1 092 600
Provisions	40 000	40 000					80 000
Payables	32 000	24 000					56 000
Tax liabilities	12 000	16 000	2	3 600	6 000	2	
					6 000	3	36 400
	84 000	80 000					172 400
Total equity and liabilities	1 089 000	633 000					1 265 000
Cash	65 000	95 000					160 000
Land	170 000	50 000					220 000
Equipment	750 000	683 000			150 000	2	1 283 000
Accumulated depreciation	(448 000)	(270 000)	2	170 000	12 000	2	(560 000)

(continued)

FIGURE 22.13 *(continued)*

Financial statements	Parent Ltd	Sub Ltd	Adjustments				Consolidation
				Dr	Cr		
Shares in Sub Ltd	500 000	—			500 000	5	—
Inventory	52 000	75 000					127 000
Patent	—	—	3	20 000			20 000
Accumulated impairment losses	—	—			5 000	3	(5 000)
Goodwill	—	—	4	25 000			25 000
Accumulated impairment losses					5 000	4	(5 000)
Total assets	1 089 000	633 000		774 600	774 600		1 265 000

22.5.3 Dividends paid/payable from subsidiary equity

Prior to May 2008, both IAS 27 *Consolidated and Separate Financial Statements* and IAS 18 *Revenue* required dividends from pre-acquisition equity to be accounted for differently from dividends from post-acquisition equity. As stated in paragraph 32 of IAS 18, dividends from pre-acquisition equity were accounted for as a reduction in the cost of the investment. In contrast, dividends from post-acquisition equity were accounted for as revenue by the parent.

In May 2008, the IASB issued amendments to IAS 27 relating to the cost of an investment in a subsidiary, jointly controlled entity or associate. These amendments:

- deleted the definition of the cost method from IAS 27
- inserted paragraph 38A into IAS 27. Paragraph 38A states:

  > An entity shall recognise a dividend from a subsidiary, jointly controlled entity or associate in profit or loss in its separate financial statements when its right to receive the dividend is established.

- removed the last two sentences of paragraph 32 of IAS 18 dealing with the accounting for dividends.

The effect of these changes is that all dividends paid or payable by a subsidiary to a parent are to be recognised as revenue by the parent. As noted in paragraph BC66H of the Basis for Conclusions to the amendments, 'the requirement to separate the retained earnings of an entity into pre-acquisition and post-acquisition components as a method for assessing whether a dividend is a recovery of its associated investment has been removed from IFRSs'.

In its response to the IASB's exposure draft on the amendments, the Australian Accounting Standards Board(AASB) made the following response to the question of whether it agreed with the proposed requirement for an investor to recognise as income dividends received from a subsidiary (see www.aasb.com.au):

> Whilst the AASB considers that the proposed changes are a departure from a conceptually pure application of the cost method, the AASB acknowledges that it is suitable on pragmatic grounds. The AASB also notes that it can be argued that the identification of particular dividends as being sourced from either pre or post-acquisition retained earnings is arbitrary in many circumstances.

Note that the AASB recognises that the amendments depart from the application of the cost method, and that its agreement with the amendments is on pragmatic grounds.

In its response to ED 160, the Institute of Chartered Accountants in Australia made the following statement in relation to the recognition of dividends by the parent as income (see www.aasb.com.au):

> We agree with the proposed requirement for an investor to recognise as income dividends received, as this aligns with the fair value basis of measurement for the investment. There are also practical benefits as it avoids the difficult and at times arbitrary process of allocating retained earnings between pre and post acquisition reserves, and also avoids the dividend trap whereby dividends paid by a subsidiary are deemed pre-acquisition and therefore not available to be passed up a group to the ultimate shareholders.

Note that the Institute's argument is based on the parent's application of fair value rather than cost in accounting for the investment in the subsidiary, as well as on pragmatic grounds.

The amendments mean that there are no effects on the pre-acquisition entry as a result of the subsidiary paying or declaring dividends. Accounting for dividends on consolidation is then treated as an intragroup transaction. Intragroup transactions are covered in chapter 23.

Bonus share dividends

Bonus share dividends involve a subsidiary issuing shares instead of cash. There are no entries in the records of the parent as a result of this transaction. Hence, the IASB's amendments to IAS 27 do not apply to this transaction. The effect to be adjusted for in the pre-acquisition entry is that this transaction results in moving pre-acquisition equity from one account to another, with no change in total pre-acquisition equity.

Assume that in the 2010–11 period the subsidiary pays a dividend of $3000 by the issue of bonus shares. The entries passed in the parent and the subsidiary as a result of the dividend are:

Parent	Subsidiary			
No entry required	Bonus Dividend Paid	Dr	3 000	
	Share Capital	Cr		3 000

No entry is required by the parent because its share of wealth in the subsidiary is unchanged by the bonus share issue. The pre-acquisition entries for the 2010–11 period are shown in figure 22.14.

Retained Earnings (1/7/10)	Dr	140 000	
Share Capital	Dr	300 000	
Business Combination Valuation Reserve	Dr	60 000	
Shares in Subsidiary	Cr		500 000
Share Capital	Dr	3 000	
Bonus Dividend Paid	Cr		3 000

FIGURE 22.14 Dividend provided for in the current period

The effect of the bonus dividend is to increase the share capital of the subsidiary by $3000 and to reduce the retained earnings by the same amount. There is no overall change in the pre-acquisition equity of the subsidiary, just a transfer from one equity account to another. Accordingly, there is no change in the balance of the investment account in the records of the parent.

The pre-acquisition entry in subsequent periods is:

Retained Earnings (opening balance)*	Dr	137 000	
Share Capital	Dr	303 000	
Business Combination Valuation Reserve	Dr	60 000	
Shares in Subsidiary	Cr		500 000
*$140 000 – $3000			

22.5.4 Pre-acquisition reserve transfers

From time to time the subsidiary may transfer retained earnings to reserves, or make transfers from reserves to retained earnings. These do not cause any change in the total pre-acquisition equity but simply change the composition of that equity. Therefore, there is no change in the investment account recorded by the parent entity. In fact, the parent is unaffected by these transfers.

Assume for the cases illustrated below that the pre-acquisition entry for the year ending 30 June 2011, apart from the effect of reserve transfers, is as follows:

Retained Earnings (1/7/10)	Dr	140 000	
Share Capital	Dr	300 000	
Business Combination Valuation Reserve	Dr	60 000	
Shares in Subsidiary	Cr		500 000

Case 1: Transfers from retained earnings to other reserves

Assume that in the 2010–11 period the subsidiary transfers $4000 to general reserve from retained earnings. The entry passed in the subsidiary as a result of the transfer is:

Transfer to General Reserve	Dr	4 000	
General Reserve	Cr		4 000

The pre-acquisition entries for the 2010–11 period are shown in figure 22.15.

Retained Earnings (1/7/10)	Dr	140 000	
Share Capital	Dr	300 000	
Business Combination Valuation Reserve	Dr	60 000	
Shares in Subsidiary	Cr		500 000
General Reserve	Dr	4 000	
Transfer to General Reserve	Cr		4 000

FIGURE 22.15 Transfer to general reserve in the current period

As both the Transfer to General Reserve and the General Reserve accounts are pre-acquisition in nature, they are eliminated as part of the pre-acquisition entry. The pre-acquisition entry in subsequent periods is:

Retained Earnings (opening balance)*	Dr	136 000	
Share Capital	Dr	300 000	
Business Combination Valuation Reserve	Dr	60 000	
General Reserve	Dr	4 000	
Shares in Subsidiary	Cr		500 000
*$140 000 – $4000			

In this case and in the following cases, the only equity account in which movements (transfers to and from) are specifically identified is Retained Earnings. Movements within the General Reserve account are not specifically noted. This is because, as illustrated in figure 22.13, the Retained Earnings account and changes therein are used to connect the statement of comprehensive income accounts and the statement of financial position accounts. In preparing the consolidated statement of changes in equity, where movements in all equity accounts are disclosed, adjustments for pre-acquisition transfers must be taken into account. Whether such adjustments are necessary can be seen from viewing the consolidation worksheet and the adjustments made to individual equity accounts. A similar issue arises in preparing other notes to the consolidated financial statements, such as for property, plant and equipment, where movements such as additions and disposals must be disclosed.

Case 2: Transfers to retained earnings from other reserves

This case uses the information in Case 1, in which a $4000 general reserve was created. Assume that in the 2011–12 period the subsidiary transfers $1000 to retained earnings from general reserve. The entry passed in the subsidiary as a result of the transfer is:

General Reserve	Dr	1 000	
Transfer from General Reserve	Cr		1 000

The pre-acquisition entries for the 2011–12 period are shown in figure 22.16.

Retained Earnings (1/7/11)	Dr	136 000	
Share Capital	Dr	300 000	
Business Combination Valuation Reserve	Dr	60 000	
General Reserve	Dr	4 000	
Shares in Subsidiary	Cr		500 000
Transfer from General Reserve	Dr	1 000	
General Reserve	Cr		1 000

FIGURE 22.16 Transfer from general reserve in the current period

Since both the Transfer from General Reserve and General Reserve accounts are pre-acquisition in nature, they are eliminated as part of the pre-acquisition entry. The pre-acquisition entry in subsequent periods is:

Retained Earnings (opening balance)*	Dr	137 000	
Share Capital	Dr	300 000	
Business Combination Valuation Reserve	Dr	60 000	
General Reserve	Dr	3 000	
Shares in Subsidiary	Cr		500 000
*$140 000 – $4000 + $1000			

22.6 REVALUATIONS IN THE RECORDS OF THE SUBSIDIARY AT ACQUISITION DATE

IFRS 3 does not discuss whether the valuation of the assets of the subsidiary at acquisition date should be done in the consolidation worksheet or in the records of the subsidiary. It is expected that most entities will make their adjustments in the consolidation worksheet, for two reasons:

- Adjustments for assets such as goodwill and inventory are not allowed in the actual records of the subsidiary. Goodwill is not allowed to be revalued because it would amount to the recognition of internally generated goodwill, and inventory cannot be written to an amount greater than cost.
- The revaluation of non-current assets in the records of the subsidiary means that the subsidiary has effectively adopted the revaluation model of accounting for those assets. As discussed in chapter 9, IAS 16 *Property, Plant and Equipment* requires the assets to be recorded at amounts not materially different from fair value. For entities wanting to measure assets using the cost model, the revaluation of subsidiary assets would be undertaken in the consolidation worksheet.

Note that the business combination valuation entries applied in the consolidation worksheet for property, plant and equipment assets in this chapter are of the same form as those applied for property, plant and equipment in chapter 9. Hence, the consolidated financial statements at acquisition date are the same regardless of whether revaluation occurs on consolidation or in the records of the subsidiary. In future periods, differences will arise because there is no requirement for valuations done in the consolidation worksheet to be updated for subsequent changes in the fair values of the assets.

22.7 DISCLOSURE

Paragraphs B64–B67 of Appendix B to IFRS 3 cover the disclosure of information about business combinations. These paragraphs require an acquirer to disclose information that enables users of its financial statements to evaluate the nature and financial effect of business combinations that occurred during the reporting period, as well as those that occur between the end of the reporting period and when the financial statements are authorised for issue. Examples of disclosures required by these paragraphs are given in figure 22.17.

FIGURE 22.17 Disclosure of business combinations

Note 4. Business combinations	**IFRS 3** *para.*
On 20 October 2010, Alborz Ltd acquired 100% of the voting shares of Bynar Ltd, a listed company specialising in the manufacture of electronic parts for sound equipment. The primary reason for the acquisition was to gain access to specialist knowledge relating to electronic systems. Control was obtained by acquisition of all the shares of Bynar Ltd.	*B64(a), (b), (c)* *B64(d)*

(continued)

FIGURE 22.17 *(continued)*

To acquire this ownership interest, Alborz Ltd issued 600 000 ordinary shares, valued at $2.50 per share, which rank equally for dividends after the acquisition date. The fair value is based on the published market price at acquisition date.	*B64(f)(iv)*
The total consideration transferred was $1 800 000 and consisted of:	*B64(f)*

	$000
Shares issued, at fair value	1 500
Cash paid	240
Cash payable in two years time	60
Total consideration transferred	1 800

The fair values and the carrying amounts of the assets acquired and liabilities assumed in Bynar Ltd as at 20 October 2010 were:	*B64(f)*

	Fair value $000	Carrying amount $000
Property, plant and equipment	1 240	1 020
Receivables	340	340
Inventory	160	130
Intangibles	302	22
Goodwill	54	0
	2 096	1 512
Payables	152	152
Provisions	103	103
Tax liabilities	41	41
	296	296
Fair value of net assets of Bynar Ltd	1 800	

Goodwill in Bynar Ltd can be attributed to the synergies existing within the company, and relate to the high level of training given to the staff as well as the professional expertise of the employees. Further, there exist in-process research activities in Bynar Ltd for which it was impossible to determine reliable fair values for the separate recognition of intangible assets.	*B64(e)*
Bynar Ltd earned a profit for the period from 20 October 2010 to 30 June 2011 of $520 000. This has been included in the consolidated statement of comprehensive income for the year ended 30 June 2011.	*B64(q)(i)*
None of the above information has been prepared on a provisional basis.	*B67*
The consolidated profit is shown in the consolidated statement of comprehensive income at $5 652 000, which includes the $520 000 contributed by Bynar Ltd from 20 October 2010 to the end of the period. If Bynar Ltd had been acquired at 1 July 2010, it is estimated that the consolidated entity would have reported:	*B64(q)(ii)*

	$000
Consolidated revenue	36 654
Consolidated profit	6 341

In relation to the business combination in the 2009–10 period when Alborz Ltd acquired all the shares in Caucasus Ltd, an adjustment was made in the current period relating to the provisional measurement of specialised equipment held by Caucasus Ltd. A loss of $250 000 was recognised in the current reporting period because of the write-down of this equipment.	*B67(a)(iii)*

FIGURE 22.17 *(continued)*

Included in the current period profit are gains on the sale of land acquired as a part of the business combination with Bynar Ltd. The gain amounted to $100 000 and arose due to an upsurge in demand for inner-city properties.	*B67(e)*

Goodwill		*B67(d)*
	$000	
Gross amount at 1 July 2010	120	
Accumulated impairment losses	15	
Carrying amount at 1 July 2010	105	
Goodwill recognised in current period	54	
Carrying amount at 30 June 2011	159	
Gross amount at 30 June 2011	174	
Accumulated impairment losses	15	
Carrying amount at 30 June 2011	159	

IAS 27 also requires disclosures in relation to a parent's interest in its subsidiaries. Figure 22.18 illustrates some of these disclosures.

Note 5. Subsidiaries	**IAS 27** *para.*
Gydon Ltd has a 40% interest in Himalaya Ltd. Although it has less than half the voting power, Gydon Ltd believes it has control of the financial and operating policies of Himalaya Ltd. Gydon Ltd is able to exercise this control because the remaining ownership in Himalaya Ltd is diverse and widely spread, with the next single largest ownership block being 11%.	*41*
Gydon Ltd has invested in a special purpose entity established by Fransipan Ltd. Fransipan Ltd established Hida Ltd as a vehicle for distributing the sailing boats it makes. Aries Ltd currently owns 60% of the shares issued by Hida Ltd. However, because of the limited decisions that the board of Hida Ltd can make owing to the constitution of that entity, Gydon Ltd believes that it does not have any real control over the operations of Hida Ltd, so it sees its role in Hida Ltd as that of an investor.	*41(b)*
Gydon Ltd has a wholly owned subsidiary, Kiso Ltd, which operates within the electricity generating industry. The end of its reporting period is 31 May. Kiso Ltd continues to use this date because the government regulating authority requires all entities within the industry to provide financial information to it based on financial position at that date.	*41(c)*
Gydon Ltd has a wholly owned subsidiary, Koryak Ltd, in the country of Mambo. Because of constraints on assets leaving the country recently imposed by the new military government, there are major restrictions on the subsidiary being able to transfer funds to Gydon Ltd.	*41(d)*

FIGURE 22.18 Disclosures concerning subsidiaries

Paragraph 43 of IAS 27 contains the disclosures required in the parent's separate financial statements:

(a) the fact that the statements are separate financial statements and the reasons why those statements are prepared if not required by law;
(b) a list of significant investments in subsidiaries . . . including the name, country of incorporation or residence, proportion of ownership interest and, if different, proportion of voting power held; and
(c) a description of the method used to account for the investments listed under (b);
and shall identify the financial statements prepared in accordance with paragraph 9 . . . to which they relate.

22.8 REVERSE ACQUISITIONS

According to IFRS 3, where a business combination is effected through an acquisition of equity interests, the acquirer is the combining entity that has the power to govern the financial and operating policies of the other entity so as to obtain benefits from its activities. A reverse acquisition occurs when the legal subsidiary has this form of control over the legal parent. The usual circumstance creating a reverse acquisition is where an entity (the legal parent) obtains ownership of the equity of another entity (the legal subsidiary) but, as part of the exchange transaction, it issues enough voting equity as consideration for control of the combined entity to pass to the owners of the legal subsidiary.

To illustrate, consider the following example, which is adapted from the Illustrative Examples to IFRS 3. Assume Entity A and Entity B agree to merge. The capital structure of each entity is:

Entity A — 100 ordinary shares
Entity B — 60 ordinary shares

Entity A issues $2\frac{1}{2}$ shares in exchange for each ordinary share of Entity B. All of Entity B's shareholders exchange their shares for Entity A shares. Entity A therefore issues 150 shares ($60 \times 2\frac{1}{2}$) for the 60 shares in Entity B. The position after the share exchange is that Entity A now owns 100% of Entity B.

Entity A is now the legal parent of the subsidiary Entity B. However, analysing the shareholding in Entity A shows that it consists of the 100 shares existing before the merger and 150 new shares held by the former shareholders in Entity B. In essence, the former shareholders of Entity B now control both Entities A and B. The former Entity B shareholders have a 60% interest in Entity A, that is, $150/(100 + 150)$. The IASB argues that there has been a reverse acquisition, and that Entity B is effectively the acquirer of Entity A.

The key accounting effect of deciding that Entity B is the acquirer is that the assets and liabilities of Entity A are to be valued at fair value. This is contrary to normal acquisition accounting, based on Entity A being the legal parent of Entity B, which would require the assets and liabilities of Entity B to be valued at fair value.

Illustrative example 22.1 demonstrates the accounting where a reverse acquisition occurs.

ILLUSTRATIVE EXAMPLE 22.1

Reverse acquisitions

This example is adapted from the illustrative example in IFRS 3, and uses the Entity A – Entity B scenario described earlier.

The statements of financial position of A Ltd and B Ltd at 30 June 2009 were as follows:

	A Ltd	B Ltd
Current assets	$ 500	$ 700
Non-current assets	1 300	3 000
Total assets	$1 800	$3 700
Share capital		
100 shares	$ 300	
60 shares		$ 600
Retained earnings	800	1 400
	1 100	2 000
Current liabilities	300	600
Non-current liabilities	400	1 100
	700	1 700
Total equity and liabilities	$1 800	$3 700

On 1 July 2009, A Ltd acquired all the issued shares of B Ltd, giving in exchange $2\frac{1}{2}$ A Ltd shares for each ordinary share of B Ltd. A Ltd thus issued 150 shares to acquire the 60 shares issued by B Ltd.

The fair value of each ordinary share of B Ltd at 1 July 2009 is $40 and the quoted market price of A Ltd's ordinary shares is $16. The fair values of A Ltd's identifiable assets and liabilities at acquisition date are the same as their carrying amounts except for the non-current assets whose fair value was $1500. The tax rate is 30%.

In acquiring the shares in B Ltd, A Ltd issued 150 shares at $16 each. Therefore, A Ltd would have raised an investment in B Ltd of $2400. However, under reverse acquisition accounting, the consideration transferred is based on what B Ltd would have paid to acquire all the shares in A Ltd, and for the former B Ltd shareholders to have a 60% interest in the combined entities. Because B Ltd has, before the acquisition date, a share total of 60, B Ltd needs to issue 40 shares to the shareholders of A Ltd in exchange for their shares in order for the former B Ltd shareholders to have a 60% interest in B Ltd. If B Ltd issued these 40 shares, it would record a consideration transferred of $1600 (i.e. 40 × $40).

The acquisition analysis then relates the imputed consideration transferred of $1600 to the fair value of A Ltd:

Fair value of A Ltd	= $300 + $800 (equity)
	+ $200(1 – 30%) (BCVR – non-current assets)
	= $1240
Consideration transferred	= $1600
Goodwill	= $360

The consolidation worksheet entries are as follows.

(1) *Change in consideration transferred*
The purpose of these entries is to eliminate the investment account actually raised by A Ltd and substitute for it the entry that B Ltd would have made if it had actually acquired the shares in A Ltd:

Share Capital – A Ltd	Dr	2 400	
Shares in B Ltd	Cr		2 400
Shares in A Ltd	Dr	1 600	
Share Capital – B Ltd	Cr		1 600

(2) *Business combination valuation entries*
These entries revalue the assets of A Ltd:

Non-current Assets	Dr	200	
Deferred Tax Liability	Cr		60
Business Combination Valuation Reserve	Cr		140
Goodwill	Dr	360	
Business Combination Valuation Reserve	Cr		360

(3) *Pre-acquisition entry*
This entry eliminates the newly created investment in A Ltd from entry (1) above against the equity of A Ltd that existed before the merger, but including any valuation reserve raised on consolidation:

Share Capital – A Ltd	Dr	300	
Retained Earnings	Dr	800	
Business Combination Valuation Reserve	Dr	500	
Shares in A Ltd	Cr		1 600

The consolidation worksheet at acquisition date is shown in figure 22.19. Note:

- the equity of A Ltd on hand at acquisition date is eliminated
- the capital that B Ltd would have issued if it had acquired the shares in A Ltd is carried forward into the statement of financial position
- it is A Ltd's assets that are revalued.

Financial statements	A Ltd	B Ltd	Adjustments				Consolidation
				Dr	Cr		
Retained earnings	800	1 400	3	800			1 400
Share capital	2 700	600	1	2 400	1 600	1	
			3	300			2 200
Business combination valuation reserve	—	—	3	500	140	2	—
					360	2	
Current liabilities	300	600					900
Deferred tax liability					60	2	60
Non-current liabilities	400	1 100					1 500
	4 200	3 700					6 060
Current assets	500	700					1 200
Shares in B Ltd	2 400	—			2 400	1	—
Shares in A Ltd			1	1 600	1 600	3	—
Non-current assets	1 300	3 000	2	200			4 500
Goodwill			2	360			360
	4 200	3 700		6 160	6 160		6 060

FIGURE 22.19 Consolidation worksheet — reverse acquisition accounting

Illustrative examples 22.2 and 22.3 are comprehensive examples demonstrating consolidation and accounting for an unrecognised intangible and liability.

ILLUSTRATIVE EXAMPLE 22.2

Consolidation

On 1 July 2009, Maoke Ltd acquired 100% of the issued shares of Schober Ltd on a *cum div.* basis. The fair value of the consideration paid was measured at $335 000. At this date, the records of Schober Ltd included the following information:

Share capital	$200 000
General reserve	5 000
Retained earnings	100 000
Dividend payable	20 000
Goodwill	5 000

The dividend liability at 1 July 2009 was paid in August 2009. At 1 July 2009, all the identifiable assets and liabilities of Schober Ltd were recorded in the subsidiary's books at fair value except for the following assets.

	Carrying amount	Fair value
Inventory	$ 40 000	$ 43 000
Plant (cost $240 000)	180 000	185 000

The inventory was all sold by 30 June 2010. The plant has a further 5-year life and is depreciated on a straight-line basis. Goodwill was not impaired in any period. When assets are sold or fully consumed, any relating business combination valuation reserve is transferred to retained earnings. The tax rate is 30%.

The summarised financial statements of the entities within the group at 30 June 2011 are as shown in figure 22.20. The transfer to general reserve in the 2010–11 period was from profits earned before acquisition date.

Required

Prepare the consolidated financial statements for Maoke Ltd at 30 June 2011.

Solution

The first step in the consolidation process is the acquisition analysis shown below. This involves comparing the net fair value of the identifiable assets and liabilities of the subsidiary with the consideration transferred, and determining the existence of goodwill or gain on bargain purchase. So it is necessary to identify:

- *the equity of the subsidiary at acquisition date:* this consists of $200 000 share capital, $5000 general reserve and $100 000 retained earnings
- *differences between the carrying amounts of recorded assets and liabilities of the subsidiary and their fair values, as well as the fair values of any unrecorded assets and liabilities of the subsidiary recognised as part of the business combination:* this consists of inventory for which there is $3000 difference (i.e. $43 000 – $40 000) and plant for which there is a $5000 difference (i.e. $185 000 – $180 000); these differences are recognised in the acquisition analysis as business combination valuation reserves, the amount being on an after-tax basis — the differences are multiplied by (1 – tax rate)
- *any goodwill recorded by the subsidiary at acquisition date:* because it is the fair value of identifiable assets being considered and goodwill is an unidentifiable asset, goodwill must be adjusted for in the calculation; in this problem, the subsidiary has goodwill of $5000.
- *dividends payable recorded by the subsidiary at acquisition date:* if dividends have been issued on an *ex div.* basis, they have no effect on the acquisition analysis. The dividends of $20 000 in this problem were issued on a *cum div.* basis. This means that the cost of the combination of $335 000 paid by the parent was for both the shares in the subsidiary and the dividends receivable. Hence, the consideration transferred must be adjusted for the amount paid for the dividends receivable, that is, $20 000.

Acquisition analysis

At 1 July 2009:

Net fair value of identifiable assets and liabilities of Schober Ltd	= $200 000 + $5000 + $100 000 (equity)
	– $5000 goodwill recorded
	+ ($5000)(1 – 30%) (BCVR – plant)
	+ ($3000)(1 – 30%) (BCVR – inventory)
	= $305 600
Consideration transferred	= $335 000 – $20 000 (dividend receivable)
	= $315 000
Goodwill	= $315 000 – $305 600
	= $9400
Unrecorded goodwill	= $9400 – $5000
	= $4400

When the net fair value of the identifiable assets and liabilities acquired is compared with the consideration transferred, it is found that the latter is the greater amount — the difference between the two numbers is goodwill. In this problem, the goodwill of the subsidiary is $9400. This is the amount that will be reported in a consolidated statement of financial position if prepared at acquisition date. As the subsidiary has already recorded goodwill of $5000, the adjustment necessary in the consolidation worksheet is $4400.

Consolidation worksheet adjustment entries at 30 June 2011
The consolidation worksheet entries should be read from the acquisition analysis, as the latter contains the information necessary to prepare the entries at acquisition date.

(1) *Business combination valuation entries at 30 June 2011*
Since the consolidated financial statements are being prepared after acquisition date, the business combination entries at 30 June 2011 are affected by changes in the assets and liabilities existing at acquisition date.

With inventory, since it has been sold by 30 June 2010, there is no longer any need to prepare a business combination valuation entry for this asset. The related valuation reserve has been transferred to retained earnings in 2010.

With the plant, it is still on hand within the group. The first adjustment entry, then, is the same as that at the acquisition date. The accumulated depreciation of $60 000 (i.e. $240 000 – $180 000) is eliminated and the plant reduced from $240 000 to fair value of $185 000, an amount of $55 000. The $5000 difference between carrying amount and fair value is split between deferred tax liability (30%) and business combination valuation reserve (70%). This entry is used in every period while the asset continues to be held by the subsidiary.

The second valuation entry reflects the fact that the plant is being depreciated on a straight-line basis over a 5-year period. Because the acquisition date was 1 July 2009 and the end of the reporting period is 30 June 2011, there is a 2-year time period between these two dates. The business combination valuation entry for equipment has to include adjustments for current period depreciation and 1-year prior period depreciation. The adjustment to the plant was $5000. Using a 20% depreciation rate, depreciation each year is $1000. The current period depreciation is adjusted via depreciation expense, whereas prior period depreciation affects retained earnings. Total depreciation is adjusted against accumulated depreciation.

As the asset is used up and benefits flow to the entity, the deferred tax liability is reversed. This can be observed via the change in the carrying amount of the asset with the recognition of accumulated depreciation. In the worksheet entry discussed in the previous paragraph, accumulated depreciation was increased by $2000. This affected the carrying amount of the asset, and caused a temporary difference between it and the tax base of the asset. This results in a reversal of the deferred tax liability raised in the first business combination valuation entry for plant. The amount of the reversal is equal to the adjustment to accumulated depreciation times the tax rate, which in this problem is $2000 × 30% = $600. The reversal affects current period income tax expense by $300 (the adjustment to depreciation expense of $1000 × the 30% tax rate) and retained earnings by $300 (the adjustment for prior period depreciation to retained earnings of $1000 × the 30% tax rate).

The final business combination valuation entry relates to the recognition of goodwill acquired in the business combination. At acquisition date, the parent acquired $9400 goodwill in the subsidiary. However, as the subsidiary had already recognised $5000 goodwill, on consolidation, an additional $4400 goodwill is recognised as having been acquired by the group.

The business combination valuation entries at 30 June 2011 are then as follows:

Accumulated Depreciation – Plant	Dr	60 000	
Plant	Cr		55 000
Deferred Tax Liability	Cr		1 500
Business Combination Valuation Reserve	Cr		3 500
Depreciation Expense	Dr	1 000	
Retained Earnings (1/7/10)	Dr	1 000	
Accumulated Depreciation	Cr		2 000
(20% × $5000 p.a. for 2 years)			

Deferred Tax Liability	Dr	600	
Income Tax Expense	Cr		300
Retained Earnings (1/7/10)	Cr		300
Goodwill	Dr	4 400	
Business Combination Valuation Reserve	Cr		4 400

(2) *Pre-acquisition entries at 30 June 2011*
The pre-acquisition entry eliminates the pre-acquisition equity of the subsidiary and the investment by the parent in the subsidiary. The pre-acquisition entry at acquisition date can be read from the acquisition analysis. The differences between carrying amounts and fair values of the subsidiary's assets and liabilities are reflected in the business combination valuation reserve. The entry at *1 July 2009* (acquisition date) is:

Retained Earnings (1/7/09)	Dr	100 000	
Share Capital	Dr	200 000	
General Reserve	Dr	5 000	
Business Combination Valuation Reserve	Dr	10 000	
Shares in Schober Ltd	Cr		315 000

(Note that there would be a further entry relating to the $20 000 dividend, but because it is paid in August 2009 it has no further effect.)

This entry changes for periods after the acquisition date because of events affecting pre-acquisition equity including movements in the business combination valuation reserve, and any impairment of goodwill. In this problem, the events between the acquisition date and the *beginning* of the current period affecting the pre-acquisition entry are that the inventory on hand at acquisition date has been sold, meaning that the related business combination valuation reserve has been transferred to retained earnings; thus, the valuation reserve has been reduced by $2100, and the retained earnings (opening balance) increased by the same amount.

The pre-acquisition entry at the beginning of the 2010–11 period is then:

Retained Earnings (1/7/10)*	Dr	102 100	
Share Capital	Dr	200 000	
General Reserve	Dr	5 000	
Business Combination Valuation Reserve**	Dr	7 900	
Shares in Schober Ltd	Cr		315 000

*$100 000 + $2100 (BCVR – inventory)
**$10 000 – $2100 (BCVR – inventory)

One further event in the *current* period that affects the balances of pre-acquisition equity is the transfer to general reserve of $15 000 made by the subsidiary in the current period — the subsidiary increased its general reserve and reduced its retained earnings using a transfer account; this affects the balances of pre-acquisition equity in specific accounts.

The extra entry required is:

General Reserve	Dr	15 000	
Transfer to General Reserve	Cr		15 000

Both the business combination valuation entries and the pre-acquisition entries are then passed through the consolidation worksheet as shown in figure 22.20.

Financial statements	Maoke Ltd	Schober Ltd	Adjustments				Consolidation
				Dr	Cr		
Revenues	125 000	90 000					215 000
Expenses	85 000	65 000	1	1 000			151 000
Profit before tax	40 000	25 000					64 000
Income tax expense	15 500	10 200			300	1	25 400
Profit for the period	24 500	14 800					38 600
Retained earnings (1/7/10)	150 000	85 000	1	1 000	300	1	132 200
			2	102 100			
	174 500	99 800					170 800
Transfer to general reserve	20 000	15 000			15 000	2	20 000
Retained earnings (30/6/11)	154 500	84 800					150 800
Share capital	500 000	200 000	2	200 000			500 000
Business combination valuation reserve	—	—	2	7 900	3 500	1	—
					4 400	1	
General reserve	50 000	20 000	2	5 000			
			2	15 000			50 000
	704 500	304 800					700 800
Available-for-sale financial assets reserve (1/7/10)	2 000	3 000					5 000
Gain on available-for-sale financial assets	12 000	10 000					22 000
Available-for-sale financial assets reserve (30/6/11)	14 000	13 000					27 000
Plant revaluation reserve (1/7/10)	8 000	5 000					13 000
Gain on plant revaluation	28 000	22 000					50 000
Plant revaluation reserve (30/6/11)	36 000	27 000					63 000
Total equity	754 500	344 800					790 800
Tax liabilities	11 000	16 000	1	600	1 500	1	27 900
Other liabilities	50 000	20 000					70 000
Total liabilities	61 000	36 000					97 900
Total equity and liabilities	815 500	380 800					888 700
Cash	25 000	5 000					30 000
Inventory	60 000	85 000					145 000
Financial assets	50 000	40 000					90 000
Plant	500 000	300 000			55 000	1	745 000
Accumulated depreciation	(160 000)	(80 000)	1	60 000	2 000	1	(182 000)
Shares in Schober Ltd	315 000	—			315 000	2	—
Fixtures and fittings	40 000	38 000					78 000
Accumulated depreciation	(14 500)	(12 200)					(26 700)
Goodwill	—	5 000	1	4 400			9 400
Total assets	815 500	380 800		397 000	397 000		888 700

FIGURE 22.20 Consolidation worksheet

The consolidated financial statements of Maoke Ltd at 30 June 2011 are as shown in figure 22.21.

FIGURE 22.21(a) Consolidated statement of comprehensive income

MAOKE LTD Consolidated Statement of Comprehensive Income for the year ended 30 June 2011	
Revenues	$215 000
Expenses	151 000
Profit before tax	**64 000**
Income tax expense	25 400
Profit for the period	$ **38 600**
Other comprehensive income	
Available-for-sale financial assets	22 000
Gain on plant revaluation	50 000
Other comprehensive income for the year net of tax	**72 000**
TOTAL COMPREHENSIVE INCOME FOR THE YEAR	$**110 600**

FIGURE 22.21(b) Consolidated statement of changes in equity

MAOKE LTD Consolidated Statement of Changes in Equity for the year ended 30 June 2011	
Total comprehensive income for the year	$110 600
Retained earnings balance at 1 July 2010	$132 200
Profit for the period	38 600
Transfer to general reserve	(20 000)
Retained earnings balance at 30 June 2011	$150 800
General reserve balance at 1 July 2010	$ 30 000
Transfer from retained earnings	$ 20 000
General reserve balance at 30 June 2011	$ 50 000
Available-for-sale assets reserve at 1 July 2010	$ 5 000
Gain for the year	22 000
Available-for-sale assets reserve at 30 June 2011	$ 27 000
Plant revaluation reserve at 1 July 2010	$ 13 000
Gain for the year	50 000
Plant revaluation reserve at 30 June 2011	$ 63 000
Share capital balance at 1 July 2010	$500 000
Share capital balance at 30 June 2011	$500 000

FIGURE 22.21(c) Consolidated statement of financial position

MAOKE LTD Consolidated Statement of Financial Position as at 30 June 2011	
EQUITY AND LIABILITIES	
Equity	
Share capital	$500 000
Other components of equity	140 000
Retained earnings	150 800
Total equity	790 800

(continued)

FIGURE 22.21(c) *(continued)*

Non-current liabilities		
Tax liabilities		27 900
Other		70 000
Total non-current liabilities		97 900
Total equity and liabilities		$888 700
ASSETS		
Non-current assets		
Plant	$ 745 000	
Accumulated depreciation	(182 000)	$563 000
Fixtures and fittings	78 000	
Accumulated depreciation	(26 700)	51 300
Goodwill		9 400
Total non-current assets		623 700
Current assets		
Cash		30 000
Inventory		145 000
Financial assets		90 000
Total current assets		255 000
Total assets		$888 700

ILLUSTRATIVE EXAMPLE 22.3

Unrecognised intangible, unrecognised liability

On 30 September 2008, Carnic Ltd acquired 80% of the shares of Dolomites Ltd for $3 per share in cash. The equity of Dolomites Ltd at that date was:

Share capital – 10 000 shares	$ 10 000
General reserve	3 000
Retained earnings	12 000

Carnic Ltd had previously acquired 20% of the shares of Dolomites Ltd for $4000. The fair value of this investment at 30 September 2008 was $6000.

At acquisition date, all the identifiable assets and liabilities of Dolomites Ltd were recorded at fair value except for machinery and inventory whose carrying amounts were each $2000 less than their fair values. All this inventory was sold by Dolomites Ltd before December 2008. The machinery had a further 5-year life. The tax rate is 30%.

In a previous period, Dolomites Ltd had purchased some goodwill that had been written down to a carrying amount of $2000 as at 30 September 2008. Dolomites Ltd had developed a business magazine containing economic indicators for the coal industry. The magazine was widely sought after. Carnic Ltd placed a value of $1500 on the masthead. The intangible asset, not recognised by Dolomites Ltd at 30 September 2008, was considered to have an indefinite life.

At 30 September 2008, Carnic Ltd had sued Dolomites Ltd for alleged damaging statements made in the magazine, and a court case was in progress. Although it considered that a present obligation for damages existed, Dolomites Ltd had not recognised any liability because it did not believe that the liability recognition criteria could be met. Carnic Ltd assessed potential damages at a fair value of $2000. In January 2010, the court handed down its decision, and Dolomites Ltd was required to pay damages of $2500.

Between 30 September 2008 and 30 June 2009 (end of the reporting period for both companies), the following movements occurred in the records of Dolomites Ltd:

- Dolomites Ltd transferred $3000 from pre-acquisition retained earnings to the general reserve.
- Dolomites Ltd had declared and paid a bonus share issue of one share for every two shares held at 1 October 2008 out of the general reserve ($3000) and partly out of the retained earnings.

Required

A. Prepare the consolidation worksheet adjustment entries for consolidation of the financial statements of Carnic Ltd and Dolomites Ltd on:
   1. 30 September 2008
   2. 30 June 2009.

B. Given no further movements in pre-acquisition equity of Dolomites Ltd, prepare the worksheet entries at 30 June 2010.

Solution

The first step is to prepare the acquisition analysis. This requires the identification of:

- *the recorded equity of the subsidiary at acquisition date:* this consists of $10 000 share capital, $3000 general reserve and $12 000 retained earnings
- *differences between carrying amounts and fair values for assets recorded by the subsidiary:* the differences arise for inventory ($2000) and plant ($2000)
- *identifiable assets and liabilities not recognised by the subsidiary but recognised as part of the business combination at their fair values:* the group recognises a masthead at $1500 fair value and a provision for damages at $2000 fair value
- *any goodwill recorded by the subsidiary at acquisition date:* the subsidiary has recorded goodwill of $2000
- *any dividends payable by the subsidiary at acquisition date:* there are none in this problem.

Acquisition analysis at 30 September 2008

Net fair value of identifiable assets and liabilities of Dolomites Ltd	= ($10 000 + $12 000 + $3000) (equity)
	+ $2000(1 – 30%) (machinery)
	– $2000 (goodwill)
	+ $2000(1 – 30%) (inventory)
	+ $1500(1 – 30%) (masthead)
	– $2000(1 – 30%) (provision for damages)
Consideration transferred	= $25 450
	= 80% × 10 000 × $3
Fair value of previously held investment	= $24 000
Aggregate amount of investment	= $6000
	= $24 000 + $6000
Goodwill acquired	= $30 000
	= $30 000 – $25 450
Unrecorded goodwill	= $4550
	= $4550 – $2 000
	$2550

The aggregate of the investment in Dolomites Ltd is $4550 greater than the net fair value of the identifiable assets and liabilities of the subsidiary. The goodwill acquired by the group is then $4550. As the subsidiary has already recorded $2000 goodwill, the consolidation adjustment is $2550.

A.1. Consolidation worksheet entries at 30 September 2008

(1) *Business combination valuation entries*

The business combination valuation entries are used to adjust the carrying amount of the subsidiary's recorded assets to fair value, and to recognise assets and liabilities not recorded by the subsidiary. These have all been identified in the acquisition analysis. In recognising the assets and liabilities at fair value, the adjustments affect the business combination valuation reserve (70% of the adjustment) and deferred tax accounts (30% of the adjustment). The entries at acquisition date are:

Machinery	Dr	2 000	
Deferred Tax Liability	Cr		600
Business Combination Valuation Reserve	Cr		1 400
Inventory	Dr	2 000	
Deferred Tax Liability	Cr		600
Business Combination Valuation Reserve	Cr		1 400
Masthead	Dr	1 500	
Deferred Tax Liability	Cr		450
Business Combination Valuation Reserve	Cr		1 050
Business Combination Valuation Reserve	Dr	1 400	
Deferred Tax Asset	Dr	600	
Provision for Damages	Cr		2 000
Goodwill	Dr	2 550	
Business Combination Valuation Reserve	Cr		2 550

Note that with the liability, there is an overall decrease in the valuation reserve, and the tax adjustment is to a deferred tax asset.

(2) *Pre-acquisition entry*

The pre-acquisition entry at acquisition date can be read from the acquisition analysis. The entry eliminates the pre-acquisition equity of the subsidiary, including the total of the business combination valuation reserve as recognised in the previous set of entries, and the investment account as recorded by the parent. The entry at acquisition date is:

Retained Earnings (30/9/08)	Dr	12 000	
Share Capital	Dr	10 000	
General Reserve	Dr	3 000	
Business Combination Valuation Reserve	Dr	5 000	
Shares in Dolomites Ltd	Cr		30 000

A.2. Consolidation worksheet entries at 30 June 2009

These entries are at the end of the first period since acquisition date, and cover a period of 9 months.

(1) *Business combination valuation entries*

The effect on the entry for machinery is that there needs to be another entry to adjust for 9 months depreciation based on the difference between carrying amount in the subsidiary and fair value. The adjustment is to current period depreciation and amounts to \$300 (i.e. $\frac{3}{4} \times 20\% \times$ \$2000) using the fact that the machinery has a further 5-year life. The recognition of depreciation changes the carrying amount of the asset. This changes the temporary difference between the carrying amount and the asset's tax base. The deferred tax liability raised on adjusting the machinery to fair value is reversed as the asset is depreciated. The reversal is \$90, that is, 30% × the depreciation charge of \$300.

Machinery	Dr	2 000	
Deferred Tax Liability	Cr		600
Business Combination Valuation Reserve	Cr		1 400

Depreciation Expense	Dr	300	
Accumulated Depreciation	Cr		300
($\frac{3}{4} \times \frac{1}{5} \times \$2000$)			
Deferred Tax Liability	Dr	90	
Income Tax Expense	Cr		90

The inventory on hand at acquisition date is all sold by December 2008. The adjustment is then made to cost of sales instead of inventory, because the cost of sales to the group is $2000 higher than that recorded by the subsidiary on sale of the inventory. On sale of the inventory, the deferred tax liability is reversed, and affects income tax expense. As the asset is sold, the group transfers the valuation reserve to retained earnings to avoid having to make adjustments to equity in future periods. The entry for inventory is:

Cost of Sales	Dr	2 000	
Income Tax Expense	Cr		600
Transfer from Business Combination Valuation Reserve	Cr		1 400

There is no change to the entry for the masthead. This entry changes only if the asset is amortised, or adjusted as a result of an impairment loss.

Masthead	Dr	1 500	
Deferred Tax Liability	Cr		450
Business Combination Valuation Reserve	Cr		1 050

There is no change to the entry for the provision for damages. This would change if the subsidiary itself recognised a liability or the liability was settled.

Business Combination Valuation Reserve	Dr	1 400	
Deferred Tax Asset	Dr	600	
Provision for Damages	Cr		2 000

There is no change to the goodwill. This would change if the goodwill were impaired.

Goodwill	Dr	2 550	
Business Combination Valuation Reserve	Cr		2 550

(2) *Pre-acquisition entries*

The pre-acquisition entry at the beginning of the period is the same as that at acquisition date:

Retained Earnings (30/9/08)	Dr	12 000	
Share Capital	Dr	10 000	
General Reserve	Dr	3 000	
Business Combination Valuation Reserve	Dr	5 000	
Shares in Dolomites Ltd	Cr		30 000

Adjustments are made to the pre-acquisition entry for events occurring in the current period that affect pre-acquisition equity balances or the goodwill balance.

In the current period, the following events affect the pre-acquisition entry at the beginning of the period:

- *$3000 transfer to general reserve from retained earnings:* this decreases retained earnings and increases the general reserve

- *$5000 bonus issue:* this increases share capital and reduces the equity accounts from which the bonus issue was made, namely $3000 from general reserve and $2000 from retained earnings, the latter affecting the bonus dividend paid account
- *the inventory on hand at acquisition date was sold in the current period:* as can be seen from the related business combination valuation reserve adjustment, on sale of the inventory the related revaluation reserve is transferred to retained earnings. Hence, at 30 June 2009, the business combination valuation reserve is reduced and retained earnings increased.

General Reserve	Dr	3 000	
Transfer to General Reserve	Cr		3 000
Share Capital	Dr	5 000	
Bonus Dividend Paid	Cr		2 000
General Reserve	Cr		3 000
Shares in Dolomites Ltd	Dr	1 500	
Dividend Receivable	Cr		1 500
Transfer from Business Combination Valuation Reserve	Dr	1 400	
Business Combination Valuation Reserve	Cr		1 400

B. Consolidation worksheet entries at 30 June 2010
This is 1 year after the last set of entries and $1\frac{3}{4}$ years since acquisition date.

(1) *Business combination valuation entries*
The adjustment entry raised at acquisition date for the machinery is still used. The depreciation now, however, is for $1\frac{3}{4}$ years since acquisition date. Current period depreciation expense is adjusted for a full year's depreciation and the prior period depreciation expense for $\frac{3}{4}$ year affects retained earnings. The using up of the asset results in changes in the carrying amount of the asset, and further results in reversing the deferred tax liability raised at acquisition date. The current period income tax expense is affected by the reversal due to the current period depreciation, and the adjustment for the previous $\frac{3}{4}$-year depreciation, affecting retained earnings, affects last year's income tax expense, also requiring an adjustment to retained earnings.

Machinery	Dr	2 000	
Deferred Tax Liability	Cr		600
Business Combination Valuation Reserve	Cr		1 400
Depreciation Expense	Dr	400	
Retained Earnings (1/7/09)	Dr	300	
Accumulated Depreciation	Cr		700
($\frac{1}{5}$× $2000 p.a.)			
Deferred Tax Liability	Dr	210	
Income Tax Expense	Cr		120
Retained Earnings (1/7/09)	Cr		90

There is still no change to the adjustment for the masthead.

Masthead	Dr	1 500	
Deferred Tax Liability	Cr		450
Business Combination Valuation Reserve	Cr		1 050

In January 2010, the court determined that the subsidiary was to pay damages of $2500. As the liability is settled, the business combination valuation reserve is transferred to retained earnings. Further, the deferred tax asset is reversed on settlement of the liability, requiring an adjustment to income tax expense. In settling the liability, the subsidiary raised a damages expense of $2500 and paid cash to external entities. Since the group recognised the liability for damages at acquisition date of $2000, the expense to the group on payment of $2500 is only $500. In other words, to the group, the $2500 outflow is a reduction in the liability of $2000 and an expense of $500. Since $2500 damages expense was recorded by the subsidiary, and the group wants to report only $500 damages expense, the consolidation adjustment is a $2000 reduction in damages expense.

Transfer from Business Combination Valuation Reserve	Dr	1 400	
Income Tax Expense	Dr	600	
Damages Expense	Cr		2 000

There is still no change to the goodwill.

Goodwill	Dr	2 550	
Business Combination Valuation Reserve	Cr		2 550

(2) *Pre-acquisition entries*

The pre-acquisition entry at the beginning of the year, 1 July 2009, is the sum of the entries made in the consolidation worksheet at 30 June 2008. However, if the worksheet entries are required for the period ending 30 June 2010, it is unnecessary to prepare the entries for each period between acquisition date and the current period. Each line in the pre-acquisition entry can be calculated by adjusting the balance at acquisition date for all events affecting that balance between acquisition date and the beginning of the current period, as follows:

Retained earnings (1/7/09):
$8400 = $12 000 (opening balance) – $3000 (transfer to general reserve) – $2000 (bonus dividend) + $1400 (transfer from BCVR – inventory)

Share capital:
$15 000 = $10 000 + $5000 (bonus dividend)

General reserve:
$3000 = zero balance at acquisition date + $3000 transfer from retained earnings

Business combination valuation reserve:
$3600 = $5000 – $1400 (transfer from BCVR – inventory)

Shares in Dolomites Ltd:
There is no change to this account.

The entry then is:

Retained Earnings (1/7/09)	Dr	8 400	
Share Capital	Dr	15 000	
General Reserve	Dr	3 000	
Business Combination Valuation Reserve	Dr	3 600	
Shares in Dolomites Ltd	Cr		30 000

Other entries are required for events occurring in the current period that affect accounts in the pre-acquisition entry. In this problem, there is only one such event. In the current period the contingent liability was settled, resulting in a transfer from business combination valuation reserve to retained earnings. The effect on the pre-acquisition entry is that the BCVR has been increased by $1400 and the retained earnings, represented by the current period transfer account, is decreased by $1400.

Business Combination Valuation Reserve	Dr	1 400	
Transfer from Business Combination Valuation Reserve	Cr		1 400

SUMMARY

This chapter covers the preparation of the consolidated financial statements for a group consisting of a parent and a wholly owned subsidiary. Because of the requirements of IFRS 3 to recognise the identifiable net assets of an acquired entity at fair value, an initial adjustment to be made on consolidation concerns any assets or liabilities for which there are differences between fair value and carrying amount at the acquisition date. Further, although some intangible assets and liabilities of the subsidiary may not have been recognised in the subsidiary's records, they are recognised as part of the business combination.

The preparation of the consolidated financial statements is done using a consolidation worksheet, the right-hand columns of which contain the financial statements of the members of the group. The adjustment columns contain the consolidation worksheet entries that adjust the right-hand columns to form the consolidated financial statements. The adjustment entries have no effect on the actual financial records of the parent and its subsidiaries.

At acquisition date, an acquisition analysis is undertaken. The key purposes of this analysis are to determine the fair values of the identifiable assets and liabilities of the subsidiary, and to calculate any goodwill or gain arising from the business combination. From this analysis, the main consolidation worksheet adjustment entries at acquisition date are the business combination valuation entries (to adjust carrying amounts of the subsidiaries' assets and liabilities to fair value) and the pre-acquisition entries.

In preparing consolidated financial statements in periods after acquisition date, the consolidation worksheet will contain valuation entries and pre-acquisition entries. However, these entries are not necessarily the same as those used at acquisition date. If there are changes to the assets and liabilities of the subsidiaries since acquisition date, or there have been movements in pre-acquisition equity, changes must be made to these entries.

Discussion questions

1. Explain the purpose of the pre-acquisition entries in the preparation of consolidated financial statements.
2. When there is a dividend payable by the subsidiary at acquisition date, under what conditions should the existence of this dividend be taken into consideration in preparing the pre-acquisition entries?
3. Is it necessary to distinguish pre-acquisition dividends from post-acquisition dividends? Why?
4. If the subsidiary has recorded goodwill in its records at acquisition date, how does this affect the preparation of the pre-acquisition entries?
5. Explain how the existence of a bargain purchase affects the pre-acquisition entries, both in the year of acquisition and in subsequent years.
6. At the date the parent acquires a controlling interest in a subsidiary, if the carrying amounts of the subsidiary's assets are not equal to fair value, explain why adjustments to these assets are required in the preparation of the consolidated financial statements.
7. How does IFRS 3 *Business Combinations* affect the acquisition analysis?
8. What is the purpose of the business combination valuation entries?
9. Using an example, explain how the business combination entries affect the pre-acquisition entries.
10. Why are some adjustment entries in the previous period's consolidation worksheet also made in the current period's worksheet?
11. Kurai Ltd has just acquired all the issued shares of Sayan Ltd. The accounting staff at Kurai Ltd has been analysing the assets and liabilities acquired in Sayan Ltd. As a result of this analysis, it was found that Sayan Ltd had been expensing its research outlays in accordance with IAS 38 *Intangible Assets*. Over the past 3 years, the company has expensed a total of \$20 000, including \$8000 immediately before the acquisition date. One of the reasons that Kurai Ltd acquired control of Sayan Ltd was its promising research findings in an area that could benefit the products being produced by Kurai Ltd.

    There is disagreement among the accounting staff as to how to account for the research abilities of Sayan Ltd. Some of the staff argue that, since it is research, the correct accounting is to expense it, and so it has no effect on accounting for the group. Other members of the accounting staff believe that it should be recognised on consolidation, but are unsure of the accounting entries to use, and are concerned about the future effects of recognition of an asset, particularly as no tax advantage remains in relation to the asset.

Required

Advise the group accountant of Kurai Ltd on what accounting is most appropriate for these circumstances.

12. Sierra Ltd has finally concluded its negotiations to take over Taurus Ltd, and has secured ownership of all the shares of Taurus Ltd. One of the areas of discussion during the negotiation process was the current court case that Taurus Ltd was involved in. The company was being sued by some former employees who were retrenched, but are now claiming damages for unfair dismissal. The company did not believe that it owed these employees anything. However, realising that industrial relations was an uncertain area, particularly given the country's current confusing industrial relations laws, it had raised a note to the accounts issued before the takeover by Sierra Ltd reporting the existence of the court case as a contingent liability. No monetary amount was disclosed, but the company's lawyers had placed a $56 700 amount on the probable payout to settle the case.

The accounting staff of Sierra Ltd is unsure of the effect of this contingent liability on the accounting for the consolidated group after the takeover. Some argue that it is not a liability of the group and so should not be recognised on consolidation, but are willing to accept some form of note disclosure. A further concern being raised is the effects on the accounts, depending on whether Taurus Ltd wins or loses the case. If Taurus Ltd wins the court case, it will not have to pay out any damages and could get reimbursement of its court costs, estimated to be around $40 000.

Required

Give the group accountant your opinion on the accounting at acquisition date for consolidation purposes, as well as any subsequent effects when the entity either wins or loses the case.

13. Toba Ltd has acquired all the shares of Tian Ltd. The accountant for Toba Ltd, having studied the requirements of IFRS 3 *Business Combinations*, realises that all the identifiable assets and liabilities of Tian Ltd must be recognised in the consolidated financial statements at fair value. Although he is happy about the valuation of these items, he is unsure of a number of other matters associated with accounting for these assets and liabilities. He has approached you and asked for your advice.

Required

Write a report for the accountant at Toba Ltd advising on the following issues:

1. Should the adjustments to fair value be made in the consolidation worksheet or in the accounts of Tian Ltd?
2. What equity accounts should be used when revaluing the assets, and should different equity accounts such as income (similar to recognition of an excess) be used in relation to recognition of liabilities?
3. Do these equity accounts remain in existence indefinitely, since they do not seem to be related to the equity accounts recognised by Tian Ltd itself?

14. When Ural Ltd acquired the shares of Stanovoi Ltd, one of the assets in the statement of financial position of Stanovoi Ltd was $15 000 goodwill, which had been recognised by Stanovoi Ltd upon its acquisition of a business from Zagros Ltd. Having prepared the acquisition analysis as part of the process of preparing the consolidated financial statements for Ural Ltd, the group accountant, Asmund Asmundson, has asked for your opinion.

Required

Provide advice on the following issues:

1. How does the recording of goodwill by the subsidiary affect the accounting for the group's goodwill?
2. If, in subsequent years, goodwill is impaired, for example by $10 000, should the impairment loss be recognised in the records of Ural Ltd or as a consolidation adjustment?

15. The accountant for Salt Ltd, Ms Finn, has sought your advice on an accounting issue that has been puzzling her. When preparing the acquisition analysis relating to Salt Ltd's acquisition of

Kirthar Ltd, she calculated that there was a gain on bargain purchase of $10 000. Being unsure of how to account for this, she was informed by accounting acquaintances that this should be recognised as income. However, she reasoned that this would have an effect on the consolidated profit in the first year after acquisition date. For example, if Kirthar Ltd reported a profit of $50 000, then consolidated profit would be $60 000. She is unsure of whether this profit is all post-acquisition profit or a mixture of pre-acquisition profit and post-acquisition profit.

Required

Compile a detailed report on the nature of an excess, how it should be accounted for and the effects of its recognition on subsequent consolidated financial statements.

STAR RATING
★ BASIC
★★ MODERATE
★★★ DIFFICULT

Exercises

Exercise 22.1 ★

CONSOLIDATION WORKSHEET ENTRIES 1 YEAR AFTER ACQUISITION DATE

At 1 July 2010, Arthur Ltd acquired all the shares of Barisan Ltd for $283 000. At this date the equity of Barisan Ltd consisted of:

Share capital – 100 000 shares	$ 200 000
General reserve	50 000
Retained earnings	20 000

All the identifiable assets and liabilities of Barisan Ltd were recorded at amounts equal to fair value except for the following assets:

	Carrying amount	Fair value
Inventory	$ 60 000	$ 65 000
Plant (cost $280 000)	200 000	210 000

The inventory was all sold by 30 June 2011. The plant has a further 5-year life, and depreciation is calculated on a straight-line basis. When revalued assets are sold or fully consumed, any related revaluation surplus is transferred to retained earnings.

The tax rate is 30%.

Required

Prepare the consolidation worksheet entries at 30 June 2011 for the preparation of the consolidated financial statements of Arthur Ltd.

Exercise 22.2 ★

ACQUISITION ANALYSIS, PARENT HOLDS PREVIOUSLY ACQUIRED SHARES IN SUBSIDIARY, WORKSHEET ENTRIES AT ACQUISITION DATE

At 1 July 2011, Crocker Ltd acquired 60% of the shares of Darling Ltd for $153 000 on a *cum div.* basis. Crocker Ltd had acquired 40% of the shares of Darling Ltd 2 years earlier for $80 000. This investment, classified as an available-for-sale investment, was recorded at a fair value on 1 July 2011 of $102 000. The changes in fair value had all been taken to other comprehensive income. At 1 July 2011, the equity of Darling Ltd consisted of:

Share capital	$160 000
Retained earnings	40 000

At this date, the identifiable assets and liabilities of Darling Ltd were recorded at fair value except for:

	Carrying amount	Fair value
Inventory	$ 40 000	$ 44 000
Plant (cost $120 000)	100 000	105 000

At 1 July 2011, Darling Ltd's assets and liabilities included a dividend payable of $5000, and goodwill of $6000 (net of $4000 accumulated impairment losses). An analysis of the unrecorded

intangibles of Darling Ltd revealed that the company had unrecorded internally generated brands, considered to have a fair value of $50 000. Further, Darling Ltd had expensed research outlays of $80 000 that were considered to have a fair value of $20 000. In its financial statements at 30 June 2011, Darling Ltd had reported a contingent liability relating to a potential claim by customers for unsatisfactory products, the fair value of the claim being $10 000.

The tax rate is 30%.

Required

Prepare the acquisition analysis at 1 July 2011, and the consolidation worksheet entries for preparation of consolidated financial statements of Crocker Ltd at that date.

Exercise 22.3

BUSINESS COMBINATION VALUATION AND PRE-ACQUISITION ENTRIES

★ On 1 July 2010, Frankland Ltd acquired all the share capital of Flinders Ltd for $218 500. At this date, Flinders Ltd's equity comprised:

Share capital – 100 000 shares	$100 000
General reserve	50 000
Retained earnings	36 000

All identifiable assets and liabilities of Flinders Ltd were recorded at fair value as at 1 July 2010 except for the following:

	Carrying amount	Fair value
Inventory	$27 000	$35 000
Land	75 000	90 000
Equipment (cost $100 000)	50 000	60 000

The equipment is expected to have a further 10-year life. All the inventory was sold by June 2011. The tax rate is 30%.

On 30 June 2011, the directors of Flinders Ltd decided to transfer $25 000 from the general reserve to retained earnings.

Required

Prepare the consolidation worksheet entries for the preparation of consolidated financial statements for Frankland Ltd and its subsidiary Flinders Ltd as at:

1. 1 July 2010
2. 30 June 2011.

Exercise 22.4

PRE-ACQUISITION ENTRIES, RECORDED GOODWILL

★ On 1 July 2012, Grampians Ltd acquired the issued shares (*cum div.*) of MacDonnell Ltd for $120 000. At that date, the financial statements of MacDonnell Ltd included the following items:

Share capital	$52 500
General reserve	45 000
Retained earnings	9 000
Dividend payable	7 500

At 1 July 2012, MacDonnell Ltd had recorded goodwill of $2000, and all its identifiable assets and liabilities were recorded at fair value. Share capital represents 75 000 shares paid to 70 cents per share. $22 500 of uncalled capital was called up on 1 October 2012. The dividend was paid on 20 October 2012. The tax rate is 30%.

Required

Prepare the pre-acquisition entries for the preparation of consolidated financial statements at:

1. 1 July 2012, immediately after combination
2. 31 December 2012.

Exercise 22.5 PARENT HOLDS PREVIOUSLY ACQUIRED INVESTMENT, CONSOLIDATION WORKSHEET

★★ On 1 December 2006, Hamersley Ltd acquired 20% of the shares of Bismarck Ltd for $10 000. These were classified as an available-for-sale investment by Hamersley Ltd. At 30 June 2010, these were recorded at a fair value of $20 400. Hamersley Ltd acquired the remaining 80% of the share capital of Bismarck Ltd for $81 600 on 1 July 2010 when the equity of Bismarck Ltd consisted of:

Share capital – 50 000 shares	$50 000
Retained earnings	30 000

All identifiable assets and liabilities of Bismarck Ltd were recorded at amounts equal to fair value, except as follows:

	Carrying amount	Fair value
Inventory	$20 000	$25 000
Plant (cost $80 000)	60 000	70 000

The plant is expected to have a further useful life of 5 years. All the inventory on hand at 1 July 2010 was sold by 31 December 2010.

The income tax rate is 30%.

At 30 June 2012, the information below was obtained from both entities.

	Hamersley Ltd	Bismarck Ltd
Profit before tax	$ 50 000	$ 40 000
Income tax expense	20 000	15 000
Profit	30 000	25 000
Retained earnings (1/7/11)	50 000	35 000
	80 000	60 000
Transfer to general reserve	20 000	5 000
Retained earnings (30/6/12)	$ 60 000	$ 55 000
Share capital	$150 000	$ 50 000
General reserve	35 000	5 000
Retained earnings	60 000	55 000
Total equity	245 000	110 000
Provisions	65 000	10 000
Payables	20 000	5 000
Total liabilities	85 000	15 000
Total equity and liabilities	$330 000	$125 000
Cash	$ 13 000	$ 14 000
Accounts receivable	30 000	25 000
Inventory	70 000	50 000
Shares in Bismarck Ltd	102 000	—
Plant	200 000	80 000
Accumulated depreciation	(85 000)	(44 000)
Total assets	$330 000	$125 000

Required

1. Prepare the consolidation worksheet entries for the preparation of consolidated financial statements for Hamersley Ltd and its subsidiary, Bismarck Ltd, as at 1 July 2010.
2. Prepare the consolidation worksheet entries and the consolidation worksheet for the preparation of consolidated financial statements for Hamersley Ltd and its subsidiary, Bismarck Ltd, as at 30 June 2012.

Exercise 22.6 ★★

RECORDED GOODWILL, UNRECORDED INTANGIBLE

On 1 July 2009, Bergamo Ltd acquired all the share capital (*cum div.*) of Ankogel Ltd, giving in exchange 50 000 shares in Bergamo Ltd, these having a fair value at acquisition date of $5 per share. Costs incurred in undertaking the acquisition amounted to $10 000. The dividend payable at the acquisition date was paid in September 2009. At 30 June 2009, the statement of financial position of Ankogel Ltd was as follows:

Statement of Financial Position as at 30 June 2009

Plant and equipment	$218 000	Share capital (150 000 shares)	$150 000
Goodwill	6 000	Retained earnings	84 000
Current assets	44 000	Dividend payable	10 000
		Other liabilities	24 000
	$268 000		$268 000

The recorded amounts of the identifiable assets and liabilities of Ankogel Ltd at the acquisition date were equal to their fair values. Ankogel Ltd had not recorded an internally developed trademark. Bergamo Ltd valued this at $20 000. It was assumed to have a 4-year life.

The tax rate is 30%.

On 31 December 2011, Ankogel Ltd paid a bonus share dividend from pre-acquisition profits, the dividend being one share for every three held.

Required

Prepare the consolidation worksheet entries for the preparation of consolidated financial statements at 30 June 2013.

Exercise 22.7 ★★

BARGAIN PURCHASE, PARENT HOLDS PREVIOUSLY ACQUIRED INVESTMENT IN SUBSIDIARY, CONSOLIDATION WORKSHEET

As part of a corporate expansion plan, Glockner Ltd acquired the remaining shares (*cum div.*) of Hafner Ltd on 1 July 2011 for $124 200 cash. At this date, it already held 10% of the shares of Hafner Ltd which it had acquired two years previously for $10 000. These available-for-sale financial instruments were recorded by Glockner Ltd at fair value. The fair value at 1 July 2011 was $13 800. The statements of financial position of both companies at 30 June 2011 were as follows:

	Glockner Ltd	Hafner Ltd
Share capital	$180 000	$ 80 000
Other components of equity	23 800	15 000
Retained earnings	58 200	30 000
Total equity	262 000	125 000
Provisions	88 000	27 000
Dividend payable	20 000	10 000
Total liabilities	108 000	37 000
Total equity and liabilities	$370 000	$162 000
Cash	$150 000	$ 10 000
Receivables	26 200	25 000
Shares in Hafner Ltd	13 800	
Inventory	55 000	42 000
Plant	190 000	100 000
Accumulated depreciation	(65 000)	(15 000)
Total assets	$370 000	$162 000

All identifiable assets and liabilities of Hafner Ltd were recorded at fair value as at 1 July 2011 except for the following:

	Carrying amount	Fair value
Inventory	$42 000	$45 000
Plant (cost $100 000)	85 000	90 000

The plant is expected to have a further useful life of 5 years. Inventory held at 1 July 2011 was all sold by 30 June 2012. The dividend payable at 1 July 2011 was paid in October 2011.

The company tax rate is 30%.

Required

1. Prepare the consolidation worksheet entries, the consolidation worksheet and the consolidated statement of financial position for Glockner Ltd and its subsidiary, Hafner Ltd, as at 1 July 2011.
2. Prepare the consolidation worksheet entries for the preparation of consolidated financial statements for Glockner Ltd and its subsidiary, Hafner Ltd, as at 30 June 2012.

Exercise 22.8 ★★

GOODWILL, GAIN ON BARGAIN PURCHASE, ADJUSTMENTS TO GOODWILL BY THE SUBSIDIARY

The statement of financial position of Albula Ltd at 30 June 2011 was as follows:

ALBULA LTD Statement of Financial Position as at 30 June 2011			
Share capital (150 000 shares)			$150 000
Retained earnings			98 000
Total equity			248 000
Dividend payable			10 000
Other liabilities			24 000
Total liabilities			34 000
Total equity and liabilities			$282 000
Inventory			$ 44 000
Non-current assets:	Plant and equipment	$ 390 000	
	Accumulated depreciation	(158 000)	
		232 000	
	Goodwill	6 000	238 000
Total assets			$282 000

The recorded amounts of the identifiable assets and liabilities of Albula Ltd at this date were equal to their fair values except for inventory and plant and equipment, whose fair values were $50 000 and $236 000 respectively. The plant and equipment has a further 5-year life. All the inventory was sold by Albula Ltd by December 2011. The tax rate is 30%.

On 1 July 2011, Plessur Ltd acquired all the shares (*cum div.*) in Albula Ltd, giving in exchange 50 000 shares in Plessur Ltd, these having a fair value at acquisition date of $5 per share. Costs incurred by Plessur Ltd in undertaking the acquisition amounted to $10 000. The dividend payable was paid in August 2011.

Required

Prepare the consolidation worksheet adjustment entries for the preparation of consolidated financial statements at 30 June 2015.

Exercise 22.9 ★★

BARGAIN PURCHASE, CONSOLIDATION WORKSHEET

Tux Ltd gained control of Stubai Ltd by acquiring its share capital on 1 January 2009. The statement of financial position of Stubai Ltd at that date showed:

Share capital	$ 60 000	Land	$ 20 000
Retained earnings	40 000	Plant and machinery	120 000
Asset revaluation reserve	20 000	Accumulated depreciation	(20 000)
Liabilities	15 000	Inventory	15 000
	$135 000		$135 000

At 1 January 2009, the recorded amounts of Stubai Ltd's assets and liabilities were equal to their fair values except as follows:

	Carrying amount	Fair value
Plant and machinery	$100 000	$102 000
Inventory	15 000	18 000

All this inventory was sold by Stubai Ltd in the following 3 months. The depreciable assets have a further 5-year life, benefits being received evenly over this period. Any business combination valuation adjustments are made on consolidation. The tax rate is 30%.

At 31 December 2009, the following information was obtained from both entities:

	Tux Ltd	Stubai Ltd
Profit before tax	$100 000	$ 15 000
Income tax expense	20 000	5 000
Profit for the year	80 000	10 000
Retained earnings (1/1/09)	103 000	40 000
	183 000	50 000
Transfer to general reserve*	10 000	4 000
Retained earnings (31/12/09)	$173 000	$ 46 000
Share capital	$445 000	$ 60 000
Retained earnings	173 000	46 000
General reserve	10 000	4 000
Asset revaluation reserve**	30 000	24 000
Liabilities	42 000	4 000
	$700 000	$138 000
Land	—	$ 20 000
Plant and machinery	$591 000	120 000
Accumulated depreciation	(20 000)	(25 000)
Inventory	15 000	23 000
Shares in Stubai Ltd	114 000	—
	$700 000	$138 000

*This transfer was from equity existing at 1 January 2009.

**This reserve relates to certain items of plant. At 1/1/09, the balances of the account were $15 000 for Tux Ltd and $20 000 for Stubai Ltd.

Required

1. Prepare the consolidated financial statements for Tux Ltd at 31 December 2009.
2. Prepare the valuation and pre-acquisition entries at 31 December 2013, assuming that, on consolidation, business combination valuation reserves are transferred to retained earnings when the related asset is sold or fully consumed.

Exercise 22.10 REVALUATION IN SUBSIDIARY'S RECORDS

★★ On 1 July 2010, Maritime Ltd acquired all the shares of Glarus Ltd (totalling $40 000) for a cash outlay of $100 000. At that date the other reserves and retained earnings of Glarus Ltd were as follows:

General reserve	$30 000
Retained earnings	20 000

All identifiable assets and liabilities of Glarus Ltd were recorded at fair value at 1 July 2010 except as follows:

	Carrying amount	Fair value
Land	$30 000	$34 000
Plant (cost $28 000)	20 000	22 000
Inventory	40 000	44 000

The plant has a further 5-year life. Of the inventory on hand at 1 July 2010, 90% was sold by 30 June 2011. Neither company had any recorded goodwill. The tax rate is 30%.

Required

1. Prepare the consolidation worksheet entries at 30 June 2011 assuming Glarus Ltd revalued the land and plant and to their fair values in its records at 1 July 2010.
2. Prepare the consolidation worksheet entries at 30 June 2011 assuming all business combination valuations are made in the consolidation worksheet.
3. If the balance of inventory was sold, what would be the business combination valuation and pre-acquisition entries at 30 June 2012, assuming requirement B above?
4. If, during June 2012, Glarus Ltd also transferred $6000 from general reserve (pre-acquisition) to retained earnings (earned before 1 July 2010), what would be the pre-acquisition entry at 30 June 2012?

Exercise 22.11 BARGAIN PURCHASE, CONSOLIDATION WORKSHEET

★★ The account balances of Balkan Ltd and Black Forest Ltd at 1 July 2013 were as follows:

	Balkan Ltd	Black Forest Ltd
	$000	$000
Share capital – 600 000 shares	600	—
– 200 000 shares	—	200
General reserve	200	50
Asset revaluation reserve	150	40
Retained earnings	200	160
Dividend payable	10	15
Provisions	320	15
	1 480	480
Land	400	200
Machinery	500	250
Accumulated depreciation	(100)	(50)
Inventory	480	75
Cash	200	5
	1 480	480

The fair values of Black Forest Ltd's assets at 1 July 2013 were:

	$000
Land	240
Machinery	220
Inventory	95

The two companies decided to combine on 1 July 2013 with Balkan Ltd issuing one share (fair value $2) and 50c cash for each share in Black Forest Ltd. Black Forest Ltd's shares were acquired *cum div.* The tax rate is 30%.

Required

1. Prepare the consolidated statement of financial position immediately after Balkan Ltd's acquisition of shares in Black Forest Ltd.
2. Prepare the consolidation worksheet entries required for the consolidation worksheet at 30 June 2014, assuming both dividends were paid during September 2013. Assume all inventory on hand at 1 July 2013 was sold in the following 3 months, and that the machinery has a further 4-year life.

Problems

Problem 22.1 ★★★

CONSOLIDATION WORKSHEET AND RESERVE TRANSFER

Financial statements	Brecon Ltd	Harz Ltd	Adjustments Dr	Adjustments Cr	Consolidation
Profit	6 000	4 000			
Retained earnings (1/7/12)	22 000	18 000			
	28 000	22 000			
Transfer from general reserve	5 000	3 000			
Retained earnings (30/6/13)	33 000	25 000			

An extract from the consolidation worksheet of Brecon Ltd and its subsidiary, Harz Ltd, as at 30 June 2013, is shown above. Brecon Ltd acquired all the share capital (*cum div.*) of Harz Ltd on 1 July 2009 for $127 000 when the equity of Harz Ltd consisted of:

Share capital	$85 000
General reserve	18 000
Retained earnings	12 000

All the identifiable assets and liabilities of Harz Ltd at 1 July 2009 were recorded at fair value except for:

	Carrying amount	Fair value
Plant (cost $100 000)	$80 000	$82 000
Inventory	6 000	7 000

The plant had a further 5-year life. All the inventory was sold by Harz Ltd by 22 September 2009. The tax rate is 30%. The liabilities of Harz Ltd included a dividend payable of $6000. Harz Ltd had not recorded any goodwill. At 1 July 2009, Harz Ltd had incurred research and development outlays of $5000, which it had expensed. Brecon Ltd placed a fair value of $2000 on this item. The project was still in progress at 30 June 2013, with Harz Ltd capitalising $3000 in the 2012–13 period. Valuation adjustments are made on consolidation.

The transfer from general reserve during the current period ending 30 June 2013 is from pre-acquisition reserves, and is the only such transfer since the acquisition date.

Required

1. Prepare the consolidation worksheet entries at 30 June 2013.
2. Complete the worksheet extract on the previous page.

Problem 22.2 ★★★

UNRECORDED LIABILITIES AND RESERVE TRANSFERS

On 1 July 2011, Tatra Ltd acquired all the share capital of Beskidy Ltd when the equity of Beskidy Ltd consisted of:

100 000 ordinary shares issued at $1, paid to 75c each	$75 000
General reserve	15 000
Retained earnings	12 000

All identifiable assets and liabilities of both companies were recorded at fair value except:

	Carrying amount	Fair value
Inventory	$20 000	$25 000
Machinery (net)	80 000	95 000

The machinery has a further 5-year life. Of the inventory on hand at 1 July 2011, 90% was sold by 31 December 2011.

At 1 July 2011, Beskidy Ltd was involved in a court case with an entity that was claiming damages from it. Beskidy Ltd had not raised a liability in relation to any expected damages. Tatra Ltd measured the fair value of the liability at $5000. By 31 December 2011, the expectation of winning the court case had improved, so the fair value was considered to be $1000.

The tax rate is 30%.

Valuation adjustments are made on consolidation.

On 1 November 2011, Beskidy Ltd transferred $6500 out of retained earnings in existence at 1 July 2011 to the general reserve account.

On 1 December 2011, Beskidy Ltd made a call of 25c per share, all call money being received by 20 December 2011.

At 31 December 2011, the statement of financial position of Tatra Ltd showed shares in Beskidy Ltd at $147 250.

Required

Prepare the consolidation worksheet entries for the preparation of the consolidated financial statements for Tatra Ltd and its subsidiary, Beskidy Ltd, as at 31 December 2011.

Problem 22.3 ★★★

BARGAIN PURCHASE, CONSOLIDATION WORKSHEET

The financial statements of Ore Ltd and its subsidiary, Pirin Ltd, at 30 June 2012 contained the following information:

	Ore Ltd	Pirin Ltd
Profit before tax	$ 3 200	$ 1 800
Income tax expense	1 300	240
Profit for the year	1 900	1 560
Retained earnings (1/7/11)	1 500	2 100
	3 400	3 660
Dividend paid	500	0
Retained earnings (30/6/12)	2 900	3 660
Share capital	25 000	10 000
General reserve	8 000	3 000
Other components of equity*	1 000	500
Liabilities	5 000	1 300
	$41 900	$18 460

	Ore Ltd	Pirin Ltd
Land	$ 8 600	$ 5 100
Plant	17 000	8 000
Accumulated depreciation	(5 000)	(1 000)
Financial assets	3 000	2 000
Inventory	3 000	4 000
Cash	300	360
Shares in Pirin Ltd	15 000	—
	$41 900	$18 460

*This relates to the available-for-sale financial assets. The balances of the accounts at 1/7/11 were $1500 (Ore Ltd) and $300 (Pirin Ltd).

Ore Ltd had acquired all the share capital of Pirin Ltd on 1 July 2010 for $15 000 when the equity of Pirin Ltd consisted of:

Share capital – 10 000 shares	$10 000
General reserve	2 000
Retained earnings	1 500

At the acquisition date by Ore Ltd, Pirin Ltd's non-monetary assets consisted of:

	Carrying amount	Fair value
Land	$4 000	$6 000
Plant (cost $6000)	5 500	6 500
Inventory	3 000	4 000

The plant had a further 5-year life. All the inventory was sold by 30 June 2011. All valuation adjustments to non-current assets are made on consolidation. The land was sold in January 2012 for $6000. The relevant business combination valuation reserves are transferred, on consolidation, to retained earnings.

The tax rate is 30%.

In September 2010, Pirin Ltd transferred $500 from its general reserve, earned before 1 July 2010, to retained earnings.

Required

Prepare the consolidated financial statements for the year ended 30 June 2012.

Problem 22.4 ★★★

CONSOLIDATION WORKSHEET, UNRECOGNISED INTANGIBLES AND LIABILITIES

Lyngen Ltd gained control of Rila Ltd by acquiring all its shares on 1 July 2010. The equity at that date was:

Share capital	$100 000
Retained earnings	35 000

At 1 July 2010, all the identifiable assets and liabilities of Rila Ltd were recorded at fair value except for:

	Carrying amount	Fair value
Inventory	$ 18 000	$ 22 000
Land	120 000	130 000
Plant (cost $120 000)	95 000	98 000

The inventory was all sold by 30 June 2011. The plant had a further 5-year life but was sold on 1 January 2013 for $50 000. The land was sold in March 2011 for $150 000.

Where revalued assets are sold or fully consumed, any associated amounts in the business combination valuation reserve are transferred to retained earnings. At 1 July 2010, Rila Ltd had guaranteed a loan taken out by Sierra Ltd. Rila Ltd had not raised a liability in relation to the guarantee but, as Sierra Ltd was not performing well, Lyngen Ltd valued the contingent liability at $5000. In January 2013, Sierra Ltd repaid the loan. Rila Ltd had also invented a special tool and patented the process. No asset was raised by Rila Ltd, but Lyngen Ltd valued the patent at $6000, with an expected useful life of 6 years. The tax rate is 30%.

Financial information for these companies for the year ended 30 June 2013 is as follows:

	Lyngen Ltd	Rila Ltd
Profit before tax	$ 50 000	$ 15 000
Income tax expense	(20 000)	(6 000)
Profit for the year	30 000	9 000
Other recognised income and expense:		
Gains on plant revaluation	6 000	0
Available-for-sale financial assets	(4 000)	(10 000)
Total recognised income and expense for the year	$ 32 000	$ (1 000)
Profit	$ 30 000	$ 9 000
Retained earnings (1 July 2012)	37 000	45 000
	67 000	54 000
Dividend paid	20 000	—
Transfer to general reserve	—	20 000
	20 000	20 000
Retained earnings (30 June 2013)	$ 47 000	$ 34 000
Share capital	$150 000	$100 000
General reserve	12 000	20 000
Asset revaluation reserve	20 000	—
Retained earnings	47 000	34 000
Other components of equity	10 000	4 000
Total equity	239 000	158 000
Payables	19 000	8 000
Loan	25 000	—
Total liabilities	44 000	8 000
Total equity and liabilities	$283 000	$166 000
Cash	$ 5 000	$ 14 000
Available-for-sale financial assets	10 000	5 000
Inventory	30 000	21 000
Plant and equipment	140 000	163 000
Accumulated depreciation	(62 000)	(37 000)
Shares in Rila Ltd	160 000	—
Total assets	$283 000	$166 000

The transfer to general reserve during the year ended 30 June 2013 was from profits earned before 1 July 2010.

Required

Prepare the consolidated financial statements for Lyngen Ltd as at 30 June 2013. Your answer should include all consolidation adjustment journal entries and a consolidation worksheet.

23 Consolidation: intragroup transactions

ACCOUNTING STANDARDS IN FOCUS

IAS 27 *Consolidated and Separate Financial Statements*

LEARNING OBJECTIVES

When you have studied this chapter, you should be able to:

- explain the need for making adjustments for intragroup transactions
- prepare worksheet entries for intragroup transactions involving profits and losses in beginning and ending inventory
- prepare worksheet entries for intragroup transactions involving profits and losses on the transfer of property, plant and equipment in both the current and previous periods
- prepare worksheet entries for intragroup transactions involving transfers from inventory to property, plant and equipment and from property, plant and equipment to inventory
- prepare worksheet entries for intragroup services such as management fees
- prepare worksheet entries for intragroup dividends
- prepare worksheet entries for intragroup borrowings.

In this chapter, the group under discussion is restricted to one where:

- there are only two entities within the group (i.e. one parent and one subsidiary)
- the parent owns all the shares of the subsidiary.

Diagrammatically, then, the group is as shown in figure 23.1.

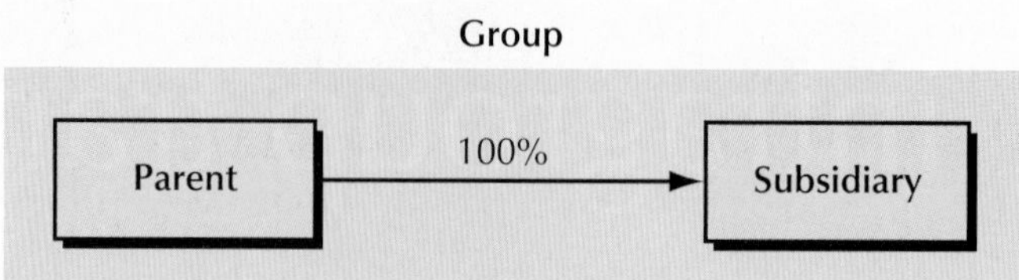

FIGURE 23.1 Group

In chapter 22, it is explained that the process of consolidation involves adding together the financial statements of a parent and its subsidiaries to reflect an overall view of the financial affairs of the group of entities as a single economic entity. It is also pointed out that two major adjustments are necessary to effect the process of consolidation:

(a) adjustments involving equity at the acquisition date, namely the business combination valuation entries (if any) and the pre-acquisition entry, eliminating the investment account in the parent's financial statements against the pre-acquisition equity of the subsidiary (see chapter 22)

(b) elimination of intragroup balances and the effects of transactions whereby profits or losses are made by different members of the group through trading with each other.

This chapter focuses on (b), adjustments for intragroup balances and transactions. The chapter analyses transactions involving inventory, depreciable assets, services, dividends and borrowings.

23.1 RATIONALE FOR ADJUSTING FOR INTRAGROUP TRANSACTIONS

Whenever related entities trade with each other, or borrow and lend money to each other, the separate legal entities disclose the effects of these transactions in the assets and liabilities recorded and the profits and losses reported. For example, if a subsidiary sells inventory to its parent, the subsidiary records a sale of inventory, including the profit on sale and reduction in inventory assets, and the parent records the purchase of inventory at the amount paid to the subsidiary. If, then, in preparing the consolidated financial statements, the separate financial statements of the legal entities are simply added together without any adjustments for the effects of the intragroup transactions, the consolidated financial statements include not only the results of the group transacting with external entities (i.e. entities outside the group) but also the results of transactions within the group. This conflicts with the purpose of the consolidated financial statements to provide information about the financial performance and financial position of the group as a result of its dealings with external entities. Hence, the effects of transactions within the group must be adjusted for in the preparation of the consolidated financial statements.

The requirement for the full adjustment for the effects of intragroup transactions is stated in paragraph 20 of IAS 27 *Consolidated and Separate Financial Statements*:

> Intragroup balances, transactions, income and expenses shall be eliminated in full.

The requirement to adjust for the full effects of the transactions is consistent with the entity concept of consolidation, as the whole of the parent and the subsidiary are within the group.

Besides adjusting for the effects of transactions occurring in the current period, it is also necessary to adjust the current period's consolidated financial statements for the ongoing effects of transactions in previous periods. Because the consolidation adjustment entries are applied in a worksheet only, and not in the accounts of either the parent or the subsidiary, any continuing effects of previous periods' transactions must be considered. This affects transactions such as loans between, say, a parent and a subsidiary where a balance owing at the end of a number of periods is reduced over time as repayments are made. Similarly, where assets such as inventory are transferred at the end of one period and then are still on hand at the beginning of the next period, consolidation adjustments are required to be made in both periods.

Some intragroup transactions do not affect the carrying amounts of assets and liabilities (e.g. where there is a management fee paid by one entity to another within the group). In that case, the items affected are fee revenue and fee expense. However, in other circumstances, there are assets and liabilities recognised by the group at amounts different from the amounts recognised by the individual legal entities. For example, consider the situation where a subsidiary sold an item of inventory to the parent for $1000, and the inventory had cost the subsidiary $800. The parent recognises the inventory at cost of $1000, whereas the cost of the inventory to the group is only $800. As is explained in more detail later in this chapter, consolidation adjustment entries are necessary to adjust for both the profit on the intragroup transaction and the carrying amount of the inventory.

Under IAS 12 *Income Taxes*, deferred tax accounts must be raised where there are temporary differences between the carrying amount of an asset or liability and its tax base. Any difference between the carrying amount of an asset or a liability and its tax base in a legal entity within the group is accounted for by the legal entity. However, on consolidation, in relation to intragroup transactions, adjustments may be made to the carrying amounts of assets and liabilities. Hence, in adjusting for intragroup transactions wherever there are changes to the carrying amounts of assets and liabilities, any associated tax effect must be considered. Paragraph 21 of IAS 27 recognises the need to apply tax-effect accounting for temporary differences arising from the elimination of profits and losses from intragroup transactions.

For example, assume an asset is recorded by a subsidiary at a carrying amount of $1000, and that the tax base is $800. In the records of the subsidiary, the application of tax-effect accounting will account for the temporary difference of $200, raising a deferred tax liability of $60, assuming a tax rate of 30%. If, on consolidation, an adjustment is made to reduce the carrying amount of the asset, say to $950, the consolidation adjustment entries must include an adjustment for the tax effect of the change in the carrying amount of the asset, namely a reduction in the deferred tax liability of $15 (i.e. 30% × $50). The consolidated financial statements then show a deferred tax liability of $45 (i.e. $60 – $15). The combination of the tax-effect entries in the subsidiaries and the tax-effect adjustments on consolidation will account for the temporary difference caused by the group showing the asset at $950 and the tax base being $800, namely a deferred tax liability of $45 (i.e. 30% × ($950 – $800)).

As can be seen in this example, in preparing the consolidation adjustments it is unnecessary to consider the tax-effect entries made in the individual entities in the group. If the appropriate tax-effect adjustments are made for changes in the carrying amounts of the assets, then the combination of those adjustments and the tax-effect entries made in the entities themselves will produce the correct answer.

In this book, it is assumed that each subsidiary is a tax-paying entity. Under the tax consolidation system in some countries, groups comprising a parent and its wholly owned subsidiaries can elect to consolidate and be treated as a single entity for tax purposes. Such entities prepare a consolidated tax return, and the effects of intragroup transactions are eliminated. Under such a scheme, the tax-effect adjustments demonstrated in this chapter would not apply.

Just as the pre-acquisition entry is used in a consolidation worksheet to eliminate the investment and to adjust for pre-acquisition equity, adjustment journal entries are prepared for intragroup transactions and are recorded in the consolidation worksheet. The same two adjustment columns are used to effect these adjustments. For example, if it were necessary to adjust downwards by $10 000 the sales revenue recorded by the legal entities, the consolidation worksheet would show the following line:

			Adjustments			
	Parent	Subsidiary		Dr	Cr		Group
Sales revenue	100 000	80 000	10 000			170 000

In the following sections of this chapter, three types of intragroup transactions are discussed — transfers of inventory, transfers of property, plant and equipment, and intragroup services. In each of the specific sections covering these transactions, the process of determining when profits are realised for the different types of transactions is discussed.

23.2 TRANSFERS OF INVENTORY

In the following examples, assume that Virgo Ltd owns all the share capital of Scorpio Ltd, and that the consolidation process is being carried out on 30 June 2010, for the year ending on that date. Assume also a tax rate of 30%. All entries shown as being for the individual entities assume the use of a perpetual inventory system, and adjustments will be made, where necessary, to cost of sales.

23.2.1 Sales of inventory

Example

On 1 January 2010, Virgo Ltd acquired $10 000 worth of inventory for cash from Scorpio Ltd. The inventory had previously cost Scorpio Ltd $8000.

In the accounting records of Scorpio Ltd, the following journal entries are made on 1 January 2010:

Cash	Dr	10 000	
Sales Revenue	Cr		10 000
Cost of Sales	Dr	8 000	
Inventory	Cr		8 000

In Virgo Ltd, the journal entry is:

Inventory	Dr	10 000	
Cash	Cr		10 000

From the viewpoint of the group in relation to this transaction, no sales of inventory were made to any party outside the group, nor has the group acquired any inventory from external entities. Hence, if the financial statements of Virgo Ltd and Scorpio Ltd are simply added together for consolidation purposes, 'sales', 'cost of sales' and 'inventory' will need to be adjusted on consolidation as the consolidated financial statements must show only the results of transactions with entities external to the group.

23.2.2 Realisation of profits or losses

Paragraph 21 of IAS 27 states that the profits and losses resulting from intragroup transactions that require consolidation adjustments to be made are those 'recognised in assets'. These profits can be described as 'unrealised profits'. The test for realisation is the involvement of an external party in relation to the item involved in the intragroup transaction. If an item of inventory is transferred from a subsidiary to the parent entity (or vice versa), no external party is involved in that transaction. The profit made by the subsidiary is unrealised to the group. If the parent then sells that inventory item to a party external to the group, the intragroup profit becomes realised to the group. For example, assume a subsidiary, Scorpio Ltd, sells inventory to its parent, Virgo Ltd, for $100, and that inventory cost Scorpio Ltd $90. The profit on this transaction is unrealised. If Virgo Ltd sells the inventory to an external party for $100, the intragroup profit is realised. The group sold inventory that cost the group $90 to an external party for $100. The group has made $10 profit. Hence, the consolidation adjustments for profits on intragroup transfers of inventory depend on whether the acquiring entity has sold the inventory to entities outside the group. In other words, the adjustments depend on whether the acquiring entity still carries some or all of the transferred inventory as ending inventory at the end of the financial period.

23.2.3 Profits in ending inventory

The following example uses the information in the example in section 23.2.1 and provides information about whether the inventory transferred is still on hand at the end of the financial period.

Example: Transferred inventory still on hand

On 30 June 2010, all the inventory sold by Scorpio Ltd to Virgo Ltd is still on hand. The adjustment entries in the consolidation worksheet at 30 June 2010 are:

Sales Revenue	Dr	10 000	
Cost of Sales	Cr		8 000
Inventory	Cr		2 000

The sales adjustment is necessary to eliminate the effects of the original sale in the current period. Scorpio Ltd recorded sales of $10 000. From the group's viewpoint, as no external party was involved in the transaction, no sales should be shown in the consolidated financial statements. To adjust sales revenue downwards, a debit adjustment is necessary. The effect of this adjustment on the consolidation process is seen in figure 23.2. Hence, an adjustment is necessary to eliminate the sales recorded by Scorpio Ltd.

Using similar reasoning as with the adjustment for sales revenue, the subsidiary has recorded cost of sales of $8000, but the group has made no sales to entities external to the group. Hence, the consolidation worksheet needs to have a reduction in cost of sales of $8000 in order to show a zero amount in the consolidation column. Note also that adjusting sales by $10 000 and cost of sales by $8000 effectively reduces consolidated profit by $2000. In other words, the $2000 profit recorded by Scorpio Ltd on selling inventory to Virgo Ltd is eliminated and a zero profit is shown on consolidation. As no external party was involved in the transfer of inventory, the whole of the profit on the intragroup transaction is unrealised. This is illustrated in figure 23.2.

			Adjustments				
	Parent	Subsidiary		Dr	Cr		Group
Sales revenue	0	10 000	*1*	**10 000**			—
Cost of sales	0	8 000			**8 000**	*1*	—
		2 000					
Tax expense	0	600			600	*2*	—
Profit		1 400					—
Inventory	10 000	—			**2 000**	*1*	8 000
Deferred tax asset	—	—	*2*	600			600

FIGURE 23.2 Extract from consolidation worksheet — profit in closing inventory

The previous explanation dealing with the effect on profit covers only the statement of comprehensive income part of the adjustment. Under the historical cost system, assets in the consolidated statement of financial position must be shown at cost to the group. Inventory is recorded in Virgo Ltd at $10 000, the cost to Virgo Ltd. The cost to the group is, however, $8000, the amount that was paid for the inventory by Scorpio Ltd to entities external to the group. Hence, if inventory is to be reported at $8000 in the consolidated financial statements, and it is recorded in Virgo Ltd's records at $10 000, a credit adjustment of $2000 is needed to reduce the inventory to $8000, the cost to the group. This effect is seen in figure 23.2.

Virgo Ltd has recorded the inventory in its records at $10 000. This amount is probably also its tax base. However, as explained in section 23.1, any difference between the tax base and the carrying amount in Virgo Ltd is accounted for in the tax-effect entries in Virgo Ltd. On consolidation, a tax-effect entry is necessary where an adjustment entry causes a difference between the carrying amount of an asset or a liability in the records of the legal entity and the carrying amount shown in the consolidated financial statements. In the adjustment entry relating to profit in ending inventory in the above example, the carrying amount of inventory is reduced downwards by $2000. The carrying amount and tax base of the inventory in Virgo Ltd is $10 000, but the carrying amount in the group is $8000. This $2000 difference is a deductible temporary difference giving rise to a deferred tax asset of $600 (i.e. 30% × $2000), as well as a corresponding decrease in income tax expense. The appropriate consolidation worksheet adjustment entry is:

Deferred Tax Asset	Dr	600	
Income Tax Expense	Cr		600

The effects of this entry are shown in figure 23.2.

The deferred tax asset recognises that the group is expected to earn profits in the future that will not require the payment of tax to the taxation office. When the inventory is sold by Virgo Ltd in a future period, this temporary difference is reversed. To illustrate this effect, assume that in the following period Virgo Ltd sells this inventory to an external entity for $11 000. Virgo Ltd will record a before-tax profit of $1000 (i.e. $11 000 – $10 000) and an associated tax expense of $300. From the consolidated group position, the profit on sale is $3000 (i.e. $11 000 – $8000). The group will show current tax payable of $300, reverse the $600 deferred tax asset, and recognise an income tax expense of $900. These effects are further illustrated below.

Example: Transferred inventories partly sold

On 1 January 2010, Virgo Ltd acquired $10 000 worth of inventory for cash from Scorpio Ltd. The inventory had previously cost Scorpio Ltd $8000. By the end of the year, 30 June 2010, Virgo Ltd had sold $7500 of the transferred inventory for $14 000 to external entities. Thus, $2500 of the inventory is on hand in Virgo Ltd at 30 June 2010.

The adjustment entry for the preparation of consolidated financial statements at 30 June 2010 is:

Sales	Dr	10 000	
Cost of Sales	Cr		9 500
Inventory	Cr		500

The total sales recorded by the *legal entities* are $24 000, i.e. $10 000 by Scorpio Ltd and $14 000 by Virgo Ltd. The sales by the *group*, being those sold to entities external to the group, are $14 000. The consolidation adjustment to sales revenue is then $10 000, being the amount necessary to eliminate the sales within the group.

The total cost of sales recorded by the *legal entities* is $15 500, i.e. $8000 by Scorpio Ltd and $7500 by Virgo Ltd (i.e. 75% × $10 000). The cost of sales to the *group*, being those to entities external to the group, is $6000, i.e. 75% × $8000. Hence, the consolidation adjustment is $9500, i.e. $15 500 (sum of recorded sales) less $6000 (group). The adjustment is that necessary to adjust the sum of the amounts recorded by the legal entities to that to be recognised by the group.

Note that the combined adjustments to sales and cost of sales result in a $500 reduction in before-tax profit. Of the $2000 intragroup profit on the transfer of inventory from Scorpio Ltd to Virgo Ltd, since three-quarters of the inventory has been sold by Virgo Ltd to an external party, $1500 of the profit is realised to the group and only $500, the profit remaining in ending inventory, is unrealised. It is the unrealised profit that is adjusted for in the worksheet entry.

The group profit is then $500 less than that recorded by the legal entities. The sum of profits recorded by the legal entities is $8500, consisting of $2000 recorded by Scorpio Ltd and $6500 (being sales of $14 000 less cost of sales of $7500) recorded by Virgo Ltd. From the group's viewpoint, profit on sale of inventory to external entities is only $8000, consisting of sales of $14 000 less cost of sales of $6000 (being 75% of original cost of $8000). Hence, an adjustment of $500 is necessary to reduce recorded profit of $8500 to group profit of $8000.

The $500 adjustment to inventory reflects the proportion of the total profit on sale of the transferred inventory that remains in the inventory on hand at the end of the period. Since 25% of the transferred inventory is still on hand at the end of the period, then 25% of the total profit on transfer of inventory, i.e. 25% × $2000, needs to be adjusted at the end of the period. The adjustment entry reduces the inventory on hand at 30 June 2010 from the recorded cost to Virgo Ltd of $2500 to the group cost of $2000 (being 25% of the original cost of $8000).

The adjustments above have been determined by comparing the combined amounts recorded by the parent and the subsidiary with the amounts that the group wants to report in the consolidated financial statements. This process could be shown in the form of a table, as follows:

	Parent	Subsidiary	Total Recorded	Group	Adjustment
Sales	14 000	10 000	24 000	14 000	Dr 10 000
Cost of sales	7 500	8 000	15 500	6 000	Cr 9 500
Profit	6 500	2 000	8 500	8 000	
Inventory	2 500	0	2 500	2 000	Cr $500

Consider the *tax effect* of this adjustment. The carrying amount of the inventory is reduced by $500, reflecting the fact that the carrying amount to the group is $500 less than the carrying amount in Virgo Ltd. This gives rise to a deductible temporary difference of $500. Hence, a deferred tax asset of $150 (i.e. 30% × $500) must be raised on consolidation with a corresponding effect on income tax expense. The expectation of the group is that, in some future period, it will recognise the remaining $500 profit in transferred inventory when it sells the inventory to an external party, but will not have to pay tax on the $500 as Scorpio Ltd has already paid the relevant tax. This expected tax saving to the group will be shown in the consolidated financial statements by a debit adjustment of $150 to the Deferred Tax Asset account.

The tax-effect adjustment entry is then:

Deferred Tax Asset	Dr	150	
Income Tax Expense	Cr		150

Example: Transferred inventory completely sold

On 1 January 2010, Virgo Ltd acquired $10 000 worth of inventory for cash from Scorpio Ltd. The inventory had previously cost Scorpio Ltd $8000. By the end of the year, 30 June 2010, Virgo Ltd had sold all the transferred inventory to an external party for $18 000.

Scorpio Ltd records a profit of	$ 2 000	(i.e. $10 000 less $8 000)
Virgo Ltd records a profit of	$ 8 000	(i.e. $18 000 less $10 000)
Total recorded profit is	$ 10 000	

Profit to the group = Selling price to external entities less cost to the group
= $18 000 – $8 000
= $10 000

Since the recorded profit equals the profit to the group, there is no need for a profit adjustment on consolidation. Further, as there is no transferred inventory still on hand, there is no need for an adjustment to inventory. Because all the inventory has been sold to an external entity, the whole of the intragroup profit is realised to the group. Note, however, that an adjustment for the sales and cost of sales is still necessary. As noted previously, the sales within the group amount to $18 000 whereas the sales recorded by the legal entities total $28 000 (i.e. $10 000 + $18 000). Hence, sales must be reduced by $10 000. The total recorded cost of sales is $18 000, being $8000 by Scorpio Ltd and $10 000 by Virgo Ltd. The group's cost of sales is the original cost of the transferred inventory, $8000. Hence, cost of sales is reduced by $10 000 on consolidation. The adjustment entry is then:

Sales	Dr	10 000	
Cost of Sales	Cr		10 000

Since there is no adjustment to the carrying amounts of assets or liabilities, there is no need for any *tax-effect* adjustment.

Where inventory is transferred in the current period and some or all of that inventory is still on hand at the end of the period, the general form of the worksheet entries is:

Sales Revenue	Dr	X	
Cost of Sales	Cr		X
Inventory	Cr		X
(The adjustment to inventory is based on the profit remaining in inventory on hand at the end of the period)			
Deferred Tax Asset	Dr	X	
Income Tax Expense	Cr		X
(The tax rate times the adjustment to ending inventory)			

23.2.4 Profits in opening inventory

Any transferred inventory remaining unsold at the end of one period is still on hand at the beginning of the next period. Because the consolidation adjustments are made only in a worksheet and not in the records of any of the legal entities, any differences in balances between the legal entities and the consolidated group at the end of one period must still exist at the beginning of the next period.

Example: Transferred inventory on hand at the beginning of the period

On 1 July 2009, the first day of the current period, Scorpio Ltd has on hand inventory worth $7000, transferred from Virgo Ltd in June 2009. The inventory had previously cost Virgo Ltd $4500. The tax rate is 30%.

In this example, in the preparation of the consolidated financial statements at *30 June 2009* the following adjustment entries for the $2500 profit in ending inventory would have been made in the consolidation worksheet:

Sales	Dr	7 000	
Cost of Sales	Cr		4 500
Inventory	Cr		2 500
Deferred Tax Asset	Dr	750	
Income Tax Expense	Cr		750
(30% × $2500)			

Since the ending inventory at 30 June 2009 becomes the beginning inventory for the next year, an adjustment is necessary in the consolidated financial statements prepared at 30 June 2010. The required adjustment is:

Retained Earnings (1/7/09)	Dr	2 500	
Cost of Sales	Cr		2 500

In making this consolidation worksheet adjustment, it is assumed that the inventory is sold to external entities in the current period. If this is not the case, then the adjustment to inventory as made at 30 June 2009 will need to be made again in preparing the consolidated financial statements at 30 June 2010.

In making a *credit adjustment* of $2500, cost of sales is reduced. The cost of sales recorded by Scorpio Ltd in the 2009–10 period is $2500 greater than that which the group wants to show, because the cost of sales recorded by Virgo Ltd is $7000, whereas the cost of sales to the group is only $4500. A reduction in cost of sales means an increase in profit. Hence, in the 2009–10 period, the group's profit is greater than the sum of the legal entities' profit.

The *debit adjustment* to the opening balance of retained earnings reduces that balance; i.e. the group made less profit in previous years than the sum of the retained earnings recorded by the legal entities. This is because, in June 2009, Virgo Ltd recorded a $2500 profit on the sale of inventory to Scorpio Ltd, this profit not being recognised by the group until the 2009–10 period.

Consider the *tax effect* of these entries. If the previous period's tax-effect adjustment were carried forward into this year's worksheet it would be:

Deferred Tax Asset	Dr	750	
Retained Earnings (1/7/09)	Cr		750

On sale of the inventory in the 2009–10 period, the deferred tax asset is reversed, with a resultant effect on income tax expense:

Income Tax Expense	Dr	750	
Deferred Tax Asset	Cr		750

On combining these two entries, the worksheet entry required is:

Income Tax Expense	Dr	750	
Retained Earnings (1/7/09)	Cr		750

In summary, the adjustment to cost of sales, retained earnings and income tax expense can be combined into one entry as follows:

Retained Earnings (1/7/09)	Dr	1 750	
Income Tax Expense	Dr	750	
Cost of Sales	Cr		2 500

Note that this entry has no effect on the closing balance of retained earnings at 30 June 2010. As the inventory has been sold outside the group, the whole of the profit on the intragroup transaction is realised to the group. There is no unrealised profit to be adjusted for at the end of the period.

Where inventory was transferred in a previous period and some or all of that inventory is still on hand at the beginning of the current period, the general form of the entries is:

Retained Earnings (opening balance)	Dr	X	
Cost of Sales	Cr		X
Income Tax Expense	Dr	X	
Retained Earnings (opening balance)	Cr		X

It can be seen that the consolidation worksheet entries for inventory transferred within the current period are different from those where the inventory was transferred in a previous period. *Before preparing the adjustment entries, it is essential to determine the timing of the transaction.*

ILLUSTRATIVE EXAMPLE 23.1

Intragroup transactions involving transfers of inventory

Pisces Ltd acquired all the issued shares of Aquarius Ltd on 1 January 2009. The following transactions occurred between the two entities:

1. On 1 June 2010, Pisces Ltd sold inventory to Aquarius Ltd for $12 000, this inventory previously costing Pisces Ltd $10 000. By 30 June 2010, Aquarius Ltd had onsold 20% of this inventory to other entities for $3000. The other 80% was all sold to external entities by 30 June 2011 for $13 000.
2. During the 2010–11 period, Aquarius Ltd sold inventory to Pisces Ltd for $6000, this being at cost plus 20% mark-up. Of this inventory, $1200 remained on hand in Pisces Ltd at 30 June 2011.

The tax rate is 30%.

Required

Prepare the consolidation worksheet entries for Pisces Ltd at 30 June 2011 in relation to the intragroup transfers of inventory.

Solution

The required consolidation worksheet entries are:

(1) *Sale of inventory in previous period*

Retained Earnings (1/7/10)	Dr	1 120	
Income Tax Expense	Dr	480	
Cost of Sales	Cr		1 600

Working:

- this is a prior period transaction
- profit after tax remaining in inventory at 1/7/10 is \$1120 (= 80% × \$2000 (1 – 30%))
- cost of sales recorded by Aquarius Ltd is \$9600 (= 80% × \$12 000); cost of sales to the group is \$8000 (= 80% × \$10 000). The adjustment is then \$1600.

(2) *Sale of inventory in current period*

Sales	Dr	6 000	
Cost of Sales	Cr		5 800
Inventory	Cr		200
Deferred Tax Asset	Dr	60	
Income Tax Expense	Cr		60

Working:

- this is a current period transaction
- sales within the group are \$6000
- cost of sales recorded by the members of the group are \$5000 for Aquarius Ltd and \$4800 (= $\frac{4}{5}$ × \$6000) for Pisces Ltd; a total of \$9800. Cost of sales for the group is \$4000 (= $\frac{4}{5}$ × \$5000). The adjustment is then \$5800
- the inventory remaining at 30 June 2011 is recorded by Pisces Ltd at \$1200. The cost to the group is \$1000 (= $\frac{1}{5}$ × \$5000). The adjustment to inventory is then \$200
- as the inventory is adjusted by \$200, the tax effect is \$60 (= 30% × \$200).

23.3 TRANSFERS OF PROPERTY, PLANT AND EQUIPMENT

Besides transferring inventory, it is possible for property, plant and equipment to be transferred within the group. The worksheet adjustment entries are shown in two parts: (1) the entries to adjust for any profit or loss on sale of the assets, and (2) the entries relating to any depreciation of the assets after sale. As realisation of the profit or loss on sale is related to the depreciation of the transferred asset, the depreciation entries are covered in section 23.3.2 in conjunction with the discussion on realisation. If a non-depreciable asset is transferred, only the first of these entries is required, and realisation of the profit or loss occurs, as with inventory, on sale of the asset to an external party.

23.3.1 Sales of property, plant and equipment

Example: Transfer in current year

Virgo Ltd sold Scorpio Ltd plant for \$18 500 cash on 1 July 2009. It had cost Virgo Ltd \$20 000 when acquired 1 year previously. Depreciation charged on plant by Virgo Ltd is 10% p.a. on cost, and Scorpio Ltd applies a rate of 6% p.a. on cost. The income tax rate is 30%.

The journal entries in the records of Virgo Ltd and Scorpio Ltd at the date of sale, 1 July 2009, are:

Virgo Ltd			
Cash	Dr	18 500	
Proceeds from Sale of Plant	Cr		18 500
Carrying Amount of Plant Sold	Dr	18 000	
Accumulated Depreciation	Dr	2 000	
Plant	Cr		20 000
Scorpio Ltd			
Plant	Dr	18 500	
Cash	Cr		18 500
The consolidation adjustment entry is:			
Proceeds from Sale of Plant	Dr	18 500	
Carrying Amount of Plant Sold	Cr		18 000
Plant	Cr		500

From the group's viewpoint, there is no sale of plant to entities external to the group. Since the legal entity Virgo Ltd recorded such a sale, the consolidation adjustment involves eliminating the effects of the sale. The adjustment entry includes a debit to revenue and a credit to the expense account, Carrying Amount of Plant Sold, to eliminate the effect of these accounts raised by Virgo Ltd. As a result of the sale, the plant is recorded by Scorpio Ltd at cost of $18 500. From the group's perspective, the cost of the asset at the time of transfer within the group is the carrying amount in the records of the selling company, Virgo Ltd, i.e. $18 000. So that the asset is reported in the consolidated financial statements at cost to the group, an adjustment entry reducing the asset from a recorded amount of $18 500 to the group's cost of $18 000 is necessary. Hence, a credit to the asset of $500 is required.

Under international accounting standards, there is no requirement to separately disclose the income on sale of property, plant and equipment, nor the carrying amounts of assets sold. Some entities may disclose on a net basis a gain or loss on sale of property, plant and equipment. In the above example, there is a gain on sale to Virgo Ltd of $500. If Virgo Ltd had recorded a gain on sale of plant, the consolidation adjustment entry would be:

Gain on Sale of Plant	Dr	500	
Plant	Cr		500

In the consolidated statement of comprehensive income, it is the gain or loss on sale of plant that is reported.

The consolidation adjustment reduces plant by $500. As with inventory, any adjustment on consolidation to the carrying amount of an asset provides a difference between the carrying amount and the tax base of the asset. Hence, there is a deductible temporary difference in relation to the plant. It is then necessary to recognise a deferred tax asset and an adjustment to income tax expense equal to the tax rate times the temporary difference, namely 30% × $500 = $150. The consolidation worksheet adjustment entry is:

Deferred Tax Asset	Dr	150	
Income Tax Expense	Cr		150
(30% × $500)			

A deferred tax asset is recognised because there is a reduction in the carrying amount of the asset. This may in fact be a reduction in a deferred tax liability raised by the legal entity if for some reason the carrying amount of the asset in the legal entity is greater than the asset's tax base. Because deferred tax assets and liabilities are netted off for disclosure purposes, a problem as to whether the adjustment is reducing a deferred tax liability or increasing a deferred tax asset is not important.

As long as the depreciable asset remains within the group, an adjustment entry is necessary to reduce Virgo Ltd's recorded prior-period profits and to reduce the cost of the asset as recorded by Scorpio Ltd. The adjustment entry in years after the year of sale of the asset is:

Retained Earnings (opening balance)	Dr	500	
Plant	Cr		500

In periods after the year of sale, as long as the asset remains on hand, the tax-effect entry is:

Deferred Tax Asset	Dr	150	
Retained Earnings (opening balance)	Cr		150

In summary, in the *year of transfer*, the general form of the consolidation worksheet entries is:

Proceeds on Sale	Dr	X	
Carrying Amount of Asset Sold	Cr		X
Property, Plant and Equipment	Cr		X
Deferred Tax Asset	Dr	X	
Income Tax Expense	Cr		X

In *years after the transfer*, the entries become:

Retained Earnings (opening balance)	Dr	X	
Property, Plant and Equipment	Cr		X
Deferred Tax Asset	Dr	X	
Retained Earnings (opening balance)	Cr		X

If a *loss* is made on transfer of property, plant and equipment, consolidation adjustments are needed to eliminate the loss in the year of transfer and bring the asset back to cost to the group. The tax-effect worksheet entry then recognises a deferred tax liability. The pro forma consolidation entries are:

Property, Plant and Equipment	Dr	X	
Proceeds on Sale	Dr	X	
Carrying Amount of Asset Sold	Cr		X
Income Tax Expense	Dr	X	
Deferred Tax Liability	Cr		X

In *years after the transfer*, the entries become:

Property, Plant and Equipment	Dr	X	
Retained Earnings (opening balance)	Cr		X
Retained Earnings (opening balance)	Dr	X	
Deferred Tax Liability	Cr		X

Paragraph 21 of IAS 27 notes that intragroup losses may indicate an impairment. In that case, an impairment loss and related accumulated impairment loss would be recognised in the consolidation worksheet.

23.3.2 Depreciation and realisation of profits or losses

Realisation of profits or losses on depreciable asset transfers

For intragroup transactions such as inventory transfers or sale of land, the determination of whether the profit on the intragroup sale is realised is simple. The profit is realised when the buying entity, say the parent, sells the transferred inventory or land to an external party. However, where transactions occur involving depreciable assets, no external party ever becomes *directly* involved in these transactions, as the transferred item remains within the group. Hence, either the profits or losses on transfer of these items are to be regarded as never being realised, or some assumption is made about the point of realisation. The former course of action is impractical because adjustments for the profit would have to be made for every year in the life of the group after the transaction occurred. In practice, the second course of action is followed.

The realisation of the profit or loss on a depreciable asset transferred within the group is *assumed* to occur when the future benefits embodied in the asset are consumed by the group. In other words, the depreciable asset transferred within the group will never be sold to an external party, but will be used up within the group to generate benefits for the group. As the asset is used up within the group, the benefits are received by the group. A useful measure of the pattern of benefits received by the group can be obtained by reference to the depreciation charged on the asset, since the depreciation allocation is related to the pattern of benefits from the use of the assets. Hence, for depreciable assets, the involvement of external entities in the transaction occurs on an indirect basis with the assumption being made that realisation occurs in a pattern consistent with the allocation of the depreciation of the non-current asset.

Assume a subsidiary sells a depreciable asset to the parent at a profit of $100, and the parent depreciates the asset on a straight-line basis of 10% p.a. On the date of sale, the unrealised profit is $100. In the first year after the sale, $10 (i.e. 10% × $100) of that profit is realised, leaving $90 unrealised profit at the end of the year. In that year the group shows $90 less profit than the sum of the profits of the parent and the subsidiary. In the second year, the group realises a further $10 profit, and shows $10 more profit than the sum of the profits of the parent and the subsidiary. The process of realisation occurs via the adjustments for the depreciation of the asset subsequent to the point of sale, and is explained in the following section on depreciation.

Depreciation

In the previous example, plant was transferred from Virgo Ltd to Scorpio Ltd for $18 500 at a before-tax gain of $500. Since the asset is transferred at the beginning of the current period, Scorpio Ltd uses the asset and charges depreciation at 6% p.a. on a straight-line basis. The adjustment for depreciation at the end of the first year after the sale is determined by comparing the depreciation charge on the cost to the legal entity with the depreciation charge on the cost to the group:

Scorpio Ltd:	Cost of asset	= $18 500
	Depreciation expense	= 6% × $18 500
		= $1 110
Group:	Cost of asset	= $18 000
	Depreciation expense	= 6% × $18 000
		= $1 080
	Adjustment	= $1 110 − $1 080
		= $30

On consolidation, depreciation is reduced by $30. The worksheet entry is:

Accumulated Depreciation	Dr	30	
Depreciation Expense	Cr		30

This adjustment increases the group's profit by $30, that is, the group has realised $30 of the $500 profit on sale of the plant. The adjustment for the gain on sale reduces the group's profit by $500, and the adjustment for depreciation results in recognising some of that profit being realised as the asset is used up. The amount of profit realised is in proportion to the depreciation charged, namely 6% p.a.

In determining whether the depreciation rate used should be Virgo Ltd's or Scorpio Ltd's, remember that Virgo Ltd sold the asset to Scorpio Ltd. The purpose of making the consolidation adjustments is not to show the financial statements as they would have been if the transaction had not occurred, but to eliminate the effects of the intragroup transactions. Within the group, the plant has been transferred from one place of use to another, namely from Virgo Ltd to Scorpio Ltd. As a result, the plant is subject to the wear and tear, life expectations and so on associated with Scorpio Ltd's assets rather than Virgo Ltd's assets. Hence, the appropriate depreciation rate for consolidation purposes is that of the entity in which the asset is used.

The difference between the carrying amount in the legal entity and that in the group at date of sale was \$500 (i.e. \$18 500 – \$18 000). At the end of the first year after sale, the difference is \$470 (i.e. by adjusting for 6% depreciation, 94% × \$18 500 less 94% × \$18 000). The reduction in the carrying amount difference is \$30, giving rise to a reversal of the initial temporary difference of \$9 (i.e. 30% × \$30). The worksheet adjustment entry for the tax effect of the depreciation adjustment is:

Income Tax Expense	Dr	9	
Deferred Tax Asset	Cr		9

The tax-effect adjustment is calculated as the tax rate times the adjustment to depreciation (i.e. 30% × \$30). This depreciation adjustment causes the carrying amount to change each period, thus reducing the temporary difference created on the initial transfer of the asset. The net effect of the depreciation and the tax-effect adjustment on the profit of the group is an increase of \$21 (i.e. \$30 – \$9). The \$350 after-tax profit on the sale of the plant is being realised at \$21 (i.e. 6% × \$350) p.a.

While the asset remains on hand, depreciation will be charged. Hence, when preparing the consolidated financial statements for the period 2010–11, the adjustment for depreciation must reflect the effects of the differences in depreciation for both the current year and the previous year. The adjustment relating to the previous period's depreciation is made against retained earnings (opening balance). The adjustment at 30 June 2011 is:

Accumulated Depreciation	Dr	60	
Depreciation Expense	Cr		30
Retained Earnings (1/7/10)	Cr		30

In this worksheet entry, both the current period's and the previous period's accounting profit is increased by the reduction in depreciation expense. From a tax-effect accounting perspective, there must be an increase in income tax expense both for the current period and for the previous period. Reversal of the deferred tax asset raised in relation to the gain on sale occurs throughout the life of the asset as it is depreciated, causing its carrying amount to fall. The consolidation adjustment entry at 30 June 2011 for the tax effect of the depreciation adjustment entry is:

Retained Earnings (1/7/10)	Dr	9	
Income Tax Expense	Dr	9	
Deferred Tax Asset	Cr		18

It can be seen that over the expected life of the asset, as it is depreciated the deferred tax asset raised on the intragroup sale of the asset is progressively being reversed.

In relation to the realisation of the profit on sale, the unrealised after-tax profit on the sale of the plant is \$350 (i.e. \$500 × (1 – 0.3)). The profit is being realised at \$21 (\$30 – \$9) p.a. At the end of the second year after the sale, a total of \$42 is realised, \$21 in the previous year and \$21 in the current year. When the asset is fully depreciated, the whole of the profit on sale is realised.

In the *year of transfer*, the general form of consolidation entries for depreciation of a transferred asset is:

Accumulated Depreciation	Dr	X	
Depreciation Expense	Cr		X
Income Tax Expense	Dr	X	
Deferred Tax Asset	Cr		X

In the *years after the transfer*, the entries are:

Accumulated Depreciation	Dr	X	
Depreciation Expense	Cr		X
Retained Earnings (opening balance)	Cr		X
Income Tax Expense	Dr	X	
Retained Earnings (opening balance)	Dr	X	
Deferred Tax Asset	Cr		X

Note that, if a loss were made on the transfer, these entries would be reversed and the tax-effect entry would reduce the deferred tax liability created as a result of the loss on transfer. Again, intragroup losses may indicate an impairment loss that requires recognition on consolidation.

23.4 TRANSFERS BETWEEN INVENTORY AND NON-CURRENT ASSETS

It is possible that an item which is regarded by one entity within the group as inventory is classified as a non-current asset by another entity. The key to determining the appropriate adjustment entries in these cases is to prepare the journal entries for the intragroup transaction in the records of the entities involved.

23.4.1 Transfers from inventory to property, plant and equipment

In this section, the situation analysed is where the selling entity regards the transferred item as inventory and the acquiring entity classifies it as a depreciable asset.

Example: Transfer from inventory to plant

Scorpio Ltd sells to Virgo Ltd an item of inventory on 1 January 2010, that is, halfway through the current accounting period, for $6000 cash. The item cost Scorpio Ltd $3000 earlier in the current year. Virgo Ltd intends to use the item as plant with a useful life of 10 years, and no estimated salvage value. A straight-line depreciation rate of 10% p.a. is applicable. The tax rate is 30%.

This transfer is examined in two stages, that is, sale and depreciation.

1. Sale

The entries in the accounts of the two entities are:

	Scorpio Ltd		
Cash	Dr	6 000	
Sales	Cr		6 000
Cost of Sales	Dr	3 000	
Inventory	Cr		3 000
	Virgo Ltd		
Plant	Dr	6 000	
Cash	Cr		6 000

Hence, from the legal entities' perspectives, there has been a sale of inventory and the acquisition of a depreciable asset, plant.

From the viewpoint of the group, there has been no sale of inventory and no acquisition of plant. Instead, the asset previously classified as inventory is now classified as plant which cost the group $3000. The three elements determining the consolidation adjustment are the profit on the sale of inventory by Scorpio Ltd, the revenue and expense items raised by Scorpio Ltd in relation to inventory, and the reporting of the plant at cost to the group.

The worksheet entry for the year ended 30 June 2010 is:

Sales	Dr	6 000	
Cost of Sales	Cr		3 000
Plant	Cr		3 000

The debit and credit to sales and cost of sales respectively remove the $3000 profit recorded by Scorpio Ltd. Note that, in comparison with the inventory-to-inventory transfers (section 23.2.1), the sales and cost of sales in the above entry are both adjustments to Scorpio Ltd's statement of comprehensive income.

The consolidation worksheet adjustment reduces the carrying amount of the plant by $3000. This gives rise to a deductible temporary difference, with the recognition of a deferred tax asset and an adjustment to income tax expense. The adjustment is equal to $900 (i.e. 30% × $3000). The consolidation worksheet adjustment entry is:

Deferred Tax Asset	Dr	900	
Income Tax Expense	Cr		900

If the acquisition by Virgo Ltd had taken place in the previous period, the sales and cost of sales of Scorpio Ltd for the current period would not be affected. Further, the profit of $3000 would be reflected in Scorpio Ltd's opening balance of retained earnings, causing the consolidation adjustment entries for the year ended 30 June 2011 to be:

Retained Earnings (1/7/10)	Dr	3 000	
Plant	Cr		3 000
Deferred Tax Asset	Dr	900	
Retained Earnings (1/7/10)	Cr		900

2. Depreciation

Virgo Ltd has recorded the asset at $6000 and charges depreciation at the rate of 10% p.a. on cost. The depreciation expense per year is, then, $600. For the half-year ended 30 June 2010, the depreciation charge is $300. From the group's viewpoint, the depreciation is based on the cost of $3000, giving depreciation for the half-year of $150. To convert the legal entity figure of $300 to the $150 required for the group, the required consolidation adjustment entry for the year ended 30 June 2010 is:

Accumulated Depreciation	Dr	150	
Depreciation Expense	Cr		150

The tax-effect entry for consolidation purposes is:

Income Tax Expense	Dr	45	
Deferred Tax Asset	Cr		45

The adjustment to depreciation expense results in a decrease in the difference between the carrying amounts of the asset to the legal entity and to the group. Income tax expense must then be increased by $45 (i.e. 30% × $150) as the credit to deferred tax asset reflects the reversal of the temporary difference.

For the year ended 30 June 2011, the consolidation adjustment entries for depreciation are:

Accumulated Depreciation	Dr	450	
Depreciation Expense	Cr		300
Retained Earnings (1/7/10)	Cr		150
Income Tax Expense	Dr	90	
Retained Earnings (1/7/10)	Dr	45	
Deferred Tax Asset	Cr		135

23.4.2 Transfers from property, plant and equipment to inventory

Assume Scorpio Ltd sold an item of plant to Virgo Ltd, which classified it as inventory. On sale of the asset, Scorpio Ltd would pass journal entries relevant to the sale of a non-current asset and Virgo Ltd would record the purchase of inventory. Further, as Virgo Ltd regards the item as inventory, no depreciation would be charged. From the group's perspective, there has been a change in the asset classification from plant to inventory.

Assuming the inventory is not still on hand at the end of the year, the form of the consolidation entries in the year of the transfer is:

Proceeds from Sale of Plant*	Dr	X	
Carrying Amount of Plant Sold*	Cr		X
Cost of Sales	Cr		X

*Instead of these two lines, a debit adjustment to the Gain on Sale of Plant account could be used.

ILLUSTRATIVE EXAMPLE 23.2

Intragroup transactions involving transfers of property, plant and equipment

Cancer Ltd owns all the issued shares of Aries Ltd. The following transactions occurred:

1. On 1 January 2009, Aries Ltd sold an item of plant to Cancer Ltd for $120 000. At time of sale, this asset had a carrying amount in the records of Aries Ltd of $115 000. The asset is depreciated on a straight-line basis at 10% p.a.
2. On 16 May 2011, Cancer Ltd sold equipment to Aries Ltd for $50 000, this asset having a carrying amount at time of sale of $40 000. The equipment was regarded by Cancer Ltd as a depreciable non-current asset, being depreciated at 10% p.a. on cost, whereas Aries Ltd records the machinery as inventory. The asset was sold by Aries Ltd before 30 June 2011.

Required

Prepare the consolidation worksheet adjustment entries for the preparation of consolidated financial statements at 30 June 2011. The tax rate is 30%.

Solution

The required journal entries are:

(1) *Sale of plant in January 2009*

Retained Earnings (1/7/10)	Dr	3 500	
Deferred Tax Asset	Dr	1 500	
Plant	Cr		5 000
(Gain on sale)			

Accumulated Depreciation	Dr	1 250	
Depreciation Expense	Cr		500
Retained Earnings (1/7/10)	Cr		750
(Depreciation at $500 p.a. for 2.5 years)			
Income Tax Expense	Dr	150	
Retained Earnings (1/7/10)	Dr	225	
Deferred Tax Asset	Cr		375
(Tax effect of depreciation adjustments)			

(2) *Sale of equipment in May 2011*

Proceeds on Sale of Equipment	Dr	50 000	
Carrying Amount of Equipment Sold	Cr		40 000
Cost of Sales	Cr		10 000
(Sale of equipment, reclassified as inventory and sold to external entity)			

23.5 INTRAGROUP SERVICES

Many different examples of services between related entities exist. For instance:

- Virgo Ltd may lend to Scorpio Ltd some specialist personnel for a limited period of time for the performance of a particular task by Scorpio Ltd. For this service, Virgo Ltd may charge Scorpio Ltd a certain fee, or expect Scorpio Ltd to perform other services in return.
- One entity may lease or rent an item of plant or a warehouse from the other.
- A subsidiary may exist solely for the purpose of carrying out some specific task, such as research activities for the parent, and a fee for such research is charged. In this situation, all service revenue earned by the subsidiary is paid for by the parent, and must be adjusted in the consolidation process.

Example: Intragroup services

During 2009–10, Virgo Ltd offered the services of a specialist employee to Scorpio Ltd for 2 months in return for which Scorpio Ltd paid $30 000 to Virgo Ltd. The employee's annual salary is $155 000, paid for by Virgo Ltd.

The journal entries in the records of Virgo Ltd and Scorpio Ltd in relation to this transaction are:

Virgo Ltd			
Cash	Dr	30 000	
Service Revenue	Cr		30 000
Scorpio Ltd			
Service Expense	Dr	30 000	
Cash	Cr		30 000

From the group's perspective there has been no service revenue received or service expense made to entities external to the group. Hence, to adjust from what has been recorded by the legal entities to the group's perspective, the consolidation adjustment entry is:

Service Revenue	Dr	30 000	
Service Expense	Cr		30 000

No adjustment is made in relation to the employee's salary since, from the group's view, the salary paid to the employee is a payment to an external party.

Since there is no effect on the carrying amounts of assets or liabilities, there is no temporary difference and no need for any income tax adjustment.

Example: Intragroup rent

Virgo Ltd rents office space from Scorpio Ltd for $150 000 p.a.

In accounting for this transaction, Virgo Ltd records rent expense of $150 000 and Scorpio Ltd records rent revenue of $150 000. From the group's view, the intragroup rental scheme is purely an internal arrangement, and no revenue or expense is incurred. The recorded revenue and expense therefore need to be eliminated. The appropriate consolidation adjustment entry is:

Rent Revenue	Dr	150 000	
Rent Expense	Cr		150 000

There is no tax-effect entry necessary as assets and liabilities are unaffected by the adjustment entry.

23.5.1 Realisation of profits or losses

With the transfer of services within the group, the consolidation adjustments do not affect the profit of the group. In a transaction involving a payment by a parent to a subsidiary for services rendered, the parent shows an expense and the subsidiary shows revenue. The net effect on the group's profit is zero. Hence, from the group's view, with intragroup services there are no realisation difficulties.

23.6 INTRAGROUP DIVIDENDS

In this section, consideration is given to dividends declared and paid after Virgo Ltd's acquisition of Scorpio Ltd. As explained in section 22.5.3, all dividends received by the parent from the subsidiary are accounted for as revenue by the parent, regardless of whether the dividends are paid from pre- or post-acquisition equity.

Three situations are considered in this section:

- dividends declared in the current period but not paid
- dividends declared and paid in the current period
- bonus share dividends from post-acquisition equity.

It is assumed that the company expecting to receive the dividend recognises revenue when the dividend is declared.

23.6.1 Dividends declared in the current period but not paid

Assume that, on 25 June 2010, Scorpio Ltd declares a dividend of $4000. At the end of the period, the dividend is unpaid. The entries passed by the legal entities are:

	Scorpio Ltd		
Dividend Declared (in retained earnings)	Dr	4 000	
Dividend Payable	Cr		4 000
	Virgo Ltd		
Dividend Receivable	Dr	4 000	
Dividend Revenue	Cr		4 000

The entry made by Scorpio Ltd both reduces retained earnings and raises a liability account. From the group's perspective, there is no reduction in equity and the group has no obligation to pay dividends outside the group. Similarly, the group expects no dividends to be received from entities outside the group. Hence, the appropriate consolidation adjustment entries are:

Dividend Payable	Dr	4000	
Dividend Declared	Cr		4000
(To adjust for the effects of the entry made by Scorpio Ltd)			
Dividend Revenue	Dr	4000	
Dividend Receivable	Cr		4000
(To adjust for the effects of the entry made by Virgo Ltd)			

In the following period when the dividend is paid, no adjustments are required in the consolidation worksheet. As there are no dividend revenue, dividend declared, or receivable items left open at the end of the period, then the position of the group is the same as the sum of the legal entities' financial statements.

23.6.2 Dividends declared and paid in the current period

Assume Scorpio Ltd declares and pays an interim dividend of $4000 in the current period. Entries by the *legal entities* are:

Virgo Ltd			
Cash	Dr	4000	
Dividend Revenue	Cr		4000
Scorpio Ltd			
Interim Dividend Paid (in retained earnings)	Dr	4000	
Cash	Cr		4000

From the outlook of the *group*, no dividends have been paid and no dividend revenue has been received. Hence, the adjustment necessary for the consolidated financial statements to show the affairs of the group is:

Dividend Revenue	Dr	4000	
Interim Dividend Paid	Cr		4000

23.6.3 Bonus share dividends

A subsidiary may occasionally pay a dividend to its parent in the form of shares rather than cash.

For example, assume a bonus share dividend of $5000 is paid by Scorpio Ltd out of post-acquisition profits. The journal entry made by Scorpio Ltd is:

Bonus Share Dividend Paid (in retained earnings)	Dr	5000	
Share Capital	Cr		5000

Since the bonus share dividend is paid by the subsidiary out of post-acquisition profits, these profits which, for consolidation purposes, are normally available for dividends have been capitalised as share capital.

In the records of Virgo Ltd, no entry is required as the bonus share dividend does not give Virgo Ltd an increased share of Scorpio Ltd; i.e. Virgo Ltd receives nothing that it did not previously own.

For consolidation purposes, two alternative adjustments are possible:

(a) Eliminate the bonus dividend paid against the share capital of Scorpio Ltd; that is, reverse the entry made by the subsidiary to record the dividend:

Share Capital	Dr	5 000	
Bonus Share Dividend Paid	Cr		5 000

If this entry is used, the fact that Scorpio Ltd has provided for a bonus dividend does not appear in the consolidated financial statements unless disclosed by way of a note. The capitalisation of Scorpio Ltd's retained earnings does not affect consolidated retained earnings, but does result in the inclusion in the consolidated retained earnings balance of those profits which have been capitalised and are not available for the payment of dividends.

(b) Do not eliminate the bonus dividend paid but set up a new capitalised profits reserve in the consolidation worksheet. The entry is:

Share Capital	Dr	5 000	
Capitalised Profits Reserve	Cr		5 000

The purpose of creating the reserve is to disclose the fact that part of the retained earnings of the group has been capitalised by the subsidiary and is therefore no longer available for payment of cash dividends to the parent.

Alternative (b) is recommended as the preferred treatment of bonus share dividends as it raises the capitalised profits reserve in the consolidated financial statements as a non-distributable reserve. From the group's viewpoint, distribution of this capitalised profits reserve to shareholders in the group is impossible and therefore is correctly treated as non-distributable.

Tax effect of dividends

Generally, dividends are tax-free. There are, therefore, no tax-effect adjustment entries required in relation to dividend-related consolidation adjustment entries.

ILLUSTRATIVE EXAMPLE 23.3

Intragroup dividends

Taurus Ltd owns all the issued shares of Orion Ltd, having acquired them for $250 000 on 1 January 2009. In preparing the consolidated financial statements at 30 June 2011, the accountant documented the following transactions:

2010	
15 Jan.	Orion Ltd paid an interim dividend of $10 000.
25 June	Orion Ltd declared a dividend of $15 000, this being recognised in the records of both entities.
1 Aug.	The $15 000 dividend declared on 25 June was paid by Orion Ltd.
2011	
18 Jan.	Orion Ltd paid an interim dividend of $12 000.
23 June	Orion Ltd declared a dividend of $18 000, this being recognised in the records of both entities.

The tax rate is 30%.

Required

Prepare the consolidation worksheet adjustment entries for the preparation of consolidated financial statements at 30 June 2011.

Solution

The required entries are:

(1) *Interim dividend paid*

Dividend Revenue	Dr	12 000	
Dividend Paid	Cr		12 000

(2) *Final dividend declared*

Dividend Payable	Dr	18 000	
Dividend Declared	Cr		18 000
Dividend Revenue	Dr	18 000	
Dividend Receivable	Cr		18 000

23.7 INTRAGROUP BORROWINGS

Members of a group often borrow and lend money among themselves, and charge interest on the money borrowed. In some cases, an entity may be set up within the group solely for the purpose of handling group finances and for borrowing money on international money markets. Consolidation adjustments are necessary in relation to these intragroup borrowings and interest thereon because, from the stance of the group, these transactions create assets and liabilities and revenues and expenses that do not exist in terms of the group's relationship with external entities.

Example: Advances

Virgo Ltd lends $100 000 to Scorpio Ltd, the latter paying $15 000 interest to Virgo Ltd. The relevant journal entries in each of the legal entities are:

Virgo Ltd			
Advance to Scorpio Ltd	Dr	100 000	
Cash	Cr		100 000
Cash	Dr	15 000	
Interest Revenue	Cr		15 000
Scorpio Ltd			
Cash	Dr	100 000	
Advance from Virgo Ltd	Cr		100 000
Interest Expense	Dr	15 000	
Cash	Cr		15 000

The consolidation adjustments involve eliminating the monetary asset created by Virgo Ltd, the monetary liability raised by Scorpio Ltd, the interest revenue recorded by Virgo Ltd and the interest expense paid by Scorpio Ltd:

Advance from Virgo Ltd	Dr	100 000	
Advance to Scorpio Ltd	Cr		100 000
Interest Revenue	Dr	15 000	
Interest Expense	Cr		15 000

The adjustment to the asset and liability is necessary as long as the intragroup loan exists. In relation to any past period's payments and receipt of interest, no ongoing adjustment to accumulated profits (opening balance) is necessary as the net effect of the consolidation adjustment is zero on that item.

Because the effect on net assets of the consolidation adjustment is zero, no tax-effect entry is necessary.

Example: Debentures acquired at date of issue

On 1 January 2010, Virgo Ltd issues 1000 $100 debentures with an interest rate of 15% p.a. payable on 1 January of each year. Scorpio Ltd, a wholly owned subsidiary of Virgo Ltd, acquires half the debentures issued.

The journal entries made by Virgo Ltd and Scorpio Ltd for the year ended 30 June 2010 are:

	Virgo Ltd			
1 Oct.	Cash	Dr	100 000	
	Debentures	Cr		100 000
	(Issue of debentures)			
30 June	Interest Expense	Dr	7 500	
	Interest Payable	Cr		7 500
	(Accrued interest payable of 15% for 6 months)			
	Scorpio Ltd			
1 Oct.	Debentures in Virgo Ltd	Dr	50 000	
	Cash	Cr		50 000
	(Debentures acquired)			
30 June	Interest Receivable	Dr	3 750	
	Interest Revenue	Cr		3 750
	(Accrued interest revenue)			

The consolidation entries to adjust for the entries recorded in the legal entities are:

Debentures	Dr	50 000	
Debentures in Virgo Ltd	Cr		50 000
Interest Payable	Dr	3 750	
Interest Receivable	Cr		3 750
Interest Revenue	Dr	3 750	
Interest Expense	Cr		3 750

Example: Debentures acquired on the open market

Virgo Ltd issued, on 1 July 2009, 1000 $100 15% debentures at nominal value. Interest is payable half-yearly on 31 December and 30 June. Debentures are to be redeemed after 10 years. Assume that Scorpio Ltd acquired 300 of these debentures cum div. on the open market for $95 on 31 March 2010.

Journal entries made by Virgo Ltd and Scorpio Ltd for the year ended 30 June 2010 are:

	Virgo Ltd			
1 July	Cash	Dr	100 000	
	Debentures	Cr		100 000
	(Issue of debentures)			
31 Dec.	Interest Expense	Dr	7 500	
	Cash	Cr		7 500
	(Interest paid on 31/12/09)			
30 June	Interest Expense	Dr	7 500	
	Cash	Cr		7 500
	(Interest paid on 30/6/10)			

	Scorpio Ltd			
31 Mar.	Debentures in Virgo Ltd	Dr	28 500	
	Cash	Cr		28 500
	(300 debentures acquired on the open market)			
30 June	Cash	Dr	2 250	
	Debentures in Virgo Ltd	Cr		1 125
	Interest Revenue	Cr		1 125
	(Interest before 31/3/10 was included in the purchase price)			

From the group's perspective, the purchase by Scorpio Ltd on the open market effectively redeemed 300 of the debentures issued by Virgo Ltd. Since the debentures were acquired cum div., the interest expense for the period 1 January to 31 March 2010 has been paid for by the group when the debentures were acquired by Scorpio Ltd. The group has redeemed 300 of the debentures at a price less than nominal value and is entitled to recognise income in the consolidation worksheet to the extent of the discount received on purchase or redemption. The consolidation adjustment entries necessary at 30 June 2010 are:

Debentures	Dr	30 000	
Debentures in Virgo Ltd	Cr		27 375*
Income on Redemption of Debentures	Cr		2 625
*$27 375 = $28 500 – $1125			
Interest Revenue	Dr	1 125	
Interest Expense	Cr		1 125

In future periods, while the debentures are still outstanding in the records of Virgo Ltd, the consolidation adjustment entries for debentures and interest must continue to be made. However, the income on redemption of debentures is considered to have occurred on 31 March 2010. Hence, in future periods, a credit entry is made to retained earnings (opening balance). To illustrate, the consolidation entries necessary at 30 June 2011 are as follows:

Debentures	Dr	30 000	
Debentures in Virgo Ltd	Cr		27 375
Retained Earnings (1/7/10)	Cr		2 625
Interest Revenue	Dr	4 500	
Interest Expense	Cr		4 500
(Full year's interest on 300 debentures)			

There is no tax effect in the group because the assets and liabilities are reduced equally.

Example: Redemption of debentures

Assume the debentures issued in the previous example are redeemed on 30 June 2018.

For the year ended 30 June 2018 the journal entries made by the legal entities are as follows:

	Virgo Ltd			
31 Dec.	Interest Expense	Dr	7 500	
	Cash	Cr		7 500
	(Interest paid)			
30 June	Interest Expense	Dr	7 500	
	Cash	Cr		7 500
	(Interest paid)			

	Debentures	Dr	100 000	
	Cash	Cr		100 000
	(Redemption of debentures)			
	Scorpio Ltd			
31 Dec.	Cash	Dr	2 250	
	Interest Revenue	Cr		2 250
30 June	Cash	Dr	2 250	
	Interest Revenue	Cr		2 250
	Cash	Dr	30 000	
	Debentures in Virgo Ltd	Cr		27 375
	Income on Redemption of Debentures	Cr		2 625

On consolidation, besides the elimination of the interest paid during the period, an adjustment is necessary to eliminate the income on redemption recorded by Scorpio Ltd. This income is not income to the group in the year ended 30 June 2018. From the group's viewpoint, the debentures were effectively redeemed when Scorpio Ltd acquired the debentures on the open market in 2009. The consolidated financial statements in that year reflected the income on redemption. The consolidation adjustment entries for the year ended 30 June 2018 are:

Interest Revenue	Dr	4 500	
Interest Expense	Cr		4 500
Income on Redemption of Debentures	Dr	2 625	
Retained Earnings (1/7/17)	Cr		2 625

Illustrative examples 23.4 and 23.5 demonstrate comprehensive examples of accounting for intragroup transfers of assets and dividends and borrowings.

ILLUSTRATIVE EXAMPLE 23.4

Intragroup transfers of assets

The following example illustrates procedures for the preparation of a consolidated statement of comprehensive income, a consolidated statement of changes in equity and a consolidated statement of financial position where the subsidiary is 100% owned. The consolidation worksheet adjustments for intragroup transactions including inventory and non-current asset transfers are also demonstrated.

Details

On 1 July 2006, Atlas Ltd acquired all the share capital of Chort Ltd for $472 000. At that date, Chort Ltd's equity consisted of the following.

Share capital	$300 000
General reserve	96 000
Retained earnings	56 000

At 1 July 2006, all the identifiable assets and liabilities of Chort Ltd were recorded at fair value.

Financial information for Atlas Ltd and Chort Ltd for the year ended 30 June 2010 is presented in the left-hand columns of the worksheet illustrated in figure 23.3. It is assumed that both companies use the perpetual inventory system.

Additional information

(a) On 1 January 2010, Chort Ltd sold merchandise costing $30 000 to Atlas Ltd for $50 000. Half this merchandise was sold to external entities for $28 000 before 30 June 2010.

(b) On 1 January 2009, Chort Ltd sold an item of inventory costing $2000 to Atlas Ltd for $4000. Atlas Ltd treated this item as part of its equipment and depreciated it at 5% p.a. on a straight-line basis.
(c) On 31 March 2010, Atlas Ltd sold plant to Chort Ltd for $6000, which was $1000 below its carrying amount to Atlas Ltd at that date. Chort Ltd charged depreciation at the rate of 10% p.a. on this item.
(d) In the 2007–08 period, Atlas Ltd sold land to Chort Ltd at $20 000 above cost. The land is still held by Chort Ltd.
(e) At 1 July 2009, there was a profit in the inventory of Atlas Ltd of $6000 on goods acquired from Chort Ltd in the previous period.
(f) The tax rate is 30%.

Required

Prepare the consolidated financial statements for the year ended 30 June 2010.

Solution

The first step is to determine the pre-acquisition entries at 30 June 2010. These entries are prepared after undertaking an acquisition analysis.

At 1 July 2006:

Net fair value of the identifiable assets and liabilities of Chort Ltd	= $300 000 + $96 000 + $56 000
	= $452 000
Consideration transferred	= $472 000
Goodwill	= $20 000

Consolidation worksheet entries

(1) *Business combination valuation entry*

As all the identifiable assets and liabilities of Chort Ltd are recorded at amounts equal to their fair values, the only business combination valuation entry required is that for goodwill.

Goodwill	Dr	20 000	
Business Combination Valuation Reserve	Cr		20 000

(2) *Pre-acquisition entry*

The entry at 30 June 2010 is the same as that at acquisition date as there have not been any events affecting that entry since acquisition date:

Retained Earnings (1/7/09)	Dr	56 000	
Share Capital	Dr	300 000	
General Reserve	Dr	96 000	
Business Combination Valuation Reserve	Dr	20 000	
Shares in Chort Ltd	Cr		472 000

The next step is to prepare the adjustment entries arising because of the existence of intragroup transactions. It is important that students classify the intragroup transactions into 'current period' and 'previous period' transactions. The resultant adjustment entries should reflect those decisions since previous period transactions would be expected to affect accounts such as retained earnings rather than accounts such as sales and cost of sales.

(3) *Profit in ending inventory*

The transaction occurred in the current period. The adjustment entries are:

Sales	Dr	50 000	
Cost of Sales	Cr		40 000
Inventory	Cr		10 000
($10 000 = $\frac{1}{2}$× [$50 000 – $30 000])			

Deferred Tax Asset	Dr	3 000	
Income Tax Expense	Cr		3 000
(30% × $10 000)			

Sales: The members of the group have recorded total sales of $78 000, being $50 000 by Chort Ltd and $28 000 by Atlas Ltd. The group recognises only sales to entities outside the group, namely the sales by Atlas Ltd of $28 000. Hence, in preparing the consolidated financial statements, sales must be reduced by $50 000.

Cost of sales: Chort Ltd recorded cost of sales of $30 000, and Atlas Ltd recorded cost of sales of $25 000 (being half of $50 000). Recorded cost of sales then totals $55 000. The cost of the sales to entities external to the group is $15 000 (being half of $30 000). Cost of sales must then be reduced by $40 000.

Inventory: At 30 June 2010, Atlas Ltd has inventory on hand from intragroup transactions, and records them at cost of $25 000 (being half of $50 000). The cost of this inventory to the group is $15 000 (being half of $30 000). Inventory is then reduced by $10 000.

Deferred tax asset/income tax expense: Under tax-effect accounting, temporary differences arise where the carrying amount of an asset differs from its tax base. In the first adjustment entry above, inventory is reduced by $10 000, that is, the carrying amount of inventory is reduced by $10 000. This then gives rise to a temporary difference, and because the carrying amount has been reduced, tax benefits are expected in the future when the asset is sold. Hence a deferred tax asset, equal to the tax rate times the change to the carrying amount of inventory (30% × $10 000), of $3000 is raised. Given there is no Deferred Tax Asset in the worksheet in figure 23.3, the adjustment is made against the Deferred Tax Liability line item.

(4) *Sale in previous period of inventory, classified as equipment*
The transfer occurred in a previous period.

Retained Earnings (1/7/09)	Dr	2 000	
Plant and Equipment	Cr		2 000
Deferred Tax Asset	Dr	600	
Retained Earnings (1/7/09)	Cr		600
(30% × $2000)			

Retained earnings: In the previous period, Chort Ltd sold inventory to Atlas Ltd at a profit of $2000 before tax. This sale did not involve entities external to the group; hence, the profit is not recognised by the group. Previous period profit must, therefore, be reduced by $2000.

Tax paid: The tax paid of $600 (30% × $2000) in relation to this profit is also not recognised by the group. Because retained earnings is an after-tax account, the net adjustment to retained earnings is $1400. The journal entry could have been made with one adjustment to retained earnings rather than two.

Plant and equipment: The transferred asset is classified as equipment by Atlas Ltd, which records it at cost of $4000. The cost to the group is $2000. Hence, the asset must be reduced by $2000.

Deferred tax asset: Deferred tax accounts for temporary differences arise where carrying amounts of assets differ from their tax bases. As the carrying amount of plant and equipment is being reduced by $2000, the temporary difference caused by this change must be accounted for. A deferred tax asset is raised in recognition of the benefits to be received by the higher depreciation deductions being allowed on the asset as it is recorded by Atlas Ltd at $4000.

(5) *Depreciation*
The asset transferred within the group is recognised as equipment by Atlas Ltd, which depreciates the asset as it is used by that entity. The consolidation adjustment entry for the depreciation is:

Accumulated Depreciation	Dr	150	
Depreciation Expense	Cr		100
Retained Earnings (1/7/09)	Cr		50

Income Tax Expense	Dr	30	
Retained Earnings (1/7/09)	Dr	15	
Deferred Tax Asset	Cr		45
($30 = 30% × $100; $15 = 30% × $50)			

Atlas Ltd records depreciation for the 1.5 years the asset is held, based on the cost of $4000. The group's depreciation is calculated at the same rate of 5% p.a. but is based on the cost to the group of $2000. A comparison of the depreciation charged by Atlas Ltd and what the group would charge is as follows:

Recorded depreciation		**Group depreciation**	
Previous period			
5% × $4000 × $\frac{1}{2}$ year	= $100	5% × $2000 × $\frac{1}{2}$ year	= $ 50
Current period			
5% × $4000	= 200	5% × $2000	= 100
	$300		$150

Accumulated depreciation: Atlas Ltd has charged a total of $300 depreciation on this asset in comparison to the group's charge of $150. Hence accumulated depreciation is reduced by $150.

Depreciation expense: In the current period, Atlas Ltd recorded depreciation expense of $200, whereas the group's depreciation is $100. Hence depreciation is reduced by $100.

Retained earnings: In the previous period, Atlas Ltd charged $100 depreciation whereas the charge to the group is $50. This difference in the previous period depreciation requires an adjustment to reduce retained earnings by $50. Retained earnings is also affected by the tax effect of the depreciation expense, resulting in a net charge of $35 to retained earnings, that is, $50(1 – 30%).

Deferred tax asset: As the adjustment to accumulated depreciation changes the carrying amount of the asset, a temporary difference arises between the carrying amount and the tax base. The deferred tax asset raised on transfer of the asset within the group is reversed as the asset is used up and depreciated within the group. The deferred tax asset is reduced by $45, that is, 30%($300 – $150), reflecting this reversal process.

(6) *Loss on sale of plant*

This is a current period transaction. The consolidation worksheet entries are:

Plant and Equipment	Dr	1 000	
Proceeds from Sale of Plant	Dr	6 000	
Carrying Amount of Plant Sold	Cr		7 000
Income Tax Expense	Dr	300	
Deferred Tax Liability	Cr		300
(30% × $1000)			

Plant and equipment: The plant is recorded by Chort Ltd at cost of $6000. The cost to the group is $7000. Hence, plant must be reduced by $1000.

Proceeds from sale: Atlas Ltd recorded proceeds on sale of the plant to Chort Ltd of $6000. Because the sale did not involve entities external to the group, the proceeds on sale must be eliminated.

Carrying amount: Atlas Ltd also recorded carrying amount of asset sold of $7000. Because this was not a sale to external entities, from the group's perspective the proceeds on sale and the carrying amount of the asset sold cannot be recognised. Hence, the carrying amount of the asset sold of $7000 must be eliminated.

Deferred tax liability: As the carrying amount of the plant sold is increased by $1000, a temporary difference between carrying amount and tax base is created. This has to be tax-effected. As the asset's carrying amount is increased, a deferred tax liability of $300 (being 30% × $1000) must be raised, reflecting the lower depreciation charge being made by the entity.

(7) *Depreciation on plant*

The transferred asset is being depreciated by Chort Ltd on a straight-line basis, at 10% p.a. The consolidation worksheet adjustment is:

Depreciation Expense	Dr	25	
Accumulated Depreciation	Cr		25
Deferred Tax Liability	Dr	8	
Income Tax Expense	Cr		8
(30% × $25 = 7.5, round to $8)			

The asset was transferred on 31 March, requiring depreciation for the remaining 3 months of the year. Chort Ltd is depreciating the asset based on cost of $6000, and the group cost is $7000. A comparison of the relative depreciation charges is:

Recorded depreciation	**Group depreciation**
10% × $6 000 × $\frac{1}{4}$ year= $150	10% × $7 000 × $\frac{1}{4}$ year = $175

Depreciation expense: As the group depreciation expense exceeds the recorded depreciation by $25, depreciation expense is increased by $25.

Accumulated depreciation: This is also increased by $25.

Deferred tax liability: The $25 adjustment to accumulated depreciation changes the carrying amount of the asset, giving rise to a temporary difference between this and the tax base. The deferred tax liability is debited for $8, that is, 30% × $25, to reflect that the depreciation being charged by the legal entity is lower than that to the group.

(8) *Profit on sale of land in previous period*

This is a previous period transaction. The consolidation worksheet entry is:

Retained Earnings (1/7/09)	Dr	20 000	
Land	Cr		20 000
Deferred Tax Asset	Dr	6 000	
Retained Earnings (1/7/09)	Cr		6 000
(30% × $20 000)			

Retained earnings: In the previous period, Atlas Ltd recorded a profit on sale of land of $20 000. This sale did not involve entities external to the group, and hence must be eliminated on consolidation. A further entry to retained earnings is required to reflect the tax on this profit. A net adjustment of $14 000 is then made to retained earnings.

Land: Chort Ltd records the land at a cost of $20 000 greater than that to the group. Hence, the land must be reduced by $20 000 so that the consolidated statement of financial position shows assets at cost to the group.

Deferred tax asset: The reduction to the carrying amount of the land creates a temporary difference between carrying amount and tax base. A deferred tax asset is raised to reflect the future tax benefits when the asset is sold.

(9) *Profit in beginning inventory*

This is a previous period transaction. The required consolidation worksheet entry is:

Retained Earnings (1/7/09)	Dr	6 000	
Cost of Sales	Cr		6 000

Income Tax Expense	Dr	1 800	
Retained Earnings (1/7/09)	Cr		1 800
(30% × $6000)			

Retained earnings: In the previous period, Chort Ltd recorded a $6000 before-tax profit, or a $4200 after-tax profit on sale of inventory within the group. Because the sale did not involve external entities, the profit must be eliminated on consolidation.

Cost of sales: In the current period, the transferred inventory is onsold to external entities. Atlas Ltd records cost of sales at $6000 greater than to the group. Hence, cost of sales is reduced by $6000. Note that this increases group profit by $6000, reflecting the realisation of the profit to the group in the current period, when it was recognised by the legal entity in the previous period.

Income tax expense: At the end of the previous period, in the consolidated statement of financial position a deferred tax asset of $1800 was raised because of the difference in cost of the inventory recorded by the legal entity and that recognised by the group. This deferred tax asset is reversed when the asset is sold. The adjustment to income tax expense reflects the reversal of the deferred tax asset raised at the end of the previous period.

Figure 23.3 shows the completed worksheet for preparation of the consolidated financial statements of Atlas Ltd and its subsidiary Chort Ltd at 30 June 2010. Once the effects of all adjustments are added or subtracted horizontally in the worksheet to calculate figures in the right-hand 'consolidation' column, the consolidated financial statements can be prepared, as shown in figure 23.4(a), (b) and (c).

FIGURE 23.3 Consolidation worksheet — intragroup transfers of assets

Financial statements	Atlas Ltd	Chort Ltd		Adjustments Dr	Adjustments Cr		Consolidation
Sales revenue	1 196 000	928 000	3	50 000			2 074 000
Cost of sales	(888 000)	(670 000)			40 000	3	(1 512 000)
					6 000	9	
Wages and salaries	(57 500)	(32 000)					(89 500)
Depreciation	(5 200)	(4 800)	7	25	100	5	(9 925)
Other expenses	(4 000)	—					(4 000)
Total expenses	(954 700)	(706 800)					(1 615 425)
	241 300	221 200					458 575
Proceeds from sale of plant	6 000	—	6	6 000			—
Carrying amount of plant sold	(7 000)	—			7 000	6	—
Gain (loss)	(1 000)	—					—
Profit before income tax	240 300	221 200					458 575
Income tax expense	(96 120)	(118 480)	5	30	3 000	3	(213 722)
			6	300	8	7	
			9	1 800			
Profit for the year	144 180	102 720					244 853
Retained earnings (1/7/09)	100 820	70 280	2	56 000	600	4	95 535
			4	2 000	50	5	
			5	15	6 000	8	
			8	20 000	1 800	9	
			9	6 000			
	245 000	173 000					340 388
Dividend paid	(80 000)	—					(80 000)
Retained earnings (30/6/10)	165 000	173 000					260 388
Share capital	500 000	300 000	2	300 000			500 000
Business combination valuation reserve			2	20 000	20 000	1	—
General reserve	135 000	96 000	2	96 000			135 000
	800 000	569 000					895 388

Financial statements	Atlas Ltd	Chort Ltd		Adjustments Dr	Cr		Consolidation
Other components of equity (1/7/09)	4 000	10 000					14 000
Available-for-sale financial assets	1 000	3 000					4 000
Other components of equity (30/6/10)	5 000	13 000					18 000
Total equity	805 000	582 000					913 388
Deferred tax liability	52 000	30 000	3	3 000	45	5	72 737
			4	600	300	6	
			7	8			
			8	6 000			
Total equity and liabilities	857 000	612 000					986 125
Shares in Chort Ltd	472 000	—			472 000	2	—
Cash	80 000	73 000					153 000
Inventory	168 000	36 000			10 000	3	194 000
Other current assets	10 000	300 000					310 000
Available-for-sale financial assets	15 000	68 000					83 000
Land	70 000	120 000			20 000	8	170 000
Plant and equipment	52 000	28 000	6	1 000	2 000	4	79 000
Accumulated depreciation	(10 000)	(13 000)	5	150	25	7	(22 875)
Goodwill	—	—	1	20 000			20 000
	857 000	612 000		588 928	588 928		986 125

ATLAS LTD Consolidated Statement of Comprehensive Income for the year ended 30 June 2010	
Revenues	$2 074 000
Expenses	1 615 425
Profit before income tax	458 575
Income tax expense	213 722
Profit for the year	$ 244 853
Other comprehensive income	
Gain on available-for-sale financial assets	4 000
TOTAL COMPREHENSIVE INCOME FOR THE YEAR	$ 248 853

FIGURE 23.4(a) Consolidated statement of comprehensive income

ATLAS LTD Consolidated Statement of Changes in Equity for the year ended 30 June 2010	
Total comprehensive income for the year	**$ 248 853**
Retained earnings at 1 July 2009	$ 95 535
Profit for the year	244 853
Dividend paid	(80 000)
Retained earnings at 30 June 2010	$ 260 388
General reserve at 1 July 2009	$ 140 000
General reserve at 30 June 2010	$ 140 000
Other components of equity at 1 July 2009	$ 14 000
Available-for-sale financial assets	4 000
Other components of equity at 30 June 2010	$ 18 000
Share capital at 1 July 2009	$ 500 000
Share capital at 30 June 2010	$ 500 000

FIGURE 23.4(b) Consolidated statement of changes in equity

ATLAS LTD
Consolidated Statement of Financial Position
as at 30 June 2010

Current assets		
Cash assets		$153 000
Inventories		194 000
Available-for-sale financial assets		83 000
Other		310 000
Total current assets		740 000
Non-current assets		
Property, plant and equipment:		
Plant and equipment	$ 79 000	
Accumulated depreciation	(22 875)	56 125
Land		170 000
Goodwill		20 000
Total non-current assets		246 125
Total assets		986 125
Non-current liabilities		
Deferred tax liabilities		72 737
Net assets		$913 388
Equity		
Share capital		$500 000
General reserve		135 000
Retained earnings		260 388
Other components of equity		18 000
Total equity		$913 388

FIGURE 23.4(c) Consolidated statement of financial position

ILLUSTRATIVE EXAMPLE 23.5

Dividends and borrowings

On 1 July 2009, Kraz Ltd acquired all the share capital of Maia Ltd and Rana Ltd for $187 500 and $150 000 respectively. At that date, equity of the three companies was:

	Kraz Ltd	Maia Ltd	Rana Ltd
Share capital	$150 000	$100 000	$100 000
General reserve	90 000	60 000	40 000
Retained earnings	20 000	17 500	10 000

At 1 July 2009, the identifiable net assets of all companies were recorded at fair values.

For the year ended 30 June 2010, the summarised financial information for the three companies show the following details:

	Kraz Ltd	Maia Ltd	Rana Ltd
Sales revenue	$ 388 500	$ 200 000	$ 150 000
Dividend revenue	9 000	—	—
Other revenue	10 000	—	—
Total revenues	407 500	200 000	150 000
Total expenses	(360 000)	(176 000)	(138 000)

	Kraz Ltd	Maia Ltd	Rana Ltd
Profit before income tax	47 500	24 000	12 000
Income tax expense	(15 000)	(10 000)	(5 000)
Profit	32 500	14 000	7 000
Retained earnings (1/7/09)	20 000	17 500	10 000
Total available for appropriation	52 500	31 500	17 000
Interim dividend paid	(7 500)	(2 500)	—
Bonus share dividend paid	—	—	4 000
Final dividend declared	(15 000)	(5 000)	(1 500)
Transfer to general reserve	(2 000)	(5 000)	—
	(24 500)	(12 500)	(5 500)
Retained earnings (30/6/10)	$ 28 000	$ 19 000	$ 11 500
Shares in Maia Ltd	$ 187 500	—	—
Shares in Rana Ltd	150 000	—	—
Dividend receivable	6 500	—	—
Loan receivable	5 000	—	—
Property, plant and equipment	18 500	$ 205 000	$ 167 000
Total assets	367 500	205 000	167 000
Final dividend payable	15 000	5 000	1 500
Loan payable	—	5 000	—
Other non-current liabilities	82 500	11 000	10 000
Total liabilities	97 500	21 000	11 500
Net assets	$ 270 000	$ 184 000	$ 155 500
Share capital	$ 150 000	$ 100 000	$ 104 000
General reserve	92 000	65 000	40 000
Retained earnings	28 000	19 000	11 500
Total equity	$ 270 000	$ 184 000	$ 155 500

Further information

- Kraz Ltd has lent $5000 to Maia Ltd, the loan having 10% interest rate attached.
- Kraz Ltd has recognised both the interim and final dividends from Maia Ltd and Rana Ltd as revenue.
- Kraz Ltd has made no entry with respect to the bonus share dividend paid by Rana Ltd.

Required

Prepare the consolidated financial statements as at 30 June 2010 for Kraz Ltd and its two subsidiaries, Maia Ltd and Rana Ltd. Assume all reserve transfers are from post-acquisition profits.

Solution

The relationship between the parent and subsidiaries may be expressed as shown in figure 23.5.

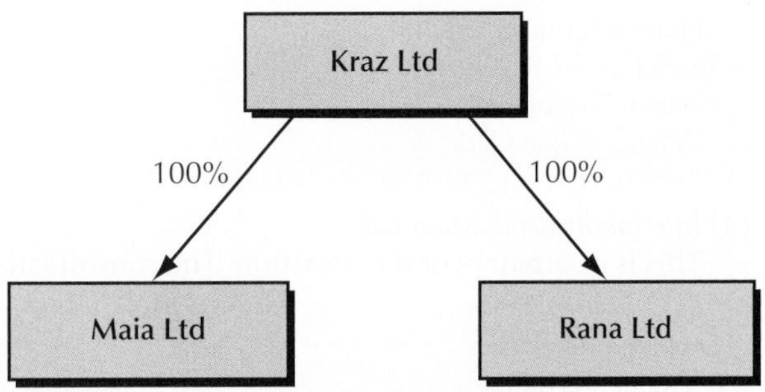

FIGURE 23.5 Relationship between parent and subsidiaries

Figure 23.6 illustrates the consolidation worksheet necessary to consolidate the financial statements of Kraz Ltd and its two subsidiaries. Detailed discussion of each adjustment is provided below.

Note that:

- no adjustment entries are made for transfers to and from reserves if post-acquisition equity only is affected
- the dividends paid and declared by the parent to its shareholders are not adjusted for in the consolidated financial statements, because these dividends are paid by the group to external entities.

Acquisition analysis: Kraz Ltd and Maia Ltd

At 1 July 2009:

Net fair value of identifiable assets and liabilities of Maia Ltd	= $100 000 + $60 000 + $17 500
	= $177 500
Consideration transferred	= $187 500
Goodwill	= $10 000

Consolidation worksheet adjustment entries

(1) *Business combination valuation entry: Kraz Ltd and Maia Ltd*

Goodwill	Dr	10 000	
Business Combination Valuation Reserve	Cr		10 000

(2) *Pre-acquisition entry: Kraz Ltd and Maia Ltd*

The pre-acquisition entry at 30 June 2010 is then:

Retained Earnings (1/7/09)	Dr	17 500	
Share Capital	Dr	100 000	
General Reserve	Dr	60 000	
Business Combination Valuation Reserve	Dr	10 000	
Shares in Maia Ltd	Cr		187 500

Acquisition analysis: Kraz Ltd and Rana Ltd

At 1 July 2009:

Net fair value of identifiable assets and liabilities of Rana Ltd	= $100 000 + $40 000 + $10 000
	= $150 000
Consideration transferred	= $150 000
Goodwill	= zero

No business combination valuation entry is required.

(3) *Pre-acquisition entry: Kraz Ltd and Rana Ltd*

The pre-acquisition entry at 30 June 2010 is then:

Retained Earnings (1/7/09)	Dr	10 000	
Share Capital	Dr	100 000	
General Reserve	Dr	40 000	
Shares in Rana Ltd	Cr		150 000

(4) *Interim dividend: Maia Ltd*

This is a current period transaction. The consolidation worksheet entry is:

Dividend Revenue	Dr	2 500	
Dividend Paid	Cr		2 500

Maia Ltd paid a dividend in cash to Kraz Ltd. Kraz Ltd recognised dividend revenue and Maia Ltd recognised dividends paid. From the group's perspective, there were no dividends paid to entities external to the group. Hence, on consolidation it is necessary to eliminate both the Dividend Paid and Dividend Revenue accounts raised by the parent and the subsidiary.

(5) *Bonus share dividend: Rana Ltd*

This is a current period transaction. In recording the bonus share dividend, Rana Ltd reduced retained earnings, recognising a bonus dividend paid and increasing share capital. Kraz Ltd made no entry. It is assumed in this solution that treatment (b) in section 23.6.3 is adopted. Hence, rather than eliminate the bonus dividend paid raised by the subsidiary, a capitalised profits reserve is raised instead to show that profits have been capitalised and dividend potential has been reduced. The share capital is reduced on consolidation.

Share Capital	Dr	4 000	
Capitalised Profits Reserve	Cr		4 000

(6) *Final dividend declared: Maia Ltd*

This is a current period transacti on. The consolidation worksheet entry is:

Final Dividend Payable	Dr	5 000	
Final Dividend Declared	Cr		5 000
Dividend Revenue	Dr	5 000	
Dividend Receivable	Cr		5 000

The subsidiary declares a dividend, recognising a liability to pay the dividend and reducing retained earnings. The parent, which expects to receive the dividend, raises a receivable asset and recognises dividend revenue. From the group's point of view, because the dividend is not receivable or payable to entities external to the group, it does not want to recognise any of these accounts. Hence, on consolidation, all the accounts affected by this transaction in the records of the parent and the subsidiary are eliminated.

(7) *Final dividend declared: Rana Ltd*

This is a current period transaction. The consolidation worksheet entry is:

Final Dividend Payable	Dr	1 500	
Final Dividend Declared	Cr		1 500
Dividend Revenue	Dr	1 500	
Dividend Receivable	Cr		1 500

The explanation for this entry is the same as that for the dividend declared by Maia Ltd.

(8) *Loan: Kraz Ltd to Maia Ltd*

The loan may have been made in a previous period or the current period. The consolidation worksheet entry is the same:

Loan Payable	Dr	5 000	
Loan Receivable	Cr		5 000

This entry eliminates the receivable raised by the parent and the payable raised by the subsidiary. From the group's point of view, there are no loans payable or receivable to entities external to the group.

(9) *Interest on loan*

The interest paid/received is a current period transaction. In some situations where interest is accrued, interest may relate to previous or future periods. The consolidation worksheet entry is:

Interest Revenue	Dr	500	
Interest Expense	Cr		500
(10% × $5000)			

The parent records interest revenue of $500 and the subsidiary records interest expense of $500. No interest was paid or received by the group from entities external to the group, so these accounts must be eliminated on consolidation.

Financial statements	Kraz Ltd	Maia Ltd	Rana Ltd	Adjustments				Group
					Dr	Cr		
Sales revenue	388 500	200 000	150 000					738 500
Dividend revenue	9 000	—	—	4	2 500			—
				6	5 000			
				7	1 500			
Other revenue	10 000	—	—	9	500			9 500
	407 500	200 000	150 000					748 000
Expenses	(360 000)	(176 000)	(138 000)			500	9	(673 500)
Profit before income tax	47 500	24 000	12 000					74 500
Income tax expense	(15 000)	(10 000)	(5 000)					(30 000)
Profit	32 500	14 000	7 000					44 500
Retained earnings (1/7/09)	20 000	17 500	10 000	2	17 500			20 000
				3	10 000			
	52 500	31 500	17 000					64 500
Interim dividend paid	(7 500)	(2 500)	—			2 500	4	(7 500)
Bonus dividend paid	—	—	(4 000)					(4 000)
Final dividend declared	(15 000)	(5 000)	(1 500)			5 000	6	(15 000)
						1 500	7	
Transfer to general reserve	(2 000)	(5 000)	0					(7 000)
	24 500	12 500	5 500					33 500
Retained earnings (30/6/10)	28 000	19 000	11 500					31 000
Share capital	150 000	100 000	104 000	2	100 000			150 000
				3	100 000			
				5	4 000			
General reserve	92 000	65 000	40 000	2	60 000			97 000
				3	40 000			
Business combination valuation reserve				2	10 000	10 000	1	—
Capitalised profits reserve						4 000	4	4 000
Final dividend payable	15 000	5 000	1 500	6	5 000			15 000
				7	1 500			
Loan payable	—	5 000	—	8	5 000			—
Other non-current liabilities	82 500	11 000	10 000					103 500
Total equity and liabilities	367 500	205 000	167 000					400 500
Shares in Maia Ltd	187 500	—	—			187 500	2	—
Shares in Rana Ltd	150 000	—	—			150 000	3	—
Dividend receivable	6 500	—	—			5 000	6	—
						1 500	7	
Loan receivable	5 000	—	—			5 000	8	—
Property, plant and equipment	18 500	205 000	167 000					390 500
Goodwill	—	—	—	1	10 000			10 000
	367 500	205 000	167 000		372 500	372 500		400 500

FIGURE 23.6 Consolidation worksheet — dividends

From figure 23.6, after all adjustments have been entered in the worksheet and amounts totalled across to the consolidation column, the consolidated financial statements can be prepared in suitable format as shown in figure 23.7(a), (b) and (c).

FIGURE 23.7(a) Consolidated statement of comprehensive income

KRAZ LTD Consolidated Statement of Comprehensive Income for the year ended 30 June 2010	
Revenues	$748 000
Expenses	673 500
Profit before income tax	74 500
Income tax expense	30 000
Profit for the year	$ 44 500
Other comprehensive income	—
TOTAL COMPREHENSIVE INCOME FOR THE YEAR	$ 44 500

FIGURE 23.7(b) Consolidated statement of changes in equity

KRAZ LTD Consolidated Statement of Changes in Equity for the year ended 30 June 2010	
Total comprehensive income for the year	**$ 44 500**
Retained earnings at 1 July 2009	$ 20 000
Profit for the year	44 500
Interim dividend paid	(7 500)
Bonus dividend paid	(4 000)
Final dividend declared	(15 000)
Transfer to general reserve	(7 000)
Retained earnings at 30 June 2010	$ 31 000
General reserve at 1 July 2009	$ 90 000
Transfer from retained earnings	7 000
General reserve at 30 June 2010	$ 97 000
Capitalised profits reserve at 1 July 2009	$ 0
Increase due to bonus dividend paid	4 000
Capitalised profits reserve at 30 June 2010	$ 4 000
Share capital as at 1 July 2009	$150 000
Share capital at 30 June 2010	$150 000

FIGURE 23.7(c) Consolidated statement of financial position

KRAZ LTD Consolidated Statement of Financial Position as at 30 June 2010	
Non-current assets	
Property, plant and equipment	$390 500
Goodwill	10 000
Total non-current assets	400 500
Total assets	400 500

(continued)

FIGURE 23.7(c) *(continued)*

Current liabilities		
Final dividend payable		15 000
Non-current liabilities		103 500
Total liabilities		118 500
Net assets		$282 000
Equity		
Share capital		$150 000
Other reserves:		
General reserve	$97 000	
Capitalised profits reserve (Note 1)	4 000	101 000
Retained earnings		31 000
Total equity		$282 000

Note 1: The capitalised profits reserve represents the non-distributable profit created by the capitalisation of profits in a subsidiary by means of a bonus share dividend.

SUMMARY

Intragroup transactions can take many forms and may involve transfers of inventory or property, plant and equipment, or they may relate to the provision of services by one member of the group to another member. To prepare the relevant worksheet entries for a transaction, it is necessary to consider the accounts affected in the entities involved in the transaction.

Intragroup transfers of inventory, property, plant and equipment, services, dividends and debentures and their adjustment in the consolidation process are associated with a need to consider the implications of applying tax-effect accounting in the consolidation process.

The basic approach to determining the consolidation adjustment entries for intragroup transfers is:

(a) Analyse the events within the records of the legal entities involved in the intragroup transfer. Determine whether the transaction is a prior period or current period event.
(b) Analyse the position from the group's viewpoint.
(c) Create adjusting entries to change from the legal entities' position to that of the group.
(d) Consider the tax effect of the adjusting entries.

Note again that there are no actual adjusting entries made in the records of the individual legal entities which constitute the group. However, if required, a special journal could be set up by the parent entity to keep a record of the adjustments made in the process of preparing the consolidated financial statements. Alternatively, the consolidation process may be performed by the use of special consolidation worksheets.

Why a particular adjustment is the correct one involves an explanation of each line in the adjustment entry including why an account was adjusted, why it was increased or decreased, and why a particular adjustment amount is appropriate. This generally involves a comparison of what accounts were affected in the records of the legal entities with the financial picture the group wants to present in the consolidated financial statements.

Discussion questions

1. Why is it necessary to make adjustments for intragroup transactions?
2. In making consolidation worksheet adjustments, sometimes tax-effect entries are made. Why?
3. Why is it important to identify transactions as current or previous period transactions?
4. Where an intragroup transaction involves a depreciable asset, why is depreciation expense adjusted?
5. Are adjustments for post-acquisition dividends different from those for pre-acquisition dividends? Explain.
6. What is meant by 'realisation of profits'?
7. When are profits realised in relation to inventory transfers within the group?

8. When are profits realised on transfers of depreciable assets within the group?
9. Virgo Ltd sold inventory to its wholly owned subsidiary, Scorpio Ltd, for $15 000. These items previously cost Virgo Ltd $12 000. Scorpio Ltd subsequently sold half the items to Norma Ltd for $8000. The tax rate is 30%.

   The group accountant for Virgo Ltd, Li Chen, maintains that the appropriate consolidation adjustment entries are as follows:

Sales	Dr	15 000	
Cost of Sales	Cr		13 000
Inventory	Cr		2 000
Deferred Tax Asset	Dr	300	
Income Tax Expense	Cr		300

   Required
   1. Discuss whether the entries suggested by Li Chen are correct, explaining on a line-by-line basis the correct adjustment entries.
   2. Determine the consolidation worksheet entries in the following year, assuming the inventory is on-sold, and explain the adjustments on a line-by-line basis.
10. At the beginning of the current period, Virgo Ltd sold a used depreciable asset to its wholly owned subsidiary, Scorpio Ltd, for $80 000. Virgo Ltd had originally paid $200 000 for this asset, and at time of sale to Scorpio Ltd had charged depreciation of $150 000. This asset is used differently in Scorpio Ltd from how it was used in Virgo Ltd; thus, whereas Virgo Ltd used a 10% p.a. straight-line depreciation method, Scorpio Ltd uses a 20% straight-line depreciation method.

    In calculating the depreciation expense for the consolidated group (as opposed to that recorded by Scorpio Ltd), the group accountant, RuiFen Xue, is unsure of which amount the depreciation rate should be applied to ($200 000, $50 000 or $80 000) and which depreciation rate to use (10% or 20%).

    Required

    Provide a detailed response, explaining which depreciation rate should be used and to what amount it should be applied.
11. The parent entity, Libra Ltd, has purchased on the open market, for an amount less than nominal value, some debentures previously issued by its wholly owned subsidiary, Gemini Ltd. The group accountant for Libra Ltd, James Cong, has stated that the adjustment in the consolidation worksheet includes the raising of an account Income on Redemption. He is unsure whether this is correct.

    Required

    What does this account represent? Would an adjustment to income, or subsequently to retained earnings, have to be made for the rest of the life of the group? If not, what event would cause the discontinuation of this adjustment entry?
12. The parent entity, Leo Ltd, has received a bonus dividend paid from its subsidiary's post-acquisition profits. The accountant for Leo Ltd, Lu Rong, is concerned that if on consolidation the total effects of this transaction have to be eliminated, then this will show a misleading financial position for the group. Her concern is that the subsidiary, by making a bonus dividend, has reduced the ability of the group to pay cash dividends. The consolidation adjustments will result in this fact not being made known to the users of the consolidated financial statements.

    Required

    Discuss whether Lu Rong has cause for concern, and what options are available for her in accounting for the bonus dividend.

STAR RATING
★ BASIC
★★ MODERATE
★★★ DIFFICULT

Exercises

Exercise 23.1

INTRAGROUP TRANSACTIONS

★ Ara Ltd owns all the share capital of Mensa Ltd. In relation to the following intragroup transactions, prepare adjusting journal entries for the consolidation worksheet at 30 June 2010. Assume an income tax rate of 30% and that all income on sale of assets is taxable and expenses are deductible.

(a) During the year ending 30 June 2010, Mensa Ltd sold $50 000 worth of inventory to Ara Ltd. Mensa Ltd recorded a $10 000 profit before tax on these transactions. At 30 June 2010, Ara Ltd has one-quarter of these goods still on hand.

(b) Mensa Ltd sold a warehouse to Ara Ltd for $100 000. This had originally cost Mensa Ltd $82 000. The transaction took place on 1 January 2009. Ara Ltd charges depreciation at 5% p.a. on a straight-line basis.

(c) During the 2009–10 period, Ara Ltd sold inventory costing $12 000 to Mensa Ltd for $18 000. One-third of this was sold to Leo Ltd for $9500 and one-third to Vela Ltd for $9000.

(d) On 1 January 2009, Mensa Ltd sold inventory costing $6000 to Ara Ltd at a transfer price of $8000. On 1 September 2009, Ara Ltd sold half these goods back to Mensa Ltd, receiving $3000 from Mensa Ltd. Of the remainder kept by Ara Ltd, half was sold in January 2010 to Pavo Ltd at a loss of $200.

(e) On 25 June 2010, Ara Ltd declared a dividend of $10 000. On the same day, Mensa Ltd declared a $5000 dividend.

(f) On 1 October 2009, Ara Ltd issued 1000 15% debentures of $100 at nominal value. Mensa Ltd acquired 400 of these. Interest is payable half-yearly on 31 March and 30 September. Accruals have been recognised in the legal entities' accounts.

(g) During the 2008–09 period, Ara Ltd sold inventory to Mensa Ltd for $10 000, recording a before-tax profit of $2000. Half this inventory was unsold by Mensa Ltd at 30 June 2009.

Exercise 23.2

INTRAGROUP TRANSACTIONS

★ Octans Ltd owns all of the share capital of Cetus Ltd. In relation to the following intragroup transactions, all parts of which are independent unless specified, prepare the consolidation worksheet adjusting entries for preparation of the consolidated financial statements as at 30 June 2011. Assume an income tax rate of 30% and that all income on sale of assets is taxable and expenses are deductible.

(a) In January 2011, Octans Ltd sells inventory to Cetus Ltd for $15 000. This inventory had previously cost Octans Ltd $10 000, and it remains unsold by Cetus Ltd at the end of the period.

(b) All the inventory in (a) above is sold to Hydra Ltd, an external party, for $20 000 on 2 February 2011.

(c) Half the inventory in (a) above is sold to Grus Ltd, an external party, for $9000 on 22 February 2011. The remainder is still unsold at the end of the period.

(d) Octans Ltd, in March 2011, sold inventory for $10 000 that was transferred from Cetus Ltd 3 years ago. It had originally cost Cetus Ltd $6000, and was sold to Octans Ltd for $12 000.

(e) Cetus Ltd sold some land to Octans Ltd in December 2010. The land had originally cost Cetus Ltd $25 000, but was sold to Octans Ltd for only $20 000. To help Octans Ltd pay for the land, Cetus Ltd gave Octans Ltd an interest-free loan of $12 000, and the balance was paid in cash. Octans Ltd has as yet made no repayments on the loan.

(f) On 1 July 2010, Octans Ltd sold a depreciable asset costing $10 000 to Cetus Ltd for $12 000. Octans Ltd had not charged any depreciation on the asset before the sale. Both entities depreciate assets at 10% p.a. on cost.

(g) On 1 July 2010, Octans Ltd sold an item of machinery to Cetus Ltd for $6000. This item had cost Octans Ltd $4000. Octans Ltd regarded this item as inventory whereas Cetus Ltd intended to use it as a non-current asset. Cetus Ltd charges depreciation at the rate of 10% p.a. on cost.

Exercise 23.3

INTRAGROUP TRANSACTIONS

★ Lyra Ltd owns all the share capital of Volans Ltd. The following transactions relate to the period ended 30 June 2011. Assuming an income tax rate of 30%, provide adjustment entries to be included in the consolidation worksheet as at 30 June 2011.

(a) On 1 July 2010, Lyra Ltd sold a motor vehicle to Volans Ltd for $15 000. This had a carrying amount to Lyra Ltd of $12 000. Both entities depreciate motor vehicles at a rate of 10% p.a. on cost.

(b) Volans Ltd manufactures items of machinery which are used as property, plant and equipment by other companies, including Lyra Ltd. On 1 January 2011, Volans Ltd sold such an item to Lyra Ltd for $62 000, its cost to Volans Ltd being only $55 000 to manufacture. Lyra Ltd charges depreciation on these machines at 20% p.a. on the diminishing value.

(c) Lyra Ltd manufactures certain items which it then markets through Volans Ltd. During the current period, Lyra Ltd sold for $12 000 items to Volans Ltd at cost plus 20%. Volans Ltd has sold 75% of these transferred items at 30 June 2011.

(d) Volans Ltd also sells second-hand machinery. Lyra Ltd sold one of its depreciable assets (original cost $40 000, accumulated depreciation $32 000) to Volans Ltd for $5000 on 1 January 2011. Volans Ltd had not resold the item by 30 June 2011.

(e) Volans Ltd sold a depreciable asset (carrying amount of $22 000) to Lyra Ltd on 1 January 2010 for $25 000. Both entities charge depreciation at a rate of 10% p.a. on cost in relation to these items. On 31 December 2010, Lyra Ltd sold this asset to Tucana Ltd for $20 000.

Exercise 23.4 ★

INTRAGROUP TRANSACTIONS

For each of the following intragroup transactions, assume that the consolidation process is being undertaken at 30 June 2010, and that an income tax rate of 30% applies. Prepare the consolidation worksheet adjustment entries for these transactions. All parts are independent unless specified. Phoenix Ltd owns all the share capital of Sagittarius Ltd.

(a) On 1 January 2010, Phoenix Ltd sold an item of plant to Sagittarius Ltd for $1000. Immediately before the sale, Phoenix Ltd had the item of plant on its accounts for $1500. Phoenix Ltd depreciated items at 5% p.a. on the diminishing balance and Sagittarius Ltd used the straight-line method over 10 years.

(b) A non-current asset with a carrying amount of $1000 was sold by Phoenix Ltd to Sagittarius Ltd for $800 on 1 January 2010. Sagittarius Ltd intended to use this item as inventory, being a seller of second-hand goods. Both entities charged depreciation at the rate of 10% p.a. on the diminishing balance on non-current assets. The item was still on hand at 30 June 2010.

(c) On 1 May 2010, Sagittarius Ltd sold inventory costing $200 to Phoenix Ltd for $400 on credit. On 30 June 2010, only half of these goods had been sold by Phoenix Ltd, but Phoenix Ltd had paid $300 back to Sagittarius Ltd.

(d) During March 2010, Sagittarius Ltd declared a $3000 dividend. The dividend was paid in August 2011.

(e) In December 2009, Sagittarius Ltd paid a $1500 interim dividend.

(f) In February 2009, Phoenix Ltd sold inventory to Sagittarius Ltd for $6000, at a mark-up of 20% on cost. One-quarter of this inventory was unsold by Sagittarius Ltd at 30 June 2009.

(g) On 1 January 2008, Sagittarius Ltd sold a new tractor to Phoenix Ltd for $20 000. This had cost Sagittarius Ltd $16 000 on that day. Both entities charged depreciation at the rate of 10% p.a. on the diminishing balance.

(h) Sagittarius Ltd rented a spare warehouse to Phoenix Ltd and also to Sagittarius Ltd during 2009–10. The total charge for the rental was $300, and Phoenix Ltd and Sagittarius Ltd both agreed to pay half of this amount to Sagittarius Ltd.

Exercise 23.5 ★★

PRE-ACQUISITION ENTRY AND INTRAGROUP TRANSACTIONS, NO FAIR VALUE — CARRYING AMOUNT DIFFERENCES AT ACQUISITION DATE

On 1 January 2007, Draco Ltd acquired all the share capital of Grater Ltd for $300 000. The equity of Grater Ltd at 1 January 2007 was:

Share capital	$200 000
Retained earnings	50 000
General reserve	20 000
	$270 000

At this date, all identifiable assets and liabilities of Grater Ltd were recorded at fair value. Goodwill is tested annually for impairment. By 31 December 2010, no impairment has occurred. At 1 January 2007, no goodwill had been recorded by Grater Ltd.

On 1 May 2010, Grater Ltd transferred $15 000 from the general reserve (pre-acquisition) to retained earnings. The current tax rate is 30%. Assuming consolidated financial statements are required for the period 1 January 2010 to 31 December 2010, provide journal entries (including the pre-acquisition entry) to show the adjustments that would be made in the consolidation worksheets. Use the following information:

(a) At 31 December 2010, Grater Ltd holds $100 000 of 7% debentures issued by Draco Ltd on 1 January 2009. All necessary interest payments have been made.

(b) At the end of the reporting period, Grater Ltd owes Draco Ltd $1000 for items sold on credit.

(c) Grater Ltd undertook an advertising campaign for Draco Ltd during the year. Draco Ltd paid $8000 to Grater Ltd for this service.

(d) The beginning and ending inventories of Draco Ltd and Grater Ltd in relation to the current period included the following unsold intragroup inventory:

	Draco Ltd	**Grater Ltd**
Beginning inventory:		
Transfer price	2 000	$1 200
Original cost	1 400	800
Ending inventory:		
Transfer price	500	900
Original cost	300	700

Draco Ltd sold inventory to Grater Ltd during the current period for $3000. This was $500 above the cost of the inventory to Draco Ltd. Grater Ltd sold inventory to Draco Ltd in the current period for $2500, recording a pre-tax profit of $800.

(e) Draco Ltd sold an item of inventory to Grater Ltd on 1 July 2010 for use as part of plant and machinery. The item cost Draco Ltd $4000 and was sold to Grater for $6000. Grater Ltd depreciated the item at 10% p.a. straight-line.

(f) Draco Ltd received dividends totalling $63 000 during the current period from Grater Ltd. All of this related to dividends paid in the current period.

Exercise 23.6 ★★

INTRAGROUP TRANSACTIONS, EXPLANATION OF RATIONALE

Lepus Ltd owns 100% of the shares of Indus Ltd. During the 2010–11 period, the following events occurred:

(a) Lepus Ltd sold inventory for $10 000 which had been sold to it by Indus Ltd in June 2010. The inventory originally cost Indus Ltd $6000 and was sold to Lepus Ltd for $9000.

(b) Lepus Ltd recorded depreciation of $10 000 on machinery sold to it by Indus Ltd on 1 January 2010. The machinery had a carrying amount in Indus Ltd at the date of sale of $80 000. Both entities apply a depreciation rate of 10% p.a. on a straight-line basis for this type of machinery.

Required

1. For *each* of the above transactions, prepare the adjustments required in the consolidation worksheet at 30 June 2011, assuming an income tax rate of 30%.
2. Explain the rationale behind *each* of the entries you have prepared.

Exercise 23.7 ★★

CONSOLIDATION WORKSHEET, INTRAGROUP TRANSACTIONS

On 1 July 2007, Pegasus Ltd acquired cum div. all the shares of Ursa Ltd, at which date the equity and liability sections of Ursa Ltd's statement of financial position showed the following balances:

Share capital (300 000 shares)	$300 000
Other reserves	30 000
Retained earnings	10 000
Other components of equity	30 000
Dividend payable	20 000

The dividend payable was subsequently paid in August 2007. A bonus dividend, on the basis of one ordinary share for every ten ordinary shares held, was paid in January 2010 out of other reserves existing at acquisition date.

On 1 July 2007, all the identifiable assets and liabilities of Ursa Ltd were recorded at fair value except for:

	Carrying amount	Fair value
Inventory	$120 000	$130 000
Machinery (cost $200 000)	160 000	165 000

The inventory was all sold by 30 November 2007. The machinery had a further 5-year life but was sold on 1 January 2010. At the acquisition date, Ursa Ltd had a contingent liability of $20 000 that Pegasus Ltd considered to have a fair value of $12 000. This liability was settled in June 2008. At 1 July 2007, Ursa Ltd had not recorded any goodwill.

On 30 June 2010, the trial balances of Pegasus Ltd and Ursa Ltd were as follows:

Trial Balances
as at 30 June 2010

	Pegasus Ltd	Ursa Ltd
Shares in Ursa Ltd	$ 396 000	$ —
Inventory	180 000	160 000
Available-for-sale financial assets	229 000	215 000
Bank	25 000	10 000
Plant and machinery	372 500	212 000
Land	154 200	65 000
Income tax expense	35 000	40 000
Dividend declared	10 000	4 000
	$ 1 401 700	$ 706 000
Share capital	$ 800 000	$ 330 000
Other components of equity	150 000	80 000
Retained earnings (1/7/09)	15 000	12 000
Profit before income tax	80 000	90 000
Debentures	100 000	40 000
Other current liabilities	34 700	40 000
Dividend payable	10 000	4 000
Accumulated depreciation – plant and machinery	212 000	110 000
	$ 1 401 700	$ 706 000

Additional information

(a) On 1 July 2008, Pegasus Ltd sold an item of plant to Ursa Ltd at a profit before tax of $4000. Pegasus Ltd depreciates this particular item of plant at a rate of 20% p.a. on cost and Ursa Ltd applies a rate of 10% p.a. on cost.

(b) At 30 June 2010, Pegasus Ltd has on hand some items of inventory purchased from Ursa Ltd in June 2009 at a profit of $500.

(c) The other components of equity relate to the available-for-sale financial assets. At 1 July 2009, the balances of this account were $140 000 (Pegasus Ltd) and $72 000 (Ursa Ltd).

(d) The tax rate is 30%.

Required

1. Prepare the adjusting journal entries for the consolidation worksheet at 30 June 2010.
2. Prepare the consolidated statement of comprehensive income, consolidated statement of changes in equity and the consolidated statement of financial position at 30 June 2010.
3. In relation to parts (a) and (b) in the *additional information*, explain why you made the consolidation adjustment worksheet entries used in preparing the consolidated financial statements at 30 June 2010.

Exercise 23.8

★★

GOODWILL, CONSOLIDATION WORKSHEET, INTRAGROUP TRANSACTIONS

Carina Ltd owns all the shares of Auriga Ltd. The shares were acquired on 1 July 2007 by Carina Ltd at a cost of $60 000. At acquisition date, the capital of Auriga Ltd consisted of 44 000 ordinary shares each fully paid at $1. There were retained earnings of $4000. All the identifiable assets and liabilities of Auriga Ltd were recorded at amounts equal to fair value, except for:

	Carrying amount	Fair value
Inventory	$12 000	$15 000
Land	60 000	70 000
Machinery (cost $100 000)	80 000	82 000

The land was sold on 1 June 2008 for $94 000. The machinery had a further 5-year life. The inventory was all sold by 31 December 2007. Auriga Ltd has not recorded any goodwill at 1 July 2007. Goodwill has not been impaired.

The trial balances of the two entities at 30 June 2009 are shown below.

Trial Balances as at 30 June 2009				
	Carina Ltd		Auriga Ltd	
	Dr	Cr	Dr	Cr
Share capital		$ 64 000		$ 44 000
Retained earnings (1/7/08)		32 000		21 000
Current liabilities		21 400		17 000
Machinery	$ 38 000		$ 71 500	
Shares in Auriga Ltd	60 000		—	
Inventory	19 000		16 400	
Receivables	5 500		8 300	
Sales revenue		43 000		52 000
Cost of sales	20 600		30 900	
Selling expenses	3 200		6 000	
Administrative expenses	5 300		2 700	
Depreciation/amortisation expenses	1 200		2 600	
Income tax expense	7 400		4 700	
Accumulated depreciation – machinery		12 200		22 300
Deferred tax assets	5 400		6 300	
Plant (net of depreciation)	8 000		7 400	
Proceeds from sale of machinery		6 000		10 000
Carrying amount of machinery sold	5 000		9 500	
	$178 600	$178 600	$166 300	$166 300

Additional information

(a) Intragroup sales of inventory for the year ended 30 June 2009 from Carina Ltd to Auriga Ltd, $14 000; and from Auriga Ltd to Carina Ltd, $3000.

(b) Intragroup inventory on hand:
 (i) at 1 July 2008: held by Auriga Ltd, purchased from Carina Ltd at a profit of $400.
 (ii) at 30 June 2009: held by Carina Ltd, purchased from Auriga Ltd at a profit of $200.

(c) Intragroup machinery on hand at 30 June 2009:
 (i) Carina Ltd: purchased from Auriga Ltd on 1 July 2008 for $10 000 at a profit to Auriga Ltd of $500. Depreciation rate is 10% p.a. on cost.
 (ii) Auriga Ltd: purchased from Carina Ltd on 1 January 2008 for $12 000, at a loss to Carina Ltd of $500. Depreciation rate is 10% p.a. on cost.

(d) Auriga Ltd had purchased from Carina Ltd an item of inventory which Carina Ltd had treated as plant. Carrying amount in Carina Ltd's records at time of sale (1 January 2009) was $5000 and it was sold at a profit of $1000. The item is still on hand in Auriga Ltd's inventory at 30 June 2009.

(e) The income tax rate is 30%.

Required
Prepare a worksheet for consolidating the financial statements of Carina Ltd and Auriga Ltd as at 30 June 2009.

Exercise 23.9

CONSOLIDATION WORKSHEET, CONSOLIDATED FINANCIAL STATEMENTS

★★ On 1 July 2008, Lacerta Ltd acquired all the shares of Crux Ltd for $160 000. The financial statements of the two entities at 30 June 2009 contained the following information:

	Lacerta Ltd	Crux Ltd
Sales revenue	$ 234 800	$ 200 000
Dividend revenue	17 000	—
Other income	6 600	—
	258 400	200 000
Cost of sales	(123 000)	(120 000)
Other expenses	(34 600)	(20 000)
	(157 600)	(140 000)
Profit before income tax	100 800	60 000
Income tax expense	(32 000)	(20 000)
Profit for the year	68 800	40 000
Retained earnings (1/7/08)	24 000	12 000
Total available for appropriation	92 800	52 000
Dividend paid from 2007–08 profit	(18 000)	(5 000)
Interim dividend paid from 2008–09 profit	(16 000)	(4 800)
Dividend declared from 2008–09 profit	(16 000)	(7 200)
Transfer to general reserve	(8 000)	—
	(58 000)	(17 000)
Retained earnings (30/6/09)	$ 34 800	$ 35 000
Current assets		
Cash	$ 1 000	$ 40
Receivables	27 000	12 100
Allowance for doubtful debts	(500)	(300)
Financial assets	20 000	10 000
Inventory	48 000	47 000
Total current assets	95 500	68 840
Non-current assets		
Plant and machinery	100 000	70 000
Accumulated depreciation	(40 000)	(26 000)
Land	102 300	190 000
Debentures in Crux Ltd	57 000	—
Shares in Crux Ltd	160 000	
Total non-current assets	379 300	234 000
Total assets	474 800	302 840
Current liabilities		
Dividend payable	16 000	7 200
Provisions	12 000	8 800
Bank overdraft	—	14 840
Current tax liabilities	11 000	10 000
Total current liabilities	39 000	40 840
Non-current liabilities		
12% mortgage debentures	—	80 000
Deferred tax liabilities	13 000	5 000
Total non-current liabilities	13 000	85 000
Total liabilities	52 000	125 840
Net assets	$ 422 800	$ 177 000

Equity	Lacerta Ltd	Crux Ltd
Share capital	$ 320 000	$ 120 000
General reserve	60 000	20 000
Retained earnings	34 800	35 000
Other components of equity	8 000	2 000
Total equity	$ 422 800	$ 177 000

Additional information

(a) At 1 July 2008, all identifiable assets and liabilities of Crux Ltd were recorded at fair values except for inventory, for which the fair value was $1000 greater than the carrying amount. This inventory was all sold by 30 June 2009. At 1 July 2008, Crux Ltd had research and development outlays that it had expensed as incurred. Lacerta Ltd measured the fair value of the in-process research and development at $8000. By 30 June 2009, it was assessed that $2000 of this was not recoverable. At 1 July 2008, Crux Ltd had reported a contingent liability relating to a guarantee that was considered to have a fair value of $7000. This liability still existed at 30 June 2009. At 1 July 2008, Crux Ltd had not recorded any goodwill.

(b) The debentures were issued by Crux Ltd at nominal value on 1 July 2007, and are redeemable on 30 June 2013. Lacerta Ltd acquired its holding ($60 000) of these debentures on the open market on 1 January 2009, immediately after the half-yearly interest payment had been made. All interest has been paid and brought to account in the records of both entities.

(c) During the 2008–09 period, Lacerta Ltd sold inventory to Crux Ltd for $40 000, at a mark-up of cost plus 25%. At 30 June 2009, $10 000 worth of inventory is still held by Crux Ltd.

(d) On 1 January 2009, Crux Ltd sold an item of inventory to Lacerta Ltd which planned to use it as a non-current asset, depreciable at 10% p.a. on cost. Lacerta Ltd paid $30 000 for this item, with Crux Ltd having manufactured it at a cost of $24 000.

(e) The Other Components of Equity account relates to the available-for-sale financial assets. For the 2008–09 period, Lacerta Ltd recorded an increase in these assets of $3000, and Crux Ltd recorded a decrease of $2000.

(f) The income tax rate is 30%.

Required

Prepare the consolidated financial statements for Lacerta Ltd and its subsidiary for the year ended 30 June 2009.

Exercise 23.10 ★★

CONSOLIDATION WORKSHEET, IMPAIRMENT OF GOODWILL

Financial information for Herwles Ltd and its 100% owned subsidiary, Lynx Ltd, for the year ended 31 December 2010 is provided below:

	Herwles Ltd	Lynx Ltd
Sales revenue	$25 000	$23 600
Dividend revenue	1 000	—
Other income	1 000	2 000
Proceeds from sale of property, plant and equipment	5 000	22 000
Total	32 000	47 600
Cost of sales	21 000	18 000
Other expenses	3 000	1 000
Carrying amount of property, plant and equipment sold	4 000	20 000
Total expenses	28 000	39 000
Profit before income tax	4 000	8 600
Income tax expense	1 350	1 950
Profit for the period	2 650	6 650
Retained earnings (1/1/10)	6 000	3 000
	8 650	9 650
Interim dividend paid	2 500	1 000
Retained earnings (31/12/10)	$ 6 150	$ 8 650

Herwles Ltd acquired its shares in Lynx Ltd at 1 January 2010, buying the 10 000 shares in Lynx Ltd for $20 000 — Lynx Ltd recorded share capital of $10 000. The shares were bought on a cum div. basis as Lynx Ltd had declared a dividend of $3000 that was not paid until March 2010.

At 1 January 2010, all identifiable assets and liabilities of Lynx Ltd were recorded at fair value except for inventory, for which the carrying amount of $2000 was $400 less than fair value. Some of this inventory has been a little slow to sell, and 10% of it is still on hand at 31 December 2010. Inventory on hand in Lynx Ltd at 31 December 2010 also includes some items acquired from Herwles Ltd during the year. These were sold by Herwles Ltd for $5000, at a profit before tax of $1000. Half the goodwill was written off as the result of an impairment test on 31 December 2010.

During March 2010, Herwles Ltd provided some management services to Lynx Ltd at a fee of $500.

On 1 July 2010, Lynx Ltd sold machinery to Herwles Ltd at a gain of $2000. This machinery had a carrying amount to Lynx Ltd of $20 000, and was considered by Herwles Ltd to have a 5-year life.

By 31 December 2010, the available-for-sale financial assets acquired by Herwles Ltd and Lynx Ltd increased by $1000 and $650 respectively.

The tax rate is 30%.

Required

1. Prepare the consolidated statement of comprehensive income for Herwles Ltd and its subsidiary, Lynx Ltd, at 31 December 2010.
2. Discuss the concept of 'realisation' using the intragroup transactions in this question to illustrate the concept.

Exercise 23.11

CONSOLIDATION WORKSHEET, CONSOLIDATED STATEMENT OF COMPREHENSIVE INCOME

★★

Financial information for Antila Ltd and Pyxis Ltd for the year ended 30 June 2009 is shown below:

	Antila Ltd	Pyxis Ltd
Sales revenue	$78 000	$40 000
Proceeds from sale of office furniture	—	3 000
Dividend revenue	4 400	1 600
Total income	82 400	44 600
Cost of sales	60 000	30 000
Other expenses	10 800	7 500
Total expenses	70 800	37 500
Profit before income tax	11 600	7 100
Income tax expense	3 000	2 200
Profit for the year	8 600	4 900
Retained earnings (1/7/08)	14 500	2 800
	23 100	7 700
Interim dividend paid	4 000	2 000
Final dividend declared	8 000	2 400
	12 000	4 400
Retained earnings (30/6/09)	$11 100	$ 3 300

Additional information

(a) On 1 July 2007, Antila Ltd purchased 100% of the shares of Pyxis Ltd for $50 000. At that date the equity of the two entities was as follows:

	Antila Ltd	Pyxis Ltd
Asset revaluation reserve	$25 000	$ 4 000
Retained earnings	14 500	2 800
Share capital	50 000	40 000

At 1 July 2007, all the identifiable assets and liabilities of Pyxis Ltd were recorded at fair value except for the following:

	Carrying amount	Fair value
Plant and equipment (cost $80 000)	$60 000	$61 000
Inventory	3 000	3 500

All of this inventory was sold by December 2007. The plant and equipment had a further 5-year life. Any valuation adjustments are made on consolidation.

(b) Antila Ltd records dividend receivable as revenue when dividends are declared.

(c) The opening inventory of Pyxis Ltd included goods which cost Pyxis Ltd $2000. Pyxis Ltd purchased this inventory from Antila Ltd at cost plus $33\frac{1}{3}$%.

(d) Intragroup sales totalled $10 000 for the year. Sales from Antila Ltd to Pyxis Ltd, at cost plus 10%, amounted to $5600. The closing inventory of Antila Ltd included goods which cost Antila Ltd $4400. Antila Ltd purchased this inventory from Pyxis Ltd at cost plus 10%.

(e) On 31 December 2008, Pyxis Ltd sold Antila Ltd office furniture for $3000. This furniture originally cost Pyxis Ltd $3000 and was written down to $2500 when sold. Antila Ltd depreciates furniture at the rate of 10% p.a. on cost.

(f) The asset revaluation reserve relates to the use of the revaluation model for land. The following movements occurred in this account:

	Antila Ltd	Pyxis Ltd
1 July 2007 to 30 June 2008	$3 000	$(500)
1 July 2008 to 30 June 2009	$2 000	$ 500

(g) The tax rate is 30%.

Required

Prepare the consolidated statement of comprehensive income for the year ended 30 June 2009.

Problems

Problem 23.1 ★★★

CONSOLIDATED WORKSHEET, CONSOLIDATED STATEMENT OF COMPREHENSIVE INCOME

On 1 April 2009, Fornax Ltd acquired all the issued ordinary shares (*cum div.*) of Dorado Ltd for $100 000. At that date, relevant balances in the records of Dorado Ltd were:

Share capital	$80 000
Asset revaluation reserve	5 000
Retained earnings	5 000
Dividend payable	4 000

All the identifiable assets and liabilities of Dorado Ltd were recorded at fair values except for the following:

	Carrying amount	Fair value
Inventory	$10 000	$12 000
Plant (cost $80 000)	50 000	53 000

Immediately after the acquisition of its shares by Fornax Ltd, Dorado Ltd revalued its plant to fair value. The plant was expected to have a further 5-year life. All the inventory on hand at 1 April 2009 was sold by the end of the financial year.

At 1 April 2009, Dorado Ltd had recorded goodwill of $2000. As a result of an impairment test on 31 March 2010, Dorado Ltd wrote goodwill down by $1500 in the consolidation worksheet.

The dividend payable was subsequently paid in June 2009.

During the period ending 31 March 2010, intragroup sales consisted of $40 000 from Fornax Ltd to Dorado Ltd at a profit to Fornax Ltd of $10 000. These were all sold to external entities by Dorado Ltd for $42 000 before 31 March 2010. Dorado Ltd also sold some inventory to Fornax Ltd for $10 000. This had cost Dorado Ltd $6000. Fornax Ltd since has sold all the items to external entities for $8000, except one batch on which Dorado Ltd recorded a $500 profit before tax (original cost to Dorado Ltd was $1000).

On 1 October 2009, Fornax Ltd sold an item, regarded by Fornax Ltd as a non-current asset, to Dorado Ltd which regarded it as inventory. At the time of sale, the carrying amount of the item to Fornax Ltd was $28 000, and it was sold to Dorado Ltd for $30 000. Fornax Ltd was using a 10% p.a. depreciation rate applied to cost. The item remains unsold by Dorado Ltd at 31 March 2010.

Both entities use the revaluation model in accounting for land. During the 2009–10 period, Fornax Ltd and Dorado Ltd both recorded revaluation increments, these being $2200 and $1100 respectively.

The following information was obtained from the companies for the year ended 31 March 2010:

	Fornax Ltd	Dorado Ltd
Sales	$ 146 000	$120 000
Dividend revenue	4 000	—
Proceeds on sale of non-current asset	30 000	—
	180 000	120 000
Cost of sales	88 000	68 000
Other expenses	44 000	19 000
	132 000	87 000
Profit before income tax	48 000	33 000
Income tax expense	12 000	14 000
Profit for the year	36 000	19 000
Retained earnings (1/4/09)	10 000	5 000
Total available for appropriation	46 000	24 000
Dividend paid	8 000	4 000
Retained earnings (31/3/10)	$ 38 000	$ 20 000

Required

1. Prepare the consolidated statement of comprehensive income as at 31 March 2010. Assume a tax rate of 30%.
2. Explain the consolidation worksheet adjustment for the sale of the non-current asset to Dorado Ltd at 1 October 2009 by Fornax Ltd.

Problem 23.2 CONSOLIDATION WORKSHEET, CONSOLIDATED FINANCIAL STATEMENTS

★★★

On 31 December 2006, Musca Ltd acquired all the issued shares of Serpens Ltd. On this date, the share capital of Serpens Ltd consisted of 200 000 shares paid to 50c per share. Other reserves and retained earnings at this date consisted of:

General reserve	$25 000
Retained earnings	20 000

At 31 December 2006, all the identifiable assets and liabilities of Serpens Ltd were recorded at fair value except for some plant and machinery. This plant and machinery, which cost $100 000, had a carrying amount of $85 000 and a fair value of $90 000. The estimated remaining useful life was 10 years. Adjustments for fair values are made on consolidation.

Immediately after acquisition, a dividend of $10 000 was declared and paid out of retained earnings. Also, 1 year after acquisition, Serpens Ltd used $20 000 from the general reserve on hand at acquisition date to partly pay the balance unpaid on the issued shares.

The trial balances of Musca Ltd and Serpens Ltd at 31 December 2011 were as shown below:

Trial Balances as at 31 December 2011		
	Musca Ltd	**Serpens Ltd**
Credits		
Share capital	$ 500 000	$ 120 000
General reserve	25 000	5 000
Asset revaluation reserve	10 000	6 000
Retained earnings (1/1/11)	40 000	65 000
Other components of equity	15 000	10 000
Current tax liabilities	22 000	18 000
Deferred tax liabilities	6 240	5 200
Payables	22 000	14 000
Sales revenue	250 000	120 000
Other income	20 000	5 000
Proceeds from sale of property, plant and equipment	14 000	50 000
	$ 924 240	$ 418 200
Debits		
Income tax expense	$ 20 000	$ 10 000
Dividend declared	10 000	8 000
Plant and machinery	425 000	337 000
Accumulated depreciation	(300 000)	(261 000)
Motor vehicles	284 200	152 600
Accumulated depreciation	(160 000)	(100 000)
Receivables	25 000	7 310
Available-for-sale financial assets	60 000	40 000
Inventory	106 440	72 000
Bank	46 900	5 990
Deferred tax assets	12 700	6 300
Shares in Serpens Ltd	160 000	—
Cost of sales	188 000	80 000
Other expenses	28 000	5 000
Carrying amount of property, plant and equipment sold	18 000	55 000
	$ 924 240	$ 418 200

Additional information

(a) During the current period, Musca Ltd sold inventory to Serpens Ltd for $20 000. This had originally cost Musca Ltd $18 200. Serpens Ltd has, by 31 December 2011, sold half this inventory for $12 310.

(b) Some of the items manufactured by Serpens Ltd are used as plant by Musca Ltd. One of the plant items held by Musca Ltd at 31 December 2011 was purchased from Serpens Ltd on 1 July 2008 for $25 000. It had cost Serpens Ltd $17 500 to manufacture this item. Musca Ltd depreciates such items at 10% p.a. on cost.

(c) At 1 January 2011, Serpens Ltd sold a machine to Musca Ltd for $50 000. This item had a carrying amount at time of sale to Serpens Ltd of $55 000. Both entities use a 5% p.a. on cost depreciation rate for this item.

(d) The tax rate is 30%.

(e) Certain specialised items of plant, considered a separate class of assets, are measured using the revaluation model. At 1 January 2010, the balances of the asset revaluation reserve were $8000 (Musca Ltd) and $7000 (Serpens Ltd).

(f) The Other Components of Equity account reflects movements in the available-for-sale financial assets. The balances of this account at 1 January 2010 were $12 000 (Musca Ltd) and $8000 (Serpens Ltd).

Required

Prepare the consolidated financial statements as at 31 December 2011.

Problem 23.3 ★★★

CONSOLIDATION WORKSHEET

On 1 July 2008, Columba Ltd acquired all the shares of Sculptor Ltd for $137 200. At acquisition date, the equity of Sculptor Ltd consisted of:

Share capital	$80 000
General reserve	16 000
Retained earnings	21 000

On this date, all the identifiable assets and liabilities of Sculptor Ltd were recorded at fair value except for the following assets:

	Carrying amount	Fair value
Inventory	$ 50 000	$56 000
Motor vehicles (cost $18 000)	15 000	16 000
Furniture and fittings (cost $30 000)	24 000	32 000
Land	18 480	24 480

The inventory and land on hand in Sculptor Ltd at 1 July 2008 were sold during the following 12 months. The motor vehicles, which at acquisition date were estimated to have a 4-year life, were sold on 1 January 2010. Except for land, valuation adjustments are made on consolidation and, on realisation of a business combination valuation reserve, a transfer is made to retained earnings on consolidation. The furniture and fittings were estimated to have a further 8-year life. At 1 July 2008, Sculptor Ltd had not recorded any goodwill.

The following trial balances were prepared for the companies at 30 June 2010:

Credits	Columba Ltd	Sculptor Ltd
Share capital	$ 170 000	$ 80 000
General reserve	41 000	22 000
Retained earnings (1/7/09)	16 000	29 500
Debentures	120 000	—
Final dividend payable	10 000	3 000
Current tax liabilities	8 000	2 500
Other payables	34 800	10 100
Advance from Columba Ltd	—	10 000
Sales revenue	85 000	65 000
Other income	23 000	22 000
Accumulated depreciation		
– Motor vehicles	4 000	2 000
– Furniture and fittings	2 000	6 000
	$ 513 800	$252 100
Debits		
Cost of sales	$ 65 000	$ 53 500
Other expenses	22 000	27 000
Shares in Sculptor Ltd	137 200	—
Land	—	24 480
Motor vehicles	28 000	22 000
Furniture and fittings	34 000	37 300
Inventory	171 580	70 320
Other assets	8 620	3 100
Income tax expense	7 200	2 000
Interim dividend paid	4 000	2 000
Final dividend declared	10 000	3 000
Deferred tax assets	16 200	7 400
Advance to Sculptor Ltd	10 000	—
	$ 513 800	$252 100

Additional information

(a) Intragroup transfers of inventory consisted of:

1/7/08 to 30/6/09:	
Sales from Columba Ltd to Sculptor Ltd	$12 000
Profit in inventory on hand 30/6/09	200
1/7/09 to 30/6/10:	
Sales from Columba Ltd to Sculptor Ltd	15 000
Profit in inventory on hand 30/6/10	
(incl. $50 from previous period sales)	1 000

(b) On 1 January 2009, Sculptor Ltd sold furniture and fittings to Columba Ltd for $8000. This had originally cost Sculptor Ltd $12 000 and had a carrying amount at time of sale of $7000. Both entities charge depreciation at the rate of 10% p.a.

(c) The tax rate is 30%.

Required

Prepare the consolidation worksheet for the preparation of the consolidated financial statements for the period ended 30 June 2010.

24 Consolidation: non-controlling interest

ACCOUNTING STANDARDS IN FOCUS

IAS 27 *Consolidated and separate financial statements*

LEARNING OBJECTIVES

When you have studied this chapter, you should be able to:

- discuss the nature of the non-controlling interest (NCI)
- explain the effects of the NCI on the consolidation process
- explain how to calculate the NCI share of equity
- explain how the calculation of the NCI is affected by the existence of intragroup transactions
- explain how the NCI is affected by the existence of a gain on bargain purchase.

24.1 NON-CONTROLLING INTEREST EXPLAINED

In chapters 22 and 23, the group under consideration consisted of two entities where the parent owned *all* the share capital of the subsidiary. In this chapter, the group under discussion consists of a parent that has only a *partial* interest in the subsidiary; that is, the subsidiary is less than wholly owned by the parent.

24.1.1 Nature of the non-controlling interest (NCI)

Ownership interests in a subsidiary other than the parent are referred to as the non-controlling interest, or NCI. Paragraph 4 of IAS 27 *Consolidated and Separate Financial Statements* contains the following definition of NCI:

> Non-controlling interest is the equity in a subsidiary not attributable, directly or indirectly, to a parent.

In figure 24.1, the group shown is illustrative of those discussed in this chapter. In this case, the parent entity owns 75% of the shares of a subsidiary. Under the entity concept of consolidation (see chapter 21 of this book), the group consists of the combined assets and liabilities of the parent and the subsidiary. There are two owners in this group — the parent shareholders and the NCI. The NCI is a contributor of equity to the group.

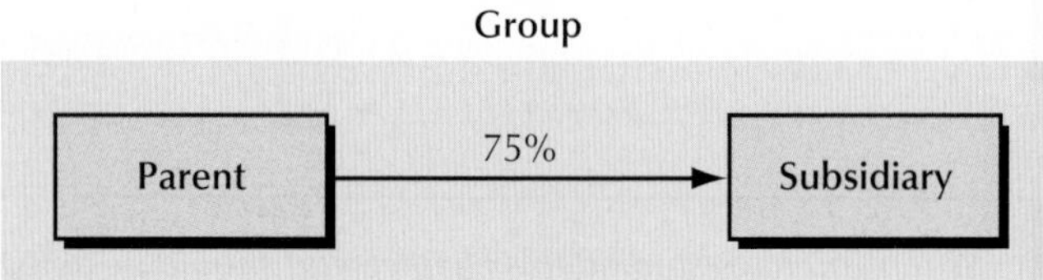

FIGURE 24.1 The group

According to paragraph 27 of IAS 27, the NCI is to be identified and presented within equity, separately from the parent shareholders' equity; that is, it is regarded as an equity contributor to the group, rather than a liability of the group. This is because the NCI does not meet the definition of a liability as contained in the *Framework*, because the group has no present obligation to provide economic outflows to the NCI. The NCI receives a share of consolidated equity, and is therefore a participant in the residual equity of the group. IAS 27, although not explicitly recognising the fact, adopts the entity concept of consolidation as it adjusts for the effects of intragroup transactions in full (paragraph 20) and categorises the NCI as equity. (See chapter 21 for a full discussion of the concepts of consolidation and the classification of NCI as equity or liability.)

Classification of the NCI as equity affects both the calculation of the NCI as well as how it is disclosed in the consolidated financial statements.

24.1.2 Calculation of the NCI share of equity

The NCI is entitled to a share of consolidated equity, because it is a contributor of equity to the consolidated group. Because consolidated equity is affected by profits and losses made in relation to transactions within the group, the calculation of the NCI is affected by the existence of intragroup transactions. In other words, the NCI is entitled to a share of the equity of the subsidiary adjusted for the effects of profits and losses made on intragroup transactions. This is discussed in more detail in section 24.4.

24.1.3 Disclosure of the NCI

According to paragraph 27 of IAS 27:

> Non-controlling interests shall be presented in the consolidated statement of financial position within equity, separately from the equity of the owners of the parent.

IAS 1 *Presentation of Financial Statements* confirms these disclosures. Paragraph 83 of requires the profit or loss for the period as well as the comprehensive income for the period to be disclosed in the statement of comprehensive income, showing separately the amounts attributable to non-controlling interest, and that attributable to owners of the parent. Figure 24.2 shows how the statement of comprehensive income may be shown. Note that in terms of the various line items in the statement, such as revenues and expenses, it is the total consolidated amount that is disclosed. It is only the consolidated profit and comprehensive income that is divided into parent share and NCI share.

ZURICH LTD
Consolidated Statement of Comprehensive Income
for the year ended 30 June 2010

	2010 $m	**2009** $m
Revenue	500	450
Expenses	280	260
Gross profit	220	190
Finance costs	40	35
	180	155
Share of after-tax profit of associates	30	25
Profit before tax	210	180
Income tax expense	28	22
PROFIT FOR THE YEAR	182	158
Other comprehensive income	31	24
TOTAL COMPREHENSIVE INCOME FOR THE YEAR	213	182
Profit attributable to:		
Owners of the parent	151	140
Non-controlling interests	31	18
	182	158
Total comprehensive income attributable to:		
Owners of the parent	179	160
Non-controlling interests	34	22
	213	182

FIGURE 24.2 Disclosure of NCI in the statement of comprehensive income

According to paragraph 106(a) of IAS 1, the total comprehensive income for the period must be disclosed in the statement of changes in equity, showing separately the total amounts attributable to owners of the parent and to non-controlling interests. Figure 24.3 provides an example of disclosures in the statement of changes of equity. Note that the only line item for which the NCI must be shown is the total comprehensive income for the period. There is no requirement to show the NCI share of each equity account.

Similarly, paragraph 54(q) of IAS 1 requires disclosure in the statement of financial position of the total NCI share of equity while paragraph 54(r) requires disclosure of the issued capital and reserves attributable to owners of the parent. The equity section of the statement of financial position could then appear as in figure 24.4 on the next page. In the statement of financial position, only the total NCI share of equity is disclosed, rather than the NCI share of the different categories of equity. The NCI share of the various categories of equity and the changes in those balances can be seen in the statement of changes in equity. Note that the consolidated assets and liabilities are those for the whole of the group; it is only equity that is divided into parent and NCI shares.

ZURICH LTD
Consolidated Statement of Changes in Equity (extract)
for the year ended 30 June 2010

	Attributable to owners of the parent					Non-controlling interest	Total equity
	Share capital	Revaluation surplus	Translation reserve	Retained earnings	Total		
	$m	$m	$m	$m	$m	$m	$m
Balance at 1 July 2009	400	120	100	250	870	130	740
Changes in accounting policy	—	—	—	—	—	—	—
Total comprehensive income for the period	—	21	10	182	213	34	179
Dividends	—	—	—	(150)	(150)	(10)	(140)
Issue of share capital	—	—	—	—	—	—	—
Balance at 30 June 2010	400	141	110	282	933	154	779

FIGURE 24.3 Disclosure of NCI in the statement of changes in equity

ZURICH LTD
Statement of Financial Position (extract)
as at 30 June 2010

	2010 $m	2009 $m
EQUITY		
Equity attributable to owners of the parent		
Share capital	400	400
Other reserves	251	220
Retained earnings	282	250
	933	870
Non-controlling interests	154	130
Total equity	779	740

FIGURE 24.4 Disclosure of NCI in the statement of financial position

24.2 EFFECTS OF AN NCI ON THE CONSOLIDATION PROCESS

Paragraph 32 of IFRS 3 states:

> The acquirer shall recognise goodwill as of the acquisition date measured as the excess of (a) over (b) below:
> (a) the aggregate of:
> (i) the consideration transferred measured in accordance with this Standard, which generally requires acquisition-date fair value (see paragraph 37);
> (ii) the amount of any non-controlling interest in the acquiree measured in accordance with this Standard; and
> (iii) in a business combination achieved in stages (see paragraphs 41 and 42), the acquisition date fair value of the acquirer's previously held equity interests in the acquiree.
> (b) the net of the acquisition-date amounts of the identifiable assets acquired and the liabilities assumed measured in accordance with this Standard.

Note that this choice is not an accounting policy choice, but is made for each business combination.

Consider a situation where A Ltd acquires 50% of the shares of B Ltd, having previously acquired 20% of the shares of B Ltd. Holding 70% of the shares of B Ltd gives A Ltd control of that entity. At acquisition date, there is an NCI of 30%. Note:

- Where the parent acquires less than all the shares of a subsidiary, it acquires only a portion of the total equity or total net assets of the subsidiary. Hence, the consideration transferred is for only a portion of the net assets of the subsidiary; in this example, 50%.
- Where the parent previously acquired an interest in the subsidiary, it will need to be accounted for as shown in chapter 22. In essence, the 20% investment held prior to the parent obtaining control must be revalued at acquisition date to fair value.

The next step is to measure the amount of the 30% non-controlling interest in the subsidiary. The problem with this step is that IFRS 3 allows alternative treatments. Paragraph 19 of IFRS 3 states:

> For each business combination, the acquirer shall measure any non-controlling interest in the acquiree *either* at fair value or at the non-controlling interest's proportionate share of the acquiree's identifiable net assets. [emphasis added]

Which alternative is chosen affects the determination of goodwill and the subsequent consolidation adjustments. Where the first alternative is used, the goodwill attributable to both the NCI and the parent is measured. Under the second alternative, only the goodwill attributable to the parent is measured. The methods are sometimes referred to as the 'full goodwill' and the 'partial goodwill' methods — see paragraph BC205 in the Basis for Conclusions on IFRS 3 for further elaboration. These terms are used in this chapter to distinguish between the two methods. The methods are demonstrated in sections 24.2.1 and 24.2.2 and the reasons for the standard setters allowing optional measurements, as well as factors to consider in choosing between the methods, is discussed in section 24.2.3.

24.2.1 Full goodwill method

Under this method, at acquisition date, the NCI in the subsidiary is measured at fair value. The fair value is determined on the basis of the market prices for shares not acquired by the parent, or, if these are not available, a valuation technique is used.

It is not sufficient to use the consideration paid by the acquirer to measure the fair value of the NCI. For example, if a parent paid \$80 000 for 80% of the shares of a subsidiary, then the fair value of the NCI cannot be assumed to be \$20 000 (i.e. $\frac{20}{80}$ × \$80 000). It may be that the acquirer paid a control premium in order to acquire a controlling interest in the subsidiary. Relating this to the nature of goodwill in chapter 11, core goodwill includes the component of combination goodwill, relating to synergies arising because of the combination of the parent and the subsidiary. The parent would increase the consideration it was prepared to pay due to these synergies. However, these synergies may result in increased earnings in the parent and not the subsidiary. In this case, the NCI does not receive any share of those synergies. Hence, the consideration paid by the parent could not be used to measure the fair value of the NCI in the subsidiary.

To illustrate the method, assume that P Ltd paid \$169 600 for 80% of the shares of S Ltd on 1 July 2010. All identifiable assets and liabilities of the subsidiary were recorded at fair value, except for land for which the fair value was \$10 000 greater than cost. The tax rate is 30%. The NCI in S Ltd was considered to have a fair value of \$42 000. At acquisition date, the equity of S Ltd consisted of:

Share capital	\$100 000
General reserve	60 000
Retained earnings	40 000

The acquisition analysis is as follows:

Net fair value of identifiable assets and liabilities of S Ltd	= \$100 000 + \$60 000 + \$40 000
	+ \$10 000(1 – 30%) (BCVR – land)
	= \$207 000

(a) Consideration transferred	= \$169 600
(b) Non-controlling interest in S Ltd	= \$42 000
Aggregate of (a) and (b)	= \$211 600
Goodwill	= \$211 600 – \$207 000
	= \$4 600
Goodwill attributable to parent:	
Net fair value acquired	= 80% × \$207 000
	= \$165 600
Consideration transferred	= \$169 600
Goodwill — parent	= \$169 600 – \$165 600
	= \$4 000
Goodwill attributable to NCI	= \$4 600 – \$4 000
	= \$600
	= \$42 000 – 20% × \$207 000

Note the following:

- BCVR refers to the business combination valuation reserve.
- Goodwill is calculated as the excess of the sum or aggregate of the consideration transferred and the fair value of the NCI over the net fair value of the identifiable assets and liabilities of the subsidiary at acquisition date. This goodwill is the goodwill of the subsidiary as a whole.
- As the fair value of the NCI (20%) is determined to be \$42 000, if P Ltd were to acquire 80% of S Ltd it would expect to pay \$168 000 (i.e. $\frac{80}{20}$ × \$42 000). As P Ltd paid \$169 600, it then paid a control premium of \$1600. Effectively, the goodwill of \$4600 is broken down into:

Control premium paid by P Ltd	\$1 600
Parent share of S Ltd's goodwill	\$2 400 [\$4 000 – \$1 600]
NCI share of S Ltd's goodwill	\$600

The control premium is recognised as part of goodwill on consolidation, but is not attributable to the NCI.

Hence, the business combination valuation reserve relating to goodwill recognised on consolidation is attributed \$4000 to the parent and \$600 to the NCI. The earnings from the control premium, namely combination goodwill, must flow into the parent's earnings and not that of the subsidiary; otherwise it would be included in the valuation of the NCI interest in the subsidiary.

The consolidation worksheet entries are as follows:

1. Business combination valuation entries			
Land	Dr	10 000	
Deferred Tax Liability	Cr		3 000
Business Combination Valuation Reserve	Cr		7 000
(Revaluation of land)			
Goodwill	Dr	4 600	
Business Combination Valuation Reserve	Cr		4 600
(Recognition of total goodwill)			
2. Pre-acquisition entry			
Retained Earnings [80% × \$40 000]	Dr	32 000	
Share Capital [80% × \$100 000]	Dr	80 000	
General Reserve [80% × \$60 000]	Dr	48 000	
Business Combination Valuation Reserve [(80% × \$7000) + \$4000]	Dr	9 600	
Shares in S Ltd	Cr		169 600

Two *business combination valuation entries* are required: one for the revaluation of the land to fair value, and the second to recognise the total goodwill of the subsidiary.

In relation to the equity on hand at acquisition date, only 80% is attributable to the parent, and 20% is attributable to the NCI. The *pre-acquisition entry* relates to the investment by the parent in the subsidiary, and thus relates to 80% of the amounts shown in the acquisition analysis. The adjustments to equity in the pre-acquisition entry are then determined by taking 80% of the recorded equity of the subsidiary, plus 80% of the business combination valuation reserves recognised as a result of differences between fair value and carrying amounts of the subsidiary's identifiable net assets at acquisition date, plus the parent's share of the goodwill.

24.2.2 Partial goodwill method

Under the second option, the NCI is measured at the NCI's proportionate share of the acquiree's identifiable net assets. The NCI therefore does not get a share of any equity relating to goodwill as goodwill is defined in Appendix A of IFRS 3 as the future economic benefits arising from assets not individually identified. The only goodwill recognised is that acquired by the parent in the business combination — hence the term 'partial' goodwill. According to paragraph 32 of IFRS 3, using the measurement of the NCI share of equity based on the NCI's proportionate share of the acquiree's identifiable net assets:

Goodwill = consideration transferred *plus* previously acquired investment by parent *plus* NCI share of identifiable assets and liabilities of subsidiary *less* net fair value of identifiable assets and liabilities of subsidiary.

As the last two items can be netted off to be the parent's share of the net fair value of the identifiable net assets of the subsidiary, the calculation of goodwill is:

Goodwill = consideration transferred *plus* previously acquired investment by parent *less* parent's share of the net fair value of the identifiable net assets of the subsidiary.

To illustrate, using the same example as in section 24.2.1, assume that P Ltd paid \$169 600 for 80% of the shares of S Ltd on 1 July 2010. All identifiable assets and liabilities of the subsidiary were recorded at fair value, except for land for which the fair value was \$10 000 greater than cost. The tax rate is 30%. At acquisition date, the equity of S Ltd consisted of:

Share capital	\$100 000
General reserve	60 000
Retained earnings	40 000

The acquisition analysis is as follows:

Net fair value of identifiable assets and liabilities of S Ltd	= \$100 000 + \$60 000 + \$40 000
	+ \$10 000(1 – 30%) (BCVR – land)
	= \$207 000
Net fair value acquired by the parent	= 80% × \$207 000
	= \$165 600
Consideration transferred	= \$169 600
Previously acquired investment by the parent	= 0
Goodwill acquired	= \$169 600 – \$165 600
	= \$4 000

Note that the $4000 goodwill is the same as the parent's share calculated in section 24.2.1. The consolidation worksheet entries are:

Business combination valuation entry			
Land	Dr	10 000	
Deferred Tax Liability	Cr		3 000
Business Combination Valuation Reserve	Cr		7 000
Pre-acquisition entry			
Retained Earnings [80% × $40 000]	Dr	32 000	
Share Capital [80% × $100 000]	Dr	80 000	
General Reserve [80% × $60 000]	Dr	48 000	
Business Combination Valuation Reserve [80% × $7000]	Dr	5 600	
Goodwill	Dr	4 000	
Shares in S Ltd	Cr		169 600

Note firstly that there is no business combination valuation entry for goodwill. This is because only the parent's share of the goodwill is recognised. A business combination valuation adjustment to recognise goodwill is only used under the full goodwill method where both the parent's and the NCI's share of goodwill is recognised.

In relation to the equity on hand at acquisition date, only 80% is attributable to the parent, and 20% is attributable to the NCI. The pre-acquisition entry relates to the investment by the parent in the subsidiary, and thus relates to 80% of the amounts shown in the acquisition analysis. The adjustments to equity in the pre-acquisition entry are then determined by taking 80% of the recorded equity of the subsidiary, plus 80% of the business combination valuation reserves recognised as a result of differences between fair value and carrying amounts of the subsidiary's identifiable net assets at acquisition date. Because only the parent's share of goodwill is recognised, this is accounted for in the pre-acquisition entry which also relates to the investment by the parent in the subsidiary.

24.2.3 Reasons for, and choosing between, the options

IFRS 3, as revised in 2008, was issued by the IASB at the same time as Statement of Financial Standards No. 141 *Business Combinations* was revised and reissued by the Financial Accounting Standards Board (FASB) in the United States. The project on determining a new standard on business combinations was conducted jointly by the FASB and the IASB in the hope of achieving convergence on the standard between the two boards. Both boards issued exposure drafts on business combinations, and, in both these documents, the full goodwill method was recommended. However, when the final standards were issued, the FASB standard required the accounting for all business combinations to use the full goodwill method; whereas, the IASB standard provided for optional treatments in the measurement of the NCI share of the subsidiary.

Paragraphs BC209–BC221 explain why the IASB chose to provide optional methods. As noted in paragraph BC210, the IASB recognises that to allow optional methods does reduce the comparability of financial statements:

> However, the IASB was not able to agree on a single measurement basis for non-controlling interests because neither of the alternatives considered (fair value and proportionate share of the acquiree's identifiable net assets) was supported by enough board members to enable a revised business combinations standard to be issued.

The IASB supports the principle of measuring all components of a business combination at fair value (paragraph BC212); however, paragraph BC213 notes some arguments against applying this to the NCI in the acquiree:

- It is more costly to measure the NCI at fair value than at the proportionate share of the net fair value of the identifiable net assets of the acquiree.
- There is not sufficient evidence to assess the marginal benefits of reporting the acquisition-date fair value of NCIs.

- Respondents to the exposure draft saw little information of value in the reported NCI, regardless of how it is measured.

One of the options considered by the IASB in writing the standard was to require the use of the fair value method for measuring the NCI but allowing entities to use the proportionate method where there exists 'undue cost or effort' in measuring the fair value. However, the IASB rejected this option as it did not think the term undue cost or effort would be applied consistently (paragraph BC215).

The IASB noted three main differences in outcome that occur where the partial goodwill method is used instead of the full goodwill method:

1. The amounts recognised for the NCI share of equity and goodwill would be lower.
2. Where IAS 36 *Impairment of Assets* is applied to a cash-generating unit containing goodwill, as the goodwill recognised by the CGU is lower, this affects the impairment loss relating to goodwill.
3. There is also an effect where an acquirer subsequently obtains further shares in the subsidiary at a later date. An explanation of this effect is beyond the scope of this book.

In choosing which method to use — full or partial goodwill — it is these three effects on the financial statements, both current and in the future, that must be taken into consideration. For example, if management has future intentions of acquiring more shares in the subsidiary (i.e. by acquiring some of the shares held by the NCI), then the potential impact on equity when that acquisition occurs will need to be considered.

24.2.4 Intragroup transactions

As noted in chapter 23, because IAS 27 adopts the entity concept of consolidation, the full effects of transactions within the group are adjusted on consolidation. In essence, the worksheet adjustment entries used in chapter 23 are the same regardless of whether the subsidiary is wholly or partly owned by its parent. The only exception to the entries used in chapter 23 is for dividends.

Where an NCI exists, any dividends declared or paid by a subsidiary are paid proportionately (to the extent of the ownership interest in the subsidiary) to the parent and proportionately to the NCI. In adjusting for dividends paid by a subsidiary, only the dividend paid or payable to the parent is eliminated on consolidation. In other words, there is a proportional adjustment of the dividend paid or declared. As with other intragroup transactions, the adjustment relates to the flow within the group. A payment or a declaration of dividends by a subsidiary reduces the NCI share of subsidiary equity because the equity of the subsidiary is reduced by the payment or declaration of dividends. In calculating the NCI share of subsidiary equity, the existence of dividends must be taken into consideration (see section 24.3.3 of this chapter). Where a dividend is declared, the NCI share of equity is reduced, and a liability to pay dividends to the NCI is shown in the consolidated statement of financial position.

To illustrate, assume a parent owns 80% of the share capital of a subsidiary. In the current period, the subsidiary pays a $1000 dividend and declares a further $1500 dividend. The adjustment entries in the consolidation worksheet in the current period are:

Dividend Revenue	Dr	800	
Dividend Paid	Cr		800
(80% × $1000)			
Dividend Payable	Dr	1 200	
Dividend Declared	Cr		1 200
(80% × $1500)			
Dividend Revenue	Dr	1 200	
Dividend Receivable	Cr		1 200
(80% × $1500)			

24.2.5 Consolidation worksheet

Because the disclosure requirements for the NCI require the extraction of the NCI share of various equity items, the consolidation worksheet is changed to enable this information to be produced. Figure 24.5 contains an example of the changed worksheet. In particular, note that two new columns are added, a *debit column* and a *credit column* for the calculation of the NCI share of equity. These two columns are not adjustment or elimination columns. Instead, they are used to divide consolidated equity into NCI share and parent entity share. The worksheet shown in figure 24.5 also contains a column showing the figures for the consolidated group. This column is shown between the adjustment columns and the NCI columns, and it is the summation of the financial statements of the group members and the consolidation adjustments. The parent figures are then determined by subtracting the NCI share of equity from the total consolidated equity of the group.

			Adjustments			Non-controlling interest		
Financial statements	**P Ltd**	**S Ltd**	**Dr**	**Cr**	**Group**	**Dr**	**Cr**	**Parent**
Profit/(loss)	5 000	4 000			9 000	400		8 600
Retained earnings (opening balance)	10 000	8 000			18 000	800		17 200
Transfer from reserves	4 000	2 000			6 000	200		5 800
Total available for appropriation	19 000	14 000			33 000			31 600
Interim dividend paid	2 000	1 500			3 500		150	3 350
Final dividend declared	4 000	2 500			6 500		250	6 250
Transfer to reserves	3 000	1 000			4 000		100	3 900
	9 000	5 000			14 000			13 500
Retained earnings (closing balance)	10 000	9 000			19 000			18 100
Share capital	50 000	40 000			90 000	4 000		86 000
Other reserves	30 000	20 000			50 000	2 000		48 000
	90 000	69 000			159 000			152 100
Asset revaluation surplus (opening balance)	4 000	5 000			9 000	500		8 500
Revaluation increments	2 000	2 000			4 000	200		3 800
Asset revaluation surplus (closing balance)	6 000	7 000			13 000			12 300
Total equity: parent								164 400
Total equity: NCI							7 600	7 600
Total equity	96 000	76 000			172 000	8 100	8 100	172 000
Current liabilities	3 000	2 000			5 000			
Non-current liabilities	8 000	6 000			14 000			
Total liabilities	11 000	8 000			19 000			
Total equity and liabilities	107 000	84 000			191 000			

FIGURE 24.5 Consolidation worksheet containing NCI columns

In figure 24.5, the amounts in the debit NCI column record the NCI share of the relevant equity item. This amount is subtracted in the consolidation process so that the consolidation column contains the parent's share of consolidated equity.

The first line in figure 24.5 is the consolidated profit/(loss) for the period. This amount is then attributed to the parent and the NCI. In all subsequent equity lines, the NCI share is recorded in the debit NCI column, and the parent's share of each equity account is calculated. The total NCI share of equity is then added to the parent column to give total consolidated equity.

The NCI share of retained earnings is increased by subsidiary profits and transfers from reserves, and decreased by transfers to reserves and payments and declarations of dividends. The total NCI share of equity is then the sum of the NCI share of capital, other reserves and retained earnings. The assets and liabilities of the group are shown in total and not allocated to the equity interests in the group — see, for example, the liabilities section in figure 24.5.

24.3 CALCULATING THE NCI SHARE OF EQUITY

According to paragraph 18(c) of IAS 27, non-controlling interests in the net assets consist of:

(i) the amount of those non-controlling interests at the date of the original combination calculated in accordance with IFRS 3; and

(ii) the non-controlling interests' share of changes in equity since the date of the combination.

In relation to part (ii), changes in equity since the acquisition date must be taken into account. Note that these changes not only are in the recorded equity of the subsidiary, but also relate to other changes in consolidated equity. As noted earlier in this chapter, the NCI is entitled to a share of consolidated equity under the entity concept of consolidation. This requires taking into account adjustments for profits and losses made as a result of intragroup transactions because these profits and losses are not recognised by the group.

The calculation of the NCI is done in two stages: (1) the NCI share of recorded equity is determined (see section 24.3.1), and (2) this share is adjusted for the effects of intragroup transactions (see section 24.4).

24.3.1 NCI share of recorded equity of the subsidiary

The equity of the subsidiary consists of the equity contained in the actual records of the subsidiary as well as any business combination valuation reserves created on consolidation at the acquisition date, where the identifiable assets and liabilities of the subsidiary are recorded at amounts different from their fair values. The NCI is entitled to a share of subsidiary equity at the end of the reporting period, which consists of the equity on hand at acquisition date plus any changes in that equity between acquisition date and the end of the reporting period. The calculation of the NCI share of equity at a point in time is done in three steps:

1. Determine the NCI share of equity of the subsidiary at acquisition date.
2. Determine the NCI share of the change in subsidiary equity between the acquisition date and the beginning of the current period for which the consolidated financial statements are being prepared.
3. Determine the NCI share of the changes in subsidiary equity in the current period.

The calculation could be represented diagrammatically, as shown in figure 24.6.

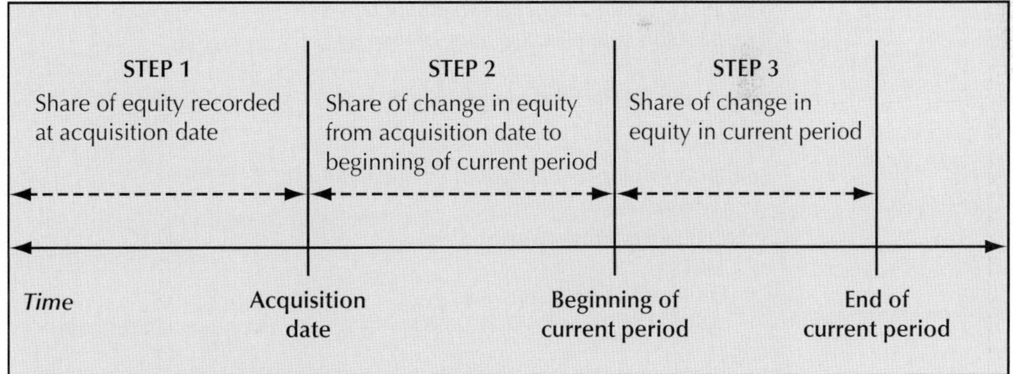

FIGURE 24.6 Calculating the NCI share of equity
Source: Based on a diagram by Peter Gerhardy, School of Commerce, Flinders University.

Note that, in calculating the NCI share of equity at the end of the current period, the information relating to the NCI share of equity from steps 1 and 2 should be available from the previous period's consolidation worksheet.

To illustrate the above procedure, consider the calculation of the NCI share of retained earnings over a 5-year period. Assume the following information in relation to Zurich Ltd:

Retained earnings as at 1 July 2006	$10 000
Retained earnings as at 30 June 2010	50 000
Profit for the 2010–11 period	15 000
Retained earnings as at 30 June 2011	65 000

Assume that Geneva Ltd had acquired 80% of the share capital of Zurich Ltd at 1 July 2006, and the consolidated financial statements were being prepared at 30 June 2011. The 20% NCI in Zurich Ltd is therefore entitled to a share of the retained earnings balance of $65 000, a share equal to $13 000. This share is calculated in three steps:

Step 1. A share of the balance at 1 July 2006 (20% × $10 000)	=	$ 2 000
Step 2. A share of the change in retained earnings from the acquisition date to the beginning of the current period (20% × [$50 000 − $10 000])	=	8 000
Step 3. A share of the current period increase in retained earnings (20% × $15 000)	=	3 000
		$13 000

The increase in retained earnings is broken into these three steps because accounting is based on time periods. The NCI is entitled to a share of the profits of past periods as well as a share of the profits of the current period. Note that, in calculating the NCI share of retained earnings for Zurich Ltd at 30 June 2012 (one year after the above calculation), the total of steps 1 and 2 for the 2012 calculation would be $13 000, as calculated above. The only additional calculation would be the share of changes in retained earnings in the 2011–12 period.

These separate calculations are not based on a division of equity into pre-acquisition and post-acquisition equity. The division of equity is based on *time* — changes in equity are calculated on a period-by-period basis for accounting purposes.

The NCI columns in the consolidation worksheet contain the amounts relating to the three steps noted above. The journal entries used in the NCI columns of the consolidation worksheet to reflect the NCI share of equity are based on the three-step approach. The form of these entries is:

Step 1: NCI at acquisition date			
Share Capital	Dr	X	
Business Combination Valuation Reserve	Dr	X	
Retained Earnings (opening balance)	Dr	X	
NCI	Cr		X
Step 2: NCI share of changes in equity between acquisition date and beginning of the current period			
Retained Earnings (opening balance)	Dr	X	
NCI	Cr		X
Step 3: NCI share of changes in equity in the current period			
NCI Share of Profit/(Loss)	Dr	X	
NCI	Cr		X
Asset Revaluation Increments	Dr	X	
NCI	Cr		X
NCI	Dr	X	
Dividend Paid	Cr		X
NCI	Dr	X	
Dividend Declared	Cr		X

The effects of these journal entries can be seen in the consolidation worksheet in figure 24.5. The above entries are illustrative only, and there may be others where there are transfers to or from reserves that affect the balances of equity in the subsidiary. The effects of these transactions are illustrated in the next section.

24.3.2 Accounting at acquisition date

This section illustrates the effects that the existence of an NCI has on the valuation entries, the acquisition analysis and the pre-acquisition entry, as well as the step 1 calculation of the NCI share of equity at acquisition date. As noted in section 24.2, the acquisition analysis and subsequent consolidation worksheet entries are affected by whether the full goodwill or partial goodwill option is used in the measurement of the NCI's share of the subsidiary at acquisition date. The choice of method affects the accounting at acquisition date but has an effect on accounting subsequent to acquisition date only if there is an impairment of goodwill or the parent changes its equity interest in the subsidiary. Neither of these events is covered in this book.

Full goodwill method

ILLUSTRATIVE EXAMPLE 24.1

Consolidation worksheet entries at acquisition date

On 1 July 2009, Basel Ltd acquired 60% of the shares (*cum div.*) of Lausanne Ltd for $45 600 when the equity of Lausanne Ltd consisted of:

Share capital	$40 000
General reserve	2 000
Retained earnings	2 000

At acquisition date, the liabilities of Lausanne Ltd included a dividend payable of $1000. All the identifiable assets and liabilities of Lausanne Ltd were recorded at fair value except for equipment and inventory:

	Carrying amount	Fair value
Equipment (cost $250 000)	$180 000	$200 000
Inventory	40 000	50 000

The tax rate is 30%. The fair value of the NCI in Lausanne Ltd at 1 July 2009 was $28 000

Acquisition analysis

Net fair value of identifiable assets and liabilities of Lausanne Ltd	= $40 000 (capital) + $2 000 (general reserve)
	+ $2 000 (retained earnings)
	+ $20 000(1 – 30%) (BCVR – equipment)
	+ $10 000(1 – 30%) (BCVR – inventory)
	= $65 000
(a) Consideration transferred	= $45 600 – (60% × $1 000) (dividend receivable)
	= $45 000
(b) Non-controlling interest in Lausanne Ltd	= $28 000
Aggregate of (a) and (b)	= $73 000
Goodwill	= $73 000 – $65 000
	= $8000
Net fair value acquired	= 60% × $65 000
	= $39 000
Consideration transferred	= $45 000
Goodwill – parent	= $45 000 – $39 000
	= $6000
Goodwill – NCI	= $8000 – $6000
	= $2000

Where an NCI exists, because the parent acquires only a part of the ownership interest of the subsidiary, the parent acquires only a proportionate share of each of the equity amounts in the subsidiary.

(1) *Business combination valuation entries*
The valuation entries are unaffected by the existence of an NCI. The purpose of these entries, in accordance with IFRS 3, is to show the assets and liabilities of the subsidiary at fair value at acquisition date. The entries for a consolidation worksheet (see figure 24.7) prepared at acquisition date are:

Accumulated Depreciation – Equipment	Dr	70 000	
Equipment	Cr		50 000
Deferred Tax Liability	Cr		6 000
Business Combination Valuation Reserve	Cr		14 000
Inventory	Dr	10 000	
Deferred Tax Liability	Cr		3 000
Business Combination Valuation Reserve	Cr		7 000
Goodwill	Dr	8 000	
Business Combination Valuation Reserve	Cr		8 000

The business combination valuation reserve is pre-acquisition equity because it is recognised on consolidation at acquisition date. The NCI is entitled to a proportionate share of this reserve, except that relating to goodwill where, in the acquisition analysis, the NCI share has been calculated as $2000. Because the reserve is recognised by the group, but not in the records of the subsidiary, this affects later calculations for the NCI share of equity.

(2) *Pre-acquisition entries*
The first pre-acquisition entry is read from the pre-acquisition analysis. The parent's proportional share of the various recorded equity accounts of the subsidiary, as well as the parent's share of the business combination valuation reserves, are eliminated against the investment account in the pre-acquisition entry. In this illustrative example, the pre-acquisition entry is:

Retained Earnings (1/7/09) [60% × $2000]	Dr	1 200	
Share Capital [60% × $40 000]	Dr	24 000	
Business Combination Valuation Reserve [60% × ($14 000 + $7000) + $6000 goodwill]	Dr	18 600	
General Reserve [60% × $2000]	Dr	1 200	
Shares in Lausanne Ltd	Cr		45 000

At acquisition date, the subsidiary has recorded a dividend payable and the parent entity a dividend receivable. An adjustment entry is required because these are not dividends receivable or payable to parties external to the group. The adjustment is a proportional one as it relates only to the amount payable within the group:

Dividend Payable	Dr	600	
Dividend Receivable [60% × $1000]	Cr		600

No further adjustment is required once the dividend has been paid.

(3) *NCI share of equity at acquisition date*
The NCI at acquisition date (the step 1 calculation) is determined as the proportional share of the equity recorded by the subsidiary at that date and the valuation reserves recorded on consolidation (see opposite).

Share capital	40% × $40 000	= $16 000
General reserve	40% × $2 000	= 800
Business combination valuation reserve	40% × ($14 000 + $7 000)	
	+ $2 000 goodwill	= 10 400
Retained earnings	40% × $2 000	= 800
		$28 000

The following entry is then passed in the NCI columns of the consolidation worksheet:

Retained Earnings (1/7/09)	Dr	800	
Share Capital	Dr	16 000	
Business Combination Valuation Reserve	Dr	10 400	
General Reserve	Dr	800	
NCI	Cr		28 000

This entry is passed as the step 1 NCI entry in *all* subsequent consolidation worksheets. It is never changed. Any subsequent changes in pre-acquisition equity are dealt with in the step 2 NCI calculation.

Figure 24.7 shows an extract from a consolidation worksheet for Basel Ltd and its subsidiary, Lausanne Ltd, at acquisition date. Only the equity section of the worksheet is shown. The worksheet entries are (1) the business combination valuation entries, (2) the pre-acquisition entries (the dividend adjustment is not shown in figure 24.7 because only an extract from the worksheet is reproduced), and (3) the NCI step 1 entry.

Financial statements	Basel Ltd	Lausanne Ltd	Adjustments				Group	Non-controlling interest				Parent
				Dr	Cr				Dr	Cr		
Retained earnings	50 000	2 000	2	1 200			50 800	3	800			50 000
Share capital	100 000	40 000	2	24 000			116 000	3	16 000			100 000
General reserve	20 000	2 000	2	1 200			20 800	3	800			20 000
Business combination valuation reserve			2	18 600	14 000	1	10 400	3	10 400			0
					7 000	1						
					8 000	1						
Total equity: parent												170 000
Total equity: NCI										28 000	3	28 000
Total equity	170 000	44 000					198 000		28 000	28 000		198 000

FIGURE 24.7 Consolidation worksheet (extract) at acquisition date

Note that, in figure 24.7, the adjustment columns eliminate the parent's share of the pre-acquisition equity accounts and the NCI columns extract the NCI share of total equity. The parent column contains only the parent's share of post-acquisition equity, which in this case, being at acquisition date, is zero.

Partial goodwill method

ILLUSTRATIVE EXAMPLE 24.2

Consolidation worksheet entries at acquisition date

On 1 July 2009, Basel Ltd acquired 60% of the shares (*cum div.*) of Lausanne Ltd for $45 600 when the equity of Lausanne Ltd consisted of:

Share capital	$40 000
General reserve	2 000
Retained earnings	2 000

At acquisition date, the liabilities of Lausanne Ltd included a dividend payable of $1000. All the identifiable assets and liabilities of Lausanne Ltd were recorded at fair value except for equipment and inventory:

	Carrying amount	Fair value
Equipment (cost $250 000)	$180 000	$200 000
Inventory	40 000	50 000

The tax rate is 30%.

Acquisition analysis

Net fair value of identifiable assets and liabilities of Lausanne Ltd	= $40 000 (capital) + $2 000 (general reserve)
	+ $2 000 (retained earnings)
	+ $20 000(1 – 30%) (BCVR – equipment)
	+ $10 000(1 – 30%) (BCVR – inventory)
	= $65 000
Net fair value acquired by Basel Ltd	= 60% × $65 000
	= $39 000
Consideration transferred	= $45 600 – (60% × $1 000) (dividend receivable)
	= $45 000
Goodwill acquired by Basel Ltd	= $6 000

Where an NCI exists, because the parent acquires only a part of the ownership interest of the subsidiary, the parent acquires only a proportionate share of each of the equity amounts in the subsidiary.

(1) *Business combination valuation entries*
The valuation entries are unaffected by the existence of an NCI. The purpose of these entries, in accordance with IFRS 3, is to show the assets and liabilities of the subsidiary at fair value at acquisition date. The entries for a consolidation worksheet (see figure 24.8) prepared at acquisition date are:

Accumulated Depreciation – Equipment	Dr	70 000	
Equipment	Cr		50 000
Deferred Tax Liability	Cr		6 000
Business Combination Valuation Reserve	Cr		14 000
Inventory	Dr	10 000	
Deferred Tax Liability	Cr		3 000
Business Combination Valuation Reserve	Cr		7 000

Note that there is no business combination valuation entry for goodwill as under the partial goodwill method; only the parent's share of goodwill is recognised, and this is done in the pre-acquisition entry. The business combination valuation reserve is pre-acquisition equity because it is recognised on consolidation at acquisition date. The NCI is entitled to a proportionate share of this reserve. Because the reserve is recognised by the group, but not in the records of the subsidiary, this affects later calculations for the NCI share of equity.

(2) *Pre-acquisition entries*
The first pre-acquisition entry is read from the pre-acquisition analysis. The parent's proportional share of the various recorded equity accounts of the subsidiary, as well as the parent's share of the business combination valuation reserves, are eliminated against the investment account in the pre-acquisition entry, and the parent's share of goodwill is recognised. In this illustrative example, the pre-acquisition entry is shown opposite.

Retained Earnings (1/7/09) [60% × $2000]	Dr	1 200	
Share Capital [60% × $40 000]	Dr	24 000	
Business Combination Valuation Reserve [60% × ($14 000 + $7000)]	Dr	12 600	
General Reserve [60% × $2000]	Dr	1 200	
Goodwill	Dr	6 000	
Shares in Lausanne Ltd	Cr		45 000

At acquisition date, the subsidiary has recorded a dividend payable and the parent entity a dividend receivable. An adjustment entry is required because these are not dividends receivable or payable to parties external to the group. The adjustment is a proportional one as it relates only to the amount payable within the group:

Dividend Payable	Dr	600	
Dividend Receivable	Cr		600
[60% × $1000]			

No further adjustment is required once the dividend has been paid.

(3) *NCI share of equity at acquisition date*

The NCI at acquisition date (the step 1 calculation) is determined as the proportional share of the equity recorded by the subsidiary at that date and the valuation reserves recorded on consolidation:

Share capital	40% × $40 000	= $ 16 000
General reserve	40% × $2 000	= 800
Business combination valuation reserve	40% × ($14 000 + $7 000)	= 8 400
Retained earnings	40% × $2 000	= 800
		$ 26 000

The following entry is then passed in the NCI columns of the consolidation worksheet:

Retained Earnings (1/7/09)	Dr	800	
Share Capital	Dr	16 000	
Business Combination Valuation Reserve	Dr	8 400	
General Reserve	Dr	800	
NCI	Cr		26 000

This entry is passed as the step 1 NCI entry in *all* subsequent consolidation worksheets. It is never changed. Any subsequent changes in pre-acquisition equity are dealt with in the step 2 NCI calculation.

Figure 24.8 shows an extract from a consolidation worksheet for Basel Ltd and its subsidiary, Lausanne Ltd, at acquisition date. Only the equity section of the worksheet is shown. The worksheet entries are (1) the business combination valuation entries, (2) the pre-acquisition entries (the dividend adjustment is not shown in figure 24.8 because only an extract from the worksheet is reproduced), and (3) the NCI step 1 entry.

Note that, in figure 24.8, the adjustment columns eliminate the parent's share of the pre-acquisition equity accounts and the NCI columns extract the NCI share of total equity. The parent column contains only the parent's share of post-acquisition equity, which in this case, being at acquisition date, is zero.

Financial statements	Basel Ltd	Lausanne Ltd		Adjustments Dr	Adjustments Cr		Group		Non-controlling interest Dr	Non-controlling interest Cr		Parent
Retained earnings	50 000	2 000	2	1 200			50 800	3	800			50 000
Share capital	100 000	40 000	2	24 000			116 000	3	16 000			100 000
General reserve	20 000	2 000	2	1 200			20 800	3	800			20 000
Business combination valuation reserve			2	12 600	14 000	1	8 400	3	8 400			0
					7 000	1						
Total equity: parent												170 000
Total equity: NCI										26 000	3	26 000
Total equity	170 000	44 000					196 000		26 000	26 000		196 000

FIGURE 24.8 Consolidation worksheet (extract) at acquisition date

24.3.3 Accounting subsequent to acquisition date

Using illustrative example 24.2, the consolidation worksheet entries at the end of the period 3 years after the acquisition date are now considered. These entries are based on the *partial goodwill* method. However, the effects of the events occurring subsequent to acquisition date on the pre-acquisition entries and business combination valuation entries are the same for the full goodwill method. Assume that:

- all inventory on hand at 1 July 2009 is sold by 30 June 2010
- the dividend payable at acquisition date is paid in August 2009
- the equipment has an expected useful life of 5 years
- goodwill has not been impaired
- in the 3 years after the acquisition date, Lausanne Ltd recorded the changes in equity shown in figure 24.9.

In preparing the consolidated financial statements at 30 June 2012, the consolidation worksheet contains the valuation entries, the pre-acquisition entries, the NCI entries and the adjustments for the dividend transactions.

	2009–10	2010–11	2011–12
Profit for the period	$ 8 000	$12 000	$15 000
Retained earnings (opening balance)	2 000	7 800	16 000
	10 000	19 800	31 000
Transfer from general reserve	—	—	500
	10 000	19 800	31 500
Transfer to general reserve	—	1 000	—
Dividend paid	1 000	1 200	1 500
Dividend declared	1 200	1 600	2 000
	2 200	3 800	3 500
Retained earnings (closing balance)	7 800	16 000	28 000
Share capital	40 000	40 000	40 000
General reserve	2 000	3 000	2 500
Other components of equity*	2 000	2 500	2 400

*Resulted from movement in fair value of available-for-sale financial assets.

FIGURE 24.9 Changes in equity over a 3-year period

(1) *Business combination valuation entries*

The valuation entries for the 2011–12 period differ from those prepared at acquisition date in that the equipment is depreciated, and the inventory has been sold. The entries at 30 June 2012 are shown opposite.

Accumulated Depreciation – Equipment	Dr	70 000	
Equipment	Cr		50 000
Deferred Tax Liability	Cr		6 000
Business Combination Valuation Reserve	Cr		14 000
Depreciation Expense	Dr	4 000	
Retained Earnings (1/7/11)	Dr	8 000	
Accumulated Depreciation	Cr		12 000
(20% × $20 000 p.a.)			
Deferred Tax Liability	Dr	3 600	
Income Tax Expense	Cr		1 200
Retained Earnings (1/7/11)	Cr		2 400
(30% × $4000 p.a.)			

(If the full goodwill method had been used, the business combination entry relating to goodwill would be included at 30 June 2012 and would be the same as that used at acquisition date.)

(2) *Pre-acquisition entries*

The pre-acquisition entries have to take into consideration the following events occurring since acquisition date:

- The dividend of $1000 on hand at acquisition date has been paid.
- The inventory on hand at acquisition date has been sold.

The entry at 30 June 2012 is:

Retained Earnings (1/7/11)*	Dr	5 400	
Share Capital	Dr	24 000	
Business Combination Valuation Reserve**	Dr	8 400	
General Reserve	Dr	1 200	
Goodwill	Dr	6 000	
Shares in Lausanne Ltd	Cr		45 000

*$1200 + (60% × $7000) (BCVR transfer – inventory)
**60% × $14 000

(3) *NCI share of equity at acquisition date (step 1)*

The NCI share of equity at acquisition date is as calculated previously. This entry is never changed from that calculated at that date — this applies whether the full goodwill or partial goodwill method is used.

Retained Earnings (1/7/11)	Dr	800	
Share Capital	Dr	16 000	
Business Combination Valuation Reserve	Dr	8 400	
General Reserve	Dr	800	
NCI	Cr		26 000

(4) *NCI share of changes in equity between acquisition date and beginning of the current period* (i.e. from 1 July 2009 to 30 June 2011) (*step 2*)

To calculate this entry, it is necessary to note any changes in subsidiary equity between the two dates. The changes will generally relate to movements in retained earnings and reserves, but changes in share capital, such as when a bonus dividend is paid, could occur.

In this example, there are four changes in subsidiary equity, as shown in figure 24.9 (p. 962).

- Retained earnings increased from $2000 to $16 000 — this will increase the NCI share of retained earnings.
- In the 2010–11 period, $1000 was transferred to the general reserve. Because the transfer has reduced retained earnings, the NCI share of retained earnings as calculated above has been reduced by this transfer; an increase in the NCI share of general reserve needs to be recognised as well as an increase in NCI in total.
- The sale of inventory in the 2009–10 period resulted in a transfer of $7000 from the business combination valuation reserve to retained earnings. Because the profits from the sale of inventory are recorded in the profits of the subsidiary, the NCI receives a share of the increased wealth relating to inventory. The NCI share of the business combination valuation reserve as recognised in step 1 must be reduced, with a reduction in NCI in total.
- Other components of equity increased by $2500, increasing the NCI share of equity by $1000.

Before noting the effects of these events in journal entry format, adjustments relating to the equipment on hand at acquisition date need to be considered. In the business combination valuation entry, the equipment on hand at acquisition date was revalued to fair value and the increase taken to the valuation reserve. By recognising the asset at fair value at acquisition date, the group recognises the extra benefits over and above the asset's carrying amount to be earned by the subsidiary. As expressed in the depreciation of the equipment (see the valuation entries above), the group expects the subsidiary to realise extra after-tax benefits of $2800 (i.e. $4000 depreciation expense less the credit of $1200 to income tax expense) in each of the 5 years after acquisition. Whereas the group recognises these extra benefits at acquisition date via the valuation reserve, the subsidiary recognises these benefits as profit in its records only as the equipment is used. Hence, the profit after tax recorded by the subsidiary in each of the 5 years after acquisition date will contain $2800 benefits from the equipment that the group recognised in the valuation reserve at acquisition date.

In calculating the NCI share of equity from acquisition date to the beginning of the current period, the NCI calculation will double-count the benefits from the equipment if there is no adjustment for the depreciation of the equipment. This occurs because the share of the NCI in equity calculated at acquisition date includes a share of the business combination valuation reserve created at that date in the consolidation worksheet. Therefore, giving the NCI a full share of the recorded profits of the subsidiary in the 5 years after acquisition date double-counts the benefits relating to the equipment. The NCI has already received a share of the valuation reserve in the step 1 calculation. Hence, in calculating the NCI share of changes in equity between acquisition date and the beginning of the current period (the step 2 calculation), there needs to be an adjustment for the extra depreciation of the equipment in relation to each of the years since acquisition date.

The adjustment for depreciation can be read directly from the valuation entry that records the depreciation on the equipment since acquisition date. In the valuation entry required for the 2011–12 consolidated financial statements (see no. (1) on the previous page), there is a net debit adjustment to retained earnings (1/7/11) of $5600 (i.e. the $8000 adjustment for previous periods' depreciation less the $2400 adjustment for previous periods' tax effect) in relation to the after-tax effects of depreciating the equipment. This reflects the extra benefits received by the subsidiary as a result of using the equipment and recorded by the subsidiary in its retained earnings account.

In this example, the only adjustment to retained earnings in the business combination valuation entry is that relating to the equipment. In other examples, there may be a number of adjustments to retained earnings depending on the number of assets being revalued. All such adjustments must be taken into account in order not to double-count the NCI share of equity. In other words, to determine the adjustments needed to avoid double counting, all adjustments to retained earnings in the valuation entries must be taken into consideration.

In illustrative example 24.2, the NCI share of changes in *retained earnings* is determined by calculating the change in retained earnings over the period, less the adjustment against retained earnings in the valuation entry relating to depreciation of the equipment. The amount is calculated as follows:

$$40\% \times (\$16\,000 - \$2\,000 - [\$8\,000 - \$2\,400]) = \$3\,360$$

The NCI is also entitled to a share of the change in *general reserve* between acquisition date and the beginning of the current period, the change being the transfer to general reserve in the 2010–11 period. As the general reserve is increased, the NCI share of that account is also increased. The calculation is:

40% × $1 000 = $400

The NCI is also entitled to a share of the movement in *other components of equity*. There was no balance in this account at acquisition date, and balance at 30 June 2011 is $2500, so the NCI's share is:

40% × $2 500 = $1 000

The NCI is also affected by the transfer on consolidation from the *business combination valuation reserve* to retained earnings as a result of the sale of inventory. The NCI share of the valuation reserve is decreased, with a reduction in NCI in total. The calculation is:

40% × $7 000 = $2 800

The consolidation worksheet entries in the NCI columns for the step 2 NCI calculation are:

Retained Earnings (1/7/11)	Dr	3 360	
NCI	Cr		3 360
(40% × [$16 000 − $2 000 − ($8 000 − $2 400)])			
General Reserve	Dr	400	
NCI	Cr		400
(40% × $1 000)			
Other Components of Equity	Dr	1 000	
NCI	Cr		1 000
(40% × $2 500)			
NCI	Dr	2 800	
Business Combination Valuation Reserve	Cr		2 800
(40% × $7 000)			

These entries may be combined as:

Retained Earnings (1/7/11)	Dr	3 360	
General Reserve	Dr	400	
Other Components of Equity	Dr	1 000	
Business Combination Valuation Reserve	Cr		2 800
NCI	Cr		1 960

(5) *NCI share of current period changes in equity (step 3)*
From figure 24.9 it can be seen that there are four changes in equity in the 2011–12 period:

- Lausanne Ltd has reported a profit of $15 000.
- There has been a transfer from general reserve of $500.
- The subsidiary has paid a dividend of $1500 and declared a dividend of $2000.
- Other components of equity has decreased by $100.

In relation to both dividends and transfer to/from reserves, from an NCI perspective note that it is irrelevant whether the amounts are from pre- or post-acquisition equity. The NCI receives a share of all equity accounts regardless of whether it existed before acquisition date or was created after that date.

The NCI share of *current period profit* is based on a 40% share of the recorded profit of $15 000. However, just as in step 2, there must be an adjustment made to avoid the double counting caused by the subsidiary recognising profits from the use of the equipment, these benefits having been recognised on consolidation in the business combination valuation reserve. Again, reference needs to be made to the valuation entries, and in particular to the amounts in these entries affecting current period profit. In the valuation entries, there is a debit adjustment to depreciation expense of $4000 and a credit adjustment to income tax expense of $1200. In other words, in the current period, Lausanne Ltd recognised in its profit an amount of $2800 from the use of the equipment that was recognised by the group in the business combination valuation reserve. Since the NCI has been given a share of the valuation reserve in step 1, to give the NCI a share of the recorded profit without adjusting for the current period's depreciation would double-count the NCI share of equity. The NCI share of current period profit is, therefore, 40% of the net of recorded profit of $15 000 less the after-tax depreciation adjustment of $2800.

The consolidation worksheet entry in the NCI columns is:

NCI Share of Profit/(Loss)	Dr	4 880	
NCI	Cr		4 880
(40% × [$15 000 – ($4000 – $1200)])			

In the current period, a change in equity is caused by the $500 *transfer from general reserve* to retained earnings. This transaction does not change the amount of equity in total because it is a transfer between equity accounts, so there is no change to the NCI in total. However, the NCI share of general reserve has decreased and the NCI share of retained earnings has increased. For the latter account, the appropriate line item is 'Transfer from General Reserve'.

The consolidation worksheet entry in the NCI columns is:

Transfer from General Reserve	Dr	200	
General Reserve	Cr		200
(40% × $500)			

The third change in equity in the current period relates to *dividends paid and declared*. Dividends are a reduction in retained earnings. The NCI share of equity is reduced as a result of the payment or declaration of dividends. Where dividends are paid, the NCI receives a cash distribution as compensation for the reduction in equity. Where dividends are declared, the group recognises a liability to make a future cash payment to the NCI as compensation for the reduction in equity. The consolidation worksheet entries in the NCI column are:

NCI	Dr	600	
Dividend Paid	Cr		600
(40% × $1500)			
NCI	Dr	800	
Dividend Declared	Cr		800
(40% × $2000)			

The fourth change in equity is the $100 reduction in *other components of equity*. This results in a reduction in the NCI share of this account that relates to available-for-sale financial assets as well as a reduction in NCI in total. The entry in the NCI columns is:

NCI	Dr	40	
Other Components of Equity	Cr		40
(40% × $100)			

(6) *Adjustments for intragroup transactions: dividends*
The entries on the next page in the adjustment columns of the worksheet are necessary to adjust for the dividend transactions in the current period — note that the amounts are based on the proportion of dividends paid within the group.

Dividend Revenue	Dr	900	
Dividend Paid	Cr		900
(60% × $1500)			
Dividend Payable	Dr	1 200	
Dividend Declared	Cr		1 200
(60% × $2000)			
Dividend Revenue	Dr	1 200	
Dividend Receivable	Cr		1 200
(60% × $2000)			

Using the figures for the subsidiary for the year ended 30 June 2012, as given in figure 24.9, and assuming information for the parent, a consolidation worksheet showing the effects of the entries developed in illustrative example 24.2 is given in figure 24.10.

Financial statements	Basel Ltd	Lausanne Ltd		Adjustments Dr	Adjustments Cr		Group		Non-controlling interest Dr	Non-controlling interest Cr		Parent
Profit /(loss) for the period	20 000	15 000	1	4 000	1 200	1	30 100	5	4 880			25 220
			6	900								
			6	1 200								
Retained earnings (1/7/11)	25 000	16 000	1	8 000	2 400	1	30 000	3	800			25 840
			2	5 400				4	3 360			
Transfer from general reserve	—	500					500	5	200			300
	45 000	31 500					60 600					51 360
Dividend paid	10 000	1 500			900	2	10 600			600	5	10 000
					300	6						
Dividend declared	5 000	2 000			1 200	6	5 800			800	5	5 000
	15 000	3 500					16 400					15 000
Retained earnings (30/6/12)	30 000	28 000					44 200					36 660
Share capital	100 000	40 000	2	24 000			116 000	3	16 000			100 000
General reserve	20 000	2 500	2	1 200			21 300	3	800	200	5	20 300
								4	400			
Business combination valuation reserve	—	—	2	8 400	14 000	1	5 600	3	8 400	2 800	4	—
	150 000	70 500					187 100					156 660
Other components of equity (1/7/11)	10 000	2 500					12 500	4	1 000			11 500
Increments/(decrements)	2 000	(100)					1 900			40	5	1 940
Other components of equity (30/6/12)	12 000	2 400					14 400					13 440
Total equity: parent												170 100
Total equity: NCI								5	600	26 000	3	31 400
								5	800	1 960	4	
								5	40	4 880	5	
Total equity	162 000	72 900					201 500		37 280	37 280		201 500

FIGURE 24.10 Consolidation worksheet with NCI columns

24.4 ADJUSTING FOR THE EFFECTS OF INTRAGROUP TRANSACTIONS

The justification for considering adjustments for intragroup transactions in the calculation of the NCI share of equity is that, under the entity concept of consolidation, the NCI is classified as a contributor of capital to the group. Thus, the calculation of the NCI is based on a share of *consolidated equity* and not equity as recorded by the subsidiary. Consolidated equity is determined as the sum of the equity of the parent and the subsidiaries after making adjustments for the effects of intragroup transactions. The NCI share of that equity must, therefore, be based on subsidiary equity after adjusting for intragroup transactions that affect the subsidiary's equity.

To illustrate, assume that during the current period a subsidiary in which there is an NCI of 20% has recorded a profit of $20 000 which includes a before-tax profit of $2000 on sale of $18 000 inventory to the parent. The inventory is still on hand at the end of the current period. In the adjustment columns of the consolidation worksheet, the adjustment entries for the sale of inventory, assuming a tax rate of 30%, are:

Sales	Dr	18 000	
Cost of Sales	Cr		16 000
Inventory	Cr		2 000
Deferred Tax Asset	Dr	600	
Income Tax Expense	Cr		600

The group does not regard the after-tax profit of $1400 as being a part of consolidated profit. Hence, in calculating the NCI share of consolidated profit, the NCI is entitled to $3720, that is, 20% × ($20 000 recorded profit – $1400 intragroup profit).

The NCI share of equity is therefore adjusted for the effects of intragroup transactions. However, note that the NCI share of consolidated equity is essentially based on a share of *subsidiary* equity. Therefore, only intragroup transactions that affect the subsidiary's equity need to be taken into consideration. Profits made on inventory sold by the parent to the subsidiary do not affect the calculation of the NCI because the profit is recorded by the parent, not the subsidiary — the subsidiary equity is unaffected by the transaction.

In section 24.3, it is explained that the NCI share of the equity recorded by the subsidiary is calculated in three steps:

1. share of equity at acquisition date
2. share of changes in equity between acquisition date and the beginning of the current period
3. share of changes in equity in the current period.

These calculations are based on the *recorded* subsidiary equity, that is, equity that will include the effects of the intragroup transactions. Having calculated the NCI as a result of the three-step process, the subsidiary needs to make further adjustments for the effects of intragroup transactions. Rather than adjust for these transactions in the NCI entries relating to the three-step process, the adjustments to the NCI are determined when the adjustments are made for the effects of the specific intragroup transactions.

For example, consider the case above where a subsidiary in which the NCI is 20% records a profit of $20 000, which includes a $2000 before-tax profit on the sale of inventory to the parent (cost $4000, selling price $6000). In the step 3 NCI calculation, the worksheet entry passed in the NCI columns is:

NCI Share of Profit/(Loss)	Dr	4 000	
NCI	Cr		4 000
(20% × $20 000 recorded profit)			

In making the adjustment for the effects of intragroup transactions to be passed in the adjustment columns of the worksheet, the following entries are made:

Profit in closing inventory: subsidiary to parent			
Sales	Dr	6 000	
Cost of Sales	Cr		4 000
Inventory	Cr		2 000
Deferred Tax Asset	Dr	600	
Income Tax Expense	Cr		600
(30% × $2000)			

As this adjustment affects the profit of the subsidiary by an amount of $1400 after tax (i.e. $2000 – $600), this triggers the need to make an adjustment to the NCI, and the following entry is passed in the NCI columns of the worksheet:

NCI	Dr	280	
NCI Share of Profit/(Loss)	Cr		280
(20% × $1400)			

[This entry is explained in more detail in illustrative example 24.3 later in this chapter.]

The combined effect of the step 3 NCI entry and this last entry is that the NCI totals $3720, i.e. $4000 less $280. Thus the NCI is given a share of recorded profit adjusted for the effects of intragroup transactions.

24.4.1 The concept of 'realisation' of profits and losses

Not all transactions require an adjustment entry for the NCI. For a transaction to require an adjustment to the calculation of the NCI share of equity, it must have the following characteristics:

- The transaction must result in the subsidiary recording a profit or a loss.
- After the transaction, the other party to the transaction (for two-company structures this is the parent) must have on hand an asset, for example, inventory, on which the unrealised profit is accrued.
- The initial consolidation adjustment for the transaction should affect both the statement of financial position and the statement of comprehensive income (including appropriations of retained earnings), unlike payments of debenture interest, which affect only the statement of comprehensive income.

In determining the transactions requiring an adjusting entry for the NCI, it is important to work out which transactions involve unrealised profit. The concept of 'realisation' is discussed in chapter 23. The test for realisation is the involvement of a party external to the group, based on the concept that the consolidated financial statements report the affairs of the group in terms of its dealings with entities external to the group. Consolidated profits are therefore realised profits as they result from dealing with entities external to the group. Profits made by transacting within the group are unrealised because no external entity is involved. Once the profits/losses on an intragroup transaction become realised, the NCI share of equity no longer needs to be adjusted for the effects of an intragroup transaction because the profits/losses recorded by the subsidiary are all realised profits.

In this section, the key point to note is when, for different types of transactions, unrealised profits on intragroup transactions become realised.

Inventory

With inventory, realisation occurs when the acquiring entity sells the inventory to an entity outside the group. Consolidation adjustments for inventory are based on the profit/loss remaining in inventory on hand at the end of a financial period. If inventory is sold in the current period by the subsidiary to the parent at a profit, giving the NCI a share of the recorded profit will overstate the NCI share of consolidated equity, because the group does not recognise the profit until the inventory is sold outside the group. Hence, whenever consolidated adjustments are made for profit remaining in inventory on hand at the end of the period, an NCI adjustment is necessary to reduce the NCI share of current period profit and the NCI total. Following the consolidation adjustment for the unrealised profit in inventory, an NCI adjustment entry is made in the NCI columns of the worksheet. The general form of the entry is:

NCI	Dr	X	
NCI Share of Profit/(Loss)	Cr		X

If there is inventory on hand at *the beginning of the current period*, the NCI share of the previous period's profit must be reduced as the subsidiary's previous year's recorded profit contains unrealised profit. As the group realises the profit in the current period when the inventory is sold to external parties, the NCI share of current period's profit must be increased. Following the worksheet adjustment for the profit remaining in beginning inventory, an NCI adjustment entry is made in the NCI columns of the worksheet. The general form of the NCI entry is:

NCI Share of Profit/(Loss)	Dr	X	
Retained Earnings (opening balance)	Cr		X

Depreciable non-current assets

With depreciable non-current assets, profit is realised as the asset is used up within the group. Realisation of the profit occurs as the future benefits embodied in the asset are consumed by the group, and occurs in proportion to the depreciation of the asset. If the subsidiary sells a non-current asset in the current period to the parent, an adjustment is made for the profit on sale, because the profit is unrealised to the group. The NCI share of current period profit must then be reduced. Following the worksheet adjustment for the profit on sale, an NCI adjustment is made in the NCI columns of the worksheet. The general form of the adjustment entry is:

NCI	Dr	X	
NCI Share of Profit/(Loss)	Cr		X

As the asset is depreciated, some of the profit becomes realised, increasing the NCI share of profit. Following the worksheet adjustment entry for depreciation, an NCI entry is made in the NCI columns of the worksheet. The general form of the entry reflecting the increased share of profit is:

NCI Share of Profit/(Loss)	Dr	X	
NCI	Cr		X

It can be seen that the NCI adjustment for the profit on sale reduces the NCI share of equity, and the NCI adjustment relating to depreciation increases the NCI share of equity. This reflects the fact that as the asset is used up the profit becomes realised.

Intragroup transfers for services and interest

For transactions involving services and interest, the group's profit is unaffected because the general consolidation adjustment reduces both expense and revenue equally. However, from the NCI's perspective, there has been a change in the equity of the subsidiary; for example, the subsidiary may have recorded interest revenue as a result of a payment to the parent entity relating to an intragroup loan. The revenue is unrealised in that no external entity has been involved in the transaction. Theoretically, the NCI should be adjusted for such transactions. However, as noted in paragraph 25 of IAS 27, it is profits and losses 'recognised in assets' that are of concern. In other words, where there are transfers between entities that do not result in the retention within the group of assets on which the profit has been accrued, it is *assumed* that the profit is realised by the group immediately on payment within the group. For transactions such as payments for intragroup services, interest and dividends, there are no assets recorded with accrued profits attached, since the transactions are cash transactions. Hence, the profit is assumed to be immediately realised. The reason for the assumption of immediate realisation of profits on these types of transactions is a pragmatic one based on the cost benefit of determining a point of realisation.

24.5 GAIN ON BARGAIN PURCHASE

This chapter has used examples of business combinations where goodwill has been acquired. In the rare case that a gain on bargain purchase may arise, such a gain has no effect on the calculation of the NCI share of equity. Further, whereas the goodwill of the subsidiary may be determined by calculating the goodwill acquired by the parent entity and then grossing this up to determine the goodwill for the subsidiary, this process is not applicable for the gain on bargain purchase. The gain is made by the parent paying less than the net fair value of the acquirer's share of the identifiable assets, liabilities and contingent liabilities of the subsidiary. The NCI receives a share of the fair value of the subsidiary, and has no involvement with the gain on bargain purchase.

To illustrate, assume a subsidiary has the following statement of financial position:

Equity	\$80 000
Identifiable assets and liabilities	\$80 000

Assume all identifiable assets and liabilities of the subsidiary are recorded at amounts equal to fair value. If a parent acquires 80% of the shares of the subsidiary for \$63 000, then the acquisition analysis, assuming the use of the partial goodwill method, is:

Net fair value of subsidiary	= \$80 000
Net fair value acquired by parent	= 80% × \$80 000
	= \$64 000
Consideration transferred	= \$63 000
Gain on bargain purchase	= \$64 000 – \$63 000
	= \$1 000

Assuming all fair values have been measured accurately, the consolidation worksheet entries at acquisition date are:

Business combination valuation entry
No entry required in this simple example.

Pre-acquisition entry			
Equity	Dr	64 000	
Gain on Bargain Purchase	Cr		1 000
Shares in Subsidiary	Cr		63 000
Non-controlling interest (step 1)			
Equity	Dr	16 000	
NCI	Cr		16 000
(20% × \$80 000)			

Note that the NCI does not receive any share of the gain on bargain purchase.

An example of the process of calculating NCI when intragroup transactions exist is given in illustrative example 24.3.

ILLUSTRATIVE EXAMPLE 24.3

NCI and intragroup transactions

Berne Ltd owns 80% of the issued shares of Lucerne Ltd. In the year ending 30 June 2010, the following transactions occurred:

(a) In July 2009, Berne Ltd sold $2000 worth of inventory that had been sold to it by Lucerne Ltd in May 2009 at a profit to Lucerne Ltd of $500.

(b) In February 2010, Berne Ltd sold $10 000 worth of inventory to Lucerne Ltd, recording a profit before tax of $2000. At 30 June 2010, 20% of this inventory remained unsold by Lucerne Ltd.

(c) In March 2010, Lucerne Ltd sold $12 000 worth of inventory to Berne Ltd at a mark-up of 20%. At 30 June 2010, $1200 of this inventory remained unsold by Berne Ltd.

(d) At 30 June 2010, Lucerne Ltd recorded depreciation of $10 000 in relation to plant sold to it by Berne Ltd on 1 July 2008. Lucerne Ltd uses a 10% p.a. straight-line depreciation method for plant. At date of sale to Lucerne Ltd, this plant had a carrying amount of $90 000 in the accounts of Berne Ltd.

Required

Given a tax rate of 30%, prepare the consolidation worksheet entries for these transactions as at 30 June 2010.

Solution

(a) *Sale of inventory in previous period: Lucerne Ltd to Berne Ltd*

The entry in the adjustment columns of the worksheet is:

Retained Earnings (1/7/09)	Dr	350	
Income Tax Expense	Dr	150	
Cost of Sales	Cr		500

Since the inventory was originally sold by the subsidiary to the parent, the entry in the NCI columns of the worksheet is:

NCI Share of Profit/(Loss)	Dr	70	
Retained Earnings (1/7/09)	Cr		70
(20% × $350)			

(b) *Sale of inventory in current period: Berne Ltd to Lucerne Ltd*

Sales	Dr	10 000	
Cost of Sales	Cr		9 600
Inventory	Cr		400
Deferred Tax Asset	Dr	120	
Income Tax Expense	Cr		120

Because the sale was from parent to subsidiary, there is no NCI adjustment required.

(c) *Sale of inventory in current period: Lucerne Ltd to Berne Ltd*

The entries in the adjustment columns of the worksheet are:

Sales	Dr	12 000	
Cost of Sales	Cr		11 800
Inventory	Cr		200
Deferred Tax Asset	Dr	60	
Income Tax Expense	Cr		60

Because the sale was from subsidiary to parent, the following entry is required in the NCI columns of the worksheet.

NCI	Dr	28	
NCI Share of Profit/(Loss)	Cr		28
(20% × $140)			

(d) *Sale of depreciable asset in prior period: Lucerne Ltd to Berne Ltd*
The entry in the adjustment columns of the worksheet is:

Retained Earnings (1/7/09)	Dr	7 000	
Deferred Tax Asset	Dr	3 000	
Plant	Cr		10 000

Since the plant was sold by the subsidiary to the parent, the entry in the NCI columns of the worksheet is:

NCI	Dr	1 400	
Retained Earnings (1/7/09)	Cr		1 400
(20% × $7000)			

Depreciation on plant
The entries in the adjustment columns of the worksheet are:

Accumulated Depreciation	Dr	2 000	
Depreciation Expense	Cr		1 000
Retained Earnings (1/7/09)	Cr		1 000
Retained Earnings (1/7/09)	Dr	300	
Income Tax Expense	Dr	300	
Deferred Tax Asset	Cr		600

The entry in the NCI column of the worksheet is:

NCI Share of Profit/(Loss)	Dr	140	
Retained Earnings (1/7/09)	Dr	140	
NCI	Cr		280
(20% × $700 p.a.)			

Illustrative example 24.4 is a comprehensive example demonstrating consolidation for an NCI.

ILLUSTRATIVE EXAMPLE 24.4

Consolidated financial statements

Lugano Ltd acquired 80% of the shares of Biel Ltd on 1 July 2006 for $540 000, when the equity of Biel Ltd consisted of:

Share capital	$ 500 000
General reserve	80 000
Retained earnings	50 000
Asset revaluation reserve	20 000

All identifiable assets and liabilities of Biel Ltd are recorded at fair value at this date except for inventory for which the fair value was $10 000 greater than carrying amount, and plant which had a carrying amount of $150 000 (net of $40 000 accumulated depreciation) and a fair value of $170 000. The inventory was all sold by 30 June 2007, and the plant had a further 5-year life with depreciation based on the straight-line method.

Financial information for both companies at 30 June 2010 is as follows:

	Lugano Ltd	Biel Ltd
Sales revenue	$ 720 000	$ 530 000
Other revenue	240 000	120 000
	960 000	650 000
Cost of sales	(610 000)	(410 000)
Other expenses	(230 000)	(160 000)
	(840 000)	(570 000)
Profit before tax	120 000	80 000
Tax expense	(40 000)	(25 000)
Profit for the period	80 000	55 000
Retained earnings at 1/7/09	200 000	112 000
	280 000	167 000
Dividend paid	(20 000)	(10 000)
Dividend declared	(25 000)	(15 000)
	(45 000)	(25 000)
Retained earnings at 30/6/10	235 000	142 000
Share capital	600 000	500 000
Asset revaluation reserve*	20 000	60 000
General reserve	80 000	100 000
Total equity	935 000	802 000
Dividend payable	25 000	15 000
Other liabilities	25 000	25 000
Total liabilities	50 000	40 000
Total equity and liabilities	$ 985 000	$ 842 000
Receivables	$ 80 000	$ 30 000
Inventory	100 000	170 000
Plant and equipment	200 000	500 000
Accumulated depreciation	(115 000)	(88 000)
Land at fair value	100 000	80 000
Shares in Biel Ltd	540 000	—
Deferred tax assets	50 000	40 000
Other assets	30 000	110 000
Total assets	$ 985 000	$ 842 000

*The balances of the reserve at 1 July 2009 were $35 000 (Lugano Ltd) and $50 000 (Biel Ltd).

The following transactions took place between Lugano Ltd and Biel Ltd:

(a) During the 2009–10 period, Biel Ltd sold inventory to Lugano Ltd for $23 000, recording a profit before tax of $3000. Lugano Ltd has since resold half of these items.

(b) During the 2009–10 period, Lugano Ltd sold inventory to Biel Ltd for $18 000, recording a profit before tax of $2000. Biel Ltd has not resold any of these items.

(c) On 1 June 2010, Biel Ltd paid $1000 to Lugano Ltd for services rendered.

(d) During the 2008–09 period, Biel Ltd sold inventory to Lugano Ltd. At 30 June 2009, Lugano Ltd still had inventory on hand on which Biel Ltd had recorded a before-tax profit of $4000.

(e) On 1 July 2008, Biel Ltd sold plant to Lugano Ltd for $150 000, recording a profit of $20 000 before tax. Lugano Ltd applies a 10% p.a. straight-line method of depreciation in relation to these assets.

Required

1. Given an income tax rate of 30%, prepare the consolidated financial statements for Lugano Ltd for the year ended 30 June 2010 using the *partial goodwill method* to measure the non-controlling interest at acquisition date.

2. What differences would occur in the consolidation worksheet entries at 30 June 2010 if the *full goodwill method* was used to calculate the non-controlling interest at acquisition date? Assume the value of the non-controlling interest in the subsidiary at acquisition date is $134 500.

Solution

A. Consolidated financial statements using partial goodwill method

The first step is to prepare the acquisition analysis. Determining the net fair value is the same as for wholly owned subsidiaries. Where an NCI exists, it is necessary to determine the net fair value acquired by the parent.

In this problem, the parent acquired 80% of the shares of the subsidiary. The net fair value of what was acquired is then compared with the consideration transferred, and a goodwill or gain is determined. Note that the goodwill or gain is only that attributable to the parent, since the residual relates to what was paid by the parent and the proportion of net fair value of the subsidiary acquired by the parent.

Acquisition analysis

Net fair value of the identifiable assets and liabilities of Biel Ltd	= $500 000 + $80 000 + $50 000 + $20 000 + $10 000(1 – 30%) (BCVR – inventory) + $20 000(1 – 30%) (BCVR – plant) = $671 000
Net fair value acquired by Lugano Ltd	= 80% × $671 000 = $536 800
Consideration transferred	= $540 000
Goodwill	= $3 200

Consolidation worksheet entries at 30 June 2010

(1) *Business combination valuation reserve entries*

The business combination entries are unaffected by the existence of an NCI. Under IFRS 3, all identifiable assets and liabilities acquired in the acquiree/subsidiary must be measured at fair value. This principle is unaffected by the existence of an NCI.

Accumulated Depreciation	Dr	40 000	
Plant	Cr		20 000
Deferred Tax Liability	Cr		6 000
Business Combination Valuation Reserve	Cr		14 000
Depreciation Expense	Dr	4 000	
Retained Earnings (1/7/09)	Dr	12 000	
Accumulated Depreciation	Cr		16 000
Deferred Tax Liability	Dr	4 800	
Income Tax Expense	Cr		1 200
Retained Earnings (1/7/09)	Cr		3 600

(2) *Pre-acquisition entry*

Retained Earnings (1/7/09)	Dr	45 600	
Share Capital	Dr	400 000	
General Reserve	Dr	64 000	
Asset Revaluation Reserve (1/7/09)	Dr	16 000	
Business Combination Valuation Reserve	Dr	11 200	
Goodwill	Dr	3 200	
Shares in Biel Ltd	Cr		540 000

These pre-acquisition entries differ from the entries prepared for a wholly owned subsidiary in that the adjustment to equity accounts is measured as the parent's share of the equity accounts. This can be seen in the acquisition analysis where the parent's share of equity (80%) is applied to the net fair value before making a comparison with the cost of the combination. Hence the adjustment to share capital is $400 000, that is, 80% of the recorded $500 000. With retained earnings (1/7/09), the adjustment is calculated as:

(80% × $50 000) (opening balance) + (80% × $7000) (BCVR – inventory)

The adjustment to the BCVR is:

80% × $14 000 (BCVR – plant)

Non-controlling interest

The next three adjustment entries relate to the calculation of the NCI. These entries are passed in the NCI columns of the worksheet, not the adjustment columns. The three entries cover the three steps used in the calculation of the NCI share of total equity.

(3) *NCI share of equity at acquisition date, 1 July 2006 (step 1)*
Step 1 is to calculate the NCI share of the equity of the subsidiary at acquisition date. This consists of the recorded equity of the subsidiary plus any reserves raised on consolidation at acquisition date, namely the business combination valuation reserve.

Pre-acquisition equity of Biel Ltd		**20%**
Retained earnings (1/7/06)	$ 50 000	$ 10 000
Share capital	500 000	100 000
General reserve	80 000	16 000
Asset revaluation reserve (1/7/06)	20 000	4 000
Business combination valuation reserve	21 000	4 200
		$134 200

The worksheet entry in the NCI columns is:

Retained Earnings (1/7/09)	Dr	10 000	
Share Capital	Dr	100 000	
General Reserve	Dr	16 000	
Asset Revaluation Reserve (1/7/09)	Dr	4 000	
Business Combination Valuation Reserve	Dr	4 200	
NCI	Cr		134 200

Note that the adjustments to the equity accounts are debits, because these amounts will be subtracted from the balances in the group column in order to determine the parent's share of equity. On the other hand, the NCI account has a credit adjustment because the NCI is classified as equity, and the balance of pre-acquisition equity is a positive amount.

(4) *NCI share of equity from 1 July 2006 to 30 June 2009 (step 2)*
In step 2, the calculation is of the NCI share of equity between the acquisition date and the beginning of the current period, that is, between 1 July 2006 and 30 June 2009. This requires the calculation of movements in the subsidiary's equity accounts between these two dates.

General reserve: The balance at 30 June 2009, read from the financial information at 30 June 2010 and noting no transfers occurred in the current period, is $100 000. The difference between this and the balance at 1 July 2006 of $80 000 is $20 000. The NCI is entitled to 20% of this increase in equity. The combination of step 1 and step 2 effectively gives the NCI a 20% share of the total $100 000 balance.

Retained earnings: The balance at 30 June 2009 is the same as the opening balance in the current period, which is read from the financial information provided, namely $112 000. The difference between this amount and the balance recorded by the subsidiary at acquisition reflects movements in the amounts recorded by the subsidiary, such as reserve transfers and dividends. What is not reflected in the difference calculated are amounts affecting retained earnings not recorded by the subsidiary but recognised on consolidation. In this problem, the transaction that needs to be taken into account is the depreciation of the plant on hand at acquisition date, as shown in the business combination valuation reserve entries. As the plant is used, the recorded profit of the subsidiary recognises the extra benefits received. The NCI in relation to retained earnings (1/7/09) is therefore:

20%[$112 000 (balance at acquisition) – $50 000 (balance at 30/6/09)
– ($12 000 – $3 600)]

Asset revaluation reserve: The balance at acquisition date is $20 000 and the balance at 30 June 2009 is $50 000. The NCI is entitled to a 20% share of the difference between these two amounts.

Business combination valuation reserve: The balance at acquisition date was $21 000. As a result of the sale of the inventory, this has been reduced at 30 June 2009 to $14 000, a reduction of $7000, because there has been a transfer from this reserve to retained earnings. Since the reserve has decreased in amount, this results in a decrease in the NCI share of this account. The total NCI in equity has not changed because the recorded retained earnings has increased by $7000 as a result of the sale of inventory by the subsidiary.

A summary of these movements is then:

	Change in equity	20%
General reserve ($100 000 – $80 000)	$20 000	$ 4 000
Retained earnings ($112 000 – $50 000 – ($12 000 – $3600))	53 600	10 720
Asset revaluation reserve ($50 000 – $20 000)	30 000	6 000
Business combination valuation reserve ($14 000 – $21 000)	(7 000)	(1 400)

The worksheet entry in the NCI columns is:

Retained Earnings (1/7/09)	Dr	10 720	
General Reserve	Dr	4 000	
Asset Revaluation Reserve	Dr	6 000	
Business Combination Valuation Reserve	Cr		1 400
NCI	Cr		19 320

(5) *NCI in equity from 1 July 2009 to 30 June 2010 (step 3)*

Steps 1 and 2 determine the NCI share of equity recorded up to the beginning of the current year. Step 3 calculates the NCI share of changes in equity in the current year — 1 July 2009 to 30 June 2010. The combination of all three steps determines the NCI share of equity at the end of the reporting period.

There are a number of changes in equity in the current period, with each change attracting its own adjustment entry in the NCI columns of the worksheet.

Profit for the period:

The NCI receives a share of recorded profit of the subsidiary. As with step 2, this is adjusted by the depreciation on the plant on hand at acquisition date. The recorded profit of the subsidiary includes benefits gained by use of the plant. The NCI share is then:

20%[$55 000 – ($4000 – $1 200)]

The worksheet entry in the NCI columns is:

NCI Share of Profit/(Loss)	Dr	10 440	
NCI	Cr		10 440

The first line in the above entry is a debit because in the consolidation worksheet this is deducted from group profit in order to calculate the parent share of profit. Note that, in later calculations, increases in the NCI share of profit require a debit adjustment to this account and decreases in the NCI share of profit require a credit adjustment.

Dividend paid:
The dividend paid by the subsidiary reduces the equity of the subsidiary. The adjustment to the NCI share of equity as a result of the dividend paid must take into consideration the full dividend paid with the effect of reducing the NCI share of total equity. The entry in the NCI columns of the worksheet is:

NCI	Dr	2 000	
Dividend Paid	Cr		2 000
(20% × $10 000)			

Dividend declared:
As with the dividend paid, the NCI has been given a full share of equity before the declaration of dividends. Because the dividend declared reduces the equity of the subsidiary, the NCI share of equity is also reduced. The entry in the NCI columns of the worksheet is:

NCI	Dr	3 000	
Dividend Declared	Cr		3 000
(20% × $15 000)			

Asset revaluation reserve:
The balance of the subsidiary's asset revaluation reserve at 1 July 2009 was $50 000. The balance at 30 June 2010 is $60 000. The NCI share of equity is increased by 20% of the change during the period. The debit adjustment is recognised in the worksheet against the Gains/Losses on Asset Revaluation as this account reflects the increase in the reserve balance. The adjustment is a debit because it reduces the group gain so that the left-hand column of the worksheet shows the parent share of the gain. The entry in the NCI columns of the worksheet is:

Gains/Losses on Asset Revaluation	Dr	2 000	
NCI	Cr		2 000
(20% × [$60 000 − $50 000])			

Intragroup transactions

(6) *Dividend paid*
The entry in the adjustment columns of the consolidation worksheet to adjust for the $10 000 dividend paid is:

Dividend Revenue	Dr	8 000	
Dividend Paid	Cr		8 000
(80% × $10 000)			

(7) *Dividend declared*
The subsidiary declared a dividend of $15 000 of which $12 000 is payable within the group.

The entries in the adjustment columns of the worksheet are:

Dividend Payable	Dr	12 000	
Dividend Declared	Cr		12 000
Dividend Revenue	Dr	12 000	
Dividend Receivable	Cr		12 000

(8) *Sale of inventory: Biel Ltd to Lugano Ltd*
The worksheet entries in the adjustment columns are:

Sales	Dr	23 000	
Cost of Sales	Cr		21 500
Inventory	Cr		1 500
(Unrealised profit on sale of inventory, 50% × $3000)			
Deferred Tax Asset	Dr	450	
Income Tax Expense	Cr		450
(Tax effect, 30% × $1500)			

(9) *Adjustment to NCI: unrealised profit in ending inventory*
The profit on sale was made by the subsidiary. The NCI is therefore affected. The total after-tax profit on the intragroup sale of inventory was $2100 (i.e. $3000 – $900 tax). However, since half the inventory is sold to an external entity, this portion is realised. The adjustment to the NCI relates only to the unrealised profits remaining in the inventory still on hand (half of $2100, or $1050). This is the same after-tax figure used to adjust profits in entry (8) above.

The transaction occurs in the current period. Therefore, it is the NCI share of current period profit that is affected. In adjustment entry (5), the NCI is given a share of the total recorded subsidiary profit for the current period. Because the realised profit is less than the recorded profit, the NCI share of equity must be reduced, specifically the NCI share of current period profit.

The worksheet entry in the NCI columns of the worksheet is:

NCI	Dr	210	
NCI Share of Profit/(Loss)	Cr		210
(20% × $1050)			

The debit adjustment shows a reduction in total equity attributable to the NCI, and the credit adjustment shows a reduction in the NCI share of current period profits.

(10) *Sale of inventory: Lugano Ltd to Biel Ltd*
The entries in the adjustment columns of the worksheet are:

Sales	Dr	18 000	
Cost of Sales	Cr		16 000
Inventory	Cr		2 000
Deferred Tax Asset	Dr	600	
Income Tax Expense	Cr		600

Because the profit on the transaction is made by the parent entity and does not affect the equity of the subsidiary, there is no need to make any adjustment to the NCI.

(11) *Payment for services: Biel Ltd to Lugano Ltd*
The entry in the adjustment columns of the worksheet is:

Other Revenues	Dr	1 000	
Other Expenses	Cr		1 000

The profit of the subsidiary is affected by the transaction even though the payment may, in effect, be from the parent to the subsidiary. However, if it is assumed that realisation occurs on payment for the services for this type of transaction, then no unrealised profit/loss exists in the subsidiary. Hence, there is no need to make any adjustment to the NCI share of equity.

(12) *Sale of inventory in previous period: Biel Ltd to Lugano Ltd*
The entries in the adjustment columns of the worksheet are:

Retained Earnings (1/7/09)	Dr	2 800	
Income Tax Expense	Dr	1 200	
Cost of Sales	Cr		4 000

(13) *Adjustment to NCI: unrealised profit in beginning inventory*
The profit on this transaction was made by the subsidiary, so an adjustment to the NCI share of equity is required. There are two effects on the NCI because the transaction affects both last year's and the current period's figures.

First, the profit made by the subsidiary in the previous period was unrealised last year. Hence, the subsidiary's retained earnings (1/7/09) account contains $2800 unrealised profit. An adjustment is necessary to reduce the NCI share of the previous period's profit:

NCI	Dr	560	
Retained Earnings (1/7/09)	Cr		560
(20% × $2800)			

Second, in relation to the current period, because the inventory transferred last period is sold in the current period to an external entity, the profit previously recorded by the subsidiary becomes realised in the current period. Since the profit is realised to the NCI in the current period but was recorded by the subsidiary last period, the NCI share of current period profit needs to be increased. The adjustment is:

NCI Share of Profit/(Loss)	Dr	560	
NCI	Cr		560
(20% × $2800)			

These two entries can be combined and passed in the NCI columns of the worksheet:

NCI Share of Profit/(Loss)	Dr	560	
Retained Earnings (1/7/09)	Cr		560

This entry has no effect on the total NCI share of equity. It simply reduces the NCI share of equity recorded last period and increases the NCI share of current period profit. This reflects the fact that the subsidiary recorded the profit in the previous period whereas the group recognised the profit in the current period.

(14) *Sale of depreciable asset in previous period: Biel Ltd to Lugano Ltd*
The sale occurred at the beginning of the previous period. The entries in the adjustment columns of the worksheet are as shown on p. 981.

Retained Earnings (1/7/09)	Dr	14 000	
Deferred Tax Asset	Dr	6 000	
Plant and Equipment	Cr		20 000

(15) *Adjustment to NCI: unrealised profit in depreciable asset in previous period*
The subsidiary recorded the profit on the transaction, so the NCI is affected. Because the transaction occurred in the previous period, the subsidiary's recorded retained earnings (1/7/09) balance contains an after-tax unrealised profit of $14 000. The NCI share of last year's profits must then be reduced by $2800 (i.e. 20% × $14 000).
The worksheet entry in the NCI columns is:

NCI	Dr	2 800	
Retained Earnings (1/7/09)	Cr		2 800

Worksheet entries relating to the sale of the asset and the associated NCI adjustment are made in each year of the asset's life. Realisation of this profit is dealt with in relation to the depreciation adjustment entry.

(16) *Depreciation on non-current asset sold*
The entries in the adjustment columns of the worksheet reflect the depreciation of the transferred asset over a 2-year period on a straight-line basis, given an overall asset life of 10 years:

Accumulated Depreciation	Dr	4 000	
Depreciation Expense	Cr		2 000
Retained Earnings (1/7/09)	Cr		2 000
(Depreciation of 10% × $20 000 p.a. for 2 years)			
Retained Earnings (1/7/09)	Dr	600	
Income Tax Expense	Dr	600	
Deferred Tax Asset	Cr		1 200

(17) *Adjustment to NCI: realisation of profit via depreciation*
The assumption made in relation to the $14 000 unrealised profit is that realisation will occur over the life of the asset as the benefits of the depreciable asset are consumed by the group. The profit is then realised in proportion to the depreciation charged on the asset. As can be seen from adjustment entry (16), the after-tax adjustment to depreciation expense is $1400 (being $2000 – $600). In other words, the $14 000 profit recognised last period by the subsidiary will be recognised as realised to the extent of $1400 p.a. over the next 10 years. Hence, $1400 is realised in the 2008–09 period, and a further $1400 is realised in the 2009–10 period. The NCI share of last year's profits is therefore increased, as is the NCI share of the current period's profits.
The worksheet entry in the NCI columns is:

NCI Share of Profit/(Loss)	Dr	280	
Retained Earnings (1/7/09)	Dr	280	
NCI	Cr		560
(20% × $1400 p.a.)			

In each of the 10 years following the transfer of the asset, the group realises an extra $1400 profit. This increases the NCI share of profit by $280 per year, and effectively reverses the reduction in the NCI share of profit relating to the gain on sale shown in entry (15). As the profit becomes realised over time, the NCI share of equity increases. Combining the effects of entries (15) and (16), the effect on NCI share of retained earnings (opening balance) over time is as shown overleaf.

NCI share of retained earnings (1/7/09)	$2 800 less $280
NCI share of retained earnings (1/7/10)	$2 800 less (2 × $280)
NCI share of retained earnings (1/7/11)	$2 800 less (3 × $280)
NCI share of retained earnings (1/7/12)	$2 800 less (4 × $280)

In the period ended 30 June 2018, the profit becomes fully realised as the asset becomes fully depreciated. In the 2018–19 period, no adjustments are necessary in relation to the transfer of the depreciable asset.

The consolidation worksheet for Lugano Ltd at 30 June 2010 is shown in figure 24.11.

FIGURE 24.11 Consolidation worksheet showing NCI and the effects of intragroup transactions

Financial statements	Lugano Ltd	Biel Ltd	Adjustments				Group	Non-controlling interest				Parent
				Dr	Cr				Dr	Cr		
Sales revenue	720 000	530 000	8	23 000			1 209 000					
			10	18 000								
Other revenues	240 000	120 000	6	8 000								
			7	12 000								
			11	1 000			339 000					
	960 000	650 000					1 548 000					
Cost of sales	(610 000)	(410 000)			21 500	8						
					16 000	10						
					4 000	12	(978 500)					
Other expenses	(230 000)	(160 000)	1	4 000	1 000	11	(391 000)					
					2 000	16						
	(840 000)	(570 000)					(1 369 500)					
Profit before tax	120 000	80 000					178 500					
Tax expense	(40 000)	(25 000)	12	1 200	1 200	1	(64 550)					
			16	600	600	10						
					450	8						
Profit	80 000	55 000					113 950	5	10 440	210	9	102 880
								13	560			
								17	280			
Retained earnings (1/7/09)	200 000	112 000	1	12 000	3 600	1		3	10 000	560	13	224 960
			2	45 600	2 000	16		4	10 720	2800	15	
			12	2 800				17	280			
			14	14 000								
			16	600			242 600					
	280 000	167 000					356 550					327 840
Dividend paid	(20 000)	(10 000)			8 000	6	(22 000)			2000	5	(20 000)
Dividend declared	(25 000)	(15 000)			12 000	7	(28 000)			3000	5	(25 000)
	(45 000)	(25 000)					(50 000)					(45 000)
Retained earnings (30/6/10)	235 000	142 000					306 550					282 840
Share capital	600 000	500 000	2	400 000			700 000	3	100 000			600 000
General reserve	80 000	100 000	2	64 000			116 000	3	16 000			96 000
								4	4 000			
Business combination valuation reserve	0	0	2	11 200	14 000	1	2 800	3	4 200	1400	4	0
	915 000	742 000					1 125 350					978 840

Financial statements	Lugano Ltd	Biel Ltd	Adjustments				Group	Non-controlling interest				Parent
				Dr	Cr				Dr	Cr		
Asset revaluation reserve (1/7/09)	35 000	50 000	1	16 000			69 000	3	4 000			59 000
								4	6 000			
Gains/losses on asset revaluation	(15 000)	10 000					(5 000)	5	2 000			(7 000)
Asset revaluation reserve (30/6/10)	20 000	60 000					64 000					52 000
Total equity: parent												1 030 840
Total equity: NCI								5	2 000	134 200	3	158 510
								5	3 000	19 320	4	
								9	210	10 440	5	
								1	2 800	2 000	5	
										560	17	
Total equity	935 000	802 000					1 189 350		182 370	182 370		1 189 350
Dividend payable	25 000	15 000	7	12 000			28 000					
Other liabilities	25 000	25 000	1	4 800	6 000	1	51 200					
Total liabilities	50 000	40 000					79 200					
Total equity and liabilities	985 000	842 000					1 268 550					
Receivables	80 000	30 000			12 000	6	98 000					
Inventory	100 000	170 000			1 500	8	266 500					
					2 000	10						
Plant and equipment	200 000	500 000			20 000	1	660 000					
					20 000	14						
Accumulated depreciation	(115 000)	(88 000)	1	40 000	16 000	1	(175 000)					
			16	4 000								
Land	100 000	80 000					180 000					
Shares in Biel Ltd	540 000	0			540 000	2	0					
Deferred tax asset	50 000	40 000	8	450	1 200	16	95 850					
			10	600								
			14	6 000								
Goodwill	0	0	2	3 200			3 200					
Other assets	30 000	110 000					140 000					
Total assets	985 000	842 000		705 050	705 050		1 268 550					

The consolidated financial statements for Lugano Ltd and its subsidiary, Biel Ltd, for the year ended 30 June 2010 are as shown in figure 24.12(a), (b) and (c).

FIGURE 24.12(a) Consolidated statement of comprehensive income

LUGANO LTD Consolidated Statement of Comprehensive Income for the year ended 30 June 2010	
Revenue:	
Sales	$ 1 209 000
Other	339 000
Total revenue	1 548 000

(continued)

FIGURE 24.12(a) *(continued)*

Expenses:	
Cost of sales	(978 500)
Other	(391 000)
Total expenses	(1 369 500)
Profit before tax	178 500
Income tax expense	(64 550)
Profit for the period	$ 113 950
Other comprehensive income	
Revaluation decrements	$ (5 000)
TOTAL COMPREHENSIVE INCOME	$ 108 950
Profit attributable to:	
Owners of the parent	$ 102 880
Non-controlling interest	11 070
	$ 113 950
Comprehensive income attributable to:	
Owners of the parent	$ 95 880
Non-controlling interest	13 070
	$ 108 950

LUGANO LTD
Consolidated Statement of Changes in Equity
for the year ended 30 June 2010

	Share capital	Retained earnings	General reserve	Asset revaluation reserve	Business combination valuation reserve	Total: Owners of the parent	Non-controlling interest	Total equity
Balance at 1 July 2009	$600 000	$224 960	$96 000	$59 000	0	$ 979 960	$150 440	$1 130 400
Total comprehensive income		102 880		(7 000)		95 880	13 070	108 950
Dividends paid		(20 000)				(20 000)	(2 000)	(22 000)
Dividends declared		(25 000)				(25 000)	(3 000)	(28 000)
Balance at 30 June 2010	$600 000	$282 840	$96 000	$52 000		$1 030 840	$158 150	$1 189 350

FIGURE 24.12(b) Consolidated statement of changes in equity

FIGURE 24.12(c) Consolidated statement of financial position

LUGANO LTD
Consolidated Statement of Financial Position
as at 30 June 2010

ASSETS	
Current assets	
Receivables	$ 98 000
Inventory	266 500
Total current assets	364 500

FIGURE 24.12(c) *(continued)*

Non-current assets	
Plant and equipment	$ 660 000
Accumulated depreciation	(175 000)
Land	180 000
Deferred tax asset	95 850
Goodwill	3 200
Other	140 000
Total non-current assets	907 250
Total assets	$ 1 268 550
LIABILITIES	
Current liabilities: Dividend payable	$ 28 000
Non-current liabilities	51 200
Total liabilities	$ 79 200
Net assets	$ 1 189 350
EQUITY	
Share capital	$ 600 000
General reserve	96 000
Asset revaluation reserve	52 000
Retained earnings	282 840
Parent interest	$ 1 030 840
Non-controlling interest	$ 158 510
Total equity	$ 1 189 350

B. Consolidation worksheet changes under full goodwill method

Under the full goodwill method, the acquisition analysis would change as goodwill is calculated by taking into consideration the fair value of the NCI in the subsidiary.

Acquisition analysis

Net fair value of the identifiable assets and liabilities of Biel Ltd	= $500 000 + $80 000 + $50 000 + $20 000 + $10 000(1 – 30%) (BCVR – inventory) + $20 000(1 – 30%) (BCVR – plant)
	= $671 000
(a) Consideration transferred	= $540 000
(b) Non-controlling interest in subsidiary	= $134 500
Aggregate of (a) and (b)	= $674 500
Goodwill	= $674 500 – $671 000
	= $3 500
Net fair value acquired by parent	= 80% × $671 000
	= $536 800
Consideration transferred	= $540 000
Goodwill – parent	= $3 200
Goodwill – NCI	= $3 500 – $3 200
	= $300

Consolidation worksheet entries at 30 June 2010

(1) *Business combination valuation reserve entries*

Because the full goodwill method is used, there will need to an extra business combination valuation entry in relation to goodwill:

Goodwill	Dr	3 500	
Business Combination Valuation Reserve	Cr		3 500

(2) *Pre-acquisition entries*

Retained Earnings (1/7/09)	Dr	45 600	
Share Capital	Dr	400 000	
General Reserve	Dr	64 000	
Asset Revaluation Reserve (1/7/09)	Dr	16 000	
Business Combination Valuation Reserve	Dr	14 400	
Shares in Biel Ltd	Cr		540 000

(3) *NCI share of equity at acquisition date, 1 July 2006 (step 1)*

Under the full goodwill method this will change as the business combination valuation reserve in relation to goodwill has been recognised. The NCI share is calculated to be:

Pre-acquisition equity of Biel Ltd		
Retained earnings (1/7/06): 20% × $50 000	=	$ 10 000
Share capital: 20% × $500 000	=	100 000
General reserve: 20% × $80 000	=	16 000
Asset revaluation reserve (1/7/06): 20% × $20 000	=	4 000
Business combination valuation reserve: $20% × $21 000 + $300 goodwill	=	4 500
		$134 500

The worksheet entry in the NCI columns is:

Retained Earnings (1/7/09)	Dr	10 000	
Share Capital	Dr	100 000	
General Reserve	Dr	16 000	
Asset Revaluation Reserve (1/7/09)	Dr	4 000	
Business Combination Valuation Reserve	Dr	4 500	
NCI	Cr		134 500

No other changes are required.

SUMMARY

Where a subsidiary is not wholly owned, the equity of the subsidiary is divided into two parts, namely the parent's share and the non-controlling interest (NCI) share. IAS 1 *Presentation of Financial Statements* requires that, with the disclosure of specific equity amounts, the parent's share and the NCI share should be separately disclosed. This affects the consolidation process. The NCI is classified as equity with the result that in statements of comprehensive income and statements of financial position where equity amounts are disclosed the parent's share and the NCI share are separately disclosed.

The existence of an NCI will have different effects on the consolidation worksheet entries used dependent on whether the full goodwill or partial goodwill method is used. Under the full goodwill method, goodwill is recognised in the business combination valuation entries, and shared between the parent and the NCI — but not necessarily on a proportionate basis. Where the partial goodwill method is used, the existence of an NCI has no effect on the business combination valuation entries. However, as a result of these entries, business combination valuation reserves are created of which the NCI has a share. With the pre-acquisition entry, the existence of an NCI has an effect as this entry is based on the parent's share of pre-acquisition equity only. Hence, a proportionate adjustment is required. The adjustments for intragroup transactions also affect the calculation of the NCI share of equity. There is no effect on the adjustment for an intragroup transaction itself — this is the same regardless of the ownership interest of the parent in the subsidiary. However, the adjustment for an intragroup transaction affects the calculation of the NCI share of equity. Since the NCI is entitled to a share of consolidated equity rather than the recorded equity of the subsidiary, where an intragroup transaction affects the equity of the subsidiary, entries in the NCI columns of the worksheet are required, affecting the calculation of the NCI. It is then necessary to observe the flow of the transaction — upstream or downstream — to determine whether an NCI adjustment is necessary. One area where the NCI is unaffected is where a gain on bargain purchase arises, because the pre-acquisition entry adjusts for the parent's share only. The gain calculated relates only to the parent and not the NCI.

Discussion questions

1. What is meant by the term 'non-controlling interest' (NCI)?
2. Explain whether the NCI is better classified as debt or equity.
3. Explain whether the NCI is entitled to a share of subsidiary equity or some other amount.
4. How does the existence of an NCI affect the business combination valuation entries?
5. How does the existence of an NCI affect the pre-acquisition entries?
6. Why is it necessary to change the format of the worksheet where an NCI exists in the group?
7. Explain how the adjustment for intragroup transactions affects the calculation of the NCI share of equity.
8. Explain whether an NCI adjustment needs to be made for all intragroup transactions.
9. What is meant by 'realisation of profit'?
10. When is profit realised on an intragroup transaction involving a depreciable asset?
11. When is profit realised on an intragroup transaction involving the parent renting a warehouse from the subsidiary?
12. If a step approach is used in the calculation of the NCI share of equity, what are the steps involved?
13. What are two events that could occur between the acquisition date and the beginning of the current period that could affect the calculation of the NCI share of retained earnings?
14. For what lines in the financial statements is it necessary to provide a break-down into parent entity share and NCI share?
15. Len Inn is the accountant for Horgen Trucks Ltd. This entity has an 80% holding in the entity Tyres-R-Us Ltd. Len is concerned that the consolidated financial statements prepared under IAS 27 may be misleading. He believes that the main users of the consolidated financial statements are the shareholders of Horgen Trucks Ltd. The key performance indicators are then the profit numbers relating to the interests of those shareholders. He therefore wants to prepare the consolidated financial statements showing the non-controlling interest in Tyres-R-Us Ltd in a category other than equity in the statement of financial performance, and for the statement of changes in equity to show the profit numbers relating to the parent shareholders only.

    Required

    Discuss the differences that would arise in the consolidated financial statements if the non-controlling interest were classified as debt rather than equity, and the reasons the standard setters have chosen the equity classification in IAS 27.

16. The consolidated financial statements of Vaud Submarine Works Ltd are being prepared by the group accountant, Raz Putin. He is currently in dispute with the auditors over the need to adjust for the NCI share of equity in relation to intragroup transactions. He understands the need to adjust for the effects of the intragroup transactions, but believes

that it is unnecessary to adjust for the NCI share of equity. He argues that the NCI group of shareholders has its interest in the subsidiary and as a result is entitled to a share of what the subsidiary records as equity. He also disputes with the auditors about the notion of 'realisation' of profit in relation to the NCI. If realisation requires the involvement of an external entity in a transaction, then in relation to transactions such as intragroup transfers of vehicles and services such as interest payments, there is never any external party involved. Those transactions are totally within the group and never involve external entities. As a result, the more appropriate accounting is to give the NCI a share of subsidiary equity and not be concerned with the fictitious involvement of external entities.

Required
Write a report to Raz convincing him that his argument is fallacious.

17. In December 2007, Valais Ltd acquired 60% of the shares of Zug Ltd. The accountant for Valais Ltd, Nikki Romanov, is concerned about the approach she should take in preparing the consolidated financial statements for the newly established group. In particular, she is concerned about the calculation of the NCI share of equity, particularly in the years after acquisition date. She has heard accountants in other companies talking about a 'step' approach, and in particular how this makes accounting in periods after the acquisition date very easy as it is then necessary to prepare only one step.

Required
Prepare a report for Nikki, explaining the step approach to the calculation of NCI and the effects of this approach in the years after acquisition date.

18. Because the Nyon Cement Works Ltd has a number of subsidiaries, Star Lin is required to prepare a set of consolidated financial statements for the group. She is concerned about the calculation of the NCI share of equity particularly where there are intragroup transactions. The auditors require that when adjustments are made for intragroup transactions the effects of these transactions on the NCI should also be adjusted for. Star has two concerns. First, why is it necessary to adjust the NCI share of equity for the effects of intragroup transactions? Second, is it necessary to make NCI adjustments in relation to *all* intragroup transactions?

Required
Prepare a report for Star, explaining these two areas of concern.

STAR RATING
★ BASIC
★★ MODERATE
★★★ DIFFICULT

Exercises

Exercise 24.1 ★

CONSOLIDATION WORKSHEET, CONSOLIDATED FINANCIAL STATEMENTS, PARTIAL GOODWILL METHOD

Cham Ltd purchased 75% of the capital of Brig Ltd for $250 000 on 1 July 2003. At this date the equity of Uster Ltd was:

Share capital	$100 000
General reserve	60 000
Retained earnings	40 000

At this date, Uster Ltd had not recorded any goodwill, and all identifiable assets and liabilities were recorded at fair value except for the following assets:

	Carrying amount	Fair value
Inventory	$ 70 000	$100 000
Plant (cost $170 000)	150 000	190 000
Land	50 000	100 000

The plant has a remaining useful life of 10 years. As a result of an impairment test, all goodwill was written off in 2006. All the inventory on hand at 1 July 2003 was sold by 30 June 2004. Differences beween carrying amounts and fair values are recognised on consolidation. The tax rate is 30%.

The trial balances of Cham Ltd and Uster Ltd at 30 June 2009 are:

	Cham Ltd	Uster Ltd
Shares in Uster Ltd	$ 250 000	—
Plant	425 500	$ 190 000
Land	110 000	50 000
Current assets	162 000	84 000
Cost of sales	225 000	35 000
Other expenses	65 000	7 000
Income tax expense	50 000	5 000
	$1 287 500	$ 371 000
Share capital	$ 400 000	$ 100 000
General reserve	60 000	80 000
Retained earnings (1/7/08)	120 000	75 000
Sales revenue	510 600	80 000
Payables	72 900	12 000
Accumulated depreciation (plant)	124 000	24 000
	$1 287 500	$ 371 000

Required

1. Prepare the consolidation worksheet entries immediately after acquisition date.
2. Prepare the consolidation worksheet entries for Cham Ltd at 30 June 2004. Assume a profit for Uster Ltd for the 2003–04 period of $40 000.
3. Prepare the consolidated financial statements as at 30 June 2009.

Exercise 24.2

CONSOLIDATION WORKSHEET ENTRIES INCLUDING NCI

★ On 1 July 2009, Jura Ltd acquired 90% of the capital of Fribourg Ltd for $290 160. The equity of Fribourg Ltd at this date consisted of:

Share capital	$200 000
Retained earnings	80 000

The carrying amounts and fair values of the assets and liabilities recorded by Fribourg Ltd at 1 July 2009 were as follows:

	Carrying amount	Fair value
Fittings	$ 20 000	$ 20 000
Land	90 000	100 000
Inventory	10 000	12 000
Machinery (net)	200 000	220 000
Liabilities	40 000	40 000

The machinery and fittings have a further 10-year life, benefits to be received evenly over this period. Differences between carrying amounts and fair values are recognised on consolidation. Jura Ltd uses the partial goodwill method.

The tax rate is 30%. All inventory on hand at 1 July 2009 is sold by 30 June 2010.

Required

1. What are the entries for the consolidation worksheet if prepared immediately after 1 July 2009?
2. What are the entries for the consolidation worksheet if prepared at 30 June 2010? Assume a profit for Fribourg Ltd for the 2009–10 period of $20 000.
3. If the non-controlling interest had a fair value of $31 800 on 1 July 2009, and the full goodwill method had been used, what entries in Parts 1 and 2 above would change? Prepare the changed entries.

Exercise 24.3 CONSOLIDATION WORKSHEET ENTRIES, BARGAIN PURCHASE, RECORDED GOODWILL

★ On 1 July 2007, Leuk Ltd acquired 75% of the shares of Ticino Ltd for $123 525. At this date, the statement of financial position of Ticino Ltd consisted of:

Share capital — 100 000 shares	$100 000	Cash	$ 5 000
General reserve	20 000	Inventories	20 000
Retained earnings	40 000	Plant (cost $100 000)	80 000
Liabilities	60 000	Fitting (cost $80 000)	50 000
		Receivables	5 000
		Land	60 000
	$220 000		$220 000

In relation to the assets of Ticino Ltd, the fair values at 1 July 2007 were:

Cash	$ 5 000
Inventories	25 000
Plant	86 000
Fittings	51 000
Receivables	4 000
Land	80 000

The inventories were all sold and the receivables all collected by 30 June 2008. The plant and fittings each have an expected useful life of 5 years. The plant was sold on 1 January 2010. The tax rate is 30%.

Additional information

(a) At 1 July 2009, the retained earnings of Ticino Ltd were $80 000, and the general reserve was $30 000.

(b) During the 2009–10 period, Ticino Ltd recorded a total comprehensive income of $18 000. This consisted of a profit of $15 000 and gains on revaluation of land of $3000.

(c) In June 2009, a dividend of $8000 was declared by Ticino Ltd, and was paid in August 2009. An interim dividend of $5000 was paid in January 2010, and a final dividend of $4000 declared in June 2010.

Required

Prepare the worksheet entries for the preparation of the consolidated financial statements of Leuk Ltd and its subsidiary, Ticino Ltd, at 30 June 2010.

Exercise 24.4 CONSOLIDATION WORKSHEET ENTRIES, MULTIPLE YEARS, PARTIAL GOODWILL METHOD

★ On 1 July 2006, Valais Ltd acquired 75% of the issued shares of Lugano Ltd for $125 750. At this date, the accounts of Lugano Ltd included the following balances:

Share capital	$80 000
General reserve	20 000
Retained earnings	40 000

All the identifiable assets and liabilities of Lugano Ltd were recorded at fair value except for the following:

	Carrying amount	Fair value
Plant (cost $50 000)	$35 000	$41 000
Land	50 000	70 000
Inventory	20 000	24 000

Adjustments for the differences between carrying amounts and fair values are to be made on consolidation except for land which is to be measured in Lugano Ltd's accounts at fair value. The plant has a further 3-year life. All the inventory was sold by 30 June 2007. Valais Ltd uses the partial goodwill method.

During the 4 years since acquisition, Lugano Ltd has recorded the following annual results:

Year ended	Profit (loss)	Total comprehensive income
30 June 2007	$10 000	$12 000
30 June 2008	23 000	28 000
30 June 2009	(6 000)	1 000
30 June 2010	22 000	22 000

The other recognised income and expense relates to gains/losses on revaluation of land.

There have been no transfers to or from the general reserve or any dividends paid or declared by Lugano Ltd since the acquisition date.

The land owned by Lugano Ltd on 1 July 2006 was sold on 1 March 2009 for $75 000. The group transfers the valuation reserves to retained earnings when an asset is sold or fully consumed. The tax rate is 30%.

Required

1. Prepare the consolidation worksheet entries as at 1 July 2006.
2. Prepare the consolidation worksheet entries for the year ended 30 June 2007.
3. Prepare the consolidation worksheet entries for the year ended 30 June 2008.
4. Prepare the consolidation worksheet entries for the year ended 30 June 2009.
5. Prepare the consolidation worksheet entries for the year ended 30 June 2010.

Exercise 24.5 ★

CONSOLIDATION WORKSHEET, CONSOLIDATED FINANCIAL STATEMENTS, FULL GOODWILL METHOD

In June 2009, Lancy Ltd made an offer to the shareholders of Vevcy Ltd to acquire a controlling interest in the company. Lancy Ltd was prepared to pay $1.50 cash per share, provided that 70% of the shares could be acquired (enough shares to gain control).

The directors of Vevcy Ltd recommended that the offer be accepted. By 1 July 2009, when the offer expired, 75% of the shares had changed hands and were now in the possession of Lancy Ltd. The statement of financial position of Vevcy Ltd on that date is shown below.

VEVCY LTD
Statement of Financial Position
as at 1 July 2009

Current assets	$368 000
Non-current assets	244 000
	$612 000
Share capital — 400 000 shares	$400 000
General reserve	50 000
Asset revaluation reserve	40 000
Other components of equity	30 000
Retained earnings	40 000
Current liabilities	52 000
	$612 000

At 1 July 2009, all the identifiable assets and liabilities of Vevcy Ltd were recorded at amounts equal to fair value. Lancy Ltd uses the full goodwill method. The fair value of the non-controlling interest at 1 July 2009 was $147 000.

The draft financial statements of the two companies on 30 June 2010 revealed the following details:

	Lancy Ltd	Vevcy Ltd
Sales revenue	$ 878 900	$ 388 900
Cost of sales	374 400	112 400
Gross profit	504 500	276 500
Other income	302 100	112 500
	806 600	389 000
Other expenses	216 200	115 800
Profit before tax	590 400	273 200
Income tax expense	112 400	50 000
Profit	478 000	223 200
Retained earnings (1/7/09)	112 000	40 000
	590 000	263 200
Dividend paid	40 000	30 000
Dividend declared	50 000	10 000
	90 000	40 000
Retained earnings (30/6/10)	500 000	223 200
Share capital	1 200 000	400 000
General reserve	24 000	50 000
Asset revaluation reserve	70 000	60 000
Other components of equity	30 000	40 000
Current liabilities	177 000	124 400
	$2 001 000	$ 897 600
Financial assets	$ 280 000	$ 204 000
Receivables	320 000	175 000
Inventory	287 500	210 600
Investments — Shares in Vevcy Ltd	450 000	—
Other investments	47 000	—
Equipment	650 000	360 000
Accumulated depreciation	(250 000)	(160 000)
Land	216 500	108 000
	$2 001 000	$ 897 600

Additional information

(a) Lancy Ltd had made an advance of $80 000 to Vevcy Ltd. This advance was repayable in June 2011.

(b) The directors of Lancy Ltd and Vevcy Ltd had declared final dividends of $50 000 and $10 000 respectively, from current period's profits.

(c) Vevcy Ltd holds at the end of the reporting period inventory purchased from Lancy Ltd during the year for $55 000. Lancy Ltd invoices goods to its subsidiary at cost plus 10%.

(d) On 1 July 2009, Vevcy Ltd sold to Lancy Ltd some display equipment for $60 000. At that date, the carrying amount of the equipment was $52 000 and the equipment was estimated to have a useful life of 10 years if used constantly over that period.

(e) Assume a tax rate of 30%.

(f) For Lancy Ltd, balances of Asset Revaluation Reserve and Other Components of Equity at 1 July 2009 were $40 000 and $25 000 respectively.

Required

Prepare the consolidated financial statements for Lancy Ltd and its subsidiary as at 30 June 2010.

Exercise 24.6 CONSOLIDATION WORKSHEET ENTRIES, DIVIDENDS, EQUITY TRANSFERS

★★

On 1 July 2007, Olten Ltd acquired 80% of the shares (*cum div.*) of Meyrin Ltd for $202 000. At this date, the equity of Meyrin Ltd consisted of:

Share capital — 100 000 shares	$100 000
General reserve	40 000
Retained earnings	50 000

The carrying amounts and fair values of the assets of Meyrin Ltd were as follows:

	Carrying amount	Fair value
Land	$70 000	$ 90 000
Plant (cost $100 000)	80 000	85 000
Fittings (cost 40 000)	20 000	20 000
Goodwill	5 000	10 000

Any adjustment for the differences in carrying amounts and fair values is recognised on consolidation. Olten Ltd uses the partial goodwill method.

Both plant and fittings were expected to have a further 5-year life, with benefits being received evenly over those periods. The plant was sold on 1 January 2010. In the year of the sale of plant, on consolidation the valuation reserve relating to the plant was transferred to retained earnings. At 1 July 2007, Meyrin Ltd had not recorded an internally generated trademark that Olten Ltd considered to have a fair value of $50 000. This intangible asset was considered to have an indefinite useful life.

Additional information

(a) The following profits were recorded by Meyrin Ltd:

For the 2007–08 period	$ 20 000
For the 2008–09 period	25 000
For the 2009–10 period	30 000

(b) In June 2009, Meyrin Ltd transferred $5000 to general reserve, and in June 2010, a further $6000 was transferred.

(c) In August 2007, the dividend payable of $5000 on hand at 1 July 2007 was paid by Meyrin Ltd.

(d) Other dividends declared or paid since 1 July 2007 are:
- $8000 dividend declared in June 2008, paid in August 2008
- $6000 dividend declared in June 2009, paid in August 2009
- $5000 dividend paid in December 2009
- $8000 dividend declared in June 2010, expected to be paid in August 2010.

Required

1. Prepare the worksheet entries for the preparation of the consolidated financial statements of Olten Ltd and its subsidiary, Meyrin Ltd, at 30 June 2010.
2. Assume Olten Ltd uses the full goodwill method and the value of the non-controlling interest at 1 July 2007 was $49 250. Prepare the entries that would differ from those in Part 1 above.

Exercise 24.7 CONSOLIDATION WORKSHEET ENTRIES, MULTIPLE YEARS, FULL GOODWILL METHOD

★★ On 1 July 2006, Prilly Ltd acquired 60% of the shares of Onex Ltd for $111 700. At this date, the equity of Onex Ltd consisted of:

Share capital	$120 000
General reserve	10 000
Retained earnings	30 000

At this date, the identifiable assets and liabilities of Onex Ltd were recorded at fair value except for the following assets:

	Carrying amount	Fair value
Equipment (cost $80 000)	$65 000	$75 000
Land	80 000	90 000
Inventory	45 000	50 000

Adjustments for the differences between carrying amounts and fair values are to be made on consolidation. The equipment has a further 5-year life. Half the inventory on hand at the acquisition date was sold by 30 June 2007, with the remainder being sold in the 2007–08 financial year. At 30 June 2009, the goodwill was written down by $3000 as the result of an impairment test.

Prilly Ltd uses the full goodwill method. The fair value of the non-controlling interest at 1 July 2006 was $74 100.

During the 3 years since acquisition, Onex Ltd has recorded the following annual results:

Year ended	Profit
30 June 2007	$15 000
30 June 2008	27 000
30 June 2009	12 000

There have been no transfers to or from the general reserve or any dividend paid or declared by Onex Ltd since the acquisition date.

The equipment owned by Onex Ltd on 1 July 2006 was sold on 1 January 2008 for $70 000. On consolidation, the group transfers the valuation reserve to retained earnings when an asset is sold or fully consumed. The tax rate is 30%.

Required

1. Prepare the consolidation worksheet entries as at 1 July 2006.
2. Prepare the consolidation worksheet entries for the year ended 30 June 2007.
3. Prepare the consolidation worksheet entries for the year ended 30 June 2008.
4. Prepare the consolidation worksheet entries for the year ended 30 June 2009.

Exercise 24.8 ★★ CONSOLIDATION WORKSHEET, UNRECORDED INTANGIBLE, DIVIDENDS, FULL GOODWILL METHOD

On 1 July 2006, Sursee Ltd acquired 70% of the shares (cum div.) of Jura Ltd for $141 950. At this date, the equity of Jura Ltd consisted of:

Share capital	$100 000
General reserve	31 000
Retained earnings	25 000
Other components of equity	9 000

Jura Ltd's records showed a dividend payable at 1 July 2006 of $10 000. The dividend was paid on 1 November 2006.

A comparison of the carrying amounts and fair values of the assets of Jura Ltd at 1 July 2006 revealed the following:

	Carrying amount	Fair value
Plant (cost $75 000)	$45 000	$60 000
Vehicles (cost $40 000)	23 000	23 000
Goodwill	10 000	

Adjustments for the differences in carrying amounts and fair values are recognised on consolidation. Both plant and vehicles were expected to have a further 5-year life, with benefits being received evenly over those periods. Jura Ltd had not recorded an internally generated brand name for an item that was considered by Sursee Ltd to have a fair value of $20 000. The brand name is regarded as having an indefinite useful life. At 30 June 2007, goodwill was considered to be impaired by $1000, and a further impairment loss of $2000 was recognised in 2008. Sursee Ltd uses the full goodwill method. The fair value of the non-controlling interest at 1 July 2006 was $57 000.

Additional information

(a) The dividends paid and declared since 1 July 2006 are:
- $10 000 dividend declared in June 2007, paid in October 2007
- $5000 dividend declared in June 2008, paid in September 2008
- $8000 dividend paid in April 2009

(b) In June 2008, Jura Ltd transferred an amount of $20 000 from the general reserve to retained earnings.

(c) The plant on hand at 1 July 2006 was sold on 30 June 2009. On consolidation, the group decided to transfer the valuation reserve relating to the plant to retained earnings.

(d) The Other Components of Equity account reflects movements in the fair values of available-for-sale financial assets. The balances of this account at 1 July 2008 were $4000 (Sursee Ltd) and $11 000 (Jura Ltd).

(e) On 30 June 2009, the financial data of both companies were:

	Sursee Ltd	Jura Ltd
Revenues	$280 000	$190 000
Expenses	220 000	140 000
Profit before tax	60 000	50 000
Income tax expense	26 000	14 000
Profit for the period	34 000	36 000
Retained earnings (1/7/08)	76 000	65 000
Total available for appropriation	110 000	101 000
Dividend paid	20 000	8 000
Retained earnings (30/6/09)	90 000	93 000
Share capital	100 000	100 000
General reserve	44 000	11 000
Other components of equity	6 000	9 000
Payables	20 000	12 000
	$260 000	$225 000
Cash	$ 22 050	$ 43 000
Financial assets	20 000	30 000
Vehicles	35 000	50 000
Accumulated depreciation	(12 000)	(30 000)
Plant and equipment	80 000	120 000
Accumulated depreciation	(50 000)	(75 000)
Land	30 000	—
Goodwill	—	10 000
Accumulated impairment	—	(3 000)
Trademarks	—	80 000
Shares in Jura Ltd	134 950	—
	$260 000	$225 000

Required

Prepare the consolidated financial statements of Sursee Ltd as at 30 June 2009.

Exercise 24.9 ★★

CONSOLIDATION WORKSHEET, CONSOLIDATED FINANCIAL STATEMENTS, FULL GOODWILL METHOD

On 1 July 2004, Baden Ltd acquired 75% of the share capital of Thun Ltd at a cost of $27 600. At this date, the capital of Thun Ltd consisted of 30 000 ordinary shares each fully paid, and retained earnings were $6000.

At 1 July 2004, Thun Ltd had not recorded any goodwill, and all the identifiable net assets of Thun Ltd were recorded at fair value. Baden Ltd uses the full goodwill method. The fair value of the non-controlling interest at 1 July 2004 was $9000.

The trial balances of the two companies as at 30 June 2009 are as shown on the next page.

Trial Balances as at 30 June 2009				
	Baden Ltd		Thun Ltd	
	Dr	Cr	Dr	Cr
Share capital		$ 40 000		$ 30 000
Retained earnings (1 July 2008)		19 000		14 500
Other components of equity		—		5 000
Current tax liability		8 500		2 900
Plant	$ 30 000		$ 60 000	
Accumulated depreciation – plant		17 000		30 500
Shares in Thun Ltd	27 600			
10% debentures in Thun Ltd	2 500			
Inventory	12 000		15 500	
Cash	14 050		500	
Financial assets	—		11 000	
Deferred tax asset	2 000		5 000	
Sales revenue		50 000		80 000
Cost of sales	34 000		58 500	
Selling expenses	4 000		6 000	
Other expenses	1 500		1 500	
Financial expenses	1 500		2 000	
Income tax expense	5 000		5 500	
Interest received from debentures		250		
Dividend revenue		1 800		
Dividend paid			2 400	
10% debentures	2 400			5 000
	$ 136 550	$136 550	$167 900	$167 900

Additional information

(a) Intragroup sales of inventory for the year ended 30 June 2009 from Thun Ltd to Baden Ltd: $19 000.

(b) Unrealised profits on inventory held at 1 July 2008: inventory held by Baden Ltd purchased from Thun Ltd at a profit before tax of $800.

(c) Unrealised profits on inventory held at 30 June 2009: inventory held by Baden Ltd purchased from Thun Ltd at a profit before tax of $1200.

(d) The Other Components of Equity account relates to available-for-sale financial assets held by Thun Ltd. The balance of this account at 1 July 2008 was $4000.

(e) The tax rate applicable is 30c in the dollar.

Required

Prepare the consolidated financial statements for the year ended 30 June 2009.

Exercise 24.10 ★★

CONSOLIDATED WORKSHEET, CONSOLIDATED FINANCIAL STATEMENTS, PARTIAL GOODWILL METHOD

On 1 July 2009, Morges Ltd acquired 80% of the share capital of Glane Ltd for $264 800. This was sufficient for Morges Ltd to gain control over Glane Ltd. On that date, the statement of financial position of Glane Ltd consisted of:

Share capital	$250 000
General reserve	10 000
Asset revaluation reserve	15 000
Retained earnings	10 000
Liabilities	180 000
	$465 000

Cash	$ 35 000
Inventories	70 000
Land	65 000
Plant and equipment	300 000
Accumulated depreciation	(130 000)
Trademark	100 000
Goodwill	25 000
	$465 000

All the identifiable assets and liabilities of Glane Ltd were recorded at fair value except for:

	Carrying amount	Fair value
Inventories	$ 70 000	$ 80 000
Land	65 000	85 000
Plant and equipment (cost $200 000)	70 000	90 000
Trademark	100 000	110 000

The plant and equipment had a further 5-year life and was expected to be used evenly over that time. The trademark was considered to have an indefinite life.

Any adjustments for differences between carrying amounts at acquisition date and fair values are made on consolidation. Morges Ltd uses the partial goodwill method.

During the year ended 30 June 2010, all inventories on hand at the beginning of the year were sold, and the land was sold on 28 February 2010 to Aigle Ltd for $80 000. Any valuation reserve created in relation to the land was transferred on consolidation to retained earnings.

The income tax rate is assumed to be 30%.

Financial information for Morges Ltd and Glane Ltd for the year ended 30 June 2010 is shown below.

	Morges Ltd	Glane Ltd
Sales revenue	$200 000	$172 000
Other income	85 000	35 000
	285 000	207 000
Cost of sales	162 000	128 000
Other expenses	53 000	31 000
	215 000	159 000
Profit before tax	70 000	48 000
Income tax expense	20 000	18 000
Profit	50 000	30 000
Retained earnings (1/7/09)	30 000	10 000
Transfer from general reserve	—	8 000
	80 000	48 000
Interim dividend paid	12 000	10 000
Final dividend declared	6 000	4 000
	18 000	14 000
Retained earnings (30/6/10)	$ 62 000	$ 34 000
Asset revaluation reserve (1/7/09)		$ 15 000
Gain on revaluation of specialised plant		5 000
Asset revaluation reserve (30/6/10)		$ 20 000

During the current year, Glane Ltd sold a quantity of inventory to Morges Ltd for $8000. The original cost of these items to Glane Ltd was $5000. One-third of this inventory was still on hand at the end of the year.

On 31 March 2010, Glane Ltd transferred an item of plant with a carrying amount of $10 000 to Morges Ltd for $15 000. Morges Ltd treated this item as inventory. The item was still on hand at the end of the year. Glane Ltd applied a 20% depreciation rate to this type of plant.

Required

1. Prepare the consolidation worksheet entries necessary for preparation of the consolidated financial statements for Glane Ltd and its subsidiary for the year ended 30 June 2010.
2. Prepare the consolidated statement of comprehensive income and statement of changes in equity for Morges Ltd and its subsidiary at 30 June 2010.

Exercise 24.11 CONSOLIDATION WORKSHEET ENTRIES

★★ On 1 July 2005, Spiez Ltd acquired 75% of the shares of Wil Ltd for $40 000. The following balances appeared in the records of Wil Ltd at this date:

Share capital	$20 000
General reserve	2 000
Retained earnings	10 000

At 1 July 2005, all the identifiable assets and liabilities of Wil Ltd were recorded at fair value except for the following:

	Carrying amount	Fair value
Machinery (cost $36 000)	$30 000	$40 000
Inventory	16 000	20 000
Receivables	20 000	18 000

The machinery, which had a remaining useful life of 5 years, was adjusted to fair value after the acquisition date in the consolidation worksheet. The machinery was sold by Wil Ltd on 1 January 2010 for $4000, with the related valuation reserve being transferred on consolidation to retained earnings. By 30 June 2006, receivables had all been collected and inventory sold.

For the year ended 30 June 2010, the following information is available:

(a) Intragroup sales were: Wil Ltd to Spiez Ltd — $40 000. The mark-up on cost of all sales was 25%.

(b) At 30 June 2010, inventory of Spiez Ltd included $2000 of items acquired from Wil Ltd.

(c) At 30 June 2009, inventory of Spiez Ltd included goods of $1000 resulting from a sale on 1 March 2009 of non-current assets by Wil Ltd at a before-tax profit of $200. These items were sold by Spiez Ltd on 1 September 2009. This class of non-current assets is depreciated using a 10% depreciation rate on a straight-line basis.

(d) On 1 January 2010, Wil Ltd sold an item of plant to Spiez Ltd for $2000 at a before-tax profit of $800. For plant assets, Wil Ltd applies a 10% p.a. straight-line depreciation rate, and Spiez Ltd uses a 2.5% p.a. straight-line method.

(e) The current tax rate is 30%.

(f) Financial information for the year ended 30 June 2010 includes the following:

	Spiez Ltd	Wil Ltd
Sales revenue	$ 88 000	$52 000
Other revenue	12 000	8 000
Total revenue	100 000	60 000
Cost of sales	58 000	26 000
Other expenses:		
Selling and administrative (including depreciation)	4 000	2 000
Financial	2 000	1 000
Carrying amount of non-current assets sold	6 000	5 000
	70 000	34 000

	Spiez Ltd	Wil Ltd
Gross profit	30 000	26 000
Dividend revenue	3 000	—
Profit before tax	33 000	26 000
Income tax expense	13 200	10 400
Profit	19 800	15 600
Retained earnings at 1 July 2009	40 000	20 000
	59 800	35 600
Transfer to general reserve	3 800	1 000
Interim dividend paid	4 000	8 000
Final dividend declared	4 000	4 000
	11 800	13 000
Retained earnings at 30 June 2010	$ 48 000	$22 600
Asset revaluation reserve (1/7/09)	$ 3 000	$ 2 000
Gains on property revaluation	1 000	500
Asset revaluation reserve (30/6/10)	$ 4 000	$ 2 500

Required

1. Prepare the consolidation worksheet entries for the preparation of the consolidated financial statements of Spiez Ltd at 30 June 2010 using the partial goodwill method.
2. Prepare the entries that would change in Part 1 above if the full goodwill method were used. The fair value of the non-controlling interest at 1 July 2005 was $12 900.

Problems

Problem 24.1

CONSOLIDATION WORKSHEET ENTRIES, RECORDED GOODWILL, LEASES

★★★

At 1 July 2008, Worb Ltd acquired 80% of the share capital of Visp Ltd for $290 000. At this date the statement of financial position of Visp Ltd, including comparative information on fair values for assets, was as shown below.

		Carrying amount	Fair value
Current assets			
Inventory		$ 60 000	$ 65 000
Receivables	$ 40 000		
Allowance for doubtful debts	5 000	35 000	35 000
Total current assets		95 000	
Non-current assets			
Plant and machinery (at cost)	200 000		
Accumulated depreciation	125 000	75 000	90 000
Vehicles (at cost)	80 000		
Accumulated depreciation	10 000	70 000	75 000
Buildings (at cost)	120 000		
Accumulated depreciation	5 000	115 000	115 000
Trademark (at valuation)		100 000	100 000
Other assets		40 000	40 000
Goodwill		20 000	
Total non-current assets		420 000	
Total assets		$515 000	
Equity			
Share capital		$200 000	
Asset revaluation reserve		50 000	
Retained earnings		50 000	
Total equity		300 000	

(continued)

	Carrying amount	Fair value
Current liabilities		
Accounts payable	40 000	
Dividend payable	20 000	
Total current liabilities	60 000	
Non-current liabilities		
Debentures	155 000	
Total liabilities	215 000	
Total equity and liabilities	$ 515 000	

At 1 July 2008, it was expected that the depreciable assets had the following remaining useful lives:

Plant and machinery	5 years
Vehicles	10 years
Trademark	100 years
Buildings	10 years

All the inventory on hand at 1 July 2008 was sold by Visp Ltd by 30 June 2009. Adjustments for differences between fair values and carrying amounts at acquisition date are made on consolidation. The tax rate is 30%.

Additional information

(a) The dividend payable in the records of Visp Ltd at 1 July 2008 was paid in September 2008.

(b) On 1 January 2011, one of the machines that was on hand in Visp Ltd at 1 July 2008 was sold for $6000. At 1 July 2008, the machine was recorded at cost of $50 000 with accumulated depreciation of $30 000, and had a fair value of $23 000. Any related revaluation reserve was transferred on consolidation to retained earnings.

(c) During the 2010–11 period, Visp Ltd transferred $10 000 from the asset revaluation surplus (on hand at 1 July 2008) to retained earnings, and transferred $20 000 to general reserve from retained earnings.

(d) Information on dividends paid and declared is as follows:

> 2008–09 period:
> paid a $5000 dividend
> 2009–10 period:
> paid a $4000 interim dividend
> declared, in June 2010, a $6000 dividend
> 2010–11 period:
> paid the $6000 dividend declared in the previous period
> paid a $5000 interim dividend
> declared, in June 2011, an $8000 dividend.

(e) Information on inventory sold by Visp Ltd to Worb Ltd at cost plus 25%:
- At 1 July 2010, Worb Ltd had $10 000 of inventory on hand.
- During the 2010–11 period, $50 000 worth of inventory was sold, with 10% still on hand in Worb Ltd at 30 June 2011.

(f) On 1 July 2010, Worb Ltd leased a machine from Visp Ltd under a direct financing lease arrangement. The fair vaue of the asset leased was $25 000, and the lease agreement had an implicit interest rate of 10%. The lease term was for the whole of the machine's useful life, being 5 years. The residual value at the end of the lease term was expected to be zero. At 30 June 2011, Worb Ltd made a lease payment to Visp Ltd of $7500, which included an amount of $1500 to cover the costs of insurance and maintenance, both supplied by Visp Ltd.

(g) The retained earnings balance at 30 June 2010 in Visp Ltd was $60 000. The total comprehensive income for the year ended 30 June 2011 was $28 000, including $3000 due to revaluation of land measured using the revaluation model. The asset revaluation reserve balance at 30 June 2010 for Visp Ltd was $55 000.

Required

1. Prepare consolidated worksheet journal entries for preparing the consolidated financial statements of Worb Ltd at 30 June 2011 using the full goodwill method. Assume the fair value of the non-controlling interest at 1 July 2008 was $67 000.
2. Prepare the entries that would change in Part 1 above if the partial goodwill method were used.

Problem 24.2 BARGAIN PURCHASE, CONSOLIDATION WORKSHEET ENTRIES

★★★ On 1 July 2005, Intertaken Ltd acquired (cum div.) a 70% interest in Aargau Ltd. The following balances appeared in the records of Aargau Ltd at this date:

Share capital — 100 000 shares	$100 000
General reserve	20 000
Retained earnings	52 000
Dividend payable	5 000

At 1 July 2005, the carrying amounts and fair values of Aargau Ltd's identifiable assets and liabilities were as shown below.

	Carrying amount	Fair value
Cash	$ 10 000	$ 10 000
Accounts receivable	28 000	26 000
Inventory	51 000	55 000
Vehicles (cost $25 000)	17 000	18 000
Plant (cost $100 000)	66 000	70 000
Furniture and fittings (cost $60 000)	34 500	34 500
	206 500	213 500
Dividend payable	5 000	5 000
Provisions	33 000	33 000
	38 000	38 000
Identifiable assets and liabilities	$168 500	$175 500

Any differences between carrying amounts at acquisition and fair values are adjusted on consolidation. The non-current assets were deemed to have the following remaining useful lives:

Vehicles	5 years
Plant	8 years
Furniture and fittings	7 years

In addition, Aargau Ltd had recorded goodwill of $3500 at 1 July 2005. Intertaken Ltd uses the partial goodwill method. The following events occurred between the acquisition date and 30 June 2008:

(a) By 30 June 2006, 80% of the inventory on hand at 1 July 2005 had been sold, and all accounts receivable deemed to be collectable at 1 July 2005 had been received.
(b) On 15 September 2005, the dividend declared as at 1 July 2005 was paid.
(c) On 15 March 2006, Aargau Ltd paid a $12 000 dividend.
(d) On 30 June 2007, Aargau Ltd transferred $15 000 from pre-acquisition retained earnings to the general reserve.

(e) On 1 January 2008, Aargau Ltd paid a bonus share dividend from the general reserve, the dividend being one share for each ten held.
(f) On 20 June 2008, Aargau Ltd declared a dividend of $5000 from pre-acquisition profits. The dividend was paid on 10 October 2008.

For the year ended 30 June 2009, the following information is available:

(a) Intertaken Ltd recognises dividend revenue when the dividends are declared by Aargau Ltd.
(b) The transfer was from pre-acquisition reserves.
(c) The balance of the Shares in Aargau Ltd account was $119380 at 30 June 2009.
(d) On 30 June 2009, vehicles on hand at the acquisition date were sold for $6500. Any related valuation reserve was transferred on consolidation to retained earnings.
(e) The company tax rate is 30%.
(f) Financial information for the year ended 30 June 2009 included the following:

	Intertaken Ltd	Aargau Ltd
Profit before tax	$42 000	$ 36 000
Income tax expense	16 800	14 400
Profit	25 200	21 600
Retained earnings (1/7/08)	55 600	66 800
Transfer from general reserve	—	10 000
Total available for appropriation	80 800	98 400
Dividend paid	15 000	8 000
Dividend declared	10 000	16 000
	25 000	24 000
Retained earnings (30/6/09)	$55 800	$ 74 400

Required

Prepare the consolidation worksheet entries for the preparation of the consolidated financial statements of Intertaken Ltd at 30 June 2009.

Problem 24.3 CONSOLIDATION WORKSHEET, REVALUATION IN SUBSIDIARY'S RECORDS, PARTIAL GOODWILL METHOD

★★★

On 1 July 2008, Aigle Ltd acquired 80% of the share capital of Sion Ltd for $198 000. At this date, the equity of Sion Ltd consisted of:

Share capital	$ 150 000
General reserve	30 000
Retained earnings	20 000

At 1 July 2008, all the identifiable assets and liabilities of Sion Ltd were recorded at fair value except for the following assets:

	Carrying amount	Fair value
Plant (cost $120 000)	$ 90 000	$100 000
Land	80 000	120 000

The plant had a further 5-year life, with benefits expected to be received evenly over that period. The land was sold by Sion Ltd in January 2010 for $150 000. Sion Ltd had revalued both these assets in its records at 1 July 2008. Aigle Ltd uses the partial goodwill method.

Financial information for these two companies at 30 June 2010 included:

	Aigle Ltd	Sion Ltd
Sales revenue	$920 000	$780 000
Other income	65 000	82 000
	985 000	862 000
Cost of sales	622 000	580 000
Other expenses	223 000	162 000
	845 000	742 000
Profit before tax	140 000	120 000
Income tax expense	30 000	40 000
Profit	110 000	80 000
Retained earnings (1/7/09)	80 000	60 000
Transfer from asset revaluation reserve		28 000
	190 000	168 000
Transfer to general reserve		15 000
Dividend paid	20 000	15 000
Dividend declared	25 000	20 000
	45 000	50 000
Retained earnings (30/6/10)	$145 000	$118 000

Additional information

(a) In the 2008–09 period, Sion Ltd transferred $10 000 from the general reserve to retained earnings. No other transfers to or from reserves took place in that period. In the 2009–10 period, the transfer from asset revaluation reserve is as a result of Sion Ltd's selling of the land on hand at 1 July 2008. The transfer to general reserve is from post-acquisition profits. The balance of Sion Ltd's asset revaluation reserve at 1 July 2009 was $50 000, with an increase of $5000 recognised at 30 June 2010.

(b) During the 2008–09 period, Sion Ltd sold some inventory to Aigle Ltd for $8000. This had originally cost Sion Ltd $6000. At 30 June 2009, 10% of these goods remained unsold by Aigle Ltd.

(c) The ending inventory of Aigle Ltd included inventory sold to it by Sion Ltd at a profit of $3000 before tax. This had cost Sion Ltd $32 000.

(d) On 1 January 2009, Sion Ltd sold an item of inventory to Aigle Ltd for $50 000. This had originally cost Sion Ltd $40 000. Aigle Ltd uses the item as a non-current asset (plant) and depreciates it on a straight-line basis over a 5-year period.

(e) The tax rate is 30%.

Required

1. Prepare the consolidation worksheet entries for the preparation of the consolidated financial statements of Aigle Ltd at 30 June 2010.
2. Prepare the consolidated statement of comprehensive income and statement of changes in equity at 30 June 2010.

Problem 24.4 ★★★

CONSOLIDATION WORKSHEET, CONSOLIDATED FINANCIAL STATEMENTS, FULL GOODWILL METHOD

Financial information at 30 June 2010 of Thalwil Ltd and its subsidiary company, Payerne Ltd included that shown on the next page.

At 1 July 2007, the date Thalwil Ltd acquired its 80% shareholding in Payerne Ltd, all the identifiable assets and liabilities of Payerne Ltd were at fair value except for the following assets:

	Carrying amount	Fair value
Plant (cost $75 000)	$50 000	$55 000
Land	30 000	38 000

The plant has an expected life of 10 years, with benefits being received evenly over that period. Differences between carrying amounts and fair values are adjusted on consolidation. The land on hand at 1 July 2007 was sold on 1 February 2008 for $40 000. Any valuation reserve in relation to the land is transferred on consolidation to retained earnings.

Thalwil Ltd uses the full goodwill method. The fair value of the non-controlling interest at 1 July 2007 was $31 500.

Additional information

(a) At the acquisition date of 80% of its issued shares by Thalwil Ltd, the equity of Payerne Ltd was:

Share capital (100 000 shares)	$100 000
General reserve	3 000
Retained earnings	37 000

(b) Inventory on hand of Payerne Ltd at 1 July 2009 included a quantity priced at $10 000 that had been sold to Payerne Ltd by its parent. This inventory had cost Thalwil Ltd $7500. It was all sold by Payerne Ltd during the year.

	Thalwil Ltd	Payerne Ltd
Sales revenue	$316 000	$220 000
Other revenue:		
Debenture interest	5 000	—
Management and consulting fees	5 000	—
Dividend from Payerne Ltd	12 000	—
Total revenues	338 000	220 000
Cost of sales	130 000	85 000
Manufacturing expenses	90 000	60 000
Depreciation on plant	15 000	15 000
Administrative	15 000	8 000
Financial	11 000	5 000
Other expenses	14 000	12 000
Total expenses	275 000	185 000
Profit before tax	63 000	35 000
Income tax expense	25 000	17 000
Profit	38 000	18 000
Retained earnings (1/7/09)	50 000	45 000
	88 000	63 000
Transfer to general reserve	3 000	—
Interim dividend paid	10 000	10 000
Final dividend declared	10 000	5 000
	23 000	15 000
Retained earnings (30/6/10)	65 000	48 000
General reserve	50 000	10 000
Other components of equity	13 000	10 000
Share capital	300 000	100 000
Debentures	200 000	100 000
Current tax liability	25 000	17 000
Dividend payable	10 000	5 000
Deferred tax liability	—	7 000
Other liabilities	90 000	12 000
	$753 000	$309 000
Financial assets	$ 50 000	$ 60 000
Debentures in Payerne Ltd	100 000	—

	Thalwil Ltd	Payerne Ltd
Shares in Payerne Ltd	131 600	—
Plant (cost)	120 000	102 000
Accumulated depreciation – plant	(65 000)	(55 000)
Other depreciable assets	76 000	55 000
Accumulated depreciation	(40 000)	(25 000)
Inventory	90 000	85 000
Deferred tax asset	85 400	30 000
Land	201 000	57 000
Dividend receivable	4 000	—
	$753 000	$309 000

(c) In Thalwil Ltd's inventory at 30 June 2008 were various items sold to it by Payerne Ltd at $5000 above cost.
(d) During the year, intragroup sales by Payerne Ltd to Thalwil Ltd were $60 000.
(e) It was also learned that Payerne Ltd had sold to Thalwil Ltd an item from its inventory for $20 000 on 1 January 2009. Thalwil Ltd had treated this item as an addition to its plant and machinery. The item was put into service as soon as received by Thalwil Ltd and depreciation charged at 20% p.a. The item had been fully imported by Payerne Ltd at a landed cost of $15 000.
(f) Management and consulting fees derived by Thalwil Ltd were all from Payerne Ltd and represented charges made for administration $2200 and technical services $2800. The latter were charged by Payerne Ltd to manufacturing expenses.
(g) All debentures issued by Payerne Ltd are held by Thalwil Ltd.
(h) Other components of equity relate to movements in the fair values of the available-for-sale financial assets. The balance of this account at 1 July 2009 was $10 000 (Thalwil Ltd) and $8000 (Payerne Ltd).
(i) The tax rate is 30%.

Required

Prepare the consolidated financial statements for Thalwil Ltd and its subsidiary, Payerne Ltd, for the year ended 30 June 2010.

DUBLIN BUSINESS SCHOOL
LIBRARY

25 Consolidation: indirect ownership interests

ACCOUNTING STANDARDS IN FOCUS

IAS 27 *Consolidated and Separate Financial Statements*

LEARNING OBJECTIVES

When you have studied this chapter, you should be able to:

- explain the difference between direct non-controlling interest (DNCI) and indirect non-controlling interest (INCI)
- calculate the NCI share of equity in a sequential acquisition situation
- explain the effects on the consolidation process where the acquisition is non-sequential
- explain the nature of reciprocal ownership between subsidiaries.

In chapter 24, the group under discussion consisted of two companies in which the parent had a partial interest in the subsidiary. Hence, in the subsidiary, there were two ownership interests: the parent and the non-controlling interest (NCI). In this chapter there are two different forms of group discussed. First, the parent may have an interest in a subsidiary that has an interest in a subsidiary of its own. This form of structure gives rise to two types of NCI: a direct non-controlling interest (DNCI) and an indirect non-controlling interest (INCI). The existence of these two types of NCI affects the consolidation process, particularly in the calculation of the NCI share of equity.

The second structure discussed in this chapter is where a parent and a subsidiary have ownership interests in each other, or where subsidiaries have ownership interests in each other. These are referred to as reciprocal ownerships. Because of the crossholdings, the calculation of the NCI share of equity is a more involved process.

25.1 DIRECT AND INDIRECT NON-CONTROLLING INTEREST

One feature of multiple subsidiary structures where a parent has an interest in a subsidiary that is itself a parent of another subsidiary is the need to classify the NCI ownership in the subsidiaries into direct non-controlling interest (DNCI) and indirect non-controlling interest (INCI). Consider the group in figure 25.1.

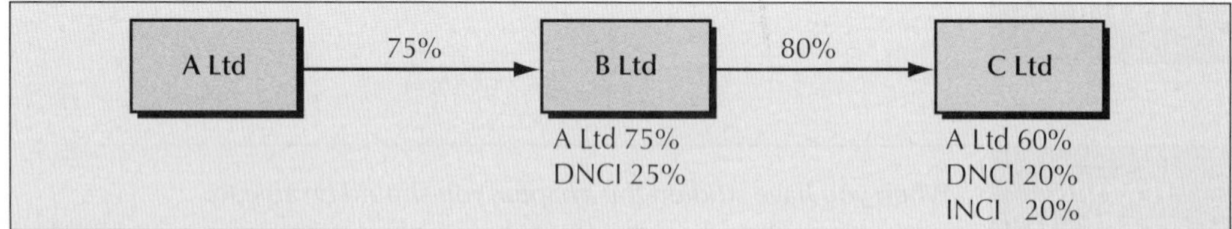

FIGURE 25.1 Group with both INCI and DNCI

In relation to B Ltd, the NCI has a direct ownership in this entity. Hence, the NCI of 25% is classified as a DNCI. In relation to C Ltd, because B Ltd owns 80% of C Ltd, there is a DNCI of 20% (i.e. an NCI that holds shares directly in C Ltd). B Ltd owns 80% of C Ltd, but B Ltd has two owners: A Ltd (75%) and the DNCI (25%). Hence, A Ltd owns 60% of C Ltd, being 75% × 80%, and the DNCI in B Ltd owns 20% of C Ltd, being 25% × 80%. The DNCI in B Ltd's ownership in C Ltd is referred to as an INCI in C Ltd because the DNCI in B Ltd does not directly own shares in C Ltd; its ownership in C Ltd is indirectly via B Ltd. It is important to note that the INCI in C Ltd is the same party as the DNCI in B Ltd.

Figure 25.2 provides another example of the existence of an INCI.

Note that, in figure 25.2, if A Ltd's ownership in B Ltd was changed to 100%, there would be no INCI in C Ltd. For an INCI to exist there has to be a DNCI in the immediate parent of that entity.

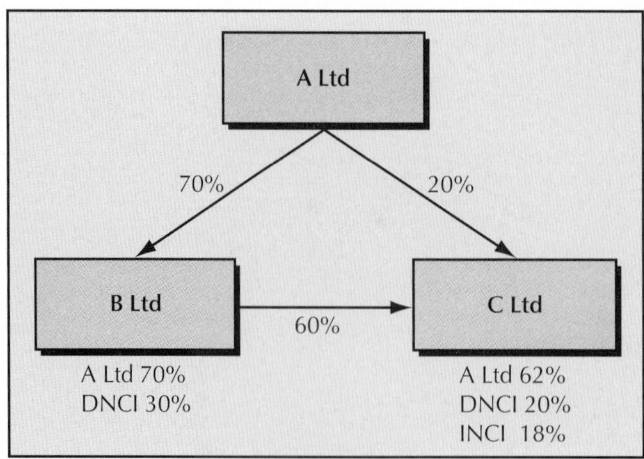

FIGURE 25.2 Indirect and direct NCI

25.2 SEQUENTIAL ACQUISITIONS

In accounting for multiple subsidiary structures, such as in figure 25.1 where A Ltd holds shares in B Ltd which holds shares in C Ltd, the accounting treatment depends on the sequence in which the acquisitions occurred. In this chapter, a sequential acquisition is one where A Ltd acquires its shares in B Ltd before B Ltd acquires its shares in C Ltd, or both acquisitions occur on the same date. A non-sequential acquisition is one where B Ltd acquires its shares in C Ltd before A Ltd acquires its shares in B Ltd. As is discussed in more detail in section 25.3, the problem with a non-sequential acquisition is that when A Ltd acquires its shares in B Ltd, one of the assets of B Ltd is 'Shares in C Ltd'; that is, the fair value of B Ltd is affected by the fair value of C Ltd.

In dealing with sequential acquisitions, what differences arise in preparing consolidated financial statements for a multiple acquisition subsidiary structure such as in figure 25.3?

FIGURE 25.3 Group with both INCI and DNCI

The steps involved in preparing the consolidation worksheet are essentially the same as outlined in previous chapters; the main difference is that there are two business combinations rather than one. The combining of P Ltd and A Ltd and the combining of A Ltd and B Ltd are analysed in exactly the same fashion as for any two-entity combination because the combination involves the two companies in the transaction. It does not matter which of the two combinations is analysed first. Hence:

- the acquisition analysis, business combination valuation entries and pre-acquisition entries for P Ltd's acquisition of A Ltd are unchanged from those demonstrated in previous chapters
- the acquisition analysis, business combination valuation entries and pre-acquisition entries for A Ltd's acquisition of B Ltd are unchanged from those demonstrated in previous chapters.

The accounting for intragroup transactions does not change from that discussed in chapter 23. If the transactions are within the group, the effects of these transactions must be adjusted for in full. This is regardless of whether B Ltd sells to P Ltd, or A Ltd sells to B Ltd or any other combination of entities is involved. The only area where a difference occurs is with dividends, and this is discussed in section 25.2.3.

The major area of difference when multiple subsidiaries are involved is the calculation of the NCI share of equity.

25.2.1 Calculation of the NCI share of equity

The difference in accounting for the NCI arises because of the existence of both a DNCI and an INCI. The basic rules are as follows:

- *Direct NCI* receives a proportionate share of all equity recorded by the subsidiary — these equity balances include both *pre-acquisition* and *post-acquisition* amounts.
- *Indirect NCI* receives a proportionate share of a subsidiary's *post-acquisition* equity only.
- In calculating the NCI share of equity, it is consolidated equity rather than recorded equity on which the NCI is calculated. Hence, in calculating both the DNCI and INCI share of equity, adjustments must be made to eliminate any unrealised profits/losses arising from transactions within the group.

The calculation of the DNCI share of equity is therefore the same as the calculation of NCI illustrated in chapter 24. The extra adjustments have to be made for the INCI as it receives a share of post-acquisition equity only. First, however, why is the INCI limited to a share of post-acquisition equity only? Consider the group of P Ltd in figure 25.4.

In analysing why the INCI receives a share of post-acquisition equity only, it is important to remember that an INCI arises only when a partly owned subsidiary holds shares in another subsidiary. In figure 25.4, the INCI arises in B Ltd only because there exists a DNCI in A Ltd. The DNCI in A Ltd is the same group of shareholders as the INCI in B Ltd.

The DNCI in A Ltd is entitled to a share of the net assets of A Ltd. This share is calculated as a 30% share of the equity of A Ltd. However, one of the assets of A Ltd is the investment Shares in B Ltd, which reflects the right of A Ltd to 60% of the net assets of B Ltd. Because the INCI in B Ltd is the same party as the DNCI in A Ltd, it would be double counting to give the INCI a share of the equity of B Ltd relating to the pre-acquisition assets of B Ltd. The double-counting issue arises because the investment, Shares in B Ltd, reflects the pre-acquisition equity and assets of B Ltd. When B Ltd earns post-acquisition equity, represented by post-acquisition assets, this equity is not reflected in A Ltd because the investment account, Shares in B Ltd, is recorded at cost. Hence, the double-counting issue does not arise in relation to B Ltd's post-acquisition equity, and the INCI is given a share of the post-acquisition equity of B Ltd.

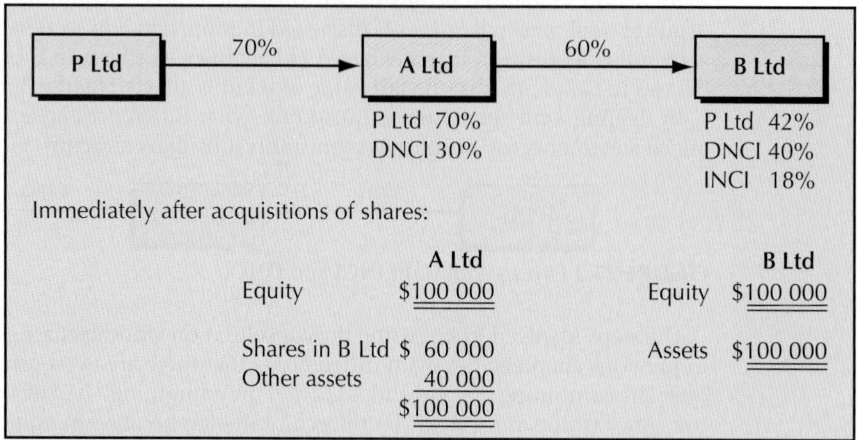

FIGURE 25.4 Group with both INCI and DNCI

In relation to the pre-acquisition equity of B Ltd, it can be seen that 60% is eliminated in the pre-acquisition entry for A Ltd's acquisition of B Ltd and the DNCI in B Ltd is given a 40% direct share. This effectively allocates all the pre-acquisition equity of B Ltd — there is none left for the INCI. This is not a problem because, as explained above, the INCI is entitled to a share of post-acquisition equity only.

As explained in previous chapters, where assets are recorded at amounts that differ from fair value, these affect *pre-acquisition* equity. In other words, as goodwill is impaired, inventory sold or non-current assets depreciated, there is an adjustment made to the balance of pre-acquisition amounts via the business combination valuation entries. As the INCI receives a share of post-acquisition equity only, the adjustment to pre-acquisition equity reflected through the pre-acquisition entry must be considered when calculating the INCI share of equity.

As explained in chapter 24, IFRS 3 allows a choice between the full goodwill and the partial goodwill methods. This choice has no effect on post-acquisition equity. Hence, the calculation of the INCI share of equity is unaffected by which goodwill method is used. *In this chapter, the partial goodwill method is used in all examples.*

As explained in chapter 24, the calculation of the NCI share of equity takes place in three steps:

- share of equity at acquisition date
- share of changes in equity from acquisition date to the beginning of the current period
- share of changes in equity in the current period.

There are only *two steps* in calculating the INCI share of equity. Since, by definition, all the equity on hand at acquisition date is *pre-acquisition*, the INCI does not receive a share of equity at that date.

ILLUSTRATIVE EXAMPLE 25.1

Calculation of the NCI share of equity

Using the example in figure 25.4, assume A Ltd pays $55 200 for its 60% interest in B Ltd when the equity of B Ltd at 1 July 2007 is:

Share capital	$40 000
General reserve	30 000
Retained earnings	15 000

All identifiable assets and liabilities of B Ltd are recorded at fair value except for the following:

	Carrying amount	Fair value
Plant	$50 000	$55 000
Inventory	20 000	25 000

The plant is expected to last a further 5 years. Of the inventory, 90% is sold by 30 June 2008 and it is all sold by 30 June 2009. The tax rate is 30%.

For the accounting period ending 30 June 2009, the profit is $10 000, and the balance of retained earnings (1/7/08) is $24 000.

Required

Prepare the consolidation worksheet entries relating to A Ltd's acquisition of B Ltd, including the NCI entries relating to B Ltd, required for the preparation of the consolidated financial statements at 30 June 2009.

Solution

Acquisition analysis

At 1 July 2007:

Net fair value of identifiable assets and liabilities of B Ltd	= $40 000 (capital) + $30 000 (general reserve)
	+ $15 000 (retained earnings)
	+ $5 000(1 – 0.3) (BCVR – plant)
	+ $5 000(1 – 0.3) (BCVR – inventory)
	= $92 000
Net fair value acquired by A Ltd	= 60% × $92 000
	= $55 200
Consideration transferred	= $55 200
Goodwill/excess	= zero

The consolidation worksheet entries at *30 June 2009* are:

(1) *Business combination valuation entries*

Plant	Dr	5 000	
Deferred Tax Liability	Cr		1 500
Business Combination Valuation Reserve	Cr		3 500
Depreciation Expense	Dr	1 000	
Retained Earnings (1/7/08)	Dr	1 000	
Accumulated Depreciation	Cr		2 000
(20% × $5 000 p.a.)			
Deferred Tax Liability	Dr	600	
Income Tax Expense	Cr		300
Retained Earnings (1/7/08)	Cr		300
Cost of Sales	Dr	500	
Income Tax Expense	Cr		150
Transfer from Business Combination Valuation Reserve	Cr		350

(2) *Pre-acquisition entries*

At 1 July 2007:

Retained Earnings (1/7/07)	Dr	9 000	
Share Capital	Dr	24 000	
General Reserve	Dr	18 000	

Business Combination Valuation Reserve	Dr	4 200	
Shares in B Ltd	Cr		55 200
(60% of equity balances)			

At 30 June 2009, the inventory has been all sold, resulting in a transfer of valuation reserve to retained earnings.

Retained Earnings (1/7/08)*	Dr	10 890	
Share Capital	Dr	24 000	
General Reserve	Dr	18 000	
Business Combination Valuation Reserve**	Dr	2 310	
Shares in B Ltd	Cr		55 200
*$10 890 = 60% × [$15 000 + 90% ($5000 – $1500) (inventory sold in previous period)]			
**$2310 = $4200 – 60%[90% ($5000 – $1500)]			
Transfer from Business Combination Valuation Reserve	Dr	210	
Business Combination Valuation Reserve	Cr		210
(60% × $350)			

(3) *NCI share of equity at acquisition date, 1 July 2007 (step 1)*
The DNCI receives a share of the equity on hand at acquisition date. Since this equity is pre-acquisition, the INCI does not receive a share. The entry in the NCI columns is:

Retained Earnings (1/7/08)	Dr	6 000	
Share Capital	Dr	16 000	
General Reserve	Dr	12 000	
Business Combination Valuation Reserve*	Dr	2 800	
NCI	Cr		36 800
(40% of balances)			
*$2800 = 40% of BCVR of $7000 at acquisition date			

(4) *NCI share of changes in equity from 1 July 2007 to 30 June 2008 (step 2)*
DNCI share:
The DNCI of 40% in B Ltd is entitled to a share of the change in equity from 1 July 2007 to 30 June 2008. The *retained earnings* balance has changed from $15 000 at acquisition date to $24 000 at 30 June 2008. To avoid double counting the NCI share of equity, an adjustment must be made for the depreciation of plant as evidenced in the valuation entry. The entry in the NCI columns of the worksheet is:

Retained Earnings (1/7/08)	Dr	3 320	
NCI	Cr		3 320
(40% × [$24 000 – $15 000 – ($1000 – $300)])			

The DNCI is also affected by the transfer on consolidation of $3150 from the business combination valuation reserve on sale of 90% of the inventory. The entry is:

NCI	Dr	1 260	
Business Combination Valuation Reserve	Cr		1 260
(40% × 90% × $3500)			

INCI share:
The INCI of 18% in B Ltd is entitled to a share of post-acquisition changes in equity over this period.

The retained earnings balance of $24 000 at 30 June 2008 contains three items relating to pre-acquisition equity:

- the $15 000 balance on hand at acquisition date
- there has been a $3150 transfer from business combination valuation reserve relating to the 90% of inventory sold
- there has been a $700 after-tax depreciation charge in relation to the plant.

In relation to the first two of these items, the effect can be read from an analysis of the pre-acquisition entry at 30 June 2009. In this entry, there is a debit adjustment to retained earnings (1/7/08) of $10 890. This amount reflects 60% (the parent's share) of the pre-acquisition subsidiary balance at 1 July 2008. The total balance of B Ltd's pre-acquisition retained earnings is then $10 890/0.6, that is, $18 150.

The post-acquisition equity in the retained earnings (1/7/08) balance is:

$$\$24\,000 - \frac{\$10\,890}{0.6} - (\$1\,000 - \$300) = \$5\,150$$

The INCI share of this is $927, being 18% × $5150. The worksheet entry at 30 June 2009 in the NCI columns is:

Retained Earnings (1/7/08)	Dr	927	
NCI	Cr		927

There is no need for any entry relating to the business combination valuation reserve. First, this is pre-acquisition equity and, second, the effects of the transfer have been taken into consideration in the grossing-up process with retained earnings.

(5) *NCI share of equity from 1 July 2008 to 30 June 2009 (step 3)*
During this period, B Ltd records a profit of $10 000.

DNCI share:
The DNCI share of profit is adjusted for the effects of the depreciation on plant and the sale of the rest of the inventory, as evidenced in the valuation entry. The entry in the NCI columns of the worksheet is:

NCI Share of Profit	Dr	3 580	
NCI	Cr		3 580
(40% × [$10 000 – ($1000 – $300) – ($500 – $150)])			

Besides the increase in equity caused by the earning of profit, the equity of B Ltd in the current period is affected by the transfer from business combination valuation reserve to retained earnings of $350 as a result of the sale of inventory that was on hand at acquisition date. This equity change is a movement within pre-acquisition equity and therefore affects only the DNCI, not the INCI. The entry in the NCI columns of the worksheet is:

Transfer from Business Combination Valuation Reserve	Dr	140	
Business Combination Valuation Reserve	Cr		140
(40% × $350)			

INCI share:

In the pre-acquisition entry at 30 June 2009, there are no adjustments to current period profit, indicating that there are no items affecting pre-acquisition equity that require an adjustment in the calculation of the INCI share of current period profit. However, as with the DNCI calculation, an adjustment must be made for the depreciation on the plant and the sale of the remaining inventory. The entry in the NCI columns is:

NCI Share of Profit	Dr	1 611	
NCI	Cr		1 611
(18% × [$10 000 – ($1000 – $300) – ($500 – $150)])			

25.2.2 The effects of intragroup transactions on the calculation of the NCI

As noted earlier, the adjustments for the effects of transactions within the group in structures such as in figure 25.5 are the same as those for the two-company structure illustrated in chapter 24. The effects of the transactions must be adjusted in full regardless of the amount of NCI existing in any entity.

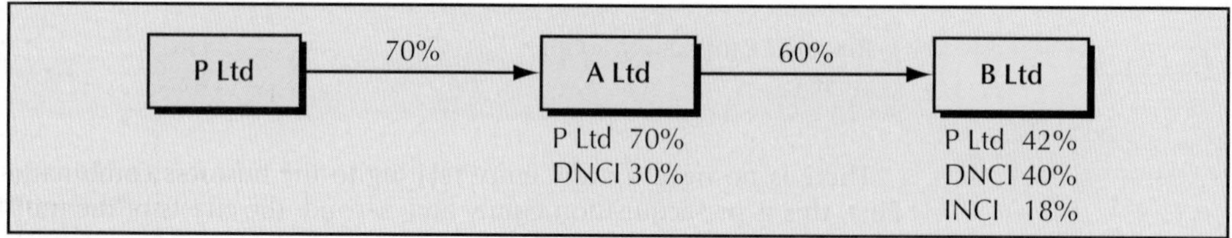

FIGURE 25.5 Group with both INCI and DNCI

What must be considered is the effect on the NCI of such adjustments. The key to this is determining which entity recorded the profit on the transaction. Using the structure in figure 25.5:

- if A Ltd earned the profit/loss — whether by selling to P Ltd or B Ltd — the NCI adjustment is based on the 30% DNCI in A Ltd
- if B Ltd made the profit/loss — whether by selling to P Ltd or A Ltd — the NCI adjustment is based on the total NCI in B Ltd of 58%, i.e. the sum of the 40% DNCI and 18% INCI.

To illustrate, assume that during the current period B Ltd sold $25 000 worth of inventory to P Ltd at a profit before tax of $5000. The inventory is still on hand at the end of the current year. The consolidation worksheet entries are:

Sale of inventory: B Ltd to P Ltd

Sales	Dr	25 000	
Cost of Sales	Cr		20 000
Inventory	Cr		5 000
Deferred Tax Asset	Dr	1 500	
Income Tax Expense	Cr		1 500

Adjustment to NCI in B Ltd

NCI	Dr	2 030	
NCI Share of Profit	Cr		2 030
([40% + 18%] × [$5000 – $1500])			

Where items of property, plant and equipment are transferred within the group, the effects of the existence of an INCI must be taken into account. For example, assume B Ltd at the beginning of the previous year sold plant to A Ltd for $800 000 at a profit before tax of $20 000, with the asset having an expected life of 5 years. The consolidation worksheet entries are:

Transfer of plant: B Ltd to A Ltd

Retained Earnings (opening balance)	Dr	14 000	
Deferred Tax Asset	Dr	6 000	
Plant	Cr		20 000

Adjustment to NCI

NCI	Dr	8120	
Retained Earnings (opening balance)	Cr		8120
([40% + 18%] × $14 000)			

Depreciation of plant

Accumulated Depreciation	Dr	8000	
Depreciation Expense	Cr		4000
Retained Earnings (opening balance)	Cr		4000
(Depreciation of 20% × $20 000 p.a.)			
Income Tax Expense	Dr	1200	
Retained Earnings (opening balance)	Dr	1200	
Deferred Tax Asset	Cr		2400

Adjustment to NCI in B Ltd

Retained Earnings (opening balance)	Dr	1624	
NCI Share of Profit	Dr	1624	
NCI	Cr		3248
([40% + 18%] × $2800 = $1624)			

25.2.3 Dividends

As explained in the calculation of NCI in chapter 24, in calculating the DNCI share of retained earnings, the DNCI is given a share of current period's profits and opening balance of retained earnings adjusted by a share of dividends paid and declared, and transfers to and from reserves. The INCI is allocated a share of the current period's post-acquisition profits, opening balance of post-acquisition retained earnings, and transfers to and from post-acquisition reserves. The INCI share of these balances is not reduced via allocation of dividend paid or declared. In this regard, consider the following consolidation worksheet in relation to dividends paid by B Ltd (using the structure in figure 25.5). An extract from the worksheet shows that the adjustment for the intragroup transaction and the allocation to the 40% DNCI in B Ltd eliminates the total balance of the dividend paid:

				Adjustments		Non-controlling interest		
Financial statements	**P Ltd**	**A Ltd**	**B Ltd**	**Dr**	**Cr**	**Dr**	**Cr**	**Consolidation**
Dividend paid	—	—	2000		1200		800	—

No dividend is paid directly to the INCI. The INCI in B Ltd receives its share through the DNCI in A Ltd receiving a share of the profit of A Ltd, which includes dividend revenue from B Ltd. When the DNCI in A Ltd receives a share of the profit of A Ltd, it receives a share of the profit of B Ltd because the dividend paid by B Ltd is a distribution of B Ltd's profit. This raises a problem of double counting, because the INCI of B Ltd, which receives a share of the profit of B Ltd, is the same party as the DNCI in A Ltd, which receives a share of the profit of B Ltd via the dividend revenue from B Ltd included in the profit of A Ltd. This problem does not arise in a two-entity situation, because any dividend paid by the subsidiary is paid to the parent of the group. With multiple subsidiaries, the problem arises when a dividend paid or declared by one subsidiary is recognised as revenue by another subsidiary, both of which contain an NCI.

The group in figure 25.5 is used to discuss the effects on the NCI of dividends paid or declared by a subsidiary whose ownership includes an INCI.

The changes in retained earnings for the period ended 30 June 2009 are:

	P Ltd	A Ltd	B Ltd
Profit for the period	$ 40 000	$28 000	$10 000
Retained earnings (opening balance)	90 000	25 000	24 000
	130 000	53 000	34 000
Dividend paid	10 000	3 000	2 000
Dividend declared	10 000	5 000	3 000
Transfer to reserves	10 000	5 000	6 000
	30 000	13 000	11 000
Retained earnings (closing balance)	$100 000	$40 000	$23 000

The DNCI of 30% in A Ltd and the DNCI of 40% in B Ltd receive their share of all equity accounts within their respective entities:

	DNCI — A Ltd 30%	DNCI — B Ltd 40%
Profit for the period	$ 8 400	$ 4 000
Retained earnings (opening balance)	7 500	9 600
	15 900	13 600
Dividend paid	900	800
Dividend declared	1 500	1 200
Transfer to reserves	1 500	2 400
	3 900	4 400
Retained earnings (closing balance)	$12 000	$ 9 200

Dividend paid in the current period

In the group illustrated in figure 25.5, the profit of A Ltd includes $1200 dividend revenue (60% × $2000), that is, A Ltd's share of the dividend paid by B Ltd from its current profit. The issue here is that, if the INCI in B Ltd is allocated a share of the profit of B Ltd and the DNCI in A Ltd is allocated a share of the profit of A Ltd (which includes the dividend revenue from B Ltd), then, because the DNCI and the INCI are the same party, the calculation of the NCI share of equity involves double counting. As noted above, in calculating the INCI share of B Ltd's equity, the INCI is not given a share of the dividend paid, which means there is no reduction in the INCI share of B Ltd's equity.

In calculating the NCI share of equity, it is necessary to make an adjustment to eliminate the double counting. This could be done by adjusting the INCI of B Ltd's equity or the DNCI share of A Ltd's equity, since the problem is caused by the fact that A Ltd has recognised some of B Ltd's profit via dividend revenue. In this book, the adjustment is made to the DNCI share of A Ltd's equity in step 3 of the calculation of the NCI share of equity, that is, in calculating the NCI share of changes in equity in the current period. Hence, when making the adjustment for the

$2000 dividend paid from B Ltd to A Ltd, there are two consolidation worksheet entries, the first adjusting for intragroup transactions and the second in step 3 of the calculation of NCI:

Dividend paid by B Ltd

Dividend Revenue	Dr	1 200	
Dividend Paid	Cr		1 200
(60% × $2000)			

Step 3: NCI calculation for A Ltd

NCI	Dr	800	
Dividend Paid	Cr		800
(40% × $2000)			
NCI	Dr	360	
NCI Share of Profit	Cr		360
(Reduction of the DNCI share of profit in A Ltd since the latter includes the dividend from B Ltd: 30% × $1200)			

Dividend declared

B Ltd has declared a $3000 dividend but not paid it by the end of the period. A Ltd will still recognise 60% of this, $1800, as dividend revenue. Hence, the same double-counting problem that arose with dividend paid also arises with dividend declared. An extra entry to overcome the double counting is again required. The consolidation worksheet entries are:

Dividend declared by B Ltd

Dividend Payable	Dr	1 800	
Dividend Declared	Cr		1 800
(60% × $3000)			
Dividend Revenue	Dr	1 800	
Dividend Receivable	Cr		1 800

Step 3: NCI calculation for A Ltd

NCI	Dr	1 200	
Dividend Paid	Cr		1 200
(40% × $3000)			
NCI	Dr	540	
NCI Share of Profit	Cr		540
(30% × $1800)			

25.3 NON-SEQUENTIAL ACQUISITIONS

Consider the group in figure 25.6 in which Y Ltd is a subsidiary of X Ltd and Z Ltd is a subsidiary of Y Ltd:

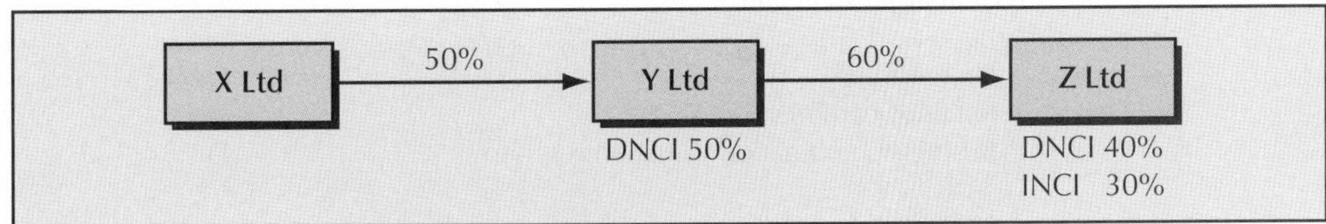

FIGURE 25.6 Group with both INCI and DNCI

The sequence in which the two acquisitions occurred was:

1 July 2008: Y Ltd acquired its interest in Z Ltd
1 July 2009: X Ltd acquired its interest in Y Ltd

The problem that the non-sequential acquisition causes is that, in relation to X Ltd's acquisition of Y Ltd, one of the assets of Y Ltd is Shares in Z Ltd. At the date of X Ltd's acquisition in Y Ltd, the fair value of the investment Shares in Z Ltd will have increased owing to the increased worth of Z Ltd. In other words, when X Ltd considers the fair value of the consideration to pay for shares in Y Ltd, it considers not only the value of Y Ltd but also the value of Z Ltd. The fair value of Y Ltd's investment in Z Ltd related to the increased wealth of Z Ltd between 1 July 2008 and 1 July 2009.

Assume Y Ltd acquired its 60% interest in Z Ltd on 1 July 2008 for \$420 when the financial position of Z Ltd was:

	Carrying amount	Fair value
Share capital	\$300	
Retained earnings	230	
	\$530	
Land	\$200	\$300
Other assets	330	330
	\$530	

The acquisition analysis of Y Ltd's acquisition of Z Ltd is then:

Net fair value of Z Ltd	= \$300 + \$230 + \$100(1 – 30%) (BCVR – land)
	= \$600
Net fair value acquired	= 60% × \$600
	= \$360
Consideration transferred	= \$420
Goodwill acquired	= \$60

The worksheet entries at acquisition date, 1 July 2008, for this acquisition are:

Business combination valuation entry — Z Ltd

Land	Dr	100	
Deferred tax liability	Cr		30
Business combination valuation reserve	Cr		70

Pre-acquisition entry

Share capital [60% × \$300]	Dr	180	
Retained earnings [60% × \$230]	Dr	138	
Business combination valuation reserve [60% × \$70]	Dr	42	
Goodwill	Dr	60	
Shares in Z Ltd	Cr		420

NCI at acquisition date

Share capital	Dr	120	
Retained earnings	Dr	92	
Business combination valuation reserve	Dr	28	
NCI	Cr		240
(40% of balances)			

On 1 July 2009, X Ltd acquires 50% of the shareholding in Y Ltd for $650 when the financial positions of Y Ltd and Z Ltd are:

Y Ltd			Z Ltd		
	Carrying amount	Fair value		Carrying amount	Fair value
Share capital	$500		Share capital	$300	
Retained earnings	600		Retained earnings	300	
Business combination valuation reserve*		$120	Business combination valuation reserve*		$140
			Liabilities*		60
Shares in Z Ltd	$420	$540	Land	$200	400
Other assets	680	680	Other assets	400	400

*These relate to the valuation of the assets, with the valuation of the land being tax-effected.

Hence, in relation to Z Ltd at 1 July 2009:

- retained earnings has increased by $70 (i.e. from $230 to $300)
- land has increased its fair value by $100 (i.e. from $300 to $400).

Worksheet entries at 1 July 2009:
Because X Ltd acquires the group consisting of Y Ltd and Z Ltd, the assets of both Y Ltd and Z Ltd are revalued at 1 July 2009.

(1) *Business combination valuation entries — Z Ltd*

Land	Dr	100	
Deferred Tax Liability	Cr		30
Business Combination Valuation Reserve	Cr		70
Land	Dr	100	
Deferred Tax Liability	Cr		30
Business Combination Valuation Reserve	Cr		70

It is useful to raise the increases in valuation separately as the NCI has to be increased by these amounts. In subsequent periods, the entries may be combined.

(2) *Pre-acquisition entry at 1 July 2009: Y Ltd and Z Ltd*
There is no change from the entry at 1 July 2008:

Share Capital [60% × $300]	Dr	180	
Retained Earnings [60% × $230]	Dr	138	
Business Combination Valuation Reserve [60% × $70]	Dr	42	
Goodwill	Dr	60	
Shares in Z Ltd	Cr		420

(3) *40% DNCI at acquisition date*
There is no change from the entry at 1 July 2008:

Share Capital	Dr	120	
Retained Earnings	Dr	92	
Business Combination Valuation Reserve	Dr	28	
NCI	Cr		240
(40% of balances)			

(4) *40% DNCI share of equity from 1 July 2008 to 1 July 2009*

Retained Earnings	Dr	28	
NCI	Cr		28
(40% × $70)			
Business Combination Valuation Reserve	Dr	28	
NCI	Cr		28
(40% × $70 land)			

The INCI of 30% receives no amount at this stage because there are no post-acquisition profits in Z Ltd. The NCI in Y Ltd (which is the same party as the INCI in Z Ltd) receives a share of the business combination valuation reserves in Y Ltd at 1 July 2009, which reflects any increase in Z Ltd's wealth between 1 July 2008 and 1 July 2009. Hence, post-acquisition equity, to which the INCI in Z Ltd is entitled to a share, occurs only after 1 July 2009.

(5) *Business combination valuation entries — Y Ltd at 1 July 2009*

Shares in Z Ltd	Dr	120	
Business Combination Valuation Reserve	Cr		120
($540 – $420)			

Note that only $420 is eliminated in the pre-acquisition entry for Y Ltd to Z Ltd. This is based on the following acquisition analysis for X Ltd and Y Ltd:

Net fair value of Y Ltd	= $500 + $600 + $120 (BCVR – Shares in Z Ltd)
	= $1220
Net fair value acquired by X Ltd	= 50% × $1220
	= $610
Consideration transferred	= $650
Goodwill acquired	= $40

(6) *Pre-acquisition entry: X Ltd and Y Ltd*

Share Capital	Dr	250	
Retained Earnings	Dr	300	
Business Combination Valuation Reserve	Dr	60	
Goodwill	Dr	40	
Shares in Y Ltd	Cr		650
Retained Earnings [60% × $70]	Dr	42	
Business Combination Valuation Reserve [60% × $70]	Dr	42	
Goodwill*	Dr	36	
Shares in Z Ltd	Cr		120

*This reflects Y Ltd's share of the extra goodwill in Z Ltd between 1 July 2005 and 1 July 2009. The goodwill of Z Ltd is not revalued at 1 July 2009; hence, there is no share of equity recognised as occurs with assets such as land.

The last entry above eliminates the extra worth in Z Ltd, which is reflected in the revaluation of Shares in Z Ltd in the accounts of Y Ltd. The whole of the fair value of this account is now eliminated on consolidation. In future worksheets this entry should be included in the valuation entries for Z Ltd because any changes in land (sale or impairment) may affect the nature of the equity accounts associated with Z Ltd.

(7) *50% DNCI in Y Ltd*

Share Capital	Dr	250	
Retained Earnings	Dr	300	
Business Combination Valuation Reserve [50% × $120]	Dr	60	
NCI	Cr		610

The consolidation worksheet at 1 July 2009 is shown in figure 25.7. For retained earnings, share capital and the business combination valuation reserve, the consolidation amounts are those for X Ltd (i.e. there are no post-acquisition subsidiary amounts in these accounts attributable to the parent).

Financial statements	X Ltd	Y Ltd	Z Ltd	Adjustments				Non-controlling interest				Consolidation
					Dr		Cr		Dr		Cr	
Retained earnings	800	600	300	*2*	138			*3*	92			800
				6	300			*4*	28			
				6	42			*7*	300			
Share capital	900	500	300	*2*	180			*3*	120			900
				6	250			*7*	250			
Business combination valuation reserve	—	—	—	*2*	42	*1*	70	*3*	28			—
				6	60	*1*	70	*4*	28			
				6	42	*5*	120	*7*	60			
Liabilities	—	—	—			*1*	30					60
						1	30					
NCI										*3*	240	906
										4	28	
										4	28	
										7	610	
	1 700	1 100	600									2 666
Shares in Y Ltd	650	—	—			*6*	650					—
Shares in Z Ltd	—	420	—	*5*	120	*2*	420					—
						6	120					
Land	—	—	200	*1*	100							400
				1	100							
Other assets	1 050	680	400									2 130
Goodwill	—	—	—	*2*	60							136
				6	40							
				6	36							
	1 700	1 100	600		1 510		1 510		906		906	2 666

FIGURE 25.7 Consolidation worksheet: non-sequential acquisition

25.4 RECIPROCAL OWNERSHIP

Reciprocal shareholdings, otherwise known as mutual holdings or crossholdings, exist when a parent and a subsidiary own shares in each other. They also exist when a parent has more than one subsidiary and two or more of the subsidiaries own shares in each other. Some illustrative structures are as shown in figures 25.8 and 25.9.

In some jurisdictions, such as Australia, subsidiaries are not allowed to hold shares in the parent entity. Hence, structures such as in figure 25.8 are not allowed to exist. However, structures such as in figure 25.9, where the crossholding is between the subsidiaries, are allowed.

The same principles, however, are applied in accounting for the structures in both figures. To simplify the explanation, the structure shown in figure 25.8 is used in this chapter for illustrative purposes.

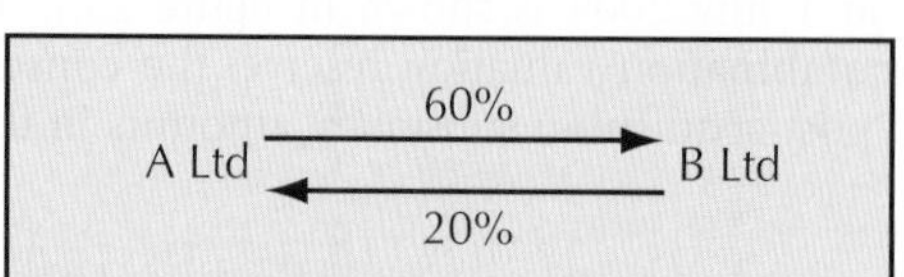

FIGURE 25.8 Reciprocal holdings

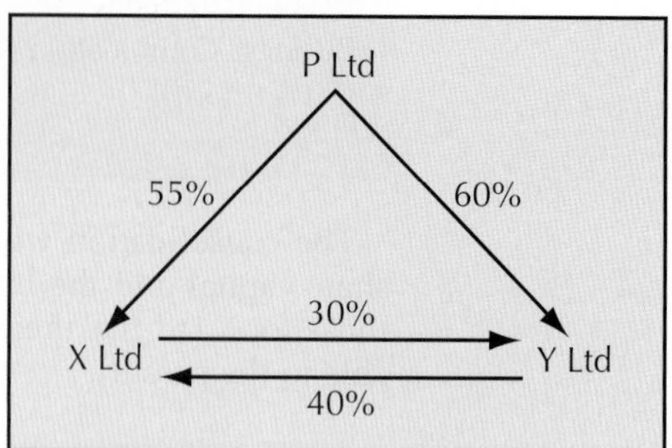

FIGURE 25.9 Reciprocal holdings

25.4.1 Pre-acquisition and valuation entries

Using the structure in figure 25.9, business combination valuation entries are necessary for both X Ltd and Y Ltd, and there are four pre-acquisition entries:

- P Ltd's acquisition of X Ltd
- P Ltd's acquisition of Y Ltd
- X Ltd's acquisition of Y Ltd
- Y Ltd's acquisition of X Ltd.

Timing of these acquisitions will affect the valuations made, and the form of the pre-acquisition entries, particularly in relation to the crossholding between X Ltd and Y Ltd. If X Ltd acquires shares in Y Ltd before Y Ltd acquires its shares in X Ltd, then in preparing the pre-acquisition/valuation entries for the latter acquisition, one of the assets of X Ltd is its investment in Y Ltd. In other words, where non-sequential acquisitions occur, particular adjustments must be taken into account, as demonstrated in section 25.3 of this chapter.

25.4.2 Non-controlling interest

Consider figure 25.10. What are the ownership interests in each entity?

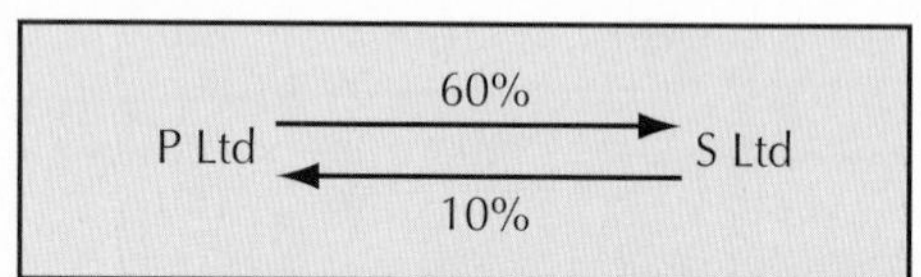

FIGURE 25.10 Reciprocal holdings

In relation to *S Ltd*, there is a DNCI of 40%. However, it is a little more difficult to determine P Ltd's interest in S Ltd because of the reciprocal holding. Similarly, in relation to P Ltd, there is an NCI in P Ltd, but its exact percentage interest is not immediately obvious.

A further factor complicating the calculation of the NCI share of equity is the timing of the various acquisitions, that is, whether P Ltd acquired its share in S Ltd before S Ltd acquired its shares in P Ltd or vice versa. The profits recorded by the two entities can be broken into three parts:

- those on hand at the first acquisition (e.g. P Ltd's acquisition of S Ltd)
- those on hand at the second acquisition (S Ltd's acquisition of P Ltd); this is the date the reciprocal ownership arises
- those earned subsequent to the point of the mutual ownership occurring. These are referred to here as *post-acquisition profits*, that is, after the point that the reciprocal holding was raised.

Allocation of pre-acquisition equity to the NCI

Some small examples containing variations in the timing of acquisitions are examined to demonstrate the approach to be taken in calculating the shares of pre-acquisition equity attributable to the parent and the NCI. The group of P Ltd and S Ltd is used in these examples. *It is assumed in these examples that no business combination valuation entries are required (i.e. all assets are at fair value and no goodwill arises on acquisition)*. Because the calculations are concerned with the allocation of *pre-acquisition* equity, only the DNCI is of concern.

Example 1: Shares acquired on the same date

On 1 July 2008, P Ltd acquired 60% of the shares of S Ltd and S Ltd acquired 10% of the shares of P Ltd. The only DNCI is the 40% in S Ltd. It is entitled to a share of all equity of S Ltd at acquisition date, 1 July 2008.

Example 2: P Ltd acquires shares in S Ltd before S Ltd acquires shares in P Ltd

Information concerning the acquisitions is as follows:

	P Ltd	S Ltd	
	1/7/09	**1/7/08**	**1/7/09**
Share capital	$40 000	$25 000	$25 000
Retained earnings	30 000	10 000	15 000
Shares in S Ltd	21 000		
Shares in P Ltd			7 300
Other assets	49 000	35 000	32 700

P Ltd acquired 60% of the shares of S Ltd for $21 000 at 1 July 2008 when the retained earnings of S Ltd were $10 000. On 1 July 2009, S Ltd acquired 10% of the shares in P Ltd for $7300. At this date, the retained earnings of S Ltd had increased by $5000 and the fair value of the Shares in S Ltd account in P Ltd increased to $24 000 (a $3000 increase, which is 60% × $5000).

The consolidation worksheet entries at 1 July 2009 are as follows:

P Ltd's acquisition of S Ltd

Pre-acquisition entry:

Share Capital [60% × $25 000]	Dr	15 000	
Retained Earnings [60% × $10 000]	Dr	6 000	
Shares in S Ltd	Cr		21 000

NCI in S Ltd at acquisition date:

Share Capital	Dr	10 000	
Retained Earnings	Dr	4 000	
NCI	Cr		14 000
(40% of balances)			

NCI share of equity from 1 July 2008 to 30 June 2009:

Retained Earnings	Dr	2 000	
NCI	Cr		2 000
(40% × [$15 000 – $10 000])			

S Ltd's acquisition of P Ltd

Valuation of P Ltd's assets:

Shares in S Ltd	Dr	3 000	
Business Combination Valuation Reserve	Cr		3 000

Pre-acquisition entries:

Share Capital [10% × $40 000]	Dr	4 000	
Retained Earnings [10% × $30 000]	Dr	3 000	
Business Combination Valuation Reserve			
[10% × $3000]	Dr	300	
Shares in P Ltd	Cr		7 300
Retained Earnings	Dr	3 000	
Shares in S Ltd	Cr		3 000
(60% × [$15 000 – $10 000])			

This last entry results in the total $15 000 of S Ltd's retained earnings now either eliminated or allocated to the NCI. The parent's share is recognised in the business combination valuation reserve.

Example 3: S Ltd acquires shares in P Ltd before P Ltd acquires shares in S Ltd

Information concerning the acquisitions is as follows:

	S Ltd	P Ltd	
	1/7/09	**1/7/08**	**1/7/09**
Share capital	$25 000	$40 000	$40 000
Retained earnings	10 000	30 000	40 000
Shares in S Ltd			21 600
Shares in P Ltd	7 000		
Other assets	28 000	70 000	58 400

On 1 July 2008, S Ltd acquired a 10% interest in P Ltd for $7000.

On 1 July 2009, P Ltd acquired a 60% controlling interest in S Ltd for $21 600. S Ltd's asset Shares in P Ltd had a fair value at this date of $8000, reflecting the increase in equity of P Ltd of $10 000. Consolidation worksheet entries at 1 July 2009 are as follows:

S Ltd's acquisition of P Ltd

Pre-acquisition entry:

Share Capital [10% × $40 000]	Dr	4 000	
Retained Earnings [10% × $30 000]	Dr	3 000	
Shares in P Ltd	Cr		7 000

P Ltd's acquisition of S Ltd

Valuation of S Ltd's assets:

Shares in P Ltd	Dr	1 000	
Business Combination Valuation Reserve	Cr		1 000
($8000 – $7000)			

Pre-acquisition entries:

Share Capital [60% × $25 000]	Dr	15 000	
Retained Earnings [60% × $10 000]	Dr	6 000	
Business Combination Valuation Reserve			
[60% × $1000]	Dr	600	
Shares in S Ltd	Cr		21 600
Retained Earnings [10% ($40 000 – $30 000)]	Dr	1 000	
Shares in P Ltd	Cr		1 000

NCI share at 1 July 2008 (note the NCI has an interest in S Ltd at this date):

Share Capital [40% × $25 000]	Dr	10 000	
Retained Earnings [40% × $10 000]	Dr	4 000	
NCI	Cr		14 000

NCI share of equity from 1 July 2008 to 1 July 2009:

Business Combination Valuation Reserve [40% × $1000]	Dr	400	
NCI	Cr		400

(Note that this reflects the increased worth of P Ltd between these two dates. The 40% DNCI in S Ltd actually has an INCI share of the equity of P Ltd between the two acquisition dates of (40% × 10%) ($40 000 – $30 000) = $400.)

Allocation of post-acquisition equity

In the above section, the NCI has been given a share of equity of both entities up to the date of the formation of the reciprocal holding. This section demonstrates the allocation of the changes in equity subsequent to the formation of the reciprocal ownership.

The difficulty in this process is that there is no easy way of determining the relative ownership interests in the entities within the group because the entities are interdependent. Consider again the following structure:

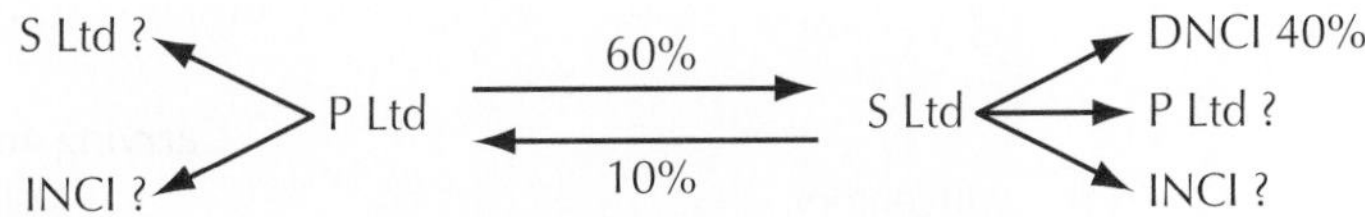

The only percentage easily calculable is the DNCI in S Ltd. There are various methods that are used to overcome the problem of interdependency. For two companies, simultaneous equations may be used. Using the group of P Ltd and S Ltd:

Let P = recorded profit of P Ltd
S = recorded profit of S Ltd
p = 'real' or 'true' profits of P Ltd
s = 'real' or 'true' profits of S Ltd.

(The 'real' profits of P Ltd consist of the recorded profits of P Ltd plus the profits of S Ltd that can be claimed by P Ltd because of its ownership interest in S Ltd.)

$$p = P + 0.6s \quad (1)$$
$$s = S + 0.1p \quad (2)$$

Substituting for p in equation (2):

$$\begin{aligned} s &= S + 0.1(P + 0.6s) \\ &= S + 0.1P + 0.06s \\ 0.94s &= S + 0.1P \\ s &= \frac{1}{0.94S} + \frac{0.1P}{0.94} \end{aligned}$$

As both P and S are known, being the recorded profits, the post-acquisition profits of P Ltd and S Ltd are calculable. The NCI share of post-acquisition profits is based on the DNCI in S Ltd of 40% receiving a share of s (i.e. a 40% share of the real post-acquisition profits of S Ltd). There is no need to calculate any INCI share of equity because, by calculating the real profits of S Ltd, the DNCI gets the appropriate share, including that from the crossholdings.

Illustrative examples 25.2 and 25.3 demonstrate the effects of intragroup transactions on the calculation of the NCI and the calculation of the NCI share of equity.

ILLUSTRATIVE EXAMPLE 25.2

Effects of intragroup transactions on the calculation of the NCI

On 1 July 2007, Tahiti Ltd acquired 60% of the shares (cum div.) of Mavi Ltd for $163 980. On the same day, Mavi Ltd acquired 75% of the shares of Jarvis Ltd for $129 050. At this date, an extract from the statement of financial position of Mavi Ltd and Jarvis Ltd disclosed the following:

	Mavi Ltd	Jarvis Ltd
Share capital	$240 000	$164 000
General reserve	8 000	—
Retained earnings	1 600	2 400
Dividend payable	14 400	—

The dividend payable by Mavi Ltd was subsequently paid. No other dividends have been paid from pre-acquisition equity.

On 1 July 2007, all the identifiable assets and liabilities of Jarvis Ltd were recorded at fair value except for the non-monetary assets. A comparison of the non-monetary assets' carrying amounts and fair values revealed the following information:

	Jarvis Ltd	
	Carrying amount	Fair value
Inventory	$ 5 000	$ 6 000
Plant (cost $160 000)	128 000	133 000
Land	56 000	60 000

The plant was expected to provide further benefits evenly over the next 5 years. All inventory was sold by 30 June 2008.

On 1 July 2007 all the identifiable assets and liabilities of Mavi Ltd were recorded at fair value except for the following:

	Mavi Ltd	
	Carrying amount	Fair value
Inventory	$ 6 000	$ 8 000
Plant (cost $147 000)	126 000	130 000

The balance of goodwill recorded at 1 July 2007 by Mavi Ltd was $6000. The financial data as at 30 June 2009 of the three companies are shown opposite.

Additional information

(a) Sales and purchases included the following transactions:
- sales by Mavi Ltd to Tahiti Ltd invoiced at cost plus 33% were $120 000
- sales by Jarvis Ltd to Tahiti Ltd invoiced at cost plus 25% were $36 000.

(b) Inventory on hand of Tahiti Ltd at 30 June 2009 included $1600 acquired from Mavi Ltd and $1200 acquired from Jarvis Ltd.

(c) Inventory of Mavi Ltd at 1 July 2008 included $160 profit on goods received from Jarvis Ltd.

(d) Receivables and payables included $3600 owing by Tahiti Ltd to Mavi Ltd.

(e) The tax rate is 30%.

Required

Based on the above information, prepare the consolidated financial statements for Tahiti Ltd and its subsidiaries as at 30 June 2009.

Solution

The *first step* in the consolidation process is to establish the structure of the group and percentage ownership of the NCI — see figure 25.11.

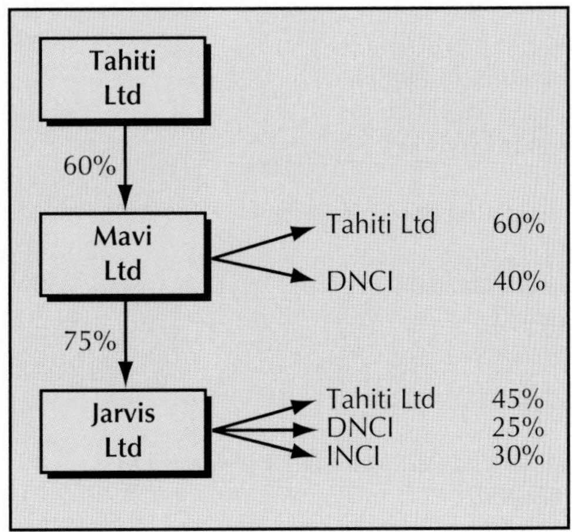

FIGURE 25.11 Structure of group

The *next step* is to choose one of the acquisitions and prepare the acquisition analysis, the business combination valuation and pre-acquisition entries, and the NCI entries.

	Tahiti Ltd	Mavi Ltd	Jarvis Ltd
Sales revenue	$675 360	$444 800	$290 000
Dividend revenue	18 720	13 200	—
Debenture interest	—	3 200	3 840
Total revenue	694 080	461 200	293 840
Cost of sales	490 400	333 600	232 000
Other expenses	44 080	42 800	20 000
Total expenses	534 480	376 400	252 000
Profit before tax	159 600	84 800	41 840
Income tax expense	64 000	32 000	16 000
Profit for the period	95 600	52 800	25 840
Retained earnings (1/7/08)	4 000	10 400	8 800
	99 600	63 200	34 640
Dividend paid	20 000	14 400	8 000
Dividend declared	30 000	16 800	9 600
	50 000	31 200	17 600
Retained earnings (30/6/09)	49 600	32 000	17 040
Share capital	420 000	240 000	164 000
General reserve	12 000	16 000	8 000
Total equity	481 600	288 000	189 040
Debentures	160 000	—	—
Provisions	20 000	29 600	16 000
Dividend payable	30 000	16 800	9 600
Current tax liability	64 400	32 000	16 000
Total liabilities	274 400	78 400	41 600
Total equity and liabilities	$756 000	$366 400	$230 640

(continued)

(continued)

	Tahiti Ltd	Mavi Ltd	Jarvis Ltd
Inventory	5 600	4 400	5 120
Receivables	21 860	15 550	1 520
Cash	28 000	10 600	21 600
Debentures in Tahiti Ltd	—	40 000	48 000
Shares in Mavi Ltd	155 340	—	—
Shares in Jarvis Ltd	—	129 050	—
Plant	500 000	147 000	160 000
Accumulated depreciation	(204 000)	(63 000)	(64 000)
Land	200 000	70 000	56 000
Deferred tax asset	32 000	6 800	2 400
Goodwill	17 200	6 000	—
Total assets	$756 000	$366 400	$230 640

Acquisition analysis: Mavi Ltd and Jarvis Ltd
At *1 July 2007*:

Net fair value of identifiable assets and liabilities of Jarvis Ltd	= $164 000 (capital) + $2400 (retained earnings)
	+ $1 000(1 – 0.3) (BCVR – inventory)
	+ $5 000(1 – 0.3) (BCVR – plant)
	+ $4 000(1 – 0.3) (BCVR – land)
	= $173 400
Net fair value acquired by Mavi Ltd	= 75% × $173 400
	= $130 050
Consideration transferred	= $129 050
Excess	= $1 000

(1) *Business combination valuation entries: Mavi Ltd and Jarvis Ltd*
At *1 July 2007*:

Inventory	Dr	1 000	
Deferred Tax Liability	Cr		300
Business Combination Valuation Reserve	Cr		700
Accumulated Depreciation – Plant	Dr	32 000	
Plant	Cr		27 000
Deferred Tax Liability	Cr		1 500
Business Combination Valuation Reserve	Cr		3 500
Land	Dr	4 000	
Deferred Tax Liability	Cr		1 200
Business Combination Valuation Reserve	Cr		2 800

At *30 June 2009*, the valuation entries for plant require adjustment to reflect depreciation of $1000 p.a., being $\frac{1}{5}$ of $5000. The inventory was all sold in the 2007–08 period. The valuation entries at 30 June 2009 are:

Accumulated Depreciation – Plant	Dr	32 000	
Plant	Cr		27 000
Deferred Tax Liability	Cr		1 500
Business Combination Valuation Reserve	Cr		3 500

Depreciation Expense	Dr	1 000	
Retained Earnings (1/7/08)	Dr	1 000	
Accumulated Depreciation	Cr		2 000
(20% × $5000)			
Deferred Tax Liability	Dr	600	
Income Tax Expense	Cr		300
Retained Earnings (1/7/08)	Cr		300
Land	Dr	4 000	
Deferred Tax Liability	Cr		1 200
Business Combination Valuation Reserve	Cr		2 800

(2) *Pre-acquisition entry: Mavi Ltd and Jarvis Ltd*
The pre-acquisition entry at *1 July 2007* is:

Retained Earnings (1/7/07)	Dr	1 800	
Share Capital	Dr	123 000	
Business Combination Valuation Reserve	Dr	5 250	
Excess – Other Income	Cr		1 000
Shares in Jarvis Ltd	Cr		129 050

The inventory is all sold in the 2007–08 period, and the related valuation reserve (75% × $700) transferred to retained earnings.

At *30 June 2009*, the entry is:

Retained Earnings (1/7/08)*	Dr	1 325	
Share Capital	Dr	123 000	
Business Combination Valuation Reserve	Dr	4 725	
Shares in Jarvis Ltd	Cr		129 050
*$1325 = $1800 – $1000 excess + (75% × $700) inventory			

(3) *NCI share of equity in Jarvis Ltd at 1 July 2007 (step 1)*

Retained Earnings (1/7/08)	Dr	600	
Share Capital	Dr	41 000	
Business Combination Valuation Reserve	Dr	1 750	
NCI	Cr		43 350

(4) *NCI share of changes in equity from 1 July 2007 to 30 June 2008*
Retained earnings of Jarvis Ltd at 30 June 2008 have increased by $6400, that is, from $2400 to $8800, but adjustments must be made for the after-tax depreciation on plant, as shown in the business combination valuation entries:

DNCI (25%):

Retained Earnings (1/7/08)	Dr	1 425	
NCI	Cr		1 425
(25% × [$6400 – ($1000 – $300)])			

INCI (30%):
The INCI receives a share of post-acquisition equity only. As the pre-acquisition entry at 30 June 2009 has a debit adjustment of $1325, then the pre-acquisition retained earnings of

Jarvis Ltd are $1767 (i.e. $1325/0.75) plus the adjustments for the depreciation of plant $700 (i.e. $1000 – $300), a total of $2467. The INCI share of post-acquisition retained earnings is:

$$30\% \times [\$8\,800 - \frac{\$1\,325}{0.75} - (\$1\,000 - \$300)] = \$1\,900$$

The worksheet entry is:

Retained Earnings (1/7/08)	Dr	1 900	
NCI	Cr		1 900

The *business combination valuation reserve* in relation to inventory has been transferred to retained earnings. This affects the DNCI only because it relates to pre-acquisition profits.

DNCI (25%):

NCI	Dr	175	
Business Combination Valuation Reserve	Cr		175
(25% × $700)			

The *general reserve* has increased from a zero balance at acquisition date to $8000, an increase of $8000. Because this has resulted from a transfer from post-acquisition retained earnings, both the DNCI and INCI are affected.

DNCI (25%) and INCI (30%):

General Reserve	Dr	4 400	
NCI	Cr		4 400
([25% + 30%] × $8000)			

(5) *NCI share of equity in Jarvis Ltd from 1 July 2008 to 30 June 2009*
Because there is no adjustment to the current period profit in the pre-acquisition entry, both the DNCI and INCI receive a share of the recorded profit of $25 840 adjusted for the depreciation of plant:

NCI Share of Profit	Dr	13 827	
NCI	Cr		13 827
([25% + 30%] × [$25 840 – ($1000 – $300)])			

Jarvis Ltd has *paid a dividend* of $8000. This affects the DNCI only.

NCI	Dr	2 000	
Dividend Paid	Cr		2 000
(25% × $8000)			

Jarvis Ltd has *declared a dividend* of $9600. Only the DNCI is affected.

NCI	Dr	2 400	
Dividend Declared	Cr		2 400
(25% × $9600)			

The *next step* is to deal with the other acquisition, Tahiti Ltd's acquisition of Mavi Ltd.

Acquisition analysis: Tahiti Ltd and Mavi Ltd

Net fair value of assets and liabilities of Mavi Ltd	= \$240 000 (capital) + \$8000 (general reserve)
	+ \$1 600 (retained earnings)
	+ \$2 000(1 – 0.3) (BCVR – inventory)
	+ \$4 000(1 – 0.3) (BCVR – plant)
	– \$6 000 (goodwill)
	= \$247 800
Net fair value acquired by Tahiti Ltd	= 60% × \$247 800
	= \$148 680
Consideration transferred	= \$163 980 – (60% × \$14 400) (dividend)
	= \$155 340
Goodwill acquired by Tahiti Ltd	= \$6 660
Non-recorded goodwill	= \$6 660 – (60% × \$6 000)
	= \$3 060

(6) *Business combination valuation entries: Tahiti Ltd and Mavi Ltd*
At *1 July 2007*:

Inventory	Dr	2 000	
Deferred Tax Liability	Cr		600
Business Combination Valuation Reserve	Cr		1 400
Accumulated Depreciation	Dr	21 000	
Plant	Cr		17 000
Deferred Tax Liability	Cr		1 200
Business Combination Valuation Reserve	Cr		2 800

The entries at 30 June 2009 take into account that the inventory is sold in 2008, and the plant is depreciated at \$1000 p.a., being $\frac{1}{4}$ of \$4000.

The entries at *30 June 2009* are:

Accumulated Depreciation	Dr	21 000	
Plant	Cr		17 000
Deferred Tax Liability	Cr		1 200
Business Combination Valuation Reserve	Cr		2 800
Depreciation Expense	Dr	1 000	
Retained Earnings (1/7/08)	Dr	1 000	
Accumulated Depreciation	Cr		2 000
Deferred Tax Liability	Dr	600	
Income Tax Expense	Cr		300
Retained Earnings (1/7/08)	Cr		300

(7) *Pre-acquisition entries*
At *1 July 2007*:

Retained Earnings (1/7/07)	Dr	960	
Share Capital	Dr	144 000	
General Reserve	Dr	4 800	
Business Combination Valuation Reserve	Dr	2 520	
Goodwill	Dr	3 060	
Shares in Mavi Ltd	Cr		155 340
Dividend Payable	Dr	8 640	
Dividend Receivable	Cr		8 640

By *30 June 2009*, the dividend has been paid and the inventory sold with the relevant valuation reserve transferred to retained earnings. The entry is:

Retained Earnings (1/7/08)	Dr	1 800	
Share Capital	Dr	144 000	
General Reserve	Dr	4 800	
Business Combination Valuation Reserve*	Dr	1 680	
Goodwill	Dr	3 060	
Shares in Mavi Ltd	Cr		155 340
*$2520 – (60% × $1400)			

(8) *NCI in equity of Mavi Ltd at 1 July 2007*

Retained Earnings (1/7/08)	Dr	640	
Share Capital	Dr	96 000	
General Reserve	Dr	3 200	
Business Combination Valuation Reserve	Dr	1 680	
NCI	Cr		101 520
(40% of balances at acquisition)			

(9) *NCI share of equity in Mavi Ltd from 1 July 2007 to 30 June 2008*
The retained earnings for Mavi Ltd have increased from $1600 to $10 400, an increase of $8800. This has to be adjusted for the after-tax depreciation on plant, $1000 – $300.

Retained Earnings (1/7/08)	Dr	3 240	
NCI	Cr		3 240
(40% × [$8800 – ($1000 – $300)])			

The *business combination valuation reserve* relating to inventory has been transferred to retained earnings:

NCI	Dr	560	
Business Combination Valuation Reserve	Cr		560
(40% × $1400)			

The *general reserve* has increased from $8000 to $16 000:

General Reserve	Dr	3 200	
NCI	Cr		3 200
(40% × $8000)			

(10) *NCI share of equity of Mavi Ltd from 1 July 2008 to 30 June 2009*
Current period profit: This is $52 800, and is adjusted for the after-tax depreciation on plant.

NCI Share of Profit	Dr	20 840	
NCI	Cr		20 840
(40% × ($52 800 – [$1000 – $300]))			

Dividend paid of $14 400:

NCI	Dr	5 760	
Dividend Paid	Cr		5 760
(40% × $14 400)			

Dividend declared of $16 800:

NCI	Dr	6 720	
Dividend Declared	Cr		6 720

Dividend revenue from Jarvis Ltd of $13 200: Jarvis Ltd paid a dividend of $8000 and declared a dividend of $9600. Mavi Ltd therefore recorded dividend revenue of $13 200 (i.e. 75% × ($8000 + $9600)). As the INCI has received a share of the profit of Jarvis Ltd, to avoid double counting the DNCI in Mavi Ltd must be adjusted in relation to the dividend revenue from Jarvis Ltd:

NCI	Dr	5 280	
NCI Share of Profit	Cr		5 280
(40% × $13 200)			

Intragroup transactions

(11) *Dividend paid — Jarvis Ltd*

Dividend Revenue	Dr	6 000	
Interim Dividend Paid	Cr		6 000
(75% × $8000)			

(12) *Dividend paid — Mavi Ltd*

Dividend Revenue	Dr	8 640	
Interim Dividend Paid	Cr		8 640
(60% × $14 400)			

(13) *Dividend declared — Mavi Ltd*

Dividend Payable	Dr	10 080	
Dividend Declared	Cr		10 080
(60% × $16 800)			
Dividend Revenue	Dr	10 080	
Dividend Receivable	Cr		10 080

(14) *Dividend declared — Jarvis Ltd*

Dividend Payable	Dr	7 200	
Dividend Declared	Cr		7 200
(75% × $9600)			
Dividend Revenue	Dr	7 200	
Dividend Receivable	Cr		7 200

(15) *Profit in ending inventory: Sales by Mavi Ltd to Tahiti Ltd*

Sales Revenue	Dr	120 000	
Cost of Sales	Cr		119 600
Inventory	Cr		400
Deferred Tax Asset	Dr	120	
Income Tax Expense	Cr		120

(16) *Adjustment to NCI in Mavi Ltd*

NCI	Dr	112	
NCI Share of Profit	Cr		112
(40% × [$400 – $120])			

(17) *Profit in ending inventory: Sales by Jarvis Ltd to Tahiti Ltd*

Sales Revenue	Dr	36 000	
Cost of Sales	Cr		35 760
Inventory	Cr		240
Deferred Tax Asset	Dr	72	
Income Tax Expense	Cr		72

(18) *Adjustment to NCI in Jarvis Ltd*

NCI	Dr	92	
NCI Share of Profit	Cr		92
([25% + 30%] × [$240 – $72])			

(19) *Profit in opening inventory: Sales by Jarvis Ltd to Mavi Ltd*

Retained Earnings (1/7/08)	Dr	112	
Income Tax Expense	Dr	48	
Cost of Sales	Cr		160

(20) *Adjustment to NCI in Jarvis Ltd*

NCI Share of Profit	Dr	62	
Retained Earnings (1/7/08)	Cr		62
([25% + 30%] × [$160 – $48])			

(21) *Intragroup balances*
Amount owing by Tahiti Ltd to Mavi Ltd is $3600.

Payables	Dr	3 600	
Receivables	Cr		3 600

(22) *Intragroup debentures*
Intragroup debentures held amount to $88 000.

8% Debentures	Dr	88 000	
Debentures in Tahiti Ltd	Cr		88 000

(23) *Debenture interest*
Interest paid by Tahiti Ltd is 8% of the sum of $40 000 and $48 000.

Debenture Interest Revenue	Dr	7 040	
Debenture Interest Expense	Cr		7 040

The consolidation worksheet is shown in figure 25.12.

FIGURE 25.12 Consolidation worksheet — indirect ownership interests

Financial statements	Tahiti Ltd	Mavi Ltd	Jarvis Ltd	Adjustments				Group	Non-controlling interest				Parent
					Dr	Cr				Dr	Cr		
Sales revenue	675 360	444 800	290 000	*15*	120 000			1 254 160					
				17	36 000								
Dividend revenue	18 720	13 200	—	*11*	6 000			—					
				12	8 640								
				13	10 080								
				14	7 200								
Debenture interest	—	3 200	3 840	*23*	7 040			—					
Total revenue	694 080	461 200	293 840					1 254 160					
Cost of sales	490 400	333 600	232 000			119 600	*15*	900 480					
						35 760	*17*						
						160	*19*						
Other expenses	44 080	42 800	20 000	*1*	1 000	7 040	*23*	101 840					
				6	1 000								
Total expenses	534 480	376 400	252 000					1 002 320					
Profit before tax	159 600	84 800	41 840					251 840					
Tax expense	64 000	32 000	16 000	*19*	48	300	*1*	111 256					
						300	*6*						
						120	*15*						
						72	*17*						
Profit for the period	95 600	52 800	25 840					140 584	*5*	13 827	5 280	*10*	111 339
									10	20 840	112	*16*	
									20	62	92	*18*	
Retained earnings (1/7/08)	4 000	10 400	8 800	*1*	1 000	300	*1*	18 563	*3*	600	62	*20*	10 820
				2	1 325	300	*6*		*4*	1 425			
				6	1 000				*4*	1 900			
				7	1 800				*8*	640			
				19	112				*9*	3 240			
	99 600	63 200	34 640					159 147					122 159

(continued)

FIGURE 25.12 *(continued)*

Financial statements	Tahiti Ltd	Mavi Ltd	Jarvis Ltd	Adjustments				Group	Non-controlling interest				Parent
					Dr	Cr				Dr	Cr		
Dividend paid	20 000	14 400	8 000			6 000	*11*	27 760			2 000	*5*	20 000
						8 640	*12*				5 760	*10*	
Dividend declared	30 000	16 800	9 600			10 080	*13*	39 120			2 400	*5*	30 000
						7 200	*14*				6 720	*10*	
	50 000	31 200	17 600					66 880					50 000
Retained earnings (30/6/09)	49 600	32 000	17 040					92 267					72 159
Share capital	420 000	240 000	164 000	2	123 000			557 000	*3*	41 000			420 000
				7	144 000				*8*	96 000			
General reserve	12 000	16 000	8 000	7	4 800			31 200	*4*	4 400			20 400
									8	3 200			
									9	3 200			
Business combination valuation reserve	—	—	—	2	4 725	3 500	*1*	2 695	*3*	1 750	175	*4*	—
				7	1 680	2 800	*1*		*8*	1 680	560	*9*	
						2 800	*6*						
Total equity: Parent													512 559
Total equity: NCI									*4*	175			170 603
									5	2 000	43 350	*3*	
									5	2 400	1 425	*4*	
									9	560	1 900	*4*	
									10	5 760	4 400	*4*	
									10	6 720	13 827	*5*	
									10	5 280	101 520	*8*	
									16	112	3 240	*9*	
									18	92	3 200	*9*	
											20 840	*10*	
Total equity	481 600	288 000	189 040					683 162		216 863	216 863		683 162

FIGURE 25.12 *(continued)*

Financial statements	Tahiti Ltd	Mavi Ltd	Jarvis Ltd	Adjustments				Group	Non-controlling interest				Parent
					Dr	Cr				Dr	Cr		
Debentures	160 000	—	—	*22*	88 000			72 000					
Provisions	20 000	29 600	16 000	*21*	3 600			62 000					
Dividend payable	30 000	16 800	9 600	*13*	10 080			39 120					
				14	7 200								
Current tax liability	64 400	32 000	16 000					112 400					
Deferred tax liabilityt	—	—	—	*1*	600	1 500	*1*	2 700					
				6	600	1 200	*1*						
						1 200	*6*						
Total liabilities	274 400	78 400	41 600					288 220					
Total equity and liabilities	756 000	366 400	230 640					971 382					
Inventory	5 600	4 400	5 120			400	*15*	14 480					
						240	*17*						
Receivables	21 860	15 550	1 520			3 600	*21*	18 050					
						10 080	*13*						
						7 200	*14*						
Cash	28 000	10 600	21 600					60 200					
Debentures in Tahiti Ltd	—	40 000	48 000			88 000	*22*	—					
Shares in Mavi Ltd	155 340	—	—			155 340	*7*	—					
Shares in Jarvis Ltd	—	129 050	—			129 050	*2*	—					
Plant	500 000	147 000	160 000			27 000	*1*	763 000					
						17 000	*6*						
Accumulated depreciation	(204 000)	(63 000)	(64 000)	*1*	32 000	2 000	*1*	(282 000)					
				6	21 000	2 000	*6*						
Land	200 000	70 000	56 000	*1*	4 000			330 000					
Deferred tax asset	32 000	6 800	2 400	*15*	120			41 392					
				17	72								
Goodwill	17 200	6 000	—	*7*	3 060			26 260					
Total assets	756 000	366 400	230 640		650 782	650 782		971 382					

The consolidated financial statements for Tahiti Ltd at 30 June 2009 are shown in figure 25.13(a), (b) and (c).

TAHITI LTD Consolidated Statement of Comprehensive Income for financial year ended 30 June 2009	
Revenues: Sales	$1 254 160
Expenses:	
Cost of sales	900 480
Other	101 840
Total expenses	1 002 320
Profit before income tax	251 840
Income tax expense	111 256
Profit for the period	140 584
Other comprehensive income	0
Total comprehensive income	$ 140 584
Attributable to:	
Owners of the parent	$ 111 339
Non-controlling interest	29 245
	$ 140 584

FIGURE 25.13(a) Consolidated statement of comprehensive income

TAHITI LTD Consolidated Statement of Changes in Equity for the year ended 30 June 2009		
Total comprehensive income for the period		$140 584
Attributable to:		
Owners of the parent		$111 339
Non-controlling interest		29 245
	Consolidated	**Parent**
Share capital		
Balance, beginning of year	$557 000	$420 000
Balance, end of year	$557 000	$420 000
General Reserve		
Balance, beginning of year	$ 31 200	$ 20 400
Balance, end of year	$ 31 200	$ 20 400
Retained earnings		
Balance, beginning of year	$ 18 563	$ 10 820
Profit for the period	140 584	111 339
Dividends paid and declared	(66 880)	(50 000)
Balance, end of year	$ 92 267	$ 72 159

FIGURE 25.13(b) Consolidated statement of changes in equity

TAHITI LTD Consolidated Statement of Financial Position as at 30 June 2009	
ASSETS	
Current assets	
Inventories	$ 14 480
Receivables	18 050
Cash	60 200
Total current assets	92 730
Non-current assets	
Plant and equipment	763 000
Accumulated depreciation	(282 000)
Land	330 000
Deferred tax assets	41 392
Goodwill	26 260
Total non-current assets	878 652
Total assets	971 382
LIABILITIES	
Current liabilities	
Provisions	62 000
Dividends payable	39 120
Current tax liabilities	112 400
Total current liabilities	213 520
Non-current liabilities	
Debentures	72 000
Deferred tax liabilities	2 700
Total non-current liabilities	74 700
Total liabilities	288 220
Net assets	$683 162
EQUITY	
Share capital	$420 000
Other reserves: General	20 400
Retained earnings	72 159
Owners interest	512 559
Non-controlling interest	170 603
Total equity	$683 162

FIGURE 25.13(c) Consolidated statement of financial position

ILLUSTRATIVE EXAMPLE 25.3

Calculation of the NCI share of equity

The following example illustrates the calculation of the NCI where reciprocal holdings exist between subsidiaries. The structure of the group is shown below:

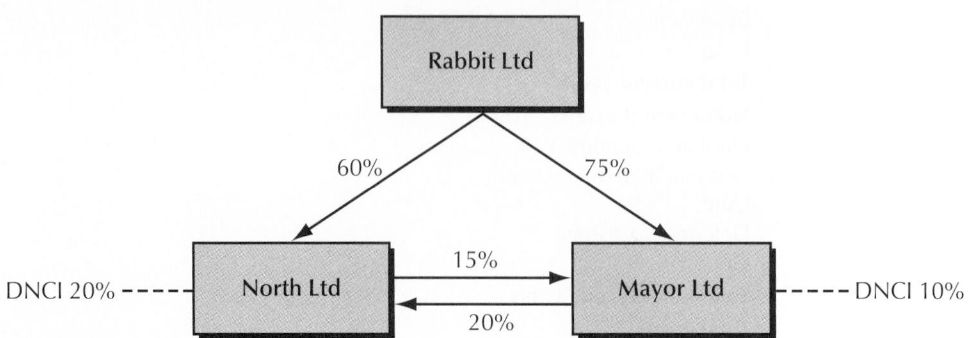

It is assumed that Rabbit Ltd had an interest in both North Ltd and Mayor Ltd prior to the occurrence of the reciprocal relationship. The pre-acquisition entries for these acquisitions will not be given here because they have no influence on the calculation of the NCI.

Assume North Ltd and Mayor Ltd acquired their shareholdings in each other on 1 July 2007:

- North Ltd paid $15 720 for 15% of Mayor Ltd's issued shares when the retained earnings of Mayor Ltd were $20 000. All the identifiable net assets of Mayor Ltd were recorded at fair value except for plant, for which the fair value was $4000 greater than carrying amount. The plant has a remaining useful life of 4 years.
- Mayor Ltd paid $30 000 for 20% of North Ltd's issued shares when the retained earnings of North Ltd were $40 000. All the identifiable net assets of North Ltd were recorded at fair value except for inventory, for which the fair value was $5000 greater than the carrying amount. The inventory was all sold within the following year.
- The tax rate is 30%, and when revalued assets are sold or consumed, any related valuation reserve relating to those assets is transferred to retained earnings.

At 30 June 2009, the financial statements of North Ltd and Mayor Ltd contained the following information:

	North Ltd	Mayor Ltd
Dividend revenue	$ 750	$ 1 000
Other income	20 000	10 000
Profit before income tax	20 750	11 000
Income tax expense	8 000	5 000
Profit for the period	12 750	6 000
Retained earnings (1/7/08)	65 000	45 000
	77 750	51 000
Dividend paid	5 000	5 000
Retained earnings (30/6/09)	72 750	46 000
Share capital	100 000	80 000
	$172 750	$126 000
Shares in North Ltd	—	$ 30 000
Shares in Mayor Ltd	$ 15 720	—
Other assets	157 030	96 000
	$172 750	$126 000

Acquisition analysis: North Ltd of Mayor Ltd

Net fair value of Mayor Ltd	= \$80 000 + \$20 000
	+ \$4 000(1 – 30%) (BCVR – plant)
	= \$102 800
Net fair value acquired by North Ltd	= 15% × \$102 800
	= \$15 420
Consideration transferred	= \$15 720
Goodwill	= \$300

Acquisition analysis: Mayor Ltd of North Ltd

Net fair value of North Ltd	= \$100 000 + \$40 000
	+ \$5 000(1 – 30%) (BCVR – inventory)
	= \$143 500
Net fair value acquired by Mayor Ltd	= 20% × \$143 500
	= \$28 700
Consideration transferred	= \$30 000
Goodwill	= \$1 300

The consolidation worksheet entries at 30 June 2006 are as follows:
(1) *Business combination valuation entries: North Ltd–Mayor Ltd*

Plant	Dr	4 000	
Deferred Tax Liability	Cr		1 200
Business Combination Valuation Reserve	Cr		2 800
Depreciation Expense	Dr	1 000	
Retained Earnings (1/7/08)	Dr	1 000	
Accumulated Depreciation	Cr		2 000
($\frac{1}{4}$ × \$4000 p.a.)			
Deferred Tax Liability	Dr	600	
Income Tax Expense	Cr		300
Retained Earnings (1/7/08)	Cr		300

(2) *Pre-acquisition entry: North Ltd–Mayor Ltd*

Share Capital	Dr	12 000	
Retained Earnings (1/7/08)	Dr	3 000	
Business Combination Valuation Reserve	Dr	420	
Goodwill	Dr	300	
Shares in Mayor Ltd	Cr		15 720

(3) *DNCI in Mayor Ltd at acquisition date (10%)*

Share Capital	Dr	8 000	
Retained Earnings (1/7/08)	Dr	2 000	
Business Combination Valuation Reserve	Dr	280	
NCI	Cr		10 280

(4) *Business combination valuation entries: Mayor Ltd–North Ltd*
There are none as the inventory has been sold.

(5) *Pre-acquisition entry: Mayor Ltd–North Ltd*

Share Capital	Dr	20 000	
Retained Earnings (1/7/08)*	Dr	8 700	
Goodwill	Dr	1 300	
Shares in North Ltd	Cr		30 000

*(20% × $40 000) + (20% × $3500) inventory sold

(6) *DNCI in North Ltd at acquisition date (20%)*

Share Capital	Dr	20 000	
Retained Earnings (1/7/08)	Dr	8 000	
Business Combination Valuation Reserve	Dr	700	
NCI	Cr		28 700

NCI share of changes in equity in Mayor Ltd and North Ltd from 1 July 2007 to 30 June 2008
In calculating the NCI share of changes in equity for both North Ltd and Mayor Ltd, simultaneous equations are used. Assume:

J = recorded profits of North Ltd
K = recorded profits of Mayor Ltd
j = real profits of North Ltd
k = real profits of Mayor Ltd

$$
\begin{aligned}
j &= J + 0.15k \\
k &= K + 0.2j \\
j &= J + 0.15(K + 0.2j) \\
&= J + 0.15K + 0.03j \\
0.97j &= J + 0.15K \\
j &= \frac{1}{0.97}J + \frac{0.15}{0.97}K
\end{aligned}
$$

This change in equity is after the date of formation of the reciprocal relationship. However, an adjustment needs to be made to the change in retained earnings in Mayor Ltd between these two dates to reflect the profits recognised by the subsidiary because of the use of the revalued plant and for the sale of inventory in relation to the retained earnings of North Ltd.

$$
\begin{aligned}
j &= \frac{1}{0.97}\left(\$65\,000 - \frac{\$8\,700}{0.2}\text{ pre-acq.}\right) \\
&\quad + \frac{0.15}{0.97}\left(\$45\,000 - \frac{\$3\,000}{0.15}\text{ pre-acq.} - [\$1\,000 - \$300]\text{ plant}\right) \\
&= \$25\,923 \\
k &= K + 0.2j \\
&= \left(\$45\,000 - \frac{\$3\,000}{0.15}\text{ pre-acq.} - [\$1\,000 - \$300]\text{ plant}\right) + (0.2 \times \$25\,923) \\
&= \$29\,485 \\
\text{NCI} &= 20\%j + 10\%k \\
&= (20\% \times \$25\,923) + (10\% \times \$29\,485) \\
&= \$8\,133
\end{aligned}
$$

The NCI entry is:

Retained Earnings (1/7/08)	Dr	8 133	
NCI	Cr		8 133

There also needs to be recognition of the fact that in North Ltd, on sale of the inventory, the business combination valuation reserve was transferred to retained earnings. The NCI entry is:

Retained Earnings (1/7/08)	Dr	700	
Business Combination Valuation Reserve	Cr		700
(20% × $3500)			

NCI share of changes in equity in North Ltd and Mayor Ltd from 1 July 2008 to 30 June 2009
The same equations as above are used for the *current period's* changes in equity:

$$j = \frac{1}{0.97}J + \frac{0.15}{0.97}K$$
$$k = K + 0.2j$$

Adjustments must be made in relation to Mayor Ltd for the continued depreciation of the plant. Further adjustments must be made in both North Ltd and Mayor Ltd for any dividend revenue recognised by either company based on dividends paid and declared by the other company to ensure no double counting of equity.

$$\begin{aligned}
j &= \frac{1}{0.97}(\$12\,750 - \$750 \text{ dividend revenue from Mayor Ltd}) \\
&\quad + \frac{0.15}{0.97}(\$6\,000 - \$1\,000 \text{ dividend revenue from North Ltd} \\
&\quad - [\$1\,000 - \$300] \text{ plant depreciation}) \\
&= \$13\,036 \\
k &= K + 0.2j \\
&= (\$6\,000 - \$1\,000 \text{ dividend revenue} - [\$1\,000 - \$300] \text{ plant} \\
&\quad \text{depreciation}) \\
&\quad + (0.2 \times \$13\,036) \\
&= \$6907 \\
\text{NCI} &= 20\%j + 10\%k \\
&= (20\% \times \$13\,036) + (10\% \times \$6\,907) \\
&= \$3\,298
\end{aligned}$$

The NCI entry is:

NCI Share of Profit	Dr	3 298	
NCI	Cr		3 298

SUMMARY

Accounting standards require the separation of consolidated equity into parent interest and non-controlling interest (NCI). One complication in the calculation of NCI is that, where a group has multiple subsidiaries, it may be necessary to classify the NCI into direct non-controlling interest (DNCI) and indirect non-controlling interest (INCI), because the calculation of the DNCI share of equity differs from that of the INCI. In particular, the INCI does not receive a share of all the equity of a subsidiary, but is entitled to a share of post-acquisition equity only. The existence of an INCI must be taken into account where dividends are paid within a group because, without adjustment for the INCI, double counting of the NCI share of equity may occur.

Where a parent has a number of subsidiaries, the timing of the acquisition of those subsidiaries is important in preparing the consolidation adjustments. Sequential acquisitions arise where the parent acquires its interest in a subsidiary before or on the same date as that subsidiary acquires an interest in its own subsidiary. Non-sequential acquisitions arise where a parent acquires an interest in a subsidiary that already is a parent, that is, has its own subsidiary. In non-sequential acquisitions, the complicating factor is that one of the assets that may have a carrying amount different from fair value is the investment in a subsidiary previously acquired. The fair value of the investment reflects increases in the worth of the underlying net assets in that subsidiary.

Separation of equity into pre-acquisition and post-acquisition amounts is important where there are reciprocal holdings within a group. The calculation of the NCI share of equity is also complicated by the timing of the acquisitions within the reciprocal holdings.

Discussion questions

1. What is the difference between direct and indirect NCI?
2. Explain the difference in the calculation of the direct and indirect NCI.
3. Why does the indirect NCI receive a share of only *post-acquisition* equity?
4. What effect does the existence of an indirect NCI have on the adjustments for intragroup transactions?
5. What effect does the existence of an indirect NCI have on the adjustments for dividends paid within a group?
6. In the pre-acquisition entry, why are only partial eliminations made when an NCI exists?
7. Why is no adjustment made for an indirect NCI when preparing consolidated financial statements immediately after acquisition?
8. Explain the effects on the consolidation process when the acquisition is non-sequential.
9. What are reciprocal ownership interests?
10. Explain how reciprocal ownership interests are accounted for on consolidation.
11. P Ltd owns 20% of B Ltd. In recent months it has been in takeover discussions with A Ltd, and agreement has finally been reached between the different parties on the acquisition by P Ltd of 60% of the issued shares of A Ltd. One of the assets of A Ltd is a 70% holding in B Ltd. The group accountant of P Ltd has been examining the new group under the control of P Ltd and considering the implications for the preparation of consolidated financial statements. One of the members of the accounting team, Mei Fen, has raised the issue of accounting for indirect non-controlling interests. According to Mei Fen, with the new group structure there are both direct and indirect non-controlling interests, and she argues that different measurements are then required. The group accountant has asked you to determine the non-controlling interests in the new group, differentiating between different non-controlling interest groups, and to explain the difference, if any, in the calculation of their interests in group equity. Prepare a report for the group accountant.
12. Andrew Brown is the group accountant for P Ltd. P Ltd owns 60% of A Ltd which owns 70% of B Ltd. He has just completed the preparation of the consolidated financial statements of the group, and discussing issues raised by the auditors. The auditors have raised concerns about the accounting for a dividend paid by B Ltd to A Ltd in the current period. They argue that further consolidation adjustments are necessary to avoid double counting the non-controlling interest's share of equity. Andrew has asked for your advice concerning the effect of the payment of such a dividend on the determination of the non-controlling interest share of equity. Write a report to Andrew explaining the non-controlling interests that exist within the group, and how the calculation of their interests is affected by payment of dividends within the group.

STAR RATING

★ BASIC

★★ MODERATE

★★★ DIFFICULT

Exercises

Note: In exercises 25.1–25.6, at the acquisition date, the identifiable assets and liabilities of the subsidiary are recorded at amounts equal to fair values. In exercises 25.7–25.14, these have carrying amounts different from fair values. The partial goodwill method is used in all questions.

Exercise 25.1 **CONSOLIDATION WORKSHEET ENTRIES, THREE COMPANIES**

★ On 1 July 2007, Tanna Ltd acquired 80% of the shares of Matthew Ltd and Matthew Ltd acquired 75% of the shares of Hunter Ltd. All shares were acquired *cum div.*

Equity of the companies at 1 July 2007 was as follows:

	Matthew Ltd	Hunter Ltd
Share capital	$80 000	$60 000
Asset revaluation reserve	5 000	—
Retained earnings	1 000	4 000
Dividend payable	8 000	5 000

At 1 July 2007, all identifiable assets and liabilities of Matthew Ltd and Hunter Ltd were recorded at fair value. No goodwill or excess arose in any of the share acquisitions.

The financial statements of the three companies at 30 June 2009 contained the following information:

	Tanna Ltd	Matthew Ltd	Hunter Ltd
Share capital	$130 000	$80 000	$60 000
Asset revaluation reserve	—	5 000	—
Retained earnings (1/7/08)	10 000	10 500	13 000
Dividend payable	13 000	8 000	6 000
Profit	4 000	2 000	1 500

The final dividends were declared out of profits for the year ended 30 June 2009.

Since 1 July 2007, the following intragroup transactions have occurred:

(a) Matthew Ltd sold to Hunter Ltd an item of machinery for $12 000 on 31 December 2007. The machinery had originally cost Matthew Ltd $14 000 and at the time of sale had been depreciated to $11 200. The group charges depreciation at 10% straight-line.

(b) During the year ended 30 June 2009, inventory was transferred by Hunter Ltd to Matthew Ltd at 25% on cost to Hunter Ltd. $4000 of this inventory is included in the inventory of Matthew Ltd as at 30 June 2009. The tax rate is 30%.

Required

Prepare the consolidation worksheet entries for the year ended 30 June 2009.

Exercise 25.2 ★

CALCULATION OF THE NON-CONTROLLING INTEREST

On 1 July 2006, Ofu Ltd acquired 75% of the shares of Rose Ltd at a cost of $280 000 and Rose Ltd acquired 80% of the shares of Swains Ltd at a cost of $135 000. At acquisition date, the equity of Rose Ltd and Swains Ltd was as follows and represented the fair values of identifiable assets and liabilities at that date:

	Rose Ltd	Swains Ltd
Share capital	$150 000	$140 000
General reserve	20 000	—
Retained earnings	50 000	20 000

On 30 June 2008, Rose Ltd transferred the general reserve back to retained earnings and declared a dividend of $20 000 which was paid on 1 November 2008.

On 30 June 2010, the companies provided the following information.

	Rose Ltd	Swains Ltd
Profit before income tax	$ 48 000	$32 000
Income tax expense	20 000	15 000
Profit	28 000	17 000
Retained earnings (1/7/09)	75 000	42 000
	103 000	59 000

	Rose Ltd	Swains Ltd
Transfer to general reserve	—	20 000
Dividend paid	10 000	—
Dividend declared	15 000	10 000
	25 000	30 000
Retained earnings (30/6/10)	$ 78 000	$29 000

Required
Calculate the non-controlling interest share of retained earnings (30/6/10) for Rose Ltd and Swains Ltd.

Exercise 25.3

★★

CONSOLIDATION WORKSHEET ENTRIES, MULTIPLE SUBSIDIARIES

On 1 July 2006, Baker Ltd acquired 70% of the shares of Chatham Ltd for $100 000 and Chatham Ltd acquired 60% of Cook Ltd for $70 000. The equity of the companies at 1 July 2006 was:

	Chatham Ltd	Cook Ltd
Share capital	$100 000	$80 000
Retained earnings	40 000	30 000

At 1 July 2006, all the identifiable assets and liabilities of both Chatham Ltd and Cook Ltd were recorded at fair value.

At 30 June 2009, the financial data of the three companies were as follows:

	Baker Ltd	Chatham Ltd	Cook Ltd
Sales revenue	$120 000	$102 000	$ 84 000
Other revenue	60 000	44 000	36 000
Total revenues	180 000	146 000	120 000
Cost of sales	90 000	80 000	72 000
Other expenses	60 000	41 000	26 000
Total expenses	150 000	121 000	98 000
Profit before income tax	30 000	25 000	22 000
Income tax expense	8 000	8 000	5 000
Profit for the period	22 000	17 000	17 000
Retained earnings (1/7/08)	55 000	46 000	25 000
Total available for appropriation	77 000	63 000	42 000
Dividend paid	15 000	10 000	5 000
Retained earnings (30/6/09)	62 000	53 000	37 000
Share capital	148 000	100 000	80 000
Net assets	$210 000	$153 000	$117 000

Since 1 July 2006, the following transactions have occurred between the three companies:

- During the current year, Chatham Ltd sold inventory valued at $20 000 to Baker Ltd, this having cost Chatham Ltd $15 000. Half of this inventory is still on hand at 30 June 2009.
- On 1 July 2008, Cook Ltd sold a motor vehicle to Chatham Ltd for $25 000. The carrying amount of the vehicle at the date of sale was $23 000. Vehicles are depreciated at 30% p.a. on a straight-line basis.

The company tax rate is 30%.

Required
Prepare the consolidation worksheet journal entries for the year ended 30 June 2009.

Exercise 25.4 ★

CALCULATION OF THE NON-CONTROLLING INTEREST SHARE OF RETAINED EARNINGS

On 1 July 2008, Austral Ltd acquired 60% of the shares of Society Ltd for $300 000, and Society Ltd acquired 80% of the shares of Tupai Ltd for $190 000.

It was considered that Austral Ltd exercised control over Society Ltd and Tupai Ltd. At acquisition date, the equity for Society Ltd and Tupai Ltd was as follows, and represented the fair values of identifiable assets and liabilities at that date:

	Society Ltd	Tupai Ltd
Share capital	$200 000	$140 000
General reserve	130 000	70 000
Retained earnings	80 000	20 000

Three years later, the companies provided the following information:

	Society Ltd	Tupai Ltd
Profit before income tax	$ 24 000	$18 000
Income tax expense	10 000	7 500
Profit	14 000	10 500
Retained earnings (1/7/10)	88 000	27 500
	102 000	38 000
Dividend declared	10 000	8 000
Retained earnings (30/6/11)	$ 92 000	$30 000

There was a transfer to reserves of $4000 from pre-acquisition profits in the period ended 30 June 2010 by Tupai Ltd.

Required

Calculate the non-controlling interest's share of retained earnings (30/6/11) of Society Ltd and Tupai Ltd.

Exercise 25.5 ★★

CONSOLIDATION WORKSHEET, CONSOLIDATED STATEMENT OF COMPREHENSIVE INCOME

Line Ltd acquired 75% of the shares of Hawaiian Ltd on 1 July 2005 for $1 900 000. The identifiable assets and liabilities of Hawaiian Ltd at fair value on the acquisition date were represented by:

Share capital	$ 500 000
General reserve	800 000
Retained earnings	1 200 000
	$2 500 000

On the same date, Hawaiian Ltd acquired 60% of Marshall Ltd for $1 100 000. The identifiable assets and liabilities of Marshall Ltd at the acquisition date at fair value were represented by:

Share capital	$ 660 000
General reserve	500 000
Retained earnings	500 000
	$1 660 000

The financial information provided by the three companies for the year ended 30 June 2010 is shown on the next page.

The following additional information was obtained:

(a) All transfers to general reserve were from post-acquisition profits.

(b) Included in the plant and machinery of Marshall Ltd was a machine sold by Hawaiian Ltd on 30 June 2007 for $75 000. The asset had originally cost $130 000 and it had been written down to $60 000. Marshall Ltd had depreciated the machine on a straight-line basis over 5 years, with no residual value.

(c) Marshall Ltd had transferred one of its motor vehicles (carrying amount of $15 000) to Line Ltd on 31 March 2009 for $12 000. Line Ltd regarded this vehicle as part of its inventory. The vehicle was sold by Line Ltd on 31 July 2009 for $17 000.

(d) The tax rate is 30%.

	Line Ltd	Hawaiian Ltd	Marshall Ltd
Sales revenue	$2 850 000	$1 100 000	$ 880 000
Other revenue	420 000	200 000	60 000
Total revenues	3 270 000	1 300 000	940 000
Cost of sales	1 410 000	520 000	380 000
Other expenses	200 000	80 000	110 000
Total expenses	1 610 000	600 000	490 000
Profit before income tax	1 660 000	700 000	450 000
Income tax expense	580 000	160 000	140 000
Profit	1 080 000	540 000	310 000
Retained earnings (1/7/09)	4 070 000	2 300 000	1 120 000
Total available for appropriation	5 150 000	2 840 000	1 430 000
Dividend paid	400 000	160 000	80 000
Dividend declared	400 000	200 000	90 000
Transfer to general reserve	100 000	50 000	40 000
	900 000	410 000	210 000
Retained earnings (30/6/10)	$4 250 000	$2 430 000	$1 220 000

Required

Prepare the consolidated statement of comprehensive income/income statement and statement of changes in equity (not including movements in the general reserve and share capital) for the group for the year ended 30 June 2010.

Exercise 25.6 ★★

CONSOLIDATED FINANCIAL STATEMENTS

On 1 July 2005, the following balances appeared in the ledgers of the following three companies:

	South Ltd	Stewart Ltd	Secretary Ltd
Retained earnings	$20 000	$10 000	$ 5 000
General reserve	8 000	2 000	1 000
Dividend payable	4 000	2 000	—
Share capital	80 000	60 000	20 000

The dividend payable on 1 July 2005 was paid in October 2005.

For the year ended 30 June 2010, the following information is available:

- Inter-company sales were:
  - Stewart Ltd to South Ltd $20 000
  - Secretary Ltd to South Ltd $15 000

  The mark-up on cost on all sales was 25%.
- At 30 June 2010, inventory of South Ltd included:
  - $1000 of goods purchased from Stewart Ltd
  - $1800 of goods purchased from Secretary Ltd.
- The current income tax rate is 30%.

- South Ltd paid $67 200 for 80% of the shares of Stewart Ltd at 1 July 2005 when all identifiable assets and liabilities of Stewart Ltd were recorded at fair value.
- Stewart Ltd paid $18 750 for 75% of the shares of Secretary Ltd at 1 July 2005 when all identifiable assets and liabilities of Secretary Ltd were recorded at fair value as below.

Receivables	$ 9 000
Inventory	10 000
Plant	20 000
Total assets	39 000
Liabilities	13 000
Net assets	$26 000

- The plant has an expected remaining useful life of 5 years. By 30 June 2006, all receivables had been collected and inventory sold.

The financial information for the year ended 30 June 2010 for all three companies was as follows:

	South Ltd	Stewart Ltd	Secretary Ltd
Sales revenue	$ 98 400	$ 48 500	$30 000
Cost of sales	61 000	29 000	13 000
Gross profit	37 400	19 500	17 000
Expenses:			
Selling and administrative (inc. depn)	10 000	5 000	3 000
Financial	3 000	1 000	1 000
	13 000	6 000	4 000
	24 400	13 500	13 000
Dividend revenue	3 200	4 500	—
Profit before income tax	27 600	18 000	13 000
Income tax expense	12 000	8 100	5 200
Profit	15 600	9 900	7 800
Retained earnings (1/7/09)	40 000	20 000	10 000
Total available for appropriation	55 600	29 900	17 800
Transfer to general reserve	4 000	1 900	—
Dividend paid	5 000	2 000	4 000
Dividend declared	5 000	2 000	2 000
	14 000	5 900	6 000
Retained earnings (30/6/10)	41 600	24 000	11 800
General reserve	12 000	3 900	1 000
Share capital	80 000	60 000	20 000
Equity	$133 600	$ 87 900	$32 800
Receivables	$ 18 000	$ 25 000	$11 000
Inventory	25 000	26 400	13 800
Shares in Stewart Ltd	65 600	—	—
Shares in Secretary Ltd	—	18 750	—
Plant	50 000	39 750	20 000
Total assets	158 600	109 900	44 800
Provisions	20 000	20 000	10 000
Dividend payable	5 000	2 000	2 000
Total liabilities	25 000	22 000	12 000
Net assets	$133 600	$ 87 900	$32 800

Required
Prepare the consolidated financial statements of South Ltd at 30 June 2010.

Exercise 25.7 ★★

CONSOLIDATION WORKSHEET ENTRIES

The statements of financial position of Florida Ltd, Solomon Ltd and Ulawa Ltd for the year ended 30 June 2009 are shown below:

	Florida Ltd	Solomon Ltd	Ulawa Ltd
Share capital	$150 000	$50 000	$21 000
Retained earnings	60 000	18 000	4 000
Dividend payable	30 000	10 000	6 000
	$240 000	$78 000	$31 000
Non-current assets	$120 000	$20 000	$10 000
Shares in Solomon Ltd	55 800	—	—
Shares in Ulawa Ltd	—	21 000	—
Inventory	10 000	25 000	20 000
Receivables	54 200	12 000	1 000
	$240 000	$78 000	$31 000

For the year ended 30 June 2009, Solomon Ltd and Ulawa Ltd recorded a profit of $2000 and $1000 respectively.

Solomon Ltd acquired 90% of the ordinary shares of Ulawa Ltd for a total consideration of $20 730. At the acquisition date, 1 July 2006, Ulawa Ltd's equity comprised:

Share capital (21 000 shares)	$21 000
Retained earnings	1 000

At this date, all identifiable assets and liabilities of Ulawa Ltd were recorded at fair value except for some plant for which the fair value of $8000 was $1000 greater than the carrying amount of $7000 (i.e. original cost of $8500 less accumulated depreciation of $1500). The plant is expected to last a further 5 years.

On the same day, the directors of Florida Ltd made a successful offer for 45 000 of Solomon Ltd's fully paid shares. The consideration was $54 990 and, at the acquisition date, Solomon Ltd's equity comprised:

Share capital (50 000 shares)	$50 000
Retained earnings	4 000

At this date, all identifiable assets and liabilities of Florida Ltd were recorded at fair value except for some machinery whose fair value was $3000 greater than its recorded amount of $6000, the latter being $10 000 cost less accumulated depreciation of $4000. The machinery is expected to have a further useful life of 3 years. When assets are sold or fully consumed, any related valuation reserves are transferred to retained earnings.

Required
Prepare the consolidation worksheet entries for the preparation of the consolidated financial statements of Florida Ltd at 30 June 2009.

Exercise 25.8 ★★

CONSOLIDATION WORKSHEET, CONSOLIDATED STATEMENT OF COMPREHENSIVE INCOME AND STATEMENT OF CHANGES IN EQUITY

On 1 July 2009, Wallis Ltd acquired 80% of the shares in Futuna Ltd (cum div.) for $44 760. At this date, Futuna Ltd had not recorded any goodwill and all its identifiable net assets were recorded at fair value except for land and inventory, as shown opposite.

	Carrying amount	Fair value
Land	$ 8 000	$10 000
Inventory	12 000	15 000

Half of this inventory still remained on hand at 30 June 2010. Immediately after the acquisition date, Futuna Ltd revalued the land to fair value. The land was still on hand at 30 June 2010.

At 1 July 2009, Futuna Ltd acquired 75% of the shares in Tuvalu Ltd for $15 300. Tuvalu Ltd had not recorded any goodwill and all its identifiable assets and liabilities were recorded at fair value except for the following:

	Carrying amount	Fair value
Inventory	$10 000	$14 000

All the inventory was sold by 30 June 2010. When assets are sold or fully consumed, any related valuation reserves are transferred to retained earnings.

At the acquisition date, the financial statements of the three companies showed the following:

	Wallis Ltd	Futuna Ltd	Tuvalu Ltd
Share capital	$80 000	$32 000	$20 000
General reserve	20 000	3 200	—
Asset revaluation reserve	16 000	6 400	—
Retained earnings	6 400	4 800	3 200 (Dr)
Dividend payable	12 000	3 200	—

The following information was provided for the year ended 30 June 2010:

	Wallis Ltd	Futuna Ltd	Tuvalu Ltd
Sales revenue	$108 000	$72 000	$54 000
Cost of sales	72 000	61 200	40 500
Gross profit	36 000	10 800	13 500
Less: Distribution and administrative expenses	9 000	2 700	2 880
	27 000	8 100	10 620
Plus: Interim dividend revenue	1 280	1 500	—
Profit before income tax	28 280	9 600	10 620
Income tax expense	8 480	1 920	2 400
Profit	19 800	7 680	8 220
Retained earnings (1/7/09)	6 400	4 800	(3 200)
	26 200	12 480	5 020
Less: Dividend paid	4 000	—	1 000
Dividend declared	4 000	1 600	1 000
	8 000	1 600	2 000
Retained earnings (30/6/10)	$ 18 200	$10 880	$ 3 020

Additional information

(a) Dividends declared for the year ended 30 June 2009 were duly paid.

(b) Intragroup purchases (at cost plus $33\frac{1}{3}$%) were:
Wallis Ltd from Futuna Ltd — $43 200; Futuna Ltd from Tuvalu Ltd — $37 800.

(c) Intragroup purchases valued at cost to the purchasing company were included in inventory at 30 June 2010, as follows:
Wallis Ltd — $5400; Futuna Ltd — $4500.

(d) The tax rate is 30%.

Required

1. Prepare the consolidation worksheet entries for the preparation of the consolidated financial statements of Wallis Ltd at 30 June 2010.
2. Prepare the consolidated statement of comprehensive income and statement of changes in equity (not including movements in share capital and other reserves) at 30 June 2010.

Exercise 25.9 CONSOLIDATION WORKSHEET ENTRIES

★★ On 1 July 2008, Guinea Ltd acquired (ex div.) 80% of the shares of Britain Ltd for $146 400. At this date, the equity of Britain Ltd consisted of:

Share capital	$100 000
General reserve	50 000
Retained earnings	20 000

In the accounts at this date, Britain Ltd had recorded a dividend payable of $5000, goodwill of $13 000, and furniture at cost of $80 000 less accumulated depreciation of $10 000. All the identifiable assets and liabilities of Britain Ltd were recorded at fair value except for the following:

	Carrying amount	Fair value
Plant (cost $120 000)	$90 000	$100 000
Inventory	40 000	45 000

The plant has a further 5-year life, and is depreciated using the straight-line method. Of the inventory, 90% was sold by 30 June 2009, the remaining 10% being sold by 30 June 2010.

During the 2008–09 period, Britain Ltd recorded a profit of $40 000. There were no changes in reserves. During the 2009–10 period, Britain Ltd recorded a profit of $36 000, and recorded a transfer to general reserve of $6000.

On 1 January 2009, Britain Ltd acquired a 50% interest in Ireland Ltd for $57 000, giving it a capacity to control that entity. At this date, the equity of Ireland Ltd consisted of:

Share capital	$ 80 000
General reserve	40 000
Retained earnings	(10 000)

The identifiable assets and liabilities of Ireland Ltd consisted of:

	Carrying amount	Fair value
Land	$50 000	$56 000
Plant (cost $110 000)	80 000	82 000
Inventory	10 000	12 000

All the inventory on hand at 1 January 2009 was sold by 30 June 2009. The plant had a further 10-year life, and was depreciated using the straight-line method. The land was sold by Ireland Ltd in the 2009–10 period.

The profit of Ireland Ltd for the period from 1 January 2009 to 30 June 2009 was $8000. There were no movements in the general reserve during this period. During the 2009–10 period, Ireland Ltd earned a $20 000 profit. Ireland Ltd also transferred $20 000 from general reserve to retained earnings during the 2009–10 period.

Assume an income tax rate of 30%. When assets are sold or fully consumed, any related valuation reserves are transferred to retained earnings.

Required

Prepare, in general journal entry format, the consolidation worksheet entries for the preparation of the consolidated financial statements of Guinea Ltd at 30 June 2010.

Exercise 25.10

★★

CONSOLIDATION WORKSHEET ENTRIES

On 1 July 2008, Rennell Ltd acquired 75% of the issued shares of Russel Ltd for $320 000. At this date the statement of financial position of Russel Ltd was as follows:

Current assets	$ 20 000
Non-current assets	500 000
	520 000
Liabilities	120 000
Net assets	$400 000
Share capital	$100 000
General reserve	100 000
Retained earnings	200 000
Total equity	$400 000

All the identifiable assets and liabilities of Russel Ltd were recorded at fair value except for some land for which the fair value was $10 000 greater than the carrying amount and some depreciable assets with a further 5-year life for which the fair value was $12 000 greater than the carrying amount. The tax rate is 30%.

On 1 July 2010, Tulagi Ltd acquired 60% of the issued shares of Rennell Ltd for $350 000. At this date, the statement of financial position of Rennell Ltd was as follows:

Current assets		$120 000
Non-current assets		
Investment in Russel Ltd	$320 000	
Other	280 000	600 000
		720 000
Liabilities		220 000
Net assets		$500 000
Share capital		$200 000
Retained earnings		300 000
		$500 000

All the identifiable assets and liabilities of Rennell Ltd were recorded at fair value except for the investment in Russel Ltd which had a fair value of $400 000. The statement of financial position of Russel Ltd at 1 July 2010 was as follows:

Current assets	$ 30 000
Non-current assets	600 000
	630 000
Liabilities	130 000
	$500 000
Share capital	$100 000
General reserve	120 000
Retained earnings	280 000
	$500 000

All the identifiable assets and liabilities of Rennell Ltd at this date were recorded at fair value except for the land held at 1 July 2008 which, at 1 July 2010, had a fair value of $20 000 greater than carrying amount, and the depreciable assets which have a further 3-year life have a fair value of $8000 greater than carrying amount.

Financial information about Tulagi Ltd, Rennell Ltd and Russel Ltd at 30 June 2011 is shown below:

	Tulagi Ltd	Rennell Ltd	Russel Ltd
Current assets	$ 200 000	$150 000	$ 35 000
Non-current assets			
Investment in Rennell Ltd	350 000	—	—
Investment in Russel Ltd	—	320 000	—
Land	100 000	50 000	40 000
Depreciable assets	500 000	400 000	620 000
Accumulated depreciation	(80 000)	(80 000)	(40 000)
	1 070 000	840 000	655 000
Liabilities	250 000	260 000	120 000
Net assets	$ 820 000	$580 000	$535 000
Share capital	$ 300 000	$200 000	$100 000
General reserve	200 000	—	120 000
Retained earnings (1/7/10)	150 000	300 000	280 000
Profit for the period	170 000	80 000	35 000
	$ 820 000	$580 000	$535 000

Required

Prepare the worksheet entries for the consolidated financial statements at 30 June 2011.

Exercise 25.11 ★★

CONSOLIDATION WORKSHEET ENTRIES, ANALYSIS OF NON-CONTROLLING INTEREST

A client of yours is the chief accountant of Kuwau Ltd which, at 30 June 2009, has two subsidiaries, Kapiti Ltd and Matakana Ltd. He is unsure how to prepare the consolidated financial statements and has asked for your help. He has provided you with the information below concerning the group, and has determined a series of questions for which he wants clear, well-written answers. Provide the answers to these questions. Assume an income tax rate of 30%.

Part A

Kuwau Ltd acquired 40% of the capital of Kapiti Ltd on 1 July 2006 for $79 400, consisting of $9400 cash and 14 000 Kuwau Ltd shares having an estimated fair value of $5 per share. The equity of Kapiti Ltd at this date is shown below.

Share capital	$100 000
General reserve	50 000
Retained earnings	40 000

All the identifiable assets and liabilities of Kapiti Ltd were recorded at fair value except for plant (carrying amount $60 000, net of $10 000 depreciation) for which the fair value was $65 000. The plant has a further 5-year life.

During January 2007, Kapiti Ltd paid a dividend of $5000. Further, in January 2007, a transfer to retained earnings of $4000 was made from the general reserve established before 1 July 2006.

Required

1. Prepare the business combination valuation and pre-acquisition entries in relation to Kuwau Ltd's acquisition of Kapiti Ltd at 30 June 2007, assuming Kapiti Ltd is a subsidiary of Kuwau Ltd at this date.
2. Explain how the calculations used in requirement A meet the requirements of IFRS 3 *Business Combinations*.
3. If Kuwau Ltd acquired its shares in Kapiti Ltd at 1 July 2006, but did not achieve control until 1 July 2007 when the retained earnings of Kapiti Ltd were $60 000 and the fair value of plant was $30 000 greater than the carrying amount, should the fair values be measured at 1 July 2006, or at 1 July 2007 when Kuwau Ltd obtained control of Kapiti Ltd? Explain your answer, referring to requirements of appropriate accounting standards to justify your answer.

4. If Kapiti Ltd earned a $10 000 profit between 1 July 2006 and 30 June 2007, determine the non-controlling interest share of Kapiti Ltd's equity at 30 June 2007.
5. Explain your calculation of the non-controlling interest share of profit in requirement D.

Part B

Kapiti Ltd acquired 75% of the issued shares of Matakana Ltd at 1 January 2007 for $137 000 when the equity of Matakana Ltd consisted of $100 000 capital and $62 000 retained earnings which included profit of $12 000, earned from 1 July 2006. At acquisition date, all the identifiable assets and liabilities of Matakana Ltd were recorded at fair value except for the following assets:

	Carrying amount	Fair value
Land	$80 000	$90 000
Plant (net of accumulated depreciation of $15 000)	60 000	65 000
Inventory	20 000	25 000

Of the inventory, 90% was sold by 30 June 2007 and the remainder by 30 June 2008. The land was sold in January 2009 for $120 000. The plant has a further 5-year life. When assets are sold or fully consumed, any related valuation reserves are transferred to retained earnings.

Required

Prepare the business combination valuation and pre-acquisition entries at 30 June 2007 and 30 June 2009.

Part C

The following transactions affect the preparation of consolidated financial statements at 30 June 2009:

(a) Sale of inventory in June 2008 from Matakana Ltd to Kuwau Ltd — the inventory cost Matakana Ltd $2000, and was sold to Kuwau Ltd for $3000. At 30 June 2009, the inventory was all sold by Kuwau Ltd.
(b) Sale of plant on 1 January 2008 from Matakana Ltd to Kuwau Ltd — the plant had a carrying amount in Matakana Ltd of $12 000 at time of sale, and was sold for $15 000. The plant had a further 5-year life.
(c) Dividend of $10 000 declared in June 2009 by Matakana Ltd to be paid in August 2009.
(d) Payment of a $4500 management fee from Matakana Ltd to Kuwau Ltd in February 2009.

Required

In relation to the preparation of the consolidated financial statements *at 30 June 2009*:

1. Provide consolidation worksheet journal entries for the above transactions, including related non-controlling interest adjustments.
2. If the retained earnings (1/7/08) of Matakana Ltd was $80 000 and the profit for the 2008–09 period was $10 000, calculate the non-controlling interests share of Matakana Ltd's equity at 30 June 2009, assuming no changes in reserves.
3. The calculation of non-controlling interest is based on the concept of sharing only those profits that are realised to the group. Explain this concept, showing how it is implemented using transactions (a), (b) and (d) in part C.
4. Explain the non-controlling interest adjustment entry in relation to transaction (c).
5. Explain the adjustment entry for transaction (a).

Exercise 25.12 ★★

CONSOLIDATED FINANCIAL STATEMENTS

On 1 July 2009, Nauru Ltd acquired 60% of the shares of Caledonia Ltd for $108 000. On the same day, Caledonia Ltd acquired 80% of the shares (cum div.) of Zealand Ltd for $71 600. At the acquisition date, Caledonia Ltd's and Zealand Ltd's financial statements showed the following balances:

	Caledonia Ltd	Zealand Ltd
Share capital	$100 000	$60 000
General reserve	30 000	20 000
Retained earnings	15 000	8 000
Dividend payable	—	5 000

The dividend of Zealand Ltd was paid later in 2009.

On 1 July 2009, all identifiable assets and liabilities of Caledonia Ltd and Zealand Ltd were recorded at fair values except for the following:

	Caledonia Ltd		Zealand Ltd	
	Carrying amount	Fair value	Carrying amount	Fair value
Plant and machinery (cost $80 000)	$60 000	$80 000	—	—
Inventory	40 000	50 000	$30 000	$40 000
Vehicles (cost $80 000)	—	—	50 000	55 000

The vehicles have an expected useful life of 4 years and the plant is expected to last a further 10 years. Benefits are expected to be received evenly over these periods. All inventory on hand at 1 July 2006 was sold by 30 June 2007. When assets are sold or fully consumed, any related valuation reserves are transferred to retained earnings.

The financial statements of the three companies at 30 June 2010 are shown below.

	Nauru Ltd	Caledonia Ltd	Zealand Ltd
Sales revenue	$520 000	$365 000	$115 000
Other revenue	160 000	105 000	58 000
	680 000	470 000	173 000
Cost of sales	410 000	190 000	86 000
Other expenses	146 000	180 000	42 000
	556 000	370 000	128 000
Profit before income tax	124 000	100 000	45 000
Income tax expense	51 000	40 000	20 000
Profit	73 000	60 000	25 000
Retained earnings (1/7/09)	24 000	15 000	8 000
	97 000	75 000	33 000
Interim dividend paid	10 000	15 000	3 000
Final dividend declared	16 000	8 000	4 000
Transfer to general reserve	25 000	6 000	4 000
	51 000	29 000	11 000
Retained earnings (30/6/10)	46 000	46 000	22 000
Share capital	250 000	100 000	60 000
General reserve	145 000	36 000	24 000
Bank overdraft	21 000	6 000	20 000
Provisions	41 000	30 000	20 000
Current tax liability	55 000	42 000	26 000
Deferred tax liability	25 000	12 000	8 000
Dividend payable	16 000	8 000	4 000
	$599 000	$280 000	$184 000
Bank	$ 49 000	$ 25 000	$ 32 000
Receivables	61 200	17 000	16 000
Inventory	108 000	41 800	68 000
Dividend receivable	4 800	3 200	—
Shares in Caledonia Ltd	105 000	—	—
Shares in Zealand Ltd	—	67 600	—
Deferred tax asset	21 000	15 400	8 000
Plant	200 000	180 000	—
Accumulated depreciation	(48 000)	(70 000)	—
Vehicles	130 000	—	100 000
Accumulated depreciation	(30 000)	—	(40 000)
	$599 000	$280 000	$184 000

Additional information

(a) Included in the ending inventory of Caledonia Ltd was inventory purchased from Zealand Ltd for $10 000. This had originally cost Zealand Ltd $8000.

(b) Nauru Ltd had sold inventory to Zealand Ltd during the period for $25 000. This had cost Nauru Ltd $20 000. Half of this has been sold to external parties by Zealand Ltd during the year for $15 000.

(c) The tax rate is 30%.

Required

Prepare the consolidated financial statements for Nauru Ltd and its subsidiaries, Caledonia Ltd and Zealand Ltd, for the period ending 30 June 2010.

Problems

Problem 25.1

★★★

CONSOLIDATED FINANCIAL STATEMENTS, RECIPROCAL SHAREHOLDINGS

On 1 July 2006, Caroline Ltd acquired 10% of the issued capital of Flint Ltd for $60 000. At this date the equity of Flint Ltd consisted of:

Share capital	$100 000
Retained earnings	450 000

All the identifiable assets and liabilities of Flint Ltd were recorded at fair value except for some machinery for which the fair value was $20 000 greater than carrying amount. The machinery had a further 5-year life, with benefits expected to be received evenly over this period.

On 1 January 2009, Flint Ltd acquired 60% of the issued capital of Caroline Ltd for $132 000, obtaining control over the financial and operating policies of Caroline Ltd. At this date the equity of Caroline Ltd consisted of:

Share capital	$100 000
Retained earnings (1/7/08)	50 000
Profit to 1/1/09	50 000

All the identifiable assets and liabilities of Caroline Ltd were recorded at fair value except for plant and machinery (expected life of 5 years) whose fair value was $5000 greater than carrying amount, and the investment account Shares in Flint Ltd which had a fair value of $70 000. The financial statements of Flint Ltd at 1 January 2009 contained the following information:

	Carrying amount	Fair value
Current assets	$120 000	$120 000
Non-current assets		
Plant and machinery	470 000	490 000
Other	200 000	200 000
	790 000	810 000
Liabilities	160 000	160 000
Net assets	$630 000	$650 000
Share capital	$100 000	
Retained earnings (1/7/08)	500 000	
Profit to 1/1/09	30 000	
Equity	$630 000	

The plant and machinery of Flint Ltd whose fair value was greater than carrying amount had a further 4-year life.

At 30 June 2009 Caroline Ltd had not disposed of its shares in Flint Ltd.

At 30 June 2009, the financial statements of Flint Ltd and its subsidiary Caroline Ltd included the following:

	Flint Ltd	Caroline Ltd
Profit before income tax	$ 50 000	$ 80 000
Income tax expense	10 000	20 000
Profit	40 000	60 000
Retained earnings at 1/7/08	500 000	50 000
	540 000	110 000
Dividends paid at 28/6/09	20 000	10 000
Retained earnings at 30/6/09	$520 000	$100 000
Current assets	$ 80 000	$ 30 000
Non-current assets		
Shares in Caroline Ltd	132 000	—
Shares in Flint Ltd	—	60 000
Plant and machinery	600 000	140 000
Accumulated depreciation	(72 000)	(20 000)
Other	80 000	50 000
Total assets	820 000	260 000
Liabilities	200 000	60 000
Net assets	$620 000	$200 000
Equity		
Share capital	$100 000	$100 000
Retained earnings	520 000	100 000
Total equity	$620 000	$200 000

Required

Prepare the consolidated financial statements at 30 June 2009. Where necessary, make calculations to the nearest dollar.

26 Consolidation: foreign subsidiaries

ACCOUNTING STANDARDS IN FOCUS

IAS 21 *The Effects of Changes in Foreign Exchange Rates*

LEARNING OBJECTIVES

When you have studied this chapter, you should be able to:

- explain the difference between functional and presentation currencies
- understand the rationale underlying the choice of a functional currency
- apply the indicators in choosing a functional currency
- translate a set of financial statements from local currency into the functional currency
- account for changes in the functional currency
- translate financial statements into the presentation currency
- prepare consolidated financial statements including foreign subsidiaries
- explain what constitutes the net investment in a foreign operation
- prepare the disclosures required by IAS 21.

26.1 TRANSLATION OF FOREIGN SUBSIDIARY'S STATEMENTS

A parent entity may have subsidiaries that are domiciled in a foreign country. In most cases, the financial statements of the foreign subsidiary are prepared in the currency of the foreign country. In order for the financial statements of the foreign operation to be included in the consolidated financial statements of the parent, it is necessary to translate the foreign operation's financial statements to the currency used by the parent entity for reporting purposes. The purpose of this chapter is to discuss the process for translating and presenting the consolidated financial statements of a parent entity where at least one of its subsidiaries is a foreign subsidiary.

The accounting standard that deals with this process is IAS 21 *The Effects of Changes in Foreign Exchange Rates*. IAS 21 was first issued by the International Accounting Standards Committee (IASC) in July 1983, revised in 1993, and further revised as a part of the Improvements project in 2003. This latter revision provided convergence with Generally Accepted Accounting Principles (GAAP) in the United States, in particular Statement of Financial Accounting Standards No. 52 (SFAS 52) *Foreign Currency Translation*. Other minor revisions have been made up to January 2009.

26.2 FUNCTIONAL AND PRESENTATION CURRENCIES

Paragraph 3 of IAS 21 notes that its two areas of application are:

- translating the results and financial position of foreign operations that are included in the financial statements of the entity by consolidation, proportionate consolidation or the equity method; and
- translating an entity's results and financial position into a presentation currency.

Note that there are two different translation processes here. In order to understand this, it is necessary to distinguish between three different types of currency: local currency, functional currency and presentation currency. Not all foreign subsidiaries experience all three currencies.

- *Local currency*. This is the currency of the country in which the foreign operation is based.
- *Functional currency*. This is defined in paragraph 8 of IAS 21 as 'the currency of the primary economic environment in which the entity operates'. As is explained in more detail later, this is the currency of the country in which the foreign operation is based. This term is not defined in IAS 21.
- *Presentation currency*. Paragraph 8 defines this as 'the currency in which the financial statements are presented'.

To illustrate, Foreign Ltd is a subsidiary of Parent Ltd. Parent Ltd is an Australian company and Foreign Ltd is based in Singapore. The operations in Singapore are to sell goods manufactured in France. In this case, Foreign Ltd would most likely maintain its accounts in Singaporean dollars, the local currency, while the functional currency could be the euro, reflecting the major economic operations in France. However, for presentation in the consolidated financial statements of Parent Ltd, the presentation currency could be the Australian dollar. As the accounts are maintained in Singaporean dollars, they may firstly have to be translated into the functional currency, the euro, and then translated again into the Australian dollar for presentation purposes. It is these two translation processes that are referred to in paragraph 3 of IAS 21.

26.3 THE RATIONALE UNDERLYING THE FUNCTIONAL CURRENCY CHOICE

This section relies heavily on the discussion in the seminal paper by Lawrence Revsine, published in 1983, in which he emphasised the need to understand the rationale underlying the choice of an exchange rate as an entity's functional currency.

As noted by Revsine (1984, p. 514):

> A much more real danger is that firms, their auditors, and outside analysts may not understand the subtle philosophy that underlies the functional currency choice. As a consequence, innocent but incorrect choices and assessments may be made, and compatibility may not be achieved.

According to paragraphs 4(a) and 4(b) of SFAS 52, the objectives of the translation process are:

1. to provide information that is generally compatible with the expected economic effects of an exchange rate change on an entity's cash flows and equity
2. to reflect in consolidated statements the financial results and relationships of the individual consolidated entities as measured in their functional currencies in conformity with US generally accepted accounting principles.

Note in particular the first objective. As the foreign subsidiary operates in another country, it is important that the financial effects on the parent entity of a change in the exchange rate are apparent from the translation process. The parent entity has an investment in a foreign operation and so has assets that are exposed to a change in the exchange rate. Capturing the extent of this exposure should be reflected in the choice of translation method. The economic relationship between the parent and the subsidiary affects the extent to which a change in exchange rate affects the parent entity. This can be seen by noting the differences in the following three cases adapted from Revsine (1984).

26.3.1 Case 1

Protea Ltd is an Australian company that wants to sell its product in Hong Kong. On 1 January 2010, when the exchange rate is A$1 = HK$5, Protea Ltd acquires a building in Hong Kong to be used to distribute the Australian product. The building cost HK$1 million, equal to A$200 000. It also deposited A$55 000 (equal to HK$275 000) in a Hong Kong bank. By 31 January 2010, the company had made credit sales in Hong Kong of HK$550 000. The exchange rate at this time was still A$1 = HK$5. The goods sold had cost A$90 000 to manufacture. The receivables were collected in February 2010 when the exchange rate was A$1 = HK$5.5. This cash receipt is transferred back to Australia immediately.

Note, in this case the company has no subsidiary but acquired an overseas asset, deposited money in an overseas bank and sold goods overseas. The company would record these transactions as follows, in Australian dollars:

Building	Dr	200 000	
Cash	Cr		200 000
Cash – HK Bank	Dr	50 000	
Cash	Cr		50 000
Receivables	Dr	110 000	
Sales	Cr		110 000
Cost of Sales	Dr	90 000	
Inventory	Cr		90 000
Foreign Exchange Loss	Dr	10 000	
Receivables	Cr		10 000
(Loss on receivables when exchange rate changed from 1:5 to 1:5.5)			
Cash	Dr	100 000	
Receivables	Cr		100 000
Foreign Exchange Loss	Dr	5 000	
Cash in HK Bank	Cr		5 000
(Loss on holding HK$55 000 when exchange rate changed from 1:5.0 to 1:5.5)			

Note two effects of this accounting procedure:

- Foreign currency transactions, whether completed (the sale) or uncompleted (the deposit), have an immediate or potentially immediate effect on the future cash flows of the parent. As a result, foreign currency gains/losses are recorded as they occur and immediately affect income.
- Non-monetary assets held in the foreign country are recorded at historical cost and are unaffected by exchange rate changes.

26.3.2 Case 2

Assume that, instead of transacting directly with customers in Hong Kong, Protea Ltd formed a subsidiary, Banksia Ltd, to handle the Hong Kong operation. As with case 1, all goods are transferred from the Australian parent to the Hong Kong subsidiary, which sells them in Hong Kong and remits profits back to the Australian parent.

Hence, Banksia Ltd is established with a capital structure of HK$1 250 000 (equal to A$250 000), an amount necessary to acquire the Hong Kong building and establish the bank account. On selling the inventory to Banksia Ltd, Protea Ltd passes the following entries:

Receivable – Banksia Ltd	Dr	110 000	
Sales Revenue	Cr		110 000
Cost of Sales	Dr	90 000	
Inventory	Cr		90 000

Assuming that the parent bills the subsidiary in Hong Kong dollars, namely HK$110 000, on receipt of the cash, the parent would pass the entry:

Foreign Exchange Loss	Dr	10 000	
Cash	Dr	100 000	
Receivable	Cr		110 000

The subsidiary will show:

Sales	HK$ 110 000
Cost of sales	110 000
Profit	—
Equity	HK$ 1 250 000
Building	HK$ 1 000 000
Cash	250 000
	HK$ 1 250 000

Note that the underlying transactions are the same in case 1 and case 2. The organisational form does not change the underlying economic effects of the transactions. The translation of the HK subsidiary must therefore show the position as if the parent had undertaken the transactions itself. This is the purpose behind the choice of the functional currency approach.

Where the subsidiary is simply a conduit for transforming foreign currency transactions into dollar cash flows, the consolidation approach treats the foreign currency statements of the subsidiary as artefacts that must be translated into the currency of the parent.

In case 2, the translation of the subsidiary's statements must show:

- the assets of the subsidiary at cost to the parent; that is, what the parent would have paid in its currency at acquisition date
- the revenues and expenses of the subsidiary at what it would have cost the parent in its currency at the date those transactions occurred
- monetary gains and losses being recognised immediately in income as they affect the parent directly.

Note, in case 2, that the functional currency of the subsidiary is the Australian dollar. It is the currency of the primary economic environment in which the entity operates. The inventories are sourced in Australian dollars, the dollars financing the subsidiary are Australian dollars, and the cash flows that influence the actions of the parent in continuing to operate in Hong Kong are Australian dollars.

The key to determining the functional currency in case 2 is the recognition of the subsidiary as an *intermediary for the parent's activities*. The alternative is for the subsidiary to act as a *free-standing unit*. Consider case 3 in this regard.

26.3.3 Case 3

Assume that Protea Ltd establishes a subsidiary in Hong Kong for HK$1 250 000, the money again being used to acquire a building and set up a bank account. However, in this case the Hong Kong operation is established to manufacture products in Hong Kong for sale in Hong Kong.

Chinese labour is used in the manufacturing process and profits are used to reinvest in the business for expansion purposes. Remittances of cash to the parent are in the form of dividends.

The economics of case 3 are different from those in case 2. The subsidiary is not just acting as a conduit for the parent. Apart from the initial investment, the cash flows, both inflows and outflows, for the subsidiary are dependent on the economic environment of Hong Kong rather than Australia. The effect of a change in the exchange rate between Australia and Hong Kong has no immediate effect on the operations of the Hong Kong subsidiary. It certainly affects the worth of the parent's investment in the subsidiary, but it has no immediate cash flow effect on the parent. In this circumstance, the functional currency is the Hong Kong dollar rather than the Australian dollar.

In analysing the success of the overseas subsidiary, the interrelationships between variables such as sales, profits, assets and equity should be the same whether they are expressed in Hong Kong or Australian dollars. In other words, the translation process should adjust all items by the same exchange rate to retain these interrelationships.

The key point of Revsine's article is that the choice of translation method should be such as to reflect the underlying economics of the situation. In particular, it is necessary to select the appropriate functional currency to reflect these underlying economic events.

26.4 IDENTIFYING THE FUNCTIONAL CURRENCY

Paragraphs 9–12 of IAS 21 provide information on determining the functional currency. As the assessment of the functional currency requires judgement, in accordance with paragraph 12 of IAS 21, management gives priority to the primary indicators in paragraph 9 before considering the indicators in paragraphs 10 and 11, which supply supporting evidence to that determined from assessment using the paragraph 9 indicators. The indicators are:

Para 9: normally the one in which it primarily *generates and expends cash*
Consider the currency:

- in which *sales prices* are denominated or which influences sales prices
- of the country whose competitive forces and regulations influence *sales prices*
- in which *input costs* — labour, materials — are denominated and settled, or which influences such costs.

Para 10: consider two factors:

- the currency in which funds from *financing activities* are generated
- the currency in which *receipts from operating activities* are retained.

Para 11: consider:

- whether the activities of the foreign operation are carried out as an *extension* of the reporting entity
- whether *transactions with the reporting entity* are a high or low proportion of the foreign operation's activities
- whether *cash flows* from the activities of the foreign operation *directly affect* the cash flows of the reporting entity and are readily available for remittance to it
- whether *cash flows* from the foreign operation are sufficient to *service existing and expected debt* obligations without funds being made available by the reporting entity.

Para 12: management should use judgement to determine which currency most faithfully reflects the economic effects of the underlying transactions and events.

These factors are not significantly different from those stated in paragraph 42 of the FASB's SFAS 52. Jeter and Chaney (2003, p. 618) provided the basis for the information provided in figure 26.1, which illustrates the functional currency indicators as set down by the FASB.

Economic indicators	Indicators pointing to local overseas currency as functional currency	Indicators pointing to parent entity's currency as functional currency
Cash flows	Primarily in the local currency and do not affect the parent's cash flows.	Directly affect the parent's cash flows on a current basis and are readily available for remittance to the parent.
Sales prices	Are not primarily responsive in the short term to exchange rate changes. They are determined primarily by local conditions.	Are primarily responsive to exchange rate changes in the short term and are determined primarily by worldwide competition.
Sales market	Active local market, although there may be significant amounts of exports.	Sales are mostly in the country of the parent entity, or denominated in the parent entity's currency.
Expenses	Production costs and operating expenses are determined primarily by local conditions.	Production costs and operating expenses are obtained primarily from parent entity sources.
Financing	Primarily denominated in the local currency, and the foreign entity's cash flow from operations is sufficient to service existing and normally expected obligations.	Primarily from parent or other parent country-denominated obligations, or the parent entity is expected to service the debt.
Intragroup transactions	Low volume of intragroup transactions and there is not an extensive interrelationship between the operations of the foreign entity and those of the parent. However, the foreign entity may rely on the parent's or affiliates' competitive advantages, such as patents and trademarks.	High volume of intragroup transactions; there is an extensive interrelationship between the operations of the parent and those of the foreign entity or the foreign entity is an investment or financing device for the parent.

FIGURE 26.1 Functional currency indicators — FASB
Source: Jeter and Chaney (2003, p. 618).

In applying the criteria shown in figure 26.1 for a parent and a single subsidiary, such as an Australian parent and a subsidiary in Hong Kong, there are three scenarios:

1. the functional currency of the subsidiary is the Australian dollar
2. the functional currency is the Hong Kong dollar
3. the functional currency is another currency, say, the Malaysian ringgit.

In relation to the choice between the first two alternatives, the extreme situations are those alluded to in the analysis of the Revsine cases. For the *Australian dollar* to be the functional currency, the expectation is that the subsidiary is a conduit for the parent entity. In the easy case, the product being sold is made in Australia, and the selling price is determined by worldwide competition. Further, because the entire product sold by the subsidiary emanates from the parent, there is significant traffic between the two entities, including cash being transferred from the subsidiary to the parent. For the *Hong Kong dollar* to be the functional currency, it is expected that the Hong Kong operation is independent of the parent entity. The products are sourced in Hong Kong and the sales prices depend on the local currency. The only regular transactions between the two entities are the annual dividends.

However, between these two scenarios there are many others where the determination of the functional currency is blurred. For example, the product being sold may require some Australian raw materials but be assembled in Hong Kong using some local raw materials. There are then material transactions between the two entities, but the subsidiary may be self-sufficient in terms of finance. In these cases, cash is generated in Hong Kong but expended in both Australia and Hong Kong. In determining the functional currency, management will need to apply judgement. The key to making a correct decision is, in accordance with Revsine, understanding what the translation process is trying to achieve in terms of reporting the underlying economic substance of the events and transactions.

In relation to the situation where another currency, such as the Malaysian ringgit, is the functional currency, this could occur where the Australian parent establishes a subsidiary in Hong Kong that imports raw materials from Malaysia and elsewhere, assembles them in Hong Kong and sells the finished product in Malaysia.

It is possible therefore for a parent entity that has a large number of foreign subsidiaries to have a number of functional currencies, particularly if the foreign subsidiaries are all relatively independent. An example of this is the US company 3M, which in 2008 was a US$24.5 billion diversified technology company that had operations in more than 60 countries, sold products in nearly 200 countries, and had 32 international companies with manufacturing operations and 35 with laboratories. The subsidiaries ran manufacturing operations ranging from small converting operations to full-scale manufacturing of multiple product lines. In the notes to its 31 December 2007 annual report (see www.3m.com), 3M's policy statement on foreign currency translation stated:

> Local currencies generally are considered the functional currencies outside the United States. Assets and liabilities for operations in local-currency environments are translated at year-end exchange rates. Income and expense items are translated at average rates of exchange prevailing during the year. Cumulative translation adjustments are recorded as a component of accumulated other comprehensive income (loss) in stockholders' equity.

As the functional currencies for the offshore operations were the local currencies, 3M had to deal with the accounting for a large number of functional currencies.

26.5 TRANSLATION INTO THE FUNCTIONAL CURRENCY

In the situation where it is determined that the Hong Kong dollar is the functional currency for the Hong Kong subsidiary, the financial statements of the subsidiary prepared in Hong Kong dollars are automatically in the functional currency. Where the Hong Kong subsidiary uses the Australian dollar as its functional currency, it is necessary to translate the Hong Kong accounts from Hong Kong dollars into Australian dollars.

The process of translating one currency into another is given in paragraphs 21 and 23 of IAS 21. Paragraph 21 deals with items reflected in the statement of comprehensive income that concern transactions occurring in the current period:

> A foreign currency transaction shall be recorded, on initial recognition in the functional currency, by applying to the foreign currency amount the spot exchange rate between the functional currency and the foreign currency at the date of the transaction.

Hence, in translating the revenues and expenses in the statement of comprehensive income, theoretically each item of revenue and expense should be translated at the spot exchange rate between the functional currency and the foreign currency on the date that the transaction occurred. However, given the large number of transactions being reported on in the statement of comprehensive income, paragraph 22 of IAS 21 provides for an averaging system to be used. A rate that approximates the actual rate at the date of the transaction can be used; for example, an average rate for a week or month might be used for all transactions within those periods. The extent to which averaging can be used depends on the extent to which there is a fluctuation in the exchange rate over a period and the evenness with which transactions occur throughout the period. For example, where the transactions are made evenly throughout a financial year — no seasonal effect, for example — and there is an even movement of the exchange rate over that year, a yearly average exchange rate could be used.

In relation to statement of financial position accounts, paragraph 23 of IAS 21 states:

> At the end of each reporting period:
> (a) foreign currency monetary items shall be translated using the closing rate;
> (b) non-monetary items that are measured in terms of historical cost in a foreign currency shall be translated using the exchange rate at the date of the transaction; and
> (c) non-monetary items that are measured at fair value in a foreign currency shall be translated using the exchange rates at the date when the value was determined.

Monetary items are defined in paragraph 8 as 'units of currency held and assets and liabilities to be received or paid in a fixed or determinable number of units of currency'. As noted in paragraph 16, examples of monetary liabilities include pensions and other employee benefits to be paid in cash and provisions to be settled in cash, including cash dividends that are recognised as a liability. Examples of monetary assets include cash and accounts receivable. All of these items are translated using the spot exchange rate at the end of the reporting period — the closing rate. As noted in case 1 previously, this reflects the amounts available in the functional currency.

For non-monetary items such as plant and equipment, IAS 16 *Property, Plant and Equipment* (see chapter 9) allows the use of the cost basis or the revaluation model of measurement. Where the cost basis is used, the appropriate translation rate is the spot rate at the date the asset was initially recorded by the subsidiary. Where the revaluation model is used, the appropriate rate is the spot rate at the date of the valuation to fair value. Paragraph 25 of IAS 21 notes that certain non-monetary assets such as inventory are to be reported at the lower of cost and net realisable value in accordance with IAS 2 *Inventory*. In such a case, it is necessary to calculate the cost, translated using the spot rate at acquisition date, and the net realisable value translated at the spot rate at the date of valuation. The lower amount is then used — this may require a write-down in the functional currency statements that would not occur in the local currency statements.

The basic principles of the translation method follow.

26.5.1 Statement of financial position items

- *Assets*. Assets should first be classified as monetary or non-monetary. Monetary assets are translated at the current rate existing at the end of the reporting period. With a non-monetary asset, the exchange rate used is that current at the date at which the recorded amount for the asset has been entered into the accounts. Hence, for non-monetary assets recorded at historical cost, the rates used are those existing when the historical cost was recorded. For non-monetary assets that have been revalued, whether upwards or downwards, the exchange rates used will relate to the dates of revaluation.
- *Liabilities*. The principles enunciated for assets apply also for liabilities. The liabilities are classified as monetary and non-monetary and, for the latter, it is the date of valuation that is important.
- *Equity*. In selecting the appropriate exchange rate two factors are important. First, equity existing at the date of acquisition or investment is distinguished from post-acquisition equity. Second, movements in other reserves and retained earnings constituting transfers within or internal to equity are treated differently from other reserves.
- *Share capital*. If on hand at acquisition or created by investment, the capital is translated at the rate existing at acquisition or investment. If the capital arises as the result of a transfer from another equity account, such as a bonus dividend, the rate is that current at the date the amounts transferred were originally recognised in equity.
- *Other reserves*. If on hand at acquisition, the reserves are translated at the rate existing at acquisition. If the reserves are post-acquisition and result from internal transfers, the rate used is that at the date the amounts transferred were originally recognised in equity. If the reserves are post-acquisition and not created from internal transfers, the rate used is that current at the date the reserves are first recognised in the accounts.
- *Retained earnings*. If on hand at acquisition, the retained earnings are translated at the rate of exchange current at the acquisition date. Any dividends paid from pre-acquisition profits are also translated at this rate. Post-acquisition profits are carried forward balances from translation of previous periods' statement of comprehensive income.

26.5.2 Statement of comprehensive income items

- *Income and expenses*. In general, these are translated at the rates current at the dates the applicable transactions occur. For items that relate to non-monetary items, such as depreciation and amortisation, the rates used are those used to translate the related non-monetary items.
- *Dividends paid*. These are translated at the rate current at the date of payment.
- *Dividends declared*. These are translated at the rate current at the date of declaration.
- *Transfers to/from reserves*. As noted earlier, if internal transfers are made, the rates applicable are those existing when the amounts transferred were originally recognised in equity.

The application of these rules will result in exchange differences. Exchange differences arise mainly from translating the foreign operation's monetary items at current rates in the same way as for the foreign currency monetary items of the entity. Because the non-monetary items are translated using a historical rate that is the same for year to year, no exchange differences arise in relation to the non-monetary items. Further, items in the statement of comprehensive income such as sales, purchases and expenses give rise to monetary items such as cash, receivables and payables. Hence, the exchange difference over the period can be explained by examining the movements in the monetary items over the period. The accounting for the exchange difference is explained in paragraph 28 of IAS 21:

> Exchange differences arising on the settlement of monetary items or on translating monetary items at rates different from those at which they were translated on initial recognition during the period, or in previous financial statements, shall be recognised in profit or loss in the period in which they arise, except as described in paragraph 32.

The exchange differences are then taken to the current period's statement of comprehensive income in the same way as movements in the exchange rates on an entity's own foreign currency monetary items. See section 26.10 of this chapter for a discussion of the paragraph 32 exception.

As stated in paragraph 34 of IAS 21, the application of the basic principles of the translation method means that when an entity keeps its records in a currency other than its functional currency all amounts are remeasured in the functional currency. This produces the same amounts in that currency as would have occurred had the items been recorded initially in the functional currency.

ILLUSTRATIVE EXAMPLE 26.1

Translation from local currency into functional currency

Sentosa Ltd, a company operating in Singapore, is a wholly owned subsidiary of Taupo Ltd, a company listed in New Zealand. Taupo Ltd formed Sentosa Ltd on 1 July 2009 with an investment of NZ$310 000. Sentosa Ltd's records and financial statements are prepared in Singaporean dollars (S$). Sentosa Ltd has prepared the financial information at 30 June 2010, as shown in figure 26.2.

SENTOSA LTD
Statement of Financial Position
as at 30 June 2010

	2010 S$
Current assets:	
Inventory	210 000
Monetary assets	190 000
Total current assets	400 000
Non-current assets:	
Land – acquired 1/7/09	100 000
Buildings – acquired 1/10/09	120 000
Plant and equipment – acquired 1/11/09	110 000
Accumulated depreciation	(10 000)
Deferred tax asset	10 000
Total non-current assets	330 000
Total assets	730 000
Current liabilities:	
Current tax liability	70 000
Borrowings	50 000
Payables	100 000
Total current liabilities	220 000

(continued)

	2010 S$
Non-current liabilities:	
Borrowings	150 000
Total liabilities	370 000
Net assets	360 000
Equity:	
Share capital	310 000
Retained earnings	50 000
Total equity	360 000

SENTOSA LTD
Statement of comprehensive income
for the year ended 30 June 2010

	2010	
	S$	S$
Sales revenue		1 200 000
Cost of sales:		
Purchases	1 020 000	
Ending inventory	210 000	810 000
Gross profit		390 000
Expenses:		
Selling	120 000	
Depreciation	10 000	
Interest	20 000	
Other	90 000	240 000
Profit before income tax		150 000
Income tax expense		60 000
Profit for the period		90 000

The only movement in equity, other than in profit, was a dividend paid during the period of S$40 000.

Additional information

(a) Exchange rates over the period 1 July 2009 to 30 June 2010 were:

	S$1.00 = NZ$
1 July 2009	1.00
1 October 2009	0.95
1 November 2009	0.90
1 January 2010	0.85
1 April 2010	0.75
30 June 2010	0.75
Average rate for year	0.85
Average rate for final quarter	0.77

(b) Proceeds of long-term borrowings were received on 1 July 2009 and are payable in four annual instalments commencing 1 July 2010. Interest expense relates to this loan.
(c) The inventory on hand at balance date represents approximately the final 3 months' purchases.
(d) Revenues and expenses are spread evenly throughout the year.
(e) Deferred tax asset relates to depreciation of the plant and equipment.
(f) The dividends were paid on 1 April 2010.

Required

The functional currency is determined to be the New Zealand dollar. Translate the financial statements of Sentosa Ltd into the functional currency.

Solution

The translation process is as shown in figure 26.2.

	S$	Rate	NZ$
Sales	1 200 000	0.85	1 020 000
Cost of sales:			
Purchases	1 020 000	0.85	867 000
Ending inventory	210 000	0.77	161 700
	810 000		705 300
Gross profit	390 000		314 700
Expenses:			
Selling	120 000	0.85	102 000
Depreciation	10 000	0.90	9 000
Interest	20 000	0.85	17 000
Other	90 000	0.85	76 500
	240 000		204 500
			110 200
Foreign exchange translation loss	0		1 000
Profit before tax	150 000		109 200
Income tax expense	60 000	0.85	51 000
Profit for the period	90 000		58 200
Retained earnings at 1/7/09	0		0
	90 000		58 200
Dividends paid	40 000	0.75	30 000
Retained earnings at 30/6/10	50 000		28 200
Share capital	310 000	1.00	310 000
Non-current borrowings	150 000	0.75	112 500
Current tax liability	70 000	0.75	52 500
Current borrowings	50 000	0.75	37 500
Payables	100 000	0.75	75 000
	730 000		615 700
Inventory	210 000	0.77	161 700
Monetary assets	190 000	0.75	142 500
Land	100 000	1.00	100 000
Buildings	120 000	0.95	114 000
Plant and equipment	110 000	0.90	99 000
Accumulated depreciation	(10 000)	0.90	(9 000)
Deferred tax asset	10 000	0.75	7 500
	730 000		615 700

FIGURE 26.2 Translation into functional currency

Exchange differences arise mainly from translating the foreign operation's monetary items at current rates in the same way as for the foreign currency monetary items of the entity. Because the non-monetary items are translated using a historical rate that is the same from year to year, exchange differences in relation to non-monetary items arise only in the periods in which they are acquired or sold. Items in the statement of comprehensive income such as sales, purchases and expenses give rise to monetary items such as cash, receivables and payables. Hence, exchange differences are going to arise by examining the movements in the monetary items over the period.

From figure 26.2, the net monetary assets of Sentosa Ltd at 30 June 2010 consist of:

	S$
Monetary assets	190 000
Deferred tax asset	10 000
Borrowings: non-current	(150 000)
Borrowings: current	(50 000)
Current tax liability	(70 000)
Payables	(100 000)
Net monetary assets at 1/7/09	(170 000)

The changes in the net monetary assets are determined from the statement of comprehensive income. The exchange differences are calculated by comparing the difference between the exchange rate used in the translation process and the current rate at the reporting date:

	S$	Current rate less rate applied	NZ$ gain (loss)
Net monetary assets at 1 July 2009	310 000	(0.75–1.00)	(77 500)
Increases in monetary assets:			
Sales	1 200 000	(0.75–0.85)	(120 000)
	1 510 000		(197 500)
Decreases in monetary assets:			
Land	100 000	(0.75–1.00)	25 000
Buildings	120 000	(0.75–0.95)	24 000
Plant	110 000	(0.75–0.90)	16 500
Purchases	1 020 000	(0.75–0.85)	102 000
Selling expenses	120 000	(0.75–0.85)	12 000
Interest	20 000	(0.75–0.85)	2 000
Other expenses	90 000	(0.75–0.85)	9 000
Dividend paid	40 000	(0.75–0.75)	—
Income tax expense*	60 000	(0.75–0.85)	6 000
	1 680 000		196 500
Net monetary assets at 30 June 2010	(170 000)		(1 000)

*The entry for the period is:

		S$	S$
Income tax expense	Dr	60 000	
Deferred tax asset	Dr	10 000	
Current tax liability	Cr		70 000

In preparing the translated financial statements for the following period, it should be noted that the balance of retained earnings at 30 June 2010, as translated in figure 26.2, is carried forward into the next period. In other words, there is no direct translation of the retained earnings (opening balance) within the translation process.

26.6 CHANGING THE FUNCTIONAL CURRENCY

In the example used in the previous section, the foreign operation in Singapore used the New Zealand dollar as its functional currency. Because of changes in the foreign operation's circumstances, such as the source of raw materials or the variables that determine the selling price of the entity's products, it may be that the functional currency changes into, for example, Japanese yen. According to paragraph 33 of IAS 21, where there is a change in the functional currency the translation procedures apply from the date of the change. Further, paragraph 35 notes that the effect of a change is accounted for prospectively.

Assume, therefore that the Singaporean operation used New Zealand dollars as the functional currency until 1 June 2011, and then decided that the Japanese yen was the appropriate functional currency. The financial statements of the Singaporean entity at the date of change, 1 June 2011, would then be translated at the rate of exchange between the Japanese yen and the Singaporean dollar. This rate would be the historical rate for all non-monetary assets held at the date of change. Any exchange differences recognised in the statements translated into New Zealand dollars would not be recognised in the new translation. These gains/losses would resurface until the parent disposed of the foreign operation, and all exchange gains/losses would be taken into account at that point.

26.7 TRANSLATION INTO THE PRESENTATION CURRENCY

Consider an Australian entity that has two subsidiaries, one in Malaysia and one in Hong Kong, and the functional currency for each of these subsidiaries is the Hong Kong dollar. The Australian parent will have to prepare a set of consolidated financial statements for the group. In which currency should the consolidated financial statements be prepared?

Theoretically, any currency could be the presentation currency. It may be the Australian dollar if management perceives it as the currency in which users prefer to read the financial statements. In that case, the two subsidiaries' financial statements would be prepared in Hong Kong dollars, which is the functional currency for them both. These would then be translated into Australian dollars and consolidated with the parent entity's statements.

It is possible that the presentation currency could be the Hong Kong dollar, for example if the majority of shareholders in the parent entity were Hong Kong residents. In that case, the parent entity's statements would be translated from the Australian dollar into the Hong Kong dollar and consolidated with those of the subsidiaries as presented in their functional currency.

Hence, having prepared the parent's and the subsidiaries' financial statements in the relevant functional currencies, a presentation currency is chosen and all statements not already in that currency are translated into the presentation currency. Obviously, a number of presentation currencies could be chosen, and multiple translations undertaken.

Paragraph 39 of IAS 21 states the principles for translating from the functional currency into the presentation currency:

> The results and financial position of an entity whose functional currency is not the currency of a hyperinflationary economy shall be translated into a different presentation currency using the following procedures:
>
> (a) assets and liabilities for each statement of financial position presented (i.e. including comparatives) shall be translated at the closing rate at the date of that statement of financial position;
>
> (b) income and expenses for each statement of comprehensive income or separate income statement presented (i.e. including comparatives) shall be translated at exchange rates at the dates of the transactions; and
>
> (c) all resulting exchange differences shall be recognised in other comprehensive income.

Paragraph 40 notes that average rates over a period for statement of comprehensive income items may be used unless exchange rates fluctuate significantly over the period.

An elaboration of these procedures for a foreign subsidiary is as follows.

26.7.1 Statement of financial position items

- *Assets*. All assets, whether current or non-current, monetary or non-monetary, are translated at the exchange rate current at the reporting date. This includes all contra-asset accounts such as accumulated depreciation and allowance for doubtful debts.
- *Liabilities*. All liabilities are translated at the same rate as assets, namely the exchange rate current at the reporting date.
- *Equity*. In selecting the appropriate rate, two factors need to be kept in mind. First, equity existing at the acquisition date or investment is distinguished from post-acquisition equity. Second, movements in other reserves and retained earnings constituting transfers within or internal to shareholders' equity are treated differently from other reserves.

- *Share capital*. If on hand at acquisition date or created by investment, this is translated at the rate current at acquisition date or investment. If created by transfer from a reserve, such as general reserve via a bonus issue, this is translated at the rate current at the date the amounts transferred were originally recognised in equity.
- *Other reserves*. If on hand at acquisition date, these are translated at the current exchange rate existing at acquisition date. If reserves are post-acquisition and created by an internal transfer within equity, they are translated at the rate existing at the date the reserve from which the transfer was made was originally recognised in the accounts. If post-acquisition and not the result of an internal transfer (e.g. an asset revaluation surplus), the rate used is that current at the date the reserve is recognised in the accounts.
- *Retained earnings*. If on hand at acquisition date, they are translated at the current exchange rate existing at acquisition. Any dividends from pre-acquisition profits are also translated at this rate. Post-acquisition profits are carried forward balances from translation of previous periods' statement of comprehensive income.

26.7.2 Statement of comprehensive income items

- *Income and expenses*. These are translated at the rates current at the applicable transaction dates. For items, such as purchases of inventory and sales, that occur regularly throughout the period, for practical reasons average or standard rates that approximate the relevant rates may be employed. This will involve considerations of materiality. In relation to items such as depreciation, which are allocations for a period, even though they may be recognised in the accounts only at year-end (because they reflect events occurring throughout the period) an average-for-the-period exchange rate may be used.
- *Dividends paid*. These are translated at the rates current when the dividends were paid.
- *Dividends declared*. These are translated at the rates current when the dividends are declared, generally at end-of-year rates.
- *Transfers to/from reserves*. As noted earlier, if these are transfers internal to equity, the rate used for the transfer and the reserve created is that existing when the amounts transferred were originally recognised in equity.

Using the example in figure 26.2 and, assuming that the functional currency of Sentosa Ltd is Singaporean dollars, the translation into New Zealand dollars as a presentation currency is shown in figure 26.3.

FIGURE 26.3 Translation into presentation currency

	S$	Rate	NZ$
Sales	1 200 000	0.85	1 020 000
Cost of sales:			
Purchases	1 020 000	0.85	867 000
Ending inventory	210 000	0.77	161 700
	810 000		705 300
Gross profit	390 000		314 700
Expenses:			
Selling	120 000	0.85	102 000
Depreciation	10 000	0.85	8 500
Interest	20 000	0.85	17 000
Other	90 000	0.85	76 500
	240 000		204 000
Profit before tax			110 700
Income tax expense	60 000	0.85	51 000
Profit for the period	90 000		59 700
Retained earnings at 1/7/09	0		0
	90 000		59 700
Dividends paid	40 000	0.75	30 000

FIGURE 26.3 *(continued)*

	S$	Rate	NZ$
Retained earnings at 30/6/10	50 000		29 700
Share capital	310 000	1.00	310 000
Non-current borrowings	150 000	0.75	112 500
Current tax liability	70 000	0.75	52 500
Current borrowings	50 000	0.75	37 500
Payables	100 000	0.75	75 000
Foreign currency translation reserve			(69 700)
	730 000		547 500
Inventory	210 000	0.75	157 500
Monetary assets	190 000	0.75	142 500
Land	100 000	0.75	75 000
Buildings	120 000	0.75	90 000
Plant and equipment	110 000	0.75	82 500
Accumulated depreciation	(10 000)	0.75	(7 500)
Deferred tax asset	10 000	0.75	7 500
	730 000		547 500

The exchange difference arising as a result of the translation is NZ$(86 500) — there has been an exchange loss over the period. This loss arises for two reasons, as explained in paragraph 41 of IAS 21:

- *The income and expense items are translated at dates of the transactions and not the closing rate:* The profit represents the net movements in income and expenses:

Profit	= S$90 000
Profit as translated	= NZ$59 700
Profit × closing rate	= S$90 000 × 0.75
	= NZ$67 500
Translation gain	= NZ$(7 800)

- *In the case of a net investment in a foreign operation, translating the opening net assets at an exchange rate different from the closing rate:*

Net investment at 1 July 2004	= S$310 000
Net investment × opening rate	= S$310 000 × 1.00
	= NZ$310 000
Net investment × closing rate	= S$310 000 × 0.75
	= NZ$232 500
Translation loss	= NZ$(77 500)

- The total translation loss is NZ$(69 700) equal to (NZ$7800 + NZ$(77 500)).

Note the following in relation to the translation into presentation currency:

- The exchange differences are not taken into current period income or expense. As explained in paragraph 41 of IAS 21, these exchange differences have little or no direct effect on the present and future cash flows from operations. The translation is for presentation only. It is the functional currency statements that recognise exchange differences in current period income and expense.
- In the Basis for Conclusions to IAS 21, in paragraphs BC10–BC14, the IASB discusses whether the standard should (a) be permitted to present its financial statements in a currency other than the functional currency, (b) be allowed a limited choice of presentation currencies or (c) be permitted to present their financial statements in any currency. The IASB concluded that

entities should be permitted to present in any currency or currencies. The IASB noted that some jurisdictions require the use of a specific presentation which will put constraints on some entities anyway. Further, many large groups have a large number of functional currencies and it is not clear which currency should be the presentation currency. In fact, in such circumstances management may prefer to use a number of presentation currencies.

When the AASB in Australia issued an exposure draft requesting responses to whether or not Australian Accounting Standards should require the use of the Australian dollar as the presentation currency, the following response was given by the Rinker Group Ltd (sourced from AASB 2003, p. 7):

> It is our view that mandated presentation currency is not now appropriate to the circumstances of Rinker and that adoption of an Australian converged standard which is identical to the proposals outlined in the improvement to IAS 21 would serve the users of our financial reports far better.
>
> While Rinker is domiciled in Australia, is listed on the Australian Stock Exchange and currently has a shareholder base which is approximately 80% Australian, it is overwhelmingly a US economic entity. Over 80% of its revenue, profit, and assets are in the US. Ninety-nine percent of its debt is in the US. The clearly stated strategy of the company is to grow in the US. One of the characteristics of the industry in which Rinker participates (heavy building materials) is that revenues and costs are totally denominated in the local currency (US revenue and costs are completely in US dollars; Australian revenue and costs are completely in Australian dollars). As a result, variances in US dollar/Australian dollar exchange rates represent purely translation variances with no economic impact on the intrinsic value of the entity . . .
>
> . . . mandated reporting in Australian dollars may provide misleading information to the users of financial reports, particularly in periods when there are significant movements in the US dollar/Australian dollar exchange rates . . .

In the AASB papers summarising these responses, the example shown in figure 26.4 was provided to illustrate the point being made by Rinker.

	2001	2002	2003
Debtors – $US	10	13	16
Actual growth	—	30%	23%
Exchange rate: A$1 = US$	0.5	0.56	0.67
Translate to presentation currency – A$			
Debtors – A$	20	23	24
Growth reported	—	15%	4%
Difference between growth rates	—	15%	19%

FIGURE 26.4 Illustration of the argument for mandated presentation currency
Source: AASB (2003, p. 4).

The financial statements in the functional currency show the financial performance and position of the entity in the currency that primarily affects the operations of that entity. The translation process should not result in a different performance/position being shown. Note the effect on the comparative analysis of the change in exchange rates. The only way that the problem is overcome is if, in comparing the 2003 results with the 2002 results, the 2002 results are translated at the 2003 exchange rate rather than the 2002 rate. In other words, comparative figures must be continuously updated for exchange rate changes. This is a similar process to that used in accounting for inflation where both the current year's and prior year's accounts must be presented in current year dollars as the buying power of the dollar changes due to inflation.

- Paragraphs BC15–BC23 of the Basis for Conclusions on IAS 21 discuss the translation method for translating from the functional currency to a different presentation currency. In paragraph BC16, the IASB emphasises that the translation process 'should not change the way in which the underlying items are measured'. Rather, the translation method should merely *express* the underlying amounts, as measured in the functional currency, in a different currency. In this regard, refer to figure 26.4. Note the following ratios:

	S$	NZ$
Current ratio	400 000/730 000 = 0.548	300 000/547 500 = 0.548
Debt to equity	370 000/360 000 = 1.03	277 500/270 000 = 1.03
Profit to sales	90 000/1 200 000 = 0.075	76 500/1 020 000 = 0.075
However, note:		
Profit to equity	90 000/360 000 = 0.25	76 500/270 000 = 0.28

The ratios are only ever going to be fully retained if all items in both the statement of comprehensive income and the statement of financial position are translated at the closing rate. Using the exchange rates at the date of transaction means that retaining the ratios will not be possible. Paragraph BC17 notes that the IASB considered the method of translating all amounts at the most recent closing rate, noting that the method is simple, does not generate exchange differences and does not change ratios such as return on assets. However, the IASB prefers the method adopted in IAS 21, arguing that this method gives the same result if you translate the foreign entity's statements first into a functional currency and then into a different presentation currency or translate them directly into the presentation currency. For example, consider a Singaporean entity that has a functional currency of Hong Kong dollars but a presentation currency of Australian dollars. In relation to, say, a S$100 sales revenue transaction on 1 January 2010, whether you translate (a) using the spot rate for Singaporean dollars to Hong Kong dollars, and then translate this amount to Australian dollars using the spot rate on 1 January 2010 for Hong Kong dollars to Australian dollars; or (b) using the spot rate on 1 January 2010 for Singaporean dollars to Australian dollars the answer is the same. This occurs because both the translation to functional currency and the translation to presentation currencies for statement of comprehensive income items use the spot rate at the date of the transaction. In contrast, if the presentation translation used the closing rate for all accounts, a different answer would be obtained. However, the translation directly into the presentation currency does not isolate the exchange differences affecting income/expense that arise under a functional currency translation; rather it includes these exchange differences and those arising on a presentation translation into one amount affecting equity rather than income/expense.

26.8 CONSOLIDATING FOREIGN SUBSIDIARIES — WHERE LOCAL CURRENCY IS THE FUNCTIONAL CURRENCY

Paragraphs 44–7 of IAS 21 deal with matters relating to the consolidation of foreign subsidiaries. As noted in paragraph 45, normal consolidation procedures as set down in IAS 27 apply to foreign subsidiaries. Where a parent establishes or sets up a subsidiary in a foreign country, the determination of what exists at acquisition date is relatively simple. This is because generally the investment recorded by the parent is equal to the initial share capital of the subsidiary. Where a parent entity obtains an overseas subsidiary by acquiring an already existing operation, the date of control determines the point of time at which historical rates for translation are determined.

For example, assume on 1 July 2009 Canberra Ltd acquires all the shares of Tokyo Ltd, a Japanese entity that has been in existence for many years. The group commences on the date of control, namely 1 July 2009. Tokyo Ltd may have some land that it acquired in 2000 for 1000 yen. The historical cost in the records of the company is 1000 yen. In other words, even though the overseas entity has held the land prior to the date that Canberra Ltd obtained control over the foreign entity, the date for measurement of the historical rate is the date of control. This is because, under IFRS 3 *Business Combinations*, all assets and liabilities of the subsidiary are measured at fair value at acquisition date.

26.8.1 Acquisition analysis

Assume that Canberra Ltd acquired all the shares of Tokyo Ltd at 1 July 2009 for A$30 000, when the exchange rate between the Australian dollar and the Japanese yen was 1:5. At acquisition date, the equity of that company consisted of:

	¥	A$
Share capital	100 000	20 000
Retained earnings	40 000	8 000

All the identifiable assets and liabilities of Tokyo Ltd were recorded at fair value except for plant, for which the fair value was ¥5000 (equal to A$1000) greater than the carrying amount. The plant has a further 5-year life. The Japanese tax rate is 20%. The Australian tax rate is 30%. At 30 June 2010, the exchange rate is A$1 = ¥6. The average rate for the year is A$1 = ¥5.5.

At acquisition date:	
Net fair value of identifiable assets and liabilities of Tokyo Ltd	= A$20 000 + $8 000 + A$1 000(1 – 20%) (BCVR – plant)
	= A$28 800
Consideration transferred	= A$30 000
Goodwill	= A$1 200
	= ¥(1 200 × 5)
	= ¥6 000

As noted in paragraph 47 of IAS 21, the goodwill is regarded as an asset of the subsidiary.

26.8.2 Business combination valuation entries

Goodwill

At acquisition date, the entry in Japanese yen is:

		¥	¥
Goodwill	Dr	6 000	
Business Combination Valuation Reserve	Cr		6 000

The valuation reserve continues to be translated at the rate at acquisition date as it is pre-acquisition equity. Assuming the functional currency is the yen, the financial statements of Tokyo Ltd would be translated into Australian dollars for presentation purposes. The goodwill is translated at the closing rate of 1:5, giving rise to a foreign currency translation loss, recognised in equity. Hence, on consolidation, the worksheet entry at 30/6/10 is:

		A$	A$
Goodwill	Dr	1 000	
Foreign Currency Translation Reserve	Dr	200	
Business Combination Valuation Reserve	Cr		1 200

Plant

Similarly to goodwill, as noted in paragraph 47 of IAS 21, any fair value adjustments to the carrying amounts of assets and liabilities at acquisition date are treated as assets and liabilities of the foreign operation.

At acquisition date, the valuation entry is:

		A$	A$
Plant (¥5000/5)	Dr	1 000	
Deferred Tax Liability	Dr		200
Business Combination Valuation Reserve	Cr		800

At 30 June 2010, the valuation reserve is translated at the exchange rate at acquisition date and, as with goodwill, a foreign exchange loss is recognised — in this case on both the plant and the deferred tax liability:

		A$	A$
Plant (¥5000/6)	Dr	833	
Foreign Currency Translation Reserve	Dr	134	
Deferred Tax Liability (20% × 833)	Cr		167
Business Combination Valuation Reserve	Cr		800

The plant is depreciated at 20% per annum. This is based on the ¥5000 adjustment, giving a depreciation of ¥1000 per annum. The plant is translated at closing rates while the depreciation is translated at average rates.

Depreciation Expense [¥1000/5.5]	Dr	182	
Accumulated Depreciation [¥1000/6.0]	Cr		167
Foreign Currency Translation Reserve	Cr		15
Deferred Tax Liability [¥200/6.0 or 20% × 167]	Dr	33	
Income Tax Expense [¥200/5.5]	Cr		36
Foreign Currency Translation Reserve	Dr	3	

26.8.3 Pre-acquisition entry

The entry at acquisition date and at 30 June 2010 is:

Retained Earnings (1/7/09)	Dr	8 000	
Share Capital	Dr	20 000	
Business Combination Valuation Reserve [800 + 1200]	Dr	2 000	
Shares in Tokyo Ltd	Cr		30 000

26.8.4 Non-controlling interest (NCI)

The NCI receives a share of the recorded equity of the subsidiary as well as the valuation reserves raised on consolidation. The NCI also receives a share of the foreign currency translation reserve raised on the translation into the presentation currency. This share will need to be adjusted for any movements in that reserve as a result of movements raised via the revaluation process.

26.8.5 Intragroup transactions

As with any transactions within the group, the effects of transactions between a parent and its foreign subsidiaries, or between foreign subsidiaries, must be eliminated in full. Neither IAS 21 nor IAS 27 provide specific guidance in relation to transactions with foreign entities. A key matter of concern is whether the adjustment should be affected by changes in the exchange rate. In this regard, note paragraphs 136 and 137 of the Basis for Conclusions relating to the US Statement of Financial Accounting Standards (SFAS) No. 52 *Foreign Currency Translation*:

> 136. An intercompany sale or transfer of inventory, machinery, etc., frequently produces an intercompany profit for the selling entity and, likewise, the acquiring entity's cost of the inventory,

machinery, etc., includes a component of intercompany profit. The Board considered whether computation of the amount of intercompany profit to be eliminated should be based on exchange rates in effect on the date of the intercompany sale or transfer, or whether that computation should be based on exchange rates as of the date the asset (inventory, machinery, etc.) or the related expense (cost of sales, depreciation, etc.) is translated.

137. The Board decided that any intercompany profit occurs on the date of sale or transfer and that exchange rates in effect on that date or reasonable approximations thereof should be used to compute the amount of any intercompany profit to be eliminated. The effect of subsequent changes in exchange rates on the transferred asset or the related expense is viewed as being the result of changes in exchange rates rather than being attributable to intercompany profit.

It needs to be emphasised that the process of making the consolidation adjustments is to eliminate the *effects* of intragroup transactions. The exchange rate change is not an effect of the transaction but an economic effect on the group resulting from having assets in foreign entities.

Example 1: Parent sells inventory to foreign subsidiary

Assume Aust Ltd, an Australian company, owns 100% of the shares of a foreign operation, F Ltd. During the current period, when the exchange rate is F1 = $2, Aust Ltd sells $10 000 worth of inventory to F Ltd, at a before-tax profit of $2000. At the end of the period, F Ltd still has all inventory on hand. At the year-end balance date, the exchange rate is F1 = $2.50. The Australian tax rate is 30%, while the tax rate in the foreign country is 20%.

Assuming the financial statements of F Ltd have been translated from the functional currency (F) to the presentation currency (Australian dollars), the consolidation worksheet adjustment entries for the intragroup transaction are:

Sales	Dr	10 000	
Cost of Sales	Cr		8 000
Inventory	Cr		2 000
Deferred Tax Asset	Dr	400	
Income Tax Expense	Cr		400
(20% × 2000)			

The above entries eliminate the sales and cost of sales as recorded by the parent. The inventory would have been recorded by F Ltd at F5000. The translation process at balance date would mean the F5000 of inventory would be translated using the closing rate of F1 = $2.50, giving a translated figure for inventory of $12 500. After passing the consolidation adjustment entry, inventory in the consolidated statement of financial position would be reported at $10 500 (i.e. $12 500 – $2000). This figure is greater than the original cost of $8000 due to the exchange rate change between the transaction date and the balance date. The US FASB would argue that no further entry is necessary as the effect of changes in the exchange rates on the transferred asset is viewed as the result of changes in exchange rates rather than intragroup profit.

Note that the tax rate used is that of the country holding the asset — in this case, the foreign country. This is because the adjustment for the tax effect is required because of the adjustment to the carrying amount of the inventory in the first journal entry. As the inventory is held by the foreign entity, it is the foreign country's tax rate that is applicable.

Example 2: Foreign subsidiary sells inventory to parent

Assume F Ltd, the foreign subsidiary, sells an item of inventory to Aust Ltd, the Australian parent, during the current period. The inventory had cost F Ltd F5000 and was sold to Aust Ltd for F7500. At the date of sale, the exchange rate was F1 = $2. The tax rate in Australia is 30%. All inventory was still on hand at the end of the period when the closing exchange rate was F1 = $2.50.

The consolidation worksheet entry is:

Sales	Dr	15 000	
Cost of Sales	Cr		10 000
Inventory	Cr		5 000
Deferred Tax Asset	Dr	1 500	
Income Tax Expense	Cr		1 500

Both sales and cost of sales as recorded by F Ltd are translated at the exchange rate existing at the date of the transaction, namely F1 = $2. The inventory sold to the parent is recorded by that entity at $15 000. The profit on sale is adjusted against inventory at the exchange rate existing at date of sale, giving an adjustment of $5000. Hence, in the consolidated statement of financial position at the end of the period, the inventory is reported at $10 000, equal to the original cost to F Ltd.

ILLUSTRATIVE EXAMPLE 26.2

Consolidation — functional currency is the subsidiary's local currency

On 1 January 2010, Kangaroos Ltd, an Australian company, acquired 80% of the shares of All Blacks Ltd, a New Zealand company, for A$2 498 000. The 2010 trial balance of All Blacks Ltd prepared in New Zealand dollars, which is also the functional currency, showed the following information:

	1 January 2010 NZ$000	1 December 2010 NZ$000
Revenue		6 450
Cost of sales		4 400
Gross profit		2 050
Expenses:		
Depreciation		280
Other		960
		1 240
Profit before income tax		810
Income tax expense		120
Profit		690
Retained earnings at beginning of year		1 440
		2 130
Dividend paid		100
Dividend declared		100
		200
Retained earnings at end of year		1 930
Cash and receivables	1 000	1 760
Inventories	1 200	1 000
Land	800	800
Buildings	2 200	2 200
Accumulated depreciation	(900)	(990)
Equipment	1 130	1 330
Accumulated depreciation	(200)	(390)
Total assets	5 230	5 710

(continued)

	1 January 2010 NZ$000	1 December 2010 NZ$000
Current liabilities	590	420
Non-current liabilities	1200	1360
Total liabilities	1790	1780
Net assets	3440	3930
Share capital	2000	2000
Retained earnings	1440	1930
Total equity	3440	3930

Additional information

1. Direct exchange rates for the New Zealand dollar are as follows:

1 January 2010	1.20
1 July 2010	1.25
1 November 2010	1.35
31 December 2010	1.40
Average for the year	1.30

2. At 1 January 2010, all the assets and liabilities of All Blacks Ltd were recorded at fair value except for the land, for which the fair value was NZ$1 000 000, and the equipment, for which the fair value was $1 010 000. The undervalued equipment had a further 4-year life. The tax rate in New Zealand is 25%.
3. Additional equipment was acquired on 1 July 2010 for NZ$200 000 by issuing a note for NZ$160 000 and paying the balance in cash.
4. Sales and expenses were incurred evenly throughout the year.
5. Dividends of NZ$100 000 were paid on 1 July 2010.
6. On 1 November 2010, All Blacks Ltd sold inventory to Kangaroos Ltd for NZ$25 000. The inventory had cost All Blacks Ltd $20 000. Half of the inventory is still on hand at 31 December 2010. The Australian tax rate is 30%.

Required

1. Translate the New Zealand financial statements into the Australian dollar, which is the presentation currency.
2. Prepare the consolidation worksheet entries for consolidating the New Zealand subsidiary into the consolidated financial statements of Kangaroos Ltd. The partial goodwill method is used.

Solution

1. Translation into presentation currency

	NZ$	Rate	A$
Revenue	6450	1/1.30	4962
Cost of sales	4400	1/1.30	3385
Gross profit	2050		1577
Depreciation	280	1/1.30	215
Other	960	1/1.30	739
	1240		954
Profit before tax	810		623
Income tax expense	120	1/1.30	92

(continued)

	NZ$	Rate	A$
Profit	690		531
Retained earnings as at 1/1/10	1 440	1/1.20	1 200
	2 130		1 731
Dividend paid	100	1/1.25	80
Dividend declared	100	1/1.40	71
	200		151
Retained earnings as at 31/12/10	1 930		1 580
Share capital	2 000	1/1.20	1 667
Non-current liabilities	1 360	1/1.40	971
Current liabilities	420	1/1.40	300
Foreign currency translation reserve			(439)
	5 710		4 079
Cash and receivables	1 760	1/1.40	1 257
Inventories	1 000	1/1.40	714
Land	800	1/1.40	572
Buildings	2 200	1/1.40	1 572
Accumulated depreciation	(990)	1/1.40	(707)
Equipment	1 330	1/1.40	950
Accumulated depreciation	(390)	1/1.40	(279)
	5 710		4 079

In relation to the foreign currency translation reserve:

- *The income and expense items are translated at dates of the transactions and not the closing rate:* The profit represents the net movements in income and expenses:

Profit	= NZ$690 000
Profit as translated	= A$530 800
Profit × closing rate	= NZ$690 000 × 1/1.40
	= A$492 857
Translation loss	= A$(37 943)
Dividend paid as translated	= A$80 000
Dividend paid at closing rate	= NZ$100 000 × 1/1.40
	= A$71 429
Translation gain	= A$8 571

- *In the case of a net investment in a foreign operation, translating the opening net assets at an exchange rate different from the closing rate:*

Net investment at 1 January 2010	= NZ$3 440 000
Net investment × opening rate	= NZ$3 440 000 × 1/1.20
	= A$2 866 667
Net investment × closing rate	= NZ$3 440 000 × 1/1.40
	= A$2 457 143
Translation loss	= A$(409 524)

- Total translation loss is A$(438 896) = (A$(37 943) + A$(409 524)) + $8 571

2. Consolidation worksheet entries: (in $000)

Net fair value of identifiable assets and liabilities of All Blacks Ltd	= A$[2 000 + 1 440 + 2 00(1 – 25%) (land) + 80(1 – 25%) (equipment)] 1/1.20
	= A$[1 667 + 1 200 + 125 + 50]
Net fair value acquired	= 80% × A$[1 667 + 1 200 + 125 + 50]
	= A$[1 334 + 960 + 100 + 40]
	= A$2 434
Consideration transferred	= A$2 498
Goodwill acquired	= A$64
	= NZ$77 (i.e. 64 × 1.20)

(i) Business combination valuation entries

Land (200/1.40)	Dr	143	
Foreign Currency Translation Reserve	Dr	18	
Business Combination Valuation Reserve (150/1.20)	Cr		125
Deferred Tax Liability (50/1.40)	Cr		36
Accumulated Depreciation (200/1.40)	Dr	143	
Equipment (120/1.40)	Cr		86
Foreign Currency Translation Reserve	Dr	7	
Deferred Tax Liability (25% × (80/1.40))	Cr		14
Business Combination Valuation Reserve (60/1.20)	Cr		50
Depreciation Expense ([1/4 × 80]/1.30)	Dr	15	
Accumulated Depreciation ([1/4 × 80]/1.40)	Cr		14
Foreign Currency Translation Reserve	Cr		1
Deferred Tax Liability ([25% × 20]/1.30)	Dr	3.5	
Income Tax Expense ([25% × 20]/1.30)	Cr		3.8
Foreign Currency Translation Reserve	Dr	0.3	

(At acquisition the deferred tax liability was NZ$20 = 25% × NZ$80)

(ii) Pre-acquisition entry

Retained Earnings (1/1/10)	Dr	960	
Share Capital	Dr	1 334	
Business Combination Valuation Reserve	Dr	140	
Goodwill	Dr	64	
Shares in All Blacks Ltd	Cr		2 498
Foreign Currency Translation Reserve	Dr	9	
Goodwill (77/1.40 – 64)	Cr		9

(iii) Non-controlling interest

Share at acquisition date

Retained Earnings (1/1/10) (20% × 1200)	Dr	240	
Share Capital (20% × 1667)	Dr	333	
Business Combination Valuation Reserve (20% [125 + 50])	Dr	35	
NCI	Cr		608

Share from 1/1/10–31/12/10

(i) Current period profit — the share is based on the translated profit of the subsidiary

NCI Share of Profit	Dr	104	
NCI	Cr		104
(20% × A$[531 – (15 – 3.8)])			

(ii) The share of the foreign currency translation reserve is based on the amount of the reserve calculated as a result of the translation process adjusted by any changes in that reserve recognised in the valuation entries

NCI	Dr	93	
Foreign Currency Translation Reserve	Cr		93
(20% [439 + 18 + 7 + 1 + 0.3])			

(iii) Dividend paid

NCI	Dr	16	
Dividend Paid	Cr		16
(20% × A$80)			

(iv) Dividend declared

NCI	Dr	14	
Dividend Declared	Cr		14
(20% × A$71)			

Intragroup transactions:

(i) Dividends

Dividend Revenue	Dr	64	
Dividend Paid	Cr		64
(80% × 100/1.25)			
Dividend Revenue	Dr	57	
Dividend Receivable	Cr		57
(80% × 100/1.40)			
Dividend Payable	Dr	57	
Dividend Declared	Cr		57

(ii) Sale of inventory: subsidiary to parent

Sales Revenue (25/1.35)	Dr	19	
Cost of Sales	Cr		17
Inventory (1/2 × 5 × 1/1.35)	Cr		2
Deferred Tax Asset (30% × 2)	Dr	0.6	
Income Tax Expense	Cr		0.6

(iii) Adjustment to NCI

NCI	Dr	0.28	
NCI Share of Profit	Cr		0.28
(20% × (2 – 0.6))			

26.9 CONSOLIDATING FOREIGN SUBSIDIARIES — WHERE FUNCTIONAL CURRENCY IS THAT OF THE PARENT ENTITY

In this circumstance, the subsidiary's financial statements are prepared in the local currency, and, as the parent's currency is the functional currency, they are translated into the parent's currency. The main difference in preparing the consolidated financial statements in this case is in the valuation entries. This is because the translation of non-monetary assets differs when the translation is for presentation purposes rather than for functional currency purposes.

Under the method described in paragraph 23 of IAS 21, the non-monetary assets of the subsidiary are translated using exchange rates at the date of the transaction (i.e. historical rates). In contrast, in illustrative example 26.2, where the translation is based on paragraph 39 of IAS 21, the non-monetary assets are translated at the closing rate.

Using the information in illustrative example 26.2:

- at acquisition date, 1 January 2010, goodwill of the subsidiary was measured to be NZ$96
- the land had a fair value-carrying amount difference of NZ$200
- the equipment had a fair value-carrying amount difference of NZ$80, with an expected remaining useful life of 25%
- the NZ tax rate is 25%
- the direct exchange rates for the NZ dollar were:

1 January 2010	1.20
1 July 2010	1.25
1 November 2010	1.35
31 December 2010	1.40
Average for the year	1.30

The business combination valuation entries are then:

The goodwill balance is translated at the historical rate:

Goodwill (96/1.20)	Dr	80	
Business Combination Valuation Reserve (96/1.20)	Cr		80

The land is translated at the historical rate, but the deferred tax liability is translated at the closing rate. As the net monetary assets held at the beginning of the period are affected by changes in the exchange rate, an exchange gain is recognised:

Land (200/1.20)	Dr	167	
Foreign Exchange Gain	Cr		6
Business Combination Valuation Reserve (150/1.20)	Cr		125
Deferred Tax Liability (50/1.40)	Cr		36

The equipment and related accumulated depreciation are translated at the historical rate, while the deferred tax liability is translated at the closing rate, giving rise to a foreign exchange gain.

Subsequent depreciation is based on the historical rate:

Accumulated Depreciation (200/1.20)	Dr	167	
Equipment (120/1.20)	Cr		100
Foreign Exchange Gain	Cr		3
Deferred Tax Liability ((25% × 80)1.40))	Cr		14
Business Combination Valuation Reserve (60/1.20)	Cr		50

Depreciation Expense ([1/4 × 80]/1.20)	Dr	17	
Accumulated Depreciation ([1/4 × 80]/1.20)	Cr		17
Deferred Tax Liability ([25% × 20]/1.40)	Dr	3.5	
Income Tax Expense ([25% × 20]/1.30)	Cr		3.8
Foreign Currency Exchange Loss	Dr	0.3	
(At acquisition the deferred tax liability was NZ$20 = 25% × NZ$80)			

26.10 NET INVESTMENT IN A FOREIGN OPERATION

Paragraph 15 of IAS 21 notes that the investment in a foreign operation may consist of more than just the ownership of shares in that operation. An entity may have a monetary item that is receivable or payable to the foreign subsidiary. According to paragraph 15, where there is an item for which settlement is neither planned nor likely to occur in the foreseeable future, it is in substance a part of the entity's net investment in that foreign operation. These items include long-term receivables and payables but not trade receivables or payables.

Consider the situation where an Australian parent entity has made a long-term loan of 100 000 yen to a Japanese subsidiary when the exchange rate is $2 = ¥1. The parent entity records a receivable of $200 000, while the subsidiary records a payable of ¥100 000. If during the following financial period the exchange rate changes to $3 = ¥1, in accordance with paragraph 28 of IAS 21 the Australian parent passes the following entry in its own records:

Loan Receivable	Dr	100 000	
Exchange Gain	Cr		100 000

This results in the receivable being recorded at $300 000. The subsidiary does not pass any entry because it still owes ¥100 000. On translation of the subsidiary into the presentation currency (the Australian dollar), the payable is translated into $300 000. On consolidation of the subsidiary, both the payable and the receivable are eliminated. However, because the receivable is regarded as part of the parent's net investment in the subsidiary, the accounting for the exchange gain is in accord with paragraph 32 of IAS 21:

> Exchange differences arising on a monetary item that forms part of a reporting entity's net investment in a foreign operation (see paragraph 15) shall be recognised in profit or loss in the separate financial statements of the reporting entity or the individual financial statements of the foreign operation, as appropriate. In the financial statements that include the foreign operation and the reporting entity (e.g. consolidated financial statements where the foreign operation is a subsidiary), such exchange differences shall be recognised initially in a separate component of equity and recognised in profit or loss on disposal of the net investment in accordance with paragraph 48.

Hence, the exchange gain of $100 000 recognised as income by the parent must, on consolidation, be reclassified to the foreign currency translation reserve raised as part of the translation process. Hence, in the consolidation worksheet the adjustment entry is:

Exchange Gain	Dr	100 000	
Foreign Currency Translation Reserve	Cr		100 000

26.11 DISCLOSURE

Paragraphs 51–57 contain the disclosure requirements under IAS 21. In particular, an entity must disclose:

- the amount of exchange differences included in profit or loss for the period
- net exchange differences classified in a separate component of equity, and a reconciliation of the amount of such exchange differences at the beginning and end of the period

- when the presentation currency of the parent entity is different from the functional currency:
  - the fact that they are different
  - the functional currency
  - the reason for using a different presentation currency
- when there is a change in the functional currency, the fact that such a change has occurred.

Some examples of accounting policies notes in relation to currency translation are given in figure 26.5.

FIGURE 26.5 Accounting policies on foreign currency translation

Example 1: Nokia Corporation, a Finnish limited liability company domiciled in Helsinki

Functional and presentation currency

The financial statements of all Group entities are measured using the currency of the primary economic environment in which the entity operates (functional currency). The consolidated financial statements are presented in Euro, which is the functional and presentation currency of the Parent Company.

Transactions in foreign currencies

Transactions in foreign currencies are recorded at the rates of exchange prevailing at the dates of the individual transactions. For practical reasons, a rate that approximates the actual rate at the date of the transaction is often used. At the end of the accounting period, the unsettled balances on non-functional foreign currency receivables and liabilities are valued at the rates of exchange prevailing at the year-end. Foreign exchange gains and losses arising from balance sheet items, as well as fair value changes in the related hedging instruments, are reported in Financial Income and Expenses.

Foreign Group companies

In the consolidated accounts all income and expenses of foreign subsidiaries are translated into Euro at the average foreign exchange rates for the accounting period. All assets and liabilities of foreign Group companies are translated into Euro at the year-end foreign exchange rates with the exception of goodwill arising on the acquisition of foreign companies prior to the adoption of IAS 21 (revised 2004) on January 1, 2005, which is translated to Euro at historical rates. Differences resulting from the translation of income and expenses at the average rate and assets and liabilities at the closing rate are treated as an adjustment affecting consolidated shareholders' equity. On the disposal of all or part of a foreign Group company by sale, liquidation, repayment of share capital or abandonment, the cumulative amount or proportionate share of the translation difference is recognized as income or as expense in the same period in which the gain or loss on disposal is recognized.

Source: Nokia (2007, p. 13–4).

Example 2: Bayer Group, which has headquarters in Germany and activities worldwide

Foreign currency translation

In the financial statements of the individual consolidated companies, all receivables and payables in currencies other than the respective functional currency are translated at closing rates, irrespective of whether they are exchange-hedged. Derivative financial instruments are stated at fair value. Exchange rate differences from valuation of balances in foreign currencies are recognized in income. The majority of consolidated companies carry out their activities financially, economically and organizationally autonomous and their functional currencies are therefore the respective local currencies.

The assets and liabilities of foreign companies at the start and end of the year are translated at closing rates. All changes occurring during the year and all income and expense items are translated at average rates for the year. Components of stockholders' equity are translated at the historical exchange rates prevailing at the respective dates of their first time recognition in Group equity.

FIGURE 26.5 *(continued)*

The differences between the resulting amounts and those obtained by translating at closing rates are reflected in other comprehensive income and stated separately in the tables in the Notes under "Exchange differences on translation of operations outside the euro zone" or "Exchange differences." When a company is deconsolidated, exchange differences recognized in stockholders' equity are removed from equity and recognized in the income statement.

The exchange rates for major currencies against the euro varied as follows:

		Closing rate		Average rate	
€1		2006	**2007**	2006	**2007**
Argentina	ARS	4.04	**4.64**	3.86	**4.27**
Brazil	BRL	2.82	**2.61**	2.73	**2.67**
China	CNY	10.28	**10.75**	10.01	**10.42**
U.K.	GBP	0.67	**0.73**	0.68	**0.68**
Japan	JPY	156.93	**164.93**	146.04	**161.23**
Canada	CAD	1.53	**1.44**	1.42	**1.47**
Mexico	MXN	14.27	**16.08**	13.69	**14.97**
Switzerland	CHF	1.61	**1.65**	1.57	**1.64**
United States	USD	1.32	**1.47**	1.26	**1.37**

Source: Bayer (2008, pp. 107–8).

Notice in figure 26.5, that both Nokia and Bayer provide information about the functional currencies of the entities within their respective groups, which relates to the disclosures required by paragraph 53 of IAS 21.

Illustrative disclosures relating to paragraph 52 of IAS 21 are given in figure 26.6.

NOTE			**IAS 21** Para.
Movements in reserves			
Foreign Currency Translation Reserve	2010	2009	*52(b)*
Balance at beginning of period	(2420)	(3020)	
Exchange differences arising on translation of overseas operations	(540)	600	
Balance at end of period	(2960)	(2420)	
Profit from operations			
	2010	2009	
Profit from operations has been arrived at after charging:			
Amortisation	X	X	
Research and development costs	X	X	
Net foreign exchange losses/(gains)	765	(346)	*52(a)*

FIGURE 26.6 Disclosures required by paragraph 50 of IAS 21

SUMMARY

A parent entity may have investments in subsidiaries that are incorporated in countries other than that of the parent. The foreign operation will record its transactions generally in the local currency. However, the local currency may not be that of the economy that determines the pricing of those transactions. To this end, IAS 21 requires the financial statements of a foreign operation to be translated into its functional currency, being the currency of the primary economic environment in which the entity operates. Determination of the functional currency is a matter of judgement, and the choice of the appropriate currency requires an analysis of the underlying economics of the foreign operation. A further problem addressed by IAS 21 is where the financial statements of the foreign operation need to be presented in a currency different from the functional currency. IAS 21 then provides principles relating to the translation of a set of financial statements into the presentation currency. Whenever a translation process is undertaken, foreign exchange translation adjustments arise. It is necessary to determine whether these adjustments are taken to current income or to a separate component of equity.

Where the foreign operation is a subsidiary, having translated the financial statements of the foreign operation into the currency in which the consolidated financial statements are to be presented, consolidation worksheet adjustments are required as a part of the normal consolidation process. In assessing the assets and liabilities held by the subsidiary at acquisition date, as well as any goodwill or excess arising as a result of the acquisition, the effects of movements in exchange rates on these assets and liabilities must be taken into consideration. The consolidation adjustments are affected by the process of translation used to translate the foreign entity's financial statements from the local currency into either the functional currency or the presentation currency.

Discussion questions[1]

1. What is the purpose of translating financial statements from one currency to another?
2. What is meant by 'functional currency'?
3. What is the rationale behind the choice of an exchange rate as an entity's functional currency?
4. What guidelines are used to determine the functional currency of an entity?
5. How are statement of comprehensive income items translated from the local currency into the functional currency?
6. How are statement of financial position items translated from the local currency into the functional currency?
7. How are foreign exchange gains and losses calculated when translating from local currency to functional currency?
8. What is meant by 'presentation currency'?
9. How are statement of comprehensive income items translated from functional currency to presentation currency?
10. How are statement of financial position items translated from functional currency to presentation currency?
11. What causes a foreign currency translation reserve to arise?
12. Why are gains/losses on translation taken to a foreign currency translation reserve rather than to profit and loss for the period?
13. In relation to the following case situations, discuss the choice of a functional currency.

    Case 1

    A Malaysian operation manufactures a product using Malaysian materials and labour. Specialised equipment and senior operations staff are supplied by its Australian parent. Reimbursement invoices for these services are denominated in the Malaysian ringgit. The product is sold in the Malaysian market at a price, denominated in Malaysian ringgit, which is determined by competition with similar locally produced products. The foreign operation retains sufficient cash to meet wages and day-to-day operating costs with the remainder being remitted to the Australian parent. The receipt of dividends from the foreign operation is important to the parent's cash management function. Long-term financing is arranged and serviced by the parent.

    Case 2

    A Korean operation is a wholly owned subsidiary of an Australian company which regards the operation as a long-term investment, and thus takes no part in the day-to-day decision making of the operation. The operation purchases parts from various non-related Australian manufacturers for assembly by Korean labour. The finished product is exported to a number of countries but Australia is the major market. Consequently, sales prices are determined by competition within Australia.

[1](*Note:* The cases in discussion questions 13–15 were used in the project by Radford (1996) to test the implementation of AASB 1012 by Australian companies.)

14. In relation to the following case situations, discuss whether you regard the reporting entity as exposed to foreign exchange gains and losses in relation to the foreign entity.

Case 1

A foreign operation extracts mineral ores that are shipped to Australia for processing at the parent entity's smelters. All senior personnel at the foreign operation are parent entity employees. Monthly invoices for ore supplied to the parent are denominated in US dollars. The parent entity pays these invoices with US dollars obtained by selling its finished product to US customers, thus taking advantage of a natural hedge. Payments to the foreign operation cover all running costs but long-term financing is provided by the parent entity.

Case 2

A foreign operation extracts a mineral product that it exports worldwide. The sales price is subject to daily fluctuations. The Australian parent regards the operation as an investment only but the extreme volatility of the foreign operation's sales prices impacts on the price of the parent's shares on the Australian stock exchange because the investment in the foreign operation is one of the parent's significant assets.

15. In relation to the following case situations, discuss which currency is the functional currency of the foreign entity.

Case 1

An Indonesian operation manufactures a product using Indonesian materials and labour. Patented processes and senior operations staff are supplied by its Australian parent. Reimbursement invoices for these services are denominated in Indonesian rupiah. The product is sold in the Indonesian market at a price, denominated in rupiah, that is determined by competition with similar locally produced products. The Indonesian operation remits all revenue to the Australian parent, retaining only sufficient cash to meet wages and day-to-day operating costs. The receipt of cash from the Indonesian operation is important to the parent's cash management function. Long-term financing is arranged and serviced by the parent.

Case 2

A New Zealand operation is a wholly owned subsidiary of an Australian company. The parent regards the operation as a long-term investment and all financial and operational decisions are made by New Zealand management. The New Zealand operation purchases parts from various non-related Australian manufacturers for assembly in New Zealand. The finished product is exported to a number of countries with Australia as the major market. Consequently, sales prices are determined by competition within Australia.

16. Foreign Ltd is a Queensland software developer that specialises in software that controls the operations of open cut mining. To exploit opportunities in the US market, the firm has established a fully owned subsidiary operating in Atlanta, Georgia. The operations of the subsidiary (Opencut Inc.) essentially involve the marketing of software initially developed in Australia but which is further developed by the US subsidiary to suit the special requirements of particular US customers. Foreign Ltd does not charge Opencut Inc. for the software successfully amended and marketed in the United States. At this stage no dividends have been paid by Opencut Inc; however, it is expected that dividends will commence within 12 months. With respect to working capital, Opencut Inc. has a 'revolving credit' agreement (overdraft facility) with the Bank of Georgia, which has been guaranteed by the Australian parent.

Discuss the process of translating the financial statements of Opencut Inc. for consolidation with Foreign Ltd.

17. The accounts listed below are for a wholly owned foreign subsidiary. In the space provided indicate the exchange rate that would be used to translate the accounts into Australian dollars. Use the following letters to indicate the appropriate exchange rate:

H — historical exchange rate
C — current exchange rate at the end of the current period
A — average exchange rate for the current period.

	Australian dollar is the functional currency	Foreign currency is the functional currency
Cash		
Prepaid expenses		
Equipment		
Goodwill		
Accounts payable		
Inventory – at cost		
Inventory – at net realisable value		
Capital		
Sales		
Depreciation expense		

18. Victory Ltd is an Australian company with two overseas subsidiaries, one in Indonesia and the other in South Korea. The Indonesian subsidiary has as its major activity the distribution in Indonesia of Victory Ltd's products. It has been agreed that the subsidiary will, for a period of time, retain all profits in order to expand its distribution network in Indonesia. In the past it has remitted most of its profits to the Australian parent company.

    The South Korean subsidiary has been established to manufacture a range of products for the South-East Asian market. There is also an expectation that it could in the future become the major manufacturing plant for Victory Ltd and provide a supply of products for the Australian market.

    Based on the above, determine the functional currency of the foreign subsidiaries. Explain your choice.
19. Discuss the differences in the translation process when translating from a local currency to a functional currency compared with translating from a functional currency to a presentation currency.
20. Discuss the use of a foreign currency translation reserve to account for movements in exchange rates compared with taking gains/losses as a result of movements in exchange rates directly to the statement of comprehensive income.
21. Explain what is meant by the 'net investment in a foreign operation'. Provide an example and explain the accounting implications.

STAR RATING
★ BASIC
★★ MODERATE
★★★ DIFFICULT

Exercises

Exercise 26.1 ★

TRANSLATION INTO FUNCTIONAL CURRENCY

Auckland Ltd is a manufacturer of sheepskin products in New Zealand. It is a fully owned subsidiary of a Hong Kong company, China Ltd. The following assets are held by Auckland Ltd at 30 June 2010:

Plant:	Cost NZ$	Useful life (years)	Acquisition date	Exchange rate on acquisition date (NZ$1 = HK$)
Tanner	40 000	5	10/8/06	5.4
Benches	20 000	8	8/3/08	5.8
Presses	70 000	7	6/10/09	6.2

Plant is depreciated on a straight-line basis, with zero residual values. All assets acquired in the first half of a month are allocated a full month's depreciation.

Inventory:
- At 1 July 2009, the inventory on hand of $25 000 was acquired during the last month of the 2008–09 period.

- Inventory acquired during the 2009–10 period was acquired evenly throughout the period. Total purchases of $420 000 was acquired during that period.
- The inventory of $30 000 on hand at 30 June 2010 was acquired during June 2010.

Relevant exchange rates (quoted as NZ$1 = HK$) are as follows:

Average for June 2009	7.2
1 July 2009	7.0
Average for 2009–10	7.5
Average for June 2010	7.7
30 June 2010	7.8

Required

1. Assuming the functional currency for Auckland Ltd is the NZ$, calculate:
   (a) the balances for the plant items and inventory in HK$ at 30 June 2010
   (b) the depreciation and cost of sales amounts in the statement of comprehensive income for 2009–10.
2. Assuming the functional currency is the HK$, calculate:
   (a) the balances for the plant items and inventory in HK$ at 30 June 2010
   (b) the depreciation and cost of sales amounts in the statement of comprehensive income for 2009–10.
3. Discuss the differences in the results achieved in parts 1 and 2 above, and why the choice of the functional currency gives a different set of accounting numbers.

Exercise 26.2 TRANSLATION INTO PRESENTATION CURRENCY

★★ January Ltd, an Australian company, acquired all the issued shares of July Ltd, a US company, on 1 January 2009. At this date, the net assets of July Ltd are shown below.

	US$
Property, plant and equipment	155 000
Accumulated depreciation	(30 000)
	125 000
Cash	10 000
Inventory	20 000
Accounts receivable	10 000
Total assets	165 000
Accounts payable	15 000
Net assets	150 000

The trial balance of July Ltd at 31 December 2009 was:

	US$ Dr	US$ Cr
Share capital		100 000
Retained earnings		50 000
Accounts payable		42 000
Sales		90 000
Accumulated depreciation – plant and equipment		45 000
Property, plant and equipment	155 000	
Accounts receivable	40 000	
Inventory	45 000	
Cash	12 000	

	US$ Dr	US$ Cr
Cost of sales	30 000	
Depreciation	15 000	
Other expenses	30 000	
	327 000	327 000

Additional information

1. No property, plant and equipment were acquired in the 2009 period.
2. All sales and expenses were acquired evenly throughout the period. The inventory on hand at the end of the year was acquired during December 2009.
3. Exchange rates were (A$1 = US$):

1 January 2009	0.52
31 December 2009	0.60
Average for December 2009	0.58
Average for 2009	0.56

4. The functional currency for July Ltd is the US dollar.

Required

1. Prepare the financial statements of July Ltd at 31 December 2009 in the presentation currency of Australian dollars.
2. Verify the translation adjustment.
3. Discuss the differences that would occur if the functional currency of July Ltd were the Australian dollar.
4. If the functional currency were the Australian dollar, calculate the translation adjustment.

Exercise 26.3

TRANSLATION OF FINANCIAL STATEMENTS INTO FUNCTIONAL CURRENCY

★★ Faber Ltd, a company incorporated in Singapore, acquired all the issued shares of Lantau Ltd, a Hong Kong company, on 1 July 2009. The trial balance of Lantau Ltd at 30 June 2010 was:

	HK$ Dr	HK$ Cr
Share capital		800 000
Retained earnings (1/7/09)		240 000
General reserve		100 000
Payables		160 000
Deferred tax liability		120 000
Current tax liability		20 000
Provisions		80 000
Sales		610 000
Proceeds on sale of land		250 000
Accumulated depreciation – plant		340 000
Plant	920 000	
Land	400 000	
Cash	240 000	
Accounts receivable	300 000	
Inventory at 1 July 2009	60 000	
Purchases	260 000	
Depreciation – plant	156 000	
Carrying amount of land sold	200 000	
Income tax expense	50 000	
Other expenses	134 000	
	2 720 000	2 720 000

Additional information

1. Exchange rates based on equivalence to HK$1 were:

	S$
1 July 2009	0.20
8 October 2009	0.25
1 December 2009	0.28
1 January 2010	0.30
2 April 2010	0.27
30 June 2010	0.22
Average during last quarter 2009–10	0.24
Average 2009–10	0.26

2. Inventory was acquired evenly throughout the year. The closing inventory of HK$60 000 was acquired during the last quarter of the year.
3. Sales and other expenses occurred evenly throughout the year.
4. The Hong Kong tax rate is 20%.
5. The land on hand at the beginning of the year was sold on 8 October 2009. The land on hand at the end of the year was acquired on 1 December 2009.
6. Movements in plant over 2009–10 were:

Plant at 1 July 2009	HK$600 000
Acquisitions – 8 October 2009	200 000
– 2 April 2010	120 000
Plant at 30 June 2010	920 000

   Depreciation on plant is measured at 20% per annum on cost. Where assets are acquired during a month, a full month's depreciation is charged.
7. The functional currency of the Hong Kong operation is the Singaporean dollar.

Required

1. Prepare the financial statements of Lantau Ltd in Singaporean dollars at 30 June 2010.
2. Verify the translation adjustment.

Exercise 26.4 ★★

CONSOLIDATION WORKSHEET ENTRIES FOR FOREIGN SUBSIDIARY

Using the information in exercise 26.3, assume that Faber Ltd acquired the shares in Lantau Ltd for HK$1 250 000. All the identifiable assets and liabilities of Lantau Ltd at acquisition date were recorded at amounts equal to fair value except for the following assets:

	HK$ Carrying amount	HK$ Fair value
Inventory	60 000	70 000
Land	200 000	250 000
Plant (cost HK$800 000)	600 000	640 000

The plant is expected to have a further 4-year life. The inventory is all sold by 30 June 2010. The tax rate in Hong Kong is 20%.

Required

Prepare the consolidation worksheet entries for the preparation of the consolidated financial statements of Faber Ltd at 30 June 2010.

Exercise 26.5 ★★

DIFFERENT FUNCTIONAL CURRENCIES, CONSOLIDATION ADJUSTMENTS

On 1 July 2009, an Australian company, Perth Ltd, acquired all the issued capital of a Swedish company, Lund Ltd, for $997 400. At the date of acquisition, the equity of Lund Ltd consisted of:

	Krona (K)
Share capital	800 000
General reserve	200 000
Retained earnings	635 000

All the identifiable assets and liabilities of Lund Ltd were recorded at fair value except for plant for which the fair value was K100 000 greater than carrying amount. The plant has a further 5-year life.

The internal financial statements of Lund Ltd at 30 June 2010 are shown below.

Statement of Comprehensive Income

		K	K
Revenues			2 585 000
Cost of sales:			
Opening stock		600 000	
Purchases		1 800 000	
		2 400 000	
Closing stock	580 000	1 820 000	
Gross profit			765 000
Expenses:			
Depreciation		125 000	
Other		270 000	395 000
Profit before income tax			370 000
Income tax expense			200 000
Profit for the period			170 000
Retained earnings as at 1 July 2009			635 000
			805 000
Dividend paid			100 000
Retained earnings as at 30 June 2010			705 000

Statement of Financial Position

1/7/09 K		30/6/10 K
	Current assets	
500 000	Cash and receivables	500 000
600 000	Inventory	580 000
1 100 000	Total current assets	1 080 000
	Non-current assets	
300 000	Land	300 000
700 000	Buildings	700 000
(100 000)	Accumulated depreciation	(130 000)
800 000	Plant	900 000
(235 000)	Accumulated depreciation	(330 000)
1 465 000	Total non-current assets	1 440 000
2 565 000	Total assets	2 520 000

1/7/09 K		30/6/10 K
350 000	Current liabilities	235 000
	Non-current liabilities	
580 000	Notes – issued September 2009	580 000
930 000	Total liabilities	815 000
1 635 000	Net assets	1 705 000
	Equity	
800 000	Share capital	800 000
200 000	General reserve	200 000
635 000	Retained earnings	705 000
1 635 000	Total equity	1 705 000

Additional information

1. Exchange rates for the Swedish krona were as follows:

	1 krona = $A
1 July 2009	0.54
Average 2009–10	0.52
January 2010	0.52
30 June 2010	0.50
Average for the last 4 months of the 2009–10 period	0.51

2. Lund Ltd acquired additional plant for K100 000 on 1 January 2010 by issuing a note for K80 000 and paying the balance in cash.
3. Sales, purchases and other expenses were incurred evenly through the year.
4. Depreciation for the period in krona was as follows:

Buildings	30 000
Plant	
– acquired before 1 July 2009	85 000
– acquired 1 January 2010	10 000

5. The inventory is valued on a FIFO basis. The opening stock was acquired when the exchange rate was 0.54, and the closing stock was acquired during the last 4 months of the 2009–10 period.
6. Dividends of K50 000 were paid on 2 July 2009 and 1 January 2010.
7. The tax rate for Lund Ltd is 25%.

Required

1. Translate the accounts of the foreign subsidiary, Lund Ltd, into Australian dollars at 30 June 2010, assuming:
   (a) the functional currency is the Swedish krona, and the presentation currency is the Australian dollar
   (b) the functional currency is the Australian dollar, as is the presentation currency.
2. Verify the translation adjustments in 1.
3. Prepare for each of (a) and (b) above the business combination valuation and pre-acquisition entries for the preparation of the consolidated financial statements at 30 June 2010.

Problems

Problem 26.1 ★★

CONSOLIDATION OF FOREIGN CURRENCY TRANSLATION RESERVE

On 1 July 2008, Kangaroo Ltd, an Australian company, acquired shares in Panda Ltd, a company based in Hong Kong. At this date, the equity of Panda Ltd was:

	HK$
Share capital	200 000
General reserve	100 000
Retained earnings	300 000

At 30 June 2009 and 2010 respectively, the retained earnings balances of Panda Ltd were HK$400 000 and HK$450 000 respectively. All transactions occurred evenly throughout these years. The internal financial statements of the two companies at 30 June 2011 were as follows:

Statement of Comprehensive Income

	Kangaroo Ltd A$	Panda Ltd HK$
Sales	700 000	595 000
Cost of sales	300 000	400 000
	400 000	195 000
Expenses	210 200	100 000
	189 800	95 000
Dividend revenue	12 000	—
Profit before income tax	201 800	95 000
Tax expense	51 800	20 000
Profit	150 000	75 000
Retained earnings as at 1/7/10	750 000	450 000
	900 000	525 000
Dividend paid	100 000	25 000
Retained earnings as at 30/6/11	800 000	500 000

Statement of Financial Position

	Kangaroo Ltd A$	Panda Ltd HK$
Current assets	311 520	250 000
Shares in Panda Ltd	288 480	—
Property, plant and equipment (net)	700 000	500 000
Patents and trademarks	100 000	150 000
Total assets	1 400 000	900 000
Liabilities	100 000	100 000
Net assets	1 300 000	800 000
Equity:		
Share capital	500 000	200 000
General reserve	—	100 000
Retained earnings	800 000	500 000
Total equity	1 300 000	800 000

Additional information
1. The dividend paid by Panda Ltd was paid on 1 May 2011.
2. Some relevant exchange rates are:

1 July 2008	HK$1 = $A0.80
Average 2008–09	0.82
1 July 2009	0.85
Average 2009–10	0.88
1 July 2010	0.90
Average 2010–11	0.85
1 May 2011	0.80
30 June 2011	0.78

Required
Translate the financial statements of Panda Ltd as at 30 June 2011 into the presentation currency of Australian dollars, assuming that the functional currency is the Hong Kong dollar.

Problem 26.2

★★★

TRANSLATION INTO PRESENTATION CURRENCY, CONSOLIDATION ADJUSTMENTS

Dragon Ltd is an international company resident in Singapore. It acquired 80% of the issued shares of an Australian company, Swan Ltd, on 1 July 2009 for A$560 000. All the identifiable assets and liabilities of Swan Ltd were recorded at fair value except for the following:

	Carrying amount A$	Fair value A$
Plant (net)	180 000	240 000
Inventory	68 000	90 000
Brand names	0	140 000

The plant is considered to have a remaining life of 5 years, with depreciation being calculated on a straight-line basis. All inventory on hand at acquisition date was sold within the following 12-month period. The brand names are considered to have an indefinite life, and are adjusted only if impaired.

At 30 June 2010, the following information was available about the two companies:

	Dragon Ltd S$	Swan Ltd A$
Share capital	560 000	350 000
Retained earnings as at 1/7/09	330 000	170 000
Provisions	45 000	30 000
Payables	14 000	40 000
Sales	620 000	310 000
Dividend revenue	6 400	0
Accumulated depreciation – plant	210 000	160 000
	1 785 400	1 060 000
Cash	92 100	30 000
Accounts receivable	145 300	115 000
Inventory	110 000	80 000
Shares in Swan Ltd	336 000	0
Buildings (net)	84 000	220 000
Plant	420 000	400 000
Cost of sales	390 000	120 000

(continued)

	Dragon Ltd S$	Swan Ltd A$
Depreciation – plant	85 000	40 000
Tax expense	23 000	15 000
Other expenses	50 000	10 000
Dividend paid	20 000	10 000
Dividend provided	30 000	20 000
	1 785 400	1 060 000

Additional information

1. Sales, purchases and other expenses were incurred evenly throughout the 2009–10 period. The dividend was paid by Swan Ltd on 1 January 2010, while the dividend was declared on 30 June 2010.
2. The tax rate in Australia is 30% and the tax rate in Singapore is 20%.
3. Swan Ltd acquired A$100 000 additional new plant on 1 January 2010. Of the depreciation charged in the 2009–10 period, A$8000 related to the new plant.
4. The rates of exchange between the Australian dollar and the Singapore dollar were (expressed as A$1 = S$0.6):

1 July 2009	0.60
1 December 2009	0.64
1 January 2010	0.68
30 June 2010	0.70
Average for the 2009–10 period	0.65

5. The functional currency of the Australian subsidiary is the Australian dollar.
6. On 1 January 2010, Swan Ltd sold some inventory to Dragon Ltd for A$20 000. The inventory had cost the subsidiary $18 000. Only 10% of this inventory remained unsold by the parent entity at 30 June 2010.

Required

1. Translate the financial statements of Swan Ltd into Singapore dollars for inclusion in the consolidated financial statements of Dragon Ltd.
2. Verify the translation adjustment.
3. Prepare the consolidation worksheet entries necessary for the preparation of the consolidated financial statements at 30 June 2010, assuming the use of the partial goodwill method.

Problem 26.3 ★★★

TRANSLATION INTO FUNCTIONAL CURRENCY, INTRAGROUP TRANSACTIONS

On 1 January 2009, Surfers Ltd formed a company, Paradise Ltd, in the United States to sell Australian products such as boomerangs and cuddly koalas and kangaroos. The initial capital was US$500 000. On 1 February 2010, a lease was signed on a shop for US$20 000, payable on the first day of each month. On 15 February, store furnishings were acquired for $448 000; these were expected to have a useful life of 4 years. On 10 June 2009, more fittings were acquired at a cost of $124 000, again with an expected life of 4 years.

Additional information

1. Where non-current assets are acquired during a month, a full month's depreciation is applied.
2. The tax rate in the United States is 20%, while the tax rate in Australia is 30%.
3. The functional currency for Paradise Ltd is the Australian dollar.
4. Exchange rates for the financial year were (A$1 = US$):

1 January 2009	0.60
1 February	0.63
15 February	0.64

10 June	0.66
30 June	0.65
Average for first half year	0.63
30 September	0.66
1 December	0.69
Average for second half year	0.65
31 December 2009	0.70

5. Sales in the first half of the year amounted to $210 000.
6. Expenses, other than depreciation, leases costs and purchases, in the first half of the year amounted to $60 000.
7. Surfers Ltd sold inventory to Paradise Ltd at cost plus 20%. Inventory transferred to Paradise Ltd during the year consisted of:

1 February	US$50 000
30 June	US$60 000
30 September	US$40 000
1 December	US$80 000

   All the inventory was sold by Paradise Ltd except for $20 000 of the stock transferred on 1 December 2009.
8. Financial information relating to Paradise Ltd for the year ending 31 December 2009 is:

	US$
Sales revenue	680 000
Closing inventory	20 000
Accumulated depreciation – furniture and fittings	120 750
Accounts payable	40 000
Share capital	500 000
	1 360 750
Lease expenses	220 000
Purchases	230 000
Inventory	20 000
Other expenses	150 000
Depreciation – furniture and fittings	120 750
Furniture and fittings	572 000
Cash	14 600
Accounts receivable	33 400
	1 360 750

Required

1. Translate the financial statements of Paradise Ltd into Australian dollars for inclusion in the consolidated financial statements of Surfers Ltd at 31 December 2009.
2. Prepare the consolidation worksheet entries for adjusting for the effects of the inventory sales from the parent to the subsidiary.

Problem 26.4 ★★★

TRANSLATION INTO PRESENTATION CURRENCY, CONSOLIDATION ENTRIES

On 1 July 2010, Cricket Ltd, an Australian company, acquired 80% of the issued shares of Baseball Ltd, a company incorporated in the United States for US$789 600 (= A$1 579 200). The draft statement of comprehensive income and statement of financial position of Baseball Ltd at 30 June 2011 are shown on the next page.

	US$	US$
Sales revenues		1 600 000
Cost of sales:		
Opening inventory	140 000	
Purchases	840 000	
	980 000	
Closing inventory	280 000	700 000
Gross profit		900 000
Expenses:		
Depreciation	90 000	
Other	270 000	360 000
Profit before income tax		540 000
Income tax expense		200 000
Profit		340 000
Retained earnings as at 1 July 2010		200 000
		540 000
Dividend paid	120 000	
Dividend declared	200 000	320 000
Retained earnings as at 30 June 2011		220 000

	2011 US$	2010 US$
Current assets:		
Inventory	280 000	140 000
Accounts receivable	20 000	130 000
Cash	20 000	570 000
Total current assets	320 000	840 000
Non-current assets:		
Patent	80 000	80 000
Plant	720 000	600 000
Accumulated depreciation	(130 000)	(80 000)
Land	500 000	300 000
Buildings	920 000	820 000
Accumulated depreciation	(120 000)	(80 000)
Total non-current assets	1 970 000	1 640 000
Total assets	2 290 000	2 480 000
Current liabilities:		
Provisions	500 000	620 000
Accounts payable	320 000	940 000
Total current liabilities	820 000	1 560 000
Non-current liabilities:		
Loan from Cricket Ltd	530 000	—
Total liabilities	1 350 000	1 560 000
Net assets	940 000	920 000
Equity:		
Share capital	720 000	720 000
Retained earnings	220 000	200 000
Total equity	940 000	920 000

Additional information

1. At acquisition date, all the assets and liabilities of Baseball Ltd were recorded at fair value except for:

	Fair value US$
Plant	540 000
Land	324 000
Inventory	182 000

   The plant was expected to have a further 5-year life. The inventory was all sold by July 2011. The US tax rate is 25%.
2. On 1 January 2011, Baseball Ltd acquired new plant for US$120 000. This plant is depreciated over a 5-year period.
3. On 1 April 2011, Baseball Ltd acquired US$200 000 worth of land.
4. On 1 October 2010, Baseball Ltd acquired US$100 000 worth of new buildings. These buildings are depreciated evenly over a 10-year period.
5. The interim dividend was paid on 1 January 2011, half of which was from profits earned prior to 1 July 2010, while the dividend payable was declared on 30 June 2011.
6. Sales, purchases and expenses occurred evenly throughout the period. The inventory on hand at 30 June 2011 was acquired during June 2011.
7. The loan of US$530 000 from Cricket Ltd was granted on 1 July 2010. The interest rate is 8% per annum. Interest is paid on 30 June and 1 January each year.
8. Cricket Ltd sold raw materials to Baseball Ltd at 20% mark-up on cost. During the 2010–11 period there were three shipments of raw materials, costing Baseball Ltd:

1 October 2010	US$120 000
1 January	US$96 000
1 April 2011	US$132 000

   At 30 June 2011, 20% of the shipment in April remains on hand in Baseball Ltd. The Australian tax rate is 30%.
9. On consolidation, the partial goodwill method is used.
10. The exchange rates for the financial year were as follows:

	US$1 = A$
1 July 2010	2.00
1 October 2010	1.80
1 January 2011	1.70
1 April 2011	1.60
30 June 2011	1.50
Average June 2011	1.52
Average for 2010–11	1.75

Required

1. If the functional currency for Baseball Ltd is the US dollar, prepare the financial statements of Baseball Ltd at 30 June 2011 in the presentation currency of the Australian dollar.
2. Verify the foreign currency translation adjustment.
3. Prepare the consolidation worksheet entries to consolidate the translated financial statements of Baseball Ltd with its parent entity at 30 June 2011.

Problem 26.5 ★★★

TRANSLATION INTO FOREIGN CURRENCY, CONSOLIDATION EFFECTS

Use the information in problem 26.4.

Required

1. If the functional currency for Baseball Ltd is the Australian dollar, prepare the financial statements of Baseball Ltd at 30 June 2011 in the functional currency.
2. Verify the foreign currency translation adjustment.
3. Prepare the consolidation worksheet entries to consolidate the translated financial statements of Baseball Ltd with its parent entity at 30 June 2011.
4. Assume on 1 January 2011, Baseball Ltd sold the patent to Cricket Ltd for US$100 000 and that Cricket Ltd depreciates this asset evenly over a 20-year period. Prepare the consolidation worksheet adjustment entries at 30 June 2011.

References

AASB 2003, *Presentation Currency of Australia Financial Reports* (Agenda paper 12.2), collation of submissions on the invitation to comment meeting of the AASB, 15–16 October, Glenelg, South Australia.

Bayer 2008, *Bayer Annual report 2008*, Bayer AG, Germany, www.bayer.com.

FASB 1981, *Foreign currency translation: Statement of Financial Accounting Standards No. 52*, Norwalk, Connecticut.

Jeter, DC & Chaney, PK 2003, *Advanced accounting*, 2nd edn, John Wiley, US.

Nokia 2007, *Nokia in 2007*, Nokia Corporation, Finland, www.nokia.com.

Radford, J 1996, *Foreign currency translation: clarity or confusion?*, project written as part of a Masters of Commerce degree, Curtin University of Technology, Perth, Western Australia.

Revsine, L 1984, 'The rationale underlying the functional currency choice', *The Accounting Review*, Vol. 59 No. 3, pp. 505–14.

27 Accounting for investments in associates

ACCOUNTING STANDARDS IN FOCUS

IAS 28 *Investments in Associates*

LEARNING OBJECTIVES

When you have studied this chapter, you should be able to:

- apply the criteria for identifying associates
- explain the rationale for the equity method and its application
- explain the basic principles of the equity method
- adjust for goodwill and fair value differences at acquisition date
- adjust for movements in equity from dividends and reserves, and the effects of dissimilar accounting policies and different ends of reporting periods
- adjust for the effects of inter-entity transactions
- account for losses recorded by the associate
- prepare the disclosures required by IAS 28.

It is a common feature of global business that entities hold investments in other entities. Accounting standards provide different methods for accounting for those investments, depending on the nature of the investments and the relationship between the investor and the investee. Traditionally, investments in other entities have been recorded using the cost model, under which the investment has been recorded at its acquisition cost. Changes to the recorded amount of the investment occur only if the asset is impaired, whereas increases in the worth of the investment are not recognised. The investor recognises revenue in relation to the investment only when the investee declares or pays a dividend from post-acquisition equity.

IAS 39 *Financial Instruments: Recognition and Measurement* provides standards on the accounting for equity investments in other entities. When a financial asset is recognised initially, it is measured at cost, which is the *fair value* of the consideration given. For the purpose of measuring a financial asset subsequent to initial recognition, IAS 39 classifies financial assets into four categories. Where financial assets are held for trading, gains and losses from changes in fair value are recognised in profit or loss for the period; for financial assets classified as available-for-sale, the changes in fair value are recognised directly in equity (except for impairment losses) until the asset is derecognised.

However, as stated in paragraph 2 of IAS 39, the standard does not apply to 'interests in subsidiaries, associates and joint ventures', except under certain conditions. Hence, investments in financial assets are accounted for under IAS 39 until they meet the criteria for classification as subsidiaries, associates or joint ventures. They are then accounted for under the relevant standard for that classification. In this book, chapters 21–26 are concerned with the accounting for subsidiaries. Because of the particular relationship that exists between a parent and a subsidiary (which is based on the control of the parent over the subsidiary), the standard setters believe that a special form of accounting other than the cost method or the fair value method is applicable, so that users of the financial statements can obtain a more informed picture of the financial position and performance of the combined economic entity or group. Hence, IAS 27 *Consolidated and Separate Financial Statements* requires the use of the *consolidation method* to account for parents and subsidiaries. The consolidation method results in the financial statements of the parent and each of its subsidiaries being combined to form the consolidated financial statements. These consolidated statements report all the assets, liabilities, revenues and expenses of these entities. The information about the entities is presented on a detailed, line-by-line basis in both the statement of comprehensive income and the statement of financial position. The accounts of the investor are not affected by the application of the consolidation method.

Just as a subsidiary is seen as having a special relationship with its parent so that a particular form of accounting is required to provide the necessary information about those companies, the relationship between an investor and its associated entities is seen as being of special significance so that a specific accounting method — the equity method of accounting — is required to provide information about the investor and its associates. As with subsidiaries, the nature of the investor–associate relationship is clearly defined, in this case in IAS 28 *Investments in Associates*, and the principles of the equity method specifically established. The accounting for investments in associates is the focus of this chapter.

27.1 IDENTIFYING ASSOCIATES

An associate is defined in paragraph 2 of IAS 28 as follows:

> An associate is an entity, including an unincorporated entity such as a partnership, over which the investor has significant influence and that is neither a subsidiary nor an interest in a joint venture.

Significant influence

The key characteristic determining the existence of an associate is that of significant influence. This term is defined in paragraph 2 of IAS 28 as follows:

> Significant influence is the power to participate in the financial and operating policy decisions of the investee but is not control or joint control over those policies.

Note the following features of this definition:

- The definition requires the investor to have the power, or the capacity, to affect the investee. As with the definition of control identifying a parent–subsidiary relationship (see chapter 21), the definition does not require the investor to actually exercise that power. Instead, the focus is on the existence of the power or capacity.

- The specific power is that of being able to participate in the financial and operating decisions of the investee. Whereas the parent–subsidiary relationship is defined in terms of the power or capacity to *dominate* the financial and operating decisions of the subsidiary, the investor–associate relationship relates to the power to *participate* in those same decisions. Hence, the investor–associate relationship is of the same nature as that existing between a parent and subsidiary, the difference being the level of control that can be exercised.
- The definition recognises three types or levels of control that one entity can exercise over another: control or dominance (relating to subsidiaries), significant influence (relating to associates), and joint control. The latter relates to joint ventures.
- In the definitions of an associate and significant influence, there is no requirement for the investor to hold any shares, or have a beneficial interest, in the associate. However, as is discussed in more detail in section 27.2 of this chapter, the application of the equity method of accounting is based on the investor owning shares in the associate. In other words, if significant influence is exercised by one entity over another by virtue of an association or contract other than from the holding of shares, then the equity method cannot be applied in relation to the associate. Even in such cases, however, some of the disclosures required by IAS 28 in relation to associates may still be required.

The assessment of the existence of significant influence requires judgement on the part of accountants. To assist in this determination, IAS 28 provides further guidance in paragraphs 6–10:

- Paragraph 6 provides that where an investor holds, directly or indirectly (e.g. through subsidiaries) 20% or more of the voting power of the investee, it is presumed that the investor has significant influence over the investee. This is a rebuttable presumption because if the investor can demonstrate that such influence does not exist, then the investee is not classified as an associate. Further, where the investor owns less than 20% of another entity, there is a presumption that the investee is *not* an associate. It is therefore possible for more than one entity to have significant influence over another entity, but there can be only one parent entity in relation to a subsidiary.
- Paragraph 7 provides a list of factors that may provide evidence of the existence of significant influence:
  (a) representation on the board of directors or equivalent governing body of the investee
  (b) participation in policy-making processes, including participation in decisions about dividends or other distributions
  (c) material transactions between the investor and the investee
  (d) interchange of managerial personnel
  (e) provision of essential technical information.

  In all the above examples, the evidence relates to actual participation. In general, the most common form of participation is that of representation on the board of directors. In other words, because of the significance of the ownership interest of the investor in the associate, the investor is able to obtain representation on the board of directors and hence influence the decision making in the investee.
- Paragraph 8 raises the issue of whether ownership of securities such as options or convertible notes should be used in assessing the existence of significant influence. This paragraph requires the potential effect of the exercise of such securities to be considered in cases where the holder currently has the ability to exercise or convert those rights. Where the rights are not exercisable because they are subject to a time constraint, they should not be taken into consideration. Note that there must be a current ability to exercise power, not a future ability to do so.

Exclusions

As noted above, where the level of influence is such that the investor has control or joint control, the investee is not regarded as an associate. Further, some entities that would meet the definition of associates are also excluded from the requirements of IAS 28. Paragraph 1 states that IAS 28 does not apply to investments in associates held by:

- venture capital organisations, or
- mutual funds, unit trusts and similar entities including investment-linked insurance funds that are classified as held for trading and accounted for at fair value in accordance with IAS 39. Such entities must recognise changes in the fair values of those investments in the current period profit or loss. According to the Basis for Conclusions on IAS 28, paragraphs BC5 and

BC6, these exclusions were made because of the lack of relevance of equity-accounted information to those entities, as well as the frequent changes in the level of ownership in these investments by such entities.

Paragraph 13 of IAS 28 also provides exclusions from the application of the equity method to associates. In particular:

- Where the investment in the associate is acquired and held exclusively with a view to its disposal within 12 months of acquisition, and the management is actively seeking a buyer, the equity method does not have to be applied to that associate. Appendix B of IFRS 5 *Non-current Assets Held for Sale and Discontinued Operations* establishes criteria for classifying assets as 'held for sale'. Such assets are required to be measured at the lower of their carrying amounts and fair values less costs to sell. According to paragraph 15 of IAS 28, if the associate is not disposed of within the requisite 12 months, the financial statements must be restated and the investment accounted for in accordance with the equity method.

  Where all these conditions apply, the entity must account for the associate as a held-for-trading investment accounted for at fair value, with changes in fair value affecting current period profit or loss.
- Where all the following apply, an investor need not apply the equity method of accounting:
  - the investor is a wholly owned subsidiary, or is a partially owned subsidiary of another entity and its owners have been informed about and do not object to the investor not applying the equity method
  - the investor's debt or equity securities are not traded in a public market such as a domestic or foreign stock exchange
  - the investor did not file, and is not in the process of filing, its financial statements with a securities commission or other regulatory organisation, for the purpose of issuing any class of securities in a public market
  - the ultimate or any intermediate parent of the investor publishes consolidated financial statements that comply with Australian Accounting Standards and thus International Financial Reporting Standards.

27.2 THE EQUITY METHOD OF ACCOUNTING: RATIONALE AND APPLICATION

Applying the equity method requires an analysis of the acquisition similar to that undertaken when accounting for subsidiaries. Whether there is any goodwill or income to be accounted for is determined by this analysis.

27.2.1 Rationale for the method

As can be seen from the discussion in relation to the identification of associates in section 27.1 above, the criterion of control used for identifying subsidiaries has similarities with the definition of significant influence used for associates. Paragraph 20 of IAS 28 states:

> Many of the procedures appropriate for the application of the equity method are similar to the consolidation procedures described in IAS 27 *Consolidated and Separate Financial Statements*. Furthermore, the concepts underlying the procedures used in accounting for the acquisition of a subsidiary are also adopted in accounting for the acquisition of an investment in an associate.

Because of the similarity with the principles and procedures used in applying the consolidation method to subsidiaries, the equity method of accounting has sometimes been described as 'one-line consolidation'. However, IAS 28 does not consistently use the consolidation principles in its application of the equity method.

IAS 28 does not justify the information, or the need for the information, provided by the application of the equity method. In paragraph 17 of IAS 28, it is argued that the cost method may be unsatisfactory for associates because the recognition of dividends may not be an adequate measure of the income earned by the investor. Further, it is argued that applying the equity method 'provides more informative reporting of the net assets and profit or loss of the investor'. However, the standard does not explain why the equity method is superior to the fair value method or other measurement methods. Similarly, where there is a departure from consolidation principles, IAS 28 does not supply a justification for the departure. This makes it difficult to evaluate the equity method on the basis of its being a one-line consolidation method or simply another measurement method competing with fair value.

Similarities and differences between the consolidation method and the equity method are noted in section 27.3 of this chapter, where the equity method is described in detail.

27.2.2 Application — consolidated or separate financial statements

Paragraph 1 of IAS 28 requires investments in associates to be accounted for by the equity method, as detailed in that standard, but it contains some exceptions to this principle. Paragraph 13 also provides some exemptions to the application of the equity method to associates.

Paragraph 35 of IAS 28 states that an investment in an associate is to be accounted for in the investor's separate financial statements in accordance with paragraphs 38–43 and 42 of IAS 27 *Consolidated and Separate Financial Statements*. Paragraph 2 of IAS 38 defines separate financial statements as the financial statements of the parent. In these statements, investments in both subsidiaries and associates are accounted for either at cost or in accordance with IAS 39 *Financial Instruments: Recognition and Measurement*. The equity method is then not used in the parent's own financial statements to account for investments in associates. For a parent entity, which will prepare consolidated financial statements, investments in associates held by the parent or its subsidiaries are accounted for in the consolidated financial statements by the equity method. Therefore, the accounting entries applying the equity method to the investment in the associate are made in the consolidation worksheet. The adjustment entries are made on a year-to-year basis, because no permanent entries for the equity accounting are made in the records of the investor.

Where the investor does not prepare consolidated financial statements — it is not a parent — the investor applies the equity method to its associates in its own accounting records. The accounts of the investor are then affected by the application of the equity method, in contrast to the situation where the equity method entries are made in the consolidation worksheet.

27.3 APPLYING THE EQUITY METHOD: BASIC METHOD

Paragraph 11 of IAS 28 provides a description of the basics of the equity method. The key steps are:

1. Recognise the initial investment in the associate at cost.
2. Increase or decrease the carrying amount of the investment by the investor's share of the profit or loss of the investee after the date of acquisition (post-acquisition profit or loss).
3. Reduce the carrying amount of the investment by distributions (such as dividends) received from the associate.
4. Increase or decrease the carrying amount of the investment for changes in the investor's share of the changes in the investee's other comprehensive income. This applies to reserves where changes in the associate's equity have not already been included in profit or loss. Hence, changes in asset revaluation and foreign currency translation reserves are recognised; but movements in general reserve, which are an appropriation from retained earnings, are not recognised.

Although potential voting rights may be used in the assessment of the existence of significant influence, they are not used in any of the above calculations (IAS 28, para. 12).

ILLUSTRATIVE EXAMPLE 27.1

Basic application of the equity method

A. Investor does not prepare consolidated financial statements

On 1 July 2010, Jack Ltd acquired 25% of the shares of Joshua Ltd for $42 500. At this date, all the identifiable assets and liabilities of Joshua Ltd were recorded at amounts equal to fair value, and the equity of Joshua Ltd consisted of:

Share capital	$100 000
General reserve	30 000
Asset revaluation reserve	20 000
Retained earnings	20 000

During the 2010–11 year, Joshua Ltd reported a profit of $25 000. The asset revaluation reserve increased by $5000, this being reported in other comprehensive income. Joshua Ltd paid a $4000 dividend and transferred $3000 to general reserve.

At 1 July 2010, Jack Ltd recorded the investment in Joshua Ltd at $42 500. At 30 June 2010, the journal entries to apply the equity method, as passed in the records of the investor, are:

(1) *Recognition of share of profit or loss of associate*

Investment in Associate	Dr	6 250	
Share of Profit or Loss of Associate	Cr		6 250
(Share of associate's profit: 25% × $25 000)			

The Share of Profit or Loss of Associate is disclosed as a separate line item in the statement of comprehensive income, as per IAS 1 paragraph 82(c).

(2) *Recognition of increase in asset revaluation reserve*

Investment in Associate	Dr	1 250	
Asset Revaluation Reserve	Cr		1 250
(Share of reserve: 25% × $5000)			

This increase is also disclosed as a separate line item in the statement of comprehensive income, as per IAS 1 paragraph 82(h) — Share of Other Comprehensive Income of Associate.

Note that there is no recognition of the increase in the general reserve because the share of the reserve has been recognised in the share of profit for the period.

(3) *Adjustment for dividend paid by associate*

Cash	Dr	1 000	
Investment in Associate	Cr		1 000
(Adjustment for dividend paid by associate: 25% × $4000)			

Because the investor has recognised its share of the equity of the associate, the dividend is simply a receipt of equity already recognised in the investment account.

At 30 June 2010, the investment in the associate is measured at $49 000 (i.e. $42 500 + $6250 + $1250 – $1000). The equity of Joshua Ltd consists of:

Share capital	$ 100 000
Asset revaluation reserve ($20 000 + $5000)	25 000
General reserve ($30 000 + 3000)	33 000
Retained earnings ($20 000 + $25 000 – $4000 – 3000)	38 000
	$ 196 000

The investor's share of the equity of the associate is 25% of $196 000, (i.e. $49 000), which is the same as the recorded amount of the investment in the associate. In other words, the equity method, in this case, is designed to show the investment in the associate at an amount equal to the investor's share of the reported equity of the associate. As explained later in this chapter, this relationship is not always achieved because of the effects of pre-acquisition equity, the existence of goodwill, and adjustments made for the effects of inter-entity transactions.

B. Investor prepares consolidated financial statements

In this circumstance, the entries are not made in the accounting records of the entities themselves but in the consolidation worksheet instead. The first two entries are the same as shown in part A of this example. The entry that differs is that for the dividend. The consolidation worksheet entry is:

(3) *Adjustment for dividend paid by associate*

Dividend Revenue	Dr	1 000	
Investment in Associate	Cr		1 000
(Adjustment for dividend paid by associate: 25% × $4000)			

When Joshua Ltd paid the $4000 dividend, Jack Ltd recorded the receipt of cash and recognised dividend revenue. The effect of the above entry on the application of the equity method is to eliminate the dividend revenue previously recognised by the investor. Because the investor recognises a share of the whole of the profit of the associate, the dividend revenue cannot also be recognised as income by the investor. However, the payment of the dividend reduces the investment in the associate.

27.4 APPLYING THE EQUITY METHOD: GOODWILL AND FAIR VALUE ADJUSTMENTS

The description of the equity method in paragraph 11 of IAS 28 refers to the recognition of *post-acquisition* equity. Further, paragraph 20 of this standard notes that many of the procedures appropriate to the application of the equity method are similar to the consolidation procedures described in IAS 27. To this end, any differences between fair values and carrying amounts of identifiable assets and liabilities acquired, as well as any goodwill or income on acquisition, must be taken into account. Paragraph 23 of IAS 28 states:

> An investment in an associate is accounted for using the equity method from the date on which it becomes an associate. On acquisition of the investment any difference between the cost of the investment and the investor's share of the net fair value of the associate's identifiable assets and liabilities is accounted for as follows:
>
> (a) goodwill relating to an associate is included in the carrying amount of the investment. Amortisation of that goodwill is not permitted.
>
> (b) any excess of the investor's share of the net fair value of the associate's identifiable assets and liabilities over the cost of the investment is included as income in the determination of the investor's share of the associate's profit or loss in the period in which the investment is acquired.
>
> Appropriate adjustments to the investor's share of the associate's profits or losses after acquisition are also made to account, for example, for depreciation of the depreciable assets, based on their fair values at the acquisition date. Similarly, appropriate adjustments to the investor's share of the associate's profits or losses after acquisition are made for impairment losses recognised by the associate, such as for goodwill or property, plant and equipment.

As with consolidated financial statements, at acquisition date the cost of the investment is compared with the net fair value of the identifiable assets and liabilities of the associate acquired by the investor in order to determine whether any goodwill is acquired or whether there is an excess to be included as income.

The purpose of this acquisition analysis is to determine the real post-acquisition equity of the associate. Because the cost of the investment is the amount paid for the net fair value of the identifiable assets and liabilities acquired and the goodwill (if any), then the recorded profits of the associate after the acquisition date are not all post-acquisition equity. They will include profits recognised and paid for by the acquiring entity at acquisition date. Hence, in determining the investor's share of post-acquisition profits of the associate, adjustments will have to be made for differences between carrying amounts and fair values at the acquisition date, as well as for any goodwill impairment or excess.

ILLUSTRATIVE EXAMPLE 27.2

Goodwill and fair value adjustments

On 1 July 2008, Lachlan Ltd acquired 25% of the shares of Riley Ltd for $49 375. At this date, the equity of Riley Ltd consisted of:

Share capital	$100 000
General reserve	50 000
Retained earnings	20 000

At the acquisition date, all the identifiable assets and liabilities of Riley Ltd were recorded at fair value, except for plant for which the fair value was $10 000 greater than its carrying amount, and inventory whose fair value was $5000 greater than its cost. The tax rate is 30%. The plant has a further 5-year life. The inventory was all sold by 30 June 2009.

In the reporting period ending 30 June 2009, Riley Ltd reported a profit of $15 000.

The acquisition analysis at 1 July 2008 is as follows:

Net fair value of the identifiable assets and liabilities of Riley Ltd	= ($100 000 + $50 000 + $20 000) (equity)
	+ $10 000(1 – 30%) (plant)
	+ $5 000(1 – 30%) (inventory)
	= $180 500
Net fair value acquired by Lachlan Ltd	= 25% × $180 500
	= $45 125
Cost of investment	= $49 375
Goodwill	= $4250
Depreciation (net of tax) of plant p.a.	= 20% × (25% × [$10 000(1 – 30%)])
	= $350
Effect of sale of inventory (net of tax)	= 25% × $5 000(1 – 30%)
	= $875

The amount of the adjustment needed in applying equity accounting to the investment in the associate at 30 June 2009 is determined as follows:

Share of profit recorded by associate (25% × $15 000)		$ 3750
Pre-acquisition adjustments:		
Depreciation of plant	$ (350)	
Sale of inventory	(875)	(1 225)
Share of post-acquisition profit of associate		$ 2 525

The journal entry to reflect the application of the equity method to the investment in the associate is:

Investment in Riley Ltd	Dr	2 525	
Share of Profit or Loss of Associate	Cr		2 525
(Recognition of share of post-acquisition profit of associate)			

This entry is the same regardless of whether the investor prepares consolidated financial statements.

These adjustments are only notional adjustments; they are not made in the records of the associate, but are made in calculating the incremental adjustment to the share of profit of the associate. Because the adjustment is made to a share of profit or loss, the adjustment is calculated on an after-tax basis. Therefore, adjustments relating to the depreciation of non-current assets or the cost of inventory sold must be calculated on an after-tax basis.

ILLUSTRATIVE EXAMPLE 27.3

Excess — income

Paragraph 23(b) of IAS 28 requires any excess of the investor's share of the net fair value of an associate's identifiable assets and liabilities over the cost of the investment to be recognised as income in the determination of the investor's share of the associate's profit or loss in the period in which the investment is acquired.

Assume in illustrative example 27.2 that the cost of the investment was $45 000. The acquisition analysis would then show:

Net fair value acquired by Lachlan Ltd	= 25% × $180 500
	= $45 125
Cost of investment	= $45 000
Excess	= $125
Depreciation (net of tax) of plant p.a.	= 20% × (25% × [$10 000(1 – 30%)])
	= $350
Effect of sale of inventory (net of tax)	= 25% × $5000(1 – 30%)
	= $875

The amount of the adjustment needed in applying equity accounting to the investment in the associate at 30 June 2009 is then as follows:

Share of profit recorded by associate (25% × $15000)		$ 3750
Pre-acquisition adjustments:		
Excess	$ 125	
Depreciation of plant	(350)	
Sale of inventory	(875)	(1 100)
Share of post-acquisition profit of associate		$ 2650

The journal entry to reflect the application of the equity method to the investment in the associate is:

Investment in Riley Ltd	Dr	2650	
Share of Profit or Loss of Associate	Cr		2650
(Recognition of share of post-acquisition profit of associate)			

27.5 APPLYING THE EQUITY METHOD: OTHER ISSUES

27.5.1 Dividends, reserves, dissimilar accounting policies and different ends of reporting periods

1. Dividends

Prior to May 2008, both IAS 27 *Consolidated and Separate Financial Statements* and IAS 18 *Revenue* required dividends from pre-acquisition equity to be accounted for differently from dividends from post-acquisition equity. As stated in paragraph 32 of IAS 18, dividends from pre-acquisition equity were accounted for as a reduction in the cost of the investment. In contrast, dividends from post-acquisition equity were accounted for as revenue by the investor.

In May 2008, the IASB issued amendments to IAS 27 relating to the cost of an investment in a subsidiary, jointly controlled entity or associate. These amendments:

- deleted the definition of the cost method from IAS 27
- inserted paragraph 38A into IAS 27 requiring entities to recognise dividends from a subsidiary, jointly controlled entity or associate in profit or loss when its right to the dividend is established
- removed the last two sentences of paragraph 32 of IAS 18 dealing with the accounting for dividends.

The effect of these changes is that all dividends paid or payable by a subsidiary to a parent are to be recognised as revenue by the parent. As noted in paragraph BC66H of the Basis for Conclusions to the amendments, 'the requirement to separate the retained earnings of an entity into pre-acquisition and post-acquisition components as a method for assessing whether a dividend is a recovery of its associated investment has been removed from IFRSs'.

When the associate pays or declares a dividend, the investor records dividend revenue. As noted earlier in this chapter, because the investment account has been adjusted for the investor's share of all post-acquisition equity, applying the equity method requires the investment account to be adjusted for dividends paid or declared.

Where no consolidated financial statements are prepared, the entry in the investor's records is:

Cash	Dr	XXX	
Investment in Associate	Cr		XXX

Where consolidated financial statements are prepared, the consolidation worksheet entry is:

Dividend Revenue	Dr	XXX	
Investment in Associate	Cr		XXX

2. Preference shares

Paragraph 28 of IAS 28 states:

> If an associate has outstanding cumulative preference shares that are held by parties other than the investor and classified as equity, the investor computes its share of profits or losses after adjusting for the dividends on such shares, whether or not the dividends have been declared.

This discussion relates only to dividends that are classified as equity because, for those preference shares classified as debt, the payments to the holders are treated as interest and deducted before calculating profit for the period. For preference shares treated as equity, the payments to holders are classified as dividends and are appropriated after the calculation of profit.

The equity attributable to the ordinary shareholders in the associate is net of dividends to the preference shareholders. Hence, in calculating the share of the current period equity attributable to the investor, adjustments need to be made for:

- preference dividends paid or declared in the current period
- preference dividends that are cumulative in the current period, but have not been paid or declared.

This applies to preference dividends relating to preference shares regardless of whether the investor owns the preference shares in the associate or other parties own the shares. The calculation is then (assuming the dollar amounts):

Profit of associate	$100
Less: Preference dividends paid/declared	20
	80
Investor's share: 20% of $80	$ 16

3. Reserves

The equity of the investee may also increase/decrease via changes in reserve balances in the associate. There are three situations to consider:

- *Where post-acquisition reserves are created by amounts taken directly to equity*
  An example of this is where the associate recognises an increase in the asset revaluation reserve — the increase in equity is recognised directly in equity. The investor's share of the asset revaluation reserve is recognised on application of the equity method via the following entry:

Investment in Associate	Dr	XXX	
Asset Revaluation Reserve	Cr		XXX

  This entry is the same regardless of whether it is made in the investor's records or in the consolidation worksheet. This increment is then disclosed as a separate line item in other comprehensive income in the statement of comprehensive income (IAS 1 paragraph 82(h)), and as a movement in the asset revaluation reserve in the statement of changes in equity.
- *Where reserves are created by the associate but reflect pre-acquisition equity*
  Reserves on hand at acquisition date may be transferred to other equity accounts after that date. As these amounts are recognised in the investor's cost of investment, and thus the carrying amount of the investment in the associate, no further adjustment is necessary on application of the equity method for movements in pre-acquisition equity.
- *Where the associate creates reserves by transferring amounts from retained earnings*
  For example, the investor may transfer an amount from retained earnings to general reserve. As the investor's share of the equity in the retained earnings account has already been recognised by the investor, there is no need to adjust for the increase in the general reserve.

4. Dissimilar accounting policies

Paragraphs 26 and 27 of IAS 28 state:

> 26. The investor's financial statements shall be prepared using uniform accounting policies for like transactions and events in similar circumstances.
> 27. If an associate uses accounting policies other than those of the investor for like transactions and events in similar circumstances, adjustments shall be made to conform the associate's accounting policies to those of the investor when the associate's financial statements are used by the investor in applying the equity method.

In the calculation of the investor's share of the profit of the associate, adjustments must then be made to the recorded profit of the associate where that figure has been measured based on policies that are different from those applied by the investor.

5. Different ends of reporting periods

Paragraph 25 of IAS 28 requires that, unless it is impracticable to do so, the associate should prepare financial statements as of the same date as the financial statements of the investor so that the equity method can be applied by the investor. Where the financial statements of the associate are prepared as of a different date, in applying the equity method, adjustments should be made for significant transactions or events that have occurred between the dates of the statements of the two entities. Paragraph 25 sets a maximum difference between the ends of the reporting periods of the investor and the associate as no more than 3 months.

ILLUSTRATIVE EXAMPLE 27.4

Dividends, reserves and dissimilar accounting policies

On 1 July 2009, Thomas Ltd acquired 40% of the shares of William Ltd for $122 400. The equity of William Ltd at acquisition date consisted of:

Ordinary share capital	$200 000
10% preference share capital	100 000
Retained earnings	80 000

At 1 July 2009, all the identifiable assets and liabilities of William Ltd were recorded at fair value except for the following:

	Carrying amount	Fair value
Machinery	$140 000	$160 000
Inventory	60 000	70 000

By 30 June 2010, the inventory on hand at 1 July 2009 had been sold by William Ltd. The machinery was expected to provide future benefits evenly over the next 2 years. The tax rate is 30%.

In relation to the preference shares, there were no arrears of dividend outstanding at 1 July 2009. However, no dividends were paid in the 2010–11 period, and the shares are cumulative. The dividends paid in the 2011–12 period included the previous period's arrears.

Dividends declared at 30 June are paid within the following 3 months, with liabilities being raised at the date of declaration.

In January 2012, William Ltd revalued furniture upwards by $6000, affecting the asset revaluation reserve.

Both companies have interests in exploring mining leases. Whereas Thomas Ltd has adopted a policy of capitalising its exploration expenditure, William Ltd has adopted a policy of expensing exploration outlays. This has resulted in William Ltd expensing $4500 and $6500 in the periods 2010–11 and 2011–12 respectively.

The financial statements of William Ltd over three periods contained the following information:

	30 June 2010	30 June 2011	30 June 2012
Profit	$ 40 000	$ 60 000	$ 70 000
Retained earnings (opening balance)	80 000	88 000	113 000
	120 000	148 000	183 000
Ordinary dividend paid	5 000	10 000	15 000
Ordinary dividend declared	7 000	15 000	20 000
Preference dividend paid	10 000	—	20 000
Transfer to general reserve	10 000	10 000	—
	32 000	35 000	55 000
Retained earnings (closing balance)	88 000	113 000	128 000

Required

Prepare the entries in the consolidation worksheet of Thomas Ltd to apply the equity method to its investment in William Ltd for each of the 3 years ending 30 June 2010, 2011 and 2012.

Solution

Acquisition analysis

Net fair value of identifiable assets and liabilities of William Ltd	= ($200 000 + $80 000) (equity)
	+ $20 000(1 – 30%) (machinery)
	+ $10 000(1 – 30%) (inventory)
	= $301 000
Net fair value acquired by Thomas Ltd	= 40% × $301 000
	= $120 400
Cost of investment	= $122 400
Goodwill	= $2 000
Depreciation of machinery p.a. after tax	= 50% × [40% × $20 000(1 – 30%)]
	= $2 800
Pre-acquisition after-tax inventory effect	= 40% × $10 000(1 – 30%)
	= $2 800

Year ended 30 June 2010: workings

Recorded profit		$ 40 000
Adjustments:		
Preference dividend paid	$(10 000)	(10 000)
		30 000
Investor's share — 40%		12 000
Pre-acquisition adjustments:		
Sale of inventory	(2 800)	
Depreciation of machinery	(2 800)	(5 600)
		$ 6 400

The journal entries in the consolidation worksheet of Thomas Ltd at 30 June 2010 are:

Investment in William Ltd	Dr	6 400	
Share of Profit or Loss of Associate	Cr		6 400
(Recognition of equity-accounted profit of associate)			
Dividend Revenue	Dr	4 800	
Investment in William Ltd	Cr		4 800
(Adjustment for ordinary dividends from associate: 40% × [$5000 + $7000])			

Note that the net increase in equity and the investment account for the year is $1600 (i.e. $6400 – $4800).

Year ended 30 June 2011: workings

Recorded profit		$60 000
Adjustments:		
Expensing of exploration outlays net of tax effect (4500 × [1 – 30%])	$ 3 150	
Preference dividend in arrears	(10 000)	(6 850)
		53 150
Investor's share — 40%		21 260
Pre-acquisition adjustments:		
Depreciation of machinery	(2 800)	(2 800)
		$ 18 460

The journal entries in the consolidation worksheet of Thomas Ltd at 30 June 2011 are:

Investment in William Ltd	Dr	1 600	
Retained Earnings (1/7/10)	Cr		1 600
(Share of previous period profits of associate)			

Note that the above entry is necessary because the equity accounting entries are made in the consolidation worksheet and not in the actual records of the investor.

Investment in William Ltd	Dr	18 460	
Share of Profit or Loss of Associate	Cr		18 460
(Recognition of equity-accounted profit of associate)			

Dividend Revenue	Dr	10 000	
Investment in William Ltd	Cr		10 000
(Adjustment for ordinary dividends from associate: 40% × [$10 000 + $15 000])			

Note that the net increase in equity and in the investment account as a result of applying the equity method is $10 060 (i.e. $1600 + $18 460 − $10 000).

Year ended 30 June 2012: workings

Recorded profit		$70 000
Adjustments:		
Expensing of exploration outlays ($6500 × [1 − 30%])	$ 4 550	
Preference dividend paid in relation to current year	(10 000)	(5 450)
		64 550
Investor's share – 40%		$25 820

The journal entries in the consolidation worksheet of Thomas Ltd at 30 June 2012 are:

Investment in William Ltd	Dr	10 060	
Retained Earnings (1/7/11)	Cr		10 060
(Share of previous period profits of associate)			
Shares in William Ltd	Dr	25 820	
Share of Profit or Loss of Associate	Cr		25 820
(Recognition of equity-accounted profit of associate)			
Dividend Revenue	Dr	14 000	
Investment in William Ltd	Cr		14 000
(Adjustment for ordinary dividends from associate: 40% × [$15 000 + $20 000])			
Investment in William Ltd	Dr	1 680	
Asset Revaluation Reserve	Cr		1 680
(Share of associate's revaluation increments: 40% × ($6000[1 − 30%])			

27.5.2 Investing in an associate in stages

Besides there being a time difference between the initial investment and the date the investee becomes an associate, a complication arises where the investor's investment in the associate is achieved in stages before obtaining a sufficient investment in the investee to wield significant influence. The accounting for this is not covered in IAS 28. The principles for business combinations involving stages, as outlined in paragraphs 41–42 of IFRS 3, must be applied. Paragraph 42 of IFRS 3 states:

> In a business combination achieved in stages, the acquirer shall remeasure its previously held equity interest in the acquiree at its acquisition-date fair values and recognise the resulting gain or loss, if any, in profit or loss. In prior reporting periods, the acquirer may have recognised changes in the value of its equity interest in the acquiree in other comprehensive income (for example, because the investment was classified as available for sale). If so, the amount that was recognised in other comprehensive income shall be recognised on the same basis as would be required if the acquirer had disposed directly of the previously held equity interest.

Hence, if an investor had previously held an investment in another entity and by a further investment that investee became an associate of the investor, at the date of the second investment:

- the previously held investment is revalued to fair value with any gain/loss being taken to profit or loss

- if the previously held investment had been measured at fair value with changes in fair value being recognised directly in equity, those amounts are transferred to current period profit and loss.

ILLUSTRATIVE EXAMPLE 27.5

Step acquisitions

Assume James Ltd acquired 10% of the shares of Ethan Ltd on 1 January 2008 for $13 000. At 31 December 2009, the end of the entity's reporting period, the fair value of the investment was $16 200. The investment was designated as available for sale.

On 1 July 2009, James Ltd acquired a further 10% of the share capital of Ethan Ltd for $17 200 (this also being the fair value of the initial investment in Ethan Ltd at this date), when the equity of Ethan Ltd consisted of:

Share capital	$100 000
Asset revaluation reserve	12 000
Retained earnings (1/1/09)	38 000
Profit (1/1/09 to 30/6/09)	8 000

The identifiable assets and liabilities of Ethan Ltd were recorded at fair value at this date except for inventory, whose fair value was $15 000 greater than carrying amount. This acquisition gives James Ltd significant influence over Ethan Ltd.

The accounting entries for these events would be determined as follows:

At 1 January 2008:
James Ltd would record its investment in Ethan Ltd at $13 000.

At 31 December 2008:
James Ltd would revalue its investment to $16 200, recognising $3200 directly in equity and reporting the increment in other comprehensive income for the 2008 period.

At 1 July 2009:
At this date Ethan Ltd becomes an associate. In accounting for its previously held investment in Ethan Ltd, James Ltd will:

(i) remeasure its investment to fair value, recognising any change in profit or loss:

Investment in Ethan Ltd	Dr	1 000	
Income: Remeasurement of Investment	Cr		1 000
(Remeasurement of investment on investee becoming an associate: $17 200 – $16 200)			

(ii) transfer any amounts previously recognised in other comprehensive income to profit or loss as a reclassification adjustment (see paragraph 93 of IAS 1):

Revaluation Reserve: Available-for-sale Financial Assets	Dr	3 200	
Income: Reclassification Adjustment	Cr		3 200
(Reclassification adjustment on investee becoming an associate: $16 200 – $13 000)			

The previously held investment is now recorded by the investor at fair value, $17 200.
At 1 July 2009, James Ltd also recognises its further investment in Ethan Ltd:

Investment in Ethan Ltd	Dr	17 200	
Cash	Cr		17 200
(Acquisition of further shares in Ethan Ltd)			

To assist in its application of the equity method to account for its investment subsequent to 1 July 2009, James Ltd would prepare the following acquisition analysis:

Net fair value of identifiable assets and liabilities of investee	= $100 000 + $12 000 + $38 000 + $8 000 + $15 000 (1 – 30%)
	= $168 500
Net fair value acquired	= 20% × $168 500
	= $33 700
Acquisition-date fair value of investment	= $34 400
Goodwill	= $34 400 – $33 700
	= $700

If Ethan Ltd then recorded a profit of $22 000 for the second half of the 2009 year, at 31 December 2009 James Ltd would recognise its 20% share of that amount, adjusted for the after-tax profit on the sale of inventory on hand at 1 July 2009 — assuming it was all sold by 31 December 2009:

Investment in Associate	Dr	2 300	
Share of Profit or Loss of Associate	Cr		2 300
(Recognition of share of post-acquisition profits of associate: 20% × [$22 000 – $15 000(1 – 30%)]			

The above entries are the same regardless of whether the equity accounting is being applied in the consolidation worksheet or in the actual accounts of the investor.

27.5.3 Becoming an associate after acquiring an ownership interest

An investor may acquire an ownership interest in an investee on a certain date, but the investee may not be classified as an associate until a later date. For example, assume Cooper Ltd acquired a 20% ownership interest in Daniel Ltd on 1 July 2009 but, because of the particular distribution of the balance of voting power, Cooper Ltd did not significantly influence the decisions of Daniel Ltd. However, on 1 January 2010, as a result of sales of certain large shareholdings in Daniel Ltd, Cooper Ltd was able to significantly influence Daniel Ltd's decisions. Hence, 1 July 2009 is the date of exchange (the date the shares were acquired), and 1 January 2010 is the acquisition date (the date significant influence is achieved).

The initial accounting for this investment is governed by IAS 39. The investor initially recognises its investment in the investee at its cost of investment, based on the fair value of what was given up to acquire the investment. Applying IAS 39, the investor classifies the investment (e.g. as a held-for-trading financial instrument) and accounts for it accordingly. If the asset is classified as held for trading, it will be measured at fair value and changes in fair value will be recognised in profit or loss for the period. If the investor obtains significant influence over the investee, the latter becomes an associate and the accounting for the investment by the investor is governed by IAS 28.

The equity method is applied at the date the investor obtains significant influence over the investee. At this date, the investor completes the following procedure:

Step 1 Remeasures the investment to fair value, taking any change to profit and loss for the period.

Step 2 Measures the fair values of the identifiable assets and liabilities of the investee.

Step 3 Measures any goodwill or income excess as the difference between the cost of the investment and the investor's share of the net fair value of the identifiable assets and liabilities acquired.

ILLUSTRATIVE EXAMPLE 27.6

Obtaining significant influence after acquiring an ownership interest

Assume James Ltd acquired 20% of the shares of Ethan Ltd on 1 January 2010 for $27 500. At 1 July 2010, James Ltd obtained significant influence over Ethan Ltd. The investment in Ethan Ltd had been classified as held for trading with movements in fair value being recognised in profit and loss for the period, and at 1 July 2010 had a fair value of $28 000. At this date, the investor measured the fair values of the identifiable assets and liabilities of Ethan Ltd at $138 000.

At 1 July 2010, the acquisition date, James Ltd would undertake an acquisition analysis:

Net fair value of identifiable assets and liabilities of Ethan Ltd	= $138 000
Net fair value acquired by James Ltd	= 20% × $138 000
	= $27 600
Acquisition-date fair value of investment previously held	= $28 000
Goodwill	= $28 000 – $27 600
	= $400

James Ltd would apply the equity method to the investment from 1 July 2010. Assume that Ethan Ltd reported a $10 000 profit for the 6 months to 31 December 2010, and that at the acquisition date there were no differences in the fair values and carrying amounts in relation to the assets and liabilities of the investee. The journal entries in the records of James Ltd to apply the equity method are:

July 1	Investment in Ethan Ltd	Dr	500	
	Income: Gain on Investment	Cr		500
	(Remeasurement of investment on adoption of equity method: $28 000 – $27 500)			
Dec. 31	Investment in Associate	Dr	2 000	
	Share of Profit or Loss of Associate	Cr		2 000
	(Share of profit of associate: 20% × $10 000)			

27.6 APPLYING THE EQUITY METHOD: INTER-ENTITY TRANSACTIONS

27.6.1 Transactions between investor and associate

Paragraph 22 of IAS 28 states:

> Profits and losses resulting from 'upstream' and 'downstream' transactions between an investor (including its consolidated subsidiaries) and an associate are recognised in the investor's financial statements only to the extent of unrelated investors' interests in the associate. 'Upstream' transactions are, for example, sales of assets from an associate to the investor. 'Downstream' transactions are, for example, sales of assets from the investor to an associate. The investor's share in the associate's profits and losses resulting from these transactions is eliminated.

As detailed in chapter 22 of this book, in the preparation of consolidated financial statements, adjustments are made to eliminate the effects of transactions between the parent and its subsidiaries, and between the subsidiaries themselves. This procedure requires the full effect of the transactions to be eliminated, and the adjustments are made against the particular accounts affected by the transactions. Under IAS 28, the adjustments for the effects of inter-entity transactions are not consistent with those used on consolidation. The principles for adjusting for the effects of inter-entity transactions under IAS 28 are as follows:

- Adjustments must be made for transactions between the associate and the investor that give rise to unrealised profits or losses. Realisation of such profits or losses occurs when the asset on which the profit or loss accrued is sold to an external party or as the future benefits embodied in the asset are consumed. Unlike consolidation, there is no need to adjust for all transactions between the investor and the associate; only the transactions where profit is affected require adjustment. Therefore, transactions such as the holding of debentures by one entity in another entity, and the payment of interest on those debentures, do not require an adjustment under equity accounting.
- Unlike adjustments for unrealised profits and losses within a consolidated group, adjustments for transactions between an investor and an associate are done on a proportional basis, determined in accordance with the investor's ownership interest in the associate. This is reasonable given that, under the equity method, only the investor's share of the equity of the associate is recognised and not the full equity of the associate.
- IAS 28 does not detail which accounts should be adjusted in this process. For example, if the associate sells an item of inventory to the investor at a profit, it is necessary to adjust the investor's share of the recorded profits of the associate. However, should the other side of the adjustment be to the inventory of the investor, because it is this asset that is affected by the inter-entity transaction? In this chapter, the adjustments are made on an after-tax basis to the accounts Investment in Associate and Share of Profit or Loss of Associate. In other words, there are no adjustments to specific asset accounts such as Property, Plant and Equipment or Inventory.

The effect of this is that the adjustments are the same for upstream and downstream transactions, because the only accounts affected by the adjustments are the carrying amount of the investment and the investor's share of profit or loss. Hence, the direction of the transaction is irrelevant in determining the accounts affected by the application of the equity method.

There are no good arguments for this method apart from simplicity. If the adjustments were consistent with those used under the consolidation method, then:

- where the investor transferred inventory to the associate, adjustments would be made to sales and cost of sales of the investor and the carrying amount of the investment in the associate, because the latter reflects the assets of the associate
- where the associate transferred inventory to the investor, the adjustments would be made to the share of profit of the associate and the inventory account of the investor.

Failing to adjust the individual accounts where appropriate departs from the approach of applying the equity method as a one-line consolidation method, and makes it more equivalent to a measurement method or valuation technique.

Another effect of the approach to adjust only the two accounts for all inter-entity transactions relating to downstream transactions is seen where the investor records a profit on the sale of inventory to an associate. Under equity accounting, an adjustment is made to the account Share of Profit or Loss of Associate. This account is affected even though the profit is made by the investor and the profits of the associate are unaffected by the transaction. The incremental change in the investment account does not therefore reflect only changes in the equity of the associate, but includes unrealised profits made by the investor.

Examples of inter-entity transactions

In the following examples, assume that the reporting period is for the year ending 30 June 2011, and that the investor, Liam Ltd, owns 25% of Noah Ltd. Liam Ltd acquired its ownership interest in Noah Ltd on 1 July 2009, when the retained earnings balance of Noah Ltd was $100 000. At this date, all the identifiable assets and liabilities of Noah Ltd were recorded at fair value. At 30 June 2010, the retained earnings balance in Noah Ltd is $140 000, and the profit recorded for the 2010–11 period is $30 000. The tax rate is 30%.

The adjustment entries may differ according to whether they are made in the consolidation worksheet or in the accounting records of the investor. Differences in particular arise where the effects of a transaction occur across 2 or more years.

Example 1: Sale of inventory from associate to investor in the current period

During the 2010–11 period, Noah Ltd sold $5000 worth of inventory to Liam Ltd. These items had previously cost Noah Ltd $3000. All the items remain unsold by the investor at 30 June 2011.

The calculations for applying the equity method are as follows:

2009–10 period	
Change in retained earnings since acquisition date:	
$140 000 – $100 000	$40 000
Investor's share — 25%	$10 000
2010–11 period	
Current period's profit	$30 000
Adjustments for inter-entity transactions:	
Unrealised after-tax profit in ending inventory	
$2000(1 – 30%)	(1 400)
	28 600
Investor's share — 25%	$ 7 150

If the investor prepares consolidated financial statements, the entries in the consolidation worksheet to apply the equity method to its associate are:

Investment in Associate	Dr	10 000	
Retained Profits (1/7/10)	Cr		10 000
Investment in Associate	Dr	7 150	
Share of Profit or Loss of Associate	Cr		7 150

If the investor does not prepare consolidated financial statements, the first of the two entries is recorded by the investor at 30 June 2010 (except that the credit is made to Share of Profit or Loss of Associate), and the second entry is recorded at 30 June 2011.

Example 2: Sale of inventory from investor to associate in the current period

Details are the same as in example 1, except that Liam Ltd sells the inventory to Noah Ltd.

The calculations and journal entries are exactly the same as in example 1. The flow of the transaction, whether upstream or downstream, does not affect the accounting for the transaction.

Example 3: Sale of inventory in the current period, part remaining unsold

During the 2010–11 period, Noah Ltd sold $5000 worth of inventory to Liam Ltd. These items had previously cost Noah Ltd $3000. Half of the items remain unsold by Liam Ltd at 30 June 2011.

The increment to the investment account is calculated in a similar way to example 1, but the adjustment is based only on the profit remaining in inventory on hand at the end of the period because it is this inventory that contains the unrealised profit. The calculations are as follows:

2009–10 period	
As for example 1:	
Increment	$10 000
2010–11 period	
Current period's recorded profit	$30 000
Adjustment for inter-entity transactions:	
Unrealised after-tax profit in ending inventory	
$1000(1 – 30%)	(700)
	29 300
Investor's share — 25%	$ 7 325

If the investor prepares consolidated financial statements at 30 June 2011, the entries in the consolidation worksheet to apply the equity method to its associate are:

Investment in Associate	Dr	10 000	
Retained Earnings (1/7/10)	Cr		10 000
Investment in Associate	Dr	7 325	
Share of Profit or Loss of Associate	Cr		7 325

If the investor does not prepare consolidated financial statements, in the 2010–11 period only the second of the above two entries is required.

Example 4: Sale of inventory in the previous period

During the 2009–10 period, Liam Ltd sold $5000 worth of inventory to Noah Ltd. These items had previously cost Liam Ltd $3000. All the items remain unsold by Noah Ltd at 30 June 2010. These were eventually sold in the following period.

The calculations for applying the equity method are as follows:

2009–10 period	
Change in retained earnings since acquisition date:	
$140 000 – $100 000	$40 000
Adjustment for inter-entity transactions:	
Unrealised after-tax profit in ending inventory	
$2000(1 – 30%)	(1 400)
	38 600
Investor's share — 25%	$ 9 650
2010–11 period	
Current period's profit	$30 000
Adjustment for inter-entity transactions:	
Realised after-tax profit in opening inventory	
$2000(1 – 30%)	1 400
	31 400
Investor's share — 25%	$ 7 850

In the 2010–11 period, the profit that was unrealised in the previous period becomes realised. Hence, the amount is added back in the calculation of the 2010–11 share of equity. The addition of the 2009–10 and the 2010–11 increments results in the inter-entity transaction having a zero effect since, by 30 June 2011, the profit on the sale is realised.

If the investor prepares consolidated financial statements at 30 June 2011, the entries in the consolidation worksheet to apply the equity method to its associate are:

Investment in Associate	Dr	9650	
Retained Earnings (1/7/10)	Cr		9650
Investment in Associate	Dr	7850	
Share of Profit or Loss of Associate	Cr		7850

If the investor does not prepare consolidated statements, the first of the above entries is recorded in the accounts of the investor at 30 June 2010 (except that the credit is made to Share of Profit or Loss of Associate), and the second entry at 30 June 2011.

Example 5: Sale of depreciable non-current asset

On 1 July 2009, Noah Ltd sold an item of plant to Liam Ltd for $8000. The carrying amount of the asset on this date in Noah Ltd's records was $3000. The plant had a remaining useful life of 5 years.

The calculations for applying the equity method are as follows:

2009–10 period	
Change in retained earnings since acquisition date	$40 000
Adjustments for inter-entity transactions:	
Unrealised after-tax profit on sale of plant	
$5000(1 – 30%)	(3 500)
Realised profit on sale of plant: $\frac{1}{5}$ × $3500	700
	37 200
Investor's share — 25%	$ 9 300

Note that the profit on the sale of the plant is unrealised because the plant was not sold to external parties. It is expected to be realised as the asset is consumed. The consumption of benefits is measured by the depreciation of the asset. Hence, as the plant is depreciated on a straight-line basis over a 5-year period, one-fifth of the profit is realised in each year after the inter-entity transfer.

2010–11 period	
Current period's recorded profit	$30 000
Adjustment for inter-entity transactions:	
Realised after-tax profit on sale of plant	
$\frac{1}{5}$ × $3500	700
	30 700
Investor's share — 25%	$ 7 675

A further one-fifth of the unrealised profit is realised in the 2010–11 period as the benefits from the asset are further consumed. After a 5-year period, the whole of the profit is realised.

If the investor prepares consolidated financial statements at 30 June 2011, the entries in the consolidation worksheet to apply the equity method to its associate are:

Investment in Associate	Dr	9300	
Retained Earnings (1/7/10)	Cr		9300
Investment in Associate	Dr	7675	
Share of Profit or Loss of Associate	Cr		7675

If the investor does not prepare consolidated statements, the first of the above entries is recorded in the accounts of the investor at 30 June 2010 (except that the credit is made to Share of Profit or Loss of Associate), and the second entry at 30 June 2011.

Example 6: Payment of interest

On 1 July 2009, Liam Ltd lent $10 000 to Noah Ltd. Interest of $1000 p.a was paid by Noah Ltd.

Although the profit of Noah Ltd includes the interest expense from this transaction, no adjustment is required because the revenue/expense on the transaction is assumed to be realised. Profits are considered to be unrealised only when there remains an asset in the investor/associate transferred at a profit or loss from the associate/investor.

27.6.2 Transactions between associates

Assume that Liam Ltd owned 25% of the shares of Noah Ltd as well as 40% of the shares of Luke Ltd. Where transactions occur between two associates, the proportional adjustment is 10% (i.e. 40% × 25%), which is the product of the ownership interests in the associate.

Example 7: Sale of inventory between associates

In the current period, Noah Ltd sold inventory to Luke Ltd at an after-tax profit of $100. The inventory remains unsold at the end of the period.

The unrealised profit on the transaction is $100. The adjustment affects Share of Profit or Loss of Associate and the carrying amount of the investment. However, is it the investment in Noah Ltd or the investment in Luke Ltd? Where transactions are between associates, the flow of the transaction is of concern. In this example, the unrealised profit relates to Noah Ltd because it was Noah Ltd who sold the inventory to Luke Ltd. Therefore, if Noah Ltd recorded a $1000 profit:

Recorded profit	$1000.0
Adjustment for inter-entity transactions:	
Unrealised profit in inventory	
(25% × 40%) × $100	10.0
	990.0
Investor's share — 25%	$ 247.5

The equity accounting entry is:

Investment in Associate – Noah Ltd	Dr	247.5	
Share of Profit or Loss of Associate – Noah Ltd	Cr		247.5
(Share of profit of associate)			

27.7 SHARE OF LOSSES OF THE ASSOCIATE

Paragraph 29 of IAS 28 discusses the accounting for losses made by an associate. In this situation, the investor recognises losses only to the point where the carrying amount of the investment reaches zero. As paragraph 29 states, the investor discontinues the use of the equity method when the share of losses equals or exceeds the carrying amount of the investment.

A further point made in paragraph 29 is that the carrying amount of the investment is not just the balance of the investment account Investment in Associate. The investor's interest in the associate also includes other long-term interests in the associate, such as preference shares or long-term receivables or loans. The base against which the losses are offset is then the investor's net investment in the associate. Where the associate incurs losses, the carrying amount of the account Investment in Associate is first reduced to zero. If losses exceed this carrying amount, they are then applied against the other components of the investor's interest in the associate in the reverse order of their seniority, or priority in liquidation. The logic is that, if the associate is making losses, then the probability of the other investments in the associate being realised is lessened.

Paragraph 30 of IAS 28 states: 'If the associate subsequently reports profits, the investor resumes recognising its share of those profits only after its share of the profits equals the share of losses not recognised.' In other words, once the equity-accounted balance of the investment returns to a positive amount, equity accounting resumes.

In situations where the associate records losses, if there are indications that the investment may be impaired, the investor should apply IAS 36 *Impairment of Assets*. Paragraph 33 of IAS 28 states that, in determining the value in use of the investment, an investor estimates:

(a) its share of the present value of the estimated future cash flows expected to be generated by the associate, including the cash flows from the operations of the associate and the proceeds on the ultimate disposal of the investment; or

(b) the present value of the estimated future cash flows expected to arise from dividends to be received from the investment and from its ultimate disposal.

Under appropriate assumptions, both methods give the same result.

ILLUSTRATIVE EXAMPLE 27.7

Share of losses of the associate

On 1 July 2006, Jacob Ltd acquired 25% of the shares of Jayden Ltd for $100 000. At that date, the equity of Jayden Ltd was $400 000, with all identifiable assets and liabilities being measured at amounts equal to fair value. Table 27.1 shows the profits and losses made by the associate over the first 5 years of operations after 1 July 2006, with their effects on the carrying amount of the investment.

TABLE 27.1 Profits and losses made by associate over first 5 years of operations

Year	Profit/(loss)	Share of profit/loss	Cumulative share	Equity-accounted balance of investment
2006–07	$ 20 000	$ 5 000	$ 5 000	$105 000
2007–08	(200 000)	(50 000)	(45 000)	55 000
2008–09	(250 000)	(62 500)	(107 500)	0
2009–10	16 000	4 000	(103 500)	0
2010–11	20 000	5 000	(98 500)	1 500

Table 27.1 shows that the investment account is initially recorded by Jacob Ltd at $100 000, and is progressively adjusted for Jacob Ltd's share of the profits and losses of Jayden Ltd. In the 2008–09 year, when the cumulative share of the losses of the associate exceed the cost of the investment, the investor discontinues recognising its share of future losses. Even though profits are recorded by the associate in the 2009–10 year, the balance of the investment stays at zero because the profits are not sufficient to offset losses not recognised.

The journal entries in the consolidation worksheets of Jacob Ltd over these periods are:

30 June 2007			
Investment in Associate	Dr	5 000	
Share of Profit or Loss of Associate	Cr		5 000
30 June 2008			
Share of Profit or Loss of Associate	Dr	50 000	
Retained Earnings (1/7/07)	Cr		5 000
Investment in Associate	Cr		45 000
30 June 2009			
Share of Profit or Loss of Associate	Dr	55 000	
Retained Earnings (1/7/08)	Dr	45 000	
Investment in Associate	Cr		100 000
30 June 2010			
Retained Earnings (1/7/09)	Dr	100 000	
Investment in Associate	Cr		100 000
30 June 2011			
Retained Earnings (1/7/10)	Dr	100 000	
Investment in Associate	Cr		98 500
Share of Profit or Loss of Associate	Cr		1 500

27.8 DISCLOSURE

Paragraphs 37–40 of IAS 28 contain the disclosures required in relation to associates.

In relation to the investment account Shares in Associate, paragraph 38 requires investments in associates accounted for using the equity method to be classified as non-current assets and disclosed as a separate item in the statement of financial position. Similarly, the account Share of Profit or Loss of Associate must be disclosed as a separate item in the statement of comprehensive income. The investor's share of any discontinuing operations of such associates must also be separately disclosed. Paragraph 39 also requires separate disclosure in the statement of comprehensive income of the investor's share of changes recognised directly in the associate's equity.

Note the following disclosure requirements:

- *Paragraph 37(c):* Where an investor holds less than 20% of the voting or potential voting power of the investee, but has applied the equity method because it believes it has significant influence, the investor must disclose the reasons the presumption that it does not have such influence is overcome.
- *Paragraph 37(d):* Where an investor holds more than 20% of the voting or potential voting power of the investee, but has not applied the equity method because it believes it does not have significant influence, the investor must disclose the reasons the presumption that it does have such influence is overcome.
- *Paragraph 37(g):* Where an investor has discontinued the application of the equity method because the associate has incurred losses, the investor must disclose the unrecognised share of losses of an associate, both for the period and cumulatively.
- *Paragraphs 37(h) and (i):* Paragraph 13 of IAS 28 provides a number of exemptions to the application of the equity method in accounting for associates. Paragraph 37(h) requires the disclosure of the fact that an associate is not accounted for under the equity method in accordance with paragraph 13. Paragraph 37(i) requires the disclosure of summarised financial information — including the amounts of total assets, total liabilities, revenues and profit or loss — either individually or in groups, of associates that are not accounted for under the equity method.

Other disclosures required in relation to associates are illustrated in figure 27.1.

Note 22: Investments in associates	**IAS 28** *para.*
The entity has a 35% interest in Tyler Ltd. The fair value of the investment at balance date is $650 000.	*37(a)*
The following information is obtained from the financial statements of Tyler Ltd at 31 December 2010:	*37(b)*
$000	
Assets 2 400	
Liabilities 900	
Revenues 10 630	
Profit 320	
The ends of the reporting periods of the company and its associate are different in that Tyler Ltd, because of legislative requirements relating to the nature of the industry it is primarily involved in, has an end of reporting period of 28 February. Any significant transactions and events occurring between the two dates have been adjusted for when applying the equity method to the investment.	*37(e)*
Because of the nature of the industry that Tyler Ltd operates in, government regulations require that Tyler Ltd notify and obtain approval from the regulatory authority before paying dividends.	*37(f)*
Tyler Ltd has recorded a contingent liability of $10 000 relating to a guarantee it has offered. The company's share of the liability incurred jointly with other investors in Tyler Ltd is $3500.	*40*

FIGURE 27.1 Disclosures concerning investments in associates

Illustrative example 27.8 is a comprehensive example demonstrating the equity method of accounting.

ILLUSTRATIVE EXAMPLE 27.8

Equity method of accounting

On 1 July 2008, Charlie Ltd paid $2 696 000 for 40% of the shares of Jake Ltd, a company involved in the manufacture of garden equipment. At that date, the equity of Jake Ltd consisted of:

Share capital — 3 000 000 shares	$3 000 000
Retained earnings	3 000 000

At 1 July 2008, all the identifiable net assets of Jake Ltd were recorded at fair value except for the following:

	Carrying amount	Fair value
Inventory	$1 000 000	$1 200 000
Plant (cost $3 200 000)	2 500 000	3 000 000

The inventory was all sold by 30 June 2009. The plant had a further expected useful life of 5 years.

Additional information

(a) On 1 July 2009, Charlie Ltd held inventory sold to it by Jake Ltd at a profit before income tax of $200 000. This was all sold by 30 June 2010.
(b) In February 2010, Jake Ltd sold inventory to Charlie Ltd at a profit before income tax of $600 000. Half of this was still held by Charlie Ltd at 30 June 2010.
(c) On 30 June 2010, Jake Ltd held inventory sold to it by Charlie Ltd at a profit before income tax of $200 000. This had been sold to Jake Ltd for $2 000 000.
(d) On 2 July 2008, Jake Ltd sold some equipment to Charlie Ltd for $1 500 000, with Jake Ltd recording a profit before income tax of $400 000. The equipment had a further 4-year life, with benefits expected to occur evenly in these years.
(e) In June 2009, Jake Ltd provided for a dividend of $1 000 000. This dividend was paid in August 2009. Dividend revenue is recognised when the dividend is provided for.
(f) The balances in the general reserve have resulted from transfers from retained earnings.
(g) The tax rate is 30%.
(h) Each share in Jake Ltd has a fair value at 30 June 2010 of $4.
(i) The consolidated financial statements of Charlie Ltd and the financial statements of Jake Ltd at 30 June 2010, not including the equity-accounted figures, are as follows:

Statements of Comprehensive Income for the year ended 30 June 2010

	Charlie Ltd	Jake Ltd
	$000	$000
Revenue	25 000	18 600
Expenses	19 200	13 600
Profit before tax	5 800	5 000
Income tax expense	2 200	1 100
Profit for the period	3 600	3 900
Other comprehensive income	0	400
Total comprehensive income	3 600	4 300

Statements of Changes in Equity for the year ended 30 June 2010

	Charlie Ltd	Jake Ltd
	$000	$000
Total comprehensive income	3600	4300
Retained earnings as at 1/7/09	4000	4000
Profit	3600	3900
	7600	7900
Transfer to general reserve	—	1000
Dividend paid	3000	1500
Dividend provided	1500	1000
	4500	3500
Retained earnings as at 30/6/10	3100	4400
Asset revaluation reserve as at 1/7/09	—	200
Increase in 2009–10		400
Asset revaluation reserve as at 30/6/10		600
General reserve as at 1/7/09	1000	1500
Increase in 2009–10	—	1000
General reserve at 30/6/10	1000	2500

Statements of Financial Position as at 30 June 2010

	Charlie Ltd	Jake Ltd
	$000	$000
EQUITY AND LIABILITIES		
Equity		
Share capital	8 000	3 000
Asset revaluation reserve	—	600
General reserve	1 000	2 500
Retained Earnings	3 100	4 400
Total equity	12 100	10 500
Total liabilities	1 500	1 400
Total equity and liabilities	13 600	11 900
ASSETS		
Non-current assets		
Property, plant and equipment	5 904	9 000
Investment in Jake Ltd	2 696	
	8 600	9 000
Current assets		
Inventory	4 000	2 000
Receivables	1 000	900
	5 000	2 900
Total assets	13 600	11 900

Required

Prepare the consolidated financial statements of Charlie Ltd at 30 June 2010, applying the equity method of accounting to the investment in Jake Ltd.

Solution

The first step is to prepare an acquisition analysis which compares at acquisition date, 1 July 2008, the cost of the investment in Jake Ltd and the share of the net fair value of the identifiable assets and liabilities of Jake Ltd. This analysis is the same as the acquisition analysis used in preparing consolidated financial statements, and results in the determination of any goodwill or income on acquisition.

Acquisition analysis
At 1 July 2008:

Net fair value of identifiable assets and liabilities of Jake Ltd	= ($3 000 000 + $3 000 000) (equity)
	+ $200 000(1 – 30%) (inventory)
	+ $500 000(1 – 30%) (plant)
	= $6 490 000
Net fair value acquired by Jake Ltd	= 40% × $6 490 000
	= $2 596 000
Cost of investment	= $2 696 000
Goodwill	= $100 000

As a result of the analysis, the effects of the adjustments to assets on hand at acquisition date can be calculated. In relation to the plant, there is a $500 000 difference between the fair value and the carrying amount at acquisition date. As a result, the recorded profits of the associate after acquisition date will include amounts that were paid for by the investor at acquisition date. The equity method recognises a share of post-acquisition equity only. The plant is being depreciated by the associate at 20% p.a. straight-line. Since the investor acquired 40% of the shares of the associate, the after-tax effect of the depreciation each year is calculated as:

Depreciation of plant p.a.	= 20% × $500 000(1 – 30%)
	= $70 000
Investor's share	= 40% × $70 000
	= $28 000

In each of the 5 years subsequent to the acquisition date, the investor's share of the recorded profit of the associate is then reduced by $28 000 p.a.

In relation to inventory, there is a $200 000 difference between fair value and carrying amount at acquisition date. When the associate sells the inventory, it will record a profit that includes pre-acquisition equity to the investor. Since the investor acquired 40% of the shares of the associate, the after-tax effect on profit on sale of the inventory is:

Pre-acquisition inventory effect	= $200 000(1 – 30%)
	= $140 000
Investor's share	= 40% × $140 000
	= $56 000

In the year of sale of the inventory, the investor's share of the recorded profit of the group is reduced by $56 000.

Consolidation worksheet entries — 30 June 2010
The investor's share of the post-acquisition equity of the associate to be recognised on consolidation is calculated in two steps: a share of post-acquisition equity between the acquisition date and the beginning of the current period, and a share of the current period's post-acquisition equity.

(1) *Share of changes in post-acquisition equity in previous periods*
The calculation is based on post-acquisition movements in the Retained Earnings account and other reserve accounts created by transfers from retained earnings, and adjusted for the effects of inter-entity transactions. The consolidation worksheet entry for the investor's

share of the associate's post-acquisition equity recognised between the date of acquisition and the beginning of the current period is calculated as follows:

	$000	$000
Retained earnings:		
Post-acquisition retained earnings from acquisition date to beginning of the current period:		
$4 000 000 – $3 000 000		$1 000
Change in general reserve in previous periods		1 500
Adjustments for inter-entity transactions:		
Inventory on hand at 30/6/10: $200 000(1 – 30%)	$ (140)	
Unrealised profit on sale of equipment:		
Original gain $400 000(1 – 30%) less depreciation p.a. of $\frac{1}{4}$ × $280 000	(210)	(350)
		2 150
Investor's share — 40%		860
Pre-acquisition adjustments:		
Depreciation of plant	(28)	
Sale of inventory	(56)	(84)
Investor's share of retained earnings at 1/7/09		776
Asset revaluation reserve:		
Share of asset revaluation reserve in previous periods: 40% × $200		80
Total increase in equity-accounted carrying amount in previous periods		$ 856

The consolidation worksheet entry in relation to previous period's equity is:

Investment in Associate – Jake Ltd	Dr	856 000	
Retained Earnings (1/7/09)	Cr		776 000
Asset Revaluation Reserve	Cr		80 000

In relation to the above entry and calculations, note the following:

Retained earnings (1/7/09):

- *Retained earnings:* The change is calculated as the difference between the recorded balance at acquisition date and the balance at the beginning of the current period.
- *General reserve:* The change in this equity amount is calculated in the same way as for retained earnings. There was no balance at acquisition date. The balance at 30 June 2010 is $2.5 million and, given a transfer to the reserve of $1 million, the balance at the beginning of the period was $1.5 million. This can be seen in the statement of changes in equity. Hence there is an increase in post-acquisition equity of $1.5 million.
- *Inter-entity transactions:* Where either the associate or the investee has recognised profits/losses on transactions with the other party, and these are not realised, adjustments are made because the recorded equity of the associate includes these unrealised profits/losses. In this problem, the Additional Information details four inter-entity transactions, only two of which relate to previous periods, namely (a) and (d):
  - (a) On 1 July 2009, the associate sold inventory to the investor at a profit before tax of $200 000. This was unrealised at 30 June 2009. The recorded change in equity is then reduced by $140 000 after-tax profit as the profit is not yet realised.
  - (d) On 2 July 2008, the associate recognised an after-tax profit of $280 000 on the sale of equipment to the investor. This profit is realised as the benefits from the asset are consumed by use. The rate of consumption is measured via depreciation. As the asset has a 4-year life, one-quarter of the profit is realised each year. Hence, the unrealised portion at 30 June 2009 is the original after-tax profit of $280 000 less $\frac{1}{4}$ of $280 000, namely $210 000.

The change in realised equity in previous periods is then $2 650 000. The investor's share (40%) is $1 060 000.

However, this is not all post-acquisition equity. The investor recognised the fair value of the assets and liabilities of the associate at acquisition date, and not the carrying amount in the associate. Where there are movements in these assets and liabilities, some of the profits recognised by the associate are pre-acquisition and not post-acquisition. There were two assets at acquisition date for which the fair value differed from carrying amount:

- *Plant:* The fair value was $500 000 greater than the carrying amount. As calculated in the acquisition analysis, since the asset has a 5-year life, in relation to the investor's share the pre-acquisition amount included in recorded equity of the associate is $180 000 p.a.
- *Inventory:* The fair value was $200 000 greater than carrying amount. As calculated in the acquisition analysis, since the asset was sold after the acquisition date, in relation to the investor's share the pre-acquisition effect is $56 000.

Hence, the investor's share of changes in retained earnings between acquisition date and the beginning of the current period is $976 000.

Asset revaluation reserve:

There was no asset revaluation reserve recognised in the associate at acquisition date. As per the statement of comprehensive income, the balance at 30 June 2009 was $200 000. Hence, the change over the period is $200 000. The investor's share of this is 40%, namely $80 000.

Investment in associate — Jake Ltd:

The investor's total share of post-acquisition equity of the associate up to the beginning of the current period is, therefore, $856 000. This amount is then added to the investment in associate account, with increases recognised in the relevant reserve accounts.

(2) *Share of profit in current period*

In part (1), the investor's share of previous period's post-acquisition equity was calculated. In this part, the calculation is of the investor's share of the post-acquisition equity of the associate relating to the current period. In this problem, increases in equity arise owing to the associate's earning a profit and recording other income as increments in the asset revaluation reserve.

The calculations and required consolidation adjustment entry is shown below:

	$000	$000
Recorded profit:		$3 900
Adjustments for inter-entity transactions:		
Realised profit in opening inventory	$ 140	
Unrealised profit in Charlie Ltd's ending inventory: $\frac{1}{2}$ × $600 000(1 – 30%)	(210)	
Unrealised profit in Jake Ltd's ending inventory: $200 000(1 – 30%)	(140)	
Realised profit on plant: $\frac{1}{4}$ × $280 000	70	(140)
		3 760
Investor's share — 40%		1 504
Pre-acquisition adjustments:		
Depreciation of plant		(28)
Investor's share of profit of associate		1 476
Other income:		
Share of increment in asset revaluation reserve: 40% × $400 000		160
Total increase in equity-accounted carrying amount in current period		$1 636

The consolidation worksheet entry is:

Investment in Associate – Jake Ltd	Dr	1 636 000	
Share of Profit or Loss of Associate	Cr		1 476 000
Asset Revaluation Reserve	Cr		160 000

In relation to these calculations and entry, note the following:

- *Share of profit or loss of associate:* The associate records an after-tax profit for the year of $3 900 000. This profit needs to be adjusted where there have been transactions between the investor and the associate and at the end of the reporting period profits/losses on these transactions are unrealised.

In this problem there are four transactions noted in the additional information that affect the current period, namely (a)–(d).

(a) The inventory on hand at 1 July 2009 is all sold by 30 June 2010. The profit on the inter-entity sale was unrealised at the beginning of the current period but is realised in the current period. The after-tax profit on sale of the inventory was $140 000. Since the profit is realised in the current period, it is added to the recorded profit of the associate. Note that $1 400 000 is subtracted in the calculation of the investor's share of previous period equity and is added to the calculation of the investor's share of current period profit. Since the profit is now realised, there is no need to make an adjustment in future periods.

(b) In February 2010, the associate sold inventory to the investor at an after-tax profit of $420 000. Since half of the inventory is still on hand at 30 June 2010, there is unrealised profit at the end of the reporting period of $210 000. This amount is subtracted from recorded profit because the investor's share relates to realised profit only.

(c) In the current period, the investor sold inventory to the associate for an after-tax profit of $140 000. Since this inventory remains on hand at the end of the reporting period, the unrealised profit is subtracted from recorded profit.

(d) The gain on sale of equipment was adjusted for in the calculation of the investor's share of previous period equity. As noted in that calculation, the unrealised profit on sale is realised as the asset is used up and depreciated. The amount realised each year is in proportion to depreciation, namely one-quarter p.a. The amount of the gain realised in the current period is then $\frac{1}{4}\times$ $280 000, that is, $70 000. Being realised profit, it is added back to recorded profit.

The total realised profit of the associate is then $3 760 000, and the investor's share (40%) is $1 504 000.

However, this profit is not all post-acquisition profit. Movements in assets and liabilities on hand at acquisition date when fair values differed from carrying amounts give rise to pre-acquisition elements in recorded profits. In the current period, because the plant on hand at acquisition date was recognised by the investor at fair value, the extra depreciation on the plant reflects pre-acquisition equity. As calculated in the acquisition analysis the pre-acquisition effect is $28 000 p.a. This is subtracted from the investor's share of realised profit to give the investor's share of realised post-acquisition profit.

- *Asset revaluation reserve:* From the statement of changes in equity, note that the asset revaluation reserve has increased by $400 000 in the current period. The investor is entitled to 40% of this, that is, $160 000.

  The investor's share of current period post-acquisition equity is then $1 636 000, which increases the investor's investment in the associate. For the profit portion, this is recognised by a separate line item in the consolidated statement of comprehensive income.

(3) *Dividends paid and provided for by associate*

A further entry is necessary to take into account reductions in the associate's equity in the current period because of dividends. In the current period, Jake Ltd paid a $1.5 million dividend and declared a $1 million dividend. Assuming the investor recognises dividend revenue in relation to the declared dividend, it would recognise dividend of $1 million (i.e. 40% × [$1.5 million + $1 million]).The following entry eliminates, on consolidation, the dividend revenue recorded by the investor. This is because in parts (1) and (2) above, the investor's equity has been increased by its share of the equity of the associate from which the dividends were paid/declared. Similarly, it is also necessary to reduce the investment in the associate as the share of equity in the associate as calculated in parts (1) and (2) has been reduced by the payment/declaration of the dividend. The consolidation worksheet entry is:

Dividend Revenue	Dr	1 000 000	
Investment in Associate – Jake Ltd	Cr		1 000 000
(40% × [$1 500 000 + $1 000 000])			

Total investment

On the basis of the above worksheet entries, the carrying amount of the investment in the associate, Jake Ltd, is:

$4 188 000 = $2 696 000 + $856 000 + $1 636 000 – $1 000 000

The consolidated financial statements of Charlie Ltd at 30 June 2010, including the investment in the associate accounted for under IAS 28, are as follows:

CHARLIE LTD
Consolidated Statement of Comprehensive Income
for year ended 30 June 2010

	$000
Revenue [$25 000 000 – $1 000 000]	24 000
Expenses	19 200
	4 800
Share of profit or loss of associate accounted for using the equity method	1 476
Profit before tax	6 276
Income tax expense	2 200
Profit for the period	4 076
Other comprehensive income:	
Share of other comprehensive income of associate accounted for using the equity method	160
Total comprehensive income	4 236

CHARLIE LTD
Consolidated Statement of Changes in Equity
for year ended 30 June 2010

	$000
Total comprehensive income	4 236
Retained earnings at 1/7/09 [$4 000 000 + $976 000]	4 776
Profit	4 076
	8 852
Dividend paid	(3 000)
Dividend provided	(1 500)
Retained earnings at 30/6/10	4 352
Asset revaluation reserve at 1/7/09	80
Revaluation increments	160
Asset revaluation reserve at 30/6/10	240
General reserve at 1/7/09	1 000
General reserve at 30/6/10	1 000

CHARLIE LTD
Consolidated Statement of Financial Position
as at 30 June 2010

	$000
EQUITY AND LIABILITIES	
Equity	
Share capital	8 000
Asset revaluation reserve	240
General reserve	1 000
Retained earnings	4 352

(continued)

EQUITY AND LIABILITIES *(continued)*	
Total equity	13 592
Total liabilities	1 500
Total equity and liabilities	15 092
ASSETS	
Non-current assets	
Property, plant and equipment	5 904
Investment in associate	4 188
	10 092
Current assets	
Inventories	4 000
Receivables	1 000
	5 000
Total assets	15 092

SUMMARY

The equity method of accounting has been used by standard setters for many years to provide information about investments in associates. However, even though the equity method is a technique used by many entities, and approved by standard setters, the theoretical bases of the method are not clear. It adopts some of the principles of consolidation, but not all. Some argue that it should be replaced with either a fair value model plus additional disclosure or a proportional consolidation method. Hence, whether the equity method will be used in the long term is debatable.

The equity method is designed to supply limited information about the performance of certain investments. The information is limited in that it provides information about earnings of the investee but not the variables underlying the earnings number or information about the assets and liabilities of the investee. The entities to which the equity method is applied are called associates. The criterion for establishing an investor–associate relationship is that of significant influence. This has some links to the control criterion used under the consolidation method, but it is even more difficult to determine whether such a relationship exists. IAS 28 makes a presumption that where an entity has more than 20% of the voting power in another entity, the latter is to be regarded as an associate.

The application of the equity method is different depending on whether it is applied in a consolidation worksheet or in the accounts of an investor. In both cases, the principle is that the investor should be allocated its share of the post-acquisition realised equity of the associate. In using the recorded equity of the associate to determine this share, adjustments must be made for pre-acquisition elements in recorded equity as well as unrealised profits/losses arising as a result of inter-entity transactions. Having made the appropriate calculations, the resultant journal entries are relatively simple, because the disclosure about associates in the investor's financial statements affects only a small number of lines. However, IAS 28 does require more extensive disclosures in the notes to the financial statements.

Discussion questions

1. What is an associate entity?
2. Why are associates distinguished from other investments held by the investor?
3. Discuss the similarities and differences between the criteria used to identify subsidiaries and that used to identify associates.
4. What is meant by 'significant influence'?
5. What factors could be used to indicate the existence of significant influence?
6. Discuss the relative merits of accounting for investments by the cost method, the fair value method and the equity method.

7. Outline the accounting adjustments required in relation to transactions between the investor and an associate. Explain the rationale for these adjustments.
8. Compare the accounting for the effects of inter-entity transactions for transactions between parent entities and subsidiaries and between investors and associates.
9. Discuss whether the equity method should be viewed as a form of consolidation or a valuation technique.
10. Explain why equity accounting is sometimes referred to as 'one-line consolidation'.
11. Explain the differences in application of the equity method of accounting where the method is applied in the records of the investor compared with the application in the consolidation worksheet of the investor.
12. Explain the treatment of dividends from the associate under the equity method of accounting.
13. The accountant of Dylan Chocolates Ltd, Ms Fraulein, has been advised by her auditors that the entity's investment in Max Milk Ltd should be accounted for using the equity method of accounting. Dylan Chocolates Ltd holds only 20.2% of the voting shares currently issued by Max Milk Ltd. Since the investment was undertaken purely for cash flow reasons based on the potential dividend stream from the investment, Ms Fraulein does not believe that Dylan Chocolates Ltd exerts significant influence over the investee.

    Required

    Discuss the factors that Ms Fraulein should investigate in determining whether an investor–associate relationship exists, and what avenues are available so that the equity method of accounting does not have to be applied.
14. The following note was attached to the annual report of the Bayer Group at 30 June 2007:

19. Investments in associates

Changes in the carrying amounts of the Group's interests in associates included at equity were as follows:

€ million	2006	**2007**
Net carrying amounts, January 1	795	532
Acquisitions	2	0
Other additions	46	28
Divestitures	(195)	0
Miscellaneous retirements	(47)	0
Reclassifications to current assets	(3)	0
Equity-method loss after taxes	(30)	(45)
Exchange differences	(36)	(31)
Net carrying amounts, December 31	532	**484**

For strategic reasons, the Bayer MaterialScience subgroup holds or is responsible for interests in companies that are included at equity in the consolidated financial statements of the Bayer Group.

In 2000, Bayer acquired the polyols business and parts of the propylene oxide (PO) production operations of Lyondell Chemicals. The strategic objective is to ensure access to patented technologies and safeguard the long-term supply of PO, a starting product for polyurethane, at reasonable prices. As part of this strategy, two joint ventures have been established to produce PO (PO JV Delaware U.S.A., Bayer's interest 44 percent and Lyondell Bayer Manufacturing Maasvlakte VOF, Netherlands, Bayer's interest 50 percent). The production facilities of both companies are operated by Lyondell. Bayer benefits from fixed long-term supply quotas/volumes of PO based on fixed price components.

The difference between the equity interest in the underlying net assets of associates and their at-equity accounting values is €12 million (2006: €12 million). It mainly relates to acquired goodwill.

The following tables present a summary of the aggregated income statement and balance sheet data for the associates included at equity in the consolidated financial statements of the Bayer Group.

Aggregated income statement data of associates included at equity	2006	**2007**
€ million		
Net sales	1 593	1 072
Gross profit	320	88
Net loss	(46)	(92)
Share of pre-tax loss	(20)	(45)
Other	(5)	0
Pre-tax loss from interests in associates included at equity (equity-method loss)	**(25)**	**(45)**

Aggregated balance sheet data of associates included at equity	Dec. 31, 2006	**Dec. 31, 2007**
€ million		
Noncurrent assets	1 100	962
Current assets	253	260
Noncurrent liabilities	10	11
Current liabilities	218	191
Stockholders' equity	1 125	1 020
Share of stockholders' equity	507	463
Other	25	21
Net carrying amount of associates included at equity	**532**	**484**

The item "miscellaneous" mainly comprises differences arising from adjustments of data to Bayer's uniform accounting policies, purchase price allocations and their amortization in income, and impairment losses.

Source: Bayer (2007, p. 148).

Required

You have been asked by a group of shareholders of Bayer to determine whether the company has met all the disclosure requirements of IAS 28. They also want you to provide some comments about the usefulness of the information provided about associates under IAS 28, using the Bayer note as an example.

15. Amalgamated Holdings Ltd provided the following information in Note 1 *Significant Accounting Policies* in its 2008 annual report:

(ii) Associates

Associates are those entities for which the Group has significant influence, but not control, over the financial and operating policies. The consolidated financial statements include the Group's share of the total recognised gains and losses of associates on an equity accounted basis, from the date that significant influence commences until the date that significant influence ceases. The Group's share of movements in reserves is recognised directly in consolidated reserves. When the Group's share of losses exceeds its interest in an associate, the Group's carrying amount is reduced to nil and recognition of further losses is discontinued except to the extent that the Group has incurred legal or constructive obligations or made payments on behalf of an associate.

In the Parent Entity's financial statements, investments in associates are initially recognised at cost, being the fair value of the consideration given and including acquisition charges associated with the investment. Where necessary, the cost is adjusted for any subsequent impairment.

(iii) Partnerships

In the consolidated financial statements, investments in partnerships are accounted for using equity accounting principles. Investments in partnerships are carried at the lower of the equity accounted amount and recoverable amount after adjustment for revisions arising from notional adjustments made at the date of acquisition.

The Group's share of partnerships' net profit or loss is recognised in the consolidated Income Statement from the date joint control commenced until the date joint control ceases. The Group's share of movements in reserves are recognised directly in consolidated reserves.

(iv) Transactions eliminated on consolidation

Intragroup balances, and any unrealised gains and losses or income and expenses arising from intragroup transactions, are eliminated in preparing the consolidated financial statements.

Unrealised gains arising from transactions with associates and partnerships are eliminated to the extent of the Group's interest in the entity.

Unrealised losses are eliminated in the same way as unrealised gains, but only to the extent that there is no evidence of impairment.

Gains and losses are recognised as the contributed assets are consumed or sold by the associates or partnerships or, if not consumed or sold by the associate or partnership, when the Group's interest in such entities is sold.

Source: Amalgamated Holdings (2008, p. 41).

Required

Some investors in Amalgamated Holdings Ltd who have limited accounting knowledge, particularly about equity accounting, have asked you to provide a report to them commenting on:

- the differences between associates and partnerships
- the determination of the date of significant influence
- realisation of profits/losses on inter-entity transactions
- recognition of losses of an associate.

STAR RATING

★ BASIC

★★ MODERATE

★★★ DIFFICULT

Exercises

Exercise 27.1 ★

ADJUSTMENTS WHERE INVESTOR PREPARES AND DOES NOT PREPARE CONSOLIDATED FINANCIAL STATEMENTS

Blake Ltd acquired a 30% interest in Isaac Ltd for $50 000 on 1 July 2008. The equity of Isaac Ltd at the acquisition date was:

Share capital	$ 30 000
Retained earnings	120 000
	$150 000

All the identifiable assets and liabilities of Isaac Ltd were recorded at fair value. Profits and dividends for the years ended 30 June 2009 to 2011 were as follows:

	Profit before tax	Income tax expense	Dividends paid
2009	$80 000	$30 000	$80 000*
2010	70 000	25 000	15 000
2011	60 000	20 000	10 000

*Includes $60 000 relating to profits earned before 1 July 2008.

Required

1. Prepare journal entries in the records of Blake Ltd for each of the years ended 30 June 2009 to 2011 in relation to its investment in the associate, Isaac Ltd. (Assume Blake Ltd does not prepare consolidated financial statements.)
2. Prepare the consolidation worksheet entries to account for Blake Ltd's interest in the associate, Isaac Ltd. (Assume Blake Ltd does prepare consolidated financial statements.)

Exercise 27.2 ★ ACCOUNTING FOR AN ASSOCIATE BY AN INVESTOR

Toby Ltd acquired a 40% interest in Owen Ltd for $170 000 on 1 July 2009. The share capital, reserves and retained earnings of Owen Ltd at the acquisition date and at 30 June 2010 were as follows:

	1 July 2009	30 June 2010
Share capital	$300 000	$300 000
Asset revaluation reserve	—	100 000
General reserve	—	15 000
Retained earnings	100 000	109 000
	$400 000	$524 000

At 1 July 2009, all the identifiable assets and liabilities of Owen Ltd were recorded at fair value.

The following is applicable to Owen Ltd for the year to 30 June 2010:

(a) Profit (after income tax expense of $11 000): $39 000
(b) Increase in reserves
- General (transferred from retained earnings): $15 000
- Asset revaluation (revaluation of freehold land and buildings at 30 June 2010): $100 000

(c) Dividends paid to shareholders: $15 000.

Additionally, depreciation is provided by Owen Ltd on the diminishing-balance method, whereas Toby Ltd uses the straight-line method. Had Owen Ltd used the straight-line method, the accumulated depreciation on non-current assets would be increased by $20 000 (2009 – $10 000). The tax rate is 30%.

Toby Ltd does not prepare consolidated financial statements.

Required

Prepare the journal entries in the records of Toby Ltd for the year ended 30 June 2010 in relation to its investment in the associate, Owen Ltd.

Exercise 27.3 ★ INTER-ENTITY TRANSACTIONS WHERE INVESTOR HAS NO SUBSIDIARIES

Bailey Ltd acquired 20% of the ordinary shares of Mitchell Ltd on 1 July 2009. At this date, all the identifiable assets and liabilities of Bailey Ltd were recorded at fair value. An analysis of the acquisition showed that $2000 of goodwill was acquired.

Bailey Ltd has no subsidiaries, and records its investment in the associate, Mitchell Ltd, in accordance with IAS 28. In the 2010–11 period, Mitchell Ltd recorded a profit of $100 000, paid an interim dividend of $10 000 and, in June 2011, declared a further dividend of $15 000. In June 2010, Mitchell Ltd had declared a $20 000 dividend, which was paid in August 2010, at which date it was recognised by Bailey Ltd.

The following transactions have occurred between the two entities (all transactions are independent unless specified):

(a) In January 2011, Mitchell Ltd sold inventory to Bailey Ltd for $15 000. This inventory had previously cost Mitchell Ltd $10 000, and remains unsold by Bailey Ltd at the end of the period.
(b) In February 2011, Bailey Ltd sold inventory to Mitchell Ltd at a before-tax profit of $5000. Half of this was sold by Mitchell Ltd before 30 June 2011.
(c) In June 2010, Mitchell Ltd sold inventory to Bailey Ltd for $18 000. This inventory had cost Mitchell Ltd $12 000. At 30 June 2010, this inventory remained unsold by Bailey Ltd. However, it was all sold by Bailey Ltd before 30 June 2011.

The tax rate is 30%.

Required

Prepare the journal entries in the records of Bailey Ltd in relation to its investment in Mitchell Ltd for the year ended 30 June 2011.

Exercise 27.4 ★

INTER-ENTITY TRANSACTIONS WHERE INVESTOR DOES NOT PREPARE CONSOLIDATED FINANCIAL STATEMENTS

Oscar Ltd owns 25% of the shares of its associate, Alex Ltd. At the acquisition date, there were no differences between the fair values and the carrying amounts of the identifiable assets and liabilities of Alex Ltd.

For 2009–10, Alex Ltd recorded a profit of $100 000. During this period, Alex Ltd paid a $10 000 dividend, declared in June 2009, and an interim dividend of $8000. The tax rate is 30%.

The following transactions have occurred between Oscar Ltd and Alex Ltd:

(a) On 1 July 2008, Alex Ltd sold a non-current asset costing $10 000 to Oscar Ltd for $12 000. Oscar Ltd applies a 10% p.a. on cost straight-line method of depreciation.

(b) On 1 January 2010, Alex Ltd sold an item of plant to Oscar Ltd for $15 000. The carrying amount of the asset to Alex Ltd at time of sale was $12 000. Oscar Ltd applies a 15% p.a. straight-line method of depreciation.

(c) A non-current asset with a carrying amount of $20 000 was sold by Alex Ltd to Oscar Ltd for $28 000 on 1 June 2010. Oscar Ltd regarded the item as inventory and still had the item on hand at 30 June 2010.

(d) On 1 July 2008, Oscar Ltd sold an item of machinery to Alex Ltd for $6000. This item had cost Oscar Ltd $4000. Oscar Ltd regarded this item as inventory whereas Alex Ltd intended to use the item as a non-current asset. Alex Ltd applied a 10% p.a. on cost straight-line depreciation method.

Required

Oscar Ltd applies IAS 28 in accounting for its investment in Alex Ltd. Assuming Oscar Ltd does not prepare consolidated financial statements, prepare the journal entries in the records of Oscar Ltd for the year ended 30 June 2010 in relation to its investment in Alex Ltd.

Exercise 27.5 ★★

INVESTOR PREPARES CONSOLIDATED FINANCIAL STATEMENTS, MULTIPLE PERIODS

On 1 July 2008, Angus Ltd purchased 30% of the shares of Jordan Ltd for $60 050. At this date, the ledger balances of Jordan Ltd were:

Capital	$150 000	Assets	$225 000
Other reserves	30 000	*Less:* Liabilities	30 000
Retained earnings	15 000		
	$195 000		$195 000

At 1 July 2008, all the identifiable assets and liabilities of Jordan Ltd were recorded at fair value except for plant whose fair value was $5000 greater than carrying amount. This plant has an expected future life of 5 years, the benefits being received evenly over this period. Dividend revenue is recognised when dividends are declared. The tax rate is 30%.

The results of Jordan Ltd for the next 3 years were:

	30 June 2009	30 June 2010	30 June 2011
Profit/(loss) before income tax	$50 000	$40 000	$(5000)
Income tax expense	20 000	20 000	—
Profit/(loss)	30 000	20 000	(5000)
Dividend paid	15 000	5 000	2000
Dividend declared	10 000	5 000	1000

Required

Prepare, in journal entry format, for the years ending 30 June 2009, 2010 and 2011, the consolidation worksheet adjustments to include the equity-accounted results for the associate, Jordan Ltd, in the consolidated financial statements of Angus Ltd.

Exercise 27.6 CONSOLIDATED WORKSHEET ENTRIES TO INCLUDE INVESTMENT IN ASSOCIATE

★★

On 1 July 2007, Harry Ltd acquired 30% of the shares of Nathan Ltd for $60 000. At this date, the equity of Nathan Ltd consisted of:

Share capital (100 000 shares)	$100 000
Asset revaluation surplus	50 000
Retained earnings	20 000

At this date, all the identifiable assets and liabilities of Nathan Ltd were recorded at fair value except for the following assets:

	Carrying amount	Fair value
Machinery	$20 000	$25 000
Inventory	10 000	12 000

The machinery was expected to have a further 5-year life, benefits being received evenly over this period. The inventory was all sold by 30 June 2008.

On 1 July 2007, the ownership interest of 30%, together with board representation and a diverse spread of remaining shareholders, was sufficient for the investor to demonstrate significant influence, and accordingly to begin accounting for the investment as an associate. At this date, the equity of Nathan Ltd consisted of:

Share capital (100 000 shares)	$100 000
Asset revaluation reserve	60 000
General reserve	10 000
Retained earnings	40 000

Dividends paid by Nathan Ltd in the 2007–08 period were $10 000, and $12 000 was paid in the 2008–09 period. In June 2009, Nathan Ltd declared a dividend of $10 000. Dividend revenue is recognised when dividends are declared.

During the period ending 30 June 2010, the following events occurred:

(a) Nathan Ltd sold to Harry Ltd some inventory, which had previously cost Nathan Ltd $8000, for $10 000. Harry Ltd still had one-quarter of these items on hand at 30 June 2010.

(b) On 1 January 2010, Harry Ltd sold a non-current asset to Nathan Ltd for $50 000, giving a profit before tax of $10 000 to Harry Ltd. Nathan Ltd applied a 12% p.a. on cost straight-line depreciation method to this asset.

(c) On 31 December 2009, Nathan Ltd paid an interim dividend of $5000.

(d) At 30 June 2010, Nathan Ltd calculated that it had earned a profit of $32 000, after an income tax expense of $8000. Nathan Ltd then declared a $5000 dividend, to be paid in September 2010, and transferred $3000 to the general reserve.

(e) The tax rate is 30%.

Required

Prepare the journal entries for the consolidation worksheet of Harry Ltd at 30 June 2010 for the inclusion of the equity-accounted results of Nathan Ltd.

Exercise 27.7 ADJUSTMENTS WHERE INVESTOR DOES AND DOES NOT PREPARE CONSOLIDATED FINANCIAL STATEMENTS

★★

On 1 July 2008, Seth Ltd acquired a 30% interest in one of its suppliers, Taj Ltd, at a cost of $13 650. The directors of Seth Ltd believe they exert 'significant influence' over Taj Ltd.

The equity of Taj Ltd at acquisition date was:

Share capital (20 000 shares)	$20 000
Retained earnings	10 000
	$30 000

All the identifiable assets and liabilities of Taj Ltd at 1 July 2008 were recorded at fair values except for some depreciable non-current assets with a fair value of $15 000 greater than carrying amount. These depreciable assets are expected to have a further 5-year life.

Additional information

(a) At 30 June 2010, Seth Ltd had inventory costing $100 000 (2009 – $60 000) on hand which had been purchased from Taj Ltd. A profit before tax of $30 000 (2009 – $10 000) had been made on the sale.

(b) All companies adopt the recommendations of IAS 12 regarding tax-effect accounting. Assume a tax rate of 30% applies.

(c) Information about income and changes in equity of Taj Ltd as at 30 June 2010 is:

Profit before tax		$360 000
Income tax expense		180 000
Profit		180 000
Retained earnings at 1/7/09		50 000
		230 000
Dividend paid	$50 000	
Dividend declared	50 000	100 000
Retained earnings at 30/6/10		$130 000

(d) All dividends may be assumed to be out of the profit for the current year. Dividend revenue is recognised when declared by directors.

(e) The equity of Taj Ltd at 30 June 2010 was:

Share capital	$ 20 000
Asset revaluation reserve	30 000
General reserve	5 000
Retained earnings	130 000
	$185 000

The asset revaluation reserve arose from a revaluation of freehold land made at 30 June 2010. The general reserve arose from a transfer from retained earnings in June 2009.

Required

1. Assume Seth Ltd does not prepare consolidated financial statements. Prepare the journal entries in the records of Seth Ltd for the year ended 30 June 2010 in relation to the investment in Taj Ltd.
2. Assume Seth Ltd does prepare consolidated financial statements. Prepare the consolidated worksheet entries for the year ended 30 June 2010 for inclusion of the equity-accounted results of Taj Ltd.

Exercise 27.8 ★★ ACCOUNTING FOR AN ASSOCIATE WITHIN — AND WHERE THERE ARE NO — CONSOLIDATED FINANCIAL STATEMENTS

On 1 July 2008, Kai Ltd purchased 40% of the shares of Logan Ltd for $63 200. At that date, equity of Logan Ltd consisted of:

Share capital	$125 000
Retained earnings	11 000

At 1 July 2008, the identifiable assets and liabilities of Logan Ltd were recorded at fair value.

Information about income and changes in equity for both companies for the year ended 30 June 2011 was as shown below.

	Kai Ltd	Logan Ltd
Profit before tax	$26 000	$23 500
Income tax expense	10 600	5 400
Profit	15 400	18 100
Retained earnings (1/7/10)	18 000	16 000
	33 400	34 100
Dividend paid	5 000	4 000
Dividend declared	10 000	5 000
	15 000	9 000
Retained earnings (30/6/11)	$18 400	$25 100

Additional information

(a) Kai Ltd recognised the final dividend revenue from Logan Ltd before receipt of cash. Logan Ltd declared a $6000 dividend in June 2010, this being paid in August 2010.

(b) On 31 December 2009, Logan Ltd sold Kai Ltd a motor vehicle for $12 000. The vehicle had originally cost Logan Ltd $18 000 and was written down to $9000 for both tax and accounting purposes at time of sale to Kai Ltd. Both companies depreciated motor vehicles at the rate of 20% p.a. on cost.

(c) The beginning inventory of Logan Ltd included goods at $4000 bought from Kai Ltd; their cost to Kai Ltd was $3200.

(d) The ending inventory of Kai Ltd included goods purchased from Logan Ltd at a profit before tax of $1600.

(e) The tax rate is 30%.

Required

1. Prepare the journal entries in the records of Kai Ltd to account for the investment in Logan Ltd in accordance with IAS 28 for the year ended 30 June 2011 assuming Kai Ltd does not prepare consolidated financial statements.
2. Prepare the consolidated worksheet entries in relation to the investment in Logan Ltd, assuming Kai Ltd does prepare consolidated financial statements at 30 June 2011.

Exercise 27.9 ★★

CONSOLIDATED FINANCIAL STATEMENTS INCLUDING INVESTMENTS IN ASSOCIATES

Caleb Ltd acquired 90% of the ordinary shares of Ashton Ltd on 1 July 2005 at a cost of $150 750. At that date the equity of Ashton Ltd was:

Share capital (100 000 shares)	$100 000
Reserve	8 000
Retained earnings	12 000

At 1 July 2005, all the identifiable assets and liabilities of Ashton Ltd were at fair value except for the following assets:

	Carrying amount	Fair value
Inventory	$10 000	$15 000
Depreciable assets	25 000	35 000

The inventory was all sold by 30 June 2006. Depreciable assets have an expected further 5-year life, with depreciation being calculated on a straight-line basis. Valuation adjustments are made on consolidation.

Caleb Ltd uses the partial goodwill method.

On 1 July 2008, Caleb Ltd acquired 25% of the capital of Brodie Ltd for $3500. All the identifiable assets and liabilities of Brodie Ltd were recorded at fair value except for the following:

	Carrying amount	Fair value
Inventory	$1 000	$1 500
Depreciable assets	6 000	7 000

All this inventory was sold in the 12 months after 1 July 2008. The depreciable assets were considered to have a further 5-year life.

Information on Brodie Ltd's equity position is as follows:

	1 July 2008	30 June 2009
Share capital	$10 000	$10 000
General reserve	—	2 000
Retained earnings	2 150	4 000

For the year ended 30 June 2010, Brodie Ltd recorded a profit before tax of $2600 and an income tax expense of $600. Brodie Ltd paid a dividend of $200 in January 2010. Caleb Ltd regards Brodie Ltd as an associated company.

During the year ended 30 June 2010, Brodie Ltd sold inventory to Ashton Ltd for $6000. The cost of this inventory to Brodie Ltd was $4000. Ashton Ltd has resold only 20% of these items. However, Ashton Ltd made a profit before tax of $500 on the resale of these items.

On 1 January 2009, Caleb Ltd sold Brodie Ltd a motor vehicle for $4000, at a profit before tax of $800 to Caleb Ltd. Both companies treat motor vehicles as non-current assets. Both companies charge depreciation at 20% p.a. on the reducing balance. Assume a tax rate of 30%.

Information about income and changes in equity for Caleb Ltd and its subsidiary, Ashton Ltd, for the year ended 30 June 2010 is as follows:

		Caleb Ltd	Ashton Ltd
Sales revenue		$200 000	$60 000
Less: Cost of sales		110 000	30 000
Gross profit		90 000	30 000
Less:	Depreciation	16 000	4 000
	Other expenses	22 000	3 000
		38 000	7 000
		52 000	23 000
Plus: Other revenue		30 000	5 000
Profit before income tax		82 000	28 000
Less: Income tax expense		20 000	10 000
Profit		62 000	18 000
Plus: Retained earnings (1/7/09)		120 000	80 000
		182 000	98 000
Less: Dividend paid		20 000	4 000
Retained earnings (30/6/10)		$162 000	$94 000

Required

1. Prepare the consolidated statement of comprehensive income and statement of changes in equity of Caleb Ltd and its subsidiary Ashton Ltd as at 30 June 2010.
2. In the consolidated statement of financial position, what would be the balance of the investment shares in Brodie Ltd?

Problems

Problem 27.1 ★★★

CONSOLIDATION WORKSHEET ENTRIES INCLUDING INVESTMENTS IN ASSOCIATES

You are given the following details for the year ended 30 June 2010:

	Cody Ltd	Joel Ltd	Jessy Ltd
Profit before tax	$100 000	$30 000	$25 000
Income tax expense	31 000	10 000	6 000
Profit	69 000	20 000	19 000
Retained earnings at 1 July 2009	20 000	12 000	11 000
	89 000	32 000	30 000
Dividend paid	14 000	6 000	2 000
Dividend declared	15 000	4 000	8 000
Transfer to general reserve (from current period's profit)	10 000	5 000	6 000
	39 000	15 000	16 000
Retained earnings at 30 June 2010	$ 50 000	$17 000	$14 000

Additional information

(a) Cody Ltd owns 80% of the participating shares in Joel Ltd and 20% of the shares in Jessy Ltd (enough to cause Cody Ltd to have significant influence over Jessy Ltd).

(b) On 1 July 2008, all identifiable assets and liabilities of Joel Ltd were recorded at fair value. Cody Ltd purchased 80% of Joel Ltd's shares on 1 July 2008, and paid $5000 for goodwill, none of which had been recorded on Joel Ltd's records. Cody Ltd uses the partial goodwill method.

(c) At the date Cody Ltd acquired its shares in Jessy Ltd, Jessy Ltd's recorded equity was:

Share capital	$100 000
General reserve	15 000
Retained earnings	5 000

All the identifiable assets and liabilities of Jessy Ltd were recorded at fair value. Cody Ltd paid $25 000 for its shares in Jessy Ltd on 1 July 2008. There was $3000 transferred to general reserve by Jessy Ltd in the year ended 30 June 2009, out of equity earned since 1 July 2008.

(d) Included in the beginning inventory of Cody Ltd were profits before tax made by Joel Ltd: $5000; Jessy Ltd: $3000.

(e) Included in the ending inventory of Joel Ltd were profits before tax made by Jessy Ltd: $4000.

(f) Jessy Ltd had recorded a profit (net of $500 tax) of $2000 in selling certain non-current assets to Cody Ltd on 1 January 2010. Cody Ltd treats the items as non-current assets and charges depreciation at the rate of 25% p.a. straight-line from that date.

(g) Cody Ltd purchased for $10 000 an item of plant from Joel Ltd on 1 September 2008. The carrying amount of the asset at that date was $7000. The asset was depreciated at the rate of 20% p.a. straight-line from 1 September 2008.

(h) During the year ended 30 June 2010, Jessy Ltd has revalued upwards one of its non-current assets by $8000. There had been no previous downward revaluations.

(i) Dividend revenue is recognised when dividends are declared.

(j) The tax rate is 30%.

Required

Prepare the consolidation worksheet entries (in general journal form) needed for the consolidated statements for the year ended 30 June 2010 for Cody Ltd and its subsidiary Joel Ltd. Include the equity-accounted results of Jessy Ltd.

Problem 27.2 ★★★

MULTIPLE ASSOCIATES, CONSOLIDATED FINANCIAL STATEMENTS

Jack Ltd has one subsidiary, Jett Ltd, and two associated companies, Jay Ltd and Jaxon Ltd, and Jett Ltd has one associated company, John Ltd.

	Jett Ltd	John Ltd	Jay Ltd	Jaxon Ltd
Share capital				
Ordinary:				
Held by group	$1 200	$ 250	$200	$ 250
Held by other interests	800	750	600	750
	$2 000	$1 000	$800	$1 000

Information about the companies for the year ended 30 June 2008 is as follows:

	Jack Ltd	Jett Ltd	John Ltd	Jay Ltd	Jaxon Ltd
Trading profit (loss)	$ 200	$1 000	$ 600	$2 400	$1 200
Dividend revenue	600	400	100	—	—
Profit before tax	800	1 400	700	2 400	1 200
Income tax expense	100	500	300	1 200	600
Profit	700	900	400	1 200	600
Dividend paid	500	500	200	1 000	200
	200	400	200	200	400
Retained earnings (1/7/07)	6 800	3 600	230	2 000	1 210
Retained earnings (30/6/08)	$7 000	$4 000	$ 430	$2 200	$1 610

	Jack Ltd	Jett Ltd	John Ltd	Jay Ltd	Jaxon Ltd
Investments	$ 4 008	$3 000	$ 800	—	—
Other non-current assets (net)	6 000	3 000	400	2 000	2 400
Current assets	1 992	2 000	800	1 600	1 000
Total assets	$12 000	$8 000	$2 000	$3 600	$3 400
Share capital	$ 1 000	$2 000	$1 000	$ 800	$1 000
Asset revaluation reserve	1 000	—	200	—	—
Retained earnings	7 000	4 000	430	2 200	1 610
Total equity	9 000	6 000	1 630	3 000	2 610
Liabilities	3 000	2 000	370	600	790
Total equity and liabilities	$12 000	$8 000	$2 000	$3 600	$3 400

Additional information

(a) *Jett Ltd:* Jack Ltd acquired a 60% interest on 30 June 2000 for $3000. Shareholders' equity at 30 June 2000 was:

Share capital	$2 000
Retained earnings	2 000
	$4 000

At the acquisition date, Jett Ltd had not recorded any goodwill. All the identifiable assets and liabilities of Jett Ltd were recorded at fair value except the following:

	Carrying amount	Fair value
Inventory	$ 500	$ 600
Non-current assets (net)	1 200	1 500

By 30 June 2000, all the inventory had been sold by Jett Ltd. The non-current assets had a further expected life of 10 years, with benefits from use being received evenly over these years. The partial goodwill method is used.

(b) *John Ltd:* Jett Ltd acquired, on 1 July 2007, 25% of the share capital for $400. Equity at 30 June 2007 was:

Share capital	$1 000
Retained earnings	230

At 30 June 2007, John Ltd had not recorded any goodwill. All the identifiable assets and liabilities were recorded at fair value except for the following:

	Carrying amount	Fair value
Inventory	$500	$600
Non-current assets (net)	200	400

By 30 June 2008, half the inventory had been sold to external parties. The non-current assets were revalued in the records of John Ltd on 1 July 2007.

(c) *Jack Ltd:* Included in current assets of Jack Ltd at 30 June 2008 is inventory that was purchased from Jett Ltd for $900. Jett Ltd sells its goods at cost plus 50% mark-up.

(d) *Jack Ltd:* Included in current assets of Jack Ltd at 30 June 2007 was inventory that was purchased from Jett Ltd for $600.

(e) *Jett Ltd:* Included in the non-current assets of Jett Ltd at 30 June 2008 is an item of plant that was sold to Jett Ltd by John Ltd on 1 July 2007 for $1200. At the date of sale, this asset had a carrying amount to John Ltd of $1000. It had an expected future useful life of 5 years, with benefits being received evenly over these years.

(f) *Jay Ltd:* Jack Ltd acquired a 25% interest on 30 June 2005 for $400. Equity at 30 June 2005 was:

Share capital	$800
Retained earnings	600

At this date, Jay Ltd had not recorded any goodwill. All the identifiable assets and liabilities of Jay Ltd were recorded at fair value except for the following assets:

	Carrying amount	Fair value
Inventory	$100	$120
Non-current assets (net)	500	600

The inventory was all sold by 30 June 2006. The non-current assets had a further useful life of 4 years.

(g) *Jaxon Ltd:* Jack Ltd acquired a 25% interest on 1 July 2007 for $600. A comparison of carrying amounts and fair values at 30 June 2007 is shown below:

	Carrying amount	Fair value
Share capital	$1 000	
Retained earnings	1 210	
Liabilities	790	$ 790
	$3 000	
Inventory	$ 800	1 000
Non-current assets:		
Plant	1 000	1 200
Equipment	1 200	1 500
	$3 000	

The plant had a further 5-year life and the equipment had a further 6-year life. By 30 June 2008, all the undervalued inventory had been sold.

(h) *Jay Ltd:* On 1 July 2006, Jay Ltd sold a non-current asset to Jack Ltd for $500. At the time of sale, this asset had a carrying amount of $450. Jack Ltd depreciated this asset evenly over a 5-year period.

(i) *Jaxon Ltd:* At 30 June 2008, Jack Ltd held inventory that was sold to it by Jaxon Ltd at a profit before tax of $200 during the previous period.

(j) *Jack Ltd:* On 30 June 2008, Jack Ltd held inventory that had been sold to it during the previous 6 months by Jay Ltd for $1000. Jay Ltd made $400 profit before tax on the sale.

(k) The tax rate is 30%.

Required

Prepare the consolidated financial statements of Jack Ltd for the year ended 30 June 2008. Include all the associates accounted for under the equity method.

References

Amalgamated Holdings 2008, *Annual report 2008*, Amalgamated Holdings Limited, www.ahl.com.au.

Bayer Group 2007, *Annual report 2007*, Bayer Group, Germany, www.bayer.com/en.

28 Interests in joint ventures

ACCOUNTING STANDARDS IN FOCUS

IAS 31 *Interests in Joint Ventures*

LEARNING OBJECTIVES

When you have studied this chapter, you should be able to:

- discuss the defining characteristics of a joint venture
- explain the different forms of a joint venture
- account for jointly controlled operations
- account for jointly controlled assets
- account for an unincorporated joint venture that is sharing output
- adjust for the effects of contributions of non-monetary assets by a joint venturer
- account for a joint venture entity sharing profit
- debate the advantages and disadvantages of using the proportionate consolidation method or the equity method
- prepare the disclosures required by IAS 31.

28.1 INVESTMENTS IN OTHER ENTITIES

In earlier chapters of this book two types of investments are analysed. First, there is the investment in a *subsidiary*, where a parent entity has the capacity to control the financial and operating policies of another entity. Where this control relationship exists, the consolidation method is used for the preparation of consolidated financial statements to report the financial performance and position of the group of entities. The consolidated financial statements provide detailed line-by-line information about the entities in the group. Second, there is the investment in an *associate*, where the investor has the capacity to significantly influence the financial and operating decisions of another entity, the associate. The accounting method used to provide information about this form of investment is the equity method, a form of one-line consolidation method where the carrying amount of the investment in the associate is adjusted for the investor's share of movements in the post-acquisition equity of the associate. Information on investments in associates as provided by applying the equity method is considerably less than that for subsidiaries resulting from applying the consolidation method.

In this chapter, another form of investment is analysed: the investment in a joint venture. As is explained in detail in the following section, the level of control that the investor has in the investee is again used to determine the existence of a joint venture. Further, both the consolidation and equity methods are used to develop a method of providing information about investments in joint ventures.

Accounting for joint ventures is dealt with in IAS 31 *Interests in Joint Ventures*, which was adopted by the IASB in 2000. The standard was originally issued by the International Accounting Standards Committee in 1990. In September 2007, the IASB issued an exposure draft, ED 9 *Joint Arrangements*, which proposes a replacement to IAS 31.

As noted in the IASB press release of 13 September 2007 announcing the issue of ED 9, the main focus of the proposals is on two aspects of the current accounting under IAS 31, namely:

- The current accounting standard follows the legal form in which the activities take place. The IASB argues that this does not always reflect the contractual rights and obligations agreed to by the parties.
- IAS 31 currently gives a choice when accounting for interests in jointly controlled entities, and ED 9 proposes to remove that choice by removing the proportionate consolidation option, and requiring additional disclosures.

The main changes proposed are to terminology, to remove the proportional consolidation method, and to disclosures.

The IASB in its press release further noted that for the majority of entities the new standard is unlikely to reshape their statement of financial position, as, in most cases, accounting for individual assets and liabilities gives the same outcome as proportionate consolidation.

This chapter focuses on the application of IAS 31 as current at the time of writing. The expected changes to IAS 31 based on ED 9 will be noted. The IASB expects to publish a new standard in the second quarter of 2009.

28.2 THE NATURE OF A JOINT VENTURE

28.2.1 Defining a joint venture

Paragraph 3 of IAS 31 *Interests in Joint Ventures* contains the following definitions:

> A *joint venture* is a contractual arrangement whereby two or more parties undertake an economic activity that is subject to joint control.
>
> A *venturer* is a party to a joint venture and has joint control over that joint venture.
>
> An *investor in a joint venture* is a party to a joint venture and does not have joint control over that joint venture.

Note first that in the definition of a joint venture reference is made to an 'economic activity'. As is explained in detail in section 28.2.2, the form of economic activity does not require the formation of another entity, and may relate to a single asset.

There are two major characteristics of a joint venture:

1. *Contractual arrangement*

   As noted in paragraph 9 of IAS 31, it is the existence of a contractual arrangement that distinguishes certain investments in associates (see chapter 27) from investments in joint ventures. The venturers are bound by the contractual arrangement that details the operation and management of the joint venture. Paragraph 10 of IAS 31 notes that the contractual arrangement may exist in a number of forms, such as a specific contract, or may be detailed in the articles or other by-laws of the joint venture. This paragraph also notes that the contractual arrangement is usually in writing and deals with such matters as:

   (a) the activity, duration and reporting obligations of the joint venture;
   (b) the appointment of the board of directors or equivalent governing body of the joint venture and the voting rights of the venturers;
   (c) capital contributions by the venturers; and
   (d) the sharing by the venturers of the output, income, expenses or results of the joint venture.

2. *Joint control*

   As noted earlier in this chapter, a parent–subsidiary relationship is evidenced by the existence of a capacity to control or dominate, while an investor–associate relationship is evidenced by the existence of significant influence. The characteristic of joint control also relies on the control relationship between the joint venturers. A single joint venturer cannot control the joint venture; otherwise that venturer would be a parent entity. It must also be a different relationship than just significantly influencing the decisions made in the joint venture.

   Joint control is defined in IAS 31, paragraph 3, as:

   the contractually agreed sharing of control over an economic activity.

   The IASB (see *IASB Update*, November 2003) expressed concern that this definition was not sufficiently explicit about the nature of the sharing of control; for example, the parties could contractually agree that all the essential strategic operating, investing and financing decisions require the consent of most of the owners. The IASB preferred the concept that all parties had to agree (i.e. unanimously consent to the decisions) to be built into the definition. As a result, there was a preference for the definition of joint control proposed in the 1999 G4+1[1] Discussion Paper ('G4-DP'), 'Reporting Interests in Joint Ventures and Similar Arrangements', principally written by Canadians J Alex Milburn and Peter D Chant (1999).

   Joint control over an enterprise exists when no one party alone has the power to control its strategic operating, investing, and financing decisions, but two or more parties can do so, and each of the parties sharing control (joint venturers) must consent.

   Paragraphs 11 and 12 of IAS 31 provide the following guidance in determining the existence of joint control:

   - no single venturer is in a position to control the activity unilaterally
   - the decisions in areas essential to the goals of the joint venture require the consent of the venturers
   - one venturer may be appointed as the manager or operator of the joint venture; however, this party acts within the financial and operating policies detailed in the contractual arrangement and consented to by the venturers.

The ownership of a majority ownership interest may often be used to indicate the existence of control because voting power is generally associated with ownership interest. However, it may be possible for joint control to exist even where there are varying ownership interests. For example, if holdings are in the proportions of 50:30:20, joint control still exists so long as the unanimous agreement of each party is necessary for strategic decisions to be made. The key factor is that no single party can unilaterally control the financial and operating decisions of the venture. Joint control might exist by each venturer being given a veto power over the strategic decisions. Note that IAS 31 distinguishes between a 'venturer' and an 'investor'. For example, where there are three parties in the venture sharing output on a 50:30:20 basis, it may be that the first party is only an investor while the other two parties are the venturers. The difference is that only the parties that have joint control are venturers — in this case, the first party would not have a veto power.

[1]The G4+1 organisation consisted of the accounting standards boards in Australia, Canada, New Zealand, the United Kingdom and the United States, as well as the International Accounting Standards Committee. G4+1 was disbanded when the International Accounting Standards Board was established.

28.2.2 Forms of joint ventures

IAS 31 identifies three forms of joint venture:

- *Jointly controlled operations* (paragraphs 13–17). As stated in paragraph 13, with a jointly controlled operation, there is no corporation, partnership or financial structure established separate from the venturers themselves. Each joint venturer uses its own assets and incurs its own expenses to create a joint product. An example is the manufacture of an aeroplane. One joint venturer makes the body, another manufactures and installs the engines while another fits out the aircraft. Each venturer is involved in its own part of the overall activity. The venturers then share the revenue on sale of the product according to the contractual arrangement.
- *Jointly controlled assets* (paragraphs 18–23). The joint venture may relate to the shared use of a single asset such as an oil or gas pipeline, a communications network or a property such as farm land. The contractual arrangement provides for each venturer to use the asset at particular periods of time or for a particular number of hours. As with the jointly owned operation, there is no specific structure created for the joint venture; the venturers simply share an asset.

  In some cases the joint venture may require the use of a number of shared assets. For example, if the joint venture is established to operate a mine, each venturer may provide an initial contribution for the establishment of the mining operation, possibly including the property, plant and equipment necessary to run the mine. The venturers then share in the output of the mine, with each party being responsible for the ultimate sale or internal use of the output. As paragraph 19 states, each venturer has control over its share of future economic benefits through its share of the jointly controlled asset.
- *Jointly controlled entities* (paragraphs 24–29). Paragraph 24 states that a jointly controlled entity is a joint venture that 'involves the establishment of a corporation, partnership or other entity in which each venturer has an interest'. Each venturer then has an interest in the entity rather than an interest in the individual assets of the joint venture. Further, as noted in paragraph 25, rather than sharing the output of the joint venture, as the joint venture earns income, the venturers share the profits of the joint venture. However, paragraph 25 notes that even in the case of a jointly controlled entity, there could be a sharing of the output.

The key difference between the first two categories (jointly controlled operations and assets) and the third category (jointly controlled entities) is that in the first two categories the venturers have an undivided interest in the assets of the joint venture. Hence, if venturers X and Y entered into a joint arrangement to extract uranium from a mine, then each venturer would hold an undivided interest in the property, plant and equipment and other assets used in the mining venture, as well as joint and several responsibility for any liabilities. With a jointly controlled entity, a separate entity is created to carry on the activity of the joint venture. The entity controls the resources contributed by the venturers, rather than the resources being controlled by the venturers, and the liabilities would be obligations of the entity itself.

Recognition that entities may have undivided interests in assets is recognised in the Statement of Financial Accounting Concepts No. 6, paragraph 185, issued by the US Financial Accounting Standards Board:

> The definition of assets focuses primarily on the future economic benefit to which an entity has access and only secondarily on the physical things and other agents that provide future economic benefits. Many physical things and other agents are in effect bundles of future economic benefits that can be unbundled in various ways, and two or more entities may have different future economic benefits from the same agent at the same time or the same continuing future economic benefit at different times. For example, two or more entities may have undivided interests in a parcel of land. Each has a right to future economic benefit that may qualify as an asset under the definition in paragraph 25, even though the right of each is subject at least to some extent to the rights of the other(s) (FASB 1985, pp. 57–8).

With jointly controlled operations, each venturer may not have any assets in which there are undivided interests because each venturer simply contributes to the overall project. With individual assets, the undivided interests could be based on time (e.g. each venturer can use the asset for a specified day of the week) or the capacity of the resource (e.g. each venturer has a proportionate share of the capacity of a pipeline).

In both the 1994 Discussion Paper 'Associates and Joint Ventures' ('UK-DP') issued by the Accounting Standards Board in the United Kingdom and the G4-DP, the question of whether joint ventures should be restricted to jointly controlled entities is raised.

In the UK-DP (paragraph 3.16), it is argued that a joint venture should be viewed as a strategic alliance in which the investor acts as a partner in the investee's business. Joint venture activities would then be limited to situations where the joint activities constituted a 'business'. Jointly controlled operations and jointly controlled assets would not be seen as giving rise to a business, and hence should not be described as joint ventures. Paragraph 3.17 of UK-DP states:

> Many joint activities stand alone as businesses in their own right. However, some joint activities amount only to a sharing of facilities. A joint activity is a shared facility rather than a business if the joint venturers derive their benefit from product or services taken in kind rather than receiving a share in the profits of trading.

The G4-DP contained similar arguments. Paragraph 2.15 states:

> . . . a joint venture must be an enterprise, that is, it must be a separate entity that carries on activities with its own assets and liabilities. The essence of the definition is that unless the joint venture is a separate entity carrying on its own activities with its own resources to achieve its own distinct purposes, it does not have a separate decision-making identity so as to be capable of independent control by external joint venturers. It may be incorporated or it may not be . . . As an example, several hospitals may set up a joint venture to provide a laundry service that is a separate entity with its own resources and decision-making identity.

The emphasis in the G4-DP is on the criterion of joint control as opposed to a shared facility. A joint venture must be an activity in which the venturers together control it, consenting to all the essential decisions. Where two parties simply share a pipeline, or similar asset, there are no strategic decisions to be made because there is no ongoing business activity. Similarly, where there are joint operations, such as the making of an aeroplane, each party manages their own contribution within a planned framework. The parties do not become involved in jointly managing a business activity.

Paragraph 2.27 of the G4-DP illustrates the nature of a joint venture:

> For example, suppose that enterprises A and B together acquire a mine and agree to share the output between them on a specified basis, to sell any surplus production, and to share costs and revenues. This activity may be set up in several different ways:
>
> (a) In some jurisdictions, A and B may hold an undivided interest in each of the assets of the mine (the mining property, buildings, equipment, working capital, etc.) and assume joint and several responsibility for any liabilities. Management is appointed to manage the mine on behalf of A and B, with costs and revenues being allocated to them for net cash settlement. (Either A or B may act as manager.) In this case, A and B will each reflect their undivided interest in the assets and share of the liabilities and will record their share of revenues and costs as an extension of its business operations. A and B would be expected to disclose the undivided interest nature of these assets and liabilities and any contingent liabilities.
>
> (b) . . .
>
> (c) A different economic arrangement could be established under which the mine is set up as a *joint venture*, that is, as a separate enterprise, as described in paragraph 2.15. In this case, rather than share costs and revenues, the joint venture would commit to acquire amounts of the output of the mine (perhaps at fixed or variable prices under a take-or-pay contract). A and B would then have a joint interest in the venture and would be entitled to share in the net profits or losses of the enterprise in accordance with their respective joint venture interests, regardless of the amount of profits or losses that resulted from each venture's transactions with the joint venture.

An alternative way of categorising the different forms of joint ventures is to make a distinction between jointly controlled assets and jointly controlled businesses. If it is agreed that a joint venture should involve a business, potentially the definition of business used in IFRS 3 *Business Combinations* could be used:

> An integrated set of activities and assets that is capable of being conducted and managed for the purpose of providing a return in the form of dividends, lower costs or other economic benefits directly to investors or other owners, members or participants.

If this is the case, then some jointly controlled assets, such as a mining operation sharing output, would be better classified as a jointly controlled entity. The term entity is normally defined to include organisational structures other than corporations and partnerships. For example, an entity is defined in the Australian concepts document SAC 1 'Definition of the Reporting Entity' as 'any legal, administrative, or fiduciary arrangement, organisational structure or other party (including a person) having the capacity to deploy scarce resources in order to achieve objectives'.

The UK FRS 9 *Associates and Joint Ventures* (1997) drew a similar conclusion, arguing that an arrangement should not be defined as a joint venture unless it constituted an entity. Paragraph 8 of FRS 9 states:

> For a joint entity arrangement to amount to an entity, it must carry on a trade or business, meaning a trade or business of its own and not just part of its participants' trades or businesses. In its activities the joint arrangement must therefore have some independence (within the objectives set by the agreement governing the joint arrangement) to pursue its own commercial strategy in its buying and selling; it must either have access to the market in its own right for its main inputs and outputs or, at least, be able to obtain them from the participants or sell them to the participants on generally the same terms as are available in the market. The following indicate that the joint activities undertaken in a joint arrangement do not amount to its carrying on a trade or business of its own — and therefore that the joint arrangement is not an entity:
> (a) the participants derive their benefit from product or services taken in kind rather than by receiving a share in the results of trading, or
> (b) each participant's share of the output or result of the joint activity is determined by its supply of key inputs to the process producing that output or result.

This definition of an entity is more narrow than the IASB definition of an entity as a 'business'. FRS 9 effectively requires a joint venture to trade and hence produce a profit or loss. It is doubtful that an entity that has inputs, processes and outputs, with the latter being distributed to the investors, is any less an entity than a trading entity.

In determining the appropriate accounting method to be used it is essential that the nature of a joint venture be clearly identified. In IAS 31, as detailed later in this chapter, jointly controlled entities are accounted for differently from jointly controlled assets and operations. However, in section 28.8, after an analysis of these methods, it is argued that joint ventures should be limited to jointly controlled businesses, while shared facilities (jointly controlled operations and assets) should be accounted for in the same way as other assets; as such they should be excluded from an accounting standard on joint ventures.

28.2.3 Proposed changes under ED 9

The title of ED 9 is *Joint Arrangements*. This is because of a change in terminology proposed in ED 9. That is, ED 9 proposes that a new IAS 31 deal with the three forms of activity covered under the current IAS 31, but that the names of the three types of joint arrangements be changed as follows:

- jointly controlled operation becomes joint operation
- jointly controlled asset becomes joint asset
- jointly controlled entity becomes joint venture.

Hence, a joint venture has a more specific meaning under ED 9. As a result, a party to a joint operation or a holder of a joint asset cannot be referred to as a 'venturer', but is referred to in ED 9 as a 'party'.

The term 'joint arrangement' is defined in Appendix A of ED 9 as:

> A contractual arrangement whereby two or more parties undertake an economic activity together and share decision-making relating to that activity.

'Shared decisions' are defined as:

> Decisions that require the consent of all of the parties to a **joint arrangement**.

An entity that participates in these shared decisions is referred to as 'party to a joint arrangement', defined in Appendix A as:

> An entity that participates in **shared decisions** relating to the **joint arrangement**.

In those joint venture arrangements that are described as joint ventures, the party becomes a 'venturer'. A venturer is defined as:

> A party to a joint venture that has **joint control** over that joint venture.

The term 'joint control' is defined as:

> The contractually agreed sharing of the power to govern the financial and operating policies of a venture so as to obtain benefits from its activities.

The term 'joint venture' is not defined in ED 9. Because of the nature of joint operations and joint assets, each party to the arrangement either uses its own assets or shares the use of an asset.

In contrast, in a joint venture there is a sharing of the governance and policy decision making in relation to a number of assets so as to obtain benefits. As noted earlier, this is in line with the notion that a joint venture is an activity in which the venturers jointly manage a business activity with strategic decisions being made by the venturers. In a joint venture, venturers do not have a direct right to individual assets. Rather, each venturer shares in the profit or loss of the joint venture.

Paragraph 5 of ED 9 compares the rights and obligations of the various entities under the different forms of joint arrangements:

> The type of joint arrangement an entity is a party to depends on the rights and obligations that arise from the contractual arrangement. A party has a joint operation or joint asset if it has contractual rights to individual assets, or contractual obligations for expenses or financing, i.e. if the contractual arrangement gives the parties an interest in individual assets and liabilities of the arrangement. An entity is a party to a joint venture if it has rights only to a share of the outcome generated by a group of assets and liabilities carrying on an economic activity.

ED 9 has then established the nature of the three forms of joint arrangements, and, in particular, the joint venture as a specific type of joint arrangement. This has clarified the nature of a joint venture and its difference from other forms of joint arrangement.

28.3 JOINTLY CONTROLLED OPERATIONS

Paragraph 15 of IAS 31 states:

> In respect of its interests in jointly controlled operations, a venturer shall recognise in its financial statements:
> (a) the assets that it controls and the liabilities that it incurs; and
> (b) the expenses that it incurs and its share of the income that it earns from the sale of goods or services by the joint venture.

As each venturer uses its own property, plant and equipment the venturer automatically includes these assets in its own records. As the venturer incurs costs in relation to a particular project, such as assisting in the manufacture of an aeroplane, the venturer accumulates those costs in a work in progress account:

Work in progress – Joint Venture	Dr	X	
Cash	Cr		X

If the venturer has to contribute towards some joint costs of the venture, these are also capitalised into work in progress.

When the aircraft is sold, the venturer receives a share of the proceeds:

Cash	Dr	X	
Revenue from Joint Venture	Cr		X

and the work in progress is recognised as cost of product sold:

Cost of Product – Joint Venture	Dr	X	
Work in Progress	Cr		X

28.4 JOINTLY CONTROLLED ASSETS

Paragraph 21 of IAS 31 details the accounting for interests in jointly controlled assets:

> In respect of its interest in jointly controlled assets, a venturer shall recognise in its financial statements:
> (a) its share of the jointly controlled assets, classified according to the nature of the assets;
> (b) any liabilities that it has incurred;

(c) its share of any liabilities incurred jointly with the other venturers in relation to the joint venture;
(d) any income from the sale or use of its share of the output of the joint venture, together with its share of any expenses incurred by the joint venture; and
(e) any expenses that it has incurred in respect of its interest in the joint venture.

Assume that a venturer has a half-share of a jointly controlled gas pipeline that cost $100 000 to construct. Each venturer will pass the following journal entry:

Pipeline – Property, Plant and Equipment	Dr	50 000	
Cash	Cr		50 000

As the pipeline is the subject of a joint control agreement, there is some debate as to whether or not each venturer should recognise its share of the pipeline as an asset. Paragraph 2.21 of G4-DP states:

> Some may argue that joint ownership of an asset (for example, a 50 percent joint interest in a mine) does not technically meet the definition of an asset, which is a resource controlled by the entity, not jointly controlled. But the distinction must be made between the mining property per se and the reporting enterprise's rights in it. The reporting enterprise's asset is its contractual joint ownership rights. The enterprise controls these rights and the benefits that flow from them. It can determine how to use them, and it may decide to sell them, hold them, or pledge them as collateral.

However, if the real asset is the rights to the pipeline, then the asset is an intangible asset, and not one of property, plant and equipment. The question of asset recognition is discussed further in section 28.8.

28.5 JOINTLY CONTROLLED ASSETS WHERE OUTPUT IS SHARED — ACCOUNTING BY THE JOINT VENTURE

Where the joint venture is undertaken outside a formal structure, such as a corporation or partnership, separate accounting records do not need to be kept for the joint venture. However, for accountability reasons it is expected that the joint venture agreement would require these records.

IAS 31 does not provide standards on accounting for the joint venture operation itself. If the joint venture does not sell the output produced, but rather distributes it to the venturers, there is no profit or loss account raised by the venture. In preparing accounts for the joint venture, the main purpose is to accumulate costs as incurred. These are capitalised into a work in progress account, which is transferred to the venturers as inventory. Further, the joint venture accounts provide information about the assets and liabilities relating to the joint venture as well as the contributions from the venturers. Hence, a statement of financial position is the joint venture's main financial statement.

Illustrative example 28.1 illustrates the accounting system within the joint venture operation. The journal entries represent the establishment of the joint venture operation and its activities throughout the year. Transactions that occur regularly throughout the year, such as payment of wages, are accumulated into one entry.

ILLUSTRATIVE EXAMPLE 28.1

Accounting by an unincorporated joint venture

On 1 July 2009, X Ltd and Y Ltd signed an agreement to form a joint venture to manufacture a product called Plasboard. This product is used in the packaging industry and has the advantages of the strength and protection qualities of cardboard as well as the flexibility and durability of plastic.

To commence the venture, both venturers contributed $1 500 000 in cash. In the example it is assumed that not all the raw materials are used during the period, and not all finished goods have been transferred to the venturers.

- *Contributions of cash by the venturers*

Cash	Dr	3 000 000	
X Ltd – Contribution	Cr		1 500 000
Y Ltd – Contribution	Cr		1 500 000
(Contributions by venturers)			

- *Use of cash and loan to buy equipment and raw materials*

Equipment	Dr	800 000	
Cash	Cr		500 000
Loan – Equipment	Cr		300 000
(Acquisition of equipment)			
Raw materials	Dr	650 000	
Trade creditors	Cr		650 000
(Acquisition of materials)			

- *Payment of wages*

Wages – Management	Dr	200 000	
Wages – Other	Dr	520 000	
Cash	Cr		700 000
Accrued wages	Cr		20 000
(Annual wages)			

- *Borrowing from the bank*

Cash	Dr	500 000	
Bank Loan	Cr		500 000
(Amount borrowed)			

- *Repayment of loan and other expenses*

Loan – Equipment	Dr	100 000	
Cash	Cr		100 000
(Part-payment for loan on equipment)			
Trade Creditors	Dr	420 000	
Cash	Cr		420 000
(Payment of trade creditors)			
Overhead Expenses	Dr	1 300 000	
Cash	Cr		1 300 000
(Payment of manufacturing expenses such as electricity)			

- *Depreciation of equipment*

Depreciation Expense	Dr	80 000	
Accumulated Depreciation	Cr		80 000
(Depreciation of equipment)			

- *Transfer of expenses to work in progress*

Work in Progress	Dr	2 580 000	
Wages	Cr		720 000
Raw Materials	Cr		480 000
Overhead Expenses	Cr		1 300 000
Depreciation Expense	Cr		80 000
(Allocating of costs to work in progress)			

- *Transfer from work in progress to inventory*

Inventory	Dr	1 800 000	
Work in Progress	Cr		1 800 000
(Allocation to finished goods)			

- *Transfer of inventory to venturers throughout the year*

X Ltd	Dr	800 000	
Y Ltd	Dr	800 000	
Inventory	Cr		1 600 000
(Delivery of output to venturers)			

The major ledger accounts of interest in relation to the joint venture are as follows:

Cash			
	$		$
Contribution – X Ltd	1 500 000	Equipment	500 000
Contribution – Y Ltd	1 500 000	Wages	700 000
Bank Loan	500 000	Loan – Equipment	100 000
		Trade Creditors	420 000
		Overhead Expenses	1 300 000
		Balance c/d	480 000
	3 500 000		3 500 000
Balance b/d	480 000		

Work in Progress			
	$		$
Wages	720 000	Inventory	1 800 000
Raw Materials	480 000		
Overhead	1 300 000		
Depreciation	80 000	Balance c/d	780 000
	2 580 000		2 580 000
Balance b/d	780 000		

The statement of financial position of the joint venture at 30 June 2010 would be:

Statement of Financial Position as at 30 June 2010			
Current assets			
Raw materials		$ 170 000	
Inventory		200 000	
Work in progress		780 000	
Cash		480 000	
Total current assets			$1 630 000
Non-current assets			
Equipment		800 000	
Accumulated depreciation		(80 000)	720 000
Total assets			2 350 000
Current liabilities			
Trade creditors		230 000	
Accrued wages		20 000	
Total current liabilities			250 000
Non-current liabilities			
Bank loan		500 000	
Loan – equipment		200 000	
Total non-current liabilities			700 000
Total liabilities			950 000
Net assets			$1 400 000
Venturers' equity			
X Ltd:	Contributions – at 1/7/09	$1 500 000	
	Cost of inventory distributed	(800 000)	$ 700 000
Y Ltd:	Contributions – at 1/7/09	1 500 000	
	Cost of inventory distributed	(800 000)	700 000
Total venturers' equity			$1 400 000

From this example, we can see that the costs of producing the output are accumulated in the joint venture operation, and the inventory, at cost, distributed to the joint venturers. In this example, all costs are capitalised into inventory. In some cases, the costs may be transferred to the venturers' accounts as expenses and matched in the records of the venturers with the revenue from sale of the output. For example, if the joint venture operation involved exploring for minerals, it may be desirable to expense the costs of exploration and evaluation rather than capitalise them for allocation to future inventory. Similarly, where depreciation is charged on non-current assets, the depreciation expense may not, as in this example, be charged in the accounts of the joint venture itself. Instead, in the records of the venturers themselves, a charge for depreciation may be made.

28.6 JOINTLY CONTROLLED ASSETS WHERE OUTPUT IS SHARED — ACCOUNTING BY A VENTURER

Theoretically, there are two methods that the venturer can use in accounting for its interest:

- *The one-line method*. Under this method, the venturer records its investment in the joint venture, adjusting only for any contributions it makes to the joint venture and any distributions or allocations made by the joint venture to the venturer. The joint venturer may provide note disclosure on the assets and liabilities underlying that investment.

- *The line-by-line method.* Under this method, the records of the venturer include, on a line-by-line basis, its share of the assets and liabilities in the joint venture.

The merits of these methods are discussed in section 28.8, with a preference being expressed for the one-line method. Because IAS 31 classifies this form of joint venture as jointly controlled assets, it requires the line-by-line method set out in paragraph 21 to be used. In illustrative examples 28.2 and 28.3, both methods are illustrated. Because paragraph 56 of IAS 31 requires disclosures of assets, liabilities, income and expenses in relation to a joint venture, in the following examples a distinction is made between joint venture elements and those belonging to the venturer. This is similar to the need to distinguish between leased assets and acquired assets.

The venturer's accounting records are affected by the nature of its contributions. The contributions can be in the form of cash, non-current assets or provision of services. In the following sections, examples of venturers' accounting records for different forms of contributions are provided.

28.6.1 Cash contributions

ILLUSTRATIVE EXAMPLE 28.2

Contribution of cash by a joint venturer

On 1 July 2009, X Ltd and Y Ltd establish a joint venture operation to manufacture a product. Each company has a 50% interest in the venture and shares output equally. To commence the venture, both companies contribute cash of $1 500 000 on 1 July 2009. Each venturer depreciates equipment at 10% p.a. on cost.

The following information was extracted from the accounts and financial statements of the joint venture operation as at 30 June 2010:

Statement of Financial Position (extract) as at 30 June 2010

Assets	
Cash	$ 420 000
Raw materials	100 000
Work in progress	650 000
Inventory	200 000
Equipment	1 500 000
Total assets	2 870 000
Liabilities	
Accounts payable (raw materials)	120 000
Accrued expenses (wages)	150 000
Bank loan	1 000 000
Total liabilities	1 270 000
Net assets	$1 600 000

Cash Receipts and Payments for the year ended 30 June 2010

	Payments	Receipts
Contributions		$3 000 000
Bank loan		1 000 000
Equipment (purchased 3/7/09)	$1 500 000	
Wages	500 000	
Accounts payable (raw materials)	380 000	
Overhead expenses	1 200 000	
	$3 580 000	$4 000 000

Costs Incurred for the year ended 30 June 2010	
Wages	$ 650 000
Raw materials	400 000
Overhead expenses	1 200 000
Less: Cost of inventory	2 250 000
Work in progress at 30/6/10	1 600 000
	$ 650 000

Required
Prepare the journal entries in the records of X Ltd and Y Ltd for the year ended 30 June 2010.

Solution
1. Line-by-line method
Records of X Ltd
At 1 July 2009, X Ltd records its interest in the joint venture, the asset cash being distinguished as an asset in a joint venture:

Cash in Joint Venture (JV)	Dr	1 500 000	
Cash	Cr		1 500 000

At 30 June 2010, the joint venture has used the cash to acquire various assets, undertake loans, incur expenses and manufacture inventory. As a contributor of 50% of the cash into the joint venture, X Ltd is entitled to 50% of all the assets, liabilities, expenses and output of the joint venture. From the statement of financial position of the joint venture, it should be noted that the net assets of the joint venture amount to $1 600 000 (i.e. $2 870 000 – $1 270 000). The inventory in the statement of financial position is $200 000. From the costs incurred information, it can be seen that the joint venture has produced $1 600 000 worth of inventory. If only $200 000 is still on hand in the joint venture, then $1 400 000 worth of inventory must have been transferred to the joint venturers: $700 000 each. The contributions section of the statement of financial position is shown below.

X Ltd:	Initial contribution	$1 500 000	
	Inventory transferred	(700 000)	$ 800 000
Y Ltd:	Initial contribution	1 500 000	
	Inventory transferred	(700 000)	800 000
			$1 600 000

At 30 June 2010, X Ltd makes the following entry in its records to replace 'Cash in JV' with a 50% share of each of the accounts in the statement of financial position of the joint venture at 30 June 2010. The entry also recognises the inventory of $700 000 transferred to X Ltd from the joint venture.

Raw Material in JV	Dr	50 000		[100 000/2]
Work in Progress in JV	Dr	325 000		[650 000/2]
Inventory in JV	Dr	100 000		[200 000/2]
Equipment in JV	Dr	750 000		[1 500 000/2]
Inventory	Dr	700 000		[1 400 000/2]
Accounts Payable in JV	Cr		60 000	[120 000/2]
Accrued Expenses in JV	Cr		75 000	[150 000/2]
Bank Loan in JV	Cr		500 000	[1 000 000/2]
Cash in JV	Cr		1 290 000	[1 500 000 – (420 000/2)]

Note that X Ltd's share of cash in the joint venture is calculated by finding the difference between the share at the beginning of the period and the share at the end of the period.

X Ltd depreciates the equipment in its own records. Therefore, having recognised an asset at $750 000, X Ltd would also pass the following entry at 30 June 2010:

Depreciation Expense Accumulated Depreciation (Depreciation on equipment in the joint venture)	Dr Cr	75 000	 75 000	[10% × 750 000]

Records of Y Ltd

As Y Ltd contributed the same asset (cash of $1 500 000) to the joint venture as X Ltd, the journal entries in the records of Y Ltd would be the same as that in X Ltd.

2. One-line method

As in the line-by-line method, each venturer records the initial contribution; however, this time as an investment in the joint venture:

Investment in Joint Venture	Dr	1 500 000	
Cash	Cr		1 500 000

On receipt of the inventory of $700 000 from the joint venture, the venturer reduces its investment in the joint venture:

Inventory	Dr	700 000	
Investment in Joint Venture	Cr		700 000

The depreciation is capitalised into the cost of the inventory:

Inventory	Dr	75 000	
Investment in Joint Venture	Cr		75 000

As the investment is recognised on a one-line basis, to provide more information about the assets and liabilities underlying the investment, the joint venturer could disclose this information in the notes to the accounts:

The investment of $725 000 in the joint venture relates to the following assets and liabilities jointly controlled within the joint venture entity:

Raw material	$ 50 000
Work in progress	325 000
Inventory	100 000
Equipment	750 000
Accumulated depreciation	(75 000)
Cash	210 000
Total assets	1 360 000
Accounts payable	60 000
Accrued expenses	75 000
Bank loan	500 000
Total liabilities	635 000
Net assets	$ 725 000

28.6.2 Contributions of non-monetary assets

Where a venturer contributes a non-current asset to the joint venture, the value of the contribution is effectively the fair value of that non-current asset. Hence, if one venturer contributed $100 000 cash and the other venturer a non-current asset, then for both parties to agree to join there would have to be agreement that the non-current asset being contributed had a fair value of $100 000. If all venturers contributed non-current assets, then some form of valuation of the contributions would need to be made by the parties involved.

Paragraph 48 of IAS 31 provides guidance on accounting for contributions of non-monetary assets provided by a venturer. It states:

> When a venturer contributes or sells assets to a joint venture, recognition of any portion of a gain or loss from the transaction shall reflect the substance of the transaction. While the assets are retained by the joint venture, and provided the venturer has transferred the significant risks and rewards of ownership, the venturer shall recognise only that portion of the gain or loss that is attributable to the interests of the other venturers. The venturer shall recognise the full amount of any loss when the contribution or sale provides evidence of a reduction in the net realisable value of current assets or an impairment loss.

Assume venturer A carries a non-current asset at fair value in its accounts; for example, an item of plant for $100 000. If this asset is contributed to a joint venture where the other venturer, B, contributes cash of $100 000, the journal entry to record the contribution in the records of venturer A under the *line-by-line method* is shown as follows.

Cash in JV	Dr	50 000		[100 000/2]
Plant in JV	Dr	50 000		[100 000/2]
Plant	Cr		100 000	

In the records of venturer B, the entry is:

Cash in JV	Dr	50 000		[100 000/2]
Plant in JV	Dr	50 000		[100 000/2]
Cash	Cr		100 000	

Note that in the records of both venturers the plant in the joint venture is recorded at the same amount — $50 000.

The accounting records of a venturer that contributes a non-current asset become more complicated when the venturer carries the contributed asset in its records at an amount less than fair value.

In contributing an asset to the joint venture, the venturer is effectively selling a proportion of that asset to the other joint venturers, and retaining a proportion for itself. Where the carrying amount of the asset is lower than the fair value, the venturer makes a profit on selling the proportion of the asset to the other venturers. The profit is the difference between the fair value and carrying amount of the proportion of the asset sold. Assume venturer A contributed a non-current asset with a fair value of $100 000, and a carrying amount of $80 000, while venturer B contributed cash of $100 000. Venturer A can then recognise a profit on sale of half the non-current asset of $10 000 (being $\frac{1}{2}$ ($100 000 – $80 000)). The entry in the records of venturer A under the line-by-line method is:

Cash in JV	Dr	50 000		[100 000/2]
Plant in JV	Dr	40 000		[80 000/2]
Carrying Amount of Plant Sold	Dr	40 000		[80 000/2]
Proceeds on Sale of Plant	Cr		50 000	[100 000/2]
Plant	Cr		80 000	

The whole of the plant at carrying amount is given up by the venturer, with half being sold to the other venturer at a profit and the other half being the asset held in the joint venture. Note that venturer A has the plant in the joint venture recorded at half of the carrying amount and not at half of the fair value.

For venturer B, under the line-by-line method, the entry in its records is:

Cash in JV	Dr	50 000		[100 000/2]
Plant in JV	Dr	50 000		[100 000/2]
Cash	Cr		100 000	

Note that venturer B has the non-current asset recorded in its records at half of fair value. Hence, venturer A and venturer B have their equal share of the plant recorded in their records at different amounts.

The fact that the venturers have the non-current asset recorded at different amounts in their records affects the calculation of the cost of the inventory distributed to the venturers from the joint venture. If the asset is depreciated, and the depreciation included in the cost of inventory, then, as the venturers have the asset recorded at different amounts, the depreciation expense for each of the venturers differs and so does the cost of inventory transferred.

Where the asset is depreciated in the joint venture's records, this depreciation is based on the fair value of the asset. For venturer B, the depreciation charge is then the appropriate one and no adjustment is necessary. However, for venturer A, an adjustment is necessary, as the depreciation charged by the joint venture is too great. As the depreciation is capitalised into inventory and work in progress in the records of the joint venture, in the accounts of venturer A, when A recognises its share of the assets of the joint venture, a further entry is necessary to reduce the balances of the inventory-related accounts. This extra entry in venturer A's records is demonstrated in illustrative example 28.3.

ILLUSTRATIVE EXAMPLE 28.3

Contribution of a non-current asset by a venturer

On 1 July 2009, X Ltd and Y Ltd established a joint venture to manufacture a product. Each company has a 50% interest in the venture and shares output equally. To commence the venture, on 1 July 2009, X Ltd contributed cash of $1 500 000 and Y Ltd contributed equipment which had a carrying amount of $1 000 000, and a fair value of $1 500 000. The equipment is depreciated in the joint venture's accounts at 10% p.a. on cost.

The following information was extracted from the joint venture's financial statements as at 30 June 2010:

Statement of Financial Position (extract) as at 30 June 2010	
Assets	
Cash	$ 420 000
Raw materials	100 000
Work in progress	800 000
Inventory	200 000
Equipment	1 500 000
Accumulated depreciation – equipment	(150 000)
Total assets	2 870 000
Liabilities	
Accounts payable	120 000
Accrued expenses (wages)	150 000
Bank loan	1 000 000
Total liabilities	1 270 000
Net assets	$1 600 000

Cash Receipts and Payments for the year ended 30 June 2010		
	Payments	**Receipts**
Contributions		$1 500 000
Bank loan		1 000 000
Wages	$ 500 000	
Accounts payable (raw materials)	380 000	
Overhead expenses	1 200 000	
	$2 080 000	$2 500 000

Costs Incurred for the year ended 30 June 2010	
Wages	$ 650 000
Raw materials	400 000
Depreciation	150 000
Overhead expenses	1 200 000
	2 400 000
Less: Cost of inventory	1 600 000
Work in progress at 30 June 2010	$ 800 000

Required

Prepare the journal entries in the records of each of the venturers for the year ended 30 June 2010.

Solution line-by-line method

Records of X Ltd

In this example, X Ltd contributes cash to the joint venture, and Y Ltd contributes equipment. At 1 July 2009, X Ltd gives up the cash contribution and recognises a share of the cash and the equipment in the joint venture. X Ltd will recognise a share of the *fair value* of the asset. The entry is:

Cash in JV	Dr	750 000		[1 500 000/2]
Equipment in JV	Dr	750 000		[1 500 000/2]
Cash	Cr		1 500 000	

At 30 June 2010, X Ltd recognises a share of the assets and liabilities in the statement of financial position of the joint venture. Note that the joint venture has produced inventory of $1 600 000, of which $1 400 000 has been transferred to the venturers. Further, the joint venture has depreciated the equipment, the depreciation being based on the fair value of the equipment. The entry at 30 June 2010 in X Ltd's accounts is shown as follows:

Raw Material in JV	Dr	50 000		[100 000/2]
Work in Progress in JV	Dr	400 000		[800 000/2]
Inventory in JV	Dr	100 000		[200 000/2]
Inventory	Dr	700 000		[1 400 000/2]
Accumulated Depreciation – Equipment in JV	Cr		75 000	[150 000/2]
Accounts Payable in JV	Cr		60 000	[120 000/2]
Accrued Expenses in JV	Cr		75 000	[150 000/2]
Bank Loan in JV	Cr		500 000	[1 000 000/2]
Cash in JV	Cr		540 000	[750 000 – (420 000/2)]

As depreciation has been based on fair value in the joint venture, and X Ltd has its share of the equipment in the joint venture recorded at fair value, the correct amount of depreciation has been capitalised into the cost of inventory. No adjusting entry is necessary.

Records of Y Ltd

At 1 July 2009, Y Ltd contributes equipment to the joint venture, this having a carrying amount in Y Ltd different from the fair value of the asset. In recording its contribution to the joint venture, Y Ltd therefore recognises a gain on selling half of the equipment to X Ltd. X Ltd's share of the equipment in the joint venture is then based on the original carrying amount of the asset. The entry is:

Cash in JV	Dr	750 000		[1 500 000/2]
Equipment in JV	Dr	500 000		[1 000 000/2]
Carrying Amount of Equipment Sold	Dr	500 000		[1 000 000/2]
Equipment	Cr		1 000 000	
Proceeds from Sale of Equipment	Cr		750 000	[1 500 000/2]

At 30 June 2010, Y Ltd recognises its share of the accounts in the statement of financial position of the joint venture as well as its share of the inventory transferred from the joint venture. The entry is:

Raw Material in JV	Dr	50 000		[100 000/2]
Work in Progress in JV	Dr	400 000		[800 000/2]
Inventory in JV	Dr	100 000		[200 000/2]
Inventory	Dr	700 000		[1 400 000/2]
Accumulated Depreciation — Equipment in JV	Cr		75 000	[150 000/2]
Accounts Payable in JV	Cr		60 000	[120 000/2]
Accrued Expenses in JV	Cr		75 000	[150 000/2]
Bank Loan in JV	Cr		500 000	[1 000 000/2]
Cash in JV	Cr		540 000	[750 000 – (420 000/2)]

Note that this entry is the same as that for X Ltd.

The depreciation recognised by X Ltd is $75 000, which is based on the fair value of the asset. However, the equipment in the joint venture has been recognised by Y Ltd at only $500 000, which is half of the original carrying amount. Y Ltd would want to recognise only $50 000 depreciation, which is 10% of $500 000. Hence, whereas the work in progress and inventory recognised by Y Ltd includes depreciation of $75 000, the real cost of these assets to Y Ltd is less, to the amount of $25 000. A further entry is necessary to reduce the accumulated depreciation recognised by Y Ltd and to reduce the cost of the work in progress and inventory relating to the joint venture. This means that the cost of these assets to Y Ltd is different from that recognised by X Ltd. This is because the cost of the equipment in the joint venture is less for Y Ltd than for X Ltd.

As the depreciation is capitalised into work in progress and inventory (both that amount still on hand in the joint venture as well as that transferred to Y Ltd), the adjustment to depreciation is proportionately allocated across these accounts:

			Share of $25 000
Work in Progress	$ 400 000	1/3	$ 8 333
Inventory in JV	100 000	1/12	2 083
Inventory	700 000	7/12	14 584
	$1 200 000		$25 000

The entry in the records of Y Ltd to adjust the accumulated depreciation and the cost of the inventory-related accounts is then:

Accumulated Depreciation — Equipment in JV	Dr	25 000		[10% × (750 000 – 500 000)]
Work in Progress in JV	Cr		8 333	
Inventory in JV	Cr		2 083	
Inventory	Cr		14 584	

28.6.3 Contributions of services

Contributions of cash and non-current assets result in the immediate provision of assets to the joint venture. With the provision of services, the venturer supplying the services raises a liability, which is the obligation to supply the services when required by the joint venture, while the joint venture recognises an asset, which is the services receivable from the venturer.

The principles established in accounting for the contributions of non-current assets where the fair value differs from the carrying amount apply to the accounting for services provided. Where a venturer has the expertise to provide services, normally the venturer supplies those services at fair value. This means that the cost of the services provided by the venturer differs from the fair value of the services. Hence:

- in providing services to the other venturers, a venturer records a profit on the supply of the services. However, the services provided to itself (i.e. its share of the joint venture) must be supplied at cost, no profit being earned.
- the joint venture will record the services receivable at fair value and capitalise the cost of the services when supplied into the cost of the work in progress and inventory. For the venturer supplying the services, an adjustment is necessary to reduce the cost of the work in progress and inventory as recorded by the joint venture back to the lower cost to the venturer.

ILLUSTRATIVE EXAMPLE 28.4

Contribution of services by a venturer

On 1 July 2009, X Ltd and Y Ltd established a joint venture to manufacture a product. Each company has a 50% interest in the venture and shares output equally. To commence the venture, on 1 July 2009, X Ltd contributed cash of $1 000 000 and Y Ltd undertook to contribute 2 years' worth of administration and production services ($1 000 000 fair value). Y Ltd estimated the cost of providing the services over the next 2 years at $750 000 (i.e. Y Ltd earning a profit on the provision of services). Each venturer depreciated equipment at 10% p.a. on cost.

The following information was extracted from the accounts and financial statements of the joint venture operation as at 30 June 2010:

Statement of Financial Position (extract)
as at 30 June 2010

Assets	
Cash	$ 20 000
Services receivable	500 000
Raw materials	100 000
Work in progress	650 000
Inventory	200 000
Equipment	800 000
Total assets	2 270 000

(continued)

Liabilities	
Accounts payable (raw materials)	120 000
Accrued expenses (wages)	50 000
Bank loan	1 500 000
Total liabilities	1 670 000
Net assets	$ 600 000

Cash Receipts and Payments
for the year ended 30 June 2010

	Payments	Receipts
Contributions		$1 000 000
Bank loan		1 500 000
Equipment (purchased 3/7/05)	$ 800 000	
Wages	100 000	
Accounts payable (raw materials)	380 000	
Overhead expenses	1 200 000	
	$2 480 000	$2 500 000

Costs Incurred
for the year ended 30 June 2010

Wages	$ 150 000
Raw materials	400 000
Services received	500 000
Overhead expenses	1 200 000
	2 250 000
Less: Cost of inventory	1 600 000
Work in progress at 30 June 2010	$ 650 000

Required
Prepare the journal entries in the records of both venturers for the year ended 30 June 2010.

Solution — Line-by-line method
Records of X Ltd
At 1 July 2010, X Ltd supplies cash to the joint venture and Y Ltd promises to provide services. The entry in X Ltd is:

Cash in JV	Dr	500 000		[1 000 000/2]
Services Receivable in JV	Dr	500 000		[1 000 000/2]
Cash	Cr		1 000 000	

The joint venture would raise an asset, Services Receivable, at $1 000 000. When the first year's services are supplied by Y Ltd, the joint venture reduces the receivable account by $500 000 and capitalises $500 000 into the work in progress account, leaving a balance of $500 000 in services receivable. This can be seen in the statement of financial position and costs incurred statement of the joint venture at 30 June 2010.

At 30 June 2010, X Ltd recognises its half share in the assets and liabilities of the joint venture and the inventory transferred from the joint venture. The entry by X Ltd is shown on the next page.

Raw Material in JV	Dr	50 000		[100 000/2]
Work in Progress in JV	Dr	325 000		[650 000/2]
Inventory in JV	Dr	100 000		[200 000/2]
Equipment in JV	Dr	400 000		[800 000/2]
Inventory	Dr	700 000		[1 400 000/2]
Accounts Payable in JV	Cr		60 000	[120 000/2]
Accrued Expenses in JV	Cr		25 000	[50 000/2]
Bank Loan in JV	Cr		750 000	[150 000/2]
Cash in JV	Cr		490 000	[500 000 – (20 000/2)]
Services Receivable in JV	Cr		250 000	[500 000 – (500 000/2)]

As the venturers depreciate the equipment in their own records, a further entry is necessary by X Ltd:

Depreciation Expense – Equipment in JV	Dr	40 000		[10% × 400 000)]
Accumulated Depreciation	Cr		40 000	

Records of Y Ltd

At 1 July 2010, Y Ltd recognises a profit on selling services to X Ltd and raises an obligation to supply services to X Ltd. It does not raise any obligation, nor recognise a profit, in relation to the supply of services to itself. Y Ltd does not, therefore, recognise a share of the services receivable account raised by the joint venture, as it cannot hold an asset in itself. The entry by X Ltd is:

Cash in JV	Dr	500 000		[1 000 000/2]
Obligation to Supply Services to JV	Cr		375 000	[750 000/2]
Gain – Supply of Services	Cr		125 000	[(1 000 000 – 750 000)/2]

During the 2009–10 period, Y Ltd supplies services to the joint venture. The cost of supplying the services to the joint venture is $375 000. Y Ltd recognises a reduction in the liability to supply services to X Ltd as well as the cost of supplying services to itself. The entry in the records of Y Ltd when the services are provided is:

Services Provided to JV	Dr	187 500		[375 000/2]
Obligation to Supply Services	Dr	187 500		[375 000/2]
Cash	Cr		375 000	[750 000/2]

At 30 June 2010, Y Ltd recognises its share of the statement of financial position accounts of the joint venture as well as the inventory transferred from the joint venture to Y Ltd. As Y Ltd did not recognise a share of the services receivable account raised by the joint venture, in recognising a share of the joint venture's accounts at 30 June 2010, it is necessary to make an adjustment for the services recognised by the joint venture. This adjustment is in two parts:

- In the accounts of the joint venture, the services provided based on their fair value have been capitalised into the cost of the work in progress and inventory. Hence, the expense account 'Services Provided to JV' raised by Y Ltd during 2009–10 needs to be eliminated — Y Ltd cannot have the cost of the services capitalised into inventory as well as recognising a period operating expense. A credit adjustment of $187 500 is then made to the 'Services provided to JV' account.

- As the amount that the joint venture has capitalised into work in progress and inventory is based on fair value, an adjustment is necessary in relation to the profit element on the provision of the services. The cost of the inventory to Y Ltd is less than that to X Ltd as Y Ltd recognises the services at cost while X Ltd pays fair value for them. The profit element on providing services must then be proportionately adjusted against the work in progress and inventory accounts recognised by the joint venture. The profit on supplying services for 1 year for one venturer is $62 500 (being $\frac{1}{2} \times \frac{1}{2} \times \$250\,000$). The allocation across the inventory-related accounts is as follows:

	Share of $62 500		
Inventory in JV	$ 100 000	100/1125	$ 5 555
Inventory	700 000	700/1125	38 890
Work in Progress in JV	325 000	325/1125	18 055
	$1 125 000		$62 500

These amounts are then credited to the appropriate accounts to eliminate the profit element on the provision of services, and hence reduce their cost to Y Ltd.

The entry at 30 June 2010 for Y Ltd is then:

Raw Material in JV	Dr	50 000		[100 000/2]
Work in Progress in JV	Dr	325 000		[650 000/2]
Inventory in JV	Dr	100 000		[200 000/2]
Equipment in JV	Dr	400 000		[800 000/2]
Inventory	Dr	700 000		[1 400 000/2]
Accounts Payable in JV	Cr		60 000	[120 000/2]
Accrued Expenses in JV	Cr		25 000	[50 000/2]
Bank Loan in JV	Cr		750 000	[1 500 000/2]
Cash in JV	Cr		490 000	[500 000 – 20 000/2]
Services Provided to JV	Cr		187 500	
Inventory in JV	Cr		5 555	
Inventory	Cr		38 890	
Work in Progress in JV	Cr		18 055	

As the venturers depreciate the equipment in their own records, a further entry is necessary in Y Ltd:

Depreciation Expense – Equipment in JV	Dr	40 000		[10% × 400 000]
Accumulated Depreciation	Cr		40 000	

28.6.4 Contributions of assets with ownership retained

In section 28.6.2, the situation analysed is where a venturer contributed a non-current asset to the joint venture, potentially to be used by the joint venture. In this section, the situation under consideration is where the non-current asset contributed to the venture is used for the life of the joint venture and then returned to the venturer. In essence, the venturer supplying the asset retains ownership of the asset and contributes some part of the benefits of the asset to the joint venture. For example, a venturer could allow the joint venture to use some land owned by a venturer, or a venturer may have a patent that the joint venture is allowed to use for a period of time.

In accounting for the contribution of such an asset, it needs to be recognised that what the venturer is contributing to the joint venture is the fair value of the benefits given up by the venturer. Assume a venturer owns an asset with a fair value of $100 000 and this is supplied to the joint venture for the next 2 years, at the end of which the fair value of the asset is $80 000. The venturer is then supplying an asset to the joint venture that has a value of $20 000. The venturer then has two assets: an asset of $80 000 and a proportionate share of the $20 000 asset in the joint venture.

ILLUSTRATIVE EXAMPLE 28.5

Contribution of a non-current asset by a venturer, with ownership retained

On 1 July 2009, X Ltd and Y Ltd established a joint venture to manufacture a product. Each company has a 50% interest in the venture and shares output equally. To commence the venture, on 1 July 2009, X Ltd contributed cash of $100 000 and Y Ltd undertook to contribute the use of equipment owned by it. At 1 July 2009, the equipment is recorded by Y Ltd at $150 000, being the fair value of the asset; the asset has a remaining 15-year life. Depreciation on the equipment is charged using a straight-line depreciation method. The asset has a fair value of $50 000 at the end of 10 years — this being the life of the joint venture.

The following information was extracted from the accounts and financial statements of the joint venture operation as at 30 June 2010:

Statement of Financial Position (extract)
as at 30 June 2010

Assets	
Cash	$ 52 000
Raw materials	1 000
Work in progress	24 000
Inventory	10 000
Equipment	100 000
Accumulated depreciation — equipment	(10 000)
Total assets	177 000
Liabilities	
Accounts payable	2 000
Accrued expenses (wages)	5 000
Total liabilities	7 000
Net assets	$170 000

Cash Receipts and Payments
for the year ended 30 June 2010

	Payments	Receipts
Contributions		$100 000
Wages	$35 000	
Accounts payable (raw materials)	3 000	
Overhead expenses	10 000	
	$48 000	$100 000

Costs Incurred
for the year ended 30 June 2010

Wages	$40 000
Raw materials	4 000
Equipment used	10 000
Overhead expenses	10 000
	64 000
Less: Inventory	40 000
Work in progress at 30 June 2010	$24 000

Required
Prepare the journal entries in the records of X Ltd and Y Ltd for the year ending 30 June 2010.

Solution line-by-line method
Records of X Ltd
As the asset has a fair value of $150 000 at 1 July 2009 and a fair value at the end of the life of the joint venture of $50 000, Y Ltd contributes an asset worth $100 000 to the joint venture. At 1 July 2009, X Ltd passes the following entry:

Equipment in JV	Dr	50 000		[100 000/2]
Cash in JV	Dr	50 000		[100 000/2]
Cash	Cr		100 000	

The joint venture recognises the equipment at $100 000 and depreciates this over the ten years at $10 000 per annum. At 30 June 2010, X Ltd recognises its share of the assets and liabilities of the joint venture and the inventory transferred to it from the joint venture. In relation to the latter, the joint venture has produced $40 000 worth of inventory, of which $30 000 has been transferred to the venturers and $10 000 remains in the joint venture. The entry at 30 June 2010 is:

Raw Material in JV	Dr	500		[1 000/2]
Work in Progress in JV	Dr	12 000		[24 000/2]
Inventory in JV	Dr	5 000		[10 000/2]
Inventory	Dr	15 000		[30 000/2]
Accounts Payable in JV	Cr		1 000	[2 000/2]
Accrued Expenses in JV	Cr		2 500	[5 000/2]
Accumulated Depreciation — Equipment in JV	Cr		5 000	[10 000/2]
Cash in JV	Cr		24 000	[50 000 – 52 000/2]

Records of Y Ltd
The accounting records of Y Ltd are very similar to those shown in illustrative example 28.3 because Y Ltd sells half of the asset to X Ltd, potentially earning a profit on the sale. The asset being sold in this example has a carrying amount of $100 000 and a fair value of $100 000, so no profit is recorded. The entry in Y Ltd at 1 July 2009 is:

Equipment in JV	Dr	50 000		[100 000/2]
Cash in JV	Dr	50 000		[100 000/2]
Carrying Amount of Equipment Sold to JV	Dr	50 000		[100 000/2]
Equipment	Cr		100 000	
Proceeds on Sale of Equipment to JV	Cr		50 000	[100 000/2]

In the records of Y Ltd there are now two assets: equipment at $50 000 and equipment in the joint venture at $50 000.

At 30 June 2010, Y Ltd recognises its share of the assets and liabilities of the joint venture as well as the inventory transferred from the joint venture. As the carrying amount of the equipment at 1 July 2009 equalled the fair value, no adjustment is necessary in relation to the carrying amount of the equipment or the cost of the work in progress and inventory. The entry is:

Raw Material in JV	Dr	500		[1 000/2]
Work in Progress in JV	Dr	12 000		[24 000/2]
Inventory in JV	Dr	5 000		[10 000/2]

Inventory	Dr	15 000		[30 000/2]
Accounts Payable in JV	Cr		1 000	[2 000/2]
Accrued Expenses in JV	Cr		2 500	[5 000/2]
Accumulated Depreciation – Equipment in JV	Cr		5 000	[10 000/2]
Cash in JV	Cr		24 000	[50 000 – 52 000/2]

This entry is the same as for X Ltd.

ILLUSTRATIVE EXAMPLE 28.6

Contribution of a non-current asset by a venturer, where the fair value is greater than the carrying amount

Assume the same information as in illustrative example 28.5, except that the equipment supplied by Y Ltd had a carrying amount of $140 000 at 1 July 2009. Hence, the equipment being supplied has, at 1 July 2009, a carrying amount of $140 000 and a fair value of $150 000, with the residual value after 10 years being $50 000.

The journal entries for X Ltd as given in the solution in illustrative example 28.5 are not affected by the carrying amount being different from the fair value at 1 July 2009. However, Y Ltd will record a gain on selling half the equipment to X Ltd and record the asset in the joint venture at half of the carrying amount. The entry in the records of Y Ltd at 1 July 2009 is:

Equipment in JV	Dr	45 000		[90 000/2]
Cash in JV	Dr	50 000		[100 000/2]
Carrying Amount of Equipment sold to JV	Dr	45 000		[90 000/2]
Equipment	Cr		90 000	
Proceeds on Sale of Equipment to JV	Cr		50 000	[100 000/2]

Y Ltd then has two assets: equipment at $50 000 and equipment in the joint venture at $45 000. In relation to the latter, the joint venture depreciates an asset that cost $100 000. The annual charge is $10 000, this being included in the cost of the work in progress and inventory accounts. For Y Ltd, the cost of these assets is less than for X Ltd as the equipment cost Y Ltd less than X Ltd. Hence, as demonstrated in illustrative example 28.3, an adjustment entry of the following form would need to be passed in the records of Y Ltd at 30 June 2010:

Accumulated Depreciation – Equipment in JV	Dr	500		[10% × (50 000 – 45 000)]
Work in Progress in JV	Cr		X	
Inventory in JV	Cr		X	
Inventory	Cr		X	

28.6.5 Management fees paid to a venturer

In section 28.6.3, the situation where a venturer supplied services as its contribution to the joint venture was discussed. In this section, the analysis is concerned with the case where a venturer supplies a service in the normal course of business to the joint venture. This includes payment to a joint venturer to act in a management capacity to the joint venture.

In accounting for these payments, the joint venture pays cash to a joint venturer, with the cost of the service being capitalised into work in progress and inventory produced by the joint venture. For a venturer that does not supply the service there are no accounting adjustments necessary because of the transaction. For the venturer that does supply the service, normally it would incur a cost to supply the service and earn a profit on the supply of that service. In accounting for its interest in the joint venture, the venturer supplying the service has to consider the following:

- As with supplying services as part of the initial contribution, a venturer cannot earn a profit on supplying services to itself.
- As the joint venture capitalises the amount paid to the venturer into the cost of work in progress and inventory, an adjustment is necessary to inventory related accounts because the cost of these items to the venturer supplying the services is less than that to the other venturer(s).

ILLUSTRATIVE EXAMPLE 28.7

Management fees paid to a venturer

X Ltd and Y Ltd have formed a joint venture and share equally in the output of the joint venture. During the current period ending 30 June 2010, the joint venture pays a management fee of $400 000 to X Ltd. The cost to X Ltd of supplying management services to the joint venture is $320 000. At the end of the current period, X Ltd's share of the inventory-related assets from the joint venture as recorded for X Ltd is:

Work in progress in JV	$300 000
Inventory in JV	200 000
Inventory	500 000

The joint venture has capitalised the management services fee of $400 000 into the cost of these assets. In the records of X Ltd at 30 June 2010, the following entries are required:

To record revenue on payment of the service fee by the joint venture

Cash	Dr	400 000	
Fee Revenue	Cr		400 000

To record the cost of supplying the services

Cost of Supplying Services	Dr	320 000	
Cash	Cr		320 000

To adjust for the profit on X Ltd supplying services to itself

The total profit to X Ltd on supplying the management service is $80 000. Half this profit is made on supplying services to Y Ltd and the other $40 000 on supplying services to itself. An adjustment is necessary to eliminate the revenue and the expense on supplying services to itself. The following entry eliminates from the fee revenue only the amount of the expense — the profit element in the revenue is eliminated in the next entry:

Fee Revenue	Dr	160 000		[320 000/2]
Cost of Supplying Services	Cr		160 000	

To adjust the cost of the inventory-related assets from the joint venture

The profit element on supplying services to itself, \$40 000, is proportionately adjusted across the inventory-related assets as follows:

		Share of \$40 000	
Inventory in JV	\$ 200 000	20%	\$ 8 000
Inventory	500 000	50%	20 000
Work in progress in JV	300 000	30%	12 000
	\$1 000 000		\$ 40 000

The entry is:

Fee Revenue	Dr	40 000	
Inventory in JV	Cr		8 000
Inventory	Cr		20 000
Work in Progress in JV	Cr		12 000

Note that the combination of this entry and the immediately preceding one results in adjusting fee revenue for a total of \$200 000, which is half the revenue paid by the joint venture to X Ltd.

If X Ltd had provided the services but the joint venture had not yet paid the fee by the end of the period, the liabilities of the joint venture need to be adjusted. Further, the fee receivable account of \$400 000 raised by X Ltd needs to be adjusted. The entry is:

Accruals in JV	Dr	200 000	
Fee Receivable	Cr		200 000

28.7 ACCOUNTING BY A VENTURER IN A JOINTLY CONTROLLED ENTITY THAT IS SHARING PROFIT

A joint venture entity that is established to generate profits to be shared between the venturers can be organised within a number of organisational structures, including corporations and partnerships. As noted in paragraph 28 of IAS 31, a jointly controlled entity maintains its own accounting records and prepares and presents financial statements in the same way as other entities in conformity with International Financial Reporting Standards.

On commencement of the joint venture, each venturer contributes cash or other assets and passes a journal entry of the following order:

Investment in Joint Venture	Dr	X	
Cash/Other Asset	Cr		X
(Initial contribution to joint venture entity)			

IAS 31 then provides two methods of accounting for jointly controlled entities.

Proportionate consolidation

Paragraph 33 of IAS 31 provides details on this method. The basic principles are:

- in its own statement of financial position, the venturer includes its share of the assets that it controls jointly and its share of the liabilities for which it is jointly responsible
- in its own statement of comprehensive income, the venturer includes its share of the income and expenses of the jointly controlled entity.

The method thus involves a line-by-line recognition of the venturer's share of the accounts of the joint venture. By taking a line-by-line approach, the method is similar to the consolidation method as applied to subsidiaries under IAS 27, but dissimilar to that method because only the venturer's share of the other entity is recognised.

Paragraph 34 of IAS 31 provides for the use of alternative reporting formats under the proportionate consolidation method. The venturer may:

- combine the share of the joint venture's activities within each line of its own financial statements, for example, the venturer's share of property, plant and equipment is included with the venturer's property, plant and equipment; or
- include separate line items for each major classification of assets, liabilities, income and expenses — this format enables the users of the venturer's financial statements to separate out the activities of the venturer from that of the joint venture. An illustration of various formats is given in figure 28.3.

Equity method

The equity method of accounting is discussed in detail in chapter 27. The basic principles of the method, as stated in the definition in paragraph 3 of IAS 31, are as follows:

- In the statement of financial position, initially record the investment in the joint venture at cost and adjust thereafter for the post-acquisition change in the venturer's share of net assets of the jointly controlled entity; the increase in net assets will equate to the profit/loss recorded by the joint venture and any increases in reserves created directly in equity.
- In the statement of comprehensive income, recognise the venturer's share of the profit or loss of the jointly controlled entity.

The equity method, as described in IAS 28, is also a consolidation technique, often being described as a one-line consolidation method.

The major difference between the two methods is that the equity method recognises the investment in the joint venture as the asset held by the venturer, whereas the proportionate consolidation method recognises the undivided interest in the individual assets and liabilities of the joint venture. The arguments for and against the two methods are discussed in section 28.8.

28.7.1 Applying the two methods of accounting for a jointly controlled entity

On 1 January 2009, Harvard Ltd signed a joint venture agreement with another venturer for the production of bottled water. One venturer had access to mineral springs and the other technical experience in manufacturing. A corporation, Princeton Ltd was established for that purpose. It was agreed that both joint venturers would initially contribute \$500 000 each, receive 100 000 \$5 shares in the new company and share profits equally.

At the end of the first year, 31 December 2009, the financial statements of the joint venture showed:

Revenues	\$ 200 000
Expenses	140 000
Profit before tax	60 000
Income tax expense	14 000
Profit for the period	46 000
Share capital	1 000 000
Payables	140 000
Provisions	150 000
	\$1 336 000
Property, plant and equipment	\$ 940 000
Accumulated depreciation	(50 000)
Inventory	250 000
Cash	36 000
Receivables	160 000
	\$1 336 000

On establishment of the joint venture and the contribution for the shares in Princeton Ltd, Harvard Ltd passed the following entry in its records:

Investment in Princeton Ltd	Dr	500 000	
Cash	Cr		500 000
(Being investment in joint venture)			

Under the proportionate consolidation method, at 31 December 2009, Harvard Ltd recognises 50% of all the accounts of Princeton Ltd. As per the consolidation method, this process requires an adjustment to eliminate the investment account in the joint venture as recorded by Harvard Ltd and the pre-acquisition equity of the joint venture. This process is shown in figure 28.1.

Financial statements	Harvard Ltd	Share of Princeton Ltd		Adjustments Dr	Adjustments Cr		Proportionate consolidation
Revenues	5 400 000	100 000					5 500 000
Expenses	4 400 000	70 000					4 470 000
Profit before tax	1 000 000	30 000					1 030 000
Tax expense	240 000	7 000					247 000
Profit	760 000	23 000					783 000
Share capital	1 500 000	500 000	*1*	500 000			1 500 000
Retained earnings	460 000						460 000
Payables	250 000	70 000					320 000
Provisions	170 000	75 000					245 000
	3 140 000	668 000					3 308 000
Property, plant and equipment	1 950 000	470 000					2 420 000
Accumulated depreciation	(350 000)	(25 000)					(375 000)
Inventory	420 000	125 000					545 000
Cash	380 000	18 000					398 000
Receivables	240 000	80 000					320 000
Investment in Princeton Ltd	500 000				500 000	*1*	
	3 140 000	668 000		500 000	500 000		3 308 000

FIGURE 28.1 Proportionate consolidation method

If the equity method is applied in the same situation, the joint venturer recognises as an increase to the carrying amount of the investment, its share of the post-acquisition profit/loss of the joint venture, in this case a 50% share of the $46 000 profit: $23 000. The adjusting journal entry passed in the worksheet is then:

Investment in Princeton Ltd	Dr	23 000	
Share of Profit of Joint Venture	Cr		23 000

The worksheet under the equity method is shown in figure 28.2.

Financial statements	Harvard Ltd		Adjustments				Equity-accounted statements
				Dr	Cr		
Revenues	5 400 000						5 400 000
Expenses	4 400 000						4 400 000
Profit before tax	1 000 000						1 000 000
Tax expense	240 000						240 000
Trading profit							760 000
Share of profit of joint venture	760 000				23 000	1	23 000
Profit for the period							783 000
Share capital	1 500 000						1 500 000
Retained earnings	460 000						460 000
Payables	250 000						250 000
Provisions	170 000						170 000
	3 140 000						3 163 000
Property, plant and equipment	1 950 000						1 950 000
Accumulated depreciation	(350 000)						(350 000)
Inventory	420 000						420 000
Cash	380 000						380 000
Receivables	240 000						240 000
Investment in Princeton Ltd	500 000		1	23 000			523 000
	3 140 000			23 000	23 000		3 163 000

FIGURE 28.2 Equity method

28.8 EQUITY METHOD VERSUS PROPORTIONATE CONSOLIDATION

In this section, the form of joint venture being analysed is the jointly controlled entity or business, and not the shared facility or jointly controlled asset. This entity may be incorporated or be an unincorporated association established by the venturers. Further, the venturers may agree to share profit or output of the venture. Where the distribution is in the form of output, the traditional equity method based upon recognition of a share of the profits of the investee is not appropriate because the joint venture does not generate a profit. In these cases, a one-line asset recognised by the joint venturer is the equivalent of the equity method for a profit-making entity. The choice being debated is effectively whether a one-line method or a proportionate multi-line method is appropriate.

Arguments for and against the two methods are given in chapter 3 of G4-DP and in chapter 4 of UK-DP. There are two main areas of debate: what assets are controllable by a joint venturer, and the need for disclosure about the assets and liabilities of the joint venture.

The control debate

The key argument here is that the proportionate consolidation method is at odds with the definition of an asset in the *Framework*. The definition of an asset in the *Framework* is:

> An asset is a resource controlled by the entity as a result of past events and from which future economic benefits are expected to flow to the entity.

There is no definition of control given in the *Framework*. In G4-DP, in paragraphs 2.8 and 2.9, definitions of control as given in accounting standards, such as IAS 31 on consolidated financial statements, are quoted. However, these definitions relate to criteria for consolidation rather than asset definition and are therefore not necessarily applicable. It is therefore questionable how much of those concepts of control can be used in determining the existence of assets.

In IAS 38 *Intangible Assets*, paragraphs 13–16 contain a discussion of control in relation to recognition of intangible assets. In paragraph 15, the following statements are made in relation to recognition of skilled staff as assets:

> The entity may also expect that the staff will continue to make their skills available to the entity. However, an entity usually has insufficient control over the expected future economic benefits arising from a team of skilled staff and from training for these items to meet the definition of an intangible asset.

It is important to note the distinction here between the ability and the right of the entity to deny access of others to the benefits of the staff skills and the ability of the entity to be able to govern or manage the extent of those benefits. While the skilled staff remain, the benefits will flow to the entity and not to other parties. However, whether the staff remain is beyond the control of the entity. In relation to an unincorporated joint venture, each venturer is entitled to a share of output. The venturer can deny or regulate the access of the other venturers to that output. However, a venturer cannot determine or regulate the extent of the production from the joint venture. It requires the consent of all venturers to make decisions on the use of the joint venture assets.

It is this element of being able to determine the policies in relation to the deployment of resources that could commonly exist between the definitions of control for consolidation purposes and for asset definition purposes. Control for asset definition purposes therefore would require the entity to be able to affect the amount of benefits to be received rather than simply having a right to the ultimate benefits.

Note the following comments in relation to leases from the G4+1 Discussion Paper (2000) entitled 'Leases: Implementation of a New Approach':

> A central feature of the definitions of assets is that past transactions or events have resulted in control over the capacity to obtain future economic benefits. [Para. 2.8]
>
> The nature of assets that arise under leases is different from those that are obtained by ownership. An owner of property is typically free to use it in any way he wishes and may sell, pledge or dispose of it. In contrast, a lessee can use the leased property only in the ways permitted by the lease contract, and usually has no rights to pledge or dispose of it. Nonetheless, the right granted by the lease to use the property is a source of economic benefits controlled by the lessee and, as such, is an asset. [Para.1.13]

The entity does not have to have an unfettered ability to do what it likes with a resource in order to have control. With leased properties, the ability of lessees to control the benefits is limited. But lessees have the capacity to make the benefits larger or smaller by their actions and by implementation of the policies they adopt for managing the leased property. If such an ability does not exist the asset is simply an investment.

Consider the notion of control in relation to the pipeline example given by Dieter and Wyatt (1978, p. 89) in their argument against proportionate consolidation:

> For example, assume a manufacturing company has a 20 percent interest in a pipeline project joint venture, organized to supply natural gas to it as a power source. Four other coventurers also have a 20 percent equity interest. The debt of the project is guaranteed, via a throughput agreement with each of the venturers, in the same proportion as their equity interests. Under these circumstances, no one venturer has direct control over the pipeline or even a portion thereof (i.e., a pipeline per se is not divisible). By combining 20 percent of the cost of the pipeline directly with the property, plant and equipment of the manufacturing operations of the investor, a reader of the investor's financial statements could be left with an erroneous impression of the amount of assets the investor's management directly controls and supervises.

These arguments are not correct. The sharing of the pipeline is no different from a number of parties leasing a taxi; one drives it in the mornings, one in the evenings and one on weekends. However, as each party has control over the manner of use and hence the extent of benefits to be received, each party has an asset. Therefore, for jointly controlled assets, or shared facilities, it is appropriate for each party to recognise its share of the resource as an asset.

If these arguments are applied to the use of proportionate consolidation for joint venture entities, then the method conflicts with the definition of an asset. This was the conclusion reached in the G4-DP, paragraph 3.12:

> There is general recognition and acceptance among the conceptual frameworks of G4+1 members that an essential condition of an asset is that it be a *resource controlled by the reporting enterprise*. Proportionate consolidation is fundamentally inconsistent with this basic economic concept because a venturer cannot control (that is, use or direct the use of) its pro rata share of individual assets in a joint venture.

Hence, to be consistent with the *Framework*, the IASB should not permit the use of proportionate consolidation or line-by-line accounting for joint venture entities. To assist in reaching the right conclusion in this area, it is necessary for the IASB to expand the *Framework* to clarify the meaning of the term 'control'. This seems to be an urgent need given the conclusions reached by Willett (1995) in his discussion of the debate on accounting for joint ventures in Canada, and by Schuetze (1993):

> The board concluded that the term 'control', as used in Section 1000, could be interpreted as dealing with the level of assurance that future economic benefits can be obtained or yielded in the future from the assets and liabilities held. The sense of the term 'control' is different from the way in which it is used in consolidations, which has more to do with 'managerial' control' (sourced from Willett 1995, p. 60).
>
> [the asset definition] is so complex, so abstract, so open-ended, so all-inclusive, and so vague that we cannot use it to solve problems (sourced from Scheutze 1993, p. 67).

The disclosure debate

Those who argue in favour of the proportionate consolidation method argue that 'the one-line method simply is uninformative in conveying the economic effects of the investment in and commitment to the joint venture by the investor in many of these joint ventures' (Dieter & Wyatt 1978, p. 90). More succinctly, the G4-DP in paragraph 3.18 stated:

> At the heart of the case of those arguing for proportionate consolidation is their strongly held belief that it is more useful accounting. They argue that portraying the venturer's share of the activities of the joint venture as part of the venturer's operations provides a broader and more comprehensive representation of the extent of venturer operations and assets and liabilities. Further, they claim that proportionate consolidation provides a better representation of the performance of enterprise management, and an improved basis for predicting the ability of the venturer to generate cash and cash equivalents in the future, particularly where a significant portion of business is conducted using joint ventures.

Some specific comments were made in the UK-DP (paragraph 4.10) concerning the disadvantages of the disclosures required by application of the equity method:

> (a) By bringing in only the net amounts for the results and assets of associates and joint ventures the equity method distorts financial ratios such as gearing and profit margin. Associates and joint venture extend the economic activities of the investor and the net amounts do not give much information on the operations of such entities and, therefore, the effect on the investor of its interests in them.
>
> (b) The net amounts shown under the equity method do not reveal the level of liabilities held by the associates and joint ventures or the structure of their financing. In general, the potential benefits and risks related to the investor's interests in strategic alliances are obscured by the presentation of net amounts.

If the one-line method is preferred, the deficiencies in relation to information disclosed in the financial statements can be overcome by providing additional disclosure. There have been a number of solutions advanced by various authors in this regard:

- *Gross equity method* (UK Financial Reporting Standard 9 'Associates and Joint Ventures' 1997)
  Under this method, the basic equity method is applied, but additional disclosure is required:
  - in the consolidated statement of comprehensive income income, the investor's share of the joint venture's turnover is separately disclosed
  - in the consolidated statement of financial position, the investor's share of the gross assets and liabilities is disclosed.

  The main criticism of this method is that it has the same shortcomings as the proportionate consolidation method because it portrays the assets and liabilities of the joint venture as being assets and liabilities of the investor.
- *The expanded equity method* (Dieter & Wyatt 1978)
  Under this method, the investor discloses its proportionate share of the assets and liabilities of the joint venture in its financial statements, but with separate disclosure and without combining the numbers with those of the investor. Dieter and Wyatt (1978) provide a number of formats. In figure 28.3, Exhibit 1 from their article is reproduced showing a comparison of the disclosures under the equity method, proportionate consolidation and two variants of the expanded equity method.

  These authors argued that the expanded equity method overcomes the objections directed at proportionate consolidation of including both controlled and jointly controlled items in the one financial statement. This is because under the expanded equity method the two types of assets and liabilities are kept separate. They argued that the expanded equity method has the advantages of:

(1) distinguishing those assets and liabilities directly owned and controlled by the investor from those represented by its interest in the joint venture's assets and liabilities and
(2) highlighting the extent of the investor's involvement in joint venture activities.

- *Summarised note disclosure* (G4-DP)
  The authors of G4-DP argued that the expanded equity method is a compromise proposal between the equity method and the proportionate consolidation method. As they noted (paragraph 3.26), the use of the expanded equity method has the same conceptual shortcomings of the proportionate consolidation method because the assets and liabilities of the joint venture are not those of the investor. If the use of the expanded equity method in the financial statements presents the joint venture's assets and liabilities as belonging to the investor, then this is conceptually incorrect. To overcome this conceptual problem, in G4-DP it was recommended (paragraph 4.4) that note disclosure be used, and the summarised financial statements of the joint venture operation be disclosed in the notes, including at least the investor's share of the following amounts:
  - current assets and long-term assets
  - current liabilities and long-term liabilities (with a maturity profile of material amounts of long-term debt)
  - revenues and expenses by major components, and net income before and after taxes
  - cash flow from operating, investing and financing activities.

Which method should be used? There seems to be general agreement that there is a need for more disclosure than required under the basic equity method. Conceptually, that information cannot be provided in the financial statements. Standard setters could move to innovative disclosure formats such as the use of different colours, as suggested by Wallman (1996), so that joint venture information was provided on the face of the financial statements but separated from the investor's own information by the use of colour. Until such innovations occur, provision of the additional disclosures in the notes would appear to be the best solution.

FIGURE 28.3 Expanded equity method

ABC JOINT VENTURE
Statement of Financial Position as at 31 December 1977

Assets		Liabilities and capital		
Current assets:		Current liabilities:		
Cash	$ 100 000	Current maturities of long-term debt		$ 200 000
Receivables	100 000	Accounts payable		100 000
Supplies	200 000	Accrued expenses		100 000
Total current assets	400 000	Total current liabilities		400 000
		Long-term debt, less current maturities:		
		Mortgage loans		$4 000 000
		Term loan		700 000
		Total long-term debt		$4 700 000
Fixed assets, at cost:			**Capital**	**Earnings**
Steam-generating facility	$6 000 000	Capital:		
Less: Accumulated depreciation	1 000 000	XYZ Corp. (30%)	$ 60 000	$ 30 000
		A Corp. (35%)	70 000	35 000
		B Corp. (35%)	70 000	35 000
Total fixed assets	$5 000 000		$200 000	$ 100 000
		Total capital		300 000
	$5 400 000			$5 400 000

(continued)

FIGURE 28.3 *(continued)*

XYZ CORPORATION Statement of Financial Position as at 31 December 1977				
	Traditional one-line equity method presentation (APB Opinion No.18)	Proportionate consolidation proposed by Reklau (1997)	Expanded equity method presentation	
			Alternative 1	Alternative 2
Current assets:				
Cash	$ 500 000	$ 530 000	$ 500 000	$ 500 000
Receivables	1 000 000	1 030 000	1 000 000	1 000 000
Inventories	3 000 000	3 060 000	3 000 000	3 000 000
Company share of current assets of joint venture	N/A	N/A	N/A	120 000
Total current assets	$4 500 000	$ 4 620 000	$ 4 500 000	$ 4 620 000
Fixed assets:				
Land	$ 100 000	$ 100 000	$ 100 000	$ 100 000
Plant	4 000 000	5 800 000	4 000 000	4 000 000
Machinery and equipment	2 000 000	2 000 000	2 000 000	2 000 000
	$6 100 000	$ 7 900 000	$ 6 100 000	$ 6 100 000
Less: Accumulated depreciation	2 100 000	2 400 000	2 100 000	2 100 000
	4 000 000	5 500 000	4 000 000	4 000 000
Company share of steam-generating plant, net, of joint venture	N/A	N/A	N/A	1 500 000
	$4 000 000	$ 5 500 000	$ 4 000 000	$ 5 500 000
Investment in equity of 30% owned joint venture	$ 90 000	—	—	—
Company share of investment in joint venture:				
Current assets	N/A	N/A	$ 120 000	N/A
Fixed assets, net			1 500 000	
			1 620 000	
Total assets	$8 590 000	$10 120 000	$10 120 000	$10 120 000
Liabilities and stockholders' equity				
Current liabilities:				
Current maturities of long-term debt	$1 000 000	$ 1 060 000	$ 1 000 000	1 000 000
Accounts payable and accrued expenses	2 000 000	2 060 000	2 000 000	2 000 000
Company share of current liabilities of joint venture	N/A	N/A	N/A	120 000
	$3 000 000	$ 3 120 000	$ 3 000 000	$ 3 120 000
Long-term debt, less current maturities:				
Mortgage loan	$3 000 000	$ 4 200 000	$ 3 000 000	$ 3 000 000
Term loan	N/A	210 000	N/A	N/A
Company share of long-term debt of joint venture	N/A	N/A	N/A	1 410 000
	$3 000 000	$ 4 410 000	$ 3 000 000	$ 4 410 000
Company share of liabilities of joint venture:				
Current liabilities			$ 120 000	
Long-term debt, less current liabilities	N/A	N/A	1410 000	N/A
			$ 1 530 000	

FIGURE 28.3 *(continued)*

	Traditional one-line equity method presentation (APB Opinion No.18)	Proportionate consolidation proposed by Reklau (1997)	Expanded equity method presentation	
			Alternative 1	Alternative 2
Stockholders' equity:				
Common stock	$1 800 000	$ 1 800 000	$ 1 800 000	$ 1 800 000
Retained earnings	790 000	790 000	790 000	790 000
	$2 590 000	$ 2 590 000	$ 2 590 000	$ 2 590 000
Total liabilities and stockholders' equity	$8 590 000	$10 120 000	$10 120 000	$10 120 000

Source: Dieter & Wyatt (1978, pp. 92–3).

28.8.1 ED 9 and the removal of proportionate consolidation

As noted earlier, ED 9 proposes to remove proportionate consolidation from the new IAS 31. Two respondents to the ED who did not agree with the removal of the proportionate consolidation method under ED 9 were BHP Billiton and Deloitte.

In its response to ED 9, BHP Billiton stated that it did not concur with the proposed removal of proportionate consolidation. It noted that, at 30 June 2007, BHP Billiton proportionately consolidated in excess of 20 of its investments in significant joint venture and petroleum operations. The company argued for use of proportionate consolidation on the following grounds:

> Application of the equity method to joint venture entities results in the public presentation of financial information in a manner contrary to BHP Billiton management's view of the business. As the substance of our joint venture arrangements mean they are a natural extension and highly integrated component of our total business structures, their financial performance is viewed and managed with a full perspective of each element. Due to the lack of transparency arising from the equity accounting method for significant joint venture entities (such as Escondida, Mozal and Panaram) analysts and shareholders required supplementary information to enable them to understand the makeup of the Group's financial result and to monitor the relationship between performance measures and their consequences. The additional disclosures provided to analysts and shareholders included:
>
> - An Underlying EBIT which represents Earnings before net finance costs and taxation, and jointly controlled entities' net finance costs and taxation and any exceptional items.
> - Revenue together with share of jointly controlled entities revenue.
> - Capital Expenditure including capital expenditure of certain jointly controlled entities.

In its response, Deloitte made the following statements.

> A simplistic argument that proportionate consolidation is inconsistent with the *Framework*, without a true and thorough analysis of accounting for joint arrangements, in our view, leaves the IASB open to criticism that it has proposed a solution only for the sake of US-GAAP convergence.
>
> . . .
>
> The IASB has indicated that it has not reconsidered the appropriateness of the equity method in developing its proposals in ED 9.[1] Instead, the IASB has focussed on the 'fundamental inconsistency with the *Framework*' that proportionate consolidation is considered to represent.[2]
>
> Equity accounting is considered by many to effectively be a 'one-line consolidation'.[3] Accordingly, this same criticism could be levelled at the use of the equity method as it in substance largely adopts a proportionate consolidation approach, but represents the outcome as a single amount in the balance sheet and income statement. In doing so, the equity method effectively conceals the detail that proportionate consolidation provides and necessitates the disclosure of detailed financial information used to perform equity accounting so that users are provided with useful and relevant information.
>
> For this reason, we have some sympathy for the proponents of proportionate consolidation that argue that this method is a practical way in which to present a venturer's interest in a joint venture.
>
> 1 Draft Basis for Conclusions, paragraph BC14.
> 2 *ibid*, paragraph BC12.
> 3 This is alluded to in IAS 27 *Consolidated Financial Statements*, para. 20.

The IASB believes that it has considered these criticisms. In paragraph BC8 of the Basis for Conclusions on ED 9, the board noted that the main problem that it had with the proportionate consolidation method was that it can lead to the recognition of assets that are not controlled and liabilities that are not obligations. Hence, it argues that the amounts recognised are not a faithful representation of an entity's assets and liabilities. Specifically, paragraph BC9 states:

> It [proportionate consolidation] could lead to a venturer recognising cash balances that it does not have the ability to direct or deploy, and from which it cannot obtain benefit, without consultation with other parties.

The IASB also considered the argument that proportionate consolidation provides more relevant information that the equity method. Paragraph BC12 states:

> Some argue that proportionate consolidation is a practical way to present a venturer's interest in a joint venture, particularly when the activities of the venture are an integral part of the venturer's operations. Despite its conceptual flaws, their view is that proportionate consolidation better meets the information needs of users of financial statements by providing a better representation of the performance of an entity's management and an improved basis for predicting future cash flows. The Board noted these arguments but concluded that the practical argument does not refute the fundamental inconsistency with the *Framework*. The Board believes that it is misleading for users of financial statements if an entity recognises as assets items that are not controlled, and as liabilities items that are not present obligations, and presents these together with items that it controls or items that are present obligations.

These arguments and differences of opinion are not new, as can be seen from the discussion in section 28.8. The IASB is currently reviewing the *Framework*, which hopefully will make clearer the definition of an asset. However, the IASB must urgently consider the place of the equity method in accounting for both associates and joint ventures. Until this is done, debate about how to account for these structures will continue to exist.

28.9 DISCLOSURES REQUIRED BY IAS 31

IAS 31 requires three types of disclosure:

- *Paragraph 54.* A venturer is required to disclose the aggregate amount of various contingent liabilities, unless the probability of loss is remote, separately from the amount of other contingent liabilities.
- *Paragraph 55.* A venturer is required to disclose the aggregate amount of various capital commitments.
- *Paragraph 56.* A venturer shall disclose a listing and description of interests in significant joint ventures and the proportion of ownership interest held in jointly controlled entities.
- *Paragraph 56.* For jointly controlled entities disclosure is required of the aggregate amounts of each of current assets, long-term assets, current liabilities, long-term liabilities, income and expenses relating to interests in joint ventures.
- *Paragraph 57.* A venturer shall disclose the method it uses to recognise its interest in jointly controlled entities.

Illustrative disclosures required by IAS 31 are provided in figure 28.4.

FIGURE 28.4 Illustrative disclosure — IAS 31

	IAS 31 Para.
Note 1: Summary of significant accounting policies Interests in jointly controlled entities are accounted for by proportionate consolidation which involves recognising a proportionate share, on a line-by-line basis, of each joint venture's assets, liabilities, income and expenses in the consolidated financial statements.	*57*
Note: Interest in joint ventures The Group has interests in the following joint venture entities: **Joint venture** — **Description** — **% interest** Mineral Valley — Oil and gas — 50 North Sea — Oil and gas — 33	*56*

FIGURE 28.4 *(continued)*

The Group's share of current assets, long-term assets, current liabilities, long-term liabilities, income and expenses of the joint venture entities which are included in the consolidated financial statements at 31 December are as follows:			
In €000	**2006**	**2005**	
Current assets	220	200	
Non-current assets	750	620	
Current liabilities	140	120	
Non-current liabilities	224	215	
Income	50	38	
Expenses	35	27	

Note: Commitments and contingencies *55*
Capital expenditure commitments *(b)*
In relation to the joint venture, North Sea, in which the Group has a 33% interest, that entity has purchase commitments for property, plant and equipment totalling €340 000 (2005 €180 000)
Contingent liabilities *54*
In relation to the joint venture Mineral Valley, in which the Group has a 50% interest, *(a)*
the parent company has guaranteed the performance of a contract for that entity for €40 000. Management does not expect a liability to arise from this guarantee.
The Group is not contingently liable for the liabilities of the other joint venturers in the *(c)*
joint ventures in which the Group has investments.

To illustrate how companies have disclosed their investments in joint ventures, figure 28.5 reproduces the note disclosures provided in the 2008 annual report of BHP Billiton in relation to its investments in jointly controlled entities.

FIGURE 28.5 Illustrative disclosures on jointly controlled entities by BHP Billiton

1. Accounting policies

Change in accounting policy

The accounting policies have been consistently applied by all entities included in the Group consolidated financial report and are consistent with those applied in all prior years presented, except for the impact of adopting AASB 2007–4 'Amendments to Australian Accounting Standards arising from ED 151 and Other Amendments'. AASB 2007–4 reinstates optional accounting treatments permitted by IFRS that were not initially available under Australian Accounting Standards. The principal impacts of AASB 2007–4 are described below.

Proportionate consolidation

As permitted by AASB 2007–4 'Amendments to Australian Accounting Standards arising from ED 151 and Other Amendments' and IAS 31 'Interests in Joint Ventures', the Group has adopted the policy of recognising its proportionate interest in the assets, liabilities, revenues ad expenses of jointly controlled entities within each applicable line item of the financial statements. All such interests were previously recognised using the equity method. The Group believes the change in policy to proportionate consolidation of jointly controlled entities provides more relevant information about the financial performance and financial position of the Group.

Following this change in policy, comparative information has been restated for all periods included in these financial statements, with the impact summarised below. There was no impact on profit after taxation, profit attributable to members of the Group, total equity or the Group's earnings per share in the current or comparative periods.

Joint ventures

The Group undertakes a number of business activities through joint ventures. Joint ventures are established through contractual arrangements that require the unanimous consent of each of the

(continued)

FIGURE 28.5 *(continued)*

venturers regarding the strategic financial and operating policies of the venture (joint control). The Group's joint ventures are of two types:

Jointly controlled entities

A jointly controlled entity is a corporation, partnership or other entity in which each participant holds an interest. A jointly controlled entity operates in the same way as other entities, controlling the assets of the joint venture, earning its own income and incurring its own liabilities and expenses. Interests in jointly controlled entities are accounted for using the proportional consolidation method, whereby the Group's proportionate interest in the assets, liabilities, revenues and expenses of jointly controlled entities are recognised within each applicable line item of the financial statements. The share of jointly controlled entities' results is recognised in the Group's financial statements from the date that joint control commences until the date at which it ceases.

Jointly controlled assets and operations

The Group has certain contractual arrangements with other participants to engage in joint activities that do not give rise to a jointly controlled entity. These arrangements involve the joint ownership of assets dedicated to the purposes of each venture but do not create a jointly controlled entity as the venturers directly derive the benefits of operation of their jointly owned assets, rather than deriving returns from an interest in a separate entity.

The financial report of the Group includes its share of the assets in such joint ventures, together with the liabilities, revenues and expenses arising jointly or otherwise from those operations. All such amounts are measured in accordance with the terms of each arrangement, which are usually in proportion to the Group's interest in the jointly controlled assets.

14. Investments in jointly controlled entities

All entities included below are subject to joint control as a result of governing contractual arrangements.

Major shareholdings in jointly controlled entities	Country of incorporation	Principal activities	Reporting date(a)	Ownership interest(a) 2008 %	2007 %
Caesar oil Pipeline Company LLC	US	Hydrocarbons transportation	31 May	**25**	25
Cleopatra Gas Gathering Company LLC	US	Hydrocarbons transportation	31 May	**22**	22
Guinea Alumina Corporation Ltd	British Virgin Islands	Bauxite mine and alumina refinery development	31 Dec	**33.3**	33.3
Mozal SARL	Mozambique	Aluminium smelting	30 June	**47.1**	47.1
Compañia Minera Antamina SA	Peru	Copper and zinc mining	30 June	**33.75**	33.75
Minera Escondida Limitata[c]	Chile	Copper mining	30 June	**57.5**	57.5
Richards Bay Minerals[b]	South Africa	Mineral sands mining and processing	31 Dec	**50**	50
Samarco Mineracao SA	Brazil	Iron ore mining	31 Dec	**50**	50
Carbones del Cerrejón LLC	Anguilla	Coal mining in Colombia	31 Dec	**33.3**	33.3
Newcastle Coal Infrastructure Group Pty Limited	Australia	New port development	30 June	**35.5**	35.5

	In aggregate 2008 US$M	In aggregate 2007 US$M	Group share 2008 US$M	Group share 2007 US$M
Net assets of jointly controlled entities				
Current assets	**7 004**	5 698	**3 325**	2 747
Non-current assets	**13 591**	12 438	**6 395**	5 744
Current liabilities	**(3 912)**	(2 516)	**(1 868)**	(1 246)
Non-current liabilities	**(4 983)**	(4 780)	**(2 388)**	(2 321)
Net assets	**11 700**	10 840	**5 464**	4 924

FIGURE 28.5 *(continued)*

	In aggregate			Group Share		
	2008 US$M	2007 US$M	2006 US$M	2008 US$M	2007 US$M	2006 US$M
Share of jointly controlled entities' profit						
Revenue	**21 704**	16 138	14 205	**10 728**	7 975	6 946
Net operating Costs	**(8 231)**	(4 307)	(4 689)	**(3 912)**	(1 985)	(2 207)
Operating profit	**13 473**	11 831	9 516	**6 816**	5 990	4 739
Net finance costs	**(181)**	(251)	(200)	**(94)**	(122)	(95)
Income tax expense	**(2 905)**	(2 477)	(1 986)	**(1 418)**	(1 201)	(950)
Profit after taxation	**10 387**	9 103	7 330	**5 304**	4 667	3 694

	2008 US$M	2007 US$M
Share of contingent liabilities and expenditure commitments of jointly controlled entities		
Contingent liabilities	**535**	417
Capital commitments	**117**	415
Other commitments	**2003**	790

(a) The ownership interest at the Group's and the jointly controlled entity's reporting date are the same. While the annual financial reporting date may be different to the Group's, financial information is obtained as at 30 June in order to report on a consistent annual basis with the Group's reporting date.

(b) Richards Bay Minerals comprises two legal entities, Tisand (Pty) Limited and Richards Bay Iron and Titanium (Pty) Limited of which the Group's ownership interest is 51 per cent (2007:51 per cent) and 49.4 per cent (2007:49.4 per cent) respectively. In accordance with the shareholder agreement between the venturers, Richards bay Minerals functions as a single economic entity. The overall profit of Richards Bay Minerals is shared equally between the venturers.

(c) While the Group legally holds a 57.5 per cent interest in Minera Escondida Limitada, the entity is subject to effective joint control due to participant and management agreements which results in the operation of an Owners' Council, whereby significant commercial and operational decisions are determined on aggregate voting interests of at least 75 per cent of the total ownership interest. Accordingly the Group does not have the ability to unilaterally control, and therefore consolidate, the investment in accordance with IAS 27/AASB 127 'Consolidated and Separate Financial Statements'.

Source: BHP Billiton (2008, pp. 191–2).

28.9.1 Disclosures required by ED 9

ED 9 proposes the following disclosures:

- *Paragraph 6*. An entity is required to provide a description of the nature and extent of its operations conducted through each of the three types of joint arrangement — joint operations, joint assets and joint ventures.
- *Paragraph 37*. Disclosure is required in relation to capital commitments.
- *Paragraph 38*. Disclosure is required concerning contingent liabilities.
- *Paragraph 39*. Disclosure is required resulting from the need to apply the equity method rather than the proportionate consolidation method. In addition to providing a list and description of interests in significant joint ventures and the proportion of ownership interest held, for each individually material joint venture, and in total for other joint ventures, summarised financial information is required, including the venturer's interest in the amount of each of:
  - current assets
  - non-current assets
  - current liabilities
  - non-current liabilities
  - revenues, and
  - profit or loss.

  Other disclosures are also required, including information on restrictions on the ability to transfer funds between the venturer and a joint venturer as well as any unrecognised share of losses.

- *Paragraph 40*. A venturer is required to disclose separately the venturer's share of the profit or loss of joint ventures accounted for using the equity method and the carrying amount of those interests. These disclosures are required to be presented in total for all joint ventures.
- *Paragraph 41*. A venturer is required to recognise in other comprehensive income its share of changes recognised in other comprehensive income by joint ventures.

SUMMARY

One of the difficult tasks faced by accounting standard setters is the determination of how to classify and account for the various investments held by one entity in another entity. Some investments are classified as subsidiaries, others as associates and others as joint ventures. In all cases, the investor has some form of special relationship with the investee relating to the involvement by the investor in the formation of the strategic policies and decisions of the investee. With joint ventures, the specific relationship between the joint venturer and the joint venture is that of joint control, requiring the joint venturer to interact with the other venturers in order for the strategic decisions about the joint venture to be made.

There is still much debate within the international community about accounting for joint ventures. The classification and definition of joint ventures is still under debate, with different opinions about the inclusion of arrangements other than entities being included in the classification of joint ventures. Debate also occurs in relation to the appropriate accounting method to be applied, particularly between those who favour proportionate consolidation and those who prefer the equity accounting method. Mixed with this is debate about the effect of the *Framework* definitions on the choice of these methods.

The IASB has proposed changes to IAS 31. However, these proposed changes have not led to a decrease in the debate about the fundamental problems in accounting for joint ventures. Until the IASB determines the place of the equity method in accounting for both associates and joint ventures, disagreement about accounting for these arrangements will continue.

Discussion questions

1. Assume Entity A owns 50% of the voting shares of Entity X, and that Entities B and C each control 25%. Discuss whether Entity A should be treated as a joint venturer in accounting for its interest in Entity X.
2. Where a venturer has joint control over another entity, it also has significant influence over that entity. It is questionable then whether the same accounting methods should be applied to associates and joint ventures. In the UK-DP, the equity accounting method was recommended for both associates and joint ventures, with additional information being provided in the notes to the accounts. Discuss whether the accounting required for joint ventures should differ from that required for associates.
3. Discuss the key difference(s) between a joint venture operation and a joint venture entity. How do these differences affect the accounting for these joint ventures?
4. Distinguish between a subsidiary, an associate, a joint venture and a partnership. Why are different accounting methods required when accounting for each of these entities?
5. IAS 31 *Interests in Joint Ventures* uses joint control as a characteristic of a joint venture. Discuss what is meant by the term joint control.
6. > The FASB's definition [of an asset] is so complex, so abstract, so open-ended, so all-inclusive, and so vague that we cannot use it to solve problems . . . Defining an asset as a probable future economic benefit is to use a high-order abstraction. Under such an approach, if an enterprise owns a truck, the truck *per se* is not the asset. The asset is the present value of the cash flows that will come from using the truck . . . (Schuetze 1993, pp. 67–8)

   Discuss whether, under the *Framework* definition of an asset, proportions of items such as cash, accounts receivable or plant held by a joint venture are assets to a joint venturer.
7. Discuss the differences in disclosures for joint venture entities under IAS 31 and the expanded entity methods raised by Reklau and Dieter and Wyatt.
8. In accounting for jointly controlled entities under IAS 31, preparers have a choice between the use of proportionate consolidation and the equity method. Explain the differences

STAR RATING

★ BASIC

★★ MODERATE

★★★ DIFFICULT

between the two methods, and the arguments for and against the use of each of the methods.

Exercises

Exercise 28.1 ★

DETERMINATION OF A JOINT VENTURE

Yale Ltd and Massachusetts Ltd decide to jointly undertake the manufacture of an electric car. They form Stanford Ltd, which undertakes the manufacture of the car. Yale Ltd and Massachusetts Ltd provide the various parts for the manufacture of the car, which is assembled by Stanford Ltd.

Yale Ltd and Massachusetts Ltd each hold 50% of the voting rights in Stanford Ltd and receive 50% of the output or profits from Stanford Ltd. The constitution of Stanford Ltd requires that the operations of the company must be in accordance with a business plan prepared annually, and to which both Yale Ltd and Massachusetts Ltd both agree. Stanford Ltd has six directors, with three being appointed by Yale Ltd and three by Massachusetts Ltd.

Required
Evaluate whether this situation should be accounted for under IAS 31.

Exercise 28.2 ★

ACCOUNTING FOR AN ASSET USED BY A NUMBER OF COMPANIES

California Ltd and Pennsylvania Ltd are companies that have newly discovered oilwells in a Middle-Eastern country. There is some distance to the nearest port and, rather than build separate pipelines, they have agreed to jointly build a pipeline to the port and share the use of the pipeline for transporting oil. Columbia Ltd also has oilwells in the area and has agreed to use any excess capacity of the pipeline.

Required
Discuss how you would account for the pipeline.

Exercise 28.3 ★

ACCOUNTING FOR A JOINTLY USED ASSET

In an area famous for its wine, it has become popular for people to retire here, establish a vineyard and grow their own grapes. Because these people have only small vineyards, they do not have the equipment to press their own grapes to extract the juice. A number of these people agreed to acquire a wine press that could be used jointly by the group. Each person in the group would have a right to use the machine for a specified number of days of the year. For those days, each person could use the machine as they saw fit, including leasing it to a third party. However, no party can sell or modify the machine. Eventual disposal or replacement of the machine is a joint decision of the group.

Required
Discuss the accounting for the wine press.

Exercise 28.4 ★

ACCOUNTING FOR DIFFERENT JOINT ARRANGEMENTS

Discuss how you would account for each of the following three situations:

1. Duke Ltd and Chicago Ltd enter into a joint arrangement to mine iron ore. Each party contributes equally to the acquisition of the necessary equipment and working capital. They assume joint and several responsibility for any liabilities that arise. A manager is appointed to run the operation. The output of the mine is distributed equally to the two companies for disposal.
2. Duke Ltd and Chicago Ltd enter into an agreement to mine iron ore. They establish a company in which they hold an equal number of shares. Both shareholders contribute an equal amount of capital to establish the company, and a manager is appointed to run the mining company. When the iron ore is extracted, it is distributed to each of the shareholders in equal proportions.
3. Duke Ltd and Chicago Ltd enter into an agreement to mine iron ore. They establish a company in which they hold an equal number of shares. Both shareholders contribute an equal amount of capital to establish the company, and a manager is appointed to run the mining company. The mining company signs contracts with the two shareholders whereby each of the shareholders agrees to acquire the output of the mine at a fixed price. The shareholders share equally in any profits or losses of the mining company.

Exercise 28.5

JOINT VENTURERS SHARE OUTPUT

★ On 1 July 2009, Dartmouth Ltd entered into a joint venture agreement with Northwestern Ltd to form an unincorporated entity to produce a new type of widget. It was agreed that each party to the agreement would share the output equally. Dartmouth Ltd's initial contribution consisted of $2 000 000 cash and Northwestern Ltd contributed machinery that was recorded in the records of Northwestern Ltd at $1 900 000. During the first year of operation both parties contributed a further $3 000 000 each.

On 30 June 2010, the venture manager provided the following statements (in $000):

Costs Incurred for the year ended 30 June 2010	
Wages	$1 840
Supplies	2 800
Overheads	2 200
	6 840
Cost of inventory	4 840
Work in progress at 30 June 2010	$2 000

Receipts and Payments for year ended 30 June 2010		
Receipts:		$2 000
Original contributions		6 000
Additional contributions		8 000
Payments:		
Machinery (2/7/09)	$ 800	
Wages	1 800	
Supplies	3 000	
Overheads	2 100	
Operating expenses	200	7 900
Closing cash balance		$ 100

Assets and Liabilities at 30 June 2010	
Assets	
Cash	$ 100
Machinery	2 800
Supplies	400
Work in progress	2 000
Total assets	5 300
Liabilities	
Accrued wages	40
Creditors	300
Total liabilities	340
Net assets	$4 960

Each venturer depreciates machinery at 20% per annum on cost.

Required

1. Prepare the journal entries in the records of Dartmouth Ltd and Northwestern Ltd in relation to the joint venture, assuming the line-by-line method of accounting is used.
2. Prepare the journal entries in the records of Northwestern Ltd assuming that the joint venture, not the venturers, had depreciated the machinery and included that expense in the cost of inventory transferred.

Exercise 28.6

UNINCORPORATED JOINT VENTURE, LINE-BY-LINE METHOD

★ On 1 July 2008, Washington Ltd entered into a joint venture agreement with Cornell Ltd to establish an unincorporated joint venture to manufacture timber-felling equipment. It was agreed that the output of the venture would be shared: Washington Ltd 60% and Cornell Ltd 40%.

To commence the venture, contributions were as follows:

- Washington Ltd: cash of $1 100 000 and equipment having a carrying amount of $300 000 and a fair value of $400 000
- Cornell Ltd: cash of $600 000 and plant having a carrying amount of $450 000 and a fair value of $400 000.

Cornell Ltd revalued the plant it contributed to the joint venture to fair value prior to its transfer to the joint venture. Plant and equipment was depreciated (to the nearest month) in the joint venture's books at 20% p.a. on cost. During December 2008, an additional $1 000 000 cash was contributed by the venturers in the same proportion as their initial contributions.

The following information, in relation to the joint venture's operations for the year ended 30 June 2009, was provided by the venture manager:

(a) *Costs incurred for the year ended 30 June 2009*

Wages	$ 400 000
Raw materials	1 200 000
Overheads	650 000
Depreciation	205 000
	2 455 000
Less: Cost of inventory	2 005 000
Work in progress at 30 June 2009	$ 450 000

(b) *Receipts and payments for year ended 30 June 2009*

	Payments	Receipts
Contributions		$2 700 000
Plant (3 January 2009)	$ 450 000	
Wages	350 000	
Accounts payable	980 000	
Overhead costs	610 000	
Operating expenses	40 000	
	$2 430 000	$2 700 000

(c) *Assets and liabilities at 30 June 2009*

	Dr	Cr
Cash	$ 270 000	
Raw materials	100 000	
Work in progress	450 000	
Inventory	255 000	
Plant and equipment	1 250 000	
Accumulated depreciation – plant and equipment		$205 000
Accounts payable		320 000
Accrued expenses – wages and overheads		90 000

Required

Prepare the journal entries in the records of Washington Ltd in relation to the joint venture for the year ended 30 June 2009, assuming the use of the line-by-line method. (Round all amounts to the nearest dollar and show all relevant workings.)

Exercise 28.7 ★★

EQUITY METHOD, PROPORTIONATE CONSOLIDATION

On 1 January 2010, Johns Ltd entered into an arrangement to establish an incorporated joint venture with Hopkins Ltd. Both entities had had previous experience in the extractives industry, and they hoped their joint skills would enable them to find an economically viable ore deposit. Under the contractual arrangement, the two parties were to share equally in the profits/losses of any viable mining venture. On 1 January 2010, they both contributed $750 000 in cash, receiving shares in the new company Brown Ltd.

One year later they had undertaken an extensive exploration program. Although no major find had been discovered, there was sufficient promise in the evaluation of their current workings to continue prospecting. All outlays for exploration had been capitalised.

At 31 December 2010, the statement of financial position of Brown Ltd showed:

Cash	$ 365 000
Land	520 000
Capitalised exploration costs	430 000
Equipment	220 000
Provisions	(35 000)
Share capital	$1 500 000

The statement of financial position of Johns Ltd at 31 December 2010 was as follows:

Current assets	
Cash	$ 100 000
Inventory	400 000
Receivables	200 000
Total current assets	700 000
Non-current assets	
Investment in joint venture	750 000
Land	600 000
Plant and equipment	1 200 000
Accumulated depreciation	(440 000)
Deferred exploration costs	840 000
Intangibles	220 000
Total non-current assets	3 170 000
Total assets	3 870 000
Current liabilities	
Payables	120 000
Provisions	320 000
Total current liabilities	440 000
Non-current liabilities	1 400 000
Total liabilities	1 840 000
Net assets	$2 030 000
Equity	
Share capital	1 200 000
Retained earnings	830 000
Total equity	$2 030 000

Required

1. Prepare the statement of financial position of Johns Ltd assuming:
   (a) the use of the equity method in accounting for the interest in the joint venture
   (b) the use of the proportionate consolidation method.
2. Explain the differences in accounting if the venturers had formed an unincorporated joint venture to undertake their activities, agreeing to share the output of the mine.

Exercise 28.8 ★★

VENTURERS SHARE OUTPUT

Rice Ltd enters into an arrangement with another venturer, Emory Ltd, to establish an unincorporated joint venture to produce a drug that assists both hay fever sufferers and those with sinus problems. To produce the drug requires a combination of the technical and pharmaceutical knowledge of both companies. Each company will receive an equal share of the output of the drug, which they will retail through their own preferred outlets, potentially under different names. Rice Ltd agrees to manage the project for a fee of $100 000 per annum. Rice Ltd estimates that it will cost $80 000 to provide the service. The management fee is capitalised into the cost of inventory produced.

The venture commences on 1 January 2010, with each venturer providing $1 million cash. At the end of the first year, the statement of financial position of the joint venture showed:

Assets:	
Vehicles	$ 200 000
Accumulated depreciation	(50 000)
Equipment	820 000
Accumulated depreciation	(60 000)
Inventory	80 000
Work in progress	320 000
Materials	210 000
Total assets	1 520 000
Liabilities:	
Provisions	80 000
Payables	40 000
	120 000
Net assets	$1 400 000
Venturers' equity	
Initial contributions	2 000 000
Inventory delivered	(400 000)
General administration costs	(200 000)
Total equity	$1 400 000

Required

1. Prepare the journal entries in the records of Rice Ltd during 2010 assuming:
   (a) the use of the line-by-line method to account for the joint venture
   (b) the use of the one-line method.
2. What differences would occur if the management fee paid to Rice Ltd were treated as general administration costs?

Problems

Problem 28.1 ★★

USE OF LINE-BY-LINE METHOD

During 2009, a group of academics were undertaking a bonding exercise in the Portadown hills. While tracking through the hills, they came across a spring of pure sweet water. They formed a company called Notre Ltd and decided to establish the extent of their find. In the process they expended funds, obtained from teaching overseas students, on equipment and employing geologists and mining experts. The general conclusion was that the find was significant and a commercially profitable business selling mineral water was feasible. As they were academics, and had no practical experience in the real world of big business, they decided to establish a joint venture with Dame Ltd who would establish a factory to produce bottled water. The joint venture agreement was signed on 1 January 2010, with Notre Ltd and Dame Ltd having a 50% share in the unincorporated joint venture.

The initial contributions by the two venturers were as follows:

Notre Ltd:	
Capitalised expenses	$ 800 000
Equipment	800 000
Cash	2 400 000
Dame Ltd:	
Cash	$4 000 000

The capitalised expenses were recorded in the books of Notre Ltd at $320 000, while the equipment was recorded at a carrying amount of $640 000. In order to supply the cash, Notre Ltd borrowed $800 000 of its required contribution. It is expected that the reserves of water will be depleted within 10 years, and the equipment is expected to have a similar useful life.

On 1 June 2010, the joint venture was ready to start producing bottles of water. The joint venture's accounts at 30 June 2011 contained the following information:

Statement of Financial Position (extract)

	2010	2011
Work in progress		$ 200 000
Capitalised costs	$ 800 000	800 000
Plant and equipment	8 360 000	7 760 000
Cash	80 000	240 000
Accounts payable – plant	(240 000)	(800 000)
Accrued expenses – wages etc.	(160 000)	(200 000)

Cash Receipts and Payments (extract)

	2011	
	Payments	Receipts
Materials and supplies	$480 000	
Administration	160 000	
Wages	560 000	
Accounts payable – plant	960 000	
Contributions from joint venturers		$2 000 000

The output of the first year's operations was distributed equally to the joint venturers. Production in the first year was estimated to be 15% of the reserves. At 30 June 2011, Notre Ltd held 10% of its share of output in inventory, having sold the rest to its customers for $2 000 000. Expenses of the joint venture incurred up to 30 June 2011 were allocated to the venturers.

At 30 June 2011, the joint venture had ordered new plant and equipment of $300 000 which had not yet arrived. Because of some damage to the environment caused by the establishment of the pumping station to extract the water, there is a potential restoration cost to be incurred at closure of the joint venture. Whether this will be required will depend on the result of current legal inquiries.

Required

1. Prepare the journal entries in the records of Notre Ltd for the periods ending 30 June 2010 and 2011, assuming the use of the line-by-line method.
2. Prepare any notes that must be attached to the accounts of Notre Ltd for the year ending 30 June 2011 in relation to the joint venture, as required by IAS 31.

Problem 28.2 VENTURERS SHARE OUTPUT, LINE-BY-LINE METHOD

★★ On 1 July 2010, Vanderbilt Ltd entered into a joint venture agreement with Berkeley Ltd to manufacture stevedoring equipment. It was agreed that each party to the agreement would share the output equally.

To commence the venture, contributions were as follows:

- Vanderbilt Ltd: cash of $2 000 000 and equipment having a $400 000 carrying amount and a fair value of $600 000
- Berkeley Ltd: cash of $1 800 000 and plant having a carrying amount of $900 000 and a fair value of $800 000.

Berkeley Ltd revalued the plant it contributed to the joint venture prior to its transfer to the joint venture.

Plant and equipment is depreciated (to the nearest month) in the joint venture's books at 20% per annum on cost.

During December 2010, both parties contributed an additional $1 500 000 cash.

The following information, in relation to the joint venture's operations for the year ended 30 June 2011, was provided by the venture manager:

(a) *Costs incurred for the year ended 30 June 2011*

Wages	$1 200 000
Raw materials	2 150 000
Overheads	1 860 000
Depreciation	470 000
	5 680 000
Less: Cost of inventory	2 580 000
Work in progress at 30 June 2011	$3 100 000

(b) *Receipts and payments for the year ended 30 June 2011*

	Payments	Receipts
Contributions		$6 800 000
Plant (10 July 2010)	$ 950 000	
Wages	1 150 000	
Accounts payable	1 980 000	
Overhead costs	1 810 000	
Operating expenses	440 000	
	$6 330 000	$6 800 000

(c) *Assets and liabilities as at 30 June 2011*

	Dr	Cr
Cash	$ 470 000	
Raw materials	360 000	
Work in progress	3 100 000	
Inventory	580 000	
Plant and equipment	2 350 000	
Accumulated depreciation — plant and equipment		$470 000
Accounts payable		530 000
Accrued expenses		100 000

Required

Prepare the journal entries in the records of Vanderbilt Ltd and Berkeley Ltd in relation to the joint venture for the year ended 30 June 2011, assuming the use of the line-by-line method.

Problem 28.3 ★★★

UNINCORPORATED JOINT VENTURE MANAGED BY ONE OF THE VENTURERS

During 2008, discussions took place between Carnegie Ltd, a company concerned with the design of specialised tools and machines, and two companies, Mellon Ltd and Georgetown Ltd, which could potentially assist in the manufacture of a new tool. The new tool is called SmartTool and is to be used in the making of high grade mining instruments. On 1 June 2009, the three companies agreed to form an unincorporated joint venture to achieve this purpose. It was agreed that the relative interests in the joint venture would be:

Carnegie Ltd	50%
Mellon Ltd	25%
Georgetown Ltd	25%

It was further agreed that Georgetown Ltd would undertake a management role in relation to the new venture, being responsible for operating decisions and for record keeping. Georgetown Ltd would be paid a management fee by the joint venture of $20 000. In establishing the joint venture, the various parties agreed to provide the following assets as their initial contribution:

- Carnegie Ltd was to provide the patent to SmartTool, which was being recorded by Carnegie Ltd at a capitalised development cost of $1 400 000. The venturers agreed that this asset had a fair value of $2 000 000, with an expected useful life of ten years.
- Mellon Ltd was to provide cash of $1 000 000.
- Georgetown Ltd was to provide the basic plant and equipment to manufacture the new tool. The plant and equipment was recorded in the books of Georgetown Ltd at $600 000, but the venturers agreed that it had a fair value of $1 000 000. The plant and equipment was estimated to have a further useful life of five years.

During the first period of the joint venture's operation, the output of the joint venture was distributed to each of the venturers in proportion to their agreed interests. By 30 June 2010, Georgetown Ltd had sold 80% of the output received from the joint venture for $300 000. The joint venture had not paid the management fee to Georgetown Ltd by 30 June 2010.

Information from the financial statements of the joint venture as at 30 June 2010 is as follows:

Assets	
Cash	$ 40 000
Plant and equipment	1 080 000
Accumulated depreciation	(208 000)
Patent	2 000 000
Accumulated depreciation	(200 000)
Office equipment	88 000
Accumulated depreciation	(8 800)
Work in progress	40 000
Liabilities	
Creditors — for materials	$ 136 000
Accruals — salaries etc, including the management fee	112 000
Cash payments	
Salaries	$ 220 000
Materials	488 000
Operating expenses	84 000

Required

1. Prepare the journal entries in the records of Carnegie Ltd and Mellon Ltd at the commencement of the joint venture, assuming the use of the line-by-line method.
2. Prepare the journal entries in the records of Georgetown Ltd for the financial year ending 30 June 2010.

Problem 28.4 ★★★

VENTURERS SHARE OUTPUT, CONTRIBUTIONS INCLUDE TANGIBLE ASSETS AND THE PROVISION OF SERVICES

Virginia Ltd, a development corporation associated with Los University, has developed and patented a new process to produce synthetic anti-ageing hormones. Due to a lack of resources, Virginia Ltd entered into a 5-year joint venture with Michigan Ltd and Angeles Ltd to produce the hormone. The venturers are to share the output equally and will contribute to the unincorporated joint venture as follows:

Virginia Ltd

Cash $400 000 and Patent $360 000. The patent is currently recorded in the records of Virginia Ltd at $240 000.

Michigan Ltd

Cash $460 000 and Services of Scientific Staff $300 000. Michigan Ltd estimates that the cost of providing the services to the joint venture will be $225 000. Additional support staff will be employed and paid by the venture.

Angeles Ltd

Cash $160 000 and a laboratory facility which has a fair value of $1 900 000 (carrying amount $1 800 000). The laboratory facility is to be returned by the joint venture at the end of the project when its expected carrying value will be $1 300 000. In addition, Michigan Ltd is to provide the joint venture with autoclaving services as a part of the normal course of business. These services are charged out at cost plus 20%.

The joint venture commenced on 1 July 2010. The joint venture's accounts at 30 June 2011 were as follows:

Cash Receipts and Payments

	Payments	Receipts
Contributions received		$1 020 000
Materials	$280 000	
Equipment**	360 000	
Administrative expenses	84 000	
Support staff wages	120 000	
Autoclaving services	36 000	

** Depreciation is to be charged by the venture at 20% p.a.; the equipment has on average been in use for 6 months during the year ended 30 June 2011.

Statement of Financial Position (extract)

Assets		
Cash		$ 140 000
Equipment	$360 000	
Accumulated depreciation	(36 000)	324 000
Patent	360 000	
Accumulated amortisation	(72 000)	288 000
Laboratory facility	600 000	
Accumulated depreciation	(120 000)	480 000
Materials inventory		30 000
Work in progress		37 000
Services receivable		240 000
		1 539 000
Liabilities		
Accounts payable (materials)		66 000
Account payable (autoclaving)		60 000
Accrued wages		30 000
		156 000
Net assets		$1 383 000

Required

1. Prepare the journal entries in the records of all venturers at the commencement of the joint venture, assuming the use of the line-by-line method.
2. Prepare the journal entries in the records of Michigan Ltd for the year ended 30 June 2011.
3. Prepare the journal entries in the records of Angeles Ltd for the year ended 30 June 2011.

Problem 28.5 JOINT VENTURERS, CONTRIBUTIONS INCLUDE NON-CURRENT ASSETS AND SERVICES

★★★

Southern Ltd has discovered a new way of providing the extra fizz to soft drinks that is necessary to capture the next generation of soft-drink consumers. To exploit this new invention, it enters into a joint agreement with two other soft-drink manufacturers, Tufts Ltd and California Ltd. The joint venture agreement was signed on 1 July 2010. The agreement contains the following specifications:

- Southern Ltd is to have a 50% interest in the joint venture, with Southern Ltd supplying the patent for the secret extra fizz to the joint venture for the next 10 years, at which point the patent will be returned to Southern Ltd. At 1 July 2010, the fair value of the patent is considered to be at $15 million. Southern Ltd has capitalised outlays during the development of the new formula for fizz and has capitalised costs of $12 million at 1 July 2010. At the end of the 10 years, it is estimated that the fair value of the patent will be $5 million. The patent is depreciated in the books of each of the venturers, and not included in the cost of inventory.
- Tufts Ltd is to have a 25% interest in the joint venture, supplying $4 million cash as well as management services to the joint venture. The services are worth $1 million and will be supplied evenly over the first 5 years of the joint venture. Tufts Ltd believes that supplying the services will cost it $750 000.
- California Ltd is to have a 25% interest in the joint venture. California Ltd is to supply plant and equipment to the joint venture at a fair value of $5 million. The plant and equipment is currently recorded in the books of California Ltd at a carrying amount of $4 million (related accumulated depreciation is $1 million). The plant and equipment has an expected remaining useful life of 5 years. California Ltd is to play a major role in the management of the joint venture, and will be paid a management fee of $200 000 per annum. The expected cost to California Ltd of supplying these services is $170 000. The fee was paid on 25 June 2011.

Information in relation to the operations of the joint venture at the end of the first year, 30 June 2011, is as follows (in $000):

Statement of Financial Position

Cash	$ 200	Venturers' equity	$14 600
Work in progress	200	Trade creditors	600
Plant and equipment	6 000	Accrued expenses	800
Accumulated depreciation	(1 200)		
Services receivable	800		
Patent	10 000		
	$16 000		$16 000

Statement of Cash Flows

Cash balance at 1/7/10		$4000
Less: Wages and salaries	$ 860	
Supplies and materials	1520	
Plant and equipment	1000	
Administration expenses	420	3800
Cash balance at 30/6/11		$ 200

Cost of Production

Wages and salaries	$1560
Supplies and materials	2120
Administration expenses	520
Services	200
Depreciation — plant and equipment	1200
	5600
Work in progress at 30 June 2011	200
Cost of inventory produced	$5400

Required
Prepare the journal entries in the records of each of the venturers for the year ending 30 June 2011, assuming the use of the line-by-line method.

Problem 28.6

PROPORTIONATE CONSOLIDATION, EQUITY METHOD, EXPANDED EQUITY METHOD

★★★ Chopel Ltd and Hill Ltd both operate in the pharmaceutical business. Both companies have been privately working on a cure for the Ross River virus, a disease carried by mosquitoes. Because of a lack of success, and after discussions between the scientists involved, the two companies agreed to establish a joint venture company, Brandeis Ltd, for the purpose of conducting joint research.

The company was established on 1 January 2010 with share capital of $800 000, with both parties contributing equally to the joint venture entity. As part of its $400 000 contribution, Chopel Ltd supplied a research laboratory to the joint venture. This laboratory was recorded by Chopel Ltd at $200 000, but was considered to have a fair value of $250 000. The laboratory was considered to have a 10-year life, and depreciated on a straight-line basis. The joint venture was to generate cash inflows by the sale of by-product drugs produced during the research process.

At 31 December 2010, the project was proceeding well. The venturers had agreed in November 2010 that Brandeis Ltd should order $400 000 worth of new computerised equipment to be delivered early in 2011. It was also agreed that the joint venture should borrow a further $500 000 in March 2011, as the laboratory facilities needed some renovations. As with the current long-term loan, both venturers agreed to act as guarantors for that loan. At 31 December 2010, the consolidated financial statements of Chopel Ltd — excluding any adjustments for the joint venture — and the financial statements of Brandeis Ltd showed the following information (in $000):

	Chapel Ltd (Group)	Brandeis Ltd
Revenues:		
Sales of products	$2600	$ 860
Dividends	30	
	2630	
Expenses:		
Wages	840	440
Depreciation – laboratories	65	25
Depreciation – equipment	95	60
Supplies	620	240
Other	120	15
	1740	780
Profit before tax	890	80
Income tax expense	210	20
Profit	680	60
Retained earnings at 1 January 2010	1450	
	2130	
Dividend paid	80	20
Retained earnings at 31 December 2010	$2050	$ 40
Current assets		
Supplies	$ 550	$ 40
Cash	80	50
Receivables	320	60
Total current assets	950	150
Non-current assets		
Laboratories	3850	250
Accumulated depreciation	(860)	(25)
Equipment	1370	420

(continued)

	Chapel Ltd (Group)	Brandeis Ltd
Accumulated depreciation	(770)	(60)
Capitalised development	2400	455
Investment in joint venture — Brandeis Ltd	400	—
Total non-current assets	5390	1030
Total assets	6340	1180
Current liabilities		
Payables	120	60
Provisions	170	80
Total current liabilities	290	140
Non-current liabilities		
Loan	1000	200
Total liabilities	1290	340
Net assets	$5050	$ 840
Equity		
Share capital	$3000	$ 800
Retained earnings	2050	40
Total equity	$5050	$ 840

Required

1. Prepare the consolidated financial statements of Chapel Ltd using:
   (a) the proportionate consolidation method
   (b) the equity method
   (c) the expanded equity method.
2. Prepare the note disclosures provided by IAS 31 in relation to the joint venture entity.

Problem 28.7 ★★★

VENTURERS SHARE OUTPUT, LINE-BY-LINE METHOD

After prospecting unsuccessfully for a number of years for gold, in November 2010 William Ltd finally found an economically viable deposit. Realising that it did not have sufficient expertise to operate a gold mine successfully, William Ltd formed an unincorporated joint venture with Mary Ltd, agreeing to share the output of the mine equally. It was agreed that the two venturers would initially contribute the following assets:

William Ltd:	
Capitalised exploration costs, including permits licences, and mining rights, currently recorded by William Ltd at $200 000	$ 800 000
Cash	700 000
Mary Ltd:	
Cash	1 500 000

The joint venture commenced on 1 January 2011. By 31 December 2011, the mine had been operating successfully. It was reliably estimated at the commencement of the project that the mine had expected reserves of 100 000 tons.

In the first year following commencement, 5000 tons of gold were extracted, while in 2012, 10 000 tons were extracted. This output was distributed to the venturers equally.

All costs except general administration costs were capitalised into the cost of the output, with depreciation of equipment and capitalised exploration costs being written off in proportion to the depletion of the reserves. General administration expenses were allocated to the venturers equally.

The financial report of the joint venture over the first 2 years of operation showed the following information:

Cash Receipts and Payments		
	2011	**2012**
Balance at 1 January	—	$ 300 000
Contributions from venturers	$2 200 000	1 200 000
	2 200 000	1 500 000
Plant and equipment	800 000	190 000
Wages	600 000	660 000
Materials	200 000	240 000
General administration	300 000	300 000
	1 900 000	1 390 000
Balance at 31 December	$ 300 000	$ 110 000

Statement of Financial Position		
	2011	**2012**
Capitalised exploration costs	$ 760 000	$ 680 000
Plant and equipment	800 000	990 000
Accumulated depreciation	(40 000)	(140 000)
Cash	300 000	110 000
Materials	50 000	40 000
	1 870 000	1 680 000
Accrued wages	10 000	20 000
Accounts payable (materials)	20 000	30 000
	30 000	50 000
Net assets	$1 840 000	$ 1 630 000
Venturers' equity:		
Contributions as at 1 January	3 000 000	1 840 000
Additional contributions		1 200 000
	3 000 000	3 040 000
Less: Output distributed	860 000	1 110 000
Allocation: general administration	300 000	300 000
	1 160 000	1 410 000
Balance at 31 December	$1 840 000	$ 1 630 000

Required

Prepare the journal entries in the records of William Ltd using the line-by-line method to record its interest in the joint venture for the years ending 31 December 2011 and 2012.

References

Accounting Standards Board 1994, 'Associates and joint ventures', Discussion Paper, Accounting Standards Board, London.

BHP Billiton 2008, *Annual report 2008, BHP Billiton*, www.bhpbilliton.com.

Dieter, R & Wyatt, AR 1978, 'The expanded equity method — an alternative in accounting for investments in joint ventures', *Journal of Accountancy*, June, pp. 89–94.

FASB 1985, *Statement of Financial Accounting Concepts No. 6*, Financial Accounting Standards Board, December, Norwalk (Connecticut), USA, www.fasb.org.

G4+1 2000, 'Leases: Implementation of a new approach', G4+1 Position Paper, published separately by the Accounting Standards Board in Australia, Canada, New Zealand, United Kingdom, United States and by the International Accounting Standards Committee.

—1999, 'Reporting interests in joint ventures and similar arrangements', 64+1 Discussion Paper, published Separately by the Accounting Standards branch in Australia, Canada, New Zealand, United Kingdom, United States and by the International Standards Committee.

IASB 2003, *IASB Update*, International Accounting Standards Committee Foundation, November, London, www.iasb.org.

Milburn, JA & Chant, PD 1999, 'Reporting interests in joint ventures and similar arrangements', published separately by the Accounting Standards Board in Australia, Canada, New Zealand, United Kingdom, United States and by the International Accounting Standards Committee.

Reklau, DL 1997, 'Accounting for investments in joint ventures — a re-examination', *Journal of Accountancy*, September, pp. 96–103.

Scheutze, WP 1993, 'What is an asset?', *Accounting Horizons*, September, pp. 66–70.

Wallman, SMH 1996, 'The future of accounting and financial reporting, Part II: the colorized approach', *Accounting Horizons*, June, pp. 138–48.

Willett, P 1995, 'Joint enterprise', *CA Magazine*, June/July, pp. 59–62.

Appendix

Fact sheets

FACT SHEET IFRS 2 *Share-based Payment*

OBJECTIVE

The objective of this standard is to specify the financial reporting by an entity when it undertakes a *share-based payment transaction*. In particular, it requires an entity to reflect in its is profit and loss and financial position the effects of share-based transactions, including expenses associated with transactions in which share options are granted to employees (para. 1).

Examples of share-based transactions include:

- purchases of goods and services with payment made in shares or options
- employees receiving shares or options as a bonus
- senior management or directors receiving cash bonuses based on share price.

KEY REPORTING REQUIREMENTS

1. For equity-settled share-based payment transactions (paras. 10–29), equity is exchanged for goods or services.
   - Where the fair value of the goods or services is known, equity is increased by a corresponding amount.
   - Where the fair value of the goods or services cannot be measured reliability, the value of the good and service is measured based on the fair value of the equity instrument provided.
   - A grant of equity instruments may be conditional (vested) on certain conditions, in which case fair value is measured by adjusting the number of equity instruments included in the transaction.
2. For cash-settled share-based payment transactions (paras. 30–33), a liability is recognised as there is a future obligation to provide cash.
   - The value of the goods or services acquired should be measured at the fair value of the liability incurred and remeasured each reporting period until settled.
3. For share-based payment transactions with cash alternatives (paras. 33–43), that is, payments for goods and services that are made with either equity or cash:
   - If the option is at the choice of the counterparty:
     - both a liability and an equity component are recognised
     - for transactions with non-employees where the fair value of the goods and services is measured directly, an equity component equal to the difference between the fair value of the goods and services provided and the fair value of the debt component is recognised
     - for other transactions, recognition is based on the terms and conditions of the agreement and settled as per the equity or cash settled transactions accordingly.
   - If the option is at the choice of the entity, a liability is recognised if the entity determines it has a present obligation to settle in cash, otherwise equity is recognised.
4. Entities are required to disclose information to allow users to understand the nature and extent of share-based payment arrangements that existed during the period, the value of these arrangements and the effect on profit and loss (paras. 44–52).
5. For the purposes of this standard, *fair value* is defined as the amount for which an asset could be exchanged, a liability could be settled, or an *equity instrument granted* could be exchanged between knowledgeable, willing parties in an arm's length transaction.

CHANGES ON THE HORIZON

The standard is expected to be revised in 2009 to clarify group-based transactions involving cash payments.

FACT SHEET IFRS 3 *Business Combinations*

OBJECTIVE

The objective of this standard is to account for the acquisition of one or more businesses by the reporting entity. The reporting of this is through the acquisition method.

KEY DEFINITIONS

A *business* is an integrated set of activities and assets that is capable of being conducted and managed for the purpose of providing a return directly to investors or other owners, members or participants.

KEY REPORTING REQUIREMENTS

1. Identification of the acquirer and the acquisition date (i.e. the date at which the controller gains control) (paras. 6–10).
2. Recognition at acquisition date as specified in paragraphs 11–31. At this date, all identifiable assets, liabilities and non-controlling interests must be:
   - separately recognised from goodwill
   - recognised in line with appropriate accounting standards and normal policies and practices
   - recognised at fair value except when another standard applies.
3. Recognition of goodwill as the aggregate of (paras. 32–44):
   - the acquisition-date fair value of the consideration transferred
   - the amount of any non-controlling interest
   - in a business combination achieved in stages, the acquisition-date fair value of the acquirer's previously held equity interest in the acquiree, and
   - the net of the acquisition-date amounts of the identifiable assets acquired and the liabilities assumed.

   If the difference above is negative, the resulting gain is recognised as a bargain purchase in profit or loss.
4. Measurement period: when provisional estimates are used at the time of acquisition or the information available is incomplete, the acquirer should retrospectively adjust any provisional amounts and add any assets or liabilities it becomes aware of for a period of 12 months (paras. 45–50).
5. The business combination only consists of assets and liabilities acquired as a part of the business combination, and assets given up in payment using the acquisition method. Any other transactions between the two parties involved should be recorded separately according to the appropriate standard (paras. 51–53).
6. Any assets or liabilities should be measured with reference to the accounting standard applying to those items post-acquisition date (paras. 54–58).
7. The acquirer shall disclose in the financial statements:
   - any business combination that occurred during the period
   - any business combination that occurred after the end of the period but before statements are released
   - enough information for users to evaluate the effects of any business combination.

CHANGES ON THE HORIZON

No changes on the horizon

FACT SHEET IFRS 6 *Exploration for and Evaluation of Mineral Resources*

OBJECTIVE

The objective of this standard is to account for the exploration for and evaluation of mineral resources, and their ongoing assessment and disclosure.

The standard applies to such things as:

- acquisition of exploration rights
- topographical and geological studies
- exploratory drilling
- activities relating to the evaluation of technical and commercial feasibility.

KEY REPORTING REQUIREMENTS

1. The standard enables a reporting entity to develop accounting policies without considering paragraphs 11 and 12 of IAS 8.
2. Recognition and measurement is at cost (para. 8).
3. Post recognition, entities can choose to apply either the revaluation model (as per IAS 16) or the cost model (para. 12).
4. A change in accounting policies in regards to the exploration and evaluation of mineral resources is allowed in accordance with IAS 8 (paras. 13 and 14).
5. Exploration and evaluation assets should be classed as either tangible (e.g. oil rigs, site infrastructure) or intangible (e.g. rights, licences) in accordance with the nature of such assets and the classification should be applied consistently (paras. 15–17).
6. If using the cost model, impairment assessment is applied as per IAS 36, except that a CGU can be no larger than an operating segment of the entity as per IFRS 8 (paras. 18–22).
7. Disclosure is required of all information that identifies and explains the amounts recognised in the financial statements resulting from applying IFRS 6, including:
   - the accounting policies for recognition of exploration and evaluation expenses and assets
   - the amounts of each asset, liability, income and expense resulting from the exploration and evaluation of mineral resources and the associated operating and investing cash flows
   - the recoverability of each area of interest either through use or sale.

   An entity must also treat exploration and evaluation assets as a separate class of assets.

CHANGES ON THE HORIZON

The IASB is currently working on a research project looking at the upstream usage of mineral resources (i.e. post exploration) and the adoption of fair value.

FACT SHEET IFRS 7 *Financial Instruments: Disclosures* , IAS 32 *Financial Instruments: Presentation*, IAS 39 *Financial Instruments: Recognition and Measurement*

OBJECTIVE

The objective of these three standards is to prescribe the accounting treatment for financial instruments; the three standards should be read and used in conjunction with each other.

IFRS 7 covers the disclose aspects of accounting for financial instruments.

IAS 32 covers how financial instruments are presented in the financial statements.

IAS 39 covers how financial instruments are recognised and measured.

KEY DEFINITIONS

A *financial instrument* is a contract that gives rise to a financial asset of one entity and a financial liability or equity instrument of another entity.

A *financial asset* is any asset that is:

1. cash
2. an equity instrument of another entity
3. a contractual right:
   - to receive cash or another financial asset from another entity, or
   - to exchange financial assets or financial liabilities with another entity under conditions that are potentially favourable to the entity
4. a contract that will or may be settled in the entity's own equity instruments and is:
   - a non-derivative for which the entity is or may be obliged to receive a variable number of the entity's own equity instruments, or
   - a derivative that will or may be settled other than by the exchange of a fixed amount of cash or another financial asset for a fixed number of the entity's own equity instruments. For this purpose the entity's own equity instruments do not include instruments that are themselves contracts for the future receipt or delivery of the entity's own equity instruments.

A *financial liability* is any liability that is:

1. a contractual obligation:
   - to deliver cash or another financial asset to another entity, or
   - to exchange financial assets or financial liabilities with another entity under conditions that are potentially unfavourable to the entity
2. a contract that will or may be settled in the entity's own equity instruments.

A *derivative* is a financial instrument:

1. whose value changes in response to the change in an underlying variable such as an interest rate, commodity or security price or index
2. that requires no initial investment, or one that is smaller than would be required for a contract with similar response to changes in market factors
3. that is settled at a future date.

An *equity instrument* is any contract that evidences a residual interest in the assets of an entity after deducting all of its liabilities.

KEY REPORTING REQUIREMENTS: IAS 39

The main requirements for the recognition and measurement of financial instruments are:

1. An entity shall classify its financial instruments as being:
   - financial assets at fair value through profit or loss, either as
     - financial instruments held for trading
     - financial instruments designated at fair value through profit or loss
   - held-to-maturity investments

- loans and receivables, or
- available-for-sale financial assets.

2. Recognition of a financial asset or financial liability is at the point the entity becomes a party to the contractual provisions of the instrument.
3. On initial recognition, a financial asset or financial liability recognised at fair value through profit or loss is measured at fair value. Other financial instruments are measured at fair value plus transaction costs that are directly attributable to the acquisition or issue of the financial asset or financial liability.
4. After initial recognition:
   - Financial assets or financial liabilities recognised at fair value through profit or loss are measured at fair value without adjustment and any change in fair value is recognised in profit and loss
   - Held-to-maturity investments as well as loans and receivables are measured at amortised cost using the effective interest method, with interest and impairment losses being recognised in profit or loss.
   - Available-for-sale financial assets are measured at fair value without adjustment. Any change in fair value is recognised directly in equity until the financial asset is sold, at which point the cumulative gain or loss previously recognised in equity is recognised in profit or loss.
   - Investments in equity instruments that do not have a quoted market price in an active market and whose fair value cannot be reliably measured, and derivatives linked to and settled by delivery of such equity instruments, are measured at cost.
   - Financial assets and financial liabilities designated as hedged items are subject to measurement under the hedge accounting requirements.
   - Financial liabilities are measured at amortised cost using the effective interest method except for those classified as financial liabilities at fair value through profit or loss.
5. Hedging — an item that is hedged can be:
   - a single recognised asset or liability, firm commitment, highly probable transaction, or a net investment in a foreign operation
   - a group of assets, liabilities, firm commitments, highly probable forecast transactions, or net investments in foreign operations with similar risk characteristics
   - a held-to-maturity investment for foreign currency or credit risk (but not for interest risk or prepayment risk)
   - a portion of the cash flows or fair value of a financial asset or financial liability
   - a non-financial item for foreign currency risk only or the risk of changes in fair value of the entire item
   - in a portfolio hedge of interest rate risk (marco hedge) only, a portion of the portfolio of financial assets or financial liabilities that share the risk being hedged.
6. Hedge accounting — to qualify for hedge accounting, the following conditions must be met:
   - Formally designated and documented, including the entity's risk management objective and strategy for undertaking the hedge, identification of the hedging instrument, the hedged item, the nature of the risk being hedged, and how the entity will assess the hedging instrument's effectiveness.
   - Expected to be highly effective in achieving offsetting changes in fair value or cash flows attributable to the hedged risk as designated and documented, and effectiveness can be reliably measured.
7. There are three types of hedging relationships:
   A. Fair value hedge — a hedge of the exposure to changes in fair value of a recognised asset or liability or an unrecognised firm commitment, or an identified portion thereof that is attributable to a particular risk and could affect profit or loss. The gain or loss from remeasuring the hedging instrument at fair value or change in hedge risk is recognised in profit or loss.
   B. Cash flow hedge — a hedge of the exposure to variability in cash flows related to the hedged item that is attributable to a particular risk associated with a recognised asset or liability or a highly probable forecast transaction and that could affect profit or loss.
   C. Hedge of a net investment in a foreign operation — the accounting treatment for this type of hedge is similar to that described for a cash flow hedge.

KEY REPORTING REQUIREMENTS: IAS 32

1. The focus of IAS 32 is when a financial instrument should be classified as either a financial liability or an equity instrument based on using substance over form at the time of recognition and does not change.

2. A financial instrument is an equity instrument only if (a) the instrument includes no contractual obligation to deliver cash or another financial asset to another entity, and (b) if the instrument will or may be settled in the issuer's own equity instruments, it is either:
   - a non-derivative that includes no contractual obligation for the issuer to deliver a variable number of its own equity instruments, or
   - a derivative that will be settled only by the issuer exchanging a fixed amount of cash or another financial asset for a fixed number of its own equity instruments.

KEY REPORTING REQUIREMENTS: IFRS 7

1. Disclosures for financial instruments fall into one of two categories:
   A. Information about the significance of financial instruments.
   B. Information about the nature and extent of risks arising from financial instruments.
2. Information about the significance of financial instruments:
   - Statement of financial position disclosure requirements:
     - each category of financial instrument as described in IAS 39 separately disclosed either in the statement or in the notes
     - when measured at fair value through the profit and loss, disclosure about credit risk, market risk and change in fair value
     - disclosure about recognition and derecognition of financial instruments
     - information regarding items pledged as, or held for, collateral
     - reconciliation for bad debts
     - financial instruments with multiple derivatives
     - breaches of loan arrangements.
   - Statement of comprehensive income disclosure requirements:
     - changes in fair value of each category of financial instruments should be recognised either in the statement or in the notes, unless recognised directly in equity (see IAS 39)
     - interest income or expense of items not measured at fair value
     - impairment of financial instruments.
   - General disclosure requirements:
     - accounting policies re financial instruments
     - details regarding hedges (type, description, gains/losses, effectiveness)
     - information about fair value, including comparable amounts and how fair value was determined or why it cannot be determined.
3. Information about the nature and extent of risks arising from financial instruments:
   - Qualitative:
     - risks for each type
     - how each risk is managed
     - changes from prior periods.
   - Quantitative:
     - summary data about risk exposure
     - disclosures about credit, market and liquidity risk
     - risk concentration.
   - Credit risk:
     - maximum exposure taking into account any collateral and description of the collateral
     - information and carrying amount of financial instruments passed due or impaired.
   - Liquidity risk:
     - a maturity analysis of financial instruments
     - a description of how the entity handles liquidity risk.

- Market risk:
  - a sensitivity analysis for each market exposed to
  - if an entity prepares a sensitivity analysis, such as value-at-risk, that reflects interdependencies between risk variables (e.g. interest rates and exchange rates) and uses it to manage financial risks, it may use that sensitivity analysis with additional disclosures on underlying assumptions and reasons for doing so.

CHANGES ON THE HORIZON

The IASB/FASB is seeking to further clarify financial instruments with the characteristics of equity, with an exposure draft due for release in 2009, and a final standard in 2011.

FACT SHEET IFRS 8 *Operating Segments*

OBJECTIVE

The objective of this standard is enable users of financial statements to access how different segments of the reporting entity are performing. This is done through an 'eye of management approach' by having the reporting entity provide both financial and descriptive information.

KEY REPORTING REQUIREMENTS

1. An *operating segment* is a component of an entity:
   - that engages in business activities from which it may earn revenues and incur expenses (including revenues and expenses relating to transactions with other components of the same entity)
   - whose operating results are regularly reviewed by the entity's chief operating decision maker to make decisions about resources to be allocated to the segment and to assess its performance
   - for which discrete financial information is available.
2. The chief operating decision maker is not a title but rather a function that allocates resources and assesses performance of different sections of the entity.
3. Not every part of a business is classified as an operating segment (such as the corporate headquarters) as certain parts may partake in activities only relating to the entity and not earn revenue.
4. Different segments may be aggregated together when they have similar economic characteristics, including:
   - the nature of the products and services
   - the nature of the production processes
   - the type or class of customer for products and services, the methods used to distribute products or provide services
   - if applicable, the nature of the regulatory environment, for example, banking, insurance or public utilities.
5. To be a reporting segment, the section in question must meet the following criteria:
   A. its reported revenue, from both external customers and inter-segment sales or transfers, is 10% or more of the combined revenue, internal and external, of all operating segments, or
   B. the absolute measure of its reported profit or loss is 10% or more of the greater, in absolute amount, of (a) the combined reported profit of all operating segments that did not report a loss, and (b) the combined reported loss of all operating segments that reported a loss, or
   C. its assets are 10% or more of the combined assets of all operating segments.
6. Entities need to make the following disclosures in relation to reporting segments:
   - General information about how the entity identified each segment and the types of products and services each provides.
   - Information about each segment's profit or loss, including certain specified revenues and expenses, assets and liabilities and the basis of measurement.
   - Reconciliations of the totals of segment revenues, reported segment profit or loss, segment assets, segment liabilities and other material items to corresponding items in the entity's financial statements.
   - Some entity-wide disclosures are required even when not part of a reportable segment, including information about each product and service.
   - Disclosures of revenues/assets by individual foreign country (if material), irrespective of the identification of operating segments.
   - Information about transactions with major customers (if material).
   - Segment information at interim reporting dates.

CHANGES ON THE HORIZON

No changes on the horizon.

FACT SHEET IAS 1 *Presentation of Financial Statements*

OBJECTIVE

The objective of this standard is to prescribe the basis for the presentation of general purpose financial statements to ensure comparability both with the entity's financial statements of previous periods and with the financial statements of other entities.

KEY REPORTING REQUIREMENTS

1. The objective of financial statements is to provide information about the financial position, financial performance and cash flows of an entity that is useful to a wide range of users in making economic decisions. To meet that objective, financial statements provide information about an entity's (para. 9):
   - assets
   - liabilities
   - equity
   - income and expenses, including gains and losses
   - other changes in equity
   - cash flows.

   That information, along with other information in the notes, assists users of financial statements in predicting the entity's future cash flows and, in particular, their timing and certainty.
2. A complete set of financial statements comprises (para. 10):
   - a statement of financial position as at the end of the period
   - a statement of comprehensive income for the period
   - a statement of changes in equity for the period
   - a statement of cash flows for the period
   - notes, comprising a summary of significant accounting policies and other explanatory information, and
   - a statement of financial position as at the beginning of the earliest comparative period when an entity applies an accounting policy retrospectively or makes a retrospective restatement of items in its financial statements, or when it reclassifies items in its financial statements.

   An entity may use titles for the statements other than those used in this standard.
3. General features:
   - Fair presentation and compliance with IFRSs (paras. 15–24):
     - Information should be presented fairly and in accordance with the definitions and recognition criteria of the elements of financial statements.
     - The application of IFRSs with additional disclosure as needed is assumed to achieve the fair presentation above.
     - In the rare case that compliance is not achieved, management can state which standard the statements do not comply with and why not, and provide adjustments to show the differences as needed.
   - Management should assess if the entity is a going concern and prepare statements accordingly (paras. 25–26).
   - Statements should be prepared using accrual accounting (paras. 27–28).
   - Similar classes of items should be reported separately if material; dissimilar items can only be aggregated when each individual item is immaterial (paras. 29–31).
   - Assets or liabilities should not be offset unless permitted by another standard (paras. 32–35).
   - An entity should report annually. If not, it should state why not and that the amounts presented may not be entirely comparable (paras. 36–37).
   - An entity should provide comparative information (normally the previous year's financial statements) (paras. 38–44).
   - Statements should be consistent from year to year unless a change would make the statements more relevant and/or reliable, or is required by a change in a standard (paras. 45–46).

- Each statement should be clearly identified and display which entity or group of entities it applies to (paras. 47–53).

4. Statement of financial position:
   - The statement can be either in current/non-current format (normal) or liquidity format (normally used by financial institutions) if more reliable.
   - Current assets are cash, cash equivalents, held for trading, or expected to be collected during the normal operating cycle (12 months).
   - Current liabilities are expected to be settled or held for trade during the normal operating cycle.
   - Information concerning share capital and reserves can be disclosed either in the statement of financial position or statement of changes in equity.
5. Statement of comprehensive income:
   - The statement can be either one statement of comprehensive income, or two separate statements showing income and other comprehensive income.
6. Statement of changes in equity.
7. Statement of cash flows (see IAS 7).
8. The notes to financial statements must show (list is in suggested order):
   - a statement of compliance with IFRSs
   - a summary of significant accounting policies applied, including:
     - the measurement basis (or bases) used in preparing the financial statements, and
     - the other accounting policies used that are relevant to an understanding of the financial statements
   - supporting information for items presented in the statement of financial position, statement of comprehensive income, income statement (if presented), statement of changes in equity and statement of cash flows, in the order in which each statement and each line item is presented, and
   - other disclosures, including:
     - contingent liabilities and unrecognised contractual commitments
     - non-financial disclosures, such as the entity's financial risk management objectives and policies
     - judgements used in applying accounting policies
     - key areas of uncertainly regarding any assumptions made
   - if not disclosed elsewhere in information published with the financial statements:
     - domicile of the enterprise
     - country of incorporation
     - address of registered office or principal place of business
     - description of the enterprise's operations and principal activities
     - name of the enterprise's parent and the ultimate parent if it is part of a group
     - details of the auditing arrangements
     - share dividends and franking credits.
9. Minimum requirements for each statement are shown in the table opposite:

CHANGES ON THE HORIZON

This is a new standard so should not have any major amendments in the near future. However, it is often subject to minor amendments due to flow on effects from changes in other standards or the introduction of new standards.

Statement of financial position	Statement of comprehensive income	Statement of changes in equity
In the statement	**In the statement**	**In the statement**
(a) property, plant and equipment (b) investment property (c) intangible assets (d) financial assets (e) investments accounted for using the equity method (f) biological assets (g) inventories (h) trade and other receivables (i) cash and cash equivalents (j) the total of assets classified as held for sale (k) trade and other payables (l) provisions (m) financial liabilities (n) liabilities and assets for current tax (o) deferred tax liabilities and deferred tax assets (p) liabilities included in disposal groups classified as held for sale (q) non-controlling interest, presented within equity	(a) revenue (b) finance costs (c) share of the profit or loss of associates and joint ventures accounted for using the equity method (d) tax expense (e) a single amount comprising the total of: (i) the post-tax profit or loss of discontinued operations, and (ii) the post-tax gain or loss recognised on the measurement to fair value less costs to sell on the disposal of the assets or disposal group(s) constituting the discontinued operation (f) profit or loss (g) each component of other comprehensive income classified by nature (h) share of the other comprehensive income of associates and joint ventures accounted for using the equity method, and (i) total comprehensive income Also (a) profit or loss for the period attributable to:	(a) total comprehensive income for the period, showing separately the total amounts attributable to owners of the parent and to non-controlling interest (b) for each component of equity, the effects of retrospective application or retrospective restatement recognised in accordance with IAS 8 (c) the amounts of transactions with owners in their capacity as owners, showing separately contributions by and distributions to owners, and (d) for each component of equity, a reconciliation between the carrying amount at the beginning and the end of the period, separately disclosing each change
(r) issued capital and reserves attributable to owners of the parent	(i) non-controlling interest, and (ii) owners of the parent, and (b) total comprehensive income for the period attributable to: (i) non-controlling interest, and (ii) owners of the parent	
Either in the statement or in the notes	**Either in the statement or in the notes**	**Either in the statement or in the notes**
Further subclassifications of line items in line with the operations of the entity	When items of income or expense are material, an entity shall disclose their nature and amount separately	The amount of dividends recognised as distributions to owners during the period, and the related amount per share

FACT SHEET IAS 2 *Inventories*

OBJECTIVE

This standard applies to the recognition and subsequent measurement of inventories until such time as the inventory is sold.

Inventories include:

- stock held for sale in the ordinary course of business
- raw materials and supplies used in the production process or rendering of services
- work in progress.

KEY REPORTING REQUIREMENTS

1. Inventories should be measured at lower of cost or net realisable value.
   - Cost includes the purchase price (including all taxes and handling costs less any rebates or discounts) and conversion costs (direct materials and labour plus an allocation of fixed and variable overhead costs) (paras. 10–14).
   - Net realisable value is the selling price less expected costs of completion and sales costs (para. 6).
   - Other costs including getting the inventory ready for use (as per IAS 23), the costs of production for service providers, and the cost of agricultural produce (as per IAS 41) can be included.
2. Where possible, the cost of inventory should be specifically identified. If this is impracticable or costly, either the first-in, first-out (FIFO) or weighted cost method should be used (paras. 21–27).
3. Inventories are to be written down to net realisable value when they are damaged, obsolete or their selling price has declined. This write-down should be done on an item-by-item basis where practicable, and consider the use of the inventory and be based on the most reliable estimate (paras. 28–33).
4. Inventories are recognised as an expense in the period they are sold. Any write-down in value is recognised as an expense in the period in which this occurs (paras. 34–35).
5. Disclosures include:
   - accounting policies used
   - the carrying amount of inventories, and the carrying amount of each subclassification (i.e. work in progress)
   - the carrying amount of inventories carried at fair value less costs to sell (see IAS 41)
   - the amount of any write-down (or reversal thereof) and the reason for it
   - the carrying amount of any inventory pledged as a security for any liabilities.

CHANGES ON THE HORIZON

No changes on the horizon.

FACT SHEET IAS 7 *Statement of Cash Flows*

OBJECTIVE

The objective of this standard is to account for the movement of cash (or cash equivalents) within an entity over its reporting period. To aid decision making, the statement of cash flows is divided into operating, investing and financing activities.

KEY DEFINITIONS

Cash comprises cash on hand and demand deposits.

Cash equivalents are short-term highly liquid investments that are readily convertible to cash and are held for the purpose of meeting short-term cash commitments.

Financing activities are activities that result in changes in the size and composition of the contributed capital and borrowings of the entity.

Investing activities are the acquisition and disposal of long-term assets and other investments not included in cash equivalents.

Operating activities are the principal revenue-producing activities of the entity and other activities that are not investing or financing activities.

KEY REPORTING REQUIREMENTS

1. Operating activities (paras. 18–20):
   - Entities are encouraged to report cash flows from operating activities using the direct method which shows each major class of gross cash receipts and gross cash payments. This information is obtained either from the accounting records of the entity or by adjusting sales, cost of sales, expenses and other items.
   - The indirect method adjusts net profit or loss for the effects of non-cash transactions or changes in accruals.
2. Cash flows from investing and financing activities (paras. 21–24):
   - These should be reported separately on a gross basis for the major classes of cash receipts and cash payments except for the following cases, which may be reported on a net basis:
     - cash receipts and payments on behalf of customers (e.g. land agents on behalf of property owners)
     - cash receipts and payments for items in which the turnover is quick, the amounts are large, and the maturities are short, generally less than 3 months (e.g. charges and collections from credit card customers)
     - for financial institutions, cash receipts and payments relating to fixed maturity deposits and cash advances and loans made to customers and repayments thereof.
3. Other issues (paras. 24–52):
   - Foreign currency transactions should be translated at the exchange rate when the transaction took place.
   - Interest and dividends should be disclosed consistently from period to period with classification usually in line with the activities of business (e.g. interest may be an operating activity for a financial institution but an investing or financing activity for other entities).
   - Cash flows resulting from income taxes are normally disclosed separately as operating activities.
   - Aggregate cash flows relating to acquisitions and disposals of subsidiaries and other business units should be presented separately and classified as investing activities, with additional disclosures.
   - Investing and financing transactions that do not require the use of cash should be separately disclosed elsewhere in the financial statements.
   - The components of cash and cash equivalents should be disclosed, and a reconciliation presented to amounts reported in the statement of financial position.

CHANGES ON THE HORIZON

No changes on the horizon.

FACT SHEET IAS 12 *Income Taxes*

OBJECTIVE

The objective of this standard is to allow the reporting entity to account for income taxes, particularly the differences between tax law and financial reporting.

KEY DEFINITIONS

A *temporary difference* is a difference between the carrying amount of an asset or liability and its tax base.

A *taxable temporary difference* is a temporary difference that will result in taxable amounts in the future when the carrying amount of the asset is recovered or the liability is settled.

A *deductible temporary difference* is a temporary difference that will result in amounts that are tax deductible in the future when the carrying amount of the asset is recovered or the liability is settled.

The *tax base* of an asset or liability is the amount attributed to that asset or liability for tax purposes.

Deferred tax assets are the amounts of income taxes recoverable in future periods in respect of:

1. deductible temporary differences
2. the carry forward of unused tax losses, and
3. the carry forward of unused tax credits.

Deferred tax liabilities are the amounts of income taxes payable in future periods in respect of taxable temporary differences.

KEY REPORTING REQUIREMENTS

1. Any unpaid current tax liability should be recognised as a liability unless there is a tax loss, in which case an asset is recognised (see below) (paras. 12–14).
2. A deferred tax liability (DTL) should be recognised for all taxable temporary differences unless it (paras. 15–23) arises from:
   - goodwill
   - the initial recognition of an asset unless it is part of a business combination or affects neither taxable profit nor accounting profit.
3. A deferred tax asset (DTA) should be recognised for all deductible temporary differences, unless it is part of a business combination and affects neither taxable profit nor accounting profit (paras. 24–45).
   - A DTA can only be recognised to the extent that it is probable that the reporting entity will have taxable income future to enable the DTA to be utilised.
4. Measurement of DTAs and DTLs are in accordance with tax laws and tax rates (in Australia this is currently 30%); that is, if a temporary difference is $1000 the corresponding DTA/DTL would be $300 (paras. 46–56).
5. Current and deferred tax should be recognised as income or expense and included in profit or loss unless it relates to a business combination or the transaction is recognised directly to equity (e.g. an asset revaluation).
6. A reporting entity can only offset DTAs and DTLs if it has a legally enforceable right to do so, and intends to settle both simultaneously.
7. Disclosures:
   - All items relating to tax should be disclosed separately in the statements.
   - Major items of tax expense should be disclosed, including:
     - current tax expense (income)
     - any adjustments of taxes of prior periods
     - amount of deferred tax expense (income) relating to the origination and reversal of temporary differences
     - amount of deferred tax expense (income) relating to changes in tax rates or the imposition of new taxes

- amount of the benefit arising from a previously unrecognised tax loss, tax credit or temporary difference of a prior period
- write-down, or reversal of a previous write-down, of a deferred tax asset, and
- amount of tax expense (income) relating to changes in accounting policies and corrections of errors.

- Items requiring separate disclosure include:
  - the aggregate of items reported directly in equity
  - tax relating to each component of other comprehensive income
  - a reconciliation of tax profit to accounting profit or a description of the differences
  - changes in tax rates
  - amounts and other details of deductible temporary differences, unused tax losses and unused tax credits
  - temporary differences associated with investments in subsidiaries, associates and branches, and
  - details of deferred tax assets.

CHANGES ON THE HORIZON

The standard is expected to be revised in 2010 to eliminate some minor differences as part of the convergence project between the IASB and the FASB. It is not expected to have any major differences.

FACT SHEET IAS 16 *Property, Plant and Equipment*

OBJECTIVE

The objective of this standard is to account for property, plant and equipment, principally its initial recognition and subsequent treatment through a choice of two methods (cost and revaluation). The standard covers most physical assets unless the asset is specifically covered by another standard (such as inventory and biological assets).

KEY REPORTING REQUIREMENTS

1. Recognition of an asset occurs when (paras. 7–10):
   - the future economic benefits associated with the asset will flow to the enterprise, and
   - the cost of the asset can be measured reliably.
2. Upon initial measurement an asset should be measured at cost (para. 13) where cost includes:
   - getting the asset ready for its intended use, such as delivery, site preparation and installation (paras. 16–22)
   - the cost of restoring a site, such as dismantling and removal (as per IAS 37)
   - interest expense if the asset is a qualifying asset (as per IAS 23).
3. Where measurable, cost is considered to be the fair value of the asset (including for non-commercial transactions and not-for-profit entities). If not measurable, cost is the carrying amount of an asset being given up (paras. 23–28).
4. Post recognition, an asset is measured using either the cost or revaluation model (para. 29).
5. Under the cost model:
   - An asset is carried at cost less any accumulated depreciation and impairment losses (para. 30).
   - In calculating depreciation, each part of the asset should be depreciated separately where feasible (paras. 43–47).
   - Depreciation expense should be included in profit and loss (paras. 48–49).
   - Depreciation should be allocated on a systematic basis over the life of the asset using a method that best reflects the use of the asset (paras. 50–62).
   - Assets should be impaired in accordance with IAS 36.
6. Under the revaluation model:
   - Revaluations should be carried out regularly, so that the carrying amount of an asset does not differ materially from its fair value at the end of the reporting period (paras. 31–34).
   - Revalued assets are depreciated in the same way as under the cost model (para. 35).
   - If an asset is revalued then all assets within that class should be revalued (paras. 36–38).
   - If a revaluation results in an increase in value, it should be credited to equity under 'Asset Surplus' unless it represents the reversal of a previous revaluation decrease of the same asset, in which case it should be recognised as income to the extent of the previous decrease (para. 39).
   - If a revaluation results in an decrease in value, it should be expensed unless it represents the reversal of a previous revaluation increase of the same asset in which case it should be debited to equity under Asset Surplus to the extent of the previous increase (para. 40).
7. Disclosures:
   - For each class of property, plant, and equipment, disclose (para. 73):
     - the basis for measuring the carrying amount
     - the depreciation method(s) used
     - the useful lives or depreciation rates
     - the gross carrying amount and accumulated depreciation and impairment losses
     - a reconciliation of the carrying amount at the beginning and the end of the period, showing all changes.
   - Also disclose (para. 74):
     - restrictions on title
     - expenditures to construct property, plant and equipment during the period
     - commitments to acquire property, plant and equipment

- compensation from third parties for items of property, plant and equipment that were impaired, lost or given up that is included in profit or loss.

- If property, plant and equipment is stated at revalued amounts, provide additional disclosures (para. 77), including:
  - the effective date of the revaluation
  - whether an independent valuer was involved
  - the methods and significant assumptions used in estimating fair values
  - the extent to which fair values were determined directly by reference to observable prices in an active market or recent market transactions on arm's length terms or were estimated using other valuation techniques
  - the carrying amount that would have been recognised had the assets been carried under the cost model
  - the revaluation surplus, including changes during the period and distribution restrictions.

CHANGES ON THE HORIZON

No changes on the horizon.

FACT SHEET IAS 17 *Leases*

OBJECTIVE

The objective of this standard is to account for and disclose operating and finance leases in the statements of the lessor and lessee.

KEY REPORTING REQUIREMENTS

1. A lease is classified as a finance lease if it transfers substantially all the risks and rewards incident to ownership from the lessor to lessee, otherwise it is an operating lease. The classification depends on the substance of the lease agreement. Situations that would normally lead to a lease being classified as a finance lease include (paras. 7–19):
   - the lease transfers ownership of the asset to the lessee by the end of the lease term
   - the lessee has the option to purchase the asset at a price that is expected to be sufficiently lower than fair value at the date the option becomes exercisable, and, at the inception of the lease, it is reasonably certain that the option will be exercised
   - the lease term is for the major part of the economic life of the asset, even if title is not transferred
   - at the inception of the lease, the present value of the minimum lease payments amounts to at least substantially all of the fair value of the leased asset
   - any other factors that indicate that the risks and benefits of ownership have transferred from the lessor to the lessee.
2. Accounting by lessees (paras. 20–35):
   - Finance leases should be recorded as an asset and a liability at the lower of the fair value of the asset and the present value of the minimum lease payments.
   - Finance lease payments should be apportioned between interest expense and the reduction of the outstanding liability.
   - The lease asset should be amortised in line with the depreciation policy for owned assets. If there is no reasonable certainty that ownership will transfer, the asset should be depreciated over the lease term.
   - Operating lease payments should be recognised as an expense over the lease term on a straight-line basis, unless another systematic basis is more appropriate.
3. Accounting by lessors (paras. 20–35):
   - Finance leases should be recorded as a receivable at an amount equal to the net investment in the lease.
   - Finance lease income should be recognised on a systemic basis over the life of the lease.
   - Manufacturers or dealer lessors should include selling profit or loss in the same period as they would have if they sold the asset.
   - Assets held for operating leases should be shown on the statement of financial position according to the nature of the asset with lease incomes recognised on a straight-line basis over the life of the lease, unless another systematic basis is more appropriate.
4. Sale and leaseback transactions:
   - For a sale and leaseback transaction that results in a finance lease, any excess of proceeds over the carrying amount is deferred and amortised over the lease term (para. 59).
   - For a transaction that results in an operating lease, if, at fair value, any profit or loss results, it should be recognised immediately; if not at fair value, any profit or loss should be amortised over the period of use.

5. Disclosures:

	Lessee	Lessor
Finance leases	• Carrying amount of asset. • Reconciliation between total minimum lease payments and their present value. • Amounts of minimum lease payments at the end of the reporting period and the present value thereof, for: – the next year – years 2–5 combined – beyond 5 years. • Contingent rent recognised as an expense. • General description of significant leasing arrangements.	• Reconciliation between gross investment in the lease and the present value of minimum lease payments. • Gross investment and present value of minimum lease payments receivable for: – the next year – years 2–5 combined – beyond 5 years. • Unearned finance income. • Unguaranteed residual values. • Accumulated allowance for uncollectable lease payments receivable. • Contingent rent recognised in income. • General description of significant leasing arrangements.
Operating leases	• Amounts of minimum lease payments at the end of the reporting period under non-cancellable operating leases for: – the next year – years 2–5 combined – beyond 5 years. • Contingent rent recognised as an expense. • General description of significant leasing arrangements.	• Amounts of minimum lease payments at the end of the reporting period under non-cancellable operating leases in the aggregate and for: – the next year – years 2–5 combined – beyond 5 years. • Contingent rent recognised as in income. • General description of significant leasing arrangements.

CHANGES ON THE HORIZON

This standard is up for review. There is suggestion that all leases may be treated as finance leases.

FACT SHEET IAS 18 *Revenue*

OBJECTIVE

The objective of this standard is to account for revenue from the sale of goods and provision of services and other common revenues.

KEY REPORTING REQUIREMENTS

1. Revenue is defined as the gross inflow of economic benefits (cash, receivables, other assets) arising from the ordinary operating activities of an enterprise (such as sales of goods, sales of services, interest, royalties and dividends) (para. 7).
2. Revenue is measured at the fair value of the consideration received or receivable (paras. 9–13):
   - In line with the conceptual *Framework*, the standard requires intangible assets to be recognised when:
     - it is probable future economic benefits will flow to the entity, and
     - the cost of the asset can be measured reliably.

     If both these conditions are met, the asset is measured at cost.
   - If not able to be identified separately, any intangible asset is included as a component of goodwill if purchased in a business combination.
3. Sale of goods revenue should be recognised when all the following conditions have been met (paras. 14–19):
   - The significant risks and rewards of ownership have been transferred to the buyer.
   - The seller retains neither continuing managerial involvement to the degree usually associated with ownership nor effective control over the goods sold.
   - The amount of revenue can be measured reliably.
   - It is probable that the economic benefits associated with the transaction will flow to the seller.
   - The costs incurred, or to be incurred, in respect of the transaction can be measured reliably.
4. Revenue arising from the provision of services should be recognised by reference to the stage of completion of the transaction at the end of the reporting period (the percentage-of-completion method), provided that all of the following criteria are met (paras. 20–28):
   - The amount of revenue can be measured reliably.
   - It is probable that the economic benefits will flow to the entity.
   - The stage of completion at the end of the reporting period can be measured reliably.
   - The costs incurred, or to be incurred, in respect of the transaction can be measured reliably.

   When the above criteria are not met, revenue arising from the rendering of services should be recognised only to the extent of the expenses recognised that are recoverable (a 'cost-recovery approach').
5. Interest, royalties and dividends revenue should be recognised provided that it is probable and measurable as follows (paras. 29–34):
   - Interest: on a time proportion basis that takes into account the effective yield.
   - Royalties: on an accruals basis in accordance with the substance of the relevant agreement.
   - Dividends: when the shareholder's right to receive payment is established.
6. An entity shall disclose (paras. 35–36):
   - all accounting polices adopted for revenue recognition
   - the amount of each category of revenue as discussed above if material, and, within each category, the amount arising from exchanges of goods and services.

CHANGES ON THE HORIZON

While there is no specific change in regards to this standard planned, any changes in the conceptual framework project in regards to the definition of income may have a flow-on effect to this standard.

FACT SHEET IAS 19 *Employee Benefits*

OBJECTIVE

The objective of this standard is to allow the reporting entity to account for payments to employees, other than share-based payments. The payments fall into four separate categories:

1. short-term employee benefits (e.g. wages)
2. post-employment benefits (e.g. employer provided pensions)
3. other long-term benefits (e.g. long service leave)
4. termination benefits (e.g. redundancy payments).

KEY DEFINITIONS

Other long-term employee benefits are employee benefits (other than post-employment benefits and termination benefits) that do not fall due wholly within 12 months after the end of the period in which the employees render the related service.

Post-employment benefits are employee benefits (other than termination benefits) that are payable after the completion of employment. There are two types of post employment benefits:

- defined contribution (such as superannuation where the employer contributes a fixed proportion of the employee's income)
- defined benefit (such as pension schemes where the benefit is based on the conditions of the pension).

Short-term employee benefits are employee benefits (other than termination benefits) that fall due wholly within 12 months after the end of the period in which the employees render the related service.

Termination benefits are employee benefits payable as a result of either:

- an entity's decision to terminate an employee's employment before the normal retirement date, or
- an employee's decision to accept voluntary redundancy in exchange for those benefits.

KEY REPORTING REQUIREMENTS

1. Measurement of short-term employee benefits, and payments expected to be made within 12 months should be undiscounted. Long-term employee benefits should be discounted using either the rate on a high quality corporate bond, or the government bond rate that matches the currency and term of the benefit.
2. Short-term employee benefits should be recognised as a liability (accrued expense) when unpaid, or as an expense when paid, unless another standard provides alternative treatment (such as IAS 16 in getting an asset ready for use).
3. An expense for a defined contribution should be recognised in the period the contribution is made (such as for superannuation payments).
4. For a defined benefit, the reporting entity must recognise the effects on both the statement of financial position and statement of comprehensive income.
   - At the end of the reporting period, the entity recognises a defined benefit liability comprising:
     - the present value of the defined benefit obligation
     - plus any actuarial gains (less any actuarial losses) not recognised
     - minus any past service cost not yet recognised
     - minus the fair value of any plan assets out of which the obligations are to be settled directly.
   - The entity recognises income or expense comprising:
     - current service cost
     - interest cost
     - expected return on plan assets and reimbursement rights
     - actuarial gains and losses.
   - Actuarial gains or losses are changed in the assumptions underpinning the calculations. These include changes in discount rates, changes in the number of people in the scheme and changes in the expected rate of return.

5. Other long-term employee benefits are recognised similarly to the recognition of a defined benefit plan; however, actuarial costs and past service cost are recognised immediately.
6. Termination benefits for either voluntary or involuntary redundancy are only recognised when there is clear formal plan to make the redundancy, with only a remote chance of the plan not being implemented.

CHANGES ON THE HORIZON

The post-employment benefits aspect of this standard is currently being reviewed by the IASB with a discussion paper released in 2008. It is expected that a new standard should be in effect in 2011.

FACT SHEET IAS 27 *Consolidated and Separate Financial Statements*

OBJECTIVE

The main objective of this standard is to specify how a group of companies under the control of a parent entity should prepare and present a single set of financial statements. The standard also provides rules for the separate financial statements of the parent entity and disclosure requirements for investments in associates when using the consolidation method.

KEY DEFINITIONS

Consolidated financial statements are the financial statements of a group presented as those of a single economic entity.

A *subsidiary* is an entity, including an unincorporated entity such as a partnership, that is controlled by another entity (known as the parent).

A *parent* is an entity that has one or more subsidiaries.

Control is the power to govern the financial and operating policies of an enterprise so as to obtain benefits from its activities.

KEY REPORTING REQUIREMENTS

1. All parent companies should prepare consolidated financial statements unless (paras. 9–11):
   - The parent is a wholly own subsidiary of another parent company, or a partly own subsidiary where other owners, when informed, do not object to the parent company not preparing consolidated statements.
   - The parent's securities are not publicly traded on the open market.
   - The parent does not file, or is in the process of filing, financial statements with a security commission or regulatory body about the issuing of securities on the open market.
   - The ultimate, or any intermediate, parent company does not produce publicly available financial statements produced in accordance with IFRSs.
2. Consolidated financial statements should be produced for the parent company and all subsidiaries it has control over. Factors indicating control include (paras. 12– 21):
   - owning more than one half of the voting rights by virtue of an agreement with other investors
   - governing the financial and operating policies of the other enterprise under a statute or an agreement
   - the ability to appoint or remove the majority of the members of the board of directors
   - the ability to cast the majority of votes at a meeting of the board of directors.
3. The consolidation process involves (paras. 22– 37):
   - combining the financial statements of the parent and its subsidiaries line by line by adding together like items of assets, liabilities, equity, income and expenses
   - eliminating the carrying amount of the parent's investment in each subsidiary and the parent's portion of equity of each subsidiary
   - eliminating intragroup balances, transactions, income and expenses in full (such as sale of inventory or provision of services between parent and subsidiary)
   - preparing statements using uniform accounting policies and reporting periods (where practicable)
   - identifying any non-controlling interests and recording these separately within equity
   - identifying any profit or loss attributable to non-controlling interests separately
   - recording changes in the parent's proportion of controlling interest as equity transactions unless it results in a loss of control
   - reporting for the subsidiary using the appropriate accounting standard if control is lost.
4. Disclosures (paras. 41–43):
   - The nature of the relationship between the parent and subsidiary when the parent does not own, directly or indirectly through subsidiaries, more than half of the voting power.
   - The reasons why the ownership, directly or indirectly through subsidiaries, of more than half of the voting or potential voting power of an investee does not constitute control.

- If a subsidiary's financial statements with a different reporting period are used to prepare the consolidated statements, the reasons for the different reporting period.
- A schedule showing any change in ownership interest.
- The nature and extent of any significant restrictions (e.g. resulting from borrowing arrangements or regulatory requirements) on the ability of subsidiaries to transfer funds to the parent in the form of cash dividends or to repay loans or advances.
- Any gain or loss resulting from a loss of control of a subsidiary.
- When consolidated financial statements are not prepared:
  - a statement to the effect and the reasons for this if not required by law
  - details of significant investments in subsidiaries, jointly controlled entities and associates, and a description of the method used to account for investments.

CHANGES ON THE HORIZON

The IASB has recently released an exposure draft strengthening and improving the requirements for control of subsidiaries.

FACT SHEET IAS 28 *Investments in Associates*

OBJECTIVE

The objective of this standard is to account for an investment in which the investor has significant influence over investee, but not full control. The exception to this is the investment is in a joint venture or subject to IAS 39.

KEY DEFINITIONS

An *associate* is an enterprise in which an investor has significant influence but not control or joint control.

Significant influence is the power to participate in the financial and operating policy decisions but not control them.

The *equity method* is a method of accounting by which an equity investment is initially recorded at cost and subsequently adjusted to reflect the investor's share of the net profit or loss of the associate (investee).

KEY REPORTING REQUIREMENTS

1. Significant influence is presumed if the investor holds 20% or more of the voting power of the investee unless proven otherwise. Less then 20% of the voting power of the investee is presumed not to hold significant influence unless it can be established looking at the following criteria (paras. 6–10):
   - representation on the board of directors or equivalent governing body of the investee
   - participation in the policy-making process
   - material transactions between the investor and the investee
   - interchange of managerial personnel
   - provision of essential technical information
   - the potential to hold votes through the conversion of options, rights or warrants.
2. The investor needs to use the equity method of accounting for investments in associates unless exempted by paragraph 13 (mainly occurs if the investment is held for disposal; other cases are rare) (paras. 13–30):
   - Under the equity method, the investment in an associate is initially recorded at cost. Subsequently, the carrying amount of the investments is increased or decreased to recognise the investor's share of the profit or loss in the investee after the date of acquisition. The investor's share of the profit or loss of the investee is recognised in the investor's profit or loss. This is adjusted by:
     - dividend or other equity distributions
     - changes in the proportion of equity caused by changes in the investee's equity that have not gone through the profit and loss (e.g. asset revaluations or foreign currency translations).
   - Post recognition, any transactions between the investee and investor are only recognised to the extent of unrelated interests, that is, the profit /loss between investor and investee is eliminated.
   - Upon loss of significant influence, the carrying amount as at that point is considered to be the cost of a financial asset in accordance with IAS 39.
   - In the advent of a loss, an investment in an associate can not fall below zero, unless it meets the definition of a liability with a clear obligation (either legal or constructive). Equity accounting resumes if the losses are recovered.
3. Impairment of investments in associates is in accordance with the impairment provisions of IAS 39 and IAS 36 (paras. 31–34).
4. Where possible, similar accounting polices and periods should be used, or disclosure made if not used (paras. 35–36).
5. Disclosures (paras. 37–40):
   - The fair value of investments in associates if published price quotations are available.
   - A summary of the associates' financial information including the aggregated amounts of assets, liabilities, revenues, and profit or loss.
   - The reasons for the existence (or non-existence if ownership is greater than 20%) of significant influence.

- The reporting date of an associate's financial statements if this date varies from the investor's reporting date, including the reason for using a different reporting period.
- The nature and extent of any significant restrictions on the ability of associates to transfer funds to the investor in the form of cash dividends or repayment of loans or advances.
- The unrecognised share of losses of an associate, both for the period and cumulatively, if an investor has discontinued recognition of its share of losses of an associate.
- Summarised financial information of associates that are not equity-accounted and the fact that an associate is not equity-accounted.
- Investments in associates that are equity-accounted should be classified as non-current assets with separate disclosure of the profit or loss of the associates, the carrying amount of the investments and the investor's share of any discontinuing operations.
- The investor's share of changes recognised directly in the associate's equity should be directly recognised in the investor's equity and should be disclosed in the statement of changes in equity.
- In accordance with IAS 37, the investor should disclose its share of contingent liabilities of an associate incurred jointly and those that arise because the investor is severally liable for all or part of the associate's liabilities.

CHANGES ON THE HORIZON

No changes on the horizon.

FACT SHEET IAS 31 *Interests in Joint Ventures*

OBJECTIVE

The objective of this standard is to allow venturers and investors to account for and present interests in joint ventures in their financial statements.

There are three main types of joint ventures:

1. jointly controlled operations
2. jointly controlled assets
3. jointly controlled entity.

KEY DEFINITIONS

A *joint venture* is a contractual arrangement whereby two or more parties undertake an economic activity that is subject to joint control.

A *venturer* is a party to a joint venture and has joint control over that joint venture.

An *investor in a joint venture* is a party to a joint venture and does not have joint control over that joint venture.

Joint control is the contractually agreed sharing of control over an economic activity such that no individual contracting party has control.

KEY REPORTING REQUIREMENTS

1. The type of accounting treatment to be used depends on the type of joint venture.
2. Jointly controlled operations:
   - In this case, the venturers use their own assets and other resources rather than establish a separate entity.
   - In its own financial statements, each venturer should recognise:
     - the assets it controls and the liabilities it incurs
     - the expenses it incurs and its share of the income earned from the sale of goods or services by the joint venture.
3. Jointly controlled assets:
   - In this case, the venturers jointly control one or more assets contributed to or acquired for the purpose of the joint venture. The asset(s) are dedicated to the purposes of the joint venture. As above, this type of joint venture does not involve the establishment of an entity separate from the venturers.
   - In its own financial statements, each venturer should recognise:
     - its share of the jointly controlled assets, classified according to the nature of the assets
     - any liabilities it has incurred and its share of jointly incurred liabilities
     - any income from the sale or use of its share of the output of the joint venture, plus its share of expenses incurred by the joint venture
     - any expenses it has incurred in respect of its interest in the joint venture.
4. Jointly controlled entity:
   - In this case, a separate entity is established in which each venturer has an interest.
   - Each venturer should recognise its interest in the jointly controlled entity using the proportionate consolidation or equity method for the period of time it has joint control in a jointly controlled entity.
   - In its own financial statements, each venture should recognise its interest in the jointly controlled entity in accordance with IAS 27 (paras. 37–42).
   - If the jointly controlled entity becomes a subsidiary or associate of a venturer, the venturer must apply IAS 27 or IAS 28 respectively.

Source: CPA Australia, *Fact Sheet AASB131 Interest in Joint Ventures* (www.cpaaustralia.com.au).

5. In jointly controlled entities, the venturer has a choice of two methods:
   - Proportionate consolidation (a choice of two formats):
     - combine its share of each of the assets, liabilities, income and expenses of the jointly controlled entity with the similar items, line by line, in its financial statements
     - include separate line items for its share of the assets, liabilities, income and expenses of the jointly controlled entity in its financial statements.
   - Equity accounting as prescribed in IAS 28, in addition:
     - If a venturer contributes or sells an asset to a jointly controlled entity, while the asset is retained by the joint venture, provided that the venturer has transferred the risks and rewards of ownership, it should recognise only the proportion of the gain attributable to the other venturers. The venturer should recognise the full amount of any loss incurred when known.
     - The requirements for recognition of gains and losses apply equally to non-monetary contributions unless the gain or loss cannot be measured, or the other venturers contribute similar assets. Unrealised gains or losses should be eliminated against the underlying assets (proportionate consolidation) or against the investment (equity method).
6. A venturer is required to disclose information about the venture in relation to:
   - contingent liabilities relating to the venture
   - its interests in joint ventures
   - a listing and description of interests in significant joint ventures and the proportion of ownership interest held in jointly controlled entities
   - the method it uses to recognise its interests in jointly controlled entities.

CHANGES ON THE HORIZON

This standard is expected to be re-released during 2009. Based on the exposure draft, the proportionate consolidation method will be removed. The new standard will also focus more on contractual rights and obligations of the joint venture rather than legal form.

FACT SHEET IAS 33 *Earnings per Share*

OBJECTIVE

The objective of this standard is to prescribe principles for the determination and presentation of earnings per share (EPS) amounts in order to improve performance comparisons between different enterprises in the same period and between different accounting periods for the same enterprise (para. 1).

KEY DEFINITIONS

An *ordinary share*, also known as a common share or common stock, is an equity instrument that is subordinate to all other classes of equity shares.

A *potential ordinary share* is a financial instrument or other contract that could result it its holder getting ordinary shares. Examples include share options and rights.

Dilution is a reduction in earnings per share or an increase in loss per share resulting from the assumption that convertible instruments are converted, that options or warrants are exercised, or that ordinary shares are issued upon the satisfaction of specified conditions.

Antidilution is an increase in earnings per share or a reduction in loss per share resulting from the assumption that convertible instruments are converted, that options or warrants are exercised, or that ordinary shares are issued upon the satisfaction of specified conditions.

KEY REPORTING REQUIREMENTS

1. Earnings per share is calculated two separate ways:
   - Basic earnings per share (EPS)

     $$\frac{\text{Profit or loss attributable to ordinary equity holders of the parent entity}}{\text{The weighted average number of ordinary shares outstanding during the period}}$$

   - Diluted EPS is the EPS adjusted for the effects of all outstanding dilutive potential ordinary shares
2. Basic earnings per share (paras. 9–29):
   - The numerator is calculated by including the profit and loss for continuing operations, and net profit and loss, and deducting non-controlling interest, tax and preference dividends.
   - The denominator is calculated by finding the weighted number of ordinary shares for the period.
3. Diluted earnings per share (paras. 30–63):
   - The numerator is calculated as the profit or loss attributable to ordinary equity holders of the parent entity, adjusted by the after-tax effect of (para. 33):
     - any dividends or other items related to dilutive potential ordinary shares are deducted in arriving at profit or loss attributable to ordinary equity holders of the parent entity
     - any interest recognised in the period related to dilutive potential ordinary shares
     - any other changes in income or expense that would result from the conversion of the dilutive potential ordinary shares.
   - The denominator is calculated as the number of shares (calculated as per the basic EPS) plus the weighted total number of ordinary shares assuming all (dilutive) potential ordinary shares are taken up.
   - Diluted earnings per shares assumes:
     - all warrant, rights and options are exercised
     - when financial instruments are issued with the choice of cash or shares, shares will be issued
     - all contingently issued shares are issued when conditions are not met (if conditions are met they are included in the basic EPS).
4. Any adjustments to these calculations should be applied retrospectively. When adjustments occur after the end of the reporting period but before the release of the statements, EPS should be calculated on the new numbers and disclosed (paras. 64–65).

5. EPS and diluted EPS should be presented in the statement of comprehensive income with equal prominence regardless of the amount (i.e. material by nature) for each class of share. For discontinued operations, EPS and diluted EPS can be either in the statements or in the notes.
6. Disclosures (para. 70):
   - The amounts used as the numerators in calculating basic and diluted EPS, and a reconciliation of those amounts to the profit or loss attributable to the parent entity for the period.
   - The weighted average number of ordinary shares used as the denominator in calculating basic and diluted EPS, and a reconciliation of these denominators to each other.
   - Instruments (including contingently issuable shares) that could potentially dilute basic earnings per share in the future, but not included in the calculation of diluted EPS because they are antidilutive for the period(s) presented.
   - A description of those ordinary share transactions or potential ordinary share transactions that occur after the end of the reporting period that would have changed significantly the number of ordinary shares or potential ordinary shares outstanding at the end of the period if those transactions had occurred before the end of the reporting period. Examples include issues and redemptions of ordinary shares, warrants and options, conversions and exercises.

CHANGES ON THE HORIZON

As part of the overall harmonisation project, this standard is expected to be re-released in the second half of 2009 moving to the simpler treasury stock method used by the FASB.

FACT SHEET IAS 36 *Impairment of Assets*

OBJECTIVE

The objective of this standard is to ensure that assets are recorded at a value that represents the future economic benefit that they represent. This is done by ensuring that their carrying amounts are not greater than their recoverable amounts.

KEY DEFINITIONS

An asset is *impaired* when its carrying amount exceeds its recoverable amount.

Carrying amount is the amount at which an asset is recognised in the statement of financial position after deducting accumulated depreciation and accumulated impairment losses.

Recoverable amount is the higher of an asset's fair value less costs to sell (sometimes called net selling price) and its value in use.

Fair value is the amount obtainable from the sale of an asset in a bargained transaction between knowledgeable, willing parties.

Value in use is the discounted present value of estimated future cash flows expected to arise from:
- the continuing use of an asset, and
- its disposal at the end of its useful life.

A *cash-generating unit (CGU)* is the smallest identifiable group of assets that generates cash inflows that are largely independent of cash flows from other assets or groups of asset.

KEY REPORTING REQUIREMENTS

1. Identifying an asset that may be impaired (paras. 7–17):
   - At the end of each reporting period, an entity should assess each asset (or CGU) for an indication that the asset may be impaired. Indications can be either external or internal:
     - External factors include a change in the market value of asset, a change in the market or economic differences, net assets being carried at more than market capitalisation.
     - Internal factors include obsolesce or physical damage, significant changes in the way the entity operates, or internal reporting identifying asset performance below expectations.
   - Irrespective of indication, the following should be tested annually:
     - assets not ready for use
     - intangible assets with indefinite useful life
     - goodwill acquired as part of a business combination.
2. Measuring recoverable amount (paras. 18–57):
   - Fair value less costs to sell is considered to be the fair value of the asset and any costs of disposals such as stamp duty or legal costs.
   - Value in use is:
     - an estimate of the future cash flows the entity expects to derive from the asset
     - expectations about possible variations in the amount or timing of those future cash flows
     - the time value of money, represented by the current market risk-free rate of interest
     - the price for bearing the uncertainty inherent in the asset
     - other factors, such as illiquidity, that market participants would reflect in pricing the future cash flows the entity expects to derive from the asset.
3. An impairment loss is recognised when the carrying amount of the asset (or CGU) is greater than recoverable (the difference is regarded as the impairment loss) (paras. 58–64).
4. Where it's not possible to determine the carrying amount of a single asset, the entity should calculate the recoverable amount of the cash-generating unit to which that asset belongs (paras. 65–108).
   - Where there is an impairment loss in a CGU, it is first allocated to goodwill (if any) then on a pro rata basis across impairable assets.
   - No asset can be impaired below either its fair value less cost to sell or its value in use (if determinable) or zero. Any excess should be allocated on a pro rata basis across the remaining assets.

5. An impairment loss can be reversed if there is an indication it no longer exists (similarly to the indicators of impairment) and can only be reversed to the extent of the carrying amount had no impairment loss existed (i.e. net of depreciation or amortisation). Impairment of goodwill cannot be reversed (paras. 109–125).
6. Disclosures:
   - Impairment losses (reversals) recognised in the statement of comprehensive income and in what line.
   - Impairment losses (reversal) by primary segments.
   - If an individual impairment loss (reversal) is material, the following also needs to be disclosed:
     - reason for the loss and amount of loss
     - individual asset: nature of and segment to which it relates
     - cash-generating unit: description, amount of impairment loss (reversal) by class of assets and segment
     - how recoverable amount was calculated and estimations used.
   - If impairment losses recognised (reversed) are material in aggregate to the financial statements as a whole, disclose (para. 131):
     - main classes of assets affected
     - main events and circumstances.

CHANGES ON THE HORIZON

Due to the number of active projects, the IASB, while recognising there are issues to be addressed, has decided not to add this standard to its project agenda at this time.

FACT SHEET IAS 37 *Provisions, Contingent Liabilities and Contingent Assets*

OBJECTIVE

The objective of this standard is to ensure recognition and measurement bases are applied consistently to provisions, contingent liabilities and contingent assets to better enable users to understand the nature, amounts and timing of these items.

Examples include:

- provisions: warranties, refund policies
- contingent liabilities: court cases where payment is required but the case is unclear
- contingent asset: court cases where the entity may be the beneficiary but the case is unclear, exploratory drilling, activities relating to the evaluation of technical and commercial feasibility.

KEY DEFINITIONS

A *provision* is a liability of uncertain timing or amount.

A *contingent liability* is:

- a possible obligation only payable contingent upon a future event not wholly in the entity's control, or
- a present obligation not currently deemed to be probable or not measurable with sufficient reliability.

A *contingent asset* is a possible asset whose existence dependant upon a future event not wholly in the entity's control.

KEY REPORTING REQUIREMENTS

1. A contingent liability is recognised when (para. 14):
   - an entity has a present obligation (paras. 15–16) as a result of a past event (paras. 17–22)
   - it is probable there will be an outflow of economic benefits to settle the obligation (paras. 23–24)
   - it can be reliably measured (paras. 25–26).
2. Contingent liabilities and assets are only disclosed not recognised (paras. 27–35).
3. Provisions are measured at the best estimate of the expenditure required to settle the present obligation at the end of the reporting period (para. 36) taking into any consideration risks and uncertainties, the present value of the obligation (if necessary), and any future events that may impact, not including a gain on disposal of assets that may be linked to the provision (paras. 37–45).
   - May be offset by a future reimbursement by a third party only when it is virtually certain the reimbursement will occur (paras. 53–58).
   - Should be reviewed at the end of each reporting period, and can only be used for their original purpose (paras. 59–62).
   - Do not cover (paras. 63–83):
     - future operating loses
     - onerous contracts
     - restructuring (unless there is a present obligation).
4. Disclosures (paras. 84–92):
   - For each class of provision, the opening and closing amounts, and the reason for any changes, as well as the nature of the obligation giving rise to the provision, the reasons for any uncertainties and what future events may impact, and any expected reimbursement.
   - For contingent liabilities and assets, an estimate of the financial effect, an indication of the uncertainties involved, and any reimbursement if possible.
   - If the above disclosures are not possible, a statement explaining the reasons why not.

CHANGES ON THE HORIZON

This standard is expected to be re-released in 2010 to eliminate differences between IFRSs and US GAAP and bring the standard in line with new conceptual *Framework* definitions.

FACT SHEET IAS 38 *Intangible Assets*

OBJECTIVE

The objective of this standard is to account for how intangible assets (non-monetary assets without physical substance) are recognised, measured (both upon and post initial recognition) and disclosed within financial statements. The standard outlines the treatment for both identifiable and non-identifiable intangible assets, as well as those generated internally and externally.

KEY REPORTING REQUIREMENTS

1. Identifying intangible assets (paras. 9–17):
   - An intangible asset can be recognised when it arises from a contract or legal right, and can be separately sold from the rest of the entity.
   - If an intangible asset cannot be separately identified, it can only be recognised when purchased as part of a business combination. In this case, it and is included in goodwill in accordance with IFRS 3.
2. Recognition of an intangible asset (paras. 18–45):
   - In line with the conceptual *Framework*, the standard requires intangible assets to be recognised when:
     - it is probable that future economic benefits will flow to the entity, and
     - the cost of the asset can be measured reliably.

     If both these conditions are met, the asset is measured at cost.
   - As noted above, if not able to be identified separately, any intangible asset is included as a component of goodwill if purchased in a business combination.
3. All internally generated intangible assets are to be expensed unless they are deemed to be development. For an entity to capitalise expenditure as development, an internally generated asset must be technically feasible, be able (and intended) to be completed and sold, be able to generate future economic benefits. The entity must also have the resources to complete and sell the asset, and its costs must be able to be reliably measured (paras. 49–71).
4. Post recognition, an intangible asset can be measured using either the cost or revaluation method. In practice, this is the same process as in IAS 16 (paras. 72–118).
5. Disclosures, for each class of intangible asset (paras. 118–122):
   - useful life or amortisation rate
   - amortisation method
   - gross carrying amount
   - accumulated amortisation and impairment losses
   - line items in the statement of comprehensive income in which amortisation is included
   - reconciliation of the carrying amount at the beginning and the end of the period showing all changes
   - basis for determining that an intangible has an indefinite life
   - description and carrying amount of individually material intangible assets
   - certain special disclosures about intangible assets acquired by way of government grants
   - information about intangible assets whose title is restricted
   - commitments to acquire intangible assets.

CHANGES ON THE HORIZON

Due to the number of active projects the IASB, while recognising there are issues to be addressed, has decided not to add this standard to its project agenda at this time.

FACT SHEET IAS 41 *Agriculture*

OBJECTIVE

The objective of this standard is to account for agricultural activity, principally self-generating and regenerating assets (SGARAs). The unique nature of these assets means that traditional valuation methods, namely cost, are not always appropriate due to factors such as:

- natural capacity to grow and/or procreate directly impacts on value
- great deal of increase in value owing to input of free goods
- great deal of cost incurred early in the asset's life but economic benefits derived much later
- production cycle might be very long
- not necessarily any relationship between expenditure and ultimate return.

The standard applies to the use of biological assets (living plant or animal) and associated produce (harvest of biological assets) through agricultural activity, that is:

- transformation of biological assets for sale (sale of cattle, sheep, etc.)
- into agricultural produce (meat, wool, logs, grapes, etc) or products (yarn, lumber, wine)
- or additional biological assets (breeding of cattle, sheep, etc.).

KEY REPORTING REQUIREMENTS

1. Recognition and measurement of biological assets and produce (paras. 10–25):
   - The standard asset definition and recognition criteria applies, that is, control of the asset through a past event bringing future economic benefits, and a cost or fair value that can be reliably measured.
   - Biological assets and produce should be measured on initial recognition at fair value less estimated costs to sell except where fair value cannot be measured reliably.
2. Gains and losses resulting from changes in the fair value less costs to sell should be included in profit and loss for the period in which they incur (paras. 26–29).
3. Inability to measure fair value reliably (paras. 33–43): the standard assumes that fair value can be measured. If not, cost is to be used less accumulated deprecation and impairment.
4. If the biological asset is associated with a government grant, the grant is recognised as income when it becomes receivable and any conditions attached to the grant are met (paras. 34–38).
5. Disclosures:
   - Aggregating gains and losses on biological assets.
   - Description of each group of biological assets including:
     - nature of each group
     - non-financial measures or estimates of quantities of each biological asset and produce.
   - Methods and assumptions used in calculating fair value and costs to sell.
   - Changes in the carrying amount of each biological asset or produce and the reason for the change.
   - Any financial commitments or risks associated with the biological asset or produce.
   - The reasons why fair value cannot be measured reliably and associated depreciation and impairment amounts and methods.

CHANGES ON THE HORIZON

No changes on the horizon.

USEFUL TERMS

Accounting estimates: Measurement judgements applied in preparing the financial statements.
Accounting policies: The specific principles, bases, conventions, rules and practices applied by an entity in preparing and presenting financial statements.
Accounting profit: Profit for a period (determined in accordance with accounting standards and statements of accounting concepts) before deducting tax expense.
Accrual basis: Recognising the effects of transactions and other events when they occur, rather than when cash or its equivalent is received or paid.
Acquirer: The entity that obtains control of the acquiree.
Acquisition date: The date on which the acquirer effectively obtains control of the acquiree.
Active market: A market in which all the following conditions exist: (a) the items traded in the market are homogeneous; (b) willing buyers and sellers can normally be found at any time; and (c) prices are available to the public.
Adjusting event after the balance sheet date: An event that provides evidence of conditions that existed at the balance sheet date
Agreement date: The date that a substantive agreement between the combining parties is reached
Agricultural produce: The harvested product of an entity's biological assets.
Allotment: The process whereby directors of the company allocate shares to applicants. Alternatively, an account recording an amount of money receivable from successful applicants once shares are allotted.
Amortisation: The systematic allocation of the depreciable amount of an intangible asset over its useful life. *See* depreciation
Amortised cost: The amount at which the financial asset or financial liability is measured at initial recognition minus principal repayments, plus or minus the cumulative amortisation using the effective interest method of any difference between that initial amount and the maturity amount, and minus any reduction (directly or through the use of an allowance account) for impairment or uncollectability.
Application: The process whereby prospective shareholders apply to the company for an allotment of shares. Alternatively, an account used to record the amount of money receivable by the company from applicants for shares.
Asset: A resource controlled by an entity as a result of past events and from which future economic benefits are expected to flow to the entity.
Associate: An entity over which the investor has significant influence and that is neither a subsidiary nor an interest in a joint venture.
Available-for-sale financial assets: Those non-derivative financial assets that are designated as available for sale or that are not classified as (a) loans and receivables, (b) held-to-maturity investments or (c) financial assets at fair value through profit or loss.
Bargain purchase option: A clause in the lease agreement allowing the lessee to purchase the asset at the end of the lease for a preset amount, significantly less than the expected residual value at the end of the lease term.
Biological asset: A living animal or plant.
Bonus issue or bonus shares: An issue of shares to existing owners as a substitute for the payment of cash, particularly as a substitute for a cash dividend.
Business: An integrated set of activities and assets that is capable of being conducted and managed for the purpose of providing a return in the form of dividends, lower costs or other economic benefits directly to investors or other owners, members or participants.
Business combination: A transaction or other event in which an acquirer obtains control of one or more businesses.
Business segment: A distinguishable component of an entity that is engaged in providing an individual product or service or a group of related products or services and that is subject to risks and returns that are different from those of other business segments.
Call: An account used to record amounts of money receivable on shares that have been allotted by shareholders whose shares were forfeited.
Carrying amount: The amount at which an asset is recognised after deducting any accumulated depreciation (amortisation) and accumulated impairment losses thereon.
Cash: Includes cash on hand, currency, cheques, money orders or electronic transfer that a bank will accept as a deposit.
Cash basis: Recognising the effects of transactions and other events when cash or its equivalent is received or paid, rather than when the transactions or other events occur.
Cash equivalents: Short-term, highly liquid investments that are readily convertible to known amounts of cash and which are subject to an insignificant risk of changes in value.
Cash flow statement: Provides information about the cash payments and cash receipts of an entity during a period.
Cash-generating unit: The smallest identifiable group of assets that generates cash inflows that are largely independent of the cash inflows from other assets or groups of assets.

Cash or settlement discount: An incentive for early payment of amounts owing on credit transactions, normally quoted as a percentage.

Cash-settled share-based payment transaction: A share-based payment transaction in which the entity acquires goods or services by incurring a liability to transfer cash or other assets to the supplier of those goods or services for amounts that are based on the price (or value) of the entity's shares or other equity instruments of the entity.

Class of assets: A category of assets having a similar nature or function in the operations of an entity, and which, for the purposes of disclosure, is shown as a single item without supplementary disclosure.

Closing rate: The spot exchange rate at the end of the reporting period.

Comparability: The quality of accounting information that results from similar accounting recognition, measurement, disclosure, and presentation standards being used by all entities.

Component of an entity: Operations and cash flows that can be clearly distinguished, operationally and for financial reporting purposes, from the rest of the entity.

Consolidated financial statements: The financial statements of a group of entities, prepared by combining the financial statements presented as those of a single economic entity.

Constructive obligation: An obligation that derives from an entity's actions where: (a) by an established pattern of past practice, published policies or a sufficiently specific current statement, the entity has indicated to other parties that it will accept certain responsibilities; and (b) as a result, the entity has created a valid expectation on the part of those other parties that it will discharge those responsibilities.

Contingency: A condition arising from past events that exists at reporting date and gives rise to either a possible asset or a possible liability, the outcome of which will be confirmed only on the occurrence of one or more uncertain future events that are outside the control of the entity.

Contingent asset: A possible asset that arises from past events and whose existence will be confirmed only by the occurrence or non-occurrence of one or more uncertain future events not wholly within the control of the entity.

Contingent consideration: Usually, an obligation of the acquirer to transfer additional assets or equity interests to the former owners of an acquiree as part of the exchange for control of the acquiree if specified future events occur or conditions are met. However, contingent consideration also may give the acquirer the right to the return of previously transferred consideration if specified conditions are met.

Contingent liability: (a) A possible obligation that arises from past events and whose existence will be confirmed only by the occurrence or non-occurrence of one or more uncertain future events not wholly within the control of the entity, or (b) a present obligation that arises from past events but is not recognised because (i) it is not probable that an outflow of resources embodying economic events will be required to settle the obligation, or (ii) the amount of the obligation cannot be measured with sufficient reliability.

Contingent rent: That part of the lease payments that is not fixed in amount but is based on the future amount of a factor that changes other than with the passage of time.

Control: The power to govern the financial and operating policies of an entity or business so as to obtain benefits from its activities.

Corporate assets: Assets other than goodwill that contribute to the future cash flows of both the cash-generating unit under review and other cash-generating units.

Corporate governance: The system by which companies are directed and managed. It influences how the objectives of the company are set and achieved, how risk is monitored and assessed, and how performance is optimised. Good corporate governance structures encourage companies to create value (through entrepreneurism, innovation, development and exploration) and provide accountability and control systems commensurate with the risks involved.

Cost: The amount of cash or cash equivalents paid or the fair value of the other consideration given to acquire an asset at the time of its acquisition or construction or, where applicable, the amount attributed to that asset when initially recognised in accordance with the specific requirements of other standards, e.g. IFRS 2 *Share-based Payment*.

Costs of conversion: Costs directly related to the units of production plus a systematic allocation of fixed and variable overheads that are incurred in converting materials into finished goods.

Costs of disposal: Incremental costs directly attributable to the disposal of an asset or cash-generating unit, excluding finance costs and income tax expense.

Costs of purchase: Costs such as purchase price, import duties and other taxes (other than those subsequently recoverable by the entity from the taxing authorities), transport, handling and other costs directly attributable to the acquisition of finished goods, materials and services.

Costs to sell: The incremental costs directly attributable to the disposal of an asset (or disposal group), excluding finance costs and income tax expense.

Cumulative: In relation to preference shares, shares on which undeclared dividends in one year accumulate to the following year/s until paid.

Current liability: A liability that (a) is expected to be settled in the normal course of the entity's operating cycle, or (b) is at call or due or expected to be settled within 12 months of the reporting date.

Current tax: The amount of income taxes payable in respect of the taxable profit for a period.

Date of exchange: The date when each individual investment is recognised in the financial report of the acquirer.

Deductible temporary differences: Temporary differences that will result in amounts that are deductible in determining taxable profit of future periods when the carrying amount of the asset or liability is recovered or settled.

Deferred tax asset: Amounts of income taxes recoverable in future periods in respect of deferred temporary differences; the carry forward of unused tax losses and the carry forward of unused tax credits.

Deferred tax liability: Amounts of income taxes payable in future periods in respect of taxable temporary differences.

Depreciable amount: The cost of an asset, or other amount substituted for cost, less its residual value.

Depreciation (amortisation): The systematic allocation of the depreciable amount of an asset over its useful life.

Derivatives: A financial instrument that derives its value from another underlying item, such as a share price or an interest rate. The definition requires all of the following three characteristics to be met: (a) its value must change in response to a change in an underlying variable such as a specified interest rate, price, or foreign exchange rate; (b) it must require no initial net investment or an initial net investment that is smaller than would be required for other types of contracts with similar responses to changes in market factors; (c) it is settled at a future date.

Development: The application of research findings or other knowledge to a plan or design for the production of new or substantially improved materials, devices, products, processes, systems or services before the start of commercial production or use.

Direct non-controlling interest (DNCI): An NCI that holds shares directly in a subsidiary.

Discontinued operation: A component of an entity that either has been disposed of or is classified as held for sale and (a) represents a separate major line of business or geographical area of operations; (b) is part of a single coordinated plan to dispose of a separate major line of business or geographical area of operations; or (c) is a subsidiary acquired exclusively with a view to resale.

Disposal group: A group of assets to be disposed of, by sale or otherwise, together as a group in a single transaction, and liabilities directly associated with those assets that will be transferred in the transaction.

Dividends: A distribution of profit to the equity holders of a company.

Economic life: Either the period over which an asset is expected to be economically useable by one or more users or the number of production or similar units expected to be obtained from the asset by one or more users.

Effective interest method: A method of calculating the amortised cost of a financial asset or a financial liability, and of allocating the interest income or interest expense over the relevant period.

Effective interest rate: The rate that exactly discounts estimated future cash payments or receipts through the expected life of the financial instrument (or, when appropriate, a shorter period) to the net carrying amount of the financial asset or financial liability.

Embedded derivative: A component of a combined (or 'hybrid') instrument that also includes a non-derivative host contract, with the effect that some of the cash flows of the combined instrument vary in a way similar to a stand-alone instrument.

Employee benefits: All forms of consideration given by an entity in exchange for services rendered by employees.

Employees and others providing similar services: Individuals who render personal services to the entity and either (a) the individuals are regarded as employees for legal or tax purposes, (b) the individuals work for the entity under its direction in the same way as individuals who are regarded as employees for legal or tax purposes, or (c) the services rendered are similar to those rendered by employees. For example, the term encompasses all management personnel, that is, those persons having authority and responsibility for planning, directing and controlling the activities of the entity, including non-executive directors.

Entity concept of consolidation: The group consists of all the assets and liabilities of the parent as well as all the assets and liabilities of the subsidiaries, and the non-controlling interest is classified as a contributor of equity to the group.

Entity-specific value: The present value of the cash flows an entity (1) expects to arise from the continuing use of an asset and from its disposal at the end of its useful life or (2) expects to incur when settling a liability.

Equity: The residual interest in the assets of the entity after deducting all its liabilities.

Equity instrument: Any contract that evidences a residual interest in the assets of an entity after deducting all of its liabilities.

Equity instrument granted: The right (conditional or unconditional) to an equity instrument of the entity conferred by the entity on another party, under a share-based payment arrangement.

Equity-settled share-based payment transaction: A share-based payment transaction in which the entity receives goods or services as consideration for equity instruments of the entity (including shares or share options).

Equity method: The method of accounting whereby the investment is initially recognised at cost and subsequently adjusted for the post-acquisition change in the investor's share of net assets of the associate. The profit or loss of the investor includes the investor's share of the profit or loss of the investee.

Errors: Omissions from or misstatements in the financial statements.

Exchange difference: The difference resulting from translating a given number of units of one currency into another currency at different exchange rates.

Exchange rate: The ratio of exchange for two currencies.

Executory contracts: Contracts under which neither party has performed any of its obligations or both parties have partially performed their obligations to an equal extent.

Executory costs: Operating amounts (including insurance, maintenance, consumable supplies, replacement parts and rates) that are paid by the lessor on behalf of the lessee.

Expenses: Decreases in economic benefits during the accounting period in the form of outflows or depletions of assets or incurrences of liabilities that result in decreases in equity, other than those relating to distributions to equity participants.

Fair value: The amount for which an asset could be exchanged, or a liability settled, between knowledgeable, willing parties in an arm's length transaction.

Fair value less costs to sell: The amount obtainable from the sale of an asset or cash-generating unit in an arm's length transaction between knowledgeable, willing parties, less the costs of disposal.

Finance lease: A lease that transfers substantially all of the risks and benefits incidental to ownership of an asset. Title may or may not eventually be transferred.

Financial asset: Any asset that is: (a) cash (b) an equity instrument of another entity (c) a contractual right: (i) to receive cash or another financial asset from another entity; or (ii) to exchange financial assets or financial liabilities with another entity under conditions that are potentially favourable to the entity; or (d) a contract that will or may be settled in the entity's own equity instruments that is: (i) a non-derivative for which the entity is or may be obliged to receive a variable number of the entity's own equity instruments; or (ii) a derivative that will or may be settled other than by the exchange of a fixed amount of cash or another financial asset for a fixed number of the entity's own equity instruments. For this purpose the entity's own equity instruments do not include instruments that are themselves contracts for the future receipt or delivery of the entity's own equity instruments.

Financial assets at fair value through profit or loss: Financial assets held for trading and measured at fair value with any gain or loss from a change in fair value recognised in profit or loss, or financial assets that upon initial recognition are designated by the entity as at fair value through profit or loss.

Financial instrument: Any contract that gives rise to a financial asset of one entity and a financial liability or equity instrument of another.

Financial liability: Any liability that is: (a) a contractual obligation: (i) to deliver cash or another financial asset to another entity; or (ii) to exchange financial assets or financial liabilities with another entity under conditions that are potentially unfavourable to the entity; or (b) a contract that will or may be settled in the entity's own equity instruments and is: (i) a non-derivative for which the entity is or may be obliged to deliver a variable number of the entity's own equity instruments; or (ii) a derivative that will or may be settled other than by the exchange of a fixed amount of cash or another financial asset for a fixed number of the entity's own equity instruments. For this purpose the entity's own equity instruments do not include instruments that are themselves contracts for the future receipt or delivery of the entity's own equity instruments.

Financial position: The assets, liabilities, and residual equity interest of an entity at a given point in time.

Financing activities: Those activities that result in changes in the size and composition of the equity capital and borrowings of the entity.

Firm commitment: A binding agreement for the exchange of a specified quantity of resources at a specified price on a specified future date or dates.

First-in, first-out (FIFO): A method of allocating cost to inventory items that assumes that the items first purchased will be the items first sold.

FOB destination: A condition of sale under which the seller pays all freight costs (FOB means 'free on board').

FOB shipping: A condition of sale under which freight costs incurred from the point of shipment are paid by the buyer (FOB means 'free on board').

Forecast transaction: An uncommitted but anticipated future transaction.

Foreign currency: A currency other than the functional currency of the entity.

Foreign operation: An entity that is a subsidiary, associate, joint venture or branch of a reporting entity, the activities of which are based or conducted in a country or currency other than those of the reporting entity.

Forfeited shares account: An account initially recording the amount of funds supplied by shareholders whose shares were forfeited.

Framework for the Preparation and Presentation of Financial Statements: The pronouncement of the International Accounting Standards Board that sets out the concepts underlying the preparation and presentation of financial statements for external users.

Functional currency: The currency of the primary economic environment in which the entity operates.

General purpose financial statements: The financial statements that a business entity prepares and presents at least annually to meet the common information needs of a wide range of users external to the entity.

Geographical segment: A distinguishable component of an entity that is engaged in providing products or services within a particular economic environment and that is subject to risks and returns that are different from those of components operating in other economic environments.

Going concern: An entity that is expected to continue in operation for the foreseeable future.

Goodwill: An asset representing the future economic benefits arising from other assets acquired in a business combination that are not individually identified and separately recognised.

Grant date: The date at which the entity and another party (including an employee) agree to a share-based payment arrangement, being when the entity and the counterparty have a shared understanding of the terms and conditions of the arrangement. At grant date the entity confers on the counterparty the right to cash, other assets, or equity instruments of the entity, provided the specified vesting conditions, if any, are met. If that agreement is subject to an approval process (e.g. by shareholders), grant date is the date when that approval is obtained.

Gross investment: For the lessor, the aggregate of the minimum lease payments receivable by the lessor under a finance lease, and any unguaranteed residual value accruing to the lessor.

Group: A parent and all its subsidiaries.

Guaranteed residual value: That part of the residual value of the leased asset guaranteed by the lessee or a third party related to the lessee.

Hedge effectiveness: The degree to which changes in the fair value or cash flows of the hedged item that are attributable to a hedged risk are offset by changes in the fair value or cash flows of the hedging instrument.

Hedged item: An asset, liability, firm commitment, highly probable forecast transaction or net investment in a foreign operation that (a) exposes the entity to risk of changes in fair value or future cash flows and (b) is designated as being hedged.

Hedging instrument: A designated derivative or (for a hedge of the risk of changes in foreign currency exchange rates only) a designated non-derivative financial asset or non-derivative financial liability whose fair value or cash flows are expected to offset changes in the fair value or cash flows of a designated hedged item.

Held-to-maturity investments: Investments that the entity has the positive intention and ability to hold to maturity (e.g. debt instruments, such as debentures held in another entity or redeemable preference shares) other than: (a) those that the entity upon initial recognition designates as at fair value through profit or loss; (b) those that the entity designates as available for sale; and (c) those that meet the definition of loans and receivables.

Highly probable: Significantly more likely than probable.

Impairment loss: The amount by which the carrying amount of an asset exceeds its recoverable amount (which is the higher of the asset's net selling price and its value in use).

Inception of the lease: The earlier of the date of the lease agreement and the date of commitment by the parties to the principal provisions of the lease.

Income: An increase in an asset or a decrease in a liability will result in income, unless the increase or decrease results from an equity contribution (such as cash raised through share capital). Because of this broad definition, income is further dissected into revenue and gains.

Incremental borrowing rate: The rate of interest the lessee would have to pay on a similar lease or, if that is not determinable, the rate that (at the inception of the lease) the lessee would incur to borrow over a similar term, and with a similar security, the funds necessary to purchase the asset.

Indirect non-controlling interest (INCI): An NCI that has an interest in a subsidiary as a result of having an interest in the parent of that subsidiary.

Initial direct costs: Incremental costs that are directly attributable to negotiating and arranging a lease, except for such costs incurred by the manufacturer or dealer lessors.

Intangible asset: An identifiable non-monetary asset without physical substance.

Interest rate implicit in the lease rate: The rate that, at the inception of the lease, causes the aggregate present value of the minimum lease payments and the unguaranteed residual value to be equal to the sum of the fair value of the leased asset and any initial direct costs of the lessor.

Intrinsic value: The difference between the fair value of the shares to which the counterparty has the (conditional or unconditional) right to subscribe or which it has the right to receive, and the price (if any) the counterparty is (or will be) required to pay for those shares. For example, a share option with an exercise price of CU15 (currency units) on a share with a fair value of CU20, has an intrinsic value of CU5.

Inventories: Assets held for sale in the ordinary course of business, in the process of production for such sale, or in the form of materials or supplies to be consumed in the production process or in the rendering of services.

Investing activities: Those activities which relate to the acquisition and disposal of long-term assets and other investments not included in cash equivalents.

Investment property: Property (land or a building, or part of a building, or both) held to earn rentals or for capital appreciation or both, rather than for (a) use in the production or supply of goods or services or for administrative purposes, or (b) sale in the ordinary course of business.

Joint control: The contractually agreed sharing of control over an economic activity that exists only when the strategic financial and operating decisions relating to the activity require the unanimous consent of the parties sharing the control (the venturers).

Joint venture: A contractual arrangement whereby two or more parties undertake an economic activity that is subject to joint control.

Lease: An agreement whereby the lessor conveys to the lessee in return for a payment or series of payments the right to use an asset for an agreed period of time.

Lease payments: The total amounts payable under the lease agreement.

Lease term: The non-cancellable period for which the lessee has contracted to lease the asset, together with any further terms for which the lessee has the option to continue to lease the asset, with or without further payment, when at the inception of the lease it is reasonably certain that the lessee will exercise the option.

Liability: A present obligation of the entity arising from past events, the settlement of which is expected to result in an outflow from the entity of resources embodying economic benefits.

Loans and receivables: Non-derivative financial assets with fixed or determinable payments that are not quoted in an active market and which the entity has no intention of trading, e.g. loan to a subsidiary.

Market condition : A condition upon which the exercise price, vesting or exercisability of an equity instrument depends that is related to the market price of the entity's equity instruments, such as attaining a specified share price or a specified amount of intrinsic value of a share option, or achieving a specified target that is based on the market price of the entity's equity instruments relative to an index of market prices of equity instruments of other entities.

Materiality: The notion of materiality guides the margin of error acceptable, the degree of precision required and the extent of the disclosure required when preparing general purpose financial reports.

Measurement: The process of determining the monetary amount at which an asset, liability, income or expense is reported in the financial statements.

Measurement date: The date at which the fair value of the equity instruments granted is measured for the purposes of this IFRS. For transactions with employees and others providing similar services, the measurement date is grant date. For transactions with parties other than employees (and those providing similar services), the measurement date is the date the entity obtains the goods or the counterparty renders service.

Minimum lease payments: The payments over the lease term that the lessee is or can be required to make, excluding contingent rent, costs for services and taxes to be paid by and reimbursed to the lessor, together with (a) for a lessee, any amounts guaranteed by the lessee or by a party related to the lessee; or (b) for a lessor, any residual value guaranteed to the lessor.

Monetary assets: Money held and assets to be received in fixed or determinable amounts of money.

Monetary items: Units of currency held and assets and liabilities to be received or paid in a fixed or determinable number of units of currency.

Net assets: Total assets minus liabilities.

Net investment in a foreign operation: The amount of the reporting entity's interest in the net assets of that operation.

Net realisable value: The estimated selling price in the ordinary course of business less the estimated costs of completion and the estimated costs necessary to make the sale.

Non-adjusting event after the balance sheet date: An event that is indicative of conditions that arose after the balance sheet date.

Non-cancellable lease: A lease that is cancellable only (a) upon the occurrence of some remote contingency; (b) with the permission of the lessor; (c) if the lessee enters into a new lease for the same or an equivalent asset with the same lessor; or (d) upon payment by the lessee of such an additional amount that, at inception of the lease, makes the continuation of the lease reasonably certain.

Non-controlling interest: The equity in a subsidiary not attributable, directly or indirectly, to a parent.

Non-sequential acquisition: Where a parent acquires its shares in a subsidiary after that subsidiary has acquired shares in its subsidiary.

Notes: Notes are prepared in accordance with IAS 1 and form part of a set of general purpose financial statements. They contain information in addition to that presented in the balance sheet, income statement, statement of changes in equity and cash flow statement. They provide narrative descriptions of the basis of preparation of the financial statements and accounting policies adopted, as well as disaggregations of items disclosed in the financial statements and information about items that do not qualify for recognition in those statements.

Obligating event: An event that creates a legal or constructive obligation that results in an entity having no realistic alternative to settling that obligation.

Onerous contract: A contract in which the unavoidable costs of meeting the obligations under the contract exceed the economic benefits expected to be received under it.

Operating activities: Those activities which relate to the main revenue-producing activities of the entity and other activities that are not investing or financing activities.
Operating lease: A lease other than a finance lease.
Parent: An entity that has one or more subsidiaries.
Participating: In relation to preference shares, shares that receive extra dividends above a fixed rate once a certain level of dividends has been paid on ordinary shares.
Performance: The ability of an entity to earn a profit on the resources that have been invested in it.
Periodic method: A system of recording inventory whereby the value of inventory is determined and recorded on a periodic basis (normally annually).
Perpetual method: A system of recording inventory whereby inventory records are updated each time a transaction involving inventory takes place.
Pre-acquisition equity: The equity of the subsidiary at acquisition date. It is not just the equity recorded by the subsidiary, but is determined by reference to the cost of the business combination.
Presentation currency: The currency in which the financial report is presented.
Private placement: An issue of shares usually to a large institutional investor such as a finance company, superannuation fund or life insurance company.
Probable: More likely than not.
Property, plant and equipment: Tangible items that (a) are held for use in the production or supply of goods or services, for rental to others, or for administrative purposes (b) are expected to be used during more than one period.
Prospective application: Means applying the change to transactions, events or other conditions occurring after the date of the change and recognising the effect in the current and future periods.
Provision: A liability of uncertain timing or amount.
Public company: A company entitled to raise funds from the public by lodging a disclosure document with ASIC and have its shares or other ownership documents traded on the stock exchange. It may be a limited company, unlimited company or no-liability company.
Reciprocal shareholdings: Where two entities hold shares in each other.
Recognition: The process of incorporating in the financial statements an item that meets the definition of an asset, liability, income or expense.
Recoverable amount: For an asset or a cash-generating unit, the higher of its fair value less costs to sell and its value in use.
Relevance: That quality of information that exists when the information influences economic decisions made by users.
Reliability: Information has the quality of reliability when it is free from material error and bias and can be depended on by users to represent faithfully that which it either purports to represent or could reasonably be expected to represent.
Reload feature: A feature that provides for an automatic grant of additional share options whenever the option holder exercises previously granted options using the entity's shares, rather than cash, to satisfy the exercise price.
Reload option: A new share option granted when a share is used to satisfy the exercise price of a previous share option.
Reportable segment: A business segment or a geographical segment identified based on the definitions for either a business segment or geographical segment.
Reporting entity: An entity in respect of which it is reasonable to expect the existence of users who rely on the entity's general purpose financial statements for information that will be useful to them for making and evaluating decisions about the allocation of scarce resources. A reporting entity can be a single entity or a group comprising a parent and all of its subsidiaries.
Research: Original and planned investigation undertaken with the prospect of gaining new scientific or technical knowledge and understanding.
Reserve: A category of equity that is not contributed capital.
Residual value: The estimated amount that an entity would currently obtain from disposal of the asset, after deducting the estimated costs of disposal, if the asset were already of the age and in the condition expected at the end of its useful life.
Revenue: The gross inflow of economic benefits during the period arising in the course of the ordinary activities of an entity when those inflows result in increases in equity, other than increases relating to contributions from equity participants.
Retrospective application: Means applying a new accounting policy to transactions, other events and conditions as if that policy had always been applied.
Revaluation decrement (increment): The amount by which the revalued carrying amount of a non-current asset as at the revaluation date is less than (exceeds) its previous carrying amount.
Rights issue: An issue of new shares giving existing shareholders the right to an additional number of shares in proportion to their current shareholdings.
Segment accounting policies: Accounting policies adopted for preparing and presenting the financial statements of the consolidated group or entity as well as those accounting policies that relate specifically to a segment.
Segment assets: Operating assets that are employed by a segment in its operating activities and that either are directly attributable to the segment or can be allocated to the segment on a reasonable basis.

Segment expense: Expense resulting from the operating activities of a segment that is directly attributable to the segment and the relevant portion of an expense that can be allocated on a reasonable basis to the segment, including expenses relating to sales to external customers and expenses relating to transactions with other segments of the same entity.

Segment liabilities: Operating liabilities that result from the operating activities of a segment and that either are directly attributable to the segment or can be allocated to the segment on a reasonable basis.

Segment result: Segment revenue less segment expense. Segment result is determined before any adjustments for minority interest.

Segment revenue: Revenue reported in the entity's income statement that is directly attributable to a segment and the relevant portion of entity revenue that can be allocated on a reasonable basis to a segment, whether from sales to external customers or from transactions with other segments of the same entity.

Separate financial statements: Statements prepared by a parent in which its investments are accounted for on the basis of the direct equity interest rather than on the basis of the reported results and net assets of the investees.

Sequential acquisition: Where a parent acquires its shares in a subsidiary before or on the same date that the subsidiary acquires shares in its subsidiary.

Share-based payment arrangement: An agreement between the entity and another party (including an employee) to enter into a share-based payment transaction, which thereby entitles the other party to receive cash or other assets of the entity for amounts that are based on the price of the entity's shares or other equity instruments of the entity, or to receive equity instruments of the entity, provided the specified vesting conditions, if any, are met.

Share-based payment transaction: A transaction in which the entity receives goods or services as consideration for equity instruments of the entity (including shares or share options), or acquires goods or services by incurring liabilities to the supplier of those goods or services for amounts that are based on the price of the entity's shares or other equity instruments of the entity.

Share buy-back: The repurchase of a company's shares by the company from its shareholders.

Share issue costs: Costs incurred on the issue of equity instruments. These include underwriting costs, stamp duties and taxes, professional advisers' fees and brokerage.

Share option: A contract that gives the holder the right, but not the obligation, to subscribe to the entity's shares at a fixed or determinable price for a specified period of time.

Significant influence: The power to participate in the financial and operating policies of the investee without having control or joint control over those policies.

Specific identification: A method of allocating cost to inventory based on identifying and aggregating all costs directly related to each individual inventory item.

Spot exchange rate: The exchange rate for immediate delivery.

Statement of changes in equity: A financial statement prepared in accordance with IAS 1 for inclusion in general purpose financial reports. The statement reports on the changes in the entity's equity for the reporting period. Changes in equity disclosed may include movements in retained earnings for the period, items of income and expense recognised directly in equity, and movements in each class of share and each reserve.

Statement of comprehensive income: A financial statement that reports on the entity's revenues and expenses for the reporting period.

Statement of financial position: A financial statement that presents assets, liabilities and equity of an entity at a given point in time.

Subsidiary: An entity, including an unincorporated entity such as a partnership, that is controlled by another entity (known as the parent).

Substance over form: The accounts will reflect the underlying economic reality of transactions and not their legal form.

Tax base: Of an asset or liability, is the amount attributed to that asset or liability for tax purposes.

Tax expense: The aggregate amount included in the determination of profit or loss for the period in respect of current tax and deferred tax.

Taxable profit: The profit for a period, determined in accordance with the rules established by the taxation authorities, upon which income taxes are payable.

Taxable temporary differences : Temporary differences that will result in taxable amounts in determining taxable profit of future periods when the carrying amount of the asset and liability is recovered or settled.

Temporary difference: The difference between the carrying amount of an asset or liability and the tax base of that asset or liability.

Trade discount: A reduction in selling prices granted to customers.

Understandability: The ability of financial information to be comprehended by financial statement users who have a reasonable knowledge of business and economic activities and accounting, and a willingness to study the information with reasonable diligence.

Underwriter: An entity which, for a fee, undertakes to subscribe for any shares not allotted to applicants as a result of an undersubscription.

Unguaranteed residual value: That part of the residual value of the leased asset, the realisation of which is not assured by the lessor or is guaranteed solely by a party related to the lessor.

Useful life: (a) the period over which an asset is expected to be available for use by an entity, or (b) the number of production or similar units expected to be obtained from the asset by an entity.

Value in use: The present value of future cash flows expected to be derived from an asset or cash-generating unit.

Venturer: A party to a joint venture that has joint control over that joint venture.

Vest: To become an entitlement. Under a share-based payment arrangement, a counterparty's right to receive cash, other assets, or equity instruments of the entity vests upon satisfaction of any specified vesting conditions.

Vesting conditions: The conditions that must be satisfied for the counterparty to become entitled to receive cash, other assets or equity instruments of the entity, under a share-based payment arrangement. Vesting conditions include service conditions, which require the other party to complete a specified period of service, and performance conditions, which require specified performance targets to be met (such as a specified increase in the entity's profit over a specified period of time).

Vesting period: The period during which all the specified vesting conditions of a share-based payment arrangement are to be satisfied.

Weighted average: A method of allocating cost to inventory items based on the weighted average of the cost of similar items at the beginning of a period and the cost of similar items purchased or produced during the period.

INDEX